CW00972486

APPLICATIONS TO WIND UP COMPANIES

APPLICATIONS TO WIND UP COMPANIES

THIRD EDITION

DEREK FRENCH

Consultant Editor
PROFESSOR STUART SIME

OXFORD
UNIVERSITY PRESS

OXFORD

UNIVERSITY PRESS

Great Clarendon Street, Oxford, OX2 6DP,
United Kingdom

Oxford University Press is a department of the University of Oxford.
It furthers the University's objective of excellence in research, scholarship,
and education by publishing worldwide. Oxford is a registered trade mark of
Oxford University Press in the UK and in certain other countries

© Derek French 2015

The moral rights of the author have been asserted

First Edition published in 1993
Third Edition published in 2015

Impression: 1

Published in the United States of America by Oxford University Press
198 Madison Avenue, New York, NY 10016, United States of America

British Library Cataloguing in Publication Data
Data available

Library of Congress Control Number: 2014959183

ISBN 978–0–19–871637–2

Printed and bound by
CPI Group (UK) Ltd, Croydon, CR0 4YY

PREFACE

This work is intended to provide a detailed statement of the law on applications to wind up companies in England and Wales. It is concerned primarily with registered companies, but also deals with all the various entities that can be wound up in the same manner as registered companies, including foreign companies, other unregistered companies and insolvent partnerships.

Many Commonwealth nations have company or corporation laws derived from United Kingdom legislation. There is still so much similarity between the law on applications to wind up companies in jurisdictions throughout the Commonwealth that court decisions from many jurisdictions can be considered together as a common law of winding up. This book focuses on English law and practice, but it is hoped that the extensive citation of jurisprudence from other jurisdictions will make the book useful elsewhere in the Commonwealth.

This edition has benefited enormously from the helpful criticism of its consulting editor, Stuart Sime, to whom I am extremely grateful. However, I am responsible for the contents of the book.

This edition, like those before it, is dedicated with love to my partner, Jennifer Strachan.

This edition is intended to state the law of England and Wales as it was thought to be on 1 September 2014. However, it has not been feasible to discuss the new s 89K of the Banking Act 2009. This came into force on 1 January 2015 and places further restrictions on petitions to wind up failing banks and other financial institutions.

Derek French
7 January 2015

CONTENTS—SUMMARY

CONTENTS

TABLE OF CASES

TABLE OF LEGISLATION

TABLE OF UK STATUTORY INSTRUMENTS

TABLE OF EUROPEAN LEGISLATION

TABLE OF INTERNATIONAL
TREATIES AND CONVENTIONS

LIST OF ABBREVIATIONS

AD   Appellate Division

CA   Court of Appeal
CFI   Court of First Instance
ChD   Chancery Division
ChDC   Divisional Court of the Chancery Division
CIC   community interest company
CIO   charitable incorporated organization
CJEU   Court of Justice of the European Union
COMI   centre of main interests
CP   Common Pleas
CPD   Common Pleas Division
CPDC   Divisional Court of the Common Pleas Division
CSess 1st Div   Court of Session First Division
CSess 2nd Div   Court of Session Second Division
CSess Extra Div Court of Session Extra Division
CSess IH   Court of Session Inner House
CSess OH   Court of Session Outer House
CVA   company voluntary arrangement

DC   Divisional Court
draft IR 2015   draft Insolvency Rules 2015

EC   European Community
EEA   European Economic Area
EEC   European Economic Community
EEIG   European economic interest grouping
EFTA   European Free Trade Area
EGTC   European grouping of territorial cooperation
ExDC   Divisional Court of the Exchequer Division

FC   Full Court
FCA   Financial Conduct Authority
FedC   Federal Court
FMI   financial market infrastructure
FSCS   Financial Services Compensation Scheme
FSMA 2000   Financial Services and Markets Act 2000

GEMA   Gas and Electricity Markets Authority

HC   High Court
HL   House of Lords

IA 1985	Insolvency Act 1985
IA 1986	Insolvency Act 1986
IPO 1994	Insolvent Partnerships Order 1994 (SI 1994/2421)
IR 1986	Insolvency Rules 1986 (SI 1986/1925)
KB	King's Bench
KBD	King's Bench Division
KBDC	Divisional Court of the King's Bench Division
LC	Lord Chancellor
LJJ	(in the Table of Cases) Lords Justices and/or Lord Chancellor forming the Court of Appeal in Chancery; (in text) Lords Justices
LLP	limited liability partnership
MiFID	Markets in Financial Instruments Directive
MR	Master of the Rolls
NHS	National Health Service
Ofcom	Office of Communications
PC	Privy Council
PD	Practice Direction supplementing the CPR
PD Insolvency Proceedings	Practice Direction—Insolvency Proceedings
PDAD	Probate Divorce and Admiralty Division
plc	public limited company
PPP	public-private partnership
PRA	Prudential Regulation Authority
QB	Queen's Bench
QBD	Queen's Bench Division
QBDC	Divisional Court of the Queen's Bench Division
SC	Supreme Court
SCA	*société en commandite par actions*
SCE	European cooperative society (*societas cooperativa europaea*)
SE	European public limited-liability company (*societas europaea*)
UNCITRAL	United Nations Commission on International Trade Law
V-C	Vice-Chancellor

1

JURISDICTION, SOURCES AND GENERAL RULES

Nature and Purpose of Compulsory Winding Up

Proceedings for Winding Up by the Court

1.1 Under the Insolvency Act 1986 (IA 1986),[1] a court with appropriate jurisdiction[2] may order the winding up of a company by the court under the provisions of the Act. This work is concerned with the process of applying for and making winding-up orders. An application for a company to be wound up by the court under IA 1986 must be made by petition.[3] The company itself, its directors, its creditors, its members (who are described as 'contributories' in IA 1986), the Secretary of State and a variety of other persons have standing to petition for it to be wound up.[4]

1.2 In its application to England and Wales, IA 1986 is principally concerned with the winding up of companies incorporated in England and Wales under the Companies Act in force at the time of registration. Petitioning for the winding up of such companies is dealt with in part 4[5] of the Act.[6] Such companies are often called 'registered companies' but they are referred to simply as 'companies' in the Act. Various other corporate business forms can be wound up as if they were registered companies.[7] IA 1986 also provides, in part 5,[8] for the winding up of other companies and associations (called 'unregistered companies'). Provision for the winding up of insolvent partnerships, and of registered companies which are members of insolvent partnerships, is made by IA 1986 as modified by the Insolvent Partnerships Order 1994 (IPO 1994).[9]

1.3 A petition for a company or other entity to be wound up by the court under IA 1986 is not sustainable unless:

---

[1] See 1.44–1.48.
[2] See 1.80–1.478.
[3] IA 1986, s 124(1).
[4] See 2.54–2.95.
[5] ss 73–219.
[6] There are relevant interpretation provisions in part 7 (ss 247–251).
[7] See 1.120–1.129.
[8] ss 220–229.
[9] SI 1994/2421; see 1.49–1.52.

(a) the company or other entity is one which can be wound up by the court under IA 1986;[10]
(b) the court to which the petition is presented has jurisdiction to hear the case under the rules of private international law;[11]
(c) there is in existence one of the circumstances in which the court may wind up the company or other entity;[12] and
(d) the petitioner has standing to petition for the company or other entity to be wound up in that circumstance.[13]

The court has very limited powers to apply the IA 1986 winding-up procedure in other situations.[14]   **1.4**

Bank insolvency is a modified form of winding up by the court which was introduced by the Banking Act 2009 to ensure that when a bank fails, depositors who are eligible claimants under the terms of the Financial Services Compensation Scheme are paid promptly from the scheme or have their accounts transferred to another financial institution. The provisions on bank insolvency have been applied (as building society insolvency) to building societies by the Building Societies Act 1986, s 90C.   **1.5**

Compulsory and Voluntary Winding Up

A winding up ordered by a court under IA 1986 is referred to in the Act as a 'winding up by the court'. It is more often referred to as a 'compulsory' (or, in North America, 'involuntary') winding up, to contrast it with a winding up effected without a court order, which is called a 'voluntary' winding up.[15] Winding up is also known as liquidation.[16]   **1.6**

Only an order of the court can initiate a winding up by the court, and the winding up is correspondingly controlled and administered by the court.[17] The same applies to bank insolvency and building society insolvency.   **1.7**

Any decision, whether of a court or not, which mandates the winding up of a company may be described as an 'order' for it to be wound up. For example, a decision of the members of a European economic interest grouping that it is to be wound up voluntarily is described in Regulation (EEC) No 2137/85, art 31(1), as a decision 'ordering' its winding up, and a company has been 'ordered to be wound up' where there is a provision in an Act of Parliament that the company shall proceed forthwith after the passing of the Act to wind up their affairs.[18]   **1.8**

---

[10] See 1.80–1.344.
[11] See 1.347–1.442.
[12] See 2.23–2.53.
[13] See 2.54–2.95.
[14] See 2.20–2.22 (power to wind up on court's own initiative), 7.551–7.568 (winding up a company despite not deciding whether a creditor has standing to petition) and 10.184 (assistance of courts in relevant countries and territories may give power to wind up foreign entities over which the court would not normally exercise jurisdiction). But see 1.80 (no general power to wind up corporations), 1.299–1.344 (entities which cannot be wound up) and 2.57 (court cannot add to statutory categories of petitioner).
[15] See IA 1986, s 84(2).
[16] Recent legislation in some Commonwealth jurisdictions uses the term 'liquidation' exclusively. See, for example, Companies Act 1993 (New Zealand); Insolvency Act 2003 (Virgin Islands), Insolvency Act 2011 (Gibraltar). In those jurisdictions, the equivalent of an order winding up a company is an order appointing a liquidator.
[17] *Donaldson v O'Sullivan* [2008] EWCA Civ 879, [2009] 1 WLR 924, per Lloyd LJ at [38].
[18] *Re Uxbridge and Rickmansworth Railway Co* (1890) 43 ChD 536.

Purposes of Compulsory Winding Up

Principal purposes

1.9 It has been said that:

> [I]t is of general public importance when the court is called on to exercise its equitable authority that it must be satisfied that there is some rational ground for its interference, a reason for incurring the costs which are the effects of making an order on the petition, and the prospect of some good being done to somebody; and if the court is satisfied of that, of course it will make an order for winding up.[19]

> But the court ought not to make a winding-up order if it is satisfied that such an order will do no good.[20]

1.10 The main purpose of winding up a company is to collect all its assets and use them to satisfy, as far as possible, its liabilities. If all liabilities can be satisfied, any surplus must be distributed to the company's members or otherwise in accordance with its constitution. It may be necessary as part of this process to establish exactly what the company's assets and liabilities are. This may involve investigating the conduct of the company's business to discover whether its officers are liable for breach of duty. The processes described so far in this paragraph constitute the 'winding up' or 'liquidation' (the terms are interchangeable) of a company. In the case of a registered company, on completion of these processes, the company is dissolved and ceases to exist as a legal person. All this is provided for in the statutory consequences of making a winding-up order set out in IA 1986, part 4.

1.11 The procedure for compulsory winding up of a company provided by IA 1986 is in practice used for three principal purposes:

(a) It enables unsecured creditors of an insolvent company to have its assets realized for their benefit[21] (and in this respect compulsory winding up has some affinity with bankruptcy). (This is not to say that a secured creditor of a company does not have standing to petition for it to be wound up.[22] However, a secured creditor of a company does not need to have it wound up in order to realize the security. In practice, of course, a secured creditor of a company in financial difficulty is likely to be also partially unsecured.)

(b) It enables members of a solvent company to have its assets realized for their benefit.[23]

(c) It enables the Secretary of State and other public officials to end a company's existence, in the public interest.[24]

1.12 In practice winding up is most often sought by creditors of insolvent companies and is usually seen primarily as an insolvency proceeding. The United Kingdom has listed winding up by the court in Regulation (EC) No 1346/2000, annex A, as an insolvency proceeding, which is defined in arts 1(1) and 2(a) as a collective proceeding which entails the partial or total divestment of a debtor and the appointment of a liquidator. Winding up by the court is also listed in annex B as a winding-up proceeding, which is defined in art 2(c) as an insolvency proceeding which involves realizing the assets of the debtor.

---

[19] *Re New Gas Generator Co* (1877) 4 ChD 874 per Bacon V-C at pp 876–7.
[20] *Re New York Exchange Ltd* (1888) 39 ChD 415 per Cotton LJ at p 422. See also *Chan Pui Chun v Leung Kam Ho* [2002] EWCA Civ 1075, [2003] BPIR 29, at [104].
[21] See chapter 7.
[22] See 7.398–7.401.
[23] See chapter 8.
[24] See chapter 9.

Other purposes may justify making a winding-up order.[25]   **1.13**

Although a winding up can be stayed or discharged in favour of a reorganization proced-   **1.14**
ure,[26] winding up is not itself conceived as a rescue or reorganization procedure, and such
a procedure (voluntary arrangement or administration) is nowadays usually put in place
before winding up.

Liquidator

From the time that a court makes an order that a company is to be wound up, the company   **1.15**
has a liquidator under IA 1986, ss 136–140. The liquidator must 'take into his custody or
under his control all the property and things in action to which the company is or appears
to be entitled'.[27]

> The functions of the liquidator of a company which is being wound up by the court are to
> secure that the assets of the company are got in, realised and distributed to the company's
> creditors and, if there is a surplus, to the persons entitled to it.[28]

The official receiver[29] is liquidator from the time that the winding-up order is made until   **1.16**
another person is appointed.[30] An appointment of a liquidator to replace the official receiver
may be made by the Secretary of State, on the official receiver's application,[31] or by meetings
of the company's creditors and contributories.[32] If a company moves from administration or
voluntary arrangement to winding up by the court, the administrator or the supervisor of
the voluntary arrangement may be appointed liquidator by the court, instead of the official
receiver, on making the winding-up order.[33]

In other jurisdictions where there is no official receiver service, the winding-up order must   **1.17**
appoint the liquidator.

From 1856 to 1890, in the United Kingdom, there was a distinction between an 'official   **1.18**
liquidator' appointed in a winding up by the court[34] and a 'liquidator' appointed in a voluntary winding up.[35] The term 'official liquidator' was replaced by 'liquidator' as from 1
January 1891 in the UK,[36] but is still used for a liquidator in a winding up ordered by the
court in Australia[37] and the Cayman Islands.[38]

---

[25] See *Re Australian Joint Stock Bank Ltd* (1897) 41 SJ 469 at 7.15; *Re Compañía Merabello San Nicholas SA*
[1973] Ch 75 at 2.129; *Re Eloc Electro-Optieck and Communicatie BV* [1982] Ch 43 at 2.129.
[26] See 6.129–6.138 and 6.151–6.157.
[27] IA 1986, s 144(1). Applied to bank insolvency by the Banking Act 2009, s 103(3), (4) and table, and
to building society insolvency by the Building Societies Act 1986, s 90C. Custody (of tangible property) or
control (of intangible property) pass to the liquidator by virtue of IA 1986, s 144(1), without any need for
action on the liquidator's part (*Katz v Bradney* [2012] EWHC 1018 (Ch), [2013] Bus LR 169).
[28] IA 1986, s 143(1).
[29] See 1.498.
[30] IA 1986, s 136(1) and (2).
[31] IA 1986, s 137.
[32] IA 1986, s 139.
[33] IA 1986, s 140.
[34] Joint Stock Companies Act 1856, s 88; Companies Act 1862, s 92.
[35] Joint Stock Companies Act 1856, s 104; Companies Act 1862, s 133.
[36] Companies (Winding up) Act 1890, s 4, which introduced the present rule in IA 1986, s 136(1) and (2),
that the official receiver becomes liquidator of a company on the making of a winding-up order.
[37] Corporations Act 2001 (Australia), s 472.
[38] Companies Law (2013 Revision) (Cayman Islands), s 105.

1.19 The official receiver is not involved in a bank or building society insolvency. Instead the bank or building society insolvency order appoints a liquidator (known as a bank liquidator or building society liquidator as appropriate).[39]

Objectives of bank and building society insolvency

1.20 A bank or building society liquidator has two objectives. Objective 1 is to work with the Financial Services Compensation Scheme (FSCS) so as to ensure that as soon as is reasonably practicable each eligible depositor[40] has the relevant account transferred to another financial institution or receives payment from (or on behalf of) the FSCS.[41] Objective 2 is to wind up the institution's affairs so as to achieve the best result for its creditors as a whole.[42] A bank or building society liquidator must begin working towards both objectives immediately upon appointment, but objective 1 takes precedence over objective 2[43] until the liquidation committee[44] passes a full payment resolution. A full payment resolution is a resolution that objective 1 has been achieved entirely or so far as is reasonably practicable.[45]

1.21 *Investigation of the company's affairs*

> But I reject the unspoken assumption that the functions of a liquidator are limited to the administration of the insolvent estate. This is only one aspect of an insolvency proceeding; the investigation of the causes of the company's failure and the conduct of those concerned in its management are another. Furthermore such an investigation is not undertaken as an end in itself, but in the wider public interest with a view to enabling the authorities to take appropriate action against those who are found to be guilty of misconduct in relation to the company.[46]

1.22 Investigation of the company's affairs is an important part of the duties of a liquidator of a company. In a winding up of a company by the court, the official receiver has a duty to investigate the promotion, formation, business, dealings and affairs of the company, and, if the company has failed, the causes of the failure.[47] The official receiver may, if he or she thinks fit, make a report to the court on these matters.[48] The official receiver must report to the Secretary of State if it appears that, as respects a person who is or has been a director of the company, the conditions for making a disqualification order are satisfied.[49] It is the duty of a liquidator who is not the official receiver to furnish information reasonably required by the official receiver, and allow the official receiver to inspect books, papers and other records, so as:

(a) to assist the official receiver in carrying out his or her functions in relation to the winding up;[50] and

---

[39] Banking Act 2009, s 94(1). Applied to building society insolvency by the Building Societies Act 1986, s 90C.
[40] Eligible depositors are depositors who are eligible for compensation under the FSCS (Banking Act 2009, s 93(2) and (3)). All provisions of the Banking Act 2009 cited in 1.20 are applied to building society insolvency by the Building Societies Act 1986, s 90C.
[41] Banking Act 2009, s 99(2).
[42] Banking Act 2009, s 99(3).
[43] Banking Act 2009, s 99(4).
[44] Which must be established under s 100.
[45] s 100(5)(a).
[46] Lord Millett in *Re Pantmaenog Timber Co Ltd* [2003] UKHL 49, [2004] 1 AC 158, at [64].
[47] IA 1986, s 132(1).
[48] IA 1986, s 132(1).
[49] Company Directors Disqualification Act 1986, s 7(3).
[50] IA 1986, s 143(2).

(b) to assist the official receiver to determine whether a director disqualification report
should be made.[51]

The official receiver is not involved in a bank or building society insolvency and so these **1.23**
provisions do not apply.

It is the duty of a liquidator who is not the official receiver to report to the official receiver if **1.24**
it appears that any past or present officer, or any member, of the company has been guilty of
any criminal offence in relation to the company.[52] In a bank insolvency, the bank liquidator
must report such suspicions to the Secretary of State.[53] In a building society insolvency the
building society liquidator must report such suspicions to the Secretary of State, who may
refer the matter to the Financial Conduct Authority (FCA) or the Prudential Regulation
Authority (PRA) for further enquiry under the Building Societies Act 1986, s 55(1).[54]

Process of Winding Up

The court order for a company's winding up does not in itself wind up the company: it does **1.25**
no more than direct that the company be wound up.[55] A winding-up by the court has been
described as an administration by the court.[56] A compulsory winding up, like a bankruptcy,
is wholly dependent on the court, and is controlled and administered by the court. It is for
the court to oversee the realization of the assets of the company and their distribution, on
the correct principles, among creditors and, where relevant, members,[57] but the acts which
IA 1986 requires to be carried out in order to wind up the company are to be performed
by the liquidator.[58] Powers of the court are delegated for exercise or performance by the
liquidator as an officer of the court, and subject to the court's control.[59] The court exercises
control and supervision of the liquidator, and exercises powers that are not delegated to the
liquidator, on applications[60] made in the winding-up proceedings. The court may remove
a liquidator.[61] In Australia, under the cooperative scheme of concurrent jurisdiction of
Supreme Courts and the Federal Court, all those courts may exercise control and supervision over the winding up of a company that has been ordered by one of them.[62]

In Australia it has been said that the steps or proceedings taken for the purpose of obtaining **1.26**
a court order that a company be wound up, which are what this work is concerned with,

---

[51] Company Directors Disqualification Act 1986, s 7(4).

[52] IA 1986, s 218(3).

[53] IA 1986, s 218(3), applied and modified by the Banking Act 2009, s 103(3), (4) and table.

[54] IA 1986, s 218(3), applied and modified by the Banking Act 2009, s 103(3), (4) and table, further
applied with modifications by the Building Societies Act 1986, s 90C, and the Building Societies (Insolvency
and Special Administration) Order 2009 (SI 2009/805), sch 1, para 13(6). One of the modifications is that
the provision does not apply in relation to offences committed by members of a building society acting in
that capacity.

[55] Per McPherson SPJ in *Re Crust 'n' Crumb Bakers (Wholesale) Pty Ltd* [1992] 2 QdR 76 at p 78; per
Branson J in *Commonwealth of Australia v Emanuel Projects Pty Ltd* (1996) 21 ACSR 36 at p 39; *Continental
Venture Capital Ltd v Amann Aviation Pty Ltd* [2001] NSWCA 476, 53 NSWLR 687.

[56] *Re Phoenix Oil and Transport Co Ltd (No 2)* [1958] Ch 565 at p 570 per Wynn-Parry J.

[57] *Donaldson v O'Sullivan* [2008] EWCA Civ 879, [2009] 1 WLR 924, per Lloyd LJ at [38].

[58] IA 1986, ss 143–146, 167 and 168.

[59] IA 1986, s 160.

[60] See 3.233–3.263.

[61] IA 1986, s 172.

[62] *Acton Engineering Pty Ltd v Campbell* (1991) 31 FCR 1; *Continental Venture Capital Ltd v Amann
Aviation Pty Ltd* [2001] NSWCA 476, 53 NSWLR 476; *Sihota v Pacific Sands Motel Pty Ltd* [2003] NSWSC
119, 56 NSWLR 721; *Maamari v Ringwood and Ply Pty Ltd* [2005] NSWSC 40, 52 ACSR 370.

are not part of the process of winding up, which does not start until a winding-up order is made.[63]

Winding Up a Company and Winding Up its Affairs or Business

1.27   In addition to powers specifically stated in IA 1986, sch 4, the liquidator of a company has power 'to do all such other things as may be necessary for winding up the company's affairs'[64] and a winding-up order occasions 'the winding up of the affairs' of a company.[65] Nevertheless, it is the company that is ordered to be wound up, not just its affairs.[66] An application to wind up a company is a proceeding against the company *in personam* not its property *in rem*.[67] These considerations were undoubtedly not in the mind of Patterson J in *Allen v Hanson*[68] when he said, at p 683, that the expressions 'winding up the business of the company' and 'the winding up of the company' were interchangeable and that the former was more apt when the company was incorporated outside the jurisdiction of the court which ordered winding up so that it would be beyond the court's power to order dissolution of the company. The equivalence of the two expressions was also the basis of the rejection by the Supreme Court of New Brunswick in *Re Cushing Sulphite Fibre Co Ltd*[69] of an argument that a winding-up order was invalid because it referred to the winding up of the company rather than the winding up of the business of the company.

1.28   In fact there is a difference between winding up a company's business and winding up a company. This became clear in cases concerning winding-up orders made under what is now the Trading with the Enemy Act 1939, s 3A(1). Such an order relates to winding up only the UK business of an enemy company, not the company itself.[70] In the winding up of a company's UK business there is no provision for distribution of any surplus after payment of creditors[71] as there is in the winding up of a company. Creditors whose debts do not arise out of transactions or dealings in relation to the UK business are not entitled to share in the distribution of the UK business's assets equally with creditors whose debts do arise out of that business[72] whereas they would share equally in the winding up of the company. In *Re Cedes Electric Traction Ltd*[73] proceedings in the winding up of a company were stayed so that its business could be wound up because the distribution of assets in the winding up of the business would be more favourable to British creditors than in a winding up of the company.

Dissolution

1.29   A registered company that has been wound up by the court is dissolved either:

---

[63] *Re Crust 'n' Crumb Bakers (Wholesale) Pty Ltd* [1992] QdR 76 per McPherson SPJ at p 78; *Joye v Beach Petroleum NL* (1996) 20 ACSR 525 per Beaumont and Lehane JJ at p 536. See 5.294–5.298.

[64] IA 1986, sch 4, para 13.

[65] *Re Oriental Bank Corporation* (1885) 54 LJ Ch 481.

[66] Per Lord Atkin in *Russian and English Bank v Baring Brothers and Co Ltd* [1936] AC 405 at p 426; per Wynn-Parry J in *Re Azoff-Don Commercial Bank* [1954] Ch 315 at pp 326–7; per Millett J in *Re International Tin Council* [1987] Ch 419 at p 446.

[67] *Re Colorado Silver Mining Co* (1884) 2 QLJ 21.

[68] (1890) 18 SCR 667.

[69] (1905) 37 NBR 254.

[70] See 9.93–9.97.

[71] *Re Fr Meyers Sohn Ltd* [1917] 2 Ch 201.

[72] *Re W Hagelberg AG* [1916] 2 Ch 503; *Re Vulcaan Coal Co* [1922] 2 Ch 60.

[73] [1918] 1 Ch 18.

(a) under IA 1986, s 202, following application to the registrar of companies by the official receiver as liquidator of the company, if it appears to the official receiver that the realizable assets of the company are insufficient to cover the expenses of winding up and that the affairs of the company do not require further investigation; or

(b) under s 205 following notification to the registrar of companies by the liquidator that the winding up is complete.

Dissolution of a registered company ends its separate legal personality and dissolves the **1.30** association between its members.

A partnership or unincorporated association may be said to be 'dissolved' as from the time **1.31** that its ending is decided on by the members or ordered by the court, and so the process of winding up the affairs of a partnership or unincorporated association may follow its 'dissolution'.

The fact that the court does not have jurisdiction to dissolve an entity other than a registered **1.32** company does not prevent the court ordering the winding up of the entity.[74]

Under s 205, dissolution does not occur until three months after the registrar has registered **1.33** the liquidator's notification that the winding up is complete. Nevertheless, the company is still 'being wound up' during those three months in that the winding up of the company continues despite completion of the winding up of its business.[75] After dissolution, though, a company is not being wound up[76] so dissolution is not an essential part of the winding-up process.

Death

In *Re Excelsior Textile Supply Pty Ltd*[77] Gillard J said, at p 578, that if a winding-up order is **1.34** made, 'it may be loosely described as ending in the capital punishment of the company'. In *Re a Company (No 00314 of 1989)*[78] Mummery J described a winding-up order as a death sentence. In *Re Hydrosan Ltd*[79] Harman J said, at p 421:

> ... if a winding-up order is made ... the company will suffer what I usually refer to as death, that is, its coming to an end and eventual dissolution.[80]

However, in *Irwin Toy Ltd v Quebec (Attorney General)*[81] it was held that s 7 of the Canadian **1.35** Charter of Rights and Freedoms, which states that 'Everyone has the right to life, liberty and security of the person and the right not to be deprived thereof except in accordance with the principles of fundamental justice', applies only to humans and not to corporations. 'To say that bankruptcy and winding-up proceedings engage s 7 would stretch the meaning of the right to life beyond recognition.'[82]

---

[74] *Re Matheson Brothers Ltd* (1884) 27 ChD 225; *Allen v Hanson* (1890) 18 SCR 667 per Patterson J at p 683.
[75] *Re Working Project Ltd* [1995] 1 BCLC 226.
[76] *Re NP Engineering and Security Products Ltd* [1998] 1 BCLC 208.
[77] [1964] VR 574.
[78] [1991] BCLC 154.
[79] [1991] BCLC 418.
[80] See his Lordship's remark in *Re Islington Metal and Plating Works Ltd* [1984] 1 WLR 14 at p 21 that 'In a liquidation an insolvent company inevitably ... dies; it is dissolved to use more formal language'.
[81] (1989) 58 DLR (4th) 577.
[82] Per Dickson CJC, Lamer and Wilson JJ at p 632.

Winding Up through Administration

Introduction

1.36 Legislation has made available various court orders which, though not winding-up orders or bank or building society insolvency orders, replace a company's directors with an independent insolvency office-holder who is at least capable of achieving the winding up of the company, that is, realizing its assets, distributing the proceeds to creditors (none of these procedures provide for a distribution to members) and having the company dissolved. The orders are various forms of administration order and the process may be described as winding up through administration. Winding up through administration is listed in Regulation (EC) No 1346/2000, annex B, as a winding-up proceeding in the United Kingdom.[83]

1.37 The official receiver is not involved in any of these procedures. There is no provision for misfeasance proceedings, other than against a present or former administrator or purported administrator, and there is no provision for making calls on or distributions to contributories.

Schedule B1 administration

1.38 An administration order under IA 1986, s 8, and sch B1, paras 10–13, is capable of achieving the winding up of a company[84] in a simple case. An administration order appoints a person as the administrator of a company[85] to manage the company's affairs, business and property.[86] An order cannot be made unless the company is, or likely to become, unable to pay its debts.[87] The court may not make an administration order in relation to a company unless it considers that the order is reasonably likely to achieve the purpose of administration.[88] In order to show that an administration order is reasonably likely to achieve the purpose of administration it is necessary to show that there is a real prospect that the purpose of administration will be achieved.[89]

1.39 The administrator of a company must perform his or her functions with the objective of:

    (a) rescuing the company as a going concern, or
    (b) achieving a better result for the company's creditors as a whole than would be likely if the company were wound up (without first being in administration), or
    (c) realising property in order to make a distribution to one or more secured or preferential creditors.

This is the 'purpose of administration'.[90]

1.40 An administrator who pursues objective (b) performs some functions which are characteristic of winding up a company. An administrator has the power to carry on the company's

---

[83] It was added by Council Regulation (EC) No 603/2005 as from 21 April 2005.
[84] For the scope of sch B1 administration see 1.242–1.244.
[85] IA 1986, sch B1, para 10.
[86] IA 1986, sch B1, para 1(1).
[87] IA 1986, sch B1, para 11(a). 'Likely' here means more likely than not (*Re AA Mutual International Insurance Co Ltd* [2004] EWHC 2430 (Ch), [2005] 2 BCLC 8). 'Unable to pay its debts' has the meaning given by s 123 (sch B1, para 111(1)).
[88] IA 1986, sch B1, para 11(b).
[89] *Re AA Mutual International Insurance Co Ltd; Hammonds v Pro-Fit USA Ltd* [2007] EWHC 1998 (Ch), [2008] 2 BCLC 159, at [24].
[90] IA 1986, sch B1, para 3(1).

business,[91] but this is not limited—as the equivalent power of a liquidator is—to carrying on the business only 'so far as may be necessary for [the company's] beneficial winding up'.[92] An administrator may make a distribution to creditors (but not members), though this requires the court's permission if creditors are neither secured nor preferential.[93] An administrator may cause the company to be dissolved.[94] However, an administrator cannot pursue objective (b) unless he or she thinks either:[95]

(a) that it is not reasonably practicable to achieve objective (a); or
(b) that objective (b) would achieve a better result for the company's creditors as a whole than objective (a).

On an application for an administration order, evidence that the order is reasonably likely   **1.41**
to achieve the purpose of administration[96] commonly shows that a particular objective can be achieved, but this cannot be used to characterize the order as being for that objective. Unless an administration order expressly limits the administrator to pursuing a particular objective, it is for the administrator to decide which objective to pursue and the administrator may alter that decision in the light of changing circumstances.[97] It follows, it is submitted, that, without such a limitation, an administration order cannot, when it is made, be an order for winding up through administration for the purposes of Regulation (EC) No 1346/2000.[98] The same applies, it is submitted, to the industry-specific administration regimes which are based on schedule B1 administration.[99] In each of these regimes, the purpose of administration specified in IA 1986, sch B1, is replaced by an objective appropriate to the particular industry.[100]

Conversion of a voluntary arrangement into winding up through administration
Under Regulation (EC) No 1346/2000, art 37, the court may order that a voluntary arrange-   **1.42**
ment in force for a company is converted into administration proceedings whose purposes are limited to the winding up of the company through administration and are to exclude the purpose contained in IA 1986, sch B1, para 3(1)(a) (rescuing the company as a going concern).[101] It would seem that this would be an order for winding up through administration for the purposes of Regulation (EC) No 1346/2000.

---

[91] IA 1986, sch B1, para 60, and sch 1, para 14.
[92] IA 1986, sch 4, para 5.
[93] IA 1986, sch B1, para 65.
[94] IA 1986, sch B1, para 84.
[95] IA 1986, sch B1, para 3(3).
[96] IA 1986, sch B1, para 11(b).
[97] *Key2Law (Surrey) LLP v De'Antiquis* [2011] EWCA Civ 1567, [2012] ICR 881, at [97]–[102].
[98] See *Key2Law (Surrey) LLP v De'Antiquis* (an administration order, when made, is not an order instituting proceedings which are analogous to bankruptcy proceedings and are instituted with a view to the liquidation of assets, for the purposes of Directive 2001/23/EC, art 5.1).
[99] See 1.262–1.294. In *Re MF Global UK Ltd* [2012] EWHC 3068 (Ch), [2013] 1 WLR 903, it was held that investment bank special administration is not 'analogous' to winding up.
[100] See, for example, Energy Act 2004, s 155, and sch 20, paras 1, 2, 3 and 4(f) (objective of an energy administration); Banking Act 2009, ss 137–140 (objectives of a bank administrator); Investment Bank Special Administration Regulations 2011 (SI 2011/245), regs 10–13 (objectives of investment bank special administration); SI 2011/245, sch 1, para 4 (objectives of special administration (bank insolvency)); SI 2011/245, sch 2, para 3 (objectives of special administration (bank administration)).
[101] IR 1986, r 1.31(1A)(a). See 10.11.

Sources of the Law on Winding Up Companies

1.43 Current Legislation

> [T]he court is dealing not with equities, but simply with statutes and rules. A liquidation is not necessarily fair.[102]

> The district judge was therefore motivated in refusing any relief on the official receiver's application by what he saw as the injustice of [provisions of IA 1986]. In my view that was an incorrect approach for him to have adopted in dealing with the application.[103]

> Mr Kaye for the Official Receiver has taken me through the Insolvency Act 1986, and the Insolvency Rules 1986 which I confess to find surprising and confusing.[104]

Insolvency Act 1986 (IA 1986)

1.44 The statute law on winding up companies is now contained principally in IA 1986, which came into force on 29 December 1986.[105]

1.45 IA 1986 is a consolidation Act, which was enacted in order to tidy up the statute book following the passing of an important amending Act, the Insolvency Act 1985. That Act amended the previous law contained in parts 18–25 of the Companies Act 1985. Apart from a few provisions which were brought into force earlier in 1986, the provisions of the Insolvency Act 1985 concerning company liquidation were brought into force on 29 December 1986[106] and were immediately replaced by IA 1986.

1.46 Transitional provisions in IA 1986, sch 11, ensure that, in general, a winding up commenced under earlier legislation continues to be governed by that legislation.

1.47 In a supplementary consolidation, a small group of sections from the Companies Act 1985 and the Insolvency 1985 were re-enacted in the Company Directors Disqualification Act 1986, which also came into force on 29 December 1986.[107]

1.48 The provisions of IA 1986 considered in this work extend to England and Wales and to Scotland,[108] but not to Northern Ireland.[109] The equivalent Northern Ireland provision is the Insolvency (Northern Ireland) Order 1989.[110] This work deals with all legislation as it applies in England and Wales.

Insolvent Partnerships Order 1994 (IPO 1994)

1.49 MR JUSTICE EVANS-LOMBE:....we now go to that dreadful piece of legislation, the Insolvent Partnerships Order. Hopefully it is going to be spirited away by the review of partnership law that is going to happen—

---

[102] Maugham J in *Re Beni-Felkai Mining Co Ltd* [1934] Ch 406.

[103] Blackburne J in *Official Receiver v Hollens* [2007] EWHC 753 (Ch), [2007] Bus LR 1402, at [24]–[25].

[104] Harman J in *Re a Company (No 001951 of 1987)* [1988] BCLC 182 at p 183. His Lordship was referring to rr 4.30 and 4.31, which were reworded a few months later by the Insolvency (Amendment) Rules 1987 (SI 1987/1919), sch, paras 43 and 44, without substantive change.

[105] IA 1986, s 443; Insolvency Act 1985 (Commencement No 5) Order 1986 (SI 1986/1924), art 3.

[106] SI 1986/1924, art 2.

[107] Company Directors Disqualification Act 1986, s 25.

[108] IA 1986, s 440.

[109] IA 1986, s 441.

[110] SI 1989/2405 (NI 19).

MR MANN: Not in the next 30 seconds.

MR JUSTICE EVANS-LOMBE: No, I am afraid not.[111]

IPO 1994 creates alternative texts of IA 1986 for use in the winding up of insolvent partner- **1.50**
ships. It applies IA 1986 to the winding up of insolvent partnerships with modifications
prescribed in IPO 1994, partly in the form of substituted provisions, partly by declaring
that certain provisions of the Act are to be applied in a particular way. It came into force on
1 December 1994, replacing the Insolvent Partnerships Order 1986.[112]

'Flat-pack' legislation, which has to be assembled by the user, such as the 1986 and 1994 **1.51**
IPOs and much of the legislation on bank and building society insolvency, is very inconven-
ient, as Evans-Lombe J made clear. The 1986 Order was described as 'somewhat tortuously
drafted' by Nicholls LJ in *Re Marr*.[113] In *Commissioners of Customs and Excise v Jack Baars
Wholesale*[114] Lindsay J complained of the difficulty of dealing with provisions which are not
in a readable form.[115]

IPO 1994 extends to England and Wales, and not to Scotland or Northern Ireland.[116] **1.52**

Banking Act 2009

The Banking Act 2009, part 2,[117] introduces the bank insolvency procedure, which is a **1.53**
modified form of winding up by the court, specially adapted to support the Financial
Services Compensation Scheme. Section 103 applies provisions of IA 1986 to bank insolvency with modifications.

Insolvency Rules 1986 (IR 1986)

Compulsory winding-up proceedings are taken under IA 1986, part 4 or part 5. IA 1986, **1.54**
s 411(1), provides for rules (called 'company insolvency rules' in the title of s 411) to be made
for the purpose of giving effect to parts 1–8[118] of the Act or Regulation (EC) No 1346/2000.
For England and Wales, rules are to be made by the Lord Chancellor with the concurrence of the Treasury and, in the case of rules that affect court procedure, the Lord Chief
Justice.[119] Without prejudice to the generality of the purpose of giving effect to the relevant
parts of IA 1986, rules may contain any such provision as is mentioned in sch 8. Paragraph
2(1) of sch 8 authorizes the inclusion in rules made under s 411 of:

> Provision for regulating the practice and procedure of any court exercising jurisdiction for
> the purposes of [IA 1986, ss 1–251] or the Companies Acts[120] so far as relating to, and to

---

[111] *Re D and D Marketing (UK) Ltd* [2002] EWHC 660 (Ch), [2003] BPIR 539. The review, by the Law
Commission and Scottish Law Commission, resulted in a report, *Partnership Law* (Cm 6015, Law Com
No 283, Scot Law Com No 192) (London: TSO, 2003). It would indeed have swept away IPO 1994, but the
government decided not to implement it.

[112] SI 1986/2142. The provisions of the 1986 Order were described in the first edition of this work.

[113] [1990] Ch 773 at p 780.

[114] [2004] EWHC 18 (Ch), [2004] BPIR 543, at [40].

[115] See also per Blackburne J in *Official Receiver v Hollens* [2007] EWHC 753 (Ch), [2007] Bus LR 1402,
at [29].

[116] IPO 1994, art 1(2).

[117] ss 90–135.

[118] ss 1–251.

[119] IA 1986, s 411(1). The obligation to consult the Lord Chief Justice was added by the Constitutional
Reform Act 2005, sch 4, para 188, with effect from 3 April 2006. Functions of the Lord Chief Justice may be
exercised by a judicial office-holder nominated by the Lord Chief Justice (IA 1986, s 411(7)).

[120] Meaning the Companies Acts (as defined in the Companies Act 2006, s 2) as they have effect in Great
Britain (IA 1986, s 436(1)).

matters connected with or arising out of, the . . . winding up of companies, being any provision that could be made by rules of court.

1.55 The Insolvency Rules 1986 (IR 1986)[121] have been made under the powers conferred by IA 1986, s 411(1). As well as companies winding up the rules deal with company voluntary arrangements, administration and administrative receivership. They are referred to in ss 1–251, as 'the rules'.[122] IR 1986 also include the individual insolvency rules, which are made under IA 1986, s 412 and sch 9, and which deal with individual voluntary arrangements, debt relief orders and bankruptcy. The provisions of IR 1986 have been extensively amended.

1.56 IR 1986 are more than just procedural regulations:[123] they enact substantive provisions of insolvency law[124] and add to the jurisdiction of the court by providing a power to review, rescind or vary its orders.[125]

1.57 Company insolvency rules are made after consultation with the Insolvency Rules Committee.[126] The Committee was established in 1976. Its members are judges and practitioners particularly concerned with insolvency matters.

Draft Insolvency Rules 2015 (draft IR 2015)

1.58 In 2006 the Insolvency Rules Committee started to review IR 1986 so as to consolidate, modernize and simplify the rules. It was intended that the new rules would come into force by the end of 2007.[127] This was wildly optimistic. A working draft of some of the new rules was put out for consultation on 26 September 2013.[128] Their working title is 'Insolvency Rules 2015' and they will be referred to as 'draft IR 2015' in this work. In June 2014 there was a stated intention to issue a further set of draft rules in early 2015 for consideration by the Committee and it was expected that the new rules would come into force in 2016.[129]

Application of the Insolvency Rules 1986

1.59 IR 1986, part 4, is devoted to companies winding up and r 4.2 states that the rules in part 4 apply whether a petition is presented under IA 1986, s 122(1) (which specifies circumstances in which the court may order the winding up of a registered company), 'or under any enactment enabling the presentation of a winding-up petition'.[130] They also apply whoever presents the petition.[131]

1.60 Where there is any conflict between IA 1986 and IR 1986, IA 1986 prevails.[132]

1.61 IR 1986 apply to England and Wales, and not to Scotland or Northern Ireland.[133]

---

[121] SI 1986/1925.
[122] IA 1986, s 251.
[123] *Poulton's Trustee v Ministry of Justice* [2010] EWCA Civ 392, [2011] Ch 1, at [70].
[124] For example, r 4.90 concerning set-off of mutual dealings and r 4.218 on priority of costs etc.
[125] r 7.47(1); see 6.14–6.43.
[126] IA 1986, s 413.
[127] 'The coming of age of the 1986 Act' (2006) 22 Insolv L & P 197.
[128] Insolvency Service, *Insolvency Rules 1986—Modernisation of Rules relating to Insolvency Law. Consultation.*
[129] Letter to Stakeholders dated 19 June 2014 from the Head of Policy, Insolvency Service.
[130] IR 1986, r 4.2(1).
[131] IR 1986, r 4.2(2).
[132] *Smith v Ian Simpson and Co* [2001] Ch 239 at p 252.
[133] IR 1986, r 0.3.

IR 1986 are applied, in more or less modified forms, to bank and building society insol- **1.62**
vency[134] and to the winding up of (and other insolvency proceedings in respect of) charitable
incorporated organizations,[135] insolvent partnerships,[136] limited liability partnerships[137]
and relevant schemes.[138]

Meaning of 'insolvency proceedings'

IR 1986, r 13.7, states that the term 'insolvency proceedings' means any proceedings under **1.63**
IA 1986 or under IR 1986. The term therefore includes winding-up proceedings taken
under IA 1986. However, IR 1986 were made only for the purposes of parts 1–11 of IA
1986,[139] so, despite what is said in r 13.7, proceedings under other parts of IA 1986 cannot
be 'insolvency proceedings' and IR 1986 do not apply to them.[140]

Bank Insolvency (England and Wales) Rules 2009 and Building Society Insolvency (England and Wales) Rules 2010

IA 1986, s 411(1A), provides for rules to be made to give effect to the Banking Act 2009, **1.64**
part 2 (bank insolvency orders), including that part as applied to building societies.[141] For
England and Wales, rules are to be made by the Lord Chancellor with the concurrence of
the Treasury and, in the case of rules that affect court procedure, the Lord Chief Justice.[142]
IA 1986, sch 8, applies to rules made under s 411(1A).[143] The rules that have been made
are the Bank Insolvency (England and Wales) Rules 2009[144] and the Building Society
Insolvency (England and Wales) Rules 2010.[145] Like IPO 1994 these Rules are in flat-pack
form giving instructions for the assembly of legislation by the user. They mostly adapt provisions of IR 1986 and expressly provide that the version of IR 1986 applied is that which
includes all amendments up to and including those made by the Insolvency (Amendment)
(No 2) Rules 2009.[146] This means that the very extensive revision of IR 1986 made by the
Insolvency (Amendment) Rules 2010[147] and the Insolvency (Amendment) (No 2) Rules
2010[148] has been ignored in the drafting of both the Bank Insolvency (England and Wales)
Rules 2009 and the Building Society Insolvency (England and Wales) Rules 2010. It is
sometimes suggested that the Interpretation Act 1978, s 20(2), requires a reference in
legislation A to a provision in legislation B to be read as referring to legislation B as amended

---

[134] See 1.64.
[135] See 1.122.
[136] See 1.145.
[137] See 1.126.
[138] See 1.168.
[139] IA 1986, ss 411(1) and 412(1).
[140] *Re Banco Nacional de Cuba* [2001] 1 WLR 2039 at p 2048 (IR 1986 do not apply to proceedings under
IA 1986, part 16); *Fourie v Le Roux* [2005] EWHC 922 (Ch), [2005] BPIR 779 (IR 1986 do not apply to
proceedings under IA 1986, s 426, which is in part 17).
[141] IA 1986, s 411(3A).
[142] IA 1986, s 411(1A). Functions of the Lord Chief Justice may be exercised by a judicial office-holder
nominated by the Lord Chief Justice (IA 1986, s 411(7)).
[143] IA 1986, s 411(2) and (2C).
[144] SI 2009/356.
[145] SI 2010/2581.
[146] SI 2009/2472. See the definition of 'the 1986 Rules' in SI 2009/356, r 3(2), and SI 2010/2581, r 3(2).
In the case of SI 2009/356, this point was added by the Bank Insolvency (England and Wales) (Amendment)
Rules 2010 (SI 2010/2579), rr 3 and 4(a)(i).
[147] SI 2010/686.
[148] SI 2010/734.

both before and after the enactment of legislation A.[149] It is submitted that, in the case of the Bank Insolvency (England and Wales) Rules 2009 and the Building Society Insolvency (England and Wales) Rules 2010, this is negatived by the express reference to the version of IR 1986 that is to be applied. In the commentary on the Bank Insolvency (England and Wales) Rules 2009 and the Building Society Insolvency (England and Wales) Rules 2010 in this work, both possibilities (reference is to IR 1986 either with or without subsequent amendments) are mentioned, because it is thought that the position is sufficiently uncertain to require the court's directions.

Civil Procedure Rules 1998 (CPR)

1.65 The Civil Procedure Rules 1998 (CPR)[150] do not apply to insolvency proceedings, except to the extent that they are applied to those proceedings by another enactment.[151] Various provisions of IR 1986 apply specific rules from the CPR to insolvency proceedings, and those particular rules apply with any necessary modifications, except so far as inconsistent with IR 1986.[152] The provisions applied are: CPR, r 2.8 (time),[153] r 3.1(2)(a) (power to extend or shorten time),[154] Part 6 (service of documents),[155] Part 18 (further information),[156] Part 29 (the multi-track),[157] Part 31 (disclosure and inspection of documents),[158] Part 37 (miscellaneous provisions about payments into court),[159] what are now rr 44.3 (basis of assessment) and 44.4 (factors to be taken into account in deciding the amount of costs),[160] Part 47 (procedure for detailed assessment of costs and default provisions)[161] and Part 52 (appeals).[162]

1.66 Some provisions of the CPR are expressly excluded from applying to insolvency proceedings. They are rr 6.30–6.47 (service of the claim form and other documents out of the jurisdiction),[163] rr 6.48–6.51 (service of documents from foreign courts or tribunals),[164] and

---

[149] See *Bennion on Statutory Interpretation*, 5th edn (London: LexisNexis, 2008), s 83. See also s 288 (presumption that updating construction to be given when a statute is to be regarded as always speaking). This view of the Interpretation Act 1978, s 20(2), cannot be used to impose a tax (*Willows v Lewis* [1982] STC 141).
[150] SI 1998/3132.
[151] CPR, r 2.1(2). This does not mean that winding-up proceedings are not civil proceedings (*Stubbs v Gonzales* [2005] UKPC 22, [2005] 1 WLR 2730).
[152] IR 1986, r 7.51A(1).
[153] IR 1986, r 12A.55(1).
[154] IR 1986, r 12A.55(2).
[155] IR 1986, rr 12A.16, 12A.17 and 12A.20. Rule 7.51A(1) states that CPR, Part 6, is applied except for rr 6.30–6.47 (service of the claim form and other documents out of the jurisdiction) and rr 6.48–6.51 (service of documents from foreign courts or tribunals). The statement that rr 6.30–6.47 are excluded is inconsistent with IR 1986, r 12A.20. It is unclear why CPR, r 6.52, which is also concerned with service of documents from foreign courts or tribunals, is not excluded. It seems that the statement of exclusions in IR 1986, r 7.51A(1), must be treated as merely (erroneously) descriptive and without substantive effect. It is treated as ineffective by PD Insolvency Proceedings 2014, para 6.7, and has been dropped from draft IR 2015. See 3.30 and 3.249–3.251.
[156] IR 1986, rr 7.60 and 9.2(3)(b).
[157] IR 1986, r 7.51A(3).
[158] IR 1986, r 7.60. Rule 7.51A(1) says that CPR, Part 31, is also applied by virtue of IR 1986, r 9.2, but that rule does not refer expressly to CPR, Part 31.
[159] IR 1986, r 7.59.
[160] IR 1986, r 7.34A(6), which still refers to the numbering of the rules in CPR, Part 44, as it was before 1 April 2013.
[161] IR 1986, r 7.34A(2)(a).
[162] IR 1986, r 7.49A (not r 7.49 as stated in r 7.51A(1)).
[163] IR 1986, r 7.51A(1). This is inconsistent with r 12A.20; see 1.65.
[164] IR 1986, r 7.51A(1). It is unclear why CPR, r 6.52, which covers the same topic, is not excluded.

all provisions for allocation questionnaires[165] and track allocation (because all insolvency proceedings must be allocated to the multi-track).[166]

All provisions of the CPR (including related practice directions) which are not either specifically applied or expressly excluded apply to proceedings under IA 1986 or IR 1986 with any necessary modifications, except so far as inconsistent with IR 1986.[167] This means that, for example, CPR, r 1.1 (the overriding objective), applies to insolvency proceedings,[168] as does r 40.12 (the slip rule),[169] but r 32.2 (evidence to be given orally unless otherwise ordered) does not apply, because it is inconsistent with IR 1986, r 7.7A (evidence to be given in writing unless otherwise ordered).[170] See also 2.9 of this work (application to winding-up petitions of CPR rules concerning statements of case) and 3.219 (security for costs). **1.67**

> The separate existence and intimidating bulk of the Insolvency Rules are in themselves strong indications that insolvency proceedings are significantly different from litigation conducted in accordance with the Rules of the Supreme Court.[171] In general, insolvency proceedings raise questions affecting not only the immediate parties to litigation, but also the financial interests of very many people who, while not parties to litigation, are vitally concerned in the efficient administration and winding up of the affairs of the insolvent company or of the bankrupt (as the case may be).[172]

PD Insolvency Proceedings

Practice Direction: Insolvency Proceedings (PD Insolvency Proceedings), came into effect on 26 April 1999, the same day as the CPR. A new version (PD Insolvency Proceedings 2014) came into force on 29 July 2014. It replaces all previous practice directions, practice statements and practice notes relating to insolvency proceedings, except PD 49B.[173] **1.68**

UNCITRAL Model Law

The UNCITRAL Model Law on Cross-Border Insolvency was adopted by UNCITRAL[174] on 30 May 1997 at its 30th session. The term 'Model Law' is used to describe a legislative document which is recommended to States for adoption, but they are under no treaty obligation to do so and may modify it if they wish. The UNCITRAL Model Law on Cross-Border Insolvency was recommended to States by the United Nations General Assembly on 15 December 1997.[175] The Insolvency Act 2000, s 14, authorized the Secretary of State to make regulations to give effect to the UNCITRAL Model Law, and this was eventually done in the Cross-Border Insolvency Regulations 2006.[176] Schedule 1 to those Regulations contains the Model Law with modifications to adapt it for application in Great Britain, and in that form it has the force of law in Great Britain.[177] **1.69**

---

[165] Allocation questionnaires have been replaced by directions questionnaires.

[166] IR 1986, r 7.51A(3).

[167] IR 1986, r 7.51A(2).

[168] *Phillips v Symes* [2006] EWHC 2595 (Ch), [2008] BPIR 212, at [8].

[169] *Re Brian Sheridan Cars Ltd* [1996] 1 BCLC 327.

[170] *Highberry Ltd v COLT Telecom Group plc* [2002] EWHC 2503 (Ch), [2003] 1 BCLC 290; *Hayes v Hayes* [2014] EWHC 2694 (Ch), LTL 16/6/2014.

[171] Now the CPR.

[172] Per Mummery J in *Re Busytoday Ltd* [1992] 1 WLR 683 at p 687.

[173] PD Insolvency Proceedings 2014, para 2.1.

[174] The United Nations Commission on International Trade Law.

[175] A/RES/52/158.

[176] SI 2006/1030. Equivalent provision has been made in Northern Ireland by the Cross-Border Insolvency Regulations 2007 (SR 2007/115).

[177] SI 2006/1030, reg 2(1).

1.70 In construing the Great Britain version of the UNCITRAL Model Law a court may[178] consider:

(a) the Model Law as adopted by UNCITRAL;
(b) documents of UNCITRAL and its working group relating to the preparation of the Model Law (*travaux préparatoires*);
(c) the Guide to the Enactment of the UNCITRAL Model Law (A/CN.9/442).

1.71 All these documents may be consulted at <http://www.uncitral.org>. Also at that website is a list of countries which have adopted legislation based on this Model Law.

1.72 Regulation (EC) No 1346/2000[179] has much in common with the UNCITRAL Model Law on Cross-Border Insolvency.

Regulation (EC) No 1346/2000

1.73 Regulation (EC) No 1346/2000 allocates jurisdiction over insolvency proceedings in the EU (apart from Denmark) and is considered at 1.361–1.407.

References in this work to legislation

1.74 In this work a reference to a provision of legislation is a reference to that provision as amended, unless the words 'as originally enacted' are used.

Case Law and Earlier Legislation

1.75 The present company winding-up procedures have been developed from those introduced in part 3[180] of the Joint Stock Companies Act 1856. Cases from the past are of great importance in interpreting the present law but they must be read in historical context. Although the outline of the statute law on petitioning for winding up companies has changed little since the Companies Act 1862, there have been changes of detail and changes in court organization and procedure which must be borne in mind when considering past cases. For the history of the winding-up legislation see 1.538–1.559. For the history of its coverage of various forms of business organization see 1.560–1.578. For the history of court jurisdiction see 1.579–1.587.

1.76 IA 1986 and IR 1986 have made many substantive changes in insolvency law. This is particularly noticeable in the provisions relating to bankruptcy, of which Nicholls LJ in *Re a Debtor (No 1 of 1987)*[181] said, at p 276:

> The new code has made many changes in the law of bankruptcy, and the court's task, with regard to the new code, must be to construe the new statutory provisions in accordance with the ordinary canons of construction, unfettered by previous authorities.

This statement was adopted, in a case on winding up a company, when considering a provision which applies to both bankruptcy and winding up, by Mummery J in *Re Busytoday Ltd*.[182] See also another bankruptcy case, *Smith v Braintree District Council*,[183] in which Lord Jauncey of Tullichettle listed the changes in specific provisions of bankruptcy law and

---

[178] SI 2006/1030, reg 2(2).
[179] See 1.73.
[180] ss 59–105.
[181] [1989] 1 WLR 271.
[182] [1992] 1 WLR 683 at pp 687–8.
[183] [1990] 2 AC 215.

in social views which justified construing the provision of IA 1986 which was in question in the case 'as a piece of new legislation without regard to 19th-century authorities or similar provisions of repealed Bankruptcy Acts'.[184] However, in relation to companies winding up IA 1986 and IR 1986 often use the same terminology and concepts as were used in earlier legislation and it is difficult to escape the assumption that Parliament reused that terminology and those concepts with the intention that they should be interpreted in the same way as before, unless the changed purposes and policies of the 1986 legislation show that a new meaning was intended.[185]

IA 1986 consolidated the statute law on both corporate and individual insolvency, which had **1.77** previously been dealt with in separate consolidations. It consolidates legislation from a number of diverse sources. Differences in the wording of sections of IA 1986 dealing with similar aspects of various insolvency procedures 'may just as well be accounted for by their different history and provenance as by an intention that they should have a different meaning or effect'.[186]

Law of other Jurisdictions

This work is concerned to set out in detail the law of England and Wales on applications **1.78** to wind up companies. The parts of IA 1986 relating to winding up companies extend to Scotland as well as to England and Wales.[187] However, procedures in the two jurisdictions are different and so IR 1986 do not extend to Scotland.[188] This work does not deal with Scots law in detail.

Company insolvency and liquidation legislation in Northern Ireland, the Republic of **1.79** Ireland and many Commonwealth countries is, or has been, largely modelled on the British legislation, both primary and secondary. Courts and lawyers in other Commonwealth jurisdictions typically pay considerable attention to English decisions on matters of company law, perhaps to a greater extent than English courts have been asked by counsel to consider Commonwealth decisions. Yet it is surely right, as Pearce LJ said in *Midland Silicones Ltd v Scruttons Ltd*,[189] that 'great common law jurisdictions should not lightly differ, more particularly on so universal a matter as commercial law'.

Entities which may be Wound Up: Introduction

An application for a winding-up order under IA 1986 cannot succeed unless the company or **1.80** other entity sought to be wound up is one of the entities which the Act gives the court power (jurisdiction) to wind up.[190] There is no inherent jurisdiction to wind up corporations,[191] but the High Court does have an inherent jurisdiction to dissolve and wind up unincorporated

---

[184] At pp 237–8.
[185] *Re a Debtor (No 784 of 1991)* [1992] Ch 554 per Hoffmann J at pp 558–9; *Re Modern Jet Support Centre Ltd* [2005] EWHC 1611 (Ch), [2005] 1 WLR 3880, at [22], [30] and [31]; *Poulton's Trustee v Ministry of Justice* [2010] EWCA Civ 392, [2011] Ch 1, at [68].
[186] *Donaldson v O'Sullivan* [2008] EWCA Civ 879, [2009] 1 WLR 924, per Lloyd LJ at [39].
[187] IA 1986, s 440.
[188] IR 1986, r 0.3.
[189] [1961] 1 QB 106 at p 128.
[190] *Re Herne Bay Pier Co, ex parte Burge* (1848) 1 De G & Sm 588 per Knight Bruce V-C at p 597 (referring to the Joint Stock Companies Winding-up Act 1848); *Davidson v Global Investments International Ltd* (1995) 19 ACSR 89.
[191] *Western Interstate Pty Ltd v Deputy Commissioner of Taxation (Cth)* (1995) 13 WAR 479; *Lunn v Cardiff Coal Co* [2002] NSWSC 1247, 171 FLR 430. Both cases declined to follow the suggestion in *Re Kalblue*

non-business associations.[192] It has been held that a statutory provision, giving the New South Wales Supreme Court 'all jurisdiction which may be necessary for the administration of justice in New South Wales',[193] allows that court to extend any statutory remedy to a case not covered by the statute.[194] It has been said that this can be applied to the statutory winding-up power.[195] This may be contrasted with the view of the English Court of Appeal that the High Court in England and Wales, despite being a court of general jurisdiction, does not have a power to make any order necessary to ensure that justice is done.[196]

1.81 Whether or not an entity is one over which the court has jurisdiction must be determined as at the date of presentation of the petition to wind it up.[197] The question must be determined in the light of the facts as they are, ignoring any estoppel.[198] Jurisdiction cannot be conferred by agreement of the parties.[199]

1.82 IA 1986, part 4, establishes the jurisdiction to wind up registered companies (referred to in the Act simply as 'companies').[200] Part 4 is applied by other legislation to the winding up of building societies,[201] charitable incorporated organizations,[202] European cooperative societies,[203] European public limited-liability companies,[204] incorporated friendly societies,[205] limited liability partnerships[206] and registered societies.[207] Part 5 is concerned with 'unregistered companies',[208] a term which has so far been found to cover a wide variety of entities[209] and can no doubt include many more as yet unknown. Modified versions of part 5 apply to insolvent partnerships.[210] Despite the wide range of these provisions the courts have decided that certain kinds of entity cannot be wound up under IA 1986 and legislation removes some entities from the jurisdiction.[211]

Pty Ltd (1994) 12 ACLC 1057 that there is such an inherent jurisdiction. The arguments advanced in *Re Kalblue Pty Ltd* are repeated by Ashley K Ehlers, 'Inherent equitable jurisdiction and the plenary power of the Supreme Court of New South Wales to order the winding up of companies' (2010) 18 Insolv LJ 52.

[192] See 1.345–1.346.
[193] Supreme Court Act 1970 (New South Wales), s 23.
[194] *Re Aldex Distributors Pty Ltd, ex parte Butterell* (1994) 12 ACLC 489 (Young J), not followed in Western Australia because there was no similar provision in the Supreme Court Act 1935 (Western Australia) (*Re Nilant* [2004] WASC 7, 28 WAR 81).
[195] *Re Kalblue Pty Ltd* (1994) 12 ACLC 1057 (Young J); *Re Botar-Tatham Pty Ltd* [2001] NSWSC 613, 52 NSWLR 680, per Young CJ in Eq at [22]; *Edwards v Attorney General* [2004] NSWCA 272, 60 NSWLR 667, per Young CJ at [63]; Ashley K Ehlers, 'Inherent equitable jurisdiction and the plenary power of the Supreme Court of New South Wales to order the winding up of companies' (2010) 18 Insolv LJ 52.
[196] *Wicks v Wicks* [1999] Fam 65 at pp 76–8 and 88–9.
[197] *Re Hercules Insurance Co* (1871) LR 11 Eq 321.
[198] *Re National Debenture and Assets Corporation* [1891] 2 Ch 505 per Kekewich J at p 510; *Re C and M Ashberg* (1990) *The Times*, 17 July 1990; *Lunn v Cardiff Coal Co* at [31].
[199] *Re C and M Ashberg.*
[200] See 1.85–1.114.
[201] See 1.120–1.121.
[202] See 1.122.
[203] See 1.123.
[204] See 1.124.
[205] See 1.125.
[206] See 1.126.
[207] See 1.127–1.129.
[208] See 1.130–1.220.
[209] See 1.137–1.138.
[210] See 1.222–1.230.
[211] See 1.299–1.344.

The fact that legislative provisions concerning the winding up of registered companies also **1.83** apply to the other types of entity referred to in 1.82 is usually not mentioned in this work, unless there is a modification of a provision when it applies to other entities.

In particular cases, the winding-up jurisdiction of the courts in England and Wales is **1.84** affected by rules which allocate jurisdiction among EU States and between EU and European Free Trade Area (EFTA) States[212] and among parts of the United Kingdom.[213]

Registered Companies

Companies Registered in England and Wales

The most significant class of entities which may be wound up under IA 1986, as it applies **1.85** in England and Wales, consists of companies registered by the Registrar of Companies in England and Wales. These are referred to simply as 'companies' in IA 1986 and the winding-up provisions of the Act are drafted primarily with reference to them. In its application to England and Wales, IA 1986, part 4,[214] provides for the winding up of any company registered (or re-registered) by the Registrar of Companies in England and Wales on or after 14 July 1856. This follows, in a rather convoluted way, from subsections (1) and (2) of s 73 (the first section in part 4), which provides:

(1) This Part applies to the winding up of a company registered under the Companies Act 2006 in England and Wales or Scotland.
(2) The winding up may be either—
    (a) voluntary (see Chapters 2 to 5), or
    (b) by the court (see Chapter 6).

As will be explained at 1.87–1.104, the term 'a company registered under the Companies **1.86** Act 2006 in England and Wales or Scotland' includes any company registered in England and Wales or Scotland since 14 July 1856. The Companies Act 2006 also provides for registration in Northern Ireland,[215] but IA 1986 does not apply to, or in relation to, companies registered in Northern Ireland.[216] In particular, part 4 applies only to companies registered in England and Wales or Scotland.[217] In IA 1986, ss 1–251, 'the court', in relation to a company, means a court having jurisdiction to wind up the company.[218] The courts of England and Wales do not have jurisdiction to wind up companies registered in Scotland[219] or Northern Ireland.[220]

Meaning of 'Company Registered under the Companies Act 2006'

UK-registered companies

In IA 1986, part 4, the term 'company' has a wider meaning than it has in the Companies **1.87** Acts. IA 1986, part 4, applies to any company that is 'registered under the Companies Act

---

[212] See 1.347–1.418.
[213] See 1.419–1.432.
[214] ss 73–219.
[215] Companies Act 2006, ss 9(6) and 1299.
[216] IA 1986, s 441(2).
[217] s 73(1).
[218] IA 1986, s 251. See 1.419–1.432 and 1.443–1.478.
[219] See 1.420–1.422.
[220] See 1.423–1.424.

2006 in England and Wales or Scotland'.[221] A company is registered under the Companies Act 2006 if it is a company formed and registered under the Companies Act 2006[222] or if it is a company registered, but not formed, under the Companies Act 2006.[223] In the Companies Acts, a company which is registered under the Companies Act 2006 is called a 'UK-registered company',[224] but only a company formed and registered under the Companies Act 2006 is called a 'company'.[225]

Companies formed and registered under Companies Acts since 1856

1.88 The Companies Act 2006, part 2,[226] provides for companies to be formed and registered under the 2006 Act.

1.89 Companies could be formed and registered in England and Wales or Scotland under the Companies Act 1985, part 1, ch 1,[227] as from 1 July 1985. Formation and registration of a company under the Companies Act 1985 have effect as if done under the Companies Act 2006,[228] and the reference in IA 1986, s 73(1), to companies registered under the Companies Act 2006 includes companies treated as so registered.[229]

1.90 The Companies Act 1985, s 735, defined what was an 'existing company' for the purposes of that Act:

> (1) ...
>> (b) 'existing company' means a company formed and registered under the former Companies Acts, but does not include a company registered under the Joint Stock Companies Acts, the Companies Act 1862 or the Companies (Consolidation) Act 1908 in what was then Ireland;
>> (c) 'the former Companies Acts' means the Joint Stock Companies Acts, the Companies Act 1862, the Companies (Consolidation) Act 1908, the Companies Act 1929 and the Companies Acts 1948 to 1983 ...
> (3) 'The Joint Stock Companies Acts' means the Joint Stock Companies Act 1856, the Joint Stock Companies Acts 1856, 1857, the Joint Stock Banking Companies Act 1857 and the Act to enable Joint Stock Banking Companies to be formed on the principle of limited liability,[230] or any one or more of those Acts (as the case may require), but does not include the Joint Stock Companies Act 1844.
> (4) The definitions in this section apply unless the contrary intention appears.

The reference in s 735(3) to 'the Joint Stock Companies Act 1856, the Joint Stock Companies Acts 1856, 1857' is tautologous, because 'the Joint Stock Companies Acts 1856, 1857' means the Joint Stock Companies Act 1856 and the Joint Stock Companies Act 1857.[231]

---

[221] IA 1986, s 73(1). See 1.85.
[222] See 1.88–1.97.
[223] See 1.98–1.102.
[224] Companies Act 2006, s 1158.
[225] Companies Act 2006, s 1(1).
[226] ss 7–16.
[227] Repealed on 1 October 2009 by the Companies Act 2006, sch 16, and the Companies Act 2006 (Commencement No 8, Transitional Provisions and Savings) Order 2008 (SI 2008/2860), art 4 and sch 1, part 1, without affecting any application for registration received by the registrar before 1 October 2009 (SI 2008/2860, sch 2, para 2(3)).
[228] Companies Act 2006, s 1297(1)–(3). See also the words in parentheses at the end of s 1(1)(b).
[229] Companies Act 2006 (Consequential Amendments, Transitional Provisions and Savings) Order 2009 (SI 2009/1941), art 3.
[230] 21 & 22 Vict, c 91.
[231] By s 2 of the 1857 Act.

Before 1 July 1985, companies were registered under the Companies Act 1948, which came **1.91**
into force on 1 July 1948.

From 1 November 1929 to 30 June 1948, companies could be registered under the **1.92**
Companies Act 1929.

From 1 April 1909 to 31 October 1929, companies could be registered under the Companies **1.93**
(Consolidation) Act 1908.

From 2 November 1862 to 31 March 1909, companies could be registered under the **1.94**
Companies Act 1862.

From 14 July 1856 to 1 November 1862, companies could be registered under the Joint **1.95**
Stock Companies Act 1856, though, by virtue of s 2 of the 1856 Act, banking companies
could not register until the Joint Stock Banking Companies Act 1857 came into force, and
insurance companies never could register under the 1856 Act (they were allowed to register
under the Companies Act 1862 and subsequent Acts). Insurance companies were excluded
from the 1856 Act so as to prevent them being registered with limited liability.

The Companies Act 1985 applied to existing companies as if they had been formed and **1.96**
registered under the Companies Act 1985, part 1.[232] So their formation and registration
now have effect as if done under the Companies Act 2006,[233] and the reference in IA 1986,
s 73(1), to companies registered under the Companies Act 2006 includes companies treated
as so registered.[234]

These provisions deal with companies which have been both registered and formed under **1.97**
the companies legislation since 14 July 1856. They mean that such companies can be wound
up as registered companies under IA 1986, part 4.[235]

Companies registered, but not formed, under Companies Acts since 1856

Since 1856 the companies legislation has provided that a company formed otherwise than **1.98**
under that legislation (an unregistered company) can register and become a registered company. Registration of a company formed otherwise than under the companies legislation
could formerly be effected under the Joint Stock Companies Act 1856, ss 110–116; the Joint
Stock Companies Act 1857, s 29; the Joint Stock Banking Companies Act 1857, s 4; the
Companies (Consolidation) Act 1908, ss 249–266; the Companies Act 1929, ss 321–336;
the Companies Act 1948, ss 382–397; and the Companies Act 1985, ss 680–690.

Registration under the Companies Act 1985, ss 680–690, now has effect as if it was registra- **1.99**
tion under the Companies Act 2006,[236] and the reference in IA 1986, s 73(1), to companies
registered under the Companies Act 2006 includes companies treated as so registered.[237]

---

[232] Companies Act 1985, s 675.
[233] Companies Act 2006, s 1297(1)–(3); Companies Act 2006 (Commencement No 8, Transitional
Provisions and Savings) Order 2008 (SI 2008/2860), sch 2, para 1(2)(a). See also the words in parentheses
at the end of s 1(1)(b).
[234] Companies Act 2006 (Consequential Amendments, Transitional Provisions and Savings) Order 2009
(SI 2009/1941), art 3.
[235] *Re Torquay Bath Co* (1863) 32 Beav 581; *Re London Indiarubber Co* (1866) LR 1 Ch App 329. The treatment of a company registered under the Joint Stock Companies Acts 1856, 1857 as an unregistered company
in *Re Great Ship Co Ltd, Parry's Case* (1863) 4 De G J & S 63 would appear to have been mistaken.
[236] Companies Act 2006, s 1297(1)–(3).
[237] Companies Act 2006 (Consequential Amendments, Transitional Provisions and Savings) Order 2009
(SI 2009/1941), art 3.

Registration under the earlier provisions listed at 1.98 took effect under the Companies Act 1985 as if it was registration under that Act,[238] and so now has effect as if it was registration under the Companies Act 2006,[239] and the reference in IA 1986, s 73(1), to companies registered under the Companies Act 2006 includes companies treated as so registered.[240]

1.100 Registration of a company formed otherwise than under the Companies Act 2006 may now be effected under ss 1040–1042 of the 2006 Act and the Companies (Companies Authorised to Register) Regulations 2009.[241] The Companies Act 2006 applies to a company registered under these provisions in the same manner as if it had been formed and registered under the 2006 Act.[242]

1.101 These provisions mean that such companies can be wound up as registered companies under IA 1986, part 4.[243]

1.102 When an unregistered company has registered, it is still the same company and so, in order to wind it up compulsorily, only one petition under IA 1986, part 4, is required: it is not necessary to petition separately for the winding up of the company in its unregistered form.[244]

Re-registration of registered joint stock companies and registration of chartered banks

1.103 The first Act enabling incorporation of companies by registration was the Joint Stock Companies Act 1844, which permitted registration as from 1 November 1844 (though it did not apply in Scotland). The system under the 1844 Act was very different from that under the 1856 Act and its successors. Accordingly, all companies registered under the 1844 Act were required to re-register under the 1856 Act on or before 3 November 1856,[245] though this was later extended to 2 November 1857 by the Joint Stock Companies Act 1857, ss 25–27. Insurance companies registered under the 1844 Act were excluded from re-registering under the 1856 Act but were required to re-register under the Companies Act 1862. Banking companies were not allowed to register under the 1844 Act, and the Joint Stock Banks Act 1844 prevented any association of more than six persons setting up a banking business without obtaining a royal charter of incorporation under the Act. All banks so chartered were required to convert themselves into registered companies by the Joint Stock Banking Companies Act 1857, s 4.

1.104 Any such company still in existence will be a company registered but not formed under the Companies Act 2006.[246]

Dissolved Registered Companies

1.105 The court does not have jurisdiction to order the compulsory winding up of a company which has been dissolved and removed from the register under IA 1986, s 201, following

---

[238] Companies Act 1985, s 676.
[239] Companies Act 2006, s 1297(1)–(3); Companies Act 2006 (Commencement No 8, Transitional Provisions and Savings) Order 2008 (SI 2008/2860), sch 2, para 1(2)(b).
[240] Companies Act 2006 (Consequential Amendments, Transitional Provisions and Savings) Order 2009 (SI 2009/1941), art 3.
[241] SI 2009/2437.
[242] SI 2009/2437, reg 18.
[243] *Re Torquay Bath Co* (1863) 32 Beav 581 at p 585.
[244] *Re Plumstead, Woolwich and Charlton Consumers Pure Water Co* (1860) 2 De G F & J 20; see also *Re Old Swan and West Derby Permanent Benefit Building Society* (1887) 57 LT 381 discussed at 6.51.
[245] Joint Stock Companies Act 1856, s 110.
[246] See 1.98–1.102.

voluntary winding up, if the company has not been restored to the register.[247] Provision for the restoration of dissolved companies to the register was introduced by the Companies Act 1907, s 31(2).[248] Before then it was suggested by James LJ that the court had power to declare that the winding up of a dissolved company was null and void in a case of fraud.[249] For an unsuccessful attempt to make out such a case, see *Re Schooner Pond Coal Co*.[250]

The court may, however, order the winding up of a company which has been struck off the register and dissolved by the registrar under the Companies Act 2006, s 1000(4)–(6) or s 1001(2)–(4).[251] Sections 1000(7)(b) and 1001(5)(b)[252] expressly provide that nothing in s 1000 or s 1001 affects the power of the court to wind up a company the name of which has been struck off the register. However, as all the property of a company dissolved under either of those sections will, under s 1012,[253] have devolved to the Crown or the duchies of Cornwall or Lancaster as though it were *bona vacantia*, there will be nothing to wind up unless the company is first restored to the register under ss 1024–1034[254] so that its property (or monetary equivalent) can be returned to it.[255] It is questionable whether a dissolved company which has not been restored to the register should be regarded as a registered company or an unregistered company. The point was not at issue in *Alliance Heritable Security Co Ltd*[256] and *Re Thompson and Riches Ltd*,[257] because the companies sought to be wound up in those cases had not been dissolved when the petitions were presented.[258] The reports of *Re Anglo-American Exploration and Development Co*[259] and *Re Waterford Improved Dwellings Co Ltd*[260] do not mention whether they were wound up as registered or unregistered companies. **1.106**

Validity of Registration

It is submitted that doubts about the validity of the registration of a company cannot affect the jurisdiction to wind it up as a registered company because the company's certificate **1.107**

---

[247] *Re Pinto Silver Mining Co* (1878) 8 ChD 273; *Re London and Caledonian Marine Insurance Co* (1879) 11 ChD 140.

[248] Last re-enacted as the Companies Act 1985, s 651. As from 1 October 2009, new provision is made by the Companies Act 2006, ss 1024–1034.

[249] *Re Pinto Silver Mining Co* at pp 283–4; *Re London and Caledonian Marine Insurance Co* at p 144.

[250] [1888] WN 70.

[251] *Alliance Heritable Security Co Ltd* (1886) 14 R 34 (in which the dissolution had occurred after the petition was presented); *Re Anglo-American Exploration and Development Co* [1898] 1 Ch 100; *Re Phoenix Extended Gold Mines Ltd (No 2)* [1903] StR Qd 183; *Re Waterford Improved Dwellings Co Ltd* [1934] IR 631; *Re Thompson and Riches Ltd* [1981] 1 WLR 682 (in which the dissolution occurred after the petition was presented and was declared to have been void after the winding-up order was made); *Re Williams United Mines Pty Ltd* (1992) 29 NSWLR 88. Provision for striking off and dissolution by the registrar was first made by the Companies Act 1880, s 7(4). The current provisions are applied in modified form (with no change to the numbering of the relevant subsections) to limited liability partnerships by the Limited Liability Partnerships (Application of Companies Act 2006) Regulations 2009 (SI 2009/1804), reg 50.

[252] First enacted in the Companies Act 1928, sch 2, as an amendment to the Companies (Consolidation) Act 1908, s 242(5).

[253] Applied in modified form to limited liability partnerships by SI 2009/1804, reg 52.

[254] Applied in modified form to limited liability partnerships by SI 2009/1804, regs 56–58.

[255] *Re Albion Machine Co* [1929] 1 DLR 274; *Re Cambridge Coffee Room Association* [1952] 1 All ER 112; *Re Thompson and Riches Ltd* [1981] 1 WLR 682.

[256] (1886) 14 R 34.

[257] [1981] 1 WLR 682.

[258] Which is the point at which status as registered or unregistered is significant: see 1.81.

[259] [1898] 1 Ch 100.

[260] [1934] IR 631.

of incorporation is conclusive evidence that the requirements of the Companies Act 2006 in respect of registration have been complied with, and that the company is duly registered under the Act.[261]

1.108 Up to 1900, the legislation stated only that a certificate of incorporation was evidence of compliance with the requirements of the Companies Act 1862, not that the company was duly registered.[262] Under that earlier legislation, courts had considered it necessary to determine whether a company was validly registered in order to determine whether there was jurisdiction to wind it up.[263] In *Re Hertfordshire Brewery Co*[264] it seems to have been conceded that the registration of a company already in voluntary winding up had been void because one of the subscribers of its memorandum of association was a minor and, on an application for directions by the voluntary liquidator, Jessel MR suggested that the company should be wound up as an unregistered company, and subsequently made a winding-up order on the petition of a creditor. It seems that in fact the registration was not improper, for when the point was argued in *Re Nassau Phosphate Co*[265] and *Re Laxon and Co (No 2)*,[266] it was held that signature of a memorandum of association by a minor is valid unless the minor has repudiated the signature before registration. All the cases mentioned so far in 1.108 were heard before the Privy Council asserted the importance of the conclusiveness of a company's certificate of incorporation in *Moosa Goolam Ariff v Ebrahim Goolam Ariff.*[267]

1.109 In *Re Dallas Horse Repository Co Ltd*[268] it was held, without reference to the certificate of incorporation, that once a company had in fact been registered it could be wound up as a registered company even if its registration was erroneous.

1.110 A company's registration can be annulled in judicial review proceedings brought by the Attorney General because the Companies Act 2006, s 15(4), does not bind the Crown.[269] For an example, see *R v Registrar of Companies, ex parte Attorney General.*[270] After annulment of a company's registration, it is submitted that it may be wound up as an unregistered company.

Effect of Events outside the Jurisdiction

Business outside the jurisdiction

1.111 A company registered in England and Wales may be wound up by the court in England and Wales even though in fact its business is carried on outside the jurisdiction.[271] If the winding up is on the ground of insolvency, this is subject to Regulation (EC) No 1346/2000.[272]

---

[261] Companies Act 2006, s 15(4).

[262] Companies Act 1862, s 18, replaced, as from 1 January 1901, by the Companies Act 1900, s 1(1).

[263] *Re Northumberland and Durham District Banking Co* (1858) 2 De G & J 357; *Princess of Reuss v Bos* (1871) LR 5 HL 176; *Re Australian Banking Co of Sydney* (1891) 12 LR (NSW) Eq 237. In all these cases, it was held that the company was properly registered.

[264] (1874) 43 LJ Ch 358.

[265] (1876) 2 ChD 610.

[266] [1892] 3 Ch 555.

[267] (1912) 28 TLR 505.

[268] (1910) 5 HKLR 194.

[269] Per Lord Parker of Waddington in *Bowman v Secular Society Ltd* [1917] AC 406 at pp 438–40 and in *Cotman v Brougham* [1918] AC 514 at p 519; *R v Registrar of Companies, ex parte Central Bank of India* [1986] QB 1114.

[270] [1991] BCLC 476.

[271] *Re Madrid and Valencia Railway Co, ex parte Turner* (1850) 2 Mac & G 169; *Princess of Reuss v Bos* (1871) LR 5 HL 176; *Re Lower Rooderpoort Ltd* (1897) 3 IWLR 250; *Re Stewart and Matthews Ltd* (1916) 26 Man R 277.

[272] See 1.113.

Registered office outside the jurisdiction

A company registered in England and Wales may be wound up by the court in England and **1.112**
Wales even though its registered office is, wrongly, outside the jurisdiction.[273] If the winding up is on the ground of insolvency, this is subject to Regulation (EC) No 1346/2000.[274]

Centre of main interests in another EU State

If the centre of main interests (COMI) of an insolvent company registered in England **1.113**
and Wales is in another EU State (other than Denmark), the courts of that other State
have exclusive jurisdiction under Regulation (EC) No 1346/2000, art 3(1), to open main
insolvency proceedings in respect of the company. Proceedings for winding up by the court
in any part of the United Kingdom, on the ground of insolvency, would be secondary or
territorial proceedings, which may be opened only if the company has an establishment
in the UK,[275] and the rules discussed at 1.419–1.432 will determine the part of the UK in
which the proceedings may be opened. If a company's registered office is in an EU State
other than the United Kingdom (or Denmark), its COMI is presumed to be in the State
where the registered office is located.[276]

Winding up outside the jurisdiction

An order made by a court outside England and Wales for the winding up of a company **1.114**
formed under the law of England and Wales does not affect the company's status in England
and Wales: it does not mean that the company is being wound up compulsorily in England
and Wales.[277] Subject to Regulation (EC) No 1346/2000[278] and the rules discussed at
1.419–1.432, it may be wound up by the court in England and Wales.[279]

Registered Companies which are Members of Insolvent Partnerships ('Corporate Members')

A registered company which is a member of an insolvent partnership is called a 'corporate **1.115**
member'.[280]

IPO 1994, art 8, provides a special procedure for petitioning for the winding up of a present **1.116**
or former corporate member of an insolvent partnership, in its capacity as such, and for the
winding up of the partnership itself as an unregistered company. An application to wind up
a corporate member under art 8 is, by art 8(4), (8) and (9), governed by the provisions of IA
1986, part 4, in so far as they relate to winding up of companies by the court in England and
Wales on a creditor's petition and as modified by IPO 1994, sch 4, part 2.

IPO 1994, art 10, provides a special procedure by which a member of an insolvent partner- **1.117**
ship can petition for the winding up of the partnership, as an unregistered company, and for
the winding up or bankruptcy of all its members in their capacity as such. An application

---

[273] *Re Baby Moon (UK) Ltd* (1984) 1 BCC 99,298.
[274] See 1.113.
[275] Regulation (EC) No 1346/2000, art 3(2).
[276] Regulation (EC) No 1346/2000, art 3(1); *Interedil Srl v Fallimento Interedil Srl* (case C-396/09) [2012] Bus LR 1582.
[277] *North Australian Territory Co v Goldsbrough, Mort and Co Ltd* (1889) 61 LT 716.
[278] See 1.113.
[279] *Re Suresnes Racecourse Co Ltd* (1890) 90 LT Jo 55; *Re Stewart and Matthews Ltd* (1916) 26 Man R 277; *Re Lancelot Investors Fund Ltd* 2009 CILR 7.
[280] IPO 1994, art 2(1).

to wind up a corporate member under art 10 is, by art 10(2), (3) and (6), governed by the provisions of IA 1986, part 4, in so far as they relate to winding up of companies by the court in England and Wales on a member's petition and as modified by IPO 1994, sch 4, part 2.

1.118 Trying to make the modifications in sch 4, part 2, apply to both art 8 and art 10 petitions is not always straightforward.

1.119 The court has jurisdiction to wind up a corporate member of an insolvent partnership on an application under art 8 or art 10 if it has jurisdiction in respect of the partnership.[281]

Entities Treated as Registered Companies

Building Societies

1.120 The Building Societies Act 1986, s 86(1), provides that a building society incorporated (or deemed to be incorporated) under the Act[282] may be wound up by the court in accordance with part 10[283] of the Act. Winding up by the court is under what the Act calls 'the applicable winding-up legislation'.[284] By s 90 and sch 15, para 1, this means, in relation to England and Wales and Scotland, parts 4, 6, 7 and 12 of IA 1986 and, in so far as they relate to offences under any of those enactments, ss 430 and 432 of and sch 10 to IA 1986, as modified by the Building Societies Act 1986, sch 15. These provisions are to apply to the winding up of building societies as they apply to the winding up of companies limited by shares and registered under the Companies Act 2006 in England and Wales or Scotland.[285]

1.121 In *Re Grosvenor House Property Acquisition and Investment Building Society*[286] the court ordered the winding up of a building society whose registration had been cancelled under what is now the Building Societies Act 1986, s 103(2)(b) (cancellation where the Financial Conduct Authority is satisfied that the society has ceased to exist).

Charitable Incorporated Organizations

1.122 IA 1986, part 4 (but not part 5), is applied to charitable incorporated organizations (CIOs) by the Charitable Incorporated Organisations (Insolvency and Dissolution) Regulations 2012,[287] sch, para 1(1) and (2)(a). So CIOs are wound up as if they were registered, not unregistered, companies. IA 1986, part 4, is applied to CIOs as it applies to companies registered in England and Wales and as modified by SI 2012/3013, sch. IR 1986 are applied with any necessary modifications to give effect to the applied provisions of IA 1986.[288] Where there is any conflict between IR 1986 and SI 2012/3013, the 2012 Regulations prevail.[289]

---

[281] See 1.146–1.149 and 1.431–1.432. IA 1986, s 117(5), as modified by IPO 1994, sch 4, para 5 (applications under art 8); IA 1986, s 117(5), as modified by IPO 1994, sch 6, para 1 (applications under art 10).
[282] See the definition of 'building society' in the Building Societies Act 1986, s 119(1).
[283] ss 86–103.
[284] s 89(1).
[285] Building Societies Act 1986, sch 15, para 2.
[286] (1902) 71 LJ Ch 748.
[287] SI 2012/3013.
[288] SI 2012/3013, sch, para 2(1) and (3)(a).
[289] SI 2012/3013, sch, para 2(2).

European Cooperative Societies

A European cooperative society (SCE) is governed by the legal provisions regarding winding up which would apply to a cooperative formed in accordance with the law of the European Economic Area (EEA) member State in which its registered office is situated.[290] The United Kingdom government considers that in the UK this is the law relating to registered societies.[291] So an SCE whose registered office is situated in Great Britain may be wound up under IA 1986, part 4, as if it were a registered company.

1.123

European Public Limited-Liability Companies

A European public limited-liability company (SE) is governed by the legal provisions regarding winding up which would apply to a public limited-liability company formed in accordance with the law of the EEA member State in which its registered office is situated.[292] So an SE whose registered office is situated in Great Britain may be wound up under IA 1986, part 4, as if it were a plc.

1.124

Incorporated Friendly Societies

The Friendly Societies Act 1992, s 22(1), provides that an incorporated friendly society may be wound up by the court under what the Act calls 'the applicable winding-up legislation'. By s 23 and sch 10, para 1, this means, in relation to England and Wales, parts 4, 6, 7, 12 and 13 of IA 1986 and, in so far as they relate to offences under any of those enactments, ss 430 and 432 of and sch 10 to IA 1986, as modified by the Friendly Societies Act 1992, sch 10. These provisions are to apply to the winding up of friendly societies as they apply to the winding up of companies registered under the Companies Act 2006.[293]

1.125

Limited Liability Partnerships

IA 1986, part 4 (but not part 5), is applied to limited liability partnerships by the Limited Liability Partnerships Regulations 2001,[294] reg 5(1)(a). So limited liability partnerships are wound up as if they were registered, not unregistered, companies. IA 1986, part 4, is applied as modified by SI 2001/1090, sch 3. IR 1986 are applied with such modifications as the context requires to give effect to the applied provisions of IA 1986.[295] Where there is any conflict between IR 1986 and the Limited Liability Partnerships Regulations 2001, the 2001 Regulations prevail.[296]

1.126

Registered Societies

A society registered, or deemed to be registered, under the Co-operative and Community Benefit Societies Act 2014, including a credit union,[297] may be wound up under IA 1986 as if it were a company,[298] that is, it can be wound up under IA 1986, part 4, as a registered

1.127

---

[290] Regulation (EC) No 1435/2003, art 63.
[291] HM Treasury, *The European Cooperative Society: A Consultation Document* (2006), para 1.8.
[292] Regulation (EC) No 2157/2001, art 63.
[293] Friendly Societies Act 1992, sch 10, para 2.
[294] SI 2001/1090.
[295] Limited Liability Partnerships Regulations 2001 (SI 2001/1090), reg 10(1)(b) and sch 6, part 2.
[296] SI 2001/1090, reg 10(2).
[297] Credit Unions Act 1979, s 1.
[298] Co-operative and Community Benefit Societies Act 2014, s 123(2).

company, not under part 5 as an unregistered company.[299] The obiter statement[300] that under the previous legislation relating to registered societies (then called industrial and provident societies) there seemed to be little doubt that a society could be wound up as an unregistered company under IA 1986, part 5, because the definition of an unregistered company[301] does not expressly exclude registered societies was, it is submitted, wrong. The general provision in IA 1986 for winding up unregistered companies did not derogate from the earlier specific provision in the Industrial and Provident Societies Act 1965, s 55, for the winding up of a particular kind of unregistered company, applying the principle, *generalia specialibus non derogant*.[302] In *Re Surrey Garden Village Trust Ltd*[303] Plowman J said that the petition before him was presented in a circumstance set out in what is now IA 1986, s 122, which relates to registered companies, rather than what is now s 221(5), which relates to unregistered companies.

1.128 The provisions relating to the winding up of registered companies have effect in relation to a registered society as if the society were such a company, with necessary changes of terminology.[304]

1.129 A society whose registration has been cancelled under the Co-operative and Community Benefit Societies Act 2014, s 5, may nevertheless be wound up by the court.[305]

Unregistered Companies

What is an Unregistered Company?

Statutory definition

1.130 IA 1986, s 221(1), provides:

> Subject to the provisions of this part,[306] any unregistered company may be wound up under this Act; and all the provisions of this Act about winding up apply to an unregistered company with the exceptions and additions mentioned in the following subsections.

The reference in s 221(1) to 'all the provisions of this Act about winding up' includes amendments to the Act made after s 221(1) was enacted,[307] for example, IA 1986, s 124A.[308]

---

[299] *Re Norse Self Build Association Ltd* [1985] BCLC 219, not following *Re Friendly Protestant Partnership Loan Fund Co* [1895] 1 IR 1. See also the discussion by Meredith MR in *Re Belfast Tailors' Co-partnership Ltd* [1909] 1 IR 49.

[300] *Re Dairy Farmers of Britain Ltd* [2009] EWHC 1389 (Ch), [2010] Ch 63, at [27].

[301] IA 1986, s 221(1). See 1.131.

[302] A general provision does not derogate from a special one. See *Bennion on Statutory Interpretation*, 5th edn (London: LexisNexis, 2008), s 88.

[303] [1965] 1 WLR 974.

[304] Co-operative and Community Benefit Societies Act 2014, s 123(2).

[305] *Re Castlecomer Co-operative Society* [1926] IR 238. The report does not state whether the society was wound up as a registered or an unregistered company, and it is not clear whether the society's registration was cancelled before or after the petition was presented. See the discussion of winding up dissolved companies at 1.105–1.106.

[306] Part 5 (ss 220–229) of IA 1986.

[307] Interpretation Act 1978, s 20(2).

[308] *Re a Company (No 007946 of 1993)* [1994] Ch 198.

The term 'unregistered company' is defined by IA 1986, s 220, to include: **1.131**

> any association and any company, with the exception of a company registered under the
> Companies Act 2006[309] in any part of the United Kingdom.

Because of the provisions for continuity of law discussed at 1.87–1.104, this definition means that no company registered in England and Wales, Scotland or Northern Ireland since 14 July 1856 is an unregistered company.[310]

According to Lewison J in *Re DAP Holding NV*,[311] an entity may be wound up under IA   **1.132**
1986, part 5, if it is within the juridical concept of a company. His Lordship mentioned that this would exclude a natural person and, as held in *Re International Tin Council*,[312] an international organization, but did not refer to any other exceptions. In fact legislation and jurisprudence have excluded several classes of entities from being wound up under IA 1986, either as registered or as unregistered companies. They are listed at 1.299–1.344. For examples of entities which have been found to be unregistered companies see 1.137–1.138.

The term 'unregistered company' is also used, with a much more restricted meaning, in the   **1.133**
Companies Act 2006, s 1043.[313]

Time at which status must be determined

The provisions of IA 1986 relating to winding up apply to an unregistered company by   **1.134**
virtue of IA 1986, s 221(1), before the company is ordered to be wound up,[314] thus giving authority for the presentation of a winding-up petition.

Whether or not an entity is an unregistered company must be determined as at the date of   **1.135**
presentation of the petition to wind it up.[315]

Unregistered companies which are to be wound up under IA 1986, part 4

There is specific legislative provision for certain types of entity to be wound up under IA   **1.136**
1986, part 4, as if they were registered companies,[316] even though they would otherwise qualify as unregistered under the definition in IA 1986, s 221(1).[317] It is submitted that the general provision in IA 1986 for winding up unregistered companies does not derogate from these specific provisions, applying the principle, *generalia specialibus non derogant*.[318] So they cannot be wound up under part 5. Part 5 is not part of the applicable winding-up legislation by which a building society or an incorporated friendly society may be wound up by the court[319] and so neither type of mutual society may be wound up as an unregistered company.

---

[309] See 1.87–1.104.
[310] *Re Torquay Bath Co* (1863) 32 Beav 581.
[311] [2005] EWHC 2092 (Ch), [2006] BCC 48, at [6].
[312] [1989] Ch 309.
[313] See 5.247.
[314] *Rudow v Great Britain Mutual Life Assurance Society* (1881) 17 ChD 600.
[315] *Re Hercules Insurance Co* (1871) LR 11 Eq 321.
[316] See 1.120–1.129.
[317] See 1.131.
[318] A general provision does not derogate from a special one. See the discussion of *Re Dairy Farmers of Britain Ltd* [2009] EWHC 1389 (Ch), [2010] Ch 63, at 1.127.
[319] See 1.120 and 1.125.

Examples of Unregistered Companies which may be Wound Up under IA 1986, Part 5

1.137   It has been held that companies of the following types may be wound up under IA 1986, part 5:

(a) Companies incorporated by royal charter.[320]
(b) Companies incorporated by private (special) Act of Parliament, such as:
  (i) a canal company,[321]
  (ii) a tramway company,[322]
  (iii) a dock company,[323]
  (iv) a ferry company,[324]
  (v) a market company.[325]
  A winding-up order does not have the effect of repealing the Act under which the company was incorporated.[326]
(c) Companies incorporated by order in council.[327]
(d) Companies incorporated by complete registration under the Joint Stock Companies Act 1844.[328]
(e) Unincorporated associations which are not partnerships, such as:
  (i) unincorporated registered friendly societies,[329]
  (ii) unincorporated joint stock companies,[330]
  (iii) unincorporated building societies,[331]

---

[320] *Re Oriental Bank Corporation* (1885) 54 LJ Ch 481; *Re Commercial Buildings Co of Dublin* [1938] IR 477. There are also reports which show that a winding-up order had been made against a chartered company but which are concerned only with later proceedings in the winding up: *Re Haytor Granite Co* (1865) LR 1 Ch App 77; *Re Commercial Bank Corporation of India and the East* (1869) LR 8 Eq 241; *Re Bank of Egypt* (1887) 3 TLR 460 (in which the charter had expired); *Re English, Scottish and Australian Chartered Bank* [1893] 3 Ch 385.

[321] *Re Proprietors of the Basingstoke Canal* (1866) 14 WR 956; *Re Wey and Arun Junction Canal Co* (1867) LR 4 Eq 197; *Re Bradford Navigation Co* (1870) LR 10 Eq 331.

[322] *Re Brentford and Isleworth Tramways Co* (1884) 26 ChD 527; *Re Borough of Portsmouth (Kingston, Fratton and Southsea) Tramways Co* [1892] 2 Ch 362; *Re South Staffordshire Tramways Co* (1894) 1 Mans 292; *Marshall v South Staffordshire Tramways Co* [1895] 2 Ch 36 at p 52; *Re Galway and Salthill Tramways Co* [1918] 1 IR 62 at p 65.

[323] *Re Exmouth Docks Co* (1873) LR 17 Eq 181.

[324] *Re Isle of Wight Ferry Co* (1865) 2 Hem & M 597.

[325] *Re South London Fish Market Co* (1888) 39 ChD 324.

[326] *Re Wey and Arun Junction Canal Co* (1867) LR 4 Eq 197 per Malins V-C at p 199.

[327] *Re Portstewart Tramway Co* [1896] IR 265.

[328] *Bowes v Hope Life Insurance and Guarantee Co* (1865) 11 HL Cas 389.

[329] *Re Independent Protestant Loan Fund Society* [1895] 1 IR 1; *Re Irish Mercantile Loan Society* [1907] 1 IR 98; *Re 20th Century Equitable Friendly Society* [1910] WN 236; *Canavan* 1929 SLT 636; *Public Prosecutor v Wong Hong Toy* [1986] 1 MLJ 133.

[330] *Aberdeen Provision Society* (1863) 2 M 385; *Re Family Endowment Society* (1870) LR 5 Ch App 118; *Re Great Britain Mutual Life Assurance Society* (1880) 16 ChD 246.

[331] *Re No 3 Midland Counties Benefit Building Society* (1864) 13 WR 399; *Re Queen's Benefit Building Society* (1871) LR 6 Ch App 815; *Re Planet Benefit Building and Investment Society* (1872) LR 14 Eq 441 (in which an order was not made); *Re Second Commercial Benefit Building Society* (1879) 48 LJ Ch 753 (in which an order was not made); *Re Bowling and Welby's Contract* [1895] 1 Ch 663; *Smith's Trustees v Irvine and Fullarton Property Investment and Building Society* (1903) 6 F 99.

(iv)   companies only provisionally registered under the Joint Stock Companies Act 1844,[332]

(v)   an unincorporated loan society registered under the Loan Societies Act 1840,[333]

(vi)   before 21 December 2002, an unincorporated association of more than 20 members which was not carrying on a business for the acquisition of gain in contravention of the provision last enacted as the Companies Act 1985, s 716,[334]

(vii)   unregistered friendly societies,[335]

(viii)   an unincorporated allotments society.[336]

Some kinds of unincorporated associations cannot be wound up as unregistered companies.[337]

(f) Foreign companies.[338]

Incorporated building societies were formerly wound up as unregistered companies.[339] **1.138**
For the present position, see 1.120. The definition of unregistered company formerly included partnerships[340] but now only insolvent partnerships and partnerships subject to the Financial Services and Markets Act 2000, s 367, can be wound up as unregistered companies.[341]

Insolvent Partnerships and Financial Services Partnerships

Types of petition against insolvent partnerships

A person with standing to do so[342] may present a petition for the winding up of an insolvent **1.139**
partnership as an unregistered company under IPO 1994 either:

(a) under art 7 (petitions other than by members) or art 9 (petitions by members) if the petitioner does not also petition for the winding up or bankruptcy of any member or former member of the partnership;

(b) under art 8 (petitions other than by members) if the petitioner also petitions for the winding up or bankruptcy of any member or former member of the partnership; or

(c) under art 10 if the petitioner is a member of the partnership who also petitions for the winding up or bankruptcy of all members of the partnership, including the petitioner, and all members consent.

Court orders for winding up an insolvent partnership other than as an unregistered com- **1.140**
pany are considered at 1.155–1.164.

---

[332] *Re Bank of London and National Provincial Insurance Association* (1871) LR 6 Ch App 421; *Re Anglo-Mexican Mint Co* [1875] WN 168.

[333] *Phillipson v Hale* (1880) 43 LT 508.

[334] *Re Belle Vue Freehold Land Society* (1882) 26 SJ 670; the Companies Act 1985, s 716, was repealed by the Regulatory Reform (Removal of 20 Member Limit in Partnerships etc) Order 2002 (SI 2002/3203), art 2, as from 21 December 2002.

[335] *Re Alfreton District Friendly and Provident Society* (1863) 7 LT 817; *Re Victoria Society, Knottingley* [1913] 1 Ch 167.

[336] *Re Osmondthorpe Hall Freehold Garden and Building Allotment Society* (1913) 58 SJ 13.

[337] See 1.331–1.344.

[338] *Re Commercial Bank of India* (1868) LR 6 Eq 517 and other cases cited at 1.169 and 1.170.

[339] See *Re Sheffield and South Yorkshire Permanent Building Society* (1889) 22 QBD 470 at pp 476–7 per Cave J and p 480 per Charles J.

[340] See 1.565–1.571.

[341] See 1.139–1.153.

[342] See 2.84–2.88.

Application and modification of IA 1986 and IR 1986

1.141 On a petition under IPO 1994, art 7 or art 9, by virtue of arts 7(1) and (2) and 9, the provisions of IA 1986, part 5, apply, as modified by IPO 1994, sch 3, part 1, except that, on a petition under art 9, IA 1986, s 221, is modified by IPO 1994, sch 5, instead of sch 3.

1.142 On a petition under art 8, by virtue of art 8(1) and (2), the provisions of IA 1986, part 5 (apart from ss 223 and 224), apply, as modified by IPO 1994, sch 4, part 1.

1.143 On a petition under art 10, by virtue of art 10(1), the provisions of IA 1986, part 5 (apart from ss 223, 224 and 226), apply, as modified by IPO 1994, sch 6 (which modifies IA 1986, s 221), and by IPO 1994, sch 4, part 1.

1.144 In particular, IA 1986, s 220, is modified by IPO 1994, sch 3, para 2 (in relation to art 7 and art 9 petitions), and sch 4, para 2 (in relation to art 8 and art 10 petitions), to read:

> For the purposes of this part,[343] the expression 'unregistered company' includes any insolvent partnership.

1.145 For the way in which IA 1986, part 4, is modified to apply to insolvent partnerships see 1.222–1.230. IR 1986 apply 'with such modifications as the context requires' for the purpose of giving effect to the provisions of IA 1986 which are applied to insolvent partnerships by IPO 1994.[344] Where there is any conflict between IR 1986 and IPO 1994, the 1994 Order prevails.[345]

Connection with the jurisdiction

1.146 In relation to petitions under IPO 1994, art 7 and art 8 (petitions other than by members), IA 1986, s 221(1), is given identical modifications by IPO 1994, sch 3, para 3 (in relation to art 7 petitions), and sch 4, para 3 (in relation to art 8 petitions). The result is that on an art 7 or art 8 petition an insolvent partnership can be wound up by the court in England and Wales if it has, or at any time had, in England and Wales, either:

(a) a principal place of business, or
(b) a place of business at which business is or has been carried on in the course of which the debt (or part of the debt) arose which forms the basis of the petition for winding up the partnership.

1.147 In relation to petitions under art 9 and art 10 (petitions by members), IA 1986, s 221(1), is given identical modifications by IPO 1994, sch 5, para 2 (in relation to art 9 petitions), and sch 6, para 4 (in relation to art 10 petitions). The result is that on an art 9 or art 10 petition an insolvent partnership can be wound up by the court in England and Wales if it has, or at any time had, a principal place of business in England and Wales.

1.148 Whichever modification of IA 1986, s 221(1), applies to an insolvent partnership the subsection is subject to s 221(2). That subsection is given identical modifications by IPO 1994, sch 3, para 3 (in relation to art 7 petitions), sch 4, para 3 (in relation to art 8 petitions), sch 5, para 2 (in relation to art 9 petitions) and sch 6, para 4 (in relation to art 10 petitions). The result is that an insolvent partnership cannot be wound up if its business has not been carried on in England and Wales at any time in the period of three years ending with the

---

[343] IA 1986, part 5.
[344] IPO 1994, art 18(1) and sch 10.
[345] IPO 1994, art 18(2).

day on which the petition is presented. IA 1986, s 221(2), as modified by IPO 1994, is in the same terms as s 265(1)(c)(ii) as originally enacted, governing jurisdiction in bankruptcy. In *Re a Debtor (No 784 of 1991)*[346] Hoffmann J held that for the purposes of s 265(1)(c)(ii), a person who has carried on business in England and Wales does not cease to carry on business in England and Wales until all the debts of that business have been paid.

1.149 IA 1986, s 221(3A), as modified by IPO 1994, sch 3, para 3, sch 4, para 3, sch 5, para 2, and sch 6, para 4, points out that IA 1986, s 221(1) and (2), as so modified, is subject to Regulation (EC) No 1346/2000.[347]

Definition of 'insolvent partnership'

1.150 The term 'insolvent partnership' is not defined in IPO 1994, but it makes provision for an insolvent partnership to be wound up if it is unable to pay its debts,[348] so this would seem to be what the term 'insolvent partnership' means. The meaning of the term 'unable to pay its debts' is discussed at 7.112–7.120.

Limited partnerships

1.151 IPO 1994 is drafted on the assumption that a limited partnership may be an insolvent partnership capable of being wound up under IPO 1994 as an unregistered company.[349] It has been held[350] that IPO 1994 applies to a Guernsey limited partnership even if its general partners have elected that it is to have legal personality.[351] But it has been held that IPO 1994 does not apply to a Luxembourg *société en commandite par actions*.[352]

Limited liability partnerships

1.152 IPO 1994 does not apply to limited liability partnerships.[353]

Financial services partnerships

1.153 The Financial Services and Markets Act 2000, s 367,[354] provides for the compulsory winding up of financial services partnerships as unregistered companies whether they are solvent or insolvent. Other partnerships can be wound up as unregistered companies only if they are insolvent.

Administration of joint estate as if a winding-up order had been made

1.154 If a winding-up or bankruptcy petition has been presented against a member of an insolvent partnership, the court may apply any provisions of IPO 1994 to the administration of the partnership's joint estate.[355] So the court may direct that the joint estate is to be administered as if a winding-up order had been made under IPO 1994, provided such an order

---

[346] [1992] Ch 554.
[347] See 1.361–1.407.
[348] See 2.39–2.44.
[349] See IA 1986, s 125A(7), inserted by IPO 1994, sch 4, para 9.
[350] *Re Kaupthing Capital Partners II Master LP Inc* [2010] EWHC 836 (Ch), [2011] BCC 338.
[351] Under the Limited Partnerships (Guernsey) Law 1995, s 9A or s 9B.
[352] *Re Hellas Telecommunications (Luxembourg) II SCA* [2009] EWHC 3199 (Ch), [2010] BCC 295.
[353] See 1.126. *Re Kaupthing Capital Partners II Master LP Inc* [2010] EWHC 836 (Ch), [2011] BCC 338, at [33].
[354] See 9.113–9.140.
[355] IA 1986, s 168(5A) and (5B) (where a winding-up petition has been presented) and s 303(2A) and (2C) (where a bankruptcy petition has been presented).

could have been made.[356] An application may be made by the official receiver, any responsible insolvency practitioner[357] or any other interested person.[358]

Court orders to wind up an insolvent partnership other than as an unregistered company

1.155   There are three types of order a court may make for the winding up of an insolvent partnership otherwise than as an unregistered company:

(a) an order under IPO 1994, art 11, for winding up in bankruptcy;[359]

(b) a direction that the joint estate of the partnership is to be administered as though an order had been made for it to be wound up under IPO 1994, art 11;[360]

(c) an order for the dissolution of the partnership under the Partnership Act 1890, s 35, and/or an order for the winding up of the business and affairs of the firm under the Partnership Act 1890, s 39, possibly supported by an order for the appointment of a receiver.[361]

Orders of type (c) can also be made in relation to solvent partnerships.

Winding up in bankruptcy on members' petition

1.156   If all partners in an insolvent partnership are individuals, and none are limited partners, they may present a joint bankruptcy petition, on which the court may adjudge all of them bankrupt and order that the trustee of their estates is also to be trustee of the partnership estate, to wind up the affairs of the partnership and administer the partnership property.[362] The partnership affairs are to be wound up and its property administered without the partnership being wound up as an unregistered company under IA 1986, part 5.[363] The partnership winding up is governed by the bankruptcy provisions of IA 1986, namely, parts 9–19 (apart from ss 273, 274 and 287), as modified by IPO 1994, sch 7.[364] The only ground on which a joint bankruptcy petition may be presented is that the partnership is unable to pay its debts.[365] If it is impracticable for all the members to join in presenting the petition, any one member may apply for an order directing that the petition is to be presented by such member or members as are specified by the court.[366] The procedure cannot be used if the partnership:[367]

(a) has permission under the Financial Services and Markets Act 2000, part 4A, to accept deposits, other than such a permission only for the purpose of carrying on another regulated activity in accordance with that permission; or

(b) continues to have a liability in respect of a deposit which was held by it in accordance with the Banking Act 1979 or the Banking Act 1987.

---

[356] *Official Receiver v Hollens* [2007] EWHC 753 (Ch), [2007] Bus LR 1402.

[357] The liquidator of a corporate member or the trustee of the estate of an individual member (IA 1986, s 436).

[358] IA 1986, ss 168(5B) and 303(2C).

[359] See 1.156.

[360] See 1.157.

[361] See 1.158–1.164.

[362] IPO 1994, art 11; IA 1986, s 264, as modified by IPO 1994, sch 7, para 2. The prescribed form of order is form 16 in IPO 1994, sch 9.

[363] IPO 1994, art 11(1).

[364] IPO 1994, art 11.

[365] IA 1986, s 272(1), as modified by IPO 1994, sch 7, para 5.

[366] IA 1986, s 266(1), as modified by IPO 1994, sch 7, para 4.

[367] IA 1986, s 264(2) and (2A), as modified by IPO 1994, sch 7, para 2.

Winding up in bankruptcy by direction of the court

If a bankruptcy petition has been presented against an individual who is a member of an **1.157** insolvent partnership, an application may be made to the court under IA 1986, s 303(2A) and (2C), for a direction that the joint estate of the partnership is to be administered as though an order had been made for it to be wound up under IPO 1994, art 11, provided an order under that article could have been made.[368] An application may be made by the official receiver, any responsible insolvency practitioner[369] or any other interested person.[370]

Orders under the Partnership Act 1890, s 39

Unlike the single order for winding up a company under IA 1986, a compulsory winding **1.158** up of a partnership in equity requires a number of orders to deal with different aspects of the process. However, to the extent that partners are willing to wind up their firm voluntarily, the full set of orders may not be required.

On the dissolution of a partnership,[371] whether solvent or insolvent, the partners have the **1.159** authority to wind up its affairs.[372] A bankrupt partner does not have this authority,[373] nor does his or her trustee in bankruptcy.[374] In the case of a limited partnership, its affairs must be wound up by the general partners unless the court orders otherwise.[375] On the dissolution of a partnership, every partner is entitled to have the partnership's property applied to pay its debts and liabilities, and to have any surplus paid to the partners in accordance with their entitlements after setting off what they owe to the firm:[376]

> The winding up of a partnership involves the realisation of the firm's assets, the ascertainment and discharge of its liabilities, and the adjustment of accounts between the partners so that the profits can be distributed to them or the losses borne by them in the appropriate shares.[377]

On the termination of a partnership, any partner or his or her representatives may apply **1.160** to the court to wind up the business and affairs of the firm,[378] but the winding-up order which the court makes on such an application is essentially only for an account to be taken of the winding up performed by the partners, so as to ascertain what is due to be paid to the claimant.[379] A winding-up order is the only legal proceeding by which a partner's share of the firm's profits and capital can be established as a liability which the other partners must pay.[380] A winding-up order will not be made on the application of a partner who is

---

[368] *Official Receiver v Hollens* [2007] EWHC 753 (Ch), [2007] Bus LR 1402.
[369] In this context, the trustee of the estate of an individual member (IA 1986, s 436).
[370] IA 1986, ss 168(5B) and 303(2C).
[371] Dissolution of a partnership means termination of the relation between the partners defined in the Partnership Act 1890, s 1(1), ie, carrying on a business in common with a view of profit. In partnership law, dissolution precedes winding up, whereas in company law, dissolution comes at the end of winding up (*Chahal v Mahal* [2005] EWCA Civ 898, [2005] 2 BCLC 655, at [27]).
[372] Partnership Act 1890, s 38.
[373] Partnership Act 1890, s 38 proviso.
[374] *Official Receiver v Hollens* [2007] EWHC 753 (Ch), [2007] Bus LR 1402, at [7].
[375] Limited Partnerships Act 1907, s 6(3).
[376] Partnership Act 1890, s 39.
[377] *Hurst v Bryk* [2002] 1 AC 185 per Lord Millett at p 197.
[378] Partnership Act 1890, s 39.
[379] *Peacock v Peacock* (1808) 16 Ves Jr 49 at pp 51–2. See David Partington, 'Partnership actions: new light on old problems' (2000) 144 SJ 606.
[380] *Hurst v Bryk* [2002] 1 AC 185 per Lord Millett at p 194.

not entitled to a share in either the capital or profits of the firm and so would not have any interest in the winding up.[381]

1.161 In a claim brought by a former member of a dissolved partnership, the court may appoint a receiver of the partnership property, if one or more partners have breached the partnership agreement or otherwise demonstrated that they cannot be trusted to carry out the winding up with proper regard to the claimant's interests.[382] The receiver may be given all powers necessary to wind up the partnership.

1.162 If the partnership has not been dissolved, it may be necessary to apply for a dissolution by the court.[383] Usually an application for dissolution also asks for a winding-up order and the appointment of a receiver.

1.163 Normally all members of a partnership must be parties to legal proceedings concerning the firm's affairs. In particular, a dissolution order cannot be made unless all the partners are before the court.[384] This rule seemed to prevent the compulsory winding up of the very large unincorporated partnerships with transferable shares (joint stock companies) which existed in the early 19th century before incorporation by registration became available. Eventually the Court of Chancery held that, if a partnership was insolvent (so the partners had no claim to a share of profits), an order for the taking of an account could be made against directors and trustees holding, or liable to account for, the company's property, and a receiver could be appointed, without a dissolution and without joining all the partners.[385] The enactment, when incorporation by registration was introduced, of a statutory procedure for winding up companies, including partnerships,[386] did not preclude the court from continuing to make orders of this kind in relation to partnerships,[387] provided no statutory winding-up order had been made.[388]

1.164 The orders discussed at 1.158–1.162 can also be used to wind up solvent partnerships.

Other Entities Identified in Legislation as Unregistered Companies

European economic interest groupings and European groupings of territorial cooperation

1.165 Winding up, in England and Wales, of a European economic interest grouping, or of a European grouping of territorial cooperation (EGTC) which has its registered office in the United Kingdom (a UK EGTC), is as an unregistered company under IA 1986, part 5.[389]

---

[381] *Peacock v Peacock* (1808) 16 Ves Jr 49 per Lord Eldon LC at p 52; *Stekel v Ellice* [1973] 1 WLR 191.

[382] *Estwick v Conningsby* (1682) 1 Vern 118; *Harding v Glover* (1810) 18 Ves Jr 281; *Blakeney v Dufaur* (1851) 15 Beav 40; *Re a Company (No 00596 of 1986)* [1987] BCLC 133 at p 135. For discussion of when appointment of a receiver is appropriate if the existence of a partnership is denied see *Floydd v Cheney* [1970] Ch 603.

[383] Partnership Act 1890, s 35.

[384] *Deeks v Stanhope* (1844) 14 Sim 57.

[385] *Wallworth v Holt* (1841) 4 My & Cr 619; *Deeks v Stanhope* (1844) 14 Sim 57.

[386] See 1.541–1.547.

[387] *Jones v Lord Charlemont* (1848) 16 Sim 271; *Clements v Bowes* (1852) 17 Sim 167; *Clements v Bowes* (1853) 1 Drew 684. These cases concerned provisionally registered railway companies which were never incorporated. The extremely brief report of *Jones v Lord Charlemont* does not mention the company's status but the full facts are in the related case of *Watson v Earl of Charlemont* (1848) 12 QB 856.

[388] *Parbury v Chadwick* (1850) 12 Beav 614.

[389] European Economic Interest Grouping Regulations 1989 (SI 1989/638), reg 8(1); European Grouping of Territorial Cooperation Regulations 2007 (SI 2007/1949), reg 7.

Collective investment schemes

The legislation on open-ended investment companies contemplates that they can be wound **1.166**
up as unregistered companies.[390] A sub-fund may be wound up as if it were an open-ended
investment company[391] and, for the purposes of the winding up, is to be treated as if it were
a separate legal person.[392]

A co-ownership scheme is a type of collective investment scheme constituted by contract **1.167**
which does not constitute a body corporate, a partnership or a limited partnership.[393] The constituting contract must be in a deed between an operator and a depositary.[394] This is the 'contractual scheme deed'.[395] The property subject to the scheme is held by, or to the order of, the
depositary on trust for the participants as tenants in common.[396] The operator acquires, man-
ages and disposes of property subject to the scheme.[397] A co-ownership scheme is one type of
'contractual scheme'.[398] If it is authorized under the Financial Services and Markets Act 2000,
s 261D(1), it is an 'authorized contractual scheme'.[399] Co-ownership schemes that are authorized contractual schemes can be either stand-alone or umbrella.[400] An umbrella scheme's
property is in separate parts and the participants are entitled to exchange rights in one part for
rights in another.[401] The arrangements constituting an umbrella co-ownership scheme, so far
as they relate to a separate part of the scheme's property, are called a 'sub-scheme'.[402]

A stand-alone co-ownership scheme or a sub-scheme of an umbrella co-ownership scheme[403] **1.168**
is called a 'relevant scheme' and may be wound up under IA 1986 as if it were an unregistered company.[404] IA 1986 applies as modified by SI 2013/1388, sch 2, parts 1, 2 and 3. IR
1986 apply as modified by SI 2013/1388, sch 3.

Foreign Companies

Foreign companies as unregistered companies

A company established under the law of a jurisdiction other than England and Wales or **1.169**
Scotland may be wound up as an unregistered company under IA 1986, part 5,[405] subject to
the rules on allocation of jurisdiction discussed at 1.347–1.432, which are especially relevant in this context. A company registered under the Companies Act 2006[406] in Northern

---

[390] Open-Ended Investment Companies Regulations (SI 2001/1228), reg 31(1).
[391] SI 2001/1228, reg 33C(1).
[392] SI 2001/1228, reg 33C(4).
[393] Financial Services and Markets Act 2000, s 235A(2) and (3)(a) and (c).
[394] Financial Services and Markets Act 2000, s 235A(3)(b).
[395] Financial Services and Markets Act 2000, s 235A(8)(a).
[396] Financial Services and Markets Act 2000, s 235A(3)(d) and (e).
[397] Financial Services and Markets Act 2000, s 235A(4)(d).
[398] Financial Services and Markets Act 2000, s 235A(1).
[399] Financial Services and Markets Act 2000, s 237(3).
[400] Financial Services and Markets Act 2000, s 237(8).
[401] Financial Services and Markets Act 2000, s 237(5) and (6).
[402] Financial Services and Markets Act 2000, s 237(7).
[403] See 1.167.
[404] Collective Investment in Transferable Securities (Contractual Scheme) Regulations 2013 (SI 2013/1388), reg 17(2).
[405] *Re Commercial Bank of India* (1868) LR 6 Eq 517; *Marshall* (1895) 22 R 697; *Russian Commercial and Industrial Bank v Comptoir d'Escompte de Mulhouse* [1925] AC 112 per Lord Wrenbury at p 149; *Inland Revenue v Highland Engineering Ltd* 1975 SLT 203; *Re a Company (No 007946 of 1993)* [1994] Ch 198 at p 203.
[406] See 1.87–1.104.

Ireland (or any other part of the United Kingdom) is not an unregistered company[407] and so cannot be wound up under IA 1986, part 5.[408] But any other association or company formed in Northern Ireland can be,[409] subject to the rules on allocation of jurisdiction.[410]

1.170 Similarly in other jurisdictions where the legislation confers power to wind up unregistered companies, for example, Victoria, before the national schemes for uniform companies legislation[411] and Hong Kong.[412] In Singapore, the definition of 'unregistered company' states expressly that it includes a foreign company.[413]

1.171 In Canada a provision in the Winding-up and Restructuring Act[414] expressly applies it to 'incorporated trading companies doing business in Canada wherever incorporated'.[415] In *Allen v Hanson*[416] this provision was held to be within the legislative capacity of the Canadian Parliament, but before the Winding-up and Restructuring Act included that express provision it was held that the Act did not authorize the winding up in Canada of an English company which was not being wound up in England.[417]

Conditions for winding up a foreign company

1.172 The court's power to wind up a foreign company is discretionary.[418] It has been accepted that three conditions must be satisfied before a foreign company can be wound up by the court in England and Wales. These conditions were stated by Knox J in *Re Real Estate Development Co*,[419] adopting the submission of counsel for the petitioner (Mark Pelling):

(1) that there must be a sufficient connection with England and Wales which may, but does not necessarily have to, consist of assets within the jurisdiction;[420]
(2) that there must be a reasonable possibility if a winding-up order is made, of benefit to those applying for the winding-up order;[421]
(3) one or more persons interested in the distribution of assets of the company must be persons over whom the court can exercise a jurisdiction.[422]

These are commonly referred to as the 'three core requirements'. If they are satisfied, a winding-up order may be made.[423]

---

[407] IA 1986, s 220.

[408] See 1.423–1.424.

[409] Adopting the argument used in *Re a Company (No 007946 of 1993)* [1994] Ch 198, 'any company' in s 220 is a 'provision expressly relating to companies incorporated elsewhere than in Great Britain' and therefore, by s 441(2), applies to companies incorporated in Northern Ireland otherwise than by registration under companies legislation. Section 441 does not prevent s 220 applying to unincorporated associations formed in Northern Ireland.

[410] See 1.427–1.430.

[411] *Re Oriental Bank Corporation* (1884) 10 VLR (E) 154; *Re Harry Rickards Tivoli Theatres Ltd* [1931] VLR 305 explaining *Re Egerton and Gordon Consolidated Gold Mines Co NL* [1908] VLR 22.

[412] *Re MKI Corp Ltd* [1998] 1 HKLRD 28.

[413] Companies Act (Singapore), s 350(1). See *Re Griffin Securities Corporation* [1999] 3 SLR 346.

[414] Which was added by 47 Vic (1884), ch 39, s 1.

[415] Winding-up and Restructuring Act, s 6. See, for example, *Re Stewart River Gold Dredging Co Ltd* (1912) 7 DLR 736; *Re Steel Realty Development Corporation* (1924) 27 OWN 37.

[416] (1890) 18 SCR 667.

[417] *Merchants' Bank of Halifax v Gillespie Moffat and Co* (1885) 10 SCR 312.

[418] *Stocznia Gdanska SA v Latreefers Inc (No 2)* [2001] 2 BCLC 116 at p 140.

[419] [1991] BCLC 210 at p 217.

[420] See 1.179–1.200.

[421] See 1.201–1.203.

[422] See 1.204–1.206.

[423] *Stocznia Gdanska SA v Latreefers Inc (No 2)* at p 141.

Jurisdiction or discretion?

There has been controversy over whether the three core requirements[424] limit the jurisdiction of the court, and so are preconditions for the existence of the discretion, or principles to be observed in considering the exercise of the discretion. This is a matter of statutory interpretation which requires the court to ask, 'Who...is within the legislative grasp, or intendment, of the statute under consideration?'[425] Usually the point is not crucial and in *Stocznia Gdanska SA v Latreefers Inc (No 2)*[426] the Court of Appeal said, at p 140, that it did not draw any distinction between jurisdiction and discretion. **1.173**

In *Re Drax Holdings Ltd*[427] the point was crucial, and it was held that the court has jurisdiction to wind up any foreign company, and the three core requirements are relevant only to whether it should exercise its discretion to do so in relation to a particular company.[428] **1.174**

In earlier cases the view that the court has jurisdiction to wind up any foreign company was expressed in *Inland Revenue v Highland Engineering Ltd*[429] per Lord Grieve; in *Re Paramount Airways Ltd*[430] per Nicholls V-C at p 240; and in *Banco Nacional de Cuba v Cosmos Trading Corporation*[431] per Scott V-C at pp 816–17. **1.175**

However, other judges have taken the view that jurisdiction is determined by the degree of connection. Thus in *Re Lloyd Generale Italiano*[432] Pearson J expressly held that the court did not have jurisdiction to wind up the company because of its lack of connection with England. Similarly, in *Re Real Estate Development Co*[433] Knox J held[434] that 'the jurisdiction simply does not exist' to make a winding-up order in respect of a company with insufficient connection with England.[435] In *Re Kailis Groote Eylandt Fisheries Pty Ltd*[436] Bray CJ said, at p 44: **1.176**

> To purport to wind up a company incorporated elsewhere is a proceeding which requires some justification of principle under the rules of private international law. I do not have a discretion to wind up any company anywhere.

In *Re Titan International Inc*[437] Peter Gibson LJ said, at pp 106–7:

> [I]t is clear from the decided cases that the English court will not assume jurisdiction over any foreign company.

---

[424] See 1.172.
[425] *Clark v Oceanic Contractors Inc* [1983] 2 AC 130 at p 152 per Lord Wilberforce. See also *Lawson v Serco Ltd* [2006] UKHL 3, [2006] ICR 250, per Lord Hoffmann at [6].
[426] [2001] 2 BCLC 116.
[427] [2003] EWHC 2743 (Ch), [2004] 1 WLR 1049.
[428] Followed in *Re OJSC ANK Yugraneft* [2008] EWHC 2614 (Ch), [2009] 1 BCLC 298, at [20]; *Re Rodenstock GmbH* [2011] EWHC 1104 (Ch), [2011] Bus LR 1245, at [23].
[429] 1975 SLT 203.
[430] [1993] Ch 223.
[431] [2000] 1 BCLC 813.
[432] (1885) 29 ChD 219.
[433] [1991] BCLC 210.
[434] At p 222.
[435] See also per Cohen J in *Re Tovarishestvo Manufactur Liudvig-Rabenek* [1944] Ch 404 at pp 407–8 and per Evershed MR in *Banque des Marchands de Moscou (Koupetschesky) v Kindersley* [1951] Ch 112 at pp 124–5.
[436] (1977) 17 SASR 35.
[437] [1998] 1 BCLC 102.

... [O]n this appeal the first and most important question is whether a sufficient connection between the company and England and Wales has been demonstrated for the English court to have jurisdiction.

In *Re HIH Casualty and General Insurance Ltd*[438] Lord Hoffmann cited *Re Drax Holdings Ltd* as authority for the statement that:

There is no doubt that an English court has jurisdiction to wind up [a foreign company] if it has assets here or some other sufficient connection with this country.

However, in *Re Drax Holdings Ltd* it was held that a different principle is correct, namely, that an English court has jurisdiction to wind up a foreign company even if it has no assets in, or other connection with, England and Wales. The difference between that principle and Lord Hoffmann's statement was not in issue in *Re HIH Casualty and General Insurance Ltd*, so Lord Hoffmann's statement is obiter.

1.177 In bankruptcy, it has been held that an English court does not have jurisdiction over an individual who is not domiciled in England and Wales and does not meet the other requirements of IA 1986, s 265, because that section prohibits the presentation of a bankruptcy petition unless those requirements are met.[439]

1.178 In *Banque des Marchands de Moscou (Koupetschesky) v Kindersley*[440] Evershed MR said:

As a matter of general principle, our courts would not assume, and Parliament should not be taken to have intended to confer, jurisdiction over matters which naturally and properly lie within the competence of the courts of other countries.

Sufficient connection with the jurisdiction

1.179 The court will not order the winding up of a foreign company unless the company has a sufficient connection with the jurisdiction[441] and there is no other more appropriate forum.[442] 'Sufficient connection' means 'sufficient to justify the court setting in motion its winding-up procedures over a body which prima facie is beyond the limits of territoriality'.[443]

1.180 In English common law the usual criterion for assuming jurisdiction over a foreign company in civil proceedings is that its business, or other corporate activity, has been carried on, either by itself or by an agent, at or from a fixed place of business in England and Wales, for more than a minimal period of time.[444] Courts have been willing to take jurisdiction to wind up foreign companies with a much less substantial connection, provided they can see some benefit from making a winding-up order.

---

[438] [2008] UKHL 21, [2008] 1 WLR 852, at [8].

[439] *North v Skipton Building Society* (2002) LTL 13/6/2002.

[440] [1951] Ch 112 at pp 125–6.

[441] *Re Compañía Merabello San Nicholas SA* [1973] Ch 75; *Re Kailis Groote Eylandt Fisheries Pty Ltd* (1977) 17 SASR 35 at p 38; *Re Scott-Brown Industries Pty Ltd* (1981) 6 ACLR 342; *Re a Company (No 00359 of 1987)* [1988] Ch 210 per Peter Gibson J at pp 225–6; *Re Paramount Airways Ltd* [1993] Ch 210 per Nicholls V-C at p 240; *Re Seagull Manufacturing Co Ltd* [1993] Ch 345 per Peter Gibson J at p 352; *Re Titan International Inc* [1998] 1 BCLC 102.

[442] *Banque des Marchands de Moscou (Koupetschesky) v Kindersley* [1951] Ch 112; *Re a Company (No 00359 of 1987)* [1988] Ch 210; *Re a Company (No 003102 of 1991)* [1991] BCLC 539; see 1.209–1.212.

[443] *Re Real Estate Development Co* [1991] BCLC 210 per Knox J at p 217.

[444] *Okura and Co Ltd v Forsback Jernverks AB* [1914] 1 KB 715; *Adams v Cape Industries plc* [1990] Ch 433.

Various factors have been said to contribute to showing that there is a sufficient connection **1.181**
with England and Wales to create jurisdiction to wind up a company. They are discussed
at 1.182–1.200. Some of these factors have been found to be enough in themselves to show
sufficient connection (see 1.182–1.184, 1.189–1.195). None of the factors is a necessary
requirement for proving sufficient connection, but the points discussed at 1.201–1.206
are necessary requirements, in addition to proof of sufficient connection, for establishing
jurisdiction.

Only office and all shareholders in the jurisdiction

The fact that a foreign company's only office is in the jurisdiction and all its shareholders are **1.182**
domiciled in the jurisdiction is in itself a sufficient connection.[445] The fact that a director or
a shareholder resides in the jurisdiction is not in itself a sufficient connection.[446]

Branch office in the jurisdiction

The presence in the jurisdiction of a branch office of a foreign company under an agent or **1.183**
manager is enough in itself to show sufficient connection.[447]

Business conducted in the jurisdiction

The fact that some business of a foreign company has been conducted within the juris- **1.184**
diction is enough in itself to show sufficient connection. In *Re Tovarishestvo Manufactur
Liudvig-Rabenek*[448] it was held that carrying on business at a place of business in the jurisdiction was a sufficient connection—the place of business in that case was the hotel at
which the company's representatives stayed when they came to England.[449]

Having office, or place of business, or doing business in jurisdiction not necessary

In some circumstances, under the rules for allocating jurisdiction discussed at 1.347–1.432, **1.185**
the courts of England and Wales will not have jurisdiction over a foreign company if it does
not have an establishment or a principal place of business here. If those rules do not apply,
jurisdiction may be established by showing a sufficient connection with England and Wales
and satisfying the other two core requirements.[450] For that purpose a sufficient connection
with England and Wales may be established by other factors without showing that the
company has its only office[451] or a branch office[452] here.[453] It is unnecessary to prove that
the company ever had a place of business in the jurisdiction,[454] or even that it carried on

---

[445] *Re Syria Ottoman Railway Co* (1904) 20 TLR 217, in which it was said, at p 218, that the company's
affairs were conducted 'as though it were an English company'.

[446] *Re Westminster Property Management Ltd (No 2)* [2001] BCC 305 at p 357.

[447] *Re Commercial Bank of India* (1868) LR 6 Eq 517; *Re Matheson Brothers Ltd* (1884) 27 ChD 225; *Re
Commercial Bank of South Australia* (1886) 33 ChD 174; *Re Federal Bank of Australia Ltd* (1893) 62 LJ Ch
561; *Re Victoria Date Co Ltd* (1898) 42 SJ 755; *Re Songvaar Salvaging Co Ltd* (1918) 14 Tas LR 92.

[448] [1944] Ch 404.

[449] For other cases in which conduct of business within the jurisdiction was one of the factors which
showed a sufficient connection with the jurisdiction see *Re Matheson Brothers Ltd* (1884) 27 ChD 225;
Banque des Marchands de Moscou (Koupetschesky) v Kindersley [1951] Ch 112; *Re a Company (No 00359 of
1987)* [1988] Ch 210; *Re a Company (No 003102 of 1991)* [1991] BCLC 539; *Re Mid East Trading Ltd* [1997]
3 All ER 481.

[450] See 1.172.

[451] See 1.182.

[452] See 1.183.

[453] *Re Compañía Merabello San Nicholas SA* [1973] Ch 75.

[454] *Re Tovarishestvo Manufactur Liudvig-Rabenek* [1944] Ch 404; *Mazur Media Ltd v Mazur Media
GmbH* [2004] EWHC 1566 (Ch), [2005] 1 BCLC 305, at [65].

business from some specific or identifiable place of business in the jurisdiction.[455] It is possible to order a foreign company to be wound up by the court even if it has never carried on business in the jurisdiction.[456]

1.186 In *Re Lloyd Generale Italiano*, the company had carried on business in England by means of agents and had creditors in England but no assets here, and had no branch office in England. Pearson J decided that the English High Court did not have jurisdiction to order the company to be wound up. In *Re Compañía Merabello San Nicholas SA*[457] Megarry J said, at p 85, that Pearson J's decision 'has subsequently been "explained" almost out of existence'.

1.187 IA 1986, s 221(3), provides that whether it is the courts of England and Wales or the courts of Scotland that have jurisdiction over a foreign company is determined by where the foreign company has a principal place of business, and deems the principal place of business to be the company's registered office. However, this does not mean that only a company with a principal place of business in Great Britain can be wound up here.[458]

Registration as an overseas company irrelevant

1.188 Jurisdiction to wind up a company incorporated outside the United Kingdom does not seem to depend on whether or not the company has complied with the duty to register at Companies House.[459] For example, winding-up orders were made in *Re NV Handelmaatschappij Wokar*,[460] *Re Compañía Merabello San Nicholas SA*[461] and *Re a Company (No 003102 of 1991)*,[462] though the companies had not registered. In *Re Atlantic Isle Shipping Co Inc*[463] Young J said that failure of a foreign company to comply with a similar registration requirement under Australian law meant that the company had carried on business in Australia illegally and that this in itself was a reason for winding up the company. See also the discussion of illegal large partnerships at 1.331–1.333. However, in England and Malaysia, it has been held that the contracts of an unregistered foreign company are not void for illegality.[464]

Assets in the jurisdiction and persons interested

1.189 The presence of assets within the jurisdiction to administer and persons subject, or at least submitting, to the jurisdiction who are concerned or interested in the proper distribution

---

[455] *Banque des Marchands de Moscou (Koupetschesky) v Kindersley* [1951] Ch 112 at pp 131–2, differing from the view expressed by Cohen J in *Re Tovarishestvo Manufactur Liudvig-Rabenek* [1944] Ch 404 at p 409 and by Pearson J in *Re Lloyd Generale Italiano* (1885) 29 ChD 219 at pp 220–1.

[456] *Re Compañía Merabello San Nicholas SA* [1973] Ch 75.

[457] [1973] Ch 75.

[458] *Banque des Marchands de Moscou (Koupetschesky) v Kindersley* [1951] Ch 112 at p 127; *Re Kailis Groote Eylandt Fisheries Pty Ltd* (1977) 17 SASR 35 at pp 40–1.

[459] Under the Companies Act 2006, s 1046, and the Overseas Companies Regulations 2009 (SI 2009/1801).

[460] [1946] Ch 98.

[461] [1973] Ch 75.

[462] [1991] BCLC 539.

[463] (1988) 14 ACLR 232.

[464] *Curragh Investments Ltd v Cook* [1974] 1 WLR 1559; *Hopewell Construction Co Ltd v Eastern and Oriental Hotel (1951) Sdn Bhd* [1988] 2 MLJ 621.

of the assets is enough in itself to show a sufficient connection with the jurisdiction.[465] The
value of the assets in the jurisdiction may be too small to justify winding up.[466]

Only assets in existence within the jurisdiction at the time the petition is presented count;[467] **1.190**
though in *Re Irish Shipping Ltd*[468] Jones J, obiter, said that it is sufficient if the petitioner
expects that assets would arrive within the jurisdiction and they are present at the time the
petition is heard. Assets which could only arise if the winding-up order were made do not
count. These are, for example, claims which it is proposed a liquidator should make under
IA 1986, s 213 (fraudulent trading) or s 214 (wrongful trading)[469] or s 423 (transactions
defrauding creditors).[470]

Present assets may be of any nature; they do not have to be 'commercial' assets or assets **1.191**
which indicate that the company formerly carried on business in the jurisdiction.[471] A right
of action is sufficient[472] unless it has no reasonable chance of success.[473] A right of action
which is subject to a contractual provision for English exclusive jurisdiction is sufficient,
regardless of where private international law would consider the right is located.[474] The
assets do not have to be distributable to creditors by the liquidator in the winding up: it
suffices if, by the making of the winding-up order, they will be of benefit to a creditor or
creditors in some other way.[475]

Provided there are assets within the jurisdiction it does not matter that all the persons con- **1.192**
cerned or interested in their proper distribution are outside the jurisdiction.[476]

In *Re American International Insurance Association*[477] a winding-up order was made against **1.193**
a company which had assets and creditors in the jurisdiction and also an office.[478] In *Kintsu
Co Ltd v Peninsular Group Ltd*[479] it was said, at p 686, that there was sufficient connection
between a foreign company and New South Wales to give the New South Wales court

---

[465] *Re NV Handelmaatschappij Wokar* [1946] Ch 98; *Banque des Marchands de Moscou (Koupetschesky)
v Kindersley* [1951] Ch 112; *Re Azoff-Don Commercial Bank* [1954] Ch 315; *Re Compañía Merabello San
Nicholas SA* [1973] Ch 75; *Re Kailis Groote Eylandt Fisheries Pty Ltd* (1977) 17 SASR 35 at p 40; *Inland
Revenue v Highland Engineering Ltd* 1975 SLT 203; *Re China Tianjin International Economic and Technical
Cooperative Corporation* [1994] 2 HKLR 327; *Flame SA v Primera Maritime (Hellas) Ltd* [2010] EWHC 2053
(Ch), LTL 16/12/2010.

[466] *Re OJSC ANK Yugraneft* [2008] EWHC 2614 (Ch), [2009] 1 BCLC 298, at [58].

[467] *Re Kailis Groote Eylandt Fisheries Pty Ltd* (1977) 17 SASR 35; *Re a Company (No 00359 of 1987)* [1988]
Ch 210; *Re Real Estate Development Co* [1991] BCLC 210.

[468] [1985] HKLR 437.

[469] *Re a Company (No 00359 of 1987)* [1988] Ch 210.

[470] *Re Real Estate Development Co* [1991] BCLC 210. A reasonable possibility that contributions could be
recovered by such a claim may show that the petitioner has a sufficient interest; see 1.201.

[471] *Re Compañía Merabello San Nicholas SA* [1973] Ch 75.

[472] *Re Compañía Merabello San Nicholas SA*.

[473] *Re Allobrogia Steamship Corporation* [1978] 3 All ER 423; *Re Real Estate Development Co* [1991]
BCLC 210.

[474] *Flame SA v Primera Maritime (Hellas) Ltd* [2010] EWHC 2053 (Ch), LTL 16/12/2010, at [19]–[20].

[475] *Re Compañía Merabello San Nicholas SA* [1973] Ch 75, in which the asset was an insurance claim
which, on the making of a winding-up order, would automatically vest in the petitioning creditors under the
Third Parties (Rights against Insurers) Act 1930.

[476] *Re Kailis Groote Eylandt Fisheries Pty Ltd* (1977) 17 SASR 35 per Bray CJ at p 42.

[477] (1963) *The Times*, 19 November 1963.

[478] See 1.183.

[479] (1998) 27 ACSR 679.

jurisdiction to wind it up when the company had assets and creditors in New South Wales and was registered as a foreign company there.[480]

1.194 The existence of persons interested in the distribution of assets over whom the court can exercise a jurisdiction (whether or not there are assets in the jurisdiction) is a separate condition for jurisdiction to order the winding up of a foreign company.[481]

1.195 Sufficient connection can be established without showing that there are assets in the jurisdiction. It is possible to order the winding up of a company which has no assets within the jurisdiction[482] and in such a case it is not necessary to show that the company was carrying on business within the jurisdiction at the time of presentation of the petition.[483]

Benefit to applicant or creditors and jurisdiction over person interested in distribution of assets

1.196 The fact that there is a person or persons within, or submitting to, the jurisdiction who will benefit from a foreign company being wound up is a factor which may, with others, show a sufficient connection.[484] In *Re Buildmat (Australia) Pty Ltd*[485] there was jurisdiction to make a winding-up order where practically all the company's creditors were within the jurisdiction and its only admitted asset was within the jurisdiction even though that asset was 'negligible'.[486]

Miscellaneous factors

1.197 The fact that a foreign company has incurred a debt under a contract negotiated, executed and performed within the jurisdiction is a factor which may, when combined with others, show a sufficient connection.[487] The presence of a creditor or creditors within the jurisdiction is not in itself sufficient.[488] The fact that a loan agreement provided that it was to be governed by the laws of Hong Kong was not in itself a sufficient connection with Hong Kong where there was no clear evidence of where the agreement had been negotiated, executed or performed.[489]

1.198 The fact that a foreign company has been advised by solicitors practising within the jurisdiction is a factor which may, when combined with others, show a sufficient connection.[490] In *Re Titan International Inc*[491] the court found no sufficient connection despite the presence of this factor.

---

[480] See 1.188.
[481] *Re Real Estate Development Co* [1991] BCLC 210 at p 217; see 1.204.
[482] *Re Eloc Electro-Optieck and Communicatie BV* [1982] Ch 43; *Re a Company (No 00359 of 1987)* [1988] Ch 210; *Re Real Estate Development Co* [1991] BCLC 210; *Re Mid East Trading Ltd* [1997] 3 All ER 481; *Stocznia Gdanska SA v Latreefers Inc (No 2)* [2001] 2 BCLC 116.
[483] *Re a Company (No 00359 of 1987)* [1988] Ch 210.
[484] *Re Eloc Electro-Optieck and Communicatie BV* [1982] Ch 43; *Re Real Estate Development Co* [1991] BCLC 210.
[485] (1981) 5 ACLR 689.
[486] AU$706 compared with secured debts of AU$905,093.
[487] *Re a Company (No 00359 of 1987)* [1988] Ch 210; *Re a Company (No 003102 of 1991)* [1991] BCLC 539.
[488] *Re Kailis Groote Eylandt Fisheries Pty Ltd* (1977) 17 SASR 35; *Re Westminster Property Management Ltd (No 2)* [2001] BCC 305 at p 357.
[489] *Re Solar Touch Ltd* [2004] 3 HKLRD 154.
[490] *Re a Company (No 003102 of 1991)* [1991] BCLC 539.
[491] [1998] 1 BCLC 102.

In *Re Atlantic Isle Shipping Co Inc*[492] the court had jurisdiction where the company had a   **1.199**
bank account within the jurisdiction and it owned a ship which was loaded in the jurisdiction 'from time to time'.

In *Re Titan International Inc*[493] the fact that persons carrying on an illegal lottery in England   **1.200**
and Wales used the funds generated by it to subscribe for shares in a foreign company which
they controlled was not in itself sufficient to give the English court jurisdiction to wind up
that foreign company.

Sufficient interest of petitioner

In *Re Real Estate Development Co*[494] Knox J, at p 217, accepted counsel's submission that   **1.201**
the second of the three core requirements for the court to order the winding up of a foreign
company is:

> that there must be a reasonable possibility if a winding-up order is made, of benefit to those
> applying for the winding-up order.

This condition was originally expressed by Megarry J in *Re Compañía Merabello San
Nicholas SA*[495] in the form:

> If it is shown that there is no reasonable possibility of benefit accruing to creditors from mak-
> ing the winding-up order, the jurisdiction is excluded.

In that form it was repeated by Peter Gibson J in *Re a Company (No 00359 of 1987)*[496] and in
Re Seagull Manufacturing Co Ltd;[497] and by Nicholls V-C in *Re Paramount Airways Ltd*.[498]
Benefit to creditors may be shown by a reasonable possibility that a liquidator could recover
contributions under IA 1986, s 213 (fraudulent trading), or s 214 (wrongful trading).[499] The
powers of investigation available to an English liquidator may be sufficient benefit to creditors.[500] Investigation by a liquidator of dealings with the company's property in another
jurisdiction is not a sufficient benefit if it is unlikely either that the liquidator would have any
powers in that other jurisdiction or that orders made by courts in the winding-up jurisdiction would have any effect there.[501] Appointment of an English insolvency practitioner as a
liquidator, who can supervise complex litigation in this country, is a sufficient advantage.[502]

In *Re Compañía Merabello San Nicholas SA* the real question was whether the petitioner   **1.202**
creditors (one of whom represented over 500 Lloyd's underwriters) would benefit and it
seems that Knox J's formulation is more appropriate in that kind of case.[503] In Knox J's

---

[492] (1988) 14 ACLR 232.
[493] [1998] 1 BCLC 102.
[494] [1991] BCLC 210.
[495] [1973] Ch 75 at p 95.
[496] [1988] Ch 210 at pp 225–6.
[497] [1993] Ch 345 at p 352.
[498] [1993] Ch 223 at p 240.
[499] *Re a Company (No 00359 of 1987)* [1988] Ch 210. In *Stocznia Gdanska SA v Latreefers Inc (No 2)* [2001]
2 BCLC 116 such claims plus a potential misfeasance claim against directors were sufficient.
[500] *Titchfield Management Ltd v Vaccinoma Inc* [2008] NSWSC 1196, 68 ACSR 448; *Flame SA v Primera
Maritime (Hellas) Ltd* [2010] EWHC 2053 (Ch), LTL 16/12/2010.
[501] *Re Solar Touch Ltd* [2004] 3 HKLRD 154.
[502] *Re OJSC ANK Yugraneft* [2008] EWHC 2614 (Ch), [2009] 1 BCLC 298, at [61].
[503] In *Re OJSC ANK Yugraneft* [2008] EWHC 2614 (Ch), [2009] 1 BCLC 298, at [60], Christopher
Clarke J said that Megarry J's formulation was fashioned to take account of the distinction between benefiting from the order and benefiting from the winding-up process.

formulation the condition is just the 'sufficient interest' test,[504] which is applied to the winding up of any company, whether incorporated locally or abroad.[505] Publicity for the petitioner's unenforceable claim against a foreign government is not sufficient.[506]

1.203 In the case of a public interest petition,[507] there must be a reasonable prospect that the public interest would be promoted by a winding-up order, rather than a benefit to the petitioner.[508]

Sufficient connection of petitioner with the jurisdiction

1.204 In *Banque des Marchands de Moscou (Koupetschesky) v Kindersley*[509] Evershed MR stated, at p 126, the following condition for the exercise of jurisdiction to wind up a foreign company:

> There must be assets here to administer and persons subject, or at least submitting, to the jurisdiction who are concerned or interested in the proper distribution of the assets.

Subsequently it was held that the exercise of the jurisdiction does not depend on the presence of assets in the jurisdiction.[510] In *Re Real Estate Development Co*[511] Knox J accepted, at p 217, counsel's submission that the third of the three core requirements for the court to order the winding up of a foreign company is:

> one or more persons interested in the distribution of assets of the company must be persons over whom the court can exercise a jurisdiction.

Knox J went on to say:

> The primary need for that connecting factor is, in my judgment, to establish that persons exist who are likely to benefit from the making of the order and who qualify for one reason or another as persons on whose behalf it would be right to set in motion the winding-up [jurisdiction] over a foreign company. Throughout the investigation into whether the court has jurisdiction, the aim is to discover a sufficient connection with this jurisdiction and that is as true in relation to the potential beneficiaries as it is in relation to the company which [is sought to be wound up].

1.205 The mere fact that a creditor of a foreign company interested in the distribution of the company's assets has petitioned the court in England and Wales, though it amounts to a submission to the jurisdiction of the court,[512] is not a sufficient connection with England and Wales to justify making a winding-up order.[513]

1.206 Sufficient connection of a petitioner with the jurisdiction may be found if the petitioner has been employed by the company in England and Wales[514] or if the petitioner is a claimant in

---

[504] *Re Eloc Electro-Optieck and Communicatie BV* [1982] Ch 43 per Nourse J at p 47.
[505] See 2.127–2.141.
[506] *Banco Nacional de Cuba v Cosmos Trading Corporation* [2000] 1 BCLC 813.
[507] See chapter 9.
[508] *Re Titan International Inc* [1998] 1 BCLC 102 per Peter Gibson LJ at p 107.
[509] [1951] Ch 112.
[510] *Re Eloc Electro-Optieck and Communicatie BV* [1982] Ch 43; *Re a Company (No 00359 of 1987)* [1988] Ch 210; *Re Real Estate Development Co* [1991] BCLC 210; *Re Mid East Trading Ltd* [1997] 3 All ER 481; *Stocznia Gdanska SA v Latreefers Inc (No 2)* [2001] 2 BCLC 116.
[511] [1991] BCLC 210.
[512] *Re Belfast Shipowners Co Ltd* [1894] 1 IR 321.
[513] *Re Real Estate Development Co* [1991] BCLC 210; *Banco Nacional de Cuba v Cosmos Trading Corporation* [2000] 1 BCLC 813 at p 817. Doubted in *Jubilee International Inc v Farlin Timbers Pte Ltd* [2005] EWHC 3331 (Ch), [2006] BPIR 765, at [73].
[514] *Re Real Estate Development Co* [1991] BCLC 210 per Knox J at p 218 explaining retrospectively *Re Eloc Electro-Optieck and Communicatie BV* [1982] Ch 43.

ongoing litigation against the company in England and Wales.[515] Registration in England and Wales of a foreign judgment obtained by the petitioner against the company is not a sufficient connection.[516]

Centre of main interests

According to *Re BRAC Rent-A-Car International Inc*,[517] Regulation (EC) No 1346/2000 has **1.207** extended the jurisdiction of United Kingdom courts, in relation to the insolvency proceedings listed for the United Kingdom in annexes A and B to the Regulation (which include winding up by the court), to every debtor whose COMI is in the United Kingdom. It is submitted at 1.394–1.406 that this interpretation is wrong,[518] but even if it is correct it would not seem to make any difference to the court's jurisdiction over foreign companies. This is because, at present, it does not seem possible for a company to have its COMI in the jurisdiction without also having one of the factors discussed at 1.179–1.200 which would establish sufficient connection with England and Wales. In particular, it would seem that in order to be found to have its COMI in England and Wales, it would need to have a place of business here.

Literature

K Lipstein, 'Jurisdiction to wind up foreign companies' (1952) 11 CLJ 198.   **1.208**

Dicey, Morris and Collins on the Conflict of Laws, 14th edn (London: Sweet & Maxwell, 2006), r 163.

Kate Dawson, 'The doctrine of "*forum non conveniens*" and the winding up of insolvent foreign companies' [2005] JBL 28.

Foreign companies: discretion whether or not to make an order: appropriate forum

Subject to the rules on allocation of jurisdiction,[519] a foreign company may be wound up by **1.209** the court in England and Wales even if it is being wound up in the place where it was incorporated.[520] The fact that a company established under the laws of another jurisdiction is not being wound up in that jurisdiction does not affect the court's power to wind it up here.[521]

The court will not order the winding up of a foreign company if winding up can be carried **1.210** out adequately in the jurisdiction of incorporation, especially if the assets in the jurisdiction of the court in which winding up is sought are very small compared with those in the jurisdiction of incorporation.[522]

Inadequacy of the judicial system in the country of incorporation may indicate that there **1.211** should also be a winding up here.[523]

---

[515] *Jubilee International Inc v Farlin Timbers Pte Ltd* [2005] EWHC 3331 (Ch), [2006] BPIR 765, at [73].

[516] *Re Real Estate Development Co* [1991] BCLC 210.

[517] [2003] EWHC 128 (Ch), [2003] 1 WLR 1421; followed in *Re TXU Europe German Finance BV* [2005] BCC 90.

[518] As was held in *Re Salvage Association* [2003] EWHC 1028 (Ch), [2004] 1 WLR 174.

[519] See 1.347–1.432.

[520] See 10.185–10.187.

[521] *Scott v Hyde* (1908) 18 Que KB 138; *Calumet Metals Ltd v Eldredge* (1914) 23 Que KB 521.

[522] *Re Halifax Sugar Refinery Co Ltd* (1889) 22 NSR 71; *Re Standard Contract and Debenture Corporation* (1892) 8 TLR 485; *Re Jarvis Conklin Mortgage Co* (1895) 11 TLR 373; *Re Steel Realty Development Corporation* (1924) 27 OWN 37; *Tong Aik (Far East) Ltd v Eastern Minerals and Trading (1959) Ltd* [1965] 2 MLJ 149, in which the company's only assets in the jurisdiction in which winding up was sought amounted to M\$52; *New Hampshire Insurance Co v Rush and Tompkins Group plc* [1998] 2 BCLC 471.

[523] *Flame SA v Primera Maritime (Hellas) Ltd* [2010] EWHC 2053 (Ch), LTL 16/12/2010 (Liberia).

1.212 In *Re Wallace Smith and Co Ltd*[524] and *Re Wallace Smith Group Ltd*,[525] petitions to wind up Ontario companies were presented by the joint liquidators of a creditor company. If the petition had succeeded they could have got themselves or their professional partners appointed liquidators of the Ontario companies and taken control of those companies' defence of proceedings brought against them by the petitioning company in Ontario. It was held that Ontario was the more appropriate jurisdiction for winding up.

Dissolved foreign corporations

1.213 The fact that a company incorporated under a foreign legal system has ceased to be a body corporate under that system does not affect the jurisdiction of an English court to order the company to be wound up.[526] In the case of a company which has been carrying on business in Great Britain and ceases to do so, this is provided expressly by IA 1986, s 225(1),[527] which reads:

> Where a company incorporated outside Great Britain which has been carrying on business in Great Britain ceases to carry on business in Great Britain, it may be wound up as an unregistered company under this Act, notwithstanding that it has been dissolved or otherwise ceased to exist as a company under or by virtue of the laws of the country under which it was incorporated.

1.214 This was enacted for the removal of doubt: it is not implied that the law was different before it was enacted.[528] In *Re Russian Commercial and Industrial Bank*[529] P O Lawrence J ordered the winding up of the bank (which had been incorporated in Russia in 1889) despite the fact that in other proceedings then before the Court of Appeal it had been asserted that the bank had ceased to exist as a separate legal entity in Russia because of Russian legislation of 1917–18 nationalizing banks.[530]

1.215 Section 225(2) points out that s 225 is subject to Regulation (EC) No 1346/2000.[531]

1.216 If a company incorporated under a foreign legal system has ceased to be a body corporate under that system, it follows that it has ceased to carry on business in Great Britain.[532]

---

[524] [1992] BCLC 970.
[525] [1992] BCLC 989.
[526] *Re Russian and English Bank* [1932] 1 Ch 663; *Re Tea Trading Co K and C Popoff Brothers* [1933] Ch 647; *Re Russian Bank for Foreign Trade* [1933] Ch 745; *Re Tovarishestvo Manufactur Liudvig-Rabenek* [1944] Ch 404; *Re Azoff-Don Commercial Bank* [1954] Ch 315; *Re Eurodis Electron plc* [2011] EWHC 1025 (Ch), [2012] BCC 57. Having been dissolved is a ground for winding up an unregistered company (IA 1986, s 221(5)(a)); see 8.119–8.130.
[527] First enacted as the Companies Act 1928, s 91.
[528] *Re Russian and English Bank* [1932] 1 Ch 663 per Bennett J at p 669; *Russian and English Bank v Baring Brothers and Co Ltd* [1936] AC 405 per Lord Atkin at pp 424–5; *Re Tovarishestvo Manufactur Liudvig-Rabenek* [1944] Ch 404 per Cohen J at p 413.
[529] (1922) 13 Ll L Rep 64.
[530] Although a majority of the Court of Appeal accepted this assertion, the House of Lords found that the burden of proving it had not been discharged (*Russian Commercial and Industrial Bank v Comptoir d'Escompte de Mulhouse* [1923] 2 KB 630, [1925] AC 112). Later, in a case involving another Russian bank, it was held that the legislation had dissolved the nationalized banks (*Re Russian Bank for Foreign Trade* [1933] Ch 745) and this was accepted as correct in *Re Russian Commercial and Industrial Bank* [1955] Ch 148 at p 149. The history of English courts' interpretation of the nationalization decrees is discussed by J E S Fawcett in 'Some foreign effects of nationalization of property' (1950) 27 BYIL 355.
[531] See 1.361–1.407.
[532] *Dairen Kisen KK v Shiang Kee* [1941] AC 373.

Status of a dissolved foreign corporation

When a dissolved foreign corporation is ordered to be wound it acquires the status of a **1.217**
company being wound up which is sufficient to enable it to bring legal proceedings in its
own name to recover property in which it was interested before its dissolution.[533] The assets
of the corporation, which might previously have been regarded as *bona vacantia*, become
available for payment of its creditors[534] and any surplus should be distributed among those
entitled to it according to the usual rules of winding up.[535] The corporation is not, however,
regarded as having been in existence as a juristic person in the period between its dissolution and the commencement of the winding up.[536] In *Re Banque des Marchands de Moscou
(Koupetschesky)*[537] it was held that a foreign corporation which had been dissolved could not
have employed a man who had provided legal services in connection with the company's
affairs between the time of its dissolution and the commencement of its winding up in
England, so he could not claim in the winding up for remuneration for those services. In
Re Russo-Asiatic Bank[538] it was held that a foreign corporation which had been dissolved
could not have been sued for a debt which became due in the period between its dissolution
and the commencement of its winding up in England, so that the limitation period for the
claim had not begun. It is difficult to reconcile the two preceding cases with the decision in
Re Russian Commercial and Industrial Bank[539] that a claim in the winding up of a dissolved
banking company by a customer for return of money on deposit with the bank at the time of
its dissolution had to be made on the basis that the relationship of banker and customer was
terminated by the winding-up order and not by the dissolution, which would imply that the
relationship continued in the period between dissolution and winding up. Similarly, in *Re
Eurodis Electron plc*[540] a company incorporated in Belgium had its COMI in England and
was put into administration here. Despite this, it was wound up by the court in Belgium
and dissolved. A year later, the company was wound up by the court in England on the
petition of the administrators. No question was raised of the appointment of the administrators ending when the company was dissolved and the court ordered that the outstanding
expenses of the administration were to be paid as an expense of the liquidation.

An order for the winding up by the court of a dissolved foreign corporation creates a com- **1.218**
pany being wound up against which claims may be made by persons who were creditors of
the corporation before it was dissolved. It seems that anticipation of this gives such persons
standing to petition as creditors for the winding up.[541]

If a foreign company is wound up by the court in England, that winding up continues **1.219**
despite the dissolution of the company in the jurisdiction in which it was incorporated.[542]
So litigation in Victoria in the name of a Western Australian company which had been

---

[533] *Russian and English Bank v Baring Brothers and Co Ltd* [1936] AC 405. There is, however, still no
company that can commence legal proceedings outside of the winding up (*United Service Insurance Co Ltd v
Lang* (1935) 35 SR (NSW) 487).
[534] *Re Banque Industrielle de Moscou* [1952] Ch 919; *Re Azoff-Don Commercial Bank* [1954] Ch 315.
[535] *Re Banque des Marchands de Moscou (Koupetschesky)* [1958] Ch 182.
[536] *Re Banque des Marchands de Moscou (Koupetschesky)* [1952] 1 All ER 1269.
[537] [1952] 1 All ER 1269.
[538] [1934] Ch 720.
[539] [1955] Ch 148.
[540] [2011] EWHC 1025 (Ch), [2012] BCC 57.
[541] See 7.557.
[542] *Re Agrenco Madeira – Comércio Internacional Lda* (2014) LTL 15/4/2014.

ordered to be wound up in Victoria could continue despite the company being dissolved in Western Australia while the Victorian winding up was in progress.[543]

Literature

1.220   M Mann, 'A note on the revivification of a dissolved foreign corporation' (1952) 15 MLR 479.

M Mann, 'The dissolved foreign corporation' (1955) 18 MLR 8.

M Mann, '*Re Russian Commercial and Industrial Bank* [1955] 2 WLR 62' (1955) 4 ICLQ 226.

L J Blom-Cooper, 'Jurisdiction to wind up a foreign company in England' (1959) 86 Journal du droit international privé 686. This article is based on an interpretation of what is now IA 1986, s 225, that is completely different from the one adopted in the discussion at 1.217–1.219.

Legislation Applied to Unregistered Companies

Unregistered Companies other than Insolvent Partnerships and European Economic Interest Groupings

1.221   IA 1986, s 221(1), provides that:

> [A]ll the provisions of this Act about winding up apply to an unregistered company with the exceptions and additions mentioned in the following subsections.

And s 229(1) provides:

> (1) The provisions of this part[544] with respect to unregistered companies are in addition to and not in restriction of any provisions in part 4 with respect to winding up companies by the court; and the court or liquidator may exercise any powers or do any act in the case of unregistered companies which might be exercised or done by it or him in winding up companies registered under the Companies Act 2006 in England and Wales or Scotland.

Insolvent Partnerships

Introduction

1.222   Compared to the provisions described at 1.221, the way in which legislation is applied to insolvent partnerships is much more complicated. As explained at 1.141–1.145, IPO 1994 provides for different versions of IA 1986, part 5, to apply to the four forms of petition that may be presented to wind up insolvent partnerships. In all versions, s 229 applies unchanged but each version has a different form of s 221.

Article 7

1.223   On a petition for the winding up of a partnership under IPO 1994, art 7 (where there is no concurrent petition for the winding up or bankruptcy of a member or former member), it is provided by IA 1986, s 221(5) and (6), as modified by IPO 1994, sch 3, para 3, that:

> (5) To the extent that they are applicable to the winding up of a company by the court in England and Wales on the petition of a creditor or of the Secretary of State, all the

---

[543] *T M Burke Estates Pty Ltd v PJ Constructions (Vic) Pty Ltd* [1991] 1 VR 610.
[544] Part 5 (ss 220–229).

provisions of this Act and the Companies Act [1985][545] about winding up apply to the winding up of an insolvent partnership as an unregistered company—

    (a) with the exceptions and additions mentioned in the following subsections of this section and in section 221A, and

    (b) with the modifications specified in part 2 of schedule 3 to [IPO 1994].[546]

(6) Sections 73(1), 74(2)(a) to (d) and (3), 75 to 78, 83, 122, 123, 176A, 202, 203, 205 and 250 shall not apply.

IA 1986, s 229, applies to IPO 1994, art 7, petitions by virtue of art 7(1).   **1.224**

Article 8

On a petition under IPO 1994, art 8 (petition to wind up a partnership with concurrent   **1.225** petitions for the winding up or bankruptcy of one or more members or former members), it is provided by IA 1986, s 221(5) and (6), as modified by IPO 1994, sch 4, para 3, that:

    (5) To the extent that they are applicable to the winding up of a company by the court in England and Wales on a creditor's petition, all the provisions of this Act and the Companies Act [1985][547] about winding up apply to the winding up of an insolvent partnership as an unregistered company—

        (a) with the exceptions and additions mentioned in the following subsections of this section, and

        (b) with the modifications specified in part 2 of schedule 4 to [IPO 1994].[548]

    (6) Sections 73(1), 74(2)(a) to (d) and (3), 75 to 78, 83, 154, 176A, 202, 203, 205 and 250 shall not apply.

Unlike IA 1986, s 221(6), as modified to apply to IPO 1994, art 7, petitions, it is unneces-   **1.226** sary to except IA 1986, ss 122 and 123, from applying to IPO 1994, art 8, petitions, because appropriate modifications are made to those sections by sch 4, paras 6(a) and 7(a). IA 1986, s 229, applies to IPO, art 8, petitions by virtue of art 8(1).

Article 9

On a petition under IPO 1994, art 9 (member's petition to wind up a partnership without   **1.227** concurrent petitions for the winding up or bankruptcy of any members), it is provided by IA 1986, s 221(5) and (6), as modified by IPO 1994, sch 5, para 2, that:

    (5) To the extent that they are applicable to the winding up of a company by the court in England and Wales on a member's petition or on a petition by the company, all the provisions of this Act and the Companies Act [1985][549] about winding up apply to the winding up of an insolvent partnership as an unregistered company—

        (a) with the exceptions and additions mentioned in the following subsections of this section and in section 221A, and

        (b) with the modifications specified in part 2 of schedule 3 to [IPO 1994].

    (6) Sections 73(1), 74(2)(a) to (d) and (3), 75 to 78, 83, 122, 123, 124(2) and (3), 176A, 202, 203, 205 and 250 shall not apply.

---

[545] The reference to the Companies Act 1985 is superfluous and should have been repealed on 1 October 2009.

[546] This provision is repeated by IPO 1994, art 7(3).

[547] The reference to the Companies Act 1985 is superfluous and should have been repealed on 1 October 2009.

[548] This provision is repeated by IPO 1994, art 8(3).

[549] The reference to the Companies Act 1985 is superfluous and should have been repealed on 1 October 2009.

1.228   IA 1986, s 229, applies to IPO, art 9, petitions by virtue of art 9(b).

Article 10

1.229   On a petition under IPO 1994, art 10 (member's petition to wind up a partnership with concurrent petitions for the winding up or bankruptcy of all members), it is provided by art 10(1)(a) that the following provisions of IA 1986 are to apply:

> sections 117, 124, 125, 221 [which is in part 5], 264, 265, 271 and 272..., modified in such manner that, after modification, they are as set out in schedule 6 to this Order.

Then it is provided in IA 1986, s 221(5) and (6), as modified by IPO 1994, sch 6, para 4, that:

> (5) To the extent that they are applicable to the winding up of a company by the court in England and Wales on a member's petition, all the provisions of this Act and the Companies Act [1985][550] about winding up apply to the winding up of an insolvent partnership as an unregistered company—
> (a) with the exceptions and additions mentioned in the following subsections of this section, and
> (b) with the modifications specified in part 2 of schedule 4 to [IPO 1994].
> (6) Sections 73(1), 74(2)(a) to (d) and (3), 75 to 78, 83, 124(2) and (3), 154, 176A, 202, 203, 205 and 250 shall not apply.

It is clear that it was intended by s 221(6) to exclude s 124(2) and (3) as originally enacted (the subsections relate specifically to contributories' petitions) and it was forgotten that IPO 1994, art 10(1)(a), replaces the whole of IA 1986, s 124, with the appropriately modified version set out in IPO 1994, sch 6, para 2. There is also a different modified version of IA 1986, s 124, in IPO 1994, sch 4, part 2, which may be applied by this version of IA 1986, s 221(5), though it is arguable that it is not applicable on a member's petition as it refers to petitions being 'presented by any creditor or creditors'.

1.230   IA 1986, s 229, applies to IPO 1994, art 10, petitions by virtue of art 10(1)(b).

European Economic Interest Groupings and European Groupings of Territorial Cooperation

1.231   Where a European economic interest grouping is wound up as an unregistered company, the provisions of IA 1986, part 5, apply with the modification[551] that s 221(1) reads:

> [A]ll the provisions of Council Regulation (EEC) No 2137/85 and of this Act about winding up apply to an unregistered company with the exceptions and additions mentioned in the following subsections.

1.232   Where a European grouping of territorial cooperation with its registered office in the United Kingdom (a UK EGTC) is wound up as an unregistered company, the provisions of IA 1986, part 5, apply with the modification[552] that s 221(1) reads:

> [A]ll the provisions of Regulation (EC) No 1082/2006 of the European Parliament and of the Council and of this Act about winding up apply to an unregistered company with the exceptions and additions mentioned in the following subsections.

---

[550] The reference to the Companies Act 1985 is superfluous and should have been repealed on 1 October 2009.

[551] Made by the European Economic Interest Grouping Regulations 1989 (SI 1989/638), reg 8(1).

[552] Made by the European Grouping of Territorial Cooperation Regulations 2007 (SI 2007/1949), sch, para 7.

Scope of other Company Insolvency Procedures

Bank and Building Society Insolvency

For the purposes of the provisions on bank insolvency, 'bank' is defined[553] as: **1.233**

> a UK institution[554] which has permission under Part 4A of the Financial Services and Markets Act 2000 to carry on the regulated activity of accepting deposits (within the meaning of section 22 of that Act, taken with Schedule 2 and any order under section 22).[555]

Part 4A permission to accept deposits can only be given to a body corporate or a **1.234** partnership.[556] The activity of accepting deposits is a PRA-regulated activity.[557] Provision is also made for banks not regulated by the PRA. An 'FCA-regulated bank' is defined as:

> a bank which does not carry on any activity which is a PRA-regulated activity for the purposes of the Financial Services and Markets Act 2000.[558]

Building societies and credit unions are not banks.[559] Nor is any institution with permission **1.235** under the Financial Services and Markets Act 2000, part 4A, to effect or carry out insurance as principal.[560]

Building society insolvency is bank insolvency applied, with modifications, to build- **1.236** ing societies by the Building Societies Act 1986, s 90C. It applies to any building society incorporated (or deemed to be incorporated) under the Building Societies Act 1986.[561] An FCA-regulated building society is a building society which does not carry on any activity which is a PRA-regulated activity for the purposes of the Financial Services and Markets Act 2000.[562]

An order may be made by the Treasury providing for the provisions on bank insolvency to **1.237** apply to credit unions.[563] The government has consulted on putting this into effect so as to create 'credit union insolvency'.[564]

---

[553] In the Banking Act 2009, s 91(1).

[554] An institution which is incorporated in, or formed under the law of any part of, the United Kingdom (Banking Act 2009, s 91(3)). The term 'institution' is not defined either in that Act or in the Financial Services and Markets Act 2000.

[555] The regulated activity of deposit taking is defined briefly as 'accepting deposits' in the Financial Services and Markets Act 2000, sch 2, para 4, and that phrase is defined in detail in the Financial Services and Markets Act 2000 (Regulated Activities) Order 2001 (SI 2001/544), arts 5–9A. Persons who are exempt from the requirement to obtain permission to accept deposits are listed in the Financial Services and Markets Act 2000 (Exemption) Order 2001 (SI 2001/1201), sch, part 2, and persons who are exempt in relation to any regulated activity are listed in part 1 of that schedule.

[556] Financial Services and Markets Act 2000, s 55B and sch 6, paras 5A and 5B.

[557] Financial Services and Markets Act 2000 (PRA-regulated Activities) Order 2013 (SI 2013/556), art 2(a).

[558] Banking Act 2009, s 129A(2).

[559] Banking Act 2009, s 91(2).

[560] Banking Act 2009 (Exclusion of Insurers) Order 2010 (SI 2010/35).

[561] Building Societies Act 1986, s 119(1), definition of 'building society'.

[562] Banking Act 2009, s 129A(2), applied by the Building Societies Act 1986, s 90C.

[563] Banking Act 2009, s 131.

[564] HM Treasury, *Industrial and Provident Societies: Growth through Co-operation* (2013).

Voluntary Arrangement

1.238 A company voluntary arrangement may be put into effect for:[565]

(a) a company registered under the Companies Act 2006[566] in England and Wales or Scotland;

(b) a company incorporated in an EEA State other than the United Kingdom; or

(c) a company not incorporated in an EEA State but having its centre of main interests[567] in an EU member State[568] other than Denmark.

1.239 A voluntary arrangement under IA 1986 cannot be proposed for a company incorporated outside the United Kingdom which has a principal place of business in Northern Ireland unless it also has a principal place of business in England and Wales and/or Scotland.[569]

1.240 The legislation on company voluntary arrangements is applied in modified form to building societies,[570] charitable incorporated organizations,[571] insolvent partnerships[572] and their corporate members,[573] limited liability partnerships[574] and registered societies.[575] An order may be made by the Treasury, with the concurrence of the Secretary of State, to extend the legislation on company voluntary arrangements (CVAs) to incorporated friendly societies and unregistered friendly societies.[576]

1.241 A moratorium in preparation for a voluntary arrangement may be obtained for a company for which a voluntary arrangement may be made,[577] and any entity to which the legislation on CVAs is applied (except a building society[578]), provided the company or other entity is eligible. Eligibility depends on the size of the entity[579] and whether it is, or has recently been, subject to another insolvency procedure.[580] An entity may be excluded from eligibility if it is a financial services company of various kinds,[581] if it is financed in certain ways,[582]

---

[565] Insolvency Act 1986, s 1(4).

[566] See 1.87–1.104.

[567] 'Centre of main interests' has the same meaning as in Regulation (EC) No 1346/2000 (IA 1986, s 1(5)). See 1.376–1.386.

[568] The term 'member State' used in IA 1986, s 1(4), means EU member State. See the European Communities Act 1972, sch 1, part 2, and the Interpretation Act 1978, sch 1, definition of 'The Communities'.

[569] IA 1986, s 1(6).

[570] Building Societies Act 1986, sch 15A.

[571] Charitable Incorporated Organisations (Insolvency and Dissolution) Regulations 2012 (SI 2012/3013), sch, para 1.

[572] IPO 1994, art 4 and sch 1.

[573] IPO 1994, art 5.

[574] Limited Liability Partnerships Regulations 2001 (SI 2001/1090), reg 5.

[575] Co-operative and Community Benefit Societies and Credit Unions (Arrangements, Reconstructions and Administration) Order 2014 (SI 2014/229), art 2(1) and sch 1, paras 1–8. A society which is a private registered provider of social housing or is registered as a social landlord under the Housing Act 1996, part 1, or the Housing (Scotland) Act 2010, part 2, is excluded (SI 2014/229, art 1(2) definition of 'relevant society' and sch 1, paras 2 and 6(b)).

[576] Enterprise Act 2002, s 255.

[577] IA 1986, s 1A and sch A1.

[578] The Building Societies Act 1986, sch 6, para 1(2)(a), excludes the application of IA 1986, s 1A, to building societies.

[579] IA 1986, sch A1, paras 2(1) and 3 (which does not apply to industrial and provident societies). In relation to insolvent partnerships, para 3 is modified by IPO 1994, sch 1, part 2.

[580] IA 1986, sch A1, paras 2(1)(a) and 4. In relation to CIOs, para 2 is substituted by SI 2012/3013, sch 1, para 1(7). In relation to insolvent partnerships, IA 1986, sch A1, para 4, is modified by IPO 1994, sch 1, part 2.

[581] IA 1986, sch A1, paras 2(1)(b), (2) and (3).

[582] IA 1986, sch A1, paras 4A, 4C to 4G and 4K. These provisions do not apply to insolvent partnerships (IA 1986, s 1A(4), as modified by IPO 1994, sch 1, part 1).

or if it is the project company of a public-private partnership project which includes step-in rights.[583]

Schedule B1 Administration

Administration under IA 1986, s 8 and sch B1, may be entered into by:[584]   **1.242**

(a) a company registered under the Companies Act 2006[585] in England and Wales or Scotland;
(b) a company incorporated in an EEA State other than the United Kingdom; or
(c) a company not incorporated in an EEA State but having its centre of main interests[586] in an EU member State[587] other than Denmark.

IA 1986, s 8 and sch B1, apply to a European public limited-liability company with a   **1.243** registered office in England and Wales or Scotland[588] and are applied in modified form to charitable incorporated organizations,[589] limited liability partnerships,[590] insolvent partnerships[591] and registered societies.[592]

An order may be made by the Treasury, with the concurrence of the Secretary of State, to   **1.244** extend the legislation on administration to incorporated friendly societies and unregistered friendly societies.[593]

Industry-specific Administration Regimes

Introduction

Various Acts have provided special administration regimes for insolvent companies which are **1.245** subject to industry-specific regulation and licensing. The earlier Acts up to 2003[594] do this by means of modified versions of IA 1986, part 2, as in force at that time. For the purposes of these modified versions, IA 1986, part 2, has been continued in force without the amendments made by the Enterprise Act 2002, s 248,[595] which came into force on 15 September 2003.[596]

---

[583] IA 1986, sch A1, paras 4B and 4H to 4K. These provisions do not apply to insolvent partnerships (IA 1986, s 1A(4), as modified by IPO 1994, sch 1, part 1).

[584] IA 1986, sch B1, para 111(1A). This provision was inserted by the Insolvency Act 1986 (Amendment) Regulations 2005 (SI 2005/879), which came into force on 13 April 2005.

[585] See 1.87–1.104.

[586] 'Centre of main interests' has the same meaning as in Regulation (EC) No 1346/2000 (IA 1986, sch B1, para 111(1B)). See 1.376–1.386.

[587] The term 'member State' used in IA 1986, sch B1, para 111(1A), means EU member State. See the European Communities Act 1972, sch 1, part 2, and the Interpretation Act 1978, sch 1, definition of 'The Communities'.

[588] Regulation (EC) No 2157/2001, art 9(1)(c)(ii).

[589] Charitable Incorporated Organisations (Insolvency and Dissolution) Regulations 2012 (SI 2012/3013), sch, para 1.

[590] Limited Liability Partnerships Regulations 2001 (SI 2001/1090), reg 5.

[591] IPO 1994, art 6 and sch 2.

[592] Co-operative and Community Benefit Societies and Credit Unions (Arrangements, Reconstructions and Administration) Order 2014 (SI 2014/229), art 2(2) and sch 1, paras 1 and 9–40. A society which is a private registered provider of social housing or is registered as a social landlord under the Housing Act 1996, part 1, or the Housing (Scotland) Act 2010, part 2, is excluded (SI 2014/229, art 1(2) definition of 'relevant society' and sch 1, paras 9, 10 and 34(b)).

[593] Enterprise Act 2002, s 255.

[594] Water Industry Act 1991; Railways Act 1993; Building Societies Act 1986 as amended by the Building Societies Act 1997; Greater London Authority Act 1999; Transport Act 2000. See 1.248–1.261.

[595] See s 249.

[596] Enterprise Act 2002 (Commencement No 4 and Transitional Provisions and Savings) Order 2003 (SI 2003/2093), art 2(1) and sch 1.

1.246   Before the scope of the administration provisions was defined in the legislation,[597] there was controversy over whether use of the word 'company' in IA 1986, part 2, meant that the administration provisions applied only to registered companies or whether adminis-tration could also be used by unregistered companies. This controversy is referred to in *Re Salvage Association*[598] by Blackburne J, who found it unnecessary to resolve the ques-tion. The adaptations made for some pre-2003 industry-specific administration regimes, expressly extending those regimes to unregistered companies, repeatedly treated IA 1986, part 2, as applying only to registered companies,[599] and the same treatment will be adopted in this work.

1.247   Legislation since 2003[600] has provided industry-specific administration regimes by means of adapted versions of IA 1986, s 8 and sch B1, as currently in force. Schedule B1 contains an express statement of its scope.[601] It seems that the earlier regimes will be converted to a sch B1 basis when a suitable legislative opportunity occurs.[602]

Water industry special administration

1.248   A special administration order[603] may be made by the High Court under the Water Industry Act 1991, s 24 or s 25, in relation to a company which holds an appointment as a water undertaker or a sewerage undertaker for an area of England and Wales under part 2, chapter 1, of the Act, or which is a qualifying licensed water supplier or a licensed infrastructure provider.[604] A qualifying licensed water supplier is defined in s 23(6) as a company which holds a combined licence[605] authorizing it to 'introduce water into a water undertaker's supply system'[606] where that introduction of water is designated as a strategic supply under s 66G or a collective strategic supply under s 66H. A licensed infrastructure provider is an infrastructure provider[607] which is the holder for the time being of a project licence granted under s 17FA.[608]

1.249   A special administration is governed by:

(a) IA 1986, part 2, without the amendments made by the Enterprise Act 2002, s 248,[609] but modified by the Water Industry Act 1991, sch 3;[610] and

(b) the Water Industry (Special Administration) Rules 2009.[611]

---

[597] By IA 1986, sch B1, para 111(1A), which came into force on 13 April 2005.

[598] [2003] EWHC 1028 (Ch), [2004] 1 WLR 174, at [7].

[599] Water Industry Act 1991, sch 3, para 1(b); Railways Act 1993, sch 6, para 1(b); Greater London Authority Act 1999, sch 13, para 1(b). And see the discussion at 1.394–1.406.

[600] See 1.262–1.294.

[601] IA 1986, sch B1, para 111(1A). See 1.242.

[602] This has been done to the Water Industry Act 1991 by the Flood and Water Management Act 2010, sch 5, para 6, which has not yet been brought into force.

[603] Defined in the Water Act 1991, s 23, which specifies the purposes of such an order.

[604] Water Industry Act 1991, s 23(1).

[605] Water Industry Act 1991, s 17A(6).

[606] Water Industry Act 1991, s 17A(5).

[607] A company designated as such under the Water Industry Act 1991, s 36D, and the Water Industry (Specified Infrastructure Projects) (English Undertakers) Regulations 2013 (SI 2013/1582), reg 8(1) (see SI 2013/1582, reg 2).

[608] SI 2013/1582, reg 2.

[609] See s 249.

[610] Applied to licensed infrastructure providers by SI 2013/1582, sch 1, para 7(4).

[611] SI 2009/2477. Applied with modifications to licensed infrastructure providers by SI 2013/1582, sch 1, para 7(7).

For the purposes of special administration orders the application of IA 1986, part 2, is **1.250**
extended to cover statutory companies as well as registered companies.[612]

When relevant provisions of the Flood and Water Management Act 2010, sch 5, para 6, **1.251**
are brought into force, special administration will be governed by an adapted version of IA
1986, sch B1, and new regulations.[613]

Protected railway companies: railway administration

A railway administration order[614] may be made by the court under the Railways Act 1993, **1.252**
s 60, 61 or 62, in relation to a protected railway company.[615] The term 'protected railway
company' is defined[616] as a company which is both:

(a) a private sector operator;[617] and
(b) the holder of:
  (i) a passenger licence or a European licence which authorizes the carriage of passen-
      gers by railway (or both); or
  (ii) a network licence, a station licence or a light maintenance depot licence.

'Company' means either a company registered under the Companies Act 2006[618] (in any **1.253**
part of the United Kingdom) or a company not registered under that Act.[619] As it applies to a
rail link service operator,[620] the definition of 'protected railway company' is modified so that
it simply means a company which is a private sector operator.[621]

A railway administration is governed by: **1.254**

(a) the Railways Act 1993, ss 59–62;
(b) IA 1986, part 2, without the amendments made by the Enterprise Act 2002, s 248,[622]
    but modified by the Railways Act 1993, sch 6; and
(c) the Railway Administration Order Rules 2001.[623]

For the purposes of railway administration orders the application of IA 1986, part 2, is **1.255**
extended to cover companies not registered under the Companies Act 2006 in England
and Wales or Scotland.[624]

---

[612] Water Industry Act 1991, sch 3, para 1(b).
[613] The Secretary of State's power to make regulations was brought into force on 1 October 2010 (Flood
and Water Management Act 2010 (Commencement No. 1 and Transitional Provisions) Order 2010 (SI
2010/2169), art 4 and sch) but none had appeared when this edition went to press.
[614] Defined in the Railways Act 1993, s 59, which states the purposes of such an order.
[615] Railways Act 1993, s 59(1).
[616] In s 59(6)(a).
[617] Which is defined in s 83(1) to mean any body of persons other than a public sector operator as defined
in s 25.
[618] See 1.87–1.104.
[619] Railways Act 1993, s 65(1).
[620] Defined in the Channel Tunnel Rail Link Act 1996, s 19(10).
[621] Channel Tunnel Rail Link Act 1996, s 19(1).
[622] See s 249.
[623] SI 2001/3352.
[624] Railways Act 1993, sch 6, para 1(b).

Administration for building societies

1.256 The administration procedure in IA 1986, part 2, without the amendments made by the Enterprise Act 2002, s 248,[625] is applied to building societies by the Building Societies Act 1986, sch 15A.[626] In that application, IA 1986, part 2, has effect with the substitution of 'building society' for 'company', so that the adapted provisions apply to a building society incorporated (or deemed to be incorporated) under the Building Societies Act 1986.[627] There is power to make rules for the purpose of giving effect, in relation to building societies, to the provisions of IA 1986, part 2,[628] but no rules have ever been made.

PPP administration

1.257 A PPP administration order[629] may be made by the court under the Greater London Authority Act 1999, s 221, 222 or 223, in relation to a PPP company.[630] A PPP company is defined[631] as a party to a PPP agreement[632] which undertakes to carry out, or secure the carrying out, of any or all of the work mentioned in s 210(3), which is work on a railway or proposed railway for London Regional Transport or Transport for London, or any of their subsidiaries.

1.258 A PPP administration is governed by:

(a) the Greater London Authority Act 1999, ss 220–224;
(b) IA 1986, part 2, without the amendments made by the Enterprise Act 2002, s 248,[633] but modified by the Greater London Authority Act 1999, sch 14; and
(c) the PPP Administration Order Rules 2007.[634]

1.259 For the purposes of PPP administration orders the application of IA 1986, part 2, is extended to cover unregistered as well as registered companies.[635]

Air traffic administration

1.260 An air traffic administration order[636] may be made by the court under the Transport Act 2000, s 28, in relation to an air traffic services licence company, referred to in the Act as a 'licence company', meaning a company which holds a licence under part 1, chapter 1, of the Act.[637] A licence under that chapter authorizes the provision of air traffic services in respect of a managed area.[638] The term 'air traffic services' is defined in s 98. The 'managed

---

[625] See s 249.
[626] Inserted by the Building Societies Act 1997, s 39, as from 1 December 1997 (Building Societies Act 1997 (Commencement No 3) Order 1997 (SI 1997/2668), art 2(1)).
[627] Building Societies Act 1986, s 119(1).
[628] Building Societies Act 1986, sch 15A, para 4(1).
[629] Defined in the Greater London Authority Act 1999, s 220, which states the purposes of such an order. 'PPP' is used in the Act as an abbreviation for 'public-private partnership'.
[630] Two were made in 2007. See Emily Springford, 'The administration of Metronet' (2007) 23 Insolv L & P 162.
[631] By s 210(5).
[632] As defined in s 210.
[633] See s 249.
[634] SI 2007/3141.
[635] Greater London Authority Act 1999, sch 13, para 1(b).
[636] Defined in the Transport Act 2000, s 29, which specifies the purposes to be achieved by the administration.
[637] ss 26(6) and 40(5).
[638] s 5(1).

areas' are the United Kingdom and any area for which the UK has undertaken to provide air traffic services.[639]

An air traffic administration is governed by the Transport Act 2000, ss 26–32, and IA 1986, **1.261** part 2, without the amendments made by the Enterprise Act 2002, s 248,[640] but modified by the Transport Act 2000, sch 1. There is power to make rules for the purpose of giving effect to the provisions of the Transport Act 2000 relating to air traffic administration orders,[641] but no rules have ever been made.

Energy administration

An energy administration order[642] may be made by the court under the Energy Act 2004, s **1.262** 157, in relation to a protected energy company, which means[643] a company holding a licence under the Gas Act 1986, s 7 (licensing of gas transporters), or the Electricity Act 1989, s 6(1) (b) or (c) (transmission and distribution licences for electricity). The objective of an energy administration is specified in the Energy Act 2004, s 155, and sch 20, paras 1, 2, 3 and 4(f).

Energy administration is governed by: **1.263**

(a) the Energy Act 2004, ss 154–159;
(b) IA 1986, sch B1, as modified by the Energy Act 2004, sch 20; and
(c) the Energy Administration Rules 2005.[644]

For the purposes of energy administration orders the application of IA 1986, sch B1, is **1.264** extended to cover unregistered as well as registered companies.[645]

Bank administration and building society special administration

Bank administration and building society special administration are modified forms of **1.265** schedule B1 administration which may be used where part of the business of a bank or building society is (a) sold to a commercial purchaser or (b) transferred to a bridge bank controlled by the Bank of England.[646] Bank administration or building society special administration will apply to the non-sold or non-transferred part of the institution, called the 'residual' bank or building society.

A bank or building society administrator has two objectives. Objective 1 is to ensure **1.266** the supply to the private sector purchaser or bridge bank of such services and facilities as are required to enable it, in the opinion of the Bank of England, to operate effectively.[647] Otherwise bank administration and building society special administration operate in the same way as schedule B1 administration.[648] Objectives 2(a) and 2(b)[649] correspond to objectives (a) and (b) of schedule B1 administration.[650] Objective 2(a) is to rescue the

---

[639] s 40(3).
[640] See the Enterprise Act 2002, s 249.
[641] Transport Act 2000, s 30(5) and (6).
[642] Defined in the Energy Act 2004, s 154.
[643] By s 154(5).
[644] SI 2005/2483.
[645] Energy Act 2004, s 171(1) definition of 'company', and sch 20, paras 33–40.
[646] Banking Act 2009, ss 11, 12 and 136. Applied to building societies by the Building Societies Act 1986, s 90C.
[647] Banking Act 2009, s 138(1); Building Societies Act 1986, s 90C.
[648] Banking Act 2009, s 137; Building Societies Act 1986, s 90C.
[649] Banking Act 2009, s 140(1); Building Societies Act 1986, s 90C.
[650] IA 1986, sch B1, para 3(1).

residual institution as a going concern. Objective 2(b) is to achieve a better result for the residual institution's creditors as a whole[651] than would be likely if the residual institution were wound up without first being in bank administration or building society special administration.[652] A bank or building society administrator must begin working towards both objectives 1 and 2 immediately upon appointment, but objective 1 takes priority over objective 2[653] until objective 1 ceases when the Bank of England gives the administrator an objective 1 achievement notice.[654] This is a notice to the administrator that the residual institution is no longer required in connection with the private sector purchaser or bridge bank. A bank administrator or building society special administrator cannot pursue objective 2(b) unless of the opinion either:[655]

(a) that it is not reasonably practicable to achieve objective 2(a); or
(b) that objective 2(b) would achieve a better result for the residual institution's creditors as a whole than objective 2(a) would.

1.267   For the definitions of 'bank' and 'building society' in this context see 1.233–1.236. The provisions on bank administration also apply to investment firms as defined in the Banking Act 2009, s 258A,[656] except firms that do not deal in any financial instruments for their own account or underwrite issues of financial instruments on a firm commitment basis.[657] 'Investment firm' is defined[658] as a UK institution[659] (apart from a bank, building society or credit union[660]) which is (or, but for the exercise of a stabilization power,[661] would be) an investment firm for the purposes of Regulation (EU) No 575/2013 (the Capital Requirements Regulation). That means[662] an institution which is subject to the requirements imposed by Directive 2004/39/EC (the Markets in Financial Instruments Directive, MiFID), excluding credit institutions,[663] local firms[664] and firms which, because of limitations on their authorization, may not at any time place themselves in debt with their clients.

---

[651] Including, in the case of a building society, all holders of shares in the society (Building Societies (Insolvency and Special Administration) Order 2009 (SI 2009/805), sch 1, para 25).

[652] Banking Act 2009, s 140(1)(b); Building Societies Act 1986, s 90C.

[653] Banking Act 2009, s 137(2); Building Societies Act 1986, s 90C.

[654] Banking Act 2009, s 139; Building Societies Act 1986, s 90C.

[655] Banking Act 2009, s 140(2); Building Societies Act 1986, s 90C.

[656] Banking Act 2009, s 159A.

[657] Banking Act 2009, s 258A(2)(b); Banking Act 2009 (Exclusion of Investment Firms of a Specified Description) Order 2014 (SI 2014/1832); Directive 2013/36/EU, art 29.

[658] Banking Act 2009, s 258A(1).

[659] An institution which is incorporated in, or formed under the law of any part of, the United Kingdom (s 258A(6), which is the same as the definition in s 91(3)).

[660] s 258A(2)(a). Section 159 authorizes the Treasury to apply the provisions on bank administration to credit unions, but this has not yet happened.

[661] The stabilization powers are defined in s 1(4) as the resolution instrument, share transfer, property transfer and third country instrument powers, with references to the sections which provide them.

[662] Regulation (EU) No 575/2013, art 4(1)(2).

[663] Defined in Regulation (EU) No 575/2013, art 4(1)(1), as an undertaking the business of which is to take deposits or other repayable funds from the public and to grant credits for its own account.

[664] Defined in art 4(1)(4) as a firm dealing for its own account on markets in financial futures or options or other derivatives and on cash markets for the sole purpose of hedging positions on derivatives markets, or dealing for the accounts of other members of those markets and being guaranteed by clearing members of the same markets, where responsibility for ensuring the performance of contracts entered into by such a firm is assumed by clearing members of the same markets.

Bank administration and building society special administration are governed by: **1.268**

(a) the Banking Act 2009, part 3;[665]
(b) IA 1986, sch B1, as applied and modified by the Banking Act 2009, s 145(2), (3), (4) and table 1;[666]
(c) other provisions of IA 1986 applied and modified by the Banking Act 2009, s 145(2), (3), (4) and table 2;[667]
(d) the Bank Administration (England and Wales) Rules 2009;[668]
(e) the Building Society Special Administration (England and Wales) Rules 2010.[669]

Investment bank special administration

An investment bank special administration order is an order appointing a person as the **1.269**
investment bank administrator of an investment bank.[670] Such an order may be made by the High Court.[671] 'Investment bank' is defined[672] as an institution incorporated in, or formed under the law of any part of, the United Kingdom,[673] which holds client assets[674] and[675] has permission under the Financial Services and Markets Act 2000, part 4A, to carry on the regulated activity of:

(a) safeguarding and administering investments;
(b) dealing in investments as principal; or
(c) dealing in investments as agent.

Permission to carry on these activities may be given to an individual, a body corporate, a **1.270**
partnership or an unincorporated association.[676]

An investment bank that is also a deposit-taking bank[677] cannot be put into special admin- **1.271**
istration if it has eligible depositors.[678] Instead, it can be put into special administration (bank insolvency)[679] or special administration (bank administration).[680]

---

[665] ss 136–168. Applied to building societies by the Building Societies Act 1986, s 90C, with the modifications made by the Building Societies (Insolvency and Special Administration) Order 2009 (SI 2009/805), sch 1.

[666] In relation to building societies, further modifications are made by SI 2009/805, sch 1, paras 26, 27, 29 and 30.

[667] In relation to building societies, further modifications are made by SI 2009/805, sch 1, para 28.

[668] SI 2009/357.

[669] SI 2010/2580.

[670] Investment Bank Special Administration Regulations 2011 (SI 2011/245), reg 4(1).

[671] The Court of Session in Scotland. The High Court in Northern Ireland. SI 2011/245, regs 2(1) and 7.

[672] Banking Act 2009, s 232.

[673] s 232(5).

[674] 'Client assets' are assets which an institution has undertaken to hold for a client (whether or not on trust and whether or not the undertaking has been complied with) (s 232(4)). 'Assets' includes money (s 232(5A)(a)), but does not include anything which the institution holds for the purposes of carrying on an insurance mediation activity (s 232(5A)(b), subject to exceptions defined in s 232(5A)(b) and (5B)). 'Insurance mediation activity' is defined in the Financial Services and Markets Act 2000, sch 6 (as originally enacted), para 2(5) and (6).

[675] Banking Act 2009, s 232(2).

[676] Financial Services and Markets Act 2000, s 40(1).

[677] A 'deposit-taking bank' is defined by SI 2011/245, reg 2(1), as an investment bank to which the definition of 'bank' in either s 2 or s 91 of the Banking Act 2009 applies. The definition in s 91 is set out at 1.233. The definition in s 2, which applies to part 1 of the Act, differs only in excluding Northern Ireland credit unions.

[678] SI 2011/245, reg 3(3)(a). For the definition of 'eligible depositor' see 1.20.

[679] See 1.275–1.277.

[680] See 1.278–1.280.

1.272   The objectives of investment bank special administration are set out in SI 2011/245, regs 10–13.

1.273   An investment bank special administration is governed by:

(a) the Investment Bank Special Administration Regulations 2011,[681] which apply IA 1986, sch B1, with modifications; and

(b) the Investment Bank Special Administration (England and Wales) Rules 2011.[682]

1.274   For the purposes of investment bank special administration orders, the application of IA 1986, sch B1, is limited to cover only registered companies.[683] However, other provisions of SI 2011/245 apply where an investment bank is a limited liability partnership[684] or a partnership.[685]

Special administration (bank insolvency)

1.275   Special administration (bank insolvency) is a modified form of investment bank special administration which incorporates some of the bank insolvency procedure. It is to be used as an alternative to bank insolvency, but only for an investment bank which is a deposit-taking bank with eligible depositors.[686] Such a bank cannot be put into investment bank special administration.[687]

1.276   In special administration (bank insolvency), the administrator's objectives are object-ive A, which is the same as objective 1 of bank insolvency,[688] and the special admin-istration objectives set out in SI 2011/1245, reg 10.[689] Objective A has priority until the objective A committee[690] has passed a full payment resolution.[691] A full payment resolution is a resolution that objective A has been achieved entirely or so far as is rea-sonably practicable.[692]

1.277   A special administration (bank insolvency) is governed by:

(a) the Investment Bank Special Administration Regulations 2011,[693] sch 1, which pro-vides that a special administration (bank insolvency) order is to be treated as an invest-ment bank special administration order, subject to the modifications set out in the schedule;[694] and

(b) the Investment Bank Special Administration (England and Wales) Rules 2011.[695]

---

[681] SI 2011/245.

[682] SI 2011/1301.

[683] IA 1986, sch B1, para 111, as applied and modified by SI 2011/245, reg 15(4), (5) and table 1.

[684] SI 2011/245, reg 24 and sch 3.

[685] SI 2011/245, reg 25 and sch 4.

[686] Investment Bank Special Administration Regulations 2011 (SI 2011/245), reg 3(3) and (4). For the definition of 'deposit-taking bank' see 1.271. For the definition of 'eligible depositor' see 1.20.

[687] SI 2011/245, reg 3(3)(a).

[688] Defined at 1.20.

[689] SI 2011/245, sch 1, para 4(1).

[690] Equivalent to the liquidation committee in bank insolvency (SI 2011/245, sch 1, para 6(2)(f)).

[691] SI 2011/245, sch 1, para 4(2).

[692] Banking Act 2009, s 100(5)(a), applied and modified by SI 2011/245, sch 1, para 6.

[693] SI 2011/245.

[694] SI 2011/245, sch 1, para 3.

[695] SI 2011/1301.

Special administration (bank administration)

Special administration (bank administration) is a modified form of investment bank special administration which incorporates some of the bank administration procedure.[696] It is to be used as an alternative to bank administration, but only for an investment bank which is a deposit-taking bank, either with or without eligible depositors.[697] If such a bank has eligible depositors, it cannot be put into investment bank special administration.[698] If it has no eligible depositors, it cannot be put into special administration (bank insolvency).[699] **1.278**

In special administration (bank administration), the administrator's objectives are objective A, which is the same as objective 1 of bank administration,[700] and the special administration objectives set out in SI 2011/1245, reg 10.[701] Objective A has priority until the Bank of England issues an objective A achievement notice.[702] Like an objective 1 achievement notice in bank administration, this is a notice that the residual bank is no longer required in connection with the private sector purchaser or bridge bank.[703] **1.279**

A special administration (bank administration) is governed by: **1.280**

(a) the Investment Bank Special Administration Regulations 2011,[704] sch 2, which provides that a special administration (bank administration) order is to be treated as an investment bank special administration order, subject to the modifications set out in the schedule;[705] and

(b) the Investment Bank Special Administration (England and Wales) Rules 2011.[706]

Postal administration

A postal administration order[707] can be made under the Postal Services Act 2011, s 71, in relation to a company which is a universal service provider by a court having jurisdiction to wind up the company.[708] 'Company' can be any registered or unregistered company which a court has jurisdiction to wind up,[709] but it is contemplated that subsidiary legislation will be necessary to extend postal administration to partnerships.[710] A universal service provider is a postal operator which has been designated as such by Ofcom.[711] Normally only one universal service provider can be designated.[712] **1.281**

The objective of a postal administration is identified in the Postal Services Act 2001, s 69. **1.282**

---

[696] See 1.265–1.268.
[697] Investment Bank Special Administration Regulations 2011 (SI 2011/245), reg 3(3) and (4). For the definitions of 'investment bank' and 'deposit-taking bank' see 1.269–1.271. For the definition of 'eligible depositor' see 1.20.
[698] SI 2011/245, reg 3(3)(a).
[699] SI 2011/245, reg 3(4).
[700] Banking Act 2009, ss 137 and 138; SI 2011/245, sch 2, para 3(1)(a).
[701] SI 2011/245, sch 2, para 3(1).
[702] SI 2011/245, sch 2, para 3(2) and (3).
[703] SI 2011/245, sch 2, para 3(2) and (3).
[704] SI 2011/245.
[705] SI 2011/245, sch 2, para 5.
[706] SI 2011/1301.
[707] Defined in the Postal Services Act 2011, s 68.
[708] Postal Services Act 2011, s 85(1) definition of 'the court'.
[709] Postal Services Act 2011, s 85(1), definitions of 'company' and 'unregistered company'.
[710] Postal Services Act 2011, s 86.
[711] Postal Services Act 2011, s 35. The term 'postal operator' is defined in s 27.
[712] Postal Services Act 2011, s 35(2)–(4).

1.283 A postal administration is governed by:

(a) the Postal Services Act 2011, part 4;[713]
(b) IA 1986, sch B1, modified by the Postal Services Act 2011, sch 10; and
(c) the Postal Administration Rules 2013.[714]

Energy supply company administration

1.284 An energy supply company is a company holding a licence under the Gas Act 1986, s 7A(1) (a) or (b) (licensing of gas suppliers and gas shippers), or the Electricity Act 1989, s 6(1) (d) (transmission and distribution licences for electricity).[715] An energy supply company administration order[716] may be made in relation to an energy supply company under the Energy Act 2004, s 157, as applied by the Energy Act 2011, s 96. It may be made by the court having jurisdiction to wind up the energy supply company or which would have such jurisdiction apart from IA 1986, s 221(2) or 441(2).[717]

1.285 The objective of an energy supply company administration is identified in the Energy Act 2011, ss 95 and 96(1) and (2)(a).

1.286 An energy supply company administration is governed by:

(a) the Energy Act 2011, ss 94–102;
(b) IA 1986, sch B1, modified by the Energy Act 2004, sch 20, and applied by the Energy Act 2011, s 96; and
(c) the Energy Supply Company Administration Rules 2013.[718]

1.287 For the purposes of energy supply company administration orders the application of IA 1986, sch B1, is extended to cover unregistered as well as registered companies.[719]

Health special administration

1.288 The Health and Social Care Act 2012 will[720] require any person who provides a health care service for the purposes of the NHS to hold a licence from Monitor (the regulator for health services),[721] unless an exemption applies.[722] The court may, on the application of Monitor, make a health special administration order in relation to a 'relevant provider',[723] meaning a company providing services to which a condition included in the company's licence under s 97(1)(i), (j) or (k) applies.[724] Such conditions are concerned with ensuring a continuing supply of services. 'Company' in this context includes a company not registered under the Companies Act 2006.[725]

---

[713] ss 68–88.
[714] SI 2013/3208.
[715] Energy Act 2011, s 94(5).
[716] Defined in the Energy Act 2011, s 94.
[717] Energy Act 2011, s 102(1).
[718] SI 2013/1046.
[719] Energy Act 2011, s 102(1).
[720] The provisions of the Act considered here have not yet been brought into force.
[721] ss 81, 85 and 87.
[722] ss 83 and 84.
[723] s 128(1) and (2).
[724] s 128(9).
[725] Health and Social Care Act 2012, s 128(9).

The objective of a health special administration is identified in the Health and Social Care   **1.289**
Act 2012, s 129.

Unusually, the primary legislation does not itself state how IA 1986, sch B1, is to apply to   **1.290**
health special administration, leaving that to regulations, which have not yet been made.[726]

FMI administration

An FMI (financial market infrastructure) company, or 'infrastructure company', is a com-   **1.291**
pany registered under the Companies Act 2006[727] which is:[728]

(a) the operator of a recognized inter-bank payment system,[729] other than a recognized
    central counterparty;[730]
(b) approved by the Bank of England under the Uncertificated Securities Regulations
    2001[731] as the operator of a securities settlement system; or
(c) designated by the Treasury under the Financial Services (Banking Reform) Act 2013,
    s 112(4), as providing services to companies (a) and (b) which, if interrupted, would have
    a serious adverse effect on their systems.

When the relevant provisions are brought into force, an FMI administration order[732] may   **1.292**
be made in relation to an infrastructure company under the Financial Services (Banking
Reform) Act 2013, s 117, by the High Court[733] on the application of the Bank of England.[734]

The objective of FMI administration is set out in the Financial Services (Banking Reform)   **1.293**
Act 2013, s 115.

An FMI administration is governed by: **1.294**

(a) the Financial Services (Banking Reform) Act 2013, part 6;[735]
(b) IA 1986, sch B1, modified by the Financial Services (Banking Reform) Act 2013,
    sch 6; and
(c) rules which have not yet been promulgated.

Administrative Receivership

The term 'administrative receiver' means:[736]   **1.295**

   (a) a receiver or manager of the whole (or substantially the whole) of a company's property
       appointed by or on behalf of the holders of any debentures of the company secured by
       a charge which, as created, was a floating charge, or by such a charge and one or more
       other securities; or
   (b) a person who would be such a receiver or manager but for the appointment of some other
       person as the receiver of part of the company's property.

---

[726] Health and Social Care Act 2012, s 130.
[727] Financial Services (Banking Reform) Act 2013, s 113(1).
[728] Financial Services (Banking Reform) Act 2013, s 112(1) and (2).
[729] A system in respect of which a recognition order under the Banking Act 2009, s 184, is in force
(Financial Services (Banking Reform) Act 2013, s 113(1)).
[730] Defined in the Financial Services and Markets Act 2000, s 285.
[731] SI 2001/3755.
[732] Defined in the Financial Services (Banking Reform) Act 2013, s 114.
[733] Financial Services (Banking Reform) Act 2013, s 127(1) definition of 'the court'.
[734] Financial Services (Banking Reform) Act 2013, s 116.
[735] ss 111–128.
[736] IA 1986, s 29(2).

1.296   In this context, 'company' means a company registered under the Companies Act 2006 in England and Wales or Scotland,[737] but 'receiver' does not include a receiver appointed under Scots law.[738] These provisions apply to limited liability partnerships[739] and to a European public limited-liability company with a registered office in England and Wales or Scotland.[740] Before the limitation to companies registered in England and Wales or Scotland came into force,[741] it was held that 'company' in the definition of 'administrative receiver' included a company incorporated outside Great Britain[742] but not a registered society.[743]

Voluntary Winding Up

1.297   Voluntary winding up is one of the two types of winding up of a company which are permitted by IA 1986, part 4, the other being winding up by the court.[744] Provisions relating to voluntary winding up are in ss 84–116. Those provisions apply to the winding up of a company registered under the Companies Act 2006 in England and Wales or Scotland.[745] They also apply to a European cooperative society,[746] a European public limited-liability company with a registered office in England and Wales or Scotland,[747] a registered society,[748] and, in modified form, to building societies,[749] charitable incorporated organizations,[750] incorporated friendly societies[751] and limited liability partnerships.[752]

1.298   Unlike winding up by the court, voluntary winding up is not available for unregistered companies, except 'in accordance with' Regulation (EC) No 1346/2000.[753] Voluntary winding up is not in itself a proceeding to which the Regulation applies, because it is not listed in annex A to the Regulation, but creditors' voluntary winding (with confirmation by the court)[754] and winding up subject to the supervision of the court[755] are listed in annexes A and B. In *Re TXU Europe German Finance BV*[756] the Chief Bankruptcy Registrar held, following *Re BRAC Rent-A-Car International Inc*,[757] that the Regulation gives any unregistered company with its COMI in the United Kingdom the power to adopt a

---

[737] IA 1986, s 28(1). See 1.87–1.104.

[738] IA 1986, s 28(2).

[739] Limited Liability Partnerships Regulations 2001 (SI 2001/1090), reg 5.

[740] Regulation (EC) No 2157/2001, art 9(1)(c)(ii).

[741] Inserted by the Companies Act 2006 (Consequential Amendments, Transitional Provisions and Savings) Order 2009 (SI 2009/1941), sch 1, para 74(1) and (2), as from 1 October 2009.

[742] *Re International Bulk Commodities Ltd* [1993] Ch 77.

[743] *Re Devon and Somerset Farmers Ltd* [1994] Ch 57. At that time registered societies were called industrial and provident societies.

[744] IA 1986, s 73(2).

[745] IA 1986, s 73(1). See 1.87–1.104.

[746] See 1.123.

[747] Regulation (EC) No 2157/2001, art 9(1)(c)(ii).

[748] See 1.127–1.128.

[749] Building Societies Act 1986, s 88 and sch 15, para 10.

[750] Charitable Incorporated Organisations (Insolvency and Dissolution) Regulations 2012 (SI 2012/3013), sch, para 1(1)–(4) and (7).

[751] Friendly Societies Act 1992, s 21 and sch 10, paras 10–17.

[752] Limited Liability Partnerships Regulations 2001 (SI 2001/1090), reg 5 and sch 3.

[753] IA 1986, s 221(4).

[754] See 10.142–10.151.

[755] Which is not currently available in the United Kingdom, see 10.152–10.154.

[756] [2005] BCC 90.

[757] [2003] EWHC 128 (Ch), [2003] 1 WLR 1421.

resolution for voluntary winding up and the court in the relevant part of the UK the juris-diction to confirm the winding up. It is submitted that *Re TXU Europe German Finance BV* must be regarded as correctly decided but for the wrong reasons. According to *Re Salvage Association*[758] (which is not referred to in the judgment in *Re TXU Europe German Finance BV*), the extension of the power to go into voluntary liquidation is derived from IA 1986, s 221(4), not from the EC Regulation.[759]

Entities which cannot be Wound Up under IA 1986

Introduction

Creation of exceptions

Legislation and jurisprudence have defined categories of entities which cannot be wound up under IA 1986. These are listed at 1.302–1.344. **1.299**

Jurisdiction allocated elsewhere

A court in England and Wales may not have jurisdiction to wind up a particular company under the rules concerning allocation of jurisdiction which are discussed at 1.347–1.432. **1.300**

Effect of Regulation (EC) No 1346/2000

According to *Re BRAC Rent-A-Car International Inc*,[760] Regulation (EC) No 1346/2000 is a source of and has extended the jurisdiction of United Kingdom courts, in relation to the insolvency proceedings listed for the UK in annexes A and B to the Regulation, to every debtor whose COMI is in the UK. However, in *Re Salvage Association*[761] it was held that the Regulation does not have this effect and it is submitted at 1.394–1.406 that this is the correct view. If, contrary to this submission, it is correct that the EC Regulation extends the jurisdiction of the United Kingdom courts, that interpretation of the Regulation would have to be applied to overrule the exceptions discussed at 1.302–1.317 and, possibly, 1.328–1.330 and 1.341, because a Regulation overrides domestic legislation and jurispru-dence.[762] For each of the categories of entity which cannot be wound up under IA 1986, the following discussion includes an estimate of the effect of the interpretation adopted in *Re BRAC Rent-A-Car International Inc*, if it is correct. **1.301**

Company already being Wound Up by the Court

A second winding-up order cannot be made against a company which is already being wound up by a court in the same jurisdiction.[763] **1.302**

---

[758] [2003] EWHC 1028 (Ch), [2004] 1 WLR 174.

[759] See 1.394–1.406.

[760] [2003] EWHC 128 (Ch), [2003] 1 WLR 1421; followed in *Re TXU Europe German Finance BV* [2005] BCC 90.

[761] [2003] EWHC 1028 (Ch), [2004] 1 WLR 174.

[762] *Politi SAS v Ministero delle Finanze* (case 43/71) [1971] ECR 1039; *SpA Marimex v Ministero delle Finanze* (case 84/71) [1972] ECR 89; *Bussone v Italian Ministry for Agriculture and Forestry* (case 31/78) [1978] ECR 2429.

[763] *Re British and Foreign Generating Apparatus Co Ltd* (1865) 12 LT 368 at 369 (MR); *Commonwealth of Australia v Emanuel Projects Pty Ltd* (1996) 21 ACSR 36; *Dewina Trading Sdn Bhd v Ion International Pty Ltd* (1996) 141 ALR 317. See 10.166–10.167.

1.303 It is submitted that this rule is not in conflict with Regulation (EC) No 1346/2000. It simply implements the principle of eliminating unnecessary legal proceedings which is essential to any legal system.

1.304 No order may be made for the winding up of a building society which is in building society insolvency.[764] But a bank in bank insolvency may be ordered to be wound up on a public interest petition.[765]

Companies for which there are Industry-Specific Administration Regimes

Schedule B1 administration

1.305 There are limited circumstances in which a winding-up order can be made during schedule B1 administration.[766] Accordingly, companies in, or preparing for schedule B1 administration are not considered here as companies which cannot be wound up at all.

Effect of Regulation (EC) No 1346/2000

1.306 If the interpretation of Regulation (EC) No 1346/2000 adopted in *Re BRAC Rent-A-Car International Inc*[767] is correct, that is, if the Regulation extends the winding-up jurisdiction of UK courts to every company which has its COMI in the UK, then this overrides the statutory exclusion of companies from winding up discussed in 1.307–1.317.[768] Though followed in *Re TXU Europe German Finance BV*,[769] this interpretation has been rejected in *Re Salvage Association*,[770] and it is submitted that the correct view is that the Regulation does not extend the jurisdiction of UK courts[771] and so does not override the exceptions discussed in 1.307–1.317.

Water companies: special administration orders

1.307 On an application to any court for the winding up of a company for which a special administration order may be made,[772] the court must not make a winding-up order, but if it is satisfied that it would be appropriate to make a winding-up order but for that prohibition, it must instead make a special administration order.[773] A special administration order may be made on the winding-up petition despite the rule that a winding-up petition must be dismissed when a special administration order is made.[774]

1.308 No winding-up order may be made when a petition for a special administration order has been presented,[775] and no winding-up order may be made while a special administration order is in force.[776]

---

[764] Building Societies (Insolvency and Special Administration) Order 2009 (SI 2009/805), sch 1, para 20(1) and (3).
[765] IA 1986, sch B1, para 42, applied by the Banking Act 2009, s 119.
[766] See 10.29–10.30.
[767] [2003] EWHC 128 (Ch), [2003] 1 WLR 1421.
[768] See 1.301.
[769] [2005] BCC 90.
[770] [2003] EWHC 1028 (Ch), [2004] 1 WLR 174.
[771] See 1.394–1.406.
[772] See 1.248–1.250.
[773] Water Industry Act 1991, s 25.
[774] IA 1986, s 11(1)(a), as applied by the Water Industry Act 1991, sch 3, para 1, and modified by para 2.
[775] IA 1986, s 10(1)(a), applied by the Water Industry Act 1991, s 24(5).
[776] IA 1986, s 11(3)(a), applied by the Water Industry Act 1991, sch 3, para 1.

Protected railway companies: railway administration

No winding-up order may be made when a petition for a railway administration order[777] has been presented,[778] except in relation to a company incorporated outside Great Britain.[779]   **1.309**

No winding-up order may be made while a railway administration order is in force,[780] except in relation to a company incorporated outside Great Britain.[781]   **1.310**

Building societies in administration

No winding-up order may be made when a petition for an administration order in relation to a building society[782] has been presented.[783]   **1.311**

No winding-up order may be made while a building society administration order is in force.[784]   **1.312**

PPP companies: PPP administration

No winding-up order may be made when a petition for a PPP administration order[785] has been presented,[786] except in relation to a PPP company incorporated outside Great Britain.[787]   **1.313**

No winding-up order may be made while a PPP administration order is in force.[788]   **1.314**

Air traffic services licence companies: air traffic administration

On an application to any court for the winding up of an air traffic services licence company,[789] the court must not make a winding-up order, but if it is satisfied that it would be appropriate to make a winding-up order but for that prohibition, it must instead make an air traffic administration order.[790] An air traffic administration order may be made on the winding-up petition despite the rule that a winding-up petition must be dismissed when an air traffic administration order is made.[791]   **1.315**

No winding-up order may be made when a petition for an air traffic administration order has been presented[792] and no winding-up order may be made while an air transport administration order is in force.[793]   **1.316**

Industry-specific administration regimes based on schedule B1 administration

In all industry-specific administration regimes based on schedule B1 administration,[794] no order can be made to wind up a company in administration and there is no exception   **1.317**

---

[777] See 1.252–1.255.
[778] IA 1986, s 10(1)(a), applied by the Railways Act 1993, s 60(5).
[779] Railways Act 1993, s 65(4)(a).
[780] IA 1986, s 11(3)(a), applied by the Railways Act 1993, sch 6, para 1.
[781] Railways Act 1993, sch 6, para 13(4)(a).
[782] See 1.256.
[783] IA 1986, s 10(1)(a), applied by the Building Societies Act 1986, sch 15A, para 1.
[784] IA 1986, s 11(3)(a), applied by the Building Societies Act 1986, sch 15A, para 1.
[785] See 1.257–1.259.
[786] IA 1986, s 10(1)(a), applied by the Greater London Authority Act 1999, s 221(5).
[787] Greater London Authority Act 1999, s 224(4)(a) and (7).
[788] IA 1986, s 11(3)(a), applied by the Greater London Authority Act 1999, sch 14, para 1.
[789] See 1.260–1.261.
[790] Transport Act 2000, s 27.
[791] IA 1986, s 11(1)(a), as applied by the Transport Act 2000, sch 1, para 2, and modified by para 4.
[792] IA 1986, s 10(1)(a), applied by the Transport Act 2000, s 30(3).
[793] IA 1986, s 11(3)(a), applied by the Transport Act 2000, sch 1, para 2.
[794] See 1.262–1.287 and 1.291–1.294.

for public interest petitions. This is provided by IA 1986, sch B1, para 42, applied with modification:

(a) to energy administration and energy supply company administration by the Energy Act 2004, sch 20, paras 1–4 and 7;[795]

(b) to bank administration, building society special administration and special administration (bank administration) by the Banking Act 2009, s 145(2), (3), (4) and table 1;[796]

(c) to investment bank special administration and special administration (bank insolvency) by the Investment Bank Special Administration Regulations 2011 (SI 2011/245), reg 15(4), (5) and table 1, and sch 1, para 5;[797]

(d) to postal administration by the Postal Services Act 2011, sch 10, paras 1, 2 and 5;

(e) to FMI administration by the Financial Services (Banking Reform) Act 2013, sch 6, paras 2 and 3 and table 1.

EEA Insurers

1.318   A winding-up order may not be made by a court in the United Kingdom in relation to an EEA insurer or any branch of an EEA insurer as an unregistered company.[798]

1.319   The term 'EEA insurer' is defined by SI 2004/353, reg 2(1), to mean an undertaking, other than a UK insurer, pursuing the activity of direct insurance,[799] which has received authorization under Directive 73/239/EEC, art 6, or Directive 2002/83/EC, art 4, from its home State regulator.[800]

1.320   A 'UK insurer' is a person who has permission under the Financial Services and Markets Act 2000, part 4A, to effect or carry out contracts of insurance, apart from a person who does so exclusively in relation to reinsurance contracts[801] and excluding Lloyd's and its members.[802]

1.321   By SI 2004/353, reg 2(1), 'branch' has the meaning given by Directive 2002/83/EC (which applies to life assurance), art 1(b), or Directive 92/49/EEC (which applies to non-life insurance), art 1(b), that is:

> an agency or branch of an assurance/insurance undertaking. Any permanent presence of an undertaking in the territory of a member State shall be treated in the same way as an agency or branch, even if that presence does not take the form of a branch or agency, but consists merely of an office managed by the undertaking's own staff or by a person who is independent but has permanent authority to act for the undertaking as an agency would.[803]

---

[795] Applied to energy supply company administration by the Energy Act 2011, s 96.

[796] Applied to building society special administration by the Building Societies Act 1986, s 90C. Applied to special administration (bank administration) by the Investment Bank Special Administration Regulations 2011 (SI 2011/245), sch 2, para 6.

[797] Applied to special administration (bank insolvency) by SI 2011/245, sch 1, para 5.

[798] Insurers (Reorganisation and Winding Up) Regulations 2004 (SI 2004/353), reg 4(1).

[799] Within the meaning of Directive 73/239/EEC (which applies to non-life insurance), art 1, or Directive 2002/83/EC (which applies to life assurance), art 2.

[800] For life assurance the references in SI 2004/353 are to Directive 79/267/EEC, which has been superseded by Directive 2002/83/EC.

[801] SI 2004/353, reg 2(1).

[802] SI 2004/353, reg 3.

[803] In Directive 92/49/EEC the second sentence is incorporated by reference to Directive 88/357/EEC, art 3.

SI 2004/353 implements Directive 2001/17/EC. Regulation (EC) No 1346/2000 does not **1.322** apply to insurance undertakings[804] and so the Regulation cannot override this exception.[805]

EEA Credit Institutions

A winding-up order may not be made by a court in the United Kingdom in relation to an **1.323** EEA credit institution or any branch of an EEA credit institution as an unregistered company.[806] The term 'EEA credit institution' means[807] an EEA undertaking, other than a UK credit institution, of the kind mentioned in Regulation (EU) No 575/2013, art 4(1)(1) and (17), and subject to the exclusion of the undertakings referred to in Directive 2013/36/EU, art 2(5)(2)–(23). Also by SI 2004/1045, reg 2(1), a 'UK credit institution' is an undertaking whose head office is in the United Kingdom and which has permission under the Financial Services and Markets Act 2000, part 4A, to accept deposits or to issue electronic money, but excluding:

(a) an undertaking which also has part 4A permission to effect or carry out contracts of insurance; and

(b) a credit union.

By SI 2004/1045, reg 2(1), 'branch' has the meaning given by Regulation (EU) No **1.324** 575/2013, art 4(1)(17), which is:

> a place of business which forms a legally dependent part of an institution and which carries out directly all or some of the transactions inherent in the business of institutions[.]

SI 2004/1045 implements Directive 2001/24/EC. Regulation (EC) No 1346/2000 does **1.325** not apply to credit institutions[808] and so the Regulation cannot override this exception.[809]

Sovereign States

A State is immune from the jurisdiction of the courts of the United Kingdom.[810] In *FG* **1.326** *Hemisphere Associates LLC v Republic of Congo*[811] Cooke J said, at [8], that no provision of the 1978 Act had been put forward to justify applying any type of insolvency proceeding to the Republic of Congo, which had failed to repay bank loans. A court must give effect to State immunity even if the State does not appear in the proceedings in question.[812]

State immunity is a general principle of international law to which EU secondary legisla- **1.327** tion must be subject, so Regulation (EC) No 1346/2000 cannot override this exception.[813]

International Organizations

In *Re International Tin Council*[814] it was held that Parliament could not have intended that **1.328** an international organization, established, by treaty, by sovereign States, should be subject

---

[804] Regulation (EC) No 1346/2000, art 1(2).
[805] See 1.301.
[806] Credit Institutions (Reorganisation and Winding Up) Regulations 2004 (SI 2004/1045), reg 3(1).
[807] SI 2004/1045, reg 2(1).
[808] Regulation (EC) No 1346/2000, art 1(2).
[809] See 1.301.
[810] State Immunity Act 1978, s 1(1), except as provided in part 1 (ss 1–17) of the 1978 Act.
[811] [2005] EWHC 3103 (Comm), *The Times*, 27 February 2006.
[812] State Immunity Act 1978, s 1(2).
[813] See 1.301.
[814] [1989] Ch 309.

to the winding-up provisions of IA 1986, and so an international organization could not be an 'association' for the purposes of the definition of an unregistered company in s 220.

1.329 Usually, the treaty establishing an international organization will require the member States to grant it immunity from legal proceedings, and where the United Kingdom is a member this will be implemented by an order under the International Organisations Act 1968, s 1. This in itself will normally confer immunity from winding-up proceedings.

1.330 Immunity of an international organization is not a general principle of international law but arises from the treaty obligations of the States which establish or join an organization. Therefore, if the European Union itself is not a member of an international organization, it is not immediately obliged to recognize the immunity of that organization in its secondary legislation. It may well be, though, that it will be found, following *Re International Tin Council*, that Regulation (EC) No 1346/2000 was not intended to apply to international organizations. If that is not the case and if the interpretation of Regulation (EC) No 1346/2000 adopted in *Re BRAC Rent-A-Car International Inc*,[815] is correct, that is, if the Regulation extends the winding-up jurisdiction of United Kingdom courts to every company which has its COMI in the UK, then this overrides the exclusion of an international organization from winding up where the EU is not a member of the organization.[816] Though followed in *Re TXU Europe German Finance BV*,[817] this interpretation has been rejected in *Re Salvage Association*,[818] and it is submitted that the correct view is that the Regulation does not extend the jurisdiction of UK courts[819] and so does not override the exception.

Illegal Associations

1.331 An association whose existence is illegal cannot be wound up under IA 1986, part 5. This was decided in cases concerning associations with more than 20 members which carried on business for gain without being incorporated contrary to the provision last enacted as the Companies Act 1985, s 716.[820] The court could not recognize such an association.[821] However, in *Re Padstow Total Loss and Collision Assurance Association* Lindley LJ said, at p 150, that this rule would not apply if the petitioner believed the association did not have more than 20 members but the association sought to prevent the winding-up order being made by claiming that in fact it did have more than 20 members. In *Re Southside Plaza Merchants' Association*[822] McLelland CJ in Equity indicated that he was willing to apply this exception but would adjourn the petition before him so that the parties could come to a compromise. See also the discussion at 1.188 of overseas companies which have not registered at Companies House In *Re Australian Banking Co of Sydney*[823] Manning J said,

---

[815] [2003] EWHC 128 (Ch), [2003] 1 WLR 1421.

[816] See 1.301.

[817] [2005] BCC 90.

[818] [2003] EWHC 1028 (Ch), [2004] 1 WLR 174.

[819] See 1.394–1.406.

[820] Which was repealed on 21 December 2002 by the Regulatory Reform (Removal of 20 Member Limit in Partnerships etc) Order 2002 (SI 2002/3203), art 2.

[821] Per Jessel MR in *Re Arthur Average Association for British, Foreign and Colonial Ships* (1875) LR 10 Ch App 545 n at pp 548–9 n; *Re Padstow Total Loss and Collision Assurance Association* (1882) 20 ChD 137; *Re South-West Milk Producers' Association* (1924) 27 WAR 27; *Re Riverton Sheep Dip* [1943] SASR 344.

[822] [1965] NSWR 1454.

[823] (1891) 12 LR (NSW) Eq 237.

at p 238, that an illegal large partnership could be wound up as a partnership by an action brought by a member, but did not explain why such an action would not also be barred by the court's refusal to recognize the illegal association (the company in the case before his Honour was not an illegal large partnership).

The only reported cases concerning winding up of illegal associations have concerned large **1.332** partnerships, which are no longer illegal. There may be other reasons why an association's existence is illegal, for example, being a proscribed organization under the Terrorism Act 2000, s 3. It may be questioned whether the doctrine of refusal to recognize and wind up illegal associations is still necessary. It may be argued that such a body should be wound up in the public interest on a petition by the Secretary of State despite the illegality of its existence, just as a company may be wound up in the public interest because it is carrying on an illegal business. There may be questions about how to distribute assets so that there is no unjust enrichment from unlawful conduct, but in practice it may well be that such cases can be dealt with using the confiscation procedures available under the Proceeds of Crime Act 2002.

Where an illegal association is unincorporated (as all proscribed organizations are) it will **1.333** not have legal personality and so cannot be a debtor for the purposes of Regulation (EC) No 1346/2000 and so the Regulation cannot override this exception.[824]

Inchoate Companies

Persons acting together to carry out the preliminary stages of formation of an incorporated **1.334** company do not constitute an association or company which may be wound up as an unregistered company,[825] nor are they in partnership.[826] However, an old-fashioned 'syndicate' formed to acquire a business or property for resale at a profit to a public company to be promoted by the syndicate is likely to be a partnership which may be wound up as such.[827]

An inchoate company is unincorporated and does not have legal personality. So it cannot be **1.335** a debtor for the purposes of Regulation (EC) No 1346/2000 and so the Regulation cannot override this exception.[828]

Clubs

As an unincorporated members' club could not be wound up under the Joint Stock **1.336** Companies Winding-up Act 1848,[829] it has been held that such a club cannot be wound up under IA 1986.[830]

---

[824] See 1.301.

[825] *Re Imperial Anglo-German Bank* (1872) 26 LT 229.

[826] *Keith Spicer Ltd v Mansell* [1970] 1 WLR 333.

[827] *Re Royal Victoria Palace Theatre Syndicate* (1873) 29 LT 668, affirmed (1874) 30 LT 3; *Re South of France Pottery Works Syndicate* (1877) 36 LT 651.

[828] See 1.301.

[829] *Re St James's Club* (1852) 2 De G M & G 383.

[830] *Re Witney Town Football and Social Club* [1994] 2 BCLC 487, though it would seem that the petitioner in the case did not have standing to petition anyway since it petitioned as a creditor but was not in fact a creditor of the club but rather of the club officials who incurred the debt. *Panter v Rowellian Football Social Club* [2011] EWHC 1301 (Ch), [2012] Ch 125, is a similar case in which an administration order could not be made.

1.337 An unincorporated members' club does not have legal personality. So it cannot be a debtor for the purposes of Regulation (EC) No 1346/2000 and so the Regulation cannot override this exception.[831]

Non-business Societies

1.338 Because IA 1986, s 221(3), provides that the location of an unregistered company's principal place of business determines which court is to have jurisdiction to wind it up, it has been held that a society which does not carry on (or has not carried on) a business cannot be wound up as an unregistered company.[832] However, the analogous argument that a foreign company cannot be wound up unless it has or has had a principal place of business within the jurisdiction on which s 221(3) can operate has been rejected.[833] Also, a non-business society which has registered as an unincorporated friendly society may be wound up as an unregistered company because it has a 'pseudo-corporate existence by virtue of the statute law which regulates [its] activities'.[834]

1.339 An unincorporated society does not have legal personality. So it cannot be a debtor for the purposes of Regulation (EC) No 1346/2000 and so the Regulation cannot override this exception.[835]

Societies with no Contractual Relationship between Members

1.340 In *Caledonian Employees' Benevolent Society*[836] it was held that the word 'association' in the definition of an unregistered company in IA 1986, s 220, means 'a society (whatever its object) based on consensual contract among its constituent members whereby their mutual relations *inter se* with regard to some common object are regulated and enforced'. This was found not to be the case with the society sought to be wound up which existed to distribute funds to employees of a particular company, all of whom were required to join the society. An unincorporated society does not have legal personality. So it cannot be a debtor for the purposes of Regulation (EC) No 1346/2000 and so the Regulation cannot override this exception.[837]

Trade Unions

1.341 A trade union is not a body corporate[838] and must not be treated as if it were one.[839] A trade union must not be registered as a company or a registered society.[840] Clearly this means that a trade union cannot be wound up as a registered company. It has also been held that a trade

---

[831] See 1.301.
[832] *Re Bristol Athenaeum* (1889) 43 ChD 236, in which it was held that an unincorporated society which was subject to the Literary and Scientific Institutions Act 1854 (and so was forbidden from distributing a surplus on dissolution to its members) could not be wound up as an unregistered company.
[833] *Banque des Marchands de Moscou (Koupetschesky) v Kindersley* [1951] Ch 112 at p 127; *Re Kailis Groote Eylandt Fisheries Pty Ltd* (1977) 17 SASR 35 at pp 40–1.
[834] *Public Prosecutor v Wong Hong Toy* [1986] 1 MLJ 133 per Wee Chong Jin CJ quoting Johnston J in *Feeney v MacManus* [1937] IR 23 at p 32.
[835] See 1.301.
[836] 1928 SC 633.
[837] See 1.301.
[838] Trade Union and Labour Relations (Consolidation) Act 1992, s 10(1)
[839] s 10(2).
[840] s 10(3).

union cannot be wound up as an unregistered company.[841] As a trade union is capable of being a debtor, it may be that this can be overridden by Regulation (EC) No 1346/2000.[842]

Unincorporated Trusts

An unincorporated trust cannot be wound up as an unregistered company.[843] An unincorporated trust does not have legal personality. So it cannot be a debtor for the purposes of Regulation (EC) No 1346/2000 and so the Regulation cannot override this exception.[844]   **1.342**

Solvent Partnerships

It is not possible to petition for the compulsory winding up under IA 1986 of a solvent partnership,[845] unless: **1.343**

(a) it has been convicted of failure to comply with a serious crime prevention order;[846] or

(b) it is a financial services partnership.[847]

Regulation (EC) No 1346/2000 does not apply to winding up on a ground other than insolvency and so cannot override this exception.[848]   **1.344**

Inherent Jurisdiction

The High Court, as a court of general jurisdiction, has an inherent jurisdiction to order the dissolution of an unincorporated association or society, which cannot be wound up under IA 1986, and order the winding up of its affairs[849] in a process analogous to the dissolution and winding up of a partnership.[850] In particular a trade union may be wound up in this way.[851] The court may appoint one or more persons to carry out the functions of a liquidator in collecting the body's assets and distributing them to members and such a person can be given the title of liquidator and such powers as are appropriate.[852] A liquidator appointed by the court in a winding up under the inherent jurisdiction cannot have all the powers of a liquidator under IA 1986 but has liberty to apply to the court to supplement or amend the powers given on appointment.[853]   **1.345**

The court may find that the association or society has already been dissolved. If that is so, no dissolution order will be made, though the court may still have to determine who is   **1.346**

---

[841] *Keys v Boulter (No 2)* [1972] 1 WLR 642; *Re National Union of Flint Glassworkers* [2006] BCC 828.
[842] See 1.301.
[843] *Gilbert Deya Ministries v Kashmir Broadcasting Corporation Ltd* [2010] EWHC 3015 (Ch), LTL 11/11/2010.
[844] See 1.301.
[845] See 1.565–1.569.
[846] See 9.9.
[847] See 1.153 and 9.121.
[848] See 1.301.
[849] *Re Lead Company's Workmen's Fund Society* [1904] 2 Ch 196; *Blake v Smither* (1906) 22 TLR 698; *Re One and All Sickness and Accident Assurance Association* (1909) 25 TLR 674; *Re Blue Albion Cattle Society* [1966] CLY 1274; *Keys v Boulter (No 2)* [1972] 1 WLR 642; *Keene v Wellcom London Ltd* [2014] EWHC 134 (Ch), [2014] WTLR 1011. In Australia, such an association may be a 'Part 5.7 body', which can be wound up under the Corporations Act 2001 (Australia), s 583 (*Re Employees of BHP Mutual Benefits Fund* [2013] NSWSC 1497).
[850] See 1.158–1.164.
[851] *Keys v Boulter (No 2)*; *Re National Union of Flint Glassworkers* [2006] BCC 828.
[852] *Butts Park Ventures (Coventry) Ltd v Bryant Homes Central Ltd* [2003] EWHC 2487 (Ch), [2004] BCC 207.
[853] *Re West Reading Social Club* (2014) LTL 31/7/2014.

entitled to the assets.[854] An unincorporated society or association may have been dissolved in accordance with its rules[855] or by unanimous agreement of all interested persons[856] or when the number of its members fell below two.[857] The court may decide that there has been a 'spontaneous' dissolution of a society or association[858] when it ceased to have any effective purpose[859] or if inactivity coupled with other circumstances shows that the society is at an end and not merely dormant.[860] Mere inactivity does not amount to dissolution.[861] Even minimal activity, such as the management of assets, is sufficient to show that spontaneous dissolution has not occurred.[862] However, cessation of all membership activities and the sale of all assets will amount to dissolution.[863]

Allocation of Jurisdiction within the EEA

Introduction

1.347 Jurisdiction over winding up of companies is allocated among EEA countries by a number of Regulations, Conventions and Directives. These may be classified:

(a) by the States and territories they cover;[864] or
(b) by whether they concern winding up on the ground of insolvency [865] or winding up on a ground other than insolvency.[866]

1.348 United Kingdom courts may be prevented by one of these instruments from winding up a company because it allocates jurisdiction to wind up that company to the courts of another State. For the argument that this does not take away jurisdiction to wind up a company, but only disables a court from exercising jurisdiction, see *Re DAP Holding NV*,[867] discussed at 1.440.

1.349 These instruments do not apply to public interest petitions.[868]

---

[854] *Re William Denby and Sons Ltd Sick and Benevolent Fund* [1971] 1 WLR 973 at pp 978–9.
[855] As in *Re Printers and Transferrers Amalgamated Trades Protection Society* [1899] 2 Ch 184.
[856] *Re William Denby and Sons Ltd Sick and Benevolent Fund* at p 978.
[857] *Re Bucks Constabulary Widows' and Orphans' Fund Friendly Society (No 2)* [1979] 1 WLR 936 at p 943; *Hanchett-Stamford v Attorney General* [2008] EWHC 330 (Ch), [2009] Ch 173.
[858] *Re GKN Bolts and Nuts Ltd (Automotive Division) Birmingham Works Sports and Social Club* [1982] 1 WLR 774.
[859] *Re William Denby and Sons Ltd Sick and Benevolent Fund*, in which it was held that this had not happened. In *Re GKN Bolts and Nuts Ltd (Automotive Division) Birmingham Works Sports and Social Club* at p 780, Megarry V-C thought the term 'loss of substratum' should not be used to describe this circumstance because of the way it is used in winding-up cases (see 8.260). However, it is really the term 'dissolution' that is used differently in the two contexts and once this is recognized, 'loss of substratum' is entirely appropriate to describe both a cause of dissolution of unincorporated societies and a reason for ordering the winding up of incorporated companies.
[860] *Re GKN Bolts and Nuts Ltd (Automotive Division) Birmingham Works Sports and Social Club* at p 780.
[861] *Re William Denby and Sons Ltd Sick and Benevolent Fund* at pp 981–2; *Re GKN Bolts and Nuts Ltd (Automotive Division) Birmingham Works Sports and Social Club* at p 779.
[862] *Keene v Wellcom London Ltd* at [20].
[863] *Re GKN Bolts and Nuts Ltd (Automotive Division) Birmingham Works Sports and Social Club*, in which it was held that dissolution occurred when the members resolved to sell the last remaining asset; *Re Woking Ex-Service Memorial Club, Working Men's Club and Institute* (2006) LTL 28/11/2006.
[864] See 1.351–1.360.
[865] See 1.361–1.407.
[866] See 1.408–1.418.
[867] [2005] EWHC 2092 (Ch), [2006] BCC 48.
[868] See 1.362 and 1.417.

A challenge to the court's jurisdiction under one of these instruments should be dealt with **1.350** swiftly and economically at the beginning of the case.[869]

Geographical Extent

EU States

Two pieces of legislation govern the allocation of jurisdiction within the EU over winding-up **1.351** proceedings:

(a) Regulation (EC) No 1346/2000[870] on insolvency proceedings; and
(b) Regulation (EU) No 1215/2012,[871] which applies to civil and commercial matters[872] excluding proceedings relating to the winding up of insolvent companies or other legal persons.[873] It therefore applies to proceedings for winding up on grounds other than insolvency.

Neither Regulation applies to Denmark.[874] However, as from 1 July 2007, Regulation **1.352** (EC) No 44/2001, which is the predecessor to Regulation (EU) No 1215/2012, applies to Denmark under an agreement between the European Community and Denmark.[875] There is no agreement between Denmark and the other EU States, or between EU and EFTA States, allocating jurisdiction for insolvency proceedings.

Aruba, French overseas departments, Gibraltar, Iceland, Norway and Switzerland

As well as Regulation (EU) No 1215/2012, allocation of jurisdiction for the winding up of **1.353** companies on grounds other than insolvency is dealt with in:

(a) the Brussels Convention on Jurisdiction and the Enforcement of Judgments in Civil and Commercial Matters 1968 (the Brussels Convention),[876] which has been replaced for most purposes by Regulation (EU) No 1215/2012, but still applies to allocate jurisdiction between, on the one hand, some EU States[877] and, on the other hand, Aruba and French overseas departments,[878] and also, in a modified form, between the United Kingdom and Gibraltar;[879] and
(b) the Lugano Convention on Jurisdiction and the Recognition and Enforcement of Judgments in Civil and Commercial Matters 2007 (the Lugano Convention

---

[869] *Cooper Tire and Rubber Co Europe Ltd v Dow Deutschland Inc* [2010] EWCA Civ 864, [2010] Bus LR 1697, at [41].

[870] In IA 1986, this is called 'the EC Regulation' (IA 1986, s 436(1)).

[871] Regulation (EU) No 1215/2012 is known as the recast Brussels I Regulation. It is a revised version of Regulation (EC) No 44/2001 (the Brussels I Regulation).

[872] Regulation (EU) No 1215/2012, art 1(1).

[873] Regulation (EU) No 1215/2012, art 1(2)(b).

[874] Regulation (EC) No 1346/2000, recital 33; *Re Arena Corporation Ltd* [2003] EWHC 3032 (Ch), [2004] BPIR 375, at [46] (point not considered on appeal); Regulation (EU) No 1215/2012, recital 41.

[875] OJ L299, 16/11/2005, pp 62–7; Council Decision 2006/325/EC, OJ L120, 5/5/2006, p 22; information concerning date of entry into force, OJ L94, 4/4/2007, p 70.

[876] Consolidated text [1998] OJ C27, 26.1.1998, p 1; also in the Civil Jurisdiction and Judgments Act 1982, sch 1–3BB.

[877] The States which were in the EU before 2000. The following States, which joined the EU after 2000, have never been parties to the Brussels Convention: Bulgaria, Croatia, Cyprus, the Czech Republic, Estonia, Hungary, Latvia, Lithuania, Malta, Poland, Romania, Slovakia and Slovenia.

[878] Regulation 44/2001, recital 23 as interpreted in the explanatory note to the Civil Jurisdiction and Judgments Regulations 2007 (SI 2007/1655).

[879] Civil Jurisdiction and Judgments Act 1982 (Gibraltar) Order 1997 (SI 1997/2602).

2007),[880] which allocates jurisdiction between all EU States[881] and Iceland, Norway and Switzerland.

Both conventions are incorporated into United Kingdom law by the Civil Jurisdiction and Judgments Act 1982.

1.354 In the Brussels Convention, the States and territories in respect of which the Convention is in force are called the Contracting States. The same terminology is used in the Civil Jurisdiction and Judgments Act 1982[882] and in the CPR.[883] In the Lugano Convention 2007 they are called 'States bound by this Convention'.[884]

1.355 The Brussels and Lugano Conventions do not apply to proceedings relating to the winding up of insolvent companies or other legal persons.[885]

EEA States

1.356 Allocation of jurisdiction within the EEA over insolvency and reorganization proceedings relating to authorized insurance undertakings and authorized credit institutions is required by two Directives.

1.357 Insurance undertakings are covered by Directive 2001/17/EC, which is extended to the whole of the EEA by the EEA Agreement, annex 9, point 13a. This Directive has been transposed into United Kingdom law by the Insurers (Reorganisation and Winding Up) Regulations 2004[886] and the Insurers (Reorganisation and Winding Up) (Lloyd's) Regulations 2005.[887]

1.358 Credit institutions are covered by Directive 2001/24/EC, which is extended to the whole of the EEA by the EEA Agreement, annex 9, point 16c. This Directive has been transposed by the Credit Institutions (Reorganisation and Winding Up) Regulations 2004.[888]

1.359 The principle of both Directives is that the only EEA State with jurisdiction over the winding up of an authorized insurance undertaking or credit institution is the home member State which authorized it and supervises it.[889]

1.360 For the interaction of these provisions with Regulation (EC) No 1346/2000, Regulation (EU) No 1215/2012, the Brussels Convention and the Lugano Convention, see 1.436–1.438.

Jurisdiction over Winding Up on the Ground of Insolvency: Regulation (EC) No 1346/2000

Scope

1.361 Regulation (EC) No 1346/2000 allocates jurisdiction for insolvency proceedings among EU States (apart from Denmark[890]). The Regulation applies to 'collective insolvency

---

[880] [2009] OJEU L147, 10.6.2009, p 5.
[881] Denmark has signed and ratified the Convention separately.
[882] s 1(3). In the 1982 Act, in relation to the Brussels Convention, a State is a Contracting State only in relation to the territories to which the Convention now applies, that is, Aruba and the French overseas territories. Gibraltar is treated as a separate Contracting State (SI 1997/2602, art 3).
[883] CPR, r 6.31(g).
[884] Lugano Convention 2007, art 1(3).
[885] Brussels Convention, art 1; Lugano Convention 2007, art 1(2)(b).
[886] SI 2004/353. See 1.318–1.322.
[887] SI 2005/1998.
[888] SI 2004/1045. See 1.323–1.325.
[889] Directive 2001/17/EC, art 8; Directive 2001/24/EC, art 9.
[890] Regulation (EC) No 1346/2000, recital 33.

proceedings which entail the partial or total divestment of a debtor and the appointment of a liquidator'.[891] Only the proceedings listed in annex A[892] are 'insolvency proceedings' for the purposes of the Regulation.[893] Proceedings listed in annex A must be regarded as coming within the scope of the Regulation.[894] These include both winding-up proceedings (which are singled out in annex B) and reorganization proceedings. The United Kingdom company winding-up proceedings listed are winding up by the court, creditors' voluntary winding up with confirmation by the court, winding up through administration, and winding up subject to the supervision of the court. Winding up subject to supervision was abolished in England and Wales and Scotland,[895] and in Northern Ireland,[896] before the Regulation came into effect, but is available in Gibraltar,[897] though it will also be abolished there by the reform of company law currently in progress.[898]

In the United Kingdom, winding up by the court is used to wind up both solvent and insol-   **1.362** vent companies, and inability to pay debts is only one of the circumstances in which winding up may be ordered. Winding-up proceedings are not within the scope of Regulation (EC) No 1346/2000 unless they are insolvency proceedings,[899] which means that the proceedings must be based on the company's insolvency and not on any other grounds.[900] This limitation is also necessary to prevent conflict with the Brussels and Lugano Conventions and Regulation (EU) No 1215/2012. The proceedings that are excluded from the scope of those instruments are 'bankruptcy, proceedings relating to the winding up of insolvent companies or other legal persons, judicial arrangements, compositions and analogous proceedings'.[901] Using the ground for the winding up rather than the solvency or insolvency of the company as the criterion for application of Regulation (EC) No 1346/2000 means that winding up in the public interest on the just and equitable ground (which can apply to both solvent and insolvent companies) is not subject to Regulation (EC) No 1346/2000, just as it is not subject to Regulation (EU) No 1215/2012 and the Brussels and Lugano Conventions.[902] But an application to a court in Belgium, made by a public official in the public interest, for a company to be declared insolvent, where the only possible ground for the declaration is the company's insolvency,[903] is subject to Regulation (EC) No 1346/2000.[904]

It has been said that Regulation (EC) No 1346/2000 must be interpreted as autonomous   **1.363** EU legislation which is not dependent on particular national legal systems, that interpretation should be teleological (purposive) and should take into account interpretative sources

---

[891] Regulation (EC) No 1346/2000, art 1(1).
[892] Which has been substituted by Regulation (EU) No 583/2011.
[893] Regulation (EC) No 1346/2000, art 2(a).
[894] *Bank Handlowy w Warszawie SA v Christianapol sp z oo* (case C-116/11) [2013] Bus LR 956 at [33].
[895] By IA 1985, s 88, on 29 December 1986.
[896] By the Insolvency (Northern Ireland) Order 1989 (SI 1989/2405 (NI 19)), sch 10, on 1 October 1991.
[897] Companies Act (1930-07) (Gibraltar), ss 298–302.
[898] Insolvency Act 2011 (Gibraltar); Companies Bill 2014 (Gibraltar).
[899] Regulation (EC) No 1346/2000, art 1(1).
[900] Virgós–Schmit report (see 1.407), point 49; *Re Marann Brooks CSV Ltd* [2003] BCC 239 per Patten J, obiter, at [32].
[901] Brussels Convention, art 2(1), quoted in Regulation (EC) No 1346/2000, recital 7, omitting, perhaps accidentally, the word 'bankruptcy'; Regulation (EU) No 1215/2012, art 1(2)(b); Lugano Convention 2007, art 1(2)(b).
[902] *Re Marann Brooks CSV Ltd* [2003] BCC 239 per Patten J, obiter, at [22]–[34].
[903] Loi sur les faillites — Faillissementswet (Law on Insolvency) of 8 August 1997 (Belgium), arts 2 and 6.
[904] *Procureur-generaal bij het hof van beroep te Antwerpen v Zaza Retail BV* (case C-112/10) [2011] ECR I-11525.

such as the recitals, decisions of the Court of Justice of the European Union (CJEU), the Virgós–Schmit report,[905] other court decisions and academic commentaries.[906] This was the approach proposed in the Virgós–Schmit report[907] and may in practice just be a summary of the CJEU's general approach to interpretation.

Jurisdiction over main, secondary and territorial insolvency proceedings

1.364 The State within the EU (apart from Denmark) in which a company's COMI[908] is situated has jurisdiction to open insolvency proceedings.[909] These are main proceedings with universal scope, aiming to encompass all the company's assets.[910]

1.365 No other State has jurisdiction to open insolvency proceedings unless it is a State in which the company has an establishment.[911] The same applies to a decision which has the same effect as a decision to open insolvency proceedings, such as a decision to join a company in insolvency proceedings against another person.[912]

1.366 To give jurisdiction to a court in the United Kingdom to order the winding up of a company whose COMI is in another EU State (apart from Denmark), the company must have an establishment in the UK when the winding-up petition is presented.[913] For the allocation of jurisdiction within the UK see 1.419–1.432. For the conditions under which a foreign company may be wound up see 1.172.

1.367 The effects of proceedings opened in a State in which the company does not have its COMI must be restricted to the company's assets situated in that State's territory.[914]

1.368 Proceedings opened in a State in which the company does not have its COMI are called 'secondary proceedings' if main proceedings have already been opened,[915] or 'territorial proceedings' if main proceedings have not been opened.[916] The time of the opening of proceedings is the time at which the judgment opening proceedings becomes effective, whether it is a final judgment or not.[917] A decision to appoint a provisional liquidator is a judgment opening insolvency proceedings.[918] Territorial proceedings become secondary proceedings when main proceedings are opened.[919]

---

[905] See 1.407.
[906] *Syska v Vivendi Universal SA* [2009] EWCA Civ 677, [2009] Bus LR 1494, at [16], per Christopher Clarke J quoting an award of an LCIA arbitral tribunal; *Re Alitalia Linee Aeree Italiane SpA* [2011] EWHC 15 (Ch), [2011] 1 WLR 2049, at [26].
[907] Virgós–Schmit report, point 43, which points out that some provisions refer to, and do not affect, national laws.
[908] See 1.376–1.386.
[909] Regulation (EC) No 1346/2000, art 3(1).
[910] Recital 12.
[911] See 1.387–1.389; art 3(2).
[912] *Rastelli Davide e C Snc v Hidoux* (case C-191/10) [2012] All ER (EC) 239 at [26]–[29].
[913] *Re Office Metro Ltd* [2012] EWHC 1191 (Ch), [2012] BPIR 1049, at [27].
[914] art 3(2).
[915] art 3(3).
[916] art 3(4).
[917] art 2(f).
[918] *Re Eurofood IFSC Ltd* (case C-341/04) [2006] Ch 508 (provisional liquidator in the Republic of Ireland); *Westwood Shipping Lines Inc v Universal Schifffahrtsgesellschaft mbH* [2012] EWHC 1394 (Comm), [2013] 1 BCLC 370 (*vorläufiger Insolvenzverwalter* in Germany).
[919] Recital 17.

Secondary proceedings must be winding-up proceedings, even if the main proceedings are **1.369** reorganization proceedings.[920]

The Regulation is not concerned with the admissibility of requests to open insolvency **1.370** proceedings, which is a matter for the law of the State which has jurisdiction under the Regulation.[921]

Recognition of judgments

Any judgment opening insolvency proceedings handed down by a court which has jurisdic- **1.371** tion to do so under the rules in Regulation (EC) No 1346/2000, art 3, must be recognized in all other EU States (apart from Denmark) from the time it becomes effective in the court's own State.[922] A court in another State may not review the jurisdiction of the court which opened the proceedings.[923] This is subject to art 26.[924]

The recognition rule is based on the principle of mutual trust, on which the system of alloca- **1.372** tion of jurisdiction depends.[925] It is inherent in that principle of mutual trust that a court hearing an application for the opening of main insolvency proceedings must check that it has jurisdiction.[926]

Refusal of recognition for public policy reasons

Regulation (EC) No 1346/2000, art 26, permits a State to refuse to recognize insolvency **1.373** proceedings opened in another member State, or to enforce a judgment handed down in such proceedings, where the effects of doing so would be manifestly contrary to its public policy, in particular, its fundamental principles or the constitutional rights and liberties of the individual. The jurisprudence on the similar provisions of Regulation (EC) No 44/2001, art 34(1) (now Regulation (EU) No 1215/2012, art 45(1)(a)), and the Brussels Convention, art 27(1), is relevant.[927]

Recognition of proceedings may be refused under art 26 where the decision to open the **1.374** proceedings was taken in flagrant breach of the fundamental right of a person concerned by the proceedings to be heard in them.[928]

Duties of communication and cooperation

If a company is subject to main insolvency proceedings in one EU State (other than **1.375** Denmark) and secondary proceedings in another (also not Denmark), the liquidators in the two proceedings have a duty to communicate information to each other.[929] Each must immediately communicate any information which may be relevant to the other proceed- ings, in particular, progress in lodging and verifying claims, and all measures aimed at terminating proceedings.[930] The liquidators have a duty to cooperate with each other.[931]

---

[920] art 3(3).
[921] *Interedil Srl v Fallimento Interedil Srl* (case C-396/09) [2012] Bus LR 1582 at [24].
[922] art 16(1).
[923] *Re Eurofood IFSC Ltd* (case C-341/04) [2006] Ch 508.
[924] See 1.373–1.374.
[925] *Re Eurofood IFSC Ltd* (case C-341/04) at [39]–[40].
[926] *Re Eurofood IFSC Ltd* (case C-341/04) at [41].
[927] *Re Eurofood IFSC Ltd* (case C-341/04) [2006] Ch 508 at [64].
[928] *Re Eurofood IFSC Ltd* (case C-341/04) [2006] Ch 508.
[929] Regulation (EC) No 1346/2000, art 31(1).
[930] art 31(1).
[931] art 31(2).

The liquidator in the secondary proceedings must give the liquidator in the main proceedings an early opportunity of submitting proposals on the liquidation or use of the assets in the secondary proceedings.[932] The duty of cooperation under the Regulation extends to courts in member States with jurisdiction in insolvency matters.[933] The court in England and Wales may seek such cooperation by issuing, under its inherent jurisdiction, letters of request.[934]

Centre of main interests

1.376 The concept of centre of main interests (COMI) in Regulation (EC) No 1346/2000 has an autonomous meaning which must be interpreted in a uniform way, independently of national legislation.[935] The concept applies to both companies and individuals, referred to generically as 'debtors'. The concept is also used in the UNCITRAL Model Law. As the Regulation and the UNCITRAL Model Law both apply in the UK, COMI must be given the same meaning in both.[936]

1.377 A debtor can have only one COMI,[937] but may move it at will.[938] A court must not take any account of movement of a debtor's COMI to another jurisdiction after a request to open insolvency proceedings in respect of the debtor has been filed.[939] If all of a company's activities have ceased at the time when a request to open insolvency proceedings is made, the last COMI before it ceased operations is the one that determines jurisdiction.[940]

1.378 Each debtor constituting a distinct legal entity has his, her or its own COMI.[941] There is no such thing as the COMI of an aggregation of debtors, such as a group of companies, and there is no rule that each debtor in an aggregation is to be assigned the COMI of them all.[942]

1.379 The Regulation does not define COMI,[943] but it contains two indications of what the term means:

(a) Recital 13 in the preamble states that the COMI of a debtor, whether an individual or a company, should correspond to the place where the debtor conducts the administration of his interests on a regular basis, and the recital asserts that this should be ascertainable by third parties. The Virgós–Schmit report[944] comments: 'Insolvency is a foreseeable

---

[932] art 31(3).
[933] *Re Nortel Networks* [2009] EWHC 206 (Ch), [2009] BCC 343.
[934] *Re Nortel Networks* [2009] EWHC 206 (Ch), [2009] BCC 343.
[935] *Re Eurofood IFSC Ltd* (case C-341/04) [2006] Ch 508 at [31]; *Interedil Srl v Fallimento Interedil Srl* (case C-396/09) [2012] Bus LR 1582.
[936] *Re Stanford International Bank Ltd* [2010] EWCA Civ 137, [2011] Ch 33, at [54].
[937] *Re BRAC Rent-A-Car International Inc* [2003] EWHC 128 (Ch), [2003] 1 WLR 1421, at [23]; *Cross Construction Sussex Ltd v Tseliki* [2006] EWHC 1056 (Ch), [2006] BPIR 888, at [5]; *Stojević v Official Receiver* [2006] EWHC 3447 (Ch), [2007] BPIR 141, at [6].
[938] *Shierson v Vlieland-Boddy* [2005] EWCA Civ 974, [2005] 1 WLR 3966.
[939] *Staubitz-Schreiber* (case C-1/04) [2006] ECR I-701, overruling on this point *Shierson v Vlieland-Boddy*. See Drazen Petkovich, 'The correct time to determine the debtor's COMI' (2006) 22 Insolv L & P 76. An SE cannot transfer its registered office to another member State if proceedings for winding up, liquidation, insolvency or suspension of payments or other similar proceedings have been brought against it (Regulation (EC) No 2157/2001, art 8(15)).
[940] *Interedil Srl v Fallimento Interedil Srl* (case C-396/09) [2012] Bus LR 1582.
[941] *Re Eurofood IFSC Ltd* (case C-341/04) [2006] Ch 508 at [30]; *Re Stanford International Bank Ltd* [2010] EWCA Civ 137, [2011] Ch 33, at [56].
[942] *Re Stanford International Bank Ltd* [2010] EWCA Civ 137, [2011] Ch 33, at [56].
[943] *Interedil Srl v Fallimento Interedil Srl* (case C-396/09) [2012] Bus LR 1582 at [47].
[944] See 1.407.

risk. It is therefore important that international jurisdiction (which ... entails the application of the insolvency laws of that ... State) be based on a place known to the debtor's potential creditors. This enables the legal risks which would have to be assumed in the case of insolvency to be calculated.'[945] Recital 13 is not a definition of COMI.[946]

(b) Article 3(1) provides that the COMI of a company is presumed to be where its registered office is, in the absence of proof to the contrary. The Virgós–Schmit report comments, 'This place normally corresponds to the debtor's head office'.[947]

According to the English text of *Interedil Srl v Fallimento Interedil Srl*[948] these statements   **1.380**
in the Regulation reflect an intention 'to attach greater importance to' the place where a company has its central administration as the criterion for jurisdiction.[949] However, the Italian original seems to express the quoted phrase better in the single word *'privilegiare'*, which would normally be translated as 'to privilege' (in the sense 'to favour'). It is also of great importance that the COMI can be ascertained by third parties. There is a presumption that the COMI is at the company's registered office,[950] which normally corresponds to the head office[951] and is also readily ascertainable by third parties as every company must state the location of its registered office in letters and order forms, whether in paper form or in any other medium, and on its websites.[952] The presumption may be rebutted if the company actually conducts its business at a head office which is not in the same jurisdiction as its registered office and has taken every practical step to inform creditors that they are to deal with the company at that head office.[953]

A court must determine where a COMI is in a way which complies with the essential pro-   **1.381**
cedural guarantees required for a fair legal process.[954] For an English court, the location of a debtor's COMI is a question of fact to which the usual civil standard of proof on balance of probabilities applies.[955] In the case of a company, this is subject to the presumption that the COMI is at its registered office.[956] That presumption can be displaced only if 'factors which are both objective and ascertainable by third parties enable it to be established that an actual situation exists which is different from' that presumption.[957] Those factors must be assessed in a comprehensive manner, taking account of the particular circumstances of each case.[958] What is ascertainable by third parties is what is in the public domain and what

---

[945] Virgós–Schmit report, point 75.
[946] *Stojević v Official Receiver* [2006] EWHC 3447 (Ch), [2007] BPIR 141, at [31]–[32].
[947] Virgós–Schmit report, point 75.
[948] *Interedil Srl v Fallimento Interedil Srl* (case C-396/09) [2012] Bus LR 1582 at [48].
[949] Citing the advocate general's opinion at [69], which in turn cites the Virgós–Schmit report, point 75.
[950] Regulation (EC) No 1346/2000, art 3(1).
[951] Virgós–Schmit report, point 75.
[952] Directive 2009/101/EC, art 5, implemented in the UK by the Companies (Trading Disclosures) Regulations 2008 (SI 2008/495), regs 6 and 7.
[953] *Re European Directories DH6 BV* [2010] EWHC 3472 (Ch), [2012] BCC 46, at [39]–[44].
[954] *Re Eurofood IFSC Ltd* (case C-341/04) at [41].
[955] *Shierson v Vlieland-Boddy*.
[956] Regulation (EC) No 1346/2000, art 3(1).
[957] *Re Eurofood IFSC Ltd* (case C-341/04) at [34]; *Re Stanford International Bank Ltd* [2010] EWCA Civ 137, [2011] Ch 33, at [56] per Morritt C with whom Hughes LJ agreed at [159]. This overrules the view of Judge Langan QC in *Re Ci4net.com Inc* [2004] EWHC 1941 (Ch), [2005] BCC 277, at [20], that the presumption that the place of a company's registered office is its COMI is not a particularly strong one and is just one of the factors to be taken into account. His Honour took the same view in *Re Parkside Flexibles SA* [2006] BCC 589 at [9].
[958] *Rastelli Davide e C Snc v Hidoux* (case C-191/10) [2012] All ER (EC) 239 at [36].

they would learn in the ordinary course of business with the company, not what can be ascertained only on enquiry.[959]

1.382 The factors to be taken into account include, in particular, all the places in which the company pursues economic activities or holds assets, so far as they can be ascertained by third parties.[960]

1.383 It has been held that the following facts do not in themselves show that a company whose registered office is in State A nevertheless has a COMI in State B:

(a) that its 'economic choices' are, or can be, controlled by a parent company in State B;[961]
(b) that it owns immovable property in State B and has entered into contracts in that State for the exploitation of the property;[962]
(c) that its property has been intermixed with the property of a person whose COMI is in State B.[963]

1.384 Earlier cases referred to criteria for determining the location of a company's COMI, such as where 'head office functions' were performed[964] or where the scale and importance of the interests administered was greatest,[965] without considering whether such matters were both objective and ascertainable by third parties. That approach should no longer be followed.[966]

1.385 If a company does not carry out any business in the State in which its registered office is located, it may be concluded that its COMI is elsewhere.[967] An example is *Re Sendo Ltd*,[968] in which it was found that a company incorporated in the Cayman Islands which had never traded there had its COMI in England where its headquarters were located and where its management and operational functions were carried out by UK-resident directors.[969] Another example is *Hans Brochier Holdings Ltd v Exner*.[970]

1.386 Using head office functions as the criterion for determining COMI seems particularly convenient for a group of companies incorporated and operating in different States, because it usually results in main proceedings for all companies in the group being administered together, which often facilitates sale of a business.[971] But even if the head

---

[959] *Re Stanford International Bank Ltd* [2010] EWCA Civ 137, [2011] Ch 33, at [56] per Morritt C with whom Hughes LJ agreed at [159]; *Interedil Srl v Fallimento Interedil Srl* (case C-396/09) [2012] Bus LR 1582 at [49].

[960] *Interedil Srl v Fallimento Interedil Srl* (case C-396/09) [2012] Bus LR 1582 at [52].

[961] *Re Eurofood IFSC Ltd* (case C-341/04) [2006] Ch 508 at [36] and [37].

[962] *Interedil Srl v Fallimento Interedil Srl* (case C-396/09) [2012] Bus LR 1582.

[963] *Rastelli Davide e C Snc v Hidoux* (case C-191/10) [2012] All ER (EC) 239 at [39].

[964] *Re Lennox Holdings plc* [2009] BCC 155.

[965] For example, *Re Daisytek-ISA Ltd* [2003] BCC 562; *Re Ci4net.com Inc* [2004] EWHC 1941 (Ch), [2005] BCC 277; *Re Aim Underwriting Agencies (Ireland) Ltd* [2004] EWHC 2114 (Ch), LTL 29/11/2004.

[966] But it was supported by Arden LJ, dissenting, in *Re Stanford International Bank Ltd* [2010] EWCA Civ 137, [2011] Ch 33, at [152]–[153].

[967] *Re Eurofood IFSC Ltd* (case C-341/04) [2006] Ch 508 at [35].

[968] [2005] EWHC 1604 (Ch), [2006] 1 BCLC 395.

[969] In *Re Sendo Ltd* the court made an administration order in relation to the Cayman Islands company relying on IA 1986, sch B1, para 111, but unaware that the paragraph had been amended by the Insolvency Act 1986 (Amendment) Regulations 2005 (SI 2005/879) (see 1.394–1.406). However, the amendment does not affect the result of the case.

[970] [2006] EWHC 2594 (Ch), [2007] BCC 127.

[971] See, for example, *Re Collins and Aikman Corporation Group* [2005] EWHC 1754 (Ch), [2006] BCC 606.

office criterion denies the States of incorporation of members of a group the opportunity of opening main proceedings, the fact that group companies operate in their States of incorporation and have establishments there will allow potentially conflicting secondary proceedings to be opened in the States of incorporation, unless they are bought off by a promise of respect for local rules on creditors' priorities etc.[972] By giving the registered office criterion primacy, the European Court of Justice in *Re Eurofood IFSC Ltd* (case C-341/04) has preferred separate main proceedings for active group members in their States of incorporation.

Establishment

The term 'establishment' is defined in Council Regulation (EC) No 1346/2000, art 2(h), to mean 'any place of operations where the debtor carries out a non-transitory economic activity with human means and goods'. The UNCITRAL Model Law also uses the concept of establishment and defines it in the same way, except that 'human means and goods' is replaced by 'human means and assets or services'. 'Human means' is a literal translation of the French '*moyens humains*', which would be better translated as 'human resources'. The human beings do not have to be employees of the debtor.[973] 'Goods' is a mistranslation of the French '*biens*', which, in legal use, means anything capable of being the subject of property rights, including movable property (*biens meubles*), land (*biens immeubles*) and intangible property (*biens incorporels*).[974]   **1.387**

The existence of an establishment must be determined on the basis of objective factors which are ascertainable by third parties.[975] The concept of an establishment requires a minimum level of organization and a degree of stability necessary for the purpose of pursuing economic activity.[976] The economic activities must be exercised 'on the market (ie externally), whether the said activities are commercial, industrial or professional'.[977] The presence of goods or a bank account does not by itself meet that requirement.[978] A dormant branch, or one which has not yet started operating, or one which has fallen into economic inactivity, will not suffice.[979] Attendance by two individuals at a branch office of a company in liquidation, only for the purposes of the liquidation and without any contact with customers is not carrying out an economic activity.[980]   **1.388**

The fact that a subsidiary company has business premises at a place does not mean that the place is an establishment of its parent company.[981]   **1.389**

---

972 *Re Collins and Aikman Europe SA* [2006] EWHC 1343 (Ch), [2006] BCC 861.

973 *Re Office Metro Ltd* [2012] EWHC 1191 (Ch), [2012] BPIR 1049, at [18].

974 *Re Office Metro Ltd* [2012] EWHC 1191 (Ch), [2012] BPIR 1049, at [19].

975 *Interedil Srl v Fallimento Interedil Srl* (case C-396/09) [2012] Bus LR 1582 at [63].

976 *Interedil Srl v Fallimento Interedil Srl* (case C-396/09) [2012] Bus LR 1582 at [64]. See also the lengthy discussion of the meaning of 'non-transitory economic activity' in *Re Office Metro Ltd* [2012] EWHC 1191 (Ch), [2012] BPIR 1049, at [28]–[33].

977 Virgós–Schmit report (see 1.407), point 71; *Trustees of the Olympic Airlines SA Pension and Life Insurance Scheme v Olympic Airlines SA* [2013] EWCA Civ 643, [2013] 2 BCLC 171, at [33] and [34].

978 *Interedil Srl v Fallimento Interedil Srl* (case C-396/09) [2012] Bus LR 1582 at [64].

979 *Trustees of the Olympic Airlines SA Pension and Life Insurance Scheme v Olympic Airlines SA* [2013] EWCA Civ 643, [2013] 2 BCLC 171, at [33].

980 *Trustees of the Olympic Airlines SA Pension and Life Insurance Scheme v Olympic Airlines SA* [2013] EWCA Civ 643, [2013] 2 BCLC 171, at [35].

981 *Telia v Hillcourt* [2002] EWHC 2377 (Ch), LTL 16/10/2002.

Companies to which the Regulation does not apply: insurance, banking and investment

1.390 Regulation (EC) No 1346/2000 does not apply to insolvency proceedings concerning insurance undertakings, credit institutions, investment undertakings which provide services involving the holding of funds or securities for third parties, or collective investment undertakings.[982] Recital 9 states these undertakings should be excluded because 'they are subject to special arrangements and, to some extent, the national supervisory authorities have extremely wide-ranging powers of intervention'. These types of enterprise cannot do business in the EEA unless authorized in accordance with Directives. In addition Directives have been adopted to allocate jurisdiction over the winding up of authorized insurance undertakings and credit institutions.[983]

1.391 Insurance undertakings are covered by Directive 2001/17/EC, which is transposed into United Kingdom law by the Insurers (Reorganisation and Winding Up) Regulations 2004[984] and the Insurers (Reorganisation and Winding Up) (Lloyd's) Regulations 2005.[985] Credit institutions are covered by Directive 2001/17/EC, which is transposed by the Credit Institutions (Reorganisation and Winding Up) Regulations 2004.[986]

1.392 It has been held in England that Regulation (EC) No 1346/2000 does apply to a company which carries on one of the businesses listed in art 1(2) without being authorized to do so.[987]

Companies to which the Regulation does not apply: COMI in Denmark or outside the EU

1.393 Regulation (EC) No 1346/2000 does not apply to Denmark[988] and so does not affect the jurisdiction of a court in England and Wales to wind up a company whose COMI is in Denmark.[989] The Regulation does not apply to insolvency proceedings relating to a debtor whose COMI is outside the EU.[990] The Regulation applies to a company whose COMI is in an EU State other than Denmark, even if the company is incorporated outside the EU.[991]

Does Regulation (EC) No 1346/2000 give an English court additional jurisdiction?

1.394 Regulation (EC) No 1346/2000, art 3, identifies which courts have jurisdiction to open insolvency proceedings. The term 'insolvency proceedings' is defined in art 2(a) to be the proceedings listed in annex A to the Regulation. For the United Kingdom, the proceedings listed in annex A which are applicable to companies are winding up by the court, winding up subject to the supervision of the court,[992] creditors' voluntary winding up with confirmation by the court, administration and voluntary arrangement. The Regulation entered into force on 31 May 2002.[993]

---

[982] Regulation (EC) No 1346/2000, art 1(2). They are called 'Article 1.2 undertakings' in draft IR 2015.
[983] See 1.356–1.360.
[984] SI 2004/353. See 1.318–1.322.
[985] SI 2005/1998.
[986] SI 2004/1045. See 1.323–1.325.
[987] *Financial Services Authority v Dobb White and Co* [2003] EWHC 3146 (Ch), [2004] BPIR 479.
[988] Recital 33.
[989] *Re Arena Corporation* [2003] EWHC 3032 (Ch), LTL 9/1/2004, at [38]–[46], point not considered on appeal.
[990] Recital 14; see, for example, *Skjevesland v Geveran Trading Co Ltd* [2002] EWHC 2898 (Ch), [2003] BCC 391.
[991] *Re BRAC Rent-A-Car International Inc* [2003] EWHC 128 (Ch), [2003] 1 WLR 1421; *Re Harley Medical Group (Ireland) Ltd* [2013] IEHC 219.
[992] See 10.152–10.154.
[993] Regulation (EC) No 1346/2000, art 47.

Before 31 May 2002, the legislation governing voluntary winding up, administration and **1.395** voluntary arrangement made those procedures available only to registered companies.[994] As from 31 May 2002, IA 1986, s 1, was amended[995] so as to extend voluntary arrangement to 'a company in relation to which a proposal for a voluntary arrangement may be made by virtue of' Regulation (EC) No 1346/2000, art 3.

At the same time, IA 1986, s 8, was amended[996] by adding a new subsection (7) which **1.396** extended administration to 'a company in relation to which an administration order may be made by virtue of' Regulation EC (No) 1346/2000, art 3. The Enterprise Act 2002, s 248, replaced IA 1986, part 2 (ss 8–27), with new provisions as from 15 September 2003.[997] In those new provisions, IA 1986, sch B1, para 111(1), extended administration to 'a company which may enter administration by virtue of' Regulation EC (No) 1346/2000, art 3.

As from 31 May 2002, IA 1986, s 221(4) was amended[998] to provide that an unregistered **1.397** company may be wound up under IA 1986 voluntarily 'in accordance with' Regulation (EC) No 1346/2000 (without specifying art 3).

The only sense in which a voluntary arrangement may be made, or a company may enter **1.398** administration, 'by virtue of' art 3 of the Regulation, or a company may be wound up voluntarily 'in accordance with' the Regulation is that the Regulation has allocated jurisdiction for opening insolvency proceedings to the courts of the United Kingdom.[999] The Regulation determines which State's courts have jurisdiction to open the insolvency proceedings which are listed in annex A, but does not specify the conditions under which those proceedings may be opened. Article 4(2) expressly states that:

> The law of the State of the opening of proceedings shall determine the conditions for the opening of those proceedings.

The only condition laid down by the Regulation is that secondary proceedings must be **1.399** winding-up proceedings.[1000] Article 3(4)(a) expressly recognizes one situation in which local laws would not permit the opening of insolvency proceedings, namely, where the debtor lacks capacity.

Despite this, in *Re BRAC Rent-A-Car International Inc*,[1001] Lloyd J accepted the argument **1.400** that the Regulation gives United Kingdom courts jurisdiction to open all the insolvency proceedings listed for the UK in annex A for every debtor whose COMI is in the UK. His Lordship made clear, at [9], that the Regulation is a source of and determines the court's jurisdiction and described the amendments made to domestic legislation by SI 2002/1240 as 'strictly speaking, unnecessary'. His Lordship held that an administration order could be made by the High Court in England in respect of a company incorporated in Delaware

---

[994] The controversy over whether administration was so limited is discussed at 1.246.

[995] By the Insolvency Act 1986 (Amendment) (No 2) Regulations 2002 (SI 2002/1240), reg 4.

[996] By SI 2002/1240, reg 5.

[997] Enterprise Act 2002 (Commencement No 4 and Transitional Provisions and Savings) Order 2003 (SI 2003/2093).

[998] By SI 2002/1240, reg 9.

[999] And the rules described at 1.419–1.432 have allocated that jurisdiction to England and Wales or Scotland.

[1000] Regulation (EC) No 1346/2000, art 3(3). Winding-up proceedings are defined by art 2(c) to be the proceedings listed in annex B.

[1001] [2003] EWHC 128 (Ch), [2003] 1 WLR 1421.

whose COMI was found to be in England. This was followed in *Re TXU Europe German Finance BV*[1002] by the Chief Bankruptcy Registrar, who confirmed creditors' voluntary liquidations of companies incorporated in the Netherlands and the Republic of Ireland.

1.401 In *Re Salvage Association*[1003] Blackburne J held, at [13], that the jurisdiction of United Kingdom courts has not been extended by the Regulation, but was extended by SI 2002/1240 to every debtor with a COMI in the UK, including a company incorporated in the UK otherwise than as a registered company. Accordingly, his Lordship held that he had jurisdiction to make an administration order in relation to a company both incorporated in and having its COMI in England, but incorporated by royal charter so that administration would not have been available to it before 31 May 2002.[1004]

1.402 The government responded with the Insolvency Act 1986 (Amendment) Regulations 2005.[1005] These reworded IA 1986, s 1, and sch B1, para 111, as from 13 April 2005, so that the extension of voluntary arrangement and administration is now[1006] to:

(a) a company registered under the Companies Act 2006 in England and Wales or Scotland;[1007]
(b) a company incorporated in an EEA State other than the United Kingdom; or
(c) a company not incorporated in an EEA State but having its COMI in a member State other than Denmark.

1.403 The explanatory note to SI 2005/879 states that it is made 'in connection with the application of' Regulation (EC) No 1346/2000. It is, therefore, odd that the provisions of SI 2005/879 refer to EEA States whereas the Regulation applies only in EU States other than Denmark. It may be argued that, in this respect, the 2005 regulations are *ultra vires*. The explanatory memorandum accompanying the 2005 regulations states the government's view that:

> The EC Regulation does not change the type of debtor to which the various insolvency proceedings of a Member State apply.

1.404 This is consistent with what Blackburne J held in *Re Salvage Association*, and it is submitted that this is the correct view. Arguments in favour of it are stated in full by Jonathan Crow in 'Which companies can be made subject to an administration order?'.[1008] It follows that the extension of jurisdiction over voluntary arrangement and administration made by SI 2005/879 (and the extension in relation to voluntary winding up made by SI 2002/1240) is made by domestic legislation, not the EC Regulation, and is limited to the companies specified in the domestic legislation, so that now voluntary arrangement and administration under IA 1986 are not available to a chartered company (thus overruling *Re Salvage*

[1002] [2005] BCC 90.
[1003] [2003] EWHC 1028 (Ch), [2004] 1 WLR 174.
[1004] In a case described by Philip Mudd and Caroline Whittington in 'Cathedral saved by CVA' (2005) 21 Insolv L & P 10, Bradford Cathedral entered into a company voluntary arrangement despite not being a registered company.
[1005] SI 2005/879.
[1006] After further amendment by the Companies Act 2006 (Consequential Amendments, Transitional Provisions and Savings) Order 2009 (SI 2009/1941), sch 1, paras 71(1) and (2) and 72.
[1007] See 1.87–1.104.
[1008] (2004) 25 Co Law 184.

Association), an ecclesiastical corporation or a Northern Ireland company.[1009] SI 2005/879, reg 3, provides that the changes made by the regulations do not affect any voluntary arrangement or appointment of an administrator taking effect before 13 April 2005. It is submitted that *Re TXU Europe German Finance BV*[1010] must be regarded as correctly decided but for the wrong reasons: according to *Re Salvage Association* (which is not referred to in the judgment in *Re TXU Europe German Finance BV*) the extension of the power to go into voluntary liquidation is derived from IA 1986, s 221(4), not from the EC Regulation.

If, contrary to this argument, the interpretation of the Regulation made in *Re BRAC Rent-A-Car International Inc* is correct, its effect on winding-up jurisdiction in England and Wales is described at 1.207 and 1.301 **1.405**

In the Republic of Ireland, judges have followed *Re BRAC Rent-A-Car International Inc* and treated Regulation (EC) No 1346/2000 as being the source of jurisdiction to wind up companies.[1011] **1.406**

Literature

Regulation (EC) No 1346/2000 is a new version of a draft Convention on Insolvency Proceedings, which it was hoped would be accepted by all EU members as an international treaty. It was opened for signature on 23 November 1995 but the United Kingdom did not sign and it lapsed. As is common with treaties of that kind an explanatory report was prepared, by Miguel Virgós and Étienne Schmit, which would have been an official commentary on the Convention, but was not required for that purpose, because the Convention never came into force. The Virgós–Schmit report (EU Council document 6500/96) has often been referred to in judgments concerning the meaning of the Regulation. It was never published in the Official Journal but is available at the website of the Archive of European Integration, <http://www.aei.pitt.edu>, and also in the book by Moss et al listed next. **1.407**

Gabriel Moss, Ian F Fletcher and Stuart Isaacs, *The EC Regulation on Insolvency Proceedings. A Commentary and Annotated Guide*, 2nd edn (Oxford University Press, 2009).

Miguel Virgós and Francisco Garcimartín, *The European Insolvency Regulation: Law and Practice* (The Hague: Kluwer Law International, 2004).

Gülin Güneysu-Güngör, 'The intra-Community effects of cross-border reorganisation and winding up of credit institutions' (2005) 26 Co Law 258.

Jurisdiction over Winding Up on a Ground other than Insolvency: Regulation (EU) No 1215/2012, Brussels and Lugano Conventions

Seat of company determines jurisdiction

If a company, or other legal person or association of natural or legal persons, has its seat in a State or territory to which Regulation (EU) No 1215/2012 (Regulation (EC) No 44/2001 in **1.408**

[1009] It is submitted that *Re 3T Telecom Ltd* [2005] EWHC 275 (Ch), [2006] 2 BCLC 137, in which an administration order was made in respect of a Northern Ireland company, was wrongly decided, possibly because, as in *Re Sendo Ltd* [2005] EWHC 1604 (Ch), [2006] 1 BCLC 395, the court was unaware of the amendment made by SI 2005/879. In *Re Sendo Ltd* the unamended text of IA 1986, sch B1, para 111, is quoted in the judgment, but in *Re 3T Telecom Ltd* the paragraph is referred to without being quoted.
[1010] [2005] BCC 90.
[1011] See *Re US Ltd* [2012] IEHC 600 at [1]; *Re Harley Medical Group (Ireland) Ltd* [2013] IEHC 219.

the case of Denmark), or the Brussels or Lugano Convention applies,[1012] the courts of that State have exclusive jurisdiction in 'proceedings which have as their object . . . the nullity or the dissolution' of the company etc.[1013] Such proceedings include winding-up proceedings[1014] on grounds other than insolvency.[1015] This applies regardless of the domicile of the company.[1016]

Location of seat

1.409   A court which must determine the location of the seat of a company or other legal person or association of natural or legal persons, in order to decide whether it has jurisdiction in winding-up proceedings, must apply its domestic rules of private international law (the law of the forum). This is required by the Convention and Regulation provisions set out in the second column of table 1.1. The legislation which prescribes the rules of United Kingdom law for this purpose is identified in the third column. The rules must resolve potential conflict between legal systems which locate the seat in the jurisdiction of incorporation or formation and those which place it where the entity's central management and control is located.[1017] All the rules make the same provision.

Table 1.1 Sources of United Kingdom rules for determining the seat of a company etc

Instrument	Provision requiring application of the law of the forum	Provision of UK law prescribing rules for that purpose
Brussels Convention	art 53	Civil Jurisdiction and Judgments Act 1982, s 43
Regulation (EC) No 44/2001	art 22(2)	Civil Jurisdiction and Judgments Order 2001 (SI 2001/3929), sch 1, para 10, without the amendments made by the Civil Jurisdiction and Judgments (Amendment) Regulations 2014 (SI 2014/2947) (see SI 2014/2947, reg 6)
Lugano Convention 2007	art 22(2)	Civil Jurisdiction and Judgments Act 1982, s 43A
Regulation (EU) No 1215/2012	art 24(2)	Civil Jurisdiction and Judgments Order 2001 (SI 2001/3929), sch 1, para 10, as amended

---

[1012]   See 1.351–1.360.

[1013]   Regulation (EC) No 44/2001, art 22(2); Brussels Convention, art 16(2); Lugano Convention 2007, art 22(2); Regulation (EU) No 1215/2012, art 24(2). The phrase 'proceedings which have as their object', as it is used in these provisions, means 'proceedings which are principally concerned with': *J P Morgan Chase Bank NA v Berliner Verkehrsbetriebe (BVG) Anstalt des öffentlichen Rechts* [2010] EWCA Civ 390, [2012] QB 176, at [83]; *Ferrexpo AG v Gilson Investments Ltd* [2012] EWHC 721 (Comm), [2012] 1 Lloyd's Rep 588, at [145].

[1014]   *Re Senator Hanseatische Verwaltungsgesellschaft mbH* [1996] 2 BCLC 562 at p 577; *Re Drax Holdings Ltd* [2003] EWHC 2743, [2004] 1 WLR 1049, at [28]; *Re Rodenstock GmbH* [2011] EWHC 1104 (Ch), [2011] Bus LR 1245, at [38].

[1015]   The Regulations and Conventions do not apply to the winding up of insolvent companies or other legal persons (Regulation (EC) No 1346/2000, art 1(2)(b); Brussels Convention, art 1; Lugano Convention 2007, art 1(2)(b); Regulation (EU) No 1215/2012, art 1(2)(b)).

[1016]   Regulation (EC) No 44/2001, art 22 introductory words; Brussels Convention, art 16 introductory words; Lugano Convention 2007, art 22 introductory words; Regulation (EU) No 1215/2012, art 24 introductory words.

[1017]   It has become a tradition among lawyers that the apparently compound term 'central management and control' is treated as grammatically singular.

Under these rules, a corporation or association which was incorporated or formed **1.410** under the law of a part of the United Kingdom has its seat in the United Kingdom,[1018] and such a corporation or association must not be regarded by a court in the United Kingdom as having its seat in any other State or territory in respect of which the Regulation or a Convention is in force.[1019] So any argument that a company incorporated or formed in the United Kingdom would be regarded by a court of such State or territory as having its seat there (because, for example, its central management and control is there) is irrelevant to the determination of the company's seat by a United Kingdom court.

If the central management and control of a corporation or association is exercised in the **1.411** United Kingdom, its seat is in the United Kingdom, even if it was not incorporated or formed in the UK.[1020] But if it was incorporated or formed in another State or territory in respect of which the Regulation or a Convention is in force, the rule stated in 1.412 will apply.

A corporation or association must be regarded as having its seat in a State or territory other **1.412** than the UK in respect of which the Regulation or a Convention is in force if it was incorporated or formed under the law of that jurisdiction, except where it is shown that the courts there would not regard it as having its seat there for this purpose.[1021] This exception applies where the other jurisdiction treats the seat as being where central management and control is exercised.

If a company was not incorporated or formed under the law of any part of the United **1.413** Kingdom and its central management and control is exercised in another State or territory in respect of which the Regulation or a Convention is in force, its seat must be regarded as being in that jurisdiction, except where it is shown that the courts there would not regard it as having its seat there for this purpose.[1022]

The *only* circumstances in which a corporation or association can be regarded as having its **1.414** seat in the United Kingdom are if it was incorporated or formed under the law of a part of the United Kingdom or if its central management and control is exercised in the United Kingdom.[1023]

[1018] SI 2001/3929, sch 1, para 10(2)(a); Civil Jurisdiction and Judgments Act 1982, ss 43(2)(a) and 43A (2)(a).

[1019] SI 2001/3929, sch 1, para 10(4)(a); Civil Jurisdiction and Judgments Act 1982, ss 43(7)(a) and 43A(4)(a).

[1020] SI 2001/3929, sch 1, para 10(2)(b); Civil Jurisdiction and Judgments Act 1982, ss 43(2)(b) and 43A(2)(b).

[1021] SI 2001/3929, sch 1, para 10(3) and (4)(b); Civil Jurisdiction and Judgments Act 1982, ss 43(6) and (7)(b) and 43A(3)(a) and (4)(b).

[1022] SI 2001/3929, sch 1, para 10(2)(a), (3)(b) and (4); Civil Jurisdiction and Judgments Act 1982, ss 43(2) (a), (6)(b) and (7), and 43A(2)(a), (3)(b) and (4)(b).

[1023] SI 2001/3929, sch 1, para 10(2); Civil Jurisdiction and Judgments Act 1982, ss 43(2) and 43A(2). A corresponding provision is made for other States and territories in respect of which the Regulation or either of the Conventions is in force by SI 2001/3929, sch 1, para 10(3), and the Civil Jurisdiction and Judgments Act 1982, s 43(6).

Where more than one State has jurisdiction

1.415 If proceedings come within the exclusive jurisdiction of several courts, the court which is first seized of the proceedings shall conduct them and the courts of other States must decline jurisdiction in favour of that court.[1024]

Forum non conveniens

1.416 If Regulation (EU) No 1215/2012 or the Brussels or Lugano Convention assigns jurisdiction over the winding up of a company to the United Kingdom, a UK court cannot decline the jurisdiction on the ground of *forum non conveniens*, even if no other State or territory in respect of which the Regulation or a Convention is in force claims jurisdiction.[1025]

Public interest petitions

1.417 Article 1 of Regulation (EU) No 1215/2012 and of the Brussels and Lugano Conventions provides that they apply 'in civil and commercial matters', and the European Court of Justice has held that this means the Brussels Convention does not apply to proceedings brought by a public authority in the exercise of its public powers.[1026] It follows that the Regulation and Conventions do not apply to a public interest petition presented by the Secretary of State under IA 1986, s 124A.[1027]

Literature

1.418 *Dicey, Morris and Collins on the Conflict of Laws*, 14th edn (London: Sweet & Maxwell, 2006), r 163.

Allocation of Jurisdiction within the UK

Civil Jurisdiction and Judgments Act 1982

1.419 The Civil Jurisdiction and Judgments Act 1982, s 16, provides that allocation of jurisdiction over civil proceedings to the different parts of the United Kingdom is to be governed by the rules in sch 4, which is a modified version of Regulation (EC) No 44/2001. The Civil Jurisdiction and Judgments Act 1982, sch 4, para 11(b), provides that 'in proceedings which have as their object...the nullity or dissolution of companies or other legal persons or associations of natural or legal persons' the courts of the part of the United Kingdom in which the company etc has its seat have exclusive jurisdiction, regardless of domicile. This is an adaptation of Regulation (EC) No 44/2001, art 22.[1028] But the Civil Jurisdiction and Judgments Act 1982, s 17(1) and sch 5, para 1, provide that sch 4 does not apply to proceedings for the winding up of a company under IA 1986 or the Insolvency (Northern Ireland) Order 1989.[1029]

[1024] Regulation (EU) No 1215/2012, art 31(1); Brussels Convention, art 23; Lugano Convention 2007, art 29.

[1025] *Owusu v Jackson* (case C-281/02) [2005] ECR I-1383, overruling *Re Harrods Buenos Aires Ltd* [1992] Ch 72.

[1026] *LTU Lufttransportunternehmen GmbH & Co KG v Eurocontrol* (case 29/76) [1976] ECR 1541; *Netherlands v Rüffer* (case 814/79) [1980] ECR 3807.

[1027] *Re a Company (No 007816 of 1994)* [1995] 2 BCLC 539 at p 541; *Re Senator Hanseatische Verwaltungsgesellschaft mbH* [1996] 2 BCLC 562.

[1028] See 1.408.

[1029] SI 1989/2405 (NI 19).

Registered Companies

Companies registered in England and Wales or Scotland

The courts of England and Wales have jurisdiction to wind up any company registered **1.420** in England and Wales.[1030] IA 1986, s 117, specifies that the High Court and the County Court have jurisdiction to wind up companies registered in England and Wales. Section 120 specifies that the Court of Session and sheriff courts have jurisdiction to wind up companies registered in Scotland. These sections (which are part of the law of both England and Wales and Scotland) must be taken to be mutually exclusive, so a court in England and Wales does not have jurisdiction under IA 1986, part 4, to wind up a company registered in Scotland.[1031] Similarly, a court in Scotland does not have jurisdiction under part 4 to wind up a company registered in England and Wales.

The jurisdiction of the County Court to wind up a registered company is further defined by **1.421** reference to the company's share capital and the location of its registered office,[1032] as is the jurisdiction of sheriff courts in Scotland.[1033]

By virtue of IA 1986, s 220, a company registered in Scotland is not an unregistered com- **1.422** pany and so cannot be wound up in England and Wales under part 5.[1034]

Companies registered in Northern Ireland

A company registered in Northern Ireland (or deemed by the Government of Ireland **1.423** (Companies, Societies, etc) Order 1922[1035] to be registered there) can be wound up by the High Court there under the Insolvency (Northern Ireland) Order 1989,[1036] part 5.

IA 1986, part 4, applies only to companies registered in England and Wales or Scotland,[1037] **1.424** so a company registered in Northern Ireland cannot be wound up under part 4. Such a company cannot be wound up under part 5 either, because it is registered in a part of the United Kingdom and so is not an unregistered company.[1038]

Republic of Ireland companies

Subject to Regulation (EC) No 1346/2000,[1039] a company registered in the Republic of **1.425** Ireland can be wound up in England and Wales under IA 1986, part 5.[1040] A company registered under the Companies (Consolidation) Act 1908 or an earlier Act in Ireland before 1 January 1922 is not a company registered under the Companies Act 2006, unless it is

---

[1030] *Princess of Reuss v Bos* (1871) LR 5 HL 176; *Re Tumacacori Mining Co* (1874) LR 17 Eq 534; *Re Baby Moon (UK) Ltd* (1984) 1 BCC 99,298, in which the company, though registered in England and Wales, wrongly had its registered office outside England and Wales.

[1031] *Re Scottish Joint Stock Trust* [1900] WN 114; *Re Helene plc* [2000] 2 BCLC 249.

[1032] See 1.444 and 1.448.

[1033] IA 1986, s 120(3) and (4).

[1034] Similarly, a company registered in England and Wales or Northern Ireland cannot be wound up in Scotland under part 5.

[1035] SR & O 1922/184.

[1036] SI 1989/2405 (NI 19).

[1037] IA 1986, s 73(1).

[1038] IA 1986, s 220, as in force from 1 October 2009. Under the wording of s 220 that was in force before 1 October 2009, it was held, controversially, that a company registered in Northern Ireland could be wound up as an unregistered company under IA 1986, part 5. See *Re a Company (No 007946 of 1993)* [1994] Ch 198 and the discussion at 1.10.2.2 in the second edition of this work.

[1039] See 1.361–1.407.

[1040] *Re Hibernian Merchants Ltd* [1958] Ch 76.

deemed to be registered in Northern Ireland.[1041] This means that such a company cannot be wound up under IA 1986, part 4, which applies only to companies registered under the Companies 2006 in England and Wales or Scotland,[1042] and such a company is also not excluded from the definition of unregistered company in IA 1986, part 5.[1043] Such a company is not registered under the Companies Act 2006,[1044] because it was not an 'existing company' for the purposes of either the Companies Act 1985,[1045] or, unless it is deemed to have been registered in Northern Ireland, the Companies (Northern Ireland) Order 1986.[1046]

European cooperative societies

1.426   The European Cooperative Society Regulations 2006[1047] distinguish between societies which have their registered offices in Great Britain[1048] and those with registered offices in Northern Ireland.[1049] Registration of a society is with the relevant competent authority.[1050] No distinction is drawn between registration in England and Wales and registration in Scotland, but, as the FCA is located in London, it is submitted that a society with a registered office in Great Britain must be treated as registered in England and Wales for the purposes of IA 1986, s 117.

Unregistered Companies, other than Insolvent Partnerships

1.427   If an unregistered company has a principal place of business in one or more parts of the United Kingdom, jurisdiction to wind it up is determined by the following rules:

(a) It may be wound up by the court in a part of the United Kingdom in which it has a principal place of business, and the principal place of business is deemed to be its registered office for all purposes of the winding up.

(b) If it has a principal place of business in one part of the United Kingdom, it cannot be wound up in another part where it does not have a principal place of business, but it can be wound up in another part where it does have a principal place of business.

1.428   These rules are the combined effect of:

(a) IA 1986, s 221(3). For England and Wales and Scotland, s 221(3) deems an unregistered company to be registered in whichever of those parts it has a principal place of business (or both parts if it has principal places of business in both parts) and deems the principal place of business to be its registered office.[1051] Then IA 1986, ss 117 and 120 (which are

---

[1041] A company whose registered office was in Northern Ireland on 1 January 1922 is deemed to be registered there by the Government of Ireland (Companies, Societies etc) Order 1922 (SR & O 1922/184), art 4.
[1042] IA 1986, s 73(1).
[1043] IA 1986, s 220.
[1044] Companies Act 2006, s 1(1).
[1045] Companies Act 1985, s 735(1)(b).
[1046] Companies (Northern Ireland) Order 1986 (SI 1986/1032 (NI 6)), art 3(1)(b).
[1047] SI 2006/2078.
[1048] For which the competent authority is the Financial Conduct Authority: reg 3(1)(a).
[1049] For which the competent authority is the Registrar of Credit Unions for Northern Ireland: reg 3(1)(b).
[1050] reg 8.
[1051] The Insolvency (Northern Ireland) Order 1989 (SI 1989/2405, NI 19), art 185(2), deems an unregistered company's principal place of business in Northern Ireland to be its registered office. Deeming an unregistered company to be a registered company is only for the purpose of determining jurisdiction, but deeming the principal place of business to be the registered office is for all purposes of the winding up.

applied to unregistered companies by s 221(1)), allocate jurisdiction to the courts of the part in which the company is deemed to be registered or the district where its deemed registered office is situated.

(b) The rule that English and Scottish jurisdiction over registered companies is mutually exclusive,[1052] which, for an unregistered company deemed to be registered, is overridden if, but only if, it has a principal place of business in both jurisdictions.[1053]

(c) IA 1986, s 221(2), and SI 1989/2405, NI 19, art 185(2), which deal with a company which has a principal place of business in Northern Ireland.

If an unregistered company has been dissolved or has otherwise ceased business, the prin- **1.429** cipal place of business referred to in these rules is the place where business was carried on before it ceased.[1054]

For a relevant scheme,[1055] these rules apply to a place of business of the scheme's depositary.[1056] **1.430**

Insolvent Partnerships

Whichever modification of IA 1986, s 221(1), applies to an insolvent partnership[1057] the **1.431** subsection is subject to s 221(3). This subsection is given identical modifications by IPO 1994, sch 3, para 3 (in relation to art 7 petitions), sch 4, para 3 (in relation to art 8 petitions), sch 5, para 2 (in relation to art 9 petitions), and sch 6, para 4 (in relation to art 10 petitions). The result is that if an insolvent partnership has a principal place of business in Scotland, a court in England and Wales does not have jurisdiction to wind it up unless the partnership had a principal place of business in England and Wales at any time in the period of one year ending with the day on which the petition is presented. If an insolvent partnership has a principal place of business in Northern Ireland, a court in England and Wales does not have jurisdiction to wind it up unless the partnership had a principal place of business in England and Wales at any time in the period of three years ending with the day on which the petition is presented.

IA 1986, s 221(3A), as modified by IPO 1994, sch 3, para 3, sch 4, para 3, sch 5, para 2, **1.432** and sch 6, para 4, points out that IA 1986, s 221(3), as so modified, is subject to Regulation (EC) No 1346/2000.[1058]

Companies Liable to be Wound Up under IA 1986

Jurisdiction to Sanction Companies' Compromises and Arrangements

The Companies Act 2006, ss 895–899, make provision for court-sanctioned compromises **1.433** and arrangements between companies and their creditors or members. In these sections, 'company' means a company 'liable to be wound up under' IA 1986.[1059] The definition has

---

[1052] See 1.420–1.422.
[1053] IA 1986, s 221(3)(b).
[1054] *Re Family Endowment Society* (1870) LR 5 Ch App 118 per Lord Hatherley LC at pp 130–1 and Giffard LJ at pp 135–6.
[1055] See 1.168.
[1056] Collective Investment in Transferable Securities (Contractual Scheme) Regulations 2013 (SI 2013/1388), reg 17(3)–(7).
[1057] See 1.146–1.149.
[1058] See 1.361–1.407.
[1059] Companies Act 2006, s 895(2)(b).

been in the same form since the provision was first enacted in 1870.[1060] At that time the provision applied only to a company in the course of being wound up, whether by the court, voluntarily or subject to the court's supervision.[1061] The definition was not changed when the provision was extended to companies not in the course of being wound up.[1062]

1.434 The definition is intended 'simply to identify the types of company and association to which the jurisdiction [to sanction a scheme or arrangement] applies'.[1063] In order to be 'liable to be wound up' for the purposes of jurisdiction to sanction a compromise or arrangement, a company must be the sort of company which is capable of being wound up under IA 1986,[1064] but it is not necessary to prove the existence of one of the circumstances in which the court may make a winding-up order.[1065] In other words, in order to show that a company 'is liable to be wound up' under IA 1986, it is not necessary to show that an immediate application to wind it up would be successful, only that such an application could not be dismissed on the ground that the court did not have jurisdiction over the company.[1066]

1.435 For these purposes at least, the three core requirements for exercising the jurisdiction to wind up a foreign company[1067] are relevant only to whether the court should exercise its discretion to wind up a particular company. They are not limits on the court's jurisdiction to wind up foreign companies, so a foreign company is liable to be wound up under IA 1986 even if the three core requirements are not satisfied.[1068] Nevertheless, the court in England and Wales will not sanction a foreign company's compromise or arrangement unless there is a sufficient connection with England and Wales.[1069] Normally the connection with England and Wales, and the reason for seeking court sanction of a compromise here, is that the company seeks to compromise debts that are governed by English law and incurred in trading here. It is almost inconceivable that the court would sanction a foreign company's compromise or arrangement with its members.[1070]

EEA Insurers and Credit Institutions

1.436 In England and Wales a company may seek a court-sanctioned compromise or arrangement with its creditors or members if it is a company which is liable to be wound up under IA 1986.[1071] An EEA insurer,[1072] or a branch of an EEA insurer, cannot be wound up by a court in the United Kingdom.[1073] But, for the purposes of jurisdiction to sanction a compromise or arrangement, an EEA insurer, or a branch of an EEA insurer, is to be treated as a company liable to be wound up under IA 1986 if it would be liable to be wound up under

[1060] Joint Stock Companies Arrangement Act 1870, s 3.
[1061] Joint Stock Companies Arrangement Act 1870, s 2.
[1062] Companies Act 1907, s 38; Companies (Consolidation) Act 1908, s 120(3).
[1063] *Re Rodenstock GmbH* [2011] EWHC 1104 (Ch), [2011] Bus LR 1245, at [56].
[1064] See 1.80–1.220.
[1065] See 2.23–2.53. *Re Drax Holdings Ltd* [2003] EWHC 2743, [2004] 1 WLR 1049, at [26]; *Re Sovereign Marine and General Insurance Co Ltd* [2006] EWHC 1335 (Ch), [2007] 1 BCLC 228, at [33].
[1066] See further 1.439–1.442.
[1067] See 1.172.
[1068] *Re Drax Holdings Ltd* [2003] EWHC 2743 (Ch), [2004] 1 WLR 1049.
[1069] *Re Drax Holdings Ltd* at [29].
[1070] *Re Drax Holdings Ltd* at [29].
[1071] Companies Act 2006, s 895(2)(b). See 1.433–1.435.
[1072] See 1.318–1.322.
[1073] Insurers (Reorganisation and Winding Up) Regulations 2004 (SI 2004/353), reg 4, implementing Directive 2001/17/EC.

that Act but for that prohibition.[1074] The same applies to an EEA credit institution[1075] and a branch of an EEA credit institution.[1076] The rules treating EEA insurers and EEA credit institutions as liable to be wound up under IA 1986 are not overridden by Regulation (EC) No 1346/2000 in relation to winding up on the ground of insolvency or Regulation (EU) No 1215/2012, the Brussels Convention or the Lugano Convention 2007 in relation to winding up on other grounds. This is because those instruments do not apply to EEA insurers or EEA credit institutions, as will be explained at 1.437–1.438.

Regulation (EC) No 1346/2000 does not apply to EEA insurers or EEA credit institu-   **1.437**
tions.[1077] So an EEA insurer or EEA credit institution which has its COMI in an EU State (apart from Denmark) other than the UK can nevertheless be treated as liable to be wound up under IA 1986, because jurisdiction to wind it up is not assigned by the Regulation to the State in which it has its COMI.[1078]

Regulation (EU) No 1215/2012, the Brussels Convention and the Lugano Convention   **1.438**
2007, which allocate jurisdiction to wind up a company to the State in which the company has its seat,[1079] do not apply to EEA insurers and EEA credit institutions. This is because the Regulation provides[1080] that it will not 'prejudice' and the Conventions provide[1081] that they will not 'affect' any provisions governing jurisdiction in specific matters contained in Community instruments or in national legislation harmonized pursuant to such instruments. So the Regulation and the Conventions do not allocate jurisdiction to wind up EEA insurers and EEA credit institutions, because this is done by the national legislation implementing Directive 2001/17/EC (insurers) and Directive 2001/24/EC (credit institutions).[1082] So an EEA insurer or EEA credit institution, which has its seat in an EU State, Iceland, Norway, Switzerland, Gibraltar, Aruba or a French overseas department, and is solvent can nevertheless be treated as liable to be wound up under IA 1986, because jurisdiction to wind it up is not allocated to the State or territory in which it has its seat.[1083]

Other EEA Companies

In England and Wales a company may seek a court-sanctioned compromise or arrange-   **1.439**
ment with its creditors or members if it is a company which is liable to be wound up under IA 1986.[1084] Special provision has been made by statutory instruments to ensure that EEA insurers and EEA credit institutions are treated as liable to be wound up under IA 1986

[1074] SI 2004/353, reg 5(1).

[1075] See 1.323–1.325.

[1076] Credit Institutions (Reorganisation and Winding Up) Regulations 2004 (SI 2004/1045), reg 3, implementing Directive 2001/24/EC; SI 2004/1045, reg 4(1).

[1077] Regulation (EC) No 1346/2000, art 1(2).

[1078] *Re La Mutuelle du Mans Assurance IARD* [2005] EWHC 1599 (Ch), [2006] BCC 11.

[1079] Regulation (EU) No 1215/2012, art 24(2); Brussels Convention, art 16(2). See 1.408.

[1080] Regulation (EU) No 1215/2012, art 67.

[1081] Brussels Convention, art 57(3); Lugano Convention 2007, art 67(1) and protocol 3, para 3.

[1082] In the UK, SI 2004/353 and SI 2004/1045.

[1083] *Re Sovereign Marine and General Insurance Co Ltd* [2006] EWHC 1335 (Ch), [2007] 1 BCLC 228, at [56]. Look Chan Ho, 'A rational basis of jurisdiction over EEA insurers' solvent schemes that the WFUM decision could be, but isn't' (2006) 22 Insolv L & P 145, argues that the Regulation does continue to apply, but without prejudice to the operation of the Community instrument or national implementing legislation. But it is difficult to see how the Regulation could be said to determine jurisdiction when that determination is made by another piece of legislation instead. See also Look Chan Ho, 'Solvent schemes for foreign insurers' (2005) 21 Insolv L & P 169.

[1084] Companies Act 2006, s 895(2)(b). See 1.433–1.435.

despite jurisdiction to wind them up being allocated to the courts of another State by Directive 2001/17/EC and Directive 2001/24/EC.[1085] But no special provision has been made legislatively to deal with jurisdiction to wind up a company being allocated to another State by the Brussels Convention, the Lugano Convention 2007, Regulation (EC) No 1346/2000 or Regulation (EU) No 1215/2012.[1086]

1.440 The court in *Re DAP Holding NV*[1087] found a way of working round the rules on allocation of jurisdiction for winding up on the ground of insolvency in Regulation (EC) No 1346/2000. It accepted an extension of the argument that a company is liable to be wound up under IA 1986 if it is the sort of company which can be wound up under that Act, regardless of whether any ground for winding it up exists at the time of determining whether it is liable to be wound up. The extension which was accepted is that a company is liable to be wound up under IA 1986 despite a present lack of jurisdiction over the company, if the company could remove that lack of jurisdiction.[1088] The possibility of removing the lack of jurisdiction need only be theoretical, not necessarily practicable. The case concerned a company incorporated in, and having its COMI in, the Netherlands. The company had no establishment in the United Kingdom. The company was not an EEA insurer or EEA credit institution. Under Regulation (EC) No 1346/2000, art 3, the courts of the United Kingdom would never have had jurisdiction (as that word is used in the Regulation) to wind up the company. Nevertheless, it was held that the company was liable to be wound up in England and Wales under IA 1986, because it could, if it wished, create an establishment here, which would give jurisdiction to the courts of England and Wales under Regulation (EC) No 1346/2000, art 3(2). There was no practical possibility of the company creating an establishment here, because it was insolvent and was not authorized to carry on its insurance business. This reasoning treats 'jurisdiction' as meaning contingent or potential jurisdiction, which seems to be a significant extension of its usual meaning. It is submitted that this decision should be regarded with caution as an ad hoc method of dealing with a statutory lacuna.

1.441 In *Re Rodenstock GmbH*[1089] Briggs J thought it more difficult to apply this reasoning in the case of a solvent company where allocation of jurisdiction is governed by Regulation (EC) No 44/2001 (now Regulation (EU) No 1215/2012). His Lordship preferred the view that neither that Regulation nor Regulation (EC) No 1346/2000 was intended to restrict the jurisdiction of the English courts over compromises and arrangements.[1090] Accordingly, for the purposes of that jurisdiction, the court can treat a solvent company whose seat is in another EU State, or an insolvent company whose COMI is in another EU State other than Denmark, in the same way as it treats an EEA insurer or credit institution. It would seem that the same argument can be applied to solvent companies for which jurisdiction to wind up is covered by the Brussels or Lugano Conventions. Another possible reason

---

[1085] See 1.436–1.438.
[1086] See 1.347–1.418.
[1087] [2005] EWHC 2092 (Ch), [2006] BCC 48.
[1088] In *Re Kailis Groote Eylandt Fisheries Pty Ltd* (1977) 17 SASR 35 it was held that a foreign company was not liable to be wound up in South Australia at a time when it did not have any assets in South Australia even though it subsequently located assets there. But the argument that potential liability to be wound up would have been sufficient was not advanced.
[1089] [2011] EWHC 1104 (Ch), [2011] Bus LR 1245, at [53].
[1090] *Re Rodenstock GmbH* at [54]. At [57]–[63] Briggs J discusses possible problems with this view, which he ruled did not affect his conclusion in the particular circumstances of the case before him.

why Regulation (EU) No 1215/2012 may not apply to a scheme of arrangement is that the Regulation is concerned with where persons domiciled in an EU State may be 'sued'[1091] and it may be argued that sanction of a compromise or arrangement does not involve any person being sued or being in the position of a defendant.[1092]

If neither of the arguments expressed in 1.441 is correct, a court in England and Wales **1.442** clearly has jurisdiction over a scheme or arrangement concerning contracts entered into by a solvent company if those contracts provide that the courts of England and Wales have jurisdiction over disputes in connection with the contracts,[1093] or if a party who could be regarded as a defendant is domiciled here,[1094] or if all parties who could be regarded as defendants have entered an appearance so as to submit to the jurisdiction.[1095]

Court Jurisdiction

Registered Companies

General rule

In England and Wales, the High Court has jurisdiction to wind up any company registered **1.443** in England and Wales.[1096] All matters involving the exercise of the High Court's jurisdiction under the enactments relating to companies are assigned to the Chancery Division by the Senior Courts Act 1981, sch 1, para 1.

If the amount of a registered company's share capital paid up or credited as paid up does not **1.444** exceed £120,000, the County Court has concurrent jurisdiction with the High Court to wind up the company,[1097] unless the company's registered office is in the London insolvency district.[1098] That district is defined[1099] to comprise the areas served by the County Court hearing centres listed in SI 2014/818, art 3. If, in the six months immediately preceding presentation of a petition to wind up a company, it has had different addresses for its registered office then it is the place which has longest been its registered office in that period which is its situation for these purposes.[1100]

The County Court has all the powers of the High Court for the purposes of exercising its **1.445** winding-up jurisdiction[1101] and accordingly is not, when exercising those powers, an inferior court subject to supervision by the High Court.[1102] A question arising in County Court

---

[1091] Regulation (EU) No 1215/2012, arts 4 and 5.
[1092] *Primacom Holdings GmbH v A Group of the Senior Lenders* [2012] EWHC 164 (Ch), [2013] BCC 201, at [10]–[13]; *Re NEF Telecom Co BV* [2012] EWHC 2944 (Comm), LTL 27/11/2012, at [38]–[39]; *Re Vietnam Shipbuilding Industry Groups* [2013] EWHC 2476 (Ch), [2014] 1 BCLC 400, at [12]; *Re Magyar Telecom BV* [2013] EWHC 3800 (Ch), 163 (7588) NLJ 20, at [31].
[1093] Regulation (EU) No 1215/2012, art 25; *Primacom Holdings GmbH v A Group of the Senior Lenders* at [14]; *Re NEF Telecom Co BV* at [41]–[42]. Jurisdiction does not have to be exclusive: *Re Vietnam Shipbuilding Industry Groups* at [15].
[1094] Regulation (EU) No 1215/2012, art 8; *Re NEF Telecom Co BV* at [43].
[1095] Regulation (EU) No 1215/2012, art 26(1); *Primacom Holdings GmbH v A Group of the Senior Lenders* at [15].
[1096] IA 1986, s 117(1).
[1097] IA 1986, s 117(2).
[1098] IA 1986, s 117(2A); High Court and County Courts Jurisdiction Order (SI 1991/724), art 6C.
[1099] By the London Insolvency District (County Court at Central London) Order 2014 (SI 2014/818).
[1100] IA 1986, s 117(2A); SI 1991/724, art 6C.
[1101] IA 1986, s 117(5).
[1102] *Re New Par Consols Ltd (No 2)* [1898] 1 QB 669; IR 1986, r 7.47(3).

winding-up proceedings may be transmitted to the High Court in the form of a special case for the opinion of the High Court, if all the parties to the proceedings, or one of them and the judge, wish to have it determined there.[1103]

1.446 Only the High Court may make a bank insolvency order.[1104]

Companies without share capital

1.447 The Companies (Winding up) Act 1890, s 1,[1105] introduced a division of jurisdiction between the High Court and county courts. It provided that a petition to wind up a company with a capital not exceeding £10,000 had to be presented in a county court and a petition for a company with a capital exceeding £10,000 had to be presented in the High Court. In *Re North of England Iron Steamship Insurance Association*[1106] it was held that the High Court still retained the jurisdiction it had under the Companies Act 1862, s 81, to wind up companies without a share capital,[1107] and in *Re Ironfounders' (Bradford Branch) Social Club and Institute*[1108] it was held that county courts did not have jurisdiction to wind up such companies. It would seem that the position is still that the County Court does not have jurisdiction to wind up a company without a share capital. Under the equivalent provision in Scotland it has been held that a sheriff court does not have jurisdiction to wind up a company without a share capital.[1109] Division of jurisdiction was replaced by the present concurrent jurisdiction of High Court and County Court by the Companies Act 1928, s 56.

County Court hearing centre

1.448 In the County Court, a petition to wind up a company may only be commenced in the County Court hearing centre which serves the area in which the company's registered office is situated,[1110] unless, for that hearing centre, SI 2014/817, sch 1, lists an alternative hearing centre, in which case the listed alternative hearing centre must be used.[1111] If, in the six months immediately preceding presentation of a petition to wind up a company, it has had different addresses for its registered office, it is the place which has longest been its registered office in that period which determines the hearing centre to be used.[1112] SI 2014/817, sch 1, lists all hearing centres, including those in the London insolvency district. The schedule identifies the hearing centres in which winding-up proceedings cannot be commenced and shows where they should be brought instead, either in an alternative hearing centre or, in the London insolvency district, in the High Court.

Building Societies

1.449 The High Court has jurisdiction to wind up any building society registered in England and Wales.[1113] Where the amount standing to the credit of shares in a building society as shown

---

[1103] IA 1986, s 119.

[1104] Banking Act 2009, s 92.

[1105] Re-enacted in the Companies (Consolidation) Act 1908, s 131.

[1106] [1900] 1 Ch 481.

[1107] See also *Re Monmouthshire and South Wales Employers Mutual Indemnity Society Ltd* [1909] WN 6.

[1108] (1923) 67 SJ 516.

[1109] *Pearce* 1991 SCLR 861.

[1110] Insolvency (Commencement of Proceedings) and Insolvency Rules 1986 (Amendment) Rules 2014 (SI 2014/817), r 2(1).

[1111] SI 2014/817, r 2(2).

[1112] SI 2014/817, r 2(3).

[1113] IA 1986, s 117(1), applied by the Building Societies Act 1986, s 90 and modified by sch 15, para 3(1)(a).

by the latest balance sheet does not exceed £120,000, the County Court has concurrent jurisdiction with the High Court to wind up the society.[1114]

Only the High Court may make a building society insolvency order.[1115]   **1.450**

Incorporated Friendly Societies

The High Court has jurisdiction to wind up any incorporated friendly society registered   **1.451**
in England and Wales.[1116] Where the amount of the contribution or subscription income of an incorporated friendly society as shown by the latest balance sheet does not exceed £120,000, the County Court has concurrent jurisdiction with the High Court to wind up the society.[1117]

Charitable Incorporated Organizations

Jurisdiction to wind up a charitable incorporated organization is assigned concurrently to   **1.452**
the High Court and the County Court.[1118]

Unregistered Companies other than Insolvent Partnerships

For the purpose of determining a court's winding-up jurisdiction, an unregistered company   **1.453**
which has a principal place of business in England and Wales is deemed to be registered in England and Wales.[1119] It follows that the High Court has jurisdiction to wind up any such company,[1120] unless that principal place of business (which is deemed to be the company's registered office for all purposes of the winding up[1121]) is in the London insolvency district.[1122] Outside the London insolvency district, the County Court has concurrent jurisdiction to wind up an unregistered company if its share capital paid up or credited as paid up does not exceed £120,000.[1123] It seems that only the High Court has jurisdiction to wind up an unregistered company that does not have a share capital.[1124]

If an unregistered company has a principal place of business in Scotland then, for the   **1.454**
purpose of determining a court's winding-up jurisdiction, it is deemed to be registered in Scotland.[1125] So it cannot be wound up in England and Wales,[1126] unless it also has a principal place of business there, in which case it is deemed to be registered in both jurisdictions[1127] and can be wound up in either of them.

[1114] IA 1986, s 117(2), as modified by the Building Societies Act 1986, sch 15, paras 3(1)(a) and (d) and 15. This provision has not yet been amended to reflect the creation of the single County Court.
[1115] Banking Act 2009, s 92, applied by the Building Societies Act 1986, s 90C.
[1116] IA 1986, s 117(1), applied by the Friendly Societies Act 1992, s 23 and modified by sch 10, para 3(1)(a).
[1117] IA 1986, s 117(2), as modified by the Friendly Societies Act 1992, sch 10, paras 3(1)(a) and 18. This provision has not yet been amended to reflect the creation of the single County Court.
[1118] IA 1986, s 117(1) and (2), as applied and modified by the Charitable Incorporated Organisations (Insolvency and Dissolution) Regulations 2012 (SI 2012/3013), sch, para 1(1), (2), (3)(a) and (7).
[1119] IA 1986, s 221(3).
[1120] IA 1986, s 117(1), applied by s 221(1).
[1121] IA 1986, s 221(3).
[1122] IA 1986, s 117(2A), applied by s 221(1). See 1.444.
[1123] IA 1986, s 117(2), applied by s 221(1). The location of the company's principal place of business is deemed to be its registered office for the purpose of determining which hearing centre (see 1.448) is to be used.
[1124] See 1.447.
[1125] IA 1986, s 221(3).
[1126] *Re Scottish Joint Stock Trust* [1900] WN 114; *Re Helene plc* [2000] 2 BCLC 249.
[1127] IA 1986, s 221(3).

1.455   If an unregistered company has been dissolved or has ceased business, the place where business was carried on before it ceased is treated as being the principal place of business for these purposes.[1128]

1.456   In England and Wales, the High Court has, but the County Court does not have, jurisdiction to wind up a European grouping of territorial cooperation which has its registered office in the United Kingdom (a UK EGTC)[1129] or a relevant scheme.[1130]

Insolvent Partnerships

Articles 7 and 8 (petitions other than by members)

1.457   In relation to a petition in accordance with IPO 1994, art 7 or art 8 (petitions other than by members), IA 1986, s 117(1) and (2), is given identical modifications by IPO 1994, sch 3, para 6 (in relation to art 7 petitions), and sch 4, para 5 (in relation to art 8 petitions). The result is that, under modified s 117(1), the High Court has jurisdiction to wind up any insolvent partnership as an unregistered company on an IPO 1994, art 7 or art 8, petition if the partnership has, or at any time had, in England and Wales, either:

(a) a principal place of business, or
(b) a place of business at which business is or has been carried on in the course of which the debt (or part of the debt) arose which forms the basis of the petition for winding up the partnership.

1.458   Alternatively, under modified IA 1986, s 117(2), an IPO 1994, art 7 or art 8, petition may be presented to the County Court hearing centre which serves the area in which the partnership has, or at any time had, either:

(a) a principal place of business, or
(b) a place of business at which business is or has been carried on in the course of which the debt (or part of the debt) arose which forms the basis of the petition for winding up the partnership.[1131]

1.459   In relation to art 7 petitions, IA 1986, s 221(7), as modified by IPO 1994, sch 3, para 6, points out that IA 1986, s 117(1) and (2), as so modified, is subject to Regulation (EC) No 1346/2000.[1132] The same point is made in relation to IPO 1994, art 8, petitions by IA 1986, s 117(9), as modified by IPO 1994, sch 4, para 5.

Articles 9 and 10 (petitions by members)

1.460   On a petition in accordance with IPO 1994, art 9 or art 10 (petitions by members), IA 1986, s 117(1) and (2), is given identical modifications by IPO 1994, sch 5, para 1 (in relation to art 9 petitions), and IPO 1994, sch 6, para 1 (in relation to art 10 petitions). The result is that the High Court has jurisdiction to wind up any insolvent partnership as an unregistered company on an art 9 or art 10 petition if the partnership has, or at any time had, a principal place of business in England and Wales.[1133] Alternatively a petition under art 9 or art 10 may be presented to

---

[1128] *Re Family Endowment Society* (1870) LR 5 Ch App 118 per Lord Hatherley LC at pp 130–1 and Giffard LJ at pp 135–6.
[1129] European Grouping of Territorial Cooperation Regulations 2007 (SI 2007/1949), sch, para 6.
[1130] Collective Investment in Transferable Securities (Contractual Scheme) Regulations 2013 (SI 2013/1388), reg 17. See 1.168.
[1131] This provision has not yet been amended to reflect the creation of the single County Court.
[1132] See 1.361–1.407.
[1133] Modified s 117(1).

the County Court hearing centre which serves the area in which the partnership has, or at any time had, a principal place of business.[1134]

In relation to art 9 petitions, IA 1986, s 221(7), as modified by IPO 1994, sch 5, para 1, points **1.461** out that s 117(1) and (2) as so modified is subject to Regulation (EC) No 1346/2000.[1135] The same point is made in relation to art 10 petitions by IA 1986, s 117(9), as modified by IPO 1994, sch 6, para 1.

Business must have been carried on in past three years

Whether a petition to wind up an insolvent partnership is presented under IPO, art 7, 8, 9 **1.462** or 10, modified IA 1986, s 117(1) and (2), is subject to modified s 117(3). This repeats the provision in modified s 221(2)[1136] that a court in England and Wales has jurisdiction to wind up an insolvent partnership only if its business has been carried on in England and Wales in the period of three years ending with the day on which the petition for winding it up is presented. The modification is made by IPO 1994, sch 3, para 6 (in relation to art 7 petitions), sch 4, para 5 (in relation to art 8 petitions), sch 5, para 1 (in relation to art 9 petitions), and sch 6, para 1 (in relation to art 10 petitions). A person who has carried on business in England and Wales does not cease to carry on business in England and Wales until all debts of that business have been paid.[1137]

Principal place of business in Scotland or Northern Ireland

Whether a petition to wind up an insolvent partnership is presented under IPO, art 7, 8, 9 **1.463** or 10, modified IA 1986, s 117(1) and (2), is subject to modified s 117(4). This repeats the provision in modified s 221(2)[1138] that a court in England and Wales does not have jurisdiction to wind up an insolvent partnership which has a principal place of business in Scotland or Northern Ireland unless it had a principal place of business in England and Wales at any time in the period of one year (if there is a principal place of business in Scotland) or three years (Northern Ireland) ending with the day on which the petition for winding it up is presented. The modification is made by IPO 1994, sch 3, para 6 (in relation to art 7 petitions), sch 4, para 5 (in relation to art 8 petitions), sch 5, para 1 (in relation to art 9 petitions), and sch 6, para 1 (in relation to art 10 petitions).

District registries cannot be used

Petitions under IPO 1994, art 8 or art 10, for the winding up of a partnership and the **1.464** bankruptcy of a member or former member cannot be presented in a district registry of the High Court.[1139]

Court of Appeal

The Court of Appeal does not have jurisdiction to hear a winding-up petition.[1140] **1.465**

[1134] Modified s 117(2). This provision has not yet been amended to reflect the creation of the single County Court.

[1135] See 1.361–1.407.

[1136] See 1.146–1.149.

[1137] *Re a Debtor (No 784 of 1991)* [1992] Ch 554.

[1138] See 1.146–1.149.

[1139] IA 1986, s 117(6), as modified by IPO 1994, sch 4, para 5 (in relation to art 8 petitions); IA 1986, s 117(6), as modified by IPO 1994, sch 6, para 1 (in relation to art 10 petitions).

[1140] *Re Dunraven Adare Coal and Iron Co* (1875) 33 LT 371.

International Jurisdiction

1.466 The rules of jurisdiction discussed at 1.443–1.465 are subject to the rules on international allocation of jurisdiction discussed at 1.347–1.432. In particular, Regulation (EC) No 1346/2000 governs jurisdiction to wind up on the ground of insolvency.[1141]

Meaning of 'the Court'

1.467 In IA 1986, ss 1–251, 'the court', in relation to a company,[1142] means a court having jurisdiction to wind up the company.[1143]

Transfer of Proceedings between Courts

1.468 Where winding-up proceedings are pending in the High Court, the court may order them to be transferred to a specified County Court hearing centre.[1144] Where winding-up proceedings are pending in a County Court hearing centre, the court may order them to be transferred either to the High Court or to another County Court hearing centre,[1145] which must be one in which proceedings to wind up companies may be commenced under IA 1986,[1146] but it does not matter that the company's paid-up capital exceeds £120,000.[1147] For transfer of proceedings commenced in the wrong court see 1.478.

1.469 A judge of the High Court may order winding-up proceedings pending in the County Court to be transferred to the High Court.[1148] It is possible to transfer part only of the proceedings.[1149]

1.470 A transfer of proceedings may be ordered:[1150]

(a) by the court of its own initiative; or
(b) on the application of the official receiver; or
(c) on the application of a person appearing to the court to have an interest in the proceedings.

1.471 An official receiver who wishes to apply for winding-up proceedings to be transferred must either obtain the petitioner's consent to the transfer or give the petitioner at least 14 days' notice of the application.[1151] The official receiver's application must be accompanied by a report setting out the reasons for the transfer and stating either that the petitioner's consent has been obtained or that the required notice has been given.[1152] If the court is satisfied from the official receiver's report that the proceedings can be conducted more conveniently in another court or County Court hearing centre, it must order the transfer of the proceedings to that court or hearing centre.[1153]

[1141] IA 1986, s 117(7). See 1.113.
[1142] Sections 1–251 deal with both registered and unregistered companies.
[1143] IA 1986, s 251.
[1144] IR 1986, r 7.11(1).
[1145] r 7.11(2).
[1146] r 7.11(3); *Re Real Estates Co* [1893] 1 Ch 398.
[1147] *Re Vernon Heaton Co Ltd* [1936] Ch 289.
[1148] r 7.11(4).
[1149] *Hall v Van der Heiden* [2010] EWHC 537 (TCC), [2010] BPIR 585.
[1150] r 7.11(5).
[1151] r 7.13(1).
[1152] r 7.13(1).
[1153] r 7.13(2).

Any other person wishing to apply for winding-up proceedings to be transferred must give at **1.472** least 14 days' notice of the application to the official receiver attached to the court or County Court hearing centre in which the proceedings are pending and to the official receiver attached to the court or hearing centre to which it is proposed they should be transferred.[1154]

The procedure to be followed by court officials following an order for transfer is set out in IR **1.473** 1986, r 7.14, and r 7.15 deals with consequential transfer of other proceedings.

There is no provision in IR 1986 for transfer from a district registry to the Royal Courts of **1.474** Justice or vice versa and so CPR, r 30.2(4), applies.[1155] In considering whether to make a transfer under r 30.2(4) the court must have regard to the criteria in r 30.3.

In *Re East Dulwich 295th Starr Bowkett Benefit Building Society*[1156] a petition to wind up a **1.475** building society, being heard in a county court, was ordered by North J to be transferred to the High Court, on the application of the society. His Lordship said that he had already dealt with proceedings concerning the affairs of the society and 'had been put in possession of facts which it would take a long time to bring to the knowledge of the county court judge'.

The fact that the parties have already agreed directions for hearing a petition in one court, **1.476** and that court has made an order based on those agreed directions, cannot prevent an order being made for transfer of the proceedings to another court if it is plainly inappropriate for the parties to be tied to their agreement.[1157]

For the transfer of parallel petitions to wind up the same company see 5.235–5.238. **1.477**

Effect of Proceeding in the Wrong Court

By IA 1986, s 118(1), nothing in s 117 invalidates a proceeding by reason of its being taken **1.478** in the wrong court.[1158] The winding up of a company by the court, or any proceedings in the winding up, may be retained in the court in which the proceedings were commenced, although it may not be the court in which they ought to have been commenced.[1159] Alternatively, where winding-up proceedings are commenced in the wrong court or County Court hearing centre, that court or hearing centre may order the transfer of the proceedings to the court or hearing centre in which they ought to have been commenced or order the proceedings to be struck out.[1160] 'Wrong' in these provisions means 'inappropriate': the effect of the provisions is that a hearing centre does not lack jurisdiction to hear a petition concerning a company whose registered office is not in its district.[1161] The court to which the petition was presented may make a winding-up order on the petition before transferring proceedings to a more appropriate court.[1162] The petitioner must pay the costs incurred by presenting the petition in the wrong court.[1163]

[1154] r 7.13(3).

[1155] See *Re Neath and Bristol Steamship Co* (1888) 58 LT 180.

[1156] (1890) 6 TLR 448.

[1157] *Re Debtors (Nos 13-MISC-2000 and 14-MISC-2000)* (2000) *The Times*, 10 April 2000.

[1158] See, for example, *Re Buller and Basset Tin and Copper Co Ltd* (1891) 35 SJ 260 and *Re Milford Haven Shipping Co* [1895] WN 16, both decided when the High Court's jurisdiction was limited under the Companies (Winding Up) Act 1890, s 1; *Re Pleatfine Ltd* [1983] BCLC 102.

[1159] IA 1986, s 118(2); IR 1986, r 7.12(b).

[1160] IR 1986, r 7.12(a) and (c).

[1161] *Re Southsea Garage Ltd* (1911) 27 TLR 295.

[1162] *Re Milford Haven Shipping Co* [1895] WN 16.

[1163] *Re Buller and Basset Tin and Copper Co Ltd* (1891) 35 SJ 260.

Judges and Court Officers

Distribution of Business between Judges and Court Officials

1.479 Anything to be done under or by virtue of IA 1986 or IR 1986 by, to or before the court may be done by, to or before a judge, district judge or the registrar.[1164] In IR 1986 'the registrar' means:[1165]

(a) a registrar in bankruptcy of the High Court; or
(b) if the proceedings are in the district registry of Birmingham, Bristol, Caernarfon, Cardiff, Leeds, Liverpool, Manchester, Mold, Newcastle upon Tyne or Preston, a district judge attached to that district registry.

In PD Insolvency Proceedings 2014, 'registrar' includes a district judge in a district registry of the High Court and a district judge in any County Court hearing centre having insolvency jurisdiction.[1166]

1.480 For the purposes of insolvency proceedings, a registrar may perform any act which CPR, r 2.4, authorizes any judge, master or district judge to perform,[1167] that is, any act which the CPR provide for the court to perform, except where an enactment, rule or practice direction provides otherwise.[1168] In the High Court, a registrar or district judge exercises the jurisdiction of the High Court, but not as a deputy judge of that court.[1169]

1.481 The 'Companies Court' is a way of describing the High Court when exercising the jurisdiction conferred on it by the Companies Act 2006 and dealing with matters originating in the chambers of the bankruptcy registrar dealing with company matters.[1170] The 'companies judge' is a way of describing a High Court judge when trying such matters.[1171] The Companies Court is not a court separate and distinct from the High Court, with its own peculiar jurisdiction.[1172] In *Re Wool Textile Employers Mutual Insurance Co Ltd*[1173] Wynn-Parry J said, at p 867:

> The phrase 'Companies Court' is a modern term introduced into the forms made pursuant to the Companies Act 1929 in place of the phrase in the previous forms 'Companies Winding-up', in order to soothe the susceptibilities of those who desired to apply to the court for some relief in the case of entirely solvent companies (as, for instance, confirmation of the reduction of the capital of a company by the return of surplus capital to its members) and who disliked that the title to the necessary proceedings should contain a reference to winding up.

[1164] IR 1986, r 13.2(1).

[1165] r 13.2(3A).

[1166] PD Insolvency Proceedings 2014, para 1.1(8).

[1167] PD Insolvency Proceedings 2014, para 7.1. District judges in the County Court have this authority under CPR, r 2.4, itself.

[1168] CPR, r 2.4.

[1169] *Re Calahurst Ltd* [1989] BCLC 140 per Harman J.

[1170] Per Wynn-Parry J in *Re Wool Textile Employers Mutual Insurance Co Ltd* [1955] 1 WLR 862 at p 867; per Brightman J in *Re Shilena Hosiery Co Ltd* [1980] Ch 219 at p 224.

[1171] Per Brightman J in *Re Shilena Hosiery Co Ltd* at p 224.

[1172] Per Wynn-Parry J in *Re Wool Textile Employers Mutual Insurance Co Ltd* at p 867; per Brightman J in *Re Shilena Hosiery Co Ltd* at p 224; *Fabric Sales Ltd v Eratex Ltd* [1984] 1 WLR 863; *Partizan Ltd v O J Kilkenny and Co Ltd* [1998] 1 BCLC 157 at p 166.

[1173] [1955] 1 WLR 862.

The judges of the Chancery Division who exercise jurisdiction in company matters also deal **1.482** with bankruptcy and can hear bankruptcy and winding-up petitions together.[1174]

The distribution of business as between judges and registrars or district judges is set out in **1.483** PD Insolvency Proceedings 2014, para 3.

The following applications in relation to the winding up of companies should always be **1.484** listed before a judge:[1175]

(a) an application for committal for contempt;

(b) an administration application;

(c) an application for an injunction to be made under the court's inherent jurisdiction, the Senior Courts Act 1981, s 37, or the County Courts Act 1984, s 38, but not an order under IA 1986 or IR 1986;

(d) an application for the appointment of a provisional liquidator; and

(e) any interim application, or application for directions or case management, after any proceedings have been referred or adjourned to the judge, except where liberty to apply to the registrar or district judge has been given.

Otherwise, all petitions, claims and applications should be listed for initial hearing before a **1.485** registrar or district judge.[1176] The registrar or district judge may refer to the judge any matter which the registrar or district judge thinks should properly be decided by the judge. The judge may either dispose of a referred matter or refer it back to the registrar or district judge with directions.[1177] The power to refer applications made to a registrar and in respect of which the registrar has jurisdiction is now very sparingly exercised. The proper use of judicial resources dictates that where the registrar has jurisdiction in respect of an application he or she should ordinarily exercise that jurisdiction.[1178] When deciding whether to hear proceedings or to refer or adjourn them to the judge, the registrar or district judge should have regard to the following factors:[1179]

(a) the complexity of the proceedings;

(b) whether the proceedings raise new or controversial points of law;

(c) the likely date and length of the hearing;

(d) public interest in the proceedings.

An application may be made direct to the judge in a proper case.[1180] Examples[1181] are where: **1.486**

(a) it is urgent and no registrar or district judge is available to hear it;[1182]

(b) it is complex or raises new or controversial points of law; or

(c) it is estimated to last longer than 30 minutes.

[1174] *Smith and Williamson v Sims Pipes* (2000) LTL 17/3/2000.

[1175] PD Insolvency Proceedings 2014, para 3.2. For details of the listing procedure see the Chancery Guide 2013, para 6.22. A judge is available to hear companies matters each day in term time, and applications to be heard by that judge may be listed for any such day (Chancery Guide 2013, para 20.8).

[1176] PD Insolvency Proceedings 2014, para 3.1; IR 1986, r 7.6A(2) and (3).

[1177] IR 1986, r 7.6A(4).

[1178] Chancery Guide 2013, para 6.23.

[1179] PD Insolvency Proceedings 2014, para 3.4.

[1180] IR 1986, r 7.6A(5).

[1181] Given in PD Insolvency Proceedings 2014, para 11.8.2, in relation to applications for validation orders.

[1182] See 3.248.

1.487 IR 1986, r 13.2(2), empowers the registrar or district judge to authorize the chief clerk or any other officer of the court acting on the chief clerk's behalf to carry out any act of a formal or administrative character which is not by statute the registrar or district judge's responsibility, in accordance with directions given by the Lord Chancellor.[1183]

Official Receivers

Appointment and functions

1.488 Official receivers attached to the High Court and/or the County Court are appointed by, and act under the general authority and directions of, the Secretary of State.[1184] The same official receiver may be attached to both courts.[1185]

1.489 The main tasks of an official receiver are to investigate the causes of insolvencies and to act as trustee in bankruptcy and as liquidator or provisional liquidator in compulsory liquidations of companies. Although the creditors of an insolvent person can put their own appointee (who must be a qualified insolvency practitioner) in place of the official receiver as trustee or liquidator, most insolvent estates are not sufficiently valuable to remunerate an insolvency practitioner.

1.490 An official receiver attached to a particular court is the person authorized to act as the official receiver in relation to every winding up falling within the jurisdiction of that court.[1186] If there are two or more official receivers attached to a particular court, the Secretary of State may provide for the distribution of their business between or among them[1187] and may also authorize an official receiver attached to one court to act as the official receiver in relation to any case or description of cases falling within the jurisdiction of the other court.[1188]

1.491 An official receiver exercises the functions of his or her office as an officer of the court in relation to which those functions are exercised.[1189]

1.492 An official receiver may be removed from office by a direction of the Secretary of State.[1190]

1.493 The Secretary of State may appoint a deputy to the official receiver attached to any court.[1191] A deputy official receiver has the same status and functions as the official receiver to whom he or she is appointed deputy, subject to directions given by the Secretary of State.[1192]

1.494 Judicial notice must be taken of the appointment of official receivers and deputy official receivers.[1193]

1.495 In case of emergency, where there is no official receiver capable of acting, anything to be done by, to or before the official receiver may be done by, to or before the registrar or district judge.[1194]

[1183] See PD Insolvency Proceedings 2014, para 12. The chief clerk is now called the court manager.
[1184] IA 1986, ss 399(2), (3), (5) and (6), and 400(2).
[1185] s 399(5).
[1186] s 399(4).
[1187] s 399(6).
[1188] s 399(6).
[1189] s 400(2).
[1190] s 399(2)(c).
[1191] s 401(1).
[1192] s 401(2).
[1193] IR 1986, r 10.1.
[1194] r 10.2(2).

Official receivers and deputy official receivers have a right of audience in winding-up proceedings, whether in the High Court or the County Court.[1195] **1.496**

An official receiver holds a statutory office, but not a Crown office. When bringing legal proceedings an official receiver does not represent the Crown. When exercising his or her right of audience in the courts an official receiver is entitled to costs as a litigant in person.[1196] **1.497**

Meaning of 'the official receiver'

For the purposes of IA 1986, 'the official receiver', in relation to any winding up, is the person **1.498**
who is authorized under s 399(4) or (6) to act as the official receiver in relation to that winding up.[1197] Any reference in IA 1986 (except in s 399(1)–(5)) to an official receiver includes a person appointed to act as the official receiver's deputy. It seems that directions under s 399(6) may authorize a deputy official receiver to act as the official receiver in relation to a winding up, and so the definition in s 399(1) of 'the official receiver' in relation to a winding up includes a person who by virtue of s 401 is authorized to act as the official receiver in relation to that winding up even though s 401(2) states that references in s 399(1) to an official receiver do not include a person appointed to act as the official receiver's deputy.

In IR 1986, any reference to the liquidator or provisional liquidator includes the official receiver **1.499**
when acting in the relevant capacity.[1198]

Effect of Order Made Erroneously or without Jurisdiction

Error over Jurisdiction

A court which hears an application to wind up a company decides, sometimes explicitly but **1.500**
much more usually implicitly, that it has jurisdiction to do so. If the court has jurisdiction to make that decision, that is, jurisdiction to decide its own jurisdiction, its decision to hear the application is valid until reversed on appeal. Any order it makes on the application is also effective until set aside.[1199] A court of general (or unlimited) jurisdiction has jurisdiction to decide its own jurisdiction.[1200] A court of limited jurisdiction may be given by statute jurisdiction to decide its own jurisdiction.[1201]

In determining whether it has jurisdiction to hear and determine an application to wind up a **1.501**
company, a court, assuming it has power to make winding-up orders, must determine whether the company is one of the types of entity which it has jurisdiction to wind up.[1202] If a court which has power to make winding-up orders against entities of a particular type orders the winding up of an entity which is not of that type, it will have made an error in finding that the facts of the case gave it jurisdiction: on appeal, that error will be corrected by setting aside

---

[1195] r 7.52(1).
[1196] *Re Minotaur Data Systems Ltd* [1999] 1 WLR 1129.
[1197] s 399(1).
[1198] IR 1986, r 13.9(2).
[1199] *Re Macks* [2000] HCA 62, 204 CLR 158; *Strachan v Gleaner Co Ltd* [2005] UKPC 33, [2005] 1 WLR 3204; *PricewaterhouseCoopers v Saad Investments Co Ltd* [2014] UKPC 35, [2014] 1 WLR 4482.
[1200] *Strachan v Gleaner Co Ltd.*
[1201] *Re Macks.*
[1202] See 1.80–1.220.

the order without inquiring into its merits.[1203] The order would have been made erroneously but not without jurisdiction and is valid until quashed on appeal.[1204]

1.502   In *Re Commercial Bank of London*[1205] a winding-up order which had been made in ignorance of the fact that the petitioner had died was treated as subsisting until discharged, so that a winding-up order made on the application of the petitioner's personal representative had to be dated after the discharge of the previous order. In *Re A B and Co (No 2)*[1206] a bankruptcy petition had been presented against a foreign partnership and, on the same day, the official receiver was appointed interim receiver of the partnership by the court. On the following day the official receiver appointed a special manager of the partnership. On hearing the bankruptcy petition it was held that the partnership was not subject to English bankruptcy law. The Court of Appeal had to consider whether the special manager was entitled to remuneration and expenses. Lindley MR said, at pp 437–8:

> [T]he Bankruptcy Court was the court which had jurisdiction to entertain bankruptcy petitions against alleged debtors; and what is called 'an order made without jurisdiction' should, in my opinion, be termed an erroneous order rather than an order made without jurisdiction. The line which divides an erroneous order from an order made without jurisdiction is a very fine one.

Collins LJ said, at p 443:

> [T]he court that made the order appointing the interim receiver had general jurisdiction over the subject matter. As part of that jurisdiction it had to deal with the case upon *ex parte* evidence; and it arrived at a decision which was ultimately found to be erroneous. Everything that was done by the officers of the court under its order was good until that order was set aside; and, being good, of course the persons who carried it out were not wrongdoers.

1.503   There are two reported Australian cases in which a provisional liquidator of a company has been appointed and the court has subsequently decided that it did not have jurisdiction to wind up the company.[1207] In both those cases it was held that the order appointing the provisional liquidator was valid and effective until rescinded. It is submitted that, in the terms used by Lindley MR in *Re A B and Co (No 2)* quoted at 1.502, these were cases of erroneous orders rather than orders made without jurisdiction.[1208]

Order Made without Jurisdiction

1.504   In one reported case, *Re Plumstead, Woolwich and Charlton Consumers Pure Water Co*,[1209] the court's error in making a winding-up order against a company was considered to be so fundamental that the order was held to be void *ab initio*. It seems that, in the terms used by Lindley MR in *Re A B and Co (No 2)*[1210] quoted at 1.502, the case was one of an order made without jurisdiction. The crucial feature seems to have been that the court which

---

[1203] *Re Padstow Total Loss and Collision Assurance Association* (1882) 20 ChD 137; *Strachan v Gleaner Co Ltd*.

[1204] *Re Padstow Total Loss and Collision Assurance Association* per Brett LJ at p 145.

[1205] [1888] WN 234.

[1206] [1900] 2 QB 429.

[1207] *Starr v Trafalgar Financial Corporation Ltd (No 2)* (1983) 8 ACLR 367; *Nationwide News Pty Ltd v Samalot Enterprises Pty Ltd* (1986) 5 NSWLR 227.

[1208] See also 4.123.

[1209] (1860) 2 De G F & J 20.

[1210] [1900] 2 QB 429.

made the winding-up order[1211] correctly identified what kind of company the order related to, but incorrectly held that it had jurisdiction to wind up that class of company. Knight Bruce LJ said[1212] that the Court of Appeal was bound to treat the winding-up order and the order appointing an official manager (the equivalent under the Joint Stock Companies Winding-up Act 1848 of a liquidator) 'as not made' and[1213] that the orders 'ought to be deemed to have had from the beginning no effectual existence'. Turner LJ[1214] described the winding-up order as 'merely null and void'. Accordingly proceedings brought by the official manager were dismissed, and in subsequent proceedings[1215] it was held that the official manager was not entitled to remuneration—Turner LJ[1216] described him as never filling the character of official manager at all.

In *Day v Mount*[1217] the Federal Court of Australia said, at p 473, that in so far as *Re Plumstead, Woolwich and Charlton Water Co, ex parte Harding* is inconsistent with *Starr v Trafalgar Financial Corporation Ltd (No 2)*[1218] (where a provisional liquidator of a company was appointed without realizing that the court did not have jurisdiction over the company, the appointment was valid until rescinded)[1219] it cannot be regarded as expressing the law in Australia. It is submitted that the two cases are on different sides of the line drawn by Lindley MR between erroneous orders (*Starr v Trafalgar Financial Corporation Ltd (No 2)*) and orders made without jurisdiction (*Re Plumstead, Woolwich and Charlton Water Co, ex parte Harding*). Nevertheless, the decision in the *Plumstead* cases that the winding-up order was void *ab initio* appears to be inconsistent with the generally accepted theory that an order of a court with jurisdiction to determine its own jurisdiction is valid until set aside[1220] and it is submitted that today the winding-up order would be found to be valid and effective until quashed on appeal. In *PricewaterhouseCoopers v Saad Investments Co Ltd* the Privy Council found that a court's order to wind up a company over which it did not have jurisdiction was valid until set aside without examining whether the order was merely erroneous.   **1.505**

In *Re Macks* the High Court of Australia dealt with a case which was clearly on the same side of Lindley MR's dividing line as the *Plumstead* litigation. The High Court held by a majority, without reference to the *Plumstead* cases, that a winding-up order made by the Federal Court was not void and was effective until set aside, even though the Federal Court had no power at all to make winding-up orders (because the statute giving it power was constitutionally invalid). Gaudron, Gummow, Hayne and Callinan JJ in the majority, and McHugh J dissenting, held that the Federal Court is a court of limited jurisdiction which, nevertheless, has a statutory power to decide whether it has jurisdiction over any matter. By hearing an application to wind up a company, it had implicitly exercised that power to   **1.506**

[1211] *Ex parte Plumstead, Woolwich and Charlton Water Co* (1858) 28 LJ Ch 163.
[1212] 2 De G F & J 20 at p 32.
[1213] At p 33.
[1214] At p 37.
[1215] *Re Plumstead, Woolwich and Charlton Water Co, ex parte Harding* (1862) 32 LJ Ch 145.
[1216] 32 LJ Ch 145 at p 147.
[1217] (1984) 53 ALR 468.
[1218] (1983) 8 ACLR 367.
[1219] See 1.503.
[1220] *Re Macks* [2000] HCA 62, 204 CLR 158; *Strachan v Gleaner Co Ltd* [2005] UKPC 33, [2005] 1 WLR 3204.

decide that it did have jurisdiction, and its duty was to adjudicate the matter and make an order accordingly, and that order must therefore be valid.[1221]

Forms, Time Limits, Notices and Service

Forms

1.507 The forms contained in sch 4 to IR 1986 must be used in and in connection with insolvency proceedings, whether in the High Court or a county court.[1222] The forms must be used with such variations, if any, as the circumstances may require.[1223] The Secretary of State, the official receiver or an insolvency practitioner may add a barcode, or other reference or recognition mark, to any form they send or receive.[1224]

Time Limits

1.508 Where by any provision of IA 1986 or IR 1986 about winding up, the time for doing anything is limited, the court may extend the time, either before or after it has expired, on such terms, if any, as it thinks fit.[1225] The court may also extend or shorten the time for compliance with anything required or authorized to be done by IR 1986, even if an application for extension is made after the time for compliance has expired.[1226]

1.509 The provisions of CPR, r 2.8, apply, as regards computation of time, to anything required or authorized to be done by IR 1986.[1227] CPR, r 2.8, does not apply when computing a time which is not a time by which an act is to be done.[1228] The provisions of r 2.8 are stated at 1.510.

1.510 Any period of time expressed as a number of days must be computed as 'clear days'.[1229] This means that if an act must be done a specified number of days before an event occurs, the day on which the act is done and the day on which the event occurs are not counted when calculating whether the required period has elapsed.[1230] If the period of time for doing any act is five days or less, the following days within the period do not count: Saturday, Sunday, a bank holiday, Christmas Day, Good Friday.[1231] Where a period for doing any act at the court offices, such as filing a document, ends on a day when the office is closed, the act will be done in time if done on the next day on which the office is open.[1232]

[1221] McHugh J, dissenting, held that only the decision to assume jurisdiction was valid: to give validity to the winding-up order would be to give effect to the constitutionally invalid power to make such orders, which should not be permitted. Gleeson CJ and Kirby J held that the Federal Court was a court of general jurisdiction.

[1222] IR 1986, r 12A.30(1).

[1223] r 12A.30(2).

[1224] r 12A.30(3).

[1225] IR 1986, r 4.3. In the Royal Courts of Justice the member of court staff in charge of the winding-up list has been authorized to deal with applications under this rule (PD Insolvency Proceedings 2014, para 12.1). In a district registry or the County Court an application must be made to a district judge (PD Insolvency Proceedings 2014, para 12.2). For examples of the operation of this rule see *Re Calmex Ltd* [1989] 1 All ER 485; *Re Virgo Systems Ltd* [1990] BCLC 34.

[1226] CPR, r 3.1(2)(a), as applied by IR 1986, r 12.9(2).

[1227] IR 1986, r 12.9(1).

[1228] *Anderton v Clwyd County Council (No 2)* [2002] EWCA Civ 933, [2002] 1 WLR 3174.

[1229] CPR, r 2.8(2).

[1230] CPR, r 2.8(3).

[1231] CPR, r 2.8(4).

[1232] CPR, r 2.8(5).

In bank or building society insolvency proceedings, where by any provision of IA 1986, **1.511**
the Banking Act 2009, the Bank Insolvency (England and Wales) Rules 2009[1233] or the
Building Society Insolvency (England and Wales) Rules 2010,[1234] the time for doing anything is limited, the court may extend the time, either before or after it has expired, on
such terms, if any, as it thinks fit.[1235] But, before the passing of a full payment resolution,
the court cannot extend time unless it is satisfied that doing so is unlikely to prejudice the
achievement of objective 1.[1236]

Meaning of 'Business Day'

In IR 1986 'business day' means[1237] any day other than a Saturday, a Sunday, Christmas **1.512**
Day, Good Friday or a day which is a bank holiday in any part of England and Wales
under or by virtue of the Banking and Financial Dealings Act 1971. This definition is applied to bank insolvency proceedings[1238] and building society insolvency
proceedings.[1239]

Notices and Service

Rules on notice and supply of documents

There are general rules on notice and supply of documents in IR 1986, rr 12A.1–12A.15. **1.513**
Those general rules are considered here at 1.514–1.523. They do not apply to the submission
of documents to the registrar of companies.[1240] In this work, all the rules relating to service of
a winding-up petition[1241] are considered at 3.1–3.41 and 8.492–8.493. All the rules relating
to service of applications, and evidence in support of applications, in insolvency proceedings[1242] are considered at 3.249–3.251 and 3.257. All the rules relating to service of a
statutory demand are considered at 7.142–7.160.

Any notice or other document that is required to be given, delivered or sent, under IA 1986 **1.514**
or IR 1986, must be in writing, subject to any order of the court.[1243] Where electronic delivery is permitted, a notice or other document in electronic form is treated as being in writing
if a copy of it is capable of being produced in legible form.[1244]

No service by the court

Except where otherwise provided by IR 1986, or required under Regulation (EU) No **1.515**
1393/2007, service of documents in insolvency proceedings is the responsibility of the parties and will not be undertaken by the court.[1245]

[1233] SI 2009/356.
[1234] SI 2010/2581.
[1235] SI 2009/356, r 6(1); SI 2010/2581, r 6(1).
[1236] SI 2009/356, r 6(2); SI 2010/2581, r 6(2). 'Objective 1' and 'full payment resolution' are defined
at 1.20.
[1237] By r 13.13(1).
[1238] Bank Insolvency (England and Wales) Rules 2009 (SI 2009/356), r 292.
[1239] Building Society Insolvency (England and Wales) Rules 2010 (SI 2010/2581), r 284.
[1240] IR 1986, rr 12A.1(3) and 12A.6(2).
[1241] To which rr 12A.1–12A.5 do not apply (r 12A.1(2)).
[1242] To which rr 12A.1–12A.5 do not apply (r 12A.1(2)).
[1243] IR 1986, rr 12A.6(1) and 12A.7.
[1244] r 12A.7.
[1245] PD Insolvency Proceedings 2014, para 6.2.

Delivery methods

1.516 Where a notice or other document is required to be given, delivered or sent, under IA 1986 or IR 1986, by any person, it may be delivered:

(a) personally;[1246] or

(b) by post in accordance with the rules on postal service in CPR, Part 6;[1247] or

(c) electronically, provided the intended recipient has consented to electronic delivery and has provided an electronic address.[1248] Consent may be general or for a specific notice or document.[1249] Where an office-holder[1250] uses electronic delivery, the notice or document must contain, or be accompanied by, a statement that the recipient may request a hard copy, which must be sent, free of charge, within five business days of receiving a request.[1251]

Options (b) and (c) are not available if, in any particular case, some other form of delivery is required by IA 1986, IR 1986 or a court order.[1252]

1.517 Delivery by post takes effect as specified in CPR, Part 6.[1253] Electronic delivery takes effect as specified in IR 1986, r 12A.10.

1.518 If it is sought to serve a document by post, the effect of addressing it to a place which is not the correct place for service of the document depends on the prejudice caused to the person on whom it was to be served.[1254]

1.519 An office-holder,[1255] who is required by any provision of IA 1986 or IR 1986 to give, deliver, furnish or send a notice or other document or information to any person, has the further option of making the notice, document or information available on a website,[1256] and sending the person a notice stating that it is available for viewing and downloading there.[1257]

[1246] IR 1986, rr 12A.1(1) and 12A.2. These rules do not apply to the service of petitions (see 3.1–3.41 and 8.492–8.493), applications to the court (see 3.249–3.251), evidence in support of petitions or applications (see 3.252–3.258), or court orders (r 12A.1(2)).

[1247] IR 1986, rr 12A.1(1) and 12A.3. These rules do not apply to the service of petitions (see 3.1–3.41 and 8.492–8.493), applications to the court (see 3.249–3.251), evidence in support of petitions or applications (see 3.252–3.258), or court orders (r 12A.1(2)).

[1248] IR 1986, r 12A.10(1). Rules 12A.10 and 12A.11 do not apply to the filing of any notice or other document with the court (r 12A.6(3)(a)) or the service of a statutory demand (r 12A.6(3)(b); see 7.142–7.160).

[1249] r 12A.10(1)(a).

[1250] In this context, 'office-holder' has the meaning defined in 1.535.

[1251] IR 1986, r 12A.11. The clear days rule in CPR, r 2.8(2) and (3), applies (see 1.510). 'Business day' is defined in IR 1986, r 13.13(1) (see 1.512).

[1252] IR 1986, rr 12A.3 and 12A.10(1).

[1253] IR 1986, r 12A.3.

[1254] *Singh v Atombrook Ltd* [1989] 1 WLR 810. The approach of the Court of Appeal in *Singh v Atombrook Ltd* is to be preferred to the less flexible attitude at first instance in *McIlhatton v John Wallace and Sons (Northern Ireland) Ltd* [1972] NI 50.

[1255] In this context, 'office-holder' means the liquidator, provisional liquidator, administrator or administrative receiver of a company, or, where a voluntary arrangement in relation to a company is proposed or has taken effect under IA 1986, part 1, the nominee or the supervisor of the voluntary arrangement (IA 1986, s 246B(3)).

[1256] IA 1986, s 246B(1).

[1257] IR 1986, r 12A.12, which sets out detailed requirements. This option does not apply to the filing of any notice or other document with the court (r 12A.6(3)(a)) or the service of a statutory demand (r 12A.6(3)(b); see 7.142–7.160).

The court may order that a single notice relating to all subsequent documents is sufficient.[1258]

Authentication and proof of sending

A document or information given, delivered or sent in hard copy form is sufficiently authen- **1.520**
ticated if it is signed by the person sending or supplying it.[1259]

A document or information given, delivered or sent in electronic form is sufficiently **1.521**
authenticated:

(a) if the identity of the sender is confirmed in a manner specified by the recipient; or
(b) where no such manner has been specified by the recipient, if the communication con-
     tains or is accompanied by a statement of the identity of the sender and the recipient has
     no reason to doubt the truth of that statement.[1260]

The giving, delivery or sending of a notice or other document may be proved by a certificate **1.522**
that it was duly given, delivered or sent.[1261]

Service on solicitor

A notice or other document which is required or authorized under IA 1986 or IR 1986 to be **1.523**
given, delivered or sent to a person may be given etc instead to a solicitor whom that person
has indicated is authorized to accept service on that person's behalf.[1262] In *Re Fletcher Hunt
(Bristol) Ltd*,[1263] the shares in the company were held by Mr Hyde (who petitioned for it to
be wound up) and by Fletcher Hunt plc and Mr Fletcher. Mr Fletcher and Fletcher Hunt plc
jointly instructed a firm of solicitors to act for the company in relation to the petition. The
solicitors acting for the petitioner, Mr Hyde, served the petition on the solicitors appointed
by Mr Fletcher. It was held that, through his solicitors acting as his agents, Mr Hyde had, by
sending the petition for service on the company to the solicitors appointed by Mr Fletcher,
joined the other members of the company in appointing those solicitors to act for the company.

Service on joint office-holders

Where there are joint office-holders in insolvency proceedings[1264] or two or more persons **1.524**
are acting jointly as the responsible insolvency practitioner[1265] in any proceedings, delivery
of a document to one of them is to be treated as delivery to them all.[1266] The same rule applies
where there are two or more persons acting jointly as a bank liquidator[1267] or building society liquidator.[1268]

[1258] IR 1986, r 12A.13.
[1259] IR 1986, r 12A.9(1).
[1260] IR 1986, r 12A.9(2).
[1261] IR 1986, r 12A.8, which specifies who may give the certificate.
[1262] IR 1986, rr 12A.5 and 13.4. 'Solicitor' includes a body recognized by the Law Society under the
Administration of Justice Act 1985, s 9 (Solicitors' Recognised Bodies Order 1991 (SI 1991/2684), arts
2(1) and 4(a) and sch 1) and a body which holds a licence issued by the Law Society which is in force under
the Legal Services Act 2007, part 5 (Legal Services Act 2007 (Designation as a Licensing Authority) (No.
2) Order 2011 (SI 2011/2866), arts 1(3) and 8 and sch 2).
[1263] [1989] BCLC 108.
[1264] See 1.535.
[1265] See 1.533–1.534.
[1266] r 13.5.
[1267] Bank Insolvency (England and Wales) Rules 2009 (SI 2009/356), r 287.
[1268] Building Society Insolvency (England and Wales) Rules 2010 (SI 2010/2581), r 279.

Registered Office

Service of documents at registered office

1.525 A document may be served on a company registered under the Companies Act 2006[1269] by leaving it at, or sending it by post to, the company's registered office.[1270] A company must at all times have a registered office.[1271] When a company is registered, its registered office is at the address which was given as the intended address of the registered office when applying for registration.[1272] A company may change the address of its registered office by giving notice to the registrar at Companies House.[1273] The change takes effect upon the notice being registered by the registrar,[1274] which will be the time that the change will come to the attention of anyone inspecting the records at Companies House. However, until the end of the period of 14 days beginning with the date of registration of the notice, a person may validly serve a document on the company at the address previously registered.[1275] These provisions are applied in modified form to limited liability partnerships[1276] by SI 2009/1804, reg 52. A slightly different definition of registered office applies to service of a winding-up petition[1277] or an application for a bank insolvency order.[1278]

False representation

1.526 It seems that if someone on behalf of a company represents to a person that the company's registered office is at a place which is not the situation determined by the statutory provisions discussed at 1.525, with the intention that the person should act on that representation, and the person serves a document at the place wrongly represented to be the registered office, then the company will be estopped from claiming that service was at the wrong place.[1279] Application of the doctrine of estoppel by representation in this context depends on accepting that a representation can be made about a matter which is in law determined by a statute. In *Comalco Aluminium Ltd v Ohtsu Tyre and Rubber Co (Aust) Pty Ltd*[1280] it was held that a company could be estopped by a false statement of the situation of its registered office in an annual return, but this was not followed in *Re Lisjam Hotels Pty Ltd*,[1281] on the basis that the Australian legislation defining the situation of a company's registered office expressly states that the definition has effect irrespective of what is stated in an annual return by the company. This provision is not made in the UK legislation but it is difficult to see what difference it makes to acceptance by the court that a representation can be made about a matter which is determined by statute.

[1269] See 1.87–1.104.

[1270] Companies Act 2006, s 1139(1). Separate provision is made in IR 1986 concerning service of a winding-up petition (see 3.9–3.16) and a statutory demand (see 7.142–7.160) at a company's registered office.

[1271] Companies Act 2006, s 86.

[1272] Companies Act 2006, ss 9(5)(a) and 16(1) and (4).

[1273] Companies Act 2006, s 87(1).

[1274] Companies Act 2006, s 87(2).

[1275] Companies Act 2006, s 87(2).

[1276] Limited Liability Partnerships (Application of Companies Act 2006) Regulations 2009 (SI 2009/1804), regs 16 (applying ss 86 and 87) and 75 (applying s 1139). For limited liability partnerships (LLPs), the equivalent of the Companies Act 2006, s 9(5)(a) is the Limited Liability Partnerships Act 2000, s 2(2)(d). There is no equivalent of the Companies Act 2006, s 16.

[1277] See 3.9–3.10.

[1278] See 3.42.

[1279] *Re Third Lojebo Pty Ltd* [1982] VR 379, in which the representation was by the company's solicitor.

[1280] (1983) 8 ACLR 330.

[1281] (1988) 14 ACLR 74.

Unauthorized change

In *Smith v Australian and European Bank*[1282] an order to wind up a company had been made **1.527**
on a petition which had been served at the place notified to the registrar as the company's
registered office, but it was alleged that the persons who had given the notification had
no authority to do so and that the true registered office was still where it had been before
the notification was given. It was held that outsiders were entitled to rely on the registrar's
records[1283] and, anyway, as the winding up of the company had been in progress for over a
year it was too late to object.

Building in multiple occupancy

If the address given for the registered office of a company is a building in multiple occupancy **1.528**
and the company has not specified the location of its registered office within the building,
it seems that service anywhere in the building is service on the company,[1284] though not if
the company's office is adequately signposted.[1285] However, if the address of the registered
office specifies a location within a building (for example, a particular suite of offices), service
elsewhere in the building, for example, at a separate letter box, is not effective.[1286] Service
at a letter box elsewhere in the building is not effective even if the box is marked as being
that of the relevant suite.[1287] In two cases, the address of the registered office named a firm
of accountants and specified a floor of a building. It was held that delivery to a place on the
specified floor bearing the firm's name was effective service.[1288]

Company no longer at its registered office

If a company has abandoned its registered office without giving notice to Companies House **1.529**
of a change of registered office, service of a document at the address which remains on the
register is effective and the company must deal with any legal proceedings that follow.[1289]
The circumstances may give rise to doubt about whether service can be effected.[1290] Care
must be taken to record the facts accurately in any certificate of service or other evidence
of service. If a document is served on a company at a location which is the address of its
registered office but is obviously occupied by another person, that fact must be stated in the
evidence of service to avoid doubt about whether the server had actually been to the location.[1291] However, a false statement in evidence of service of a winding-up petition that it
had been handed to an employee of the company's accountants purporting to be a servant

---

[1282] (1882) 8 VLR (M) 23.
[1283] Compare *Re Specialty Laboratories Asia Pte Ltd* [2001] 2 SLR 563, in which a company controlled by
the man who had registered the unauthorized change could not rely on the registrar's record.
[1284] *Quicksafe Freightlines Pty Ltd v Shell Co of Australia Ltd* (1984) 10 ACLR 161; *Golden Orchid Pty Ltd
v Comax Pty Ltd* (1995) 17 ACSR 442; *Wily v Terra Cresta Business Solutions Pty Ltd* [2008] NSWSC 805.
[1285] *Technology Licensing Ltd v Climit Pty Ltd* [2001] QSC 84, [2002] 1 QdR 566.
[1286] *Jin Xin Investment and Trade (Australia) Pty Ltd v ISC Property Pty Ltd* [2006] NSWSC 7, 196 FLR
350. *Re Emeritus Pty Ltd* [1968] 1 NSWR 458 is to the contrary and must be questionable.
[1287] *James v Ash Electrical Services Pty Ltd* [2008] NSWSC 1112, 73 NSWLR 95.
[1288] *Saferack Pty Ltd v Marketing Heads Australia Pty Ltd* [2007] NSWSC 1143, 214 FLR 393 (in-tray
bearing the firm's name at the reception desk of a suite of offices occasionally visited by the firm's principal);
Career Training on Line Pty Ltd v BES Training Solutions Pty Ltd [2010] NSWSC 460 (document pushed
under external door bearing the firm's name).
[1289] *A/S Cathrineholm v Norequipment Trading Ltd* [1972] 2 QB 314. See 3.17–3.19, 6.37–6.38 and
7.153–7.159.
[1290] In *A/S Cathrineholm v Norequipment Trading Ltd* the building was being demolished.
[1291] See *von Risefer v Mainfreight International Pty Ltd* [2009] VSCA 179, 25 VR 366, in which the evidence of service was rejected.

or agent of the company at a place which in fact had ceased to be the company's registered office 18 months previously was held not to vitiate the winding-up order made on the petition in the company's absence.[1292]

1.530 Usually, a company which has been served with originating process at a registered office which it has abandoned must apply for a court order made in its absence to be set aside. Normally this involves showing that the company would have a reasonable prospect of success at a fresh hearing.[1293]

1.531 In Australia it has been said that if, after serving originating process on a company at its registered office, a litigant becomes aware that it may not have been effective to bring the document to the company's attention, the litigant is under a duty to apply to the court for directions.[1294] Moreover, if there is a failure to do this, or to provide in some other way what is usually described as 'fair notice', any order obtained in the absence of the company is irregular and will be set aside as of right.[1295] Most statements of the doctrine of fair notice say that it applies only if the litigant's inaction amounts to an abuse of process and it is the abuse which is the reason for setting aside judgment rather than any defect in service.[1296] It may be that the doctrine is limited to cases in which a document does not come to the notice of the party to be served because of deliberate suppression or some other improperly motivated conduct of the serving party.[1297]

Principal office of a building society

1.532 In the Building Society Insolvency (England and Wales) Rules 2010[1298] 'principal office' means:[1299]

(a) the place which is specified in the building society's memorandum sent to the Financial Conduct Authority (FCA) under the Building Societies Act 1986, sch 2, para 1(1)(c), as the address of its principal office; or

(b) if notice has been given by the building society to the FCA under sch 2, para 11(2) (change of principal office), the place specified in that notice or, as the case may be, in the last such notice.

Responsible Insolvency Practitioner; Office-holder

1.533 The term 'responsible insolvency practitioner' is used in IR 1986 with the following meaning:[1300]

[1292] *Re Nicholls Pty Ltd* (1982) 7 ACLR 76.

[1293] CPR, r 39.3(5); *A/S Cathrineholm v Norequipment Trading Ltd*. See 6.36–6.40.

[1294] *Re Gasbourne Pty Ltd* [1984] VR 801 at p 858; *Re Rustic Homes Pty Ltd* (1988) 49 SASR 41 at p 45.

[1295] *Re Gasbourne Pty Ltd* at p 858; *Deputy Commissioner of Taxation v Abberwood Pty Ltd* (1990) 19 NSWLR 530. In *A/S Cathrineholm v Norequipment Trading Ltd* there was no indication to the party which obtained judgment that service had not informed the defendant company of the proceedings.

[1296] See, for example, *Re Future Life Enterprises Pty Ltd* (1994) 33 NSWLR 559 per McLelland CJ in Eq at pp 564–5; *Lane Cove Council v Geebung Polo Club Pty Ltd (No 2)* [2002] NSWSC 118, 167 FLR 175, at [51]–[53].

[1297] *Lane Cove Council v Geebung Polo Club Pty Ltd (No 2)* at [53]; *Re Art Pacific Pty Ltd* [2013] VSC 330 at [39].

[1298] SI 2010/2581.

[1299] SI 2010/2581, r 3(2).

[1300] IR 1986, r 13.9.

(a) the person (other than the official receiver) acting in a company insolvency, as supervisor of a voluntary arrangement under part 1[1301] of [IA 1986], or as administrator, administrative receiver, liquidator or provisional liquidator;

(b) the person (other than the official receiver) acting in an individual insolvency, as the supervisor of a voluntary arrangement under part 8[1302] of [IA 1986], or as trustee or interim receiver.

In bank insolvency proceedings, the term means the person acting in the bank insolvency as the bank liquidator or provisional bank liquidator.[1303] In relation to a building society insolvency, it means the person acting in the building society insolvency as the building society liquidator or provisional building society liquidator.[1304]   **1.534**

In IR 1986, in relation to insolvency proceedings, 'office-holder' means any person who, by virtue of any provision of IA 1986 or IR 1986, holds office in relation to those proceedings.[1305]   **1.535**

Formal Defects

IR 1986, r 7.55, provides: **1.536**

> No insolvency proceedings shall be invalidated by any formal defect or by any irregularity, unless the court before which objection is made considers that substantial injustice has been caused by the defect or irregularity, and that the injustice cannot be remedied by any order of the court.

This rule cannot be used to cure a lack of jurisdiction.[1306]   **1.537**

History

History of the Legislation

Before the introduction of incorporation by registration

Before 1844 business associations in Britain could be incorporated individually by royal charter or Act of Parliament: sometimes both a charter and an Act were needed in order to confer all the powers required by the business. The Crown and Parliament could only be persuaded to incorporate companies for purposes of general public importance and in circumstances which would be appropriate to the dignity of the institution conferring incorporation. Other business associations were not incorporated and so the law of partnership applied to them. However, the law of partnership was developed to deal with arrangements between a small number of partners who associated together more or less permanently on a basis of mutual trust and confidence with all partners participating in the management of the business. An increasing number of unincorporated partnerships in the late 18th and early 19th centuries were associations of large numbers of people who merely contributed   **1.538**

[1301] ss 1–7B.
[1302] ss 252–263.
[1303] Bank Insolvency (England and Wales) Rules 2009 (SI 2009/356), r 289.
[1304] Building Society Insolvency (England and Wales) Rules 2010 (SI 2010/2581), r 281.
[1305] IR 1986, r 13.9A.
[1306] *Re Bridgend Goldsmiths Ltd* [1995] 2 BCLC 208, in which an application concerning individual voluntary arrangements had been made to the High Court, which held that the application could only be heard by a county court. It has subsequently been held that the High Court does have jurisdiction in such a case (*Clarke v Coutts and Co* [2002] EWCA Civ 943, [2002] BPIR 916; *Commissioners of HM Revenue and Customs v Earley* [2011] EWHC 1783 (Ch), [2011] BPIR 1590).

capital (the 'joint stock') to an enterprise run by professional managers. A notable feature of these joint stock companies was that they were formed on the basis that members could leave the association and new members could join at any time: membership was a matter of investment and it had to be possible to sell one's membership at any time in order to realize the capital value of the investment.

1.539 Bankruptcy law was capable of dealing with insolvent small partnerships: the partners could be made jointly or individually bankrupt. It took some time to develop adequate methods of dealing with insolvent joint stock companies and corporations. The difference that incorporation made to the liability of the members of an association was clear. John George, in *A View of the Existing Law Affecting Unincorporated Joint Stock Companies*,[1307] put it this way, at p 29:[1308]

> The great distinction in contemplation of law, between common Joint Stock Companies or partnerships, and corporations, is, that in the first, the law looks to the individuals of whom the partnership is composed, and knows the partnership no otherwise than as being such a number of individuals; while in the second, it sees only the creature of the charter, the body corporate, and knows not the individuals. Hence on a judgment against a corporation, execution can only be levied on the corporate effects, or supposing a trading corporation to become wholly insolvent, the individual members or proprietors will only lose their stock or share in the capital of the body corporate, and do not become answerable for the debts in their individual capacities. But…it is far otherwise with the members of unincorporated partnerships, who may be made answerable for the debts of the firm, to use a recent expression of the Lord Chancellor,[1309] 'even to their last shilling and their last acre'.

1.540 Chartered companies have been extensively studied by W R Scott, *The Constitution and Finance of English, Scottish and Irish Joint-Stock Companies to 1720*[1310] and A DuBois, *The English Business Company after the Bubble Act 1720–1800*.[1311] DuBois confirms that members of a chartered company could not be sued for the company's debts, and judgments against the company could not be executed against the members' property.[1312] There was no 'simple and efficient method of liquidation' of incorporated companies.[1313] The bankruptcy laws could not be used.[1314] This is all the more surprising in that several companies had spectacular financial difficulties which caused widespread problems in the business world.

Joint Stock Companies Act 1844

1.541 When Parliament introduced incorporation by registration with the registrar of companies in the Joint Stock Companies Act 1844 (7 & 8 Vic, c 110), it insisted that the members of the new companies should have unlimited liability as if the company were not incorporated.[1315] On the same day as c 110 was enacted, a separate Act (7 & 8 Vic, c 111)[1316] was enacted introducing a procedure for winding up the new registered companies and also all chartered

[1307] London: Sweet, 1825.
[1308] The original wording and punctuation are retained in this quotation.
[1309] Lord Eldon was Lord Chancellor from 1801–1806 and 1807–1827.
[1310] Cambridge: Cambridge University Press, 1910–12.
[1311] New York: The Commonwealth Fund; London: Oxford University Press, 1938.
[1312] pp 93–104; and see per Baggallay LJ in *Re Oriental Bank Corporation* (1885) 54 LJ Ch 481 at p 483.
[1313] DuBois, *The English Business Company after the Bubble Act 1720–1800*, p 374.
[1314] p 431, n 214, and p 432, n 218; contemporary books on bankruptcy did not mention corporations.
[1315] s 25.
[1316] Sometimes called Lord Dalhousie's Act. The 10th Earl (later 1st Marquess) of Dalhousie was Vice President of the Board of Trade in 1844.

and statutory commercial and trading companies. The latter Act was mainly concerned to apply bankruptcy procedure to companies[1317] by providing that a bankruptcy petition could be presented against a company if it committed an act of bankruptcy. Only creditors could petition but the directors of a company could render it open to a petition by making a declaration of insolvency (that is, a declaration that the company 'is unable to meet its engagements'), because making such a declaration was an act of bankruptcy.[1318] Failing to pay a judgment debt within 14 days of being served with a notice to pay was another act of bankruptcy.[1319]

The procedure under the 1844 Act was complicated in that the petition and adjudication **1.542** of bankruptcy were in the Bankruptcy Court, which dealt with the establishment of claims against the company and getting in the company's assets apart from contributions from its members. But getting in members' contributions and finally winding up the affairs of the company had to be the subject of separate proceedings in Chancery.[1320]

The Joint Stock Companies Winding-up Act 1848 introduced a procedure by which any **1.543** contributory[1321] of a company could petition directly to the Lord Chancellor or the Master of the Rolls for the company to be wound up, provided bankruptcy proceedings had not been started by a creditor in the Bankruptcy Court.[1322] The conditions under which a contributory could petition were that:[1323]

(a) the company had committed an act of bankruptcy; or
(b) the directors had filed a declaration of insolvency; or
(c) a judgment debt had not been paid 10 days after demand; or
(d) a debt remained unpaid (and no defence had been entered) three weeks after service of notice of a writ; or
(e) the company was 'dissolved' (which, as in partnership law, meant that the members had decided to end their association) or ceased business;
(f) 'Or if any other Matter or Thing shall be shown which in the Opinion of the court shall render it just and equitable that the Company should be dissolved'.

Even though a company was being wound up in Chancery on a contributory's petition, **1.544** it could be the subject of separate bankruptcy proceedings in the Bankruptcy Court.[1324] Once a bankruptcy petition had been presented against a company, only the creditors' assignee could petition for it to be wound up, and only if directed to do so by the Court of Bankruptcy.[1325] However, a winding-up order could be made on a contributory's petition presented before a bankruptcy petition.[1326]

[1317] See ss 1–11.
[1318] s 4.
[1319] s 5.
[1320] See *Re Royal British Bank, Aitchison v Lee* (1856) 3 Drew 637.
[1321] The contributories of a company include its present members; see 8.18–8.50.
[1322] ss 5 and 6.
[1323] s 5.
[1324] *Re London and Eastern Banking Corporation* (1858) 2 De G & J 484.
[1325] Joint Stock Companies Winding-up Act 1848, s 6.
[1326] *Re Port of London Shipowners' Loan and Assurance Co, ex parte Collingridge* (1850) 19 LJ Ch 234; *Re Mitre General Life Assurance etc Association* (1860) 29 Beav 1.

1.545 The Joint Stock Companies Winding-up Amendment Act 1849 made extensive detailed amendments to the 1848 Act and[1327] extended its coverage to all companies, partnerships and associations of seven or more members, but railway companies were excluded:[1328]

> ... very little good has been effected by the Winding-up Acts, but a great deal of harm.[1329]
>
> Kindersley V-C said that during the whole progress of this case the idea had pressed upon him more and more that it would be most beneficial for all parties if the petition stood over for some time, say three months, to see if some unexceptionable persons could not be found to wind up this company without the intervention of the Winding-up Acts, of which, from experience, he had a morbid horror.[1330]

1.546 Amendments were made by the Joint Stock Companies Winding-up Amendment Act 1857 but the system of winding up governed by these Acts was by then being phased out because it did not apply to companies registered under the Joint Stock Companies Act 1856.[1331]

1.547 The Limited Liability Act 1855 permitted registered companies to limit the liability of their members and the limited liability company became the normal form of registered company.

Joint Stock Companies Act 1856

1.548 The whole of the law governing registered companies was revised in the Joint Stock Companies Act 1856, and companies registered under the 1844 Act were required to re-register under the new Act. Part 3[1332] of the 1856 Act provided a new system of winding up to apply only to companies registered or re-registered under the 1856 Act, and that system is the origin of the winding-up provisions of IA 1986. Petitioning for the bankruptcy of a registered company was ended, and since the 1856 Act it has been inappropriate to use the term 'bankruptcy' in connection with registered companies in England and Wales.[1333] Under the 1856 Act, either a creditor or a contributory of a company could petition for it to be wound up but a creditor could petition only on the ground that the company was unable to pay its debts.[1334] A contributory could petition on that ground and also if:[1335]

(a) the company had adopted a special resolution that it should be wound up by the court;
(b) the company had not commenced its business within a year from its incorporation or had suspended its business for a year;
(c) the number of shareholders was less than seven;
(d) three-quarters of the company's capital had been lost or become unavailable.

1.549 All these circumstances, except impairment of capital, have continued ever since to be circumstances in which a winding up may be ordered, though the minimum number of members has been reduced in line with reductions in the minimum number required to register a company.

[1327] s 1.
[1328] See 1.572–1.577.
[1329] Per Knight Bruce V-C in *Re Tirhoot Co* (1850) 16 LT OS 189.
[1330] *Re Newcastle Commercial Banking Co* (1856) 5 WR 31 at p 32.
[1331] Joint Stock Companies Act 1856, s 59.
[1332] ss 59–105.
[1333] In North America, bankruptcy laws still apply to both corporations and individuals. In Canada, there is a parallel regime for winding up corporations but it is nowadays used more by contributories than by creditors. In the USA there is no separate procedure for winding up corporations.
[1334] s 69.
[1335] s 67.

The 1856 Act also introduced a statutory procedure for the voluntary winding up of regis- **1.550**
tered companies.[1336]

The Joint Stock Companies Act 1857 introduced winding up subject to the supervision of **1.551**
the court.[1337] This form of winding up, in which the court could require a voluntary liquidator to obtain the court's sanction before exercising any or all of his powers, was popular in
the 19th century but fell into disuse and has been abolished in the United Kingdom and
the Republic of Ireland.

Further amendments to the law on winding up registered companies were made by the Joint **1.552**
Stock Companies Amendment Act 1858.

Companies Act 1862

All the Acts mentioned so far were repealed and replaced by the Companies Act 1862. **1.553**

> [The Companies Act 1862] is, I believe, as perfect a scheme as any we are acquainted with.
> It intends—and in my opinion it does accomplish the object for which it was passed—to
> provide a general law applicable to all joint stock companies, and to provide above all for
> their winding up. They are to be wound up in case their creditors require it, or in case their
> shareholders require it.[1338]

The 1862 Act listed five circumstances in which a registered company could be wound up.[1339] **1.554**
They were the same as those in the 1856 Act,[1340] except that the just and equitable ground
(taken from the 1848 Act) was substituted for the impairment of capital ground in the 1856
Act. The 1862 Act permitted both creditors and contributories to petition in any of these
five circumstances. Section 170 of the 1862 Act provided for the Lord Chancellor to make
'rules concerning the mode of proceeding to be had for winding up a company'. Rules under
this provision were made as an order of court dated 11 November 1862, amended by a general order and rules dated 21 March 1868, and replaced by the Companies (Winding-up)
Rules 1890.

The 1862 Act introduced provisions for the winding up of 'unregistered companies' to cover **1.555**
the types of company which could previously be wound up under the 1848 and 1849 Acts.

IA 1986

Further consolidations of the legislation on companies, including winding up, occurred in **1.556**
the Companies (Consolidation) Act 1908, the Companies Act 1929, the Companies Act
1948 and the Companies Act 1985. There was then a substantial revision of company insolvency and liquidation law and of bankruptcy law made by IA 1985 and consolidated in IA
1986. This followed a detailed study of the existing law by a committee which was appointed
in 1977 by the Secretary of State for Trade and chaired by the noted insolvency practitioner
Sir Kenneth Cork.[1341] This introduced the 'rescue culture', in which continuation of an
insolvent person's business as a going concern is preferred wherever possible to a mere sale
of assets. Two new insolvency procedures were introduced: administration (for registered
companies) and voluntary arrangement (in separate forms for registered companies and

---

[1336] ss 102–105.
[1337] s 19. See 10.152–10.154.
[1338] *Re Star and Garter Ltd* (1873) 42 LJ Ch 374 per Bacon V-C at p 377.
[1339] s 79.
[1340] See 1.548.
[1341] See *Insolvency Law and Practice. Report of the Review Committee* (Cmnd 8558), London: HMSO, 1982.

for individuals). For the first time since 1856, the legislation on companies winding up (IA 1986) and the rest of companies legislation (the remaining provisions of the Companies Act 1985) were in separate Acts. For the first time ever, a single Act, IA 1986, dealt with both companies winding up (in England and Wales and Scotland) and bankruptcy (in England and Wales only). Secondary legislation, of unprecedented length and detail, included IR 1986 and IPO 1986,[1342] which, for the first time, made detailed provision for the winding up of partnerships. IPO 1986 was replaced by IPO 1994.

1.557 The Water Industry Act 1991 was the first of a series of Acts introducing industry-specific administration regimes for utility companies.[1343]

1.558 IA 2000 introduced a moratorium to allow preparation of a company voluntary arrangement. This procedure is available, as an alternative to administration, for small companies.

1.559 The law on administration was completely revised and replaced by the Enterprise Act 2002, s 248.

History of the Jurisdiction

Earliest registered companies

1.560 The first winding-up statute, 7 & 8 Vict c 111, enacted at the same time as the first statute providing for incorporation of companies by registration (the Joint Stock Companies Act 1844), was expressed by its first section to apply to:

(a) any commercial or trading company incorporated by charter or Act of Parliament;
(b) any commercial or trading company granted privileges under the Chartered Companies Act 1837 or by any Act of Parliament;
(c) any commercial or trading company provisionally or completely registered under the Joint Stock Companies Act 1844;
(d) any existing joint stock company as that term was defined in the Joint Stock Companies Act 1844, s 2 (that is, every partnership with freely transferable shares, every insurance company, including friendly societies, and every partnership with more than 25 members).

The statute 7 & 8 Vict c 111 provided only for petitions by creditors.

1.561 Provision for petitions by contributories was introduced by the Joint Stock Companies Winding-up Act 1848, which was expressed by its first section to apply to all companies within the provisions of 7 & 8 Vict c 111 and to all future companies, associations and partnerships with freely transferable shares. The second section of the Act extended its scope to all associations or companies formed for the purposes of working mines or minerals and to benefit building societies not duly certified and enrolled.

1.562 The Joint Stock Companies Winding-up Amendment Act 1849, s 1, declared that, notwithstanding anything in the 1848 Act 'importing a more limited application thereof' it was to be applied to all incorporated or unincorporated partnerships, associations and companies with not less than seven members except railway companies incorporated by Act of Parliament.[1344]

[1342] SI 1986/2142.
[1343] See 1.245–1.294.
[1344] See 1.572–1.577.

The 1848 and 1849 Acts were held to apply to: **1.563**

(a) a provisionally registered company formed to make a railway;[1345]
(b) a foreign corporation;[1346]
(c) an unincorporated loan society not registered under the Loan Societies Act 1840;[1347]
(d) a certified and enrolled unincorporated building society whose shares were freely transferable;[1348]
(e) a society formed under the Industrial and Provident Societies Act 1852.[1349]

But it was held that the Acts did not apply to an unincorporated members' club not trading for profit[1350] or (remarkably) to a pier company incorporated by special Act of Parliament.[1351]

Joint Stock Companies Act 1856

The Joint Stock Companies Act 1856 established the present-day system of registration of   **1.564**
companies, and part 3[1352] of the Act provided for the winding up of companies registered
or re-registered under the Act, but not any other companies.[1353] The winding up of a company re-registered under the Act included the winding up of the company as it was before
re-registration.[1354]

Companies Act 1862 to the present

The Companies Act 1862 repealed all the preceding Acts. It introduced the present format   **1.565**
of one part, part 4,[1355] devoted to the winding up of registered companies and another part,
part 8,[1356] for unregistered companies, a term introduced in the Act and defined in s 199 to
mean 'any partnership, association, or company, except railway companies incorporated by
Act of Parliament, consisting of more than seven members, and not registered under this
Act'. It was held that companies registered under the Joint Stock Companies Act 1856 were
not unregistered companies.[1357]

This format was repeated in the various consolidations down to IA 1986.   **1.566**

Partnerships: general partnerships

The statutory provisions on winding up companies, from the Joint Stock Companies   **1.567**
Winding-up Act 1848 to the Companies Act 1985, used to extend to partnerships, whether
solvent or insolvent, unless they were small partnerships.[1358] The Joint Stock Companies

---

[1345] *Re London and Manchester Direct Independent Railway Co (Remington's Line), ex parte Barber* (1849) 1 Mac & G 176; *Bright v Hutton* (1852) 3 HL Cas 341 at p 370. As a provisionally registered company was not incorporated, the Court of Chancery could alternatively order an account to be taken, which could be cheaper than a winding up (see 1.163).
[1346] *Re Dendre Valley Railway and Canal Co* (1850) 19 LJ Ch 474.
[1347] *Re Sherwood Loan Co* (1851) 1 Sim NS 165: the point was left undecided in the earlier case of *Re Crown and Cushion Loan Fund Society* (1850) 14 Jur 874.
[1348] *Re St George's Building Society* (1857) 4 Drew 154.
[1349] *Re National Industrial and Provident Society* (1861) 30 LJ Ch 940.
[1350] *Re St James's Club* (1852) 2 De G M & G 383.
[1351] *Re Herne Bay Pier Co, ex parte Burge* (1848) 1 De G & Sm 588.
[1352] ss 59–105.
[1353] s 59.
[1354] *Re Plumstead, Woolwich and Charlton Consumers Pure Water Co* (1860) 2 De G F & J 20; *Re Liverpool Tradesman's Loan Co Ltd, ex parte Stevenson* (1862) 32 LJ Ch 96.
[1355] ss 74–173.
[1356] ss 199–204.
[1357] *Re Torquay Bath Co* (1863) 32 Beav 581; *Re London Indiarubber Co* (1866) LR 1 Ch App 329.
[1358] See 1.571.

Winding-up Act 1848 had been extended in 1849 to all partnerships with not less than seven members.[1359] The Companies Act 1985 re-enacted the provision first made in the Companies Act 1862 that the term 'unregistered company' included any partnership with eight members or more.[1360] Under these provisions, the following types of entity, which perhaps should be regarded as types of partnership, have been wound up as unregistered companies:

(a) unincorporated joint stock companies;[1361]

(b) companies only provisionally registered under the Joint Stock Companies Act 1844.[1362]

1.568 There is a concurrent jurisdiction to wind up under partnership law, which applies to both solvent and insolvent partnerships.[1363] In practice, insolvent partnerships are usually dealt with by making the partners bankrupt.[1364]

1.569 IA 1985 deleted the reference to partnerships in the definition of unregistered companies.[1365] Instead, separate provision was made for winding up insolvent (but not solvent) companies as unregistered companies by the Insolvent Partnerships Order 1986,[1366] which is now replaced by IPO 1994. The concurrent jurisdiction to wind up under partnership law still continues.

Partnerships: limited partnerships

1.570 The Limited Partnerships Act 1907, s 6(4), provided that the provisions of the Companies Acts 1862–1900 relating to the winding up of companies by the court were to apply to the winding up by the court of limited partnerships. This was re-enacted in the Companies (Consolidation) Act 1908, s 268(1)(vii).[1367] The 1908 Act also provided[1368] that any limited partnership was an unregistered company. Under the 1908 Act, a limited partnership could be wound up as an unregistered company whatever the number of members.[1369] In England and Wales, limited partnerships were withdrawn from the winding-up jurisdiction and instead made liable to bankruptcy proceedings by the Bankruptcy and Deeds of Arrangement Act 1913, s 24. This repealed in England and Wales all provisions of the 1908 Act relating to the winding up of limited partnerships.[1370] Instead, limited partnerships were to be treated as ordinary (general) partnerships and subject to bankruptcy law.[1371] The latter provision was re-enacted in the Bankruptcy Act 1914, s 127.[1372] In the Companies

---

[1359] Joint Stock Companies Winding-up Amendment Act 1849, s 1.

[1360] Companies Act 1862, s 199, Companies Act 1985, s 665.

[1361] *Aberdeen Provision Society* (1863) 2 M 385; *Re Family Endowment Society* (1870) LR 5 Ch App 118; *Re Great Britain Mutual Life Assurance Society* (1880) 16 ChD 246.

[1362] *Re Bank of London and National Provincial Insurance Association* (1871) LR 6 Ch App 421; *Re Anglo-Mexican Mint Co* [1875] WN 168.

[1363] See 1.158–1.164.

[1364] See 1.156–1.157.

[1365] IA 1985, sch 10, part 4, which came into force on 29 December 1986 (Insolvency Act 1985 (Commencement No 5) Order 1986 (SI 1986/1924), art 2).

[1366] SI 1986/2142.

[1367] The Limited Partnerships Act 1907, s 6(4), was repealed by the Companies (Consolidation) Act 1908, sch 6, part 1.

[1368] In s 267.

[1369] See 1.571. For examples, see *Re Hughes and Co* [1911] 1 Ch 342 and *Muirhead v Borland* 1925 SC 474.

[1370] s 24(2).

[1371] s 24(1).

[1372] The Bankruptcy and Deeds of Arrangement Act 1913, s 24, was repealed by the Bankruptcy Act 1914, s 168(1) and sch 6.

Acts 1929, 1948 and 1985 it was declared that the term 'unregistered company' included limited partnerships but it was also provided that limited partnerships registered in England and Wales or Northern Ireland were not unregistered companies,[1373] so that only Scottish limited partnerships could be wound up as unregistered companies. In Scotland it ceased to be possible to wind up limited partnerships as unregistered companies after amendments made to the Companies Act 1985, s 665, by the Bankruptcy (Scotland) Act 1985, sch 8, came into force on 1 April 1986.[1374] All references to limited partnerships in the provisions relating to unregistered companies were repealed, along with the reference to general partnerships, by IA 1985, sch 10, part 4, which came into force on 29 December 1986.[1375] The Bankruptcy Act 1914, s 127, was repealed by IA 1985, sch 10, part 2, which also came into force on 29 December 1986.

Partnerships: small partnerships

From 2 November 1862 (when the Companies Act 1862 came into force) until 28 December **1.571** 1986 (after which IA 1986 came into force under s 443 and SI 1986/1924, art 3), a partnership, association or company with fewer than eight members could not be wound up as an unregistered company.[1376] Under the Companies Acts 1929, 1948 and 1985 this limit did not apply to a foreign partnership, association or company[1377] and under the Companies (Consolidation) Act 1908 it did not apply to a limited partnership.[1378] The Companies Act 1985, s 665(c), was repealed by IA 1985, sch 10, part 4.

Incorporated railway companies

The Abandonment of Railways Act 1850 introduced a special procedure for winding up **1.572** railway companies, which were usually statutory companies incorporated individually by local Acts of Parliament. A revised procedure was substituted by the Transport Act 1962, s 83. The essence of the procedure under these Acts was that a railway company could not be wound up as an unregistered company until it had obtained a warrant of abandonment under the 1850 Act or an abandonment order under the 1962 Act. A warrant of abandonment or abandonment order could be obtained only after making satisfactory arrangements for terminating the obligations imposed on the company by its incorporating Act.[1379] A railway company incorporated by Act of Parliament was forced to follow this special procedure by statutes which provided that the winding-up legislation did not apply to such a company,[1380] unless a warrant had been obtained for the abandonment of the whole of its

---

[1373] Companies Act 1929, s 337(4); Companies Act 1948, s 398(d); Companies Act 1985, s 665(d).

[1374] Bankruptcy (Scotland) Act 1985 (Commencement) Order 1985 (SI 1985/1924), art 4; *Smith* 1999 SLT (Sh Ct) 5.

[1375] Insolvency Act 1986 (Commencement No 5) Order 1986 (SI 1986/1924).

[1376] Companies Act 1862, s 199; Companies (Consolidation) Act 1908, s 267; Companies Act 1929, s 337(3); Companies Act 1948, s 398(c); Companies Act 1985, s 665(c); *Re Bolton Benefit Loan Society* (1879) 12 ChD 679; *Re Bowling and Welby's Contract* [1895] 1 Ch 663; *Re New York and Continental Line* (1909) 54 SJ 117.

[1377] Companies Act 1928, sch 2; Companies Act 1929, s 337(3); Companies Act 1948, s 398(c); Companies Act 1985, s 665(c).

[1378] Companies (Consolidation) Act 1908, s 267 as originally enacted. The Bankruptcy and Deeds of Arrangement Act 1913, s 24, ended the application to limited partnerships of companies winding-up provisions.

[1379] Law Commission, *Statute Law Repeals: Consultation Paper: Abortive Railway Projects – Proposed Repeals* (SLR 01/09), pp vii–x; Law Commission and Scottish Law Commission, *Statute Law Repeals: Nineteenth Report* (Cm 8330, Law Com No 333, Scot Law Com No 227), paras 9.5–9.12.

[1380] From 1 August 1849, even before the 1850 Act was enacted, the Joint Stock Companies Winding-up Act 1848 ceased to apply to railway companies incorporated by Act of Parliament (Joint Stock Companies

railway.[1381] Under the 1850 Act and the Railway Companies Act 1867 only a shareholder of a railway company which had obtained a warrant of abandonment could petition for its winding up,[1382] but this was altered by the Abandonment of Railways Act 1869 so that anyone with standing to petition for the winding up of a company could petition in the case of a railway company.

1.573 Under the Transport Act 1962, s 83, the undertakers, or a creditor of the undertakers, of any railway undertaking in Great Britain, other than the nationalized railways, could obtain an abandonment order from the Secretary of State for Transport which would release the undertakers from any statutory obligation to construct, maintain or operate their railway. A railway company incorporated by Act of Parliament whose railway was the subject of an abandonment order could be wound up as an unregistered company.[1383]

1.574 Alternatively, it was held in Ireland that a railway company which was not a registered company could register under what is now the Companies Act 2006, ss 1040–1042, and then be wound up as a registered company,[1384] though in *Re Uxbridge and Rickmansworth Railway Co*[1385] Lindley LJ said, at p 566, that whether this procedure was allowable was 'well known to be one of those thorny points which have not been decided'.

1.575 The provisions for making abandonment orders were repealed (except in relation to Scotland) by the Transport and Works Act 1992, sch 4.

1.576 The restrictions on winding up railway companies as unregistered companies were held not to apply to tramway companies,[1386] or to a company which was incorporated to construct docks and a branch railway, which was held to be a dock company rather than a railway company.[1387]

1.577 The Railways Act 1993 introduced railway administration.[1388]

Trustee savings banks

1.578 In the Companies Acts from 1908 to 1985, and in IA 1986, s 220(1), as originally enacted, trustee savings banks were included in the definition of unregistered companies but the reference to trustee savings banks was repealed as from 5 July 1988 by virtue of IA 1986, s 220(2), and the Trustee Savings Banks Act 1985 (Appointed Day) (No 4) Order 1986.[1389]

Winding-up Amendment Act 1849, s 1). From 1862 such companies were excluded from the definition of unregistered company by the Companies Act 1862, s 199; Companies (Consolidation) Act 1908, s 267; Companies Act 1929, s 337(1); Companies Act 1948, s 398(a); Companies Act 1985, s 665(a); and IA 1986, s 220(1)(a). IA 1986, s 220(1)(a), was repealed by the Transport and Works Act 1992, s 65(1)(f) and sch 4, brought into force in that respect on 1 January 1993 by the Transport and Works Act 1992 (Commencement No 3 and Transitional Provisions) Order 1992 (SI 1992/2784).

[1381] Abandonment of Railways Act 1850, s 31; Railway Companies Act 1867, s 31. For an example of a winding up under these provisions see *Re Skipton and Wharf Dale Railway Co* (1869) 20 LT 359.

[1382] *Re North Kent Railway Extension Railway Co* (1869) LR 8 Eq 356.

[1383] Transport Act 1962, s 83(6), repealed by the Transport and Works Act 1992, sch 4.

[1384] *Re Ennis and West Clare Railway Co* (1879) 3 LR Ir 94.

[1385] (1890) 43 ChD 536.

[1386] *Re Brentford and Isleworth Tramways Co* (1884) 26 ChD 527; *Re Portstewart Tramway Co* [1896] IR 265.

[1387] *Re Exmouth Docks Co* (1873) LR 17 Eq 181.

[1388] See 1.252–1.255.

[1389] SI 1986/1223.

History of Court Jurisdiction

Registered and unregistered companies

Under the Joint Stock Companies Act 1856, s 60, jurisdiction to wind up a limited company **1.579** registered in England was assigned to the Court of Bankruptcy having jurisdiction in the place where the company's registered office was situated. Other registered companies (the Act did not deal with unregistered companies) were to be wound up by the High Court of Chancery unless they were subject to the stannaries jurisdiction. The Court of Bankruptcy had jurisdiction over unlimited companies re-registered as limited.[1390]

Under the Companies Act 1862, s 81, the High Court was given jurisdiction over all com- **1.580** panies registered in England, but after making a winding-up order against a company, the High Court could direct that all further proceedings in the winding up be taken in the Court of Bankruptcy having jurisdiction where the company's registered office was situated. The Companies Act 1867, s 41, provided that subsequent proceedings could be referred to a county court instead of the Court of Bankruptcy. This reflected the transfer of jurisdiction from the Country District Courts of Bankruptcy (outside London) to county courts initiated in the Bankruptcy Act 1861 and completed by the Bankruptcy Act 1869, s 130. The jurisdiction of the London Bankruptcy Court was transferred to the High Court by the Bankruptcy Act 1883, s 93. In relation to unregistered companies, the Companies Act 1862, s 199(1), made the same provisions as are now in IA 1986, s 221(3).

The Companies (Winding up) Act 1890, s 1, re-enacted in the Companies (Consolidation) **1.581** Act 1908, s 131, provided that a petition to wind up a company with a paid-up capital not exceeding £10,000 had to be presented in a county court and a petition for a company with a paid-up capital exceeding £10,000 had to be presented in the High Court. An order of the Lord Chancellor dated 29 November 1890 and made under the Companies (Winding up) Act 1890, s 1(5), established the system by which many county courts (now County Court hearing centres) do not have jurisdiction in winding up and their districts are attached to other county courts or, in the London area, to the High Court.[1391] This followed the rules already in operation for the bankruptcy jurisdiction of county courts. The present concurrent jurisdiction of High Court and County Court was introduced by the Companies Act 1928, s 56.

Building societies and registered societies

Under the Building Societies Act 1874, s 4, the court with jurisdiction to wind up an incor- **1.582** porated building society was the county court of the district in which the chief office or place of meeting for the business of the society was situated. Similarly, under the Industrial and Provident Societies Act 1862, s 17, and the Industrial and Provident Societies Act 1876, s 17(1), the county courts were given exclusive jurisdiction over what are now called registered societies. Although the exclusive jurisdiction of the county courts was conferred by the legislation only in relation to societies registered under the Act, it was held that the exclusivity extended to societies which were entitled to register but had not done so.[1392] This

---

[1390] *Re Plumstead, Woolwich and Charlton Consumers Pure Water Co* (1860) 2 De G F & J 20; *Re Liverpool Tradesman's Loan Co Ltd, ex parte Stevenson* (1862) 32 LJ Ch 96.

[1391] *Re Court Bureau Ltd* (1891) 7 TLR 223.

[1392] *Re Rotherhithe Co-operative and Industrial Society* (1862) 32 Beav 57; *Re Midland Counties Benefit Building Society* (1864) 12 WR 661; *Re Chatham Co-operative Industrial Society* (1864) 4 NR 481.

meant that a society had to be registered in order to be wound up.[1393] The exclusive jurisdiction of county courts over building societies and registered societies was not affected by the Companies (Winding up) Act 1890[1394] but was ended by the Industrial and Provident Societies Act 1893, s 58, and the Building Societies Act 1894, s 8.

Stannary courts

1.583 The stannaries are the tin-mining areas of Cornwall and Devon. From the 13th century until 1896, stannary courts exercised jurisdiction over matters relating to mining in the stannaries.[1395] The Vice-Warden's Court exercised equity jurisdiction.[1396] Stewards' courts exercised common law jurisdiction, but in 1836 the jurisdiction of the four Cornwall stewards' courts was transferred to its vice-warden.[1397] This resulted in just one stannary court for Cornwall, which is variously referred to as the Court of Stannaries in Cornwall, the Court of the Vice-Warden of the Stannaries or the Vice-Warden's Court. Originally the jurisdiction of stannary courts was confined to tin-mining, but jurisdiction was extended to mining for other metals[1398] and then to mixed mines extracting both metallic and non-metallic material.[1399] Before limited liability became generally available for registered companies, investment in a mine was through the medium of a cost-book company, which was an unincorporated partnership[1400] with freely transferable shares. In early times the members of a cost-book mining company (often called the 'adventurers') actually worked the mine themselves. They appointed a 'purser', who acted as treasurer. The purser's accounts formed the company's 'cost book', which was balanced usually six times a year to show profits that could be divided or losses which the adventurers had to meet and for which they had unlimited liability. By the 19th century, most of the members of cost-book mining companies were investors who usually did not take part in the management or working of the mine, but still had unlimited personal liability for the company's debts.[1401]

1.584 By the 1830s a procedure known as a creditor's suit in the Vice-Warden's Court had developed into a procedure for winding up a cost-book company on a creditor's petition.[1402] There was no similar procedure for shareholders. All that a shareholder could do was to petition against all the other shareholders for a general account and contribution.[1403] The Joint Stock Companies Winding-up Act 1848 introduced a procedure by which a contributory of a company could petition for it to be wound up by the Court of Chancery, but it was declared that nothing in the Act was to affect the jurisdiction of the Court of Stannaries in Cornwall.[1404] This was clarified by the Joint Stock Companies Winding-up

---

[1393] This point was not raised in *Re Alfreton District Friendly and Provident Society* (1863) 7 LT 817.

[1394] *Re London and Suburban Bank* [1892] 1 Ch 604 (industrial and provident societies); *Re Real Estates Co* [1893] 1 Ch 398 (building societies).

[1395] See Robert R Pennington, *Stannary Law* (Newton Abbot: David & Charles, 1973).

[1396] There were separate vice-wardens for Cornwall and Devon, but from 1836, the legislation referred to only one Vice-Warden's Court—that in Cornwall—and its jurisdiction was extended to Devon by the Stannaries Act 1855, s 32. For the history of the court and its procedure up to that time see the 'Introductory notice' in *Procedure in the Court of the Vice Warden of the Stannaries* (London: Sweet, 1856).

[1397] Stannaries Act 1836.

[1398] Stannaries Act 1836, s 4.

[1399] Stannaries Act 1855, s 1.

[1400] *Re Nance, ex parte Ashmead* [1893] 1 QB 590 per Lindley LJ at p 594.

[1401] Pennington, *Stannary Law*, ch 5.

[1402] Pennington, *Stannary Law*, pp 174–7.

[1403] Argument in *Re Tretoil and Messer Mining Co* (1862) 2 John & H 421 as reported at 6 LT 154.

[1404] Joint Stock Companies Winding-up Act 1848, s 2. The Vice-Warden's Court was by then the only stannaries court in Cornwall.

Amendment Act 1849, which provided that nothing in the 1848 or 1849 Acts was to extend to cost-book companies within the stannaries in Cornwall and within the jurisdiction of the Vice-Warden's Court.[1405] However, the 1849 Act did provide that the owners of 10 per cent (in value) of the shares of a cost-book company in the stannaries could present a petition to the Lord Chancellor or the Master of the Rolls (in the Court of Chancery) for the company to be wound up under the 1848 Act, and proceedings under such a winding up could be referred to the Court of Stannaries.[1406]

When the Joint Stock Companies Act 1856 introduced a separate winding-up regime **1.585** for registered companies, the Vice-Warden's Court was given jurisdiction to wind up registered companies engaged in working any mine within and subject to the stannaries jurisdiction.[1407]

The Joint Stock Companies Winding-up Amendment Act 1857 introduced a new restriction **1.586** tion on contributories' petitions for winding up unincorporated cost-book companies. No such petition could be presented in the Court of Chancery, under the 1848 Act, unless it was shown that the company could not be effectually dissolved or wound up in the Vice-Warden's Court or the Vice-Warden had certified that his Court's powers were insufficient.[1408] In practice, permission to present a petition in the Court of Chancery was given for shareholders' petitions to wind up cost-book companies, because of the inadequacy of procedures in the Vice-Warden's Court; in particular, because that court had no power to restrain proceedings by an unincorporated company's creditors against contributories personally.[1409]

The Companies Act 1862 repealed the 1848, 1849, 1856 and 1857 Acts.[1410] It introduced **1.587** the current system that the provisions relating to the winding up of registered companies apply to unregistered companies such as cost-book mining companies.[1411] It gave the Vice-Warden's Court exclusive jurisdiction over the winding up of companies engaged in working mines within and subject to the jurisdiction of the stannaries, except where the Vice-Warden certified that in his opinion a company within his court's jurisdiction would be more advantageously wound up in the High Court of Chancery.[1412] The Stannaries Act 1887, s 28,[1413] made the Vice-Warden's Court the only court in which a petition could be presented for the winding up of a company formed for working mines within the stannaries,[1414] unless it could be shown that the company was actually working mines, or engaged in any other undertaking, beyond the limits of the stannaries, or had entered into a contract

---

[1405] Joint Stock Companies Winding-up Amendment Act 1849, s 1. This provision was not applied to Devon when the jurisdiction of the Vice-Warden's court was extended there (*Re South Lady Bertha Mining Co* (1862) 2 John & H 376).

[1406] Joint Stock Companies Winding-up Amendment Act 1849, s 1.

[1407] Joint Stock Companies Act 1856, s 60; Companies Act 1862, ss 68 and 81.

[1408] Joint Stock Companies Winding-up Amendment Act 1857, s 12.

[1409] *Re Wheal Anne Mining Co* (1862) 30 Beav 601, more fully reported at 10 WR 330; *Re Tretoil and Messer Mining Co* (1862) 2 John & H 421; *Re South Lady Bertha Mining Co* (1862) 2 John & H 376.

[1410] Companies Act 1862, s 205 and sch 3, part 1.

[1411] Companies Act 1862, s 199.

[1412] Companies Act 1862, s 81.

[1413] Re-enacted in the Companies (Winding Up) Act 1890, s 1(4).

[1414] According to Vaughan Williams J during argument in *Re New Terras Tin Mining Co* [1894] 2 Ch 344 at p 347, the change of wording from 'engaged in working' to 'formed for working' restored the jurisdiction which had been decided in *Re East Botallack Consolidated Mining Co Ltd* (1864) 34 LJ Ch 81 but disapproved in *Re Silver Valley Mines* (1881) 18 ChD 472.

to do so.[1415] The Vice-Warden's power to allow the transfer of the case to what by then was the Chancery Division of the High Court was repealed.[1416] Following a decline in its business, the jurisdiction of the Vice-Warden's Court was transferred to the Cornwall County Court.[1417] The Companies Act 1928 gave concurrent jurisdiction over companies formed for working mines within the stannaries to the court exercising stannaries jurisdiction and the High Court.[1418] The last active cost-book mining company converted to a registered company in 1920.[1419] All references in the Companies Acts to stannaries and cost-book companies were repealed, as obsolete, on 1 July 1985 following a recommendation by the Law Commission.[1420] But there is still a reference in IA 1986, s 226(3), to winding up unregistered companies engaged in or formed for working mines within the stannaries.

[1415] *Dunbar v Harvey* [1913] 2 Ch 530 confirmed that the Vice-Warden's Court had exclusive jurisdiction.
[1416] Companies (Winding Up) Act 1890, sch 2.
[1417] Stannaries Court (Abolition) Act 1896; Order of the Lord Chancellor dated 16 December 1896 (SR & O 1896/1106). Now the County Court (Stannaries Court (Abolition) Act 1896, s 1(1A)).
[1418] Companies Act 1928, s 56(4); Companies Act 1929, s 163(4); Companies Act 1948, s 218(4).
[1419] Pennington, *Stannary Law*, p 195.
[1420] Companies Consolidation (Consequential Provisions) Act 1985, s 28; Law Commission, *Statute Law Revision: Eleventh Report. Obsolete Provisions in the Companies Act 1948* (Law Com No 135, Cmnd 9236) (London: HMSO, 1984).

2

PRESENTATION OF A WINDING-UP PETITION

Winding-up Petitions

Compulsory Winding Up must be Ordered under IA 1986

2.1 Court orders which have the effect of winding up companies' affairs but which are not winding-up orders or comparable insolvency procedures[1] have been deprecated. A winding

---

[1] See 1.36–1.42.

up which is not ordered under one of those procedures will not be carried out under the extensive provisions of the Insolvency Act 1986 (IA 1986) and the Insolvency Rules 1986 (IR 1986), which provide important safeguards for all interested parties.

In *Bakal v Petursson*[2] a member of a company had brought a derivative action[3] (to which **2.2** the company was formally a co-defendant) to recover assets which had been fraudulently transferred. The Manitoba Court of Appeal had appointed a receiver of the company to collect those assets, realize them and distribute the proceeds to the shareholders. The Supreme Court of Canada varied this order limiting the receiver's task to taking charge of the company's assets and protecting the company's property. Locke J observed, at p 458, that the Court of Appeal's order had assigned to the receiver functions properly exercisable by a liquidator upon the winding up of a company and proceeded on the assumption that the company was not to continue its business, which was a matter to be determined by the shareholders not a court hearing an action[4] against the company. In *Re Swallow Footwear Ltd*[5] an order made by the Queen's Bench Division, on the application of a person claiming to be an unsecured creditor of the company, appointing a receiver of the company and ordering the receiver to sell all the company's assets and bring the proceeds into court was described as an irregular substitute for a winding-up order by Roxburgh J, who made a winding-up order on the petition of another creditor. In *Re Brian Cassidy Electrical Industries Pty Ltd*[6] McLelland J refused to sanction an arrangement between a company and its creditors because the scheme would have taken the place of a winding up. In *Re Full Cup International Trading Ltd*[7] a member of a company, who had presented a petition for the relief of unfairly prejudicial conduct of the company's affairs, had been appointed receiver of the company by the court. On hearing the unfair prejudice petition, Ferris J declined to make any order under what is now the Companies Act 2006, s 996, but indicated that he would make a winding-up order if the petition were amended to ask for one, but added[8] that he was not willing 'to continue the receivership indefinitely as an alternative to winding up'. His Lordship gave leave for the petition to be amended to ask for a winding-up order, and a provisional liquidator was appointed about a month later. The petitioner appealed, saying that he did not want a winding up, but the appeal was dismissed.[9]

There is an exception when a winding-up or bankruptcy petition has been presented against **2.3** a member of an insolvent partnership. The court may apply any provisions of the Insolvent Partnerships Order 1994 (IPO 1994) to the administration of the joint estate of the partnership.[10] So the court may direct that the joint estate is to be administered as if a winding-up order had been made under IPO 1994, provided such an order could have been made.[11] An

---

[2] [1953] 4 DLR 449.

[3] Derivative actions are now called derivative claims in the United Kingdom.

[4] What in England and Wales would now be called a Part 7 claim.

[5] (1956) *The Times*, 23 October 1956.

[6] (1984) 9 ACLR 140.

[7] [1995] BCC 682.

[8] At p 694.

[9] Sub nom *Antoniades v Wong* [1997] 2 BCLC 419.

[10] IA 1986, s 168(5A) and (5B) (where a winding-up petition has been presented), and s 303(2A) and (2C) (where a bankruptcy petition has been presented).

[11] *Official Receiver v Hollens* [2007] EWHC 753 (Ch), [2007] Bus LR 1402.

application may be made by the official receiver, any responsible insolvency practitioner[12] or any other interested person.[13]

Originating Process for a Winding-up Order

2.4 An application for an order that a company be wound up by the court under IA 1986 must be made by petition[14] and, if winding up is ordered, it will normally be deemed to have commenced when the petition was presented.[15] Winding up may not be sought among other remedies in an ordinary claim.[16] As the requirement for application by petition is imposed by statute, the court has no power under the Civil Procedure Rules 1998 (CPR) to waive a failure to comply with it.[17]

2.5 There are three exceptions to the requirement for a petition:

(a) A court hearing an administration application, energy administration application, energy supply company administration application, postal administration application or FMI administration application may treat the application as a winding-up petition and make a winding-up order on it.[18]

(b) An application by a member State liquidator to convert a voluntary arrangement or an administration into a winding up by the court is made by application notice.[19]

(c) On an application (which must be made by Part 8 claim form) under the Companies Act 2006, s 758, the court may, in certain circumstances, make an order for the compulsory winding up of a company which has contravened the prohibition on public offers by private companies.[20]

All these exceptions involve bypassing the requirements for gazetting and payment of a deposit for the official receiver's fee which apply to an application by petition.

2.6 In *Deputy Commissioner of Taxation v Woodings*[21] Wallwork J interpreted a general power in the Corporations Act 2001 (Australia), s 447A(1), to 'make such order as [the court] thinks appropriate about how [a part of the Act dealing with administration] is to operate in relation to a particular company' as including a power to order a company in administration to be wound up on the application of a creditor. It is questionable whether a power given to facilitate the implementation of the administration procedure can be used to implement winding up and it is unlikely that the similar provision in IA 1986, sch B1, para 74, would be interpreted in that way. However, it is possible that the powers given to the court to 'make

---

[12] The liquidator of a corporate member or the trustee of the estate of an individual member (IA 1986, s 436).

[13] IA 1986, ss 168(5B) and 303(2C).

[14] IA 1986, s 124; *McRae v Western Ice and Cold Storage Ltd* (1962) 38 WWR NS 484; *Rymark (Australia) Development Consultants Pty Ltd v Mahoney's Constructions Pty Ltd* [1972] VR 735; *Re Brooke Marine Ltd* [1988] BCLC 546.

[15] IA 1986, s 129(2); see 5.277–5.302.

[16] *Mirras v Chronis* [1939] 1 WWR 158; *McDougall v Gamble* [1942] OWN 303; *Tung Ah Leek v Perunding DJA Sdn Bhd* [2005] 3 MLJ 667.

[17] *Re Osea Road Camp Sites Ltd* [2004] EWHC 2437 (Ch), [2005] 1 WLR 760.

[18] IA 1986, sch B1, para 13(1)(e); Energy Act 2004, s 157(1)(e), applied to energy supply company administration by the Energy Act 2011, s 96; Postal Services Act 2011, s 71(1)(e); Financial Services (Banking Reform) Act 2013, s 117(3)(e).

[19] See 10.23 and 10.64.

[20] See 8.519–8.521.

[21] (1995) 13 WAR 189.

any order it thinks appropriate' when ending administration[22] may include a power to make a winding-up order, as these powers are not limited to making orders for the purposes of the administration.[23] A court considering exercising the power in this way must consider whether it is appropriate to bypass the requirements for gazetting and payment of a deposit for the official receiver's fee which apply to an application by petition.

Petitions

According to *Odgers on High Court Pleading and Practice*,[24] at pp 386–7:   **2.7**

> A petition is a written application, in the nature of a pleading, setting out a party's case in detail and made[25] in open court. . . .
>
> It . . . sets out the facts upon which the petitioner relies in consecutively numbered paragraphs in the manner of a statement of claim.

A petition must contain all necessary allegations in a form which is sufficient to enable the **2.8** court to make the requisite findings and consider the appropriate order.[26] See 2.186–2.239.

A petition is not a 'statement of case' for the purposes of the CPR.[27] Similarly, a petition **2.9** was not a 'pleading' for the purposes of the Rules of the Supreme Court 1965.[28] But the provisions of the CPR and related practice directions concerning statements of case apply to winding-up petitions[29] with any necessary modifications, except so far as inconsistent with IR 1986.[30] See 3.69 (striking out), 3.135 (supply of documents to a non-party from court records), 3.207 (amendment of petition) and 8.480 (verification of contributory's petition). A petition of any kind is a 'claim' for the purposes of CPR, Part 6.[31] However, as far as winding-up petitions are concerned, apart from the provisions on service out of the jurisdiction,[32] Part 6 only applies to contributories' petitions.[33]

A winding-up petition can refer to only one company because a winding-up order can refer **2.10** to only one company.[34] A petitioner seeking to wind up a group of companies must present a separate petition for each company in the group.[35] However, the rules permit the petitioner to provide one statement of truth verifying several petitions.[36] There must be a photocopy for each petition and the statement of truth must refer to all the companies by name.

---

[22] IA 1986, sch B1, paras 79(4)(d) and 81(3)(d).

[23] *Re Mark One (Oxford Street) plc* [1999] 1 WLR 1445.

[24] 23rd edn by D B Casson (London: Sweet & Maxwell, 1991).

[25] That is, put before the court which is hearing the case.

[26] *Re Richard Pitt and Sons Pty Ltd* (1979) 4 ACLR 459 at p 478; *Re Jinro (HK) International Ltd* [2004] 2 HKLRD 221 at pp 224–5.

[27] CPR, r 2.3(1); *Investment Invoice Financing Ltd v Limehouse Board Mills Ltd* [2006] EWCA Civ 9, [2006] 1 WLR 985, at [36].

[28] RSC, ord 1, r 4(1), definition of 'pleading'; *Re Unisoft Group Ltd (No 3)* [1994] 1 BCLC 609 at p 613. Nor is it a 'pleading' for the purposes of the Rules of the High Court (Hong Kong) (*Re Jinro (HK) International Ltd* [2004] 2 HKLRD 221 at p 224).

[29] And administration and bankruptcy petitions.

[30] IR 1986, r 7.51A(2). See *Paulin v Paulin* [2009] EWCA Civ 221, [2010] 1 WLR 1057, at [44].

[31] CPR, r 6.2(c).

[32] See 3.3 and 3.30.

[33] See 8.492.

[34] *Re Shields Marine Insurance Co, Lee and Moor's Case* (1867) 17 LT 308.

[35] *Re a Company* [1984] BCLC 307; *Tam Shuk Yin Anny v Choi Kwok Chan* [2005] 4 HKLRD 375. The court should be asked to direct that the petitions are heard together or consecutively.

[36] IR 1986, r 4.12(7).

2.11 The court handles a large number of winding-up petitions each year and the work can be done efficiently only if parties adhere to the rules of procedure. Parties who do not comply with the rules may be ordered to pay other parties' costs or, if petitioning, may have their petitions struck out.[37]

Juridical Classification of Winding-up Petitions

Action, claim, suit, proceeding

2.12 An application for a winding-up order is a 'proceeding'.[38] It is a 'civil proceeding'.[39] It is a proceeding under IA 1986 and so winding-up petitions are 'insolvency proceedings' for the purposes of IR 1986.[40] Describing winding-up proceedings as insolvency proceedings does not allow for the fact that the proceedings may be taken against solvent as well as insolvent companies.

2.13 The phrase 'suit and legal process'[41] comprehends presentation of a petition for a winding-up order.[42]

2.14 In England, although a power to 'sue' did not include a power to apply for a commission in bankruptcy,[43] it has been held that a person petitioning for the winding up of a company is 'suing'[44] so that a winding-up petition is a 'suit'.[45] But in Victoria it has been held that a winding-up petition is not a suit[46] and in New Zealand that presenting a winding-up petition is not suing.[47] In England the phrase 'commence... actions, suits and other proceedings', commonly used in powers of attorney, was held to cover commencing proceedings in bankruptcy by signing a petition,[48] but in Victoria it was held that a winding-up petition is not a proceeding that is *ejusdem generis* with an action or suit.[49]

2.15 An application to wind up a company is not an 'action'.[50] In particular, it is not an 'action' as that word is defined in the Senior Courts Act 1981, s 151 ('any civil proceedings commenced by writ or in any other manner prescribed by rules of court'), because the manner in which it is presented is prescribed by IA 1986, s 124, not by rules of court.[51]

---

[37] Per Nourse J in *Re Shusella Ltd* [1983] BCLC 505.

[38] *Re Laxon and Co* [1892] 3 Ch 31; *Re Auckland Piano Agency Ltd* [1928] GLR 249; *Re Excelsior Textile Supply Pty Ltd* [1964] VR 574; *Re Testro Bros Consolidated Ltd* [1965] VR 18; *Re Laceward Ltd* [1981] 1 WLR 133; *Re Cayman Capital Trust Co* [1988–9] CILR 444; *Re Unisoft Group Ltd (No 1)* [1993] BCLC 1292.

[39] *Jaska v Jaska* (1996) 141 DLR (4th) 385.

[40] IR 1986, r 13.7.

[41] Which is regularly used in statutory instruments conferring immunities and privileges on international organizations.

[42] *Re International Tin Council* [1987] Ch 419, point not considered on appeal.

[43] *Guthrie v Fisk* (1824) 3 B & C 178. But the phrasal verb 'sue out' was usually used at that time for obtaining a commission of bankruptcy, as it was for obtaining a commission of lunacy or a writ of execution.

[44] *Re Waterloo Life etc Assurance Co (No 1)* (1862) 31 Beav 586.

[45] Shakespeare referred to petitioners (for love) 'suing' in *Venus and Adonis*, line 356. Whether Shakespeare knew enough about the law to use its terminology with technical accuracy has long been the subject of lively debate. For recent discussion see B J Sokol and Mary Sokol, *Shakespeare's Legal Language* (London: Continuum, 2004).

[46] *Re Provincial and Suburban Bank Ltd* (1879) 5 VLR (E) 159 at pp 166–7.

[47] *Re Gilbert Machinery Co (No 1)* (1906) 26 NZLR 47.

[48] *Re Wallace, ex parte Wallace* (1884) 14 QBD 22.

[49] *Re Provincial and Suburban Bank Ltd* (1879) 5 VLR (E) 159 at pp 166–7.

[50] *Re National Funds Assurance Co Ltd* (1876) 4 ChD 305.

[51] *Re Simpkin Marshall Ltd* [1959] Ch 229 per Wynn-Parry J at p 233.

Likewise, an application for an individual to be made bankrupt is not an action.[52] But the extent of a power to recover money by 'action' depends on the purpose for which the power is given, and, if given for the purpose of collecting taxes, it includes a power to petition for bankruptcy.[53] In the CPR the term 'action' is replaced by 'claim'. A winding-up petition is not a claim or counterclaim,[54] except for the purposes of CPR, Part 6.[55]

Where 'action' is defined as 'any civil proceeding', an application for a winding-up order is an action because it is a civil proceeding.[56] In the Limitation Act 1980, s 38(1), 'action' is defined as including 'any proceeding in a court of law', unless the context otherwise requires. Depending on the nature of the debt on which a creditor's winding-up petition is based, the petition may be an action founded on simple contract for the purposes of s 5[57] or an action to recover a sum for the purposes of s 9(1).[58] It is submitted that, by analogy, a winding-up petition based on a specialty debt is an action on a specialty for the purposes of s 8. But a winding-up petition cannot be an action upon a judgment for the purposes of s 24(1). This is because s 24(1) is concerned only with fresh proceedings brought in respect of a claim on which judgment has already been obtained and brought for the purpose of obtaining a second judgment which can be executed. An application for a winding-up order does not serve this purpose and therefore is not an action upon a judgment as that term is used in s 24(1).[59]

2.16

In some contexts, 'action', though not expressly defined, may be construed as having a wide meaning[60] which includes a winding-up or bankruptcy petition. This is the case with the Solicitors Act 1974, s 61 (enforcement of contentious business agreements)[61] and s 69 (action to recover solicitor's costs).[62]

2.17

It would seem, therefore, that a winding-up petition may be properly described as a proceeding or as a legal process, and, at least in England and Wales, as a suit, but not as a claim or counterclaim. Whether it is an action depends on the context in which that term is used.

2.18

Against the company

An application for an order that a company be wound up by the court, unless it is made by the company itself, is a proceeding 'against the company',[63] though not against the members of the company.[64] However, a creditor's petition is not a *lis inter partes*[65] for the benefit of the petitioner as against the company: it is the invoking of a class remedy

2.19

---

[52] *Ex parte Sutton* (1805) 11 Ves Jun 163; *Ex parte Steele* (1809) 16 Ves Jun 161 at p 166; *Re Howell, ex parte Howell* (1812) 1 Rose 312; *Re Ford, ex parte Ford* (1838) 3 Deac 494.

[53] *Re Smith* (1908) 8 SR (NSW) 246.

[54] *Best Beat Ltd v Rossall* [2006] EWHC 1494 (Comm), [2006] BPIR 1357; *Salford Estates (No 2) Ltd v Altomart Ltd* [2014] EWCA Civ 1575, LTL 9/12/2014.

[55] CPR, r 6.2(c); see 2.9.

[56] *Jaska v Jaska* (1996) 141 DLR (4th) 385.

[57] *Re Cases of Taffs Well Ltd* [1992] Ch 179 at p 188.

[58] *Re Karnos Property Co Ltd* [1989] BCLC 340.

[59] *Ridgeway Motors (Isleworth) Ltd v ALTS Ltd* [2005] EWCA Civ 92, [2005] 1 WLR 2871.

[60] *Bradlaugh v Clarke* (1883) 8 App Cas 354 at p 361; *Re Smith* (1908) 8 SR (NSW) 246 at p 249.

[61] *Wilson v Specter Partnership* [2007] EWHC 133 (Ch), [2007] BPIR 649, at [12].

[62] *Re a Debtor (No 88 of 1991)* [1993] Ch 286 at p 291; see Angharad J T Start, 'Fees by statutory demand' (1992) 142 NLJ 1121.

[63] *Re Excelsior Textile Supply Pty Ltd* [1964] VR 574; *Re Testro Bros Consolidated Ltd* [1965] VR 18 at p 31.

[64] *Four Pillars Enterprises Co Ltd v Beiersdorf AG* [1999] 1 SLR 737.

[65] Lawsuit between parties.

for the benefit of the petitioner and other members of the class.[66] A contributory's petition under s 122(1)(g), the just and equitable clause, 'is not in truth hostile litigation by a shareholder against a company. It is in truth a claim by a shareholder based upon wrongful acts by other shareholders or directors which have amounted to some equitable mal-doing'.[67] Often such a petition is just as much adversarial litigation *inter partes*, between two shareholders or groups of shareholders, as any claim in the Commercial Court.[68]

Winding-up Order on Court's Own Initiative

2.20 It has been held that in a thoroughly exceptional case, the court may make a winding-up order on its own initiative in proceedings where no winding-up petition (or application which can be treated as a winding-up petition) has been presented.[69] A winding-up order may be made where a petition has not been presented if:

> the circumstances are so plain, and the inevitability, appropriateness and urgency of a winding-up order are so clear, that it would be a denial of justice, and a waste of time and money, for the court to refuse to make an order there and then.[70]

It may be done where it is:

> virtually inconceivable that anyone would even consider opposing it, and, even if there was opposition, [it would be] inconceivable that the court would do anything other than make a winding-up order.[71]

It follows that the court should not make a winding-up order without a winding-up petition, which has been publicly notified, unless all parties to the proceedings agree that a winding-up order should be made. Persons who are entitled to object to the making of a winding-up order are entitled to assume that an order cannot be made without public notification of the petition for the order so that they will have an opportunity to raise their objections in court.[72]

2.21 The claimed source of the power to order the winding up of a company without a winding-up petition is that IA 1986, s 122, states the circumstances in which a registered company may be wound up by the court, so if the court finds those circumstances exist it may make a winding-up order, and the provisions for presentation and hearing of winding-up petitions do not preclude the court from making an order of its own motion.[73] But it may be objected that there is a more fundamental principle that the court has no jurisdiction to exercise a statutory power except on the application of a person qualified by the statute to make it,[74] and IA 1986 is drafted in the context of that principle; and if Parliament intended to give the court power to make an order on the court's own motion, that power would have been

---

[66] *Re Southbourne Sheet Metal Co Ltd* [1992] BCLC 361 per Harman J at p 364.

[67] Per Harman J in *Re Hydrosan Ltd* [1991] BCLC 418 at p 421.

[68] *Re Harrods (Buenos Aires) Ltd* [1992] Ch 72 per Dillon LJ at p 108; see also per Stocker LJ at pp 120–1 and Bingham LJ at p 127.

[69] *Lancefield v Lancefield* [2002] BPIR 1108 (Neuberger J).

[70] *Lancefield v Lancefield* at p 1112.

[71] *Lancefield v Lancefield* at p 1112. For examples see *Re BTR (UK) Ltd* [2012] EWHC 2398 (Ch), [2012] BCC 864, at 10.36–10.37 and *Re Marches Credit Union Ltd* [2013] EWHC 1731 (Ch), LTL 2/7/2013, at 11.14.

[72] *Lancefield v Lancefield* at p 1112.

[73] *Lancefield v Lancefield* at pp 1110–12.

[74] *Deloitte & Touche AG v Johnson* [1999] 1 WLR 1605 per Lord Millett at p 1611.

expressly stated.[75] Moreover, there is no provision for payment of a deposit for the official receiver's fee if there is no petition.[76]

In earlier cases, judges stated that, in their view, a company involved in proceedings before **2.22** them should be wound up, but said that this was not possible because they were not proceedings on a winding-up petition and clearly the judges did not consider that the court could have a power to make a winding-up order of its own motion.[77] Those cases would anyway not satisfy the criteria set out in 2.20 for making a winding-up order of the court's own motion as there was neither urgency nor absence of controversy. It may be appropriate for the judge in such a situation to refer the papers in the case to the Secretary of State or an appropriate regulatory authority.

Circumstances in which a Winding-up Order may be Made

Prescribed Circumstances must Exist

For all the various types of entity which may be wound up by the court under IA 1986, **2.23** the relevant legislation specifies the circumstances in which that type of entity may be wound up.[78] These are usually called the 'grounds' for winding up. The court does not have authority to wind up a company in any other circumstances. As James LJ said in *Re Irrigation Co of France*:[79] 'A compulsory winding up can only be given in one of the cases pointed out by the statute'.[80] The lists usually state a number of specific circumstances, such as being unable to pay debts, in which an entity may be wound up and end with the circumstance that 'the court is of the opinion that it is just and equitable that the company should be wound up'. This 'just and equitable clause' allows a petitioner to invite the court to find that other circumstances exist which make it just and equitable that the company should be wound up. Whether it is just and equitable that a company should be wound up is an inference of law from the facts of the situation.[81] How the just and equitable clause is applied in practice is discussed at 8.131–8.431 (contributories' petitions) and 9.19–9.71 (public interest petitions).

One, at least, of the specific circumstances prescribed in the relevant legislation, or the **2.24** circumstances which make it just and equitable that the company should be wound up, must exist at the time of hearing the petition.[82] It should also have existed at the time of

---

[75] See, for example, IA 1986, s 251M(7)(b) (power given to the court to make one kind of order under the section on the court's own motion, if particular circumstances arise).

[76] See 2.254–2.256.

[77] *Hammond v Ontario Silver Black Foxes Ltd* (1924) 27 OWN 303 (company was 'a bare-faced fraud' but could not be wound up in an ordinary action); *Re Mascot Home Furnishers Pty Ltd* [1970] VR 593 at p 594 (on an application to sanction a scheme of arrangement which involved the company continuing in business despite being insolvent, so that it could be sold as a tax loss, the court could not order the company to be wound up). Gillard J in *Re Mascot Home Furnishers Pty Ltd* at p 594 expressly stated that a court cannot wind up a company on its own initiative (*sua sponte*, by itself).

[78] See 2.27–2.53.

[79] (1871) LR 6 Ch App 176 at p 184.

[80] See also per Kindersley V-C in *Re London Conveyance Co* (1853) 1 Drew 465 and Lord Mackay in *Galbraith v Merito Shipping Co Ltd* 1947 SC 446 at p 458.

[81] Per Jessel MR during argument in *Re Rica Gold Washing Co* (1879) 11 ChD 36.

[82] *Re Fildes Bros Ltd* [1970] 1 WLR 592; *Syd Mannix Pty Ltd v Leserv Constructions Pty Ltd* [1971] 1 NSWLR 788.

petitioning since the petition must state the facts from which it may be concluded that the circumstance or circumstances exist[83] and must be verified by a statement of truth,[84] and, if a winding up is ordered, it is, in most cases, deemed to commence at the time of presentation of the petition.[85] But it is possible to make a winding-up order on a ground that was introduced by amendment after the petition was presented.[86] The view that only the circumstances at the time of presentation of the petition are relevant[87] is wrong: in particular, the legislation expresses some of the circumstances in the present tense[88] showing that they must exist at the time of the hearing.[89]

2.25   It may be possible to amend a petition to state a ground for seeking the winding-up order which has arisen only since the petition was presented.[90]

2.26   The fact that a petition to wind up a company has been dismissed does not prevent the court hearing another petition presented by a different petitioner submitting different evidence.[91]

Registered Companies

Insolvency Act 1986, s 122(1)

2.27   The circumstances in which a registered company may be wound up by the court are listed in IA 1986, s 122(1):

> A company may be wound up by the court if—
> (a) the company has by special resolution resolved that the company be wound up by the court,[92]
> (b) being a public company which was registered as such on its original incorporation, the company has not been issued with a trading certificate under section 761 of the Companies Act 2006 (requirement as to minimum share capital) and more than a year has expired since it was so registered,[93]
> (c) it is an old public company, within the meaning of Schedule 3 to the Companies Act 2006 (Consequential Amendments, Transitional Provisions and Savings) Order 2009,[94]
> (d) the company does not commence its business within a year from its incorporation or suspends its business for a whole year,[95]
> (e) [*repealed*]
> (f) the company is unable to pay its debts,[96]

---

[83] See 2.202–2.212.

[84] See 2.218–2.223.

[85] *Re Catholic Publishing and Bookselling Co Ltd* (1864) 2 De G J & S 116 per Turner LJ at p 120; *Syd Mannix Pty Ltd v Leserv Constructions Pty Ltd* [1971] 1 NSWLR 788; *Re Kailis Groote Eylandt Fisheries Pty Ltd* (1977) 17 SASR 35; *Comalco Aluminium Ltd v Ohtsu Tyre and Rubber Co (Aust) Pty Ltd* (1983) 8 ACLR 330; *Dallhold Investments Pty Ltd v Gold Resources Australia Ltd* (1991) 31 FCR 587 at pp 589–90.

[86] See 2.25.

[87] *Re North Sydney Investment and Tramway Co Ltd* (1892) 3 BC (NSW) 81.

[88] For example, IA 1986, s 122(1)(c), (f) and (g).

[89] *Re Fildes Bros Ltd* [1970] 1 WLR 592 per Megarry J at p 597.

[90] *Re Richbell Strategic Holdings Ltd* [1997] 2 BCLC 429; see 3.209.

[91] *Re Manitoba Commission Co* (1913) 9 DLR 436.

[92] See 8.91–8.92 and 11.4–11.6.

[93] See 8.93–8.95.

[94] SI 2009/1941. Because of an error in SI 2009/1941, its provisions relating to old public companies in England and Wales and Scotland had to be re-enacted and the relevant definition is now in the Companies Act 2006 (Consequential Amendments and Transitional Provisions) Order 2011 (SI 2011/1265), sch 1, para 1. See 8.96–8.97.

[95] See 8.98–8.104.

[96] See 7.74–7.308.

(fa) at the time at which a moratorium for the company under [IA 1986, s 1A] comes to an end, no voluntary arrangement approved under [IA 1986, part 1] has effect in relation to the company,

(g) the court is of the opinion that it is just and equitable that the company should be wound up.[97]

Corporate members of insolvent partnerships

In relation to a petition for the winding up of an insolvent partnership together with the **2.28** winding up of a corporate member or former corporate member,[98] IA 1986, s 122, is modified,[99] so that it refers only to the circumstances in which a corporate member or former corporate member[100] may be wound up.[101] IA 1986, s 122, as modified, is applied to the winding up of a corporate member or former corporate member by IPO 1994, art 8(4), (5), (8) and (9), and art 10(2), (3) and (6). Under IA 1986, s 122, as modified, the only circumstances in which a corporate member or former corporate member may be wound up on a petition under IPO 1994, art 8 or art 10, are:

(a) if it is unable to pay its debts;[102] or

(b) if there is a creditor, by assignment or otherwise, to whom the insolvent partnership is indebted and the corporate member or former corporate member is liable in relation to that debt and at the time at which a moratorium for the insolvent partnership under s 1A[103] comes to an end, no voluntary arrangement approved under part 1 has effect in relation to the insolvent partnership.[104]

Entities Treated as Registered Companies

Building societies

IA 1986, s 122, does not apply to building societies.[105] A building society may be wound **2.29** up in the circumstances set out in the Building Societies Act 1986, s 89(1), which reads as follows:

A building society may be wound up under the applicable winding-up legislation by the court on any of the following grounds in addition to the grounds referred to or specified in section 37(1), that is to say, if—

(a) the society has by special resolution resolved that it be wound up by the court;

(b) the number of members is reduced below ten;

(c) the number of directors is reduced below two;

(d) being a society registered as a building society under [the Building Societies Act 1986] or the [Building Societies Act 1962 or the Building Societies Act 1874 or, in relation to Northern Ireland, the Building Societies Act (Northern Ireland) 1967], the society has

---

[97] See 8.131–8.431.
[98] Such a petition may be presented by a non-member under IPO 1994, art 8, or by a member under art 10. An art 8 petition can ask for the winding up of a former corporate member, but an art 10 petition cannot.
[99] By IPO 1994, sch 4, para 6(a).
[100] In relation to art 8 petitions only.
[101] IA 1986, s 221(5), as modified by IPO 1994, sch 4, para 3 (in relation to art 8 petitions); IA 1986, s 221(5), as modified by IPO 1994, sch 6, para 4 (in relation to art 10 petitions).
[102] See 7.117.
[103] Which is applied to insolvent partnerships by IPO 1994, art 4(1). IA 1986, s 1A, is applied to insolvent partnerships as modified by IPO 1994, sch 1.
[104] See 10.17.
[105] Building Societies Act 1986, sch 15, para 16.

not been given permission under Part 4A of the Financial Services and Markets Act 2000 to accept deposits and more than three years has expired since it was so registered;

(e) the society's permission under Part 4A of the Financial Services and Markets Act 2000 to accept deposits has been cancelled (and no such permission has subsequently been given to it);

(f) the society exists for an illegal purpose;

(g) the society is unable to pay its debts; or

(h) the court is of the opinion that it is just and equitable that the society should be wound up.

For the meaning of 'the applicable winding-up legislation' see 1.120. The purpose or principal purpose of a building society established under the Building Societies Act 1986 must, by s 5(1)(a) of the Act, be that of making loans which are secured on residential property and are funded substantially by its members. Section 89(4) specifies that s 89(1)(f) (society existing for an illegal purpose) is satisfied if a building society exists after its purpose or principal purpose has ceased to be that required by s 5(1)(a).

2.30   Although the opening words of s 89(1) refer to 'the grounds referred to or specified in section 37(1)', it is submitted that s 37(1) does not specify additional circumstances in which the court may wind up a building society but rather circumstances in which the Financial Conduct Authority (FCA) or the Prudential Regulation Authority (PRA) may petition for winding up, and it is therefore considered at 9.100–9.103.

Charitable incorporated organizations

2.31   Charitable incorporated organizations (CIOs) may be wound up as if they were registered companies.[106] In the application of IA 1986, part 4, to CIOs, the following is substituted for s 122(1):

(1)   A CIO may be wound up by the court if—

   (a) the members of the CIO have passed a resolution that the CIO be wound up by the court ('resolution for court winding up');

   (b) the CIO does not commence its business within a year of its registration in the register of charities or suspends its business for a whole year;

   (c) the CIO is unable to pay its debts;

   (d) at the time when a moratorium for the CIO under section 1A comes to an end, no voluntary arrangement approved under Part 1 has effect in relation to the CIO;

   (e) it is just and equitable in the opinion of the court that the CIO should be wound up.

European cooperative societies

2.32   A European cooperative society (SCE) with a registered office in Great Britain is treated as a registered company for the purposes of winding up.[107] So a winding-up order may be made in the circumstances listed in IA 1986, s 122(1),[108] so far as they are applicable to an SCE, and also in the circumstances listed in Regulation (EC) No 1435/2003. Those are:

(a) breach of art 2(1) (which defines the ways in which an SCE may be formed) and/or art 3(2) (which requires an SCE's subscribed capital to be at least €30,000);[109]

(b) formation of an SCE by merger without scrutiny of legality.[110]

---

[106]   See 1.122.

[107]   See 1.123.

[108]   See 2.27.

[109]   art 73(1).

[110]   arts 34 and 73(1).

European public limited-liability companies

A European public limited-liability company (SE) whose registered office is situated in **2.33**
Great Britain may be wound up as if it were a registered company.[111]

Incorporated friendly societies

IA 1986, s 122, does not apply to incorporated friendly societies.[112] An incorporated friendly **2.34**
society may be wound up in the circumstances set out in the Friendly Societies Act 1992,
s 22(1), which reads as follows:

> An incorporated friendly society may be wound up under the applicable winding-up legisla-
> tion by the court on any of the following grounds, that is to say, if—
> (a) the society has by special resolution resolved that it be wound up by the court;
> (b) the number of members is reduced below seven;
> (c) the number of members of the committee of management is reduced below two;
> (d) the society has not commenced business within a year from its incorporation or has
>   suspended its business for a whole year;
> (e) the society exists for an illegal purpose;
> (f) the society is unable to pay its debts; or
> (g) the court is of the opinion that it is just and equitable that the society should be
>   wound up.

For the meaning of 'the applicable winding-up legislation' see 1.120.

Limited liability partnerships

In the application of IA 1986 to limited liability partnerships,[113] s 122(1) is substituted[114] **2.35**
so that it reads:

> (1) A limited liability partnership may be wound up by the court if—
>   (a) the limited liability partnership has determined that the limited liability partner-
>   ship be wound up by the court,
>   (b) the limited liability partnership does not commence its business within a year from
>   its incorporation or suspends its business for a whole year,
>   (c) the number of members is reduced below two,
>   (d) the limited liability partnership is unable to pay its debts[,]
>   (da) at the time at which a moratorium for the limited liability partnership under sec-
>   tion 1A comes to an end, no voluntary arrangement approved under Part I has
>   effect in relation to the limited liability partnership, [or]
>   (e) the court is of the opinion that it is just and equitable that the limited liability
>   partnership should be wound up.

Registered societies

Registered societies, including credit unions, may be wound up as if they were registered **2.36**
companies.[115] So a winding-up order may be made in the circumstances listed in IA 1986,
s 122(1).[116]

---

[111] See 1.124.
[112] Friendly Societies Act 1992, sch 10, para 19.
[113] By the Limited Liability Partnerships Regulations 2001 (SI 2001/1090), reg 5.
[114] By SI 2001/1090, sch 3, as amended by the Limited Liability Partnerships (Amendment) Regulations
2005 (SI 2005/1989), sch 2, para 6, which, surely by mistake, deletes the comma at the end of para (d) and
does not provide an 'or' at the end of para (da).
[115] See 1.127–1.129.
[116] See 2.27.

Unregistered companies

2.37   IA 1986, s 122, does not apply to unregistered companies.[117] The circumstances in which an unregistered company may be wound up by the court are listed in s 221(5):

> The circumstances in which an unregistered company may be wound up are as follows:
> (a) if the company is dissolved, or has ceased to carry on business, or is carrying on business only for the purpose of winding up its affairs;[118]
> (b) if the company is unable to pay its debts;[119]
> (c) if the court is of opinion that it is just and equitable that the company should be wound up.[120]

2.38   For a relevant scheme,[121] s 221(5)(a) is omitted and para (b) is replaced by:[122]

> (b) if the operator of a relevant scheme is unable to pay the debts of that scheme out of the property subject to it[.]

Insolvent Partnerships

Articles 7 and 9

2.39   The circumstances in which an order to wind up an insolvent partnership may be made on a petition under IPO 1994, art 7 or art 9 (where the petitioner does not also petition for the winding up or bankruptcy of any member or former member of the partnership), are listed in IA 1986, s 221(7), as modified by IPO 1994, sch 3, para 3 (in relation to art 7 petitions), and IA 1986, s 221(7), as modified by IPO 1994, sch 5, para 2 (in relation to art 9 petitions). They are:

(a) if the partnership is dissolved, or has ceased to carry on business, or is carrying on business only for the purpose of winding up its affairs;[123]

(b) if the partnership is unable to pay its debts;[124]

(c) if the court is of the opinion that it is just and equitable that the partnership should be wound up.[125]

2.40   IA 1986, s 122, does not apply to an art 7 or art 9 petition.[126]

Article 8

2.41   The only circumstances in which an order to wind up an insolvent partnership may be made on a petition under IPO 1994, art 8 (where the petitioner also petitions for the winding up or bankruptcy of any member or former member of the partnership), are:[127]

(a) that the partnership is unable to pay its debts;[128]

---

[117] *Re Trans Pacific Insurance Corporation* [2009] NSWSC 308, 71 ACSR 569.
[118] See 8.119–8.130.
[119] See 7.74–7.308.
[120] See 8.131–8.431.
[121] See 1.168.
[122] Collective Investment in Transferable Securities (Contractual Scheme) Regulations 2013 (SI 2013/1388), sch 2, paras 3, 5(a) and part 3.
[123] See 8.119–8.130.
[124] See 7.112–7.115.
[125] See 8.131–8.431.
[126] IA 1986, s 221(6), as modified by IPO 1994, sch 3, para 3 (in relation to art 7 petitions); IA 1986, s 221(6), as modified by IPO 1994, sch 5, para 2 (in relation to art 9 petitions).
[127] IA 1986, s 221(8), as modified by IPO 1994, sch 4, para 3.
[128] See 7.116.

(b) at the time at which a moratorium for the insolvent partnership under IA 1986, s 1A,[129] comes to an end, no voluntary arrangement approved under part 1 has effect in relation to the insolvent partnership.[130]

In relation to an IPO 1994, art 8, petition, IA 1986, s 122, is modified[131] so that it concerns **2.42** only a corporate member or former corporate member.[132]

Article 10

The only circumstance in which an order to wind up an insolvent partnership may be made **2.43** on a petition under IPO 1994, art 10 (where the petitioner, who must be a member of the partnership, also petitions for the winding up or bankruptcy of all members of the partnership), is that the partnership is unable to pay its debts.[133]

In relation to an IPO 1994, art 10, petition, IA 1986, s 122, is modified[134] so that it concerns **2.44** only a corporate member or former corporate member.[135]

European Economic Interest Groupings

Circumstances in which an EEIG may be wound up

A European economic interest grouping (EEIG) is an unregistered company and may be **2.45** wound up under IA 1986, part 5.[136] Where an EEIG is wound up as an unregistered company under IA 1986, part 5, s 221(1) will be modified to provide that all the provisions of Regulation (EEC) No 2137/85 about winding up apply.[137] Accordingly an EEIG, like any unregistered company, can be wound up in the circumstances listed in IA 1986, s 221(5),[138] and also the circumstances listed in Regulation (EEC) No 2137/85. Those are:

(a) infringement of art 3;[139]

(b) infringement of art 12;[140]

(c) infringement of art 31(3);[141]

(d) on the application of a member, 'on just and proper grounds',[142] which, it is submitted, is equivalent to IA 1986, s 221(5)(c) (court's opinion that it is just and equitable to order winding up);[143]

(e) under 'national laws governing insolvency and cessation of payments', which are applied by Regulation (EEC) No 2137/85, art 36, confirming that an EEIG is liable to

---

[129] Which is applied to insolvent partnerships by IPO 1994, art 4(1). IA 1986, s 1A, is applied to insolvent partnerships as modified by IPO 1994, sch 1.

[130] See 10.16.

[131] By IPO 1994, sch 4, para 6(a).

[132] See 2.28.

[133] IA 1986, s 221(8), as modified by IPO 1994, sch 6, para 4. See 7.120.

[134] By IPO 1994, sch 4, para 6(a), as applied by IA 1986, s 221(5)(b), as modified by IPO 1994, sch 6, para 4.

[135] See 2.28.

[136] European Economic Interest Grouping Regulations 1989 (SI 1989/638), reg 8(1).

[137] SI 1989/638, reg 8(1).

[138] See 2.37.

[139] art 32(1). See 2.47.

[140] art 32(1). See 2.48.

[141] art 32(1). See 2.49.

[142] art 32(2).

[143] See 8.131.

be wound up as an unregistered company under IA 1986, s 221(5)(b), where it is unable to pay its debts.

2.46 Also, an EEIG which has its official address in Great Britain may be wound up in the public interest on the application of the Secretary of State.[144]

Infringement of Regulation (EEC) No 2137/85, art 3

2.47 The court must order the winding up of an EEIG in the event of infringement of Regulation (EEC) No 2137/85, art 3, unless its affairs can be and are put in order before the court has delivered a substantive ruling.[145] Article 3 provides that an EEIG must not:

(a) have an activity which is more than ancillary to the economic activities of its members;[146]

(b) exercise, directly or indirectly, a power of management or supervision over its members' own activities or over the activities of another undertaking, in particular in the fields of personnel, finance and investment;[147]

(c) directly or indirectly, on any basis whatsoever, hold shares of any kind in a member undertaking;[148]

(d) hold shares in another undertaking, except so far as is necessary for the achievement of the grouping's objects and on its members' behalf;[149]

(e) employ more than 500 persons;[150]

(f) be used by a company to make a loan to a director of a company, or any person connected with a director, in contravention of national law;[151]

(g) be used for the transfer of any property, movable or immovable, between a company and a director, or any person connected with a director, except to the extent allowed by national laws governing companies;[152]

(h) be a member of another EEIG.[153]

Infringement of Regulation (EEC) No 2137/85, art 12

2.48 The court must order the winding up of an EEIG in the event of infringement of Regulation (EEC) No 2137/85, art 12, unless its affairs can be and are put in order before the court has delivered a substantive ruling.[154] Article 12 provides that an EEIG's official address must be situated in the EU and must be either where the grouping has its central administration or where one of its members has its central administration (or, in the case of a natural person, his or her principal activity), provided the grouping carries on an activity there.

---

[144] European Economic Interest Grouping Regulations 1989 (SI 1989/638), reg 7(2) and (2A), exercising the member State option provided in Regulation (EEC) No 2137/85, art 32(3). See 9.10.

[145] Regulation (EEC) No 2137/85, art 32(1).

[146] art 3(1).

[147] art 3(2)(a).

[148] art 3(2)(b).

[149] art 3(2)(b).

[150] art 3(2)(c).

[151] art 3(2)(d), in which 'the making of a loan' includes entering into any transaction or arrangement of similar effect. See the Companies Act 2006, ss 197–214, for restrictions on loans by companies to directors or connected persons.

[152] Regulation (EEC) No 2137/85, art 3(2)(d); see the Companies Act 2006, ss 190–196, for restrictions on substantial property transactions between a company and a director or connected person.

[153] Regulation (EEC) No 2137/85, art 3(2)(e).

[154] Regulation (EEC) No 2137/85, art 32(1).

Infringement of Regulation (EEC) No 2137/85, art 31(3)

The court must order the winding up of an EEIG in the event of infringement of Regulation **2.49**
(EEC) No 2137/85, art 31(3), unless its affairs can be and are put in order before the court
has delivered a substantive ruling.[155] Article 31(3) requires the members or remaining member of an EEIG to wind it up voluntarily if the conditions laid down in art 4(2) are no longer
fulfilled. Those conditions require an EEIG to have at least two members, who must have
their central administrations (or, in the case of a natural person, principal activity) in different member States.

European Groupings of Territorial Cooperation

A European grouping of territorial cooperation which has its registered office in the United **2.50**
Kingdom (a UK EGTC) is an unregistered company and may be wound up under IA 1986,
part 5.[156] Where a UK EGTC is wound up as an unregistered company under IA 1986,
part 5, s 221(1) will be modified to provide that all the provisions of Regulation (EC) No
1082/2006 about winding up apply.[157] Accordingly a UK EGTC, like any unregistered
company, can be wound up in the circumstances listed in IA 1986, s 221(5),[158] and also the
circumstances listed in Regulation (EC) No 1082/2006. Those are:

(a) the EGTC no longer complies with the requirements laid down in art 1(2) (objective of
an EGTC);[159]
(b) the EGTC no longer complies with the requirements laid down in art 7 (tasks), in particular, it is acting outside the confines of the tasks laid down in art 7.[160]

The court must order winding up if it finds that a UK EGTC no longer complies with any of **2.51**
these requirements.[161] It may allow the EGTC time to rectify the situation, but if the EGTC
fails to do so in the time allowed, the court must order it to be wound up.[162]

Lloyd's Reorganization

For the special circumstances in which a member or former member of Lloyd's may be **2.52**
wound up when a Lloyd's market reorganization order is in force see 10.73–10.77.

Bank and Building Society Insolvency

The court may make a bank insolvency order in respect of a bank, or a building society **2.53**
insolvency order in respect of a building society, if satisfied that:[163]

(a) the bank or building society has eligible depositors;[164] and

---

[155] Regulation (EEC) No 2137/85, art 32(1).
[156] European Grouping of Territorial Cooperation Regulations 2007 (SI 2007/1949), reg 7.
[157] SI 2007/1949, sch, para 7.
[158] See 2.37.
[159] art 14(1).
[160] art 14(1).
[161] art 14(1).
[162] art 14(2).
[163] Banking Act 2009, s 97(1) and (2). Section 97(1) is applied to building society insolvency by the Building Societies Act 1986, s 90C, and the Building Societies (Insolvency and Special Administration) Order 2009 (SI 2009/805), sch 1, para 11.
[164] For the definition of 'eligible depositor' see 1.20.

(b) if the applicant is the Bank of England or the PRA,[165] either:
  (i) the bank or building society is unable, or likely to become unable, to pay its debts (referred to in the legislation[166] as Ground A); or
  (ii) the winding up of the bank or building society would be fair (Ground C); or
(c) in relation to a bank only, if the applicant is the Secretary of State, the winding up of the bank would be in the public interest (Ground B) and would be fair (Ground C).

The word 'fair' is used as a shorter modern equivalent of the expression 'just and equitable'[167] and is not intended to exclude jurisprudence concerning the application of that expression.[168]

Persons with Standing to Petition

Need for Standing

Principle

2.54 The general principle is that a court will not order the winding up of a company unless the person applying for the order is given standing to do so by the legislation that applies to the company.[169] In *Re MTI Trading Systems Ltd*[170] Saville LJ said, at p 403:

> before the court will bring the company to an end, it will have to be satisfied, save perhaps in a wholly exceptional case, that the person seeking to achieve that objective has the requisite status to petition the court. Whether that can be described as a limitation on the jurisdiction of the court, or as an obvious common-sense rule of practice, does not to my mind really matter.

2.55 Subsequently, the Privy Council (per Lord Millett) said,[171] in relation to the statutory power to order the removal of a liquidator:

> This goes to the jurisdiction of the court, for the court has no jurisdiction to exercise a statutory power except on the application of a person qualified by the statute to make it.

2.56 The Privy Council also identified a general rule that a person asking the court to exercise any power must show a legitimate interest in the relief sought.[172]

2.57 The persons who are given standing by the various legislative provisions are listed in 2.69–2.89. The court cannot extend standing to anyone else.[173] In particular, it has no inherent jurisdiction to override a statutory provision that only certain persons have

---

[165] The FCA in the case of an FCA-regulated bank or building society (Banking Act 2009, s 129A, applied by the Building Societies Act 1986, s 90C). For the definitions of 'FCA-regulated bank' and 'FCA-regulated building society' see 1.233–1.236.
[166] Banking Act 2009, s 96(1). Applied to building society insolvency with modifications by the Building Societies Act 1986, s 90C, and the Building Societies (Insolvency and Special Administration) Order 2009 (SI 2009/805), sch 1, para 10.
[167] As used in IA 1986, ss 122(1)(g) and 221(5)(c); see 8.131–8.257.
[168] Banking Act 2009, s 93(8). Applied to building society insolvency by the Building Societies Act 1986, s 90C.
[169] *Mann v Goldstein* [1968] 1 WLR 1091 at p 1094.
[170] [1998] BCC 400.
[171] *Deloitte & Touche AG v Johnson* [1999] 1 WLR 1605 at p 1611.
[172] See 2.127–2.141.
[173] *Re H L Bolton Engineering Co Ltd* [1956] Ch 577; *Re Parmalat Capital Finance Ltd* 2006 CILR 480 at p 491.

standing.[174] But in a thoroughly exceptional case, the court may make a winding-up order on its own initiative.[175]

A person is not given standing to petition for the winding up of a company merely because a circumstance exists in which a winding-up order may be made, for example, the company is insolvent.[176]   **2.58**

The Crown has no general right (other than as a creditor or contributory) to petition for companies to be wound up,[177] but various public bodies and officers have limited statutory powers to petition.[178]   **2.59**

The rules in IR 1986, part 4, apply to a winding-up petition whoever presents it.[179]   **2.60**

In some cases it has been said that a petitioner must have standing at the time the petition is presented.[180] Subsequently, though, it has been said that a petition presented by a person without standing to do so is not void but will be struck out as an abuse of process[181] or dismissed at its hearing,[182] unless a person who does have standing is substituted as petitioner[183] or the original petitioner's lack of standing is cured.[184] The court retains a discretion to make a winding-up order on such a petition, but will do so only in a wholly exceptional case.[185] The only cases reported so far have been ones in which a winding-up order has been made on a creditor's petition despite an unresolved dispute about the petitioner's standing.[186]   **2.61**

For procedural aspects of disputes about standing see 2.93–2.95.   **2.62**

Corporate petitioners

A petitioner does not have to be a natural person: a company may petition.[187] A petition presented in the name of a company must be authorized by those with power to conduct the company's litigation (normally the company's board of directors[188]).[189]   **2.63**

---

[174] *Western Interstate Pty Ltd v Deputy Commissioner of Taxation (Cth)* (1995) 13 WAR 479, disagreeing with *Re Kalblue Pty Ltd* (1994) 12 ACLC 1057, which was also doubted in *Re University of Newcastle Union Ltd* [2008] NSWSC 1361 at [16]. The statutory provision in question is the Corporations Act 2001 (Australia), s 462(5).

[175] See 2.20–2.22.

[176] *Mann v Goldstein* [1968] 1 WLR 1091 at pp 1094–5; *CVC Investments Pty Ltd v P and T Aviation Pty Ltd* (1989) 18 NSWLR 295 at p 302.

[177] *Re Testro Bros Consolidated Ltd* [1965] VR 18 at p 31.

[178] See 2.69 (designated officers of magistrates' courts, the Secretary of State, official receivers) and 2.75.

[179] r 4.2(2).

[180] *Re H L Bolton Engineering Co Ltd* [1956] Ch 577 at p 581; *Re Kailis Groote Eylandt Fisheries Pty Ltd* (1977) 17 SASR 35; *Bital Holdings Ltd v Middleditch* [1992] MCLR 323 at pp 328 and 330.

[181] *Re a Company (No 001259 of 1991)* [1991] BCLC 594.

[182] *Re William Hockley Ltd* [1962] 1 WLR 555; *Torsir Pty Ltd v Maxgrow Developments Pty Ltd* (1995) 121 FLR 170.

[183] IR 1986, r 4.19; see 3.181–3.206. Substitution is not possible if the petition was presented as a contributory's petition.

[184] *Re Cooling Equipment Wholesale Ltd* [2002] EWHC 678 (Ch), [2002] 2 BCLC 745. But in *Re Kailis Groote Eylandt Fisheries Pty Ltd* (1977) 17 SASR 35 at p 42 Bray CJ said that a petitioner's lack of standing when presenting a petition cannot be cured between presentation and hearing.

[185] See the remarks of Saville LJ in *Re MTI Trading Systems Ltd* [1998] BCC 400 quoted at 2.54.

[186] See 7.551–7.568.

[187] *Re Federal Land Co Ltd* (1889) 15 VLR 135.

[188] See *Mayson, French and Ryan on Company Law*, 31st edn (Oxford: Oxford University Press, 2014), 15.10.3.

[189] *Re Cygnet Ltd* [1926] GLR 332; *Re Kinward Holdings* [1962] CLY 357; *R v Robinson* [1990] BCC 656.

Petition by solicitor on behalf of client

2.64 The fact that a petition is expressed to be presented by a solicitor on behalf of another person does not make it the petition of the solicitor instead of the petition of the person on whose behalf it is presented.[190]

2.65 A solicitor should not act for both the petitioner and the company sought to be wound up, if they are different persons.[191]

Death of petitioner

2.66 If an individual petitions as creditor or contributory but dies after presenting the petition, the court may substitute the petitioner's personal representatives as petitioners.[192]

2.67 An executor may petition before probate has been obtained but must have obtained probate before the order is made.[193]

Loss of standing while petition is pending

2.68 In Australia it has been held that the court has a discretion to make a winding-up order on a petition even if the petitioner loses standing before the petition is heard and no other person is substituted as petitioner.[194] There is no reported case in which a winding-up order has been made in those circumstances. It is very difficult to see how any court could make an order in any kind of legal proceedings after deciding that no party to the proceedings is presently entitled to apply for the order. It is submitted that if a court has decided that the person who presented a winding-up petition no longer has standing to do so, and no other person has been substituted as petitioner, the only order the court can make is to dismiss the petition,[195] unless it is one of the thoroughly exceptional cases in which the court may make a winding-up order on its own initiative.[196]

Standing in relation to any Registered or Unregistered Company

2.69 A petition for the compulsory winding up, under IA 1986, of any registered company, or some other incorporated entities that may be wound up as a registered company,[197] may be presented by the following persons:

(a) any creditor or creditors of the company (including any contingent or prospective creditor or creditors);[198]

(b) any contributory or contributories of the company;[199]

---

[190] *Re New Zealand Gum-Machines Co Ltd* [1922] NZLR 93.

[191] *Re Lennox Publishing Co Ltd* (1890) 61 LT 787.

[192] CPR, r 19.2(4); *Re Dynevor Duffryn Collieries Co* [1878] WN 199; *Re Commercial Bank of London* [1888] WN 214, 234.

[193] *Re Masonic and General Life Assurance Co* (1885) 32 ChD 373.

[194] *Motor Terms Co Pty Ltd v Liberty Insurance Ltd* (1967) 116 CLR 177 (in which the petitioner was held, on appeal, to have had standing when the winding-up order was made); *Deputy Commissioner of Taxation v Guy Holdings Pty Ltd* (1994) 14 ACSR 580; *Deputy Commissioner of Taxation v Visidet Pty Ltd* [2005] FCA 830 at [5]–[6]; *Australian Beverage Distributors Pty Ltd v The Redrock Co Pty Ltd* [2007] NSWSC 966, 213 FLR 450, at [33].

[195] See per Vos JA in *Re GFN Corporation Ltd* 2009 CILR 650 at [102], quoted at 7.555.

[196] See 2.20–2.22.

[197] Charitable incorporated organizations (see 1.122), European cooperative societies (see 1.123), European public limited-liability companies (see 1.124), limited liability partnerships (see 1.126) and registered societies (see 1.127–1.129).

[198] IA 1986, s 124(1); see chapter 7, especially 7.309–7.430.

[199] IA 1986, s 124(1); see chapter 8, especially 8.18–8.66.

(c)   a liquidator or temporary administrator appointed in main proceedings in relation to the company in another EU State (apart from Denmark);[200]

(d)   the company itself;[201]

(e)   the directors of the company;[202]

(f)   a supervisor of a voluntary arrangement of the company;[203]

(g)   the designated officer for a magistrates' court (if the company has failed to pay a fine);[204]

(h)   all or any of the parties listed in (a)–(g) together or separately;[205]

(i)   the Secretary of State;[206]

(j)   an official receiver (though only if the company is already in voluntary winding up);[207]

(k)   an administrator of the company,[208] including an administrator appointed under an industry-specific administration regime;[209]

(l)   an administrative receiver of the company;[210]

(m)   a receiver (other than an administrative receiver) appointed under a charge on property of the company, if the charge was created as a floating charge and IA 1986, s 176A (share of assets for unsecured creditors), applies;[211]

(n)   a foreign representative appointed in a foreign main proceeding or a foreign non-main proceeding.[212]

2.70   Points (a)–(k) in 2.69 apply to unregistered companies.[213] Points (f) and (k) apply only to the limited categories of unregistered companies for which voluntary arrangement (point (f))[214] and administration (point (k)) are available.[215] Point (l) does not apply to unregistered companies.[216] Point (n) applies to unregistered companies.

2.71   For certain types of company, other persons also have standing to petition for winding up.[217] There are separate rules for building societies,[218] incorporated friendly societies[219] and insolvent partnerships.[220]

2.72   In practice, the most important classes of petitions are those by creditors and those by contributories (though, in Britain, about 95 per cent of petitions are by creditors). The significant

---

[200]   Regulation (EC) No 1346/2000, arts 29(a) and 38; IA 1986, s 124(1); see 10.188–10.193.

[201]   IA 1986, s 124(1); see 11.1–11.13.

[202]   IA 1986, s 124(1); see 11.14–11.16.

[203]   IA 1986, s 7(4)(b); see 10.6–10.10 (does not apply to European cooperative societies or registered societies, for which company voluntary arrangements are not available).

[204]   IA 1986, s 124(1) (does not apply to charitable incorporated organizations); see 11.18–11.19.

[205]   IA 1986, s 124(1).

[206]   IA 1986, s 124(4) (does not apply to charitable incorporated organizations); see 9.1–9.87.

[207]   IA 1986, s 124(5); see 10.134–10.138.

[208]   IA 1986, sch B1, para 60, and sch 1, para 21 (does not apply to European cooperative societies or registered societies, for which administration is not available).

[209]   See 10.51–10.58.

[210]   IA 1986, s 42(1) and (2); sch 1, para 21; see 10.68–10.70.

[211]   IR 1986, rr 3.39 and 3.40. See 10.71–10.72.

[212]   Cross-Border Insolvency Regulations 2006 (SI 2006/1030), sch 1, art 11; see 10.202–10.205. SI 2006/1030 does not apply to some classes of company; see 10.200.

[213]   To which IA 1986, s 124(1), is applied by s 221(1). *Re Trans Pacific Insurance Corporation* [2009] NSWSC 308, 71 ACSR 569; *Re Trans Pacific Insurance Corporation* [2009] NSWSC 554, 72 ACSR 327, at [20].

[214]   IA 1986, s 1(4), (5) and (6).

[215]   IA 1986, sch B1, para 111(1A)(b) and (c) and (1B).

[216]   IA 1986, s 28(1).

[217]   See 2.74–2.81.

[218]   See 2.82.

[219]   See 2.83.

[220]   See 2.84–2.88.

difference between these two classes of petitions is that, in general, creditors petition to wind up insolvent companies, whereas contributories petition to wind up solvent companies.

2.73 When winding up subject to the supervision of the court was available,[221] a petition for a company to be wound up in that way could be presented only by a person who would have had standing to petition for the company's compulsory winding up.[222]

Additional Standing in Relation to Particular Types of Company

Introduction

2.74 For certain types of company, other persons have standing to petition for winding up in addition to the persons listed in 2.69–2.73. See 2.75–2.81.

Specific types of company: public bodies and officers

2.75 The following persons exercising public functions have standing to petition for the winding up of specific types of registered and unregistered companies in defined circumstances which are discussed in chapter 9:

- the Attorney General: charitable companies;[223]
- the Board of Trade: enemy companies;[224]
- the Charity Commission: charitable companies;[225]
- the FCA: building societies,[226] credit unions,[227] European cooperative societies,[228] financial services companies and partnerships,[229] friendly societies,[230] registered societies;[231]
- the Office for Tenants and Social Landlords (the Regulator of Social Housing): registered providers of social housing;[232]
- the PRA: building societies,[233] credit unions,[234] financial services companies and partnerships,[235] friendly societies,[236] registered societies;[237]
- the Regulator of Community Interest Companies: community interest companies;[238]
- the Secretary of State: European economic interest groupings,[239] European public limited-liability companies,[240] enemy companies;[241]
- the Welsh Ministers: registered social landlords.[242]

---

[221] See 10.152.
[222] *Re Pen-y-Van Colliery Co* (1877) 6 ChD 477.
[223] See 9.104.
[224] See 9.93–9.97.
[225] See 9.105–9.107.
[226] See 9.99–9.103.
[227] See 9.110–9.111.
[228] See 9.112.
[229] See 9.113–9.140.
[230] See 9.141–9.142.
[231] See 9.145–9.146.
[232] See 9.143.
[233] See 9.99–9.103.
[234] See 9.110–9.111.
[235] See 9.113–9.140.
[236] See 9.141–9.142.
[237] See 9.145–9.146.
[238] See 9.109.
[239] See 9.10 and 9.88–9.89.
[240] See 9.90–9.92.
[241] See 9.93–9.97.
[242] See 9.144.

European cooperative societies

Any person with a legitimate interest has standing under Regulation (EC) No 1435/2003, **2.76** art 73(1), to petition for the winding up of an SCE on either of the following grounds:

(a) there has been a breach of art 2(1) (which defines the ways in which an SCE may be formed), and/or art 3(2) (which requires an SCE's subscribed capital to be at least €30,000); or

(b) the SCE was formed by merger without scrutiny of legality.[243]

For petitions by the FCA see 9.112. **2.77**

European economic interest groupings

'Any person concerned' may apply under Regulation (EEC) No 2137/85, art 32(1), for an **2.78** order that a European economic interest grouping be wound up by the court for infringement of art 3, 12 or 31(3).[244] For petitions by the Secretary of State see 9.10 and 9.88–9.89.

European groupings of territorial cooperation

'Any competent authority with a legitimate interest' may apply under Regulation (EC) **2.79** No 1082/2006, art 14(1), for an order that a European grouping of territorial cooperation which has its registered office in the United Kingdom (a UK EGTC) be wound up by the court for no longer complying with art 1(2) or art 7.[245] The government has interpreted this as meaning 'any person with a legitimate interest'.[246]

Lloyd's and its members

While a Lloyd's market reorganization order[247] is in force, a reorganization controller has **2.80** standing to petition for the winding up of any underwriting member or former member of Lloyd's or Lloyd's itself.[248]

Open-ended investment companies

A petition for the winding up of an open-ended investment company or a sub-fund may be **2.81** presented by its depositary as well as by any person authorized under IA 1986, ss 124 and 124A.[249]

Building Societies

IA 1986, s 124, does not apply to building societies.[250] A petition for the winding up of a **2.82** building society may be presented by:

(a) the FCA or the PRA;[251]

---

[243] art 34.

[244] See 2.47–2.49.

[245] See 2.50–2.51.

[246] Explanatory Memorandum to the European Grouping of Territorial Cooperation Regulations 2007 (SI 2007/1949), annex.

[247] Under the Insurers (Reorganisation and Winding Up) (Lloyd's) Regulations 2005 (SI 2005/1998).

[248] See 10.73–10.78.

[249] Open-Ended Investment Companies Regulations 2001 (SI 2001/1228), reg 31(2), applied to sub-funds by reg 33C(1), (5) and (6).

[250] Building Societies Act 1986, sch 15, para 16.

[251] Building Societies Act 1986, ss 37, 89(2)(a) and 119(1) (definition of 'appropriate authority'); see 9.99–9.103.

(b) the building society or its directors;[252]

(c) any creditor or creditors (including any contingent or any prospective creditor);[253]

(d) any contributory or contributories;[254]

(e) all or any of those parties, together or separately;[255]

(f) a supervisor of a voluntary arrangement of the society;[256]

(g) an administrator of the society.[257]

Incorporated Friendly Societies

2.83   IA 1986, s 124, does not apply to incorporated friendly societies.[258] Under the Friendly Societies Act 1992, s 22(2), a petition for the winding up of an incorporated friendly society may be presented by:

(a) the FCA or the PRA;

(b) the society or its committee of management;

(c) any creditor or creditors (including any contingent or any prospective creditor); or

(d) any contributory or contributories;

(e) all or any of those parties, together or separately.

Insolvent Partnerships

Article 7

2.84   IPO 1994, art 7, provides for a petition to wind up an insolvent partnership, other than by a member of the partnership, where the petitioner does not also petition for the winding up or bankruptcy of any member or former member of the partnership. A petition under art 7 for the winding up of a partnership may be presented by:

(a) a creditor;[259]

(b) the Secretary of State;[260]

(c) the liquidator of a present or former corporate member of the partnership (a 'responsible insolvency practitioner');[261]

(d) the administrator of a present or former corporate member of the partnership;[262]

(e) the administrator of the partnership;[263]

(f) the trustee of a present or former individual member's estate;[264]

---

[252] s 89(2)(b).

[253] s 89(2)(c).

[254] s 89(2)(d).

[255] s 89(2).

[256] IA 1986, s 7(4)(b), as applied by the Building Societies Act 1986, sch 15A, paras 1 and 2—see 10.13.

[257] IA 1986, s 14(1), and sch 1, para 21, as continued in force by the Enterprise Act 2002, s 249, and applied by the Building Societies Act 1986, sch 15A, para 1—see 10.45–10.46.

[258] Friendly Societies Act 1992, sch 10, para 20.

[259] IPO 1994, art 7(1); IA 1986, s 124(1), as applied by the modified form of s 221(5) set out in IPO 1994, sch 3, para 3.

[260] IPO 1994, art 7(1); IA 1986, s 124(4), as applied by the modified form of s 221(5) set out in IPO 1994, sch 3, para 3.

[261] IPO 1994, art 7(1); IA 1986, s 221A(1)(a), inserted by IPO 1994, sch 3, para 3. A corporate member is a member of an insolvent partnership which is a registered company and a liquidator of a corporate member is called a responsible insolvency practitioner (IPO 1994, art 2(1)).

[262] IA 1986, s 221A(1)(a), inserted by IPO 1994, sch 3, para 3.

[263] IA 1986, s 221A(1)(b), inserted by IPO 1994, sch 3, para 3; IA 1986, sch B1, para 60, and sch 1, para 19, as applied by IPO 1994, art 6(1), and modified by sch 2, para 43.

[264] IA 1986, s 221A(1)(c), inserted by IPO 1994, sch 3, para 3.

(g) the supervisor of a voluntary arrangement approved under IA 1986, part 1,[265] in relation to the partnership;[266]

(h) the supervisor of a voluntary arrangement approved under IA 1986, part 1, in relation to a corporate member of the partnership, or under part 8 in relation to an individual member;[267]

(i) a liquidator or temporary administrator appointed in main proceedings in relation to the company in another EU State (apart from Denmark).[268]

IPO 1994, art 7(1), also refers to 'the petition…of any other person other than a member'. **2.85** It is submitted that 'any other person' must mean 'any other person who is given standing to petition for the winding up of an insolvent partnership'. All the persons who have that standing but are not mentioned in art 7(1) are given standing to petition under art 7 by IA 1986, s 221A.[269] A member of an insolvent partnership has standing to petition for it to be wound up but can petition under IPO 1994, art 9 or art 10 only.

Article 8

IPO 1994, art 8, provides for a petition for the winding up of an insolvent partnership to **2.86** be presented in conjunction with a petition or petitions for the bankruptcy or winding up of one or more present or former members of the partnership. A petition under art 8 may be presented only by:

(a) a creditor or creditors to whom the partnership and the present or former member or members sought to be wound up or adjudged bankrupt are indebted in respect of a liquidated sum payable immediately;[270]

(b) a liquidator or temporary administrator appointed in main proceedings in relation to the partnership in another EU State (apart from Denmark).[271]

Article 9

IPO 1994, art 9, provides for a petition for the winding up of an insolvent partnership to be **2.87** presented by a member of the partnership who does not also petition for the bankruptcy or winding of any other member of the partnership. If the partnership has eight members or more, any member may present an art 9 petition.[272] If the partnership has fewer than eight members, a member may present an art 9 petition only after applying for and obtaining the leave of the court.[273] The court cannot give leave unless it is satisfied that the member has paid, other than out of partnership money, a joint debt or debts exceeding £750 due from the partnership and that the following events have occurred:

(a) The member has served a demand for the money in form 10 in IPO 1994, sch 9. Service must be:

    (i) by leaving the demand at a principal place of business of the partnership in England and Wales; or

---

[265] Which is applied to insolvent partnerships by IPO 1994, art 4(1), in the modified form set out in sch 1.
[266] IA 1986, s 221A(1)(d), inserted by IPO 1994, sch 3, para 3; IA 1986, s 7(4)(b), as applied by IPO 1994, art 4(1), and modified by sch 1, part 1. See 10.18–10.20.
[267] IA 1986, s 221A(1)(d), inserted by IPO 1994, sch 3, para 3.
[268] Regulation (EC) No 1346/2000, arts 29(a) and 38; IPO 1994, art 7(1).
[269] Inserted by IPO 1994, sch 3, para 3.
[270] IA 1986, s 124(2), as modified by IPO 1994, sch 4, para 8.
[271] Regulation (EC) No 1346/2000, arts 29(a) and 38; IPO 1994, art 8(1).
[272] IA 1986, s 221A(1), as modified by IPO 1994, sch 5, para 2.
[273] IA 1986, s 221A(2), as modified by IPO 1994, sch 5, para 2.

    (ii) by delivering it to an officer of the partnership; or

    (iii) in such manner as the court may approve or direct.

(b) The partnership has for three weeks after the service of the demand neglected to pay the sum or to secure or compound for it to the member's satisfaction.[274]

(c) The member has obtained a judgment, decree or order of any court against the partnership for reimbursement of the amount, and all reasonable steps (other than insolvency proceedings) have been taken to enforce that judgment, decree or order.

Article 10

2.88 IPO 1994, art 10, provides for a petition for the winding up of an insolvent partnership to be presented by a member of the partnership at the same time as petitions for the winding up or bankruptcy of all members of the partnership, including the petitioner. All members must consent to being the subject of a bankruptcy or winding-up order.[275] Only a member may present an art 10 petition.

Collective Investment Schemes

2.89 The persons who may petition for the winding up of a relevant scheme[276] are:[277]

(a) the operator of the relevant scheme;

(b) a creditor of the relevant scheme;

(c) the FCA;

(d) the Secretary of State.

Restrictions on who has Standing in Certain Circumstances

During a moratorium for preparation of a voluntary arrangement

2.90 While a moratorium under IA 1986, s 1A (moratorium when directors propose a voluntary arrangement), is in force for a company, only the Secretary of State, the FCA or the PRA may present a petition for it to be wound up.[278] The same applies to limited liability partnerships[279] and insolvent partnerships.[280] While a moratorium is in force for a charitable incorporated organization, only the Attorney General and the Charity Commission may petition.[281]

Standing to apply for opening of territorial proceedings

2.91 If a company's centre of main interests (COMI) is in another EU State (apart from Denmark) and no main insolvency proceedings have been opened in that State, a petition for the company to be wound up by the court in England and Wales on the ground that it

---

[274] See 7.180–7.201.

[275] IA 1986, s 124(2)(b), as modified by IPO 1994, sch 6, para 2. The court may permit petitions relating to only some of the members if satisfied that it would be impracticable to petition against them all (IA 1986, s 124(3), as modified by IPO 1994, sch 6, para 2).

[276] See 1.168.

[277] Collective Investment in Transferable Securities (Contractual Scheme) Regulations 2013 (SI 2013/1388), reg 17(9).

[278] See 10.3.

[279] See 10.11.

[280] See 10.14.

[281] See 10.12.

is unable to pay its debts would be a request for the opening of territorial proceedings.[282] The circumstances in which such a request may be made are restricted by Regulation (EC) No 1346/2000, art 3(4), which must be interpreted strictly.[283] As it applies in England and Wales, art 3(4) normally means that a petition can be presented only by a creditor whose domicile, habitual residence or registered office is in the United Kingdom, or whose claim arises from the operation of the company's establishment in the UK.[284] A public official cannot request the opening of territorial proceedings in the public interest if the request is not made as a creditor, or in the name, or on behalf, of creditors.[285] In England, though, it has been held that a public official may petition for the opening of territorial proceedings on the just and equitable ground.[286]

The effect of art 3(4) is that a petition may be presented by any other person with standing   **2.92**
to do so under English law only if main insolvency proceedings cannot be opened because of the conditions laid down by the law of the State in which the company's COMI is situated.[287] This is limited to a situation in which the law of the COMI State prevents insolvency proceedings being opened at all and does not cover a situation in which insolvency proceedings cannot be opened because of the specific circumstances in which the opening is requested.[288] In particular, the fact that the COMI State's law does not give the proposed petitioner standing to request the opening of main proceedings, but does give other persons standing, does not mean that main proceedings cannot be opened.[289]

Disputes about Standing to Petition for Winding Up

If there is a dispute about a petitioner's standing to petition, that dispute should be decided   **2.93**
before any other issue,[290] unless the case is a wholly exceptional one in which the court will make a winding-up order despite the dispute about standing being unresolved.[291] However, as answering a question of standing may bring an end to proceedings, it may be raised at any stage, either at first instance or on appeal.[292] A company which decides to challenge standing at a substantive rather than an interim hearing must be prepared at the hearing to answer all allegations in the petition as well as arguing against the petitioner's standing: it cannot rely on being granted an adjournment to prepare the rest of its case should the question of standing be decided against it.[293]

The mere fact that a petition has been presented does not prove that the person who pre-   **2.94**
sented it has standing to petition, and the fact that the court is willing, exceptionally, to

---

[282] See 1.364–1.370.

[283] *Procureur-generaal bij het hof van beroep te Antwerpen v Zaza Retail BV* (case C-112/10) [2011] ECR I-11525 at [29].

[284] Regulation (EC) No 1346/2000, art 3(4)(b).

[285] *Procureur-generaal bij het hof van beroep te Antwerpen v Zaza Retail BV* (case C-112/10) [2011] ECR I-11525.

[286] *Re Marann Brooks CSV Ltd* [2003] BCC 239.

[287] Regulation (EC) No 1346/2000, art 3(4)(a).

[288] *Procureur-generaal bij het hof van beroep te Antwerpen v Zaza Retail BV* (case C-112/10) [2011] ECR I-11525.

[289] *Procureur-generaal bij het hof van beroep te Antwerpen v Zaza Retail BV* (case C-112/10) [2011] ECR I-11525.

[290] *Strata Welding Alloys Pty Ltd v Henrich Pty Ltd* (1980) 5 ACLR 442 at p 447.

[291] See 7.551–7.568.

[292] *Westford Special Situations Fund Ltd v Barfield Nominees Ltd* (HCVAP 2010/014) at [26].

[293] *Re Tanganyika Produce Agency Ltd* [1957] EA 241.

determine in the winding-up proceedings whether or not that person has standing does not in itself confer standing on the petitioner.

2.95 In proceedings on a creditor's winding-up petition, the court will not normally decide a dispute about the existence of the creditor's claimed debt, even though that is a dispute about the creditor's standing to petition.[294] The court's usual practice is to dismiss such a petition.[295] The court may restrain presentation of such a petition as an abuse of process.[296] The court is more willing to decide disputes about standing in proceedings on a contributory's petition.[297]

Bank and Building Society Insolvency

2.96 An application for a bank insolvency order may be made by the Bank of England, the PRA[298] or the Secretary of State.[299] There are three grounds for applying:[300]

(a) Ground A is that a bank is unable, or likely to become unable, to pay its debts,
(b) Ground B is that the winding up of a bank would be in the public interest, and
(c) Ground C is that the winding up of a bank would be fair.

The Bank of England or the PRA[301] can apply on either Ground A or Ground C.[302] The Secretary of State can apply only on Ground B.[303]

2.97 An application for a building society insolvency order may be made by the Bank of England or the PRA.[304] There are two grounds for applying:[305]

(a) Ground A is that a building society is unable, or likely to become unable, to pay its debts, and
(b) Ground C is that the winding up of a building society would be fair.

The word 'fair' is used as a shorter modern equivalent of the expression 'just and equitable'[306] and is not intended to exclude jurisprudence concerning the application of that expression.[307]

---

[294] See 7.515–7.527.

[295] See 7.529–7.535.

[296] See 2.165–2.166.

[297] See 8.2–8.4.

[298] The FCA in the case of an FCA-regulated bank (Banking Act 2009, s 129A). The term 'FCA-regulated bank' is defined at 1.234.

[299] Banking Act 2009, s 95(1).

[300] s 96(1).

[301] The FCA in the case of an FCA-regulated bank (Banking Act 2009, s 129A).

[302] Banking Act 2009, s 96(2)(b)(ii) and (3)(b)(iii).

[303] s 96(4)(b).

[304] Banking Act 2009, s 95(1), applied to building society insolvency with modifications by the Building Societies Act 1986, s 90C, and the Building Societies (Insolvency and Special Administration) Order 2009 (SI 2009/805), sch 1, para 9. In the case of an FCA-regulated building society, the FCA replaces the PRA (Banking Act 2009, s 129A, applied by the Building Societies Act 1986, s 90C).

[305] Banking Act 2009, s 96(1), applied to building society insolvency with modifications by the Building Societies Act 1986, s 90C, and the Building Societies (Insolvency and Special Administration) Order 2009 (SI 2009/805), sch 1, para 10.

[306] As used in IA 1986, ss 122(1)(g) and 221(5)(c); see 8.131–8.257.

[307] Banking Act 2009, s 93(8). Applied to building society insolvency by the Building Societies Act 1986, s 90C.

The primary objective of bank and building society insolvency is the protection of eligible **2.98** depositors.[308] So an application for a bank or building society insolvency order cannot be made in relation to an institution unless the applicant is satisfied that it has eligible depositors.[309]

The PRA[310] and the Bank of England cannot apply for a bank insolvency order in relation **2.99** to a bank, or a building society insolvency order in relation to a building society, unless the PRA is satisfied that the institution is failing or likely to fail (Condition 1)[311] and the Bank of England is satisfied that, having regard to timing and other relevant circumstances, it is not reasonably likely that (ignoring the stabilization powers) action will be taken by or in respect of the bank that will result in Condition 1 ceasing to be met (Condition 2)[312] If the PRA is satisfied of Condition 1 and the Bank of Condition 2, the Bank, on being informed of the PRA's opinion, may either make the application itself[313] or consent to the PRA making the application.[314]

Before applying for a bank or building society insolvency order in relation to an **2.100** FCA-regulated institution:[315]

(a) The FCA must consult the PRA.
(b) The Bank of England must consult the PRA if a PRA-authorized person[316] is a member of the institution's immediate group.[317]

Permission, Consent or Prior Notice Required

Administration

Interim moratorium

While an interim moratorium, in preparation for schedule B1 administration, is in force for **2.101** a company, no person, other than the Secretary of State, the FCA or the PRA, may present a petition for it to be wound up unless they have the court's permission or the petition is for the purpose of proceedings under the default rules of exchanges and clearing houses in financial markets described in 10.67.[318]

---

[308] For the definition of 'eligible depositor' see 1.20.
[309] Banking Act 2009, s 96(2)(b)(i), (3)(b)(ii) and (4)(a). Applied to building society insolvency by the Building Societies Act 1986, s 90C.
[310] In the case of an FCA-regulated bank or building society, all references to the PRA in 2.99 are to be treated as references to the FCA (Banking Act 2009, s 129A, applied by the Building Societies Act 1986, s 90C).
[311] Banking Act 2009, ss 7(2) and 96(2)(a). See s 1(4) for 'stabilization powers'.
[312] Banking Act 2009, ss 7(3) and 96(3)(b)(i).
[313] Banking Act 2009, s 96(2). Applied to building society insolvency by the Building Societies Act 1986, s 90C.
[314] Banking Act 2009, s 96(3). Applied to building society insolvency by the Building Societies Act 1986, s 90C.
[315] Banking Act 2009, s 96, as modified by s 129A. Applied to building society insolvency by the Building Societies Act 1986, s 90C.
[316] See 9.114.
[317] 'Immediate group' is defined in the Financial Services and Markets Act 2000, s 421ZA.
[318] See 10.26 (schedule B1 administration), 10.38 (limited liability partnerships) and 10.59 (insolvent partnerships).

2.102 While an application is pending for an administration order to be made in respect of a company under any of the industry-specific administration regimes based on schedule B1 administration,[319] the court's permission is required for the presentation of any winding-up petition.[320]

During administration

2.103 When a company is in schedule B1 administration, no person may present a petition for it to be wound up without the administrator's consent or the court's permission unless the petition is for the purpose of proceedings under the default rules of exchanges and clearing houses in financial markets described in 10.67.[321]

2.104 While an industry-specific administration order[322] is in force in relation to a company, no person may present a petition for the company to be wound up without the administrator's consent or the court's permission.[323]

Receiver

2.105 A receiver (other than an administrative receiver) appointed under a charge on a company's property must notify the company's creditors whether he or she proposes to petition for the company to be wound up.[324]

Air Traffic Services Licence Companies

2.106 A person other than the Secretary of State may not present a petition to wind up an air traffic services licence company[325] without giving the Secretary of State and the Civil Aviation Authority at least 14 days' notice of intention to do so.[326]

Residual Banks and Building Societies

2.107 The PRA or the FCA must give notice to the Bank of England before petitioning for the winding up of a residual bank or building society.[327]

Lloyd's Reorganization

2.108 While a Lloyd's market reorganization order is in force, no person may present a winding-up petition without the court's permission against an affected market participant, Lloyd's, or a Lloyd's subsidiary to which the reorganization order applies.[328] An 'affected market participant' means[329] any of the following to whom the reorganization order applies:

---

[319] See 1.262–1.287 and 1.291–1.294.

[320] See 10.42–10.44.

[321] See 10.29 (schedule B1 administration), 10.38 (limited liability partnerships), 10.60 (insolvent partnerships).

[322] See 1.245–1.294.

[323] See 10.45–10.50.

[324] IR 1986, r 3.39(2)(c). See 10.71–10.72.

[325] See 1.260–1.261.

[326] Transport Act 2000, s 26(4).

[327] Banking Act 2009, s 157. Applied to building societies by the Building Societies Act 1986, s 90C. For the meaning of 'residual' in this context see 1.265.

[328] Insurers (Reorganisation and Winding Up) (Lloyd's) Regulations 2005 (SI 2005/1998), reg 8(1) and (2)(b)(i).

[329] SI 2005/1998, reg 2(1).

(a) an underwriting member of Lloyd's;

(b) a former member, meaning a person who has ceased to be an underwriting member of Lloyd's, whether by resignation or otherwise, in accordance with the Lloyd's Act 1982, or any predecessor of that Act which was in force at the time of cessation of membership;

(c) a managing agent, as defined in the Financial Services and Markets Act 2000 (Regulated Activities) Order 2001;[330]

(d) a members' agent, meaning a person who carries out the activity of advising a person to become, or continue or cease to be, a member of a particular Lloyd's syndicate;

(e) a Lloyd's broker, as defined in the Lloyd's Act 1982, s 2(1);

(f) an approved run-off company, meaning a company having the permission of Lloyd's to perform executive functions, insurance functions or administrative and processing functions on behalf of a managing agent;

(g) a coverholder, meaning a company or partnership authorized by a managing agent to enter into, in accordance with the terms of a binding authority, a contract or contracts of insurance to be underwritten by the members of a syndicate managed by that managing agent.

'Contract of insurance' is defined in SI 2001/544, reg 3(1), which must be read with the Financial Services and Markets Act 2000, s 22 and sch 2, but does not include a reinsurance contract.[331]

If the petition is against an underwriting member or former member of Lloyd's, and the **2.109** petitioner wants the court to disapply SI 2005/1998, reg 13(2) (which applies SI 2004/353 to the company sought to be wound up as if it were a UK insurer, and also applies to it SI 2005/1998 and the Financial Services and Markets Act 2000 (Administration Orders Relating to Insurers) Order 2002[332]), the petitioner must apply to the court before presenting the petition,[333] notify the application to the reorganization controller,[334] and state in the petition whether the court has made an order.[335]

Reserve and Auxiliary Forces

A judgment creditor of a company must obtain leave to present a petition to wind up the **2.110** company from the court in which the judgment was obtained if the court has made a declaratory order under the Reserve and Auxiliary Forces (Protection of Civil Interests) Act 1951, s 3(1)(c), or the company has applied for such an order and its application has not been disposed of, or has given written notice to the creditor of intention to apply for such an order.[336]

---

[330] SI 2001/544.

[331] Insurers (Reorganisation and Winding Up) Regulations 2004 (SI 2004/353), reg 2(4), applied by SI 2005/1998, reg 2(2).

[332] SI 2002/1242. This has been revoked and replaced by the Financial Services and Markets Act 2000 (Administration Orders Relating to Insurers) Order 2010 (SI 2010/3023).

[333] SI 2005/1998, reg 13(4)(a).

[334] reg 13(5).

[335] reg 13(4)(b).

[336] Reserve and Auxiliary Forces (Protection of Civil Interests) Act 1951, ss 2(1) and 3(1) and (9); Reserve and Auxiliary Forces (Protection of Civil Interests) Rules 1951 (SI 1951/1401), rr 3 and 7.

Enemy Companies

2.111 If an order has been made under the Trading with the Enemy Act 1939, s 3A(1), in respect of a business carried on by a company,[337] a petition for the winding up of the company must not be presented without the consent of the Board of Trade or the Secretary of State.[338]

Purpose, Motive and Interest

Purpose of Petitioner; Abuse of Process

Benefit for all creditors and contributories

2.112 A winding-up order operates in favour of all creditors and contributories of the company.[339] It is an abuse of process for a person to petition for a company's compulsory liquidation otherwise than for the purpose of providing for all its creditors and contributories the benefits that the liquidation will produce (though no doubt self-interest will be the petitioner's primary concern).[340] In *Re Southbourne Sheet Metal Co Ltd*[341] Harman J said, at p 364:

> a winding-up petition is not a *lis inter partes*[342] for the benefit of A as against B. It is the invoking by A of a class remedy for the benefit of himself and other members of the class. Nonetheless, it is (a) based upon a commercial interest of the person invoking the remedy, and (b) it is for the benefit of himself, amongst other members of the class.

2.113 If other members of the petitioner's class are of opinion that it is not expedient to pursue the common benefit, the court will consider their views when deciding whether to exercise its discretion to make a winding-up order.[343] The idea of a petitioner as a representative of a class applies primarily to creditors' petitions.

2.114 There are two types of case:

(a) where the petitioner does not expect the company to be wound up at all, but is using the threat or embarrassment of the proceedings to coerce the company into settling another dispute (see 2.115–2.118);

(b) where the petitioner wants the company to be wound up but for a collateral purpose (see 2.119–2.123).

Coercion to settle another dispute

2.115 In *Ebbvale Ltd v Hosking*[344] Lord Wilson, giving the judgment of the Privy Council in an appeal from the Bahamas, said:

---

[337] See 9.93–9.97.

[338] Trading with the Enemy Act 1939, s 3A(8); Secretary of State for Trade and Industry Order 1970 (SI 1970/1537), arts 2(1) and 7(4). The continuing responsibilities of the Board of Trade in this respect are explained at 9.97.

[339] IA 1986, s 130(4).

[340] *Re Wheal Lovell Mining Co* (1849) 1 Mac & G 1 per Lord Cottenham LC at p 22; *Re a Company (No 001573 of 1983)* [1983] BCLC 492; *Tang Choon Keng Realty (Pte) Ltd v Tang Wee Cheng* [1992] 2 SLR 1114 at p 1137.

[341] [1992] BCLC 361.

[342] Lawsuit between parties.

[343] See 7.698–7.733 (creditors' petitions) and 8.194–8.199 (contributories' petitions).

[344] [2013] UKPC 1, [2013] 2 BCLC 204, at [26].

Sometimes a petitioner who presents, or threatens to present, a winding-up petition seeks not to obtain an actual order but rather, by the application of pressure on the company and in particular through the prospect of damaging publicity as a result of the requisite advertisement of the petition, to cause it to act in a particular way. Such is a classic example of abuse of the process of the court, which will lead it to accede to an application by the company to stay[345] the petition or, by injunction, to preclude its presentation.

The first example cited by Lord Wilson, *Cadiz Waterworks Co v Barnett*,[346] concerned the most common type of improper purpose—pressurizing a company into paying a disputed debt: this is considered in more detail at 7.603–7.608.[347]   **2.116**

In *Cadiz Waterworks Co v Barnett*[348] Malins V-C said, at p 196:   **2.117**

> if [this court] sees a petition to wind up presented, not for a bona fide purpose of winding up the company, but for some collateral and sinister object, on that ground it will be dismissed with costs . . . the object of this court is to restrain the assertion of doubtful rights in a manner productive of irreparable damage.

Other examples of coercive petitions are: **2.118**

• *Re a Company*[349] (contributory's petition intended to pressurize company into settling a claim which seems to have had no legal basis at all);
• *Charles Forte Investments Ltd v Amanda*[350] (contributory's petition intended to pressurize directors to approve the petitioner's transfer of his shares);
• *Re Bellador Silk Ltd*[351] (contributory's petition intended to pressurize the company into repaying a loan owed to another company in which the petitioner was interested);
• *Re Senson Auto Supplies Sdn Bhd*[352] (contributories' petition intended to pressurize company to settle claim for rescission of allotment of shares);
• *RCB v Thai Asia Fund Ltd*[353] (contributory's petition as part of a 'vulture fund' policy of harassing management of mutual funds to persuade them to repurchase shares at a premium, a practice known as 'greenmail');
• *Wangsini Sdn Bhd v Grand United Holdings Bhd*[354] (creditor's petition for payment of a larger sum than was due to it under a court-sanctioned scheme of arrangement by which it was bound).

Improper collateral purpose

For examples of improper collateral purposes see: **2.119**

• *Re Patent Bread Machinery Co Ltd*[355] (contributory's petition—if company were wound up, its most valuable asset would revert to the petitioner);

---

[345] In England and Wales now, strike out; see 3.60–3.61.
[346] (1874) LR 19 Eq 182.
[347] See also 7.660 for pressurizing a company to pay a debt free of a set-off.
[348] (1874) LR 19 Eq 182.
[349] (1917) 34 DLR 396.
[350] [1964] Ch 240.
[351] [1965] 1 All ER 667.
[352] [1988] 1 MLJ 326.
[353] 1996 CILR 9.
[354] [1998] 5 MLJ 345.
[355] (1866) 14 LT 582.

- *Re National Financial Corporation*[356] (petitioner held shares in a company which was being amalgamated with the company sought to be wound up and wished to prevent that amalgamation);
- *Anglo-American Brush Electric Light Corporation Ltd v Scottish Brush Electric Light and Power Co Ltd*[357] (contributory's petition presented so as to invalidate any further allotment of shares in the company which would dilute the petitioner's interest);
- *Re Surrey Garden Village Trust Ltd*[358] (contributories' petition to wind up a society with the real purpose of making it impossible for the society to enforce a restrictive covenant preventing the petitioners from making a lucrative disposal of their land);
- *Re a Company (No 001573 of 1983)*[359] (creditor's petition brought in order to activate a forfeiture clause in the company's lease so that the petitioner would be granted a new lease of the premises);
- *Re Tellsa Furniture Pty Ltd*[360] (tax collector's policy was to apply for winding up of slow-paying companies and allow the application to remain pending until the tax was paid);
- *Re Kolback Group Ltd*[361] (contributory's petition to wind up holding company of company which the contributory was suing; contributory had only nominal shareholding and did not put forward any proof of its allegation that the company was insolvent);
- *Re J E Cade and Son Ltd*[362] (contributory's petition brought to end the company's security of tenure of agricultural land owned by the petitioner);
- *Re Wallace Smith and Co Ltd*[363] and *Re Wallace Smith Group Ltd*[364] (creditor's petition presented so as to obtain the appointment of a friendly liquidator who would discontinue the company's defence to proceedings brought by the petitioner in another jurisdiction); but a desire to secure the appointment of an independent liquidator who will evaluate professionally how to conduct the company's litigation against the petitioner in the interests of all creditors is not an abuse of process;[365]
- *Euro Systems and Equipment (NZ) Ltd v Bainbridge Panel and Paint Ltd*[366] (petition to wind up a company which owned half of the shares in the petitioning creditor company, which the holders of the other shares hoped to be able to buy cheaply in the liquidation);
- *Re Leigh Estates (UK) Ltd*[367] (creditor's petition presented by local authority in the belief that if the company were put into liquidation its incumbent administrative receiver would become liable for paying rates on property occupied by the company, there being no other funds from which the rates could be paid);
- *Re Lo Siong Fong*[368] (contributory's petition coupled with application to appoint a provisional liquidator so as to impede a petition by other members for relief of oppressive conduct of the company's affairs);

---

[356] (1866) 14 LT 749.
[357] (1882) 9 R 972.
[358] [1965] 1 WLR 974.
[359] [1983] BCLC 492.
[360] (1985) 81 FLR 185.
[361] (1991) 4 ACSR 165.
[362] [1992] BCLC 213.
[363] [1992] BCLC 970.
[364] [1992] BCLC 989.
[365] *Ebbvale Ltd v Hosking* [2013] UKPC 1, [2013] 2 BCLC 204.
[366] [1993] MCLR 516.
[367] [1994] BCC 292.
[368] [1994] 2 MLJ 72.

- *Re Millennium Advanced Technology Ltd*[369] (creditor's petition seeking a winding up in the public interest);
- *Lai Shit Har v Lau Yu Man*[370] (contributory's petition to hamper the company's pursuit of a claim against him);
- *Re Goode Concrete*[371] (creditor's petition to hamper the company's pursuit of a claim against it).

Although a creditor's petition to wind up a company has an improper collateral purpose **2.120** it may nevertheless be permitted to proceed if the winding up would, to a material extent, serve the petitioner's interest as a creditor, even if that is not the petitioner's principal purpose.[372] It would seem that a similar principle could apply to contributories' petitions, but in that context it would be subject to the rule that the court does not wind up a company simply to realize a contributory petitioner's investment.[373]

It is not improper to petition at a particular time in order to render a particular past transac- **2.121** tion liable to adjustment: adjustment of past transactions is part of the process of winding up and is done for the benefit of all creditors and contributories.[374]

The mere fact that the petitioner is an agent for another person who is engaged in separate **2.122** litigation with the company does not show that the petitioner has an ulterior purpose.[375]

The fact that a company was fraudulently redomiciled in a jurisdiction so as to be wound up **2.123** there would not make the winding-up proceedings an abuse of process.[376]

Motive of Petitioner

Motive (in the sense of a psychological process which induces a person to act in a certain way **2.124** by influencing that person's volition) is irrelevant if a petitioner has standing to petition and has established the existence of a circumstance in which the court has jurisdiction to order winding up.[377] As Gibbs J said in *IOC Australia Pty Ltd v Mobil Oil Australia Ltd*,[378] 'it is not the law that only a creditor who feels goodwill towards his debtor is entitled to a winding-up order'. The fact that the petitioner is a commercial rival whose business will benefit from eliminating the company sought to be wound up is not in itself a reason for not making a winding-up order.[379]

In *Mann v Goldstein*,[380] Ungoed-Thomas J said, at p 1095: **2.125**

> It seems to me that to pursue a substantial claim in accordance with the procedure provided and in the normal manner, even though with personal hostility or even venom, and from

---

[369] [2004] EWHC 711 (Ch), [2004] 1 WLR 2177.
[370] [2008] SGCA 33, [2008] 4 SLR 348.
[371] [2012] IEHC 439.
[372] *Re Millennium Advanced Technology Ltd* at [42]; *Ebbvale Ltd v Hosking* [2013] UKPC 1, [2013] 2 BCLC 204, at [33(d)].
[373] See 8.184–8.188.
[374] *Dallhold Investments Pty Ltd v Gold Resources Australia Ltd* (1991) 31 FCR 587.
[375] *Re Bydand Ltd* [1997] BCC 915.
[376] *Re Electric Mutual Liability Insurance Co Ltd* [1996] Bda LR 62.
[377] *Re Amalgamated Properties of Rhodesia (1913) Ltd* [1917] 2 Ch 115; *Re A I Levy (Holdings) Ltd (No 2)* (1965) 109 SJ 209; *Bryanston Finance Ltd v De Vries (No 2)* [1976] Ch 63; *Tele-Art Inc v Nam Tai Electronics Inc* (1999) 57 WIR 76; *Ebbvale Ltd v Hosking* [2013] UKPC 1, [2013] 2 BCLC 204, at [28].
[378] (1975) 2 ACLR 122 at p 131.
[379] *Fuji Photo Film Co Ltd v Jazz Photo (Hong Kong) Ltd* [2005] 1 HKLRD 530.
[380] [1968] 1 WLR 1091.

some ulterior motive, such as the hope of compromise or some indirect advantage, is not an abuse of the process of the court or acting mala fide but acting bona fide in accordance with the process. And certainly no authority suggesting otherwise has been brought to my attention.

2.126 In *Pembinaan KSY Sdn Bhd v Lian Seng Properties Sdn Bhd*[381] the petitioner was guarantor of a debt of the company under an on-demand guarantee (under which the amount guaranteed must be paid on demand whether it is owed or not), and had paid its liability under the guarantee, apparently after asking the principal creditor to make demand. It was held entitled to petition as a creditor. *Morgan Guaranty Trust Co of New York v Lian Seng Properties Sdn Bhd*[382] is a similar case.

Sufficient Interest of Petitioner: Companies without Assets

Petitioner must have sufficient interest

2.127 The court will not, in its discretion, make a winding-up order if it is shown that the petitioner does not have a 'sufficient interest' in having a winding up.[383] The interest that a petitioner must show is a potential benefit from the making of the winding-up order. The fundamental principle[384] is that the court will not wind up a company if there is no likelihood that any advantage will be achieved by the petitioner.[385] '[A] petition is only presented if it is bona fide in pursuit of some interest of the petitioner arising from his particular status as such'.[386] This is an example of the general principle that a person asking the court to exercise any power must show a legitimate interest in the relief sought.[387] But see 2.141.

2.128 The requirement for a sufficient interest applies to all types of petitioner, not just creditors.[388] The sufficient interest that a contributory must have in order to petition is usually called a 'tangible interest'.[389]

What constitutes a sufficient interest?

2.129 In the case of a creditor's or contributory's petition, the most obvious interest which a petitioner may claim in having a company wound up is a share in the company's assets which may be distributed to the petitioner as a creditor or, if the company is solvent, as a contributory. Even if there is no possibility of the petitioner sharing in the company's assets, the court may make a winding-up order if it is shown that the order will benefit the petitioner in some other way. In particular, it is sufficient if the likely benefit to the petitioner will flow from the making of the order rather than the winding-up process.[390] However, in order to

---

[381] [1991] 1 MLJ 100.

[382] [1991] 1 MLJ 95.

[383] *Re London Permanent Benefit Building Society* (1869) 21 LT 8; *Re Rica Gold Washing Co* (1879) 11 ChD 36 per Jessel MR at p 43. For what may constitute a sufficient interest see 2.129–2.131.

[384] Nourse J in *Re Eloc Electro-Optieck and Communicatie BV* [1982] Ch 43 at p 47.

[385] Per Bowen LJ in *Re Chapel House Colliery Co* (1883) 24 ChD 259 at p 269; *Re Company or Fraternity of Free Fishermen of Faversham* (1887) 36 ChD 329; *Re Compañía Merabello San Nicholas SA* [1973] Ch 75; per Nourse J in *Re Eloc Electro-Optieck and Communicatie BV* [1982] Ch 43 at p 47; *Joint v Stephens (No 2)* [2008] VSC 69.

[386] *Re Millennium Advanced Technology Ltd* [2004] EWHC 711 (Ch), [2004] 1 WLR 2177, at [31].

[387] *Deloitte & Touche AG v Johnson* [1999] 1 WLR 1605 at p 1611.

[388] *Re Millennium Advanced Technology Ltd*.

[389] See 8.67–8.86.

[390] *Re Australian Joint-Stock Bank Ltd* (1897) 41 SJ 469, the facts of which are given at 8.424; *Re Compañía Merabello San Nicholas SA* [1973] Ch 75, in which the order brought into operation the Third Parties (Rights

be a sufficient interest, a benefit to a creditor or contributory petitioner must relate to the petitioner's position as one of the company's creditors or contributories.[391] In *Re Chesterfield Catering Co Ltd*[392] the fact that if a winding-up order were made, a liquidator would be appointed from whom the petitioner (who petitioned as a contributory) could purchase the company's property was not a sufficient interest. A person who has guaranteed a debt of a company may have difficulty in demonstrating any interest in having the company wound up, because of the rule against double proof, which requires that a guaranteed debt must be paid in full before the guarantor can prove in the principal debtor's insolvency.[393] But on a petition presented jointly by a creditor and a contributory to wind up a Russian company, appointment of an English insolvency practitioner as liquidator, to supervise complex litigation in this country, for the benefit of all creditors and contributories, was a sufficient advantage.[394]

The fact that the benefit sought by the petitioner could be achieved by other means may, depending on the circumstances, be a reason for the court to exercise its discretion not to make a winding-up order.[395]   **2.130**

A public interest petition by the Secretary of State[396] is necessarily brought not in the Secretary of State's own interest but in the interests of the public at large.[397]   **2.131**

Onus

The onus is on those opposing the petition to show that the petitioner does not have a sufficient interest,[398] except where the petition is by a contributory in which case the burden of proving a sufficient interest is on the petitioner.[399]   **2.132**

Petition costs not a sufficient interest

Nineteenth-century judges said that they would not make winding-up orders which would benefit only the professionals who would recover their costs.[400]   **2.133**

---

against Insurers) Act 1930 to vest in the petitioner the company's claim against an insurer (see also the similar case of *Re Allobrogia Steamship Corporation* [1978] 3 All ER 423); *Re Eloc Electro-Optieck and Communicatie BV* [1982] Ch 43, in which the making of the order entitled the petitioners to claim their unpaid wages from the Secretary of State under what is now the Employment Rights Act 1996, part 12.

[391] *Re Millennium Advanced Technology Ltd* [2004] EWHC 711 (Ch), [2004] 1 WLR 2177.

[392] [1977] Ch 373.

[393] *Sugar Hut Brentwood Ltd v Norcross* [2008] EWHC 2634 (Ch), LTL 12/12/2008; *Re La Plagne Ltd* [2011] IEHC 91, [2012] 1 ILRM 203.

[394] *Re OJSC ANK Yugraneft* [2008] EWHC 2614 (Ch), [2009] 1 BCLC 298, at [61].

[395] *Re OJSC ANK Yugraneft* [2008] EWHC 2614 (Ch), [2009] 1 BCLC 298, at [60].

[396] See 9.5–9.8 and 9.11–9.86.

[397] Per Megarry J in *Re Lubin, Rosen and Associates Ltd* [1975] 1 WLR 122 at pp 128–9; per Harman J in *Re Xyllyx plc (No 2)* [1992] BCLC 378 at p 380; per Finn J in *Australian Securities Commission v AS Nominees Ltd* (1995) 133 ALR 1 at p 59.

[398] *Re Company or Fraternity of Free Fishermen of Faversham* (1887) 36 ChD 329 per Cotton LJ at p 339; *G P Gardner and Co v Link* (1894) 21 R 967; *Re Crigglestone Coal Co Ltd* [1906] 2 Ch 327 per Collins MR at p 337 and per Romer LJ at p 338; *Re Compañía Merabello San Nicholas SA* [1973] Ch 75 at p 89; *Re Datadeck Ltd* [1998] BCC 694, in which the company did not raise the point, see at p 707. In *Re Georgian Bay Ship Canal and Power Aqueduct Co* (1898) 29 OR 358 those opposing the winding up were unable to show that there were no free assets.

[399] *Re Lancashire Brick and Tile Co Ltd* (1865) 34 LJ Ch 331.

[400] *Re General Provident Assurance Co* (1868) 19 LT 45 per Malins V-C; *Re New Gas Generator Co* (1877) 4 ChD 874 per Bacon V-C; *Re Diamond Fuel Co* [1878] WN 11 per Jessel MR; *Re Cab Company of Graham and Co Ltd* (1884) 1 TLR 46 per Bacon V-C; *Re Company or Fraternity of Free Fishermen of Faversham* (1887) 36 ChD 329 per Fry LJ at p 344.

2.134   If a registered company does not have any affairs to be wound up but it is desired to have it dissolved, its directors may apply for the company to be struck off the register.[401] Alternatively, the registrar of companies may strike the company off the register.[402] These procedures had not been introduced when *Re New Gas Generator Co*[403] was heard and in that case the court dismissed a petition for the compulsory winding up of the company, accepting the opposition of contributories with partly paid shares: as the company had no affairs to be wound up, the only effect of a winding-up order would have been to force the contributories to pay calls to pay the costs of the winding up.

Companies without free assets

2.135   The court must not refuse to order the winding up of a company on the ground only that the company's assets have been mortgaged to an amount equal to or in excess of those assets, or that the company has no assets.[404] The word 'only' is important.[405] This provision does not take away the court's discretion to refuse to wind up a company with no free assets, where there is some reason other than the absence of assets for refusing to order winding up. If the absence of assets means that the petitioner does not have a sufficient interest in having the company wound up, the court will exercise its discretion not to make an order for the reason that the petitioner does not have a sufficient interest rather than because there are no assets.[406] Similarly, the court may refuse to order the winding up of a company with no assets on a creditor's petition if the company has a substantial cross-claim against the petitioner.[407] But if the petitioner has a sufficient interest despite the absence of assets, IA 1986, s 125(1), enables the court to make an order.[408]

Absence of free assets and absence of any other interest

2.136   If it is shown that a company has no assets available for the payment of unsecured creditors, and the petitioner cannot demonstrate any other interest in having the company wound up, the court may, in the exercise of its discretion, dismiss the petition.[409] In the past this was particularly the case where all the company's assets were charged to secure payment of a debt exceeding their value.[410] However, this was before the introduction of the statutory

---

[401]   Companies Act 2006, ss 1003 to 1011.

[402]   Companies Act 2006, s 1000.

[403]   (1877) 4 ChD 874.

[404]   IA 1986, s 125(1). This provision does not apply to petitions to wind up building societies or incorporated friendly societies (Building Societies Act 1986, sch 15, para 18(1); Friendly Societies Act 1992, sch 10, para 21(1)). The provision was first enacted as the Companies Act 1907, s 29, but it stated the existing practice of the court (*Re Belfast Tailors' Co-partnership Ltd* [1909] 1 IR 49 per Meredith MR at p 54). In 1902 Buckley J held that a petition for the winding up of a company had to allege that the company had, or would have, assets for distribution to the petitioner (Practice Note [1902] WN 77). This seems to have been a surprise to practitioners and the practice of requiring this allegation was abandoned soon after (*Re Chic Ltd* [1905] 2 Ch 345 at p 348).

[405]   Per Megarry J in *Re Compañía Merabello San Nicholas SA* [1973] Ch 75 at p 88.

[406]   *Re Eastern Minerals and Trading (1959) Ltd* [1964] MLJ 451. See 2.136–2.138 and 8.67–8.70. This point was not taken in *Re Albion Enterprises Ltd* [2012] IEHC 115, where the court took the view that it was constrained to make a winding-up order despite it being contrary to common sense.

[407]   *Re Goode Concrete* [2012] IEHC 439. See 7.618–7.665.

[408]   See 2.139–2.141.

[409]   See *Re Chapel House Colliery Co* (1883) 24 ChD 259 per Cotton LJ at pp 268–9, Bowen LJ at p 269; *Re United Stock Exchange Ltd* (1884) 51 LT 687; *Re Company or Fraternity of Free Fishermen of Faversham* (1887) 36 ChD 329; *Re Crigglestone Coal Co Ltd* [1906] 2 Ch 327.

[410]   See *Re London Health Electrical Institute Ltd* (1897) 76 LT 98; *Re Edgbaston Brewery Co Ltd* (1893) 68 LT 341; *Re Okell and Morris Fruit Preserving Co Ltd* (1902) 9 BCR 153; *Re Eastern Minerals and Trading (1959) Ltd* [1964] MLJ 451, in which the petitioner's claim that it could get the charge set aside was rejected.

share of floating charge assets to be set aside to pay unsecured creditors under IA 1986, s 176A, which came into force on 15 September 2003.

The onus of proving that the petitioner does not have a sufficient interest is on those oppos- **2.137**
ing the making of a winding-up order.[411]

The practice of dismissing a petition because the petitioner has no interest in a winding up **2.138**
is not affected by IA 1986, s 125(1).[412]

Recovery of further assets by liquidator

Absence of assets at the time of hearing the winding-up petition will not lead to the conclu- **2.139**
sion that the petitioner does not have a sufficient interest in having the company wound up
if it appears to the court that there is a reasonable possibility that a liquidator would recover
further assets.[413] A winding-up order may be made despite an absence of assets if it appears
that it would be in the petitioner's interest for there to be an investigation of the company's
affairs.[414] In *Re Lacey and Co Ltd*[415] a winding-up order was made on a creditor's petition
against a company with assets of only £7: the report does not state what account the judge
took of the petitioner's claim that money might be recovered from directors in misfeasance
proceedings. In *Re Ilfracombe Permanent Mutual Benefit Building Society*[416] there was an
absence of assets because the affairs of the company had already been wound up; the court
found that recovery of 'substantial' further assets was unlikely and dismissed the petition.
In *Re Alexander Dunbar and Sons Co*[417] a winding-up order was made despite a claim by
chargees that there were no free assets, but the judge's reasoning is not reported.

Representation of unsecured creditors' interests

If assets have been heavily mortgaged, winding up may be ordered so that a liquidator can **2.140**
represent the interests of unsecured creditors vis-à-vis secured creditors.[418]

Unsecured creditors' interest: feeding a floating charge

At the beginning of the 20th century there were instances of the holders of a floating charge **2.141**
over a company's assets, whose secured debt exceeded the value of the assets, allowing the
company to continue trading while insolvent so that it would acquire goods on credit which
would be caught by the floating charge. In three reported cases in which this had happened
the court made a winding-up order on an unsecured creditor's petition on the just and

---

[411] *Re Company or Fraternity of Free Fishermen of Faversham* (1887) 36 ChD 329 per Cotton LJ at p 339;
G P Gardner and Co v Link (1894) 21 R 967; *Re Crigglestone Coal Co Ltd* [1906] 2 Ch 327 per Collins MR at
p 337 and per Romer LJ at p 338; *Re Datadeck Ltd* [1998] BCC 694, in which the company did not raise the
point, see at p 707. In *Re Georgian Bay Ship Canal and Power Aqueduct Co* (1898) 29 OR 358 those opposing
the winding up were unable to show that there were no free assets.

[412] See 2.135.

[413] *Re Diamond Fuel Co* (1879) 13 ChD 400 (contributory's petition); *Re Krasnapolsky Restaurant and
Winter Gardens Co* [1892] 3 Ch 174 (creditor's petition); *Re International Commercial Co Ltd* (1897) 75 LT
639 (creditor's petition); *Re a Company (No 00359 of 1987)* [1988] Ch 210 (creditor's petition); *Clendon
Plumbing Ltd v Tamstone Holdings Ltd* [1994] MCLR 393.

[414] *Re Zirceram Ltd* [2000] 1 BCLC 751; *Re Parmalat Capital Finance Ltd* 2006 CILR 480.

[415] (1877) 46 LJ Ch 660.

[416] [1901] 1 Ch 102.

[417] (1910) 9 ELR 217.

[418] *Re Crigglestone Coal Co Ltd* [1906] 2 Ch 327; *Re Marlborough Sealink Ltd* (1985) 3 NZCLC 99,501;
Bell Group Finance (Pty) Ltd v Bell Group (UK) Holdings Ltd [1996] 1 BCLC 304; but not in *Re Northern
Developments (Holdings) Ltd* (1977) 128 NLJ 86.

equitable ground, despite the fact that the petitioner would get nothing from the winding up.[419] In *Re Clandown Colliery Co* Astbury J said, at p 373:

> This is a state of affairs that is not reasonable or proper in the interests of innocent unsecured creditors, and it ought not to be allowed to go on.

Injunction against Presenting a Petition

Injunction to Prevent Abuse of Process

Principle

2.142   The court may grant a *quia timet* injunction to prevent presentation of a winding-up petition which it considers would be an abuse of process. An application to prevent a petition proceeding invokes the inherent jurisdiction of a court to prevent an abuse of its process.[420]

2.143   If it is found that a petition which has been presented is an abuse of process, the court will, on the company's application, restrain gazetting of the petition and strike it out.[421]

Conditions for granting a quia timet *injunction*

2.144   A *quia timet* injunction is granted to prevent a threatened and intended injury to the applicant.

2.145   Threat and intention to present a petition may be found, for example, in a solicitor's letter[422] or in the service of a statutory demand.[423]

2.146   It is easy to expect injury to a company's credit and prospects from presentation of a petition to wind it up, and this is usually described as 'irreparable damage',[424] adopting a locution used by Malins V-C in *Cadiz Waterworks Co v Barnett*.[425]

2.147   The legal right which a company is seeking to protect by an injunction to prevent presentation of a winding-up petition is the right not to be involved in litigation which would constitute an abuse of the process of the court.[426] So it must be proved that the petition would be an abuse of process.[427]

---

[419]   *Re Chic Ltd* [1905] 2 Ch 345; *Re Alfred Melson and Co Ltd* [1906] 1 Ch 841; *Re Clandown Colliery Co* [1915] 1 Ch 369.

[420]   *Charles Forte Investments Ltd v Amanda* [1964] Ch 240 per Willmer LJ at p 250 and Danckwerts LJ at 259; *Bryanston Finance Ltd v De Vries (No 2)* [1976] Ch 63 per Stephenson LJ at p 79; *Bina Satu Sdn Bhd v Tan Construction* [1998] 1 MLJ 533; *Re a Company (No 0012209 of 1991)* [1992] 1 WLR 351 at p 354.

[421]   See 3.60–3.89.

[422]   For example, *Niger Merchants Co v Capper* (1877) 18 ChD 557 n; *Cercle Restaurant Castiglione Co v Lavery* (1881) 18 ChD 555; *Charles Forte Investments Ltd v Amanda* [1964] Ch 240.

[423]   For example, *Merchant Banking Co of London v Hough* [1874] WN 230; *New Travellers' Chambers Ltd v Cheese and Green* (1894) 70 LT 271; *Stonegate Securities Ltd v Gregory* [1980] Ch 576 per Goff LJ at p 588; *Instrumech Engineering Sdn Bhd v Sensorlink Sdn Bhd* [2001] 1 MLJ 127; *Dynaworth Shipping Sdn Bhd v Ling Chung Ann* [2001] 3 MLJ 399; *Moorside Investments Ltd v DAG Construction Ltd* [2007] EWHC 3490 (Ch), LTL 18/12/2007, at [65].

[424]   See, for example, *Charles Forte Investments Ltd v Amanda* [1964] Ch 240 at p 252.

[425]   (1874) LR 19 Eq 182 at p 196.

[426]   *Bryanston Finance Ltd v De Vries (No 2)* [1976] Ch 63 per Buckley LJ at p 76.

[427]   *Bryanston Finance Ltd v De Vries (No 2)* per Buckley LJ at p 76; *Coulon Sanderson and Ward Ltd v Ward* (1985) 2 BCC 99,207; *Re Leasing and Finance Services Ltd* [1991] BCC 29; *Southern Cross Group plc v Deka Immobilien Investment GmbH* [2005] BPIR 1010 at [30]; repeated in *Re Pan Interiors Ltd* [2005] EWHC 3241 (Ch), LTL 14/7/2005, at [36].

Alternative basis: petition must fail

The criterion for granting an injunction to prevent presentation of a winding-up petition is **2.148** sometimes stated with reference to the petition being bound to fail. For example, in *Charles Forte Investments Ltd v Amanda*[428] Willmer LJ said that the company had to prove that:

> this is a petition which is bound to fail and amounts in the circumstances to an abuse of the process of the court.

In *Re a Company (No 003028 of 1987)*[429] Scott J described abuse of process and inevitable fail- **2.149** ure as alternative but associated grounds for striking out. In *Bryanston Finance Ltd v De Vries (No 2)*[430] Buckley LJ said that the company had to prove that the petition would be an abuse of process, while Stephenson LJ[431] said the company had to prove the petition would be bound to fail, or perhaps that there is a suitable alternative remedy.

It is submitted that it is unnecessary to consider abuse of process and inevitable failure as separate **2.150** ate criteria for granting an injunction. Litigation which is bound to fail is a waste of court resources and therefore an abuse of process. So a petition which is bound to fail is an abuse of process.[432] The fact that a petition is bound to fail is therefore an indication that it is an abuse of process. But it is not the only possible indicator of abuse of process.[433]

The result of finding that a petition which has been presented is an abuse of process is that the **2.151** court will almost inevitably prevent the petition proceeding,[434] so it will fail. In that sense, inevitable failure and abuse of process are equivalent. However, finding that a petition is an abuse of process does not depend on finding that it is bound to fail.[435]

Sometimes the criterion of inevitable failure is interpreted as referring specifically to inevitabil- **2.152** ity of failure as a matter of law or because of lack of evidence.[436] This has been in the context of submissions, which the courts have rejected, that whether or not a threatened petition is 'bound to fail' in this restricted sense is the sole criterion for granting an injunction to prevent presentation of a creditor's petition.[437] The fact that a threatened petition is bound to fail in that restricted sense is not the sole criterion for preventing its presentation. The fact that it would, for some other reason, be an abuse of process[438] also justifies granting an injunction.[439]

---

[428] [1964] Ch 241 at p 252.
[429] [1988] BCLC 282.
[430] [1976] Ch 63 at p 76.
[431] *Bryanston Finance Ltd v De Vries (No 2)* at p 80.
[432] *Bryanston Finance Ltd v De Vries (No 2)* per Buckley LJ at p 77.
[433] *Camulos Partners Offshore Ltd v Kathrein and Co* 2010 (1) CILR 303 at [56]–[57]. This proviso was not included in the discussion of this point in the second edition of this work, which left that discussion open to an unintended misinterpretation which had to be corrected by the Cayman Islands Court of Appeal in *Camulos Partners Offshore Ltd v Kathrein and Co.*
[434] *Stuart v Goldberg* [2008] EWCA Civ 2, [2008] 1 WLR 823, at [24] per Lloyd LJ.
[435] See per Chadwick P in *Camulos Partners Offshore Ltd v Kathrein and Co* 2010 (1) CILR 303 at [78] commenting on a less sophisticated version of this statement in the second edition of this work.
[436] See 2.174.
[437] *Fortuna Holdings Pty Ltd v Deputy Federal Commissioner of Taxation* [1978] VR 83; *Pembinaan Lian Keong Sdn Bhd v Yip Fook Thai* [2005] 5 MLJ 786; *Metalform Asia Pte Ltd v Holland Leedon Pte Ltd* [2007] SGCA 6, [2007] 2 SLR 268.
[438] See 2.165–2.173 and 2.175.
[439] In *Pembinaan Lian Keong Sdn Bhd v Yip Fook Thai* an injunction was granted on the ground that presentation of the threatened petition would be an abuse of process. The intending petitioner claimed to be a creditor but the company disputed the debt. It was found, at [56], that the petition was threatened for the purpose of putting improper or undue pressure on the company to abandon the dispute; see 2.167–2.168 and 7.603–7.608.

Procedure

2.153   An application[440] for an order restraining presentation of a winding-up petition must be made to a court having jurisdiction to wind up the company.[441] An application for an injunction against presentation of a petition to wind up a company on the ground that it is unable to pay its debts is a proceeding relating to the winding up of an insolvent company and is therefore excepted from the operation of Regulation (EU) No 1215/2012,[442] the Brussels Convention and the Lugano Convention.[443] The application must be listed before a judge.[444] It is usual to ask[445] for the hearing to be held in private, on the ground that publicity would defeat the object of the hearing[446] and/or that the hearing involves confidential information and publicity would damage that confidentiality.[447] However, unless the court expressly prohibits publication of information heard in a private hearing, it is not contempt of court to make that information public.[448]

2.154   Before IR 1986 the practice was to issue a writ claiming an injunction, and then to apply by motion seeking an interlocutory injunction to restrain the presentation of the threatened winding-up petition until the trial of the writ action. As the decision on this motion effectively disposed of the issue, there was never a trial of the action. It was recognized that this two-stage procedure was inefficient, which is why the modern practice involves just the one stage of issuing an application for the injunction.

2.155   The application must be supported by written evidence, usually in witness statements and exhibits.[449]

2.156   Consideration must be given to whether the application is sufficiently urgent to justify applying without notice to the likely petitioner.[450] A hearing date for the application is given when the application is issued.[451] Judges are available to hear companies matters every day during term time.[452] Sufficient time should be allowed for service if the application is to be dealt with on notice.[453] Service is effected by the applicant.[454] Paragraphs 7.2–7.38 of the Chancery Guide 2013 on hearings before judges should be complied with. These require:

(a)   the advocates for all the parties to deliver a time estimate for the hearing as soon as possible after the papers have been lodged;[455]

---

[440]   See 3.233–3.263.

[441]   IR 1986, r 4.6A(a).

[442]   art 1(2)(b). *Citigate Dewe Rogerson Ltd v Artaban Public Affairs SPRL* [2009] EWHC 1689 (Ch), [2011] 1 BCLC 625.

[443]   Article 1 of each Convention.

[444]   PD Insolvency Proceedings 2014, para 3.2(3).

[445]   Under CPR, r 39.2(3).

[446]   CPR, r 39.2(3)(a).

[447]   CPR, r 39.2(3)(c).

[448]   *A F Noonan (Architectural Practice) Ltd v Bournemouth and Boscombe Athletic Community Football Club Ltd* [2007] EWCA Civ 848, [2007] 1 WLR 2614.

[449]   IR 1986, r 7.7A.

[450]   See IR 1986, r 7.4(6).

[451]   IR 1986, r 7.4(2).

[452]   Chancery Guide 2013, para 20.8.

[453]   IR 1986, r 7.4(5), requires service at least 14 days before the hearing.

[454]   IR 1986, r 7.4(3); PD Insolvency Proceedings 2014, para 6.2.

[455]   Chancery Guide 2013, para 7.5.

(b) bundles, which should be agreed if possible, and prepared in accordance with Practice Direction (PD) 39A, para 3, to be lodged by 10 am on the morning preceding the day of the hearing unless the court otherwise directs;[456]

(c) that consideration is given to lodging a core bundle if the papers are voluminous;[457]

(d) that a further time estimate, reading list, and estimate for the time needed to read the documents on the reading list, be lodged with the bundles;[458]

(e) that skeleton arguments be lodged by 10 am on the day before the hearing;[459] and

(f) unless photocopies are provided, lists of authorities should be supplied to the usher by 9 am on the day of the hearing.[460]

An order made by the court on an application to restrain presentation of a petition is not **2.157** made in the exercise of its jurisdiction to wind up companies, and therefore cannot be reviewed, rescinded or varied by it under IR 1986, r 7.47.[461]

Whether a petition to wind up a company should be prevented is a separate question from **2.158** whether the company should be wound up, and is the only issue decided on the application to halt the petition.[462]

Condition for granting a temporary injunction

On an application for a temporary order, pending a full hearing, restraining presentation **2.159** of a petition, whether on notice to other parties or not, the company must prove a prima facie case that the petition would be an abuse of process.[463] The court might make a very short-term order on an application without notice, to allow evidence to be prepared.[464]

Stay of injunction

If an injunction against presentation of a winding-up petition has been granted, the court is **2.160** unlikely to stay it pending appeal.[465] However, if the court has refused an injunction against presentation of a petition and the petition has been presented, it may grant an injunction to prevent the petition proceeding until an appeal against its first decision has been dealt with.[466]

The Court's Approach

In order to obtain an injunction preventing presentation of a winding-up petition, it must **2.161** be shown that the petition would be an abuse of process.[467] Whether or not to halt proceedings because they are an abuse of process is a matter of discretion, but whether or not there is an abuse of process is not decided by exercising a discretion: it is a question to which there

---

[456] Chancery Guide 2013, paras 7.9, 7.11, 7.15 and 7.16.
[457] Chancery Guide 2013, para 7.14.
[458] Chancery Guide 2013, para 7.30.
[459] Chancery Guide 2013, para 7.22.
[460] Chancery Guide 2013, para 7.33.
[461] *Re Portedge Ltd* [1997] BCC 23 at p 27.
[462] *Bryanston Finance Ltd v De Vries (No 2)* [1976] Ch 63 per Buckley LJ at p 76; *Australian Mid-Eastern Club Ltd v Elbakht* (1988) 13 NSWLR 697.
[463] *Coulon Sanderson and Ward Ltd v Ward* (1985) 2 BCC 99,207; *Pink Pages Publications Ltd v Team Communications Ltd* [1986] 2 NZLR 704.
[464] *Coulon Sanderson and Ward Ltd v Ward*.
[465] *Paganelli Sdn Bhd v Care-Me Direct Sales Sdn Bhd* [1999] 2 MLJ 464.
[466] *Celcom (Malaysia) Bhd v Inmiss Communication Sdn Bhd* [2003] 3 MLJ 178.
[467] See 2.142–2.152.

can be only one right answer.[468] It is only in very unusual circumstances that the court would not strike out proceedings that are an abuse of process.[469] The court should be cautious in finding reasons why an application to wind up a company would be an abuse of process, because it must exercise great circumspection before deciding to prevent a person petitioning the court.[470]

> The right to petition the court for a winding-up order in appropriate circumstances is a right conferred by statute. A would-be petitioner should not be restrained from exercising it except on clear and persuasive grounds.[471]

2.162 Allowing presentation of a petition but forbidding giving notice of it was described as a *via media* by Buckley LJ,[472] though it has the disadvantage for the company that an application must be made for a validation order to permit it to continue business.[473]

2.163 For examples of petitions which the court has found to be an abuse of process see 2.165–2.175.

2.164 Whether or not to prevent presentation of a winding-up petition should not be decided by the principles governing applications for interim injunctions, in particular, the principles outlined in *American Cyanamid Co v Ethicon Ltd*.[474] This was established[475] on the ground that granting such an injunction finally disposes of the dispute[476] or on the ground that injunctions to restrain winding-up petitions, like other anti-suit injunctions, are special cases which are not governed by the *American Cyanamid* guidelines. See also the view of Woodhouse P and McMullin J in *Anglian Sales Ltd v South Pacific Manufacturing Co Ltd*[477] that the question whether a winding-up petition should not be heard: 'ought not to rest simply on the balance of convenience considerations which may be relevant for an interim injunction. Something more than that is required.'[478]

Examples

Disputed debt petitions

2.165 The court's practice is to dismiss a creditor's petition to wind up a company if the company disputes, on substantial grounds, the existence of the debt on which the petition

---

[468] *Aldi Stores Ltd v WSP Group plc* [2007] EWCA Civ 1260, [2008] 1 WLR 748, at [16]; *Stuart v Goldberg* [2008] EWCA Civ 2, [2008] 1 WLR 823, at [24] and [81]; *Aktas v Adepta* [2010] EWCA Civ 1170, [2011] QB 894, at [53].
[469] *Stuart v Goldberg* at [24] per Lloyd LJ.
[470] *Tench v Tench Bros Ltd* [1930] NZLR 403; *Charles Forte Investments Ltd v Amanda* [1964] Ch 240 per Willmer LJ at p 250; *Bryanston Finance Ltd v De Vries (No 2)* [1976] Ch 63; *Truck and Machinery Sales Ltd v Marubeni Komatsu Ltd* [1996] 1 IR 12.
[471] *Bryanston Finance Ltd v De Vries (No 2)* per Buckley LJ at p 78.
[472] *Bryanston Finance Ltd v De Vries (No 2)* per Buckley LJ at p 78.
[473] Under IA 1986, s 127.
[474] [1975] AC 396.
[475] In *Bryanston Finance Ltd v De Vries (No 2)* [1976] Ch 63 shortly after *American Cyanamid Co v Ethicon Ltd* was decided. Affirmed in *Re Leasing and Finance Services Ltd* [1991] BCC 29 at p 30. Followed in Malaysia: *Sri Binaraya Sdn Bhd v Golden Approach Sdn Bhd* [2000] 3 MLJ 465; *JB Kulim Development Sdn Bhd v Great Purpose Sdn Bhd* [2002] 2 MLJ 298; *Pembinaan Lian Keong Sdn Bhd v Yip Fook Thai* [2005] 5 MLJ 786; but not in *Malayan Flour Mill Bhd v Raja Lope and Tan Co* [2000] 6 MLJ 591. A different view is taken in Australia—see 7.609–7.612.
[476] See per Sir John Pennycuick in *Bryanston Finance Ltd v De Vries (No 2)* at pp 80–1; per Megarry J in *Re Euro Hotel (Belgravia) Ltd* [1975] 3 All ER 1075 at p 1085; per Vincent Ng J in *Pembinaan Lian Keong Sdn Bhd v Yip Fook Thai* [2005] 5 MLJ 786 at [9]–[12].
[477] [1984] 2 NZLR 249 at p 252.
[478] See also *Re Pureway Corporation Nigeria Ltd* 1978 (2) ALR Comm 214; *Truck and Machinery Sales Ltd v Marubeni Komatsu Ltd* [1996] 1 IR 12.

is based.[479] The court will restrain presentation of such a petition because that rule of practice means the petition would be bound to fail and so would be an abuse of process.[480] A cross-claim is treated in the same way.[481] In the case of a dispute about the existence of the debt claimed by an intending petitioner or an assertion that the company has a cross-claim against the intending petitioner, it must be shown that the dispute or cross-claim is sufficiently substantial to make dismissal of the petition inevitable, were it to be presented[482] not whether a claim for the intending petitioner's debt (which is a different issue) would be bound to fail.[483] The court may have to deal with an assertion by the intending petitioner that, exceptionally, the court would determine the dispute about the debt in proceedings on the petition[484] or would make a winding-up order despite the dispute or cross-claim,[485] so that presenting the petition would not be an abuse of process.

There is an overlap between disputed debt or cross-claim cases and the suitable alternative **2.166** remedy category described at 2.171–2.173, in that the Companies Court usually refuses to deal with disputed debt petitions because there is the better alternative of having the dispute on the debt determined in a common law claim.

Oppression

An injunction may be granted to prevent presentation of a petition to wind up a company, **2.167** because the petition would be an abuse of process, if it would be oppressive or unfair or, as it is often expressed, would put improper or undue pressure on the company to accede to the intending petitioner's demands.[486] In *Cadiz Waterworks Co v Barnett* Malins V-C said, at p 194:

> And I beg to express my opinion that this Court ought not, and I think will not—at all events I will not until I am controlled by higher authority—permit this winding-up process to be made a vehicle of oppression.

It is not oppressive for a creditor to commence a claim for the debt and also present a petition **2.168** to wind up the company based on the same debt.[487]

Collateral purpose

An injunction may be granted to prevent presentation of a petition to wind up a company, **2.169** because it would be an abuse of process, if the primary purpose of presenting it would not be to get the company wound up for the benefit of the intending petitioner's class.[488] Commonly, as in *Cadiz Waterworks Co v Barnett*, the collateral purpose is to put improper pressure on the company.[489] Other examples are given at 2.119–2.123.

---

[479] See 7.529–7.535.
[480] *Cadiz Waterworks Co v Barnett* (1874) LR 19 Eq 182 at p 194; see 2.148–2.152.
[481] See 7.618–7.665.
[482] See 7.444–7.514, 7.573 and 7.627–7.630.
[483] See *Pembinaan Lian Keong Sdn Bhd v Yip Fook Thai* [2005] 5 MLJ 786; *Metalform Asia Pte Ltd v Holland Leedon Pte Ltd* [2007] SGCA 6, [2007] 2 SLR 268.
[484] See 7.523–7.527.
[485] See 7.551–7.568, 7.621 and 7.631–7.643.
[486] *Cadiz Waterworks Co v Barnett* (1874) LR 19 Eq 182 at pp 194–7; *Fletcher Development and Construction Ltd v New Plymouth Hotels Holdings Ltd* [1986] 2 NZLR 302. See 7.603–7.608.
[487] *Re Leasing and Finance Services Ltd* [1991] BCC 29.
[488] See 2.112–2.123. *Cadiz Waterworks Co v Barnett* (1874) LR 19 Eq 182 at pp 195–6.
[489] See 2.167–2.168.

2.170   In *Re First Western Corporation Ltd*[490] Virtue SPJ said, at p 138, that he thought a petition could not be prevented from proceeding unless it was proved 'that the sole motive of the petitioners in presenting the petition is an ulterior motive and that it is an abuse of the process of the court', but in *Mincom Pty Ltd v Murphy*[491] G N Williams J pointed out that in practice a petitioner may have more than one purpose and it must always be a question of degree whether or not one can conclude that a petition has not been presented with the genuine object of obtaining a winding-up order.

Suitable alternative remedy

2.171   An injunction may be granted to prevent presentation of a petition to wind up a company, because it would be an abuse of process, if the intending petitioner is seeking to wind up the company instead of pursuing an alternative and more appropriate remedy.[492] For discussion of the circumstances in which it may or may not be found that a petition would be an abuse of process, because there is an alternative remedy, see 7.46–7.50 (petition by unpaid undisputed creditor), 7.572–7.575 (disputed debt and cross-claim petitions), 8.216–8.247 (contributories' petitions), 9.17–9.18 (public interest petitions) and 10.83–10.84 (company in voluntary liquidation).

2.172   Commonly, as in *Cadiz Waterworks Co v Barnett*,[493] the intending petitioner is seeking to put improper pressure on the company to accede to the petitioner's claim[494] without having it established in the suitable alternative proceedings, which will constitute a collateral purpose.[495]

2.173   It cannot be said to be an abuse of process to apply for a company to be wound up by the court if winding up is the only remedy available to meet the wrong of which the petitioner complains, unless the petition is bound to fail.[496]

Bound to fail as a matter of law or because of lack of evidence

2.174   An injunction will be granted to prevent presentation of a petition to wind up a company if the petition would be bound to fail as a matter of law or because of lack of evidence.[497] As Buckley LJ pointed out in *Bryanston Finance Ltd v De Vries (No 2)*,[498] no one knows what will or will not be in a petition until it is presented.

Further cases

2.175   The cases pointed out in 2.165–2.174 are only examples: there is no basis for confining the doctrine of abuse of process to any particular factual circumstances.[499] See also the discussion of striking out at 3.60–3.86.

---

[490] [1970] WAR 136.

[491] [1983] 1 QdR 297.

[492] *Charles Forte Investments Ltd v Amanda* [1964] Ch 240; *Fortuna Holdings Pty Ltd v Deputy Federal Commissioner of Taxation* [1978] VR 83; *Mincom Pty Ltd v Murphy* [1983] QdR 297; *CVC/Opportunity Equity Partners Ltd v Demarco Almeida* [2002] UKPC 16, [2002] 2 BCLC 108, at [53].

[493] (1874) LR 19 Eq 182.

[494] See 2.167–2.168.

[495] See 2.169–2.170.

[496] *Camulos Partners Offshore Ltd v Kathrein and Co* 2010 (1) CILR 303 at [62].

[497] *Tench v Tench Bros Ltd* [1930] NZLR 403 per Smith J at p 410 and Kennedy J at p 412; *Charles Forte Investments Ltd v Amanda* [1964] Ch 240, in which it is not clear whether it was law or evidence or both which the intending petitioner lacked.

[498] [1976] Ch 63 at p 78.

[499] *Kapeleris v Bytenet Pty Ltd* (1997) 24 ACSR 668 per Beaumont J at p 676.

Costs

Orders as to costs of an application for an injunction to restrain presentation of a petition **2.176** are at the discretion of the court but will normally follow the event.[500] A person who has threatened to present a winding-up petition which would be an abuse of process is adopting 'a high risk strategy' and may be ordered to pay the company's costs of restraining presentation of the petition on an indemnity basis.[501]

Tortious Petitions

Malicious Presentation or Continuation

Definition of tort

It is a tort to petition maliciously and without reasonable or probable cause for a company **2.177** to be wound up.[502] Presentation of a winding-up petition is one of the few civil proceedings to which the tort of malicious prosecution, which is primarily concerned with malicious institution of criminal proceedings, has been extended in English law.[503] Only three kinds of damages may be recovered in a claim for malicious prosecution of proceedings:

(a) damage to reputation;
(b) damage to the person, for example, from loss of liberty;
(c) charges and expenses, limited to the cost of defending the proceedings.[504]

Unlike the position in relation to criminal proceedings, where damage must be proved, it may be assumed that presenting a petition to wind up a company necessarily damaged the company's reputation, and no other damage need be proved.[505] In order to succeed in a claim for this tort, the company must show:

(a) that proceedings on the petition ended in its favour;
(b) that there was absence of reasonable cause for presenting the petition; and
(c) that there was malice or improper motive.[506]

In *Tibbs v Islington London Borough Council*[507] the Court of Appeal doubted whether a **2.178** substituted petitioner or a supporting creditor could be sued for malicious prosecution.[508]

---

[500] *Cannon Screen Entertainment Ltd v Handmade Films (Distributors) Ltd* (1988) 5 BCC 207.
[501] *Re a Company (No 0012209 of 1991)* [1992] 1 WLR 351; *Baillieu Knight Frank (NSW) Pty Ltd v Ted Manny Real Estate Pty Ltd* (1992) 30 NSWLR 359. See also 7.597–7.602.
[502] *Quartz Hill Consolidated Gold Mining Co v Eyre* (1883) 11 QBD 674.
[503] See *Gregory v Portsmouth City Council* [2000] 1 AC 419 at pp 427–8. Presentation of a bankruptcy petition is another (*Johnson v Emerson* (1871) LR 6 Ex 329). The Privy Council (in an appeal from the Cayman Islands) has now extended the tort to all civil proceedings (*Crawford Adjusters v Sagicor General Insurance (Cayman) Ltd* [2013] UKPC 17, [2014] 1 AC 366).
[504] *Savill v Roberts* (1698) 12 Mod 208; *Quartz Hill Consolidated Gold Mining Co v Eyre* at p 683; *Land Securities plc v Fladgate Fielder* [2009] EWCA Civ 1402, [2010] Ch 467. The Privy Council has removed this restriction (*Crawford Adjusters v Sagicor General Insurance (Cayman) Ltd* [2013] UKPC 17, [2014] 1 AC 366).
[505] *Quartz Hill Consolidated Gold Mining Co v Eyre*. Apparently, this does not apply to malicious presentation of a bankruptcy petition (*Jacob v Vockrodt* [2007] EWHC 2403 (QB), [2007] BPIR 1568, at [43]).
[506] *Radivojevic v LR Industries Ltd* (22 November 1984, Court of Appeal, unreported) quoted in *Business Computers International Ltd v Registrar of Companies* [1988] Ch 229; also cited in *Partizan Ltd v O J Kilkenny and Co Ltd* [1998] 1 BCLC 157.
[507] [2002] EWCA Civ 1682, [2003] BPIR 743.
[508] Simon Brown LJ, at [21], thought that a supporting creditor could not be liable.

Proceedings ended in the company's favour

2.179   A claim for malicious prosecution can only be made in respect of proceedings which actually ended in the claimant's favour. A claim cannot be made on the basis that new evidence will show that the proceedings should have ended in the claimant's favour.[509] The fact that a creditor is found to be entitled to prove for considerably less than the amount initially claimed does not mean that the proceedings have ended in the company's favour.[510]

Reasonable or probable cause

2.180   In *Quartz Hill Consolidated Gold Mining Co v Eyre*[511] it was said to be necessary to show that the petitioner did not have reasonable or probable cause. It seems that the adjectives 'reasonable' and 'probable' are used synonymously in the cases. In *'Seaspray' Steamship Co Ltd v Tenant*[512] Lord Salvesen used the phrases 'reasonable cause' and 'probable cause' as if they were interchangeable. In *Aitchison and Sons Ltd v M'Ewan*[513] Lord Low spoke only of 'want of probable cause'. In the leading case on maliciously petitioning for bankruptcy, *Johnson v Emerson*,[514] the judges used the phrase 'reasonable *and* probable cause', and this phrase is commonly used in cases on malicious prosecution: it was also used by Brett MR in *Quartz Hill Gold Mining Co v Eyre* and at p 687 his Lordship used the phrases 'want of reasonable and probable cause' and 'want of reasonable or probable cause' in successive sentences. In the context of malicious prosecution, Hawkins J said in *Hicks v Faulkner*:[515]

> Now I should define reasonable and probable cause to be, an honest belief in the guilt of the accused based upon a full conviction, founded upon reasonable grounds, of the existence of a state of circumstances, which, assuming them to be true, would reasonably lead any ordinarily prudent and cautious man, placed in the position of the accuser, to the conclusion that the person charged was probably guilty of the crime imputed.

This definition was approved by Lord Atkin in *Herniman v Smith*.[516] Absence of reasonable or probable cause for petitioning for winding up means 'a want of genuine belief by [the petitioner], based on reasonable grounds, that there were good grounds in law for presenting the petition'.[517] The fact that the petitioner has acted on professional legal advice will usually show that the petitioner had reasonable or probable cause,[518] though there may be difficulty if the advice is incompetent or negligent and the crucial factor is always the information and belief of the petitioner.[519] A creditor's petition presented by a person knowing that the claim on which the petition is based is disputed is nevertheless presented with reasonable or probable cause if the petitioner believes that the dispute is ill-founded.[520] A petitioner who petitioned in reliance on a state of affairs which did not in fact exist may nevertheless be found to have acted with reasonable or probable cause on showing both an

---

[509] *Tibbs v Islington London Borough Council* [2002] EWCA Civ 1682, [2003] BPIR 743.
[510] *Tibbs v Islington London Borough Council.*
[511] (1883) 11 QBD 674.
[512] (1908) 15 SLT 874.
[513] (1902) 10 SLT 501.
[514] (1871) LR 6 Ex 329.
[515] (1878) 8 QBD 167 at p 171.
[516] [1938] AC 305 at p 316.
[517] *Partizan Ltd v O J Kilkenny and Co Ltd* [1998] 1 BCLC 157 per Rimer J at p 170.
[518] *QIW Retailers Ltd v Felview Pty Ltd* [1989] 2 QdR 245.
[519] *Jacob v Vockrodt* [2007] EWHC 2403 (QB), [2007] BPIR 1568.
[520] *Partizan Ltd v O J Kilkenny and Co Ltd* [1998] 1 BCLC 157.

honest belief that the state of affairs did exist and reasonable care in ascertaining what the state of affairs was.[521]

In *Partizan Ltd v O J Kilkenny and Co Ltd*[522] Rimer J found that the petition had not been **2.181** presented without reasonable or probable cause, but, in case this should be overturned on appeal, assessed general damages for loss of reputation at £5,000.

Malice

'Malice' means 'improper or wrongful motive of some kind'[523] or 'an undue and improper **2.182** motive'.[524] In *Gibbs v Rea*[525] the majority of the Privy Council said, at p 797, that the true foundation of the tort of malicious prosecution is 'intentional abuse of the processes of the court' and 'Malice in this context has the special meaning common to other torts and covers not only spite and ill-will but also improper motive'. Absence of reasonable cause may be evidence of malice, but is not sufficient evidence.[526] The fact that a creditor's petition was based on a debt which was disputed on substantial grounds does not show that the petitioner was intentionally abusing the court's process if the petitioner did not know or believe that the debt was disputed on substantial grounds.[527]

Malicious continuation of proceedings

If the circumstances that would make presentation of a petition malicious arise only after it **2.183** is presented, continuation of the proceedings is a tort.[528]

Collateral Abuse of Process

It is a tort to institute proceedings for a purpose, or to effect an object, beyond that which **2.184** the legal process offers.[529] Unlike malicious prosecution[530] it is not necessary to show that there was a favourable end to the proceedings or that there was an absence of reasonable cause. It is, however, necessary to show that the improper purpose was the dominant purpose. The tort is rarely claimed and its ambit should be the same as that of malicious prosecution, with the same limits on the kinds of damages that can be claimed.[531] It is perhaps a statistical anomaly that two reported successful claims concern winding-up petitions. In *Allure Sportswear Inc v Beiner*[532] damages of C$900 were awarded against an individual who maliciously caused a company he controlled to petition as creditor. In *QIW Retailers Ltd v Felview Pty Ltd*[533] damages of AU$10,000 were awarded.

---

[521] *Quartz Hill Consolidated Gold Mining Co v Eyre* (1884) 50 LT 274.
[522] [1998] 1 BCLC 157.
[523] Per Rimer J in *Partizan Ltd v O J Kilkenny and Co Ltd* [1998] 1 BCLC 157 at p 173.
[524] *Johnson v Emerson* (1871) LR 6 Ex 329 per Cleasby B at p 332.
[525] [1998] AC 786.
[526] *Quartz Hill Gold Mining Co v Eyre* (1883) 11 QBD 674 per Brett MR at p 687 and per Bowen LJ at p 694; *Gibbs v Rea* [1998] AC 786 at p 798.
[527] *Jacob v Vockrodt* [2007] EWHC 2403 (QB), [2007] BPIR 1568.
[528] *Jacob v Vockrodt* [2007] EWHC 2403 (QB), [2007] BPIR 1568, at [35].
[529] *Grainger v Hill* (1838) 4 Bing NC 212; *Williams v Spautz* (1992) 174 CLR 509, in which the tort is called collateral abuse of process.
[530] See 2.177.
[531] *Land Securities plc v Fladgate Fielder* [2009] EWCA Civ 1402, [2010] Ch 467.
[532] [1960] Que SC 628.
[533] [1989] 2 QdR 245.

Procedure

2.185 A claim for damages on the ground that a petition to wind up a company was presented tortiously must be made separately: such damages cannot be awarded on the hearing of the petition.[534] Under the English court procedure before the CPR it was held in *Partizan Ltd v O J Kilkenny and Co Ltd*[535] that a claim for damages for tortiously presenting a winding-up petition could not be made by ordinary application in the winding-up proceedings, because the Rules of the Supreme Court 1965, ord 5, r 2, required such a claim to be begun by writ. It is submitted that the position is similar under the CPR, which are based on the principle that all proceedings are to be started by issuing a claim form, unless some other method is expressly prescribed, as is the case for winding-up proceedings. In *Partizan Ltd v O J Kilkenny and Co Ltd* the claim was permitted to proceed under the old Rules of the Supreme Court 1965, ord 2, r 1 (which provided that a failure to comply with the rules when purporting to begin proceedings was not to nullify the proceedings), as the petitioner had failed to apply within a reasonable time to set aside the proceedings. It is likely that the court would exercise its discretion in the same way under CPR, r 3.10.

Form and Contents of Petition

Prescribed Form of Petition[536]

2.186 Under IR 1986, r 4.7, the prescribed form of petition for the winding up of a company, if the petitioner is not a contributory, is form 4.2 in sch 4 to the Rules.[537]

2.187 There are special forms prescribed for certain types of petitions under IPO 1994.

2.188 If a petition under IPO 1994, art 7 (petition for the winding up of a partnership, other than by a member of the partnership with no accompanying petition for the winding up or bankruptcy of a present or former member of the partnership), is presented by one of the insolvency practitioners authorized to petition by IA 1986, s 221A, as inserted by IPO 1994, sch 3, para 3, the prescribed form of petition is form 3 in sch 9 to IPO 1994.

2.189 The prescribed form of a petition under IPO 1994, art 8, to wind up an insolvent partnership is form 5 in sch 9 to IPO 1994 and the prescribed form for an accompanying petition to wind up a present or former corporate member of the partnership is form 6 in that schedule.[538]

2.190 The prescribed form of a petition under IPO 1994, art 10, to wind up an insolvent partnership is form 11 in sch 9 to IPO 1994 and the prescribed form for an accompanying petition to wind up a corporate member of the partnership is form 12 in that schedule.[539]

2.191 There is no prescribed form of application for a bank or building society insolvency order.

---

[534] *Si and Si Sdn Bhd v Hazrabina Sdn Bhd* [1996] 2 MLJ 509.
[535] [1998] 1 BCLC 157.
[536] The material in 2.186–2.191 does not apply to a petition to wind up a company presented by a contributory or contributories of the company or at the instance of the company's administrator or voluntary arrangement supervisor (IR 1986, rr 4.2(4) and 4.7(9)). Such petitions are discussed at 8.469–8.518.
[537] As substituted by the Insolvency (Amendment) Rules 2002 (SI 2002/1307), sch, part 2.
[538] IA 1986, s 124(1), as modified by IPO 1994, sch 4, para 8.
[539] IA 1986, s 124(1), as modified by IPO 1994, sch 6, para 2.

Contents of Petition[540]

Prescribed contents

A winding-up petition must be headed:[541]   **2.192**

> IN THE MATTER OF [name of company sought to be wound up]
> AND IN THE MATTER OF THE INSOLVENCY ACT 1986

Deviation from the prescribed form of citation of the statute is not permitted.[542]   **2.193**

The petition must be addressed to Her Majesty's High Court of Justice or to the County Court.   **2.194**
It must state the full name and address of the petitioner.

The prescribed paragraphs of a petition to wind up a company in form 4.2 state: **2.195**

(1) The full name, registered number[543] and date of incorporation of the company, and which Companies Act it was registered under.

(2) The address of its registered office and, in the case of an overseas company, the address of any establishment registered at Companies House.[544]

(3) Its nominal capital (otherwise known as authorized share capital)[545] and how that is divided into shares, and its paid-up capital. PD Insolvency Proceedings 2014, para 11.2(5), says that what should be given is:

   (a) In the case of companies incorporated under any of the Companies Acts prior to the Companies Act 2006, a statement of the nominal capital of the company, the manner in which its shares are divided up and the amount of the capital paid up or credited as paid up.

   (b) In the case of any other companies, a statement of the known issued share capital of the company, the manner in which its shares are divided up and the amount of the capital paid up or credited as paid up.

(4) The principal objects of the company.[546] PD Insolvency Proceedings 2014, para 11.2(6), says that what should be given is:

   (a) In the case of companies incorporated under any of the Companies Acts prior to the Companies Act 2006, brief details of the principal objects for which the company was

---

[540] The material in 2.192–2.217 does not apply to a petition to wind up a company presented by a contributory or contributories of the company or at the instance of the company's administrator or voluntary arrangement supervisor (IR 1986, rr 4.2(4) and 4.7(9)). Such petitions are discussed at 8.469–8.518.

[541] PD Insolvency Proceedings 2014, para 4.2.

[542] *Re Frith House Paper Mills Co Ltd* (1880) 24 SJ 690; cf *Re Marezzo Marble Co Ltd* (1874) 43 LJ Ch 544 discussed at 3.152.

[543] Every company is allocated a registered number by the registrar of companies under the Companies Act 2006, s 1066. PD Insolvency Proceedings 2014, para 11.2(2), emphasizes that 'any registered number/s of the company' must be given.

[544] Under the Companies Act 2006, s 1046, and the Overseas Companies Regulations 2009 (SI 2009/1801). PD Insolvency Proceedings 2014, para 11.2(4).

[545] As from 1 October 2009, a registered company is no longer required to have an authorized share capital. Any provision of the old-style memorandum of a company registered before 1 October 2009 stating the amount of its authorized share capital is treated on or after that day as a provision of its articles setting the maximum amount of shares that may be allotted by the company (Companies Act 2006 (Commencement No 8, Transitional Provisions and Savings) Order 2008 (SI 2008/2860), sch 2, para 42).

[546] As from 1 October 2009, the objects of a registered company are unrestricted, unless specifically restricted by its articles (Companies Act 2006, s 31).

established followed, where appropriate, by the words 'and other objects stated in the memorandum of association of the company'.[547]

(b) In the case of companies incorporated under the Companies Act 2006, either:

(i) a statement confirming that its objects are unrestricted pursuant to the Companies Act 2006, s 31(1); or alternatively

(ii) a statement confirming that its objects are restricted by its articles of association and brief details of such restrictions.

(5) The 'grounds on which a winding-up order is sought'.[548]

(6) A statement of whether the company is or is not one of the types of company to which Regulation (EC) No 1346/2000 (called the EC Regulation in form 4.2) does not apply.[549]

(7) A statement that, for the reasons stated in the written evidence filed in support of the petition, it is considered that Regulation (EC) No 1346/2000 will or will not apply, and, if the Regulation does apply, whether the proceedings will be main, secondary or territorial proceedings.[550]

(7A) A statement, if applicable, that the reasons why more than four months have elapsed since a statutory demand was served on the company are set out in the statement of truth filed in support of the petition.

(8) A statement that: 'In the circumstances it is just and equitable that the company should be wound up'.

2.196 There is then a prayer that the company named may be wound up by the court under the provisions of IA 1986 or that such other order may be made as the court thinks fit. A note states that it is intended to serve the petition on the company (if that is the case) and gives the names and addresses of all other persons on whom it is intended to serve the petition.[551]

2.197 It is very important that items (1)–(3) correspond exactly with the data on the company's file at Companies House. If the company is not a registered company, information which is only relevant to a registered company can be omitted,[552] but as much similar information as is available should be given.[553]

2.198 The prescribed forms of petition end with a section headed 'endorsement'. This has spaces to be filled in by a court official with the venue for hearing the petition[554] and spaces to be filled in with the name, address and telephone number of the petitioner's solicitors and their reference number and equivalent details of their London agents. The information about the petitioner's solicitors must be completed before the petition is filed.

2.199 The prescribed paragraphs may be left blank if it is not possible to obtain the information.[555]

2.200 It is not necessary for a petition to be signed or sealed by the petitioner.[556]

---

[547] The old-style memorandum of a company registered before 1 October 2009 was required to state the company's objects. On and after that day, the statement is treated as a provision of the company's articles (Companies Act 2006, s 28).

[548] See 2.202–2.212.

[549] See 1.390–1.392 and 2.234–2.237.

[550] See 2.234–2.237.

[551] See 3.1–3.48 for the requirements relating to service.

[552] IR 1986, r 12A.30(2).

[553] PD Insolvency Proceedings 2014, para 11.2 introductory words.

[554] See 2.243.

[555] *Re Standard Contract and Debenture Corporation* (1892) 8 TLR 485.

[556] *Osborne v Gaunt* (1872) 3 AJR 47; *Re Federal Land Co Ltd* (1889) 15 VLR 135; *Re Root Hog Gold Mining Co Ltd* (1890) 1 BC (NSW) 32; *Re Testro Bros Consolidated Ltd* [1965] VR 18; but *Re Lemay Ltd* (1924)

Settlement system

If the subject of a winding-up petition or an application for a bank or building society **2.201** insolvency order is a participant in a designated system, the petition or application must contain details needed by the court to notify the order, if it makes one.[557] The petition or application must state that it concerns a participant in a designated system and identify the system operator of the relevant designated system, the relevant designating authority, and the email or other addresses to which the court will be required to send notice.[558]

Grounds

In para 5 of the prescribed form of petition, the petitioner alleges the existence of one **2.202** or more of the circumstances in which the court may make a winding-up order (usually called 'grounds' for winding up, see 2.23–2.53) and states the facts from which it may be concluded that the alleged circumstance or circumstances exist. A creditor's petition to wind up a company on the ground that it is unable to pay its debts must include:[559]

(a) details of the basis on which it is contended that the company is insolvent including, where a debt is relied on, sufficient particulars of the debt (the amount, nature and approximate date(s) on which it was incurred) to enable the company and the court to identify the debt; and
(b) a statement that the company is insolvent and unable to pay its debts.

A petitioner is not limited to relying on only one ground.[560] The legislative provision defining **2.203** each ground relied on should be identified precisely.[561] A petition is bound to fail if it does not allege any facts from which it may be concluded that at least one of the prescribed circumstances exists.[562]

In winding-up proceedings the petitioner's case must be stated in the petition (though **2.204** amendment may be allowed): the petitioner cannot leave it to the hearing to establish the ground for the petition. At the hearing the petitioner will be limited to the grounds stated in the petition.[563] The court will not 'travel outside' the allegations in the petition.[564]

---

26 OWN 443 at p 444, saying that a petition by a company not under the corporate seal or signed by the president and secretary must be disregarded, is to the contrary.

[557] See 5.274.
[558] PD Insolvency Proceedings 2014, paras 19.1 and 19.2.
[559] PD Insolvency Proceedings 2014, para 11.2(7) and (8).
[560] *Emporium Jaya (Bentong) Sdn Bhd v Emporium Jaya (Jerantut) Sdn Bhd* [2002] 1 MLJ 182.
[561] In Malaysia it has been said that a petition which does not do this will be struck out (*Wong Thai Kuai v Kansas Corp Sdn Bhd* [2007] 4 MLJ 33).
[562] *Re Wear Engine Works Co* (1875) LR 10 Ch App 188; *Re National Petroleum Ltd* [1958] QdR 482; *Re Eastern Minerals and Trading (1959) Ltd* [1964] MLJ 451; *Hollands Printing Ltd v San Michele Ltd* [1992] 3 NZLR 469, in which it was said that such a petition would be an abuse of process; *Securum Finance Ltd v Camswell Ltd* [1994] BCC 434, in which it was said that such a petition would be an abuse of process; *Datuk Mohd Sari bin Datuk Hj Nuar v Idris Hydraulic (M) Bhd* [1997] 5 MLJ 377. See also *Nomura International plc v Granada Group Ltd* [2007] EWHC 642 (Comm), [2008] Bus LR 1 (it is an abuse of process to issue a claim form when incapable of stating grounds for the claim).
[563] *Re Spence's Patent Non-conducting Composition and Cement Co* (1869) LR 9 Eq 9; *Re Michael P Georgas Ltd* [1948] 2 DLR 602; *Re Fildes Bros Ltd* [1970] 1 WLR 592; *Re Armvent Ltd* [1975] 1 WLR 1679 at p 1683; *Datuk Mohd Sari bin Datuk Hj Nuar v Idris Hydraulic (M) Bhd* [1997] 5 MLJ 377; *Fairview Schools Bhd v Indrani a/p Rajaratnam (No 2)* [1998] 1 MLJ 110.
[564] *Re Lundie Brothers Ltd* [1965] 1 WLR 1051 per Plowman J at p 1058.

A winding-up petition should be *secundum allegata et probanda* (in accordance with what is alleged and proved).[565] In *Re Fildes Bros Ltd*[566] Megarry J said, at p 598:

> In cases in which there are no normal pleadings, it seems to me important that those who oppose a winding up should know, in time to prepare their case, what are the allegations that they have to meet. If after a petition has been presented the petitioner wishes to broaden his attack, let him first amend his petition.

2.205 A petitioner cannot rely on disclosure and inspection of documents[567] or cross-examination of the company's witnesses[568] to reveal facts to support the petition.

2.206 Paragraph 5 of a winding-up petition must state the circumstances which give the petitioner standing to petition: merely describing the petitioner as, for example, 'creditor' or 'contributory' is not sufficient.[569]

2.207 The grounds on which a winding up is sought must be stated in the petition itself: it is not sufficient to state them in an accompanying witness statement.[570] In *Re a Company (No 007936 of 1994)*[571] a statement in a petition that 'The petitioners will rely on the substantial correspondence exhibited to the affidavit verifying this petition, as the particulars are too numerous to be conveniently set out here' was described by Roger Kaye QC (sitting as a deputy High Court judge) as 'completely unacceptable'.[572] Mr Kaye went on to say:

> Any averment in a petition that expects the respondent and its advisers to trawl through a mass of indigestible correspondence, minutes and other documents in order to find out what the case is against them in a material respect is to be regarded, in my view, as bad.

2.208 A petition which fails to allege enough for the court to act on used to be described as 'demurrable'.[573]

2.209 In *Re Richard Pitt and Sons Pty Ltd*,[574] Cosgrove J said:

> opposition to the petitioner's claim is to be demonstrated by filing one or more affidavits[575] in reply. The petitioner may also file affidavits. The whole procedure envisages trial by affidavit, subject to cross-examination of the deponents. A petition, therefore, must contain all necessary allegations in a form which is sufficient to enable the court to make the requisite findings, and consider the appropriate order. The allegation must condescend to particulars to that extent.

2.210 Nevertheless, the primary purpose of a petition is to state the factual allegations supporting the petitioner's plea, rather than the evidence which will be used to prove those allegations. As Waddell J said in *Re Media Press Pty Ltd*:[576]

> a petition [is required by the rules and usage of the court] to set out the material facts on which the petitioner relies for the relief claimed and particulars of these facts which are

---

[565] *Re Wear Engine Works Co* (1875) LR 10 Ch App 188.
[566] [1970] 1 WLR 592.
[567] *Re a Company, ex parte Burr* [1992] BCLC 724 per Vinelott J at p 736 and on appeal sub nom *Re Saul D Harrison and Sons plc* [1995] 1 BCLC 14 per Hoffmann LJ at p 22.
[568] *Re a Company* (1917) 34 DLR 396.
[569] *Re Palais Cinema Ltd* [1918] VLR 113.
[570] *Re Buzolich Patent Damp-Resisting and Anti-Fouling Paint Co Ltd* (1884) 10 VLR (E) 276; *Re Palais Cinema Ltd* [1918] VLR 113.
[571] [1995] BCC 705.
[572] At p 716.
[573] *Re Wear Engine Works Co* (1875) LR 10 Ch App 188.
[574] (1979) 4 ACLR 459 at p 478.
[575] In England and Wales, evidence is now given in witness statements rather than affidavits.
[576] (1980) 4 ACLR 867, at p 870.

sufficient to make clear the precise nature of the case made by the petitioner. The petition should not contain a statement of the evidence by which those facts are to be proved because to do so would be likely to mislead as to the true nature of the petitioner's case.

His Honour struck out a 25-page narrative from a petition, saying, at p 872:

> The paragraphs objected to do not, in general, state material facts or particulars of such facts but facts which may or may not be evidence from which an inference might be drawn of the existence of some fact material to the relief of the kind sought. Even considered as evidence the great bulk of the paragraphs are ambiguous and incomplete and are not capable of leading to any relevant conclusion of fact.

Re Netsor Pty Ltd [577] is another case in which a long narrative was struck out of a winding-up petition. **2.211**

The fact that a petition contains an untrue statement about a person who is not a party to the winding-up proceedings does not entitle that person to have the statement struck out, provided it is relevant.[578] **2.212**

Prayer

In the prescribed form of petition, the prayer is that the company named in the petition be wound up by the court or 'that such other order may be made as the court thinks fit'. As will be explained at 5.127–5.134 the court's power under IA 1986, s 125(1), on hearing a winding-up petition to make any other order that it thinks fit is limited to making ancillary orders in furtherance of or otherwise in connection with a present or prospective winding-up order: the court is not authorized to order some remedy other than winding up. Therefore a winding-up petition cannot pray for any alternative or additional remedy.[579] **2.213**

The full name and registered number of the company must be stated in the prayer, and the name as stated there will be inserted in the winding-up order, if made. Therefore, it is most important that the name is stated correctly in the prayer. **2.214**

Company struck off the register

A petition for the winding up of a registered company which has been struck off the register of companies should state that fact and include as part of the relief sought an order that it be restored to the register. Save where the petition has been presented by a minister of the Crown or a government department, evidence of service on the Treasury Solicitor or the Solicitor for the affairs of the Duchy of Lancaster or the Solicitor to the Duchy of Cornwall (as appropriate) should be filed exhibiting the *bona vacantia* waiver letter.[580] **2.215**

Insolvent partnerships

Where petitions are presented under IPO 1994, art 8, for the winding up of an insolvent partnership and the bankruptcy or winding up of one or more present or former members of the partnership, each petition must contain particulars of other petitions being presented in relation to the partnership, identifying the partnership and members concerned.[581] **2.216**

---

[577] (1981) 6 ACLR 114.
[578] *Re Indian Kingston and Sandhurst Gold Mining Co Ltd* (1882) 26 SJ 671.
[579] *See Teow Guan v Kian Joo Holdings Sdn Bhd* [1995] 3 MLJ 598; *Aznor bin Abdul Karim v Kemasrunding Sdn Bhd* [1998] 5 MLJ 572.
[580] PD Insolvency Proceedings 2014, para 11.4.
[581] IA 1986, s 124(5), as modified by IPO 1994, sch 4, para 8.

2.217 Where petitions are presented under IPO 1994, art 10, for the winding up of a partnership and the winding up or bankruptcy of every one of its members, each petition must contain particulars of other petitions being presented in relation to the partnership, identifying the partnership and members concerned[582] and each petition for the winding up of a member must contain a statement that the member is willing for a winding-up order to be made against it.[583]

Verification of Petition[584]

Requirement for verification

2.218 A winding-up petition must be verified by a statement of truth[585] in accordance with CPR, Part 22.[586] The statement of truth should be made no more than ten business days before the date of issue of the petition.[587]

2.219 The statement of truth verifying a winding-up petition must state whether, in the opinion of the petitioner, Regulation (EC) No 1430/2000 (the EC Regulation) applies and, if it does, whether the proceedings will be main, secondary or territorial proceedings.[588] If a creditor's petition is in respect of debts due to different creditors, the debts to each creditor must be separately verified.[589]

2.220 If the statement of truth is not contained in or endorsed on the petition which it verifies, it must be sufficient to identify the petition and must specify:

(a) the name and registered number of the company,

(b) the name of the petitioner, and

(c) the court in which the petition is to be presented.[590]

2.221 Proceedings for contempt of court may be brought against a person who makes, or causes to be made, a false statement in a document verified by a statement of truth without an honest belief in its truth.[591]

2.222 A petition for the winding up of an insolvent partnership must be verified by an affidavit in form 2 in sch 9 to IPO 1994.[592]

---

[582] IA 1986, s 124(5), as modified by IPO 1994, sch 6, para 2.

[583] IA 1986, s 124(2), as modified by IPO 1994, sch 6, para 2; a drafting error raises doubt about whether this provision is effective; see 1.229.

[584] The material in 2.218–2.237 applies as far as possible to a petition to wind up a company presented by a contributory or contributories of the company or at the instance of the company's administrator or voluntary arrangement supervisor. See 8.480.

[585] IR 1986, rr 4.7(1) and 4.12(1).

[586] IR 1986, r 13.13(17).

[587] PD Insolvency Proceedings 2014, para 11.3.

[588] IR 1986, r 4.12(8). See 2.234–2.237.

[589] IR 1986, r 4.12(2).

[590] IR 1986, r 4.12(3A). For a petition to wind up a relevant scheme (see 1.168), this paragraph is modified by the Collective Investment in Transferable Securities (Contractual Scheme) Regulations 2013 (SI 2013/1388), sch 3.

[591] CPR, r 32.14(1), applied by IR 1986, r 7.51A(4). For procedure see CPR, rr 81.17 and 81.18.

[592] IA 1986, s 221(8), as modified by IPO 1994, sch 3, para 3 (in relation to petitions under art 7 of the Order); IA 1986, s 221(9), as modified by IPO 1994, sch 4, para 3 (in relation to art 8 petitions); IA 1986, s 221(8), as modified by IPO 1994, sch 5, para 2 (in relation to art 9 petitions); IA 1986, s 221(9), as modified by IPO 1994, sch 6, para 4 (in relation to art 10 petitions).

Until 25 April 1999, verification of any winding-up petition except a contributory's petition **2.223** had to be by affidavit in prescribed form. From 26 April 1999, verification could be by a witness statement instead of an affidavit,[593] but this option was not made available to petitions for the winding up of insolvent partnerships. The current rule requiring verification by statement of truth came into force on 6 April 2010,[594] but the requirement for an affidavit in the case of an insolvent partnership was not revoked.

Who may verify

The statement of truth verifying a winding-up petition must be authenticated by:[595]   **2.224**

(a) the petitioner (or if there are two or more petitioners, any one of them), or
(b) some person such as a director, company secretary or similar company officer, or a solicitor, who has been concerned in the matters giving rise to the presentation of the petition, or
(c) some responsible person who is duly authorized to authenticate the statement of truth and has the requisite knowledge of those matters.

In cases (b) and (c) the person verifying the petition must state the capacity in which, and **2.225** the authority by which, he or she does so, and the means of knowing the matters being verified.[596] In *Handlingair Douglas Ltd v Aetna Casualty and Surety Co*[597] a winding-up order had been made on a petition verified by an affidavit which did not contain this statement. On appeal against the winding-up order it was said that the defect could be cured by a supplementary affidavit.[598] In r 4.12(4)(b) 'solicitor' does not include a body recognized by the Law Society under the Administration of Justice Act 1985, s 9,[599] or a body which holds a licence issued by the Law Society which is in force under the Legal Services Act 2007, part 5.[600]

The court has a discretion to accept verification from a person not mentioned in r 4.12(4).[601] **2.226**

Position under earlier rules

IR 1986, r 4.12(4)(c), provides that a winding-up petition may be verified by some respon- **2.227** sible person who is duly authorized to do so and has the requisite knowledge of the matters giving rise to the presentation of the petition. This provision is new to the 1986 rules and appears to have considerably widened the class of people declared by the rules to be capable of verifying a petition. Under the previous rules, affidavits from agents for petitioners who were individuals outside the jurisdiction had been accepted[602] and a petition by the Crown

---

[593] IR 1986, r 7.57(5).
[594] The change was made by the Insolvency (Amendment) Rules 2010 (SI 2010/686).
[595] IR 1986, r 4.12(4).
[596] IR 1986, r 4.12(5).
[597] 1986–87 CILR 441.
[598] An affidavit cannot be amended, which is why a second affidavit was required.
[599] Solicitors' Recognised Bodies Order 1991 (SI 1991/2684), arts 2(1) and 4(a) and sch 1.
[600] Legal Services Act 2007 (Designation as a Licensing Authority) (No. 2) Order 2011 (SI 2011/2866), arts 1(3) and 8 and sch 2.
[601] *Re African Farms Ltd* [1906] 1 Ch 640.
[602] *Re Fortune Copper Mining Co* (1870) LR 10 Eq 390; *Re Carrara Marble Co* [1896] WN 87 (affidavit by clerk to the solicitors acting for the petitioners who had full knowledge of the proceedings leading to the petitioners being judgment creditors); *Re African Farms Ltd* [1906] 1 Ch 640; but not in *Re Charterland Stores and Trading Co* [1900] 2 Ch 870.

could be verified by a fit and proper person.[603] It was emphasized in *Re African Farms Ltd*[604] that the person who made the affidavit knew the facts better than the absent petitioner. In *Re Andre's Piquenique Basket Pty Ltd*[605] and *Re R and G Publishing Pty Ltd*,[606] affidavits from officers employed by the Deputy Commissioner of Taxation were accepted as verifying petitions presented by the Deputy Commissioner, because those officers knew the facts better than the petitioner.

2.228   The 1862 rules did not make any provision for a petitioner being a company (except where a company was petitioning for its own winding up), but affidavits of officers of petitioning companies were accepted in *Re Cakemore Causeway Green and Lower Holt United Brickworks and Colliery Co Ltd*[607] (affidavit of petitioner's general manager), *Re Birmingham Concert Halls Ltd*[608] (affidavit of petitioner's secretary) and *Bahama Islands Lakefront Estates Ltd v Exuma Services Ltd*.[609]

2.229   The Companies Winding-up Rules 1890 provided for a petition being presented by a company other than the petitioner but required the petition of a company to be verified by 'some director, secretary, or other principal officer thereof'.[610] In Practice Note [1937] WN 350 it was said that an assistant secretary of the petitioning company was not a principal officer. In *Re Vic Groves and Co Ltd*,[611] one of 32 divisional managers of a large petrol company was held not to be a principal officer of the company—it made no difference that the company had given him a power of attorney to make affidavits on its behalf to verify its winding-up petitions. In *Re Action Waste Collections Pty Ltd*[612] the affidavit of the compulsory liquidator of the principal shareholder of the petitioning company was not acceptable. However, in *Re Martmel (No 17) Pty Ltd*[613] it was said that a company's application could be verified by an affidavit from a person other than a director, secretary or principal officer of the company if it was proved that the person making the affidavit was a fit and proper person with knowledge of the facts, and in *Re Beauretta Pty Ltd*[614] it was accepted that an employee of the liquidator of the applicant company was within that description. In *Re Review Publishing Co*[615] the petitioning company was itself in liquidation and also a receiver had been appointed by the court: an affidavit from the receiver's manager was accepted (either the receiver or the manager—the statement in the report is ambiguous—was one of the liquidators). In England and Wales the class of persons authorized by the rules to swear a verifying affidavit on behalf of a corporation was enlarged by the Companies (Winding-up) (Amendment)

---

[603] *Re Brandy Distillers Co* (1901) 17 TLR 272 (Attorney General's petition for non-payment of income tax verified by affidavit of the Solicitor to the Inland Revenue); *Re Golden Chemical Products Ltd* [1976] Ch 300 (Secretary of State's public interest petition verified by Inspector of Companies); *Jamincorp International Merchant Bank v Minister of Finance* (1987) 36 WIR 313 (government minister's public interest petition verified by affidavit of official).

[604] [1906] 1 Ch 640.

[605] (1987) 11 ACLR 456.

[606] [1989] VR 457.

[607] (1880) 28 WR 299.

[608] [1890] WN 91.

[609] [1971–6] 1 LRB 140.

[610] r 36.

[611] [1964] 1 WLR 956.

[612] (1976) 2 ACLR 253.

[613] [1994] 1 QdR 588.

[614] [1994] 2 QdR 3.

[615] [1893] WN 5.

Rules 1967,[616] r 2, to any 'person who has been concerned in the matter on behalf of the corporation'.

It is submitted that the persons who made the affidavits in *Re Charterland Stores and Trading Co*;[617] Practice Note [1937] WN 350 and *Re Vic Groves and Co Ltd*[618] could nowadays verify petitions under IR 1986, r 4.12(4)(c). Now that r 4.12(4)(b) refers to a 'similar company officer' rather than a 'principal officer', it may be that a person in the position of the manager in *Re Vic Groves and Co Ltd* would be within r 4.12(4)(b)—see *Handlingair Douglas Ltd v Aetna Casualty and Surety Co*,[619] in which it was said that a divisional manager of the petitioning company who reported to one of the company's 100–200 vice-presidents might be within r 4.12(4)(b). **2.230**

Time of verification

As verification of a winding-up petition must be filed with the petition it may be made before the petition is filed.[620] However, it should be made no more than ten business days before the date of issue of the petition.[621] If there is an interval of more than ten business days, the court will usually require re-verification.[622] **2.231**

Under the 1862 Rules[623] and subsequent rules up to the 1949 Rules,[624] the verifying affidavit had to be sworn after the petition was presented. If a winding-up order had been made on a petition verified by an affidavit sworn before it was presented, the affidavit had to be re-sworn and the order re-dated with the date of filing of the re-sworn affidavit, with the permission of the court to extend the time for filing.[625] The requirement that the verifying affidavit be sworn after the petition was not removed until 1 April 1979.[626] **2.232**

Verification of more than one petition

If there are simultaneous petitions to wind up several companies (for example, all companies in a group) it is permissible to make one statement of truth referring to all the companies and submit a photocopy with each petition.[627] **2.233**

Application of the EC Regulation

Paragraph 7 of the prescribed form of winding-up petition[628] requires the statement of truth filed in support of the petition to give evidence for the petitioner's consideration, stated in para 7, and in the statement of truth,[629] of: **2.234**

(a) whether or not Regulation (EC) No 1430/2000 (the EC Regulation) applies; and
(b) if it does, whether the proceedings will be main, secondary or territorial proceedings.

---

[616] SI 1967/1341.
[617] [1900] 2 Ch 870.
[618] [1964] 1 WLR 956.
[619] 1986–87 CILR 441.
[620] *Re Martmel (No 17) Pty Ltd* [1994] 1 QdR 588.
[621] PD Insolvency Proceedings 2014, para 11.3.
[622] Chancery Guide 2013, para 20.20.
[623] General Order and Rules of the High Court of Chancery to Regulate the Mode of Proceeding under the Companies Act 1862 (11 November 1862), r 4.
[624] Companies (Winding-up) Rules 1949 (SI 1949/330), r 30.
[625] *Re Western Benefit Building Society* (1864) 33 Beav 368; *Bahama Islands Lakefront Estates Ltd v Exuma Services Ltd* [1971–6] 1 LRB 140; *Delta Drive (M) Sdn Bhd v Hong Leong Finance Bhd* [2008] 4 MLJ 400.
[626] Companies (Winding-up) (Amendment) Rules 1979 (SI 1979/209), r 4.
[627] IR 1986, r 4.12(7).
[628] IR 1986, sch 4, form 4.2.
[629] IR 1986, r 4.12(8). See 2.219.

2.235 The Regulation does not apply to the types of company listed in art 1(2).[630] Paragraph 6 of form 4.2 lists these types and requires the petitioner to state whether the company sought to be wound up is one of them. If para 6 states that the company is in one of the excluded classes, para 7 will state that the Regulation does not apply and the supporting statement of truth will have to state the reason for concluding that the company is in one of the excluded classes.

2.236 If the company sought to be wound up is not in any of the excluded classes, the Regulation will apply if the company has its COMI in an EU State (including the UK, but excluding Denmark), even if it is incorporated in Denmark or outside the EU.[631] For the determination of where a company's COMI is located see 1.376–1.386. The most important point is that a company's COMI is presumed to be at its registered office, in the absence of proof to the contrary.[632] So the supporting statement of truth should state where the registered office of the company is located. If it is necessary to claim that the COMI is in a different jurisdiction, evidence sufficient to rebut the presumption must be presented in the supporting statement of truth.

2.237 If it is considered that the EC Regulation does apply, the proceedings will be main proceedings if the company's COMI is in the UK. If that is the case, no further evidence will be required in the supporting statement of truth, because it will already have established that the COMI is in the UK for the purpose of establishing that the Regulation applies. If the company's COMI is not in the UK, winding-up proceedings can be opened here only if it has an establishment[633] in the UK.[634] So evidence will be required in the supporting statement of truth of the existence of such an establishment. It will also be necessary to state whether main proceedings have been opened in another EU State (other than Denmark), for this determines whether the English winding up will be territorial proceedings (opened before main proceedings) or secondary proceedings (opened after main proceedings).

Verification of a bank or building society insolvency application

2.238 An application for a bank or building society insolvency order must have attached to it a witness statement stating that the statements in the application are true, or are true to the best of the applicant's knowledge, information and belief.[635] The witness statement must:[636]

(a) identify the person making it;
(b) include the capacity in which the person makes the statement; and
(c) include the basis for that person's knowledge of the matters set out in the application.

The witness statement is, unless proved otherwise, evidence of the statements in the application.[637]

---

[630] See 1.390–1.392.
[631] See 1.393.
[632] art 3(1).
[633] See 1.387–1.389.
[634] art 3(2).
[635] Bank Insolvency (England and Wales) Rules 2009 (SI 2009/356), r 11(1) and (2); Building Society Insolvency (England and Wales) Rules 2010 (SI 2010/2581), r 11(1) and (2).
[636] SI 2009/356, r 11(3); SI 2010/2581, r 11(3).
[637] SI 2009/356, r 11(4); SI 2010/2581, r 11(4).

Further Witness Statement

The prescribed contents of a petition[638] are required in all cases but may not be sufficient.[639] **2.239**
This is because the court has a discretion whether or not to make a winding-up order and
may exercise its discretion against making one if there is nothing more than the prescribed
statements in a case where the petition levels grave charges against individuals or is one
of complexity turning upon the conduct of individuals.[640] The facts of an alleged fraud
must be stated in the petition[641] and in the written evidence.[642] When any additional or
supplementary evidence is filed by the petitioner, notice of the filing must be given to the
company.[643] For the company's evidence in opposition, see 3.178–3.180.

Filing, Venue and Track Allocation[644]

General Rules on Filing and Fixing of Venue

Filing a petition

Before presenting a petition for the winding up of a company, a search must be conducted **2.240**
of the central registry of winding-up petitions[645] to ensure that no petition for the winding
up of that company is already pending. Save in exceptional circumstances a second petition
should not be presented while a prior petition is pending.[646]

A petition for the winding up of a company (with the verification described at 2.218–2.237) **2.241**
must be filed in court.[647] A petition is 'presented' when it is filed, not when it is issued.[648]
'Filing' a document is defined as delivering the document, by post or otherwise, to the
court office.[649] A petition cannot be filed unless the receipt for the deposit for the official
receiver's administration fee is produced with it.[650] The date on which the petition is filed
at court will be recorded on it by a seal or receipt stamp.[651] Particulars of the petition and
the title of the proceedings will be entered in court records[652] and in the central registry of
winding-up petitions.

---

[638] See 2.192–2.217.

[639] *Re St David's Gold Mining Co Ltd* (1866) 14 LT 539.

[640] *Re ABC Coupler and Engineering Co Ltd (No 2)* [1962] 1 WLR 1236.

[641] *Re Rica Gold Washing Co* (1879) 11 ChD 36.

[642] *Re South Staffordshire Tramways Co* (1894) 1 Mans 292; *Re London and Hull Soap Works Ltd* [1907]
WN 254; *Re Whitla Holdings Pty Ltd* (1982) 7 ACLR 348.

[643] *Re British Cycle Manufacturing Co Ltd* (1898) 77 LT 683.

[644] The material in 2.240–2.247 does not apply to a petition to wind up a company presented by a contributory or contributories of the company or at the instance of the company's administrator or voluntary
arrangement supervisor (IR 1986, rr 4.2(4) and 4.7(9)). Such petitions are discussed at 8.469–8.518.

[645] By personal attendance at the ground floor, Royal Courts of Justice, Rolls Building, 7 Rolls Buildings,
Fetter Lane, London EC4A 1NL, or by telephone on 0906 754 0043.

[646] PD Insolvency Proceedings 2014, para 11.1.

[647] IR 1986, r 4.7(1).

[648] *Re Blights Builders Ltd* [2006] EWHC 3549 (Ch), [2007] Bus LR 629, which concerned the meaning
of 'presented' in IA 1986, sch B1, para 25.

[649] CPR, r 2.3(1).

[650] IR 1986, r 4.7(2); see 2.255.

[651] PD 5, para 5.1.

[652] PD 5, para 5.2.

2.242 An application for a bank or building society insolvency order must be filed in court,[653] but the official receiver is not involved in bank or building society insolvency so no deposit for an official receiver's fee is required.

Fixing a venue

2.243 When a petition for the winding up of a company, or an application for a bank or building society insolvency order, is filed in court, the court must fix a venue for hearing it.[654] 'Venue' means the time, date and place for the hearing.[655] The court must endorse the venue on every copy issued to the petitioner or applicant.[656] In fixing a venue for an application for a bank or building society insolvency order, the court must have regard to the desirability of the application being heard as soon as reasonably practicable and the need to give the institution a reasonable opportunity to attend.[657]

Number of copies to be filed: winding-up petition

2.244 IR 1986, r 4.7, requires copies of the petition, which are required for service on various persons, to be filed with it. These copies are sealed by the court, endorsed with the venue for the hearing and issued to the petitioner.[658]

2.245 Unless the petition is presented by the company itself, it must be accompanied by a copy for service on the company.[659] (If the company is the petitioner, service on the company is not required.)

2.246 Whether the petition is presented by the company itself or not, r 4.7(4) requires copies of the petition to be filed with it in the following circumstances:

(a) If the company is in course of being wound up voluntarily, and a liquidator has been appointed, one copy of the petition to be sent to the voluntary liquidator.[660] Sending this copy is required by r 4.10(1) if, to the petitioner's knowledge, the company is being wound up voluntarily.

(b) If the company is in administration, one copy to be sent to the administrator.[661] Sending this copy is required by r 4.10(2) if, to the petitioner's knowledge, the company is in administration.

(c) If an administrative receiver has been appointed in relation to the company, one copy to be sent to that administrative receiver.[662] Sending this copy is required by r 4.10(2) if, to the petitioner's knowledge, an administrative receiver has been appointed in relation to the company.

---

[653] Bank Insolvency (England and Wales) Rules 2009 (SI 2009/356), r 7(1); Building Society Insolvency (England and Wales) Rules 2010 (SI 2010/2581), r 7(1).

[654] IR 1986, r 4.7(6); Bank Insolvency (England and Wales) Rules 2009 (SI 2009/356), r 7(3); Building Society Insolvency (England and Wales) Rules 2010 (SI 2010/2581), r 7(3).

[655] IR 1986, r 13.6.

[656] IR 1986, r 4.7(6); Bank Insolvency (England and Wales) Rules 2009 (SI 2009/356), r 7(4); Building Society Insolvency (England and Wales) Rules 2010 (SI 2010/2581), r 7(4).

[657] SI 2009/356, r 7(3); SI 2010/2581, r 7(3).

[658] IR 1986, r 4.7(5) and (6).

[659] IR 1986, r 4.7(3).

[660] IR 1986, r 4.7(4)(a).

[661] IR 1986, r 4.7(4)(b).

[662] IR 1986, r 4.7(4)(c).

(d) If there is in force for the company a voluntary arrangement under IA 1986, part 1,[663] one copy for the supervisor of the arrangement.[664] Sending this copy is required by r 4.10(3) if, to the petitioner's knowledge, there is in force for the company a voluntary arrangement.

(e) If a member State liquidator has been appointed in main proceedings in relation to the company, one copy to be sent to him or her.[665] Sending this copy is required by r 4.10(3A) if, to the petitioner's knowledge, there is a member State liquidator appointed in main proceedings in relation to the company.[666]

(f) If the company is an authorized deposit-taker or former authorized deposit-taker and the petitioner is not the FCA or the PRA, one copy for each of those Authorities.[667] An authorized deposit-taker is a person with permission under the Financial Services and Markets Act 2000, part 4A, to accept deposits.[668] A former authorized deposit-taker is a person who is not an authorized deposit-taker, but was formerly an authorized institution under the Banking Act 1987, or formerly a recognized bank or a licensed institution under the Banking Act 1979, and continues to have liability in respect of any deposit for which it had liability at a time when it was an authorized institution, recognized bank or licensed institution.[669] Sending this copy is required by IR 1986, r 4.10(4), which has not been amended to refer to the 2000 Act.

There are three other circumstances, not picked up in IR 1986, in which legislation requires a copy of a winding-up petition to be served: **2.247**

(g) If a petition is presented for the winding up of an authorized person[670] which has permission to effect or carry out contracts of insurance, or which is a reclaim fund,[671] and the petitioner is not the FCA or the PRA, the petitioner must serve a copy of the petition on the FCA and, if the petition is for the winding up of a PRA-authorized person, the PRA.[672] If either the FCA or the PRA presents a petition for the winding up of a PRA-authorized person which has permission to effect or carry out contracts of insurance, or which is a reclaim fund, it must serve a copy of the petition on the other regulator.[673]

(h) If a petition is presented for the winding up of an open-ended investment company or a sub-fund by a person other than the FCA, a copy of the petition must be served on the FCA.[674]

(i) While a Lloyd's market reorganization order is in force, if a petition is presented for the winding up of Lloyd's, and the petitioner is not the reorganization controller, the petitioner must serve a copy of the petition on the reorganization controller.[675]

---

[663] ss 1–7B.

[664] IR 1986, r 4.7(4)(d).

[665] IR 1986, r 4.7(4)(da).

[666] Rule 4.7(4)(da) does not mention that this copy is not required if the member State liquidator is the petitioner (r 4.10(3A)).

[667] IR 1986, r 4.7(4)(e).

[668] IR 1986, r 13.12A(1).

[669] IR 1986, r 13.12A(2).

[670] See 9.113.

[671] 'Reclaim fund' is defined as a company whose objects are restricted to dealing with dormant bank and building society accounts in specified ways (Dormant Bank and Building Society Accounts Act 2008, s 5(1)).

[672] Financial Services and Markets Act 2000, ss 369(1) and (3) and 369A(1), (3) and (4).

[673] ss 369(4) and 369A(5).

[674] Open-Ended Investment Companies Regulations 2001 (SI 2001/1228), reg 31(3), applied to sub-funds by reg 33C(1) and (5)(a).

[675] Insurers (Reorganisation and Winding Up) (Lloyd's) Regulations 2005 (SI 2005/1998), reg 30(1) and (2).

Number of copies to be filed: application for a bank or building society insolvency order

2.248 An application for a bank or building society insolvency order must be filed with copies as required by the rules.[676] These copies will be sealed by the court, endorsed with the venue, date and time of the hearing and issued to the applicant.[677] Copies are required for:

(a) service on the institution;[678]

(b) attachment to the proof of service;[679]

(c) the proposed bank or building society liquidator;[680]

(d) the Bank of England, if it is not the applicant;[681]

(e) the FCA, if it is not the applicant;[682]

(f) the PRA, if it is not the applicant and if the institution is a PRA-authorized person;[683]

(g) the Financial Services Compensation Scheme;[684]

(h) any person who has given notice in respect of the bank under the Banking Act 2009, s 120, or the building society under the Building Societies Act 1986, s 90D (which require notice to be given to the FCA and/or the PRA of an application for an administration order, a petition for a winding-up order, a resolution for voluntary winding up or a proposed appointment of an administrator);[685]

(i) if a voluntary arrangement is in force for the institution, the supervisor,[686] and the court to which the nominee's report under IA 1986, s 2, was submitted, if that is not the court in which the application for the insolvency order is filed;[687]

(j) any administrative receiver of the institution.[688]

Special Rules for Petitions to Wind Up Insolvent Partnerships

2.249 IPO 1994, art 8, provides for a petition for the winding up of an insolvent partnership to be presented in conjunction with a petition or petitions for the bankruptcy or winding up of one or more present or former members of the partnership. All the petitions must be presented to the same court and, except as the court otherwise permits or directs, on the same day.[689] The court must fix a venue for the hearing of the petition to wind up the partnership in advance of that fixed for the hearing of any petition against an insolvent member.[690] After presenting a petition under art 8 the petitioner may apply to the court for leave to add other members or former members of the partnership as parties to the proceedings in relation to the insolvent partnership and the court may give leave on such terms as it thinks just.[691]

---

[676] Bank Insolvency (England and Wales) Rules 2009 (SI 2009/356), r 7(2); Building Society Insolvency (England and Wales) Rules 2010 (SI 2010/2581), r 7(2).

[677] SI 2009/356, r 7(4); SI 2010/2581, r 7(4).

[678] SI 2009/356, r 7(2)(a); SI 2010/2581, r 7(2)(a).

[679] SI 2009/356, r 7(2)(b); SI 2010/2581, r 7(2)(b).

[680] SI 2009/356, r 10(1)(a); SI 2010/2581, r 10(1)(a).

[681] SI 2009/356, r 10(1)(b); SI 2010/2581, r 10(1)(b).

[682] SI 2009/356, r 10(1)(c); SI 2010/2581, r 10(1)(c) (see r 3(2) for the definition of 'the appropriate regulator').

[683] SI 2009/356, r 10(1)(ca); SI 2010/2581, r 10(1)(c) (see r 3(2) for the definition of 'the appropriate regulator').

[684] SI 2009/356, r 10(1)(d); SI 2010/2581, r 10(1)(d).

[685] SI 2009/356, r 10(1)(e); SI 2010/2581, r 10(1)(e).

[686] SI 2009/356, r 10(1)(f); SI 2010/2581, r 10(1)(f).

[687] SI 2009/356, r 7(5); SI 2010/2581, r 7(5).

[688] SI 2009/356, r 10(1)(g); SI 2010/2581, r 10(1)(g).

[689] IA 1986, s 124(3)(a), as modified by IPO 1994, sch 4, para 8.

[690] IA 1986, s 124(6), as modified by IPO 1994, sch 4, para 8.

[691] IA 1986, s 124(4), as modified by IPO 1994, sch 4, para 8.

IPO 1994, art 10, provides for a petition for the winding up of an insolvent partnership to **2.250** be presented by a member of the partnership in conjunction with a petition or petitions for the bankruptcy or winding up of all members of the partnership (including the petitioner). All the petitions must be presented to the same court and, except as the court otherwise permits or directs, on the same day.[692] The court must fix a venue for the hearing of the petition to wind up the partnership in advance of that fixed for the hearing of any petition against an insolvent member.[693] If the court is satisfied that it would be impracticable to present petitions against every member, it may, on the application of any member, direct that petitions be presented against the partnership and such member or members as it specifies.[694]

The rules on providing copies of the petition for other persons[695] apply to a petition for the **2.251** winding up of an insolvent partnership.

Track Allocation

All insolvency proceedings, including winding-up petitions, are allocated to the multi-track[696] **2.252** and so the provisions of the CPR concerning directions questionnaires and track allocation do not apply.[697] The same provision is made for bank insolvency proceedings[698] and building society insolvency proceedings.[699]

Fee and Deposit

On presentation of a winding-up petition, a court fee of £280 must be paid.[700] **2.253**

The petitioner must deposit £1,250 as security for the administration fee which will become **2.254** payable to the official receiver if a winding-up order is made and transmitted to the official receiver.[701] In the case of a public interest petition presented by the Secretary of State under IA 1986, s 124A, the deposit is £5,000.[702]

A petition cannot be filed unless the receipt for the deposit is produced,[703] unless the Secretary **2.255** of State has given written notice (which has not been revoked) that the petitioner has made other arrangements for paying deposits to the official receiver.[704]

The deposit is security for the official receiver's administration fee and must be used to dis- **2.256** charge that fee to the extent that the company's assets are insufficient.[705] The administration

---

[692] IA 1986, s 124(4)(a), as modified by IPO 1994, sch 6, para 2.
[693] IA 1986, s 124(6), as modified by IPO 1994, sch 6, para 2.
[694] IA 1986, s 124(3), as modified by IPO 1994, sch 6, para 2. Unfortunately IA 1986, s 221(6), as modified by IPO 1994, sch 6, para 4, accidentally provides that s 124(3) does not apply to an art 10 petition; see 1.229.
[695] See 2.240–2.247.
[696] See CPR, part 29.
[697] IR 1986, r 7.51A(3).
[698] Bank Insolvency (England and Wales) Rules 2009 (SI 2009/356), r 227(2).
[699] Building Society Insolvency (England and Wales) Rules 2010 (SI 2010/2581), r 220(2).
[700] Civil Proceedings Fees Order 2008 (SI 2008/1053), sch 1, fee 3.3.
[701] IA 1986, s 414(4); Insolvency Proceedings (Fees) Order 2004 (SI 2004/593), art 6(1)(a).
[702] SI 2004/593, art 6(1)(aa).
[703] IR 1986, r 4.7(2).
[704] IR 1986, r 4.7(2), (2A) and (2B).
[705] SI 2004/593, art 6(2).

fee is £2,400[706] or £5,000 in the case of an s 124A petition.[707] The court must transmit the deposit to its official receiver.[708] If a winding-up order is made, any part of the deposit which is not required to pay the administration fee must be returned.[709] If the petition is dismissed or withdrawn, the whole of the deposit must be repaid.[710] The court fee is not repayable. The principal danger for a petitioner is that the company's assets will not be sufficient to repay the deposit: in the order of priority of expenses,[711] it is only item (g).

2.257 Where petitions are presented under IPO 1994, art 8 or art 10, for the winding up of a partnership and the winding up or bankruptcy of one or more of its present or former members, only one court fee is payable[712] and a deposit is required only in respect of the petition for the winding up of the partnership but is treated as a deposit in respect of all the petitions.[713]

2.258 Production of any receipt for the sum deposited upon presentation of a petition for winding up a partnership shall suffice for the filing in court of a petition for the winding up or bankruptcy of an insolvent member of the partnership.[714]

2.259 The court fee on presentation of an application for a bank or building society insolvency order is £480,[715] but no deposit is required for an official receiver's fee.

No Undertaking as to Damages

2.260 Despite the great inconvenience that can be caused by the presentation of an unsuccessful winding-up petition, a petitioner is never required to give an undertaking in damages unless there is an application for the appointment of a provisional liquidator.[716]

Court Files

Court Files

2.261 When a winding-up petition is presented to a court, or an application is made for an injunction prohibiting presentation of a petition, the court must open and maintain a file and place on it all documents filed with the court under IA 1986 or IR 1986.[717]

2.262 The court must open and maintain a file for each bank or building society insolvency and (subject to the direction of the registrar) all documents relating to that insolvency shall be placed on that file.[718]

---

[706] SI 2004/593, sch 2, fee W1.
[707] SI 2004/593, sch 2, fee W1A.
[708] SI 2004/593, art 11(3).
[709] SI 2004/593, art 11(5).
[710] SI 2004/593, art 11(4).
[711] IR 1986, r 4.218(3).
[712] SI 2008/1053, sch 1, note following fee 3.3.
[713] IPO 1994, art 13(1).
[714] IPO 1994, art 13(2).
[715] SI 2008/1053, sch 1, fee 1.5.
[716] *Re Highfield Commodities Ltd* [1985] 1 WLR 149.
[717] IR 1986, r 7.31A(1) and (2).
[718] Bank Insolvency (England and Wales) Rules 2009 (SI 2009/356), r 209(1); Building Society Insolvency (England and Wales) Rules 2010 (SI 2010/2581), r 203(1).

Inspection and Copying

Winding up

The following may inspect a court file relating to a winding-up petition, or, on payment of **2.263** any prescribed fee, obtain from the court a copy of the file or a copy of any document or documents on the file:

(a) The office-holder in the proceedings.[719]

(b) The Secretary of State.[720]

(c) Any person who is a creditor of the company to which the proceedings relate if that person provides the court with written confirmation of being a creditor.[721] In relation to the file on a winding-up petition, a member State liquidator appointed in main proceedings in relation to the company has the same right as a creditor.[722]

(d) An officer or former officer of the company to which the proceedings relate.[723]

(e) A member of the company or a contributory in its winding up.[724]

(f) A person authorized by any of the persons in (a)–(e) to exercise on their behalf their right to inspect or obtain copies.[725]

(g) Any person who has the permission of the court.[726]

An application may be made to the court for a direction that a file, a document, part of a **2.264** document, a copy of a document, or a copy of part of a document, must not be made available to persons in (a)–(f) without the court's permission.[727] The application may be made by the official receiver, the office-holder in the proceedings or any person appearing to the court to have an interest.[728] It may be made without notice to any other party, but the court may direct that notice must be given to any person who would be affected by its decision.[729]

A person who does not need the court's permission to inspect a court file relating to a **2.265** winding-up petition may inspect it at any reasonable time,[730] but must file with the court a written request, and pay the prescribed fee, in order to obtain a copy of a document.[731]

The court must comply with any request by the Secretary of State or the official receiver for **2.266** transmission of the file of any insolvency proceedings, provided:

(a) the file is required for the purposes of powers conferred by IA 1986 or IR 1986;

(b) the file is not for the time being in use for the court's own purposes.[732]

---

[719] IR 1986, r 7.31A(3)(a); see 1.535. For a petition to wind up a relevant scheme (see 1.168), r 7.31A is modified by the Collective Investment in Transferable Securities (Contractual Scheme) Regulations 2013 (SI 2013/1388), sch 3.

[720] r 7.31A(3)(b).

[721] r 7.31A(3)(c).

[722] r 7.64(2).

[723] r 7.31A(4)(a)(i).

[724] r 7.31A(4)(a)(ii).

[725] r 7.31A(5).

[726] r 7.31A(6).

[727] r 7.31A(7).

[728] r 7.31A(8).

[729] r 7.31A(11).

[730] r 7.31A(9)(b).

[731] r 7.31A(10)(b).

[732] r 7.31A(12).

Bank or building society insolvency

2.267   The following have the right to inspect a court file for a bank or building society insolvency:

(a) The liquidator.[733]

(b) Any person who is a creditor of the institution to which the insolvency relates if that person provides the court with written confirmation of being a creditor.[734]

(c) A member of the bank or building society.[735]

(d) Any person who is, or at any time has been, a director or officer of the institution to which the insolvency relates.[736]

(e) Any person who is a contributory of the institution to which the insolvency relates.[737]

(f) The Bank of England.[738]

(g) The FCA and, if the institution is a PRA-authorized person, the PRA.[739]

(h) The Financial Services Compensation Scheme.[740]

(i) A person authorized by any of the persons in (a)–(h) to exercise on their behalf their right to inspect or obtain copies.[741]

(j) Any person who has the permission of the court.[742]

2.268   An application may be made to the court for a direction that a document or part of a document is not to be open to inspection without the court's permission.[743] The application may be made by the liquidator or any person appearing to the court to have an interest in the insolvency.[744]

2.269   A person who does not need the court's permission to inspect a court file relating to a bank insolvency may inspect it at any reasonable time.[745]

2.270   The court must comply with any request by the Secretary of State for transmission of the file on a bank or building society insolvency, provided:

(a) the file is required for the purposes of powers conferred by IA 1986, the Banking Act 2009 or (as appropriate) the Bank Insolvency (England and Wales) Rules 2009 or the Building Society Insolvency (England and Wales) Rules 2010;

(b) the file is not for the time being in use for the court's own purposes.[746]

Application for Permission to Inspect or Copy a Court File

Winding-up proceedings

2.271   If the court's permission is required to inspect or copy all or part of a court file, it must be asked for by filing an application notice.[747] This may be done without notice to any other

---

[733] Bank Insolvency (England and Wales) Rules 2009 (SI 2009/356), r 209(2)(a); Building Society Insolvency (England and Wales) Rules 2010 (SI 2010/2581), r 203(2)(a).

[734] SI 2009/356, r 209(2)(b); SI 2010/2581, r 203(2)(b).

[735] SI 2009/356, r 209(2)(c); SI 2010/2581, r 203(2)(c).

[736] SI 2009/356, r 209(2)(d); SI 2010/2581, r 203(2)(d).

[737] SI 2009/356, r 209(2)(e); SI 2010/2581, r 203(2)(e).

[738] SI 2009/356, r 209(2)(f); SI 2010/2581, r 203(2)(f).

[739] SI 2009/356, r 209(2)(f); SI 2010/2581, r 203(2)(f).

[740] SI 2009/356, r 209(2)(f); SI 2010/2581, r 203(2)(f).

[741] SI 2009/356, r 209(3); SI 2010/2581, r 203(3).

[742] SI 2009/356, r 209(4); SI 2010/2581, r 203(4).

[743] SI 2009/356, r 209(5); SI 2010/2581, r 203(5).

[744] SI 2009/356, r 209(6); SI 2010/2581, r 203(6).

[745] SI 2009/356, r 209(2); SI 2010/2581, r 203(2).

[746] SI 2009/356, r 209(7); SI 2010/2581, r 203(7).

[747] IR 1986, r 7.31A(9)(a) and (10)(a).

party, but the court may direct that notice must be given to any person who would be affected by its decision.[748]

A good case must be made out for obtaining permission.[749] The purpose for which inspection or copying is permitted is 'to enable persons who have a legitimate interest in a particular insolvency proceeding to discover what has taken place'.[750] Inspection may be allowed for the purpose of obtaining evidence for use in other proceedings.[751] **2.272**

Applications to inspect all the records, for example, to produce a mailing list[752] or to create a commercially exploitable duplicate of the court's records,[753] are not for a proper purpose and will be refused. If a commercial organization created a duplicate of the court's records, the court would lose control over the inspection of them. **2.273**

In *Ex parte Austintel Ltd*[754] Ward LJ said, obiter, that it is legitimate for a person to inspect for the purpose of establishing whether a winding-up petition had been presented against a company with which that person is contemplating doing business, even if notice has not yet been given of the petition, or it has not yet been served on the company, so that the company has not had the opportunity to prevent the petition proceeding. His Lordship thought it is also legitimate to employ an agent to inspect for such a purpose, and suggested ways in which a business such as Austintel's could be granted permission to inspect on behalf of clients. In the light of this judgment, systematic multiple inspections by a firm of insolvency practitioners have been permitted, subject to a number of undertakings, but this facility cannot be used to create mailing lists for advertising the firm's services.[755] **2.274**

Bank and building society insolvency proceedings

In bank and building society insolvency proceedings, the Bank Insolvency (England and Wales) Rules 2009[756] and the Building Society Insolvency (England and Wales) Rules 2010[757] apply IR 1986 without the amendments made by the Insolvency (Amendment) Rules 2010.[758] In particular, they apply IR 1986, rr 7.27 (court records) and 7.28 (inspection of records),[759] which were replaced in the 2010 revision.[760] So the rules try to apply to bank and building insolvency a system of records of insolvency proceedings which no longer exists, which would seem to be unworkable. As explained at 1.64, it is uncertain whether the provisions of SI 2009/356 and SI 2010/2581 can be treated as applying IR 1986 with the **2.275**

---

[748] IR 1986, r 7.31A(11).
[749] *Mansell v Acton* [2005] EWHC 3048 (Ch), [2006] BPIR 778.
[750] *Re an Application under the Insolvency Rules 1986* [1994] 2 BCLC 104 per Millett J at p 105.
[751] *Franbar Holdings Ltd v Patel* [2008] EWHC 1534 (Ch), [2009] 1 BCLC 1 (where the application was made in the other proceedings).
[752] *Re an Application under the Insolvency Rules 1986.*
[753] *Ex parte Creditnet Ltd* [1996] 1 WLR 1291.
[754] [1997] 1 WLR 616 at pp 622–4.
[755] *Re Haines Watts* [2004] EWHC 1970 (Ch), [2005] BPIR 798.
[756] SI 2009/356.
[757] SI 2010/2581.
[758] SI 2010/686. See the definition of 'the 1986 Rules' in SI 2009/356, r 3(2), and SI 2010/2581, r 3(2).
[759] Rules 7.27 and 7.28 are discussed in the second edition of this work at 2.12. They are applied to bank insolvency by SI 2009/356, rr 207 and 208, and modified by r 3(3)(b) and (4)(h). They are applied to building society insolvency by SI 2010/2581, rr 201 and 202, and modified by r 3(5)(b) and (6)(j).
[760] SI 2010/686, sch 1, para 457.

2010 amendments, and it is thought that the court should be asked to give directions on the point. If SI 2009/356 and SI 2010/2581 are to be treated as applying IR 1986 with the 2010 amendments, the position is that what is said at 2.271–2.274 applies to bank and building society insolvency proceedings.[761]

Office Copies of Documents on the Court File

2.276 Any person who, under IR 1986, has a right to inspect the court file of insolvency proceedings[762] may require the court to provide an office copy of any document from the file.[763] A requisition may be made by the person's solicitor.[764] An office copy will be in such form as the registrar thinks appropriate and must bear the court's seal.[765] The same applies to bank insolvency proceedings[766] and building society insolvency proceedings.[767]

---

[761] Treating the references in SI 2009/356, r 208, and SI 2010/2581, r 202, to IR 1986, r 7.28, as references to r 7.31A(10) and (11), and ignoring SI 2009/356, r 207, and SI 2010/2581, r 201. The applied provision of IR 1986 would be modified by SI 2009/356, r 3(3)(b) and (7), or SI 2010/2581, r 3(5)(b) and (10), as appropriate.

[762] See 2.263.

[763] r 7.61(1).

[764] r 7.61(2).

[765] r 7.61(3).

[766] Bank Insolvency (England and Wales) Rules 2009 (SI 2009/356), r 233.

[767] Building Society Insolvency (England and Wales) Rules 2010 (SI 2010/2581), r 226.

3

BETWEEN PRESENTATION AND HEARING

Service of Petition[1]

Service on the Company Sought to be Wound Up

General rule

3.1   Unless a petition to wind up a company is the company's own petition, a copy of the petition must be served on the company.[2] This must be a copy which was filed in court with the petition and issued to the petitioner, sealed by the court and endorsed with the venue for the hearing of the petition.[3] It must be served at least seven business days *before* notice of it appears by gazetting or otherwise as the court orders,[4] and the notice must appear at least seven business days before the hearing date.[5] There is no requirement for service of a copy of a separate statement of truth.[6]

3.2   Service is the responsibility of the petitioner and will not be undertaken by the court.[7]

---

[1]   The material in 3.1–3.59 does not apply to a petition to wind up a company presented by a contributory or contributories of the company or at the instance of the company's administrator or voluntary arrangement supervisor (IR 1986, rr 4.2(4) and 4.7(9)). Such petitions are discussed at 8.469–8.518.

[2]   IR 1986, rr 4.7(3) and 4.8.

[3]   IR 1986, r 4.7(3), (5) and (6).

[4]   See 3.120.

[5]   IR 1986, r 4.11(4)(b). 'Business day' is defined in r 13.13(1) (see 1.512).

[6]   *Timbunan Alam Development Sdn Bhd v Platicorp Holding (M) Sdn Bhd* [2000] 2 MLJ 636. This is so in England and Wales even though the verification is now filed with the petition instead of afterwards, as is still the case in Malaysia (see 2.231–2.232).

[7]   PD Insolvency Proceedings 2014, para 6.2.

Part 6 of the Civil Procedure Rules (CPR) does not apply to the service of a winding-up **3.3** petition within the jurisdiction.[8] Instead there are complicated provisions in the Insolvency Rules 1986 (IR 1986) about service on a company of a petition to wind it up.[9]

A certificate of service must be filed in court.[10] The company itself is not required to commu- **3.4** nicate with the court: acknowledgment of service and filing a defence have no place in proceedings on a winding-up petition, though the company may file evidence in opposition.[11]

A petition to wind up a relevant scheme[12] must be served on the scheme's operator and on **3.5** its depositary.[13]

A winding-up order made on a petition that has not been served is fundamentally defective **3.6** and will normally be set aside.[14] Under the CPR, setting aside is at the court's discretion, which must be exercised in a way that furthers the overriding objective.[15] So the court can properly refuse to set aside the order only if there is no prejudice to the company or a third party.[16] Inexcusable delay in applying to set aside the order after learning of it may be a reason for refusing to set it aside.[17]

In *Re Victorian Street Railway Co*,[18] on hearing a petition, the court upheld an objection by **3.7** contributories that service had not been effected properly and adjourned the hearing for the error to be corrected: the fact that the contributories had appeared was held not to be a waiver of service. In two cases under the Joint Stock Companies Winding-up Act 1848 and the Joint Stock Companies Winding-up Amendment Act 1849 the court made winding-up orders despite failure to serve the petition on the companies.[19] In each case the company had appeared to consent to the order. In the first case the court required service on the company before the order could be drawn up.

Service on solicitor

If a company has indicated that its solicitor is authorized to accept service on its behalf, service **3.8** may be effected on the solicitor instead of the company.[20] In *Re Fletcher Hunt (Bristol) Ltd* the shares in the company were held by Mr Hyde (who petitioned as a creditor for it to be wound up) and by Fletcher Hunt plc and Mr Fletcher. Mr Fletcher and Fletcher Hunt plc jointly

---

[8] IR 1986, rr 12A.16(2)(a) and 12A.17. CPR, Part 6, does apply to service outside the jurisdiction; see 3.30.

[9] They are set out at 3.9–3.33.

[10] IR 1986, r 4.9A. See 3.34–3.40.

[11] See 3.178–3.180. As there is no requirement to acknowledge service or file a defence, default judgment under CPR, Part 12, is not possible.

[12] See 1.168.

[13] IR 1986, r 4.8, as applied and modified by the Collective Investment in Transferable Securities (Contractual Scheme) Regulations 2013 (SI 2013/1388), sch 3.

[14] *Craig v Kanssen* [1943] KB 256; *White v Weston* [1968] 2 QB 647; *Re Samoana Press Co Ltd* (1987) 4 NZCLC 64,119; *Nelson v Clearsprings (Management) Ltd* [2006] EWCA Civ 1252, [2007] 1 WLR 962. See 6.8–6.9.

[15] CPR, r 1.1. *Nelson v Clearsprings (Management) Ltd* at [49].

[16] *Nelson v Clearsprings (Management) Ltd* at [50].

[17] *Nelson v Clearsprings (Management) Ltd* at [50].

[18] (1865) 2 W W & A'B (E) 132.

[19] *Re Tring, Reading and Basingstoke Railway Co* (1849) 3 De G & Sm 10; *Re Great Western Railway Co of Bengal, ex parte Wolesey* (1849) 3 De G & Sm 101.

[20] IR 1986, r 13.4; *Re Regent United Service Stores* (1878) 8 ChD 75; *Re Fletcher Hunt (Bristol) Ltd* [1989] BCLC 108 per Knox J at p 113; *Re Griffin Securities Corporation* [1999] 3 SLR 346; *Re Bezier Acquisitions Ltd* [2011] EWHC 3299 (Ch), [2012] Bus LR 636.

instructed a firm of solicitors to act for the company in relation to the petition. The solicitors acting for the petitioner, Mr Hyde, served the petition on the solicitors appointed by Mr Fletcher. It was held that, through his solicitors acting as his agents, Mr Hyde had, by sending the petition for service on the company to the solicitors appointed by Mr Fletcher, joined the other members of the company in appointing those solicitors to act for the company.

Service at the registered office of a registered company

3.9   If service of a petition to wind up a registered company is not to be on the company's solicitor, the petition must be served at the company's registered office, if it has one.[21] IR 1986, r 4.8(2), specifies that 'the company's registered office' means:

(a) the place which was given as the intended address of the registered office when applying for registration,[22] and which became the company's registered office when the company was registered;[23] or

(b) if notice has been given by the company to the registrar of companies of a change of address of its registered office,[24] 'the place specified in that notice or, as the case may be, in the last such notice'.

3.10   No mention is made in IR 1986, r 4.8(2), of the provision that the change of address takes effect upon the notice being registered by the registrar, but, until the end of the period of 14 days beginning with the date of registration of the notice, a person may validly serve a document on the company at the address previously registered.[25]

3.11   A petition for a registered company to be wound up may be served at the company's registered office in any of the following ways:[26]

(a) it may be handed to a person who there and then acknowledges him or herself to be, or to the best of the server's knowledge, information and belief is, a director or other officer, or employee, of the company; or

(b) it may be handed to a person who there and then acknowledges him or herself to be authorized to accept service of documents on the company's behalf; or

(c) in the absence of any such person as is mentioned in (a) or (b), it may be deposited at or about the registered office in such a way that it is likely to come to the notice of a person attending at the office (it seems there is no requirement that this is to be a person who has any connection with the company).

3.12   If option (c) in 3.11 is used, the certificate of service must state that no director, officer or employee of the company, or person authorized to accept service on the company's behalf was present at the registered office, referring to every one of these categories.[27] It must also state where in the registered office the petition was deposited and how, so as to indicate why it would be likely to come to the notice of a person attending at the office. It will not, for example, suffice simply to post the petition under a wooden door, because there can be no

---

[21] IR 1986, r 4.8(2).
[22] Companies Act 2006, s 9(5)(a).
[23] Companies Act 2006, s 16(1) and (4).
[24] Companies Act 2006, s 87(1).
[25] Companies Act 2006, s 87(2).
[26] IR 1986, r 4.8(3).
[27] *Re Hatcham Motor Garage Co Ltd* [1916] WN 152; *MUI Bank Bhd v Golden Hornbill Hotel Sdn Bhd* [1993] 1 MLJ 290.

certainty that the petition is visible. It might, for example, have become lodged underneath the carpet or mat on the other side of the door. Posting a petition under a glass door is sufficient if the process server can see that the petition is clearly visible in the premises and cannot easily be removed from outside the premises. If it is necessary to affix a petition to an external door of the registered office, it should be securely fastened in a waterproof envelope to protect against rain making it illegible. In these circumstances, the manner of service (together, crucially, with the level of detail provided by way of evidence of service) must be given careful consideration.

Handing the petition, at the registered office, to an individual, who is not a director, officer **3.13** or employee of the company and is not authorized to accept service, so that the individual can send it to a company officer is not valid service.[28]

For service at a registered office in a building in multiple occupancy see 1.528. **3.14**

It is clear from r 4.8(6) that service at the registered office may not be effected in any **3.15** other way (for example, by post) without the court's approval or direction. Postal service of a winding-up petition was not permitted under the Companies (Winding-up) Rules 1949, r 29.[29]

The company's solicitor is not, as such, an officer of the company and is not an employee **3.16** unless actually engaged under a contract of employment, and so cannot be served as an officer or employee.[30] Service on the company's solicitor is proper only if the solicitor is instructed to accept service.[31]

Where service at registered office will not bring the petition to the company's attention

If it is apparent that service of a petition to wind up a company at its registered office is **3.17** unlikely to bring the petition to the company's attention, an application may be made to the court for directions.[32]

In *Re London and Westminster Wine Co Ltd*[33] the registered office was found to be shut up **3.18** and there was no person to take in letters but the petitioner knew where the company's solicitors and directors were. The court directed that the petition could be put in the letter box at the company's registered office and copies served on the solicitors and one of the directors. In *Re Stewart and Brother*[34] the company sought to be wound up was in voluntary winding up and no one was present at its registered office when an attempt was made to serve the petition. It was held that service on the voluntary liquidator was sufficient (there was at the time no rule corresponding to the present IR 1986, r 4.10(1), requiring a copy of a petition for the winding up of a company in voluntary winding up to be sent to the voluntary liquidator, unless the petition was for the continuation of the voluntary winding up under the supervision of the court). This seems to be inconsistent with the ruling in *Re*

---

[28] *Sterling Hay Corporate Risks Ltd v Wasu* [2003] EWHC 748 (Ch).
[29] *Re a Company* [1985] BCLC 37 per Nourse J at pp 42–3.
[30] *Re Trent Valley and Chester and Holyhead Continuation Railway Co, ex parte Dale* (1849) 3 De G & Sm 11.
[31] See 3.8.
[32] For the view that not making such an application may be an abuse of process see 1.531.
[33] (1863) 9 LT 321.
[34] [1880] WN 15.

Petroleum Co[35] that service on the liquidator of a company in voluntary winding up was not sufficient and that service had to be on the company secretary.

3.19 For rescission of a winding-up order where the petitioner was unaware that the company had left the registered office given in the registrar's records see 6.37–6.38.

Service at principal place of business or on officer of company

3.20 IR 1986, r 4.8(4), specifies methods for serving a winding-up petition on the company sought to be wound up if:

(a) the company is a registered company but service at its registered office is not practicable, or
(b) the company is a registered company but has no registered office, or
(c) the company is an unregistered company.

3.21 In any of those cases the petition may be served on the company by:

(a) leaving it at the company's last known principal place of business in such a way that it is likely to come to the attention of a person attending there,[36] or
(b) delivering it to the secretary or some director, manager or principal officer of the company, wherever that person may be found.

3.22 Option (a) only authorizes service at a place of business within the jurisdiction.[37]

3.23 If there is no known principal place of business within the jurisdiction, option (a) is not available, so option (b) must be followed or an order for alternative service sought under r 4.8(6).[38] It would seem that the same applies if the registered office or only known place of business of the company has been demolished.[39] A petition for the winding up of a dissolved company may be served on the company under r 4.8(4) by leaving it at the company's last known principal place of business within the jurisdiction, or at some place within the jurisdiction at which it has carried on business.[40] However, in *Re Unity General Assurance Association*[41] the petitioner said that the former directors of a dissolved unregistered company were well-known and the court ordered service on any five of them. Similarly, in *Re Anglo-American Exploration and Development Co*,[42] service on a former director and chairman of a dissolved registered company was accepted, though Vaughan Williams J pointed out, at p 102, that, because the company was dissolved, a former director was no longer an agent of the company and it would have been better to serve a shareholder if one could have been found within the jurisdiction. In the similar case of *Re Phoenix Extended Gold Mines Ltd*[43]

---

[35] (1866) 15 LT 169.
[36] As in *Re City of London and Colonial Financial Association Ltd* (1867) 36 LJ Ch 832 where an unregistered company no longer had an office and the petition was left at what had been its office.
[37] *Re Tea Trading Co K and C Popoff Brothers* [1933] Ch 647 at p 651.
[38] See 3.27–3.29. *Re National Credit and Exchange Co Ltd* (1862) 7 LT 817; *Re Inventors' Association Ltd* (1865) 13 WR 1015; *Re Thames Mutual Club Insurance Co* (1866) 15 LT 263. These cases were decided before option (b) was made available.
[39] See *Re Manchester and London Life Assurance and Loan Association* (1870) LR 9 Eq 643 (in which service on a workman at the site of the demolished office was held to be insufficient: another petition had been served on the company's two remaining directors) and *Re Vron Slate Co* [1878] WN 70 (which is discussed at 3.29). These cases were decided before option (b) was made available.
[40] *Re Tea Trading Co K and C Popoff Brothers* [1933] Ch 647, which concerned an unregistered company.
[41] (1863) 8 LT 160.
[42] [1898] 1 Ch 100.
[43] [1903] QWN 41.

the petition was ordered to be served on the chairman and a director who was also the largest shareholder in the jurisdiction.

In two Malaysian cases the court has excused[44] service made erroneously at a company's **3.24** principal place of business when the company did have a registered office and service there would have been practicable.[45] In both cases there was no prejudice to the company.

The Joint Stock Companies Winding-up Act 1848, s 10, provided that a petition for the **3.25** winding up of a company under that Act could be served on 'any member, officer or servant of the company'. For an example of service of a petition under that Act on a member of a company which did not have an office see *Re Brighton, Lewes, and Tonbridge Wells Direct Railway Co*.[46] With the widespread adoption of limited liability for members of companies after 1855 it ceased to be appropriate to allow service on members generally.

Overseas companies

A petition for the winding up of an overseas company (a company incorporated outside the **3.26** United Kingdom[47]) which has been registered at Companies House[48] may be served on the company in any manner provided for by the Companies Act 2006, s 1139(2).[49]

Alternative service

If for any reason it is impracticable to effect service as provided by IR 1986, r 4.8(2)–(5), **3.27** the petition may be served in such other manner as the court may approve or direct.[50] An application[51] for the court's approval of an alternative method of service[52] may be made without notice to any other party.[53] The application must be accompanied by a witness statement setting out what steps have been taken to comply with r 4.8(2)–(5) and the reasons why it is impracticable to effect service as provided in those paragraphs.[54] If an order is made and service is effected under the order, a sealed copy of the order must be exhibited to the certificate of service.[55]

In *Re Great Cwmsymtoy Silver Lead Co*[56] and *Re Velletri and Terracina Co Ltd*[57] the court **3.28** ordered service on the subscribers of the company's memorandum of association. In both cases there appeared to be no other persons connected with the companies and neither company had a registered office or place of business. In *Re Inventors' Association Ltd*[58]

---

[44] Under the Malaysian equivalent of IR 1986, r 7.55.
[45] *Ann Joo Metal Sdn Bhd v Pembenaan MY Chahaya Sdn Bhd* [2000] 5 MLJ 708; *Bank Industri dan Teknologi Malaysia Bhd v Alom Building Systems Sdn Bhd* [2006] 4 MLJ 405.
[46] (1849) 1 De G & Sm 604. It seems that the spelling of what is now known as Tunbridge Wells had not been settled at that time.
[47] Companies Act 2006, s 1044.
[48] Under the Companies Act 2006, s 1046, and the Overseas Companies Regulations 2009 (SI 2009/1801).
[49] IR 1986, r 4.8(5). See *Blackstone's Civil Practice 2015*, 15.47.
[50] IR 1986, r 4.8(6).
[51] See 3.233–3.263.
[52] For example, service by post at the company's registered office or service on a director or other officer of the company.
[53] IR 1986, r 4.8(7).
[54] IR 1986, r 4.8(7).
[55] IR 1986, r 4.9A(3).
[56] (1868) 17 LT 463.
[57] (1868) 18 LT 350.
[58] (1865) 13 WR 1015.

the company (which was in voluntary winding up) was said to have no office or place of business when the petition was presented, and the court directed service on the nine surviving subscribers of the memorandum (who had all acted as directors) and on 'three or four of the principal shareholders'. In *Re Imperial Deposit Bank, Building and Investment Co of Queensland Ltd*[59] the company was in voluntary winding up and had no registered office—the court ordered service on the voluntary liquidator, who was also a member of the company.

3.29   The present rules make wider provision for service than previous rules did, and most of the reported applications for directions are no longer relevant because the situations which gave rise to the applications are now covered by the rules. For example, in *Re Vron Slate Co*[60] it was not practicable to serve the petition at the company's registered office because it had been pulled down and it appeared that the company did not have a place of business: the court ordered service on the company's secretary at the office of the company's solicitors and also on a member of that firm of solicitors—nowadays, it would be sufficient to serve the petition on the company's secretary under r 4.8(4) without applying to the court. *Re Thames Mutual Club Insurance Co*[61] and *Re Keswick Old Brewery Co Ltd*[62] are similar. In *Re South Essex Estuary and Reclamation Co Ltd*[63] the company apparently had no registered office or place of business and service on the company's solicitors and one of its directors was ordered: again service on the director would now be sufficient under r 4.8(4). In *Re Petroleum Co*[64] the company had no registered office or place of business and service on the company's secretary was ordered (which would nowadays be sufficient under r 4.8(4)), but as the company was in voluntary winding up it may be questioned whether the secretary still held office: service on the voluntary liquidator was held to be insufficient, which appears to be inconsistent with *Re Stewart and Brother*.[65]

Service outside the jurisdiction

3.30   Service outside England and Wales of a winding-up petition, or a document relating to a petition, is governed by CPR, Part 6 (service of documents), with such modifications as the court may direct,[66] treating the petition as a claim form.[67] Service in another EU State must be carried out under Regulation (EU) No 1393/2007 (the Service Regulation).[68] CPR, r 6.36 (service of the claim form where the permission of the court is required) and r 6.37(1) and (2) (application for permission to serve the claim form out of the jurisdiction), do not

---

[59] (1901) 10 QLJ NC 1.

[60] [1878] WN 70.

[61] (1866) 15 LT 263.

[62] (1886) 55 LT 486.

[63] (1868) 18 LT 178.

[64] (1866) 15 LT 169.

[65] [1880] WN 15.

[66] IR 1986, rr 7.51A(1), 12A.16(1) and 12A.20. Rule 12A.20 is inconsistent with the statement in r 7.51A(1) that CPR, rr 6.30–6.47 (service of the claim form and other documents out of the jurisdiction), do not apply to insolvency proceedings. It seems that the statement in IR 1986, r 7.51A(1), must be treated as merely (erroneously) descriptive and without substantive effect. It has been dropped from draft IR 2015.

[67] IR 1986, r 12A.16(3).

[68] *Re Baillies Ltd* [2012] EWHC 285 (Ch), [2012] BCC 554. In *Re Anderson Owen Ltd* [2009] EWHC 2837 (Ch), [2010] BPIR 37, service of misfeasance proceedings in Germany otherwise than under the Service Regulation was validated under IR 1986, r 7.55, as there was no prejudice to the person served.

apply in insolvency proceedings.[69] Instead, a petition or a document relating to a petition cannot be served outside the jurisdiction without the court's permission.[70] An application for permission to serve out of the jurisdiction must be supported by a witness statement setting out:[71]

(a) the nature of the petition and the relief sought;
(b) that the applicant believes that the petition has a reasonable prospect of success; and
(c) the address of the person to be served or, if not known, in what place or country that person is, or is likely, to be found.

Permission is not required for service elsewhere in the EU of a petition presented, in the exercise of a statutory power under the Insolvency Act 1986 (IA 1986), by an office-holder who has been appointed in insolvency proceedings in respect of a company with its centre of main interests within the jurisdiction.[72]   **3.31**

Permission is not required for service on a member State liquidator of a copy of a petition.[73]   **3.32**

In *Re Baby Moon (UK) Ltd*[74] a company had been registered in England and Wales with a memorandum which stated its registered office was to be in England, but the statement of intended situation of the registered office said it was to be in Livingston, which is in Scotland and was where an office of the company was in fact situated. Harman J held that the certificate of incorporation was conclusive evidence that the company was registered in England and Wales and so could be wound up by the High Court, and gave leave for service of the petition outside the jurisdiction at the company's Livingston office.   **3.33**

Proof of service

Service of a winding-up petition must be proved by a certificate of service.[75] This must be sufficient to identify the petition served and must specify:[76]   **3.34**

(a) the name and registered number of the company,
(b) the address of the registered office of the company,
(c) the name of the petitioner,
(d) the court in which the petition was filed and the court reference number,
(e) the date of the petition,
(f) whether the copy served was a sealed copy,
(g) the date on which service was effected, and
(h) the manner in which service was effected.

If substituted service has been ordered, the certificate of service must have attached to it a sealed copy of the order.[77]   **3.35**

---

[69] PD Insolvency Proceedings 2014, para 6.7. This provision would be unnecessary if the statement in IR 1986, r 7.51A(1), that CPR, rr 6.30–6.47, are excluded from applying to insolvency proceedings had substantive effect.
[70] PD Insolvency Proceedings 2014, para 6.4.
[71] PD Insolvency Proceedings 2014, para 6.6.
[72] PD Insolvency Proceedings 2014, para 6.5.
[73] PD Insolvency Proceedings 2014, para 6.5.
[74] (1984) 1 BCC 99,298.
[75] IR 1986, r 4.9A(1). For a petition to wind up a relevant scheme (see 1.168), this rule is modified by the Collective Investment in Transferable Securities (Contractual Scheme) Regulations 2013 (SI 2013/1388), sch 3.
[76] r 4.9A(2).
[77] r 4.9A(3).

3.36 A certificate of service must be verified by a statement of truth[78] in accordance with CPR, Part 22.[79]

3.37 The certificate of service must be filed in court as soon as reasonably practicable after service, and in any event not less than five business days before the hearing of the petition.[80]

3.38 The manner of service must be described in sufficient detail to establish that service was in accordance with the rules. For example, evidence of service under r 4.8(3)(a) must state how it was established that the individual to which the petition was handed was a director, other officer or employee of the company. Evidence of service under r 4.8(3)(c) must give the details described at 3.12.

3.39 Obvious difficulties in effecting service, for example, the fact that the address of a company's registered office is in fact occupied by another person,[81] should be recorded so as to avoid suspicion that the server never actually attended the place of service.[82] In *Re Nicholls Pty Ltd*[83] the company had omitted to file notification of the change of situation of its registered office, which had occurred 18 months before a winding-up petition was presented. The petition was served by leaving it at the old office, but the evidence of service included the false statement that the petition had been handed to an employee of the company's accountants purporting to be a servant or agent of the company. It was held that the false statement did not vitiate the winding-up order made on the petition in the company's absence.

3.40 There is no requirement for acknowledgment of service of a winding-up petition.

Service at the wrong place

3.41 Attempted service of a winding-up petition at the wrong place is an error of procedure within CPR, r 3.10,[84] or a formal defect or irregularity under IR 1986, r 7.55.[85] It does not invalidate the proceedings unless, under CPR, r 3.10, there has been prejudice to the company or a third party,[86] or, under IR 1986, r 7.55, it has caused substantial injustice. If there has not been prejudice or substantial injustice, the court may make an order under CPR, r 3.10, or IR 1986, r 7.55, to remedy the error.

Application for a bank or building society insolvency order

3.42 An application for a bank insolvency order 'shall' be served on the bank by personal service at its registered office,[87] but service at the registered office 'may be effected' in the same way as service of a winding-up petition.[88] An application for a building society insolvency order

---

[78] r 13.13(16).

[79] IR 1986, r 13.13(17).

[80] r 4.9A(4). The clear days rule in CPR, r 2.8(2) and (3), applies (see 1.510). 'Business day' is defined in IR 1986, r 13.13(1) (see 1.512).

[81] See 1.529.

[82] *Von Risefer v Mainfreight International Pty Ltd* [2009] VSCA 179, 25 VR 366, in which evidence of service was rejected.

[83] (1982) 7 ACLR 76.

[84] *Nelson v Clearsprings (Management) Ltd* [2006] EWCA Civ 1252, [2007] 1 WLR 962, at [48].

[85] See *Ann Joo Metal Sdn Bhd v Pembenaan MY Chahaya Sdn Bhd* [2000] 5 MLJ 708 and *Bank Industri dan Teknologi Malaysia Bhd v Alom Building Systems Sdn Bhd* [2006] 4 MLJ 405 discussed at 3.24.

[86] *Nelson v Clearsprings (Management) Ltd* at [50].

[87] Bank Insolvency (England and Wales) Rules 2009 (SI 2009/356), r 8(2). 'Registered office' is defined in r 8(3) in the same terms as the definition in IR 1986, r 4.8(2), which is discussed at 3.9–3.10.

[88] See 3.9–3.16. SI 2009/356, r 7(3).

must be served on the building society at its principal office[89] in the same way as service of a winding-up petition.[90]

Methods of personal service are specified in CPR, r 6.5.[91] Personal service of a document on **3.43** a company or other corporation is effected by leaving the document with a person holding a senior position within the company or corporation.[92]

If, for any reason, it is impractical to effect service in the prescribed way, an application may **3.44** be made to the court for an order approving or directing an alternative method of service.[93]

SI 2009/356 and SI 2010/2581 apply IR 1986 without the amendments made by the **3.45** Insolvency (Amendment) Rules 2010.[94] In particular, they apply IR 1986, r 4.9 (proof of service),[95] which was replaced by r 4.9A in the 2010 revision.[96] As explained at 1.64, it is uncertain whether the provisions of SI 2009/356 and SI 2010/2581 should be treated as applying IR 1986 with the 2010 amendments, and it is thought that the court should be asked to give directions on the point. If SI 2009/356 and SI 2010/2581 are to be treated as applying IR 1986 with the 2010 amendments, the position is that what is said at 3.34–3.40 of this edition applies to an application for a bank or building society insolvency order.[97]

Copies of Winding-up Petition for other Persons

Insolvency office-holders

On the next business day after a winding-up petition is served on the company, copies **3.46** must be sent[98] to the following persons, if, to the petitioner's knowledge, they exist:[99] the company's voluntary liquidator, administrative receiver or administrator, a supervisor of a voluntary arrangement in force in relation to the company, or a member State liquidator appointed in main proceedings in relation to the company (unless that liquidator is the petitioner).[100]

Financial Conduct Authority and Prudential Regulation Authority

Legislation requires that a copy of a petition for the winding up of certain types of **3.47** entity must be supplied to the Financial Conduct Authority (FCA) (unless it is the

---

[89] Building Society Insolvency (England and Wales) Rules 2010 (SI 2010/2581), r 8(2). 'Principal office' is defined at 1.532.

[90] SI 2010/2581, r 8(3).

[91] CPR, r 6.5, applies to applications for bank insolvency orders by r 6.5(1) and the definition of 'personal service' in SI 2009/356, r 3(2).

[92] CPR, r 6.5(3). PD 6A, para 6.2, identifies who holds a senior position.

[93] SI 2009/356, r 8(5) and (6); SI 2010/2581, r 8(4) and (5). The procedure is the same as for an application for alternative service of a winding-up petition, see 3.27–3.29.

[94] SI 2010/686. See the definition of 'the 1986 Rules' in SI 2009/356, r 3(2), and SI 2010/2581, r 3(2).

[95] Rule 4.9 is described in the second edition of this work at 3.1.1.9. It is applied to bank insolvency by SI 2009/356, r 9, and modified by r 3(3)(b) and (4)(c) and (j). It is applied to building society insolvency by SI 2010/2581, r 9, and modified by r 3(5)(b) and (6)(d) and (l).

[96] Insolvency (Amendment) Rules 2010 (SI 2010/686), sch 1, para 144.

[97] Treating the references in SI 2009/356, r 9, and SI 2010/2581, r 9, to IR 1986, r 4.9, as references to r 4.9A as modified by SI 2009/356, r 3(3)(b) and (4)(j) and (k) or SI 2010/2581, r 3(5)(b) and (6)(l) and (m) respectively.

[98] For permitted methods of delivery see 1.516–1.519.

[99] IR 1986, r 4.10(1), (2), (3), (3A) and (5). 'Business day' is defined in r 13.13(1) (see 1.512).

[100] See also 2.244–2.247.

petitioner) and Prudential Regulation Authority (PRA) (unless it is the petitioner). The types of entity are:

(a) What the relevant rule[101] still refers to as 'an authorised institution or former authorised institution within the meaning of the Banking Act 1987',[102] which should have been amended to refer to an authorized deposit-taker or former authorized deposit-taker:[103] a copy of the petition must be sent[104] to the FCA and the PRA on the next business day after the petition is served on the company.[105]

(b) An authorized person[106] which has permission to effect or carry out contracts of insurance, or which is a reclaim fund:[107] a copy of the petition must be served on the FCA and, if the petition is for the winding up of a PRA-authorized person, the PRA.[108] If either the FCA or the PRA presents a petition for the winding up of a PRA-authorized person which has permission to effect or carry out contracts of insurance, or which is a reclaim fund, it must serve a copy of the petition on the other regulator.[109]

(c) An open-ended investment company or a sub-fund: a copy of the petition must be served on the FCA.[110]

(d) A relevant scheme:[111] a copy of the petition must be sent to the FCA.[112]

Lloyd's reorganization

3.48 While a Lloyd's market reorganization order is in force, if a petition is presented for the winding up of Lloyd's and the petitioner is not the reorganization controller, the petitioner must serve a copy of the petition on the reorganization controller.[113]

Notice of Petition

Companies for which industry-specific administration regimes are possible

3.49 If a company is eligible for one of the industry-specific administration orders discussed at 1.245–1.294 (except those for banks and building societies[114] and water companies), notice of a petition to wind up the company must be given to the regulator or minister who could apply for an administration order, so as to give time to make such an application. The requirements, which do not apply to a petition presented by the Secretary of State (in the

---

[101] IR 1986, r 4.10(4).

[102] The Banking Act 1987 has been repealed by the Financial Services and Markets Act 2000 (Consequential Amendments and Repeals) Order 2001 (SI 2001/3649), art 3(1)(d).

[103] As in IR 1986, r 4.7(4)(e); see 2.246.

[104] For permitted methods of delivery see 1.516–1.519.

[105] IR 1986, r 4.10(5). 'Business day' is defined in r 13.13(1) (see 1.512).

[106] 'Authorized person' is defined in 9.113.

[107] 'Reclaim fund' is defined as a company whose objects are restricted to dealing with dormant bank and building society accounts in specified ways (Dormant Bank and Building Society Accounts Act 2008, s 5(1)).

[108] Financial Services and Markets Act 2000, ss 369(1) and (3) and 369A(1), (3) and (4).

[109] ss 369(4) and 369A(5).

[110] Open-Ended Investment Companies Regulations 2001 (SI 2001/1228), reg 31(3), applied to sub-funds by reg 33C(1) and (5)(a).

[111] See 1.168.

[112] IR 1986, r 4.10, as applied and modified by the Collective Investment in Transferable Securities (Contractual Scheme) Regulations 2013 (SI 2013/1388), sch 3.

[113] Insurers (Reorganisation and Winding Up) (Lloyd's) Regulations 2005 (SI 2005/1998), reg 30(1) and (2).

[114] See 3.50–3.54.

case of a PPP company, the Mayor of London, in the case of a financial market infrastructure company, the Bank of England), are:

(a) For protected railway companies:[115] notice must be served on the appropriate national authority,[116] which means:[117]

    (i) in relation to a Scottish protected railway company,[118] or a company in railway administration which was a Scottish protected railway company when the order was made, the Scottish Ministers;

    (ii) in any other case, the Secretary of State.

    A winding-up order cannot be made unless at least 14 days have elapsed since service of the notice.[119]

(b) For PPP companies:[120] notice must be served on the Mayor of London.[121] A winding-up order cannot be made unless at least 14 days have elapsed since service of the notice.[122]

(c) For air traffic services licence companies:[123] notice must be given before presenting the petition.[124]

(d) For protected energy companies[125] and energy supply companies:[126] notice must be given both to the Secretary of State and to the Gas and Electricity Markets Authority (GEMA).[127] A winding-up order cannot be made unless at least 14 days have elapsed since service of the last of those notices[128] nor can a provisional liquidator be appointed.[129]

(e) For a universal service provider (of postal services):[130] notice must be served on the Secretary of State and Ofcom, and the court cannot make a winding-up order or exercise any other power under IA 1986, s 125 (apart from adjourning the proceedings), or appoint a provisional liquidator unless at least 14 days have elapsed since the service of the last of those notices.[131]

(f) For a financial market infrastructure company:[132] the Bank of England must be notified, and the petition may not be determined unless 14 days have elapsed since the Bank received the notice.[133]

---

[115] See 1.252–1.255.
[116] Railways Act 1993, s 61(1)(a).
[117] s 59(6)(za).
[118] Defined in s 59(6)(c).
[119] s 61(1)(b).
[120] See 1.257–1.259.
[121] Greater London Authority Act 1999, s 222(1)(a).
[122] s 222(1)(b).
[123] See 1.260–1.261.
[124] See 2.106.
[125] See 1.262–1.264.
[126] See 1.284–1.287.
[127] Energy Act 2004, s 160(1) and (2)(a), applied to energy supply companies by the Energy Act 2011, s 96.
[128] Energy Act 2004s 160(1), (2)(b) and (4)(a), applied to energy supply companies by the Energy Act 2011, s 96.
[129] Energy Act 2004, s 160(4)(b), applied to energy supply companies by the Energy Act 2011, s 96.
[130] See 1.281–1.283.
[131] Postal Services Act 2011, s 74(2).
[132] See 1.291–1.294.
[133] Financial Services (Banking Reform) Act 2013, s 122(1).

Table 3.1 Notification to financial regulators

Type of institution	Petitioner must notify	Regulator must inform
Bank	PRA and Bank of England[1]	–
FCA-regulated bank	FCA and Bank of England[2]	–
Building society which is a PRA-authorized person	FCA, PRA and Bank of England[3]	–
Building society which is not a PRA-authorized person	FCA and Bank of England[4]	–
Investment bank which is a PRA-authorized person and is not a deposit-taking bank	FCA and PRA[5]	If the Bank of England has made special bail-in provision for the institution by a resolution instrument under the Banking Act 2009, s 12A, in the three months ending with the date on which the FCA receives notification of the petition, the FCA must inform the Bank.[6]
Investment bank which is not a PRA-authorized person and is not a deposit-taking bank	FCA[7]	
Recognized clearing house	Bank of England[8]	–
Relevant firm	FCA (PRA if PRA-authorized) and Bank of England[9]	–

[1] Banking Act 2009, s 120(2) and (5)(b).
[2] Banking Act 2009, s 120(2) and (5)(b), as modified by s 129A.
[3] Building Societies Act 1986, s 90D(2) and (5)(b).
[4] Building Societies Act 1986, s 90D(2) and (5)(b).
[5] SI 2011/245, reg 8(2), (5)(a) and (8).
[6] SI 2011/245, reg 8(6A), as modified by the Financial Services (Banking Reform) Act 2013, sch 2, para 33.
[7] SI 2011/245, reg 8(2), (5)(a) and (8).
[8] Financial Services and Markets Act 2000, sch 17A, para 34(2) and (5)(b).
[9] See the Banking Act 2009, s 120A.

Banks, building societies, investment banks and clearing houses

3.50 A petitioner for a winding-up order in respect of a bank,[134] a building society, an investment bank that is not a deposit-taking bank[135] or a recognized clearing house[136] must:

(a) notify the appropriate regulator (see table 3.1) that the petition has been presented; and

(b) file with the court a copy of the notice, which the court must make available for public inspection.[137]

---

[134] For the definitions of 'bank' and 'FCA-regulated bank' in this context see 1.233–1.234.
[135] For the definitions of 'investment bank' and 'deposit-taking bank' see 1.269–1.271.
[136] A body is a recognized clearing house if there is in force a recognition order made under the Financial Services and Markets Act 2000 (FSMA 2000), s 290 or s 292, declaring that the body is a recognized central counterparty or a recognized clearing house which is not a recognized central counterparty (FSMA 2000, ss 285(1)(b), 290(1), 292(2), 313(1) and 417(1)).
[137] Banking Act 2009, s 120(2), (5)(b) and (6) (s 120(5) is modified by s 129A when it applies to FCA-regulated banks); Building Societies Act 1986, s 90D(2), (5)(b) and (6); SI 2011/245, reg 8(2), (5)(a) and (b) and (8); Financial Services and Markets Act 2000, sch 17A, para 34(2) and (6).

Table 3.2 Clearance by regulator which will permit a petition to proceed

Type of institution	Clearance required
Bank or building society	The PRA[1] and the Bank of England have each informed the petitioner that they do not intend to apply for a bank or building society insolvency order (or, in the case of an investment bank that is a deposit-taking bank, an investment bank special administration order), and
	the Bank of England has also declared that it does not intend to exercise a stabilization power under the Banking Act 2009, part 1.[2]
	(The PRA[3] and the Bank of England have a duty to inform the petitioner, within the seven-day period, whether they intend to take any of these steps.[4])
Investment bank that is not a deposit-taking bank	The FCA and, if the investment bank is a PRA-authorized person, the PRA have informed the petitioner that they consent to proceedings on the petition going ahead.[5]
Recognized clearing house	The Bank of England has informed the petitioner that:
	(a) it has no objection to the winding-up order being made, and
	(b) it does not intend to exercise a stabilization power under the Banking Act 2009, part 1.[6]

[1] The FCA in the case of an FCA-regulated bank. No provision is made for FCA-regulated building societies.
[2] Banking Act 2009, s 120(7)(b) (modified by s 129A when it applies to FCA-regulated banks); Building Societies Act 1986, s 90D(7); SI 2011/245, reg 9 and sch 1, para 7(a).
[3] The FCA in the case of an FCA-regulated bank.
[4] Banking Act 2009, s 120(10)(b) and (c) (modified by s 129A when it applies to FCA-regulated banks); Building Societies Act 1968, s 90D(10)(b) and (c) and (11)(b); SI 2011/245, reg 9 and sch 1, para 7(c) and (d). Also within that time, the PRA or the Bank of England must inform the petitioner if it decides to apply for a special administration (bank insolvency) order (Banking Act 2009, s 120(10)(b) and (c), as modified by SI 2011/245, reg 9 and sch 1, para 7(c) and (d)).
[5] SI 2011/245, reg 8(5)(c) and (8).
[6] Financial Services and Markets Act 2000, sch 17A, para 34(7)(b).

3.51 The regulators must, within seven days, inform the petitioner if they intend to take certain steps in relation to the institution (see table 3.2) and must serve the petitioner with a copy of an application for any of the relevant industry-specific administration or insolvency orders (see 3.113–3.115).

3.52 Points (a) and (b) in 3.50 are two of four conditions[138] (three in the case of a clearing house) which must be satisfied before the petition may be determined.[139] Condition 3[140] is that either:

[138] Five when the Banking Act 2009, s 12A, applies; see 3.54.
[139] Banking Act 2009, s 120(2); Building Societies Act 1986, s 90D(2); SI 2011/245, reg 8(2); Financial Services and Markets Act 2000, sch 17A, para 34(2).
[140] Banking Act 2009, s 120(7); Building Societies Act 1986, s 90D(7); SI 2011/245, reg 8(5)(c); Financial Services and Markets Act 2000, sch 17A, para 34(7).

(a) the period of seven days, beginning with the day on which notice is received, has ended;[141] or

(b) positive clearance has been given by the appropriate regulator (see table 3.2).

3.53 Condition 4 (which does not apply to clearing houses) is that no application for a bank or building society insolvency order, an investment bank special administration order or a special administration (bank insolvency) order in respect of the company is pending.[142]

3.54 Condition 5[143] applies only to a petition for the winding up of an institution for which the Bank of England has made special bail-in provision by a resolution instrument under the Banking Act 2009, s 12A,[144] in the three months ending with the date on which the appropriate regulator receives notification of the petition. In that case, the petition cannot be determined until the Bank of England has informed the petitioner (and the appropriate regulator if the institution is an investment bank) that it consents to the petition going ahead.[145] The Bank must inform the petitioner, within two weeks of receiving the notice (for an investment bank, within two weeks of the appropriate regulator receiving the notice), whether or not it consents.[146]

Registered providers of social housing and registered social landlords

3.55 In England, presentation of a petition for the winding up of a registered provider of social housing[147] which is a registered society or a registered company is ineffective unless the petitioner has given notice of it to the Regulator of Social Housing.[148] Presentation of the petition starts a period of moratorium on disposal of land held by the provider,[149] during which the regulator may appoint an interim manager[150] and/or make proposals about the future ownership and management of the land.[151]

3.56 In Wales, presentation of a petition for the winding up of a registered social landlord[152] which is a registered society or a registered company (including a company which is a

---

[141] Banking Act 2009, s 120(7)(a); Building Societies Act 1986, s 90D(7)(a); SI 2011/245, reg 8(5)(c)(i); Financial Services and Markets Act 2000, sch 17A, para 34(7)(a).

[142] Banking Act 2009, s 120(8); Building Societies Act 1986, s 90D(8); SI 2011/245, reg 8(5)(d); Banking Act 2009, s 120(8), as modified by SI 2011/245, reg 9 and sch 1, para 7(b). The winding-up petitioner has to be served with a copy of any such application; see 3.113–3.115.

[143] For an investment bank, this is modified condition 3.

[144] Which came into force on 31 December 2014.

[145] Banking Act 2009, s 120(8A); SI 2011/245, reg 8(5)(c), as modified by the Financial Services (Banking Reform) Act 2013, sch 2, para 33.

[146] Banking Act 2009, s 120(10)(d); SI 2011/245, reg 8(6B), as modified by the Financial Services (Banking Reform) Act 2013, sch 2, para 33.

[147] Provision for registration with the Office for Tenants and Social Landlords (the Regulator of Social Housing) is made in the Housing and Regeneration Act 2008, ss 110–121.

[148] Housing and Regeneration Act 2008, s 144, which does not apply if the regulator is the petitioner. Notice is also required by s 145(2) to be given by the petitioner to the regulator 'as soon as is reasonably practicable' but s 145(3) provides that failure to give this notice does not invalidate the presentation of the petition.

[149] ss 145–150. The period ends (unless extended or cancelled) 28 working days after receiving notice given under s 145(2) (s 146(2)). In addition, if a winding-up order is made, IA 1986, s 127(1), makes any disposition after presentation of the petition void unless the court orders otherwise.

[150] Housing and Regeneration Act 2008, s 151.

[151] ss 152–154.

[152] Provision for registration of social landlords in Wales is made in the Housing Act 1996, ss A1–6.

registered charity) is ineffective unless the petitioner has given notice of it to the Welsh Ministers.[153]

European groupings of territorial cooperation

If an application is made for the winding up of a European grouping of territorial cooper-   **3.57**
ation (EGTC), the court must inform all the member States under whose law the members
of the EGTC have been formed.[154]

Copies of Bank or Building Society Insolvency Application for other Persons

Copies of an application for a bank or building society insolvency order must be sent by the   **3.58**
applicant to:

(a) the proposed liquidator;[155]
(b) the Bank of England, if it is not the applicant;[156]
(c) the FCA, if it is not the applicant;[157]
(d) the PRA, if it is not the applicant and if the institution is a PRA-authorized person;[158]
(e) the Financial Services Compensation Scheme;[159]
(f) any person who has given notice in respect of the bank under the Banking Act 2009, s 120, or the building society under the Building Societies Act 1986, s 90D (which require notice to be given to the FCA and/or the PRA of an application for an administration order, a petition for a winding-up order, a resolution for voluntary winding up or a proposed appointment of an administrator);[160]
(g) if a voluntary arrangement is in force for the institution, the supervisor,[161] and the court to which the nominee's report under IA 1986, s 2, was submitted, if that is not the court in which the application for the insolvency order is filed;[162]
(h) any administrative receiver of the institution.[163]

One copy must be sent electronically as soon as practicable and another (sealed) copy must   **3.59**
be sent by first class post on the business day on which the application is served on the
institution.[164]

---

[153] Housing Act 1996, s 40. See also 5.264.
[154] Regulation (EC) No 1082/2006, art 14(1).
[155] Bank Insolvency (England and Wales) Rules 2009 (SI 2009/356), r 10(1)(a); Building Society Insolvency (England and Wales) Rules 2010 (SI 2010/2581), r 10(1)(a).
[156] SI 2009/356, r 10(1)(b); SI 2010/2581, r 10(1)(b).
[157] SI 2009/356, r 10(1)(c); SI 2010/2581, r 10(1)(c) (see r 3(2) for the definition of 'the appropriate regulator').
[158] SI 2009/356, r 10(1)(ca); SI 2010/2581, r 10(1)(c) (see r 3(2) for the definition of 'the appropriate regulator').
[159] SI 2009/356, r 10(1)(d); SI 2010/2581, r 10(1)(d).
[160] SI 2009/356, r 10(1)(e); SI 2010/2581, r 10(1)(e).
[161] SI 2009/356, r 10(1)(f); SI 2010/2581, r 10(1)(f).
[162] SI 2009/356, r 7(5); SI 2010/2581, r 7(5).
[163] SI 2009/356, r 10(1)(g); SI 2010/2581, r 10(1)(g).
[164] SI 2009/356, r 10(1) and (2); SI 2010/2581, r 10(1) and (2). This does not apply to the copy for the voluntary arrangement court. The term 'business day' is defined in IR 1986, r 13.13(1) (see 1.512), which is applied by SI 2009/356, r 292, and SI 2010/2581, r 284. There is no requirement that the application must be served on the bank or building society on a business day.

Restraint of Gazetting and Striking Out

Principle

3.60 If the court considers that a petition to wind up a company is an abuse of process, or is bound to fail,[165] it will normally restrain gazetting of the petition and strike it out.[166]

3.61 In the old procedure in which an interim injunction was obtained until trial,[167] the interim injunction stayed all further proceedings on the petition[168] or restrained the taking of any further steps to prosecute the petition.[169] A stay should not be sought as a final order instead of striking out,[170] because of the court's policy of not allowing winding-up petitions to remain pending indefinitely.[171]

3.62 Usually the company's immediate concern is to prevent gazetting. The court has jurisdiction to restrain not only gazetting but also any publicization of the fact that a petition has been presented.[172] The court should be reluctant to restrain only gazetting of a petition without also stopping other proceedings on the petition.[173]

3.63 A petition may be struck out even if it has been gazetted,[174] but the court must be aware that, as a result of gazetting, someone may apply to be substituted as petitioner.[175]

3.64 A company may have to invoke this jurisdiction if it has been unable to obtain an injunction to restrain presentation of a petition, and the discussion at 2.142–2.176 is relevant to what is said here. If the court has refused an injunction against presentation of a petition and the petition has been presented, it may grant an injunction to prevent the petition proceeding until an appeal against its first decision has been dealt with.[176] On the other hand, if an injunction against presentation has been granted, the court is unlikely to stay it pending appeal.[177]

3.65 In Malaysia, the Court of Appeal has warned against using strike-out applications as a delaying tactic.[178]

---

[165] For inevitability of failure as an indicator of abuse of process see 2.148–2.152.

[166] *Re a Company (No 00315 of 1973)* [1973] 1 WLR 1566; *Re a Company (No 001573 of 1983)* [1983] BCLC 492; *Re a Company (No 4079 of 2003)* [2003] EWHC 1879 (Ch), LTL 1/10/2003.

[167] See 2.154.

[168] *Re a Company (No 0089 of 1894)* [1894] 2 Ch 349.

[169] *Mann v Goldstein* [1968] 1 WLR 1091; *James Dolman and Co Ltd v Pedley* [2003] EWCA Civ 1686, [2004] BCC 504, at [10].

[170] *Re a Company (No 00928 of 1991)* [1991] BCLC 514 per Harman J at p 518.

[171] See 5.113–5.116 and 5.119.

[172] *Re a Company (No 007339 of 1985)* [1986] BCLC 127.

[173] *Re Murph's Restaurants Ltd* [1979] ILRM 141 at p 144.

[174] *Re CDPD* [1975] CLY 322.

[175] See 3.181–3.206.

[176] *Celcom (Malaysia) Bhd v Inmiss Communication Sdn Bhd* [2003] 3 MLJ 178.

[177] *Paganelli Sdn Bhd v Care-Me Direct Sales Sdn Bhd* [1999] 2 MLJ 464.

[178] *Maril-Rionebel (M) Sdn Bhd v Perdana Merchant Bankers Bhd* [2001] 4 MLJ 187; *Tan Kim Hor v Tan Heng Chew* [2003] 1 MLJ 492.

In England and Wales, the court has a power to direct that a petition is not to be gazetted.[179] **3.66**
In Malaysia, the court does not have this power and it has been held that this means that the
court cannot issue an injunction restraining advertisement.[180]

Procedure

Inherent jurisdiction

An application to the court for an order striking out a petition or restraining gazetting and **3.67**
further proceedings invokes the court's inherent jurisdiction to prevent abuse of its process.[181]

In *Re Martin Coulter Enterprises Ltd*[182] Vinelott J said at p 19: **3.68**

> The power to strike out a proceeding on the ground that it is an abuse of the process of the
> court is founded on the principle that parties are not to be harassed by frivolous, vexatious
> or hopeless litigation.

Application

The court's power to strike out a statement of case if it is an abuse of process is in CPR, **3.69**
r 3.4.[183] A petition is not a statement of case[184] but the provisions of the CPR for striking
out a statement of case if it is an abuse of process apply to winding-up petitions and do not
require any modification.[185]

An application[186] to stop proceedings on a petition that has already been presented is **3.70**
made to the court in which the petition is pending.[187] An application for an injunction to
restrain gazetting of a petition must be listed before a judge.[188] It is usual to ask[189] for the
hearing to be held in private, on the ground that publicity would defeat the object of the
hearing[190] and/or that the hearing involves confidential information and publicity would
damage that confidentiality.[191] However, unless the court expressly prohibits publication of information heard in a private hearing, it is not contempt of court to make that
information public.[192]

Temporary order

On an application for a temporary order, pending a full hearing, restraining gazetting of a peti- **3.71**
tion, whether on notice to other parties or not, the company must prove a prima facie case that

---

[179] IR 1986, r 4.11(1). See 3.126–3.129.
[180] *Malaysian Resources Corporation Bhd v Juranas Sdn Bhd* [2002] 3 MLJ 169; *Azman and Tay Associates Sdn Bhd v Sentul Raya Sdn Bhd* [2002] 4 MLJ 390.
[181] *Re a Company (No 0089 of 1894)* [1894] 2 Ch 349 at p 350; *Mann v Goldstein* [1968] 1 WLR 1091 at p 1094; *Re a Company (No 003079 of 1990)* [1991] BCLC 235 at p 236; *Ngan Tuck Seng v Ngan Yin Hoi* [1999] 5 MLJ 509; *Sri Binaraya Sdn Bhd v Golden Approach Sdn Bhd* [2000] 3 MLJ 465; *James Dolman and Co Ltd v Pedley* [2003] EWCA Civ 1686, [2004] BCC 504, at [10].
[182] [1988] BCLC 12.
[183] See r 3.4(2)(b).
[184] See 2.9.
[185] IR 1986, r 7.51A(2); *Paulin v Paulin* [2009] EWCA Civ 221, [2010] 1 WLR 1057, at [44].
[186] See 3.233–3.263.
[187] IR 1986, r 4.6A(b).
[188] PD Insolvency Proceedings 2014, para 3.2(3).
[189] Under CPR, r 39.2(3).
[190] CPR, r 39.2(3)(a).
[191] CPR, r 39.2(3)(c).
[192] *A F Noonan (Architectural Practice) Ltd v Bournemouth and Boscombe Athletic Community Football Club Ltd* [2007] EWCA Civ 848, [2007] 1 WLR 2614.

the petition would be an abuse of process.[193] In *Re Wizard Co Ltd* [194] a temporary injunction restraining a creditor of a company from continuing with a petition to wind it up was granted on an application without notice supported by an affidavit stating that the company was solvent and the petitioner's debt was disputed. The controllers of the company then decamped taking all its movable property and the petition was allowed to continue.

3.72   In *Re a Company (No 003640 of 1989)*[195] an interim order restraining advertisement of a petition to wind up the company had been made on the company undertaking 'to make and file an affidavit by a responsible officer of the company exhibiting evidence from the company's bankers or its auditors as to its solvency and ability to pay its debts as they fell due'. The affidavit filed in pursuance of that undertaking exhibited two letters from the company's auditors which merely expressed belief that the company's assets exceeded its liabilities but said that the auditors had not examined accounts since the end of the company's last financial year. Hoffmann J held that this was a sufficient compliance with the undertaking but expressed doubt whether the letters would be sufficient to enable him to make a final order to strike out the petition. (The company's fate is not reported.)

The Court's Approach

3.73   As the court prevents from being presented winding-up petitions which it would dismiss if they were presented, the types of petition which the court will prevent from proceeding are essentially the same as those which the court will prevent from being presented.[196] Where the indication that a petition will be an abuse of process is that the petition is bound to fail, it must be perfectly clear that it cannot succeed.[197]

3.74   The hearing of an application to prevent a petition proceeding is conducted on the basis that assertions of fact made by the petitioner can be proved at trial,[198] and that bona fide conflicts of fact are resolved in favour of the petitioner.[199]

Examples

Disputed debt petitions

3.75   The court's practice is to dismiss a creditor's petition to wind up a company if the petition is based on the company's failure to pay a debt whose existence it disputes.[200] This rule of practice means that such a petition is bound to fail and so is an abuse of process. The court will, therefore, restrain gazetting of and strike out such a petition. A cross-claim is treated in the same way.[201] To obtain an order halting proceedings on a petition because there is a dispute about the existence of the debt or because there is a cross-claim, it must be shown that the dispute or cross-claim is sufficiently substantial to make dismissal of the petition

---

[193] *SN Group plc v Barclays Bank plc* [1993] BCC 506, following *Coulon Sanderson and Ward Ltd v Ward* (1985) 2 BCC 99,207; see 2.159.
[194] (1897) 41 SJ 817.
[195] [1990] BCLC 201.
[196] See 2.165–2.175 and 3.75–3.86.
[197] *Virdi v Abbey Leisure Ltd* [1990] BCLC 342 per Balcombe LJ at p 347; *Re Copeland and Craddock Ltd* [1997] BCC 294 per Dillon LJ at p 297; *North Holdings Ltd v Southern Tropics Ltd* [1999] 2 BCLC 625 per Aldous LJ at p 633; *Greenacre Publishing Group v The Manson Group* [2000] BCC 11.
[198] *Re a Company (No 003028 of 1987)* [1988] BCLC 282 at p 283.
[199] *North Holdings Ltd v Southern Tropics Ltd* [1999] 2 BCLC 625 per Aldous LJ at p 633.
[200] See 7.529–7.535.
[201] See 7.618–7.665.

inevitable,[202] not whether a claim for the petitioner's debt (which is a different issue) would be bound to fail.[203] The court may have to deal with an assertion by the petitioner that, exceptionally, the court would determine the dispute about the debt in proceedings on the petition[204] or would make a winding-up order despite the dispute or cross-claim,[205] so that presenting the petition would not be an abuse of process.

There is an overlap between disputed debt and cross-claim cases and the suitable alternative **3.76** remedy category described at 3.79–3.80, in that the Companies Court refuses to deal with disputed debt petitions because there is the better alternative of having the dispute on the debt determined in a common law claim.

Oppression

The court may prevent a petition to wind up a company proceeding because it is an abuse of **3.77** process if it is oppressive or unfair or will put improper pressure on the company to accede to the petitioner's demands.[206] In *Re Norper Investments Pty Ltd*[207] the collector of taxes petitioned for the winding up of the company for non-payment of an assessment against which the company had lodged an appeal which appeared to be unanswerable because of a tribunal decision in another case with identical facts. The revenue authority had appealed against the tribunal decision and the collector relied on provisions of Australian tax legislation which provide that the fact that an appeal is pending against an assessment shall not affect the assessment and that tax may be recovered as if no appeal were pending. Needham J described the petition as oppressive and an abuse of process and dismissed it with costs.

Collateral purpose

The court may prevent a petition to wind up a company proceeding, because it is an abuse **3.78** of process, if the primary purpose of presenting it is not to get the company wound up for the benefit of the intending petitioner's class.[208]

Suitable alternative remedy

The court may prevent a petition to wind up a company proceeding because it is an abuse **3.79** of process if the intending petitioner is unreasonably seeking to wind up the company instead of pursuing an alternative and more appropriate remedy.[209] This is especially so where the petitioner is actually pursuing alternative and more appropriate legal proceedings.[210] For discussion of the circumstances in which it may or may not be found that a petition would be an abuse of process, because there is an alternative remedy,

---

[202] See 7.444–7.514 and 7.573.

[203] See *Pembinaan Lian Keong Sdn Bhd v Yip Fook Thai* [2005] 5 MLJ 786; *Metalform Asia Pte Ltd v Holland Leedon Pte Ltd* [2007] SGCA 6, [2007] 2 SLR 268.

[204] See 7.523–7.527.

[205] See 7.551–7.568, 7.621 and 7.631–7.643.

[206] *Re a Company (No 0089 of 1894)* [1894] 2 Ch 349; *SN Group plc v Barclays Bank plc* [1993] BCC 506.

[207] (1977) 15 ALR 603.

[208] *Tang Choon Keng Realty (Pte) Ltd v Tang Wee Cheng* [1992] 2 SLR 1114 at p 1137. See 2.112–2.123 and 2.169–2.170.

[209] *Charles Forte Investments Ltd v Amanda* [1964] Ch 240; *Re Forbes Enterprises (1975) Ltd* (1978) 1 BCR 178; *Re Trocadero Ltd* [1988] 2 HKLR 443. All these were contributories' petitions.

[210] *Re a Company (No 003028 of 1987)* [1988] BCLC 282 (an unusual case in which a contingent creditor petitioned on grounds usually relied on by contributories); *Bank of New Zealand v Rada Corporation Ltd* (1989) 5 NZCLC 66,221 (a creditor's petition, in relation to which this ground for striking out was not sustained); *Lai Kim Loi v Dato Lai Fook Kim* [1989] 2 MLJ 290 (a member's petition seeking winding up as a remedy for oppression); *Re Essentially Yours (HK) Ltd* (2000) HCCW378/2000 (a contributory's petition).

see 7.46–7.50 (petition by unpaid undisputed creditor), 7.572–7.575 (disputed debt and cross-claim petitions—in practice the most important category), 8.216–8.247 (contributories' petitions), 9.17–9.18 (public interest petitions) and 10.83–10.84 (company in voluntary liquidation).

3.80 Commonly, the petitioner is seeking to put improper pressure on the company to accede to the petitioner's claim[211] without having the claim established in the suitable alternative proceedings, and that in itself will constitute a collateral purpose.[212]

Bound to fail as a matter of law or because of lack of evidence

3.81 The court may prevent a petition to wind up a company proceeding because it is an abuse of process if the petition would be bound to fail as a matter of law or because of lack of evidence, for example, because the petition fails to allege sufficient grounds for the court to make a winding-up order[213] or the petitioner does not have standing.[214]

3.82 In *Re a Company (No 003096 of 1987)*[215] Peter Gibson J said, at p 81:

> It is trite law that an application to strike out will fail unless it is plain and obvious that the petition will not succeed. If the court, on a review of the material that has properly been put before it, finds that there are facts in dispute which are or may be material to a determination in the petitioners' favour of the petition, then it must let the petition go to trial. On the other hand, if the facts which must be taken to be true or (where evidence is admissible) are established by evidence which is not disputed, lead the court to the clear view that the petition is bound to fail, then it would be pointless to allow the petition to go to a hearing and thereby to protract the uncertainty that hangs over the company.

This was adopted by Warner J in *Re a Company (No 001363 of 1988)*.[216] In *Seapark Group Ltd v Convertech Group Ltd*[217] the company sought to be wound up failed to establish that the petition was bound to fail. In *Ngan Tuck Seng v Ngan Yin Hoi*[218] a contributory's petition was struck out.

3.83 Whether or not a petition is bound to fail is to be determined in the light of the circumstances existing at the time of hearing the application to stop it.[219] If circumstances exist at the time of hearing the application which would persuade the court to stop the petition, it is irrelevant that the petitioner did not know of those circumstances when presenting the petition.[220]

3.84 Whether or not it is 'plain and obvious' that the petition will fail may only become apparent after extensive argument.[221] Where lengthy argument is required, the court should hear

---

[211] See 3.77.
[212] See 3.78.
[213] *Re Trocadero Ltd* [1988] 2 HKLR 443; *Hollands Printing Ltd v San Michele Ltd* [1992] 3 NZLR 469; *Re Saul D Harrison and Sons plc* [1995] 1 BCLC 14; *RCB v Thai Asia Fund Ltd* 1996 CILR 9.
[214] *Re a Company (No 001259 of 1991)* [1991] BCLC 594.
[215] (1987) 4 BCC 80.
[216] [1989] BCLC 579.
[217] (1990) 5 NZCLC 66,975.
[218] [1999] 5 MLJ 509.
[219] *Re a Company (No 002567 of 1982)* [1983] 1 WLR 927 at p 934.
[220] *Re a Company (No 003079 of 1990)* [1991] BCLC 235.
[221] *Re Johnson Corporation Ltd* (1980) 5 ACLR 227 at p 234.

that argument if it appears to be possible that the petition will be struck out, because striking it out would obviate the necessity for hearing the petition.[222] As Sir Gordon Willmer said in *Drummond-Jackson v British Medical Association*:[223]

> The question whether a point is plain and obvious does not depend upon the length of time it takes to argue. Rather the question is whether, when the point has been argued, it has become plain and obvious that there can be but one result.

Petition prohibited by or under statute

The court will strike out a petition that is prohibited by or under a statute.[224]   **3.85**

Petitioner contractually bound not to petition

A contractual obligation of a creditor not to apply for winding up will be enforced by the   **3.86** court, if necessary by striking out, and is not contrary to public policy.[225] But a company's articles of association cannot remove its members' statutory right to apply as contributories for it to be wound up.[226]

Effect of Delay

Whether an application to prevent further proceedings on a petition should be dismissed   **3.87** for being made too late will depend on the facts of the case.[227] Five months between the presentation of the petition and the application for it to be struck out was not considered too long in *Jurupakat Sdn Bhd v Kumpulan Good Earth (1973) Sdn Bhd*,[228] in which the application was successful.

Costs

Orders as to costs of applying for an order restraining giving notice of, and further pro-   **3.88** ceedings on, a petition or striking out are at the discretion of the court but will normally follow the event.[229] A person who has presented a winding-up petition which is an abuse of process may be ordered to pay the company's costs of halting the petition on an indemnity basis.[230]

Adjournment pending Appeal

In *Re Hong Kong Construction (Works) Ltd*[231] the court refused an application to adjourn   **3.89** proceedings on a winding-up petition pending an appeal against the court's refusal to strike out the petition. No new ground of opposition to the petition had been raised.

---

[222] *Williams and Humbert Ltd v W and H Trade Marks (Jersey) Ltd* [1986] AC 368; *Smith v Croft (No 2)* [1988] Ch 114.
[223] [1970] 1 WLR 688, at p 700.
[224] *Re Laceward Ltd* [1981] 1 WLR 133, in which the petition was prohibited by what is now the Solicitors' (Non-contentious Business) Remuneration Order 1994 (SI 1994/2616), art 6.
[225] See 7.426.
[226] *Re Peveril Gold Mines Ltd* [1898] 1 Ch 122.
[227] *Re St Piran Ltd* [1981] 1 WLR 1300 at p 1302: in *Re St Piran Ltd* the application was heard and eventually adjourned so that the petition could be amended.
[228] [1988] 3 MLJ 49.
[229] *Re Pendigo Ltd* [1996] 2 BCLC 64.
[230] *Re a Company (No 0012209 of 1991)* [1992] 1 WLR 351; *Re a Company (No 00751 of 1992)* [1992] BCLC 869. See also 7.597–7.602.
[231] (13/01/2003, HCCW 670/2002).

Starting other Insolvency Proceedings

Moratorium for Preparation of a Voluntary Arrangement

3.90 If, after presentation of a petition to wind up a company, a moratorium under IA 1986, s 1A, for preparation of a voluntary arrangement comes into effect, no proceedings against the company may be continued.[232] By analogy with the administration moratorium provisions, this prohibition applies to a winding-up petition and means that the petition cannot be gazetted.[233] The court should not extend this statutory moratorium to a company which is not eligible to invoke it.[234] In any case, a company cannot give an undertaking that a company voluntary arrangement (CVA) will be approved so that the court can issue a *quia timet* injunction as it can where administration is proposed.[235]

3.91 These provisions[236] are applied to charitable incorporated organizations[237] and limited liability partnerships (LLPs).[238] The same provisions are made for insolvent partnerships.[239]

3.92 It is very difficult to envisage a case in which a voluntary arrangement which was likely to result in creditors, or some of them, receiving less than they would in a winding up would not be found to be unfairly prejudicial under IA 1986, s 6.[240]

Preparation for Administration

Interim moratorium before administration

3.93 If, after presentation of a petition to wind up a company, an interim moratorium[241] comes into effect, no legal process may be continued against the company without the court's permission.[242] This applies to a winding-up petition[243] and means that the petition must not be gazetted without the court's permission.[244] An order restraining the petitioner from gazetting the petition will be made.[245] A restraining order will be made as a *quia timet* injunction on the application of a person intending to put the company into administration (or make an administration application), provided an undertaking to do so is given.[246]

---

[232] IA 1986, sch A1, para 12(1)(h).
[233] *Re a Company (No 001448 of 1989)* [1989] BCLC 715 at p 716; *Re Arucana Ltd* [2009] EWHC 3838 (Ch), LTL 21/6/2012.
[234] *Re a Company* [2010] EWHC 3814 (Ch), [2012] BCC 289.
[235] *Re a Company* [2010] EWHC 3814 (Ch), [2012] BCC 289.
[236] IA 1986, s 1A, and sch A1, para 12(1)(h).
[237] Charitable Incorporated Organisations (Insolvency and Dissolution) Regulations 2012 (SI 2012/3013), sch, para 1.
[238] Limited Liability Partnerships Regulations 2001 (SI 2001/1090), reg 5, and sch 3.
[239] IPO 1994, art 4, and IA 1986, sch A1, para 12(1)(h), as modified by IPO 1994, sch 1.
[240] *Re T & N Ltd* [2004] EWHC 2361 (Ch), [2005] 2 BCLC 488, at [82].
[241] Under IA 1986, sch B1, para 44.
[242] IA 1986, sch B1, para 43(6), applied and modified by para 44(5).
[243] *Re Arucana Ltd* [2009] EWHC 3838 (Ch), LTL 21/6/2012.
[244] *Re a Company (No 001448 of 1989)* [1989] BCLC 715 at p 716.
[245] *Re a Company (No 001992 of 1988)* [1989] BCLC 9; *Re Manlon Trading Ltd* (1988) 4 BCC 455 at p 456.
[246] *Re Manlon Trading Ltd* (1988) 4 BCC 455 per Harman J at p 456; *Re a Company (No 001448 of 1989)* [1989] BCLC 715.

The rules[247] are applied to charitable incorporated organizations[248] and limited liability **3.94** partnerships,[249] and the same provision is made for insolvent partnerships.[250]

Presentation of a petition or application for an industry-specific administration order

If, after presentation of a petition to wind up a company, a petition or application for one of **3.95** the industry-specific administration orders discussed at 1.245–1.294 is presented, proceedings on the winding-up petition cannot be continued without the court's leave. In particular, the petition cannot be gazetted without the court's leave.[251] For forms of administration based on IA 1986, part 2, without the amendments made by the Enterprise Act 2002, s 248,[252] this is provided by IA 1986, s 10(1)(c), as continued in force by the Enterprise Act 2002, s 249, and applied:

(a) to special administration of water companies by the Water Industry Act 1991, s 24(5);

(b) to railway administration by the Railways Act 1993, s 60(5);

(c) to administration of building societies by the Building Societies Act 1986, sch 15A, paras 1, 2 and 12;

(d) to PPP administration by the Greater London Authority Act 1999, s 221(5);

(e) to air traffic administration by the Transport Act 2000, s 30(3).

For industry-specific administration regimes based on schedule B1 administration,[253] the **3.96** provision is made by IA 1986, sch B1, paras 43(6) and 44(1) and (5), as applied:

(a) to energy administration and energy supply company administration by the Energy Act 2004, sch 20, paras 1–4 and 8;[254]

(b) to bank administration, building society special administration and special administration (bank administration) by the Banking Act 2009, s 145(2), (3), (4) and table 1;[255]

(c) to investment bank special administration and special administration (bank insolvency) by the Investment Bank Special Administration Regulations 2011 (SI 2011/245), reg 15(4), (5) and table 1;[256]

(d) to postal administration by the Postal Services Act 2011, sch 10, paras 1, 2 and 6;

(e) to FMI administration by the Financial Services (Banking Reform) Act 2013, sch 6, paras 2 and 3 and table 1.

In some administration regimes, when deciding whether to give permission, the court must **3.97** have regard to the following objectives:

(a) in bank administration and building society special administration, the objectives set out in the Banking Act 2009, s 137;[257]

---

[247] In IA 1986, sch B1, paras 43(6) and 44(5).

[248] Charitable Incorporated Organisations (Insolvency and Dissolution) Regulations 2012 (SI 2012/3013), sch, para 1.

[249] Limited Liability Partnerships Regulations 2001 (SI 2001/1090), reg 5, and sch 3.

[250] IPO 1994, art 6, and IA 1986, sch B1, paras 43(5) and 44(5), as modified by IPO 1994, sch 2.

[251] *Re a Company (No 001448 of 1989)* [1989] BCLC 715 at p 716.

[252] See 1.248–1.261.

[253] See 1.262–1.287 and 1.291–1.294.

[254] Applied to energy supply company administration by the Energy Act 2011, s 96.

[255] Applied to building society special administration by the Building Societies Act 1986, s 90C. Applied to special administration (bank administration) by the Investment Bank Special Administration Regulations 2011 (SI 2011/245), sch 2, para 6.

[256] Applied to special administration (bank insolvency) by SI 2011/245, sch 1, para 5.

[257] IA 1986, sch B1, para 43, as modified by the Banking Act 2009, s 145, table 1.

(b) in special administration (bank administration), objective A and the special administration objectives;[258]

(c) in special administration (bank insolvency), objective A.[259]

3.98 The cases cited at 3.93 also apply to industry-specific administration.

Going into Administration

Appointment of administrator by court

3.99 When the court makes an administration order, it must dismiss any pending winding-up petition.[260] This applies to charitable incorporated organizations,[261] insolvent partnerships[262] and limited liability partnerships.[263]

3.100 When the court makes any of the industry-specific administration orders discussed at 1.245–1.294, it must dismiss any pending winding-up petition, unless it is making the administration order on the winding-up petition[264] (which is not possible in the case of building societies). For industry-specific administration regimes based on IA 1986, part 2, without the amendments made by the Enterprise Act 2002, s 248,[265] this is provided by IA 1986, s 11(1)(a), as continued in force by the Enterprise Act 2002, s 249, and applied:

(a) to special administration of water companies by the Water Industry Act 1991, sch 3, paras 1 and 2;

(b) to railway administration by the Railways Act 1993, sch 6, paras 1 and 2;

(c) to administration of building societies by the Building Societies Act 1986, sch 15A, paras 1, 2 and 13;

(d) to PPP administration by the Greater London Authority Act 1999, sch 14, paras 1 and 2;

(e) to air traffic administration by the Transport Act 2000, sch 1, paras 1–4.

3.101 For industry-specific administration regimes based on schedule B1 administration,[266] the provision is made by IA 1986, sch B1, para 40(1)(a), as applied:

(a) to energy administration and energy supply company administration by the Energy Act 2004, sch 20, paras 1–4 and 6;[267]

(b) to bank administration, building society special administration and special administration (bank administration) by the Banking Act 2009, s 145(2), (3), (4) and table 1;[268]

---

[258] IA 1986, sch B1, para 43, as modified by the Banking Act 2009, s 145, table 1, and further modified by SI 2011/245, sch 2, para 6(2)(f). For the objectives of special administration (bank administration) see 1.279.

[259] SI 2011/245, sch 1, para 5(2). For the objectives of special administration (bank insolvency) see 1.276.

[260] IA 1986, sch B1, para 40(1)(a).

[261] Charitable Incorporated Organisations (Insolvency and Dissolution) Regulations 2012 (SI 2012/3013), sch, para 1.

[262] IPO 1994, art 6.

[263] Limited Liability Partnerships Regulations 2001 (SI 2001/1090), reg 5, and sch 3.

[264] See 5.68–5.70.

[265] See 1.248–1.261.

[266] See 1.262–1.287 and 1.291–1.294.

[267] Applied to energy supply company administration by the Energy Act 2011, s 96.

[268] Applied to building society special administration by the Building Societies Act 1986, s 90C. Applied to special administration (bank administration) by the Investment Bank Special Administration Regulations 2011 (SI 2011/245), sch 2, para 6.

(c) to investment bank special administration and special administration (bank insolvency) by the Investment Bank Special Administration Regulations 2011 (SI 2011/245), reg 15(4), (5) and table 1;[269]

(d) to postal administration by the Postal Services Act 2011, sch 10, paras 1, 2 and 4;

(e) to FMI administration by the Financial Services (Banking Reform) Act 2013, sch 6, paras 2 and 3 and table 1.

The rule that a winding-up petition must be dismissed on the making of an administration order does not apply if the petition was presented for the purpose of proceedings under the default rules of exchanges and clearing houses in financial markets described in 10.67.[270] **3.102**

Appointment of administrator by holder of floating charge

If, after presentation of a petition to wind up a company, the holder of a qualifying floating charge in respect of the company's property appoints an administrator,[271] the petition 'shall be suspended'.[272] This does not apply[273] to a petition presented by: **3.103**

(a) the Secretary of State as a public interest petition under IA 1986, s 124A;[274]

(b) the Secretary of State in respect of a European public limited-liability company under s 124B;[275] or

(c) the Financial Conduct Authority or the Prudential Regulation Authority under the Financial Services and Markets Act 2000, s 367.[276]

It also does not apply if the petition was presented for the purpose of proceedings under the default rules of exchanges and clearing houses in financial markets described in 10.67.[277]

IA 1986 does not explain the idea of suspending a petition, but it has been held that it means that the existence of the petition is without legal effect for the period of the administration.[278] It is not clear how this provision interacts with sch B1, para 43(6), which prohibits the continuation of legal process against a company in administration, unless it is with the administrator's consent or the court's permission. **3.104**

The rules[279] apply to insolvent partnerships[280] and limited liability partnerships.[281] They are also applied to charitable incorporated organizations,[282] for which IA 1986, sch B1, para 40(2), is substituted[283] so as to provide that the only petition which is not suspended by the **3.105**

---

[269] Applied to special administration (bank insolvency) by SI 2011/245, sch 1, para 5.
[270] Companies Act 1989, s 161(4); Enterprise Act 2002, s 249.
[271] Under IA 1986, sch B1, para 14.
[272] IA 1986, sch B1, para 40(1)(b).
[273] IA 1986, sch B1, para 40(2).
[274] See 9.5–9.8 and 9.11–9.86.
[275] See 9.90–9.92.
[276] See 9.113–9.140.
[277] Companies Act 1989, s 161(4); Enterprise Act 2002, s 249.
[278] *Re J Smiths Haulage Ltd* [2007] BCC 135.
[279] In IA 1986, sch B1, paras 40(1)(b) and (2), and 43(6).
[280] IPO 1994, art 6, and IA 1986, sch B1, para 40(1)(b) and (2), and para 43(5), as modified by IPO 1994, sch 2, para 18.
[281] Limited Liability Partnerships Regulations 2001 (SI 2001/1090), reg 5, and sch 3.
[282] Charitable Incorporated Organisations (Insolvency and Dissolution) Regulations 2012 (SI 2012/3013), sch, para 1.
[283] By SI 2012/3013, sch, para 1(7).

appointment of an administrator, by the holder of a floating charge, is one presented by the Attorney General or the Charity Commission.[284]

Appointment of administrator by company or directors

3.106 If a petition to wind up a company has been presented, neither the company nor its directors can appoint an administrator[285] until the petition has been disposed of.[286] The government has proposed adding to the legislation a provision that appointment of an administrator by the company or its directors will be possible if notice of intention to appoint was filed with the court before the winding-up petition was presented,[287] unless it is a public interest petition.[288]

3.107 If a petition to wind up a limited liability partnership has been presented, the limited liability partnership cannot appoint an administrator[289] until the petition has been disposed of.[290]

3.108 If a petition to wind up an insolvent partnership has been presented, the partnership cannot appoint an administrator[291] until the petition has been disposed of.[292]

3.109 Provided they are unaware that a winding-up petition has been presented and not disposed of, a company or its directors, an LLP or an insolvent partnership can give a notice of intention to appoint an administrator[293] and file it in court.[294] The notice is effective to start an interim moratorium.[295] If the petition is withdrawn within the period of ten business days beginning with the date of filing the notice, an administrator can be appointed. If not, the court's permission to withdraw the notice of intention should be sought by the person who filed it.[296]

Bank and Building Society Insolvency

3.110 When the court makes a bank or building society insolvency order, it must dismiss any pending winding-up petition.[297]

---

[284] Under the Charities Act 2011, s 113.

[285] Under IA 1986, sch B1, para 22.

[286] IA 1986, sch B1, para 25(a).

[287] Without the permission required by IA 1986, sch B1, para 43(6), as applied and modified by para 44(5).

[288] Deregulation Bill (2014 HL Bill 33), sch 6, paras 4 and 5. This settles the problem raised in *Re Arucana Ltd* [2009] EWHC 3838 (Ch), LTL 21/6/2012, by using the solution adopted in *Re Ramora UK Ltd* [2011] EWHC 3959 (Ch), [2012] BCC 672.

[289] Under IA 1986, sch B1, para 22, as applied by the Limited Liability Partnerships Regulations 2001 (SI 2001/1090), reg 5, and modified by sch 3.

[290] IA 1986, sch B1, as applied by SI 2001/1090, reg 5, and sch 3.

[291] Under IA 1986, sch B1, para 22, as modified by IPO 1994, sch 2, para 9.

[292] IA 1986, sch B1, para 25(a), as applied by IPO 1994, art 6.

[293] IA 1986, sch B1, paras 22 and 26.

[294] IA 1986, sch B1, para 27. The person who proposes to make the appointment is required by para 27(2), (3), and (4) to make a statutory declaration that, so far as he is able to ascertain, the appointment is not prevented by, *inter alia*, para 25(a).

[295] IA 1986, sch B1, para 44(4); *Re Business Dream Ltd* [2011] EWHC 2860 (Ch), [2013] 1 BCLC 456.

[296] *Re Business Dream Ltd.*

[297] IA 1986, sch B1, para 40(1)(a), applied by the Banking Act 2009, s 119; Building Societies (Insolvency and Special Administration) Order 2009 (SI 2009/805), sch 1, para 20(1) and (2).

Applications for other Insolvency Processes

If, when making an application for an administration order in respect of a company, the applicant knows that a petition for the winding up of the company has been presented: **3.111**

(a) details of the winding-up petition (and any other insolvency proceedings in relation to the company), so far as within the immediate knowledge of the applicant, must be given in the witness statement supporting the administration application;[298] and
(b) a copy of the administration application must be served on the winding-up petitioner.[299]

This also applies to charitable incorporated organizations,[300] insolvent partnerships[301] and limited liability partnerships.[302]

If, when petitioning or applying for a water industry special administration order, a railway administration order, a PPP administration order, an energy administration order, an energy supply company administration order or a postal administration order to be made in respect of a company, the petitioner or applicant knows that a petition for the winding up of the company has been presented: **3.112**

(a) details of the winding-up petition must be given in the affidavit[303] supporting the administration petition or application;[304] and
(b) a copy of the administration petition or application must be served on the winding-up petitioner.[305]

If a petitioner for a winding-up order in respect of a bank, a building society or an investment bank that is not a deposit-taking bank, has notified the appropriate regulator:[306] **3.113**

(a) the witness statement supporting an application for a bank administration, building society special administration or special administration (bank administration) order must specify the notified winding-up petition or any other insolvency proceedings which have been instituted in respect of the institution;[307] and

---

[298] IR 1986, r 2.4(2)(a).
[299] IR 1986, r 2.6(3)(b).
[300] Charitable Incorporated Organisations (Insolvency and Dissolution) Regulations 2012 (SI 2012/3013), sch, para 2.
[301] IPO 1994, art 18 and sch 10.
[302] Limited Liability Partnerships Regulations 2001 (SI 2001/1090), reg 10(1)(b) and sch 6, part 2, para 3.
[303] Witness statement for an energy supply company administration application or postal administration application.
[304] Water Industry (Special Administration) Rules 2009 (SI 2009/2477), r 8(5)(a) (details to the best of the deponent's knowledge and belief); Railway Administration Order Rules 2001 (SI 2001/3352), r 2.3(5)(a) (details so far as within the immediate knowledge of the deponent); PPP Administration Order Rules 2007 (SI 2007/3141), r 5(5)(a) (ditto); Energy Administration Rules 2005 (SI 2005/2483), r 6(3)(c) (details so far as within the immediate knowledge of the applicant); Energy Supply Company Administration Rules 2013 (SI 2013/1046), r 6(3)(c) (ditto); Postal Administration Rules 2013 (SI 2013/3208), r 6(3)(c) (ditto).
[305] Water Industry (Special Administration) Rules 2009 (SI 2009/2477), r 11(1) and (2)(e); Railway Administration Order Rules 2001 (SI 2001/3352), r 2.6(2)(c); PPP Administration Order Rules 2007 (SI 2007/3141), r 8(2)(d); Energy Administration Order Rules 2005 (SI 2005/2483), r 8(3)(c); Energy Supply Company Administration Rules 2013 (SI 2013/1046), r 8(3)(c); Postal Administration Rules 2013 (SI 2013/3208), r 8(3)(c).
[306] See 3.50.
[307] Bank Administration (England and Wales) Rules 2009 (SI 2009/357), r 12(1)(e); Building Society Special Administration (England and Wales) Rules 2010 (SI 2010/2580), r 12(1)(e); Investment Bank Special Administration (England and Wales) Rules 2011 (SI 2011/1301), r 39(1)(e). Clearly this information should

(b) the winding-up petitioner must be served with a copy of any application for a bank or building society insolvency order, a bank administration order, a building society special administration order, an investment bank special administration order, a special administration (bank insolvency) order or a special administration (bank administration) order in respect of the institution sought to be wound up.[308]

3.114 For an administration application, or an application or petition for a water industry special administration order, a railway administration order, a PPP administration order, an energy administration order, an energy supply company administration order or a postal administration order, what is to be served on the winding-up petitioner is a copy of the application or petition which has been issued to the applicant or petitioner by the court, sealed by the court and endorsed with the date and time of filing and the venue for its hearing, together with the supporting witness statement or affidavit and the documents attached to the application or petition.[309] For an application for a bank or building society insolvency order or a special administration (bank insolvency) order, one copy of the application must be sent electronically as soon as practicable and a paper copy which has been sealed by the court and endorsed with the venue, date and time for the hearing must be sent by first class post.[310] For an application for a bank administration order, a building society special administration order, an investment bank special administration order, or a special administration (bank administration) order, a copy of the application and its accompanying documents, sealed by the court and endorsed with the date and time of filing and the venue for its hearing, must be served.[311]

3.115 In all cases, the winding-up petitioner may appear or be represented at the hearing of the application or petition for the other insolvency process.[312]

3.116 If, after making an administration application, or an application or petition for a water industry special administration order, a railway administration order, a PPP administration order, an energy administration order, an energy supply company administration order or a postal administration order, in relation to a company, the applicant or petitioner becomes aware of a winding-up petition (or any other insolvency proceedings) against the company, the applicant must notify the court in writing.[313]

---

also be given in an application for a bank or building society insolvency order, investment bank special administration order or special administration (bank insolvency) order.

[308] Bank Insolvency (England and Wales) Rules 2009 (SI 2009/356), r 10(1)(e); Building Society Insolvency (England and Wales) Rules 2010 (SI 2010/2581), r 10(1)(e); Bank Administration (England and Wales) Rules 2009 (SI 2009/357), r 15(d); Building Society Special Administration (England and Wales) Rules 2010 (SI 2010/2580), r 15(d); Investment Bank Special Administration (England and Wales) Rules 2011 (SI 2011/1301), rr 10(1)(c), 20(1)(e) and 41(1)(c).

[309] IR 1986, rr 2.5(1)–(3) and 2.6(1); SI 2009/2477, rr 9(1)–(3) and 11(1); SI 2001/3352, rr 2.5(1)–(3) and 2.6(1); SI 2007/3141, rr 7(1)–(3) and 8(1); SI 2005/2483, rr 7(1)–(3) and 8(1); SI 2013/1046, rr 7(1)–(3) and 8(1); SI 2013/3208, rr 7(1)–(3) and 8(1).

[310] SI 2009/356, rr 3(2) definition of 'sealed', 7(1)–(4) and 10(2); SI 2010/2581, rr 3(2) definition of 'sealed', 7(1)–(4) and 10(2); SI 2011/1301, rr 17(2) and (4) and 20(1) and (2).

[311] SI 2009/357, rr 13, 14 and 16; SI 2010/2580, rr 13, 14 and 16; SI 2011/1301, rr 9(1) and (4), 10(2), 40 and 41(2).

[312] IR 1986, r 2.12(1)(e); SI 2009/2477, r 14(a); SI 2001/3352, r 2.10(1)(f); SI 2007/3141, r 12(1)(f); SI 2005/2483, r 12(1)(f); SI 2013/1046, r 12(1)(f); SI 2009/356, r 10(3); SI 2010/2581, r 10(3); SI 2009/357, r 22(f); SI 2010/2580, r 22(f); SI 2011/1301, rr 13(f), 20(3) and 44(f); SI 2013/3208, r 12(1)(f).

[313] IR 1986, r 2.5(4); SI 2009/2477, r 13; SI 2001/3352, r 2.5(4); SI 2007/3141, r 7(4); SI 2005/2483, r 7(4); SI 2013/1046, r 7(4); SI 2013/3208, r 7(4).

Publicization of Petition[314]

Gazetting

Requirement

A winding-up order is a collective remedy and the order operates in favour of all creditors   **3.117**
and contributories,[315] each of whom can appear at the hearing of the petition to support
or oppose it. Therefore, unless the court otherwise directs, notice of a winding-up petition
must be given by the petitioner.[316] The notice must be given by 'gazetting',[317] that is, by one
advertisement in the *London Gazette*.[318] If gazetting is not reasonably practicable, notice
must be given in such other manner as the court thinks fit.[319] The notice serves to invite
creditors and contributories to appear on the hearing of the petition and submit their views
to the court: the notice is a substitute for, and renders unnecessary, service of the petition on
them.[320] Further, if the original petitioner abandons the petition, any creditor or contributory may ask to be substituted as petitioner.[321]

Conversely, if notice has not been given of a petition, by gazetting or otherwise as ordered by   **3.118**
the court, no creditor or contributory has standing to appear at the hearing[322] so that, until
notice is given, the only parties to it are the petitioner and the company.[323]

Until 5 April 2009, the rules referred to advertising rather than giving notice of a peti-   **3.119**
tion.[324] Until 1979 the rules required a second advertisement of a winding-up petition in a
newspaper other than the *London Gazette*.[325]

Timing

The notice of a petition, by gazetting or otherwise as ordered by the court, must appear at   **3.120**
least seven business days *before* the date appointed for the hearing, and, unless the company
itself is the petitioner, must not appear until at least seven business days *after* service of the
petition on the company.[326] The date of publication of an advertisement in a periodical is
the date that copies of the periodical are actually available to the public, not a nominal issue
date, if that is different.[327]

---

[314] The material in 3.117–3.154 does not apply to a petition to wind up a company presented by a contributory or contributories of the company or at the instance of the company's administrator or voluntary arrangement supervisor (IR 1986, rr 4.2(4) and 4.7(9)). Such petitions are discussed at 8.469–8.518.
[315] IA 1986, s 130(4).
[316] IR 1986, r 4.11(1).
[317] IR 1986, r 4.11(2).
[318] IR 1986, r 13.13(4) and (4A).
[319] IR 1986, r 4.11(3).
[320] *Re National Credit and Exchange Co Ltd* (1862) 7 LT 817; *Re Marlborough Club Co* (1865) LR 1 Eq 216;
Re New Gas Co (1877) 5 ChD 703.
[321] See 3.181–3.206.
[322] *Re United Stock Exchange Ltd, ex parte Philp and Kidd* (1884) 28 ChD 183.
[323] *Re a Company Incorporated in the Australian Capital Territory* (1980) 35 ACTR 36.
[324] The change of terminology was made by the Insolvency (Amendment) Rules 2009 (SI 2009/642),
which came into force on 6 April 2009.
[325] See the Companies (Winding-up) Rules 1949 (SI 1949/330), r 28, as originally made and as amended
by the Companies (Winding-up) (Amendment) Rules 1979 (SI 1979/209), r 3.
[326] IR 1986, r 4.11(4). 'Business day' is defined in r 13.13(1) (see 1.512). The clear days rule in CPR, r 2.8(2)
and (3), applies (see 1.510).
[327] *Re NKM Holdings Sdn Bhd* [1985] 2 MLJ 390, [1987] 1 MLJ 39.

Filing

3.121 A copy of the notice given of a petition, by gazetting or otherwise as ordered by the court, must be filed in court with the certificate of compliance required by IR 1986, r 4.14.[328] If filing a copy of the notice is not reasonably practicable, a description of the form and content of any notice given is to be filed.[329] A copy or description of the notice must be lodged as soon as possible after publication and in any event not later than five business days before the hearing of the petition.[330] This applies even if the notice is defective in any way (for example, if it was published at the wrong time or has omitted or misprinted important words) or if the petitioner is not pursuing the petition (for example, because the petition debt has been paid).[331]

Notice not in accordance with the rules

3.122 If notice of a winding-up petition is not given in accordance with IR 1986, r 4.11, the petition may be dismissed.[332] This applies where no notice at all is given.[333] It applies to notice that is given for the purpose of complying with r 4.11, but is given at the wrong time or is wrongly worded,[334] but it does not apply to any notification of the petition that is not made for the purpose of complying with r 4.11.[335]

3.123 By providing that the court 'may' dismiss a petition if notice is not given in accordance with the rules, r 4.11(6) contemplates that the court may, at its discretion, allow an incorrectly notified petition to proceed, presumably directing, under r 4.11(1), that notice of the petition need not be given in accordance with the rules. The costs of a non-complying notification may be disallowed. The 1862 rules gave the court an express power to dispense with advertising[336] and this was used in *Re Land and Sea Telegraph Co*[337] (advertisement appeared correctly in newspapers but too late in the *Gazette*) and *Re McLean and Co*[338] (advertisement appeared correctly in the *Gazette* but too late in newspapers), the latter case not following *Re London and Westminster Wine Co*,[339] in which a fresh advertisement was required to correct the same error.

3.124 The period of seven business days between service of the petition on the company and giving notice of the petition is required so that the company may, depending on the circumstances: (a) apply for the petition to be struck out; (b) pay the debt on a creditor's petition; (c) consider its position generally with regard to the petition; (d) if necessary, make an application under IA 1986, s 127, for an anticipatory validation order.[340] However, if it is clear that the company cannot have been prejudiced because it could not have resisted the winding-up petition, the petitioner will not be penalized for failing to provide the company

---

[328] See 3.156–3.162.
[329] IR 1986, r 4.14(2).
[330] PD Insolvency Proceedings 2014, para 11.5.2.
[331] PD Insolvency Proceedings 2014, para 11.5.2.
[332] IR 1986, r 4.11(6).
[333] See 3.125.
[334] See 3.141–3.152.
[335] See 3.136–3.140.
[336] r 53.
[337] (1870) 18 WR 1150.
[338] [1881] WN 8.
[339] (1863) 1 Hem & M 561.
[340] *Re Signland Ltd* [1982] 2 All ER 609 per Slade J at p 609; *Re Bill Hennessey Associates Ltd* [1992] BCC 386 per Judge Leonard Bromley at p 387.

with an opportunity it did not need.[341] The power to dismiss a prematurely notified petition to wind up a company is a discretionary disciplinary power and might not be exercised on the company's application if the company does not show that it has been prejudiced, for example, by showing on a creditor's petition that it could have paid the debt.[342]

Failure to give notice

The timely notification of a creditor's petition to wind up a company is important to ensure **3.125** that the class remedy of winding up by the court is available to all creditors, and is not used as a means of putting improper pressure on the company to pay the petitioner's debt or costs.[343] The court may dismiss a petition if notice of it has not been given in accordance with IR 1986, r 4.11.[344] If a petition has not been advertised by the time set for its first hearing, the court may dismiss it summarily at that hearing, unless good reason is shown for the failure.[345] Good reason would include an undertaking or direction not to give notice, or an injunction against giving notice.[346] If, instead of dismissing the petition, the court grants an adjournment, this will usually be on condition that notice of the petition is given in accordance with the rule in due time for the adjourned hearing.[347] No further adjournment for the purpose of giving notice will normally be granted.[348]

Court's direction not to give notice

IR 1986, r 4.11(1), refers to the possibility of the court directing that notice is not to be given **3.126** of a winding-up petition. On an application[349] by a company for a direction that notice is not to be given of a petition for it to be wound up, it is for the company to show sufficient reason for departure from the normal practice of giving notice of petitions other than contributories' petitions,[350] but it is not necessary for the company to show that the petition is bound to fail.[351]

One function of gazetting notice (which may, of course, be taken up by credit reference **3.127** agencies and other news media) of presentation of a petition to wind up a company is to alert the public that if they deal with the company, they will be dealing with a company against which a winding-up petition has been presented and which has not obtained an order restraining gazetting.[352] Accordingly, if the company has not obtained an order under IA 1986, s 127, validating dispositions in the ordinary course of the company's business, the

[341] *Re Roselmar Properties Ltd* (1986) 2 BCC 99,156; *Re DR Electrical and Engineering Pty Ltd* (1989) 15 ACLR 700; *Melcann Ltd v Marmlon Holdings Pty Ltd* (1991) 4 ACSR 736; *Dikwa Holdings Pty Ltd v Oakbury Pty Ltd* (1992) 36 FCR 274.
[342] *Re Roselmar Properties Ltd* (1986) 2 BCC 99,156; *Re Corbenstoke Ltd* [1989] BCLC 496; *Re Garton (Western) Ltd* [1989] BCLC 304.
[343] PD Insolvency Proceedings 2014, para 11.5.1.
[344] IR 1986, r 4.11(6).
[345] PD Insolvency Proceedings 2014, para 11.5.1.
[346] *Re Five Oaks Construction Ltd* (1968) 112 SJ 86; *Re a Company (No 002791 of 1986)* (1986) 2 BCC 99,281.
[347] PD Insolvency Proceedings 2014, para 11.5.1.
[348] PD Insolvency Proceedings 2014, para 11.5.1.
[349] See 3.233–3.263.
[350] *Re a Company (No 007946 of 1993)* [1994] Ch 198; *Re a Company (No 007923 of 1994)* [1995] 1 WLR 953.
[351] *Re a Company (No 007923 of 1994)* [1995] 1 WLR 953.
[352] See 3.60–3.89. *Applied Data Base Ltd v Secretary of State for Trade and Industry* [1995] 1 BCLC 272 per Lightman J at p 274.

court will not direct that notice is not to be given of the petition, other than in exceptional circumstances.[353]

3.128   In *Commissioner of State Revenue of Victoria v Roy Morgan Research Centre Pty Ltd*[354] the court directed the applicant for a winding-up order not to advertise the application but to notify members and creditors that it had been brought and of their right to support or oppose it. This was ordered on the company's application 'on the ground that [advertisement] might cause unnecessary harm to the [company], without necessarily serving any particularly useful purpose'.[355] However, it is difficult to see what advantage there could be to the company from the procedure directed by the court.

3.129   In *Re a Company (No 007020 of 1996)*[356] the company had issued an application to restrain advertisement of a creditor's petition and the creditor had undertaken not to advertise it until the date fixed for hearing the application. There was not time to hear it on the date fixed and the court indicated that it would be heard the next morning, but there was no application to continue the undertaking. The petitioner arranged for the petition to be advertised in the next day's *Gazette*. This was held to be an abuse of process and the petition was struck out.

Public interest petitions

3.130   For gazetting public interest petitions see 9.78–9.83.

Contents of Notice

3.131   The contents of the advertisement of a winding-up petition in the *London Gazette* are specified in IR 1986, rr 4.11(5), 12A.33, 12A.34 and 12A.36.[357] The prescribed form of an advertisement is form 4.6 in sch 4. The contents of a notice of a petition that is advertised in any other way are specified in rr 4.11(5), 12A.38, 12A.39 and 12A.41.[358]

3.132   The advertisement must have a heading corresponding with the heading of the petition—that is:

> IN THE MATTER OF [name of company sought to be wound up]
> AND IN THE MATTER OF THE INSOLVENCY ACT 1986

3.133   Descriptive matter such as 'trading as...' may not be added. Tendentious or illustrative matter must not be introduced on any pretext.[359]

3.134   Where petitions are presented under IPO 1994, art 8 or art 10, for the winding up of a partnership and the winding up or bankruptcy of one or more of its present or former members, the prescribed form of advertisement for the winding-up petitions is form 8 in IPO 1994, sch 9.[360]

---

[353] *Applied Data Base Ltd v Secretary of State for Trade and Industry* [1995] 1 BCLC 272 per Lightman J at pp 274–5.

[354] (1997) 24 ACSR 73.

[355] At p 77.

[356] [1998] 2 BCLC 54.

[357] See r 13.13(4B)(a).

[358] See r 13.13(4B)(b).

[359] Practice Note [1948] WN 481.

[360] IA 1986, s 124(3)(b), as modified by IPO 1994, sch 4, para 8 (in respect of art 8 petitions); IA 1986, s 124(4)(b), as modified by IPO 1994, sch 6, para 2 (in respect of art 10 petitions).

Provision of Copies of the Petition

When a petition has been presented for the winding up of a company, the petitioner (or the   **3.135**
petitioner's solicitor, if there is one) must, on request, supply to any director, contributory or
creditor of the company a copy of the petition. A copy must be supplied within two business
days[361] of being applied for and a fee of 15p per A4 or A5 page (30p per A3 page) may be
charged.[362] In Bermuda it has been held that any person who claims in good faith to be an
actual, contingent or prospective creditor is entitled to a copy under this rule. The evidential
threshold is very low indeed and the petitioner or the court is not required to resolve any dispute raised by the company about the requester's standing.[363] As a copy of the petition may
be requested before it has been served on the company or publicly notified, there may be a
danger of breaching the principle that a petition may not be publicized before it has been
publicly notified.[364] The court may restrain the petitioner from complying with a request
for a copy of the petition, as part of its jurisdiction to restrain gazetting of, and strike out,
a petition.[365] Alternatively, it may extend the time for complying with a request.[366] Either
order is, of course, discretionary. A petition is not a statement of case,[367] but the provisions
of the CPR concerning the supply of documents to a non-party from court records[368] apply
to winding-up petitions with any necessary modifications.[369]

Other Publicization of the Petition

Publicity for a winding-up petition, given otherwise than for the purpose of complying   **3.136**
with IR 1986, r 4.11, is not 'notice' for the purposes of that rule and, in particular, r 4.11(6)
(which provides a power to dismiss a petition for failure to comply with r 4.11) does not
apply.[370] However, in *Re FSA Business Software Ltd*[371] Warner J said, at p 468:

> It is at least a breach of the spirit of the rules of this court for publicity to be given to a
> winding-up petition before it has been advertised.

The court may dismiss a petition if a third party is informed of its existence before the   **3.137**
expiry of seven business days from service on the company and informing the third party
was intended to put pressure on the company: such an action is an abuse of process.[372] In
SN Group plc v Barclays Bank plc[373] it was found that the publicization of the petition was

---

[361] The clear days rule in CPR, r 2.8(2) and (3), applies (see 1.510). 'Business day' is defined in IR 1986,
r 13.13(1) (see 1.512).
[362] IR 1986, rr 4.13 and 13.11(b). For a petition to wind up a relevant scheme (see 1.168), r 4.13 is modified by the Collective Investment in Transferable Securities (Contractual Scheme) Regulations 2013 (SI
2013/1388), sch 3.
[363] *Re IPOC Capital Partners Ltd* [2007] Bda LR 33 at [93(ii)].
[364] See 3.136–3.140.
[365] See 3.60–3.89. *Re IPOC Capital Partners Ltd* [2007] Bda LR 33 at [93(iii)].
[366] IR 1986, r 4.3. *Re IPOC Capital Partners Ltd* [2007] Bda LR 33 at [93(iii)].
[367] See 2.9.
[368] CPR, r 5.4C.
[369] IR 1986, r 7.51A(2).
[370] *Re a Company (No 0013925 of 1991)* [1992] BCLC 562; *SN Group plc v Barclays Bank plc* [1993] BCC
506; *Secretary of State for Trade and Industry v North West Holdings plc* [1999] 1 BCLC 425, overruling *Re a
Company (No 001127 of 1992)* [1992] BCC 477.
[371] [1990] BCC 465.
[372] *Re Bill Hennessey Associates Ltd* [1992] BCC 386, where a copy of the petition was faxed to the company's bank on the same day as it was served on the company; *Re a Company (No 001127 of 1992)* [1992] BCC
477, in which the petitioner informed the company's bank and many of its suppliers by letter that a petition
had been presented.
[373] [1993] BCC 506.

not designed to put pressure on the company (which was found to be insolvent) and the company's application to have the petition dismissed was rejected. In Australia it has been held that a winding-up application may be dismissed if premature publicity has caused harm, or if the reasonable inference open to the court is that it must have caused harm.[374]

3.138 Publicization of an intention to present a petition may be an abuse of process which may be punished by striking out the petition when it is presented.[375]

3.139 In *Ex parte Creditnet Ltd*[376] it was held that the court will not provide credit reference agencies with information about pending petitions which may not yet have been advertised. However, in further proceedings in the same case,[377] Ward LJ said, obiter, at pp 623–4, that a credit reference agency could inspect the register for such a purpose as agent for a specific client.[378]

3.140 Publication of a winding-up petition, other than in accordance with IR 1986, will be a criminal contempt of court, for which there is strict liability, if it creates a serious risk that the course of justice in the winding-up proceedings will be seriously impeded or prejudiced.[379] If the Contempt of Court Act 1981, s 2, does not apply, there may be a contempt of court if intention to commit one can be proved. In two 19th-century cases contempt was found. They were decided at a time when it was considered that there was strict criminal liability for publication of any one-sided account of a pending claim. In *Re Cheltenham and Swansea Railway Carriage and Wagon Co*[380] an entire petition by a contributory, containing grave charges of fraud and misconduct against directors, had been published as a news item in a newspaper. In *Re Crown Bank*[381] the publisher of a newspaper was fined for contempt after publishing articles adopting allegations of fraud made in a contributory's petition while the petition was pending.

Errors in Notices

Effects of an error

3.141 If there is an error or inaccuracy in an advertisement in the *London Gazette* then, unless the court waives it, the person who was responsible for giving the notice must, as soon as reasonably practicable, cause a further entry to be made in the *Gazette* for the purpose of correcting the error or inaccuracy.[382] The court has a discretion to waive an error.[383]

3.142 If an error in the notice of the petition is discovered after the winding-up order has been made and the error cannot be waived, fresh proceedings with fresh notice will be permitted: there is no issue estoppel.[384]

---

[374] *Australian Beverage Distributors Pty Ltd v Evans and Tate Premium Wines Pty Ltd* [2007] NSWCA 57, 61 ACSR 441, in which a press release stating that an application for winding up had been filed against a company whose shares were publicly traded concluded by expressing the applicant's view that the shares were worthless.

[375] *Re Doreen Boards Ltd* [1996] 1 BCLC 501.

[376] [1996] 1 WLR 1291.

[377] *Ex parte Austintel Ltd* [1997] 1 WLR 616.

[378] For some information about an order of that kind see *Re Haines Watts* [2004] EWHC 1970 (Ch), [2005] BPIR 798.

[379] Contempt of Court Act 1981, s 2.

[380] (1869) LR 8 Eq 580.

[381] (1890) 44 ChD 649.

[382] IR 1986, r 12A.37(3).

[383] *Re Worthing Royal Sea House Hotel Co* [1872] WN 74.

[384] *Re Army and Navy Hotel* (1886) 31 ChD 644.

Misdescription of the company sought to be wound up

If notice, by gazetting or otherwise as ordered by the court, of a petition to have a company **3.143** wound up does not give the company's name correctly, it will be completely ineffective and there will have to be fresh notice,[385] unless the mistake was one that the court can waive because it is not significant and will not have misled anyone.[386] In *Re Vidiofusion Ltd*, the advertisement incorrectly gave the company's name as 'Videofusion Ltd' ('e' instead of 'i'). Megarry J waived the mistake and said that, normally, an error would be waived if four conditions are satisfied:

(a) There must be no other company on the register with a similar name.
(b) The true name and the misspelt name should have substantially the same pronunciation.[387]
(c) There should be no marked visual difference between the true name and the misspelt name (so that 'Jaxen' for 'Jackson' would not be waived despite the similarity of pronunciation).
(d) The error must not materially affect the alphabetical order of the names.

The practice of waiving misspellings continues, but it is submitted that it is time to review it, **3.144** now that there are over three million British registered companies and now that banks and other persons checking whether they deal with companies which are the subject of winding-up petitions use computer searches which are usually not capable of recognizing such errors.[388]

In *Re J and P Sussman Ltd*[389] the name of the company intended to be wound up was J and P **3.145** Sussmann Ltd, but in the advertisement (and throughout the proceedings) it had been referred to as J and P Sussman Ltd. Vaisey J amended the order and waived the error in the advertisement. In *Re Army and Navy Hotel*,[390] the fact that Army and Navy Hotel Ltd had been misdescribed as 'Army and Navy Hotel Co Ltd' was not waived. In *Re London and Provincial Pure Ice Manufacturing Co*[391] omission of the word 'Ltd' from the company's name was not waived. However, in *Re L'Industrie Verrière Ltd*[392] the misspelling of the word 'Industrie' as 'Industre' was waived, and in *Re E S Snell and Son Ltd*,[393] the description of the company as 'E S Snell and Son Ltd' when its correct name was 'E S Snell and Sons Ltd' was waived (the report in *The Times* does not make it clear whether the error was in the advertisement or only in the petition but, according to Astbury J in *Re L'Industrie Verrière Ltd*, the error was in both).

In *Re Samuel Birch Co Ltd*[394] the fact that 'Samuel Birch and Co Ltd' was misdescribed as **3.146** 'The Samuel Birch Co Ltd' was not waived.

---

[385] *Re City and County Bank* (1875) LR 10 Ch App 470 per James LJ at p 477.
[386] *Re L'Industrie Verrière Ltd* [1914] WN 222; *Re J and P Sussman Ltd* [1958] 1 WLR 519; *Re Vidiofusion Ltd* [1974] 1 WLR 1548.
[387] Subsequently, his Lordship described this as a benevolent application of the doctrine of *idem sonans* (sounding the same): *A New Miscellany-at-Law* (Oxford: Hart Publishing, 2005), p 224.
[388] See, for example, *Re MTB Motors Ltd* [2010] EWHC 3751 (Ch), [2012] BCC 601, where an online search in the Financial Services Register for 'M.T.B. Motors Ltd' did not find the company which had been entered on that register as 'MTB Motors Ltd'.
[389] [1958] 1 WLR 519.
[390] (1886) 31 ChD 644.
[391] [1904] WN 136.
[392] [1914] WN 222.
[393] (1911) *The Times*, 20 December 1911.
[394] [1907] WN 31.

3.147 However, in *Re Newcastle Machinists Co*[395] the company consented to waiver of being described as 'The Newcastle Machinists Co Ltd' instead of 'The Newcastle-upon-Tyne Machinists Co Ltd'. The winding-up order had already been made in the wrong name when the error was discovered and so the court corrected the error in the order[396] but required a new advertisement of the making of the order.

3.148 The petition in *Re Consolidated Minera Lead Mining Co Ltd*[397] was presented at a time when a petition had to be advertised in two newspapers as well as in the *London Gazette*. In one newspaper the word 'Minera' had been printed as 'Mineral' and in another as 'Minerva'. Correcting advertisements were published the following day but it would seem that the correcting advertisements were published too late, though there is no comment on this fact in the reports. A winding-up order was made notwithstanding the errors. It may be assumed that the advertisement in the *Gazette* was correct but the reports do not state what effect this had on the decision.

3.149 In *Re Professional and Trade Papers Ltd*[398] the name of the company intended to be wound up was Professional and Trade Papers Ltd, but in the order (and throughout the proceedings) it had been referred to as Professional and Trades Papers Ltd. Buckley J allowed amendment of the petition and required publication of an advertisement stating the error that had been made and that the winding-up order would be drawn up seven days after the issue of the advertisement.

Other errors

3.150 In *Re Bull, Bevan and Co*[399] the fact that the advertisement gave the wrong date for the date of presentation of the petition was waived by the court. In *Re Broad's Patent Night Light Co*,[400] *Re Saul Moss and Sons Ltd*[401] and *Re Obie Pty Ltd*[402] the court waived an erroneous statement of the date by which notices of appearance had to be given.[403] In the first case no one claimed to have been misled. In the second case notices had been given and dealt with after the erroneous date. In *Re Dublin Grains Co Ltd*[404] the fact that the advertisement had given the wrong date for the hearing of the petition was waived—the advertised date was in fact a public holiday. But in *Re Joint Stock Companies Winding-up Act*[405] the court required a new advertisement when it heard on Thursday 20 December 1849 a petition which had been advertised as to be heard on Saturday 20 December 1849 (the court did sit on Saturdays in those days).

3.151 In *Re Hille India Rubber Co*[406] part of the prescribed advertisement had been omitted because of the misleading way the form had been printed in the rules. The court refused

---

[395] [1888] WN 246 and [1889] WN 1.
[396] See 6.1–6.6.
[397] (1876) 25 WR 36.
[398] (1900) 44 SJ 740.
[399] [1891] WN 170.
[400] [1892] WN 5.
[401] [1906] WN 142.
[402] (1983) 8 ACLR 439.
[403] See 5.32–5.36.
[404] (1886) 17 LR Ir 512.
[405] (1849) 13 Beav 434.
[406] [1897] WN 6.

to waive the error and required a new advertisement, making it clear that the waiver of the same error in *Re Mont de Piété of England*[407] was exceptional.

In *Re Marezzo Marble Co Ltd*[408] the heading of the advertisement referred to the Companies **3.152** Act 1862 instead of the Companies Acts 1862 and 1867 as required by the rules of the time. The court refused to waive the error.

Dispensing with Gazetting

The court may dispense with gazetting of a winding-up petition.[409] See also 9.78–9.83 for **3.153** dispensing with gazetting of public interest petitions.

In Australia it has been considered unnecessary to advertise applications to wind up dereg- **3.154** istered companies.[410]

Bank or Building Society Insolvency Application

There is no requirement for gazetting of an application for a bank or building society insol- **3.155** vency order. Every contributory or creditor of the institution is entitled to a copy of the application on request to the applicant.[411] The applicant must respond to any request for a copy of the application as soon as reasonably practicable, on payment of 15p per A4 or A5 page, or 30p per A3 page.[412]

Certificate of Compliance[413]

Before the date appointed for the hearing of a winding-up petition, the petitioner or the **3.156** petitioner's solicitor must file in court a certificate of compliance with the rules relating to service and gazetting.[414] A certificate must:[415]

(a) State the date of presentation of the petition.
(b) State the date fixed for hearing it.
(c) State the date or dates on which the petition was served and notice of it was given, by gazetting or otherwise as ordered, in compliance with the rules.
(d) Be accompanied by a copy of the notice. If filing a copy of the notice is not reasonably practicable, a description of the form and content of any notice given is to be filed.

The certificate of compliance must be filed at least five business days before the hearing of **3.157** the petition.[416]

---

[407] [1892] WN 166.
[408] (1874) 43 LJ Ch 544.
[409] IR 1986, r 4.11(1).
[410] *Re Sparad Ltd* (1993) 12 ACSR 12; *Scott v Janniki Pty Ltd* (1994) 14 ACSR 334.
[411] Bank Insolvency (England and Wales) Rules 2009 (SI 2009/356), r 12(1); Building Society Insolvency (England and Wales) Rules 2010 (SI 2010/2581), r 12(1).
[412] SI 2009/356, rr 12(2) and 290; SI 2010/2581, rr 12(2) and 282.
[413] The material in 3.156–3.162 does not apply to a petition to wind up a company presented by a contributory or contributories of the company or at the instance of the company's administrator or voluntary arrangement supervisor (IR 1986, rr 4.2(4) and 4.7(9)). Such petitions are discussed at 8.469–8.518.
[414] IR 1986, r 4.14(1). The prescribed form of certificate is form 4.7 in IR 1986, sch 4.
[415] IR 1986, r 4.14(2).
[416] IR 1986, r 4.14(1). The clear days rule in CPR, r 2.8(2) and (3), applies (see 1.510). 'Business day' is defined in IR 1986, r 13.13(1) (see 1.512).

3.158 Failure to file a certificate of compliance is a ground on which the court may, if it thinks fit, dismiss the petition.[417] In practice, the court will not make a winding-up order unless and until a certificate of compliance is filed. The Privy Council has, however, said that the rule requiring a certificate is directory not mandatory: it is primarily an administrative provision for the benefit of the court.[418] Failure to file a certificate is not tantamount to abandoning the petition.[419] In *Re J Lang and Co Ltd*[420] North J thought that a petition should not be dismissed for failure to file a certificate of compliance unless the failure had caused substantial injustice which could not be remedied by an order of the court.

3.159 A copy or description of the notice must be filed even if it was defective in some way, for example, because it was published at the wrong time or omitted or misprinted important words.[421] If the petition has not been notified because of an undertaking or direction not to notify, or an injunction against notification, the certificate prescribed in form 4.7 should be adapted to state the reason for not notifying.[422] Failure to notify a petition for such a reason is not in itself a ground for dismissing the petition.[423]

3.160 A petitioner who has given notice of the petition but has decided not to pursue it should, nevertheless, file a copy or description of the notice[424] and a certificate of compliance so as to be entitled to costs.

3.161 When it was first introduced,[425] this provision simply required a petitioner to satisfy the registrar that the petition had been duly advertised and other rules had been complied with. Soon after, the judges added the requirement that the petitioner should give a certificate.[426]

3.162 The rule in IR 1986 on filing a certificate of compliance is applied to an application for a bank or building society insolvency order,[427] with three modifications:

(a) The period for filing is as soon as reasonably practicable before the hearing of the application.[428]

(b) It is not necessary to file a copy of a notice, because an application for a bank insolvency order is not publicly notified.[429]

(c) A witness statement by the proposed liquidator must be filed with the certificate of compliance stating that he or she is qualified to act as an insolvency practitioner in accordance with IA 1986, s 390, and consents to act as the liquidator.[430] The court cannot make a bank insolvency order unless this statement has been filed.[431]

---

[417] IR 1986, r 4.14(3).

[418] *Jamincorp International Merchant Bank v Minister of Finance* (1987) 36 WIR 313 at p 316.

[419] *Jamincorp International Merchant Bank v Minister of Finance*.

[420] (1892) 36 SJ 271.

[421] PD Insolvency Proceedings 2014, para 11.5.2.

[422] See *Re a Company (No 002791 of 1986)* (1986) 2 BCC 99,281.

[423] *Re Five Oaks Construction Ltd* (1968) 112 SJ 86; *Re a Company (No 002791 of 1986)* (1986) 2 BCC 99,281.

[424] PD Insolvency Proceedings 2014, para 11.5.2.

[425] As the Companies Winding-up Rules (February) 1891, r 1.

[426] *Re Kershaw and Pole Ltd* [1891] WN 202.

[427] IR 1986, r 4.14 applied by the Bank Insolvency (England and Wales) Rules 2009 (SI 2009/356), r 13(1), and the Building Society Insolvency (England and Wales) Rules 2010 (SI 2010/2581), r 13(1).

[428] SI 2009/356, r 13(2); SI 2010/2581, r 13(2).

[429] SI 2009/356, r 13(3); SI 2010/2581, r 13(3).

[430] SI 2009/356, r 13(3); SI 2010/2581, r 13(4).

[431] SI 2009/356, r 16(1); SI 2010/2581, r 16(1).

Permission to Withdraw a Petition

Withdrawal under IR 1986

In England and Wales the initiator of legal proceedings may withdraw them before judgment only in accordance with rules of court.[432] **3.163**

A person petitioning for a company to be wound up may make an application[433] to the court without notice to other parties for permission to withdraw the petition.[434] The following conditions must be satisfied: **3.164**

(a) The petition must not have been advertised[435] and no notices with reference to the petition (whether in support of or in opposition to it) must have been received by the petitioner, either under r 4.16[436] or otherwise.[437]

(b) The company must consent to the court giving permission to withdraw the petition.[438]

(c) The parties must have agreed who is to pay costs. If there has been no agreement, the petition must be heard so that the court can make an order, but then the petition must be gazetted.[439]

(d) The application must be made at least five business days before the day fixed for hearing the petition.[440]

The prescribed form of order for permission to withdraw a petition is form 4.8 in sch 4 to IR 1986. **3.165**

The procedure in r 4.15 is used, for example, when a creditor who has petitioned for winding up is paid the debt before gazetting the petition. **3.166**

Rule 4.15 does not apply to a petition to wind up a company presented by a contributory or contributories of the company or at the instance of the company's administrator or voluntary arrangement supervisor.[441] **3.167**

If permission is given to a petitioner to withdraw the petition, another person may be substituted as petitioner.[442] **3.168**

---

[432] *Fox v Star Newspaper Co Ltd* [1900] AC 19 (High Court); *Gilham v Browning* [1998] 1 WLR 682 (County Court).

[433] See 3.233–3.263.

[434] IR 1986, r 4.15. In the Royal Courts of Justice the member of court staff in charge of the winding-up list has been authorized to deal with applications under this rule (PD Insolvency Proceedings 2014, para 12.1). In a district registry or the County Court an application must be made to a district judge (PD Insolvency Proceedings 2014, para 12.2).

[435] IR 1986, r 4.15(a); *Re an Insurance Company* (1875) 33 LT 49; *Re Five Oaks Construction Ltd* (1968) 112 SJ 86.

[436] See 5.32–5.36.

[437] IR 1986, r 4.15(b); *Re Wavern Engineering Co Ltd* (1986) 3 BCC 3.

[438] IR 1986, r 4.15(c); *Re a Company* [1986] CLY 337. For a petition to wind up a relevant scheme (see 1.168), r 4.15(c) is modified by the Collective Investment in Transferable Securities (Contractual Scheme) Regulations 2013 (SI 2013/1388), sch 3, to require the consent of the depositary and the operator.

[439] *Re Shusella Ltd* [1983] BCLC 505.

[440] IR 1986, r 4.15. The clear days rule in CPR, r 2.8(2) and (3), applies (see 1.510). 'Business day' is defined in IR 1986, r 13.13(1) (see 1.512).

[441] IR 1986, r 4.2(4); see 8.505.

[442] IR 1986, r 4.19; see 3.181–3.206.

3.169 When giving permission to withdraw a petition the court should not give liberty to the petitioner to restore it, because this would be the same as an adjournment of the petition, which is generally deprecated.[443]

3.170 The rule in IR 1986 on withdrawal of a winding-up petition is applied to an application for a bank or building society insolvency order, with the following modifications:[444]

(a) As there is no public notification of applications for bank or building society insolvency orders, the requirement that advertisement must have occurred does not apply.

(b) There is no time limit for applying for permission to withdraw.

Simultaneous Petitions in respect of an Insolvent Partnership and its Members

3.171 Where petitions are presented under IPO 1994, art 8 or art 10, for the winding up of a partnership and the winding up or bankruptcy of one or more of its present or former members, the legislation contemplates that normally the petitioner cannot withdraw one of the petitions without withdrawing all of them.[445] Withdrawal has to take place 'at the hearing' and the petitioner must give the court notice of intention to withdraw at least three days before the date appointed for that hearing.[446] It would seem to follow that notice to withdraw a petition which involves the withdrawal of all the petitions must be given at least three days before the first hearing (which must be of the petition to wind up the partnership).

3.172 The court may permit the petitioner to withdraw one petition without withdrawing all of them if the court is satisfied, on an application made to it by the petitioner, that continuance of that petition would be likely to prejudice or delay the proceedings on one of the other petitions.[447] Prejudice or delay justifying such permission may be caused by difficulties in serving the petition sought to be withdrawn or for any other reason. It would seem that the court can rule at any time that the petitioner can withdraw one petition without withdrawing all of them, even though permission to withdraw can only be given at the time appointed for hearing the petition to be withdrawn.

3.173 Having received notice to withdraw an art 8 petition (which can be presented only by a creditor), the court can substitute another creditor as petitioner in all the petitions relating to the partnership, and then none of the petitions will be withdrawn.[448]

---

[443] See 5.113–5.116 and 5.119. *Re Sailport Pty Ltd* [1990] 2 QdR 395; *RHB Bank Bhd v Oilangas Shipping Services (M) Sdn Bhd* [1999] 1 MLJ 446; in both cases leave to withdraw was given on condition that the applicant should not, without leave, make a further application to wind up the same company based on the same or similar grounds. The fear expressed in *Re Sailport Pty Ltd* that dismissing a petition instead of giving permission to withdraw it would create an estoppel under the principle of *res judicata* does not apply in England and Wales, where it is established that an order dismissing proceedings does not create any estoppel if it was made without any consideration of the merits, admission or default amounting to admission (*Pople v Evans* [1969] 2 Ch 255; *Birkett v James* [1978] AC 297).

[444] IA 1986, r 4.15, applied by the Bank Insolvency (England and Wales) Rules 2009 (SI 2009/356), r 14, and modified by rr 3(3)(b) and (4)(f), (j) and (k) and 14, and also applied by the Building Society Insolvency (England and Wales) Rules 2010 (SI 2010/2581), r 14, and modified by rr 3(5)(b) and (6)(h), (l) and (m) and 14.

[445] IA 1986, s 124(9)(a), as modified by IPO 1994, sch 4, para 8 (in respect of art 8 petitions); IA 1986, s 124(9)(a), as modified by IPO 1994, sch 6, para 2 (in respect of art 10 petitions).

[446] IA 1986, s 124(9)(b), as modified by IPO 1994, sch 4, para 8 (in respect of art 8 petitions); IA 1986, s 124(9)(b), as modified by IPO 1994, sch 6, para 2 (in respect of art 10 petitions).

[447] IA 1986, s 124(10), as modified by IPO 1994, sch 4, para 8 (in respect of art 8 petitions); IA 1986, s 124(10), as modified by IPO 1994, sch 6, para 2 (in respect of art 10 petitions).

[448] IA 1986, s 124(11), as modified by IPO 1994, sch 4, para 8.

Inherent Jurisdiction

Outside England and Wales it seems to have been recognized that a court has an inherent **3.174**
jurisdiction to give permission to withdraw a winding-up petition.[449]

In Australia it has been held that the court cannot require the company to prove its solvency **3.175**
as a condition of giving permission to withdraw a petition by agreement.[450]

In *J N Taylor Finance Pty Ltd v BCF (Bond Corporation Finance) Ltd (No 2)*[451] the court gave **3.176**
permission to withdraw an application to wind up a company, after approving a compromise of proceedings brought by the petitioner against the company, where all persons who
had given notice of appearing at the hearing of the application agreed to the withdrawal.

Notice of Appearance

Persons wishing to appear on the hearing of a winding-up petition must give notice to the **3.177**
petitioner or the petitioner's solicitor by 4:00 pm on the business day before the hearing,
and a list of persons who have given notice must be prepared and given to the court before
commencement of the hearing.[452]

Company's Evidence in Opposition[453]

If a petition to wind up a company has been presented and it is to be opposed by the com- **3.178**
pany, the company's witness statement in opposition must be filed in court not less than
five business days before the day fixed for hearing the petition.[454] A copy of the evidence
must be sent to the petitioner as soon as reasonably practicable after filing.[455] Rule 4.18 is
the only provision in IR 1986 putting a time limit on the filing of evidence and it applies
only to the *company's* evidence in opposition, not to evidence in opposition presented
by other persons.[456] Written evidence in response to the company's evidence filed under
r 4.18 cannot be filed unless the court directs the filing of further evidence or otherwise
gives permission.[457] The court has a general power under CPR, r 32.1(1), to give directions
on the way in which evidence is to be placed before the court.

---

[449] *Re Mackay Sawmills Pty Ltd* [1951] QWN 24, which concerned a contributory's petition.
[450] *Re Alexanders Securities Ltd (No 1)* [1983] 2 QdR 629.
[451] (1991) 5 ACSR 49.
[452] IR 1986, rr 4.16 and 4.17. See 5.32–5.37.
[453] The material in 3.178–3.180 does not apply to a petition to wind up a company presented by a contributory or contributories of the company or at the instance of the company's administrator or voluntary
arrangement supervisor (IR 1986, rr 4.2(4) and 4.7(9)). Such petitions are discussed at 8.469–8.518.
[454] IR 1986, r 4.18(1). The clear days rule in CPR, r 2.8(2) and (3), applies (see 1.510). 'Business day' is
defined in IR 1986, r 13.13(1) (see 1.512). For a petition to wind up a relevant scheme (see 1.168), r 4.18 is
modified by the Collective Investment in Transferable Securities (Contractual Scheme) Regulations 2013
(SI 2013/1388), sch 3, to refer to the scheme operator's evidence in opposition, which can be filed only with
the depositary's consent.
[455] IR 1986, r 4.18(2). For what constitutes 'sending' see 1.516–1.519.
[456] *Re Piccadilly Property Management Ltd* [1999] 2 BCLC 145 at p 153.
[457] *Re Multicultural Media Centre for the Millennium Ltd* [2001] EWCA Civ 1687, *The Times*, 16
November 2001.

3.179 In practice, if it appears on first hearing a petition that it will be opposed, the court will adjourn it and give directions for evidence to be filed by the company and the petitioner, and it does not matter that no evidence was filed before the first hearing.[458]

3.180 A similar rule applies to evidence in opposition to an application for a bank or building society insolvency order.[459] In relation to a bank or building society insolvency application, though, the only time limit is that the evidence must be filed in court and served before the hearing,[460] but the fact that evidence in opposition has not been filed in court does not prevent the institution from being heard at the hearing of the application.[461] Evidence in opposition to a bank or building society insolvency application may be served by personal service[462] or by electronic means.[463] It must be served on the applicant[464] and on the persons listed in SI 2009/356, r 10(1), or SI 2010/2581, r 10(1) (to whom a copy of the application should have been sent and who are entitled to attend and be heard at the hearing of the application).[465]

Substitution of Petitioner[466]

Introduction

3.181 IR 1986, r 4.19, is of great importance in the procedure for petitioning for winding up, particularly on creditors' petitions. Its effect is that if a person who has presented a petition is not after all going to ask for a winding-up order then 'any creditor or contributory who in [the court's] opinion would have a right to present a petition, and who is desirous of prosecuting it'[467] may be substituted by the court as petitioner. Without provision for substitution, an insolvent company could delay being wound up by paying off petitioning creditors one by one, forcing other creditors to present and gazette new petitions, then waiting until a petition by each creditor was at or near hearing before paying that creditor off too.[468] In order to counter these tactics, several creditors would have to present petitions simultaneously. As Needham J said in *DMK Building Materials Pty Ltd v C B Baker Timbers Pty Ltd*:[469]

---

[458] Chief Registrar Baister, 'The hearing of the petition' (2008) 1 Corporate Rescue and Insolvency 115. A different view was taken in Malaysia in *Crocuses and Daffodils (M) Sdn Bhd v Development and Commercial Bank Bhd* [1997] 2 MLJ 756, in which it was held that the fact that a hearing is adjourned does not cure a failure to file evidence in opposition in time before the date originally set for the hearing. However, this seems to ignore the court's power to extend or shorten time (*Dato Ting Check Sii v Datuk Haji Mohamad Tufail bin Mahmud* [2007] 7 MLJ 618).

[459] Bank Insolvency (England and Wales) Rules 2009 (SI 2009/356), r 15; Building Society Insolvency (England and Wales) Rules 2010 (SI 2010/2581), r 15.

[460] SI 2009/356, r 15(2) and (4); SI 2010/2581, r 15(2) and (4).

[461] SI 2009/356, r 15(5); SI 2010/2581, r 15(5).

[462] Methods of personal service are specified in CPR, r 6.5, which applies by r 6.22(3) and the definition of 'personal service' in SI 2009/356, r 3(2), and SI 2010/2581, r 3(2).

[463] SI 2009/356, r 15(3) and (4); SI 2010/2581, r 15(3) and (4).

[464] SI 2009/356, r 15(2); SI 2010/2581, r 15(2).

[465] SI 2009/356, r 15(4); SI 2010/2581, r 15(4). The persons are listed at 5.30.

[466] The material in 3.181–3.206 does not apply to a petition to wind up a company presented by a contributory or contributories of the company or at the instance of the company's administrator or voluntary arrangement supervisor (IR 1986, rr 4.2(4) and 4.7(9)). Such petitions are discussed at 8.469–8.518.

[467] IR 1986, r 4.19(2).

[468] This explanation quoted with approval by Laffoy J in *Re Lycatel (Ireland) Ltd* [2009] IEHC 264, [2009] 3 IR 736.

[469] (1985) 10 ACLR 16, at p 19.

The purpose of substitution, in my opinion, is to ensure that once a prima facie right to the winding up of a company has arisen, the company should not escape from that position except upon the basis of fair dealing with all its creditors, not merely by paying off the particular [applicant].

What substitution does is to reduce the delay between hearings to approximately two weeks **3.182** (the time needed to amend and gazette the existing petition) instead of the six weeks or more needed for presentation of a new petition.

In IR 1986, references to 'the petitioner' or 'the petitioning creditor' include any person **3.183** who has been substituted as such.[470]

Substitution was first allowed by rules made on 29 March 1893.[471]   **3.184**

Before substitution was introduced, a petitioning creditor was said to be *dominus litis*[472] and **3.185** entitled to ask for the petition to be dismissed at the hearing despite other creditors appearing to support it.[473] Thus a company could, for a protracted period, avoid winding up by paying petitioning creditors one by one.

For the special rules on substitution of petitioners in relation to a creditor's petition **3.186** for the winding up of an insolvent partnership with simultaneous petitions for the winding up or bankruptcy of two or more insolvent members of the partnership, see 3.171–3.173.

Circumstances in which a Substitution may be Made

If a person has presented a petition (other than as a contributory) for the compulsory **3.187** winding up of a company, a contributory, or another creditor, may be substituted as petitioner if:[474]

(a) The original petitioner is subsequently found not entitled to petition (it was held in *Re Charles Ltd*[475] that substitution was not possible in this situation under an earlier version of the rule which did not expressly provide for it, though in *Re Fernlake Pty Ltd*[476] W C Lee J thought that it was unnecessary to provide for the situation expressly, considering that this was one of the difficulties the rule was designed to overcome).

(b) The original petitioner fails to advertise the petition, within the time prescribed by IR 1986[477] or such extended time as the court may allow.

(c) The original petitioner 'consents' to withdraw the petition. It seems that 'consents' here means 'agrees with the company', but it is not clear whether an application to withdraw[478] is necessary.

(d) The original petitioner consents to allow the petition to be dismissed.

---

[470] IR 1986, r 13.10.
[471] General Rules Made Pursuant to Section 26 of the Companies (Winding-up) Act 1890 (29 March 1893), r 2.
[472] The principal in the lawsuit.
[473] *Re Home Assurance Association* (1871) LR 12 Eq 59; *Re Hereford and South Wales Waggon and Engineering Co* (1874) LR 17 Eq 423.
[474] IR 1986, r 4.19.
[475] (1906) 51 SJ 101.
[476] [1995] 1 QdR 597.
[477] See 3.120.
[478] See 3.163–3.169.

(e) The original petitioner consents to an adjournment of the petition. This applies even if the petitioner's consent is given because of a practical impediment to proceeding with the petition.[479]

(f) The original petitioner fails to appear in support of the petition when it is called on in court on the day originally fixed for the hearing or on a day to which it is adjourned (early versions of the rule did not allow for this situation[480]).

(g) The original petitioner appears when the petition is called on in court but does not apply for an order in the terms of the prayer of the petition.

3.188 If the company is the subject of main proceedings in which a member State liquidator has been appointed and the member State liquidator wishes to prosecute the petition, the court may substitute him or her as petitioner, on such terms as it thinks just.[481]

3.189 Substitution may be ordered under these rules whether or not the petition has been gazetted.[482]

3.190 Sometimes, substitution has been allowed in circumstances other than those set out in the rules, for example:

(a) after a winding-up order has been made,[483]

(b) after a petition has been adjourned without the petitioner's consent,[484]

(c) after a winding-up order has been set aside on appeal.[485]

However, in *Maldon Minerals NL v McLean Exploration Services Pty Ltd*[486] the petition had been dismissed without the petitioner's consent and it was said at first instance that as none of the situations set out in the rules was present an order for substitution could not be made, and there was no appeal on that point.

3.191 If the petition was originally a creditor's petition, the fact that the original petitioner's debt has been paid does not affect the fact that the petition is still before the court: therefore substitution of another petitioner is still possible[487] but the original petitioner cannot be substituted so as to petition on the ground of non-payment of another debt.[488] Substitution of the original petitioner is now expressly allowed by the Australian legislation.[489]

3.192 There may be two or more successive substitutions[490] though this may lead to a similar situation of a company paying off its creditors slowly one by one which substitution was supposed to put a stop to.[491] If a winding-up order is eventually made, all payments since the petition was presented will be void under IA 1986, s 127.

---

[479] *Re People's Parkway Development Pte Ltd* [1992] 1 SLR 413.

[480] *Re Vanguard Motorbus Co Ltd* (1908) 24 TLR 526.

[481] IR 1986, r 4.19(2A).

[482] *Re Lycatel (Ireland) Ltd* [2009] IEHC 264, [2009] 3 IR 736.

[483] *Re Cedes Electric Traction Ltd* [1918] 1 Ch 18.

[484] *Re Peter Martin Builders Ltd* (1986) 3 NZCLC 99,632.

[485] *Re Goldthorpe and Lacey Ltd* (1987) 3 BCC 595.

[486] (1992) 9 ACSR 265.

[487] *DMK Building Materials Pty Ltd v C B Baker Timbers Pty Ltd* (1985) 10 ACLR 16.

[488] *Re Mercantile Developments Ltd* (1980) Butterworths Current Law Digest 1979–1983 216.

[489] Corporations Act 2001, s 465B(3).

[490] *Re Bostels Ltd* [1968] Ch 346 at p 350.

[491] *Re Bart Engineering Co (Chch) Ltd* (1987) 3 NZCLC 100,257; *Re Brackland Magazines Ltd* [1994] 1 BCLC 190.

Procedure

Substitution may be asked for at a hearing of a petition when it is clear that one of cir- **3.193**
cumstances (a)–(g) listed at 3.187 has occurred. As an application is made in immediate
response to one of those circumstances, it is not required to be in writing and no notice
of it is required. The company should be aware of the possibility that substitution may
be ordered at any hearing without notice and cannot complain about substitution being
ordered at a hearing which it chose not to attend.[492]

In circumstances (b) and (c) listed at 3.187, substitution may be ordered at any time[493] on **3.194**
an application[494] otherwise than at a hearing of the petition. The potential respondents to
the application are the original petitioner and any other person who has given the original
petitioner notice of intention to appear when the petition is heard.[495] If the application is
with the consent of the original petitioner, it should be accompanied by a letter indicating
that the original petitioner has not, and does not intend to, gazette the petition, or that the
original petitioner has agreed to withdraw the petition, as the case may be. A person who
has given notice of intention to appear may wish to be substituted instead of the applicant.

A substitution order may be made on such terms as the court thinks just.[496] The usual **3.195**
terms are:

(a) that the petition is amended to identify the substituted petitioner and solicitors, and
    state the substituted petitioner's grounds for petitioning;
(b) that the amended petition is verified;
(c) that the amended petition is served on the company, unless the company was rep-
    resented when the substitution order was made, in which case sending a copy of the
    amended petition to the company is sufficient;
(d) that the amended petition is gazetted, unless the court considers that gazetting the
    original petition is sufficient;
(e) that the original petitioner continues to be a supporting creditor for the purpose of seek-
    ing costs if a winding-up order is made.

Who may be Substituted

Any creditor or contributory who, in the court's opinion, would have a right to present a **3.196**
petition, and who is desirous of prosecuting it, may be substituted.[497] The rule permits the
substitution as petitioner of any creditor or contributory with a right to present *a* petition,
not *the* petition that is being relinquished by its petitioner. Thus the substituted petitioner
may have different grounds for petitioning and need not be from the original petitioner's
class. In *Re Bryant Investment Co Ltd*[498] two contributories were substituted as petitioners
for a creditor when the court decided it had not been proved that the company was unable

---

[492] *Bank Industri dan Teknologi Malaysia Bhd v Alom Building Systems Sdn Bhd* [2006] 4 MLJ 405.
[493] IR 1986, r 4.19(3).
[494] See 3.233–3.263. In the Royal Courts of Justice the member of court staff in charge of the winding-up
list has been authorized to deal with applications under this rule (PD Insolvency Proceedings 2014, para 12.1).
In a district registry or the County Court an application must be made to a district judge (PD Insolvency
Proceedings 2014, para 12.2).
[495] See 5.32–5.36.
[496] IR 1986, r 4.19(2).
[497] IR 1986, r 4.19(2).
[498] [1974] 1 WLR 826.

to pay its debts. In *Re Fernlake Pty Ltd*[499] a contributory and director of a company was substituted as applicant for the company itself. However, in *Re Xyllyx plc (No 1)*[500] Harman J refused to substitute two contributories for the Secretary of State, saying that a contributories' petition was very different from a public interest petition. Substitution of a creditor for a contributory occurred in *Re Creative Handbook Ltd*[501] and in *Re Commercial and Industrial Insulations Ltd*,[502] but there is now no provision in IR 1986 for substitution on a contributory's petition.[503]

3.197 A creditor who is substituted need not have been a creditor at the time the petition was originally presented.[504]

3.198 A person who does not have standing to petition will not be substituted as petitioner.[505] It has been held in Malaysia that the court should not adjourn an application to be substituted to allow the applicant time to become qualified to present a petition.[506]

3.199 If a petitioning creditor's debt is assigned after the petition is presented, the assignee will normally be substituted as petitioner.[507]

3.200 It has been held in New Zealand that the person to be substituted cannot be the person who was petitioner before the substitution,[508] but this is now expressly allowed by the Australian legislation.[509]

Effect of Substitution

3.201 A petition is a single proceeding from presentation to order notwithstanding that there may have been one or more substitutions.[510] Substitution of the petitioner and amendment of the petition do not mean that a new petition is presented.[511] This means that if a winding-up order is made, the date of commencement of the winding up (if there was no prior voluntary winding up) is the date the petition was presented by its original petitioner.[512] The original petitioner is to be regarded as having been a party to the proceedings and so entitled to the costs of presenting and advertising the petition.[513] It is not necessary for the original petitioner to appear at subsequent hearings in order to maintain the right to be awarded costs.[514]

---

[499] [1995] 1 QdR 597.

[500] [1992] BCLC 376.

[501] [1985] BCLC 1.

[502] [1986] BCLC 191.

[503] See IR 1986, rr 4.2(4) and 4.24.

[504] *Re Starting Gate Ltd* (1985) 2 NZCLC 99,416; *Perak Pioneer Ltd v Petrolium Nasional Bhd* [1986] AC 849; *Re Richbell Strategic Holdings Ltd* [1997] 2 BCLC 429 at p 455; the contrary was assumed in *Deputy Commissioner of Taxation v Sun Heating Pty Ltd* [1983] 2 NSWLR 78.

[505] *Perak Pioneer Ltd v Petroliam Nasional Bhd* [1986] AC 849 at p 857; and see 7.669–7.670.

[506] *Lindeteves-Jacoberg (Malaya) Sdn Bhd v Electrical Switchgears Automation (M) Sdn Bhd* [1999] 5 MLJ 530.

[507] *Perak Pioneer Ltd v Petroliam Nasional Bhd* [1986] AC 849.

[508] *Re Mercantile Developments Ltd* (1980) Butterworths Current Law Digest 1979–1983 216.

[509] Corporations Act 2001 (Australia), s 465B(3).

[510] *Re Bostels Ltd* [1968] Ch 346 at p 351.

[511] *Re Western Welsh International System Buildings Ltd* (1984) 1 BCC 99,296.

[512] See 5.279.

[513] *Re Castle Coulson and MacDonald Ltd* [1973] Ch 382. This may be stated expressly in the substitution order.

[514] *Re Castle Coulson and MacDonald Ltd.*

Discretion of the Court

3.202 IR 1986, r 4.19(2), confers a discretion on the court whether to order substitution or not.[515] Substitution may be on such terms as the court thinks just.

3.203 In *Commissioner of Inland Revenue v Bemelman Engineering Ltd*,[516] in relation to an application by a creditor to be substituted, Master Towle said, at p 66,495:

> I believe a court in exercising its discretion must have regard to all the circumstances of the particular case in order to form a view of what it may think just. One of those circumstances must be the details of the debt or the ground on which reliance is placed by the [creditor applying to be substituted], but other relevant circumstances would include the existence of supporting creditors, the trading position of the company, the attitude of the company to the application for substitution and any other special circumstances affecting the parties which may arise.

The learned master refused to substitute an applicant claiming to be a creditor of a company whose claim was disputed, and it is unlikely that such an applicant would ever be substituted.[517]

3.204 In *Re Ron Winters Glazing Services Ltd*[518] Holland J refused to substitute a supporting creditor who, though represented at each hearing, had stood by and allowed several adjournments of the petition for the purpose of agreeing a compromise with the petitioner.

3.205 In *Re Clutha Leathers Ltd*[519] the company sought to be wound up was in receivership but was apparently trading successfully. The original petitioning creditor had agreed to withdraw its petition, and other creditors had indicated that they wished the company to continue trading in receivership. The company seeking to be substituted as petitioner and the original petitioner were both subsidiaries of the same holding company. The court refused to allow the substitution and awarded the company costs against the company seeking to be substituted. In fact this is the same result as would have occurred if the creditor seeking substitution had been substituted and its petition had been heard: it would have been prosecuting a petition knowing that it was opposed by other creditors on reasonable grounds, and so its petition would have been dismissed with costs.[520]

3.206 Where more than one creditor seeks to be substituted, it is usual to give precedence to the one with the largest debt.

Amendment of Petition

Applicable Rules

3.207 A petition is not a statement of case[521] but the provisions of the CPR for amendments to statements of case[522] apply to winding-up petitions with any necessary modifications, except so far as inconsistent with IR 1986.[523]

---

[515] *Re Calsil Ltd* (1982) 6 ACLR 515.
[516] (1990) 5 NZCLC 66,494.
[517] See 7.669–7.670.
[518] (1988) 4 NZCLC 64,294.
[519] (1987) 4 NZCLC 64,160.
[520] See 5.188.
[521] See 2.9.
[522] CPR, Part 17.
[523] IR 1986, r 7.51A(2).

3.208   The court may require an amended petition to be served on the company and also may require the petitioner to gazette it.

Introduction of a New Ground

3.209   A petition may be amended to state a ground for seeking the winding-up order which has arisen only since the petition was presented.[524] The test for giving permission to make such an amendment is not more stringent than the test for a claimant seeking to amend a statement of claim so as to introduce a cause of action which arose after the claim was issued.[525] It is not necessary for the petitioner to show that some relief would have been granted at the hearing of the original petition.[526] In *Re Richbell Strategic Holdings Ltd* Neuberger J said that permission to introduce a post-presentation ground might not be granted if:

(a) the petition had been presented unfairly or without warning;
(b) it had been presented speculatively in the hope that something might turn up after presentation to justify a winding-up order; or
(c) the company would not have an adequate opportunity to respond to the amended petition.

3.210   In *Re Sutherland Manure Co Ltd*,[527] at the hearing of a contributory's petition it was found that the petition did not allege facts which would justify a winding-up order and the petitioner was refused permission to amend the petition to allege fraud by the directors. In *Re White Star Consolidated Gold Mining Co*,[528] though, the objection that the petition did not allege sufficient facts was not made until the evidence had been gone into, and the petitioner was allowed to amend the petition. The same happened in *Re Eastern Fur Finance Corp Ltd*[529] and *Hassgill Investments Pty Ltd v Newman Air Charter Pty Ltd*.[530]

3.211   In *Re Queen's Benefit Building Society*[531] a contributory of an unregistered company appealed against the making of an order for the company to be wound up, claiming that the petitioner's debt was unenforceable because incurring it was beyond the capacity of the company. The Court of Appeal gave permission to the petitioner to amend his petition to allege only an enforceable debt and dismissed the appeal.

3.212   In *Re Burgundy Royale Investments Pty Ltd*[532] a construction company erecting a building for an owner petitioned for the winding up of the owner alleging non-payment of a progress payment. The progress payment was then paid with interest. The petition had not been advertised. The petitioner sought leave to amend the petition to allege that the owner was unable to pay its debts 'if regard is had to the contingent liabilities of the company'—the contingent liabilities in question being future progress payments to the petitioner. Permission to amend was refused.

---

[524] *Re Richbell Strategic Holdings Ltd* [1997] 2 BCLC 429.
[525] *Re Richbell Strategic Holdings Ltd.*
[526] *Re Richbell Strategic Holdings Ltd.*
[527] (1892) 11 NZLR 460.
[528] (1883) 48 LT 815.
[529] [1934] 1 DLR 611.
[530] (1991) 5 WAR 165.
[531] (1871) LR 6 Ch App 815.
[532] (1984) 75 FLR 114.

Correction of the Company's Name

In *Pro-Image Productions (Vic) Pty Ltd v Catalyst Television Productions Pty Ltd*[533] proceedings **3.213**
to wind up Catalyst TV Productions Pty Ltd mistakenly named the company as 'Catalyst
Television Productions Pty Ltd'. Amendment of the name was permitted. In both *Re Army and
Navy Hotel*[534] and *Re J and P Sussman Ltd*[535] amendment of the name of the company sought
to be wound up was permitted after a winding-up order had been made in the wrong name.[536]

Correction of the Petitioner's Name

If the petitioner has been misnamed in the petition, permission to correct the name will be **3.214**
given as a matter of course, if the mistake has not prejudiced other parties.[537]

Further Information and Disclosure

Any party to insolvency proceedings may apply to the court under IR 1986, r 7.60, for fur- **3.215**
ther information to be given by another party under CPR, part 18, or to obtain disclosure
and inspection of documents under CPR, part 31. Such an application[538] may be made
without notice being served on any other party.[539] But, on a creditor's petition for the winding up of a company the court is very unlikely to order the company to give disclosure to
the petitioner. This is because a petition should not be presented unless it can be supported
by evidence which, if accepted at the hearing, would found a claim for relief: it is improper
to present a petition in the hope that evidence to support it may be found by disclosure.[540]

The predominant view expressed in the reported cases is that the court will not order a com- **3.216**
pany to give disclosure of documents to a creditor petitioning for the company's winding
up unless there are exceptional circumstances.[541] A different view was taken in *Re Auckland
Piano Agency Ltd*[542] (in which the English cases were not cited), and the point was left open
in *Re Bunarba Pastoral Co Pty Ltd*.[543]

In *Nationwide Produce Holdings Pty Ltd v Franklins Ltd*[544] a company was relieved from **3.217**
complying with a notice to produce virtually all of its internal accounting records to a creditor applying for it to be wound up, because the creditor had not established even a prima
facie case that the company was insolvent.

---

[533] (1988) 14 ACLR 303.
[534] (1886) 31 ChD 644.
[535] [1958] 1 WLR 519.
[536] See 6.1–6.6.
[537] *Re Goldthorpe and Lacey Ltd* (1987) 3 BCC 595 per Slade LJ at p 602.
[538] See 3.233–3.263.
[539] IR 1986, r 7.60(2).
[540] *Re a Company, ex parte Burr* [1992] BCLC 724 per Vinelott J at p 736 and on appeal sub nom *Re Saul
D Harrison and Sons plc* [1995] 1 BCLC 14 per Hoffmann LJ at p 22.
[541] *Re European Assurance Society* (1869) 18 WR 9 at p 12; *Re Hoover Hill Gold Mining Co* (1883) 27 SJ 434
in which Chitty J quoted 'the late Master of the Rolls' (Sir George Jessel) as saying that 'he was not going to
assist a man to wreck a company by ransacking its documents'; *Re West Devon Great Consols Mine* (1884) 27
ChD 106 per Lindley LJ at p 110; *Highberry Ltd v COLT Telecom Group plc* [2002] EWHC 2503 (Ch), [2003]
1 BCLC 290; *PNP Realty Pty Ltd v Bluechip Development Corporation (Cairns) Pty Ltd* [2009] ACTSC 97.
[542] [1928] GLR 249.
[543] [1958] SR (NSW) 23.
[544] [2001] NSWSC 1120, 20 ACLC 309.

3.218 IR 1986, r 7.60, is applied to bank and building society insolvency proceedings,[545] but, before the passing of a full payment resolution, the court cannot grant an order for disclosure unless it is satisfied that doing so is unlikely to prejudice the achievement of objective 1.[546]

Security for Costs

Applicable Rules

3.219 The normal rules of court relating to security for costs apply in winding-up proceedings.[547] No provision for security for costs is made in IR 1986 or Practice Direction (PD) Insolvency Proceedings 2014 and so the relevant rules are CPR, rr 25.12–25.15,[548] with, as 'necessary modifications',[549] 'claim' changed to 'petition',[550] 'defendant' to 'company' and 'claimant' to 'petitioner'.

Examples

Petitioner resident outside the jurisdiction

3.220 A petitioner who is resident outside the jurisdiction, and not in the EU, Iceland, Norway or Switzerland, may be required to give security for costs.[551] In a previous version of this rule the criterion was ordinary residence rather than residence. A petitioning company is ordinarily resident where its central management and control abides.[552]

3.221 In *Banco Econômico SA v Allied Leasing and Finance Corporation*[553] the Cayman Islands Grand Court decided not to order a petitioning company resident in Brazil to give security for costs, partly because the court had heard enough of the case when considering other applications to see that the petition had merit, and partly because, although the petitioner was in liquidation, the liquidator was appointed by the Brazilian government which the court should assume would meet its obligations. In *Re Cybervest Fund*[554] the Grand Court refused to order security partly because the contributory petitioner was an agency of the government of Kuwait which could be assumed to meet its obligations and partly because the petitioner's own shares in the company were within the jurisdiction and could be used to meet any liability for costs and, according to the company, were very valuable.

3.222 A petitioner cannot ask the court to order a person who has a right to appear on the hearing of the petition, but who resides outside the jurisdiction, to give security for costs.[555]

---

[545] Bank Insolvency (England and Wales) Rules 2009 (SI 2009/356), r 232(1), with modification by r 3(3)(b) and (4)(h); Building Society Insolvency (England and Wales) Rules 2010 (SI 2010/2581), r 225(1), with modification by r 3(5)(b) and (6)(j).

[546] SI 2009/356, r 232(2); SI 2010/2581, r 225(2). 'Objective 1' and 'full payment resolution' are defined at 1.20.

[547] *Re Pretoria Pietersburg Railway Co (No 2)* [1904] 2 Ch 359.

[548] IR 1986, r 7.51A(2).

[549] r 7.51A(2).

[550] A petition is not a claim; see 2.15.

[551] CPR, r 25.13(2)(a); *Re Royal Bank of Australasia, ex parte Latta* (1850) 3 De G & Sm 186; *Re Home Assurance Association (No 2)* (1871) LR 12 Eq 112.

[552] *Re Little Olympian Each Ways Ltd* [1995] 1 WLR 560; *Charter View Holdings (BVI) Ltd v Corona Investments Ltd* [1998] 1 HKLRD 469.

[553] 1998 CILR 102.

[554] 2006 CILR 80.

[555] *Re Percy and Kelly Nickel, Cobalt, and Chrome Iron Mining Co* (1876) 2 ChD 531; *Re Co-operative Development Funds of Australia Ltd* (1977) 2 ACLR 284.

Impecunious company

Security for costs may be ordered if the petitioner is a company or other body (whether **3.223**
incorporated inside or outside Great Britain) and there is reason to believe that it will be
unable to pay the costs of the company sought to be wound up, if ordered to do so.[556] This
provision applies to both limited and unlimited companies as petitioners.[557] The court is
not required to decide finally whether or not the petitioner will be unable to pay the costs.[558]

Petitioner failing to give an address

In *Re Sturgis (British) Motor Power Syndicate Ltd* [559] a petitioner who refused to give his **3.224**
address was ordered to give security for costs.[560]

Nominal claimant

In *Re Carta Para Mining Co*[561] the petitioner was an insolvent individual who had himself **3.225**
petitioned for the liquidation of his own affairs by arrangement. He was ordered to give
security for costs following a supposed principle that a litigant in his position will hold
the fruits of the litigation for his or her creditors and is therefore to be classed as a nominal
claimant.[562] But in *Rhodes v Dawson*[563] the Court of Appeal held that such a litigant is not
correctly classed as a nominal claimant and the general rule is that poverty is not a reason
for requiring an individual litigant to give security for costs.

Effect of Delay in Applying

When considering whether to grant an order for security for costs the court will take into **3.226**
account whether delay in applying for the order has prejudiced the party against whom the
order is sought.[564] In *Loreva Pty Ltd v Cefa Associated Agencies Pty Ltd*[565] an application that
the petitioner should give security for costs was refused because it was not made until three
months after the petition was presented and the petitioner had already incurred costs.

Petition against Member of Insolvent Partnership

If a winding-up petition has been presented against an entity that is a member of an insol- **3.227**
vent partnership, the court may, on having its attention drawn to that fact, make an order
as to the future conduct of the insolvency proceedings.[566] The court's order may apply any
provisions of IPO 1994 with any necessary modifications.[567] An application for an order
under s 168(5A) may be made by the official receiver, the liquidator of the partnership or
of a corporate member of the partnership, the trustee of the partnership or of an individual
member of the partnership, or any other interested person.[568] The court's order may provide

---

[556] CPR, r 25.13(2)(c).
[557] *Jirehouse Capital v Beller* [2008] EWCA Civ 908, [2009] 1 WLR 751.
[558] *Jirehouse Capital v Beller* [2008] EWCA Civ 908, [2009] 1 WLR 751.
[559] (1885) 53 LT 715.
[560] See CPR, r 25.13(2)(e).
[561] (1881) 19 ChD 457.
[562] CPR, r 25.13(2)(f).
[563] (1886) 16 QBD 548.
[564] *Jenred Properties Ltd v Ente Nazionale Italiano per il Turismo* (1985) *Financial Times*, 29 October 1985.
[565] (1982) 7 ACLR 164.
[566] IA 1986, s 168(5A).
[567] IA 1986, s 168(5A).
[568] IA 1986, s 168(5B).

for the administration of the joint estate of the partnership, and in particular how it and the separate estate of any member are to be administered.[569]

Inordinate Delay and Negligence

Inordinate Delay

3.228 Delay in prosecuting legal proceedings, however long, inordinate and inexcusable, is not in itself an abuse of process,[570] but it may be if it is caused by, for example:

(a) having no intention to bring the proceedings to a conclusion;[571] or
(b) complete, total or wholesale disregard of the rules of court with full awareness of the consequences.[572]

3.229 In *Birkett v James*,[573] it was confirmed that proceedings may be struck out where inordinate and inexcusable delay will give rise to a substantial risk that it is not possible to have a fair trial of the issues or is likely to cause or to have caused serious prejudice to the defendant. However, it seems that the principle established in *Birkett v James*, that proceedings cannot be dismissed for want of prosecution if the limitation period has not expired (because the proceedings can legitimately be started again), applies to a winding-up petition, where there is no limitation period and so the proceedings can legitimately be recommenced.[574]

3.230 In *Re Pek Chuan Development Pte Ltd*[575] the company sought to have a contributory's winding-up petition, which had been presented almost four years previously, dismissed for want of prosecution. It was found that both the company and the petitioner had been guilty of delay and so the striking-out application was dismissed with no order as to costs. In *C G and L Investment Ltd v Gala Land Investment Co Ltd*[576] it was sought to have a contributories' petition presented six years earlier struck out for want of prosecution but it was held that there was no substantial risk to the possibility of a fair trial and that no serious prejudice had been caused to the company, which in fact had transacted no business while the petition was pending.

3.231 A winding-up petition may be dismissed if notice of it is not duly given by gazetting or as otherwise ordered by the court[577] or if the petitioner does not file a certificate of compliance.[578] This does not apply to a petition presented by a contributory or contributories of the company or at the instance of the company's administrator or voluntary arrangement supervisor.[579] If, at a hearing of a winding-up petition, there is no appearance for the petitioner and no one is substituted as petitioner, the petition will be dismissed.[580]

---

[569] IA 1986, s 168(5B).
[570] *Habib Bank Ltd v Jaffer* [2000] CPLR 438 at [10]–[11].
[571] *Grovit v Doctor* [1997] 1 WLR 640; *Icebird Ltd v Winegardner* [2009] UKPC 24, LTL 3/6/2009, at [7].
[572] *Habib Bank Ltd v Jaffer* [2000] CPLR 438 at [10]–[11]; *Wearn v HNH International Holdings Ltd* [2014] EWHC 3542 (Ch), LTL 6/11/2014.
[573] [1978] AC 297.
[574] *Re Pek Chuan Development Pte Ltd* [1988] 3 MLJ 140, in which it was not necessary to decide the point.
[575] [1988] 3 MLJ 140.
[576] [1992] 2 HKLR 23.
[577] IR 1986, r 4.11(6). See 3.125.
[578] IR 1986, r 4.14(3). See 3.158.
[579] IR 1986, rr 4.2(4) and 4.7(9).
[580] *Re Royal Mutual Benefit Building Society* [1960] 1 WLR 1143; *Re Aim Investments (Holdings) Ltd* [2004] 2 HKLRD 201.

Negligent Conduct of Petition

It is not possible to recover damages for the negligent conduct of proceedings on a peti- **3.232** tion from the petitioner.[581] For circumstances in which presentation or continuation of a winding-up petition may be tortious see 2.177–2.185.

Applications in Insolvency Proceedings

Procedural Rules

Applications in insolvency proceedings are governed by IR 1986, rr 7.1–7.10. Those rules **3.233** apply, according to r 7.1, to any application made to the court under IA 1986 or IR 1986, apart from a petition for a winding-up order, an administration application and a bankruptcy petition. They do, however, apply to applications made within, or in anticipation of, proceedings on a winding-up petition etc.

Form

The prescribed form for an application in insolvency proceedings is form 7.1A (application **3.234** notice) in IR 1986, sch 4. It is necessary to state on this form whether or not the application is in insolvency proceedings which are already before the court. Before 6 April 2010 a distinction was drawn between ordinary applications (which were in insolvency proceedings already before the court) and originating applications (which were not). There used to be different forms for the two kinds of application.

Applications that are made in insolvency proceedings which are already before the court **3.235** include any interim application while a winding-up petition is pending, and any interim application while an appeal against a decision made in the proceedings is pending.

Applications that are not made in insolvency proceedings which are already before the **3.236** court include an application for an injunction against presentation of a winding-up petition[582] and any application in a voluntary winding up.[583]

Use of the wrong form to bring an application is a formal defect or irregularity which does **3.237** not invalidate the application unless it has caused substantial injustice which cannot be remedied by any order of the court.[584]

Where there are two joined matters between the same parties, one of which is an insolvency **3.238** application and the other requires a different form of originating process, both may be commenced by the insolvency application.[585]

---

[581] *Business Computers International Ltd v Registrar of Companies* [1988] Ch 229.
[582] See 2.153–2.158.
[583] *Re Continental Assurance Co of London plc (No 2)* [1998] 1 BCLC 583.
[584] IR 1986, r 7.55; *Re Continental Assurance Co of London plc (No 2)* [1998] 1 BCLC 583 (use of an ordinary application instead of an originating application had not caused injustice, because the information about the grounds for the application, which did not have to be disclosed in an ordinary application but would have been required in an originating application, had been given in points of claim); *Phillips v McGregor-Paterson* [2009] EWHC 2385 (Ch), [2010] 1 BCLC 72 (use of an ordinary claim form instead of an ordinary application had not caused injustice even though it meant that an application for summary judgment was not heard by a registrar but by a master, whose decision was reversed on appeal).
[585] CPR, r 7.3; *Re Prestige Grindings Ltd* [2005] EWHC 3076 (Ch), [2006] 1 BCLC 440.

Contents of an Application

3.239 An application must be in writing.[586] It must state:

(a) that it is made under the Insolvency Act 1986;[587]

(b) the names of the parties;[588]

(c) the name of the bankrupt, or the debtor who or company which is the subject of the insolvency proceedings to which the application relates;[589]

(d) the court (and where applicable, the division or district registry of that court) in which the application is made;[590]

(e) where the court has previously allocated a number to the insolvency proceedings within which the application is made, that number;[591]

(f) the nature of the remedy or order applied for or the directions sought from the court;[592]

(g) the names and addresses of the persons (if any) on whom it is intended to serve the application or that no person is intended to be served;[593]

(h) where IA 1986 or IR 1986 require that notice of the application is to be given to specified persons, the names and addresses of all those persons (so far as known to the applicant);[594] and

(i) the applicant's address for service.[595]

3.240 The application must be signed by the applicant, if acting in person, or by, or on behalf of, the applicant's solicitor.[596]

Filing and Fee

3.241 An insolvency application must be filed with the court, accompanied by one copy in any event, plus enough copies for service on every person who is to be served.[597]

3.242 If an application is not in insolvency proceedings which are already before the court, the court fee is £280.[598] The court fee for an application in proceedings which are before the court is £50 if the application is by consent or without notice,[599] or £155 if it is with notice.[600]

Venue, Directions, Track Allocation

3.243 When an application is filed, the court must fix a venue for it to be heard unless:[601]

(a) it considers it not appropriate to do so—the court may, for example, direct that no venue is to be fixed before service and may set a time limit for service;[602]

(b) the rule under which the application is brought provides otherwise; or

---

[586] IR 1986, r 7.3(1).
[587] r 7.3(1)(a).
[588] r 7.3(1)(aa).
[589] r 7.3(1)(ab).
[590] r 7.3(1)(ac).
[591] r 7.3(1)(ad).
[592] r 7.3(1)(b).
[593] r 7.3(1)(c).
[594] r 7.3(1)(d).
[595] r 7.3(1)(e).
[596] r 7.3(3).
[597] IR 1986, r 7.4(1).
[598] Civil Proceedings Fees Order 2008 (SI 2008/1053), sch 1, fee 3.5.
[599] SI 2008/1053, sch 1, fee 3.11.
[600] SI 2008/1053, sch 1, fee 3.12.
[601] IR 1986, r 7.4(2).
[602] *Re Continental Assurance Co of London plc (No 2)* [1998] 1 BCLC 583.

(c) the relevant provisions of IA 1986 or IR 1986 do not require service of the application on, or notice of it to be given to, any person, in which case the court may either fix a venue or hear the application as soon as reasonably practicable without fixing a venue.[603]

Any application should be made, in the High Court, to the registrar,[604] and in the County Court, to the district judge, unless:[605] **3.244**

(a) a direction to the contrary has been given;[606] or
(b) the registrar or district judge does not have power to make the order required.[607]

If the registrar or district judge thinks that the application should properly be decided by the judge, it may be referred up.[608]

The court may at any time give such directions as it thinks fit concerning service or notice **3.245** of the application, the procedure on the application, and evidence.[609]

All insolvency proceedings are allocated to the multi-track,[610] and so the provisions of the **3.246** CPR concerning directions questionnaires and track allocation do not apply.

The hearing of an application is in open court, unless the court orders otherwise.[611] **3.247**

The registrars and district judges operate urgent applications lists for urgent and time-critical **3.248** applications and may be available to hear urgent applications at other times.[612] A party asking for an application to be dealt with in the urgent applications list or urgently at any other time must complete the certificate set out in PD Insolvency Proceedings 2014, para 9.1. Appropriate sanctions may be imposed for misuse of this service.[613]

Service

A sealed copy of an insolvency application must be served on the respondent named in it[614] **3.249** at least 14 days before the date fixed for the hearing,[615] unless:[616]

(a) the provision of IA 1986 or IR 1986 under which the application is made specifies a different period; or
(b) the application is urgent, in which case the court may hear it immediately, even without notice to, or attendance by, other parties, or may authorize a period of service shorter than 14 days.[617]

---

603 r 7.5A.
604 District judge in a district registry (r 13.2(3A)).
605 r 7.6A(2) and (3).
606 See PD Insolvency Proceedings 2014, para 12.
607 See PD 2B.
608 IR 1986, r 7.6A(4).
609 IR 1986, rr 7.4(4) and 7.10(2) and (3).
610 IR 1986, r 7.51A(3).
611 IR 1986, r 7.6A(1). For the circumstances in which a hearing may be in private see CPR, r 39.2, and PD 39A, paras 1.1–1.15.
612 PD Insolvency Proceedings 2014, para 9.1.
613 PD Insolvency Proceedings 2014, para 9.1.
614 IR 1986, r 7.4(3).
615 IR 1986, r 7.4(5). The clear days rule in CPR, r 2.8(2) and (3), applies (see 1.510). For rules on service see 1.513–1.524.
616 IR 1986, r 7.4(5).
617 r 7.4(6).

3.250 Service in England and Wales of an application, or a document relating to an application, is governed by CPR, Part 6 (service of documents), with such modifications as the court may direct,[618] treating an application against a respondent as a claim form.[619] Where there are joint office-holders in insolvency proceedings[620] service on one of them is to be treated as service on all of them.[621]

3.251 The rules on service outside England and Wales of an application, or a document relating to an application, are the same as for a winding-up petition. See 3.30–3.33.

Evidence

3.252 Further information and disclosure may be obtained under IR 1986, r 7.60.[622] In relation to applications in insolvency proceedings, if the court is satisfied that it is desirable in the interests of justice to do so, it will order disclosure of documents. In general terms disclosure will be ordered unless it is unduly burdensome, oppressive or not necessary for the disposal of the issue before the court.[623] For an application in the course of proceedings on a creditor's winding-up petition, this is subject to the policy of refusing to order disclosure by the company to the petitioner.[624]

3.253 Unless the court directs otherwise, evidence in insolvency proceedings must be given by witness statement[625] or by a report of an official receiver or insolvency office-holder.[626]

3.254 The following individuals may file a report in court instead of a witness statement:[627]

(a) the official receiver or a deputy official receiver,
(b) an administrator,
(c) a liquidator,
(d) a provisional liquidator,
(e) a special manager,
(f) a trustee in bankruptcy, an interim receiver or an insolvency practitioner appointed under IA 1986, s 273(2).

3.255 A report is to be treated as if it were a witness statement.[628] The official receiver or a deputy may file a report instead of a witness statement in any case.[629] The other persons in the list in 3.254 are not permitted to file reports instead of witness statements if the application involves other parties or if the court otherwise orders.[630] A report does not have to be the work of the person who files it.[631]

---

[618] IR 1986, rr 7.51A(1), 12A.16(1) and 12A.17.
[619] IR 1986, r 12A.16(3).
[620] See 1.535.
[621] IR 1986, r 12A.19.
[622] See 3.215–3.218.
[623] *Re Primlaks (UK) Ltd (No 2)* [1990] BCLC 234 per Harman J at p 239.
[624] See 3.216.
[625] IR 1986, r 7.7A(1); PD Insolvency Proceedings 2014, para 5.1.
[626] IR 1986, r 7.9; see 3.254–3.255.
[627] IR 1986, r 7.9.
[628] IR 1986, r 7.9(2).
[629] IR 1986, r 7.9(1)(a).
[630] IR 1986, r 7.9(1)(b).
[631] *Re Homes Assured Corporation plc* [1994] 2 BCLC 71 at pp 78–9.

An applicant who intends to rely, at the first hearing, on evidence in a witness statement **3.256** must file the statement with the court, and serve a copy on the respondent, not less than 14 days before the day fixed for the hearing.[632] A respondent to an application who intends to oppose it, and to rely for that purpose on evidence in a witness statement, must file the statement with the court, and serve a copy on the applicant, not less than five business days before the date fixed for the hearing.[633]

The rules on service of a witness statement (as a document relating to an application) are the **3.257** same as for service of an application.[634]

Oral evidence and cross-examination on witness statements should not normally be allowed **3.258** in interim proceedings.[635] However, cross-examination will usually be ordered if there is a challenge to the contents of written evidence and if the decision in the proceedings will finally dispose of the matter (apart from any question of appeal).[636]

Adjournment

The court may adjourn the hearing of an application on such terms as it thinks fit.[637] It may **3.259** give directions about the manner in which evidence is to be adduced at a resumed hearing.[638]

Striking Out

The court has an inherent jurisdiction to strike out an application which is frivolous, vexa- **3.260** tious or otherwise an abuse of process.[639]

Applications in Bank and Building Society Insolvency Proceedings

An application made to the court under the Banking Act 2009, part 2, or under the Bank **3.261** Insolvency (England and Wales) Rules 2009[640] (apart from an application for a bank insolvency order) is governed by SI 2009/356, rr 188–199.[641] An application made to the court under the Banking Act 2009, part 2, as applied to building society insolvency or under the Building Society Insolvency (England and Wales) Rules 2010[642] (apart from an application for a building society insolvency order) is governed by SI 2010/2581, rr 182–193.[643]

The provisions in both SI 2009/356 and SI 2010/2581 apply[644] IR 1986, rr 7.2–7.8 **3.262** and 7.10,[645] as they were before the substantial amendments made by the Insolvency (Amendment) Rules 2010.[646] As explained at 1.64, it is uncertain whether the provisions

---

[632] IR 1986, r 7.8(1)(a).
[633] IR 1986, r 7.8(1)(b).
[634] See 3.249–3.251.
[635] *Re Whitemark Pty Ltd* (1992) 7 WAR 54.
[636] *Re Bank of Credit and Commerce International SA (No 5)* [1994] 1 BCLC 429.
[637] IR 1986, r 7.10(1).
[638] r 7.10(3).
[639] *Port v Auger* [1994] 1 WLR 862.
[640] SI 2009/356.
[641] SI 2009/356, r 188.
[642] SI 2010/2581.
[643] SI 2010/2581, rr 3(4)(a) and 182.
[644] With the modifications of terminology made by SI 2009/356, r 3(3)(b) and (4), and SI 2010/2581, r 3(5)(b) and (6).
[645] IR 1986, r 7.9, is replaced by SI 2009/356, r 198, and SI 2010/2581, r 192.
[646] SI 2010/686. See the definition of 'the 1986 Rules' in SI 2009/356, r 3(2), and SI 2010/2581, r 3(2).

of SI 2009/356 and SI 2010/2581 can be treated as applying IR 1986 with the 2010 amendments, and it is thought that the court should be asked to give directions. The rules without the 2010 amendments are discussed in the second edition of this work at 3.15. If SI 2009/356 and SI 2010/2581 are to be treated as applying IR 1986 with the 2010 amendments, the position is that the following provisions of IR 1986 which have been discussed in this edition are applied[647] to applications in bank and building society insolvency proceedings: r 7.3 (form and contents of application, see 3.239–3.240),[648] r 7.4 (filing and service of application, see 3.241, 3.245 and 3.249),[649] r 7.5A (hearings without notice, see 3.243),[650] r 7.6A (hearing of application, see 3.244 and 3.247),[651] r 7.7A (witness statements—general, see 3.253),[652] r 7.8 (filing and service of witness statements, see 3.256)[653] and r 7.10 (adjournment of hearing, directions, see 3.259).[654]

3.263 In relation to evidence in bank and building society insolvency proceedings, the persons who may file a report instead of a witness statement[655] are the bank or building society liquidator, the provisional bank or building society liquidator and the special manager.[656]

Protecting a Company's Property while a Winding-up Petition is Pending

3.264 If a winding-up order is made against a company on a winding-up petition,[657] the winding up is deemed to have commenced at the time when the petition was presented, or the time the company went into voluntary liquidation, if earlier.[658] All claims against the company are fixed as at the commencement of winding up, and it is necessary to prevent specific unsecured creditors recovering payment of debts at the expense of the other unsecured creditors. (The winding up of a company does not, in general, affect security interests in the company's property.) Provision is made:

(a) for stay of other proceedings against the company while the petition is pending;[659]
(b) for all dispositions of the company's property to be void unless validated by the court;[660]

---

[647] With the modifications of terminology made by SI 2009/356, r 3(3)(b) and (4), and SI 2010/2581, r 3(5)(b) and (6).

[648] SI 2009/356, r 190; SI 2010/2581, r 184.

[649] SI 2009/356, r 192; SI 2010/2581, r 186.

[650] SI 2009/356, r 194; SI 2010/2581, r 188—treating the references in both provisions to IR 1986, r 7.5, as references to r 7.5A.

[651] SI 2009/356, r 195; SI 2010/2581, r 189—treating the references in both provisions to IR 1986, r 7.6, as references to r 7.6A.

[652] SI 2009/356, r 196; SI 2010/2581, r 190—treating the references in both provisions to IR 1986, r 7.7, as references to r 7.7A.

[653] SI 2009/356, r 197; SI 2010/2581, r 191.

[654] SI 2009/356, r 199; SI 2010/2581, r 193.

[655] See 3.254–3.255.

[656] SI 2009/356, r 198; SI 2010/2581, r 192.

[657] Rather than an administration application or an energy, energy supply company or postal administration application.

[658] IA 1986, s 129; see 5.277–5.302.

[659] IA 1986, s 126.

[660] IA 1986, s 127.

(c) for executions and attachments put in before commencement, but not completed, to be given up;[661] and

(d) for any execution, attachment, sequestration or taking control of goods put in after commencement to be void.[662]

The liability of contributories is also fixed as at the commencement of winding up, and so **3.265** alterations in the status of the company's members cannot be made without the approval of the court.[663]

If no winding-up order is made on a petition, the provisions listed at 3.264 (other than (a)) **3.266** do not come into effect, but the court's sanction for dispositions of property (b) can be given while a petition is pending (an 'anticipatory validation order').

Sometimes it may be necessary for control of a company to be taken away from its directors **3.267** while a winding-up petition is pending, and for this purpose a provisional liquidator may be appointed.[664]

These provisions apply to any other entity that may be wound up as a registered com- **3.268** pany,[665] to unregistered companies,[666] to insolvent partnerships[667] and, in modified form, to relevant schemes.[668] Apart from the provision for stay of other proceedings against the company while the petition is pending, they are applied to bank insolvency[669] and building society insolvency.[670]

While a winding-up or unfair prejudice petition is pending against a company, the peti- **3.269** tioner may be granted an injunction to prevent dissipation of the company's assets.[671] It must be shown that the petitioner's interests are in jeopardy, which they will not be if there is no suggestion that those in control of the company intend to act improperly.[672] If the petitioner expects that the company or its liquidator will have a claim against another person, and believes that a freezing injunction should be obtained against that person, the appointment of a provisional liquidator should be sought.[673] Although the court has jurisdiction to grant the petitioner an injunction against such a person, it should not do so, other than in wholly exceptional circumstances, because the petitioner does

---

[661] IA 1986, ss 183 and 184.

[662] IA 1986, s 128.

[663] IA 1986, s 127.

[664] See chapter 4.

[665] Building societies (see 1.120–1.121), charitable incorporated organizations (see 1.122), European cooperative societies (see 1.123), European public limited-liability companies (see 1.124), incorporated friendly societies (see 1.125), limited liability partnerships (see 1.126) and registered societies (see 1.127–1.129).

[666] IA 1986, s 221(1).

[667] See 1.222–1.230.

[668] See 1.168. IA 1986, ss 183 and 184, are not applied to relevant schemes. Sections 126 and 127 are modified by the Collective Investment in Transferable Securities (Contractual Scheme) Regulations 2013 (SI 2013/1388), sch 2, paras 3 and 5(d), (g) and (i), and part 3. See also SI 2013/1388, reg 17(10)(c).

[669] Banking Act 2009, s 103(3), (4) and table.

[670] Building Societies Act 1986, s 90C.

[671] *Riener v Gershinson* [2004] EWHC 76 (Ch), [2004] 2 BCLC 376, at [102]; *Her Majesty's Revenue and Customs v Egleton* [2006] EWHC 2313 (Ch), [2007] Bus LR 44, at [20]–[21].

[672] *Walter Developments Pty Ltd v Roberts* (1995) 16 ACSR 280.

[673] See chapter 4.

not have standing to commence the claim thought to be available, whereas the provisional liquidator does have that standing and can give the usual undertaking to commence the claim.[674]

3.270 After a petition for its winding up has been presented, an SE cannot transfer its registered office to another member State.[675]

---

[674] *Her Majesty's Revenue and Customs v Egleton* [2006] EWHC 2313 (Ch), [2007] Bus LR 44; *Fourie v Le Roux* [2007] UKHL 1, [2007] 1 WLR 320.
[675] Regulation (EC) No 2157/2001, art 8(15).

4

APPOINTMENT OF A PROVISIONAL LIQUIDATOR

Purpose of Appointment

Function of a Provisional Liquidator

Power to appoint

4.1 A provisional liquidator of a company, also referred to as a 'liquidator appointed provisionally', may be appointed by the court under the Insolvency Act 1986 (IA 1986), s 135. Either the official receiver or any other fit person may be appointed.[1]

4.2 The court may appoint a provisional liquidator of a company at any time in the period between presentation of a petition for the compulsory winding up of the company and the court's disposal of the petition (by making a winding-up order, dismissing the petition or striking it out).[2] This is an interim remedy.[3]

4.3 Section 135 applies to any other entity that may be wound up as a registered company.[4] Section 135 is applied to unregistered companies by s 221(1),[5] to insolvent partnerships[6] and to relevant schemes.[7]

4.4 A provisional liquidator may be appointed to a company already in voluntary liquidation.[8]

4.5 A provisional bank liquidator may be appointed at any time after the making of an application for a bank insolvency order.[9] A provisional building society liquidator may be appointed at any time after the making of an application for a building society insolvency order.[10]

4.6 On hearing an administration application, the court may[11] treat it as a winding-up petition and make any order which it could make under IA 1986, s 125. The court's treatment of an administration application as a winding-up petition, will, for the purposes of s 135, turn it into a winding-up petition that has been presented and so the court can appoint

---

[1] IA 1986, s 135(2).

[2] IA 1986, s 135(1) and (2); *Re a Company (No 00315 of 1973)* [1973] 1 WLR 1566.

[3] *Commissioners of HM Revenue and Customs v Rochdale Drinks Distributors Ltd* [2011] EWCA Civ 1116, [2012] 1 BCLC 748, at [109].

[4] Building societies (see 1.120–1.121), charitable incorporated organizations (see 1.122), European cooperative societies (see 1.123), European public limited-liability companies (see 1.124), incorporated friendly societies (see 1.125), limited liability partnerships (see 1.126) and registered societies (see 1.127–1.129).

[5] For examples of appointment to foreign companies see *Re Scott-Brown Industries Pty Ltd* (1981) 6 ACLR 342; *Re a Company (No 00359 of 1987)* [1988] Ch 210; *Re Atlantic Isle Shipping Co Inc* (1988) 14 ACLR 232; *Re Latreefers Inc* [1999] 1 BCLC 271; *Re New Cap Reinsurance Corporation Holdings Ltd* (1999) 32 ACSR 234.

[6] See 1.222–1.230.

[7] See 1.168.

[8] See, for example, *Re P Turner (Wilsden) Ltd* [1987] BCLC 149; *Securities and Investments Board v Lancashire and Yorkshire Portfolio Management Ltd* [1992] BCLC 281; *Re Pinstripe Farming Co Ltd* [1996] 2 BCLC 295.

[9] IA 1986, s 135, applied by the Banking Act 2009, s 103(3), (4) and table.

[10] IA 1986, s 135, applied and modified by the Banking Act 2009, s 103(3), (4) and table, and the Building Societies Act 1986, s 90C.

[11] IA 1986, sch B1, para 13.

a provisional liquidator.[12] Before the power to treat an administration application as a winding-up petition was created, it was held that the court could not appoint a provisional liquidator under the power to make an interim order on an administration petition.[13]

It would seem that there is no power to appoint a provisional liquidator on an unfair-prejudice **4.7** petition with an alternative prayer for winding up. On such a petition in *Re a Company (No 00596 of 1986)*[14] there was serious dissension among directors resulting in a high degree of difficulty in managing the company properly. A receiver was appointed under the Senior Courts Act 1981, s 37, pending the hearing of further interim applications.

Object of appointment

The usual object of the appointment of a provisional liquidator is that an independent **4.8** person will take charge of the company's affairs, maintain the status quo and prevent prejudice either to those supporting the winding-up petition or to those against it, pending the court's decision on the petition.[15] There may be other circumstances which would justify an appointment.[16]

Provisional liquidators are independent persons operating under the direction of the court **4.9** for a purpose that is one entirely of preservation during an interim period: a provisional liquidator does not represent any one group of creditors.[17]

In some cases a provisional liquidator has been appointed so as to provide a period (which **4.10** may be expected to be several years) of independent management of an insolvent company where administration would not be appropriate. This has been done, for example, to organize a scheme of arrangement of an insurance company,[18] to protect a long-term stream of income,[19] to protect a foreign company's assets in this country which it could not deal with because of United Nations economic sanctions,[20] and in jurisdictions where there is no equivalent to the British administration procedure.[21] A provisional liquidator may be appointed for the purpose of facilitating a restructuring proposal.[22] A lengthy period of provisional liquidation is obtained by repeated adjournment of the winding-up petition so that the court can review the need for continuation of the provisional liquidation. Lengthy provisional liquidation is appropriate only in exceptional cases where special circumstances exist.[23]

---

[12] *Data Power Systems Ltd v Safehosts (London) Ltd* [2013] EWHC 2479 (Ch), [2013] BCC 721.
[13] *Re W F Fearman Ltd* (1987) 4 BCC 139. At that time, the power was in IA 1986, s 9(4). It is now in IA 1986, sch B1, para 13(1)(d).
[14] [1987] BCLC 133.
[15] Per Lord President Clyde in *Levy v Napier* 1962 SC 468 at p 477; per Street J in *Re Carapark Industries Pty Ltd* (1966) 86 WN (Pt 1) (NSW) 165 at p 171; per McPherson J in *South Downs Packers Pty Ltd v Beaver* (1984) 8 ACLR 990 at p 994.
[16] Per Kelly J in *Re Lockyer Valley Fresh Foods Co-operative Association Ltd* (1980) 5 ACLR 282.
[17] *Re Bank of Credit and Commerce International SA (No 2)* [1992] BCLC 579.
[18] See *Smith v UIC Insurance Co Ltd* [2001] BCC 11; *Jacob v UIC Insurance Co Ltd* [2006] EWHC 2717 (Ch), [2007] Bus LR 568. The provisional liquidation of UIC Insurance Co Ltd lasted ten years.
[19] *MHMH Ltd v Carwood Barker Holdings Ltd* [2004] EWHC 3174 (Ch), [2006] 1 BCLC 270.
[20] *Re Rafidain Bank* (2000) LTL 23/3/2000.
[21] *Re Fruit of the Loom Ltd* 2000 CILR N-7.
[22] *Re Luen Cheong Tai International Holdings Ltd* [2003] 2 HKLRD 719; *Re I-China Holdings Ltd* [2003] 1 HKLRD 629.
[23] *Re Coolfadda Developers Ltd* [2009] IESC 54, [2010] 1 ILRM 342.

Alternative appointment of receiver

4.11   A provisional liquidator has a similar role to a receiver *pendente lite*.[24] In *McGuiness v Black*[25] the petitioner, who was a contributory, asked for the appointment of a provisional liquidator but Lord McCluskey preferred to appoint an interim judicial factor, as requested by the only other contributory. The fact that a receiver has been appointed by the court in other proceedings is something that weighs against appointing a provisional liquidator.[26]

4.12   In *Re United Medical Protection Ltd*[27] the judge asked counsel to consider whether the appointment of a receiver and manager would be more appropriate, but decided that it would not have any practical advantage over appointing a provisional liquidator.

4.13   In a case in Malaysia it was held that there is no power to appoint a receiver instead of a provisional liquidator,[28] but the court did not have cited to it *Hwang Chin Hor v Song Seng Sdn Bhd*,[29] in which such an appointment was made.

Liquidation, insolvency and winding up

4.14   The name 'provisional liquidator' is misleading because the one thing that a provisional liquidator of a company does not do is carry out the liquidation of the company.[30] In Regulation (EC) No 1346/2000, the term 'liquidator' is given, by art 2(b), the extended meaning of a person or body whose function is to administer or liquidate assets of which the debtor has been divested or to supervise the administration of his affairs. With this meaning, the term 'liquidator' can and does include a British provisional liquidator.[31]

4.15   It cannot be said that a company 'begins to be wound up' when a provisional liquidator is appointed[32] or that the appointment is in, or commences, 'the course of the winding up of the company'.[33] However, a provisional liquidator of a company can be appointed only after a petition has been presented for the compulsory liquidation of the company.[34] An order for the appointment of a provisional liquidator may therefore be regarded as an order in connection with the winding up of a company[35] and should be seen as part of the compulsory liquidation process.

4.16   In IA 1986, a group of sections[36] dealing with, among other matters, provisional liquidators has been given the title 'Miscellaneous provisions applying to companies which are insolvent or in liquidation'. Again this is somewhat misleading: it is not necessary for the appointment of a provisional liquidator of a company that the company be insolvent: a provisional liquidator may be appointed in connection with a contributory's petition to

---

[24] *Re Club Mediterranean Pty Ltd* (1975) 11 SASR 481 per Bright J at p 483.
[25] 1990 SC 21.
[26] *Re Brylyn No 2 Pty Ltd* (1987) 12 ACLR 697 at p 703.
[27] [2002] NSWSC 413, 41 ACSR 623.
[28] *Kok Fook Sang v Juta Vila (M) Sdn Bhd* [1996] 2 MLJ 666.
[29] [1990] 2 MLJ 105.
[30] *Levy v Napier* 1962 SC 468; *Re Carapark Industries Pty Ltd* (1966) 86 WN (Pt 1) (NSW) 165 per Street J at p 171; *Re Obie Pty Ltd* [1985] 1 QdR 464; *Ashborder BV v Green Gas Power Ltd* [2005] EWHC 1031 (Ch), LTL 1/2/2005.
[31] See 4.26.
[32] *Re Scobie* (1995) 95 ATC 4525.
[33] *Re Overnight Ltd* [2009] EWHC 601 (Ch), [2009] Bus LR 1141, at [27].
[34] IA 1986, s 135(1).
[35] *Capita Financial Group Ltd v Rothwells Ltd* (1989) 18 NSWLR 306.
[36] ss 230–246.

wind up a solvent company.[37] Furthermore, when a provisional liquidator of a company is appointed the company is usually not actually in liquidation because the appointment is made between the time of presenting a petition for compulsory liquidation and the disposal of the petition and the company will not at that stage be in liquidation unless it is in voluntary liquidation.[38]

Effect on Company Governance and Contracts

The appointment of a provisional liquidator of a company terminates the powers of its **4.17** directors as effectively as does the making of a winding-up order.[39] The directors do, however, have standing to apply for the provisional liquidator's appointment to be discharged,[40] or to apply for an administration order to be made in relation to the company[41] or to apply to dismiss or otherwise resist the petition.[42]

Where a provisional liquidator of a company has been appointed, the directors of the com- **4.18** pany do not have power to allot and issue shares of the company.[43]

The appointment of a provisional liquidator of a company terminates the actual authority **4.19** of all the company's agents,[44] but the authority of an agent is not terminated until the agent has notice of the appointment of the provisional liquidator.[45]

Apart from the effects on the company's directors and agents noted at 4.17–4.19, the **4.20** appointment of a provisional liquidator of a company has no effect on its contracts, though a particular contract may make provision, either expressly or by implication, for what is to happen if there is such an appointment.[46] In particular, the appointment of a provisional liquidator of a company does not terminate the contracts of employment of its employees.[47]

Effect on Litigation

After a petition to wind up a company has been presented, the appointment of a provisional **4.21** liquidator of the company has a significant effect on actions or proceedings against it. If no provisional liquidator is appointed, actions or proceedings may continue unless restrained by the court under IA 1986, s 126. After a provisional liquidator is appointed, s 130(2) provides that actions or proceedings cannot continue or commence unless the court gives leave. The same provision is made in IA 1986, s 130(3), with respect to actions and proceedings against any contributory of a company registered but not formed under the Companies Act 2006[48] which has been ordered to be wound up. IA 1986, s 130(3), is also expressed to apply to actions and proceedings against the company but this seems to be superfluous

---

[37] For example, *Levy v Napier* 1962 SC 468; *South Downs Packers Pty Ltd v Beaver* (1984) 8 ACLR 990; *Re Nerang Investments Pty Ltd* (1985) 9 ACLR 646.

[38] See 5.294–5.298.

[39] *Re Mawcon Ltd* [1969] 1 WLR 78.

[40] *Re Union Accident Insurance Co Ltd* [1972] 1 WLR 640; *Taman Sungai Dua Development Sdn Bhd v Goh Boon Kim* [1997] 2 MLJ 526.

[41] *Re Gosscott (Groundworks) Ltd* [1988] BCLC 363 per Mervyn Davies J at p 366.

[42] *Ashborder BV v Green Gas Power Ltd* [2005] EWHC 1031 (Ch), LTL 1/2/2005, at [62].

[43] *Anfrank Nominees Pty Ltd v Connell* (1989) 1 ACSR 365.

[44] *Pacific and General Insurance Co Ltd v Hazell* [1997] BCC 400.

[45] *Re Oriental Bank Corporation, ex parte Guillemin* (1884) 28 ChD 634.

[46] *Bank of Credit and Commerce International SA v Malik* [1996] BCC 15.

[47] *Donnelly v Gleeson* (1978) Irish Company Law Reports 406.

[48] See 1.98–1.102.

since they would be covered by s 130(2). Section 130(2) applies to any other entity that may be wound up as a registered company[49] and to unregistered companies,[50] including foreign companies.[51]

4.22   IA 1986, s 130(2) and (3), are applied to bank insolvency[52] and building society insolvency.[53]

Effect on Administration

4.23   If a provisional liquidator of a company has been appointed, an administrator may not be appointed either by the holder of a floating charge[54] or by the company or its directors.[55] It is, however, possible for the court to make an administration order.

No Deemed Insolvency; Opening of Insolvency Proceedings

4.24   The appointment of a provisional liquidator of a company is not an event that will cause the company to be deemed to be insolvent or to have become insolvent for the purposes of the Company Directors Disqualification Act 1986 or IA 1986. It also does not activate provisions of the Employment Rights Act 1996, part 12 (payment of employees' wages from the National Insurance Fund), or the Third Parties (Rights against Insurers) Act 1930. It is, though, a judgment opening insolvency proceedings if the proceedings are subject to Regulation (EC) No 1346/2000.[56]

Is a Provisional Liquidator a Liquidator?

In British legislation

4.25   The description in IA 1986, s 135(1), of a provisional liquidator as 'a liquidator' appointed provisionally raises the question whether legislative provisions relating to liquidators also apply to provisional liquidators. Some sections of IA 1986 are expressed to apply to both liquidators and provisional liquidators.[57] Some sections are expressed to apply when a winding-up order is made or when a provisional liquidator is appointed.[58] In one section,[59] it is provided that in sch 8 to the Act (provisions capable of inclusion in company insolvency rules), 'liquidator' includes a provisional liquidator. In *Re Overnight Ltd*[60] it was held that unless express provision is made in IA 1986, the term 'liquidator' does not include a provisional liquidator. In particular, s 213, which authorizes a liquidator to apply to the court for a declaration of liability for fraudulent trading, does not authorize a provisional liquidator to make such an application. It has been opined, obiter, that 'liquidator' in what is now the

---

[49]   Building societies (see 1.120–1.121), charitable incorporated organizations (see 1.122), European cooperative societies (see 1.123), European public limited-liability companies (see 1.124), incorporated friendly societies (see 1.125), limited liability partnerships (see 1.126) and registered societies (see 1.127–1.129).

[50]   IA 1986, ss 221(1) and 229(1).

[51]   *Mazur Media Ltd v Mazur Media GmbH* [2004] EWHC 1566 (Ch), [2005] 1 BCLC 305, at [67]. For an example of s 130(2) being used in the English winding up of a foreign company see *Queensland Mercantile and Agency Co Ltd v Australasian Investment Co Ltd* (1888) 15 R 935.

[52]   Banking Act 2009, s 103(3), (4) and table.

[53]   Building Societies Act 1986, s 90C.

[54]   IA 1986, sch B1, para 17(a).

[55]   sch B1, para 25(a), which comes into effect when a winding-up petition is presented.

[56]   *Re Eurofood IFSC Ltd* (case C-341/04) [2006] Ch 508.

[57]   ss 144(1) and 234(1).

[58]   ss 130(2), 131(1) and 144(1).

[59]   s 411(3).

[60]   [2009] EWHC 601 (Ch), [2009] Bus LR 1141, at [25].

Companies Act 2006, s 859H(3) (unregistered charge void against liquidator), does not include a provisional liquidator.[61]

In Regulation (EC) No 1346/2000

For the purposes of Regulation (EC) No 1346/2000, the term 'liquidator' is defined by art **4.26** 2(b) to mean a person or body whose function is to administer or liquidate assets of which the debtor has been divested or to supervise the administration of his affairs. Those persons and bodies are listed in annex C. As a provisional liquidator appointed by a court in the United Kingdom is listed in annex C, a provisional liquidator is a liquidator for the purposes of the Regulation. This means, in particular, that a provisional liquidator appointed by a court in the UK has the following powers in relation to insolvency proceedings in other EU States (apart from Denmark):

(a) a provisional liquidator appointed in main proceedings may request the opening of secondary proceedings;[62]

(b) a provisional liquidator in either main or secondary proceedings may participate in other proceedings on the same basis as a creditor;[63]

(c) a provisional liquidator in main proceedings may request a stay of secondary proceedings;[64]

(d) a provisional liquidator in main proceedings may propose a rescue plan, a composition or a comparable measure which will close secondary proceedings;[65]

(e) a provisional liquidator in main proceedings may require insolvency proceedings which are not winding-up proceedings to be converted into winding-up proceedings.[66]

In Australia

Courts in Australia have concluded that it is necessary to consider each provision of the **4.27** Australian corporations legislation in context to determine whether 'liquidator' includes provisional liquidator.[67] Australian courts have decided that a provisional liquidator is a liquidator for the purposes of:

(a) the Corporations Act 2001 (Australia), s 462(2)(d) (standing to apply for the company to be wound up by the court);[68]

(b) s 468(2) (exemption for dispositions by a liquidator from the rule that dispositions after commencement of liquidation are void; the subsection has subsequently been amended to refer expressly to provisional liquidators);[69]

(c) a provision like IA 1986, s 168(3), empowering a liquidator to apply to the court for directions;[70]

---

[61] *Re Namco UK Ltd* [2003] EWHC 989 (Ch), [2003] 2 BCLC 78, at [16].
[62] art 29.
[63] art 32(3).
[64] art 33.
[65] art 34.
[66] art 37.
[67] *Newmont Pty Ltd v Laverton Nickel NL* [1978] 2 NSWLR 325; *Capita Financial Group Ltd v Rothwells Ltd* (1989) 18 NSWLR 306.
[68] *Zempilas v J N Taylor Holdings Ltd (No 5)* (1991) 5 ACSR 22.
[69] *Re Breseden Pty Ltd* (1989) 17 NSWLR 513; *Re Charodell Corporation Pty Ltd* (1991) 24 NSWLR 343—these cases were decided before the rules on commencement of compulsory winding up were changed in Australia.
[70] *Newmont Pty Ltd v Laverton Nickel NL* [1978] 2 NSWLR 325.

(d) a provision with the same wording as IA 1986, s 167(3) (control by the court of a liquidator's exercise of powers), except for omitting the words 'in a winding up by the court'.[71]

4.28 Australian courts have decided that a provisional liquidator is not a liquidator for the purposes of:

(a) the Income Tax Assessment Act 1936 (Australia);[72]
(b) a provision of subordinate legislation in the same terms as the English Companies (Winding-up) Rules 1949,[73] r 195(1);[74]
(c) a provision since repealed that the appointment of a liquidator ends the official management of a company.[75]

In former British legislation

4.29 The problem of whether a provisional liquidator is a liquidator also occurred under the old system in which the official receiver was referred to as the provisional liquidator of a company on the making of a winding-up order.[76]

Applying for Appointment

Who may Apply

4.30 When a petition has been presented for the compulsory liquidation of a company, an application to appoint a provisional liquidator may be made by:[77]

(a) the petitioner;
(b) a creditor of the company;
(c) a contributory of the company;
(d) the company itself;
(e) the Secretary of State;
(f) a temporary administrator;
(g) a member State liquidator appointed in main proceedings;
(h) any person who would, under any enactment, be entitled to present a petition to wind up the company.

4.31 The equivalent rule in the Companies (Winding-up) Rules 1949,[78] namely, r 32, referred only to applications by a creditor, a contributory or the company, but it is clear that this did not limit the circumstances in which an appointment could be made.[79]

---

[71] *Re Bayswood Pty Ltd* (1981) 6 ACLR 107.
[72] *Re Obie Pty Ltd* [1985] 1 QdR 464; *Re Rothercroft Pty Ltd* (1986) 4 NSWLR 673; *Deputy Commissioner of Taxation v Access Finance Corporation Pty Ltd* (1987) 8 NSWLR 557.
[73] SI 1949/330.
[74] *Re W T and M E Peterie Pty Ltd* [1979] 1 NSWLR 708.
[75] *Re GC Distributors Pty Ltd* [1974] 1 NSWLR 155.
[76] See 4.59; *Re English Bank of the River Plate* [1892] 1 Ch 391; *Re ABC Coupler and Engineering Co Ltd (No 3)* [1970] 1 WLR 702.
[77] IR 1986, r 4.25(1).
[78] SI 1949/330.
[79] *Re Highfield Commodities Ltd* [1985] 1 WLR 149; *Re Pacific Syndicates (NZ) Ltd* (1977) 1 BCR 95, in which it was said, obiter, that the court could make an appointment of its own motion.

The persons who may apply for the appointment of a provisional liquidator of a relevant **4.32** scheme[80] are the operator of the scheme, its depositary, the Financial Conduct Authority (FCA) and a creditor of the scheme.[81]

When an application has been made for a bank or building society insolvency order, an **4.33** application to appoint a provisional bank liquidator or provisional building society liquidator may be made by:[82]

(a) the Bank of England;
(b) the FCA (with the consent of the Bank of England);
(c) if the institution is a PRA-authorized person, the Prudential Regulation Authority (PRA) (with the consent of the Bank of England); or
(d) in the case of a bank insolvency only, the Secretary of State.

Application Procedure

Form of application

An application to the court[83] for the appointment of a provisional liquidator of a company **4.34** must be supported by a witness statement stating:[84]

(a) The grounds for the appointment.
(b) If the proposed provisional liquidator is not the official receiver, that the person proposed has consented to act and that he or she is, to the best of the applicant's knowledge, a qualified insolvency practitioner.[85]
(c) Whether or not the official receiver has been informed of the application and, if so, whether a copy of the application has been sent to the official receiver.[86]
(d) Whether, to the applicant's knowledge:
  (i) There has been proposed, or is in force, for the company a voluntary arrangement.
  (ii) An administrator or administrative receiver is acting in relation to the company.
  (iii) A voluntary liquidator has been appointed.
(e) The applicant's estimate of the value of the assets in respect of which the provisional liquidator is to be appointed.

There are similar requirements for a witness statement accompanying an application to **4.35** appoint a provisional bank or building society liquidator.[87] In that case the witness statement must state the functions the applicant wishes to be carried out by the provisional liquidator in relation to the institution's affairs.[88]

---

[80] See 1.168.
[81] IR 1986, r 4.25(1), as applied and modified by the Collective Investment in Transferable Securities (Contractual Scheme) Regulations 2013 (SI 2013/1388), sch 3.
[82] Bank Insolvency (England and Wales) Rules 2009 (SI 2009/356), r 20(2); Building Society Insolvency (England and Wales) Rules 2010 (SI 2010/2581), r 20(1) (see r 3(2) for the definition of 'the appropriate regulator').
[83] See 3.233–3.263.
[84] IR 1986, r 4.25(2).
[85] See 4.67–4.68.
[86] See 4.37.
[87] Bank Insolvency (England and Wales) Rules 2009 (SI 2009/356), r 20(3); Building Society Insolvency (England and Wales) Rules 2010 (SI 2010/2581), r 20(2).
[88] SI 2009/356, r 20(3)(f); SI 2010/2581, r 20(2)(f).

4.36 In *Re W F Fearman Ltd*,[89] in view of the urgency of the case, Harman J appointed a provisional liquidator on an application which was not in writing and did not conform to any of the relevant procedural requirements.

Notice

4.37 Whether or not it is proposed that the official receiver should be the provisional liquidator, a copy of the application and supporting witness statement must be sent to the official receiver, who may attend the hearing and make representations.[90] If it is not possible to send these copies, the official receiver must at least be informed of the application in time to attend the hearing.[91]

4.38 If the company is an authorized person[92] which has permission to effect or carry out contracts of insurance, or which is a reclaim fund,[93] and the applicant is not the FCA or the PRA, the applicant must serve a copy of the application on the FCA and, if the company is a PRA-authorized person, the PRA.[94] If either the FCA or the PRA applies for the appointment of a provisional liquidator of a PRA-authorized person which has permission to effect or carry out contracts of insurance, or which is a reclaim fund, it must serve a copy of the petition on the other regulator.[95]

Hearing

4.39 An application for the appointment of a provisional liquidator must be listed before a judge.[96] An application may be heard in private[97] if it is necessary, in order to protect the company, its creditors and its shareholders, to prevent the appointment of a provisional liquidator becoming known.[98] However, unless the court expressly prohibits publication of information heard in a private hearing, it is not contempt of court to make that information public.[99]

The court's order

4.40 The court may make the appointment applied for, on such terms as it thinks fit, if satisfied that sufficient grounds are shown for the appointment.[100]

4.41 The court may make alternative orders instead of appointing a provisional liquidator.[101]

---

[89] (1987) 4 BCC 139.
[90] IR 1986, r 4.25(3).
[91] IR 1986, r 4.25(3).
[92] See 9.113.
[93] 'Reclaim fund' is defined as a company whose objects are restricted to dealing with dormant bank and building society accounts in specified ways (Dormant Bank and Building Society Accounts Act 2008, s 5(1)).
[94] Financial Services and Markets Act 2000, ss 369(1) and (3) and 369A(1), (3) and (4).
[95] ss 369(4) and 369A(5).
[96] PD Insolvency Proceedings 2014, para 3.2(4).
[97] CPR, r 39.2(3).
[98] *Re London and Norwich Investment Services Ltd* [1988] BCLC 226.
[99] *A F Noonan (Architectural Practice) Ltd v Bournemouth and Boscombe Athletic Community Football Club Ltd* [2007] EWCA Civ 848, [2007] 1 WLR 2614.
[100] IR 1986, r 4.25(4); Bank Insolvency (England and Wales) Rules 2009 (SI 2009/356), r 20(4); Building Society Insolvency (England and Wales) Rules 2010 (SI 2010/2581), r 20(3). See further 4.1–4.16 and 4.75–4.109.
[101] *Re Senator Hanseatische Verwaltungsgesellschaft mbH* [1996] 2 BCLC 562, in which injunctions were issued to prevent a foreign company which administered a pyramid investment scheme recruiting new members or remitting cash abroad but, on appeal [1997] 1 WLR 515, Millett LJ and Lord Woolf MR at pp 526–7 said that it would have been better to appoint a provisional liquidator.

If the company has insufficient free assets to pay the applicant's costs, the court will not give **4.42** those costs priority over the rights of secured creditors.[102]

In *J C Scott Constructions v Mermaid Waters Tavern Pty Ltd*[103] the plaintiff had petitioned **4.43** for the winding up of the defendant without wanting a winding up but only so as to obtain the appointment of a provisional liquidator as part of its efforts to obtain payment of a judgment debt. The application for the appointment was adjourned pending an appeal by the defendant against refusal of a stay of judgment. The judgment debt was paid when that appeal was dismissed, and the plaintiff asked for its application for appointment of a provisional liquidator to be dismissed. The court made no order as to costs on the application.

Undertaking in damages

Unless an application is made in the public interest,[104] the court will not normally appoint **4.44** a provisional liquidator unless the applicant gives an undertaking in damages. This is an undertaking to compensate the company for any loss caused to it by the appointment of the provisional liquidator if it should turn out that the appointment was wrongly made.[105] The practice in England and Wales is to require an undertaking in damages if an application for an appointment is made without notice to the company and the court has no opportunity to hear the company's views, but an undertaking in damages is not usually required if the company had an opportunity to give the court its views on the application.[106] In Australia an undertaking is required whether the company was represented at the hearing or not, unless there are appropriate reasons for not requiring an undertaking.[107] In Hong Kong it has been said that whether an undertaking in damages is required when the company is represented depends on the circumstances of the case.[108]

Application in the public interest

If an applicant for the appointment of a provisional liquidator of a company is carrying **4.45** out its public duty to enforce the law in the public interest, rather than to protect its own proprietary rights, an undertaking in damages will not be required, unless it is fair to do so in the particular circumstances of a case.[109] An applicant from outside the jurisdiction may be treated in this way, at least if the lawbreaking being dealt with is transnational.[110]

---

[102] *Caxton Products Ltd v Packaging House Ltd* (1990) 5 NZCLC 66,611.

[103] (1983) 8 ACLR 687.

[104] See 4.45.

[105] This is similar to the undertaking (traditionally called a 'cross-undertaking in damages') required on granting an interim injunction.

[106] *Re Highfield Commodities Ltd* [1985] 1 WLR 149 at p 155.

[107] *Re Property Corporate Services Pty Ltd* [2004] FCA 175, 48 ACSR 508, at [51]. In *Lubavitch Mazal Pty Ltd v Yeshiva Properties No 1 Pty Ltd* [2003] NSWSC 535, 47 ACSR 197, an undertaking was not required because there was no practical possibility of damage.

[108] *Re Prudential Enterprise Ltd (No 2)* [2003] 3 HKLRD 136 per Chu J at pp 155–6. For a case in which an undertaking was required see *Re Jinro (HK) International Ltd* [2003] 3 HKLRD 459.

[109] *Re Highfield Commodities Ltd* [1985] 1 WLR 149; *Re City Vintners Ltd* (2001) LTL 21/2/2002; *Australian Securities and Investments Commission v ACN 102 556 098 Pty Ltd* [2003] NSWSC 1253, 48 ACSR 50. See also cases concerning interim injunctions: *Kirklees Metropolitan Borough Council v Wickes Building Supplies Ltd* [1993] AC 227; *Securities and Investments Board v Lloyd-Wright* [1993] 4 All ER 210; *Financial Services Authority v Sinaloa Gold plc* [2013] UKSC 11, [2013] 2 AC 28. An undertaking in damages was required in the unusual circumstances of *Commissioners of Customs and Excise v Anchor Foods Ltd* [1999] 1 WLR 1139 (freezing injunction), where not giving the defendant that protection would have been oppressive.

[110] *United States Securities and Exchange Commission v Manterfield* [2009] EWCA Civ 27, [2010] 1 WLR 172.

According to Etherton J in *Re City Vintners Ltd* the Secretary of State should draw expressly to the judge's attention:

(a) that an undertaking in damages is not being offered;
(b) why an alternative course, such as the appointment of a receiver or the acceptance of under-takings, is not considered appropriate;
(c) why it is not considered appropriate to give the company notice;
(d) why it is not considered appropriate to give the company an opportunity to be heard.

This has been described as the 'Etherton protocol'. Failure to follow it is not a ground for discharging the appointment of a provisional liquidator.[111]

Application without Notice to the Company

When can a provisional liquidator be appointed without notice?

4.46 An application for the appointment of a provisional liquidator of a company clearly affects the company but may be made without notice to the company.[112]

4.47 According to Hoffmann J in *Re First Express Ltd*[113] and *Re Secure and Provide plc*,[114] an order should not be made without notice to the company unless:

(a) giving the company an opportunity to be heard appears likely to cause injustice to the applicant, because of:
(i) the delay involved, or
(ii) action which it is likely will be taken before the order can be made; and
(b) the court is satisfied that any damage which the company may suffer from the appointment of the provisional liquidator may be compensated through the applicant's undertaking in damages or that the risk of incompensable loss is clearly outweighed by the risk of injustice to the applicant if the order is not made.

4.48 According to Lewison LJ in *Commissioners of HM Revenue and Customs v Rochdale Drinks Distributors Ltd*:[115]

A judge should not entertain an application of which no notice has been given unless either giving notice would enable the defendant to take steps to defeat the purpose of the remedy (as in the case of a freezing or search and seizure order) or there has been literally no time to give notice before the remedy is required to prevent the threatened wrongful act.

4.49 The applicant must provide evidence to justify applying without notice.[116]

Applicant's duty of disclosure

4.50 As with any application without notice, the applicant has a duty to make 'a full and fair disclosure of all the material facts'.[117] The court may discharge an order made without notice,

---

[111] *Mishcon de Reya v Barrett* [2006] EWHC 952 (Ch), [2007] 1 BCLC 153.
[112] *Emporium Jaya (Bentong) Sdn Bhd v Emporium Jaya (Jerantut) Sdn Bhd* [2002] 1 MLJ 182.
[113] [1991] BCC 782 at p 785.
[114] [1992] BCC 405.
[115] [2011] EWCA Civ 1116, [2012] 1 BCLC 748, at [111].
[116] *Commissioners of HM Revenue and Customs v Rochdale Drinks Distributors Ltd* at [111]. But Rimer LJ, at [106], thought that the seriousness of a case could itself justify making the application without notice.
[117] *R v Kensington Income Tax Commissioners, ex parte Princess Edmond de Polignac* [1917] 1 KB 486 per Scrutton LJ at p 514.

without examining the merits of the case, if material facts have not been disclosed,[118] and this may make the applicant liable on an undertaking in damages. However, the court may also make a fresh order. Discharge for material non-disclosure may not be appropriate, especially where the non-disclosure was innocent.[119] The question is not whether an order was obtained as a result of misrepresentation or non-disclosure but whether the information not disclosed was material to be taken into account in deciding whether or not to grant relief without notice and if so on what terms.[120]

For examples of discharge, for material non-disclosure, of an appointment of a provisional liquidator made on an application without notice to the company, see *Pac Asian Services Pte Ltd v European Asian Bank AG*;[121] *Securities and Futures Commission v Mandarin Resources Corporation Ltd*,[122] in which a fresh order reappointing the provisional liquidator was made; and *Re OJSC ANK Yugraneft*.[123]   **4.51**

Application to set aside appointment

An application under IR 1986, r 7.47(1), to set aside an appointment of a provisional liquidator made without notice to the company should be made promptly after becoming aware of the order. In *Re QRP Construction Pty Ltd*[124] two directors of the company had known of the order appointing joint provisional liquidators on the day it was made and apparently offered no objection. The company applied three weeks later to discharge the appointment and this was held to be too late, though it was also found that no reason had been shown for discharging the order.   **4.52**

Restrictions on Appointing Provisional Liquidators to Certain Types of Companies

Air traffic services licence companies

The court must not appoint a provisional liquidator of an air traffic services licence company.[125]   **4.53**

Protected energy companies, energy supply companies, universal service provider

On a petition for the winding up of a protected energy company,[126] energy supply company[127] or universal service provider (of postal services),[128] presented by a person other than the Secretary of State, a provisional liquidator cannot be appointed until at least 14 days have elapsed since service of notice of the petition on the Secretary of State and, as appropriate, on the Gas and Electricity Markets Authority (GEMA) or Office of Communications (Ofcom).[129]   **4.54**

---

[118] *R v Kensington Income Tax Commissioners, ex parte Princess Edmond de Polignac* per Scrutton LJ at p 514.

[119] See *Brink's Mat Ltd v Elcombe* [1988] 1 WLR 1350 and *Re OJSC ANK Yugraneft* [2008] EWHC 2614 (Ch), [2009] 1 BCLC 298, in which the principles are thoroughly reviewed.

[120] *Re Stanford International Bank Ltd* [2010] EWCA Civ 137, [2011] Ch 33, per Morritt C at [83].

[121] [1987] SLR 1.

[122] [1997] HKLRD 405.

[123] [2008] EWHC 2614 (Ch), [2009] 1 BCLC 298.

[124] [1973] QdR 157.

[125] See 1.260–1.261. Transport Act 2000, s 27(3).

[126] See 1.262–1.264.

[127] See 1.284–1.287.

[128] See 1.281–1.283.

[129] Energy Act 2004, s 160(1), (2) and (4)(b) (requiring service on GEMA), applied to energy supply companies by the Energy Act 2011, s 96; Postal Services Act 2011, s 74(1), (2) and (4)(b) (requiring service on Ofcom).

EEA insurers

4.55 A court in the United Kingdom must not appoint a provisional liquidator in relation to an EEA insurer[130] or any branch of an EEA insurer.[131]

EEA credit institutions

4.56 A court in the United Kingdom must not appoint a provisional liquidator in relation to an EEA credit institution[132] or any branch of an EEA credit institution.[133]

Changes in Practice

4.57 Under the Companies Act 1862, in the compulsory liquidation of a company, the court was empowered to appoint one or more persons to be 'official liquidators' of the company[134] and had power to make such an appointment provisionally at any time after presentation of a petition.[135] It was normal practice for the court to make an appointment provisionally soon after presentation of a petition if the company itself was the petitioner or otherwise admitted that a winding-up order should be made[136] but not if the winding-up petition was contested[137] and not on the *ex parte* application of a creditor.[138]

4.58 The liquidator appointed provisionally expected to be confirmed as official liquidator on the making of the order, and it became the practice to give the provisional liquidator all the powers of an official liquidator.[139] Hence there was a strong incentive to obtain appointment as a provisional liquidator as soon as possible.[140]

4.59 The Companies (Winding up) Act 1890 changed the system. First the title 'official liquidator' was changed to 'liquidator';[141] secondly, it was enacted that the official receiver was to be liquidator ex officio on the making of the winding-up order and would act until a creditors' meeting was held which could either confirm the official receiver as liquidator or appoint another person as liquidator.[142] The court no longer had any power to appoint a liquidator on making a winding-up order.[143] Confusingly, the official receiver, while acting as liquidator between the making of the winding-up order and the creditors' meeting was called a 'provisional liquidator'[144] and the court was sometimes required to decide whether

---

[130] See 1.318–1.322.

[131] Insurers (Reorganisation and Winding Up) Regulations 2004 (SI 2004/353), reg 4(1)(b).

[132] See 1.323–1.325.

[133] Credit Institutions (Reorganisation and Winding Up) Regulations 2004 (SI 2004/1045), reg 3(1)(b).

[134] s 92.

[135] s 85.

[136] Per Lord Romilly MR in *Re London, Hamburg and Continental Exchange Bank, Emmerson's Case* (1866) LR 2 Eq 231 at pp 236–7, and on the same day in *Re Railway Finance Co Ltd* (1866) as reported in 14 LT 507; *Re West Worthing Waterworks, Baths, and Assembly Rooms Co Ltd* (1868) 18 LT 849 (appointment on creditor's petition with company's agreement).

[137] Per Lord Romilly MR in further proceedings in *Re Railway Finance Co Ltd* (1866) as reported in 14 WR 754.

[138] *Re London and Manchester Industrial Association* (1875) 1 ChD 466.

[139] *Re Rochdale Property and General Finance Co* (1879) 12 ChD 775.

[140] See also *Re Cilfoden Benefit Building Society* (1868) LR 3 Ch App 462; *Re General Financial Bank* (1882) 20 ChD 276.

[141] s 4(3).

[142] s 4(1), (2) and (6).

[143] *Re John Reid and Sons Ltd* [1900] 2 QB 634.

[144] This secondary use of the term 'provisional liquidator' ended when the Companies Act 1985, s 533(2), was repealed by IA 1985, sch 10, part 2.

the term 'liquidator' in legislation covered this kind of provisional liquidator.[145] Between the presentation of the petition and the making of the order the court still retained the power to appoint any person provisional liquidator under the Companies Act 1862, s 85.[146] However, the fact that the official receiver would act as liquidator ex officio on the making of a winding-up order inclined the court to appoint the official receiver rather than anyone else as provisional liquidator before an order was made.[147] Presumably this reduced the number of applications for an appointment to be made before the winding-up order motivated only by a desire to secure appointment as liquidator permanently.

Two cases can be seen as the origin of the modern practice in the appointment of provisional liquidators. In *Re Marseilles Extension Railway and Land Co*[148] Malins V-C appointed a provisional liquidator where it was 'apprehended that part of the assets of the company might be made away with before the petition could be heard'. In *Re Hammersmith Town Hall Co*[149] Jessel MR made an order on the application of petitioning creditors 'to protect the company's assets'. **4.60**

Who will be Appointed

Independence

Either the official receiver or any other fit person may be appointed provisional liquidator.[150] A provisional liquidator of a company must be independent of the persons with interests in the company's affairs.[151] In particular there may be doubts about the impartiality of a person who has previously advised the directors of the company about their liabilities.[152] But previous advice about the company's financial position and the possibility of restructuring is unlikely to be a disqualification[153] and familiarity with the company's circumstances may be an advantage, though every case will depend on its own facts.[154] **4.61**

In *Re Southern Cross Airlines Holdings Ltd*[155] it was found to be convenient to appoint as provisional liquidator a person who had been acting as court-appointed receiver: it was stressed that this was appropriate only because the receiver had not been appointed to enforce a security. **4.62**

It is in principle wrong for different groups of creditors to apply for their own nominees to be appointed joint provisional liquidators: a provisional liquidator is an independent person who does not represent any particular interest.[156] **4.63**

---

[145] See *Re English Bank of the River Plate* [1892] 1 Ch 391.

[146] *Re North Wales Gunpowder Co* [1892] 2 QB 220.

[147] *Re Mercantile Bank of Australia* [1892] 2 Ch 204 per North J at p 210.

[148] [1867] WN 68.

[149] (1877) 6 ChD 112.

[150] IA 1986, s 135(2).

[151] *Re West Australian Gem Explorers Pty Ltd* (1994) 13 ACSR 104.

[152] *Re Club Superstores Australia Pty Ltd* (1993) 10 ACSR 730. See also *Re Giant Resources Ltd* [1989] 1 QdR 107 discussed at 4.161.

[153] *Re Luen Cheong Tai International Holdings Ltd* [2003] 2 HKLRD 719.

[154] See *Re Maxwell Communications Corporation plc* [1992] BCC 372, which concerned the appointment of an administrator.

[155] (1993) 10 ACSR 466.

[156] *Re Bank of Credit and Commerce International SA* [1992] BCC 83.

4.64 Before the official receiver can be appointed as the provisional liquidator of a company, a deposit for remuneration and expenses must be paid or secured.[157]

4.65 The official receiver cannot be appointed as a provisional bank liquidator[158] or provisional building society liquidator.[159]

4.66 Whether or not an application for the appointment of a provisional liquidator asks for the official receiver to be appointed, a copy of the application and supporting evidence must be sent to the official receiver, who may attend the hearing and make representations.[160] If it is not possible to send these copies, the official receiver must at least be informed of the application in time to attend the hearing.[161] The court will not appoint a person other than the official receiver as provisional liquidator if the official receiver objects.[162] A copy of an order appointing a provisional liquidator must be sent by the court to the official receiver (even if the official receiver is not the person appointed).[163]

Qualification

4.67 It is an offence triable either way for someone other than an official receiver to act as the provisional liquidator of a company when not qualified to act as an insolvency practitioner in relation to the company.[164] However, the acts of a provisional liquidator are valid notwithstanding any defect in his or her qualifications.[165]

4.68 The evidence supporting an application for the appointment of someone other than an official receiver as a provisional liquidator must state that the person proposed is, to the best of the applicant's belief, qualified to act as an insolvency practitioner in relation to the company and that he or she has consented to act.[166]

4.69 Only a person who is qualified to act as an insolvency practitioner, and who consents to act, may be appointed as a provisional bank liquidator[167] or provisional building society liquidator.[168] The witness statement accompanying an application to appoint a provisional bank or building society liquidator must state that the person to be appointed has consented to act[169] and is qualified to act as an insolvency practitioner.[170]

---

[157] IR 1986, r 4.27; see 4.135.

[158] IA 1986, s 135, as applied and modified by the Banking Act 2009, s 103(3), (4) and table.

[159] IA 1986, s 135, as applied and modified by the Banking Act 2009, s 103(3), (4) and table as further applied and modified by the Building Societies Act 1986, s 90C.

[160] IR 1986, 4.25(3).

[161] IR 1986, 4.25(3).

[162] *Re a Company (No 003102 of 1991)* [1991] BCLC 539 per Harman J at p 542.

[163] IR 1986, r 4.26(2)(a) and (b).

[164] IA 1986, ss 388(1)(a) and (5) and 389. In addition, subsections (4) and (5) of s 230 state that a provisional liquidator must be a qualified insolvency practitioner unless he or she is an official receiver. Provisions about qualification are in ss 390–398.

[165] IA 1986, s 232.

[166] IR 1986, r 4.25(2)(b).

[167] IA 1986, s 135, as applied and modified by the Banking Act 2009, s 103(3), (4) and table.

[168] IA 1986, s 135, as applied and modified by the Banking Act 2009, s 103(3), (4) and table, and further applied and modified by the Building Societies Act 1986, s 90C.

[169] Bank Insolvency (England and Wales) Rules 2009 (SI 2009/356), r 20(3)(b); Building Society Insolvency (England and Wales) Rules 2010 (SI 2010/2581), r 20(2)(b).

[170] SI 2009/356, r 20(3)(c); SI 2010/2581, r 20(2)(c).

In proceedings on petitions under the Insolvent Partnerships Order 1994 (IPO 1994), art 8   **4.70**
or art 10, a person who is not an official receiver may not be appointed provisional liquidator of a partnership and of a corporate member of the partnership unless he or she is, at the time of the appointment, qualified to act as an insolvency practitioner both in relation to the insolvent partnership and in relation to any corporate member in respect of which he or she is appointed.[171]

A person who is subject to a disqualification order or undertaking commits an offence triable either way if he or she acts as provisional liquidator of a company.[172] When an administration order against an individual under the County Courts Act 1984, part 6, is revoked, an order may be made under IA 1986, s 429, applying that section and the Company Directors Disqualification Act 1986, s 12, to that individual. It is then a criminal offence for the individual to act as liquidator of a company, except with the leave of the court which made the order under IA 1986, s 429.[173] It is submitted that this is one context in which a statutory reference to a 'liquidator' should be read as including a reference to a provisional liquidator.[174]   **4.71**

A person who is not an official receiver must provide security for the due performance of his or her duties as provisional liquidator and may be removed from office for failing to keep up the security.[175]   **4.72**

Groups of Companies

If insolvency proceedings are being taken against several related companies together, normally, the same insolvency practitioner should be appointed to deal with them all: where the companies have conflicting interests in mutual dealings, an application may be made to the court for instructions, but the insolvency practitioner should not be regarded as disqualified by a conflict of interest.[176]   **4.73**

Insolvent Partnerships

When a petition to wind up an insolvent partnership is presented by an insolvency office-holder of the partnership or a member of the partnership under IA 1986, s 221A(1),[177] the court is authorized by s 221A(4) to appoint the office-holder provisional liquidator of the partnership under s 135.   **4.74**

---

[171] IA 1986, s 230(3), as modified by IPO 1994, sch 4, para 26; probably applied to art 10 petitions by IA 1986, s 221(5), as modified by IPO 1994, sch 6, para 4; see 1.229.

[172] Company Directors Disqualification Act 1986, ss 1(1)(b), 13 and 22(3); IA 1986, s 388(1)(a). Such a person is, in any case, not qualified to act as an insolvency practitioner (IA 1986, s 390(4)(b)).

[173] Company Directors Disqualification Act 1986, ss 12 and 13.

[174] See 4.25.

[175] IR 1986, rr 4.28 and 4.29. Applied to bank insolvency by SI 2009/356, rr 23 and 24, and modified by r 3(3)(b) and (4)(l) and (o). Applied to building society insolvency by SI 2010/2581, rr 23 and 24, and modified by r 3(5)(b) and (6)(n) and (q).

[176] *Re Bruton Pty Ltd* (1990) 2 ACSR 277; *Re Arrows Ltd* [1992] BCC 121; *Re Luen Cheong Tai International Holdings Ltd* [2003] 2 HKLRD 719; *Macquarie University Union Ltd v Venues at Macquarie Pty Ltd* [2007] FCA 721, 62 ACSR 353; *Parmalat Capital Finance Ltd v Food Holdings Ltd* [2008] UKPC 23, [2009] 1 BCLC 274.

[177] Inserted by IPO 1994, sch 3, para 3; see 8.9–8.10.

When an Appointment will be Made

Winding-up Order is Likely to be Made

4.75 A provisional liquidator of a company may be appointed only after a petition to wind up the company compulsorily has been presented,[178] but the court's power to make an appointment following the presentation of a petition ceases if the petition is struck out,[179] so the applicant must show that it is likely that a winding-up order will be made when the petition is heard.[180]

4.76 In *Re Mercantile Bank of Australia*[181] North J said, at p 210, that: 'The appointment of a provisional liquidator implies that, in all probability, a winding-up order will afterwards be made'. Nevertheless, the appointment of a provisional liquidator does not mean that a winding-up order *must* be made.[182] See, for example, *Day v Mount*,[183] in which the winding-up petition was dismissed; *Ah Toy v Registrar of Companies (NT)*,[184] in which the winding-up petition was eventually dismissed because of the petitioner's lack of standing; *Re a Company (No 001951 of 1987)*,[185] in which the winding-up petition was dismissed but made on appeal.[186] The fact that the winding-up petition under which a provisional liquidator was appointed has been dismissed does not invalidate the court's order appointing the provisional liquidator.[187]

4.77 On a creditor's petition, showing that the petition is based on a debt which is disputed on substantial grounds will demonstrate that it is not likely that a winding-up order will be made.[188]

4.78 Unusually, in *Re Denilikoon Nominees (No 2) Pty Ltd*[189] it was hoped that investigations by the provisional liquidator would facilitate payment of the petitioning creditor's debt so that it would be unnecessary to make a winding-up order. However, it turned out that there were no funds to pay for the investigation and so a winding-up order was made.[190]

---

[178] IA 1986, s 135(1).

[179] *Re a Company (No 00315 of 1973)* [1973] 1 WLR 1566.

[180] *Commissioners of HM Revenue and Customs v Rochdale Drinks Distributors Ltd* [2011] EWCA Civ 1116, [2012] 1 BCLC 748, at [77]. This replaces the former criterion that there must be a good prima facie case for making a winding-up order: *Re Union Accident Insurance Co Ltd* [1972] 1 Lloyd's Rep 297; *Teague* 1985 SLT 469; *PT Anekapangan Dwitama v Far East Food Industries Sdn Bhd* [1995] 1 MLJ 21. The likelihood threshold criterion had already been adopted in Australia: *Re McLennan Holdings Pty Ltd* (1983) 7 ACLR 732 at p 738; *Rural Industries Co-operative Society Ltd v Porky Pigs Pty Ltd* (1988) 12 ACLR 794; *Re Qintex Ltd (No 3)* (1990) 2 ACSR 627; *Natwest Australia Bank Ltd v Glen Pacific Pty Ltd* (1992) 6 ACSR 711; though see *Emanuele v Australian Securities Commission* (1995) 141 ALR 506 discussed at 4.98. In Scotland, the test established in *Purewal Enterprises Ltd* [2008] CSOH 127, 2008 GWD 37-555, that there is a good arguable case, may need to be reconsidered.

[181] [1892] 2 Ch 204.

[182] *Levy v Napier* 1962 SC 468; *Teague* 1985 SLT 469.

[183] (1984) 53 ALR 468.

[184] (1986) 72 ALR 107 at pp 115–21.

[185] [1988] BCLC 182.

[186] *Re Walter L Jacob and Co Ltd* [1989] BCLC 345.

[187] *Day v Mount* (1984) 53 ALR 468.

[188] As in *Natwest Australia Bank Ltd v Glen Pacific Pty Ltd* (1992) 6 ACSR 711.

[189] (1981) 6 ACLR 262.

[190] *Re Denilikoon Nominees (No 2) Pty Ltd* (1982) 6 ACLR 509.

If the application is made on a contributory's petition under the just and equitable clause, **4.79**
it will not be refused on the company's assertion that the petitioner has an alternative
remedy.[191]

If the court does not have jurisdiction to wind up a company, it does not have jurisdiction **4.80**
to appoint a provisional liquidator.[192]

Once it has been established that it is likely that a winding-up order will be made, the **4.81**
second stage is to consider whether in the circumstances of the particular case, it is—as a
matter of judicial discretion—right that a provisional liquidator should be appointed.[193]
There is no limit to the circumstances in which an appointment may be made.[194] The second
stage is discussed at 4.82–4.87 (application supported by the company) and 4.88–4.109
(application not supported by the company).

Application Supported by the Company

Appointment not automatic

The pre-1890 position[195] was that an unopposed application for the appointment of a provi- **4.82**
sional liquidator of a company made by, or with the agreement of, the company itself would
be granted automatically. Although judges in more recent times, in obiter reviews of the
law, have repeated that position,[196] it is submitted that the better view is that the fact that it
is the company itself which is seeking appointment of a provisional liquidator is a relevant
and often persuasive consideration,[197] but is not conclusive.[198] The court will not automatically appoint a provisional liquidator of a company when asked for by the company.[199] There
must be 'a situation of jeopardy inimical to the proper maintenance of the status quo pending determination of the winding-up application'.[200]

Application by directors

If an application to appoint a provisional liquidator of a company is made by the company's **4.83**
directors, the court should consider whether the appointment is in the interests of the company's members.[201]

---

[191] *Teague* 1985 SLT 469; *Re Brylyn No 2 Pty Ltd* (1987) 12 ACLR 697.

[192] *Starr v Trafalgar Financial Corporation Ltd (No 2)* (1983) 8 ACLR 367; *Davidson v Global Investments International Ltd* (1995) 19 ACSR 89.

[193] *Commissioners of HM Revenue and Customs v SED Essex Ltd* [2013] EWHC 1583 (Ch), [2013] BVC 314, at [11].

[194] *Re Union Accident Insurance Co Ltd* [1972] 1 Lloyd's Rep 297 at p 300; *Re Club Mediterranean Pty Ltd* (1975) 11 SASR 481 at p 484; *Re Lockyer Valley Fresh Foods Co-operative Association Ltd* (1980) 5 ACLR 282 at p 289; *Securities and Futures Commission v Mandarin Resources Corporation Ltd* [1997] HKLRD 405; *Re Stewardship Credit Arbitrage Fund Ltd* (2008) 73 WIR 136 at [36].

[195] See 4.57–4.58.

[196] Per Bright J in *Re Club Mediterranean Pty Ltd* (1975) 11 SASR 481 at p 484; per Plowman J in *Re Union Accident Insurance Co Ltd* [1972] 1 Lloyd's Rep 297 at p 300.

[197] *Re United Medical Protection Ltd* [2002] NSWSC 413, 41 ACSR 623, at [16].

[198] See Edward Husband, 'Application by a petitioning creditor for the appointment of a provisional liquidator: recent clarification of the basis on which an appointment will be made' (2000) 16 Insolv L & P 3.

[199] *Re T and L Trading (Aust) Pty Ltd* (1986) 10 ACLR 388; *Re McLennan Holdings Pty Ltd* (1983) 7 ACLR 732; *Re New Cap Reinsurance Corporation Holdings Ltd* (1999) 32 ACSR 234.

[200] *Telfer v Astarra Securities Pty Ltd* [2010] NSWSC 682 at [12].

[201] *Re United Medical Protection Ltd* [2002] NSWSC 413, 41 ACSR 623, at [3].

Where there are no directors

4.84   The fact that there are no directors capable of acting and no prospect of any being appointed is a reason for appointing a provisional liquidator.[202]

Appointment to manage company's run-down

4.85   In *Re W F Fearman Ltd*[203] the company, which carried on business as building contractors, was obviously insolvent and it was clear that it was not a suitable case for making an administration order. Joint provisional liquidators were appointed in order to manage an orderly withdrawal from the company's construction sites. But in two other reported cases, courts have not been convinced that provisional liquidation for the purpose of completing a construction company's contracts would be in the interest of creditors.[204]

4.86   In *Re Tamaris plc*[205] the court refused to appoint a provisional liquidator to manage a company in financial difficulty so as to relieve the directors of potential liability for wrongful acts.

Appointment so as to stay litigation

4.87   Usually the court will not appoint a provisional liquidator of a company merely for the purpose of activating IA 1986, s 130(2), to impose a stay on proceedings against the company.[206] The company should instead apply for a stay under s 126(1).[207]

Application not Supported by the Company

The court's attitude

4.88   If an application for the appointment of a provisional liquidator is made which is not supported by the company, the applicant must show circumstances justifying the appointment.[208] However, as an interim remedy, it is granted by the court before the facts of the case have been determined, and it is:

> one of the most intrusive interim remedies in the court's armoury. In many, if not most, cases its effect will be to stop the company trading; and to cause the company's employees to lose their jobs.[209]

4.89   The need to make the appointment must overtop its serious consequences.[210] Appointment of a provisional liquidator is not an order to be made lightly and requires most anxious consideration by the court.[211] As with granting an interim injunction, the basic or overriding principle is that the court should take whichever course seems likely to cause the

---

[202] *CIC Insurance Ltd v Hannan and Co Pty Ltd* [2001] NSWSC 437, 38 ACSR 245; *Telfer v Astarra Securities Pty Ltd* [2010] NSWSC 682.

[203] (1987) 4 BCC 139.

[204] *Deputy Commissioner of Taxation v Status Constructions Pty Ltd* (1987) 12 ACLR 689; *Re Coolfadda Developers Ltd* [2009] IESC 54, [2010] 1 ILRM 342.

[205] (ChD 15 December 1999) discussed in Edward Husband, 'Application by a petitioning creditor for the appointment of a provisional liquidator: recent clarification of the basis on which an appointment will be made' (2000) 16 Insolv L & P 3.

[206] *Re McLennan Holdings Pty Ltd* (1983) 7 ACLR 732; *Re Namco UK Ltd* [2003] EWHC 989 (Ch), [2003] 2 BCLC 78.

[207] *Re Namco UK Ltd*.

[208] *Re Hammersmith Town Hall Co* (1877) 6 ChD 122; *Re Union Accident Insurance Co Ltd* [1972] 1 Lloyd's Rep 297 at p 300; *Re Trinbar Ltd* (1978) 13 Barb LR 184.

[209] *Commissioners of HM Revenue and Customs v Rochdale Drinks Distributors Ltd* [2011] EWCA Civ 1116, [2012] 1 BCLC 748, at [109].

[210] *Re Highfield Commodities Ltd* [1985] 1 WLR 149 per Megarry V-C at p 159.

[211] *Commissioners of HM Revenue and Customs v Rochdale Drinks Distributors Ltd* at [76] and [110].

least irremediable prejudice to one party or the other. Among the matters which the court may take into account are the prejudice which the claimant may suffer if the remedy is not granted or the defendant may suffer if it is; the likelihood of such prejudice actually occurring; the extent to which it may be compensated by an award of damages or enforcement of the undertaking in damages; the likelihood of either party being able to satisfy such an award; and the likelihood that the remedy will turn out to have been wrongly granted or withheld, that is to say, the court's opinion of the relative strength of the parties' cases.[212]

4.90 The court may need to consider the commercial realities which may prompt the appointment of a provisional liquidator, the degree of urgency, the need established by the applicant and the balance of convenience.[213] An appointment should not be made if other measures would be adequate to preserve the status quo.[214]

4.91 Stronger evidence is required if the application is without notice to the company than if the company is represented.[215]

4.92 It is an unusual and drastic step to appoint a provisional liquidator of a solvent company.[216]

4.93 The court must consider all the circumstances of the case.[217] Sometimes it is necessary to balance many conflicting considerations, as in *Re Adnot Pty Ltd*;[218] *Clemada Pty Ltd v Hire It Pty Ltd (No 2)*;[219] and *Constantinidis v JGL Trading Pty Ltd*,[220] in which Kirby P emphasized that a decision has to be made quickly which may mean not exploring all the arguments fully.

4.94 From some of the reported cases a generalized description of some particular circumstances justifying appointment of a provisional liquidator may be drawn to serve as a guide in future cases.[221]

Protection of assets

4.95 On a creditor's winding-up petition, a provisional liquidator will probably be appointed if it is shown that the assets of the company are being, or are likely to be, dissipated to the detriment of the company's creditors or it is otherwise necessary to protect the assets.[222]

---

[212] *National Commercial Bank Jamaica Ltd v Olint Corpn Ltd* [2009] UKPC 16, [2009] 1 WLR 1405, at [17]–[18]; *Commissioners of HM Revenue and Customs v Rochdale Drinks Distributors Ltd* at [109].
[213] *Re Club Mediterranean Pty Ltd* (1975) 11 SASR 481 at pp 483–4; *Re Five Lakes Investment Co Ltd* [1985] HKLR 273 at p 284; *Re I-China Holdings Ltd* [2003] 1 HKLRD 629 at p 634; *Re Jinro (HK) International Ltd* [2003] 3 HKLRD 459 at p 463; *Lubavitch Mazal Pty Ltd v Yeshiva Properties No 1 Pty Ltd* [2003] NSWSC 535, 47 ACSR 197.
[214] *Zempilas v J N Taylor Holdings Ltd (No 2)* (1990) 55 SASR 103 at p 106.
[215] *Re Club Mediterranean Pty Ltd* (1975) 11 SASR 481; *Riviana (Aust) Pty Ltd v Laospac Trading Pty Ltd* (1986) 10 ACLR 865.
[216] *Re Yick Fung Estates Ltd* [1986] HKLR 240; *Broadby v Vecon Pty Ltd* [1982] TasR 91.
[217] *Re Stewardship Credit Arbitrage Fund Ltd* (2008) 73 WIR 136.
[218] (1982) 7 ACLR 212.
[219] (1990) 3 ACSR 202.
[220] (1995) 17 ACSR 625.
[221] See 4.95–4.107.
[222] *Re Marseilles Extension Railway and Land Co* [1867] WN 68; *Re Hammersmith Town Hall Co* (1877) 6 ChD 112; *Re Milford Co-operative Store Society Ltd* (1901) 7 IWLR 55; *Re Scott-Brown Industries Pty Ltd* (1981) 6 ACLR 342; *United States Surgical Corporation v Ballabil Holdings Pty Ltd* (1985) 9 ACLR 904; *Ah Toy v Registrar of Companies (NT)* (1986) 72 ALR 107 at pp 115–21; *Re a Company (No 00359 of 1987)* [1988] Ch 210; *Re Norfolk Island Shipping Line Pty Ltd* (1988) 14 ACLR 229; *Robert Bryce and Co Ltd v Chicken and Food Distributors Ltd* (1990) 5 NZCLC 66,648; *Re a Company (No 003102 of 1991)* [1991] BCLC 539;

A provisional liquidator may be appointed to protect assets which are outside the jurisdiction.[223] In *Re a Company (No 003102 of 1991)*[224] Harman J said, at p 542:

> If there is a risk of assets being dissipated—that is made away with other than by the rateable distribution amongst all the company's creditors at the date of presentation of the winding-up petition—there must be a good case for the court appointing its own officers, for that is what provisional liquidators are, to try and get in and secure the assets so that if, at the end of the day, the company is put into compulsory liquidation,... then there will be assets available and they will not have been dissipated. It is not a dissipation in the *Mareva* sense of deliberately making away with the assets[225] but any serious risk that the assets may not continue to be available to the company.

4.96 An example of a risk of assets becoming unavailable to creditors is where an insolvent company continues to trade without an anticipatory validation order.[226]

4.97 On a contributory's winding-up petition, a provisional liquidator will probably be appointed if it is shown that the assets of the company are being, or are likely to be, dissipated to the detriment of the petitioner.[227] In *Re Trinbar Ltd*[228] allegations of past misappropriations were insufficient to justify appointment of a provisional liquidator. In *Re Back 2 Bay 6 Pty Ltd*[229] there was a sufficient circumstantial case to satisfy the court that independent supervision was necessary to protect the contributory's interest in the company where the judge had discerned 'irrational and possibly hysterical attitudes on both sides' of the dispute.[230] A provisional liquidator who finds that concerns of this kind are unfounded may apply to be discharged.[231]

4.98 On an application to wind up a company in a group by a liquidator of another company in the group, where there are inevitably inter-company debts and cross-guarantees, if there is a risk of assets being dissipated, it may not be necessary to show it is likely that a winding-up order will be made,[232] though it is submitted that in these circumstances the appointment is made on the assumption, based on experience, that during the provisional liquidation evidence will be found to justify a winding-up order.

Protection of persons dealing with the company

4.99 On a creditor's petition, a provisional liquidator will probably be appointed if it is shown that the company is insolvent and a provisional liquidator should be appointed to protect

---

PT Anekapangan Dwitama v Far East Food Industries Sdn Bhd [1995] 1 MLJ 21; *Commonwealth v Hendon Industrial Park Pty Ltd* (1995) 17 ACSR 358; *Emanuele v Australian Securities Commission* (1995) 141 ALR 506; *Re I-China Holdings Ltd* [2003] 1 HKLRD 629.

[223] *Re a Company (No 00359 of 1987)* [1988] Ch 210; *Re a Company (No 003102 of 1991)* [1991] BCLC 539.

[224] [1991] BCLC 539.

[225] At the time of this judgment, freezing injunctions were called *Mareva* injunctions or orders after *Mareva Compañía Naviera SA v International Bulk Carriers SA* [1980] 1 All ER 213. For the limitation of *Mareva* injunctions to prevention of deliberate removal see *Searose Ltd v Seatrain UK Ltd* [1981] 1 WLR 894 at p 897.

[226] *Commissioners of HM Revenue and Customs v Rochdale Drinks Distributors Ltd* [2011] EWCA Civ 1116, [2012] 1 BCLC 748, at [99].

[227] *Levy v Napier* 1962 SC 468; *Teague* 1985 SLT 469; *South Downs Packers Pty Ltd v Beaver* (1984) 8 ACLR 990; *Re Nerang Investments Pty Ltd* (1985) 9 ACLR 646; *Re Bike World (Wholesale) Pty Ltd* (1992) 6 ACSR 681.

[228] (1978) 13 Barb LR 184.

[229] (1994) 12 ACSR 614.

[230] At p 616.

[231] *Re Back 2 Bay 6 Pty Ltd* at p 616.

[232] *Emanuele v Australian Securities Commission* (1995) 141 ALR 506.

persons who deal with the company[233] especially where it appears that the company's directors should not be allowed to continue to have control of it.[234] These circumstances also justify appointment of a provisional liquidator on a public interest petition.[235]

Investigation

On a creditor's petition, if there are significant concerns about the integrity of the company's management and the quality of its accounting and record-keeping, a provisional liquidator may be appointed to take control of books and records and investigate the company's transactions.[236]   **4.100**

In *Re Latreefers Inc*[237] Lloyd J, on a creditor's petition, appointed a provisional liquidator of a foreign company to investigate whether there was a reasonable possibility that a liquidator could recover contributions under IA 1986, s 213 (fraudulent trading) and/or s 214 (wrongful trading), which would determine whether a winding-up order could be made. This seems to be a notable extension of the circumstances in which a provisional liquidator may be appointed.   **4.101**

Deadlock

On a contributory's petition, a provisional liquidator will probably be appointed if it is shown that there is deadlock in the company's management.[238] In *Bulktec Pty Ltd v Geothetis Pty Ltd*[239] the application to appoint a provisional liquidator prompted the warring parties to cooperate in carrying out essential administrative tasks rather than waste the company's funds on employing a provisional liquidator.   **4.102**

Administrative vacuum

In *Re Qintex Ltd (No 3)*[240] a decision was urgently required on an important contract with the company but the company did not have sufficient directors to form a quorum. Although all the company's assets were under the control of an administrative receiver, a provisional liquidator was appointed on the application of a creditor petitioner and a supporting creditor so that there would be a person with authority to deal with the contract on behalf of the company.   **4.103**

To provide alternative management

In *Hongkong and Shanghai Banking Corporation Ltd v Kemajuan Bersatu Enterprise Sdn Bhd*[241] provisional liquidators were appointed to a property development company so that   **4.104**

---

[233] *Re London Trading Bank Ltd* (1910) *The Times*, 28 November 1910; *Wine Grapes Marketing Board for the City of Griffith and the Shires of Leeton, Carrathool and Murrumbidgee v Griffith Vintners Pty Ltd* (1989) 1 ACSR 88.

[234] *Re Brackland Magazines Ltd* [1994] 1 BCLC 190, in which the directors were ordered to pay the costs of the application for the appointment of a provisional liquidator; *Re Global SDR Technologies Pty Ltd* [2004] VSC 402, 51 ACSR 42.

[235] *Australian Securities Commission v Solomon* (1996) 19 ACSR 75.

[236] *Commissioners of HM Revenue and Customs v Rochdale Drinks Distributors Ltd* [2011] EWCA Civ 1116, [2012] 1 BCLC 748, at [100] and [113].

[237] [1999] 1 BCLC 271.

[238] *Re Five Lakes Investment Co Ltd* [1985] HKLR 273; *Re Bike World (Wholesale) Pty Ltd* (1992) 6 ACSR 681.

[239] (1994) 13 ACSR 716.

[240] (1990) 2 ACSR 627.

[241] [1992] 2 MLJ 370.

development of an abandoned housing estate could be restarted in cooperation with a government-sponsored agency which refused to deal with the company's former directors.

Danger of prejudice to contributory petitioner

4.105 On a contributory's petition, a provisional liquidator will probably be appointed if it is shown that the persons with de facto control of the company could act to the prejudice of the petitioner.[242] In *Kelly v Tsakirios and Kelly Pty Ltd*[243] the applicant failed to prove this circumstance. The independence and neutrality of the person appointed will usually be sufficient guard against factional advantage but the court will avoid making an appointment that would give an unjustified procedural or tactical advantage to one faction.[244] In *Re Fan Bostic Construction Ltd*[245] allegations that the personal relationship in a quasi-partnership company had broken down were insufficient to justify appointment of a provisional liquidator: the court observed that the company had been extremely successful and could be embarrassed by an appointment.

Public interest

4.106 On a public interest winding-up petition, a provisional liquidator will probably be appointed if it is shown that it is in the public interest for an independent person to take control of the company's affairs.[246] An appointment sought on this ground was refused in *Re Forrester and Lamego Ltd*:[247]

> [T]he public interest must be given full weight, though it is not to be regarded as being conclusive.[248]

Removal of voluntary liquidator

4.107 On a creditor's petition, a provisional liquidator will probably be appointed if it is shown that a voluntary liquidator of the company presently in office should be displaced,[249] and similarly on a public interest petition.[250]

Applicant's private advantage not enough

4.108 In *Natwest Australia Bank Ltd v Glen Pacific Pty Ltd*[251] the company was, in separate proceedings, disputing the debt claimed by the applicant for the winding-up order. The applicant asked for the appointment of a provisional liquidator in the hope that the provisional liquidator would discontinue the proceedings disputing its debt. The court refused to

---

[242] *McCabe v Andrew Middleton (Enterprises) Ltd* 1969 SLT (Sh Ct) 29; *Re Commercial Pacific Lumber Exports Pty Ltd* [1971–72] P&NGLR 178; *Re Centre Restaurant Pty Ltd* (1982) 6 ACLR 481; *Rural Industries Co-operative Society Ltd v Porky Pigs Pty Ltd* (1988) 12 ACLR 794; *Zempilas v J N Taylor Holdings Ltd (No 2)* (1990) 55 SASR 103.

[243] (1992) 110 FLR 202.

[244] *Re Hill and Plummer (Merchants) Ltd* [1956] NZLR 979.

[245] (1981) 16 Barb LR 97.

[246] *Re Union Accident Insurance Co Ltd* [1972] 1 Lloyd's Rep 297; *McCormack v Landbase Nominees Ltd* (1988) 4 NZCLC 64,631; *Securities and Investments Board v Lancashire and Yorkshire Portfolio Management Ltd* [1992] BCLC 281; *Re Pinstripe Farming Co Ltd* [1996] 2 BCLC 295; *Securities and Futures Commission v Mandarin Resources Corporation Ltd* [1997] HKLRD 405; *Re a Company (No 7151 of 2000)* (2000) LTL 27/11/2000; *Re Treasure Traders Corporation Ltd* [2005] EWHC 2774 (Ch), LTL 8/12/2005.

[247] [1997] 2 BCLC 155.

[248] *Re Highfield Commodities Ltd* [1985] 1 WLR 149 per Megarry V-C at p 159.

[249] *Re P Turner (Wilsden) Ltd* [1987] BCLC 149. See 10.108.

[250] *Securities and Investments Board v Lancashire and Yorkshire Portfolio Management Ltd* [1992] BCLC 281; *Re Pinstripe Farming Co Ltd* [1996] 2 BCLC 295; *Re a Company (No 007070 of 1996)* [1997] 2 BCLC 139.

[251] (1992) 6 ACSR 711.

appoint a provisional liquidator observing (a) that the petition, being a disputed debt petition, was unlikely to succeed, and (b) as the applicant had already appointed an administrative receiver of the company, it was unlikely that the company's resources would be used to pursue the proceedings against the applicant.

In *Re TransTec Automotive (Campsie) Ltd*[252] there was an attempt to get a provisional liquidator of a company appointed in the hope that he would charge a lower price to the applicant for the company's product than its administrative receivers were seeking. The attempt failed as the court pointed out that it was the duty of both the administrative receivers and a provisional liquidator to try to obtain the best price. **4.109**

Order of Appointment

Form of Order

The order appointing a provisional liquidator of a company should be in form 4.15 in sch 4 to IR 1986 and it must specify the functions to be carried out by the provisional liquidator in relation to the company's affairs.[253] The appointment of a provisional liquidator may be made on such terms as the court thinks fit.[254] **4.110**

The order appointing a provisional bank or building society liquidator may be made on such terms as the court thinks fit[255] and must specify the functions to be carried out by the provisional liquidator in relation to the institution's affairs.[256] **4.111**

The appointment of a provisional liquidator takes effect from the first moment of the day on which it is made.[257] **4.112**

In *Re Latreefers Inc*[258] Lloyd J appointed a provisional liquidator on a creditor's petition and refused to exclude from the provisional liquidator's powers the conduct of the company's litigation against the petitioner, saying, at p 284, that dealing with conflicting opposed interests 'is something which insolvency practitioners can and do cope with'. **4.113**

Transmission

Having made an order appointing a provisional liquidator of a company, the court must, as soon as reasonably practicable, give notice of the appointment to the official receiver.[259] If the appointed provisional liquidator is not the official receiver, the court must send a copy of the notice to the appointee.[260] The court will send a sealed copy of the order to the person appointed as provisional liquidator, and (if the person appointed is not the official receiver) to the official receiver, and to the company's administrative receiver, if there is **4.114**

---

[252] [2001] BCC 403.
[253] IR 1986, r 4.26(1).
[254] r 4.25(4).
[255] Bank Insolvency (England and Wales) Rules 2009 (SI 2009/356), r 20(4); Building Society Insolvency (England and Wales) Rules 2010 (SI 2010/2581), r 20(3).
[256] SI 2009/356, r 22(1); SI 2010/2581, r 22(1).
[257] *Sayer v Capital Aviation Ltd* (1993) 6 NZCLC 68,372 at p 68,374.
[258] [1999] 1 BCLC 271.
[259] IR 1986, r 4.25A(1).
[260] r 4.25A(2).

one.[261] Further sealed copies are provided to the provisional liquidator to be sent to the company (or to its voluntary liquidator, if there is one) and to Companies House.[262]

4.115 An order appointing the official receiver provisional liquidator cannot be issued until the amount directed by the court to cover the official receiver's remuneration and expenses is deposited or secured.[263]

4.116 When a provisional bank or building society liquidator has been appointed, the court must notify the applicant and the person appointed.[264] Immediately after the order is made, the court must send four sealed copies of the order (or more if requested by the provisional liquidator) to the provisional liquidator[265] and must, if practicable, immediately send a copy electronically.[266] The provisional liquidator must serve one of the sealed copies on the institution at its registered office if it is a bank or its principal office if it is a building society and, if the email address is known, send an electronic copy.[267] Other sealed copies must be sent to the Bank of England, the FCA, the PRA if the institution is a PRA-authorized person and the Financial Services Compensation Scheme,[268] to the registrar of companies (bank insolvency only),[269] to any administrative receiver of the institution[270] and the supervisor of any voluntary arrangement.[271] The electronic copy must be sent as soon as practicable and the sealed copy must be sent by first class post on the business day on which the order is served on the institution.[272]

Public Notification

4.117 A provisional liquidator must, unless the court orders otherwise, gazette[273] notice of his or her appointment, as soon as reasonably practicable after receiving the notice of appointment given by the court.[274] The appointment may also be advertised in such other manner as the provisional liquidator thinks fit.[275] The same applies to a provisional bank liquidator[276] and a provisional building society liquidator.[277] The contents of a notice of appointment in the *London Gazette* are specified in IR 1986, rr 4.25A(4), 12A.33, 12A.34 and 12A.36.[278] The contents of a notice that is advertised in any other way are specified in rr 4.25A(4), 12A.38, 12A.39 and 12A.41.[279]

---

[261] IR 1986, r 4.26(2).

[262] r 4.26(2) and (3).

[263] r 4.27(1); see 4.135.

[264] Bank Insolvency (England and Wales) Rules 2009 (SI 2009/356), r 21(1); Building Society Insolvency (England and Wales) Rules 2010 (SI 2010/2581), r 21(1).

[265] SI 2009/356, r 22(2); SI 2010/2581, r 22(2).

[266] SI 2009/356, r 22(3); SI 2010/2581, r 22(3).

[267] SI 2009/356, r 22(4); SI 2010/2581, r 22(4). 'Registered office' of a bank is defined in SI 2009/356, r 8(3) (see 3.42), only for the purposes of r 8(2). 'Principal office' of a building society is defined at 1.532.

[268] SI 2009/356, r 22(5)(a) (see r 3(2) for the definition of 'the appropriate regulator'); SI 2010/2581, r 22(5)(a)–(c) (see r 3(2) for the definition of 'the appropriate regulator').

[269] SI 2009/356, r 22(5)(b).

[270] SI 2009/356, r 22(5)(c); SI 2010/2581, r 22(5)(e).

[271] SI 2009/356, r 22(5)(d); SI 2010/2581, r 22(5)(d).

[272] SI 2009/356, r 22(6); SI 2010/2581, r 22(6).

[273] 'Gazette' means advertise once in the *London Gazette* (IR 1986, r 13.13(4) and (4A)).

[274] r 4.25A(3). Notice is given by the court under r 4.25A(1); see 4.114.

[275] r 4.25A(3)(b).

[276] SI 2009/356, r 21(2).

[277] SI 2010/2581, r 21(2).

[278] See r 13.13(4B)(a).

[279] See r 13.13(4B)(b).

A sealed copy of the order appointing a provisional liquidator must be forwarded by the **4.118** appointee to Companies House.[280]

If the winding-up proceedings in which a provisional liquidator is appointed are subject **4.119** to Regulation (EC) No 1346/2000, the appointment is a judgment opening insolvency proceedings[281] and the provisional liquidator is a liquidator.[282] Accordingly the notification provisions of arts 21, 22 and 40 apply.[283]

The provisions for notification discussed at 5.265–5.273 apply when a United Kingdom **4.120** court appoints a provisional liquidator of a UK insurer, third country insurer, UK credit institution or third country credit institution.

Joint Provisional Liquidators

If two or more persons are appointed joint provisional liquidators of a company, the order **4.121** of appointment must state whether any act required or authorized under any enactment to be done by the provisional liquidator is to be done by all or any one or more of the persons for the time being holding the office.[284]

Defective Appointment

The acts of an individual as provisional liquidator of a company are deemed to be valid **4.122** despite any defect in his or her appointment.[285] In applying a provision of this type it is necessary to distinguish between an appointment in which there is a defect and no appointment at all.[286]

If a court erroneously decides that it has jurisdiction to appoint a provisional liquidator **4.123** when it does not, the appointment is valid until rescinded or reversed on appeal.[287] The provisional liquidator is validly appointed until the appointment is set aside.[288] In *Re Deisara Pty Ltd*[289] the Supreme Court of the Northern Territory had somehow been persuaded to appoint a Mr Jackson as 'liquidator' of a company even though no application had been made to wind up the company. Mildren J held that Mr Jackson must have been appointed as provisional liquidator, and held that the appointment was valid, and Mr Jackson's acts were valid, until the appointment was rescinded. Furthermore the Australian equivalent of IA 1986, s 232, applied because the appointment was not void *ab initio*. Accordingly Mr Jackson actually was a provisional liquidator and so was entitled to remuneration under a statutory provision that 'A provisional liquidator is entitled to receive such remuneration by way of percentage or otherwise as is determined by the court'. On the remuneration point *Re Deisara Pty Ltd* did not follow *Starr v Trafalgar Financial Corporation Ltd (No 2)*, but was

---

[280] IR 1986, r 4.26(2) and (3).
[281] *Re Eurofood IFSC Ltd* (case C-341/04) [2006] Ch 508.
[282] art 2(b) and annex C.
[283] See 5.256–5.258.
[284] IA 1986, s 231.
[285] IA 1986, s 232.
[286] *Morris v Kanssen* [1946] AC 459, dealing with what is now the Companies Act 2006, s 161, concerning defective appointments of directors.
[287] *Strachan v Gleaner Co Ltd* [2005] UKPC 33, [2005] 1 WLR 3204. See 1.504–1.506.
[288] *Starr v Trafalgar Financial Corporation Ltd (No 2)* (1983) 8 ACLR 367, in which the court had appointed a provisional liquidator of a company which it did not have jurisdiction to wind up.
[289] (1992) 107 FLR 235.

followed in *Davidson v Global Investments International Ltd*,[290] in which the court had not had jurisdiction to wind up the company.

4.124 If a provisional liquidator is appointed by a court before it has had an opportunity to consider a claim that it does not have jurisdiction, the appointment would, it is submitted, be valid, as in *Re A B and Co (No 2)*,[291] which is discussed at 1.502.

Remuneration and Expenses

Provisional Liquidator Other than the Official Receiver

Fixing remuneration

4.125 The remuneration of a provisional liquidator who is not the official receiver will be fixed by the court, from time to time, on the provisional liquidator's application.[292] When a provisional liquidator's appointment terminates, the court may give such directions as it thinks fit with respect to the accounts of his or her administration.[293] These rules also apply to a provisional bank or building society liquidator.[294] Remuneration does not include expenses. A provisional liquidator is entitled to reimbursement of his or her expenses and the amounts do not have to be fixed by the court, though they may be challenged.[295] Remuneration and expenses may be reviewed either when fixing remuneration or when reviewing accounts on termination of appointment.[296]

4.126 Remuneration can only be reasonable remuneration.[297] A provisional liquidator must justify a claim to remuneration by reference to adequate records of work done.[298] In fixing remuneration the court must take into account:[299]

(a) the time properly given by the provisional liquidator and his or her staff in attending to the company's affairs;
(b) the complexity (or otherwise) of the case;
(c) any respects in which, in connection with the company's affairs, there falls on the provisional liquidator any responsibility of an exceptional kind or degree;
(d) the effectiveness with which the provisional liquidator appears to be carrying out, or to have carried out, his or her duties; and
(e) the value and nature of the property with which the provisional liquidator has to deal.

---

[290] (1996) 19 ACSR 332.
[291] [1900] 2 QB 429.
[292] IR 1986, r 4.30(1). In Hong Kong it has been held that the court also has an inherent jurisdiction (*Re Peregrine Investments Holdings Ltd (No 4)* [1999] 2 HKLRD 722; *Re Express Builders Co Ltd* [2005] 1 HKLRD 92).
[293] IR 1986, r 4.31(2).
[294] IR 1986, rr 4.28 and 4.29, applied by the Bank Insolvency (England and Wales) Rules 2009 (SI 2009/356), rr 25 and 26, and modified by r 3(3)(b) and (4)(f), (i), (l) and (o). IR 1986, rr 4.28 and 4.29, applied by the Building Society Insolvency (England and Wales) Rules 2010 (SI 2010/2581), rr 23 and 24, and modified by r 3(5)(b) and (6)(h), (k), (n) and (q).
[295] *Venetian Nominees Pty Ltd v Conlan* (1998) 20 WAR 96.
[296] *Jacob v UIC Insurance Co Ltd* [2006] EWHC 2717 (Ch), [2007] Bus LR 568.
[297] *Venetian Nominees Pty Ltd v Conlan* (1998) 20 WAR 96 at p 99 ('fair and reasonable'); *Jacob v UIC Insurance Co Ltd* [2006] EWHC 2717 (Ch), [2007] Bus LR 568, per Peter Smith J at [73].
[298] *Jacob v UIC Insurance Co Ltd* [2006] EWHC 2717 (Ch), [2007] Bus LR 568, at [76].
[299] IR 1986, r 4.30(2).

A self-employed consultant is not a member of the provisional liquidator's staff.[300]   **4.127**

The requirement to take account of the provisional liquidator's effectiveness does not mean   **4.128**
that the provisional liquidator is entitled to a success fee and is not a reason for awarding
remuneration that has been claimed but has not been justified.[301]

There is a detailed statement of the court's practice in Practice Direction (PD) Insolvency   **4.129**
Proceedings 2014, para 21.[302]

There was formerly a practice of ordering, very shortly after appointing a provisional liquid-   **4.130**
ator, that he or she could draw remuneration on a time cost basis in accordance with his or
her normal hourly rates. This is no longer done.[303]

Payment of remuneration

If a winding-up order is made, the provisional liquidator's remuneration and expenses must   **4.131**
be paid as an expense of the liquidation, 'in the prescribed order of priority'.[304] In fact
there is a prescribed priority only for the provisional liquidator's remuneration,[305] not the
expenses. 'Expenses' in r 4.30(3) means expenses paid by the provisional liquidator out of
his or her own pocket or for which he or she is personally liable.[306]

In *Re Grey Marlin Ltd*[307] the learned deputy judge held that the expenses of a provisional   **4.132**
liquidator of a company which was being wound up by the court and had insufficient assets
to satisfy its liabilities were expenses incurred in the winding up to which IA 1986, s 156,
applied. Under s 156 the court could make an order concerning the payment out of the
assets of the expenses in such order of priority as the court thought just. The order made
was that expenses incurred by the provisional liquidator in preserving, realizing or getting in any of the company's assets ranked before item (a) in the list in IR 1986, r 4.218(3),
and other necessary disbursements ranked before item (f). It is submitted that the result
achieved by the order in *Re Grey Marlin Ltd* was correct. However, the decision has been
put in doubt, because it was not cited to the House of Lords in *Re Toshoku Finance UK
plc*,[308] in which Lord Hoffmann (with whom the other Law Lords agreed) said that r 4.218
sets out a complete list of the expenses which are payable out of the assets of a company in
liquidation, subject only to other provisions of IR 1986, and the court's only power under
IA 1986, s 156, is to modify the order of priority of items in the list, not to add items to it. It
may be argued that Lord Hoffmann's view on this point is obiter, but it leaves the status of

---

[300] *Jacob v UIC Insurance Co Ltd* [2006] EWHC 2717 (Ch), [2007] Bus LR 568.
[301] *Jacob v UIC Insurance Co Ltd* [2006] EWHC 2717 (Ch), [2007] Bus LR 568.
[302] See Stephen Baister, 'Remuneration, the insolvency practitioner and the courts' (2006) 22 Insolv L &
P 50. PD Insolvency Proceedings 2014, para 21, was formerly Practice Statement: The Fixing and Approval
of the Remuneration of Appointees [2004] BCC 912, [2004] BPIR 953. For the history of attempts by the
court to control insolvency office-holders' remuneration see *Brook v Reed* [2011] EWCA Civ 331, [2012] 1
WLR 419.
[303] *Re Goodwill Merchant Financial Services Ltd* [2001] 1 BCLC 259; *Re Independent Insurance Co Ltd*
[2002] EWHC 1577 (Ch), [2002] 2 BCLC 709; *Jacob v UIC Insurance Co Ltd* [2006] EWHC 2717 (Ch),
[2007] Bus LR 568, at [73].
[304] IR 1986, r 4.30(3).
[305] Item (f) in the list in r 4.218(3).
[306] *Re Grey Marlin Ltd* [2000] 1 WLR 370.
[307] [2000] 1 WLR 370.
[308] [2002] UKHL 6, [2002] 1 WLR 671.

provisional liquidators' expenses unnecessarily uncertain. IR 1986 should be amended to reflect the decision in *Re Grey Marlin Ltd.*

4.133 A more general approach is that payment of the remuneration and expenses of an individual who is or has been a provisional liquidator of a company is secured by an equitable lien on the company's assets that he or she has administered.[309]Accordingly, if the company is subsequently ordered to be wound up, the provisional liquidator can realize his or her security in priority to all unsecured creditors, and payment from the assets subject to the lien is not governed by IR 1986, r 4.218. If assets of the company are recovered after the provisional liquidator's appointment has ended, those assets will not be subject to the provisional liquidator's lien.

Official Receiver

Fixing of remuneration

4.134 The remuneration of the official receiver as provisional liquidator is fixed by the Insolvency Regulations 1994,[310] reg 35.

Payment of remuneration

4.135 An order appointing the official receiver provisional liquidator cannot be issued until an amount directed by the court to cover the official receiver's remuneration and expenses is deposited with the official receiver, or is otherwise secured to the official receiver's satisfaction.[311] On an application by the Secretary of State in connection with a public interest winding-up petition, the practice is not to require a deposit.[312]

4.136 From time to time the official receiver may apply to the court to order a further amount to be deposited or secured, and if the order is not complied with within two business days of service the court may discharge the official receiver's appointment as provisional liquidator.[313]

4.137 If, after an order appointing the official receiver provisional liquidator of a company is made, the company is ordered to be wound up by the court and the assets available for payment of the expenses of the liquidation are insufficient for payment of the provisional liquidator's remuneration and expenses, they must be paid out of the deposit paid to the official receiver.[314] If the deposit is not required for the payment of the provisional liquidator's remuneration and expenses, it must be repaid to the person who lodged it (or as that person may direct).[315] The prescribed order of priority for this repayment is item (g) in r 4.218(3), that is, it ranks after the remuneration of the provisional liquidator.

No Winding-up Order Made

4.138 If no winding-up order is made, a provisional liquidator's remuneration and expenses must be paid out of the property of the company, subject to any order of the court as to costs.[316]

---

[309] *Re Pac-Asian Services Pte Ltd* [1987] SLR 542; *Shirlaw v Taylor* (1991) 102 ALR 551.
[310] SI 1994/2507.
[311] IR 1986, r 4.27(1).
[312] *Re a Company (No 001951 of 1987)* [1988] BCLC 182.
[313] IR 1986, r 4.27(2). The clear days rule in CPR, r 2.8(2) and (3), applies (see 1.510). 'Business day' is defined in IR 1986, r 13.13(1) (see 1.512).
[314] rr 4.27(3) and 4.30(3).
[315] r 4.27(3).
[316] IR 1986, r 4.30(3)(a).

Remuneration and expenses payable out of the company's property are part of the company's costs of the proceedings on the petition.[317] However, they must be paid by the company, even if the petition is dismissed, unless there are circumstances in which it is right to order that they are to be paid by the petitioner (or whoever else is ordered to pay the company's costs).[318] The fact that the petitioner did not have standing to present the petition may be a reason for including a provisional liquidator's remuneration and expenses in the costs payable by the petitioner.[319] Unless the court otherwise directs, the provisional liquidator may retain out of the company's property such sums or property as are or may be required for meeting his or her remuneration and expenses.[320] The official receiver may, it seems, be paid out of the deposit if the company's assets are insufficient, though since this would mean that the company was unable to pay its debts it would be unlikely that a winding-up order would not be made. The rules do not explicitly provide for the return of the deposit if a winding-up order is not made but, of course, it is paid to the official receiver for a specific purpose and if not used for that purpose is held on trust for the depositor.

Appointment Ended before Substantive Hearing of Petition

If a provisional liquidator's appointment is discharged before the fate of the petition is determined, the court has power under IR 1986, r 4.31(2), to direct that the provisional liquidator's expenses and remuneration are to be paid out of the company's assets.[321] **4.139**

Functions and Powers of a Provisional Liquidator

If a provisional liquidator is thought of as a liquidator appointed provisionally[322] then a provisional liquidator would be entitled to exercise all the powers of a liquidator acting after a winding-up order has been made,[323] but most of those powers are appropriate for the actual liquidation of a company rather than for the maintenance of the status quo which is the primary purpose of appointing a provisional liquidator. **4.140**

The powers conferred on a compulsory liquidator by IA 1986, s 167, would, in any case, seem to be not available to a provisional liquidator because the section is expressed to apply 'where a company is being wound up by the court'[324] and this will not be the situation until a winding-up order is made.[325] **4.141**

A provisional liquidator carries out such functions as are conferred by the court[326] and those functions are to be specified in the court's order of appointment,[327] and that order may limit **4.142**

---

[317] *Graham v John Tullis and Son (Plastics) Ltd (No 2)* 1992 SLT 514. In Scotland, costs are called judicial expenses.

[318] IR 1986, r 4.30(3)(a); *Re a Company (No 001951 of 1987)* [1988] BCLC 182.

[319] *Graham v John Tullis and Son (Plastics) Ltd (No 2)* 1992 SLT 514.

[320] IR 1986, r 4.30(3A).

[321] *Re UOC Corporation* [1997] 2 BCLC 569.

[322] See 4.25.

[323] *Re Chateau Hotels Ltd* [1977] 1 NZLR 381.

[324] s 167(1).

[325] See 5.294–5.298.

[326] IA 1986, s 135(4). Applied to provisional bank liquidators by the Banking Act 2009, s 103(3), (4) and table, and to provisional building society liquidators by the Building Societies Act 1986, s 90C.

[327] IR 1986, r 4.26(1). The same provision is made in relation to provisional bank insolvency liquidators by the Bank Insolvency (England and Wales) Rules 2009 (SI 2009/356), r 22(1), and in relation to

the provisional liquidator's powers.[328] When a provisional liquidator is appointed on an application made without notice to the company, powers are usually limited so that nothing irreversible (such as dismissing employees or selling non-perishable assets) can be done.

4.143 On appointment, a provisional liquidator of a company must take into his or her custody or under his or her control all the property and things in action to which the company is or appears to be entitled.[329] Legal title to this property is not vested in the provisional liquidator.[330] Normally the order of appointment forbids the provisional liquidator from distributing or parting with assets.[331]

4.144 A provisional liquidator may, if necessary, be given power to carry on the company's business.[332] Alternatively, power may be given to apply for the appointment of a special manager.[333]

4.145 In *Coffey v DFC Financial Services Ltd*[334] the New Zealand Court of Appeal, obiter, questioned whether a provisional liquidator of a company could be given power to control the shareholding, management and directorship of any subsidiary of the company, including power to remove any directors or employees of any subsidiary.

4.146 The powers conferred on a provisional liquidator on appointment may be added to or amended at any time thereafter.[335] This may be done on the application of a creditor[336] or the provisional liquidator.[337] The court's order of appointment may state that the provisional liquidator may apply for an amendment of his or her powers. Otherwise, it would seem that such an application may be made because the provisional liquidator was appointed by the court and is entitled, if necessary, to seek the assistance of and directions from the court in exercising the powers and functions conferred by the court.[338] It would seem that such an application is not made under IA 1986, s 168(3), which empowers a 'liquidator' to apply to the court for directions, since s 168 applies only in the case of a company 'which is being wound up by the court'.[339] In New South Wales it has been held that such an amendment is made under the court's inherent jurisdiction.[340]

4.147 The court is usually anxious to limit a provisional receiver's role to being a neutral holder of the company's property pending determination of the winding-up petition. Thus it may be

---

provisional building society liquidators by the Building Society Insolvency (England and Wales) Rules 2010 (SI 2010/2581), r 22(1).

[328] IA 1986, s 135(5). Applied to provisional bank liquidators by the Banking Act 2009, s 103(3), (4) and table, and to provisional building society liquidators by the Building Societies Act 1986, s 90C.

[329] IA 1986, s 144(1). Applied to provisional bank liquidators by the Banking Act 2009, s 103(3), (4), and table, and to provisional building society liquidators by the Building Societies Act 1986, s 90C.

[330] *Shirlaw v Taylor* (1991) 102 ALR 551 at p 553.

[331] See the standard first paragraph of the list of functions quoted in *Equitas Ltd v Jacob* [2005] EWHC 1440 (Ch), [2005] BPIR 1312, at [7].

[332] As in *Re Dry Docks Corporation of London* (1888) 39 ChD 306; *Wilson* (1912) 50 SLR 161; and *Re Centre Restaurant Pty Ltd* (1982) 6 ACLR 481.

[333] IA 1986, s 177; *Re Bound and Co* [1893] WN 21.

[334] (1990) 5 NZCLC 66,757.

[335] *Equitas Ltd v Jacob* at [14].

[336] As in *Equitas Ltd v Jacob*.

[337] As in *Re Highfield Commodities Ltd* [1985] 1 WLR 149 at p 163.

[338] *Re P R Clark Holdings Pty Ltd* (1977) 2 ACLR 416; *Re Rothwells Ltd* (1989) 15 ACLR 142 at p 146.

[339] s 168(1).

[340] *Re Ryan* [2006] NSWSC 297, 57 ACSR 172.

in order for a provisional liquidator of a company to close one of its branch offices and discharge the staff of that office in order to reduce unnecessary expenditure[341] but not to discontinue the company's entire business.[342] On a contributory's petition to wind up a solvent company, a provisional liquidator may be authorized to enter into a substantial transaction involving a disposition of the company's assets if all contributories agree.[343]

As an independent person preserving the status quo, a provisional liquidator should not pursue proceedings in the company's name which would determine the position of parties contesting control of the company.[344] In *Garden Mews-St Leonards Pty Ltd v Butler Pollnow Pty Ltd*[345] Butler Pollnow Pty Ltd was in provisional liquidation but Mr Pollnow, who was interested in the company, wanted it to defend the winding-up application and take action against various persons alleged to have injured it. As the substance of the claims in the action would also be the defence to the winding-up application and as the provisional liquidator could not defend the winding-up application, it was also inappropriate for him to pursue the action, so the court appointed Mr Pollnow receiver of the company's rights of action. By contrast, in *Christianos v Aloridge Pty Ltd*,[346] in which the contributory petitioner wanted the company to sue its directors and others, it was unnecessary to appoint a receiver of the company's cause of action because there was no intention to defend the winding-up application so control of the litigation could be left to a liquidator who was likely to be appointed shortly. **4.148**

In *Re P R Clark Holdings Pty Ltd (No 2)*[347] the provisional liquidator wanted to continue running the company for a further six months to show creditors that they should accept a scheme of arrangement. The court clearly disapproved of such enthusiastic involvement and made a winding-up order. **4.149**

By IA 1986, ss 234(1) and 236(1), a provisional liquidator may apply under s 236 for an order for a private examination of any of the persons listed in s 236(2). Such an order will be discharged if the petition by virtue of which the provisional liquidator has been appointed is dismissed.[348] **4.150**

It is not part of the task of the provisional liquidator of a company to oppose the winding-up petition under which he or she was appointed.[349] **4.151**

Effect of Administrative Receivership

If an administrative receiver is acting in relation to a company when an application is made for the appointment of a provisional liquidator, the fact must be stated in the evidence supporting the application[350] and if it makes an order, the court will send a sealed copy of it to **4.152**

---

[341] *Re Union Accident Insurance Co Ltd* [1972] 1 Lloyd's Rep 297.

[342] *Re ML Industries Pty Ltd* (1981) 5 ACLR 769, in which the application to the court for permission to discontinue the business was made five days before the hearing of the winding-up petition and was refused.

[343] *Re London Authorities Mutual Ltd* [2009] EWHC 3920 (Ch), LTL 16/12/2009.

[344] *Re Chateau Hotels Ltd* [1977] 1 NZLR 381; *Garden Mews-St Leonards Pty Ltd v Butler Pollnow Pty Ltd* (1984) 9 ACLR 91.

[345] (1984) 9 ACLR 91.

[346] (1995) 131 ALR 129.

[347] (1977) 3 ACLR 67.

[348] *Re Kingscroft Insurance Co Ltd* [1994] BCC 343.

[349] See 5.21.

[350] IR 1986, r 4.25(2)(d)(ii).

the administrative receiver.[351] The appointment of a provisional liquidator of a company after an administrative receiver has been appointed makes no difference to the receiver's responsibility for the company's preferential debts under IA 1986, s 40.

4.153   In *Re Colonial Trusts Corporation, ex parte Bradshaw*[352] it was held that the appointment of a provisional liquidator crystallized a floating charge on the company's assets because the company ceased to carry on its business when the provisional liquidator was appointed. However, a contrary view has been taken in Australia.[353]

4.154   If an administrative receiver is appointed of a company when there is already a provisional liquidator acting, the receiver will be responsible, under IA 1986, s 40, for paying the company's preferential debts as at the date of being appointed (unless the company had gone into voluntary liquidation before that date, in which case the receiver may be called upon to pay preferential debts in liquidation under s 175(2)(b)).

Vacation of Office

4.155   A provisional liquidator vacates office:

(a) On death.

(b) On removal from office by order of the court.[354]

(c) If not the official receiver, on ceasing to be qualified to act as an insolvency practitioner in relation to the company.[355] The office is vacated by virtue of the cessation of qualification alone: there is no need for any action by the provisional liquidator.[356]

(d) On discharge of the order of appointment.[357]

(e) When a liquidator takes office.[358] Under IA 1986, the official receiver becomes liquidator on the making of a winding-up order.[359]

(f) If the winding-up petition under which the provisional liquidator was appointed is dismissed either without a substantive hearing[360] or at a substantive hearing.[361]

4.156   There is no provision for resignation as such, but a provisional liquidator may make his or her own application for a removal order.[362]

4.157   An application to the court for an order removing a provisional liquidator from office may be made by the provisional liquidator or by anyone who has standing to apply for the appointment of a provisional liquidator.[363]

---

[351]   r 4.26(2)(c).

[352]   (1879) 15 ChD 465.

[353]   *Re Obie Pty Ltd* [1984] 1 QdR 371, point not considered on appeal; *Re Alspar Pty Ltd* (1990) 101 FLR 212.

[354]   IA 1986, s 172(2).

[355]   s 172(5).

[356]   See *Re A J Adams Builders Ltd* [1991] BCC 62 and *Re Stella Metals Ltd* [1997] BCC 626 on the identically worded provision in s 171(4) relating to a liquidator in a voluntary winding up.

[357]   *Re Deisara Pty Ltd* (1992) 107 FLR 235 at p 237.

[358]   *Shirlaw v Taylor* (1991) 102 ALR 551 at p 553.

[359]   IA 1986, s 136(1) and (2). See 5.141.

[360]   *Re Laverton Nickel NL* (1979) 3 ACLR 945.

[361]   IR 1986, r 4.31(2).

[362]   *Day v Mount* (1984) 53 ALR 468; *Re Kingscroft Insurance Co Ltd* [1994] BCC 343.

[363]   See 4.30–4.33. IR 1986, r 4.31(1).

The appointment of a bank or building society provisional liquidator may be terminated **4.158** by the court on the application of the provisional liquidator or any person who has standing to apply for the appointment of a provisional liquidator.[364] The appointment of a bank or building society provisional liquidator terminates on the making of a bank or building society insolvency order.[365]

Where someone is the provisional liquidator of a partnership and of a corporate member of the **4.159** partnership, appointed in proceedings on petitions under IPO 1994, art 8 or art 10, provision for removal from or vacation of office is made by IA 1986, s 172, as modified by IPO 1994, sch 4, para 21. Under the modified section, removal from or vacation of office relates to all offices held in the proceedings relating to the partnership.[366] A partnership provisional liquidator may be removed from office only by an order of the court.[367] A partnership provisional liquidator who is not an official receiver vacates office if he or she ceases to be a person who is qualified to act as an insolvency practitioner in relation to the insolvent partnership or any insolvent member of it against which a winding-up or bankruptcy order has been made.[368]

In *Re United Medical Protection Ltd*[369] it was said, at [33], that on an application to end a **4.160** provisional liquidator's appointment (that is, to take a company out of provisional liquidation), the court should consider:

(a) whether the purposes for which the appointment was made have been exhausted, and whether there is a reasonable prospect that matters may arise in the future with which the provisional liquidator should deal;
(b) whether the termination might put at risk the interests of creditors, contributories and the provisional liquidator; and
(c) whether it is in the public interest that the appointment be terminated.

Re Giant Resources Ltd[370] involved a public listed company with numerous subsidiaries **4.161** and worldwide interests. Initially two members of the firm KPMG Peat Marwick were appointed provisional liquidators, but, almost inevitably, that firm or its overseas associates had had dealings with some of the companies involved in the case. On an application by two banks, which were major creditors of Giant Resources Ltd and which were dissatisfied with the work of the provisional liquidators, the court removed the provisional liquidators and appointed someone regarded as more independent. *Aboriginal and Torres Strait Island Commission v Jurnkurakurr Aboriginal Resource Centre Aboriginal Corporation*[371] is a similar case. In *Re West Australian Gem Explorers Pty Ltd*[372] the court refused to dismiss

---

[364] IR 1986, r 4.31(1), applied by the Bank Insolvency (England and Wales) Rules 2009 (SI 2009/356), r 26(1), and modified by r 3(3)(b) and (4)(l) and (7), so that the reference to IR 1986, r 4.25(1), is a reference to SI 2009/356, r 20(2). IR 1986, r 4.31(1), applied by the Building Society Insolvency (England and Wales) Rules 2010 (SI 2010/2581), r 26(1), and modified by r 3(5)(b) and (6)(n) and (10), so that the reference to IR 1986, r 4.25(1), is a reference to SI 2010/2581, r 20(2).
[365] IR 1986, r 4.31(3), inserted by SI 2009/356, r 26(2); IR 1986, r 4.31(2A), inserted by SI 2010/2581, r 26(2).
[366] s 172(1).
[367] Modified s 172(2).
[368] Modified s 172(4).
[369] [2003] NSWSC 1031, 47 ACSR 705.
[370] [1989] 1 QdR 107.
[371] (1992) 110 FLR 1.
[372] (1994) 13 ACSR 104.

the provisional liquidator it had appointed a month earlier and replace him with someone who had acted as administrator of the company, and who it was claimed had familiarized himself with the company's affairs, but who was clearly biased in favour of the directors of the company who were proposing his appointment.

4.162 In *Re UOC Corporation*[373] the appointment of a provisional liquidator was terminated, on his application, because he had incurred expenses and remuneration of £56,000 but had been able to get in only just over £4,000 of the company's assets.

4.163 On termination of a provisional liquidator's appointment, the court may give such directions as it thinks fit with respect to the accounts of the provisional liquidator's administration or any other matters which it thinks appropriate.[374]

4.164 A provisional liquidator must, unless the court otherwise directs, gazette[375] notice of termination of his or her appointment, as soon as reasonably practicable.[376] Termination of the appointment may also be advertised in such other manner as the provisional liquidator thinks fit.[377]

4.165 The court may discharge an order appointing the official receiver as provisional liquidator of a company if an additional sum to cover remuneration and expenses is not deposited or secured within two business days of service of an order requiring it.[378] An order appointing someone other than an official receiver as provisional liquidator of a company may be discharged if his or her security is not kept up.[379]

---

[373] [1997] 2 BCLC 569.
[374] IR 1986, r 4.31(2).
[375] 'Gazette' means advertise once in the *London Gazette* (IR 1986, r 13.13(4) and (4A)).
[376] r 4.31(3) inserted by the Insolvency (Amendment) Rules 2009 (SI 2009/642), r 23.
[377] IR 1986, r 4.31(3)(b), inserted by SI 2009/642, r 23.
[378] IR 1986, r 4.27(2)—see 4.136.
[379] IR 1986, r 4.29.

5

HEARING THE PETITION AND MAKING THE ORDER

Judge

Judicial Nature of Decision

The power to make a winding-up order under IA 1986 is a judicial rather than an executive **5.1** power,[1] just like the power to make a bankruptcy order[2] or a debt relief order.[3] According to Gaudron J in *Gould v Brown*, at [68], the proceedings are:

> essentially judicial in the sense that they usually involve parties...and invariably require proof of factual matters by application of the rules of evidence in proceedings conducted in accordance with judicial procedures. Moreover, the power to order the winding up of a company...is exercised by 'the application of legal principles to proved states of fact and not upon considerations of policy or expediency'.[4]

Judge

A winding-up petition is heard in the first instance by a registrar or district judge, who may **5.2** give any necessary directions and may, in the exercise of his or her discretion, either hear and determine it or refer it to the judge.[5] The practice is for opposed petitions to be referred to the judge and for the registrar or district judge to hear all unopposed petitions.

In *Re Dollar Land (Feltham) Ltd*[6] the registrar heard, and made a winding-up order on, a **5.3** creditor's petition when no other creditors appeared to oppose it, though the company asked for an adjournment so that the possibility of a voluntary arrangement could be explored. A report by insolvency practitioners on the possible voluntary arrangement was put in evidence. On appeal against the winding-up order, Blackburne J had 'some doubt' whether it was appropriate for the registrar to deal with the matter personally rather than referring it to the judge, because opposition to the making of a winding-up order was implicit in the company's request for an adjournment and its evidence. However, Blackburne J refused to overrule the registrar's exercise of discretion.

Management with Related Proceedings

It is possible for proceedings in the Companies Court to be managed so that they are heard **5.4** at the same time as related proceedings in the Chancery Division.[7] For an example see *Interoil Trading v Watford Petroleum*,[8] which concerned a petition for relief of unfairly prejudicial conduct of the company's affairs. The judgment in *Re R A Noble and Sons (Clothing) Ltd*[9] deals with both a contributory's winding-up petition and a claim against the company.

In practice it will rarely, if ever, be appropriate to hamper the progress of a creditor's petition **5.5** for the winding up of a company by joining it to other proceedings which are not insolvency

---

[1] *Gould v Brown* [1998] HCA 6, 193 CLR 346, per Brennan CJ and Toohey J at [31], Gaudron J at [68], Kirby J at [324]–[330].

[2] *R v Davison* (1954) 90 CLR 353.

[3] *R (Howard) v Official Receiver* [2013] EWHC 1839 (Admin), [2014] QB 930.

[4] *R v Davison* (1954) 90 CLR 353 at p 383 per Kitto J.

[5] PD Insolvency Proceedings 2014, para 3.1; IR 1986, r 7.6A(2) and (3).

[6] [1995] 2 BCLC 370.

[7] Chancery Guide 2013, para 20.26.

[8] [2002] EWHC 2108 (Ch), LTL 31/10/2002.

[9] [1983] BCLC 273.

proceedings: the winding-up proceedings concern the company and all of its members and creditors and should be dealt with quickly,[10] whereas other proceedings are likely to involve only the company and a small number of other parties.[11] It is, though, not uncommon for a winding-up petition presented against a company to be adjourned pending the hearing of an administration application concerning the same company.

5.6 Consolidation[12] of a petition and a claim under Civil Procedure Rules (CPR), Part 7 or Part 8, was described as 'a theoretical impossibility' by Pumfrey J in *Interoil Trading v Watford Petroleum*. Under earlier rules consolidation of an action and a winding-up petition was refused in *Lovatt v Oxfordshire Ironstone Co.*[13] Nevertheless, consolidation of an action and a petition was at least contemplated in *Garden Mews-St Leonards Pty Ltd v Butler Pollnow Pty Ltd*[14] and in *Barrett v Duckett*,[15] though in the latter case the action was struck out by the Court of Appeal.[16]

Who may be Heard?

Right to be Heard

Petitioner

5.7 If there is no appearance for the petitioner at a hearing of a winding-up petition, it will be dismissed.[17]

Persons capable of being parties

5.8 The court hearing a petition for the compulsory winding up of a company has a discretion to hear anyone who can assist the court, as advocate to the court,[18] but only persons capable of being parties to the petition have a right to be heard.[19] Before the Insolvency Rules 1986 (IR 1986) came into force, the prescribed form of advertisement of a petition for the winding-up of a company invited its creditors and contributories to appear at the hearing, and it was concluded that they were the only persons (apart from the company and the petitioner) with a right to appear. In *Re SBA Properties Ltd*[20] (a public interest petition presented by the Board of Trade) Pennycuick J said at p 802:

> It is not in dispute that the only persons entitled to appear upon the hearing of a winding-up petition are the company, its creditors and its contributories.[21]

---

[10] See 5.113–5.116 and 5.119.

[11] *Re National Computers Systems and Services Ltd* (1991) 6 ACSR 133; *Wimborne v Brien* (1997) 23 ACSR 576 at p 578.

[12] Under CPR, r 3.1(2)(g).

[13] (1886) 30 SJ 338.

[14] (1984) 9 ACLR 91 at p 95.

[15] [1995] 1 BCLC 73 at p 83.

[16] [1995] 1 BCLC 243.

[17] *Re Royal Mutual Benefit Building Society* [1960] 1 WLR 1143; *Re Aim Investments (Holdings) Ltd* [2004] 2 HKLRD 201.

[18] *Re Bradford Navigation Co* (1870) LR 5 Ch App 600; *Re Hughes King (Nigeria) Ltd* 1970 (2) ALR Comm 35; *Re Gasbourne Pty Ltd* (1984) 79 FLR 394.

[19] *Re St Kilda and Brighton Railway Co* (1864) 1 W W & A'B 157 at p 160; *Re Bradford Navigation Co* (1870) LR 5 Ch App 600.

[20] [1967] 1 WLR 799.

[21] Clearly the petitioner is also entitled to appear.

A foreign creditor has the same rights regarding participation in proceedings as creditors **5.9** in Great Britain.[22]

IR 1986 altered the rules for advertising petitions. The invitation to persons to appear at the **5.10** hearing of the petition is not now limited to creditors and contributories of the company. It is questionable whether this change has affected rights to appear on the hearing of a winding-up petition.

A different view was taken in the Supreme Court of Victoria by Nicholls J in *Re Gasbourne Pty* **5.11** *Ltd*.[23] His Honour held that the true rule is that any person whose interests may be affected by the making of a winding-up order may appear at the hearing of the petition for it (though his Honour also held that the party in question had standing as a contingent creditor).

Where the sole reason given in the petition for winding up a foreign company was to obtain **5.12** an order requiring its auditors to produce books and papers, the auditors' partnership had a right to be joined as a party to the proceedings on the petition.[24] In *Teck Yow Brothers Hand-Bag Trading Co v Maharani Supermarket Sdn Bhd*,[25] after a creditor of the company sought to be wound up had presented its winding-up petition, the company's landlord dis-trained against the company's goods for unpaid rent. The sale of the seized goods yielded enough to pay the rent but if a winding-up order were to be made on the petition, the dis-tress would be void under the Malaysian equivalent of IA 1986, s 128. It was held that the landlord had standing to appear at the hearing of the petition and object to the order being made as it had an interest in the subject matter of the winding up. It could be argued that the landlord was a contingent creditor.

A person is entitled to appear at the hearing of a winding-up petition by virtue of the gazet- **5.13** ting of the petition: it does not matter that the person has not been served with a copy of the petition.[26]

Examples of persons the court has refused to hear

In *Re SBA Properties Ltd*[27] a person against whom the company had a claim was held not **5.14** to have standing to appear on the hearing of the petition. Pennycuick J was willing to hear its counsel anyway but it withdrew from the proceedings. In *Re Craven Insurance Co Ltd*[28] Pennycuick J refused to consider an affidavit from the Member of Parliament for the area where the company's offices were situated outlining the grave consequences for employees if an order were made on the petition. In *Re Azoff-Don Commercial Bank*[29] a man who claimed that the liquidator in the winding up in France of a Russian company had assigned to him most of the company's assets in England was held not to have standing to appear on the hearing of a petition for the company to be wound up in England. Wynn-Parry J, at p 322, described the man's claim as being 'outside any liquidation' so that it would be unaf-fected by any winding-up order made as a result of the hearing.

---

[22] Cross-Border Insolvency Regulations 2006 (SI 2006/1030), sch 1, art 13(1).
[23] [1984] VR 801.
[24] *PricewaterhouseCoopers v Saad Investments Co Ltd* [2014] UKPC 35, [2014] 1 WLR 4482 at [38]–[39].
[25] [1989] 1 MLJ 101.
[26] *Re Patent Cocoa Fibre Co* (1876) 1 ChD 617; *Re New Gas Co* (1877) 5 ChD 703.
[27] [1967] 1 WLR 799.
[28] [1968] 1 WLR 675.
[29] [1954] Ch 315.

5.15   A committee of creditors (in the sense of a committee to whom a number of creditors have entrusted representation of their interests), as opposed to a creditor or creditors as such, has no right to be heard.[30] The same would apply to a shareholders' committee or action group and to bodies such as a liquidation committee in creditors' voluntary winding up or a creditors' committee in administrative receivership.[31]

Secured creditors

5.16   Secured creditors may appear: a secured creditor does not have to elect between resting on the security and taking part in the liquidation until after the winding-up order is made.[32]

The company's officers

5.17   As part of their general management powers conferred, for example, by art 3 of the model articles of association for private companies limited by shares and for public companies,[33] the directors of a company sought to be wound up have power to instruct solicitors and counsel to appear for the company, even if the company is in administrative receivership[34] or a provisional liquidator has been appointed[35] or the directors have been interned as enemy aliens.[36] However, the managing director of a company does not have implied authority to make crucial decisions following the presentation of a petition to wind up the company, and, in particular, does not have implied authority to instruct solicitors to oppose the petition.[37]

The company's insolvency office-holder

5.18   An administrator of a company has a power to defend a petition to wind up the company.[38] An administrator of a partnership has power to defend a petition for the winding up of the partnership under the Insolvent Partnerships Order 1994 (IPO 1994).[39]

5.19   An administrative receiver of a company has a power to defend a petition to wind up the company.[40] It may be questioned whether this power is given so that the receiver can represent the company's interests or the interests of the creditor who appointed the receiver. In *Bank of New Zealand v Essington Developments Pty Ltd*[41] a similar provision of Australian law was interpreted to mean that the receiver could assume the carriage of the proceedings on the company's behalf but could not actively resist the petition. If the receiver exercised

---

[30]   *Re Mid Kent Fruit Co* (1892) 36 SJ 389, 398.
[31]   *Re Testro Bros Consolidated Ltd* [1965] VR 18 at p 20.
[32]   *Re Carmarthenshire Anthracite Coal and Iron Co* (1875) 45 LJ Ch 200.
[33]   Companies (Model Articles) Regulations 2008 (SI 2008/3229), sch 1 and sch 3.
[34]   *Re Reprographic Exports (Euromat) Ltd* (1978) 122 SJ 400; *Australian Securities and Investments Commission v Lanepoint Enterprises Pty Ltd* [2006] FCA 1163, 60 ACSR 217. But see the discussion of administrative receivership at 5.19.
[35]   *Re Union Accident Insurance Co Ltd* [1972] 1 WLR 640; *Re Surplus Trader Ltd* [2005] 4 HKLRD 436 at [16].
[36]   *Re Polack Tyre and Rubber Co Ltd* [1918] WN 17.
[37]   *Re Qintex Ltd (No 2)* (1990) 2 ACSR 479; *Nece Pty Ltd v Ritek Incorporation* (1997) 24 ACSR 38. The managing director of Qintex Ltd had instructed solicitors to oppose a petition for its compulsory winding up. The court held that he had no authority to do so and therefore it could not hear counsel instructed by those solicitors. The board of Qintex Ltd was unable to ratify the managing director's acts because there were no longer enough directors to form a quorum.
[38]   IA 1986, s 14(1) and sch 1, para 21.
[39]   IA 1986, s 14(1) and sch 1, para 19, as modified by IPO 1994, sch 2, paras 8 and 10.
[40]   IA 1986, s 42 and sch 1, para 21.
[41]   (1991) 5 ACSR 86.

the power then this would supersede the directors' power to defend the petition. Accordingly, the receiver should only choose to exercise the power if the purposes of the receivership would be best served by the company going into compulsory winding up. It is submitted that if an administrative receiver is opposed to a winding-up petition, the creditor who appointed the receiver should appear to state that opposition, not the receiver. In *Re Thames Freightlines Ltd*[42] Greig J observed that a receiver appearing to oppose a petition (without statutory power to do so) could either be regarded as representing the creditor by whom he or she was appointed or as a creditor for the costs and expenses of the receivership.

5.20   If a petition is presented to wind up a company in voluntary winding up, the voluntary liquidator may instruct counsel to appear for the company: there should not be separate appearances for the liquidator and the company.[43] The appearance should be for the purpose of providing information and arguing the company's case: the liquidator should not take sides in an argument among creditors or between contributories and creditors.[44] If the petition criticises the liquidator's conduct of the voluntary winding up, the liquidator should answer the criticisms fully.[45]

5.21   If a provisional liquidator has been appointed, he or she does not, it seems, have a right to appear at the hearing of the winding-up petition[46] but if heard as advocate to the court will be awarded the costs of appearing out of the company's assets.[47]

5.22   If the petition is subject to Regulation (EC) No 1346/2000 and there are main or secondary proceedings in relation to the company in another EU State (apart from Denmark), the liquidator in those proceedings may participate in the English proceedings on the same basis as a creditor.[48] If the company is subject to a foreign proceeding which has been recognized,[49] the foreign representative is entitled to participate in the English winding-up proceedings.[50]

Contributories

5.23   A person wishing to appear as a contributory must admit to being a contributory.[51]

5.24   Appearance of a person as a contributory is not permitted unless:

(a) the person has a tangible interest[52] in the winding up of the company;[53] or

---

[42] (1981) 1 NZCLC 98,112.
[43] *Re A W Hall and Co Ltd* (1885) 53 LT 633; *Re Mont de Piété of England* [1892] WN 166; *Re William Adler and Co Ltd* [1935] Ch 138.
[44] *Re Medisco Equipment Ltd* [1983] BCLC 305; *Re Roselmar Properties Ltd (No 2)* (1986) 2 BCC 99,157; *Re Arthur Rathbone Kitchens Ltd* [1997] 2 BCLC 280.
[45] *Re Arthur Rathbone Kitchens Ltd*; *Re Leading Guides International Ltd* [1998] 1 BCLC 620.
[46] *Re General International Agency Co Ltd* (1865) 36 Beav 1; *Re Laverton Nickel NL* (1979) 3 ACLR 945 at p 947.
[47] *Re Times Life Assurance and Guarantee Co* (1869) LR 9 Eq 382; *Re Laverton Nickel NL*.
[48] art 32(3).
[49] See 10.206–10.210.
[50] Cross-Border Insolvency Regulations 2006 (SI 2006/1030), sch 1, art 12. In the absence of the provision made by the UNCITRAL Model Law a person holding office under foreign insolvency proceedings can appear only as an advocate to the court (*Re Orient Networks Holdings Ltd* 2004-05 CILR 540).
[51] *Re Eastern Counties Junction and Southend Railway Co* (1850) as reported at 14 LT OS 369; *Charit-email Technology Partnership LLP v Vermillion International Investments Ltd* [2009] EWHC 388 (Ch), [2009] BPIR 762.
[52] See 8.67–8.86.
[53] *Re Rodencroft Ltd* [2004] EWHC 862 (Ch), [2004] 1 WLR 1566; *Secretary of State for Business, Innovation and Skills v World Future Ltd* [2013] EWHC 723 (Ch), LTL 29/7/2013.

(b) the appearance is to argue that the company could become solvent if the petition were adjourned or dismissed;[54] or

(c) there are exceptional circumstances.[55]

Contributories' petitions

5.25 Before IR 1986 came into force, because a contributory's petition was advertised, a creditor was entitled to appear at the hearing of it,[56] though there was a different rule under the Joint Stock Companies Act 1856.[57]

5.26 Under IR 1986 contributories' petitions are not usually gazetted and creditors no longer have a right to a copy of a pending contributory's petition. It is questionable whether this change has affected rights to appear on the hearing of a winding-up petition.

Financial Conduct Authority and Prudential Regulation Authority

5.27 The Financial Conduct Authority (FCA) and/or the Prudential Regulation Authority (PRA) are entitled to be heard on the hearing of a petition to wind up a body, if either of them could have petitioned for the body's winding up.[58] In any particular case, the regulator entitled to appear is called the 'appropriate regulator'. The FCA is an appropriate regulator in any case, and the PRA is also an appropriate regulator if the body is a PRA-regulated person.[59] This provision does not confer entitlement to be heard on a petitioner,[60] because a petitioner has that entitlement anyway.

5.28 If a petition is presented for the winding up of an open-ended investment company or a sub-fund by a person other than the FCA, then the FCA is entitled to be heard on the petition.[61]

Insolvent partnerships

5.29 On the hearing of a petition to wind up a partnership presented under IPO 1994, art 8 or art 10 (concurrent petitions for the winding up of a partnership and the winding up or bankruptcy of one or more of its present or former members), any person against whom a

---

[54] *Re Camburn Petroleum Products Ltd* [1980] 1 WLR 86.

[55] *Secretary of State for Business, Innovation and Skills v World Future Ltd*, where the learned deputy judge said that he could not think of any such circumstances.

[56] *Re New Gas Co* (1877) 5 ChD 703.

[57] *Re Maresfield Patent Gunpowder Co Ltd, ex parte Sharpe* (1858) 32 LT OS 51, in which it was held that a creditor could not appear at the hearing of a contributory's petition to oppose the petition; *Re Cumberland Black Lead Mining Co Ltd, ex parte Bell* (1862) 6 LT 197, in which a creditor was permitted to appear at the hearing of a contributory's petition for the compulsory winding up of a company in voluntary winding up only for the purpose of objecting to adoption of the proceedings in the voluntary winding up.

[58] Financial Services and Markets Act 2000, s 371(2)(a), which applies when a person presents a petition for the winding up of a body listed in s 371(1). The bodies listed there are the same as those listed in s 367(1) as bodies which may be the subject of a petition by the FCA or the PRA (see 9.116). However, s 371 does not provide that solvent partnerships are included, as is provided in s 367(2), (6) and (7). This is presumably because only a regulator can petition for a solvent partnership to be wound up under IA 1986, so a power to appear on another person's petition is unnecessary.

[59] Financial Services and Markets Act 2000, s 371(6)(a). For the definition of 'PRA-regulated person' see 9.115.

[60] Financial Services and Markets Act 2000, s 371(7).

[61] Open-Ended Investment Companies Regulations 2001 (SI 2001/1228), reg 31(3), applied to sub-funds by reg 33C(1), (5) and (6).

winding-up or bankruptcy petition has been presented in relation to the insolvent partnership is entitled to appear and to be heard.[62]

Bank or building society insolvency application

There is no advertisement of an application for a bank or building society insolvency order. **5.30** A copy of the application must be sent to the following persons[63] and any of them have the right to attend and be heard at the hearing of the application:[64]

(a) the proposed bank or building society liquidator;[65]

(b) the Bank of England, if it is not the applicant;[66]

(c) the FCA, if it is not the applicant;[67]

(d) the PRA, if it is not the applicant and if the institution is a PRA-authorized person;[68]

(e) the Financial Services Compensation Scheme;[69]

(f) any person who has given notice in respect of the bank under the Banking Act 2009, s 120, or the building society under the Building Societies Act 1986, s 90D (which require notice to be given to the FCA and/or the PRA of an application for an administration order, a petition for a winding-up order, a resolution for voluntary winding up or a proposed appointment of an administrator);[70]

(g) if a voluntary arrangement is in force for the institution, the supervisor,[71]

(h) any administrative receiver of the institution.[72]

The institution is entitled to be heard at the hearing despite not filing a witness statement in **5.31** opposition.[73] The court may make a bank or building society insolvency order in the absence of the institution or its legal representatives if it is satisfied that the application has been properly served on the institution.[74]

Notice of Appearance or Permission to be Heard

Notice of appearance

Any person wishing to appear on the hearing of a winding-up petition is required by IR 1986, **5.32** r 4.16 to give notice[75] to the petitioner or the petitioner's solicitor to arrive not later than 4:00 pm on the business day before the date appointed for the hearing (or the date of an adjournment).[76] If the company which is sought to be wound up intends to oppose the petition, it must file, and

---

[62] IA 1986, s 124(8), as modified by IPO 1994, sch 4, para 8 (in respect of art 8 petitions); IA 1986, s 124(8), as modified by IPO 1994, sch 6, para 2 (in respect of art 10 petitions).

[63] Bank Insolvency (England and Wales) Rules 2009 (SI 2009/356), r 10(1); Building Society Insolvency (England and Wales) Rules 2010 (SI 2010/2581), r 10(1).

[64] SI 2009/356, r 10(3); SI 2010/2581, r 10(3).

[65] SI 2009/356, r 10(1)(a); SI 2010/2581, r 10(1)(a).

[66] SI 2009/356, r 10(1)(b); SI 2010/2581, r 10(1)(b).

[67] SI 2009/356, r 10(1)(c); SI 2010/2581, r 10(1)(c) (see r 3(2) for the definition of 'the appropriate regulator').

[68] SI 2009/356, r 10(1)(ca); SI 2010/2581, r 10(1)(c) (see r 3(2) for the definition of 'the appropriate regulator').

[69] SI 2009/356, r 10(1)(d); SI 2010/2581, r 10(1)(d).

[70] SI 2009/356, r 10(1)(e); SI 2010/2581, r 10(1)(e).

[71] SI 2009/356, r 10(1)(f); SI 2010/2581, r 10(1)(f).

[72] SI 2009/356, r 10(1)(g); SI 2010/2581, r 10(1)(g).

[73] SI 2009/356, r 15(5); SI 2010/2581, r 15(5).

[74] SI 2009/356, r 8(7); SI 2010/2581, r 8(6).

[75] For permitted methods of delivery see 1.516–1.519.

[76] IR 1986, r 4.16. 'Business day' is defined in r 13.13(1) (see 1.512).

send to the petitioner, a witness statement in opposition not less than five business days before the hearing,[77] but notice under r 4.16 is not required from the company.[78]

5.33 As winding-up petitions are heard in public, there is no need to give a notice of appearance merely in order to attend the hearing. A person who has given notice of appearance, unlike a member of the public attending the hearing, may address the court,[79] and becomes a party to the proceedings.[80] In practice most persons giving notice of appearance do not wish to be heard by the court but are content that their support for or opposition to the petition is registered in the list of appearances.

5.34 A notice of appearance must be in form 4.9 in IR 1986, sch 4, and must state whether the appearance will be to support or oppose the petition.[81] A commitment to one side or the other must be made at this stage rather than waiting to see who wins and then claiming to be on the winning side so as to get costs: if there is no statement of the position being taken, costs will not be awarded.[82] The notice must also state the name and address of the person giving it, and any telephone number and reference which may be required for communication with that person or with any other person (to be also specified in the notice) authorized to speak or act on behalf of the person giving the notice.[83] The address is essential; it is not enough to give the address of solicitors acting for the giver of the notice.[84] The notice must also state the amount and nature of the debt claimed by the person giving the notice[85]— clearly this applies only if the person is a creditor.

5.35 Notice of appearance cannot be given by a committee of creditors (in the sense of a committee to whom a number of creditors have entrusted representation of their interests), only by a creditor or creditors as such.[86] The same would apply to a shareholders' committee.[87]

5.36 The notice of a winding-up petition which is gazetted must state the name and address of the petitioner and of the petitioner's solicitor (if any), and must state that any person wishing to appear at the hearing of the petition must give notice in accordance with r 4.16.[88]

List of persons intending to appear

5.37 The petitioner must prepare for the court a list of persons who have given notice of intention to appear, stating whether they support or oppose the petition, and must hand a copy of the list to the court before the commencement of the hearing.[89]

---

[77] IR 1986, r 4.18. See 3.178–3.180. The clear days rule in CPR, r 2.8(2) and (3), applies (see 1.510).
[78] *Sun Microsystems (M) Sdn Bhd v KS Eminent Systems Sdn Bhd* [2000] 4 MLJ 565; *Eastool Industries Sdn Bhd v Getfirms Electronics (M) Sdn Bhd* [2001] 2 MLJ 641.
[79] *Re Piccadilly Property Management Ltd* [1999] 2 BCLC 145 at pp 152–3.
[80] *Four Pillars Enterprises Co Ltd v Beiersdorf AG* [1999] 1 SLR 737.
[81] r 4.16(2)(b).
[82] *Re Green, McAllan and Fielden Ltd* [1891] WN 127.
[83] r 4.16(2)(a).
[84] *Re Descours, Parry and Co Ltd* [1909] WN 50.
[85] r 4.16(2)(c).
[86] *Re Mid Kent Fruit Co* (1892) 36 SJ 389, 398.
[87] See 5.15.
[88] IR 1986, r 4.11(5)(c), (f) and (g).
[89] IR 1986, r 4.17; the prescribed form is 4.10 in sch 4. It is known as 'the list'. If no notices to appear are received, and no permission is given to appear without notice, form 4.10 should be handed in with 'The list is negative' written on it (Chief Registrar Baister, 'The hearing of the petition' (2008) 1 Corporate Rescue and Insolvency 115).

Permission of the court to appear without notice to the petitioner

A person who has not given notice in accordance with IR 1986, r 4.16, may appear on the **5.38** hearing of the petition only with the permission of the court.[90] See *Re M McCarthy and Co (Builders) Ltd*[91] for an example of a supporter given permission at the hearing of the petition. (Under the rules in force at that time, 'special leave' was required, but the court apparently did not consider the significance of the difference between 'leave' and 'special leave'. In *Re Property Growth Securities Ltd*[92] it was held that special leave could be given only if there were special reasons for giving it.) Following *Re M McCarthy and Co (Builders) Ltd*,[93] Practice Note (Winding up: Appearance)[94] was issued, indicating that an application to be added to a list of appearances out of time would normally be granted provided the applicant undertakes not to apply for the costs of the application, though the applicant might be released from this undertaking once the petition is disposed of. An earlier practice note stated that a person added to the list of appearances who merely supports a point of view represented by a person who was in time will not be awarded costs.[95] This advice has not been repeated in PD (Practice Direction) Insolvency Proceedings 2014, which replaces all previous practice notes relating to insolvency proceedings, but it must be unlikely that the court's attitude has changed.

In *Re Xyllyx plc (No 1)*[96] two contributories of the company applied at the hearing of the peti- **5.39** tion for permission to appear at the hearing, so that they could be substituted as petitioners. Harman J indicated that he would refuse to allow the substitution and, perhaps from an abundance of caution, refused permission to appear as well.

The petitioner must add to the list required by IR 1986, r 4.17, the name of anyone given **5.40** permission by the court to appear without having given proper notice.[97]

Security for Costs

A petitioner cannot ask the court to order a person who has a right to appear on the hearing **5.41** of the petition, but who resides outside the jurisdiction, to give security for costs.[98]

Evidence

Written and Oral Evidence

Written evidence preferred

The hearing of an application to wind up a company, like any insolvency proceeding, is on **5.42** the basis of written evidence, subject to a power to call a deponent for cross-examination. Unless the court directs otherwise, evidence in insolvency proceedings must be given by

---

[90] r 4.16(5).
[91] [1976] 2 All ER 338.
[92] (1991) 4 ACSR 783.
[93] [1976] 2 All ER 338.
[94] [1976] 1 WLR 515.
[95] Practice Note [1930] WN 78.
[96] [1992] BCLC 376.
[97] r 4.17(4).
[98] *Re Percy and Kelly Nickel, Cobalt, and Chrome Iron Mining Co* (1876) 2 ChD 531; *Re Co-operative Development Funds of Australia Ltd* (1977) 2 ACLR 284.

witness statement[99] or by a report of an official receiver or insolvency office-holder.[100] The court may order the maker of any witness statement to attend for cross-examination.[101] This is the reverse of CPR, r 32.2, which requires evidence to be given orally in public unless the court orders otherwise and so r 32.2 does not apply to insolvency proceedings.[102]

Verified petition

5.43 A creditor's petition to wind up a company on the ground of insolvency, containing all relevant prescribed particulars and verified by a statement of truth,[103] can be, and if unopposed normally is, sufficient to persuade the court to make a winding-up order.

Other evidence

5.44 Further witness statements may be required from the petitioner to deal with allegations of fraud or other serious misconduct.[104] For the company's evidence in opposition see 3.178–3.180.

Contributories' petitions

5.45 IR 1986 introduced a separate regime for contributories' petitions. On or after the return day for a contributory's petition, under r 4.23(1)(d), the court gives such directions as it thinks appropriate with respect to the manner in which any evidence is to be adduced at any hearing before the judge and in particular:

(a) the taking of evidence wholly or in part by witness statement or orally;
(b) the cross-examination of any persons authenticating witness statements; and
(c) the matters to be dealt with in evidence.

See 8.494–8.501.

Cross-examination

5.46 Before the CPR came into force the court had a discretion to order the maker of an affidavit to attend for cross-examination.[105] If the maker of an affidavit failed to attend for cross-examination when ordered to do so, the affidavit could not be put in evidence unless the court gave leave.[106] Cases on this old rule may be relevant to the court's exercise of discretion under CPR, r 32.1, to direct how evidence is to be presented, and under r 32.5 to order that a witness who has made a witness statement need not give oral evidence.

5.47 In *Rover International Ltd v Cannon Films Sales Ltd*[107] Harman J said, at p 1604:

> [Proceedings on a contributory's petition to wind up a company on the just and equitable ground] raise hotly contested issues of fact. They are always conducted upon affidavit in the first instance, but in my universal experience of those matters, the direction is always given by the judge on the petition that the parties are to have liberty at trial to cross-examine the deponents to affidavits and, if a deponent is not then produced for cross-examination, his affidavit shall not be read.

---

[99] IR 1986, r 7.7A(1); PD Insolvency Proceedings 2014, para 5.1.
[100] IR 1986, r 7.9; see 3.254–3.255.
[101] r 7.7(1).
[102] IR 1986, r 7.51(1); *Highberry Ltd v COLT Telecom Group plc* [2002] EWHC 2503 (Ch), [2003] 1 BCLC 290.
[103] See 2.218–2.237.
[104] See 2.239.
[105] Rules of the Supreme Court 1965, ord 38, r 2(3), now revoked.
[106] Rules of the Supreme Court 1965, ord 38, r 2(3).
[107] [1987] 1 WLR 1597.

Cross-examination was refused if the matters sought to be raised were not relevant to   **5.48**
whether or not the company should be wound up.[108]

In a number of cases applications to cross-examine a deponent were refused because no   **5.49**
affidavit controverting the deponent's had been filed and no doubt had been cast on what
was said in the affidavit. See *Re Canton Trust and Commercial Bank Ltd (No 2)*,[109] in which
cross-examination of the maker of the affidavit verifying the petition was refused; and *Re
London Fish Market and National Fishing Co Ltd*[110] and *Re Hughes King (Nigeria) Ltd*,[111] in
both of which contributory petitioners were refused permission to cross-examine opponents. However, in *Re Bank of Credit and Commerce International SA (No 6)*[112] Nicholls V-C
said, at p 453:

> I am unable to accept that there is a rule of universal application that, failing some contrary
> sworn evidence, cross-examination of a deponent will not be ordered. The court will always
> be concerned to see that an order for cross-examination is not made needlessly or when it
> would be oppressive. The purpose sought to be achieved when cross-examination is ordered
> is that this is necessary for fairly disposing of the particular issue. Whether it is so necessary
> will necessarily depend on the circumstances of the particular case. In cases where the other
> party is in a position to give evidence contrary to the deponent's case and he chooses not to
> do so, the court no doubt will be slow to order cross-examination. The party who seeks cross-
> examination can be expected to put forward his own account of the facts in dispute of which
> he himself has knowledge. If he chooses not to do so, and declines himself to give evidence
> and expose himself thereby to an application for cross-examination, the court may well be
> disinclined to order cross-examination of the deponent who has given evidence. But even in
> such a case no absolute rule can be laid down. The court retains a discretion, and it would be
> unwise to say that in such a case cross-examination will never be ordered. There must always
> be the exceptional case.

In *Banco Econômico SA v Allied Leasing and Finance Corporation*[113] an application to cross-
examine the maker of an affidavit verifying a petition containing allegations of fraud was
refused after the petitioner undertook to withdraw it and submit a new affidavit omitting
the allegations, which were not made in the petition itself.

In *Tay Bok Choon v Tahansan Sdn Bhd*[114] Lord Templeman, giving the judgment of the   **5.50**
Privy Council, said, at pp 418–19:

> The court [hearing a winding-up petition] cannot give a direction about evidence unless one
> of the litigants desires such direction to be made. [In England and Wales the position is now
> different under CPR, r 32.1.] Of course a judge may indicate to a petitioner that unless he
> calls oral evidence or applies to cross-examine the deponents of the opposition so as to prove
> a disputed fact, his petition is likely to fail. The judge may equally indicate to a respondent
> that unless he calls oral evidence or applies to cross-examine the petitioner's deponents for
> the purposes of disproving an allegation made by the petitioner, then the petitioner is likely
> to succeed. At the end of the day the judge must decide the petition on the evidence before
> him. If allegations are made in affidavits by the petitioner and those allegations are credibly

---

[108] *Re SBA Properties Ltd* [1967] 1 WLR 799, in which the person seeking to cross-examine was held not
to have standing to appear.
[109] [1965] HKLR 591.
[110] (1883) 27 SJ 600.
[111] 1971 (2) ALR Comm 221.
[112] [1994] 1 BCLC 450.
[113] 1998 CILR 92.
[114] [1987] 1 WLR 413.

denied by the respondent's affidavits, then in the absence of oral evidence or cross-examination, the judge must ignore the disputed allegations. The judge must then decide the fate of the petition by consideration of the undisputed facts.

5.51 For an application of this principle see *Yai Yen Hon v Lim Mong Sam*,[115] in which the undisputed facts showed that the petitioner's case was not proved. A dispute about facts revealed in affidavits can be resolved only by oral evidence: it is not permissible to take the latest uncontradicted affidavit as the best evidence.[116]

Only allegations in petitions may be heard

5.52 At the hearing of a winding-up petition, the petitioner is limited to the allegations made in the petition.[117] A winding-up petition should be *secundum allegata et probanda* (in accordance with what is alleged and proved).[118] In *Re Fildes Bros Ltd*,[119] Megarry J said at p 598:

> In cases in which there are no normal pleadings, it seems to me important that those who oppose a winding up should know, in time to prepare their case, what are the allegations that they have to meet. If after a petition has been presented the petitioner wishes to broaden his attack, let him first amend his petition.

5.53 Evidence of matters not alleged in the petition will not be allowed if objected to in time.[120] If such evidence is given without objection, though, the petitioner may be allowed to amend the petition to allege the facts introduced by the evidence.[121]

5.54 In *Re Turf Enterprises Pty Ltd*,[122] the petition alleged a failure to comply with a statutory demand. It was found that the debt demanded was not owed to the person who made the demand so that there was no neglect to comply with it. However, in a lengthy hearing with oral evidence, the company's insolvency was admitted in cross-examination. It was held that this evidence was admissible because it was relevant. The person who was found to be the true creditor was substituted as petitioner and permission was given to amend the petition so that a winding-up order could be made. But in *Ng Tai Tuan v Chng Gim Huat Pte Ltd*,[123] in which the petition alleged only failure to comply with a statutory demand, the court refused to consider an affidavit alleging the company's general insolvency which had been filed too late for the company to have an adequate opportunity to rebut.

5.55 In *Re a Company*[124] the petition alleged no facts to support the allegation that 25 per cent of the company's capital was lost and was not likely to be restored within one year (a circumstance in which a winding-up order may be made in Canada). The petitioner sought to establish relevant facts by cross-examining the company's president but leave to cross-examine was refused.

[115] [1997] 2 MLJ 190.
[116] *National Bank of Nigeria Ltd v Are Brothers (Nigeria) Ltd* 1977 (1) ALR Comm 123.
[117] *Re Spence's Patent Non-conducting Composition and Cement Co* (1869) LR 9 Eq 9; *Re Fildes Bros Ltd* [1970] 1 WLR 592; *Re Armvent Ltd* [1975] 1 WLR 1679 at p 1683; *Banco Econômico SA v Allied Leasing and Finance Corporation* 1998 CILR 92.
[118] *Re Wear Engine Works Co* (1875) LR 10 Ch App 188.
[119] [1970] 1 WLR 592.
[120] *Re Londonderry Ltd* (1921) 21 SR (NSW) 263 at p 265.
[121] *Re White Star Consolidated Gold Mining Co* (1883) 48 LT 815; *Re Eastern Fur Finance Corp Ltd* [1934] 1 DLR 611; *Hassgill Investments Pty Ltd v Newman Air Charter Pty Ltd* (1991) 5 WAR 165.
[122] [1975] QdR 266.
[123] [1991] 1 MLJ 338.
[124] (1917) 34 DLR 396.

Views of Creditors and/or Contributories other than the Petitioner

Whether or not a winding-up order is to be made is one of the matters relating to the wind- **5.56** ing up of a company in relation to which the court may have regard to the wishes of the creditors or contributories under IA 1986, s 195.[125] The court is not bound to accede to the wishes of creditors[126] or contributories.[127]

In the case of creditors, regard must be had to the value of each creditor's debt.[128] This **5.57** means the amount claimed, not the amount likely to be realized in the winding up.[129] In the case of contributories, regard must be had to the number of votes conferred on each contributory.[130]

The wishes of creditors and/or contributories may be proved by any sufficient evidence.[131] **5.58** In *Re English, Scottish and Australian Chartered Bank*[132] A L Smith LJ explained[133] that the phrase 'as proved to [the court] by any sufficient evidence':

> is put in for the purpose of enlarging the powers of the judge who has to adjudicate in these winding-up matters. It clearly abrogates the necessity of his acting upon strict legal evidence. That is quite clear. It allows him to act upon secondary evidence if he thinks fit; and… it empowers the judge in matters of winding up, when he wants to ascertain what are the wishes of creditors or contributories, to act upon any evidence which he thinks sufficient for the purpose of arriving at the truth with regard to their wishes.

The way in which the views of creditors and/or contributories are to be proved is a matter for **5.59** the judge hearing the petition.[134] The court may direct meetings of the creditors to be called, held and conducted in such manner as the court directs for the purposes of ascertaining the wishes of the creditors and may appoint a chair of any such meeting to report the result of it to the court.[135] However, it is unnecessary for the court to direct a meeting if it has sufficient evidence otherwise.[136]

---

[125] *Re Factage Parisien Ltd* (1864) 34 LJ Ch 140 (MR), 11 LT 556 (LC); *Re Imperial Mercantile Credit Association, Coleman's, M'Andrew's, Figdor's and Doyle's Cases* (1866) 12 Jur NS 739; *Re Brighton Hotel Co* (1868) LR 6 Eq 339; *Re Langley Mill Steel and Iron Works Co* (1871) LR 12 Eq 26; *Re Western of Canada Oil Lands and Works Co* (1873) LR 17 Eq 1 per Lord Selborne LC at pp 5–6; *Re St Thomas' Dock Co* (1876) 2 ChD 116; *Re Uruguay Central and Hygueritas Railway Co of Monte Video* (1879) 11 ChD 372; *Re Great Western (Forest of Dean) Coal Consumers' Co* (1882) 21 ChD 769 per Fry J at p 773; *Re Chapel House Colliery Co* (1883) 24 ChD 259; *Re Crigglestone Coal Co Ltd* [1906] 2 Ch 327 per Buckley J at p 332; *Re Belmont Land Co* (1913) 32 NZLR 864; *Deputy Commissioner of Taxation v Cye International Pty Ltd (No 1)* (1985) 10 ACLR 303; *Re DTX Australia Ltd* (1987) 11 ACLR 444. The contrary view has been taken in Canada in *Re Mid-West Glass Co Ltd* (1931) 40 Man R 289.

[126] *Re Cushing Sulphite Fibre Co Ltd* (1905) 37 NBR 254; *Re George Downs and Co Ltd* [1943] IR 420; see also *Re Bank of Credit and Commerce International SA (No 3)* [1993] BCLC 1490.

[127] *Re Imperial Mercantile Credit Association, Coleman's, M'Andrew's, Figdor's and Doyle's Cases* (1866) 12 Jur NS 739 per Wood V-C at p 739.

[128] IA 1986, s 195(2).

[129] *Re Manakau Timber Co Ltd* (1895) 13 NZLR 319.

[130] IA 1986, s 195(3).

[131] IA 1986, s 195(1)(a).

[132] [1893] 3 Ch 385.

[133] At p 417.

[134] *Adebayo v Official Receiver of Nigeria* [1954] 1 WLR 681.

[135] s 195(1)(b); for an example see *Re Investment Bank of London Ltd* (1910) 130 LT Jo 149 in which the court ordered a meeting, to be summoned by newspaper advertisements, of creditors holding bearer securities to consider a proposed external reconstruction.

[136] *Re West Hartlepool Ironworks Co* (1875) LR 10 Ch App 618; *Re Langley Mill Steel and Iron Works Co* (1871) LR 12 Eq 26; *Re Leonard Spencer Pty Ltd* [1963] QdR 230.

5.60 The views of creditors and/or contributories may be established to the satisfaction of the court by a meeting convened by the company,[137] by the court under IA 1986, s 195,[138] or by a provisional liquidator,[139] or by appearances in support of or opposition to the petition when it is heard.[140] In *Re Leonard Spencer Pty Ltd*[141] a meeting had been held at which the voting was 51.2 per cent against winding up but between the meeting and the hearing two creditors representing 4.3 per cent of the total votes changed their minds and appeared to support the petition: Gibbs J decided the case on the basis that there was a majority in favour of winding up. The court should not convene a meeting of creditors to determine their views unless there is some reasonable proposition which creditors, voting as business people, could favour in preference to winding up.[142] In *Re Regent Street Ltd*,[143] the court refused to pay attention to the views of creditors which had allegedly been expressed at meetings to which the petitioner was not invited and which were reported to the court only by affidavit of the company secretary, no opposing creditors appearing at the hearing.

5.61 Misleading creditors or contributories into opposing compulsory winding up may be a contempt of court.[144] Opposition which the company has obtained by circulating misleading information will not persuade the court.[145]

Inspectors' Reports and other Investigative Materials

5.62 Parliament has established investigatory processes for providing the Secretary of State with reports, information or documents on which an opinion may be based that it is expedient in the public interest that a company should be wound up.[146] It follows that the Secretary of State may use the relevant report etc as evidence in support of a petition to wind up the company despite the rule against evidence of findings of fact, conclusions and evaluative judgments.[147] Such evidence may also be adduced on a contributory's petition.[148]

Report on Petitions against Members of Insolvent Partnership

5.63 On the day appointed for the hearing of a petition to wind up an insolvent partnership presented under IPO 1994, art 8 or art 10 (concurrent petitions for the winding up of a partnership and the winding up or bankruptcy of one or more of its present or former members), before the hearing, the petitioner must hand to the court a notice of the current state of proceedings on the petitions against the members of the partnership: the prescribed form for the notice is form 9 in sch 9 to IPO 1994.[149]

---

[137] *Re Langley Mill Steel and Iron Works Co* (1871) LR 12 Eq 26; *Re Chapel House Colliery Co* (1883) 24 ChD 259.
[138] *Re Belmont Land Co* (1913) 32 NZLR 864.
[139] *Re Leonard Spencer Pty Ltd* [1963] QdR 230.
[140] *Re West Hartlepool Ironworks Co* (1875) LR 10 Ch App 618.
[141] [1963] QdR 230.
[142] *Deputy Commissioner of Taxation v Cye International Pty Ltd (No 1)* (1985) 10 ACLR 303.
[143] [1933] GLR 329.
[144] As in *Re Septimus Parsonage and Co* [1901] 2 Ch 424.
[145] *Re Chreon Electronics Ltd* (1984) 2 NZCLC 99,131.
[146] IA 1986, s 124A(1). See 9.11.
[147] See 9.27–9.32.
[148] See 8.516.
[149] IA 1986, s 124(7), as modified by IPO 1994, sch 4, para 8 (in respect of art 8 petitions); IA 1986, s 124(7), as modified by IPO 1994, sch 6, para 2 (in respect of art 10 petitions).

Orders the Court may Make

Orders Available to the Court

General

On hearing a winding-up petition the court may, at its discretion,[150] dismiss it, or adjourn   **5.64**
the hearing conditionally or unconditionally, or make an interim order, or any other order
that it thinks fit.[151]

The court thus has the following options on the hearing of a winding-up petition: **5.65**

(a) make the winding-up order applied for;
(b) dismiss the petition;
(c) adjourn the hearing conditionally;
(d) adjourn the hearing unconditionally;
(e) make an interim order;
(f) make any other order that it thinks fit.

In Australia it has been held that these options are available whether the hearing is interim   **5.66**
or final.[152]

In New Zealand it has been held that the court cannot both dismiss a petition and make   **5.67**
another order that it thinks fit.[153]

Companies which may not be wound up

On an application to any court for the winding up of a company for which a water industry   **5.68**
special administration order[154] or an air traffic administration order[155] may be made, the
court must not make a winding-up order. If it is satisfied that it would be appropriate to
make a winding-up order but for that prohibition, it must instead make an appropriate
industry-specific administration order.[156] A water industry special administration order or
an air traffic administration order may be made on the winding-up petition despite the rule
that a winding-up petition must be dismissed when such an order is made.[157]

Exercising powers on industry-specific administration application

If a petition for a railway or PPP administration order, or an energy, energy supply company   **5.69**
or postal administration application, is presented after a petition for the winding up of the
same company, the court may, on hearing the winding-up petition, exercise the powers
available to it on hearing the administration petition or application instead of its powers
under IA 1986, s 125.[158]

---

[150] *Re Bayoil SA* [1999] 1 WLR 147.
[151] IA 1986, s 125(1).
[152] *Alati v Wei Sheung* (2000) 34 ACSR 489.
[153] *Nippon Credit Australia Ltd v Girvan Corporation New Zealand Ltd* (1991) 5 NZCLC 67,498.
[154] See 1.248–1.251.
[155] See 1.260–1.261.
[156] Water Industry Act 1991, s 25; Transport Act 2000, s 27.
[157] IA 1986, s 11(1)(a), as applied by the Water Industry Act 1991, sch 3, para 1, and modified by para 2, and as applied by the Transport Act 2000, sch 1, para 2, and modified by para 4.
[158] Railways Act 1993, s 61(2) and (3); Greater London Authority Act 1999, s 222(2) and (3); Energy Act 2004, s 160(3) (applied to energy supply company administration by the Energy Act 2011, s 96); Postal Services Act 2011, s 74(3). There is no equivalent provision for FMI administration.

Alternative orders for financial institutions

5.70 On a petition for a winding-up order in respect of a bank, building society or investment bank, the court may instead make a bank insolvency order,[159] a building society insolvency order,[160] an investment bank special administration order,[161] a special administration (bank insolvency) order[162] or a special administration (bank administration) order[163] as appropriate. All these orders can only be made on the application of particular regulators, as set out in table 5.1.

Table 5.1 Permitted applicants for alternative orders

Alternative order	Only permitted applicant(s)
Bank insolvency order (other than for an FCA-regulated bank)	• PRA with the consent of the Bank of England and the FCA, or • Bank of England[1]
Bank insolvency order for an FCA-regulated bank	• FCA with the consent of the Bank of England, or • Bank of England[2]
Building society insolvency order for a PRA-authorized person	• PRA with the consent of the Bank of England, or • Bank of England[3]
Building society insolvency order for a building society which is not a PRA-authorized person	• FCA with the consent of the Bank of England, or • Bank of England[4]
Investment bank special administration order for a PRA-authorized person	PRA[5]
Investment bank special administration order for an investment bank which is not a PRA-authorized person	FCA[6]
Special administration (bank insolvency) order for a PRA-authorized person	• PRA with the consent of the Bank of England, or • Bank of England[7]
Special administration (bank insolvency) order for an investment bank which is not a PRA-authorized person	• FCA with the consent of the Bank of England, or • Bank of England[8]
Special administration (bank administration) order for a PRA-authorized person	PRA[9]
Special administration (bank administration) order for an investment bank which is not a PRA-authorized person	FCA[10]

[1] Banking Act 2009, s 117(2).
[2] Banking Act 2009, s 117(2), as modified by s 129A.
[3] Building Societies Act 1986, s 89A(2) (see s 119(1) for the definition of 'appropriate authority').
[4] Building Societies Act 1986, s 89A(2).
[5] SI 2011/245, reg 22(3).
[6] SI 2011/245, reg 22(3).
[7] SI 2011/245, regs 3(3), 9 and 22(3) and sch 1, para 3.
[8] SI 2011/245, regs 3(3), 9 and 22(3) and sch 1, para 3.
[9] SI 2011/245, regs 3(3) and (4), 9 and 22(3) and sch 2, para 5.
[10] SI 2011/245, regs 3(3) and (4), 9 and 22(3) and sch 2, para 5.

---

[159] Banking Act 2009, s 117(1).
[160] Building Societies Act 1986, s 89A(1).
[161] Investment Bank Special Administration Regulations 2011 (SI 2011/245), reg 22(1) and (2). See 1.269–1.274.
[162] SI 2011/245, regs 3(3), 9 and 22(1) and (2) and sch 1, para 3. See 1.275–1.277.
[163] SI 2011/245, regs 3(3) and (4), 9 and 22(1) and (2) and sch 2, para 5. See 1.278–1.280.

Winding-up Order: the Court's Discretion Whether to Make an Order or Not

Principle

The court may order the winding up of a company on application made by petition under **5.71**
IA 1986, s 124, if one or more of the circumstances in which a company of its type may be
wound up[164] exists. For the form of a winding-up order, see form 4.11 in sch 4 to IR 1986.

The rules in IR 1986, part 4, apply whether a petition is presented under IA 1986, s 122(1), **5.72**
'or under any enactment enabling the presentation of a winding-up petition'.[165]

The fact that a foreign government may possibly claim an interest in some of the company's **5.73**
assets does not prevent the court making a winding-up order.[166]

When an order takes effect

The general rule is that an order takes effect from the day on which it is given or made.[167] It **5.74**
has been said that a winding-up order is effective from the first moment of the day on which
it is made,[168] applying a rule that is supposed to hold for any judicial act, but it has also been
doubted whether there is such a general rule.[169] In *Re Exhall Coal Mining Co Ltd*[170] Knight
Bruce LJ thought that an event which took place on the same day as a winding-up order was
made, but earlier in the day, occurred before the company was being wound up. See also
Merchants Bank v Roche Percee Coal Co[171] where it was held[172] that an event taking place on
the same day as a winding-up order was made did not occur after the order. The court has
power to post-date a winding-up order,[173] but cannot backdate one.[174] Because of the wording of the statutory provision,[175] an administration order can be backdated, though this has
never been argued adversarially.[176]

Discretion of court

The fact that one or more of the circumstances in which a company may be compulsorily **5.75**
wound up exists does not mean that a winding-up order will be made as a matter of course.[177]
The court's power to order the winding up of a company is discretionary, both in relation to
registered companies—IA 1986, s 122(1), says that a registered company '*may* be wound up
by the court' in the circumstances specified in the subsection—and in relation to unregistered
companies—s 221(1) says that any unregistered company '*may* be wound up' under IA 1986
subject to the provisions of part 5[178] of the Act.

---

[164] See 2.23–2.53.
[165] IR 1986, r 4.2(1).
[166] *Re Russian Bank for Foreign Trade* [1933] Ch 745; State Immunity Act 1978, s 6(3).
[167] CPR, r 40.7.
[168] *Re Red Robin Milk Bar Ltd* [1968] NZLR 28; *Re Blackburn Industries Pty Ltd* [1980] QdR 211 per
Dunn J at pp 224–5; *Dunecar Pty Ltd v Colbron* [2001] NSWSC 1181, 40 ACSR 342, at [4].
[169] *Re Palmer* [1994] Ch 316.
[170] (1864) 4 De G J & S 377 at p 379.
[171] (1897) 3 Terr LR 463.
[172] At p 464.
[173] CPR, r 40.7(1); *Re Doncaster Permanent Benefit Building and Investment Society* (1863) 11 WR 459.
[174] CPR, r 40.7(1); *Smith v Dha* [2013] EWHC 838 (QB), LTL 12/4/2013. This point was not raised in *Re
People's Restaurant Group Ltd* (2012) LTL 6/2/2013, where it was sufficient that the winding-up order could
not be backdated earlier than the deemed date of commencement of the winding up (at [4]).
[175] IA 1986, sch B1, para 13(2)(a).
[176] *Re Care Matters Partnership Ltd* [2011] EWHC 2543 (Ch), [2012] 2 BCLC 311, at [1]–[9].
[177] *Re London Conveyance Co* (1853) 1 Drew 465; *Re Metropolitan Railway Warehousing Co Ltd* (1867) 36
LJ Ch 827 per Lord Cairns LJ at p 829.
[178] ss 220–229.

5.76 For judicial confirmation that the power is discretionary in relation to registered companies, see *Re Langley Mill Steel and Iron Works Co*,[179] in which Malins V-C said, at pp 29–30, 'I am of opinion that the court has...complete discretion in all cases of winding up, and must exercise that discretion with reference to all the surrounding circumstances'; *Re P and J Macrae Ltd*;[180] *Fallis v United Fuel Investments Ltd*;[181] *Re Southard and Co Ltd*[182] per Buckley LJ at p 1203 and Bridge LJ at p 1207; *Malayan Plant (Pte) Ltd v Moscow Narodny Bank Ltd*,[183] in which Lord Edmund-Davies said[184] that what is now s 122(1) 'serves to vest in the court a wide discretion'; *Re Derrygarrif Investments Pty Ltd*;[185] *Re Bula Ltd*,[186] in which McCarthy J said at p 448 that it was 'a true discretion which should be exercised in a principled manner that is fair and just'; *Re Armour Insurance Co Ltd*;[187] *Pilecon Engineering Bhd v Remaja Jaya Sdn Bhd*;[188] *Montgomery v Wanda Modes Ltd*.[189]

5.77 In relation to unregistered companies, see *Re Planet Benefit Building and Investment Society*,[190] where Lord Romilly MR said, 'there is no right which I consider more clear than that which the court has of exercising its discretion and judgment with respect to the effect of winding up a company'; *Re Second Commercial Benefit Building Society*[191] per Jessel MR at p 754; *Banque des Marchands de Moscou (Koupetschesky) v Kindersley*[192] per Evershed MR at p 126; *Re Hibernian Merchants Ltd*[193] per Roxburgh J at p 78; *Morshead Management Ltd v Capital Entertainment Establishment*;[194] *Stocznia Gdanska SA v Latreefers Inc (No 2)*;[195] *Re Trans Pacific Insurance Corporation*.[196]

5.78 The position was the same under the Joint Stock Companies Winding-up Acts 1848 and 1849.[197]

Discretion must be exercised judicially

5.79 The discretion whether or not to make a winding-up order must be exercised judicially,[198] but the very existence of discretion means that no rules can be laid down concerning the exercise of the discretion.[199]

---

[179] (1871) LR 12 Eq 26.
[180] [1961] 1 WLR 229.
[181] (1963) 40 DLR (2d) 1 at p 8.
[182] [1979] 1 WLR 1198.
[183] [1980] 2 MLJ 53.
[184] At p 54.
[185] (1982) 6 ACLR 751.
[186] [1990] 1 IR 440.
[187] [1993] 1 HKLR 179.
[188] [1997] 1 MLJ 808.
[189] [2002] 1 BCLC 289 at p 292.
[190] (1872) LR 14 Eq 441 at p 450.
[191] (1879) 48 LJ Ch 753.
[192] [1951] Ch 112.
[193] [1958] Ch 76.
[194] (1999) LTL 28/3/2000 (in relation to IA 1986, s 221(5)(a)).
[195] [2001] 2 BCLC 116 at p 140.
[196] [2009] NSWSC 554, 72 ACSR 327, at [43].
[197] *Re Union Bank of Calcutta, ex parte Watson* (1850) 3 De G & Sm 253; *Re Monmouthshire and Glamorganshire Banking Co* (1851) 15 Beav 74; *Re British Alkali Co, ex parte Guest* (1852) 5 De G & Sm 458; *Bright v Hutton* (1852) 3 HL Cas 341 at p 370. See also *Re Greta Collieries Ltd* (1894) 4 BC (NSW) 47; *Re Strathy Wire Fence Co* (1904) 8 OLR 186; *Marsden v Minnekahda Land Co Ltd* (1918) 40 DLR 76.
[198] Per Lord Cairns LJ in *Re Metropolitan Railway Warehousing Co Ltd* (1867) 36 LJ Ch 827 at p 830.
[199] Per Buckley LJ in *Re Southard and Co Ltd* [1979] 1 WLR 1198 at pp 1204–5.

In *Re P and J Macrae Ltd*[200] Upjohn LJ said, at p 237:   **5.80**

> a judicial or textbook gloss upon the terms of the discretion are apt to mislead if they are
> treated as a complete statement of the law. Reported cases can only be quoted as examples of
> the way in which in the past judges have thought fit to exercise the discretion, and judicial
> decision cannot fetter or limit the discretion conferred by statute or even create a binding
> rule of practice.

Harman LJ concurred with this in *Re J D Swain Ltd*,[201] and in *Re LHF Wools Ltd*[202] where **5.81**
he paraphrased Upjohn LJ as having said that other cases about discretion could be 'no more
than guides or signposts along the road'.

In *Re Bayoil SA*[203] Ward LJ, speaking of the discretion conferred by IA 1986, s 125(1), said, **5.82**
at p 156:

> Like every wide discretion, this one conferred by the Act must be exercised judicially. It is not
> unusual, indeed it is salutary and proper, for the court, especially this court,[204] on occasions
> to give guidance to the judges as to how judicially they will ordinarily be expected to pro-
> ceed. Consistency of approach leading to certainty in the litigation process is a virtue. That
> was the concern of Edmund Davies LJ in . . . his judgment in *Re LHF Wools Ltd*:[205]
>
> > . . . I am a little nervous, accordingly, about any decision which appears to lay down
> > almost as a statement or proposition of law that that discretion has to be exercised in any
> > particular direction.
>
> The guidance which may be given serves therefore to establish the principle by which the
> discretion is generally to be exercised, recognising, however, that the rule is *always* subject
> to the exception that, in order not to fetter the discretion, special circumstances, which the
> judge should explain if his exercise of discretion is to be upheld on appeal, will always justify
> a departure from the rule.

The court must assess all the material evidence and consider all relevant issues.[206] In relation **5.83**
to petitions under s 122(1)(g) (the just and equitable clause) Nicholls LJ said, in *Re Walter
L Jacob and Co Ltd*:[207]

> In considering whether or not to make a winding-up order under s 122(1)(g), the court has
> regard to all the circumstances of the case as established by the material before the court at
> the hearing . . . The court will consider those matters which constitute reasons why the com-
> pany should be wound up compulsorily, and those which constitute reasons why it should
> not. The court will carry out a balancing exercise, giving such weight to the various factors as
> is appropriate in the particular case.

Some factors that may apply to all types of company are discussed at 5.87–5.90 and some **5.84**
that apply to particular types of company are discussed at 5.91–5.99. Factors that apply to
particular types of petition are discussed in chapters 7–9, especially at 7.674–7.741 (exercise
of the court's discretion on hearing creditors' petitions) and 8.216–8.247 (contributory's
petition, alternative remedy).

---

[200] [1961] 1 WLR 229.
[201] [1965] 1 WLR 909 at p 911.
[202] [1970] Ch 27 at p 36.
[203] [1999] 1 WLR 147.
[204] The Court of Appeal.
[205] [1970] Ch 27 at p 42.
[206] *Lai Shit Har v Lau Yu Man* [2008] SGCA 33, [2008] 4 SLR 348, at [20].
[207] [1989] BCLC 345 at pp 351–2.

5.85 Where the issue in a case is the exercise of the court's discretion it is particularly important that reasons should be given for the court's decision so that the parties will know which factors were taken into account and which were not.[208]

5.86 Whether or not a winding-up order is to be made is one of the matters relating to the winding up of a company in relation to which the court may have regard to the wishes of the creditors or contributories under s 195.[209]

No assets

5.87 The fact that a company has no assets or that its assets have been mortgaged to an amount equal to or in excess of those assets[210] is not in itself a ground for refusing to order the company to be wound up.[211]

Duration, cost and complexity of winding up

5.88 The fact that winding up a company will take a long time is not a reason for not making a winding-up order.[212] The cost of winding up a company will rarely, if ever, be sufficient, on its own, to persuade the court to exercise its discretion against the making of a winding-up order.[213] Cost and complexity of liquidation could be a reason for not making a winding-up order only in exceptional cases.[214]

5.89 Where the purpose of a petition to wind up a company is to hamper its pursuit of a claim against the petitioner, and imposing the costs of winding up on the company is part of that plan, cost will be a factor in refusing to make a winding-up order.[215]

Small number of members

5.90 In the early days, when the minimum number of members required to form a company was seven, the court took the view that winding up by the court was inappropriate for a company with a small number of members.[216] This view followed the rule in the Companies Act 1862, s 199, that a partnership or association with fewer than eight members could not be wound up as an unregistered company.[217] The view was expressed before the popularity of private companies and before the minimum number of members required to form a company was reduced from seven to two[218] (and subsequently to one for private limited companies[219] and now for all companies[220]). *Re Sanderson's Patents Association*[221] marks the abandonment of this view. In *Re Second Commercial Benefit Building Society*[222] Jessel MR said, at pp 755–6,

---

[208] *Carter-Knight v Peat* (2000) *The Times*, 11 August 2000.
[209] See 5.56–5.61.
[210] *J Speirs and Co v Central Building Co Ltd* 1911 SC 330.
[211] IA 1986, s 125(1); see 2.135.
[212] *Re Universal Tontine Life Insurance Co, ex parte Dee* (1849) 3 De G & Sm 112.
[213] *Pham Tai Duc v PTS Australian Distributor Pty Ltd* [2005] NSWSC 98 at [16].
[214] *Re Oryx Natural Resources* 2007 CILR N6.
[215] *Lai Shit Har v Lau Yu Man* [2008] SGCA 33, [2008] 4 SLR 348.
[216] *Re Natal etc Co Ltd* (1863) 1 Hem & M 639, in which the court refused to order the winding up of a company with nine members; *Re Sea and River Marine Insurance Co* (1866) LR 2 Eq 545, no winding-up order for company with seven members.
[217] See 1.571.
[218] Companies Act 1907, s 37(4).
[219] Companies (Single Member Private Limited Companies) Regulations 1992 (SI 1992/1699).
[220] Companies Act 2006, s 7(1).
[221] (1871) LR 12 Eq 188.
[222] (1879) 48 LJ Ch 753.

that the small number of members was not the sole reason for refusing to make orders in *Re Natal etc Co Ltd* and *Re Sea and River Marine Insurance Co*: the cost of a compulsory winding up compared to the amount of assets involved was in his Lordship's view the principal reason.

Mandatory winding-up orders

On an application for the winding up of a European economic interest grouping under Regulation (EEC) No 2137/85, art 32(1) (infringement of any of various conditions in the Regulation, see 2.45–2.49), if an infringement is proved, the court must order the EEIG to be wound up, unless its affairs can be and are put in order before the court has delivered a substantive ruling. **5.91**

On an application for the winding up of a European cooperative society under Regulation (EC) No 1435/2003, art 73(1), the court must order the SCE to be wound up if it finds: **5.92**

(a) a breach of art 2(1) (which defines the ways in which an SCE may be formed) and/or art 3(2) (which requires an SCE's subscribed capital to be at least €30,000); or

(b) that the SCE was formed by merger without scrutiny of legality,[223]

and the SCE has failed to rectify the situation within a time allowed by the court.

On an application for the winding up of a European grouping of territorial cooperation (EGTC) under Regulation (EC) No 1082/2006, art 14(1), the court must order the EGTC to be wound up if it finds that it no longer complies with the requirements of art 1(2) (objective of an EGTC) or art 7 (tasks) of the Regulation, and has failed to rectify the situation within a time (if any) allowed by the court. **5.93**

Requirement that notice must have been given

There are rules forbidding the making of an order to wind up certain types of companies unless notice of the petition has been given to a person with power to apply for an industry-specific administration order. For the rules relating to protected railway companies, PPP companies, protected energy companies, energy supply companies, a universal service provider (of postal services), and (financial market) infrastructure companies see 3.49. For the rules relating to banks and building societies see 3.50–3.54. For the rules relating to registered providers of social housing and registered social landlords see 3.55–3.56. **5.94**

Companies incorporated for public purposes

Where a company providing a public utility is in financial difficulties, winding it up may not be appropriate if it will involve ending the provision of services on which the public rely. **5.95**

In *Re Exmouth Docks Co*,[224] which concerned an unregistered company, Malins V-C said that one of the grounds for not ordering the winding up of the company was because: **5.96**

> the legislature has declared it to be a work of public importance, and subsequent experience has not been, in my opinion, sufficient, considering in whose hands this property has been, to pronounce it worthless.

In *Re Company or Fraternity of Free Fishermen of Faversham*[225] Fry LJ thought that one reason for not ordering the winding up of the company was that 'we ought not to put an end **5.97**

---

[223] art 34.
[224] (1873) LR 17 Eq 181.
[225] (1887) 36 ChD 329 at p 345.

to a public benefit which was in the mind of the Legislature for the purpose of satisfying private demands of creditors'. The fact that if a company which has been incorporated for a public purpose is wound up the liquidator may have to obtain an Act of Parliament to authorize disposition of the company's undertaking may persuade the court that winding up is not worthwhile.[226]

5.98   From 1862 to 1992 there was legislation to prevent railway companies being wound up, by excepting them from the definition of unregistered companies.[227] Other utility companies were subject to the winding-up jurisdiction and, despite the misgivings expressed in the cases cited at 5.96–5.97, the courts did make orders winding up utility companies, though it was appreciated that the liquidator might have to obtain an Act of Parliament to authorize disposition of the company's undertaking.[228]

5.99   Since the 1990s extensive statutory provision has been made to provide alternatives to winding up for utility companies in the form of industry-specific administration regimes,[229] but only water companies[230] and air traffic services licence companies[231] are exempted from being wound up.

Juridical Classification of a Winding-up Order

Finality

5.100   A winding-up order is a final order.[232] In subsequent proceedings in the winding up, the court will not consider whether the order was properly made:[233] that can be considered only on an appeal against the order[234] or on an application to rescind it.[235] In *Re Mexican and South American Mining Co, Barclay's Case*[236] a person who was sought to be placed on the list of contributories was said to be not a party to the proceedings on the petition but was required to put his challenge to the validity of the winding-up order at a rehearing of the petition[237] and not in the proceedings for settling the list of contributories.

5.101   A winding-up order may be challenged in other proceedings on the ground that the court which made it did not have jurisdiction. In *Re Plumstead, Woolwich and Charlton*

---

[226] *Re Exmouth Docks Co; Re St Kilda and Brighton Railway Co* (1864) 1 W W & A'B 157.

[227] See 1.572–1.577.

[228] See *Re Electric Telegraph of Ireland* (1856) 22 Beav 471, decided under the Joint Stock Companies Winding-up Act 1848; *Re Bradford Navigation Co* (1870) LR 10 Eq 331, (1870) LR 5 Ch App 600; *Re Ennis and West Clare Railway Co* (1879) 3 LR Ir 94; *Re Barton-upon-Humber and District Water Co* (1889) 42 ChD 585; *Re Borough of Portsmouth (Kingston, Fratton and Southsea) Tramways Co* [1892] 2 Ch 362; *Re South Staffordshire Tramways Co* (1894) 1 Mans 292; and *Re Woking Urban District Council (Basingstoke Canal) Act 1911* [1914] 1 Ch 300. All the cases cited concerned unregistered companies except *Re Ennis and West Clare Railway Co*.

[229] See 1.245–1.294.

[230] See 1.248–1.251.

[231] See 1.260–1.261.

[232] *Re National Funds Assurance Co* (1876) 4 ChD 305; *Re Michael P Georgas Co Ltd* [1948] OR 708; *Re Reliance Properties Ltd* [1951] 2 All ER 327.

[233] *Re Universal Salvage Co, Sharpus's Case* (1849) 3 De G & Sm 49; *Re Overend, Gurney and Co Ltd, ex parte Oakes and Peek (No 2)* (1867) 36 LJ Ch 413; *Re London Marine Insurance Association* (1869) LR 8 Eq 176; *Re Cosmopolitan Life Association* (1893) 15 Ont PR 185; *Re Mid East Trading Ltd* [1998] 1 All ER 577.

[234] See 6.44–6.85.

[235] See 6.24–6.43.

[236] (1858) 26 Beav 177.

[237] Rehearings were allowed in the Chancery practice of that time, see 6.158–6.162.

Consumers Pure Water Co[238] a winding-up order was challenged by a person being sued by the liquidator, who questioned whether the liquidator had standing to bring proceedings. In *Re Bowling and Welby's Contract*[239] a purchaser of land from a company in liquidation questioned a liquidator's ability to convey good title to the land.[240] In *Banque des Marchands de Moscou (Koupetschesky) v Kindersley*[241] a person being sued by a company which had been dissolved in a foreign country questioned whether an English winding-up order had been properly made to give the company personality to sue.

The only ground on which a court could ignore a winding-up order would be that the proceedings had been void *ab initio* (for example, because of lack of jurisdiction of the court which made the order).[242]   **5.102**

In rem *or* in personam

The terms '*in rem*' (relating to a thing) and '*in personam*' (relating to a person) are used in several different ways to describe legal proceedings. An application to wind up a company is a proceeding against the company *in personam* not its property *in rem*.[243] Although a winding-up order, like a bankruptcy order, determines the status of a person, it is not an *in rem* order which binds strangers: a winding-up order only binds the company and its members.[244] The Privy Council has used the terms *in rem* and *in personam* in a different way, saying[245] that: **5.103**

> Judgments *in rem* and *in personam* are judicial determinations of the existence of rights: in the one case, rights over property and in the other, rights against a person.

The purpose of a winding-up order is not to determine or establish the existence of rights. Rather, it provides a mechanism for the enforcement of creditors' existing rights, though those rights may, incidentally, have to be determined in the insolvency proceedings.[246] The Privy Council concluded from this that the rules of private international law concerning the enforcement of judgments *in rem* and *in personam* do not apply to a winding-up or bankruptcy order, which, for the purposes of those rules, is in neither class.[247] But the United Kingdom Supreme Court has held that in English law there are no exceptions to the enforcement rules.[248]

Dismissal of Petition

It is wrong to dismiss a petition conditionally, leaving those affected by the petition to check whether the dismissal has taken effect.[249] If a condition is to be fulfilled before a   **5.104**

---

[238] (1860) 2 De G F & J 20.

[239] [1895] 1 Ch 663.

[240] See also *Butts Park Ventures (Coventry) Ltd v Bryant Homes Central Ltd* [2003] EWHC 2487 (Ch), [2004] BCC 207, where the winding up was under the court's inherent jurisdiction instead of IA 1986.

[241] [1951] Ch 112.

[242] *R v Robinson* [1990] BCC 656.

[243] *Re Colorado Silver Mining Co* (1884) 2 QLJ 21.

[244] *Re Bowling and Welby's Contract* [1895] 1 Ch 663.

[245] *Cambridge Gas Transport Corporation v Official Committee of Unsecured Creditors of Navigator Holdings plc* [2006] UKPC 26, [2007] 1 AC 508, at [13].

[246] *Cambridge Gas Transport Corporation v Official Committee of Unsecured Creditors of Navigator Holdings plc* at [14]–[15].

[247] *Cambridge Gas Transport Corporation v Official Committee of Unsecured Creditors of Navigator Holdings plc.*

[248] *Rubin v Eurofinance SA* [2012] UKSC 46, [2013] 1 AC 236.

[249] *Maldon Minerals NL v McLean Exploration Services Pty Ltd* (1992) 9 ACSR 265.

petition is dismissed then the petition must be adjourned to the time by which the condition is to be fulfilled. In *Maresca v Brookfield Development and Construction Ltd*[250] Norris J said he would order that if the company were to pay the petitioner the amount it owed her (£10,000) by a certain date then she was bound to transfer her share in the company to its other shareholder and the company was not to be wound up. This would appear to be a conditional dismissal, but the wording of the order is not known.

5.105   In Hong Kong, in *Re Shop Clothing Ltd*,[251] the petitioning creditors and the company asked for the petition to be dismissed and no party opposed that request. Nevertheless, it was held that the court had a discretion whether or not to dismiss the petition and, as the company was insolvent, decided to make a winding-up order. But in Australia it has been held that the court must dismiss a petition if all parties to it ask for dismissal.[252]

5.106   If, at a hearing of a winding-up petition, there is no appearance for the petitioner and no one is substituted as petitioner, the petition will be dismissed.[253]

Adjournment

Principle

5.107   On hearing a winding-up petition the court may adjourn the hearing conditionally or unconditionally.[254] At the first hearing of a winding-up petition, which is to be defended, it is usual to adjourn it and give directions for filing evidence.[255]

5.108   The petitioner must, forthwith, send notice of an adjournment to the company and to any creditor who has given notice of appearance[256] but was not present at the hearing at which the adjournment was ordered.[257] The notice must state the venue for the adjourned hearing.[258]

5.109   Usually, adjournment of a creditor's petition which has not been served or has been served but not gazetted will be granted only on condition that those steps are completed in time for the adjourned hearing.[259] If the required steps have not been completed and a certificate of compliance has not been filed by the time of the adjourned hearing, no further adjournment for that purpose will be granted and the petition will generally be dismissed.[260] The fact that negotiations are in progress is not a reason for departing from this practice.[261] If protracted negotiations are envisaged, the petition should be gazetted so as to inform other creditors and remove the use of the threat of publicity as a bargaining point.

---

[250]   [2013] EWHC 3151 (Ch), LTL 5/11/2013.
[251]   [1999] 2 HKLRD 280.
[252]   *Re Laverton Nickel NL* (1979) 3 ACLR 945; *Re Alexanders Securities Ltd (No 1)* [1983] 2 QdR 629.
[253]   *Re Royal Mutual Benefit Building Society* [1960] 1 WLR 1143; *Re Aim Investments (Holdings) Ltd* [2004] 2 HKLRD 201.
[254]   IA 1986, s 125(1).
[255]   Chief Registrar Baister, 'The hearing of the petition' (2008) 1 Corporate Rescue and Insolvency 115.
[256]   See 5.32–5.36.
[257]   IR 1986, r 4.18A.
[258]   IR 1986, r 4.18A.
[259]   PD Insolvency Proceedings 2014, para 11.5.1; Chief Registrar Baister, 'The hearing of the petition' (2008) 1 Corporate Rescue and Insolvency 115.
[260]   PD Insolvency Proceedings 2014, para 11.5.1; Chief Registrar Baister, 'The hearing of the petition' (2008) 1 Corporate Rescue and Insolvency 115.
[261]   Chief Registrar Baister, 'The hearing of the petition' (2008) 1 Corporate Rescue and Insolvency 115.

Before the era of active case management and strict timetables, it was held[262] that an **5.110** adjournment could be *sine die*.[263] Alternatively the court may order an indefinite stay of proceedings under its power to make any other order that it thinks fit.[264]

Sometimes adjournments have been ordered subject to conditions which the court has con- **5.111** sidered it is imposing under its power to make any other order that it thinks fit.[265]

During the period of adjournment of one petition, another may be presented by another **5.112** petitioner.[266] This may be one of the exceptional circumstances in which a second petition may be presented while an earlier one is still pending, but consideration should first be given to making an application to be substituted as petitioner in the earlier petition.[267]

Policy against long or repeated adjournments

The court has a strong and well-established policy of discouraging long or repeated adjourn- **5.113** ments of winding-up petitions.[268] Before the era of active case management and strict time- tables, it was said that a winding-up petition presented by a creditor did not give rise to a true *lis* between petitioner and company which those parties could deal with as they like, for example, agreeing between themselves to repeated adjournments.[269]

In *Re Metropolitan Railway Warehousing Co Ltd*[270] (which concerned a contributory's peti- **5.114** tion) Cairns LJ said, at p 830:

> I am averse to adjourning or suspending the petition, for this reason, that I think it is always
> a very inconvenient thing for a company to have a pending petition for a winding-up order
> hanging over their heads, I think the court should, as far as possible, either make an order
> upon the petition for the winding up of the company, if it is a fit case, or, if not, dismiss
> the petition. There are many cases in which it cannot be done; but where that can be done,
> I think that is the better course, and the more so, because it is well known, if the petition is
> adjourned, it is adjourned with this consequence imminent over the company, if the wind-
> ing-up order is made, the winding up will date back to the presentation of the petition, and
> avoid, therefore, or imperil anything that has been done by the company in the mean time.

In Practice Note (Companies: Winding up) [1977] 1 WLR 1066[271] Brightman J said: **5.115**

> [Repeated and lengthy unopposed adjournments of creditors' petitions] are often undesirable
> because the winding-up order, if made, dates back to the presentation of the petition, and the
> adjournments may make the process of liquidation more complex. The books of the company
> tend to get out of date, and sometimes they are lost, quite apart from any dishonesty. Officers
> and employees who could provide valuable information sometimes leave and cannot be traced.
> Further, dispositions made between the presentation of the petition and the making of the

---

[262] *Re R J Jowsey Mining Co Ltd* [1969] 2 OR 549.
[263] Without a day being appointed, ie, indefinitely.
[264] *Re Rudyard Developments Ltd* (1977) 1 BCR 100.
[265] See 5.130.
[266] *Re Scott and Jackson Ltd* (1893) 38 SJ 59; *Electrical Equipment Ltd v Sibmark Pty Ltd* (1991) 22 NSWLR 732.
[267] See 5.225.
[268] *Re a Debtor (No 544/SD/98)* [2000] 1 BCLC 103 at pp 116–17 per Robert Walker LJ.
[269] See *Re Argentine Loan and Mercantile Agency Co Ltd* (1892) 36 SJ 541; *Re Pentasia (Pte) Ltd* [1979] 2 MLJ 59; *Re a Company (No 001573 of 1983)* [1983] BCLC 492 per Harman J at p 495; *Re Pleatfine Ltd* [1983] BCLC 102 per Harman J at p 103; *Re Boston Timber Fabrications Ltd* [1984] BCLC 328; *Re X10 Ltd* [1989] 2 HKLR 306; *Re Par Excellence Co Ltd* [1990] 2 HKLR 277.
[270] (1867) 36 LJ Ch 827.
[271] Not repeated in PD Insolvency Proceedings.

winding-up order have to be examined to see if they are justifiable, and delay both increases the number of these transactions and makes their examination more difficult.

3. Whatever may be the rights of the parties to agree on deferring the hearing of ordinary litigation, the special considerations which apply to creditors' winding-up petitions require as a general rule that they should be heard promptly. No rigid timetable can or should be laid down, but in normal cases where the debt is admitted, a period of four weeks from the date of the first hearing ought to suffice to enable the petitioning creditor, if still unpaid, to decide whether to press for a winding-up order, or whether to rely on other arrangements. Usually this period should also suffice to enable the company to decide whether or not to promote a moratorium or other scheme of arrangement.

4. It is recognised that in some cases there will be special factors which will justify longer agreed adjournments, or more adjournments than one; an example is where a receiver has been appointed and is realising the assets. But those practising in the Companies Court should realise that in future the court is likely to be reluctant to grant long or repeated adjournments, even with the consent of all concerned, unless there are shown to be cogent grounds for the application.

5. This statement does not apply to contributories' petitions. Different considerations apply to these, and there will normally be no objection to long or repeated adjournments by consent.

5.116 There have been exceptional cases in which the court has accepted adjournments for several years so that a company's assets could be protected by a provisional liquidator without the company being wound up.[272]

Related criminal proceedings

5.117 The fact that criminal proceedings are pending in respect of matters to be raised in the winding-up proceedings does not in itself mean that the winding-up proceedings should be adjourned until the completion of the criminal proceedings.[273] The old rule that civil proceedings could not be taken in respect of a felony until after a criminal prosecution, unless good reason was shown for not prosecuting, has not survived the abolition by the Criminal Law Act 1967, s 1, of special rules of law and practice relating to felonies.

5.118 In *Re Electric Mutual Liability Insurance Co Ltd*[274] a Massachusetts company had been redomiciled in Bermuda and had presented its own petition to be wound up by the court there. A creditor claimed that the redomiciliation was fraudulent. The court refused to determine this allegation in proceedings on the winding-up petition because it was irrelevant. The creditor had started judicial review proceedings making the same claim and applied for proceedings on the petition to be adjourned pending the outcome of the judicial review. It was held that the question of adjournment should be decided on the balance of convenience[275] and that the balance was against granting an adjournment. The company undertook that it would not, in the judicial review proceedings, rely on the making of a winding-up order.

---

[272] See 4.10. In *Re Rafidain Bank* (2000) LTL 23/3/2000 provisional liquidators had already been in office for nine years.

[273] *Rowe v Brandon Packers Ltd* (1961) 29 DLR (2d) 246, which concerned a contributory's petition and in which it was emphasized that the interests of the company should be considered.

[274] [1996] Bda LR 62.

[275] *American Cyanamid Co v Ethicon Ltd* [1975] AC 396.

Application by petitioner opposed by other creditors

If it appears that a compromise can be reached shortly, for example, by paying a creditor peti- **5.119**
tioner's debt, it is better to adjourn the petition than to make an order which the petitioner may
not want to be perfected.[276] But a supporting creditor who intends to apply to be substituted
as petitioner if the original petitioning creditor is paid should object to an adjournment for
the purpose of paying or agreeing a compromise with the petitioner so that the winding-up
proceedings are not prolonged unnecessarily and no void disposition of the company's assets is
made to the original petitioner.[277]

Application by company or contributory

On a creditor's petition to wind up a company the court is unlikely to grant an application for **5.120**
an adjournment made by the company[278] or a contributory[279] if the application is opposed by
the petitioner and not supported by other creditors. But an adjournment should be ordered
where the company has been led to believe that adjournment would not be opposed by the
petitioner because negotiations are in progress.[280] A mere assertion by counsel for the company
that, given time, it was hoped to obtain evidence to establish that the petitioner did not have
standing was not enough to obtain an adjournment in *E G and H Nominees Pty Ltd v General
Mutual Insurance Co Ltd.*[281] For adjournments of disputed debt petitions see 7.541–7.549.

On a public interest petition, the court must be very careful before refusing an adjournment **5.121**
to give an opportunity for evidence to be put in against making the winding-up order.[282]
But an adjournment will be refused if the court can see that the evidence would not be
persuasive.[283] In *Re a Company (No 005448 of 1996)*[284] it was found to be just to allow an
adjournment so that two companies sought to be wound up in the public interest could put
in further evidence, but the companies were required to pay the costs thrown away by the
adjournment forthwith on an indemnity basis.

Application by other creditors on creditor's petition

The court may be more sympathetic to an application for adjournment of a creditor's peti- **5.122**
tion by creditors opposing the petition. There is no rule that a supporting creditor is entitled
to insist that the petition be heard or dismissed.[285] Applications by opposing creditors for
adjournments are decided on the same principles as opposing creditors' applications for
dismissal[286] and those principles will be dealt with at 7.698–7.733. Opposing creditors must
produce reasons for adjourning and must not assume that an adjournment will be granted
for them to organize their case.[287]

---

[276] *Re Baker Tucker and Co* (1894) 38 SJ 274.
[277] *Re Ron Winters Glazing Services Ltd* (1988) 4 NZCLC 64,294.
[278] *Re Morgan Shipping Corporation Ltd* (1986) 3 NZCLC 99,876.
[279] *Re Camburn Petroleum Products Ltd* [1980] 1 WLR 86.
[280] *Visage Continental Sdn Bhd v Smooth Track Sdn Bhd* [2008] 1 MLJ 101.
[281] (1976) 50 ALJR 460.
[282] *Re ForceSun Ltd* [2002] EWHC 443 (Ch), [2002] 2 BCLC 302.
[283] *Re ForceSun Ltd.*
[284] [1998] 1 BCLC 98.
[285] *Re Margate Hotel Co* [1888] WN 73.
[286] *Re D W Crompton and Co Ltd* (1975) 1 BCR 51; *Re Airfast Services Pty Ltd* (1976) 11 ACTR 9; *Re
Nationwide Air Ltd* (1978) 1 BCR 208; *Re DTX Australia Ltd* (1987) 11 ACLR 444; see also *Re Leonard
Spencer Pty Ltd* [1963] QdR 230, in which a provisional liquidator had been appointed.
[287] *Southern World Airlines Ltd v Auckland International Airport Ltd* [1992] MCLR 210.

5.123 Sometimes, on a creditor's petition that is opposed by other creditors, the opposers ask for a lengthy adjournment (typically six months) instead of dismissal of the petition, though in practice the court sees opposition as a reason for dismissing rather than adjourning because it disapproves of lengthy adjournments of petitions other than contributories' petitions.[288]

5.124 A long adjournment may be on the terms of a '*St Thomas' Dock* order', that is, an undertaking by the company not to consent to a winding-up order on the petition of any other creditor, or to a voluntary winding up.[289] The petitioner may be asked to agree to share costs with any further petitioner.[290]

Building societies

5.125 On adjourning a petition to wind up a building society the court may, under the Building Societies Act 1986, sch 15, para 18(2), impose conditions for securing:

(a) that the building society be dissolved by consent of its members under the Building Societies Act 1986, s 87, or

(b) that the society amalgamates with, or transfers its engagements to, another building society under the Building Societies Act 1986, s 93 or s 94, or

(c) that the society transfers its business to a company under the Building Societies Act 1986, s 97.

The court may also include conditions for securing that any default which occasioned the petition be made good and that the costs of the proceedings on the petition be defrayed by the person or persons responsible for the default.

Incorporated friendly societies

5.126 On adjourning a petition to wind up an incorporated friendly society the court may, under the Friendly Societies Act 1992, sch 10, para 21(2), impose conditions for securing:

(a) that the friendly society be dissolved by consent of its members under the Friendly Societies Act 1992, s 20, or

(b) that the society amalgamates with, or transfers all or any of its engagements to, another friendly society under the Friendly Societies Act 1992, s 85 or s 86, or

(c) that the society converts itself into a company under the Friendly Societies Act 1992, s 91.

The court may also include conditions for securing that any default which occasioned the petition be made good and that the costs of the proceedings on the petition be defrayed by the person or persons responsible for the default.

Interim or other Order; Alternative Remedies

Scope of an interim or other order

5.127 The power given to the court by IA 1986, s 125(1), to make an interim or other order is limited to making ancillary orders in furtherance of or otherwise in connection with a present

---

[288] *Re Chapel House Colliery Co* (1883) 24 ChD 259.

[289] *Re St Thomas' Dock Co* (1876) 2 ChD 116; *Re International Cable Co* (1890) 2 Meg 183 (in which the adjournment was for three months and a winding-up order was made at the end of that period—see 8 TLR 307 at p 308); *Re Joseph Bull Sons and Co* (1892) 36 SJ 557; *Re St Neots Water Co* (1905) 93 LT 788; *Re Mosbert Finance (Australia) Pty Ltd* (1976) 2 ACLR 5.

[290] *Re Scott and Jackson Ltd* [1893] WN 184.

or prospective winding-up order: the subsection does not empower the court to order some remedy other than winding up.[291]

The power to make any other order the court thinks fit is at the end of a list of powers in s **5.128** 125(1) and is subject to the *ejusdem generis* rule:[292] it does not, for example, empower the court to direct that the company's claim for damages for petitioning maliciously be heard in the winding-up proceedings.[293] It does not empower the court to direct how the winding up is to be conducted, by, for example, ordering assets to be distributed in kind,[294] giving a direction disapplying some part of the statutory winding-up scheme[295] or ordering the liquidator to carry on the company's business and preserve its assets so that they can be handed over to named individuals.[296]

A different view has been taken in cases discussed at 8.221. **5.129**

The court is empowered to adjourn a winding-up application and give directions, and it **5.130** may make the adjournment conditional upon compliance with the directions, provided it is contemplated that a winding-up order will be made if the directions are not complied with (so that the order is in connection with a winding up, not a substitute for one).[297] The order proposed in *Re R J Jowsey Mining Co Ltd* was that the winding-up application would be adjourned *sine die* subject to continuation of the application on failure to comply with the specified condition (the majority of the court, though agreeing that there was jurisdiction to make such an order, decided not to make it). However, in *Pilecon Engineering Bhd v Remaja Jaya Sdn Bhd*[298] the court ordered that if conditions were not fulfilled by a specified day, the company would be deemed to be wound up, and described the petition as 'stayed' until that time, but it is respectfully submitted that such an order introduces undesirable uncertainty about a company's status for persons dealing with it, as they will not know whether the condition has been fulfilled, and the court does not have jurisdiction to make what is in effect a conditional winding-up order.

In *Re Rudyard Developments Ltd*[299] the court ordered an indefinite stay of proceedings. **5.131**

A claim for damages on the ground that a petition to wind up a company was presented **5.132** tortiously must be sought in separate proceedings: they cannot be awarded on the hearing of the petition.[300]

---

[291] *Re Wheal Lovell Mining Co* (1849) 1 Mac & G 1; *Re R J Jowsey Mining Co Ltd* [1969] 2 OR 549; *Re Humber Valley Broadcasting Co Ltd* (1978) 19 Nfld & PEIR 230; *Rafuse v Bishop* (1979) 34 NSR (2d) 70 at pp 82–3; *Idugboe v Oilfield Supply Ltd* 1979 (1) ALR Comm 1; *Maldon Minerals NL v McLean Exploration Services Pty Ltd* (1992) 9 ACSR 265; *See Teow Guan v Kian Joo Holdings Sdn Bhd* [1995] 3 MLJ 598; *Kok Fook Sang v Juta Vila (M) Sdn Bhd* [1996] 2 MLJ 666; *Aznor bin Abdul Karim v Kemasrunding Sdn Bhd* [1998] 5 MLJ 572.

[292] *Re Bank of Credit and Commerce International SA (No 10)* [1997] Ch 213 at p 239.

[293] *Partizan Ltd v O J Kilkenny and Co Ltd* [1998] 1 BCLC 157.

[294] *See Teow Guan v Kian Joo Holdings Sdn Bhd* [1995] 3 MLJ 598.

[295] *Re Bank of Credit and Commerce International SA (No 10)* [1997] Ch 213 at p 239.

[296] *Fairview Schools Bhd v Indrani a/p Rajaratnam (No 2)* [1998] 1 MLJ 110.

[297] *Re R J Jowsey Mining Co Ltd* [1969] 2 OR 549.

[298] [1997] 1 MLJ 808.

[299] (1977) 1 BCR 100.

[300] *Si and Si Sdn Bhd v Hazrabina Sdn Bhd* [1996] 2 MLJ 509.

5.133   A petition for the compulsory winding up of a company in voluntary winding up cannot ask alternatively for removal and replacement of the voluntary liquidator.[301]

5.134   For the appointment of a liquidator on making a winding-up order see 5.141–5.154.

Provisions in winding-up order for conduct of the winding up

5.135   A court ordering the winding up of an insolvent partnership on the ground that it is unable to pay its debts may make an order as to the future conduct of the winding-up proceedings, and any such order may apply any provisions of IPO 1994 with any necessary modifications.[302]

5.136   Otherwise the court cannot add to a winding-up order any conditions about how the winding up is to be conducted: 'The court has a discretion in relation to the making of an order, but none as to its operation when made'.[303] It is not desirable to insert any special provision in an order winding up a foreign company limiting the liquidator's powers[304] though this was done in early cases.

5.137   When in office, a liquidator may apply to the court for directions in relation to any matter arising in the winding up.[305] A supervisor of a voluntary arrangement or an administrator who, when petitioning for winding up, seeks appointment as liquidator under IA 1986, s 140,[306] may simultaneously apply under s 168(3) for directions.[307]

Alternative remedy for insurers

5.138   There is statutory provision for an alternative remedy where an insurer has been proved to be unable to pay its debts. Under the Financial Services and Markets Act 2000, s 377, the court may, if it thinks fit, instead of making a winding-up order, reduce the value of one or more of the insurer's contracts, on such terms and subject to such conditions as the court thinks fit. For the purposes of this provision 'insurer' is defined in the Financial Services and Markets Act 2000 (Insolvency) (Definition of 'Insurer') Order 2001,[308] but the provision does not apply to EEA insurers (which cannot be wound up in the United Kingdom anyway, see 1.318–1.322).[309]

5.139   Under earlier legislation, the court could reduce the amount of the contracts of an insurance company.[310] It was held that a scheme under which policyholders were to exchange their policies for new less valuable policies issued by another insurer was not within that earlier provision[311] nor was a scheme under which different policyholders suffered disproportionate reductions.[312]

---

[301] *Re Cork Shipping and Mercantile Co Ltd* (1879) 7 LR Ir 148; *Re Provincial and Suburban Bank Ltd* (1879) 5 VLR (E) 159 at p 164.

[302] IA 1986, s 168(5C).

[303] Per Roxburgh J in *Re Banque des Marchands de Moscou (Koupetschesky)* [1958] Ch 182 at p 193.

[304] *Re Hibernian Merchants Ltd* [1958] Ch 76.

[305] IA 1986, s 168(3).

[306] See 5.143–5.150.

[307] As in *Re WW Realisation 1 Ltd* [2010] EWHC 3604 (Ch), [2012] 1 BCLC 405.

[308] SI 2001/2634.

[309] Insurers (Reorganisation and Winding Up) Regulations 2004 (SI 2004/353), reg 4(7).

[310] Last re-enacted as the Insurance Companies Act 1982, s 58.

[311] *Re Nelson and Co* [1905] 1 Ch 551.

[312] *Re Nelson and Co.*

Interim costs

Interim costs may be awarded.[313] **5.140**

Appointment of a Liquidator

The official receiver

Normally when a winding-up order is made against a company, the official receiver[314] **5.141**
becomes the liquidator of the company, by virtue of his or her office, on the making of
the order.[315] The court does not have any power to appoint anyone other than the official
receiver as liquidator when making a winding-up order,[316] except where the enactments
discussed at 5.143–5.150 apply.

In the Republic of Ireland, where there is no provision for automatic appointment of a pub- **5.142**
lic official as liquidator, a winding-up order cannot be made unless it appoints a liquidator,
putting the onus on the petitioner to find someone willing to act.[317]

Administrator or supervisor of voluntary arrangement

Where a winding-up order is made immediately upon the appointment of an administrator **5.143**
ceasing to have effect, the administrator whose appointment has ceased can be appointed
liquidator.[318]

Where a winding-up order is made at a time when there is a supervisor of a voluntary arrange- **5.144**
ment approved under IA 1986, part 1,[319] the supervisor can be appointed liquidator.[320]

Where a partnership is ordered to be wound up on a petition under IPO 1994, art 7 (where **5.145**
there is no concurrent petition for the winding up or bankruptcy of a member or former
member of the partnership), presented by one of the insolvency practitioners listed in IA 1986,
s 221A(1),[321] the practitioner who presented the petition may be appointed liquidator.[322] The
insolvency practitioners concerned are:

(a) the liquidator or administrator of a present or former corporate member of the partnership;
(b) the administrator of the partnership;
(c) the trustee of a present or former individual member's estate;
(d) the supervisor of a voluntary arrangement approved under IA 1986, part 1, in relation
     to a corporate member or the partnership, or under part 8 in relation to an individual
     member.

IA 1986, s 140(1), is modified by IPO 1994, sch 4, para 15, to provide that where a partnership **5.146**
is ordered to be wound up and winding-up and/or bankruptcy orders are made against one
or more of its members or former members on petitions under IPO 1994, art 8, immediately

---

[313] *Re Hillcrest Housing Ltd* (1992) 94 DLR (4th) 165 affirming (1992) 97 Nfld & PEIR 124—the case
concerned a contributory's petition which had been litigated for ten years.
[314] See 1.498.
[315] IA 1986, s 136(1) and (2).
[316] *Re North Wales Gunpowder Co* [1892] 2 QB 220; *Sayer v Capital Aviation Ltd* (1993) 6 NZCLC 68,372.
[317] *Re Davis Joinery Ltd* [2013] IEHC 353.
[318] IA 1986, s 140(1).
[319] ss 1–7B.
[320] s 140(2).
[321] Inserted by IPO 1994, sch 3, para 3.
[322] IA 1986, s 221A(5), inserted by IPO 1994, sch 3, para 3.

upon the discharge of an administration order in respect of the partnership, the court may appoint as liquidator or trustee, as appropriate, of all the persons against whom orders are made, the former administrator of the partnership. IA 1986, s 140(2), is similarly modified. Both modified provisions also apply where orders are made on IPO 1994, art 10, petitions for the winding up of a partnership and the winding up or bankruptcy of all its members.[323]

5.147   The fact that the current administrator or supervisor was appointed by the court as a replacement is not in itself a reason for not appointing the current administrator or supervisor as liquidator.[324]

5.148   If the court chooses to act under any of these provisions, it can appoint as liquidator only the person mentioned in the relevant provision: it has no power to appoint an additional liquidator to act with that person.[325]

5.149   An administrator or supervisor seeking appointment under IA 1986, s 140, must notify creditors of the company, either in writing or at a creditors' meeting, that he or she intends to seek appointment.[326] The administrator or supervisor must, at least two business days[327] before the return day, file in court a report giving details of any response from creditors to the notification (including any objections to his or her appointment) and stating the date on which the creditors were notified, which must be at least seven business days before the date of filing the report.[328]

5.150   The court's order making an appointment under s 140 must not issue unless and until the person appointed has filed in court a statement to the effect that he or she is an insolvency practitioner, who is duly qualified under IA 1986 to be the liquidator, and that he or she consents to act.[329]

Insurers

5.151   Where the court is considering whether to appoint a liquidator of an insurer under IA 1986, s 140,[330] the manager of the Financial Services Compensation Scheme may appear and make representations to the court concerning the person to be appointed.[331] In this context, 'insurer' is defined[332] by the Financial Services and Markets Act 2000 (Insolvency) (Definition of 'Insurer') Order 2001.[333]

Building societies and incorporated friendly societies

5.152   The provisions of IA 1986, s 140,[334] do not apply to building societies[335] or incorporated friendly societies.[336]

---

[323] IA 1986, s 221(5), as modified by IPO 1994, sch 6, para 4.
[324] *Landsman v De Concilio* [2005] EWHC 267 (Ch), LTL 25/1/2005.
[325] *Re Exchange Travel (Holdings) Ltd* [1993] BCLC 887.
[326] IR 1986, r 4.7(10).
[327] The clear days rule in CPR, r 2.8(2) and (3), applies (see 1.510). 'Business day' is defined in IR 1986, r 13.13(1) (see 1.512).
[328] IR 1986, r 4.7(10). The seven days must also be clear days.
[329] IR 1986, r 4.102(1) and (2).
[330] See 5.143–5.150.
[331] Insurers (Winding Up) Rules 2001 (SI 2001/3635), r 4.
[332] SI 2001/3635, r 2(1).
[333] SI 2001/2634.
[334] See 5.143–5.150.
[335] Building Societies Act 1986, sch 15, para 22.
[336] Friendly Societies Act 1992, sch 10, para 25.

Bank and building society insolvency orders

A bank insolvency order is an order appointing a person as the bank liquidator of a bank.[337] **5.153**
A building society insolvency order is an order appointing a person as the building society
liquidator of a building society.[338] A bank or building society insolvency order may be made
only if the person who is to be appointed liquidator has consented to act.[339] Electronic and
hard copies of an application for a bank or building society insolvency order must be sent
to the proposed liquidator,[340] and a witness statement by the proposed liquidator must be
filed stating that he or she is qualified to act as an insolvency practitioner in accordance with
IA 1986, s 390, and consents to act as the liquidator.[341] The court cannot make a bank or
building society insolvency order unless this statement has been filed.[342]

History

Until the Companies (Winding up) Act 1890, no one became liquidator of a company on the **5.154**
making of a winding-up order. Instead it was left to the person (normally the successful petitioner) who had what was known as the 'carriage and prosecution' of the order to 'carry it in'
to the master's office and take out a summons to appoint what was then known as an 'official
liquidator'. As only the persons who had appeared at the hearing of the petition could appear
on the summons to appoint a liquidator, and a liquidator did not have to be either professionally qualified or independent of the company, a petitioner associated with those who had
controlled the company could obtain the appointment of a liquidator who would not investigate its affairs. Alternatively, if the controllers of the company satisfied the petitioner's claim
so that the petitioner did not proceed any further, winding up could be delayed for months
until someone noticed that nothing was happening and applied to take over carriage of
the order.[343] The Companies (Winding up) Act 1890 introduced the idea that the official
receiver would take up office as what was then called 'provisional liquidator', but at first this
still depended on the person who had carriage of the order taking the necessary steps to have
it drawn up: if that person declined to have the order drawn up, another interested person had
to apply to the court for liberty to draw up the order.[344] The Companies Winding-up Rules
1892 introduced the present system[345] under which the court draws up orders.

Interaction with other Insolvency Proceedings

Winding Up a Company Already Subject to an Insolvency Proceeding

The question whether a winding-up order may be made in respect of a company which is **5.155**
already subject to an insolvency proceeding is dealt with in chapter 9.

---

[337] Banking Act 2009, s 94(1).
[338] Banking Act 2009, s 94(1), applied and modified by the Building Societies Act 1986, s 90C.
[339] Banking Act 2009, s 94(3), applied and modified by the Building Societies Act 1986, s 90C.
[340] Bank Insolvency (England and Wales) Rules 2009 (SI 2009/356), r 10(1)(a); Building Society
Insolvency (England and Wales) Rules 2010 (SI 2010/2581), r 10(1)(a).
[341] IR 1986, r 4.14(2), as applied and modified by SI 2009/356, r 13(3); IR 1986, r 4.14(2A), inserted by SI
2010/2581, r 13(4). The statement must be filed with the certificate of compliance, see 3.162.
[342] SI 2009/356, r 16(1); SI 2010/2581, r 16(1).
[343] See, for example, *Re Larne, Belfast and Ballymena Railway Co* (1850) 3 De G & Sm 242.
[344] *Re South Metropolitan Brewing and Bottling Co* [1891] WN 51.
[345] See 5.243.

Administration Applications

Reference to winding-up petition in administration application and service on winding-up petitioner

5.156 See 3.111 and 3.114–3.116.

On making an administration order

5.157 On making an administration order in respect of a company, a petition for its winding up must be dismissed.[346] This provision is applied to limited liability partnerships[347] and to insolvent partnerships.[348]

Treating an administration application as a winding-up petition

5.158 On hearing an administration application, the court may[349] treat it as a winding-up petition and make any order which it could make under IA 1986, s 125.[350] This provision is applied to limited liability partnerships[351] and to insolvent partnerships.[352]

5.159 If the court finds that administration is likely to achieve a better result for the company's creditors as a whole than would be likely if the company went into liquidation directly, it will make an administration order rather than a winding-up order, even if the company's affairs require investigation.[353]

Making a bank or building society insolvency order on an administration application or petition

5.160 The provisions for making alternative orders (including, as appropriate, bank and building society insolvency orders) on petitions to wind up banks, building societies and investment banks, discussed at 5.70, also apply to an application for an administration order in respect of a bank[354] or an investment bank,[355] or a petition for an administration order in respect of a building society.[356]

Petitions and Applications for Industry-Specific Administration Orders

Petition or application pending for industry-specific administration order

5.161 While a petition or application for an industry-specific administration order in relation to a company is pending, an order to wind up the company cannot be made. For forms of administration based on IA 1986, part 2, without the amendments made by the Enterprise Act 2002, s 248,[357] this is provided by IA 1986, s 10(1)(a), as continued in force by the Enterprise Act 2002, s 249, and applied:

(a) to water industry special administration by the Water Industry Act 1991, s 24(5);

---

[346] IA 1986, sch B1, para 40(1)(a).
[347] Limited Liability Partnerships Regulations 2001 (SI 2001/1090), reg 5.
[348] IPO 1994, art 6.
[349] By IA 1986, sch B1, para 13(1)(e).
[350] See 5.64–5.67.
[351] Limited Liability Partnerships Regulations 2001 (SI 2001/1090), reg 5.
[352] IPO 1994, art 6.
[353] *Quality Kebab Ltd v Danbury Foods* [2006] EWHC 1764, LTL 4/8/2006.
[354] Banking Act 2009, s 117.
[355] Investment Bank Special Administration Regulations 2011 (SI 2011/245), reg 22.
[356] Building Societies Act 1986, s 89A.
[357] See 1.248–1.261.

(b) to railway administration by the Railways Act 1993, s 60(5), with an exception in s 65(4)(a) for a company incorporated outside Great Britain;

(c) to administration of building societies by the Building Societies Act 1986, sch 15A, paras 1, 2 and 12;

(d) to PPP administration by the Greater London Authority Act 1999, s 221(5), with an exception in s 224(4)(a) for a company incorporated outside Great Britain;

(e) to air traffic administration by the Transport Act 2000, s 30(3).

For industry-specific administration regimes based on schedule B1 administration,[358] the **5.162** provision is made by IA 1986, sch B1, paras 42(3) and 44(1) and (5), as applied:

(a) to energy administration and energy supply company administration by the Energy Act 2004, sch 20, paras 1–4, 7 and 8;[359]

(b) to bank administration, building society special administration and special administration (bank administration) by the Banking Act 2009, s 145(2), (3), (4) and table 1;[360]

(c) to investment bank special administration and special administration (bank insolvency) by the Investment Bank Special Administration Regulations 2011,[361] reg 15(4), (5) and table 1;[362]

(d) to postal administration by the Postal Services Act 2011, sch 10, paras 1, 2, 5 and 6;

(e) to FMI administration by the Financial Services (Banking Reform) Act 2013, sch 6, paras 2 and 3 and table 1.

Contents of administration application and service on winding-up petitioner
See 3.112–3.116.   **5.163**

Treating a winding-up petition as an application for an industry-specific administration order
See 5.68–5.70.   **5.164**

Treating an energy, energy supply company, postal or FMI administration application as a winding-up petition
On hearing an energy, energy supply company, postal or FMI administration application, **5.165** the court may[363] treat it as a winding-up petition and make any order which it could make under IA 1986, s 125.[364]

Dismissal of winding-up petition on making an industry-specific administration order
If an industry-specific administration order is made in respect of a company on an adminis- **5.166** tration petition or application, a pending petition for its winding up must be dismissed. For forms of administration based on IA 1986, part 2, without the amendments made by the

---

[358] See 1.262–1.287 and 1.291–1.294.

[359] Applied to energy supply company administration by the Energy Act 2011, s 96.

[360] Applied to building society special administration by the Building Societies Act 1986, s 90C. Applied to special administration (bank administration) by the Investment Bank Special Administration Regulations 2011 (SI 2011/245), sch 2, para 6.

[361] SI 2011/245.

[362] Applied to special administration (bank insolvency) by SI 2011/245, sch 1, para 5(1).

[363] Energy Act 2004, s 157(1)(e), applied to energy supply company administration by the Energy Act 2011, s 96; Postal Services Act 2011, s 71(1)(e); Financial Services (Banking Reform) Act 2013, s 117(3)(e).

[364] See 5.64–5.67.

Enterprise Act 2002, s 248,[365] this is provided by IA 1986, s 11(1)(a), as continued in force by the Enterprise Act 2002, s 249, and applied:

(a) to water industry special administration by the Water Industry Act 1991, sch 3, paras 1 and 2;

(b) to railway administration by the Railways Act 1993, sch 6, paras 1 and 2;

(c) to administration of building societies by the Building Societies Act 1986, sch 15A, paras 1, 2 and 13;

(d) to PPP administration by the Greater London Authority Act 1999, sch 14, paras 1 and 2;

(e) to air traffic administration by the Transport Act 2000, sch 1, paras 1–4.

5.167 For industry-specific administration regimes based on schedule B1 administration,[366] the provision is made by IA 1986, sch B1, para 42(3), as applied:

(a) to energy administration and energy supply company administration by the Energy Act 2004, sch 20, paras 1–4 and 7;[367]

(b) to bank administration, building society special administration and special administration (bank administration) by the Banking Act 2009, s 145(2), (3), (4) and table 1;[368]

(c) to investment bank special administration and special administration (bank insolvency) by the Investment Bank Special Administration Regulations 2011,[369] reg 15(4), (5) and table 1;[370]

(d) to postal administration by the Postal Services Act 2011, sch 10, paras 1, 2 and 5;

(e) to FMI administration by the Financial Services (Banking Reform) Act 2013, sch 6, paras 2 and 3 and table 1.

Concurrent Petitions against an Insolvent Partnership and One or More Members

5.168 Where concurrent petitions are presented under IPO 1994, art 8 or art 10, for the winding up of a partnership and the winding up or bankruptcy of one or more of its members or former members, IA 1986, s 125, is replaced by a modified s 125 and a new s 125A.[371] The modifications made in relation to art 8 and art 10 petitions are identical except that the art 8 version of s125A has a subsection (8) which does not appear in the art 10 version. Section 125A(8) states that the court's power to authorize the amendment of a petition, by the omission of any creditor or debt, is not prejudiced by anything in ss 125, 125A, 267 or 268. This is the only current mention in legislation of a power to permit amendment of a winding-up petition.[372]

5.169 Under the modified s 125(1), as under s 125(1) as originally enacted,[373] on hearing an art 8 or art 10 petition against a partnership or any of its insolvent members, the court may

---

[365] See 1.248–1.261.

[366] See 1.262–1.287 and 1.291–1.294.

[367] Applied to energy supply company administration by the Energy Act 2011, s 96.

[368] Applied to building society special administration by the Building Societies Act 1986, s 90C. Applied to special administration (bank administration) by the Investment Bank Special Administration Regulations 2011 (SI 2011/245), sch 2, para 6.

[369] SI 2011/245.

[370] Applied to special administration (bank insolvency) by SI 2011/245, sch 1, para 5(1).

[371] IPO 1994, sch 4, para 9 (in relation to art 8 petitions) and sch 6, para 3 (in relation to art 10 petitions).

[372] See 3.207.

[373] See 5.64–5.67.

dismiss it, or adjourn the hearing conditionally or unconditionally, or make any other order that it thinks fit, but it does not have power to make an interim order. Also under the modified s 125(1) the court must not refuse to make a winding-up order against a partnership or a corporate member on the ground only that the partnership property or (as the case may be) the member's assets have been mortgaged to an amount equal to or in excess of that property or those assets, or that the partnership has no property or the member no assets.[374] Under the modified s 125(2), if the court hears an art 8 or art 10 petition for the winding up of an insolvent partnership, and a bankruptcy or winding-up order has already been made against a member of the partnership, the court's order under s 125(1) may contain directions as to the future conduct of any insolvency proceedings in existence against that insolvent member.

On the hearing of an art 8 or art 10 petition against a member of an insolvent partnership, **5.170** the petitioner must draw the court's attention to the result of the hearing of the winding-up petition against the partnership (which must be heard before any petition against a member).[375]

If, on the petition against the partnership, the court has neither made a winding-up order **5.171** nor dismissed the petition, it may adjourn the petition against the member until either of those events has occurred.[376]

If the court has ordered the partnership to be wound up, it may order the winding up or **5.172** bankruptcy, as appropriate, of the member.[377] IPO 1994 makes special provision for the joint administration of the insolvencies of the partnership and its members, provided a winding-up or bankruptcy order is made against at least one of them within 28 days of making the partnership winding-up order. If that does not happen, the insolvency proceedings against the partnership are conducted as if the order had been made on a petition under art 7 (creditor's petition for winding up of a partnership with no concurrent petition against any member), and any subsequent winding-up or bankruptcy of a member is conducted under IA 1986 without the modifications made by IPO 1994 apart from the insertion of ss 168(5A), (5B) and (5C) and 303(2A), (2B) and (2C).[378]

If the court has dismissed the petition against the partnership, it may dismiss the petition **5.173** against the member.[379] If it does order the winding up or bankruptcy of the member, it is conducted under IA 1986 without the modifications made by IPO 1994 apart from the insertion of ss 168(5A), (5B) and (5C) and 303(2A), (2B) and (2C).[380]

If the court has ordered the winding up of the partnership, it may dismiss the petition **5.174** against the member if it considers it just to do so because of a change of circumstances since the making of the winding-up order against the partnership.[381]

---

[374] See 2.135.
[375] IA 1986, s 125A(1).
[376] s 125A(2); the court has power anyway under s 125(1) to adjourn a petition against a member conditionally.
[377] s 125A(3).
[378] IA 1986, s 125A(4).
[379] IA 1986, s 125A(5); the court has power anyway under s 125(1) to dismiss a petition against a member.
[380] IA 1986, s 125A(5).
[381] s 221A(6); the court has power anyway under s 125(1) to dismiss a petition against a member.

5.175   The court may, under s 221A(7), dismiss an art 8 or art 10 petition against a limited partner if:[382]

    (a) it lodges in court for the benefit of the creditors of the partnership sufficient money or security to the court's satisfaction to meet its limited liability for the debts and obligations of the partnership; or

    (b) it satisfies the court that it is no longer under any liability in respect of the debts and obligations of the partnership.

5.176   If a partnership has been ordered to be wound up on an art 8 or art 10 petition and, in the course of hearing a winding-up petition presented against a member of the partnership (whether under art 8 or art 10 or not), the court is satisfied that an application has been or will be made under IA 1986, s 147(1), as modified by IPO 1994, sch 4, para 19, to stay proceedings in the partnership winding up,[383] the court may adjourn the petition against the insolvent member, either conditionally or unconditionally.[384] If the court then stays the partnership winding up, it may dismiss the petition against the member.[385]

Costs

5.177   I see that Vice-Chancellor Knight Bruce has made an observation to this effect with regard to the Winding-up Acts, namely, that if those Acts were as beneficial to the rest of Her Majesty's subjects as they are to the profession of the law, they would be a great achievement in legislation.[386]

General

5.178   In relation to a winding-up petition, as with any court proceedings, the question of costs is always at the discretion of the court.[387] The general rule is that the unsuccessful party will be ordered to pay the costs of the successful party, but the court may make a different order.[388] Paragraphs 5.180–5.214 state how the costs of various parties to winding-up proceedings would normally be dealt with by the court.

5.179   If a company is ordered to be wound up, and it is ordered to pay the costs of the petitioner or any person appearing on the petition, the court may 'allow' those costs as expenses of the liquidation.[389] The company itself is a 'person appearing on the petition' for these purposes.[390]

---

[382] IA 1986, s 125A(7).

[383] See 6.90. IA 1986, s 147(1), as modified by IPO 1994, sch 4, para 19, is probably applied to petitions under art 10 of the 1994 Order by IA 1986, s 221(5), as modified by IPO 1994, sch 6, para 4; see 1.229.

[384] IA 1986, s 147(2), as modified by IPO 1994, sch 4, para 19.

[385] IA 1986, s 147(3)(a), as modified by IPO 1994, sch 4, para 19. The court has power to do these things anyway under IA 1986, s 125(1).

[386] Per Lord Cranworth V-C in *Re Sherwood Loan Co* (1851) 1 Sim NS 165 at p 177.

[387] Senior Courts Act 1981, s 51(1); CPR, r 44.2(1); *Re Albion Bank Ltd* (1866) 15 LT 346 per Stuart V-C at p 347; *Re Criterion Gold Mining Co* (1889) 41 ChD 146 per Kay J at p 148.

[388] CPR, r 44.4(2).

[389] IR 1986, r 4.218(3)(h). See 5.215–5.217.

[390] *Re Portsmouth City Football Club Ltd* [2012] EWHC 3088 (Ch), [2013] Bus LR 374, at [115]; [2013] EWCA Civ 916, [2013] Bus LR 1152.

Petitioner

If a winding-up order is made

The petitioner's costs of a successful petition are normally ordered to be paid by the com- **5.180**
pany as an expense of the liquidation.[391] The petitioner is also entitled to the costs of any
interim applications, unless there is good reason to the contrary.[392] For allowance of costs
as expenses of a liquidation see 5.179.

If a petition succeeds after substitution of the petitioner, the original petitioner's costs of **5.181**
presenting and gazetting the petition will be ordered to be paid as an expense of the liquidation,[393] even if the original petitioner does not appear at the hearing as a supporter.[394]

In *Re Lennox Publishing Co Ltd*[395] the same solicitor had acted for both the creditor peti- **5.182**
tioner and the company. Kay J marked his disapproval by disallowing the petitioner's costs
and giving carriage of the winding up[396] to a supporting creditor.

If the effective opposition to a successful petition came from a party other than the com- **5.183**
pany itself, that party may be ordered to pay the petitioner's costs.[397] The power to order
a non-party to pay costs can be exercised if, in all the circumstances, it is just to do so.[398]

A non-party costs order may be made against a person who caused a company to defend **5.184**
a winding-up petition unsuccessfully if that person did not believe bona fide (a) that the
company had an arguable case and (b) that it was in the interests of the company (or if the
company was insolvent, its creditors) to pursue that case to the extent that it did.[399]

In *Re Interdisciplinary Health Consultancy Pty Ltd*[400] a successful contributory petitioner **5.185**
had given an indemnity for the liquidator's remuneration and expenses, and sought an order
that the only other contributory should share any payment required under this indemnity,
but the order was refused as the other contributory had not appeared to oppose the winding
up and it was doubtful whether such an order could be made.

If a winding-up order is not made and the petition debt has not been paid

Normally, if a petition is unsuccessful, the petitioner must pay the company's costs,[401] one **5.186**
set of costs to opposing creditors and one set to opposing contributories.[402] The position is

---

[391] *Re Humber Ironworks Co* (1866) LR 2 Eq 15; *Re Bostels Ltd* [1968] Ch 346 at p 350; *Re a Company (No 004055 of 1991)* [1991] 1 WLR 1003 at p 1005; Senior Courts Costs Office Guide 2013, para 2.14.
[392] *Re Ryan Developments Ltd* [2002] EWHC 1121 (Ch), [2002] 2 BCLC 792.
[393] *Re Bostels Ltd* [1968] Ch 346.
[394] *Re Castle Coulson and MacDonald Ltd* [1973] Ch 382.
[395] (1890) 61 LT 787.
[396] See 5.154.
[397] *Re Co-operative Development Funds of Australia Ltd (No 3)* (1978) 3 ACLR 437, in which the controllers of a number of companies had appeared in person as contributories to oppose public interest winding-up petitions (which the companies did not appear to oppose) and were ordered to pay the petitioner's costs—the hearings had lasted for eight weeks; *Re Worldhams Park Golf Course Ltd* [1998] 1 BCLC 554 (contributory's petition opposed by another contributory); *Stocznia Gdanska SA v Latreefers Inc (No 2)* [2001] 2 BCLC 116 (company's parent company, acting in its own interest, funded the company's opposition to a creditor's petition when the company was insolvent); *Re Datacom Wire and Cable Co Ltd* [2000] 1 HKLRD 526 (creditor's petition opposed by contributory who misrepresented the company's ability to pay its debts so as to obtain an adjournment).
[398] *Re Aurum Marketing Ltd* [2000] 2 BCLC 646 at p 654.
[399] *Re Aurum Marketing Ltd*; *Re North West Holdings plc* [2001] EWCA Civ 67, [2001] 1 BCLC 468.
[400] (1993) 12 ACSR 185.
[401] See 5.199–5.200.
[402] See 5.208–5.210.

different if a creditor's petition achieves payment of the petition debt and no winding-up order is asked for at the hearing.[403]

5.187 Before substitution of petitioners was introduced, there were cases in which, at the hearing of a petition, the petitioner merely asked for it to be dismissed so that the court never had an opportunity to determine its merits. In such cases the petitioner was normally ordered to pay the costs of opposing creditors[404] and might be ordered to pay the costs of both supporting and opposing creditors and contributories[405] as well as the company's costs.[406] The rule was not invariable. The contributory petitioner in *Re District Bank of London*[407] was not ordered to pay other parties' costs. In *Re North Brazilian Sugar Factories Ltd*[408] the contributory petitioner was ordered to pay the costs of each person appearing.

5.188 If the petition of an unpaid creditor whose debt is undisputed is refused only because the court accepts the view of opposing creditors that there should not be a compulsory winding up, no order as to costs will be made, unless the petitioner was acting unreasonably, for example, where the petitioner ought to have known that the petition would fail.[409] In *Re Arrow Leeds Ltd*[410] the company was ordered to pay the petitioner's costs because it did not become clear that the majority of creditors opposed winding up until the petition had been adjourned twice.

5.189 In some cases, a costs penalty has been imposed on a company for not giving timely information to a petitioner about the circumstances which would lead to dismissal of the petition. In *Re M McCarthy and Co (Builders) Ltd (No 2)*[411] the company sought to be wound up had been incorporated with the same name as a company which had earlier been struck off the register and apparently by the people who controlled the old company. The petitioner was a creditor of the old company who did not realize that the new company was a different entity. The petition was dismissed but the new company was ordered to pay the petitioner's costs. In *Re Lanaghan Bros Ltd*,[412] payment by the company sought to be wound up of the creditor petitioner's costs on dismissing the petition was ordered where the company had allowed the creditor to obtain judgment by default and had not disputed the debt or had the judgment set aside until after the petition was presented. In *Re Mailrite Pty Ltd*[413] the petitioning creditor was a company in liquidation. The debt had arisen before the liquidation and the debtor company may have indicated then that it was disputed, but failed to tell the

---

[403] See 5.192–5.193.
[404] *Re Patent Cocoa Fibre Co* (1876) 1 ChD 617.
[405] *Re Anglo-Virginian Freehold Land Co* [1880] WN 155; *Re Peckham etc Tramways Co* (1888) 57 LJ Ch 462; *Re Paper Bottle Co* (1888) 40 ChD 52; *Re British Electric Street Tramways* [1903] 1 Ch 725.
[406] *Re A E Hayter and Sons (Porchester) Ltd* [1961] 1 WLR 1008 at p 1011.
[407] (1887) 35 ChD 576.
[408] (1887) 56 LT 229.
[409] *Re Chapel House Colliery Co* (1883) 24 ChD 259; *Re East Kent Colliery Co Ltd* (1914) 30 TLR 659; *Re R W Sharman Ltd* [1957] 1 WLR 1008; *Re Research Industries Ltd* [1959] SASR 290; *Re A E Hayter and Sons (Porchester) Ltd* [1961] 1 WLR 1008; *Re Sklan Ltd* [1961] 1 WLR 1013; *Re Riviera Pearls Ltd* [1962] 1 WLR 722; *Re Lockyer Valley Fresh Foods Co-operative Association Ltd* (1980) 5 ACLR 455; *Re Jakab Industries Pty Ltd* (1982) 6 ACLR 784; see also *Re Clutha Leathers Ltd* (1987) 4 NZCLC 64,160 discussed at 3.205.
[410] [1986] BCLC 538.
[411] [1976] 2 All ER 339.
[412] [1977] 1 All ER 265.
[413] (1985) 9 ACLR 863.

liquidator there was any dispute despite being asked for payment on several occasions over a period of four months. No order as to costs was made when the petition was dismissed.

In *Re Xyllyx plc (No 2)*[414] Harman J ruled that if a public interest petition to wind up a company is unsuccessful then the company may nevertheless be ordered to pay the petitioner's costs if the petition was properly presented on the basis of information available to the petitioner. However, in *Re Southbourne Sheet Metal Co Ltd*[415] the Court of Appeal said that Harman J's idea that litigants bringing civil proceedings in the public interest should not have to pay a successful party's costs if there were good reasons for bringing the proceedings is wrong. Subsequent cases have shown that, in costs orders generally, no special advantage should be given to a party merely because it has acted in the public interest.[416] *Re Xyllyx plc (No 2)*[417] is therefore unlikely to be followed. **5.190**

The report of *Re Tyneside Permanent Benefit Building Society*[418] states that a petitioner whose petition is dismissed will never be awarded costs, but the cases cited at 5.187–5.189 show that this statement is too rigid and there are inevitably exceptions as costs are always at the discretion of the court. **5.191**

Creditor's petition achieving payment of the petitioner's debt

If a creditor petitioner's debt is paid before the hearing and no winding-up order is asked for at the hearing then, provided the petition has been gazetted, the petition will be dismissed and the company will be ordered to pay the petitioner's costs[419] even if the company does not appear.[420] This is so even if only part of the amount demanded was paid, it being conceded that the balance is disputed[421] or that the petition overstated the debt.[422] The petitioner is also entitled to the costs of any interim applications, unless there is good reason to the contrary.[423] If the petition has not been gazetted by the time of the initial hearing, the court will make an order for costs only if the company consents to the petition being dismissed on terms that the costs are paid.[424] Otherwise, the petitioner may ask for an adjournment for gazetting and for filing a certificate of compliance. The court will not waive the requirement for gazetting in these circumstances for fear of encouraging creditors to use the court as a debt collecting service.[425] But in practice the threat of gazetting the petition, and adding the costs of doing that, and of applying for a costs order, to the costs payable, should persuade a company to pay the petitioner's costs as well as the petition debt without requiring an order for costs. The Irish High Court has decided not to make advertising the petition a condition of granting a costs order, on the ground that advertising is an unnecessary cost.[426] But the inability of the company to pay the costs raises the probability that the petition will have to **5.192**

[414] [1992] BCLC 378.
[415] [1993] 1 WLR 244.
[416] *R (Bahta) v Secretary of State for the Home Department* [2011] EWCA Civ 895, [2011] 5 Costs LR 857.
[417] [1992] BCLC 378.
[418] [1885] WN 148.
[419] *Re Alliance Contract Co* [1867] WN 218; *Re Flagstaff Silver Mining Co of Utah* (1875) LR 20 Eq 268; *Re Nowmost Co Ltd* [1996] 2 BCLC 492.
[420] *Re Shusella Ltd* [1983] BCLC 505.
[421] *International Factors (Singapore) Pty Ltd v Speedy Tyres Pty Ltd* (1991) 5 ACSR 250.
[422] *Hydratek Fluid Power Ltd v Transglobal Freight Management Ltd* [2002] EWHC 2498 (Ch).
[423] *Re Ryan Developments Ltd* [2002] EWHC 1121 (Ch), [2002] 2 BCLC 792.
[424] Chief Registrar Baister, 'The hearing of the petition' (2008) 1 Corporate Rescue and Insolvency 115.
[425] *Re Shusella Ltd*.
[426] *Re MCR Personnel Ltd* [2011] IEHC 319.

go ahead anyway, possibly with a substituted petitioner, and should, therefore, be gazetted to inform other creditors.

5.193 Costs are awarded because the petitioner is regarded as having effectively succeeded.[427] However, the court may make no order as to part or all of the petitioner's costs as a penalty for unreasonable pre-action behaviour[428] or unreasonable rejection of an offer of payment.[429] Such a penalty may be reduced because of the company's own unreasonable behaviour.[430]

Travelling and subsistence

5.194 The petitioner's travelling and subsistence expenses may be allowed by the costs officer.[431]

The Company

If a winding-up order is made

5.195 The 'usual compulsory order' made on a winding-up petition includes provision for the payment of the company's costs of preparing for and appearing at the hearing of a successful winding-up petition as an expense of the liquidation.[432] But the court has jurisdiction to order that the company's costs are not to be paid out of its assets in the liquidation.[433] The company's assets available for distribution to its creditors should not be used to pay for its unjustified opposition to the petition. Where there has been unjustified opposition, the court may:

(a) order the company's costs to be paid by a person who instigated the company's unjustifiable opposition; and

(b) order that the company's costs are not to be paid until all unsecured creditors have been paid in full.[434]

5.196 The first order is in the nature of a third party costs order and the person against whom such an order is sought must be given an opportunity to submit a response and, if necessary, put in evidence, before the order is made.[435] It orders the third party to pay to the company the amount of costs that must be paid as an expense of the liquidation. It is intended to ensure that those costs are not paid with money that should otherwise go to the unsecured creditors. All the reported cases in which such an order has been made have been public interest petitions. The order has been made[436] in favour of a

---

[427] *Re Nowmost Co Ltd* [1996] 2 BCLC 492.

[428] CPR, r 44.2(4)(a) and (5)(a). See 7.8–7.21.

[429] *Holmes v Mainstream Ventures Ltd* [2009] EWHC 3330 (Ch), [2010] 1 BCLC 651.

[430] *Holmes v Mainstream Ventures Ltd*.

[431] IR 1986, r 7.41(2).

[432] *Re Humber Ironworks Co* (1866) LR 2 Eq 15; *Re Wiarton Beet Sugar Co* (1904) 3 OWR 393; *Re Gibbons Radio and Electrical Ltd* [1962] NZLR 353; *Re Bostels Ltd* [1968] Ch 346 at p 350; *Re a Company (No 004055 of 1991)* [1991] 1 WLR 1003 at p 1005; IR 1986, r 4.218(3)(h).

[433] *Re Bathampton Properties Ltd* [1976] 1 WLR 168.

[434] *Re a Company (No 004055 of 1991)* [1991] 1 WLR 1003 (in principle, an order of type (a) may be made but an order of type (b) may not be made); *Re Aurum Marketing Ltd* [2000] 2 BCLC 645 (orders of both kinds made); *Secretary of State for Trade and Industry v Liquid Acquisitions Ltd* [2002] EWHC 180 (Ch), [2003] 1 BCLC 375 (orders of both kinds made). *Re a Company (No 004055 of 1991)* was a creditor's petition; the other two cases were public interest petitions.

[435] *Re AB Developments Pty Ltd* (1982) 6 ACLR 654; *Re a Company (No 004055 of 1991)* [1991] 1 WLR 1003; *Re Land and Property Trust Co plc (No 4)* [1994] 1 BCLC 232.

[436] Or, in *Re a Company (No 004055 of 1991)*, allowed to be made.

company (and in the interest of its creditors), on an application by the petitioner, where the company has been represented by the person against whom the order is sought. It is an open question whether this practice could be extended to permit any other application for costs in favour of a party who is not the applicant.[437] The second order (known as a '*Bathampton* order'[438]) has been said to ensure that the person ordered to pay the company's costs cannot claim an indemnity from the company in competition with unsecured creditors.[439] Before the jurisdiction to make third-party costs orders was established, only *Bathampton* orders were made,[440] but this would have deprived the solicitors concerned of their fees and disbursements and it would be unfair to do that on grounds which have no necessary connection with the conduct of the solicitors themselves.[441] The correct mechanism for depriving solicitors of fees is by assessment or a wasted costs order.

Factors in favour of allowing costs of opposing a successful petition are:[442]   **5.197**

(a) the solicitors were duly instructed on behalf of the company;
(b) those directing the affairs of the company at the relevant time considered that it was in the best interests of the company for the company to oppose the winding up petition in the way, and on the grounds on which, it did;
(c) those directing the company were not acting in their own interests in a way which was in conflict with the best interests of the company;
(d) the work done by the solicitors on behalf of the company was in fact in the best interests of the company;
(e) there is no factor which would justify the court in refusing to allow the company's costs to be an expense of the liquidation.

The company's costs allowable as expenses of the liquidation may include the costs of   **5.198** unsuccessfully applying for the petition to be struck out, the costs of advice on applying for a validation order under IA 1986, s 127, and costs relating to a parallel petition,[443] but not the costs of other proceedings which might establish a cross-claim against the petitioner.[444]

If a winding-up order is not made

The company's costs of opposing an unsuccessful winding-up petition must be paid by the   **5.199** petitioner unless there are exceptional circumstances[445] or the petition has achieved payment

[437] *Re Portsmouth City Football Club Ltd* [2012] EWHC 3088 (Ch), [2013] Bus LR 374, at [62]–[66]; [2013] EWCA Civ 916, [2013] Bus LR 1152.
[438] *Re Bathampton Properties Ltd* [1976] 1 WLR 168.
[439] *Secretary of State for Trade and Industry v Liquid Acquisitions Ltd* at [11].
[440] *Re Bathampton Properties Ltd*; *Re Reprographic Exports (Euromat) Ltd* (1978) 122 SJ 400; *Re a Company (No 004055 of 1991)* [1991] 1 WLR 1003; *Allied Leasing and Finance Corporation v Banco Econômico SA* 2001 CILR 93.
[441] *Re a Company (No 004055 of 1991)* at p 1006.
[442] *Re Portsmouth City Football Club Ltd* [2012] EWHC 3088 (Ch), [2013] Bus LR 374, at [128]; [2013] EWCA Civ 916, [2013] Bus LR 1152.
[443] See 5.224–5.241.
[444] *Re Portsmouth City Football Club Ltd* [2012] EWHC 3088 (Ch), [2013] Bus LR 374, at [113]–[136]; [2013] EWCA Civ 916, [2013] Bus LR 1152.
[445] *Re Humber Ironworks Co* (1866) LR 2 Eq 15; *Re Tuglow Investments Pty Ltd* (1977) 77 ATC 4,245; *Re Fernforest Ltd* [1990] BCLC 693.

of the petitioner's debt.[446] This rule applies if a creditor's petition is dismissed because the petition debt is disputed, and the costs will not be reserved to the hearing of a claim to establish the debt[447] or ordered to be costs in that claim.[448] See 7.597–7.602. The company will be awarded its costs against the petitioner if the petition is dismissed for failure to file a certificate of compliance.[449]

5.200 In *Re Xyllyx plc (No 2)*[450] Harman J ruled that if a public interest petition to wind up a company is unsuccessful, the company may nevertheless be ordered to pay the petitioner's costs if the petition was properly presented on the basis of information available to the petitioner. However, in *Re Southbourne Sheet Metal Co Ltd*[451] the Court of Appeal said that Harman J's idea that litigants bringing civil proceedings in the public interest should not have to pay a successful party's costs if there were good reasons for bringing the proceedings is wrong. *Re Xyllyx plc (No 2)*[452] is therefore unlikely to be followed.

Voluntary liquidator

5.201 A voluntary liquidator of a company may appear on a petition to wind up the company but the company and the voluntary liquidator will not both be awarded costs.[453]

Company petitioning for its own winding up

5.202 If a company petitions for its own winding up, its solicitor's bill of costs must give credit for any deposit on account of the costs and expenses to be incurred in respect of the filing and prosecution of the petition.[454]

Supporting Creditors and Contributories

If a winding-up order is made

5.203 When a winding-up order is made, creditors who appeared to support the petition will be awarded one set of costs between them to be paid as an expense of the liquidation, and a second set of costs will be awarded on the same basis to supporting contributories.[455] The earlier view of Lord Romilly MR in *Re Humber Ironworks Co*[456] that only one set of costs should be awarded to be shared between both creditors and contributories has not been acted on nor has the view of Vaughan Williams J in *Re New British Iron Co Ltd*[457] that costs would be awarded to supporters only if they reasonably supposed that there would be a contest about some question affecting their interests. It is an invariable rule that only one set of costs is awarded to successful supporting

---

[446] See 5.192–5.193.
[447] *GlaxosmithKline Export Ltd v UK (Aid) Ltd* [2003] EWHC 1383 (Ch), [2004] BPIR 528.
[448] *Re Fernforest Ltd* [1990] BCLC 693.
[449] *Re Royal Mutual Benefit Building Society* [1960] 1 WLR 1143.
[450] [1992] BCLC 378.
[451] [1993] 1 WLR 244.
[452] [1992] BCLC 378.
[453] *Re A W Hall and Co Ltd* (1885) 53 LT 633; *Re Mont de Piété of England* [1892] WN 166.
[454] IR 1986, r 7.37(1).
[455] *Re European Banking Co* (1866) LR 2 Eq 521; *Re Peckham etc Tramways Co* (1888) 57 LJ Ch 462 per Chitty J at 463; *Re Bostels Ltd* [1968] Ch 346 at p 350; Senior Courts Costs Office Guide 2013, para 2.14 (which does not mention contributories).
[456] (1866) LR 2 Eq 15.
[457] (1892) 93 LT Jo 202.

creditors,[458] even if several persons legitimately appear to present separate views.[459] They must arrange among themselves how to divide up the costs. The limit of one set of costs is adopted to discourage appearances merely for the sake of making costs, and also, when the petition succeeds, to protect the assets of the company inasmuch as the costs then come out of those assets.[460]

5.204 Secured creditors are as entitled to costs as unsecured creditors: a secured creditor does not have to elect between resting on the security and taking part in the liquidation until after the winding-up order is made.[461]

5.205 Supporters who instruct the same solicitors as the petitioner are not allowed separate costs, and solicitors instructed in such circumstances should not instruct counsel to represent the supporters in addition to counsel instructed to represent the petitioner.[462]

If a winding-up order is not made

5.206 Supporters of an unsuccessful petition are not entitled to costs.[463] If permission is granted at the hearing of a petition for the petition to be withdrawn, no order will be made for the costs of those appearing to support the petition[464] unless they give their consent to the withdrawal of the petition only on condition that their costs are paid.[465]

Opposing Creditors and Contributories

If a winding-up order is made

5.207 Creditors or contributories appearing to oppose a successful petition are not entitled to costs.[466]

If a winding-up order is not made

5.208 Creditors who appear to oppose an unsuccessful petition may be given one set of costs between them from the petitioner and so may opposing contributories if their interests are distinct from the company's.[467] A shareholder against whom a personal charge is made and who is vindicated will be awarded costs against the petitioner.[468] The view taken in *Re Ibo Investment Trust Ltd*,[469] which concerned a contributory's petition, that it is the company which should defend a winding-up petition so that other shareholders should not be given

---

[458] *MBf Finance Bhd v Sri Hartamas Development Sdn Bhd* [1994] 2 MLJ 709.

[459] *Re Esal (Commodities) Ltd* [1985] BCLC 450.

[460] *Re Peckham etc Tramways Co* (1888) 57 LJ Ch 462 per Chitty J at p 463. In Victoria, each supporting creditor is allowed costs reasonably incurred: *Re Property Growth Securities Ltd* (1991) 4 ACSR 783 at pp 792–3.

[461] *Re Carmarthenshire Anthracite Coal and Iron Co* (1875) 45 LJ Ch 200.

[462] *Re Military and General Tailoring Co Ltd* (1877) 47 LJ Ch 141; *Re Brighton Marine Palace and Pier Co Ltd* (1897) 13 TLR 202.

[463] *Re Humber Ironworks Co* (1866) LR 2 Eq 15.

[464] *Re Jablochkoff Electric Light and Power Co Ltd* (1883) 49 LT 566.

[465] *Re Nacupai Gold Mining Co* (1884) 28 ChD 65.

[466] *Re Humber Ironworks Co* (1866) LR 2 Eq 15 at p 18; *Re Criterion Gold Mining Co* (1889) 41 ChD 146 at p 149; *Re Leonard Spencer Pty Ltd* [1963] QdR 230 at p 237; *Re Bathampton Properties Ltd* [1976] 1 WLR 168 at p 171.

[467] *Re European Banking Co* (1866) LR 2 Eq 521; *Re Anglo-Egyptian Navigation Co* (1869) LR 8 Eq 660; *Re Heaton's Steel and Iron Co* [1870] WN 85; *Re Carnarvonshire Slate Co Ltd* (1879) 40 LT 35; *Re Peckham etc Tramways Co* (1888) 57 LJ Ch 462 per Chitty J at p 463; not following *Re Humber Ironworks Co* (1866) LR 2 Eq 15.

[468] *Re Humber Ironworks Co* (1866) LR 2 Eq 15; *Re Londonderry Ltd* (1921) 21 SR (NSW) 263 at p 272.

[469] [1904] 1 Ch 26.

the costs of defending charges made against them, would probably not be followed now in relation to contributories' petitions which the court recognizes to be litigation between members which the company itself should not pay for.[470] A contributory whose interests are not distinct from the company's will not be awarded costs.[471] Costs will be awarded to opposing creditors on an unsuccessful contributory's petition just as on an unsuccessful creditor's petition.[472] In *Re Albion Bank Ltd*[473] the court ordered the petitioner to pay the costs of three separate groups of opposing contributories.

5.209 If opposing creditors and contributories instruct the same solicitors, they will be awarded only one set of costs between them.[474]

5.210 Opposers who instruct the same solicitors as the company are not allowed separate costs.[475]

Opposer subject to a freezing injunction

5.211 A creditor or contributory of a company who wishes to oppose a petition for the compulsory winding up of the company but whose assets are subject to a freezing injunction should normally be permitted to spend money on preparing that opposition even if the freezing injunction was obtained in proceedings brought by the company itself.[476] The principle that the company's assets available for distribution to its creditors should not be expended unjustifiably does not apply in such a case though if the company has a specific claim to any assets then expenditure will not be permitted out of those assets.

Where there is both a Winding-up Petition and an Administration Application

5.212 Where a company has been subject to both a winding-up petition and an administration application, and either winding up or administration is ordered, the court has a discretion to order that the costs of applying for the insolvency process that has not been put in place are to be paid as expenses of the process that has been put into effect.[477] The person applying for the costs order must make out a case for it.[478]

5.213 When a winding-up order has been made there have been sharply differing views on how the discretion should be exercised in respect of the costs of an administration application. On one side it has been said that such costs should be allowed if the application was made in good faith, reasonably and on professional advice.[479] On the other side it has been said that

---

[470] See 8.508–8.512.
[471] *Re Times Life Assurance and Guarantee Co, ex parte Nunneley* (1870) LR 5 Ch App 381.
[472] *Re New Gas Co* (1877) 5 ChD 703; *Re Diamond Fuel Co* [1878] WN 11.
[473] (1866) 15 LT 346.
[474] *Re Silberhütte Supply Co Ltd* [1910] WN 81.
[475] *Re Brighton Marine Palace and Pier Co Ltd* (1897) 13 TLR 202.
[476] *Investment and Pensions Advisory Service Ltd v Gray* [1990] BCLC 38.
[477] *Re Gosscott (Groundworks) Ltd* [1988] BCLC 363 (costs of administration application to be paid as expenses of winding up); *Irish Reel Productions Ltd v Capitol Films Ltd* [2010] EWHC 180 (Ch), [2010] Bus LR 854 (costs of winding-up petition to be paid as expenses of administration). *Re Gosscott (Groundworks) Ltd* is analysed in *Re Portsmouth City Football Club Ltd* [2012] EWHC 3088 (Ch), [2013] Bus LR 374, at [74]–[76].
[478] See *Unadkat and Co (Accountants) Ltd v Bhardwaj* [2006] EWHC 2785 (Ch), [2007] BCC 452, at [17].
[479] *Re Gosscott (Groundworks) Ltd* [1988] BCLC 363.

the fact that an application has been made in good faith, reasonably and on professional advice is not a reason for making the creditors pay for it.[480]

Where an appointment out of court of an administrator of a company by the holder of a floating **5.214** charge suspends a petition for the winding up of the company, the costs thus far of the petition cannot be expenses of the administration.[481]

Order of Payment out of the Company's Assets

Costs of a successful winding-up petition ordered to be paid out of the company's estate to **5.215** any person cannot be set off against any debts owed to the company by that person,[482] not even costs which that person is ordered to pay the company in subsequent proceedings in the winding up.[483]

IA 1986, s 156, provides that if, in the winding up of a company, its assets are insufficient to **5.216** satisfy its liabilities, the court may make an order for the payment of the expenses of the winding up of the company 'out of the assets' in such order of priority as the court thinks just. IR 1986, r 4.218, gives a general rule on the order of priority for the payment of expenses 'out of the assets' but, by r 4.220(1), this is subject to the court's power to make orders under IA 1986, s 156, where the assets are insufficient to satisfy the liabilities. The court has no power under s 156 to change the priority of payments that are not listed in IR 1986, r 4.218.[484] The assets out of which expenses are payable are defined in detail in IR 1986, r 4.218(2), which reflects the provision in IA 1986, s 176ZA, that expenses of winding up have priority over any claims to property comprised in or subject to a floating charge, in so far as the expenses cannot be paid out of assets available for payment of general creditors.[485]

The petitioner's costs rank after a number of other items in the order of priority of pay- **5.217** ments set out in IR 1986, r 4.218(3) (where they are item (h)). Costs ordered to be paid to supporting creditors and contributories rank equally with the petitioner's costs in the order of priority of payments set out in r 4.218(3). In *Re Audley Hall Cotton Spinning Co*[486] Lord Romilly MR said, at p 247, that in the exercise of what is now IA 1986, s 156, 'the petitioner is entitled to have his costs paid first'. However, this was before any provision like IR 1986, r 4.218, was made.

Witnesses

An officer of the company who attends as a witness is not to be made any 'allowance as a **5.218** witness' (meaning, presumably, the travelling expenses and compensation for loss of time

---

[480] *Re W F Fearman Ltd (No 2)* (1987) 4 BCC 141; *EPIS Services Ltd v Commissioners of HM Revenue and Customs* [2007] EWHC 3534 (Ch), LTL 30/4/2010.
[481] *Re Portsmouth City Football Club Ltd* [2012] EWHC 3088 (Ch), [2013] Bus LR 374; [2013] EWCA Civ 916, [2013] Bus LR 1152.
[482] *Re General Exchange Bank* (1867) LR 4 Eq 138; *Re Equestrian and Public Buildings Co* (1888) 1 Meg 115 (in which the petitioner was admittedly insolvent); *Re Beer, Brewer and Bowman* (1915) 113 LT 990.
[483] *Re Scott, Sibbald and Co Pty Ltd* (1907) 7 SR (NSW) 634; *Re Beer, Brewer and Bowman.*
[484] *Re MT Realisations Ltd* [2003] EWHC 2895 (Ch), [2004] 1 WLR 1678.
[485] This overturns *Buchler v Talbot* [2004] UKHL 9, [2004] 2 AC 298, which had overruled *Re Barleycorn Enterprises Ltd* [1970] Ch 465 and *Re Portbase Clothing Ltd* [1993] Ch 388.
[486] (1868) LR 6 Eq 245.

referred to in CPR, r 34.7), except as directed by the court.[487] The petitioner, though, is not treated as a witness and is allowed travelling and subsistence expenses.[488]

Assessment

5.219 The court may order costs of proceedings on a winding-up petition to be decided by detailed assessment.[489] If costs of a successful petition to wind up a company are payable as an expense out of the insolvent estate, they must be decided by detailed assessment unless agreed between the liquidator and the person entitled to payment.[490] In the absence of agreement, the liquidator may serve notice requiring detailed assessment proceedings to be commenced by the person entitled to payment.[491] Such a notice must be served if required by the liquidation committee.[492] Detailed assessment proceedings must be commenced in the court to which the winding-up proceedings are allocated.[493]

5.220 In bank and building society insolvency proceedings, the Bank Insolvency (England and Wales) Rules 2009[494] and the Building Society Insolvency (England and Wales) Rules 2010[495] apply IR 1986 without the amendments made by the Insolvency (Amendment) Rules 2010.[496] In particular, they apply IR 1986, rr 7.34 (requirement to assess costs by the detailed procedure),[497] which was replaced by r 7.34A in the 2010 revision.[498] As explained at 1.64, it is uncertain whether the provisions of SI 2009/356 and SI 2010/2581 should be treated as applying IR 1986 with the 2010 amendments, and it is thought that the court should be asked to give directions on the point. If SI 2009/356 and SI 2010/2581 are to be treated as applying IR 1986 with the 2010 amendments, the position is that IR 1986, r 7.34A, as described at 5.219, with suitable adaptations, applies to bank and building society insolvency.

5.221 For an example of an assessment (then called taxation) of a petitioner's costs see *Re A and N Thermo Products Ltd*.[499]

5.222 A costs officer's final costs certificate is final and conclusive on all matters which have not been objected to in accordance with the rules of court.[500] If the costs are not to be paid by

---

[487] IR, r 7.41(1). Applied to an officer of a bank who is a witness in bank insolvency proceedings by the Bank Insolvency (England and Wales) Rules 2009 (SI 2009/356), r 218, and modified by r 3(3)(b) and (4)(f). Applied to an officer of a building society who is a witness in building society insolvency proceedings by the Building Society Insolvency (England and Wales) Rules 2010 (SI 2010/2581), r 211, and modified by r 3(5)(b) and (6)(h). For a petition to wind up a relevant scheme (see 1.168), applied to the operator and depositary of the scheme or any of their employees by the Collective Investment in Transferable Securities (Contractual Scheme) Regulations 2013 (SI 2013/1388), sch 3.

[488] IR 1986, r 7.41(2).

[489] IR 1986, r 7.34A(5).

[490] IR 1986, r 7.34A(1).

[491] r 7.34A(2)(a).

[492] r 7.34A(2)(b).

[493] r 7.34A(3).

[494] SI 2009/356, rr 207 and 208.

[495] SI 2010/2581, rr 201 and 202.

[496] SI 2010/686. See the definition of 'the 1986 Rules' in SI 2009/356, r 3(2) and SI 2010/2581, r 3(2).

[497] Rule 7.34 is discussed in the second edition of this work at 4.6.8. It is applied to bank insolvency by SI 2009/356, r 212, and modified by r 3(3)(b) and (4)(h) and (j). It is applied to building society insolvency by SI 2010/2581, r 205, and modified by r 3(5)(b) and (6)(j) and (l).

[498] SI 2010/686, sch 1, para 457.

[499] [1963] 1 WLR 1341.

[500] IR 1986, r 7.42(1). Applied to bank insolvency by SI 2009/356, r 219. Applied to building society insolvency by SI 2010/2581, r 212.

the company, the costs officer must note on the final certificate who is to pay them, or how they are to be paid.[501]

Any amount disallowed from the company's solicitor's bill on detailed assessment under r 7.34 of what is payable from one party to another is nevertheless a debt owed by the company to the solicitor for which the solicitor may prove in the liquidation, subject to detailed assessment as between solicitor and client.[502]   **5.223**

Parallel Petitions

Only One Petition Necessary

> I entirely agree with what was said many times by Lord Romilly—namely, that if every bona fide creditor were to be allowed to present a winding-up petition, it would be the interest of every solicitor who had such a creditor for a client to get him to present that petition, and thus the expenses of a winding up, which are already very great, would be enormously increased. My experience is that the expenses of a winding up are already out of proportion to the advantages which it secures for creditors, and I should very much lament anything which would tend to increase the cost of it.[503]   **5.224**

If two or more persons wish to petition for a company to be wound up, only one petition need be presented. They may petition jointly[504] or one may petition and the other or others appear to support the petition—and if the one who petitions abandons the petition, a supporter may be substituted as petitioner. A person who believes that an existing petitioner does not have standing should give notice to appear and, if necessary, ask to be substituted as petitioner.[505] There is no rule against presentation of more than one petition to wind up the same company,[506] but: **5.225**

> it is the usual, if not invariable, practice of this court to ensure that the winding up of a company is the subject of one petition only and not the subject of two or more petitions.[507]

It may be that adjournment of one petition and refusal to consent to substitution of petitioner in that petition may justify presentation of a second petition.

PD Insolvency Proceedings 2014, para 11.1, gives the following advice: **5.226**

> Before presenting a winding-up petition the creditor must conduct a search[508] to ensure that no petition is already pending. Save in exceptional circumstances a second winding-up petition should not be presented whilst a prior petition is pending. A petitioner who presents his own petition while another petition is pending does so at risk as to costs.[509]

---

[501] IR 1986, r 7.38. Applied to bank insolvency by SI 2009/356, r 215. Applied to building society insolvency by SI 2010/2581, r 208.

[502] *Re C B and M (Tailors) Ltd* [1932] 1 Ch 17.

[503] Jessel MR in *Re Norton Iron Co* (1877) 47 LJ Ch 9 at p 10.

[504] IA 1986, s 124(1).

[505] *Re Russian and English Bank* [1932] Ch 663 at p 665.

[506] *Re European Banking Co, ex parte Baylis* (1866) LR 2 Eq 521 per Kindersley V-C at p 522; *Maril-Rionebel (M) Sdn Bhd v Perdana Merchant Bankers Bhd* [2001] 4 MLJ 187.

[507] Per Mervyn Davies J in *Re Creative Handbook Ltd* [1985] BCLC 1 at p 2.

[508] See 5.227.

[509] The advice is repeated in the Chancery Guide 2013, para 20.19.

5.227   The Companies Court in London maintains a central registry of winding-up petitions presented in all courts in England and Wales. This includes the names of the companies sought to be wound up and the solicitors acting for petitioners. Whether or not a petition has been presented in respect of a particular company may be checked by searching this central registry by personal attendance at the ground floor, Royal Courts of Justice, Rolls Building, 7 Rolls Buildings, Fetter Lane, London EC4A 1NL, or by telephone on 0906 754 0043. The court will not provide this information in bulk for use by credit reference agencies because this would remove the protection from publicity for seven business days after a petition is presented which is provided by IR 1986, r 4.11(4).[510]

Consolidation

5.228   If (as is now very unlikely) two or more petitions to wind up the same company are presented in the same court, they may be consolidated by the court using the power given by CPR, r 3.1(2)(g).

5.229   If two or more petitions to wind up a company are heard together by a court and the court decides to make a winding-up order, it is possible for the order to be made on all the petitions,[511] but the general rule is that the court gives priority to the petition presented first.[512]

Historical

5.230   Before the Companies (Winding up) Act 1890 it was significant to determine who had the 'carriage and prosecution' of a winding-up order[513] and in some cases where more than one petition was heard, the winding-up order was made on all the petitions but carriage of the order was given to the petitioner who was first in time.[514] This practice developed even though in an earlier case it was said that the better practice was to make the order on the petition presented first and dismiss the others.[515] If a winding-up order is made on two or more petitions, all the successful petitioners are entitled to be paid costs as an expense of the liquidation[516] though it may be that they have to share one set of costs between them.[517]

5.231   In the 19th century it was sometimes alleged that a petition was a 'friendly' petition presented by someone associated with the controllers of the company in order to get carriage of the order and so obtain the appointment of a friendly liquidator. If it was found that an earlier

---

[510] *Ex parte Creditnet Ltd* [1996] 1 WLR 1291, but see the obiter remarks of Ward LJ in *Ex parte Austintel Ltd* [1997] 1 WLR 616 at pp 622–4 and *Re Haines Watts* [2004] EWHC 1970 (Ch), [2005] BPIR 798.

[511] *Re British and Foreign Generating Apparatus Co Ltd* (1865) 12 LT 368 at 369 (V-C).

[512] *Re Commercial Discount Co Ltd* (1863) 32 Beav 198; *Re London and Australian Agency Corporation Ltd* (1873) 29 LT 417; *Re Storforth Lane Colliery Co* (1879) 10 ChD 487; *Re Provincial and Suburban Bank Ltd* (1879) 5 VLR (E) 159; *Re Building Societies' Trust Ltd* (1890) 44 ChD 140; *Re Federal Bank of Australia Ltd* (1893) 62 LJ Ch 561 at p 562 (ChD); *Re Bamford Ltd* [1910] 1 IR 390; *Re Simpson and Hunter Ltd* (1916) 10 WWR 922; *Re Obie Pty Ltd* (1983) 8 ACLR 439.

[513] See 5.154.

[514] *Re London and Australian Agency Corporation Ltd* (1873) 29 LT 417; *Re Storforth Lane Colliery Co* (1879) 10 ChD 487; *Re General Financial Bank* (1882) 20 ChD 276; and see *Re Constantinople and Alexandria Hotels Co Ltd* (1865) 13 WR 851, the report of which does not explain why one of the petitioners was given carriage of the order, and *Re Lundy Granite Co* (1868) 17 WR 91 discussed at 7.556.

[515] See per Stuart V-C in *Re Accidental and Marine Insurance Co Ltd, ex parte Rasch* (1866) 36 LJ Ch 75.

[516] *Re London and Australian Agency Corporation Ltd* (1873) 29 LT 417; *Re Owen's Patent Wheel, Tire and Axle Co Ltd* (1873) 29 LT 672; *Re General Financial Bank* (1882) 20 ChD 276.

[517] *Re Owen's Patent Wheel, Tire and Axle Co Ltd* (1873) 29 LT 672 headnote; *Re General Financial Bank* (1882) 20 ChD 276 per Jessel MR at p 279.

petition was not bona fide, priority would be given to the next in time.[518] In *Re International Electric Co*[519] a judgment creditor of a company failed to get a winding-up order made on the company's own petition set aside and an order made on its petition instead as there was no complaint about the reliability or good faith of the liquidator.

In *Re United Ports and General Insurance Co*[520] three winding-up petitions were presented **5.232** but the order was made on the last to be presented, James V-C saying that it was the date of advertisement which determined priority, but that has not been adopted as a rule in other reported cases, and it was pointed out by Chitty J in *Re Building Societies' Trust Ltd*[521] that the two earlier petitions in *Re United Ports and General Insurance Co* were described as 'apparently friendly petitions' in the headnote to the report of the case so that decision could just as well be explained by the rule established in *Re Norton Iron Co*.

In *Re Enterprise Hosiery Co*[522] a friendly petitioner managed to get an order made on her **5.233** petition before an earlier petition in the same court was heard and without informing the judge that another petition was pending. On objection by the other petitioner the order was not drawn up and an order was made on the earlier petition.

Petitions in Different Courts

Priority of petition heard first

If (as is now very unlikely) one court hears a petition while other petitions are pending in **5.234** other courts it may make an order on the petition before it, even if that petition was not the first to be presented.[523] The earlier petition will then be redundant, because if one court has ordered a company to be wound up, another court in the same jurisdiction cannot make a second winding-up order.[524]

Transfer

There are numerous possible varieties of case involving factors such as dates of gazetting, **5.235** dates of hearing and collusion to delay creditors. An application to transfer may therefore give rise to what Roxburgh J in *Re Filby Bros (Provender) Ltd*[525] described[526] as a knotty problem. In *Re Filby Bros (Provender) Ltd* a petition had been presented in a county court before one was presented in the High Court. Before the county court petition was heard, Roxburgh J ordered the proceedings in the county court to be transferred to the High Court. In *Re Audio Systems Ltd*,[527] a petition was presented in the High Court and then a

---

[518] *Re Lundy Granite Co* (1868) 17 WR 91; *Re Norton Iron Co* (1877) 47 LJ Ch 9; *Re General Financial Bank* (1882) 20 ChD 276; *Re Estates Ltd* (1904) 8 OLR 564; see also *Re Building Societies' Trust Ltd* (1890) 44 ChD 140, in which the second petitioner failed to show that the first petition was not bona fide.

[519] (1911) 18 OWR 476.

[520] (1869) 39 LJ Ch 146.

[521] (1890) 44 ChD 140.

[522] (1904) 4 OWR 56.

[523] *Re British and Foreign Generating Apparatus Ltd* (1865) 12 LT 368; *Re Trades Bank Co* [1877] WN 268 as explained in *Re Building Societies' Trust Ltd* (1890) 44 ChD 140; *Re Wynaad Gorddu Lead Mining Co* (1882) 31 WR 226; *Re Official Co-operative Society* (1888) 21 LR Ir 385.

[524] *Re British and Foreign Generating Apparatus Co Ltd* (1865) 12 LT 368 at 369 (MR); *Commonwealth of Australia v Emanuel Projects Pty Ltd* (1996) 21 ACSR 36; *Dewina Trading Sdn Bhd v Ion International Pty Ltd* (1996) 141 ALR 317.

[525] [1958] 1 WLR 683.

[526] At p 686.

[527] [1965] 1 WLR 1096.

second one was presented in a county court. Pennycuick J ordered the proceedings on the county court petition to be transferred to the High Court and then stayed all further proceedings on that petition.

5.236   Evidence must be provided of the fact that a petition has been presented in another court and the state of proceedings in that court: they are not matters for judicial notice.[528]

5.237   *Re Filby Bros (Provender) Ltd* was decided at a time when only the High Court could order a transfer of proceedings from a county court to the High Court. Accordingly, Roxburgh J held that only the High Court could deal adequately with the problem of parallel petitions in different courts. Now, under IR 1986, r 7.11(2), the County Court can order a transfer of proceedings to the High Court or to another County Court hearing centre but it cannot transfer proceedings to itself from the High Court. It would seem that the High Court is still the proper place for sorting out parallel petitions in that court and the County Court.

5.238   Both *Re Filby Bros (Provender) Ltd* and *Re Audio Systems Ltd* were decided before the central register of petitions was established. In both cases the second petitioner petitioned in ignorance of the first petition because it had not been advertised and the second petitioner was allowed costs up to the time of transfer of proceedings. This type of case should be much rarer now.

Costs of rejected petitions when order is made on earlier petition

5.239   If there are two or more parallel petitions and a winding-up order is made but only on the first petition, then the second and any subsequent petitioners are entitled to costs up to the time of knowing that there is a prior petition[529] or up to the time when this would have been discovered if inquiries had been made which should reasonably have been made.[530] They may be entitled to share in the costs of supporting creditors.[531] Costs up to the hearing will be allowed out of the company's assets to a second petitioner if the court finds that there was justification for pursuing the second petition despite the existence of the first[532] or alternatively the court may make an order on more than one petition.[533]

Costs of rejected petitions when order is made on later petition

5.240   If a person presents a petition for the winding up of a company and, before the petition is heard, the company itself petitions and obtains a winding-up order, no costs may be allowed to the company or its solicitor out of the company's estate, unless the court considers that the estate has benefited by the company's conduct or there are other special circumstances justifying the allowance of costs.[534]

---

[528]   *Re Filby Bros (Provender) Ltd* at pp 685–6.
[529]   *Re Marron Bank Paper Mill Co Ltd* (1878) 38 LT 140; *Re General Financial Bank* (1882) 20 ChD 276; *Re Building Societies' Trust Ltd* (1890) 44 ChD 140; *Re Manitoba Milling etc Co* (1891) 8 Man R 426; *Re Sheringham Development Co Ltd* (1893) 37 SJ 175; *Re Federal Bank of Australia Ltd* (1893) 62 LJ Ch 561 at p 562 (ChD); *Re Algoma Commercial Co* (1904) 3 OWR 140; *Re Dramstar Ltd* (1980) 124 SJ 807.
[530]   *Re Minpro Pty Ltd* (1981) 6 ACLR 235. For inquiries which should be made see 5.226.
[531]   *Re Building Societies' Trust Ltd* (1890) 44 ChD 140; *Re Manitoba Milling etc Co* (1891) 8 Man R 426.
[532]   *Re Scott and Jackson Ltd* [1893] WN 184.
[533]   See 5.228–5.229.
[534]   IR 1986, r 7.37(2) and (3).

If a person presents a petition for the winding up of a company and, before the petition is **5.241**
heard, another petition is presented and a winding-up order is made on the later petition,
the court will order the first petitioner's costs to be paid by the company.[535]

Notice to Official Receiver and Perfection of Order

When a winding-up order is made the court will give notice to its official receiver as soon as **5.242**
reasonably practicable.[536] Unless someone else has been appointed as liquidator, the official
receiver may begin acting as liquidator immediately on being notified that a winding-up
order has been made and need not wait until the order is perfected.[537]

The petitioner, and every person who appeared on the hearing of the petition, must, not **5.243**
later than the business day after the order is made, leave at the court all documents necessary to enable the order to be completed.[538] It is not normally necessary to appoint a time
for settlement of the order.[539] The court will draw up the order.[540] This procedure was
introduced by the Companies Winding-up Rules 1892 to avoid delays caused by successful
petitioners declining to have orders drawn up.[541]

Public Notification of a Winding-up Order

The Official Receiver, the Company, Companies House

When a winding-up order has been made in relation to a company, the court sends three **5.244**
sealed copies to the official receiver.[542] Only two copies are required in the case of a European
grouping of territorial cooperation which has its registered office in the United Kingdom
(a UK EGTC).[543] The official receiver sends one of the copies by post to the company at
its registered office.[544] A second copy is forwarded to the registrar of companies, who must
enter it in the records at Companies House relating to the company.[545] If the company is
a community interest company, the registrar of companies must provide the Regulator of
Community Interest Companies with a copy of the order.[546] The requirement to forward a
copy of a winding-up order to the registrar of companies does not apply to UK EGTCs.[547]
For building societies, incorporated friendly societies and registered societies, it is replaced
by a requirement to give notice of the order, or forward a copy of it, to the FCA and, in some

---

[535] *Re British and Foreign Generating Apparatus Co Ltd* (1865) 12 LT 368 at 369 (V-C).
[536] IR 1986, r 4.20(1).
[537] *Smith and Williamson v Sims Pipes* (2000) LTL 17/3/2000.
[538] r 4.20(2). 'Business day' is defined in r 13.13(1) (see 1.512).
[539] r 4.20(3).
[540] PD Insolvency Proceedings 2014, para 8.1.
[541] See 5.154.
[542] IR 1986, r 4.21(1).
[543] European Grouping of Territorial Cooperation Regulations 2007 (SI 2007/1949), sch, para 9.
[544] IR 1986, r 4.21(2). If there is no registered office, the company's copy may be sent to the company's
principal, or last known principal, place of business, or be served on such person or persons as the court
directs (r 4.21(2)).
[545] IA 1986, s 130(1); IR 1986, r 4.21(3).
[546] Community Interest Company Regulations 2005 (SI 2005/1788), reg 35(2).
[547] European Grouping of Territorial Cooperation Regulations 2007 (SI 2007/1949), sch, para 8.

cases, the PRA.[548] For a charitable incorporated organization the second copy must be forwarded to the Charity Commission instead of the registrar of companies.[549] For a relevant scheme,[550] the operator must forward the second copy to the FCA.[551] Otherwise, the requirement applies to both registered and unregistered companies[552] (even an unregistered company for which the registrar has no file) and to limited liability partnerships.[553]

5.245   If a winding-up order made against a registered company has been erroneously made against the wrong company, it may be rescinded and the registrar of companies may be ordered to correct the records at Companies House.[554]

5.246   When a bank or building society insolvency order has been made, the court must immediately send five sealed copies (or more if requested by the liquidator) to the liquidator.[555] It must also, if practicable, send a copy to the liquidator electronically.[556] The liquidator must serve one of the sealed copies on the institution at its registered office (in the case of a bank) or principal office (in the case of a building society) and, if the email address is known, send an electronic copy.[557] The liquidator must also send a sealed copy and an electronic copy to the Bank of England, the FCA,[558] the PRA if the institution is a PRA-authorized person, and the Financial Services Compensation Scheme,[559] to the registrar of companies (bank insolvency only), who must enter it in the records at Companies House relating to the bank,[560] and to the supervisor of any voluntary arrangement[561] and any administrative receiver.[562] The electronic copy must be sent as soon as practicable and the sealed copy must be sent by first class post on the business day on which the order is served on the institution.[563]

Official Notification

5.247   The registrar of companies must give public notice of receipt of a copy of a winding-up order in respect of a registered company.[564] This requirement is applied[565] to any company which

---

[548]   See 5.261–5.262.

[549]   Charitable Incorporated Organisations (Insolvency and Dissolution) Regulations 2012 (SI 2012/3013), sch, para 1(3)(e).

[550]   See 1.168.

[551]   Collective Investment in Transferable Securities (Contractual Scheme) Regulations 2013 (SI 2013/1388), sch 2, paras 3, 4 and 5(k) and part 3.

[552]   IA 1986, s 221(1) (unregistered companies generally); IA 1986, s 434E (any overseas company that is required to register particulars under the Companies Act 2006, s 1046).

[553]   Limited Liability Partnerships Regulations 2001 (SI 2001/1090), reg 5.

[554]   *Re Calmex Ltd* [1989] 1 All ER 485.

[555]   Bank Insolvency (England and Wales) Rules 2009 (SI 2009/356), r 16(2); Building Society Insolvency (England and Wales) Rules 2010 (SI 2010/2581), r 16(2).

[556]   SI 2009/356, r 16(3); SI 2010/2581, r 16(3).

[557]   SI 2009/356, r 16(4); SI 2010/2581, r 16(4). 'Registered office' of a bank is defined in SI 2009/356, r 8(3) (see 3.42), only for the purposes of r 8(2). 'Principal office' of a building society is defined at 1.532.

[558]   In the case of a building society, the FCA must place the copy of the order on the public file of the society (IA 1986, s 130(1), as applied and modified by the Banking Act 2009, s 103(3), (4) and table, and further applied and modified by the Building Societies Act 1986, s 90C, and the Building Societies (Insolvency and Special Administration) Order 2009 (SI 2009/805), sch 1, para 3(d) and (i)).

[559]   SI 2009/356, r 16(5)(a) (see r 3(2) for the definition of 'the appropriate regulator'); SI 2010/2581, r 16(5)(a)–(c) (see r 3(2) for the definition of 'the appropriate regulator').

[560]   IA 1986, s 130(1), applied and modified by the Banking Act 2009, s 103(3), (4) and table.

[561]   SI 2009/356, r 16(5)(c); SI 2010/2581, r 16(5)(d).

[562]   SI 2009/356, r 16(5)(d); SI 2010/2581, r 16(5)(e).

[563]   SI 2009/356, r 16(5A); SI 2010/2581, r 16(6).

[564]   Companies Act 2006, ss 1077 and 1078(1) and (2), implementing Directive 68/151/EEC, arts 2 and 3(4).

[565]   By the Unregistered Companies Regulations 2009 (SI 2009/2436), sch 1, para 19.

is an unregistered company for the purposes of the Companies Act 2006, s 1043, and the Unregistered Companies Regulations 2009.[566] Those provisions apply to[567] any body corporate incorporated in, and having a principal place of business in, the United Kingdom, other than:

(a) a body incorporated by, or registered under, a public general Act of Parliament;
(b) a body not formed for the purpose of carrying on a business that has for its object the acquisition of gain by the body or its individual members;
(c) a body for the time being exempted from s 1043 by direction of the Secretary of State;
(d) an open-ended investment company.

The notice must state the name and registered number of the company, the description of the document and the date of receipt.[568] At present, these notices are published in weekly supplements to the *London Gazette*. The Companies Act 2006, s 1116, will give the Secretary of State power to provide for publication by electronic means, but there is no intention to use this power yet. **5.248**

Publication of notice of receipt of a winding-up order constitutes 'official notification' of the making of the order for the purposes of the Companies Act 2006, s 1079.[569] Under s 1079 a company cannot rely, against another person, on the making of a winding-up order if, at the material time, it had not been officially notified, unless the company can prove that the other person knew that the order had been made.[570] In addition, if the material time was on or before the 15th day after official notification (or the next business day if the 15th day is not a business day), the company will not be able to rely on the making of the order if it is shown that the other person was unavoidably prevented from knowing of it at that time.[571] **5.249**

These provisions apply to limited liability partnerships.[572] **5.250**

Gazetting and Advertisement

Having received copies of a winding-up order the official receiver must, as soon as reasonably practicable, cause the order to be gazetted.[573] The official receiver may also advertise notice of the order in such other manner as he or she thinks fit.[574] The contents of a notice of a winding-up order in the *London Gazette* are specified in IR 1986, rr 4.21(5), 12A.33, 12A.34 and 12A.36.[575] The contents of a notice that is advertised in any other way are specified in rr 4.21(5), 12A.38, 12A.39 and 12A.41.[576] A copy of the *Gazette* containing the notice of the order may, in any proceedings, be produced as conclusive evidence that the order was made on the date specified in the notice.[577] **5.251**

---

[566] SI 2009/2436.
[567] Companies Act 2006, s 1043(1); SI 2009/2436, reg 2(a).
[568] Companies Act 2006, s 1077(2).
[569] Companies Act 2006, s 1079(4)(b).
[570] Companies Act 2006, s 1079(1) and (2)(d).
[571] Companies Act 2006, s 1079(3).
[572] Limited Liability Partnerships (Application of Companies Act 2006) Regulations 2009 (SI 2009/1804), reg 63.
[573] IR 1986, r 4.21(4)(a). 'Gazetted' means advertised once in the *London Gazette* (r 13.13(4) and (4A)).
[574] r 4.21(4)(b).
[575] See r 13.13(4B)(a).
[576] See r 13.13(4B)(b).
[577] IR 1986, r 12A.37(2).

5.252 If a winding-up order that has been gazetted is varied by the court, the official receiver must, as soon as reasonably practicable, cause the variation of the order to be gazetted.[578] If an order has been erroneously or inaccurately gazetted, the official receiver must, as soon as reasonably practicable, cause a further entry to be made in the *Gazette* for the purpose of correcting the error or inaccuracy.[579]

5.253 If the making of a winding-up order has been advertised with the company erroneously named, because it was misnamed in the petition, the court may require a new advertisement with the correct name.[580]

5.254 In an old Australian case it was held that failure to advertise an order to wind up a company (then the responsibility of the petitioner) caused the order to lapse so that a new petition could be presented and a fresh order made to wind up the same company.[581]

5.255 After receiving copies of a bank or building society insolvency order, the liquidator must, as soon as reasonably practicable, cause the order to be gazetted, and may advertise the order in such other manner as he or she thinks fit.[582]

Notification in other EU States

5.256 If Regulation (EC) No 1346/2000 applies to proceedings in which a winding-up order is made, the court having jurisdiction, or the liquidator appointed by it, must immediately inform known creditors who have their habitual residences, domiciles or registered offices in other EU member States (apart from Denmark).[583] The information must be provided by an individual notice[584] and must include:[585]

(a) time limits;
(b) penalties laid down in regard to those time limits;
(c) the body or authority empowered to accept the lodgment of claims; and
(d) whether creditors whose claims are preferential or secured *in rem* need lodge claims.

5.257 The liquidator may request that notice of the winding-up order and the decision appointing him or her be published in any other member State (apart from Denmark) in accordance with the publication procedures provided for in that State.[586] The notice must name the liquidator and state whether the court's jurisdiction to open the proceedings arose under art 3(1) or 3(2), that is, whether the proceedings are main, secondary or territorial.[587] If the proceedings are main proceedings, the liquidator may also request that the winding-up order be registered in

---

[578] r 12A.37(3).
[579] r 12A.37(3).
[580] *Re Newcastle Machinists Co* [1888] WN 246 and [1889] WN 1, decided at a time when the petitioner was responsible for advertising the order.
[581] *Re Cognac Co, Dwyer and Kelly's Case* (1877) 3 VLR Eq 146.
[582] Bank Insolvency (England and Wales) Rules 2009 (SI 2009/356), r 16(6); Building Society Insolvency (England and Wales) Rules 2010 (SI 2010/2581), r 16(7). 'Gazetted' means advertised once in the *London Gazette* (IR 1986, r 13.13(4) and (4A), applied by SI 2009/356, r 292, and SI 2010/2581, r 284).
[583] art 40(1).
[584] art 40(2).
[585] art 40(2).
[586] art 21(1).
[587] art 21(1).

the land register, trade register and any other public register kept in other member States.[588] Member States may make publication and registration mandatory.[589]

The English court may provide an insolvency office-holder with a declaration of his or **5.258** her statutory powers to match the lists of powers commonly provided when appointing office-holders in other EU jurisdictions.[590] In administration proceedings, this is provided in a schedule to the administration order.[591]

Company's Documents and Websites

Every invoice, order for goods or services, business letter or order form issued by or on **5.259** behalf of a company being wound up, or by or on behalf of a liquidator of the company or a receiver or manager of its property (including an administrative receiver) must state that it is being wound up.[592] This applies whether the documents are in hard copy, electronic or any other form.[593] All the company's websites must contain a statement that the company is being wound up.[594] If there is default in complying with this provision then the company, and any officer of the company, liquidator, receiver or manager who knowingly and wilfully authorized the default may be fined.[595] It is usual to satisfy this requirement by putting '(in liquidation)' after the company's name.

If a receiver or manager of the company's property has been appointed, there must also be a **5.260** statement of that appointment.[596]

Building Societies, Incorporated Friendly Societies and Registered Societies

If a winding-up order is made in respect of a building society or incorporated friendly soci- **5.261** ety, the society must, within 15 days, give notice of the order to the FCA and, if the society is a PRA-authorized person, the PRA.[597] Failure to do so is a summary offence for which the society and any officer who is also guilty of the offence may be fined.[598] The FCA must keep the notice in the public file of the society.[599] Neither the society nor the official receiver[600] is required to forward a copy of the order to the registrar of companies.[601]

If a winding-up order is made in respect of a body registered, or deemed to be registered, **5.262** under the Co-operative and Community Benefit Societies Act 2014, the court will send

---

[588] art 22(1).
[589] arts 21(2) and 22(2). Early experience suggested that the Regulation should make publication and registration compulsory. See Glen Flannery, 'Registration and publication of judgments opening insolvency proceedings under the EC Regulation (with reference to the *Crisscross Communications* case)' (2005) 21 Insolv L & P 57; Brian Rawlings, 'Recognition of administration proceedings under the EC Regulation—the Rover experience' (2005) 21 Insolv L & P 159.
[590] Brian Rawlings, 'Recognition of administration proceedings under the EC Regulation—the Rover experience' (2005) 21 Insolv L & P 159.
[591] *Re MG Rover España SA* [2006] BCC 599; *Re Collins and Aikman Europe SA* [2006] EWHC 1343 (Ch), [2007] 1 BCLC 182, at [6]–[7].
[592] IA 1986, s 188(1).
[593] s 188(1).
[594] s 188(1).
[595] s 188(2) and sch 10.
[596] s 39.
[597] Building Societies Act 1986, sch 15, para 21(3); Friendly Societies Act 1992, sch 10, para 24(3).
[598] Building Societies Act 1986, sch 15, para 21(4); Friendly Societies Act 1992, sch 10, para 24(4).
[599] Building Societies Act 1986, sch 15, para 21(3); Friendly Societies Act 1992, sch 10, para 24(3).
[600] Under IA 1986, s 130(1), and IR 1986, r 4.21(3).
[601] Building Societies Act 1986, sch 15, para 21(2); Friendly Societies Act 1992, sch 10, para 24(2).

three sealed copies to the official receiver,[602] who must forward one of them to the FCA, which must register the order in its records relating to the society.[603]

European Economic Interest Groupings

5.263 By Regulation No 2137/85, art 7(f), a judicial decision ordering the winding up of a European economic interest grouping in accordance with art 32 of the Regulation must be filed at the registry where the grouping is registered (which will be in the EU State in which the grouping has its official address). A grouping with its official address in England or Wales is registered at the registry of companies in England and Wales.[604] A decision ordering the winding up of an EEIG whose official address is in the United Kingdom must be filed with form EE MP01 within 15 days of 'the event to which [it] relates'.[605] If a grouping fails to deliver this document as required by reg 13, the grouping, and any officer of it who intentionally authorizes or permits the default, is guilty of an offence and liable on summary conviction to a fine not exceeding level 3 on the standard scale.[606] There is also provision for punishment of default which continues after conviction.[607] The registrar must publish in the *London Gazette* a notice of receipt of the decision.[608]

Registered Social Landlords

5.264 If an order is made for the winding up of a registered social landlord[609] which is a registered society or a registered company, the petitioner must give notice of the order to the Welsh Ministers.[610] Giving the notice starts a 28-day moratorium on disposal of land held by the landlord,[611] during which the Welsh Ministers may make proposals for the future ownership and management of the land.[612] Failure to give notice does not affect the validity of the winding-up order, but the moratorium period does not begin to run until the notice has been given.[613]

Insurers and Credit Institutions

5.265 If a court makes an order for the winding up of a UK insurer or a third country insurer, a UK credit institution or a third country credit institution, it must immediately inform the FCA, or cause the FCA to be informed, of the order.[614] If the insurer or credit institution is a PRA-authorized person,[615] the PRA must also be informed.[616] It is not necessary to inform a regulator which has been represented at all hearings in connection with the petition on which the winding-up order was made.[617] The FCA or PRA must, as soon as is practicable after

---

[602] IR 1986, r 4.21(1).
[603] IA 1986, s 130(1), and IR 1986, r 4.21(3), applied and modified by the Co-operative and Community Benefit Societies Act 2014, s 123(2).
[604] European Economic Interest Grouping Regulations 1989 (SI 1989/638), reg 9.
[605] SI 1989/638, reg 13(1), (1A) and (1B).
[606] reg 13(3).
[607] reg 13(3).
[608] reg 15(1).
[609] Provision for registration of social landlords in Wales is made in the Housing Act 1996, ss A1–6.
[610] Housing Act 1996, s 41.
[611] ss 42 and 43.
[612] s 44.
[613] s 41(5).
[614] Insurers (Reorganisation and Winding Up) Regulations 2004 (SI 2004/353), regs 8, 9, 48 and 49; Credit Institutions (Reorganisation and Winding Up) Regulations 2004 (SI 2004/1045), regs 7, 9 and 37.
[615] See 9.114.
[616] SI 2004/353, regs 8, 9, 48 and 49; SI 2004/1045, regs 7, 9 and 37.
[617] SI 2004/353, reg 9(6) and (6A); SI 2004/1045, reg 9(5) and (5A).

the order is made (if the regulator was present) or after being informed of it, inform its counterparts in every other EEA State that the order has been made and, in general terms, its effect on an insurer's business and the rights of policyholders[618] or a credit institution's business.[619]

The insurer or credit institution's liquidator must, as soon as is reasonably practicable, publish, **5.266** or cause to be published, in the *Official Journal of the European Union*, a notice summarizing the terms of the order, and identifying him or herself and the statutory provisions under which the order was made.[620] In the case of a credit institution the notice must also be published in two national newspapers in each EEA State in which the institution has a branch.[621] Failure to comply is a criminal offence[622] but does not invalidate the winding-up order.[623]

All known creditors of the insurer or credit institution must be notified by its liquidator, as soon **5.267** as is reasonably practicable, in accordance with SI 2004/353, reg 12, or SI 2004/1045, reg 14.

A 'UK insurer' is a person who has permission under the Financial Services and Markets Act **5.268** 2000, part 4A, to effect or carry out contracts of insurance, apart from a person who does so exclusively in relation to reinsurance contracts[624] and excluding Lloyd's and its members.[625] A 'third country insurer' is a person who has permission under the 2000 Act to effect or carry out contracts of insurance, whose head office is not in the UK or any other EEA State.[626]

These provisions of SI 2004/353 also apply, with necessary changes, if the court makes an **5.269** order reducing the value of a UK or third country insurer's contracts[627] or appoints a provisional liquidator of a UK insurer.[628]

These provisions of SI 2004/353 also apply, while a Lloyd's market reorganization order is **5.270** in force, when an order is made for the winding up of an underwriting member or former member of Lloyd's which is treated as a UK insurer by the Insurers (Reorganisation and Winding Up) (Lloyd's) Regulations 2005,[629] reg 13(2), except where that provision has been disapplied by a court order which has not been revoked.[630]

A 'UK credit institution' is[631] an undertaking whose head office is in the United Kingdom **5.271** and which has permission under the Financial Services and Markets Act 2000, part 4A, to accept deposits or to issue electronic money, but excluding:

(a) an undertaking which also has part 4A permission to effect or carry out contracts of insurance; and
(b) a credit union.

---

[618] SI 2004/353, reg 10(1).
[619] SI 2004/1045, reg 10(1).
[620] SI 2004/353, reg 11; SI 2004/1045, reg 12.
[621] SI 2004/1045, reg 12(3).
[622] SI 2004/353, reg 11(9); SI 2004/1045, reg 12(9).
[623] SI 2004/353, reg 11(10); SI 2004/1045, reg 12(10).
[624] SI 2004/353, reg 2(1).
[625] reg 3.
[626] reg 48(1)(b) and (2).
[627] See 5.138–5.139.
[628] See chapter 4.
[629] SI 2005/1998.
[630] regs 32–36.
[631] By SI 2004/1045, reg 2(1).

5.272 A 'third country credit institution' is a person who has permission under the 2000 Act to accept deposits or to issue electronic money and whose head office is not in the UK or another EEA State.[632]

5.273 These provisions of SI 2004/1045 also apply when a UK court appoints a provisional liquidator of a UK or third country credit institution.

Settlement Systems

5.274 Under the Financial Markets and Insolvency (Settlement Finality) Regulations 1999,[633] if a winding-up order, bank insolvency order or building society insolvency order is made against a participant in a designated system,[634] the court must forthwith notify both the system operator of that designated system and the designating authority.[635] The designating authority is either the FCA or the Bank of England.[636] Following receipt of the notification, the designating authority must forthwith inform the Treasury.[637] The United Kingdom government must immediately notify the European Systemic Risk Board, other EEA States and the European Securities and Markets Authority.[638] The details needed by the court to make this notification must be included in the petition or application.[639]

Public Notification of Dismissal of a Petition[640]

5.275 When a winding-up petition is dismissed, the petitioner must give notice of the dismissal, unless the court otherwise directs.[641] Notice must be given as soon as reasonably practicable.[642] It must either be gazetted,[643] or advertised in accordance with the court's directions.[644] The contents of a notice of dismissal of a petition in the *London Gazette* are specified in IR 1986, rr 4.21B(2), 12A.33, 12A.34 and 12A.36.[645] The contents of a notice that is advertised in any other way are specified in rr 4.21B(2), 12A.38, 12A.39 and 12A.41.[646]

5.276 If the petitioner has not given notice within 21 days of the date of the hearing at which the petition was dismissed, the company may give notice itself, by gazetting.[647]

---

[632] reg 36(1)(b) and (2).

[633] SI 1999/2979, implementing Directive 98/26/EC.

[634] The terms 'designated system' and 'participant' are defined in SI 1999/2979, reg 2(1).

[635] SI 1999/2979, reg 22(1), applied to bank insolvency by the Banking Act (Parts 2 and 3 Consequential Amendments) Order 2009 (SI 2009/317), art 3(1) and (2)(e), and applied to building society insolvency by the Building Societies (Insolvency and Special Administration) Order 2009 (SI 2009/805), art 18 and sch 2, paras 1(a) and 3(a); Directive 98/26/EC, art 6(1) and (2).

[636] SI 1999/2979, reg 2(1).

[637] SI 1999/2979, reg 22(2).

[638] Directive 98/26/EC, art 6(3).

[639] PD Insolvency Proceedings 2014, paras 19.1 and 19.2. See 2.201.

[640] The material in 5.275–5.276 does not apply to a petition to wind up a company presented by a contributory or contributories of the company or at the instance of the company's administrator or voluntary arrangement supervisor (IR 1986, rr 4.2(4) and 4.7(9)). Such petitions are discussed at 8.469–8.518.

[641] IR 1986, r 4.21B(1).

[642] IR 1986, r 4.21B(1).

[643] 'Gazetted' means advertised once in the *London Gazette* (r 13.13(4) and (4A)).

[644] r 4.21B(1).

[645] See r 13.13(4B)(a).

[646] See r 13.13(4B)(b).

[647] r 4.21B(3), which does not apply if the company was the petitioner.

Commencement of Winding Up, Going into Liquidation etc

Commencement

Introduction

'Commencement of winding up' is a technical phrase or term of art.[648] It is defined in **5.277**
legislation which deals with four classes of case:

(a) the commencement of voluntary winding up;[649]
(b) the commencement of compulsory winding up when a winding-up order is made on a
petition presented after a company has adopted a resolution for voluntary winding up;[650]
(c) the commencement of compulsory winding up when a winding-up order is made on an
administration application;[651]
(d) any other case in which a winding-up order is made.[652]

In addition, for the purposes of IA 1986, s 185 (which is concerned with the effect of diligence **5.278**
under Scots law on the estate or effects of a company being wound up), the phrase 'the commencement of the winding up of the company' is given a special meaning by s 185(3).

Company not in voluntary winding up when petition presented and order not made on an administration application

If an order for a company to be wound up by the court is made on a winding-up petition (and **5.279**
not an administration application or an energy, energy supply company or postal administration application[653]), and the company did not adopt a resolution for voluntary winding up
before the petition was presented, the winding up of the company by the court is deemed to
have commenced at the time when the petition was presented.[654] This is not at the beginning
of the day on which the petition was presented but at the moment of presentation, because
s 129(2) refers to the time rather than the date of presentation of the petition.[655] Nevertheless,
a period of time expressed as a number of days after presentation of a winding-up petition
would normally be interpreted as a number of calendar days after the day on which the petition is presented, not a number of 24-hour periods starting at the time of presentation.[656]

In Australia the time of presentation of the winding-up petition was formerly the com- **5.280**
mencement of the winding up but, with effect from 23 June 1993, winding up is deemed to
commence when the winding-up order is made.[657] In New Zealand, since 26 April 1999,
the liquidation of a company commences on the date on which, and at the time at which,
the liquidator is appointed.[658]

---

[648] Per McPherson SPJ in *Re Crust 'n' Crumb Bakers (Wholesale) Pty Ltd* [1992] 2 QdR 76 at p 78.
[649] See 5.282–5.288.
[650] See 5.289–5.292.
[651] See 5.293.
[652] See 5.279–5.281.
[653] See 5.293.
[654] IA 1986, s 129(2).
[655] *Re London and Devon Biscuit Co* (1871) LR 12 Eq 190; *Re Blackburn Industries Pty Ltd* [1980] QdR
211 per D M Campbell J at p 217 and Dunn J at p 224; see also the latter case on appeal sub nom *Wilde v
Australian Trade Equipment Co Pty Ltd* (1981) 145 CLR 590.
[656] *Cerissi Design and Marketing Ltd v Australian Rugby Union Ltd* [1997] 3 NZLR 208.
[657] Corporations Act 2001 (Australia), s 513A.
[658] Companies Act 1993 (New Zealand), s 241(5).

5.281   If a winding-up order is made on two or more petitions heard together[659] and they were presented when the company was not in voluntary winding up, the commencement of winding up is the time of presentation of the earliest petition on which the order is made.[660]

Commencement of voluntary winding up

5.282   A company can go into voluntary winding up under IA 1986, part 4, in three ways:

(a) by adopting a resolution for voluntary winding up;[661]

(b) by moving from schedule B1 administration, energy administration, energy supply company administration or postal administration to creditors' voluntary winding up under IA 1986, sch B1, para 83;[662]

(c) by conversion of a voluntary arrangement[663] by a court order under IR 1986, r 1.33(3), or conversion of an administration[664] by a court order under r 2.132(3), providing that the company be wound up as if a resolution for voluntary winding up under IA 1986, s 84, were passed on the day on which the order is made.

5.283   If a company adopts a resolution for voluntary winding up, the voluntary winding up is deemed to commence at the time when the resolution was adopted.[665] By analogy with the decisions on commencement of winding up by the court,[666] it is submitted that this means the moment of adoption of the resolution, not the beginning of the day on which it is adopted.

5.284   There is disagreement over whether the members of a company can adopt a resolution for voluntary winding up which is to take effect at a later date and thus postpone the commencement of the winding up.[667]

5.285   The fact that a liquidator was not appointed when a resolution for voluntary winding up was adopted does not mean that the voluntary winding up did not commence then.[668]

5.286   If a company moves to creditors' voluntary winding up, under IA 1986, sch B1, para 83, the voluntary winding up is deemed to commence at the beginning of the day on which the administrator's notice is registered at Companies House.[669]

---

[659]   See 5.228–5.229.

[660]   *Kent v Freehold Land and Brick-making Co* (1868) LR 3 Ch App 493.

[661]   s 84(1) and (2).

[662]   Which is applied to energy administration by the Energy Act 2004, sch 20, paras 1–4 and 19; to energy supply company administration by the Energy Act 2011, s 96; to postal administration by the Postal Services Act 2011, sch 10, paras 1, 2 and 18. The provision is not applied to other industry-specific administration regimes based on IA 1986, sch B1, so far promulgated.

[663]   See 10.21–10.25.

[664]   See 10.62–10.66.

[665]   IA 1986, s 86.

[666]   See 5.279.

[667]   In *Re Dino Music Ltd* [2000] BCC 696 it was held that a resolution may be adopted to take effect on a later date, but in *Re Norditrack (UK) Ltd* [2000] 1 WLR 343, in which *Re Dino Music Ltd* was not cited, it was held that this is not possible.

[668]   *Thomas v Patent Lionite* Co (1881) 17 ChD 250.

[669]   sch B1, para 83(8)(b); applied to energy administration by the Energy Act 2004, sch 20, paras 1–4; applied to energy supply company administration by the Energy Act 2011, s 96; applied to postal administration by the Postal Services Act 2011, sch 10, paras 1 and 2. The provision is not applied to other industry-specific administration regimes based on IA 1986, sch B1, so far promulgated.

It is submitted that the resolution for voluntary winding up referred to in IA 1986, s 86, should include the notional resolution in a conversion order which provides that a company is to be wound up as if a resolution for winding up had been passed on the day of the order. Provision to that effect is made in s 247(3)(b)[670] and could be made, as a consequential provision, in a conversion order.[671] **5.287**

Under earlier law, if a company was put into voluntary liquidation by a special resolution which had to be confirmed at a second, separately convened meeting (the necessity for confirmation was abolished by the Companies Act 1928, s 25), the voluntary winding up commenced when the confirmatory resolution was adopted.[672] **5.288**

Company in voluntary winding up when petition presented

If an order for the winding up of a company is made on a petition presented after a resolution for voluntary winding up under IA 1986, part 4, has been adopted by the company, the winding up by the court is deemed to have commenced at the time when that resolution was adopted.[673] Again it is submitted that this means the moment of adoption, not the beginning of the day on which it is adopted.[674] **5.289**

If an order for the winding up of a company is made on a petition presented after the company has moved, under sch B1, para 83, from schedule B1 administration, energy administration, energy supply company administration or postal administration to creditors' voluntary winding up, the winding up by the court is deemed to have commenced at the beginning of the day on which the administrator's notice was registered at Companies House.[675] **5.290**

It is submitted that the resolution for voluntary winding up referred to in s 129(1) should include the notional resolution in a conversion order which provides that a company is to be wound up as if a resolution for winding up had been passed on the day of the order. Provision to that effect is made in s 247(3)(b).[676] **5.291**

Section 129(1) was first enacted in the Companies Act 1928, s 57(1). Before then the Court of Appeal had held that, in general, if an order to wind up a registered company was made on a petition presented when the company was in voluntary winding up, the winding up by the court commenced when the petition was presented.[677] However, in relation to two statutory provisions, the time of commencement of the winding up in those circumstances was held to be when the resolution for voluntary winding up was adopted.[678] **5.292**

---

[670] See 5.304.

[671] IR 1986, rr 1.33(2) and 2.132(2).

[672] *Re China Steam Ship Co, Dawes's Case* (1868) LR 6 Eq 232; *Re Imperial Land Co of Marseilles, ex parte Colborne and Strawbridge* (1871) LR 11 Eq 478; *Re Emperor Life Assurance Society* (1885) 31 ChD 78.

[673] s 129(1).

[674] See 5.279 and 5.283, and compare sch B1, para 83(8)(e), discussed at 5.290, which expressly refers to the beginning of the day.

[675] sch B1, para 83(8)(e); applied to energy administration by the Energy Act 2004, sch 20, paras 1–4; applied to energy supply company administration by the Energy Act 2011, s 96; applied to postal administration by the Postal Services Act 2011, sch 10, paras 1 and 2. The provision is not applied to other industry-specific administration regimes based on IA 1986, sch B1, so far promulgated.

[676] See 5.304.

[677] *Re Taurine Co* (1883) 25 ChD 118, disagreeing with the assumption in *Re United Service Co* (1868) LR 7 Eq 76 that it would begin when the voluntary winding up commenced.

[678] *Thomas v Patent Lionite Co* (1881) 17 ChD 250 and *Re Stanley and Co Ltd* (1923) 155 LT Jo 233, both of which concerned what is now IA 1986, s 128(1); *Re Havana Exploration Co Ltd* [1916] 1 Ch 8, which

Winding-up order made on administration application

5.293 If a winding-up order is made on hearing an administration application, the winding up is deemed to commence on the making of the order.[679] The same applies to a winding-up order made on an energy, energy supply company or postal administration application.[680] It seems that this applies even if the company was in voluntary winding up when the application was presented.

While winding-up petition is pending

5.294 A compulsory winding up is deemed to have commenced before the winding-up order is made, but this deeming provision does not come into effect until the order is made.[681] There is no commencement of the compulsory winding up of a company unless a winding-up order is made. In the period between presentation of a petition to wind up a company and the court's decision on hearing the petition, there is no winding up by the court of the company[682] (which is, therefore, not being wound up by the court[683]), and, unless the company is in voluntary liquidation:

(a) the company is not 'being wound up',[684]

(b) winding up is not in progress,[685] and

(c) nothing occurring in that period happens in 'the course of the winding up' of the company.[686]

See also 1.26 (steps taken to apply for a winding-up order are not part of the process of winding up).

5.295 If a petition is presented for the compulsory winding up of a registered company and, before the petition is heard, the company adopts a resolution for voluntary winding up (or had adopted such a resolution before the petition was presented), it would seem that the company is 'being wound up' as from the time of adoption of the resolution. But, for the purposes of IA 1986, s 40 (which requires a receiver appointed under a floating charge on a company's assets to pay the company's preferential debts if the company is not in course of being wound up), a company which has adopted a resolution for voluntary winding up is not 'in the course of being wound up' until a liquidator has been appointed.[687]

---

concerned what is now IA 1986, s 387(3)(c), which was reworded by the Companies Act 1947, s 91(7), to make it clear that the commencement of voluntary winding up is the relevant time.

[679] IA 1986, s 129(1A).

[680] IA 1986, s 129(1A), applied and modified by the Energy Act 2004, sch 20, paras 41 and 45; Energy Act 2011, s 96(1) and (3)(f); Postal Services Act 2011, sch 10, paras 40 and 45.

[681] IA 1986, s 129 (see 5.279–5.281 and 5.289–5.292), unless the order is made on an administration application or an energy, energy supply company or postal administration application (see 5.293).

[682] *Equitas Ltd v Jacob* [2005] EWHC 1440 (Ch), [2005] BPIR 1312, at [11].

[683] *Secretary of State for Business, Innovation and Skills v Top Choice Wholesale Ltd* [2012] EWHC 1262 (Ch), BAILII.

[684] *Re Exhall Coal Mining Co Ltd* (1864) 4 De G J & S 377 per Knight Bruce LJ at p 379 (but obiter because irrelevant to the case before his Lordship: see *Re Traders' North Staffordshire Carrying Co, ex parte North Staffordshire Railway Co* (1874) LR 19 Eq 60 per Jessel MR at p 64); *Re Tumacacori Mining Co* (1874) LR 17 Eq 534 at p 537; *Re Christonette International Ltd* [1982] 1 WLR 1245; *Object Design Inc v Object Design Australia Pty Ltd* (1997) 78 FCR 60.

[685] *Re Miles Aircraft Ltd* [1948] Ch 188 per Vaisey J at p 191.

[686] *Wightman v Bennett* [2005] BPIR 470; *Re Overnight Ltd* [2009] EWHC 601 (Ch), [2009] Bus LR 1141. The contrary decision in *Re Dynamics Corporation of America* [1973] 1 WLR 63 was for the purposes of a provision in the Companies Act 1948, s 276(1). That provision is now IA 1986, s 426(1), where it has been reworded so that it no longer refers to 'the course of winding up'. See 5.297.

[687] *Re Christonette International Ltd* [1982] 1 WLR 1245.

In Malaysia, however, it has been held that, after a winding-up application has been pre- **5.296**
sented, there is a commencement of a winding up by the court even though the petition has
not yet been heard.[688] The same was assumed in Australia[689] before the commencement of
winding up by the court was moved forward to the time of making the winding-up order.
The curious result of these Malaysian and Australian cases is that there can be a commencement of a winding up by the court even though no winding up by the court occurs.

In the interval between presentation and hearing of a petition to wind up a company it is **5.297**
possible for actions and proceedings against the company to be stayed under IA 1986, s 126,
and in *Re Dynamics Corporation of America*,[690] Templeman J held that an order made under
s 126 is made 'in the course of winding up a company' even though it does not necessarily
follow that a winding-up order will be made when the petition is heard. His Lordship made
this rather strained interpretation in the context of a statutory provision[691] which has since
been reworded so that it no longer refers to 'the course of winding up'.[692]

In *Newmont Pty Ltd v Laverton Nickel NL*,[693] though, Needham J held that the actions of **5.298**
a provisional liquidator of a company in the period after a winding-up petition has been
presented but before the court has finally disposed of it are actions in the winding up of
the company, and said he thought that this was not 'straining language'. It seems that his
Honour was assuming that a winding-up order would be made, creating a winding up
which would commence when the petition was presented.

Building societies

If an order is made to wind up a building society and, before the petition was presented, **5.299**
an instrument of dissolution under the Building Societies Act 1986, s 87, was placed in the
society's public file, the winding up is deemed to have commenced on the date on which the
instrument was placed in the file.[694]

Incorporated friendly societies

If an order is made to wind up an incorporated friendly society and, before the petition was **5.300**
presented, an instrument of dissolution under the Friendly Societies Act 1992, s 20, was
placed in the society's public file, the winding up is deemed to have commenced on the date
on which the instrument was placed in the file.[695]

Unregistered companies

If an order is made for the compulsory winding up of an unregistered company that is already **5.301**
being wound up under its own rules or under legislation applying to it, the commencement

---

[688] *Tye Chwee Hoon v Cayman Commodities (M) Sdn Bhd* [1990] 2 MLJ 23; *Pembinaan KSY Sdn Bhd v Lian Seng Properties Sdn Bhd* [1992] 1 MLJ 571; *Kredin Sdn Bhd v Development and Commercial Bank Bhd* [1995] 3 MLJ 304; Samsar Kamar bin Hj Ab Latif, 'Recent developments in company liquidation' [1996] 3 MLJ xciii.
[689] *Re Barrier Reef Finance and Land Pty Ltd* [1989] 1 QdR 252; though *Fleet Motor and General Insurance (Aust) Pty Ltd v Tickle* [1984] 1 NSWLR 210 is to the contrary.
[690] [1973] 1 WLR 63.
[691] Companies Act 1948, s 276(1).
[692] See IA 1986, s 426(1).
[693] [1978] 2 NSWLR 325.
[694] Building Societies Act 1986, sch 15, para 20.
[695] Friendly Societies Act 1992, sch 10, para 23.

of the winding up by the court is, under IA 1986, s 129(2), the time of presentation of the petition.[696]

Open-ended investment companies

5.302 An open-ended investment company must give written notice to the FCA of any proposal to wind up its affairs, or a sub-fund, otherwise than by the court, and must not give effect to the proposal unless the FCA has given its approval or, after one month since the notice was given, the FCA has failed to give a warning notice that it proposes to refuse approval.[697] If an order is made for the winding up by the court of an open-ended investment company, or a sub-fund, that is already being wound up otherwise than by the court, the winding up by the court is deemed to have commenced either:[698]

(a) at the time when the FCA gave its approval to the proposal to wind up; or
(b) if the proposal was implemented because of a failure by the FCA to give a warning notice within one month, on the day following the end of the one-month period.

Winding up under the supervision of the court

5.303 A voluntary winding up under the supervision of the court[699] commences when the voluntary winding up commenced, whether the petition was presented after the voluntary winding up commenced[700] or before[701] and even if a provisional liquidator was appointed before the voluntary winding up commenced.[702]

Going into Liquidation

5.304 IA 1986 uses the phrase 'go into liquidation'. By s 247(2) and (3), a company goes into liquidation when:[703]

(a) it adopts a resolution for voluntary winding up;
(b) Companies House registers a notice given by the company's administrator, that sch B1, para 83 (moving from administration to creditors' voluntary liquidation), applies;
(c) the court, under IR 1986, r 1.33(3) or r 2.132(3), orders that the company is to be wound up as if a resolution for voluntary winding up had been passed;[704]

---

[696] *Re Sick and Funeral Society of St John's Sunday School, Golcar* [1973] Ch 51 at pp 57–8.

[697] Open-Ended Investment Companies Regulations 2001 (SI 2001/1228), reg 21 ('the Authority' in that regulation is the FCA, see reg 2).

[698] SI 2001/1228, reg 31(4), applied to sub-funds by reg 33C(1), (5) and (6) ('the Authority' is the FCA, see reg 2).

[699] See 10.152–10.165. This form of winding up is no longer available in the United Kingdom.

[700] *Re Traders' North Staffordshire Carrying Co, ex parte North Staffordshire Railway Co* (1874) LR 19 Eq 60; *Re Thurso New Gas Co* (1889) 42 ChD 486; though *Re Dublin Exhibition Palace and Winter Garden Co Ltd* (1868) IR 2 Eq 158 is to the contrary.

[701] Per Lord Romilly MR during argument in *Hodgkinson v Kelly* (1868) LR 6 Eq 496; *Re Smith, Knight and Co, Weston's Case* (1868) LR 4 Ch App 20.

[702] *Re Emperor Life Assurance Society* (1885) 31 ChD 78; *Re West Cumberland Iron and Steel Co* (1889) 40 ChD 361. In *Marshall v Glamorgan Iron and Coal Co* (1868) LR 7 Eq 129, *Re Imperial Land Co of Marseilles, ex parte Colborne and Strawbridge* (1871) LR 11 Eq 478, *Re Artistic Colour Printing Co, ex parte Fourdrinier* (1882) 21 ChD 510 and *Re London, Windsor and Greenwich Hotels Co, Quartermaine's Case* [1892] 1 Ch 639, it was accepted that the winding up under supervision commenced when the voluntary winding up commenced but the reports of the cases do not state the date of presentation of the petitions.

[703] Even though the section uses 'if' instead of 'when' (*Re Walter L Jacob and Co Ltd* [1993] BCC 512).

[704] See 10.21–10.25 and 10.62–10.66 (conversion of voluntary arrangement or administration into creditors' voluntary winding up with confirmation by the court).

(d) an order for its winding up is made (unless any of events (a), (b) or (c) has occurred, in which case the date of their occurrence is the date of going into liquidation).

The same definition applies to the Company Directors Disqualification Act 1986.[705]

Point (b) in 5.304 also applies to a notice of moving to creditors' voluntary liquidation given by an energy, energy supply company or postal administrator.[706] **5.305**

For the construction of the term 'go into liquidation' in contracts see *Emo Oil Ltd v Sun Alliance and London Insurance Co.*[707] **5.306**

Summary

Where a winding-up order is made on a petition, the times of commencement of winding up and going into liquidation depend on the sequence of events as shown in table 5.2. **5.307**

Commencement of Bank or Building Society Insolvency

A bank or building society insolvency order takes effect from when the application for the order was made, unless the application was made in the two weeks following notification to the PRA that an administration application[708] or winding-up petition had been presented,[709] in which case it takes effect from the date of presentation of that administration application or winding-up petition.[710] **5.308**

Table 5.2 Commencement of winding up and going into liquidation

Sequence of events	Commencement of winding up; time of going into liquidation
Sequence 1	
1 Presentation of petition	Commencement of winding up by the court
2 Winding-up order made	Company goes into liquidation
Sequence 2	
1 Resolution for voluntary winding up, or going from voluntary arrangement or administration to voluntary winding up	Company goes into liquidation and commencement of winding up by the court
2 Presentation of petition	
3 Winding-up order made	
Sequence 3	
1 Presentation of petition	Commencement of winding up by the court
2 Resolution for voluntary winding up	Company goes into liquidation
3 Winding-up order made	

---

[705] Company Directors Disqualification Act 1986, s 22(3).
[706] Energy Act 2004, sch 20, paras 1–4, 19 and 41; Energy Act 2011, s 96; Postal Services Act 2011, sch 10, paras 1, 2, 18 and 40.
[707] [2009] IESC 2.
[708] Petition in the case of a building society.
[709] See 3.50.
[710] Banking Act 2009, s 98(1), (2) and (3). Applied to building societies by the Building Societies Act 1986, s 90C, and modified by the Building Societies (Insolvency and Special Administration) Order 2009 (SI 2009/805), sch 1, para 12. For an FCA-regulated bank, references to the PRA are to be treated as references

5.309   While a bank or building society insolvency order has effect the institution may be described as being 'in bank insolvency' or 'in building society insolvency' as appropriate.[711]

Becoming Insolvent

5.310   If a company goes into liquidation[712] at a time when its assets are insufficient for the payment of its debts and other liabilities and the expenses of the winding up, it 'becomes insolvent' for the purposes of the Company Directors Disqualification Act 1986, ss 6 and 7.[713] But, for the purposes of the Employment Rights Act 1996, s 166 (claiming redundancy payments from the Secretary of State) and part 12 (insolvency of employers), an employer which is a company 'has become insolvent' if a winding up order has been made, or a resolution for voluntary winding up has been passed, with respect to the company, regardless of its financial position.[714] And in those circumstances the employer is to be 'taken to be insolvent' for the purposes of the Pension Schemes Act 1993, part 7, chapter 2 (payment by Secretary of State of unpaid scheme contributions),[715] and the Pensions Act 1995, ss 81–85 (compensation provisions).[716]

5.311   The Company Directors Disqualification Act 1986 is applied to insolvent partnerships[717] with some of its provisions modified.[718] A partnership 'becomes insolvent' for the purposes of modified ss 6 and 7 if it is ordered to be wound up by the court as an unregistered company at a time when its assets are insufficient for the payment of its debts and other liabilities and the expenses of the winding up.[719]

5.312   A bank which becomes subject to a bank insolvency order or a bank administration order 'becomes insolvent' for the purposes of the Company Directors Disqualification Act 1986,

---

to the FCA (Banking Act 2009, s 129A). There is no express reference to notification to the FCA in the case of a building society that is not a PRA-authorized person.

[711] Banking Act 2009, s 94(4)(b). Applied to building societies by the Building Societies Act 1986, s 90C.

[712] See 5.304–5.305.

[713] Company Directors Disqualification Act 1986, ss 6(2)(a) and 22(3). The other ways of becoming insolvent for these purposes are specified in the rest of s 6(2). For the purposes of ss 6 and 7 'company' means a company registered under the Companies Act 2006 in Great Britain or an unregistered company that may be wound up under IA 1986, part 5 (Company Directors Disqualification Act 1986, s 22(2)). The term also includes a building society (s 22A(2)), an incorporated friendly society (s 22B(2)), an NHS foundation trust (s 22C(2)), an open-ended investment company (s 22D(1)), a registered society (s 22E(1) and (3)) and a limited liability partnership (Limited Liability Partnerships Regulations 2001 (SI 2001/1090), reg 4(2)(a)).

[714] Employment Rights Act 1996, ss 166(5)(b) and (7)(a) and 183(1)(b) and (3)(a). 'Company' includes a charitable incorporated organization (ss 166(9) and 183(5)) but is otherwise undefined. For a limited liability partnership, a voluntary winding up is determined rather than resolved (ss 166(5)(c) and (8)(a) and 183(1)(c) and (4)(a)). The other ways in which an employer may become insolvent for these purposes are listed in the rest of ss 166 and 183. Simply being unable to pay one's debts is not enough (*Secretary of State for Trade and Industry v Key* [2004] BPIR 214). It has been held that, for these purposes, if an employer goes through two or more insolvency procedures (such as voluntary arrangement followed by winding up), it has become insolvent only once, at the time of the first procedure (*Secretary of State for Business, Innovation and Skills v McDonagh* [2013] ICR 1177).

[715] Pension Schemes Act 1993, s 123(1)(c)(i).

[716] Pensions Act 1995, s 81(3) and (8). Other circumstances in which an employer is to be taken to be insolvent in England and Wales are listed in the remainder of the Pension Schemes Act 1993, s 123(1).

[717] By IPO 1994, art 16.

[718] As set out in IPO 1994, sch. 8.

[719] Company Directors Disqualification Act 1986, s 6(2)(a)(i), as modified by IPO 1994, sch 8. Entering administration is the only other way in which a partnership can become insolvent for those purposes (s 6(2)(a)(ii) as so modified).

ss 6 and 7.[720] The same applies to an investment bank which becomes subject to an investment bank special administration order[721] and a building society which becomes subject to a building society insolvency order or a building society special administration order.[722]

The fact that a company has been ordered to be wound up does not in itself prove that it is **5.313** insolvent.[723] There are exceptions:

(a) If the winding-up proceedings are main proceedings subject to Regulation (EC) No 1346/2000, the company will be presumed to be insolvent for the purposes of opening secondary proceedings elsewhere in the EU (apart from Denmark).[724]

(b) If the winding-up proceeding is a main proceeding under the UNCITRAL Model Law, there will be a rebuttable presumption that the company is insolvent for the purposes of opening non-main proceedings in another State which has enacted the law.[725]

(c) A winding-up order is prima facie evidence that, in any action or other legal proceeding in which the company is claimant, it would be unable to pay the defendant's costs so that it should be ordered to give security under CPR, r 25.13(2)(c).[726]

(d) The Employment Rights Act 1996, s 166, discussed at 5.310.

Is Wound Up

Whether a company 'is wound up' when a winding-up order is made or when the winding **5.314** up is completed depends on the context.[727]

---

[720] Banking Act 2009, ss 121(1) and (2)(c) and 155(1) and (2)(c).

[721] Investment Bank Special Administration Regulations 2011 (SI 2011/245), reg 23(1)(c).

[722] Building Societies Act 1986, s 90E(1) and (2)(c).

[723] *Re New Zealand Banking Corporation, Hickie and Co's Case* (1867) LR 4 Eq 226.

[724] art 27; see 10.188.

[725] UNCITRAL Model Law, art 31.

[726] *Northampton Coal Iron and Waggon Co v Midland Waggon Co* (1878) 7 ChD 500 per Jessel MR at 503; *North-West Timber Co v McMillan* (1886) 3 Man R 277; *Pure Spirit Co v Fowler* (1890) 25 QBD 235; *Grand Pacific Hotel Ltd v Leung Kai Man* [2004] 1 HKLRD 1015.

[727] *General Share and Trust Co v Wetley Brick and Pottery Co* (1882) 20 ChD 260.

6

REVIEW OF ORDERS

Correction of Slips

6.1 The court may at any time correct an accidental slip or omission in a judgment or order.[1] The court may vary an order so as to make its meaning and intention clear.[2]

6.2 There have been several cases in which the court has been asked to correct a misspelling in a winding-up order of the name of the company to be wound up. The court has a power to amend the title of proceedings, even after judgment, if the nature of the proceedings or judgment is not altered by the change.[3] For example, in *Re J and P Sussman Ltd*[4] the name of the company intended to be wound up was J and P Sussmann Ltd, but in the order (and throughout the proceedings) it had been referred to as J and P Sussman Ltd. The company had not objected to the misspelling of its name in earlier proceedings brought against it by the petitioner. The petitioner applied to amend the spelling of the company's name in the petition and Vaisey J allowed that amendment and also made a new winding-up order with the company's correct name. *Swift Canadian Co v Island Creamery Association*[5] is a similar case. In *Re Cork Constitution Co Ltd*[6] an order had been made to wind up a company called Cork Constitution Ltd but misnaming it Cork Constitution Co Ltd and on the application of a purchaser of the company's property the court ordered that the petition and winding-up order be amended.

6.3 If the making of a winding-up order has been advertised with the company erroneously named, the court may require a new advertisement with the correct name.[7]

6.4 In *Re Professional and Trade Papers Ltd*[8] the name of the company intended to be wound up was Professional and Trade Papers Ltd, but in the order (and throughout the proceedings) it had been referred to as Professional and Trades Papers Ltd. Buckley J allowed amendment of the petition and required publication of an advertisement stating the error that had been made and that the winding-up order would be drawn up seven days after the issue of the advertisement.

6.5 In *Re Shields Marine Insurance Co*[9] the court had wrongly made one order winding up two separate companies and it regarded making new separate orders as rectifying a slip.

---

[1] CPR, r 40.12, the 'slip rule'.
[2] *Swindale v Forder* [2007] EWCA Civ 29, [2007] 1 FLR 1905.
[3] *Pearlman (Veneers) SA (Pty) Ltd v Bernhard Bartels* [1954] 1 WLR 1457.
[4] [1958] 1 WLR 519.
[5] (1912) 10 DLR 833.
[6] (1882) 9 LR Ir 163.
[7] *Re Newcastle Machinists Co* [1888] WN 246 and [1889] WN 1, decided at a time when the petitioner was responsible for advertising the order.
[8] (1900) 44 SJ 740.
[9] [1867] WN 296.

An application for permission to amend an error in a petition discovered after the **6.6** winding-up order has been made should be made to the member of court staff in charge of the winding-up list in the Royal Courts of Justice or to a district judge in any other court.[10] PD Insolvency Proceedings 2014 gives the following details:

> 11.6.2 Where the error is an error in the name of the company, the member of court staff in charge of the winding-up list in the Royal Courts of Justice or a district judge in any other court may make any necessary amendments to ensure that the winding-up order is drawn up with the correct name of the company inserted. If there is any doubt, for example, where there might be another company in existence which could be confused with the company to be wound up, the member of court staff in charge of the winding-up list will refer the application to a registrar at the Royal Courts of Justice and a district judge may refer it to a judge.

> 11.6.3 Where it is discovered that the company has been struck off the register of companies prior to the winding-up order being made, the matter must be restored to the list as soon as possible to enable an order for the restoration of the name to be made as well as the order to wind up and, save where the petition has been presented by a minister of the Crown or a government department, evidence of service on the Treasury Solicitor or the Solicitor for the Affairs of the Duchy of Lancaster or the Solicitor to the Duchy of Cornwall (as appropriate) should be filed exhibiting the *bona vacantia* waiver letter.

Recall or Setting Aside of an Order Made on a Winding-up Petition

Recall

As a general rule a court may recall, vary or alter a judgment or proposed order, up to the time **6.7** that the order is perfected[11] and even after judgment has been delivered.[12] Subject to the overriding objective,[13] a court may hear further argument after a judgment has been delivered or order made but not drawn up.[14] In exceptional circumstances,[15] further evidence may be heard and a statement of case may be amended.[16]

Setting Aside

Fundamentally defective order

Under the court's inherent jurisdiction to control its own procedure, it may set aside an order **6.8** which it has made if the order is so fundamentally defective that it ought not to have been

---

[10] PD Insolvency Proceedings 2014, para 11.6.1.

[11] *Millensted v Grosvenor House (Park Lane) Ltd* [1937] 1 KB 717; *Re Harrison's Share under a Settlement* [1955] Ch 260; *Re XL Petroleum Pty Ltd* [1971] VR 560; *Pittalis v Sherefettin* [1986] QB 868; *Hyde and South Bank Housing Association v Kain* (1989) 133 SJ 1578; *Royal Brompton Hospital NHS Trust v Hammond* [2001] EWCA Civ 778, [2001] BLR 317, at [4].

[12] *Re L (Children) (Preliminary Finding: Power to Reverse)* [2013] UKSC 8, [2013] 1 WLR 634.

[13] CPR, r 1.1, especially the requirement to allocate an appropriate share of the court's resources to the case; *Royal Brompton Hospital NHS Trust v Hammond* [2001] EWCA Civ 778, [2001] BLR 317.

[14] *Taylor v Williamsons* [2002] EWCA Civ 1380, *The Times*, 9 August 2002.

[15] *Stewart v Engel* [2000] 1 WLR 2268.

[16] *Charlesworth v Relay Roads Ltd* [2000] 1 WLR 230.

made.[17] The court may refuse an application to set aside if it has not been made promptly.[18] In *Re K W and L M Powell Ltd*[19] an application was made but there was no evidence of any miscarriage of justice calling for the exercise of the jurisdiction.

6.9 An application to set aside an order should be made as an application for rescission of the order under the Insolvency Rules 1986 (IR 1986), r 7.47(1).[20]

Company's failure to attend hearing

6.10 An application to set aside an order made against a party to insolvency proceedings on the ground that it was made at a hearing which the party did not attend must be made as an application for the order to be rescinded under IR 1986, r 7.47(1),[21] rather than an application for it to be set aside under the Civil Procedure Rules (CPR), r 39.3(3).[22]

6.11 A provision in rules of court for setting aside a judgment by default was used when there was no power to review or rescind winding-up orders.[23] In Australia and New Zealand it has been held that a winding-up order which has been made against a company in its absence can be set aside under a rule of court giving power to set aside an order made at a trial which a party did not attend.[24]

6.12 The statutory provisions in Malaysia for appealing against a winding-up order and staying proceedings in a winding up exhaustively state the means of reviewing perfected winding-up orders so that there is no jurisdiction to set aside an order made in default of appearance.[25]

Other reasons for setting aside

6.13 An application by creditors of a company to set aside an order to wind up the company on the ground that they were being defrauded by the liquidator was described as 'entirely misconceived' in *Re Standard Cobalt Co.*[26]

---

[17] *Re South African Syndicate Ltd* (1883) 28 SJ 152, in which a contributory's petition had been presented by a person who was in fact disqualified from petitioning by what is now IA 1986, s 124(2); *Re Blatt Ray Inc* (1939) 20 CBR 447, in which a contributory's petition had been presented by a person who was not a contributory; *Re Samoana Press Co Ltd* (1987) 4 NZCLC 64,119, in which the petition had not been served on the company; *Double Bay Newspapers Pty Ltd v The Fitness Lounge Pty Ltd* [2006] NSWSC 226, 57 ACSR 131, in which a creditor's application for a winding-up order was continued by mistake after agreement to compromise the applicant's debt.

[18] *Re Morning Star Gold Mining Co* (1879) 2 SCR NS (NSW) Eq 14; *Smith v Australian and European Bank* (1882) 8 VLR (M) 23; *Wilson v Specter Partnership* [2007] EWHC 133 (Ch), [2007] BPIR 649, at [24].

[19] (1983) 1 NZCLC 98,704.

[20] *Re Calmex Ltd* [1989] 1 All ER 485; *Re Dollar Land (Feltham) Ltd* [1995] 2 BCLC 370. See 6.24–6.43.

[21] See 6.24–6.43.

[22] *Papanicola v Humphreys* [2005] EWHC 335 (Ch), [2005] 2 All ER 418, at [37]; *Brown v Button* [2012] EWHC 195 (Ch), LTL 22/2/2012.

[23] *Re Aston Hull Coal and Brick Co Ltd* (1882) 45 LT 676.

[24] In Australia: *Re Swiftcrete Pty Ltd* (1977) 2 ACLR 411; *Re Rick Wilson Pty Ltd* (1982) 7 ACLR 354 per McLelland J at pp 356–7; *Nationwide News Pty Ltd v Samalot Enterprises Pty Ltd* (1986) 5 NSWLR 227; *George Ward Steel Pty Ltd v Kizkot Pty Ltd* (1989) 15 ACLR 464; *Registrar of Aboriginal Corporations v Murnkurni Women's Aboriginal Corporation* (1995) 137 ALR 404. It must be shown that the company is solvent (*Double Bay Newspapers Pty Ltd v The Fitness Lounge Pty Ltd* [2006] NSWSC 226, 57 ACSR 131). In New Zealand: *Bridon New Zealand Ltd v Tent World Ltd* [1992] 3 NZLR 725, disagreeing with *Kensington Swan v NZ Fisheries Ltd* (1989) 5 NZCLC 66,186.

[25] *Perdana Merchant Bankers Bhd v Maril Rionebel (M) Sdn Bhd* [1996] 4 MLJ 343.

[26] (1910) 1 OWN 875.

Review, Rescission or Variation

Power to Review, Rescind or Vary an Order

Principle

A court which has made an order in the exercise of its jurisdiction under the Insolvency Act **6.14** 1986 (IA 1986), parts 1–4, and IR 1986, parts 1–4, may review, rescind or vary that order.[27] Rescission of a winding-up order is considered at 6.24–6.43. The same provision is made in relation to orders made by the court in the exercise of its bankruptcy jurisdiction.[28]

The High Court may review, rescind or vary any order made by it in the exercise of its juris- **6.15** diction under the Banking Act 2009, part 2.[29]

Who may exercise the power

Any Chancery Division judge may review, rescind or vary an order made by another **6.16** Chancery Division judge, because IR 1986, r 7.47(1), provides that the 'court' may review etc its decisions,[30] but there has been doubt about who can review etc a decision of a bankruptcy registrar. Formerly it had been held that the registrars in bankruptcy did not form a separate court within the Chancery Division.[31] However, the creation by what is now IR 1986, r 7.47(2)(a), of a procedure for appealing from a registrar to a judge[32] appeared to constitute the registrars as a separate court, and it was held in *Re SN Group plc*[33] that a decision made by a registrar could be reviewed etc only by the registrar, though the registrar could adjourn the matter to be heard by the judge.[34] In *Re Piccadilly Property Management Ltd*,[35] though, it was held, that the registrars are not a separate court and that a decision of a registrar may be reviewed etc by the registrar or by a judge.[36] This means that when an order has been made by a registrar it is possible both to apply to the judge to rescind or review the order and to appeal against it, though this should be rare.[37]

In the County Court a judge cannot review, rescind or vary a decision of a district judge, **6.17** or vice versa.[38]

After a transfer of proceedings from one court to another, the transferee court may review, **6.18** rescind or vary a decision of the previous court.[39]

---

[27] IR 1986, r 7.47(1).

[28] IA 1986, s 375(1).

[29] Bank Insolvency (England and Wales) Rules 2009 (SI 2009/356), r 224(1); Building Society Insolvency (England and Wales) Rules 2010 (SI 2010/2581), r 217(1).

[30] *Re W and A Glaser Ltd* [1994] BCC 199 at p 206.

[31] *Re Rolls Razor Ltd (No 2)* [1970] Ch 576 at pp 590–1.

[32] See 6.45–6.48.

[33] [1994] 1 BCLC 319.

[34] As in *Re Dollar Land (Feltham) Ltd* [1995] 2 BCLC 370.

[35] [1999] 2 BCLC 145.

[36] Followed in *Inland Revenue v O'Brien* (1999) LTL 29/7/99.

[37] *Re Piccadilly Property Management Ltd*. Laddie J thought it at least arguable that this would be an abuse of process (*Smurthwaite v Simpson-Smith (No 1)* [2005] EWHC 447 (Ch), 2005 WL 669854, at [20]).

[38] *Re Maugham* (1888) 21 QBD 21; *Re Clifton* (1890) 7 Morr 59 at pp 62–3; *Re a Debtor (No 39 of 1974)* [1977] 1 WLR 1308.

[39] *Re a Debtor (No 2A of 1980)* [1981] Ch 148.

Nature of process

6.19 The power to review, rescind or vary is unfettered but must be exercised judicially.[40] It is not to be used in order to hear an appeal against a decision of a judge of coordinate jurisdiction, save in the most exceptional circumstances.[41] Such an exceptional circumstance might be where the court is satisfied that there has been something amounting to a miscarriage of justice which cannot be corrected by the ordinary process of appeal.[42] The distinction between an appeal and an application to review, rescind or vary is that the question on an appeal against a decision is whether the decision was right or wrong or was otherwise unjust through a serious procedural or other irregularity, whereas the question on an application to review, rescind or vary is whether the original order ought to remain in force in the light of changed circumstances or further evidence.[43]

6.20 An application to review, rescind or vary a decision must not be used merely to obtain a rehearing[44] or merely to restate the applicant's case in what is hoped to be a more persuasive way.[45]

The court's approach

6.21 In *Papanicola v Humphreys*[46] Laddie J summarized the principles on which the court will exercise its discretion to review, rescind or vary orders under IA 1986, s 375(1), in bankruptcy. As the power to review, rescind or vary is conferred by s 375(1) in the same terms as IR 1986, r 7.47(1), his Lordship's remarks are equally applicable to winding-up proceedings. Among the points made by his Lordship are:

(2) The onus is on the applicant to demonstrate the existence of circumstances which justify exercise of the discretion [to review, rescind or vary] in his favour.

(3) Those circumstances must be exceptional.[47]

(4) The circumstances relied on must involve a material difference to what was before the court which made the original order. In other words there must be something new to justify the overturning of the original order.[48]

(5) There is no limit to the factors which may be taken into account. They can include, for example, changes which have occurred since the making of the original order and significant facts which, although in existence at the time of the original order, were not brought to the court's attention at that time.

(6) Where the new circumstances relied on consist of or include new evidence which could have been made available at the original hearing, that, and any explanation . . . the applicant gives for the failure to produce it then or any lack of such explanation, are factors which can be taken into account in the exercise of the discretion.

---

[40] *Mond v Hammond Suddards* [2000] Ch 40 per Chadwick LJ at p 49.

[41] *Mond v Hammond Suddards* at p 49.

[42] *Re a Debtor (No 32 of 1991) (No 2)* [1994] BCC 524 per Vinelott J at p 528.

[43] Per Millett J in *Re a Debtor (No 32-SD-1991)* [1993] 1 WLR 314 at p 319 and (as Millett LJ) in *Fitch v Official Receiver* [1996] 1 WLR 242 at p 246; *Mond v Hammond Suddards* [2000] Ch 40 at p 49 per Chadwick LJ; CPR, r 52.11(3). For the use of further evidence see 6.22–6.23.

[44] *Egleton v Commissioners of Inland Revenue* [2003] EWHC 3226, [2004] BPIR 476.

[45] *RWH Enterprises Ltd v Portedge Ltd* [1998] BCC 556; *Re Thirty-Eight Building Ltd (No 2)* [2000] 1 BCLC 201; *Papanicola v Humphreys* [2005] EWHC 335 (Ch), [2005] 2 All ER 418, at [26].

[46] [2005] EWHC 335 (Ch), [2005] 2 All ER 418, at [25].

[47] His Lordship rejected a challenge to this point in *Smurthwaite v Simpson-Smith (No 1)* [2005] EWHC 447 (Ch), 2005 WL 669854, at [21]. Another way of putting this point is that the jurisdiction to review must be exercised extremely cautiously (*Re Thirty-Eight Building Ltd (No 2)* [2000] 1 BCLC 201 at p 206).

[48] The need for something new may be irrelevant in exceptional cases where it is necessary to correct an obvious injustice (*Re Thirty-Eight Building Ltd (No 2)* [2000] 1 BCLC 201 at p 206).

In relation to point (4), there is a material difference if the party seeking review etc of an order was not present or represented when the order was made, but is now.[49]

Fresh evidence

Further evidence may be adduced both on an appeal against a decision and on an application to review, rescind or vary it. Before the CPR came into force evidence could not be adduced on appeal if, with reasonable diligence, it could have been obtained for use at the hearing below.[50] In *Re a Debtor (No 32-SD-1991)*[51] Millett J held, at p 319, that evidence could be heard on an application to review etc whether or not it could have been obtained at the original hearing. But where the evidence might and should have been obtained at the original hearing that will be a factor for the court to take into account.[52] In *Fitch v Official Receiver*[53] Millett LJ suggested, at p 246, that fresh evidence could be presented on an application to review etc only if it could not be presented on an appeal. **6.22**

Under the CPR the discretion to admit new evidence on an appeal must be exercised in accordance with the overriding objective,[54] using the *Ladd v Marshall* principles as persuasive guidelines rather than strict rules.[55] It seems that, on an application to review, rescind or vary, those principles are less significant. **6.23**

Rescission of a Winding-up Order

Who may apply

An application[56] under IR 1986, r 7.47(1),[57] to rescind a winding-up order may be made only by a creditor or a contributory, though the company may join in an application.[58] The costs of an unsuccessful application will be paid by the creditor or contributory applicant even when the company has been joined.[59] **6.24**

Time limit

An application for rescission of a winding-up order must be made within five business days of the date on which the order was made[60] though this time limit may be extended by the court under r 4.3.[61] An application for extension of time should be made with the application for rescission[62] and the witness statement supporting the application should include reasons for the failure to apply within five business days.[63] **6.25**

---

[49] *Holtham v Kelmanson* [2006] EWHC 2588 (Ch), [2006] BPIR 1422. See 6.36–6.40.
[50] *Ladd v Marshall* [1954] 1 WLR 1489.
[51] [1993] 1 WLR 314
[52] *Re a Debtor (No 32-SD-1991)* [1993] 1 WLR 314 at p 319; see also per Peter Gibson LJ in *RWH Enterprises Ltd v Portedge Ltd* [1998] BCC 556 at p 559 and per Patten J in *Ahmed v Mogul Eastern Foods Ltd* [2005] EWHC 3532 (Ch), [2007] BPIR 975, at [24].
[53] [1996] 1 WLR 242.
[54] *Evans v Tiger Investments Ltd* [2002] EWCA Civ 161, [2002] 2 BCLC 185.
[55] *Hertfordshire Investments Ltd v Bubb* [2000] 1 WLR 2318.
[56] See 3.233–3.263.
[57] See 6.14–6.24.
[58] PD Insolvency Proceedings 2014, para 11.7.3; *Re Mid East Trading Ltd* [1997] 3 All ER 481.
[59] PD Insolvency Proceedings 2014, para 11.7.4.
[60] IR 1986, r 7.47(4). The clear days rule in CPR, r 2.8(2) and (3), applies (see 1.510). 'Business day' is defined in IR 1986, r 13.13(1) (see 1.512).
[61] As in *Re Calmex Ltd* [1989] 1 All ER 485 and *Re Virgo Systems Ltd* [1990] BCLC 34.
[62] PD Insolvency Proceedings 2014, para 11.7.2.
[63] PD Insolvency Proceedings 2014, para 11.7.3.

6.26 In a case of any complexity before 1 April 2013, an application for extension of time had to be treated as an application under CPR, r 3.9, for relief from a sanction.[64] An application to rescind a winding-up order must be made promptly because the order affects all creditors of the company and gives the official receiver authority to act immediately as liquidator and the possibility of rescission at any time would give rise to unwelcome uncertainty.[65]

6.27 An extension of time is unlikely to be granted if liquidators have incurred expense in investigating the company's insolvency.[66] A delay of three and a half to four and a half months, after learning of the order and the grounds for rescinding it, is 'very large'[67] and 'significant'.[68] There can be no conceivable justification for an application made more than three years after the winding-up order which, at the time it was made, the applicant had accepted was properly made.[69]

6.28 If an application is made within five business days of the order being made, the order will not have been drawn up and sealed.

Notice of application

6.29 Notice of an application to rescind a winding-up order must be given to the petitioner, any supporting or opposing creditor and the official receiver.[70]

The court's approach

6.30 The general principles set out at 6.21 will be applied by the court to an application to rescind a winding-up order. The position has been summarized by Barling J as follows:[71]

(1) The power to rescind is discretionary and is only to be exercised with caution;[72]
(2) the onus is on the applicant to satisfy the court that it is an appropriate case in which to exercise the discretion;
(3) it will only be an appropriate case where the circumstances are exceptional and those circumstances must involve a material difference from those before the court that made the original order;[73]
(4) there is no limit to the factors that the court can take into account, and they may include changes since the original order was made, and significant facts which, although in existence at the time of the original order, were not brought to the court's attention at that time;[74] but where that evidence could have been made available, any explanation the applicant gives for the failure to produce it then or any lack of such an explanation, are factors to be taken into account;

---

[64] *Sayers v Clarke Walker* [2002] EWCA Civ 645, [2002] 1 WLR 3095; *Re Metrocab Ltd* [2010] EWHC 1317 (Ch), [2010] 2 BCLC 603. See *Blackstone's Civil Practice 2015*, ch 48.

[65] *Re Metrocab Ltd* [2010] EWHC 1317 (Ch), [2010] 2 BCLC 603, at [17].

[66] *Re Mid East Trading Ltd* [1997] 3 All ER 481 at p 489, in which the application was about 14 months late.

[67] *Wilson v Specter Partnership* [2007] EWHC 133 (Ch), [2007] BPIR 649, at [23].

[68] *Re Metrocab Ltd* [2010] EWHC 1317 (Ch), [2010] 2 BCLC 603, at [19].

[69] *Leicester v Stevenson* [2002] EWHC 2831 (Ch), [2003] 2 BCLC 97, in which the applicant was warned that he could be treated as a vexatious litigant.

[70] PD Insolvency Proceedings 2014, para 11.7.2.

[71] *Credit Lucky Ltd v National Crime Agency* [2014] EWHC 83 (Ch), LTL 5/2/2014, at [31], based on *Re Metrocab Ltd* [2010] EWHC 1317 (Ch), [2010] 2 BCLC 603, at [36], based in turn on the passage from *Papanicola v Humphreys* [2005] EWHC 335 (Ch), [2005] 2 All ER 418, that is quoted and annotated at 6.21.

[72] *Re Dollar Land (Feltham) Ltd* [1995] 2 BCLC 370; *Wilson v Specter Partnership* [2007] EWHC 133 (Ch), [2007] BPIR 649, at [23].

[73] Or, in exceptional circumstances, where justice demands rescission (*Re Turnstem Ltd* [2004] EWHC 1765 (Ch), [2005] 1 BCLC 388, at [71], per Lawrence Collins J). See, for example, 6.41–6.42.

[74] See 6.22–6.23.

(5) the circumstances in which the court's power will be exercised will vary but generally where the rescission application involves dismissal of the winding up petition, so that the company is free to resume trading, the court will wish to be satisfied:

    (a) that the debt of the petitioning creditor has been paid, or will be paid, that the costs of the official receiver or any liquidator can be paid, and that the company is solvent at least on the basis that it can pay its debts as they fall due;

    (b) that the application has not been presented in a misleading way and the court is in possession of all the material facts and has not been left in doubt;

    (c) that the trading operations of the company have been fair and above board, and there is nothing that requires investigation of the affairs of the company.

The court requires 'very cogent reasons' for rescinding a winding-up order, with no cogent reason for not rescinding it,[75] but it is submitted that this does not mean that there is a special standard of proof.[76] The fact that those in control of the company deliberately decided not to oppose the winding-up petition and have now changed their minds is not an exceptional circumstance which justifies rescission.[77]   **6.31**

Evidence

An application to rescind a winding-up order must be accompanied by a witness statement which should include details of assets and liabilities.[78]   **6.32**

At the discretion of the court, fresh evidence may be adduced on an application to rescind an order.[79]   **6.33**

Attendance

The hearing of an application to rescind a winding-up order is a rehearing of the petition on which the order was made and that petition is restored to the court. Accordingly, any person who might have been heard on the hearing of the petition may appear on the hearing of the application to rescind and IR 1986, r 4.16 (which requires notice of intention to appear or the leave of the court[80]), applies.[81]   **6.34**

If the company is to resume business

Usually, if all the creditors of a company in liquidation have been paid and there is a desire that the company should cease being wound up, the appropriate order to ask for is an order staying proceedings in the winding up[82] not an order rescinding the winding-up order.[83]   **6.35**

Company unaware of the winding-up proceedings against it

An application to set aside an order made against a party to company insolvency proceedings on the ground that the order was made at a hearing which the party did not attend must be made as an application for the order to be rescinded under IR 1986, r 7.47(1), rather than   **6.36**

---

[75] *Re Piccadilly Property Management Ltd* [1999] 2 BCLC 145 at p 163.
[76] See 6.106.
[77] *Re Turnstem Ltd* [2004] EWHC 1765 (Ch), [2005] 1 BCLC 388.
[78] PD Insolvency Proceedings 2014, para 11.7.3.
[79] See 6.22–6.23.
[80] See 5.32–5.40.
[81] *Re Dollar Land (Feltham) Ltd* [1995] 2 BCLC 370.
[82] See 6.86–6.150.
[83] *Re Baxters Ltd* [1898] WN 60; *Re Lyric Syndicate Ltd* (1900) 17 TLR 162.

an application for it to be set aside under CPR, r 39.3(3).[84] Nevertheless, the philosophy underlying CPR, r 39.3(3)–(5), applies.[85] This means:[86]

(a) the applicant must act promptly on learning that the order has been made;
(b) the applicant must have had a good reason for not attending the hearing at which the order was made; and
(c) the applicant must have a reasonable prospect of success at a fresh hearing.

6.37   In *Re Virgo Systems Ltd*[87] the company had been acquired off the shelf but the registrar of companies had never been notified of a change of registered office. Accordingly, a statutory demand and, after that was not complied with, a winding-up petition, were served on the company at its registered office at the premises of the registration agent. The company did not appear at the hearing of the petition and a winding-up order was made. When the company learned that the order had been made, the company applied for rescission. The court extended the time limit for applying, noting that the company had applied within seven days of being informed of the existence of the order. The order was rescinded on the company demonstrating its solvency, undertaking to pay all creditors promptly and to pay the official receiver's costs.

6.38   The court may set aside a winding-up order made on a petition served at a registered office which the company had left if neither the petitioner nor the company were aware that the registrar had not registered the company's notice of change of address.[88]

6.39   In *Re a Company (No 1344 of 2003)*[89] a delay of six or eight weeks after learning of the winding-up order was enough for the court to refuse an application to extend time for applying to rescind.

6.40   If an extension of time for applying to rescind a winding-up order is refused, a solvent company may apply for a stay of all proceedings in the winding up.[90]

Order made against the wrong company

6.41   If a winding-up order is made against the wrong company, it may be rescinded under IR 1986, r 7.47(1), and the registrar of companies may be ordered to correct the records at Companies House.[91] The company wrongly ordered to be wound up will not be able to recover damages for the negligence of the petitioner.[92]

Petitioner unaware of company's voluntary liquidation

6.42   In *Re Cuerden Timber and Joinery Ltd*[93] a winding-up order was made without knowing that the company was already in voluntary liquidation (why this was not known is not

---

[84] *Papanicola v Humphreys* [2005] EWHC 335 (Ch), [2005] 2 All ER 418, at [37]; *Brown v Button* [2012] EWHC 195 (Ch), LTL 22/2/2012.
[85] *Papanicola v Humphreys* at [37].
[86] CPR, r 39.3(5).
[87] [1990] BCLC 34.
[88] *Deputy Commissioner of Taxation v Media Press Computer Supplies Pty Ltd* [2004] NSWSC 1271, 53 ACSR 517, in which it appeared that the registrar had lost the notice.
[89] [2003] EWHC 2807 (Ch), [2004] 2 BCLC 404.
[90] See 6.86–6.150.
[91] *Re Calmex Ltd* [1989] 1 All ER 485.
[92] *Business Computers International Ltd v Registrar of Companies* [1988] Ch 229.
[93] (2006) LTL 9/3/2007.

mentioned in the judgment). The voluntary liquidator (as a creditor for his fees) successfully applied for the winding-up order to be rescinded. The official receiver, the petitioner and supporting creditors expressed agreement to the rescission.

History

After the Supreme Court of Judicature Act 1873 but before IR 1986 came into force, a **6.43** winding-up order could be rescinded before it was perfected,[94] but not after.[95] However, in *Bridon New Zealand Ltd v Tent World Ltd*[96] Thomas J held that the court has an inherent power to rescind a winding-up order whenever it would be in the interest of justice to do so. For the position before the Supreme Court of Judicature Act 1873 see 6.158–6.162.

Appeal

Tribunal and Permission to Appeal

Permission to appeal

In a civil matter in proceedings under IA 1986, parts 1–4, and IR 1986, parts 1–4, or in **6.44** bank or building society insolvency proceedings, an appeal may be brought against an order of a court only with the permission of the court which made the decision or the permission of the court which has jurisdiction to hear the appeal.[97]

From first-instance decision by a High Court registrar or the County Court

An appeal from an order made by the County Court or a registrar of the High Court lies to **6.45** a single judge of the High Court.[98] Permission to appeal must be obtained from the judge or registrar who made the decision being appealed or from the High Court.[99]

For the purposes of IR 1986, r 7.47(2), an order made by a district judge sitting in the **6.46** County Court is an order made by that court and so the only appeal is under r 7.47(2) to a single judge of the High Court, not to the circuit judge or to the Court of Appeal under the Access to Justice Act 1999 (Destination of Appeals) Order 2000,[100] arts 3(2) and 4(b).[101]

On an appeal from a registrar to a single judge, the appeal is regarded as being heard by **6.47** a tribunal higher in the hierarchy of courts than the registrar, rather than in the same court.[102]

---

[94] *Re Crown Bank* (1890) 44 ChD 634 at pp 647–9; *Re Century Stores* [1964] CLY 482; *Re G and W Automatics Ltd (No 2)* (1969) 113 SJ 51; *Bridon New Zealand Ltd v Tent World Ltd* [1992] 3 NZLR 725.

[95] *Re Lyric Syndicate Ltd* (1900) 17 TLR 162; *Re Intermain Properties Ltd* [1986] BCLC 265.

[96] [1992] 3 NZLR 725.

[97] IR 1986, rr 7.47(2) and 7.49A(1) and (3), applying CPR, r 52.3; Bank Insolvency (England and Wales) Rules 2009 (SI 2009/356), r 224(2) and (3); Building Society Insolvency (England and Wales) Rules 2010 (SI 2010/2581), r 217(2) and (3); PD Insolvency Proceedings 2014, para 20.3.

[98] IR 1986, r 7.47(2)(a); *Re Calahurst Ltd* [1989] BCLC 140; *Midrome Ltd v Shaw* [1994] 1 BCLC 180; Bank Insolvency (England and Wales) Rules 2009 (SI 2009/356), r 224(2); Building Society Insolvency (England and Wales) Rules 2010 (SI 2010/2581), r 217(2); PD Insolvency Proceedings 2014, para 20.1.

[99] IR 1986, r 7.49A(1); SI 2009/356, r 224(2); SI 2010/2581, r 217(2). The requirement for permission is also imposed by IR 1986, r 7.49A(3), and PD Insolvency Proceedings 2014, para 20.3, applying CPR, r 52.3 (see the parenthesis at the end of r 52.3(1)).

[100] SI 2000/1071.

[101] *Re Langley Marketing Services Ltd* [1992] BCC 585.

[102] *Re Industrial and Commercial Securities plc* (1988) 5 BCC 320.

6.48 A decision by a High Court judge on a first appeal may be appealed to the Court of Appeal (a 'second appeal'), but only with the permission of that court.[103]

From first-instance decision by a High Court judge

6.49 An appeal from an order made by a High Court judge is to the Court of Appeal in the normal way.[104]

6.50 In *Re Dunraven Adare Coal and Iron Co*[105] the Court of Appeal was due to hear an appeal against the dismissal of one creditor's petition when another creditor presented a second petition. All parties wished the Court of Appeal to hear the second petition together with the appeal against the dismissal of the first petition, but it was held that the Court of Appeal had no jurisdiction to hear a petition at first instance, and hearing the second petition would not be for purposes of or incidental to the hearing and determination of the appeal on the first petition, so as to give the Court of Appeal jurisdiction under what is now the Senior Courts Act 1981, s 15(3).

6.51 If there are inadequate transitional provisions in legislation, re-registration of a company may render an appeal against dismissal of a winding-up petition nugatory. In *Re Old Swan and West Derby Permanent Benefit Building Society*[106] a petition to wind up an unincorporated building society as an unregistered company was presented to the Chancery Court of the County Palatine of Lancaster but was dismissed. The petitioner appealed to the Court of Appeal. Before the appeal was heard, the building society was incorporated by registration under the Building Societies Act 1874, in which provision was made for incorporated building societies to be wound up only by county courts. The Court of Appeal held that it did not have jurisdiction to hear the appeal because of the change of status of the society.

Procedure

Rules

6.52 The procedural rules and practice which apply to appeals in insolvency proceedings are CPR, Part 52, and PD 52A, PD 52B and PD 52C,[107] except for:[108]

(a) PD 52A, paras 4.3, 4.4 and 4.5 (judges hearing appeals; for the provision that is made in this regard by PD Insolvency Proceedings 2014 see 6.55–6.56); and
(b) PD 52B, section II (venue for appeals and filing of notices; for the provision that is made in this regard see 6.54).

Time limit

6.53 Unless the lower court directs some other period for filing an appellant's notice, the time limit for doing that is 21 days from the date of the decision being appealed.[109]

---

[103] Access to Justice Act 1999, s 55; CPR, r 52.13; PD Insolvency Proceedings 2014, para 20.4.
[104] IR 1986, 7.47(2)(b); Bank Insolvency (England and Wales) Rules 2009 (SI 2009/356), r 224(3); Building Society Insolvency (England and Wales) Rules 2010 (SI 2010/2581), r 217(3); PD Insolvency Proceedings 2014, para 20.2.
[105] (1875) 33 LT 371.
[106] (1887) 57 LT 381.
[107] IR 1986, r 7.49A(3); SI 2009/356, r 225; SI 2010/2581, r 218; PD Insolvency Proceedings 2014, para 20.9.3. See *Blackstone's Civil Practice 2015*, chapters 74 and 75.
[108] PD Insolvency Proceedings 2014, para 20.9.4.
[109] IR 1986, r 7.49A(2); CPR, r 52.4.

Appellant's notice

An appeal from a registrar in bankruptcy must be filed at the Royal Courts of Justice in **6.54**
London.[110] An appeal from a district judge sitting in a district registry may be filed either at
the RCJ or in that district registry.[111] An appeal from the County Court must be filed at the
designated court centre for the circuit.[112]

Judge

An appeal, or application for permission to appeal, from a decision of the County Court or **6.55**
of a registrar or district judge in the High Court, may be heard or considered by:

(a) a High Court judge, or
(b) any person authorized under the Senior Courts Act 1981, s 9, to act as a judge of the
    High Court in the Chancery Division,[113] but this alternative is limited to a person
    authorized under paras (1), (2) or (4) of the table in s 9(1) if the appeal or application
    concerns a decision of a recorder or circuit judge.[114]

Other applications in any appeal or application for permission to appeal may be heard or **6.56**
considered and directions may be given by a High Court judge or by any person authorized
under s 9 to act as a judge of the High Court in the Chancery Division.[115]

Standing to Appeal

Any person with standing to appeal against a decision in winding-up proceedings or bank **6.57**
or building society insolvency proceedings must obtain permission to appeal.[116]

Any person who was a party on the record to the proceedings has standing to appeal. Any **6.58**
other person who is either bound by the order or is aggrieved by it, or is prejudicially affected
by it may appeal if the appeal tribunal gives permission.[117] A creditor or contributory who
was entitled to appear at the hearing of a winding-up petition but did not do so cannot
appeal without permission.[118] In *Re Securities Insurance Co* Lindley LJ said, at p 413:

> It does not require much to obtain leave. If a person alleging himself to be aggrieved by an
> order can make out even a prima facie case why he should have leave he will get it.

However, 120 years later the Privy Council said that permission should be given only in
exceptional circumstances and the fact that a winding-up order will detrimentally affect a
person's rights is not enough to justify allowing that person to appeal against the order.[119]

---

[110] PD Insolvency Proceedings 2014, para 20.5.1.
[111] PD Insolvency Proceedings 2014, para 20.5.2.
[112] PD Insolvency Proceedings 2014, para 20.6, which lists the centres.
[113] PD Insolvency Proceedings 2014, paras 20.7(1) and 20.8.
[114] PD Insolvency Proceedings 2014, para 20.7(2).
[115] PD Insolvency Proceedings 2014, paras 20.7(3) and 20.8.
[116] IR 1986, r 7.49A(1) and (3), applying CPR, r 52.3; Bank Insolvency (England and Wales) Rules
2009 (SI 2009/356), r 224(2) and (3); Building Society Insolvency (England and Wales) Rules 2010 (SI
2010/2581), r 217(2) and (3); PD Insolvency Proceedings 2014, para 20.3.
[117] *Re Securities Insurance Co* [1894] 2 Ch 410; *Re Rick Wilson Pty Ltd* (1982) 7 ACLR 354. In Malaysia
it has been held that only the company may appeal (*Kotabato Corporation (M) Sdn Bhd v Wisma Central
Management Corporation* [2003] 4 MLJ 473), which seems to be inconsistent with *Fairview Schools Bhd v
Indrani a/p Rajaratnam (No 1)* [1998] 1 MLJ 99.
[118] *Re Securities Insurance Co*; *Re Rick Wilson Pty Ltd*; *Fairview Schools Bhd v Indrani a/p Rajaratnam
(No 1)*.
[119] *PricewaterhouseCoopers v Saad Investments Co Ltd* [2014] UKPC 35, [2014] 1 WLR 4482, at [36]–[37.

In the case before the Privy Council, permission to appeal could, if necessary have been given to the company's auditors where the sole reason given in the petition for winding up a foreign company was to obtain an order requiring the auditors to produce books and papers.

6.59 In *Fairview Schools Bhd v Indrani a/p Rajaratnam (No 1)* the Malaysian Court of Appeal said, at p 107, that 'Wilful failure to participate in the proceedings and acquiescing in the order made will provide grounds for refusal of leave'. The applicants in the case had not explained why they had not appeared at the hearing of the petition and permission for them to appeal was refused.

6.60 For an example of creditors of a company appealing against its winding up see *Re Eldorado Union Store Co*,[120] in which execution creditors appealed so as to save the proceeds of their executions.

6.61 A person who appeared as advocate to the court at the hearing is not entitled to appeal.[121]

6.62 A company that has been ordered to be wound up has standing to appeal against the order.[122] Whoever launches an appeal against a winding-up order, the company which has been ordered to be wound up must be a party to the appeal.[123]

6.63 As part of their general management functions conferred, for example, by art 3 of the model articles of association for private companies limited by shares and for public companies,[124] the directors of a company that has been ordered to be wound up by the court may instruct solicitors and counsel, in the company's name, to appeal against the order: the question whether they have power to do so depends on whether the winding-up order has been correctly made, and that is the very matter under appeal.[125] In Australia, directors of a company subject to a winding-up order are now required by statute to obtain the approval of the court or the liquidator before exercising any powers, including launching an appeal in the company's name against the winding-up order.[126]

6.64 If an order is made for a company in voluntary winding up to be wound up by the court, the voluntary liquidator may cause the company to appeal, but may not appeal in his or her own name.[127] It is submitted that, as with directors, the question whether the voluntary liquidator should still be in office is the very question that is to be determined on an appeal against the winding-up order, and therefore the voluntary liquidator should have standing to appeal the order that the company be wound up by the court. The voluntary liquidator does not, however, have standing to appeal only the part of the winding-up order which appoints a liquidator.[128]

---

[120] (1886) 18 NSR 514.

[121] *Re Bradford Navigation Co* (1870) LR 5 Ch App 600.

[122] *Southern World Airlines Ltd v Auckland International Airport Ltd* [1992] MCLR 210.

[123] *Re Rick Wilson Pty Ltd* (1982) 7 ACLR 354 at p 355.

[124] Companies (Model Articles) Regulations 2008 (SI 2008/3229), sch 1 and sch 3.

[125] *Re Diamond Fuel Co* (1879) 13 ChD 400; *Ripon Press and Sugar Mill Co Ltd v Gopal Chetti* (1931) LR 58 Ind App 416; *Re Union Accident Insurance Co Ltd* [1972] 1 WLR 640 per Plowman J at p 642; *Re G and W Automatics Ltd* (1968) 113 SJ 51 is to the contrary but see *Re G and W Automatics Ltd (No 2)* (1969) 113 SJ 51.

[126] Corporations Act 2001 (Australia), s 471A(1); *Re Rock Bottom Fashion Market Pty Ltd* [1997] QCA 399, [2000] 2 QdR 573; *Brolrik Pty Ltd v Sambah Holdings Pty Ltd* [2001] NSWSC 1171, 40 ACSR 361; *HVAC Construction (Qld) Pty Ltd v Energy Equipment Engineering Pty Ltd* [2002] FCA 1638, 44 ACSR 169. The statutory provision was overlooked in *Aetna Properties Ltd v GA Listing and Maintenance Pty Ltd* (1994) 13 ACSR 422 and *Emanuele v Australian Securities Commission* (1995) 141 ALR 506.

[127] *Robert H Barber and Co Ltd v Simon* (1914) 19 CLR 24.

[128] *International Professionals Ltd v Billes* 2000 CILR 429.

Security for Costs

If there is an appeal against the making of a winding-up order, an application by the **6.65**
petitioner, under CPR, r 25.15, for security for costs of the appeal must normally seek
security from the person who is instigating the appeal, not from the company, and the
security should be in the nature of an indemnity. This is because, normally, the costs
of an unsuccessful appeal should not be borne by the creditors or contributories of the
company but by the person instigating the appeal.[129] In *Re Yue Hing Co Ltd*,[130] unusually, the court refused to make the directors who had instigated an unsuccessful appeal
by the company against its winding-up order responsible for the petitioner's costs: no
application had been made before the appeal was heard for them to give security for
those costs.

Stay of Proceedings in a Winding-up pending Appeal

Unless the appeal court or the lower court orders otherwise, an appeal does not oper- **6.66**
ate as a stay of any order or decision of the lower court.[131] The directors of a company
which is subject to a winding-up order have a residual power to apply in its name for a
stay of proceedings in the winding up pending appeal against the order.[132] In England
and Wales, it is not the practice of the court to stay proceedings in the winding up of a
company pending determination of an appeal against the winding-up order,[133] though
there have been exceptions. Proceedings were stayed (on the order of the Court of
Appeal) pending appeal in *Re British Liquid Air Co Ltd*[134] (the petition was subsequently
dismissed by consent on terms agreed between the parties: 126 LT Jo 77). Proceedings
were stayed, pending appeal, on a winding-up order made on a contributory's petition
in *Re Westbourne Galleries Ltd*:[135] the Court of Appeal set aside the winding-up order
but it was reinstated by the House of Lords.[136] Proceedings were also stayed in *Re
Industrial and Commercial Securities plc*,[137] where the petitioner's debt had been paid
after the winding-up order was made. It may be that this payment would, in itself,
have justified a stay of proceedings. Stay pending appeal was ordered in *Re Dollar Land
(Feltham) Ltd*.[138]

---

[129] *Re Photographic Artists' Co-operative Supply Association* (1883) 23 ChD 370 (creditor's petition); *Re
Consolidated South Rand Mines Deep Ltd* [1909] WN 66 (contributory's petition); *Re E K Wilson and Sons
Ltd* [1972] 1 WLR 791 (contributory's petition); *Tricorp Pty Ltd v DCT (WA)* (1992) 6 ACSR 706 (creditor's
petition).

[130] (1916) 11 HKLR 82.

[131] CPR, r 52.7.

[132] *Arafura Finance Corporation Pty Ltd v Kooba Pty Ltd (No 2)* (1987) 52 NTR 52; *Aetna Properties
Ltd v GA Listing and Maintenance Pty Ltd* (1994) 13 ACSR 422, in which it was not noticed that in
Australia directors of a company subject to a winding-up order now need the court's approval before
exercising any powers, see *Re Rock Bottom Fashion Market Pty Ltd* [1997] QCA 399, [2000] 2 QdR 573,
and *HVAC Construction (Qld) Pty Ltd v Energy Equipment Engineering Pty Ltd* [2002] FCA 1638, 44
ACSR 169.

[133] *Re A and BC Chewing Gum Ltd* [1975] 1 WLR 579 at pp 592–3; per Harman J in *Re Calahurst Ltd*
[1989] BCLC 140 at p 141; *Re BLV Realty II Ltd* [2010] EWHC 1791 (Ch), LTL 17/9/2010.

[134] (1908) 126 LT Jo 7.

[135] [1971] Ch 799. See at p 813.

[136] [1973] AC 360 sub nom *Ebrahimi v Westbourne Galleries Ltd*.

[137] (1988) 5 BCC 320.

[138] [1995] 2 BCLC 370. See at p 378.

6.67 The English practice has been followed in the Cayman Islands,[139] Malaysia[140] and New Zealand, also with exceptions.[141] However, no general rule is recognized in Australia.[142] In Malaysia it has been said that the paramount consideration governing an application for a stay is that the appeal, if successful, should not be rendered nugatory.[143]

Nature of Appeal Process

6.68 The hearing of an appeal from a decision at first instance is limited to a review of that decision,[144] unless the court considers that it is in the interests of justice to hold a rehearing.[145]

6.69 Unless it orders otherwise, the appeal court will not receive oral evidence or evidence which was not before the lower court.[146] Unless the ground of an appeal against the decision made on hearing a winding-up petition is that there was a serious procedural or other irregularity which made the decision unjust, the question for the appeal court is whether the decision was right or wrong.[147] The original decision is presumed to be correct and the onus is on the appellant to show that it was wrong.[148] As Thesiger LJ said in *Re Diamond Fuel Co*:[149]

> we have not to decide the case as if it was a matter coming before us in the first instance, but must dismiss the appeal unless we are satisfied that the [tribunal at first instance] has been led to a wrong conclusion.

6.70 In deciding whether or not to make a winding-up order the court of first instance was exercising a discretion.[150] On hearing an appeal against an exercise of discretion, as Lord Diplock said in *Hadmor Productions Ltd v Hamilton*:[151]

> the function of an appellate court ... is not to exercise an independent discretion of its own. It must defer to the judge's exercise of his discretion and must not interfere with it merely upon the ground that the members of the appellate court would have exercised the discretion differently. The function of the appellate court is initially one of review only.

6.71 This is so even when a single judge of the High Court is hearing an appeal from a decision of the registrar exercising the jurisdiction of the same court, because IR 1986, r 7.49, requires such an appeal to be conducted in the same way as an appeal from the High Court to the Court of Appeal.[152]

---

[139] *Re Parmalat Capital Finance Ltd* 2007 CILR 1.

[140] *KTL Sdn Bhd v Azrahi Hotels Sdn Bhd* [2003] 5 MLJ 503.

[141] *Vujnovich v Vujnovich (No 2)* (1988) 4 NZCLC 64,557; *Kensington Swan v NZ Fisheries Ltd* (1990) 5 NZCLC 66,289.

[142] See, for example, *Brinds Ltd v Offshore Oil NL (No 2)* (1985) 10 ACLR 242; *Arafura Finance Corporation Pty Ltd v Kooba Pty Ltd (No 2)* (1987) 52 NTR 52; *Bernhardt v Beau Rivage Pty Ltd* (1989) 15 ACLR 160 at p 166; *Aetna Properties Ltd v GA Listing and Maintenance Pty Ltd* (1994) 13 ACSR 422.

[143] *See Teow Guan v Kian Joo Holdings Sdn Bhd* [1995] 3 MLJ 598 at p 610.

[144] CPR, r 52.11(1).

[145] CPR, r 52.11(1).

[146] CPR, r 52.11(2).

[147] CPR, r 52.11(3); *Re Industrial and Commercial Securities plc* (1988) 5 BCC 320 per Knox J at p 325.

[148] Per Edmund Davies LJ in *Re LHF Wools Ltd* [1970] Ch 27 at p 43.

[149] (1879) 13 ChD 400 at p 411.

[150] See 5.71–5.99.

[151] [1983] 1 AC 191 at p 220.

[152] *Re Industrial and Commercial Securities plc* (1988) 5 BCC 320; *Re Gilmartin* [1989] 1 WLR 513; *Re a Debtor (No 2389 of 1989)* [1991] Ch 326 per Vinelott J at pp 336–7; *Re Probe Data Systems Ltd (No 3)* [1991] BCLC 586, [1992] BCLC 405; *Re Tasbian Ltd (No 3)* [1991] BCLC 792, [1993] BCLC 297 at p 301.

When the decision of the court of first instance has depended on its assessment of the **6.72** credibility of witnesses and that assessment turns on their manner and demeanour, the appeal tribunal must always be guided by the impression made on the judge who saw the witnesses.[153]

If the appeal tribunal decides that the decision appealed against is wrong, it can exercise its **6.73** own discretion to make any order the tribunal appealed from could have made.[154]

The fact that circumstances have changed since a winding-up order was made is not a rea- **6.74** son for setting aside the order on appeal.[155] It is a ground for rescinding the order,[156] but an application for rescission must be made promptly.[157] There is no process for the annulment of a winding-up order as there is for a bankruptcy order under IA 1986, s 282. If it is too late for rescission, the most that can be done when there is a change of circumstances is to stay the proceedings in the winding up under s 147.[158]

The grounds on which an appeal tribunal can reverse a decision on the hearing of a **6.75** winding-up petition have been considered in several cases. In *Re P and J Macrae Ltd*[159] Willmer LJ said, at p 236, that the appeal tribunal should not reverse the judge's decision:

> unless he misdirected himself by failing to take into consideration matters which he should, or by taking into consideration matters which he should not.

In *Re J D Swain Ltd*[160] Harman LJ said, at p 911, that there should not be reversal of **6.76** the judge's decision 'unless he has made some error in law'. In *Bateman Television Ltd v Coleridge Finance Co Ltd*[161] Lord Upjohn said, at p 932, that the judge's decision was not to be reversed:

> unless it is shown to be exercised on some wrong principle, or that the judge relied on some fact irrelevant for the purpose, or omitted consideration of a relevant fact or finally that he was wholly wrong.

In *Re LHF Wools Ltd*[162] Harman LJ said, at p 36: **6.77**

> one has to find, if this court [the Court of Appeal] is going to upset what [the judge at first instance] decided, that he exercised his judgment on some wrong principle—that is to say, either that he took too much account of something put to him or that he took no account of something else which he ought to have taken into account.

In *Re Gilmartin*[163] Harman J said, at p 838, that on an appeal to a single judge of the High **6.78** Court from a decision of the registrar, it is for the appellant to show that the registrar:

> has erred in principle or erred in law in the way in which he has applied or exercised his discretion.

---

153 *Coghlan v Cumberland* [1898] 1 Ch 704.
154 Senior Courts Act 1981, s 15(3); CPR, r 52.10.
155 *Re Industrial and Commercial Securities plc* (1988) 5 BCC 320.
156 See 6.30.
157 See 6.25–6.28.
158 See 6.86–6.150.
159 [1961] 1 WLR 229.
160 [1965] 1 WLR 909.
161 [1971] NZLR 929.
162 [1970] Ch 27.
163 [1989] 2 All ER 835.

6.79   In *Re Walter L Jacob and Co Ltd*[164] Nicholls LJ said, at p 351, that the Court of Appeal:

> is not entitled, still less required, to intervene and set aside the order made by the judge in the exercise of the discretion conferred on him by the statute unless satisfied that, when exercising his discretion, the judge misdirected himself on the law or the evidence, or that his decision is so plainly wrong that he must have exercised his discretion wrongly.

6.80   In other contexts it has been said that a judge's exercise of discretion will not be reversed 'unless he has declined to exercise his discretion, or has manifestly proceeded on a wrong ground'[165] but that if a 'decision will result in injustice being done [an appellate court] has both the power and the duty to remedy it'.[166]

Role of the Liquidator

6.81   If there is an appeal against a winding-up order, the liquidator appointed in the winding up should adopt a position of complete impartiality but should be ready to provide information to the appeal tribunal about any facts and circumstances in relation to the company's affairs which the tribunal asks for or which, in the liquidator's judgment, the tribunal ought to know.[167]

Setting Aside Winding-up Order not Practicable

6.82   In *Ripon Press and Sugar Mill Co Ltd v Gopal Chetti*[168] the Privy Council decided not to set aside a winding-up order because of the extraordinary delay (six-and-a-half years) since the order was made. In *Nutectime International Pty Ltd v Timentel Pty Ltd*[169] the New South Wales Court of Appeal held that a winding-up order should not have been made two years earlier under the specific statutory provision invoked[170] but that winding up of the company had been inevitable anyway because of its insolvency. The court ordered the setting aside of the winding-up order unless, within 14 days, the parties signed a consent order confirming the winding up.

Costs

6.83   The normal principles that costs are discretionary and that usually costs follow the event[171] apply to an appeal. In *Re Ibo Investment Co*[172] it was held that if a petitioner appeals and opposing contributories or creditors appear and the appeal is dismissed then, provided there is no appeal against the costs ordered at first instance, only one set of costs will be awarded to opposing contributories and one set to opposing creditors.

6.84   Normally, the costs of opposing an unsuccessful appeal by a company against an order winding it up should be borne by those who instigated the appeal: such persons may be ordered to give security for such costs.[173] In *Re Yue Hing Co Ltd*[174] no such security was

---

[164] [1989] BCLC 345.
[165] *Crowther v Elgood* (1887) 34 ChD 591 per Cotton LJ at p 697.
[166] Per Lord Atkin in *Evans v Bartlam* [1937] AC 473 at p 481.
[167] *Ripon Press and Sugar Mill Co Ltd v Gopal Chetti* (1931) LR 58 Ind App 416 at p 428.
[168] (1931) LR 58 Ind App 416.
[169] [2011] NSWCA 257, 85 ACSR 570.
[170] See 8.461.
[171] CPR, r 44.2.
[172] [1903] 2 Ch 373.
[173] See 6.65.
[174] (1916) 11 HKLR 82.

asked for, and, after the appeal failed, the court refused the petitioner's application for an order that the directors who instigated the appeal should pay his costs, which instead had to be paid out of the company's assets.

If an appeal against a winding-up order is successful, the liquidator is entitled to his or her **6.85** remuneration and expenses. The court will not reduce the amount payable on the ground that the remuneration and expenses would not have been incurred if the court had not made the decision which has been overturned.[175]

Stay

Enactments under which Stay may be Ordered

Winding up by the court, bank and building society insolvency

There are two provisions, one general and one particular, under which the court may **6.86** make an order staying all proceedings in the winding up of a company. Both provisions are applied to bank and building society insolvency. The general provision is that on proof to the satisfaction of the court that it ought to do so, the court may make an order staying all proceedings in a winding up, either altogether or for a limited time, on such terms and conditions as the court thinks fit.[176] The particular provision is that if a decision to approve a voluntary arrangement has effect under IA 1986, s 4A,[177] for a company being wound up, the court may stay all proceedings in the winding up.[178]

These provisions are applied to limited liability partnerships.[179]   **6.87**

The court does not have power under IA 1986, s 147(1), to stay only some of the proceed- **6.88** ings in a winding up: an application to stay part of the proceedings should be made under s 167(3).[180]

Voluntary winding up

In a voluntary winding up under IA 1986, the liquidator, or any contributory or creditor, **6.89** may apply under s 112(1) and (2) for the court to exercise its power under s 147(1) of staying all proceedings in the winding up, and if the court is satisfied that exercising the power will be just and beneficial, it may accede wholly or partially to the application on such terms and conditions as it thinks just, or it may make such other order as it thinks just.[181] A resolution for voluntary winding up cannot be revoked or rescinded.[182]

---

[175] *Re Joseph Phillips Ltd* [1964] 1 WLR 369.
[176] IA 1986, s 147(1). Applied to bank insolvency by the Banking Act 2009, s 103(3), (4) and table, and to building society insolvency by the Building Societies Act 1986, s 90C.
[177] Applied to building societies by the Building Societies Act 1986, s 90A and sch 15A.
[178] IA 1986, s 5(1) and (3). Applied to bank insolvency by the Banking Act 2009, s 113(6), and to building society insolvency by the Building Societies Act 1986, s 90C. See 6.132–6.138.
[179] Limited Liability Partnerships Regulations 2001 (SI 2001/1090), reg 5.
[180] *Re European Assurance Society* [1872] WN 85.
[181] *Re Schanschieff Electric Battery Syndicate Ltd* [1888] WN 166; *Re Steamship 'Titian' Co Ltd* (1888) 58 LT 78; *Re Calgary and Edmonton Land Co Ltd* [1975] 1 WLR 355.
[182] *Ross v P J Heeringa Ltd* [1970] NZLR 170; *Re Houto Farms Ltd* (1991) 5 NZCLC 67,184.

Insolvent partnerships

6.90 At any time after a partnership has been ordered to be wound up on a petition under the Insolvent Partnerships Order 1994 (IPO 1994), art 8 or art 10, the court may make an order staying all proceedings in the winding up, either altogether or for a limited time, on such terms and conditions as the court thinks fit.[183] If a decision to approve a voluntary arrangement has effect under IA 1986, s 4A,[184] for an insolvent partnership being wound up as an unregistered company, the court may stay all proceedings in the winding up, including any related insolvency proceedings of a member of the partnership qua member.[185]

Effect of Stay

General effect

6.91 Sections 5(3) and 147(1) of IA 1986 provide for the stay of 'all proceedings in the winding up' of a company, which means the whole process and activity of winding up the company's affairs, not just (in the case of a company being wound up by the court) the court proceedings.[186] While proceedings in the winding up of a company are stayed, the company is not 'being wound up' and it does not have to comply with IA 1986, s 188 (notification of liquidation on company documents),[187] and its business activities are not restricted to those necessary for beneficial winding up.[188]

Effect on directors

6.92 Australian courts have taken the view that when a winding-up order is made, the directors remain in office but their powers are removed, and therefore if proceedings in the winding up are stayed, the directors continue in office and their powers are returned to them.[189] This view has now been adopted in the Corporations Act 2001 (Australia), s 471A, which provides that while a company is being wound up in insolvency or by the court, a person cannot perform or exercise, and must not purport to perform or exercise, a function or power as an officer (other than a liquidator or administrator) of the company, except with the approval of the liquidator or the court.

Effect on the winding-up order

6.93 The effect of an order staying proceedings altogether is that the court's winding-up order becomes inoperative without being revoked.[190] Proceedings are not ended by a stay though nothing can be done to pursue them without a further court order.[191] In *Krextile Holdings Pty Ltd v Widdows*[192] Gillard J said, at p 694, that the effect of a permanent stay is 'to say

---

[183] IA 1986, s 147(1), as modified by IPO 1994, sch 4, para 19; IA 1986, s 147(1), as modified by IPO 1994, sch 4, para 19, is probably applied to art 10 petitions by IA 1986, s 221(5), as modified by IPO 1994, sch 6, para 4.

[184] As applied by IPO 1994, art 4(1), and modified by sch 1, part 1.

[185] IA 1986, s 5(1) and (3), as applied by IPO 1994, art 4(1), and modified by sch 1, part 1.

[186] *Krextile Holdings Pty Ltd v Widdows* [1974] VR 689 at p 693.

[187] *Krextile Holdings Pty Ltd v Widdows* at p 693.

[188] *Krextile Holdings Pty Ltd v Widdows* at pp 693–4.

[189] *Re Country Traders Distributors Ltd* [1974] 2 NSWLR 135; *Austral Brick Co Pty Ltd v Falgat Constructions Pty Ltd* (1990) 21 NSWLR 389; *McAusland v Deputy Commissioner of Taxation* (1993) 118 ALR 577.

[190] *Krextile Holdings Pty Ltd v Widdows* [1974] VR 689 at p 694.

[191] Cf *Rofa Sport Management AG v DHL International (UK) Ltd* [1989] 1 WLR 902 on the difference between staying and discontinuing proceedings commenced by writ.

[192] [1974] VR 689.

the least ... somewhat paradoxical'. In *Re Kim Maxwell Ltd*[193] Tipping J said, at p 75, that it seemed to him that a permanent stay 'amounts in reality to a contradiction in terms: the winding up remains but is permanently stayed', but said in *Re Bell Block Lumber Ltd*[194] that these ambiguities must be recognized and accepted. This may be compared with the effect of rescinding[195] or discharging[196] a winding-up order.

In Australia, the court may now make an order 'terminating the winding up on a day speci-   **6.94**
fied in the order'.[197] In *McAusland v Deputy Commissioner of Taxation*[198] French J said, at p 592, that a termination order 'prospectively extinguishes the winding-up order' but his Honour doubted whether there was any practical difference between a termination and a permanent stay. Despite French J's reference to prospective effect, a termination order may be backdated. In *Re Buddies Investments Pty Ltd*[199] a winding up was ordered to be termin-ated as from the date on which the winding-up order was made.

On an application to stay proceedings in a winding up, the court does not have power to   **6.95**
vary the costs order made at the time of the original winding-up order.[200]

Effect on previous proceedings in the winding up
In Canada it has been held that a provision like IA 1986, s 147, does not empower the court   **6.96**
to reverse anything done in the liquidation up to the time of the stay.[201]

In Malaysia, in *Mookapillai v Sri Saringgit Sdn Bhd*[202] the company had been ordered to be   **6.97**
wound up on a contributory's petition alleging oppression of the minority. About 18 months after the winding-up order was made, all the members realized that the break-up of the very valuable assets of the company was a financial disaster for them and they asked for a stay of proceedings and for reversal of the liquidator's sales, which had nearly all been completed. The court refused to interfere with the liquidator's sales because this would be a breach of commercial morality, and refused to order a stay of proceedings because the liquidation was almost complete.

Stay for a fixed period
When a stay for a fixed period expires, the company is once again being wound up and the   **6.98**
winding up still has the same commencement date as it did before the stay, but persons who became creditors of the company during the stay can prove in the winding up.[203]

Application for a Stay
Who may apply
An application under IA 1986, s 147, for a stay of all proceedings in a winding up may be   **6.99**
made either by the liquidator or the official receiver or any creditor or contributory.[204] The

---

193 [1992] 1 NZLR 69.
194 [1992] MCLR 190 at p 192.
195 See 6.24–6.43.
196 See 6.151–6.157.
197 Corporations Act 2001 (Australia), s 482(1). Similar provision is made in the Companies Act 1993 (New Zealand), s 250.
198 (1993) 118 ALR 577.
199 [1997] 2 QdR 453.
200 *Re GT Motor Inns Pty Ltd* (1980) 4 ACLR 881.
201 *Re Red Gold Mining Co* [1950] Que KB 47.
202 [1981] 2 MLJ 114.
203 *Re Kim Maxwell Ltd* [1992] 1 NZLR 69.
204 s 147(1).

company itself does not have standing to apply.[205] A person who was a contributory when the winding up commenced but has subsequently become bankrupt does not have standing to apply for a stay, because the trustee in bankruptcy will have replaced the bankrupt as a contributory under s 82. This lack of standing continues even after discharge from bankruptcy.[206] A person whose status as a contributory of a company is not admitted or has not been proved does not have standing to apply for a stay.[207] A person with a disputed claim against a company is not a creditor with standing to apply for a stay.[208] If the court is otherwise persuaded that there should be a stay, it may require the liquidator, as an officer of the court, to make the application.[209]

6.100 An application for a stay of all proceedings in a bank or building society insolvency may be made only by:[210]

(a) the bank or building society liquidator;

(b) the PRA;

(c) the Bank of England;

(d) the Financial Services Compensation Scheme; or

(e) a creditor or contributory, but only if the liquidation committee has passed a full payment resolution.[211]

6.101 The court may direct that the application is to be served on creditors and contributories.[212] Normally it is sufficient if all creditors and contributories are given notice of the application for a stay giving adequate opportunity for them to consider whether to object.[213]

Evidence

6.102 An application for a stay of all proceedings in a winding up should be accompanied by evidence of:[214]

(a) whether creditors, the liquidator and contributories agree to the stay;

(b) the circumstances in which the company was wound up;

(c) the company's business and financial position;

(d) how any failures of directors to comply with regulatory requirements will be addressed.

6.103 Australian courts have often been critical of the quality of evidence of financial position and have called for the 'fullest and best' evidence including proper verification of assets and

---

[205] *Re Bell Block Lumber Ltd* [1992] MCLR 190.

[206] *Re Wolverhampton Steel and Iron Co Ltd* [1977] 1 WLR 860.

[207] *Re Continental Bank Corporation* (1867) 16 LT 112, [1867] WN 178.

[208] *Watta Battery Industries Sdn Bhd v Uni-Batt Manufacturing Sdn Bhd* [1993] 1 MLJ 149.

[209] *PricewaterhouseCoopers v Saad Investments Co Ltd* [2014] UKPC 35, [2014] 1 WLR 4482, at [34].

[210] IA 1986, s 147, as modified by the Banking Act 2009, s 103(3), (4) and table. Applied to building society insolvency by the Building Societies Act 1986, s 90C.

[211] 'Full payment resolution' is defined at 1.20.

[212] IR 1986, rr 7.4(4) and 7.10(2).

[213] *Re Worcester, Tenbury and Ludlow Railway Co* (1850) 3 De G & Sm 189; *Re Bank of Queensland Ltd* (1870) 2 QSCR 113; principle 2 in the quotation at 6.123 from *Re Warbler Pty Ltd* (1982) 6 ACLR 526 at p 533.

[214] See 6.106–6.123.

liabilities.[215] Evidence given only by a director with no independent verification is unlikely to be sufficient.[216]

Before making an order staying all proceedings in a compulsory winding up, the court may **6.104** require the official receiver to report on any facts or matters which are, in the official receiver's opinion, relevant to the application.[217] This does not apply to an application for a stay of proceedings in a voluntary winding up.[218]

Insolvent partnerships

An application for the winding up of an insolvent partnership to be stayed may be made by the **6.105** liquidator of the partnership, the official receiver or any creditor or contributory.[219] The court may call for a report from the official receiver.[220]

The Court's Approach

Onus

The jurisdiction to order a stay is discretionary and the onus is on the applicant to make out a **6.106** sufficient case.[221] The applicant 'must make out a case that carries conviction',[222] but this does not mean that there is a special standard of proof: the ordinary standard of satisfying the judge, whether on evidence or other material, applies.[223]

Interests to be considered

The court must consider the rights and interests of persons who may be affected by its deci- **6.107** sion.[224] Depending on the circumstances, they may include the company's present creditors, persons who may become creditors in the future, its liquidator and its contributories (members, shareholders), and there may be a public interest which must be considered.[225] There may be other persons whose rights and interests are to be considered.[226] There is no absolute right to full protection of the position which any person has in the winding up:

> What is reasonable protection for any person with an interest must depend on the nature of that interest, the nature of any other interests and the whole other circumstances of the particular case.[227]

---

[215] For example, *QBE Workers' Compensation Pty Ltd v P Russell Enterprises Pty Ltd* [2005] NSWSC 1128 at [26]. The phrase 'fullest and best' is taken from *Commonwealth Bank of Australia v Begonia Pty Ltd* (1993) 11 ACSR 609 at p 617.

[216] *Deputy Commissioner of Taxation v Sydney Concrete Steel Fixing Pty Ltd* [1999] NSWSC 494, 17 ACLC 972.

[217] IA 1986, s 147(2).

[218] *Re Serene Shoes Ltd* [1958] 1 WLR 1087.

[219] IA 1986, s 147(1), as modified by IPO 1994, sch 4, para 19; IA 1986, s 147(1), as modified by IPO 1994, sch 4, para 19, is probably applied to art 10 petitions by IA 1986, s 221(5), as modified by IPO 1994, sch 6, para 4.

[220] See 6.104. IA 1986, s 147(4), as modified by IPO 1994, sch 4, para 19.

[221] *Krextile Holdings Pty Ltd v Widdows* [1974] VR 689; *Re Calgary and Edmonton Land Co Ltd* [1975] 1 WLR 355; *Vijayalakshmi Devi d/o Nadchatiram v Dr Mahadevan s/o Nadchatiram* [1995] 2 MLJ 709; *McGruther v James Scott Ltd* 2004 SC 514 at p 522.

[222] *Re Calgary and Edmonton Land Co Ltd* [1975] 1 WLR 355 per Megarry J at pp 358–9.

[223] *McGruther v James Scott Ltd* at p 522.

[224] *McGruther v James Scott Ltd* at p 522.

[225] *Re Golden Butterfly Gold Mining Co NL* [1916] SALR 177 per Murray CJ, who did not mention the liquidator; *Re Calgary and Edmonton Land Co Ltd* [1975] 1 WLR 355 per Megarry J at p 360; *McGruther v James Scott Ltd* 2004 SC 514 at p 522. The interest of persons who may become creditors of the company in the future is often regarded as an aspect of the public interest.

[226] *McGruther v James Scott Ltd*.

[227] *McGruther v James Scott Ltd* at p 522.

Creditors

6.108 The interests of the present creditors of a company which is applying for a stay of proceedings in its winding up are best served by being paid in full.[228] Agreeing to be bound by a composition or arrangement may, however, be the best that can be achieved.[229] In *Re Hafna Mining and Smelting Co Ltd*[230] all claims against the company had been released. Evidence that there would be unspecified satisfactory provision for payment was accepted in *Re Condes Co of Chili Ltd*.[231]

6.109 The court is reluctant to stay a winding up if the stay would result in a creditor being deprived of rights which it would have if the winding up proceeded, especially if this would affect one creditor rather than others.[232]

6.110 There is no absolute rule that the winding up of a company cannot be stayed unless all its present debts are discharged.[233] However, the winding up of a company should not be stayed if continuing liability to repay present debts would endanger the interests of persons who might become creditors in the future. The court must be assured that the 'company will have additional financial strength and stability to provide confidence that it can continue without an appreciable risk of returning to liquidation'.[234] So the winding up of a company will not be stayed if its liabilities substantially exceed its assets, unless the court is assured that payment of existing debts, especially if they are owed to persons associated with the company, will not be detrimental to persons who may become creditors in the future.[235] The same applies where a company is technically solvent but likely to become insolvent.[236] A mere agreement between the creditors and the company to subordinate debts is not sufficient, because it may be varied at will or simply ignored by the company.[237] Appropriate undertakings to the court by creditors may be sufficient,[238] but the court may be concerned that there is no effective way of monitoring compliance.[239] A short-term undertaking may be accepted if there is an obvious commercial incentive to comply with it.[240] In Australia, the courts have usually required debts to be capitalized (that is, the creditors are issued with

---

[228] As in *Re Worcester, Tenbury and Ludlow Railway Co* (1859) 3 De G & Sm 189.

[229] *Re Nardell Coal Corporation Pty Ltd* [2004] NSWSC 281, 49 ACSR 110. See 6.132–6.138.

[230] (1888) 84 LT Jo 403.

[231] (1892) 36 SJ 593.

[232] *Tecma Pty Ltd v Solah Blue Metal Pty Ltd (No 2)* (1988) 14 ACLR 539.

[233] *Mercy and Sons Pty Ltd v Wanari Pty Ltd* [2000] NSWSC 756, 35 ACSR 70 (winding up by the court); *Re Nardell Coal Corporation Pty Ltd* [2004] NSWSC 281, 49 ACSR 110 (voluntary winding up).

[234] *Re Living Creatively Exhibitions Pty Ltd* [2013] NSWSC 717 at [7].

[235] *Re Mascot Home Furnishers Pty Ltd* [1970] VR 593; *Re Denistone Real Estate Pty Ltd* [1970] 3 NSWR 327; *Re Data Homes Pty Ltd* [1972] 2 NSWLR 22; *Re Falcon Concrete Contractors Ltd* (1983) 1 NZCLC 98,696; *Re Skay Fashions Pty Ltd* (1986) 10 ACLR 743 at p 746; *Timaru Rental Cars Ltd v Mutual Rental Properties Ltd* [1992] MCLR 296; *Re Nature Springs Pty Ltd* (1994) 13 ACSR 50; *Remiliotis v Tenth Anemot Pty Ltd* (1994) 13 ACSR 650; *Ting Yuk Kiong v Mawar Biru Sdn Bhd* [1995] 2 MLJ 700. The earlier of these Australian cases and *Re Falcon Concrete Contractors Ltd* involved schemes to exploit companies' losses for taxation purposes. It was held in *Commissioner of Inland Revenue v Eden Electroplaters Ltd* (2006) 10 NZCLC 264,243 that such tax avoidance will not prevent a stay (in New Zealand, termination) being ordered provided the burden of its debts will not make the company a hazard to those with whom it may trade.

[236] *Anderson v Palmer* [2002] NSWSC 192 at [6].

[237] *Re Nature Springs Pty Ltd* (1994) 13 ACSR 50; followed in *Sutherland v Rahme Enterprises Pty Ltd* [2003] NSWSC 673, 46 ACSR 458.

[238] *Re Lowston Ltd* [1991] BCLC 570; *Brolrik Pty Ltd v Sambah Holdings Pty Ltd* [2001] NSWSC 1171, 40 ACSR 361.

[239] *Owners Strata Plan 70294 v LNL Global Enterprises Pty Ltd* [2006] NSWSC 1386, 60 ACSR 646, at [25].

[240] *Pine Forests of Australia (Canberra) Pty Ltd* [2010] NSWSC 1296, 80 ACSR 377, at [17].

shares in consideration for abandoning their claims).[241] This will be required even if the company is a trustee.[242]

In *Re Wiltull Ltd*[243] proceedings in the compulsory winding up of a group of companies **6.111** were stayed so that another company could take control of them, for a price, and obtain the benefit of their licences to prospect for coal, even though unsecured creditors would not be paid in full immediately. The deal as a whole was beneficial to creditors and would not have gone through without a stay of the winding up.

The present creditors whose interests the court must consider on an application for a stay are **6.112** only creditors whose debts or claims have been proved in the winding up.[244] But this does not apply where the liquidator has not yet had time to consider claims and creditors generally will benefit if a stay is ordered immediately.[245]

The liquidator

The liquidator's remuneration, and the costs, charges and expenses of the liquidation must **6.113** be paid or adequately provided for, because that is the basis on which the liquidator accepted appointment.[246]

A stay which is required for the purposes of interfering with the exercise by a liquidator **6.114** of his or her discretion will not be ordered.[247] A desire to save the expense of a liquidator's remuneration is not in itself a good reason for staying proceedings in a winding up.[248]

Members

The members must agree to the stay and any dissentients must be given the opportunity to **6.115** receive what they would have received if the liquidation had been completed.[249] If necessary a scheme of arrangement must be approved under the Companies Act 2006, ss 895–901. Before the procedure in ss 895–901 for making a compromise or arrangement binding when approved by a three-quarters majority at a meeting was enacted, considerable effort had to be expended in trying to contact apathetic members so as to satisfy the court that they had been given adequate opportunity to consider whether to object to a stay.[250]

Public interest

The court must also consider the public interest and whether a stay would be conducive or **6.116** detrimental to commercial morality.[251] If it is proposed that the company should return to being managed by the same people who were running it when it went into liquidation, the

---

[241] *Collins v G Collins and Sons Pty Ltd* (1984) 9 ACLR 58; *Sutherland v Rahme Enterprises Pty Ltd* [2003] NSWSC 673, 46 ACSR 458.
[242] *Owners Strata Plan 70294 v LNL Global Enterprises Pty Ltd* [2006] NSWSC 1386, 60 ACSR 646.
[243] (1979) 4 ACLR 225.
[244] *Sri Binaraya Sdn Bhd v Golden Approach Sdn Bhd* [2002] 6 MLJ 632.
[245] *Tecma Pty Ltd v Solah Blue Metal Pty Ltd (No 2)* (1988) 14 ACLR 539.
[246] *Re Calgary and Edmonton Land Co Ltd* [1975] 1 WLR 355 at p 360.
[247] *Re Hockerill Athletic Club Ltd* [1990] BCLC 921.
[248] *Anderson v Palmer* [2002] NSWSC 192 at [43].
[249] *Re South Barrule Slate Quarry Co* (1869) LR 8 Eq 688; *Re Steamship Chigwell Ltd* (1888) 4 TLR 308; *Re Calgary and Edmonton Land Co Ltd* [1975] 1 WLR 355 at p 363; *Ting Yuk Kiong v Mawar Biru Sdn Bhd* [1995] 2 MLJ 700.
[250] *Re Worcester, Tenbury and Ludlow Railway Co* (1850) 3 De G & Sm 189; *Re Bank of Queensland Ltd* (1870) 2 QSCR 113.
[251] *Re Telescriptor Syndicate Ltd* [1903] 2 Ch 174; *City Realties (Holdings) Ltd v Investment Finance Corporation Ltd* (1989) 5 NZCLC 66,213; *Chan v Austgrove Enterprises Pty Ltd* (1993) 12 ACSR 427.

court is unlikely to agree to a stay if their conduct appears to be at fault, especially if they have failed to deliver a statement of affairs or have otherwise failed to cooperate with the liquidator.[252] Director disqualification proceedings may deal with the court's concerns.[253] The court will not agree to stay proceedings in the winding up of a company if it appears that the affairs of the company should be investigated by a liquidator.[254] Even if all present debts can be paid, the court will not order a stay if it appears that the company will be mismanaged again and become insolvent.[255] 'It is wrong to order a stay if there is any real or substantial risk that the restored company may have a brief life and may incur debts which it cannot meet.'[256]

6.117   The public interest in the completion of a housing project being developed by the company in liquidation was considered to outweigh those of a disputed creditor in *Sri Binaraya Sdn Bhd v Golden Approach Sdn Bhd*.[257]

Where there will be a surplus

6.118   In *Re Calgary and Edmonton Land Co Ltd*[258] Megarry J observed, at p 360, that in normal circumstances, where there is sufficient to pay all creditors and liquidation expenses and there will be a surplus for the members:

(a) Creditors cannot object to a stay if they have been paid in full, or satisfactory provision for payment in full has been, or will be, made.

(b) There should be payment or sufficient security for payment of the liquidator's expenses, because that was the basis on which the liquidator accepted appointment.

(c) A stay should not be ordered unless members consent or there is secured for them the right to receive all that they would have received had the liquidation proceeded to its conclusion.

6.119   Creditors and/or members may be bound by a compromise or arrangement to accept something different.

6.120   In New Zealand it has been accepted that these are appropriate criteria in the general run of cases where there is a surplus for members.[259]

Outstanding disputes

6.121   A stay has been refused where a claim against the company was still being disputed by the liquidator[260] and where misfeasance proceedings were pending.[261]

6.122   It is not necessary to stay proceedings in the winding up of a company so that it can pursue litigation which the liquidator refuses to carry on: an application should instead be made

---

[252] *Re Telescriptor Syndicate Ltd* [1903] 2 Ch 174; *Re SN Group plc* [1994] 1 BCLC 319, in which it also appeared that an undischarged bankrupt had acted as a director of the company.

[253] *Re Asean Interests Ltd* [2005] 4 HKLRD 665.

[254] *Re Allebart Pty Ltd* [1971] 1 NSWLR 24; *Lai Kam-hung v Guangdong (HK) International Co Ltd* [1995] 2 HKLR 211.

[255] *Re Skay Fashions Pty Ltd* (1986) 10 ACLR 743.

[256] *Re Welsh Highland Railway Light Railway Co* [1993] BCLC 338 per Vinelott J at p 358.

[257] [2002] 6 MLJ 632.

[258] [1975] 1 WLR 355.

[259] *Re Bell Block Lumber Ltd* [1992] MCLR 190.

[260] *Re Dover and Deal Railway, Cinque Ports, Thanet and Coast Junction Co, Cases of Clifton and Others* (1854) 5 De G M & G 743.

[261] *Vijayalakshmi Devi d/o Nadchatiram v Dr Mahadevan s/o Nadchatiram* [1995] 2 MLJ 709.

for a contributory or other interested person to be authorized to conduct the litigation in the company's name.[262]

Australian list of eight principles

In Australia a court giving judgment on an application for a stay of proceedings in a wind-   **6.123**
ing up usually refers to a list of eight principles stated by Master Lee QC in the Queensland Supreme Court in *Re Warbler Pty Ltd*.[263] The list was intended to show which points had not been dealt with in evidence[264] in the case before the learned master and was not intended to be exhaustive. The principles are:

1. The granting of a stay is a discretionary matter, and there is a clear onus on the applicant to make out a positive case for a stay.[265] [See 6.106.]
2. There must be service of notice of the application for a stay on all creditors and contributories, and proof of this.[266] [See 6.101.]
3. The nature and extent of the creditors must be shown, and whether or not all debts have been discharged.[267] [See 6.108–6.112.]
4. The attitude of creditors, contributories and the liquidator is a relevant consideration.[268] [See 6.118–6.120.]
5. The current trading position and general solvency of the company should be demonstrated. Solvency is of significance when a stay of proceedings in the winding up is sought.[269] [See 6.108–6.112.]
6. If there has been non-compliance by directors with their statutory duties as to the giving of information or furnishing a statement of affairs, a full explanation of the reasons and circumstances should be given.[270] [See 6.116–6.117.]
7. The general background and circumstances which led to the winding-up order should be explained.[271] [See 6.116–6.117.]
8. The nature of the business carried on by the company should be demonstrated, and whether or not the conduct of the company was in any way contrary to 'commercial morality' or the 'public interest'.[272] [See 6.116–6.117.]

For a review of mostly unreported Australian cases which elaborate on these points see the judgment of Ward J in *Re Yelin Group Pty Ltd, Li v Jin*.[273]

Stay in Favour of other Winding-up Proceedings

It is possible to stay proceedings in a compulsory winding up so that the company can go   **6.124**
into voluntary winding up.[274]

---

[262] *Credit Lucky Ltd v National Crime Agency* [2014] EWHC 83 (Ch), LTL 5/2/2014.

[263] (1982) 6 ACLR 526 at p 533.

[264] See 6.102–6.103.

[265] *Re Calgary and Edmonton Land Co Ltd* [1975] 1 WLR 355 at pp 358–9 per Megarry J. See also the Companies Act 1961 (Queensland), s 243 [equivalent to IA 1986, s 147].

[266] *Re South Barrule Slate Quarry Co* (1869) LR 8 Eq 688; *Re Bank of Queensland Ltd* (1870) 2 QSCR 113.

[267] *Krextile Holdings Pty Ltd v Widdows* [1974] VR 689; *Re Data Homes Pty Ltd* [1972] 2 NSWLR 22.

[268] Companies Act 1961 (Queensland), s 243(1) [equivalent to IA 1986, s 147(1)]; *Re Calgary and Edmonton Land Co Ltd.*

[269] *Re a Private Company* [1935] NZLR 120; *Re Mascot Home Furnishers Pty Ltd* [1970] VR 593 at p 598.

[270] *Re Telescriptor Syndicate Ltd* [1903] 2 Ch 174.

[271] *Krextile Holdings Pty Ltd v Widdows.*

[272] *Krextile Holdings Pty Ltd v Widdows*; *Re Data Homes Pty Ltd.*

[273] [2012] NSWSC 74 at [8]–[20].

[274] *Re Bristol Victoria Pottery Co* [1872] WN 85, in which the voluntary winding up was under the supervision of the court.

6.125 In *Re Orthomere Ltd*[275] the court stayed proceedings in a compulsory winding up based on one petition so that it could make an order on the basis of another petition which had been presented earlier. The effect was to backdate the commencement of winding up so as to render certain transactions of the company liable to be impeached as preferences.

6.126 In *Re Intermain Properties Ltd*[276] proceedings were stayed under a winding-up order which was so fundamentally defective that it should be treated as null, and Hoffmann J suggested that another petition to wind up the company could then be presented and another order made. (A fundamentally defective winding-up order may now be rescinded under the power to rescind given by IR 1986, r 7.47(1), which is discussed at 6.14–6.43.[277])

6.127 In *Re Cedes Electric Traction Ltd*[278] proceedings in a winding up of an enemy company were stayed so that the Board of Trade could order the winding up of the UK business of the company under what is now the Trading with the Enemy Act 1939, s 3A(1), because the distribution of assets under such an order would be more advantageous to British creditors than in a winding up by the court.

6.128 A stay may be ordered if it is more convenient to wind up the company in another jurisdiction.[279]

Stay in Favour of Administration

6.129 When the court makes an administration order in relation to a company in compulsory winding up, the legislation requires the court to discharge the winding-up order rather than stay the winding-up proceedings.[280] However, this does not apply to industry-specific administration regimes or to bank or building society insolvency.

6.130 If a company is eligible for water industry special administration or air traffic administration, it cannot be wound up by the court.[281] So, for such companies there cannot be a move from compulsory winding up to an industry-specific administration regime. It is not possible to make an energy administration order, energy supply company administration order or postal administration order in respect of a company in liquidation.[282] It seems that there is no statutory bar to making a railway administration order or a PPP administration order in respect of a company in liquidation, and such an order would necessitate a stay of all proceedings in the winding up. However, it is unlikely that this could occur in practice, because there should be ample opportunity to consider administration before a winding-up order is made. Similarly, although a move from winding up of a bank to bank administration, or winding up of a building society to administration or building society special administration, is possible, those options, and bank or building society insolvency, should have been considered first.

[275] (1981) 125 SJ 495.
[276] [1986] BCLC 265.
[277] *Re Calmex Ltd* [1989] 1 All ER 485.
[278] [1918] 1 Ch 18.
[279] *Re Oriental Bank Corporation* (1884) 10 VLR (E) 154; *Re Stewart and Matthews Ltd* (1916) 26 Man R 277. In both cases no creditor objected. But see 1.416.
[280] See 6.151–6.157.
[281] Water Industry Act 1991, s 25; Transport Act 2000, s 27.
[282] Energy Act 2004, s 157(4)(b), applied to energy supply company administration by the Energy Act 2011, s 96; Postal Services Act 2011, s 71(4)(b).

404

A bank or building society liquidator who thinks that administration would achieve a bet- **6.131**
ter result for the institution's creditors as a whole than bank insolvency may apply to the
court (in the case of a bank) or petition the court (in the case of a building society) for an
administration order,[283] provided three conditions are satisfied:[284]

(a) The liquidation committee must have passed a full payment resolution.[285]
(b) The liquidation committee must have resolved that moving to administration might:
   (i) in the case of a bank, enable the rescue of the bank as a going concern;[286]
   (ii) in the case of a building society, enable the survival of the society, and the whole or
    any part of its undertaking, as a going concern.[287]
(c) The bank or building society liquidator must be satisfied, as a result of arrangements
   made with the Financial Services Compensation Scheme, that any depositors still
   eligible for compensation under the scheme will receive their payments or have their
   accounts transferred during administration.[288]

Making an administration order in these circumstances necessarily entails staying all proceedings in the bank or building society insolvency.

Stay when Voluntary Arrangement has been Approved

Registered companies

If meetings of the members and creditors of a company being wound up have approved a **6.132**
voluntary arrangement, the court may, by order, stay all proceedings in the winding up and/
or give such directions with respect to the conduct of the winding up as it thinks appropriate for facilitating the implementation of the approved voluntary arrangement.[289] The
court must not make an order staying proceedings until the end of the period of 28 days
beginning with the first day on which each of the reports of the chairmen of the members'
and creditors' meetings has been made to the court.[290] That is the period during which
the voluntary arrangement may be challenged by an application to the court made by the
liquidator, the nominee or any person entitled to vote at either meeting.[291] If an application
challenging approval of the arrangement is made, the court must not order a stay while the
application is pending, or during the period within which an appeal in respect of such an
application may be brought, or while such an appeal is pending.[292]

Entry into a compromise or scheme of arrangement with creditors does not in itself termin- **6.133**
ate the winding up of a company: there must be a court order.[293]

---

[283] Banking Act 2009, s 114(1). Applied to building societies by the Building Societies Act 1986, s 90C.
[284] Banking Act 2009, s 114(2). Applied to building societies by the Building Societies Act 1986, s 90C.
[285] Banking Act 2009, s 114(3). Applied to building societies by the Building Societies Act 1986, s 90C.
'Full payment resolution' is defined at 1.20.
[286] Banking Act 2009, s 114(4).
[287] Banking Act 2009, s 114(4), applied to building societies by the Building Societies Act 1986, s 90C,
and modified by the Building Societies (Insolvency and Special Administration) Order 2009 (SI 2009/805),
sch 1, para 15(b).
[288] Banking Act 2009, s 114(5). Applied to building societies by the Building Societies Act 1986, s 90C.
[289] IA 1986, s 5(1) and (3).
[290] IA 1986, s 5(4)(a). The reports are required by s 4(6).
[291] IA 1986, s 6(1), (2) and (3)(a).
[292] s 5(4)(b).
[293] *Mercy and Sons Pty Ltd v Wanari Pty Ltd* [2000] NSWSC 756, 35 ACSR 70.

6.134 In *Re Belding Lumber Co Ltd*[294] a stay of compulsory winding-up proceedings was ordered so that the company's affairs could be dealt with by an assignment for the benefit of creditors generally (controlled by statutory provisions which have no equivalent in England) as this was the course preferred by the great majority of creditors.

Limited liability partnerships

6.135 What is said in 6.132–6.134 applies to limited liability partnerships, except that when a limited liability partnership proposes an arrangement, there is only one meeting (of creditors) instead of two.[295]

Building societies

6.136 What is said in 6.132–6.134 also applies to a building society which is being wound up.[296]

Insolvent partnerships

6.137 What is said in 6.132–6.134 also applies to an insolvent partnership which is being wound up, with the court having the additional power to stay, and/or give appropriate directions with respect to the conduct of, any related insolvency proceedings concerning a member of the partnership.[297]

Bank and building society insolvency

6.138 What is said in 6.132–6.134 also applies to an institution in bank insolvency or building society insolvency.[298] Directions which the court may give include an order suspending the bank or building society insolvency, rather than staying it.[299] The bank or building society liquidator has the power to apply to the court to lift the suspension when the voluntary arrangement is terminated.[300]

Company in Voluntary Liquidation Resuming Business

6.139 In several cases a stay of a creditors' voluntary winding up of a company has been ordered where the members have changed their minds about winding up after the company traded out of difficulties.[301]

6.140 A members' voluntary winding up has been stayed where the company's remaining asset, previously overlooked, would provide benefits to the company only in the long term.[302]

---

[294] (1911) 23 OLR 255.

[295] Limited Liability Partnerships Regulations 2001 (SI 2001/1090), reg 5 and sch 3.

[296] Building Societies Act 1986, sch 15A, paras 1 and 2.

[297] IA 1986, s 5(3), as modified by IPO 1994, sch 1.

[298] IA 1986, s 5(3), applied to bank insolvency by the Banking Act 2009, s 113(6), and to building society insolvency by the Building Societies Act 1986, s 90C.

[299] Banking Act 2009, s 113(8), applied to building society insolvency by the Building Societies Act 1986, s 90C.

[300] Banking Act 2009, s 113(9), applied to building society insolvency by the Building Societies Act 1986, s 90C.

[301] See *Re Steamship 'Titian' Co Ltd* (1888) 58 LT 78 (in which there was evidence that all creditors consented to the stay); *Re Steamship Chigwell Ltd* (1888) 4 TLR 308; *Re Filshie Broadfoot and Co Ltd* [1913] QWN 46 (in which the creditors consented to the stay and the company's prospects were said to be very promising); *Re Golden Butterfly Gold Mining Co NL* [1916] SALR 177; *Re Stephen Walters and Sons Ltd* (1926) 70 SJ 953 (in which the court also sanctioned a scheme of arrangement with creditors); *Re Backhouse Pty Ltd* [1946] QWN 4; *Re Barr-Brown Construction Co Ltd* [1946] NZLR 333.

[302] *McKern v Pacific Edge Corporation Pty Ltd* [2004] NSWSC 1150, 51 ACSR 602.

Wrongly Made Winding-up Order

An assertion that a winding-up order was wrongly made should be pursued in an appeal **6.141**
against the order[303] or an application for it to be rescinded[304] rather than an application
for a stay.[305] Nevertheless, in *Re Nicholls Pty Ltd*[306] the company applied for a permanent
stay of proceedings in its winding up on the ground that the winding-up order had been
obtained by a creditor whose debt was disputed. The court found that there was not a 'bona
fide dispute on good and substantial grounds' which would have been sufficient to warrant
dismissing the petition on hearing it,[307] but adjourned the application for 28 days to allow
the company to make arrangements to pay the petitioner's debt and reapply for a stay on
the ground that it was solvent. And in *Stubbs Enterprises Ltd v Springfield Acres Ltd*[308] a contributory applied for a stay of proceedings in the winding up of a company and also for the
setting aside of a summary judgment obtained by the petitioning creditor, but the application to set aside the judgment was dismissed and the application for a stay was described as
an abuse of process.

Making an Order to Stay

Incidental directions

When ordering a stay of all proceedings under IA 1986, s 147(1), the court has an inher- **6.142**
ent jurisdiction to give incidental directions such as directions for the holding of a general
meeting to appoint directors.[309] See, for example, *Re Backhouse Pty Ltd*.[310] Remarkably,
the majority of the court in *McAusland v Deputy Commissioner of Taxation*[311] interpreted
the direction to convene such a meeting as a condition precedent to the termination of the
winding up so that as the meeting was not held the winding up never terminated.

In *BSN Commercial Bank (M) Bhd v River View Properties Sdn Bhd*[312] the court added to an **6.143**
order staying all proceedings in the winding up of a company an order that the company's
directors could only dispose of its assets in the day-to-day running of the company, and
then had to interpret the order to prevent difficulties for the company's bank.

Further conditions: building societies

On staying proceedings in the winding up of a building society the court may[313] impose **6.144**
conditions for securing:

(a) that the building society be dissolved by consent of its members under the Building
     Societies Act 1986, s 87, or

---

[303] See 6.44–6.85.
[304] See 6.24–6.43.
[305] *Re Empire Builders Ltd* (1919) 88 LJ Ch 459, which concerned a now superseded procedure for winding
up enemy companies.
[306] (1982) 7 ACLR 76.
[307] See 7.528.
[308] [1993] MCLR 185.
[309] *McAusland v Deputy Commissioner of Taxation* (1993) 118 ALR 577 per French J at p 593.
[310] [1946] QWN 4. Apparently, this is not the practice in New South Wales, per French J in *McAusland v
Deputy Commissioner of Taxation* (1993) 118 ALR 577 at p 591 citing an ambiguous remark by Mahoney J in
Re Country Traders Distributors Ltd [1974] 2 NSWLR 135 at p 139.
[311] (1993) 118 ALR 577.
[312] [1996] 1 MLJ 872.
[313] Under the Building Societies Act 1986, sch 15, paras 18(2) and 24.

(b) that the society amalgamates with, or transfers its engagements to, another building society under s 93 or s 94, or

(c) that the society transfers its business to a company under s 97.

6.145 The court may also include conditions for securing that any default which occasioned the petition be made good and that the costs of the proceedings on the petition be defrayed by the person or persons responsible for the default.

Further conditions: incorporated friendly societies

6.146 On staying proceedings in the winding up of an incorporated friendly society the court may[314] impose conditions for securing:

(a) that the friendly society be dissolved by consent of its members under the Friendly Societies Act 1992, s 20, or

(b) that the society amalgamates with, or transfers all or any of its engagements to, another friendly society under s 85 or s 86, or

(c) that the society converts itself into a company under s 91.

6.147 The court may also include conditions for securing that any default which occasioned the petition be made good and that the costs of the proceedings on the petition be defrayed by the person or persons responsible for the default.

Further order: insolvent partnerships

6.148 If the court stays proceedings in a partnership winding up and a member of the partnership has been ordered to be wound up on a petition presented under IPO 1994, art 8 or art 10, the court may rescind the winding-up order against the member.[315]

Notification of stay

6.149 If the court makes an order staying proceedings in the winding up of a registered company, the company must forward a copy of the order forthwith to the registrar of companies.[316] A copy of an order staying proceedings in the winding up of a building society, incorporated friendly society or registered society must be sent to the Financial Conduct Authority.[317] The court may, in an order staying a winding up, require the company to notify creditors and contributories of the stay.[318]

Effect of Staying a Stay

6.150 In *Vijayalakshmi Devi d/o Nadchatiram v Jegadevan s/o Nadchatiram*[319] it was held that if an order staying all proceedings in a winding up is itself stayed pending appeal, the winding-up court should nevertheless hear no further applications in the winding up and

---

[314] Under the Friendly Societies Act 1992, sch 10, paras 21(2) and 27.

[315] IA 1986, s 147(3)(b), as modified by IPO 1994, sch 4, para 19; IA 1986, s 147(1), as modified by IPO 1994, sch 4, para 19, is probably applied to art 10 petitions by IA 1986, s 221(5), as modified by IPO 1994, sch 6, para 4.

[316] IA 1986, s 112(3) (voluntary winding up); s 147(3) (compulsory winding up).

[317] Building Societies Act 1986, sch 15, para 3(1)(b); Friendly Societies Act 1992, sch 10, para 3(1)(c); Co-operative and Community Benefit Societies Act 2014, s 123(2).

[318] IR 1986, r 4.48(2). Applied to bank insolvency by the Bank Insolvency (England and Wales) Rules 2009 (SI 2009/356), r 39, and modified by rr 3(3)(b) and (4)(f) and 39. Applied to building society insolvency by the Building Society Insolvency (England and Wales) Rules 2010 (SI 2010/2581), r 39, and modified by rr 3(5)(b) and (6)(h) and (v) and 39.

[319] [1995] 1 MLJ 830.

should not make further orders because such orders would become nullities if the order staying the winding up were to be affirmed on appeal. This seems to have been a pragmatic solution to a paradox.

Discharge on Making an Administration Order

A company being wound up by the court can be put into administration only[320] by an **6.151** administration order applied for:

(a) by the holder of a qualifying floating charge in respect of the company's property;[321] or
(b) by the company's liquidator.[322]

If the court makes an administration order in relation to a company which is in liquidation **6.152** by virtue of a winding-up order, it must discharge the winding-up order.[323] The effect of discharge of a winding-up order is that the order ceases to have effect as from the time of discharge and the winding up is terminated. It does not mean that the order is to be treated as never having been made.[324]

Where the court makes an administration order in relation to a company in compulsory **6.153** liquidation, it must[325] include in the order:

(a) details concerning the release of the liquidator;
(b) provision for payment of the expenses of the liquidation;
(c) provisions regarding any indemnity given to the liquidator;
(d) provisions regarding the handling or realization of any of the company's assets in the hands of or under the control of the liquidator;
(e) such provision as the court thinks fit with respect to matters arising in connection with the liquidation; and
(f) such other provisions as the court shall think fit.

The court may make consequential provisions, including specifying modification to the **6.154** operation of sch B1 in the administration, and must specify which powers under sch B1 are to be exercisable by the administrator.[326]

The witness statement in support of an application for an administration order to be made **6.155** in relation to a company which is in liquidation must[327] contain:

(a) full details of the existing insolvency proceedings, the name and address of the liquidator, the date he or she was appointed and by whom;
(b) the reasons why it has subsequently been considered appropriate that an administration application should be made;

---

[320] IA 1986, sch B1, para 8(1)(b) and (3).
[321] IA 1986, sch B1, para 37.
[322] IA 1986, sch B1, para 38.
[323] IA 1986, sch B1, paras 37(3)(a) and 38(2)(a).
[324] *Re Albany Building Ltd* [2007] BCC 591.
[325] IR 1986, r 2.13.
[326] IA 1986, sch B1, paras 37(3)(c), (d) and (e) and 38(2)(c), (d) and (e).
[327] IR 1986, r 2.11(1).

(c) all other matters that would, in the opinion of the applicant, assist the court in considering the need to make provisions in respect of matters arising in connection with the liquidation; and

(d) the details required in rr 2.4(2) and (4) (which apply to all administration applications).

6.156 If the application is by the holder of a qualifying floating charge, the supporting witness statement must set out sufficient evidence to satisfy the court that the applicant charge holder is entitled to appoint an administrator under IA 1986, sch B1, para 14.[328]

6.157 In *Re SN Group plc*[329] the court refused an application to stay proceedings on a winding-up order made one month previously so that an application could be made for an administration order. The application to stay was refused because the creditor who had petitioned for the winding up objected and it appeared that no other creditors had been consulted.

History

6.158 In the pre-1875 Court of Chancery, a party against whom a decree or order had been made, but not enrolled, could petition for it to be reheard by the judge who made it or by his successor in office.[330] In the case of a decree or order of the Master of the Rolls or a Vice-Chancellor, this was in addition to a right to appeal to the Lord Chancellor[331] or, from 1851, to the Court of Appeal in Chancery.[332]

6.159 The party who had obtained a decree or order could preclude rehearing or appeal to the Lord Chancellor by having the decree or order signed by the Lord Chancellor and enrolled, but it was possible to enter a caveat to prevent enrolment for 28 days. After enrolment, there could be an appeal to the House of Lords[333] or an originating process called a bill of review could be filed in the Court of Chancery asking for reconsideration of the decree or order by the court, either because of an error of law or because of new evidence which could not have been adduced at the original hearing.

6.160 The Joint Stock Companies Winding-up Act 1848, s 101, provided that an order made under the Act by the Master of the Rolls or a Vice-Chancellor could be reheard by the Lord Chancellor and that such a rehearing could be sought by motion. A motion was a cheaper and less elaborate process than a petition.[334] This route of appeal to the Lord Chancellor could be blocked by having the order enrolled.[335] The Vice-Chancellors and the Master of the Rolls retained their power to rehear their own first-instance decisions, and so discharge

---

[328] IR 1986, r 2.11(2).

[329] [1994] 1 BCLC 319.

[330] The description of the rehearing process here is taken from *Re St Nazaire Co* (1879) 12 ChD 88 per Jessel MR at pp 97–8; John Newland, *The Practice of the High Court of Chancery*, 3rd edn (London: Saunders & Benning, 1830), vol 1, ch 10; John Sidney Smith, *A Treatise on the Practice of the Court of Chancery* (London: Saunders & Benning, 1835), vol 2, ch 1–4.

[331] Such an appeal was itself by way of rehearing.

[332] *Brown v Higgs* (1803) 8 Ves Jr 561; *Blackburn v Jepson* (1814) 2 Ves & B 359.

[333] The House would not hear an appeal against a decree or order that was not enrolled (*Broadhurst v Tunnicliff* (1842) 9 Cl & F 71).

[334] For an example of an appeal against a winding-up order using this provision see *Re Borough of St Marylebone Joint Stock Banking Co, ex parte Walker* (1848) 1 H & Tw 100.

[335] *Re Direct London and Exeter Railway Co* (1849) 1 H & Tw 587.

of a winding-up order could be sought by a petition for rehearing which was heard by the judge who had made the order or his successor.[336] Usually a petition for discharge of a winding-up order asked alternatively for the court to vary the order as it thought fit. From 1854 it became usual to apply to discharge or vary a winding-up order by motion, unless there were complicated facts which ought to be recorded in a petition.[337]

No time limit was prescribed for an application for a rehearing to discharge or vary a **6.161** winding-up order,[338] but such an application would be dismissed if there was delay in making it.[339] In *Re Direct Exeter, Plymouth and Devonport Railway Co, ex parte Woolmer*[340] an application to discharge a winding-up order was refused because the applicants had originally concurred in petitioning for the order.

The Supreme Court of Judicature Act 1873 transferred the Court of Chancery's rehearing **6.162** jurisdiction to the Court of Appeal.[341] In bankruptcy proceedings, however, the London Bankruptcy Court and county courts continued to have a statutory power to review, rescind or vary their orders,[342] and this remained after the jurisdiction of the London Bankruptcy Court was transferred to the High Court.[343] Apart from statute and rules of court, the Chancery Division of the High Court now has no powers to rehear its own decisions other than the power that all divisions of the court have to set aside a decision obtained by the fraud of a party.[344]

---

[336] *Re Ipswich, Norwich and Yarmouth Railway Co, ex parte Barnett* (1849) 1 De G & Sm 744; *Re Cambrian Junction Railway Co, ex parte Coleman* (1849) 3 De G & Sm 139; *Re Anglo-Californian Gold Mining Co* (1861) 1 Drew & Sm 628; *Re London and Mediterranean Bank Ltd* (1866) 15 LT 153. A petition for rehearing was also the procedure for reversing dismissal of a winding-up petition (*Re North Wales Slate Supply Co* (1870) 21 LT 818).

[337] *Re Metropolitan Carriage Co, Clarke's Case* (1854) 1 Kay & J 22; *Re Patent Floor-Cloth Co* (1869) LR 8 Eq 664; *Re National Permanent Benefit Building Society, ex parte Williamson* (1869) LR 5 Ch App 309; Joseph S Taylor, *A Manual on the Winding Up of Companies* (London: William Amer, 1865), p 128.

[338] *Re Direct Exeter, Plymouth and Devonport Railway Co, ex parte Besley* (1851) 3 Mac & G 287; *Re Anglo-Californian Gold Mining Co* (1861) 1 Drew & Sm 628.

[339] *Re Chepstow, Gloucester and Forest of Dean Railway Co* (1851) 2 Sim NS 11; *Re Metropolitan Carriage Co, Clarke's Case* (1854) 1 Kay & J 22; *Re Anglo-Californian Gold Mining Co, ex parte Baldy* (1862) 6 LT 340. In all three cases the delay was more than a year. But in *Re National Permanent Benefit Building Society, ex parte Williamson* (1869) LR 5 Ch App 309 a delay of similar length was held not to preclude discharge of the winding-up order.

[340] (1852) 2 De G M & G 665.

[341] *Re St Nazaire Co* (1879) 12 ChD 88; *Re Barrell Enterprises* [1973] 1 WLR 19; *Cinpres Gas Injection Ltd v Melea Ltd* [2008] EWCA Civ 9, [2008] Bus LR 1157.

[342] Bankruptcy Act 1869, s 71.

[343] Bankruptcy Act 1883, s 104; Bankruptcy Act 1914, s 108(1).

[344] *Re Barrell Enterprises* [1973] 1 WLR 19; *Cinpres Gas Injection Ltd v Melea Ltd* [2008] EWCA Civ 9, [2008] Bus LR 1157; *Roult v North West Strategic Health Authority* [2009] EWCA Civ 444, [2009] PIQR P18.

7

PETITIONS BY CREDITORS

Standing of Creditors to Petition and Circumstances in which they may Petition

Creditor or Creditors

7.1 A petition for the compulsory winding up of a registered or unregistered company may be presented by any creditor[1] or creditors (including any contingent or prospective creditor[2] or creditors) of the company.[3] The same applies to building societies,[4] incorporated friendly societies[5] and any other entity that may be wound up as a registered company.[6] The same applies to a petition to wind up an insolvent partnership as an unregistered company,[7] but there are restrictions on which creditors may petition concurrently for the winding up of a partnership and the winding up or bankruptcy of a member or former member of the partnership.[8] A creditor of a relevant scheme[9] may petition for it to be wound up.[10]

7.2 In *Dolvelle Pty Ltd v Australian Macfarms Pty Ltd*[11] Santow J referred, at p 724, to a:

> long-settled practice... that if there are two or more creditors in respect of separate debts, only one creditor is to make the application to wind up... and does so in a representative capacity. Any others... would simply file a notice of intention to appear and otherwise seek leave to be substituted in appropriate circumstances.

---

[1] See 7.309–7.430.

[2] See 7.318–7.358.

[3] IA 1986, s 124(1), applied to unregistered companies by s 221(1).

[4] Building Societies Act 1986, s 89(2)(c).

[5] Friendly Societies Act 1992, s 22(2)(c).

[6] Charitable incorporated organizations (see 1.122), European cooperative societies (see 1.123), European public limited-liability companies (see 1.124), limited liability partnerships (see 1.126) and registered societies (see 1.127–1.129).

[7] IPO 1994, art 7. IA 1986, s 124(1), as applied by the modified form of s 221(5) set out in IPO 1994, sch 3, para 3.

[8] IPO 1994, art 8. See 7.431–7.432.

[9] See 1.168.

[10] Collective Investment in Transferable Securities (Contractual Scheme) Regulations 2013 (SI 2013/1388), reg 17(9)(a).

[11] (1998) 43 NSWLR 717.

A petition presented by a creditor must state how the petitioner came to be a creditor: merely **7.3** describing the petitioner as 'creditor' is not sufficient.[12]

In *O'Neill v New Zealand Concrete Printers Ltd*[13] an application for the winding up of a **7.4** company was brought in the form of a derivative claim by a member of a company which was alleged to be a creditor of the company sought to be wound up, but it was held that the circumstances did not come within any exceptions to the proper claimant principle[14] and so the applicant did not have standing to make the winding-up application.

Grounds

In principle, a creditor (present, contingent or prospective) is entitled to present a petition **7.5** on any of the grounds set out in the Insolvency Act 1986 (IA 1986), s 122(1) (in relation to a registered company), or s 221(5) (in relation to an unregistered company).[15] In particular, a creditor may petition under s 122(1)(g) or s 221(5)(c), the just and equitable clause.[16] The same applies to the separate lists of circumstances set out for some entities that are treated as registered companies[17] and relevant schemes[18] (all of which include the just and equitable clause) or the additional circumstances available for other entities.[19]

Only a creditor (or creditors) may petition on the ground that a moratorium has not resulted **7.6** in an approved voluntary arrangement.[20]

In practice a creditor usually relies on the company's inability to pay its debts.[21] Under the **7.7** Joint Stock Companies Act 1856, s 69, this was the only circumstance in which a creditor of a company could petition, but this restriction did not appear in the Companies Act 1862 and has not been revived in subsequent Acts. Inability to pay debts must exist at the time of hearing the petition[22] and should also have existed at the time of petitioning since the existence of the circumstances relied on must be verified by a statement of truth, and if a winding up is ordered, it is deemed, in most cases, to commence at the time of presentation of the petition.[23] However, the view that it is only necessary to prove inability to pay debts at

---

[12] *Re Palais Cinema Ltd* [1918] VLR 113; *Garden Mews-St Leonards Pty Ltd v Butler Pollnow Pty Ltd* (1984) 9 ACLR 91 at p 93; though *Re Barrier Reef Trading Co Ltd* [1929] StR Qd 177, obiter, at p 182, is to the contrary.

[13] (1989) 4 NZCLC 65,262.

[14] The rule in *Foss v Harbottle* (1843) 2 Hare 461.

[15] *Re a Company (No 006794 of 1983)* [1986] BCLC 261 at p 263; *Re a Company (No 003028 of 1987)* [1988] BCLC 282. For s 122(1) see 2.27. For s 221(5) see 2.37.

[16] *Re Australian Joint-Stock Bank Ltd* (1897) 41 SJ 469; *Re Squashland Southport Pty Ltd* (1980) 5 ACLR 47; *Re a Company (No 003028 of 1987)* [1988] BCLC 282; *Deputy Commissioner of Taxation v Casualife Furniture International Pty Ltd* [2004] VSC 157, 55 ATR 599; *Macquarie Bank Ltd v TM Investments Pty Ltd* [2005] NSWSC 608, 223 ALR 148; and see *Re Sparad Ltd* (1993) 12 ACSR 12 and *Deputy Commissioner of Taxation v Action Workwear Pty Ltd* (1996) 132 FLR 345, discussed at 8.296.

[17] Building societies (see 2.29–2.30), charitable incorporated organizations (see 2.31), incorporated friendly societies (see 2.34) and limited liability partnerships (see 2.35).

[18] See 2.38.

[19] European cooperative societies (see 2.32), European economic interest groupings (see 2.45–2.49) and European groupings of territorial cooperation (see 2.50–2.51).

[20] IA 1986, ss 122(1)(fa) and 124(3A); IA 1986, ss 122(1)(da) and 124(3A), as modified by SI 2001/1090, sch 3; IA 1986, ss 122(1)(d) and 124(3A), as modified by the Charitable Incorporated Organisations (Insolvency and Dissolution) Regulations 2012 (SI 2012/3013), sch, para 1(5) and (7).

[21] IA 1986, s 122(1)(f) or s 221(5)(b).

[22] *Syd Mannix Pty Ltd v Leserv Constructions Pty Ltd* [1971] 1 NSWLR 788.

[23] *Re Catholic Publishing and Bookselling Co Ltd* (1864) 2 De G J & S 116 per Turner LJ at p 120; *Syd Mannix Pty Ltd v Leserv Constructions Pty Ltd* [1971] 1 NSWLR 788. See 5.277–5.302.

the time of presentation of the petition, and that the position of the company at the time of hearing the petition is irrelevant[24] is wrong, because IA 1986, ss 122(1)(f) and 221(5)(b), are in the present tense showing that the circumstance must exist at the time of the hearing.[25]

Reasonable Pre-action Conduct

Reasonable pre-action conduct required

7.8 There is no specific pre-action protocol for creditors' winding-up petitions. So reasonable pre-action conduct is required by Practice Direction (PD) Pre-action Conduct, paras 6.1–8.4, before a person claiming a debt from a company applies for the company to be wound up by the court.[26] The court may take into consideration whether there has been reasonable pre-action conduct when deciding how to exercise its discretion to make a winding-up order[27] and when making orders about who should pay costs.[28] Reasonable pre-action conduct is required so as to give the company an opportunity to dispute the claimed debt. Equally, a company cannot claim that a petition based on a debt which it disputes has been pursued unreasonably if it has not promptly informed the petitioner that the debt is disputed and set out the nature of the dispute.[29]

Informing the company of the claimed debt

7.9 Before a creditor's petition to wind up a company is presented, the intending petitioner and the company should:[30]

(a) exchange sufficient information about the matter to allow them to understand each other's position and make informed decisions about settlement and how to proceed;
(b) make appropriate attempts to resolve the matter without starting proceedings, and in particular consider the use of an appropriate form of alternative dispute resolution (ADR) in order to do so.[31]

7.10 Before presenting a petition:[32]

(a) the intending petitioner should set out the details of the debt claimed in writing to the company; and
(b) the company should give a full written response within a reasonable period.

7.11 Written details of the debt claimed may be given either in a statutory demand for the debt[33] or in a letter before claim. A statutory demand may be used only for an undisputed debt which is presently payable.[34] A letter before claim may be appropriate where the claim has

---

[24] *Re North Sydney Investment and Tramway Co Ltd* (1892) 3 BC (NSW) 81.
[25] See *Re Fildes Bros Ltd* [1970] 1 WLR 592 per Megarry J at p 597 on the just and equitable clause.
[26] See *Blackstone's Civil Practice 2015*, 8.12–8.14.
[27] *Commissioners of Customs and Excise v Anglo Overseas Ltd* [2004] EWHC 2198 (Ch), LTL 6/10/2004, at [41].
[28] CPR, r 44.3(4)(a) and (5)(a); PD Pre-action Conduct, para 4.1.
[29] *Re Merc Property Ltd* [1999] 2 BCLC 286; *Jacob v Vockrodt* [2007] EWHC 2403 (QB), [2007] BPIR 1568.
[30] PD Pre-action Conduct, para 6.1.
[31] See Susan Blake, Julie Browne and Stuart Sime, *The Jackson ADR Handbook* (Oxford: Oxford University Press, 2013).
[32] PD Pre-action Conduct, para 7.1.
[33] See 7.125–7.247.
[34] See 7.161–7.165 and 7.213–7.216.

not yet been acknowledged by the company or is not yet quantified.[35] If it is known that the existence of the debt claimed is disputed on substantial grounds, presentation of a winding-up petition would normally be an abuse of process[36] and other more appropriate proceedings should be contemplated. The letter before claim for a disputed debt should be in accordance with PD Pre-action Conduct, annex A. Claimant and company may have different views on whether a claim is disputed.

If a company fails to comply with a statutory demand within 21 days, it will be deemed to be **7.12** unable to pay its debts, and the claimant may present a winding-up petition. But there is no failure to comply if the demanded debt is disputed on a substantial ground.[37] The company should, therefore, advise the claimant within the 21 days that the debt is disputed, though this may be too short a time to give the kind of detailed written response contemplated by PD Pre-action Conduct. If the claimant refuses to undertake not to present a petition before a detailed written response is provided, the company may apply for an injunction to prevent presentation.[38] If there is a dispute on substantial grounds about the existence of the debt, the claimant should undertake not to present a petition at all until the dispute is resolved: an undertaking to give 14 days' notice of intention to present a petition is not adequate.[39]

Letter before claim

A letter before claim sent by a creditor of a company, who is not aware that the company dis- **7.13** putes the existence or amount of the debt, is not required to follow PD Pre-action Conduct, annex A.[40] However, the requirements of annex A can be adapted to suggest what a letter before claim for an undisputed debt should contain. The letter should give details of the claimed debt which are concise but sufficient to enable the recipient to understand and investigate the claim without extensive further information.[41] It should include:[42]

(a) the creditor's full name and address;
(b) a statement that the company is indebted to the creditor;
(c) a clear summary of the facts which have given rise to the debt;
(d) an explanation of how the amount owed has been calculated; and
(e) a statement that the creditor requires the company to pay the debt.

The letter should also:[43]   **7.14**

(a) list the essential documents on which the creditor intends to rely;
(b) set out the form of ADR (if any) that the creditor considers the most suitable and invite the company to agree to this (as the creditor believes the debt is undisputed, it is likely that the creditor will not think any form of ADR is appropriate); and

---

[35] The creditor should have no doubt that at least £750 is owed; see 7.392.
[36] See 7.572.
[37] See 7.198–7.201.
[38] See 7.569–7.608.
[39] *Sleetree Ltd v Reston Ltd* [2006] EWHC 2489 (Ch), LTL 3/11/2006.
[40] PD Pre-action Conduct, annex A, does not apply where it is not disputed that the money is owed (PD Pre-action Conduct, para 2.5(1) and annex A, para 1.1).
[41] PD Pre-action Conduct, annex A, para 2.1.
[42] PD Pre-action Conduct, annex A, para 2.1.
[43] PD Pre-action Conduct, annex A, para 2.2.

(c) state the date by which the creditor considers it reasonable for a full response to be provided by the company. It is suggested that 21 days after receipt of the letter should be allowed as this is the time that the company would have to comply with a statutory demand. However, PD Pre-action Conduct, para 7.2(2), says that 14 days is normally sufficient in the case of an undisputed debt.

7.15 Unless the company is known to be legally represented, the letter before claim should:[44]

(a) refer the company to PD Pre-action Conduct and in particular draw attention to para 4 concerning the court's powers to impose sanctions for failure to comply with the practice direction; and

(b) inform the company that ignoring the letter before claim may lead to the creditor starting proceedings and may increase the company's liability for costs.

Company's full response or acknowledgment

7.16 The company should normally provide a full written response to the creditor's letter before claim within the period specified in the letter.[45] The response should, as appropriate, accept that the debt is payable, in whole or in part (stating which part), or deny that it is payable.[46] A response which states that all or part of the claimed debt is not payable should:[47]

(a) give reasons why the claim is not accepted, identifying which facts and which parts of the claim (if any) are accepted and which are disputed, and the basis of that dispute;

(b) state whether the company intends to make a counterclaim against the claimant (and, if so, provide information equivalent to a claimant's letter before claim);

(c) state whether the company alleges that the claimant was wholly or partly to blame for the problem that led to the dispute and, if so, summarize the facts relied on;

(d) state whether the company agrees to the claimant's proposals for ADR and if not, state why not and suggest an alternative form of ADR (or state why none is considered appropriate);

(e) list the essential documents on which the company intends to rely; and

(f) identify and ask for copies of any further relevant documents, not in the company's possession and which the company wishes to see.

7.17 If it is not possible to provide a full written response within 14 days, a written acknowledgment should be given within that time,[48] stating whether an insurer is, or may be, involved,[49] and when a full response will be provided.[50] If the date given is later than the date specified in the letter before claim, the company should give reasons for requiring a longer period.[51] The acknowledgment may request further information to enable the company to provide a full response.[52]

---

[44] PD Pre-action Conduct, annex A, para 2.3.
[45] PD Pre-action Conduct, para 7.2(2).
[46] PD Pre-action Conduct, annex A, para 4.1.
[47] PD Pre-action Conduct, annex A, para 4.2.
[48] PD Pre-action Conduct, annex A, para 3.1.
[49] PD Pre-action Conduct, annex A, para 3.2(1).
[50] PD Pre-action Conduct, annex A, para 3.2(2).
[51] PD Pre-action Conduct, annex A, para 3.3.
[52] PD Pre-action Conduct, annex A, para 3.2(3).

Cases outside the CPR

Before the Civil Procedure Rules (CPR) introduced pre-action protocols, there were cases **7.18**
in which creditor petitioners were penalized for presenting a petition precipitately. In *Re
Edric Audio Visual Ltd*[53] the petitioner obtained judgment in default of defence and, without any further communication with the debtor, presented and advertised a winding-up
petition. The debt was paid in full four days after advertisement. The Court of Appeal held
that there should be no order as to costs up to the time the petition was served, but the company should pay the petitioner's costs thereafter. In Queensland, in *Re Great Barrier Reef
Flying Boats Pty Ltd*[54] no order for costs was made where the petitioner knew the amount
of the debt had been disputed for over six months, and the petitioner agreed to a compromise immediately after the petition was served. In *Re a Company (No 001573 of 1983)*[55] a
creditor's petition was dismissed as an abuse of process, in part because it was presented on
the same day as the creditor's debt was created by a court order for payment of costs to be
assessed. As the amount had not been assessed there was obviously a dispute about the size
of the debt.

In *Frank Saul (Fashions) Ltd v Commissioners of HM Revenue and Customs*[56] the court made **7.19**
no order as to costs where a company had taken (and been allowed) more than a year to
provide the creditor with information it required to verify the company's assertion that the
petition debt was not owed. The court found that both sides were at fault in not giving the
matter proper attention.

The onus is on the company to show why it should not be ordered to pay the petitioner's **7.20**
costs, but the company's evidence about the circumstances in which the petition was presented may be given to the court informally, unless the petitioner objects, in which case
there must be an adjournment.[57]

See also 7.597–7.602.   **7.21**

Should a creditor be required to obtain judgment and attempt execution?

In general, a creditor of a company whose debt is not disputed is not required to exhaust all **7.22**
other legal means of enforcing payment of the debt, or any specific means, before resorting
to a winding-up petition.[58] But judges have sometimes remarked that a creditor of a company whose debt is not disputed should obtain a judgment for the debt and attempt execution, and should not petition for the company to be wound up until execution has failed.[59]
This is inconsistent with (or requires the creditor to ignore) the rule that a company's failure
to pay one debt is evidence that it is unable to pay its debts.[60] The common theme of these

---

[53] (1981) 125 SJ 395.
[54] (1982) 6 ACLR 820.
[55] [1983] BCLC 492.
[56] [2012] EWHC 1603 (Ch), [2012] BPIR 985.
[57] *Re Nowmost Co Ltd* [1996] 2 BCLC 492.
[58] See 7.46–7.50.
[59] Per Needham J in *Suave International (1980) Pty Ltd v Salson Pty Ltd* (1982) 7 ACLR 87, in which the
company said that it disputed the petitioner's debt but that it was uneconomic to litigate the dispute; per
Harman J in *Re a Company (No 001573 of 1983)* [1983] BCLC 492 at p 495; per Young J in *Westeq Ltd v
Challenger Mining Corp NL* (1988) 13 ACLR 627 at p 629.
[60] See 7.272–7.281.

remarks is that a winding-up petition should not be used to collect a debt from a solvent company, but this assumes that a company which does not pay an admitted debt is nevertheless solvent. It is submitted that the correct view is that held by Harman J in *Cornhill Insurance plc v Improvement Services Ltd*.[61] This is that a creditor who is undoubtedly owed a sum of money by a company and is not paid must suspect that the company cannot pay. Therefore the creditor can properly sign a statement of truth that the company is unable to pay its debts and can properly present a winding-up petition.

7.23 It is a notable feature of IA 1986 that it provides that a creditor of an *individual* must serve a statutory demand for the debt, or obtain judgment for it and attempt execution, before petitioning for the individual's bankruptcy,[62] but the same restrictions are not imposed by the Act on a petition for the winding up of a *company*. This is a deliberate difference between the treatment of companies, which are artificial entities, and the treatment of individuals. Exposure to winding-up proceedings brought by a creditor who has not obtained judgment for the debt and has not attempted execution is, like filing accounts for public inspection[63] and liability to investigation,[64] one of the prices which Parliament has imposed for the privilege of trading through the medium of an artificial incorporated entity with limited liability.

Must proceedings on a creditor's petition be stayed in favour of arbitration?

7.24 On the application of a party to an arbitration agreement, a court must stay legal proceedings brought against that party (whether by way of claim or counterclaim) in respect of a matter which, under the arbitration agreement, is to be referred to arbitration.[65] In *Best Beat Ltd v Rossall*[66] Park J held that proceedings brought by winding-up petition are not covered by this provision, because they are neither a claim nor a counterclaim. It was also held that the dispute, which was alleged to be about the company's liability under a clearly indisputable statutory obligation to the creditor petitioner, was not covered by an arbitration clause in a lease.

7.25 The questions for determination by the court on a creditor's petition to wind up a company on the ground that it is unable to pay its debts are: (a) whether the company is unable to pay its debts, and (b) whether the company should be wound up. Neither of these is a dispute or difference concerning the petitioner's debt[67] and so is not covered by an arbitration agreement in the contract under which the debt arose.[68] A dispute about the existence of the debt claimed by the petitioner will not normally be decided in proceedings on the petition,

---

[61] [1986] 1 WLR 114 at p 118, in effect answering his earlier remark in *Re a Company (No 001573 of 1983)* [1983] BCLC 492 at p 495. See also *Re a Company (No 003079 of 1990)* [1991] BCLC 235 at pp 235–6; *Forsayth NL v Juno Securities Ltd* (1991) 4 WAR 376.

[62] IA 1986, ss 267 and 268.

[63] Companies Act 2006, ss 444–447.

[64] Companies Act 1985, part 14.

[65] Arbitration Act 1996, s 9.

[66] [2006] EWHC 1494 (Comm), [2006] BPIR 1357. Confirmed by *Salford Estates (No 2) Ltd v Altomart Ltd* [2014] EWCA Civ 1575, LTL 9/12/2014.

[67] As required for an effective reference to arbitration by the Arbitration Act 1996, ss 6(1) and 82(1). See Susan Blake, Julie Browne and Stuart Sime, *The Jackson ADR Handbook* (Oxford: Oxford University Press, 2013), para 25.05.

[68] *Community Development Pty Ltd v Engwirda Construction Co* (1969) 120 CLR 455; *Re Sanpete Builders (S) Pte Ltd* [1989] 1 MLJ 393; *Hollmet AG v Meridian Success Metal Supplies Ltd* [1997] HKLRD 828.

whether the dispute is covered by an arbitration agreement or not. The usual practice of the court is to dismiss (or, sometimes, adjourn) a creditor's winding-up petition if there is a dispute on substantial grounds about the existence of the petitioner's debt, leaving the petitioner to establish the debt in other more appropriate proceedings,[69] which will be arbitration in the case of a dispute covered by an arbitration agreement. Even where there is an arbitration agreement, this practice is not followed if the court finds that there are no substantial grounds for the dispute.[70]

Limitation

If the limitation period for claiming a debt incurred by a company has not expired, it is inter- **7.26**
rupted, and time stops running, when the creditor presents a petition, as a creditor in respect of the debt, for the company to be wound up, at least where the debt is a simple contract debt,[71] a sum recoverable by statute[72] or, it is submitted, a specialty debt.[73] However, until a winding-up order is made,[74] presentation of a winding-up petition has no effect on the limitation periods of the company's other creditors,[75] even, it seems, if they give notice of intention to support the petition.[76] For the purposes of the Limitation Act 1980, a winding-up petition is brought before the end of a limitation period if it is received, together with the necessary fees, in the appropriate court office, during opening hours, before the limitation period has ended.[77] If the court office is closed on the day on which a limitation period ends, the period is extended to the next day on which the office is open.[78] A person whose claim against a company is statute-barred does not have standing to petition as a creditor for it to be wound up.[79]

Nature of Creditors' Petitions to Wind Up Insolvent Companies

Function of Creditors' Petitions which Allege Inability to Pay Debts

Individual and collective remedy

A creditor's winding-up petition alleging inability to pay debts has a dual function as both **7.27**
an individual remedy provided by statute to enforce payment of the petitioner's debt and a collective remedy which enables all unsecured creditors to obtain payment of their debts at the same rate. It is also sometimes said that there is a public interest in ensuring that insolvent companies do not continue in business causing a hazard to those who deal with them.[80]

---

[69] See 7.528–7.549.

[70] *Salford Estates (No 2) Ltd v Altomart Ltd* [2014] EWCA Civ 1575, LTL 9/12/2014.

[71] Limitation Act 1980, s 5; *Re Cases of Taffs Well Ltd* [1992] Ch 179 at p 188.

[72] Limitation Act 1980, s 9; *Re Karnos Property Co Ltd* [1989] BCLC 340.

[73] Limitation Act 1980, s 8.

[74] *Re Cases of Taffs Well Ltd* [1992] Ch 179.

[75] *Re Cases of Taffs Well Ltd* [1992] Ch 179 at pp 188–9.

[76] *Re Cases of Taffs Well Ltd* [1992] Ch 179 at p 189.

[77] PD 7, para 5.1; *St Helens Metropolitan Borough Council v Barnes* [2006] EWCA Civ 1372, [2007] 1 WLR 879.

[78] *Pritam Kaur v S Russell and Sons Ltd* [1973] QB 336.

[79] *Motor Terms Co Pty Ltd v Liberty Insurance Ltd* (1967) 116 CLR 177 (in which it was held that the petitioner's debt was not statute-barred); *Re Karnos Property Co Ltd* [1989] BCLC 340; criticized by A McGee, 'Who is a creditor?' (1989) 10 Co Law 235.

[80] *Melbase Corporation Pty Ltd v Segenhoe Ltd* (1995) 17 ACSR 187; *Scolaro's Concrete Construction Pty Ltd v Schiavello Commercial Interiors (Vic) Pty Ltd* (1996) 62 FCR 319 at p 323; *South East Water Ltd v Kitoria Pty Ltd* (1996) 21 ACSR 465; *Bozell Asia (Holding) Ltd v CAL International Ltd* [1997] HKLRD 1; *Re Shop Clothing Ltd* [1999] 2 HKLRD 280; and see 2.141.

And that there is a public interest that on a creditor's petition a solvent company should not be put into liquidation causing a waste of money on fees and expenses.[81] These are opposing public interests which have to be balanced.[82]

7.28 In *Re Lines Bros Ltd*[83] Brightman LJ said, at p 20:

> The liquidation of an insolvent company is a process of collective enforcement of debts for the benefit of the general body of creditors. Although it is not a process of execution, because it is not for the benefit of a particular creditor, it is nevertheless akin to execution because its purpose is to enforce, on a *pari passu* basis, the payment of the admitted or proved debts of the company. When therefore a company goes into liquidation a process is initiated which, for all creditors, is similar to the process which is initiated, for one creditor, by execution.

7.29 The *pari passu* (with equal steps) basis is that all unsecured creditors are paid the same proportion of their debts. This basis is considerably modified in three ways. First there is a legislative system of preferential treatment for expenses of the liquidation,[84] for pension scheme contributions, employees' remuneration etc and amounts due to the FSCS and bank depositors.[85] Unsecured creditors who do not qualify for preferential treatment are not paid anything until the preferential debts are paid in full, but after that has happened, if there are insufficient assets to pay them in full, they must be paid *pari passu*.[86] Secondly there is a general principle of set-off of mutual debts,[87] which normally benefits a creditor of a company being wound up who is also a debtor of the company. Thirdly, some unsecured debts are postponed, either by legislation[88] or by court order.[89] Any agreement by a company that an asset is to be distributed to creditors in a way that is inconsistent with these rules becomes void on the commencement of the company's winding up.[90] This is subject to two exceptions. First, a charge on a company's property remains effective despite winding up, provided there has been compliance with requirements for registration of the charge.[91] Secondly, a company may agree that its lease or licence to use another person's property may be terminated by that person if the company is wound up.

7.30 In *Oakes v Turquand*[92] Lord Cranworth said, at p 363:

> The winding up is but a mode of enforcing payment. It closely resembles a bankruptcy, and a bankruptcy has been called, not improperly, a statutable execution for the benefit of all creditors. The same description may be given to a winding up.

---

[81] *Kekatos v Holmark Construction Co Pty Ltd* (1995) 18 ACSR 199 per Young J at p 200.
[82] *Switz Pty Ltd v Glowbind Pty Ltd* [2000] NSWCA 37, 48 NSWLR 661, at pp 673–4.
[83] [1983] Ch 1.
[84] IA 1986, ss 175(2)(a) and 176ZA; IR 1986, rr 4.21A and 4.218–4.220.
[85] IA 1986, ss 175 and 386 and sch 6, which also still accords preference to levies payable to the now defunct European Coal and Steel Community.
[86] IR 1986, r 4.181.
[87] IR 1986, r 4.90.
[88] IA 1986, s 189 (post-liquidation interest); Companies Act 2006, s 735(6) (payments for redemption or purchase of own shares); IA 1986, s 74(2)(f) (debts owed to members or past members in their character as members); IR 1986, r 4.61(4) (expenses of summoning and holding a contributories' meeting on the requisition of contributories).
[89] Under IA 1986, s 215(4) (postponement of debt owed to a person made liable for fraudulent or wrongful trading); or as part of a costs order (*Bathampton* order, see 5.195–5.196).
[90] *British Eagle International Airlines Ltd v Compagnie Nationale Air France* [1975] 1 WLR 758.
[91] Companies Act 2006, part 25. A charge may be cancelled by the court, if it is a transaction at an undervalue (IA 1986, s 238) or a preference (s 239). A floating charge may be invalid under s 245.
[92] (1867) LR 2 HL 325.

A company cannot be adjudged bankrupt because, by definition,[93] a bankruptcy order is an **7.31** order adjudging an *individual* bankrupt, and IA 1986, s 264(1), refers only to a bankruptcy order being made against an individual.

The two functions of a creditor's winding-up petition as both an individual and a collective **7.32** remedy may conflict. Sometimes, courts focus on the individual remedy,[94] and sometimes on the collective remedy.[95] The conflict between the two functions is most apparent in:

(a) the question whether a creditor of a solvent company may apply for it to be wound up, and whether the court would order its winding up if it refused to pay the creditor's debt;[96] and

(b) the problem of dealing with different creditors' disagreements about the expediency of putting an insolvent company into compulsory liquidation.[97]

Focus on individual remedy

At first the courts seem to have given preference to the individual remedy. In *Re National* **7.33** *Permanent Benefit Building Society*[98] Giffard LJ said:

The winding-up petition is in the nature of an execution against the company.

And in *Re General Company for the Promotion of Land Credit*[99] he said:

[An order to wind up] is neither more nor less than the mode of execution which this court gives to a creditor against a company unable to pay its debts.

The most significant consequence of treating a winding-up order on a creditor's petition as **7.34** an individual remedy was the view that an unpaid undisputed creditor of a company was entitled to an order *ex debito justitiae* (as a matter of right).[100]

As was mentioned in 7.22, courts have sometimes expressed disapproval of what they see **7.35** as creditors using winding-up petitions to collect debts from solvent companies. In *Re International Electric Co Ltd, McMahan's Case*[101] Meredith CJCP said, at p 454, that he would not grant a winding-up order when sought for the sole purpose of enforcing a single creditor's claim in a case where such claims could be as well enforced by execution. In *Visto Do Mar Ltd v Julien Parcou and Co*[102] the Seychelles Court of Appeal said, at p 396:

Where the aim is simply to recover a comparatively small sum and there is a reasonable prospect that it can be recovered by an ordinary action for debt, it would, we think, be undesirable and likely to bring discredit on the administration of justice, if the courts were to encourage creditors not to proceed in the ordinary way but to seek immediately a winding-up order.

In *Re a Company (No 001573 of 1983)*[103] Harman J said, at p 495:

it is trite law that the Companies Court is not, and should not be used as (despite the methods in fact often adopted) a debt-collecting court. The proper remedy for debt

---

[93] IA 1986, s 381(2).
[94] See 7.33–7.39.
[95] See 7.40–7.42.
[96] See 7.43–7.45.
[97] See 7.698–7.733.
[98] (1869) LR 5 Ch App 309.
[99] (1870) LR 5 Ch App 363.
[100] See 7.680–7.682.
[101] (1914) 20 DLR 451.
[102] 1978 (2) ALR Comm 389.
[103] [1983] BCLC 492.

collection is an execution upon a judgment, a distress,[104] a garnishee order,[105] or some such procedure.

7.36 In the New South Wales Supreme Court Young J said that the court 'exercising its jurisdiction to wind up companies, is not a court to provide a debt-collecting service'.[106] In the same court, Needham J expressed a similar opinion in *Suave International (1980) Pty Ltd v Salson Pty Ltd*.[107] In *Arundel v Designers International Ltd*[108] Barker J, at p 438, expressed concern 'that for relatively minor amounts the winding-up procedure continues to be invoked not because it is alleged that the defendant is insolvent, but to short-circuit the normal processes of obtaining judgment through the proper channels'.

7.37 These remarks ignore the fact that a failure by a company to pay an undisputed debt is evidence that the company is unable to pay its debts, as was subsequently recognized by Harman J.[109]

7.38 The contention that it is an abuse of process to use the winding-up procedure (specifically, the statutory demand procedure) as a debt-collection device has been described as:

> too sweeping a generalisation. Clearly one of the objects of the winding-up procedure is the realisation of the company's assets and the distribution of them in discharge of its liabilities. It has long been recognised that the winding-up procedure may properly be used with the aim of at least getting paid in part.[110]

This identifies the dual function of a creditor's winding-up petition.[111]

7.39 Focus on individual remedy can also be seen in cases in which disclosure by the Commissioners of HM Revenue and Customs to a liquidator of confidential information about taxpayers has been permitted because it enabled the liquidator to recover money owed to the Commissioners.[112]

Focus on collective remedy

7.40 As an alternative to the attention paid to using winding-up petitions as a means of obtaining payment of one creditor's debt, the courts have focused attention on the collective benefit that a winding-up order is supposed to confer on all creditors. In *Cambridge Gas Transport Corporation v Official Committee of Unsecured Creditors of Navigator Holdings plc*[113] the Privy Council, per Lord Hoffmann at [14], described bankruptcy and company winding up as:

> a mechanism of collective execution against the property of the debtor by creditors whose rights are admitted or established.

---

[104] Now commercial rent arrears recovery.

[105] Now a third party debt order.

[106] *Westeq Ltd v Challenger Mining Corp NL* (1988) 13 ACLR 627 at p 629.

[107] (1982) 7 ACLR 87.

[108] [1994] MCLR 433.

[109] *Cornhill Insurance plc v Improvement Services Ltd* [1986] 1 WLR 114 at p 118. See 7.22.

[110] *Bluehaven Transport Pty Ltd v Deputy Commissioner of Taxation* [2000] QSC 268, 157 FLR 26, at [23].

[111] See 7.27–7.32.

[112] *Silversafe Ltd v Hood* [2006] EWHC 1849 (Ch), [2007] STC 871; *Re ABC Ltd* [2010] EWHC 1645 (Ch), [2010] BPIR 1297.

[113] [2006] UKPC 26, [2007] 1 AC 508.

As Bowen LJ said in *Re Chapel House Colliery Co*:[114]

> The power of winding up [on a creditor's petition] was given for the benefit of a particular class, and is entrusted to the court for their benefit.

In *Re Crigglestone Coal Co Ltd*[115] Buckley J said, at pp 331–2, in relation to a creditor's petition:

> the order which the petitioner seeks is not an order for his benefit, but an order for the benefit of a class of which he is a member. The right *ex debito justitiae*[116] is not his individual right, but his representative right.

In *Re a Company (No 001573 of 1983)*[117] Harman J said, at p 495, 'The true position is that a creditor petitioning the Companies Court is invoking a class right'. In *Re Pleatfine Ltd*[118] his Lordship said, at p 103:

> winding-up petitions are a somewhat special class of litigation. There is not a true *lis* in which the petitioning creditor and the company are able to deal with the matter as they see fit. A petition invokes a class right, and the court is concerned at all times with the interests of all the members of the relevant class and the interests of the company.

In *Re Southbourne Sheet Metal Co Ltd*[119] his Lordship said, at p 364:

> a winding-up petition is not a *lis inter partes*[120] for the benefit of A as against B. It is the invoking by A of a class remedy for the benefit of himself and other members of the class. Nonetheless, it is (a) based upon a commercial interest of the person invoking the remedy, and (b) it is for the benefit of himself, amongst other members of the class.

This identifies the dual function of a creditor's winding-up petition.[121]

7.41 Although one unpaid creditor of a company has standing to petition, the actual winding-up order is made or not made at the discretion of the court in the interest of all creditors.[122]

7.42 However, in *Re Cases of Taffs Well Ltd*[123] Judge Paul Baker QC said, at p 189, that the provision for other creditors to give notice of appearance specifying whether they support or oppose the petition[124] is inconsistent with the idea of a creditor's petition as a class action. In Judge Baker's view:

> A petitioning creditor does not petition for the general good but rather in the hope of recovering his own debt or part of it.

Unpaid creditor of a solvent company

7.43 Provided there is reasonable pre-action conduct,[125] an unpaid creditor of even a substantial and prosperous company, whose debt is not disputed, is entitled to petition for its winding

---

114 (1883) 24 ChD 259 at p 270.
115 [1906] 2 Ch 327.
116 See 7.34 and 7.680–7.682.
117 [1983] BCLC 492.
118 [1983] BCLC 102.
119 [1992] BCLC 361.
120 Lawsuit between parties.
121 See 7.27–7.32.
122 See 7.698–7.733.
123 [1992] Ch 179.
124 IR 1986, r 4.16. See 5.32–5.36.
125 See 7.8–7.21.

up, even if owed only a small debt.[126] This is because a failure by a company to pay one debt is evidence that the company is unable to pay its debts.[127] Such a petition is not an abuse of process, and an application to prevent presentation or continuation of such a petition will be dismissed.[128]

7.44 It would seem to follow that a solvent company which persisted in refusing to pay an admitted creditor would be wound up compulsorily on that creditor's petition.[129] In *Re Rosbro Holdings Ltd*[130] the company refused to pay the petitioner's admitted debt because it had a cross-claim against the petitioner but it was held that in New Zealand this was not a reason for refusing a winding-up order, and the court would have made one had the company not then paid the petitioner's debt. On the other hand, in *Re Fabo Pty Ltd*[131] a full court of the Victoria Supreme Court said, at p 436, that a company will not be wound up on a creditor's petition, even if it neglects to comply with a valid statutory demand, if it establishes by independent evidence that it is solvent.[132] This did not apply in the case before the full court where the company had put in no evidence and had not participated in the proceedings in any way. In *Commissioner of State Revenue of Victoria v Roy Morgan Research Centre Pty Ltd*[133] it was accepted by the party applying for the winding-up order, that if it was clear that a company was solvent, the court would strike out an application to wind it up as an abuse of process. However, it was not clear that the company in this case was solvent and the application was allowed to proceed.

7.45 There seems to be no reported case in which a company which the court has accepted is solvent has been ordered to be wound up because it refused to pay an undisputed debt.[134] Refusal by a company to pay its debts is not a circumstance in which a company may be wound up by the court[135] and there is no point in alleging it in a winding-up petition.[136] However, there is also no reported case in which a solvent company has been able to get a winding-up petition dismissed and maintain its refusal to pay the petitioner's undisputed debt.

---

[126] *Re a Company* (1950) 94 SJ 369; *Cornhill Insurance plc v Improvement Services Ltd* [1986] 1 WLR 114; *Elite Motor Campers Australia v Leisureport Pty Ltd* (1996) 22 ACSR 235. The court's usual practice is to dismiss a creditor's winding-up petition if the existence of the petition debt is disputed on substantial grounds; see 7.529–7.535.

[127] See 7.272–7.281.

[128] *Re a Company* (1950) 94 SJ 369; *Mann v Goldstein* [1968] 1 WLR 1091 per Ungoed-Thomas J at p 1096; *Cornhill Insurance plc v Improvement Services Ltd* [1986] 1 WLR 114; *Elite Motor Campers Australia v Leisureport Pty Ltd* (1996) 22 ACSR 235.

[129] *Cowan v Scottish Publishing Co* (1892) 19 R 437; *Re South East Corporation Ltd* (1915) 23 DLR 724; *Re Barrier Reef Finance and Land Pty Ltd* [1989] 1 QdR 252. A solvent individual who fails to pay a debt may be made bankrupt (*Johnson v Tandrige* [sic] *District Council* [2007] EWHC 3325 (Ch), [2008] BPIR 405).

[130] (1987) 3 NZCLC 100,131.

[131] [1989] VR 432.

[132] Adopted by the Malaysian Federal Court in *Malaysia Air Charter Co Sdn Bhd v Petronas Dagangan Sdn Bhd* [2000] 4 MLJ 657 at p 668.

[133] (1997) 24 ACSR 73.

[134] This may be what happened in *Re Solfire Pty Ltd (No 2)* [1999] 2 QdR 182 (see p 196), in which the winding up was stayed on condition that the petitioner's debt was paid in full. There are two reported cases in which the court has ordered the winding up of a company which was in members' voluntary liquidation and therefore presumed to be solvent, but in both cases the solvency was doubted. See *Re Surplus Properties (Huddersfield) Ltd* [1984] BCLC 89 and *Re Leading Guides International Ltd* [1998] 1 BCLC 620 discussed at 10.101.

[135] IA 1986, s 122(1).

[136] *Re Bond Corporation Holdings Ltd* (1990) 1 ACSR 488 at pp 491–2.

Unnecessary to try other means of enforcement

A creditor of a company whose debt is not disputed is not required to exhaust all other **7.46** legal means of enforcing payment of the debt, or any specific means, before resorting to a winding-up petition.[137] In particular, if there are no substantial grounds for disputing a debt owed by a company, the creditor is not required to obtain a judgment for it before presenting a winding-up petition.[138] A judgment creditor is not required to attempt execution of the judgment.[139] There is no rule that a creditor's petition can only be based on non-compliance with a statutory demand.[140]

It follows from 7.46 that presentation of a winding-up petition based on non-payment of an **7.47** undisputed debt cannot be opposed by asserting that it is an abuse of process because the petitioner has a suitable alternative remedy.[141]

There is an exception in the conditions under which a member of a partnership with fewer **7.48** than eight members may be given leave to petition under the Insolvent Partnerships Order 1994 (IPO 1994), art 9, for the winding up of the partnership without also petitioning for the winding up or bankruptcy of all the partnership's members. The applicant member must have obtained a judgment, decree or order of a court against the partnership for reimbursement of a joint debt which the applicant has paid other than out of partnership property, and must have taken all reasonable steps (other than insolvency proceedings) to enforce that judgment, decree or order.[142]

Another possible exception concerns a decision of an adjudicator under the Housing **7.49** Grants, Construction and Regeneration Act 1996.[143] The appropriate way of enforcing an adjudicator's decision is by bringing enforcement proceedings seeking summary judgment under the expedited procedure in the Technology and Construction Court.[144] In the case of a decision requiring a payment by an individual, it has been said that this procedure should be followed rather than issuing a statutory demand with a view to presenting a bankruptcy petition.[145]

---

[137] *Re Mid-West Glass Co Ltd* (1931) 40 Man R 289; *Re Roma Industries Pty Ltd* (1976) 1 ACLR 296 at p 298; *Re Hong Huat Realty (M) Sdn Bhd* [1987] 2 MLJ 502 (petitioner not required to wait to see how much would be realized by enforcing its security interests in the company's property); *Re Sanpete Builders (S) Pte Ltd* [1989] 1 MLJ 393 at p 399; *Wine Grapes Marketing Board for the City of Griffith and the Shires of Leeton, Carrathool and Murrumbidgee v Griffith Vintners Pty Ltd* (1989) 1 ACSR 88 (petitioner not required to exercise its right to repossess goods it had sold subject to reservation of title).
[138] *Cornhill Insurance plc v Improvement Services Ltd* [1986] 1 WLR 114; *Re a Company (No 003079 of 1990)* [1991] BCLC 235 at pp 235–6; *Forsayth NL v Juno Securities Ltd* (1991) 4 WAR 376; *Bluehaven Transport Pty Ltd v Deputy Commissioner of Taxation* [2000] QSC 268, 157 FLR 26; *Imbangan Utama Sdn Bhd v Lotan Engineering Sdn Bhd* [2002] 2 MLJ 313; *Bank Industri dan Teknologi Malaysia Bhd v Alom Building Systems Sdn Bhd* [2006] 4 MLJ 405.
[139] *Re a Company* (1950) 94 SJ 369. *Re Stock and Share Auction and Advance Co* (1885) 2 TLR 2 is to the contrary, though in that case the debt was disputed. See 7.22.
[140] *L and D Audio Acoustics Pty Ltd v Pioneer Electronic Australia Pty Ltd* (1982) 7 ACLR 180 at p 185; *Teck Yow Brothers Hand-Bag Trading Co v Maharani Supermarket Sdn Bhd* [1989] 1 MLJ 101; *Taylors Industrial Flooring Ltd v M and H Plant Hire (Manchester) Ltd* [1990] BCLC 216. The contrary view in *Re Hunza Investments Ltd* [1988–9] CILR 1 is, with respect, wrong.
[141] *Cornhill Insurance plc v Improvement Services Ltd* [1986] 1 WLR 114 at p 118.
[142] IA 1986, s 221A(2), as modified by IPO 1994, sch 5, para 2. See 2.87.
[143] See Susan Blake, Julie Browne and Stuart Sime, *The Jackson ADR Handbook* (Oxford: Oxford University Press, 2013), chapter 26.
[144] Technology and Construction Court Guide, section 9.
[145] *Harlow and Milner Ltd v Teasdale* [2006] EWHC 54 (TCC), BAILII.

7.50   For the position where the company disputes the petitioner's debt on substantial grounds, or has a cross-claim against the petitioner which is based on substantial grounds, see 7.433–7.672.

Creditor petitioning for winding up and taking other proceedings to recover the debt

7.51   A claim seeking an order that a company is to pay a sum of money to the claimant and an application by that claimant for the company to be wound up by the court do not involve the same cause of action, for the purposes of Regulation (EU) No 1215/2012, art 29, which is concerned with parallel uncompleted proceedings in different States.[146]

7.52   If a creditor petitioner's debt is disputed on substantial grounds,[147] that dispute cannot normally be resolved in proceedings on the petition[148] and the court's usual practice is to dismiss the petition.[149] The fact that the petitioner has commenced other proceedings claiming the debt may show that it is disputed on substantial grounds.[150]

7.53   A claim for payment of an *undisputed* debt and presentation of a winding-up petition by the creditor are not mutually exclusive alternatives between which an election must be made: they can be pursued simultaneously.[151] If the winding-up order is made, the other claim against the company cannot be proceeded with unless the court gives leave.[152] The essential question, therefore, is whether there is a dispute on a substantial ground about the existence of the petitioner's debt.[153] In Australia, the court may not be able to take cognizance of a dispute where the Corporations Act 2001 (Australia), s 459S, applies.[154] So it has been necessary there to assert that it is always an abuse of process to make a claim against a company for a debt and also apply for the company to be wound up in insolvency, though applications for winding up have been dismissed on this ground only where there has in fact been a larger cross-claim by the company against the applicant[155] or a dispute about the applicant's debt.[156]

7.54   Courts have differed over whether a creditor of a company can petition for it to be wound up even though the money owed is also the subject of matrimonial proceedings between the creditor and another shareholder.[157] In one case the winding-up application was seen

---

[146]   *Citigate Dewe Rogerson Ltd v Artaban Public Affairs SPRL* [2009] EWHC 1689 (Ch), [2011] 1 BCLC 625, at [29].

[147]   See 7.444–7.514.

[148]   See 7.515–7.527.

[149]   See 7.529–7.535.

[150]   For example, *Bank of New Zealand v Rada Corporation Ltd* (1989) 5 NZCLC 66,221. See 7.498–7.511.

[151]   *Re Hong Huat Realty (M) Sdn Bhd* [1987] 2 MLJ 502; *Re Leasing and Finance Services Ltd* [1991] BCC 29; *Roy Morgan Research Centre Pty Ltd v Wilson Market Research Pty Ltd (No 2)* (1996) 20 ACSR 170; *Radiancy (Sales) Pty Ltd v Bimat Pty Ltd* [2007] NSWSC 962, 25 ACLC 1216; *Citigate Dewe Rogerson Ltd v Artaban Public Affairs SPRL* [2009] EWHC 1689 (Ch), [2011] 1 BCLC 625, at [35].

[152]   IA 1986, s 130(2).

[153]   *Citigate Dewe Rogerson Ltd v Artaban Public Affairs SPRL* [2009] EWHC 1689 (Ch), [2011] 1 BCLC 625, at [36]. See 7.433–7.672.

[154]   See 7.243.

[155]   *Murphy v Teakbridge Pty Ltd* [1999] NSWSC 1231, in which, it seems, the court did not realize that, because it was found that the statutory demand had not been served, s 459S did not apply, so the court could have found that there was a cross-claim and dismissed the application for winding up on that ground alone.

[156]   *Milano Construction Pty Ltd v JD Holdings Pty Ltd* [2001] NSWSC 899.

[157]   Such a petition was permitted in the New Zealand case of *Tracy Properties Ltd v Tracy* (1988) 3 BCR 1, but dismissed as an abuse of process in the New South Wales case of *Roberts v Wayne Roberts Concrete Constructions Pty Ltd* [2004] NSWSC 734, 185 FLR 315.

as an attempt to forestall the decision in the matrimonial proceedings.[158] But in another case it was observed that any property recovered by the petitioner in the winding up would have to be brought into account in the matrimonial proceedings.[159] It may be essential to conduct a winding up as well as matrimonial proceedings if there are third-party interests in the company.

Exceptionally, winding up cannot be applied for under a liability order in respect of a **7.55** non-domestic rate, council tax or BID levy[160] while steps by way of taking control of goods or, in relation to council tax, charging (or other remedies which do not appear to be applicable to companies) are being taken against the company.[161] The same provision was made in relation to community charges.[162] Where a company is one of two or more persons jointly liable for non-domestic rate or BID levy, and a liability order has been made against the company and one or more of the other persons jointly liable, and a warrant of commitment is issued against (or a term of imprisonment is fixed in the case of) one of the other persons, no steps may be taken by way of winding up against the company in relation to the amount for which the warrant was made.[163]

Undisputed creditor may petition to force settlement

It is not an abuse of process for an unpaid undisputed creditor of a company to petition for **7.56** its compulsory winding up knowing that it is likely that the matter will be settled without a winding-up order being made. In *Re St Thomas' Dock Co*[164] Jessel MR said, at pp 118–19, that presenting a winding-up petition for an undisputed debt 'with the idea... of getting paid by reason of the company not daring to meet the threat or risk of being wound up' was not the 'primary use' of a winding-up petition, though his Lordship would not say that it was an illegitimate use.

Juridical Classification of Creditors' Petitions Alleging Inability to Pay Debts

Juridical classification of winding-up petitions

For discussion of the juridical classification of winding-up petitions generally see 2.12–2.19. **7.57**

Not a claim for payment of a debt

The view of a creditor's winding-up petition alleging inability to pay debts as an individual **7.58** remedy is a description of one aspect of the proceeding rather than a legal categorization of it. Presentation of a winding-up petition by a creditor does not raise substantially the same question or issue as a claim for payment of the debt and therefore should not be characterized as a duplication of proceedings, implying that the winding-up petition should be stayed in favour

---

[158] *Roberts v Wayne Roberts Concrete Constructions Pty Ltd.*
[159] *Tracy Properties Ltd v Tracy* at p 5.
[160] BID levy is imposed in a business improvement district in which BID arrangements are in force under the Local Government Act 2003, part 4.
[161] Non-Domestic Rating (Collection and Enforcement) (Local Lists) Regulations 1989 (SI 1989/1058), reg 19(2); Council Tax (Administration and Enforcement) Regulations 1992 (SI 1992/613), reg 52(2); Business Improvement Districts (England) Regulations 2004 (SI 2004/2443), sch 4, para 9; Business Improvement Districts (Wales) Regulations 2005 (SI 2005/1312), sch 4, para 9.
[162] Community Charges (Administration and Enforcement) Regulations 1989 (SI 1989/438), reg 46(2).
[163] Non-Domestic Rating (Collection and Enforcement) (Miscellaneous Provisions) Regulations 1990 (SI 1990/145), reg 4(9); SI 2004/2443, sch 4, para 13(8); SI 2005/1312, sch 4, para 13(8). It is unclear why the same provision is not made in relation to council tax.
[164] (1876) 2 ChD 116.

of the claim: the issues on the winding-up petition are whether the company is unable to pay its debts and whether the court should in its discretion make a winding-up order; the issue in the claim is whether the company owes the debt.[165] It makes no difference that the company has a cross-claim against the petitioner which will be a factor which the court hearing the winding-up petition will have to take into consideration and also will be considered by the court hearing the claim on an application to stay judgment.[166]

7.59   A winding-up petition is not a claim or counterclaim[167] and does not seek a money judgment[168] or a judgment which can be executed.[169] Proceedings to obtain a judgment ordering a company to pay money and a petition to wind up the company for not complying with the judgment are different actions, causes or matters.[170]

Not execution or enforcement

7.60   A creditor's winding-up petition is 'not infrequently misdescribed as a form of debt enforcement'.[171] Presenting a petition to wind up a company is not in any meaningful sense a proceeding to enforce an obligation of the company.[172] The presentation by a company's judgment creditor of a petition to wind up the company is not a proceeding to execution on a judgment or order, nor is it an enforcement of a judgment or order, because a winding-up order is for the benefit of all creditors and may be obtained whether the petitioner has a judgment or not.[173] A judgment creditor's petition is not a writ of execution to enforce the judgment and so does not require permission under CPR, r 83.2.[174] Therefore a stay of execution of a judgment against a company does not preclude the judgment creditor from petitioning for the company to be wound up[175]—a judgment debt is still due despite a stay of execution.[176]

7.61   The presentation of a petition to wind up a company based on non-payment of an arbitration award against the company in the petitioner's favour is not an enforcement of the arbitration award[177] and so does not require leave under the Arbitration Act 1996, s 66.[178]

7.62   An application by a secured creditor of a company to wind up the company is not an action to enforce the security.[179]

---

[165] *Re Leasing and Finance Services Ltd* [1991] BCC 29.

[166] *Re Leasing and Finance Services Ltd*.

[167] *Best Beat Ltd v Rossall* [2006] EWHC 1494 (Comm), [2006] BPIR 1357.

[168] *Her Majesty's Revenue and Customs v Egleton* [2006] EWHC 2313 (Ch), [2007] Bus LR 44, at [15].

[169] *Re a Company (No 00928 of 1991)* [1991] BCLC 514 at p 517.

[170] *Re Peretz Co Ltd* [1965] Ch 200.

[171] *HM Revenue and Customs v Egleton* [2006] EWHC 2313 (Ch), [2007] Bus LR 44, per Briggs J at [15].

[172] *Satinland Finance Sàrl v BNP Paribas Trust Corporation UK Ltd* [2010] EWHC 3062 (Ch), [2011] Bus LR D96, at [42].

[173] *Re World of Golf Ltd* (1914) 59 SJ 7; *Re a Company (No 0022 of 1915)* [1915] 1 Ch 520; *Re Parker Davies and Hughes Ltd* [1953] 1 WLR 1349; *Maril-Rionebel (M) Sdn Bhd v Perdana Merchant Bankers Bhd* [2001] 4 MLJ 187; but it is deemed to be so for the purposes of ss 2 and 3(3) of the Reserve and Auxiliary Forces (Protection of Civil Interests) Act 1951 by s 3(9) of that Act.

[174] *Wangsini Sdn Bhd v Grand United Holdings Bhd* [1998] 5 MLJ 345.

[175] *Deputy Commissioner of Taxation (WA) v Mobile Homes of Australia Pty Ltd* (1986) 19 ATR 183; *Australian Beverage Distributors Pty Ltd v Evans and Tate Premium Wines Pty Ltd* [2007] NSWCA 57, 61 ACSR 441; *Mikien Sdn Bhd v Woolley Development Sdn Bhd* [2008] 1 MLJ 823.

[176] *Woodley v Woodley (No 2)* [1994] 1 WLR 1167; *Australian Beverage Distributors Pty Ltd v Evans and Tate Premium Wines Pty Ltd* [2007] NSWCA 57, 61 ACSR 441.

[177] *Re Ghelani Impex Ltd* [1975] EA 197; *Re International Tin Council* [1989] Ch 309.

[178] *Re Ghelani Impex Ltd* [1975] EA 197.

[179] *Australian Cherry Exports Ltd v Commonwealth Bank of Australia* (1996) 132 FLR 266.

In Singapore in *Re Makin Nominees Pte Ltd*[180] Lim Teong Qwee JC questioned the con- **7.63**
clusion reached in *Re a Company (No 0022 of 1915)*[181] and said that the better view is that
whether or not a winding-up petition by a judgment creditor infringes a rule forbidding
enforcement of the judgment depends on the construction of the rule.

Not an action on a judgment

A petition by a judgment creditor is not an action upon the judgment for the purposes of **7.64**
the Limitation Act 1980, s 24.[182]

Founded on, but not enforcement of, a contract under which the petition debt was incurred

The petition of a creditor whose debt is a simple contract debt is an action founded on simple **7.65**
contract for the purposes of the Limitation Act 1980, s 5.[183]

Presentation of a petition by a creditor of a company whose debt arose under a contract is **7.66**
not an enforcement of the contract,[184] though Canadian courts have differed on whether it
is 'in respect of' the contract.[185]

Presentation of a petition by a creditor of a company whose debt arose under a contract in **7.67**
which there is an arbitration clause is not the commencement of an action upon a dispute
or difference about a matter arising under the contract which must be referred to arbitration: the petition is presented because the company is unable to pay its debts, not because
of a dispute over the contract.[186]

Means of obtaining payment

The interest that a person who is owed a debt by a company has in petitioning for its winding **7.68**
up is the possibility that some or all of the debt will be paid, by a dividend in the winding
up or to prevent the petition proceeding. A winding-up petition is, therefore, a means of
obtaining payment of a debt,[187] in the sense that it is one of the options afforded by the law
to a creditor who cannot obtain payment.[188] It is an option that can be used when other
processes (such as execution) are unproductive.[189]

Remedy

A creditor's winding-up petition is a 'remedy' for a debt which is transferred by legal assign- **7.69**
ment of the debt under the Law of Property Act 1925, s 136(1).[190]

---

[180] [1994] 3 SLR 429.
[181] [1915] 1 Ch 520.
[182] *Ridgeway Motors (Isleworth) Ltd v ALTS Ltd* [2005] EWCA Civ 92, [2005] 1 WLR 2871, overruling *Re
a Debtor (No 50A-SD-1995)* [1997] Ch 310 and *Bruton v Commissioners of Inland Revenue* [2000] BPIR 946.
[183] *Re Cases of Taffs Well Ltd* [1992] Ch 179 at p 188.
[184] *FCOS Finance Ltd v Colway Farms Ltd* (1990) 5 NZCLC 66,888 at p 66,902.
[185] In *Re Nelson Ford Lumber Co* (1908) 1 Sask LR 108 and in *Re Canadian Fibre Wood and Manufacturing
Co Ltd* (1913) 4 OWN 1183 it was held that it is; in *Re Nelson Ford Lumber Co* (1908) 8 WLR 546 it was held
that it is not. Remarkably, the two *Nelson Ford Lumber Co* cases seem to be about different petitions against
one company by the same creditor.
[186] See 7.25.
[187] *Re a Company (No 0022 of 1915)* [1915] 1 Ch 520; *Investment Invoice Financing Ltd v Limehouse Board
Mills Ltd* [2006] EWCA Civ 9, [2006] 1 WLR 985, at [40].
[188] *Re Roma Industries Pty Ltd* (1976) 1 ACLR 296 at p 298.
[189] *Re South East Corporation Ltd* (1915) 23 DLR 724 at p 725.
[190] *Re Premier Permanent Building Land and Investment Association, ex parte Stewart* (1890) 16 VLR 20.

Recovery

7.70 A power to 'recover' money owed by a company is normally a power to obtain satisfaction of the debt through any available legal proceedings, and so includes a power to apply for the company to be wound up by the court.[191] A winding-up petition by a person owed a sum recoverable by statute (for example, rates) is a proceeding to 'recover' that sum for the purposes of the Limitation Act 1980, s 9(1).[192] A petition by a solicitor based on unpaid costs is a proceeding to recover the costs, even where they are subject to assessment.[193] A person given power of attorney to 'recover' a debt owed by a company may do so by petitioning for its winding up.[194] But a winding-up petition is not recovery by proceedings in which summary judgment may be sought.[195]

7.71 Petitioning for a debtor company to be wound up falls within taking possession of, collecting and protecting the creditor's assets.[196]

Giving effect to judgment or order

7.72 It has been held that bankruptcy proceedings brought by a judgment creditor against the judgment debtor 'give effect to' the judgment because they give the creditor an opportunity to obtain at least partial payment of the judgment debt.[197] Clearly the same applies to winding-up proceedings.

In respect of the creditor's debt

7.73 A petition by a creditor is 'in respect of' the creditor's debt, even if the petition is under the just and equitable clause.[198]

Proof of Inability to Pay Debts

Meaning of 'Unable to Pay its Debts'

Legislative definition of inability to pay debts

7.74 A company may be wound up by the court if it is 'unable to pay its debts'.[199] IA 1986, s 123 (in relation to registered companies) and ss 222–224 (in relation to unregistered companies), state a number of circumstances in which a company is deemed unable to pay its debts. The phrase 'unable to pay its debts' is used in the British legislation on winding up companies rather than the term 'insolvent', though that term is used (without definition) in IPO 1994 and was used in the Life Assurance Companies Act 1870, s 21. In Australia, the term 'unable to pay its debts' was replaced by 'insolvent' by the Corporate Law Reform Act 1992 (Australia)[200] and a company is defined to be insolvent if it is not able to pay all its debts as and when they become due and payable.[201]

---

191 *Bluehaven Transport Pty Ltd v Deputy Commissioner of Taxation* [2000] QSC 268, 157 FLR 26.
192 *Re Karnos Property Co Ltd* [1989] BCLC 340.
193 *Re Laceward Ltd* [1981] 1 WLR 133.
194 *Re Gilbert Machinery Co (No 1)* (1906) 26 NZLR 47.
195 *Re a Company (No 00928 of 1991)* [1991] BCLC 514 at p 517.
196 *Re Emeritus Pty Ltd* [1968] 1 NSWR 458.
197 *Re a Debtor (No 68/SD/97)* [1998] 4 All ER 779, which concerned an order for costs.
198 *Re Peter Dynes Esq International Ltd* (1988) 4 NZCLC 64,906.
199 IA 1986, s 122(1)(f) (registered companies) and s 221(5)(b) (unregistered companies).
200 See now the Corporations Act 2001 (Australia), ss 95A and 459A.
201 Corporations Act 2001 (Australia), s 95A.

Which debts must be considered?

In relation to the winding up of a company, 'debt' is defined in the Insolvency Rules 1986 **7.75**
(IR 1986), r 13.12, as follows:

13.12 'Debt', 'liability' (winding up)
(1) 'Debt', in relation to the winding up of a company, means (subject to the next paragraph) any of the following—
  (a) any debt or liability to which the company is subject—
    (i) in the case of a winding up which was not immediately preceded by an administration, at the date on which the company went into liquidation;[202]
    (ii) in the case of a winding up which was immediately preceded by an administration, at the date on which the company entered administration;
  (b) any debt or liability to which the company may become subject after that date by reason of any obligation incurred before that date; and
  (c) any interest provable as mentioned in Rule 4.93(1).[203]
(2) For the purposes of any provision of [IA 1986] or [IR 1986] about winding up, any liability in tort is a debt provable in the winding up, if either—
  (a) the cause of action has accrued—
    (i) in the case of a winding up which was not immediately preceded by an administration, at the date on which the company went into liquidation;
    (ii) in the case of a winding up which was immediately preceded by an administration, at the date on which the company entered administration; or
  (b) all the elements necessary to establish the cause of action exist at that date except for actionable damage.
(3) For the purposes of references in any provision of [IA 1986] or [IR 1986] about winding up to a debt or liability, it is immaterial whether the debt or liability is present or future, whether it is certain or contingent, or whether its amount is fixed or liquidated, or is capable of being ascertained by fixed rules or as a matter of opinion; and references in any such provision to owing a debt are to be read accordingly.
(4) In any provision of [IA 1986] or [IR 1986] about winding up, except in so far as the context otherwise requires, 'liability' means (subject to paragraph (3) above) a liability to pay money or money's worth, including any liability under an enactment, any liability for breach of trust, any liability in contract, tort or bailment, and any liability arising out of an obligation to make restitution.
(5) This Rule shall apply where a company is in administration and shall be read as if—
  (a) references to winding up were references to administration,
  (b) references to administration were references to winding up,
  (c) references to going into liquidation were references to entering administration, and
  (d) references to entering administration were references to going into liquidation.

The definition, apart from para (5), also applies to a bank insolvency[204] and a building **7.76**
society insolvency.[205] In relation to a relevant scheme,[206] a reference to a debt or liability
of a company is to be read as a reference to a debt or liability of the relevant scheme;[207] a

---

[202] Unless it is already in voluntary liquidation, a company goes into liquidation when a winding-up order is made; see 5.304–5.305.
[203] Interest payable on a proved debt up to the date the company went into liquidation or administration.
[204] Bank Insolvency (England and Wales) Rules 2009 (SI 2009/356), r 291. Necessary terminological adaptations are made by r 3(3)(b) and (4)(a), (b), (f), (g) and (m).
[205] Building Society Insolvency (England and Wales) Rules 2010 (SI 2010/2581), r 283. Necessary terminological adaptations are made by r 3(5)(b) and (6)(a), (b), (c), (h), (i) and (o).
[206] See 1.168.
[207] SI 2013/1388, sch 3, part 1, para 2(h).

reference to a debt is a reference to any debt or obligation incurred for the purposes of, or in connection with, the acquisition, management or disposal of property subject to the relevant scheme;[208] and a reference to a liability is a reference to any liability (including any contingent or prospective liability) of the participants in the relevant scheme for a debt of the relevant scheme.[209]

7.77 Debts due to members of the company must be taken into account,[210] but share capital contributed by members is not a debt due from the company to the members.[211] A preference dividend, though in arrear, is not a liability until it is declared.[212]

7.78 In an article, Chief Registrar Baister has said that IR 1986, r 13.12, applies for the purpose of determining whether a company is unable to pay its debts.[213] However, it might be argued that the rule is expressed to apply to the winding up of a company and that the hearing of a winding-up petition is not part of the winding up.[214] Nevertheless, it is difficult to see how a company can persuade a court to ignore anything comprehended by r 13.12 when determining whether the company is unable to pay its debts. In particular, the court is expressly required to take into account contingent and prospective liabilities.[215] The company can require the court to value future and contingent debts to reflect their futurity and contingency and in practice it may be so difficult to do this rationally that a petitioner relying on future and contingent debts to show insolvency will be unable to discharge the burden of proof.[216] Usually, the court can determine that a company is unable to pay its debts using statutory tests which require consideration of only one debt, namely the one that has not been paid to the petitioner, and that debt must be one that is presently due and payable.[217] See further 7.309–7.432.

Rates, council tax, BID levy and community infrastructure levy

7.79 Where a liability order in respect of a non-domestic rate has been made against a company, the 'amount due' is deemed to be a debt for the purposes of IA 1986, s 122(1)(f) and s 221(5)(b).[218] In this context, 'amount due' means 'an amount equal to any outstanding sum which is or forms part of the amount in respect of which the liability order was made'.[219] These provisions are applied to the enforcement of BID levy.[220] The same

---

[208] SI 2013/1388, reg 17(1)(b)(ii).

[209] SI 2013/1388, reg 17(1)(b)(iii).

[210] *Re G Minerals Ltd* (1967) 10 CBR NS 281.

[211] *Re United Canneries of British Columbia Ltd* (1903) 9 BCR 528; *Re Great West Brick and Coal Co Ltd* (1916) 9 Sask LR 240; and see 8.110–8.111.

[212] *Re Farmers' Oil and Supply Co Ltd* [1944] 3 WWR 110.

[213] Chief Registrar Baister, 'Winding up: the basics' (2008) 1 Corporate Rescue and Insolvency 7.

[214] For what may not be part of the winding up of a company see 1.26 and 5.294–5.298.

[215] See 7.81–7.82.

[216] See *BNY Corporate Trustee Services Ltd v Eurosail-UK 2007-3BL plc* [2013] UKSC 28, [2013] 1 WLR 1408.

[217] IA 1986, ss 123(1)(a) and 222(1) (failure to comply with a statutory demand; see 7.125–7.247) and 123(1)(b) and 224(1)(a) (unsatisfied execution; see 7.248–7.253).

[218] Non-Domestic Rating (Collection and Enforcement) (Local Lists) Regulations 1989 (SI 1989/1058), reg 18(2) as amended by the Non-Domestic Rating (Collection and Enforcement) (Miscellaneous Provisions) Regulations 1990 (SI 1990/145), reg 7(4).

[219] SI 1989/1058, reg 18(3).

[220] Business Improvement Districts (England) Regulations 2004 (SI 2004/2443), sch 4, para 9; Business Improvement Districts (Wales) Regulations 2005 (SI 2005/1312), sch 4, para 9.

provisions are made in relation to council tax[221] and community infrastructure levy,[222] and were made in relation to community charges.[223] These provisions do not mean that amounts due are not debts for any other purposes.[224] Due and unpaid non-domestic rates, BID levy and council tax are debts for the purposes of IA 1986, ss 122(1)(f) and 221(5)(b), even if a liability order has not been made.[225]

Where a liability order for non-domestic rate or BID levy is made against partners in their **7.80** firm name SI 1989/1058, reg 18(2), has effect as if the reference to a company included a reference to the partnership and the reference to IA 1986, s 221(5)(b), were a reference to the equivalent point in s 221 as modified by IPO 1994.[226] The equivalent provisions are IA 1986, s 221(7)(b), as modified by IPO 1994, sch 3, para 3 (petition under art 7 of the Order), and IA 1986, s 221(8), as modified by IPO 1994, sch 4, para 3 (petition under art 8 of the Order).

Future and contingent debts

Unless the meaning of the phrase 'is unable to pay its debts' is expanded by legislation, the **7.81** phrase refers only to debts presently due and payable, not debts payable in the future.[227] In *Re European Life Assurance Society* James V-C said, at p 127:

> I apprehend that [counsel for the company sought to be wound up] is right in his construction, that inability to pay debts must refer to debts absolutely due—that is to say, debts for which a creditor may go at once to the company's office and demand payment.

Since *Re European Life Assurance Society* was decided, the lists of circumstances in which a **7.82** company is deemed unable to pay its debts have been expanded. Now a company is deemed unable to pay its debts if it is proved to the satisfaction of the court that the company is unable to pay its debts *as they fall due*,[228] and to decide this the court may take into account the company's ability to pay debts payable in the reasonably near future[229] though not, it seems, contingent debts.[230] And a company is deemed unable to pay its debts if it is proved that the value of its assets is less than the amount of its liabilities, taking into account its prospective and contingent liabilities.[231] The effect of these provisions is that a company can be deemed to be unable to pay its debts by taking into account prospective or contingent debts which could otherwise not be taken into account.

---

[221] Council Tax (Administration and Enforcement) Regulations 1992 (SI 1992/613), reg 49(2) and (3).
[222] Community Infrastructure Levy Regulations 2010 (SI 2010/948), reg 105.
[223] Community Charges (Administration and Enforcement) Regulations 1989 (SI 1989/438), reg 43(2) and (3), though these regulations did not mention IA 1986, s 221(5)(b).
[224] *Preston Borough Council v Riley* [1995] BCC 700.
[225] *Bolsover District Council v Ashfield Nominees Ltd* [2010] EWCA Civ 1129, [2011] Bus LR 492, at [10].
[226] Non-Domestic Rating (Collection and Enforcement) (Miscellaneous Provisions) Regulations 1990 (SI 1990/145), reg 5(5), where the references are to IPO 1986 and must be further adapted to refer to IPO 1994 by applying the Interpretation Act 1978, ss 17(2)(a) and 23(1) and (2); SI 2004/2443, sch 4, para 14(5); SI 2005/1312, sch 4, para 14(5), where the references are erroneous, apparently because the paragraph is a copy of SI 1990/145, reg 5(5), with only the date of the IPO changed (the same error in SI 2004/2443 has been corrected by amendment).
[227] *Re European Life Assurance Society* (1869) LR 9 Eq 122; *Re a Debtor (No 17 of 1966)* [1967] Ch 590.
[228] IA 1986, s 123(1)(e) (registered companies) and s 224(1)(d) (unregistered companies); see 7.254–7.283.
[229] *BNY Corporate Trustee Services Ltd v Eurosail-UK 2007-3BL plc* [2013] UKSC 28, [2013] 1 WLR 1408, at [37].
[230] *JSF Finance and Currency Exchange Co Ltd v Akma Solutions Inc* [2001] 2 BCLC 307.
[231] IA 1986, s 123(2) (in relation to registered companies); s 224(2) (in relation to unregistered companies). See 7.284–7.292.

Tests

7.83 Various tests are used by accountants to assess an accounting entity's ability to pay its debts. Two factors have to be considered: the size of the debts and the time at which they must be paid.

7.84 The so-called 'balance sheet test' considers whether the entity's assets as recorded in its balance sheet for a particular date are less than its liabilities as so recorded: if assets are less than liabilities, the entity is unable to pay its debts on the balance sheet test. Using this test, a company may be deemed to be unable to pay its debts under IA 1986, s 123(2) (if it is a registered company) or s 224(2) (if it is unregistered).[232]

7.85 The balance sheet of a company which a creditor may inspect at Companies House is inevitably a historical document describing the company's financial position at the end of the last financial year, or the one before last. Unless a creditor of a company can persuade its directors to disclose more up-to-date management accounts (or has a contractual right to insist on receiving copies), it is impossible to discover whether or not a company is currently unable to pay its debts on the balance sheet test. Generally, the only indication that persons dealing with a company have of its inability to pay its debts is that it actually ceases to pay them.

7.86 Accordingly IA 1986 allows for inability to pay debts to be assessed either by the 'cash flow test'—inability to pay debts as they fall due (also known as the 'liquidity test')—or the more stringent 'non-payment test'—failure to pay one due debt when demanded.

7.87 IA 1986 makes the liquidity and non-payment tests available in winding-up proceedings by provisions under which a company is deemed to be unable to pay its debts if it is unable to pay its debts as they fall due[233] or if it fails to pay one due debt when demanded.[234] It has also been held that failure to pay one debt when due is proof of inability to pay debts as they fall due.[235] This makes the non-payment test a substitute for the liquidity test, and, in practice, the non-payment test is the one normally relied on to demonstrate that a company is unable to pay its debts.

7.88 The balance sheet test also has the disadvantage that the value of assets recorded in the balance sheet is only an estimate which may not be achieved if it is necessary to liquidate the assets in order to pay debts. The non-payment test is therefore the crucial test, and a company may be wound up for failing to meet the non-payment test even though it is apparently solvent on the balance sheet test.[236]

7.89 In *Re National Funds Assurance Co Ltd*[237] Jessel MR referred, at p 1066, to 'the ordinary commercial meaning' of the term 'insolvent' (as used in the Life Assurance Companies Act 1870, s 21) 'that [an insolvent company] is unable to meet the current demands of its

---

[232] See 7.284–7.292.

[233] s 123(1)(e) (registered companies); s 224(1)(d) (unregistered companies).

[234] s 123(1)(a)–(d) (registered companies); ss 222, 223 and 224(1)(a)–(c) (unregistered companies).

[235] *Taylors Industrial Flooring Ltd v M and H Plant Hire (Manchester) Ltd* [1990] BCLC 216; see 7.272–7.281.

[236] *Re Gem Sapphires (Aust) Pty Ltd* (1974) 8 ACLR 225; *Re Sunshine Securities (Pte) Ltd* [1978] 1 MLJ 57; *Sri Hartamas Development Sdn Bhd v MBf Finance Bhd* [1992] 1 MLJ 313; *Re Minrealm Ltd* [2007] EWHC 3078 (Ch), [2008] 2 BCLC 141.

[237] (1876) 24 WR 1066.

creditors'. This is a version of the liquidity test using ability to pay demanded debts rather than due debts and it acknowledges the commercial reality that creditors often do not demand payment of debts until after they are due for payment. Inability to meet current demands is often described as 'commercial insolvency'.

Burden of Proof

On the hearing of a winding-up petition alleging inability to pay debts, the onus is on **7.90** the petitioner to prove that the company is unable to pay its debts (to the civil standard of proof on balance of probabilities), not on the company to prove its solvency.[238] Therefore, the petitioner must provide evidence of the company's inability to pay its debts: an unsupported assertion in the petition that the company is unable to pay its debts is insufficient.[239] The company's evidence that it is solvent would ordinarily be sufficient to rebut such a bare assertion.[240] The court must allow the company a proper chance to prepare and present its case, if necessary directing a provisional liquidator to allow access to the company's accounting records.[241]

Failure of a company to appear at the hearing of a petition to wind it up on the ground of its **7.91** inability to pay its debts may be evidence that it is unable to pay its debts.[242] In practice, if the company does not contact the court office seeking an opportunity to file evidence, and there is no attendance on the company's behalf when the petition is heard, the company will be wound up unless there is a defect in the proceedings that the court is not prepared to waive.

Methods of Proving a Company is Unable to Pay its Debts

Registered companies

IA 1986, s 123, states a number of circumstances in which a registered company 'is deemed **7.92** unable to pay its debts'. The circumstances mentioned in s 123(1)(a)–(d) are circumstances which will have occurred before the presentation of the petition (or its subsequent amendment by a substituted petitioner) and which must be proved to have occurred by evidence to the court. Deemed inability to pay debts occurs under s 123(1)(e) or (2) when insolvency is proved to the satisfaction of the court at the hearing.

The text of s 123 is as follows: **7.93**

123 Definition of inability to pay debts
(1) A company is deemed unable to pay its debts—

---

[238] *Re Wheal Lovell Mining Co* (1849) 1 Mac & G 1 per Lord Cottenham LC at p 21; *La Société des Arts du Canada v Prévost* (1910) 20 Que KB 227 at p 234; *Tecma Pty Ltd v Solah Blue Metal Pty Ltd* (1988) 14 ACLR 358 per Young J at p 360; *Australian Mid-Eastern Club Ltd v Yassim* (1989) 1 ACSR 399 at p 404; *Lim Tok Chiow v Dian Tong Credit and Development Sdn Bhd* [1994] 2 MLJ 345 at p 348; *Commonwealth Bank of Australia v Individual Homes Pty Ltd* (1994) 119 ACTR 1 at p 7; *BNY Corporate Trustee Services Ltd v Eurosail-UK 2007-3BL plc* [2013] UKSC 28, [2013] 1 WLR 1408, at [37].
[239] Per Lord Craighill in *Macdonell's Trustees v Oregonian Railway Co Ltd* (1884) 11 R 912 at p 920; *Re Eldorado Union Store Co* (1886) 18 NSR 514.
[240] *Re Gold Hill Mines* (1883) 23 ChD 210 per Lindley LJ at pp 214–15; *National Mutual Life Association of Alasia Ltd v Oasis Developments Pty Ltd* (1983) 7 ACLR 758 at pp 761–2; *General Welding and Construction Co (Qld) Pty Ltd v International Rigging (Aust) Pty Ltd* (1983) [1983] 2 QdR 568.
[241] *Re Armour Insurance Co Ltd* [1993] 1 HKLR 179.
[242] *Re Vendas (Wholesale) Pty Ltd* (1991) 5 ACSR 447.

(a) if a creditor (by assignment or otherwise) to whom the company is indebted in a sum exceeding £750 then due has served on the company, by leaving it at the company's registered office, a written demand (in the prescribed form) requiring the company to pay the sum so due and the company has for three weeks thereafter neglected to pay the sum or to secure or compound for it to the reasonable satisfaction of the creditor, or

(b) if, in England and Wales, execution or other process issued on a judgment, decree or order of any court in favour of a creditor of the company is returned unsatisfied in whole or in part, or

(c) if, in Scotland, the induciae of a charge for payment on an extract decree, or an extract registered bond, or an extract registered protest, have expired without payment being made, or[243]

(d) if, in Northern Ireland, a certificate of unenforceability has been granted in respect of a judgment against the company, or

(e) if it is proved to the satisfaction of the court that the company is unable to pay its debts as they fall due.

(2) A company is also deemed unable to pay its debts if it is proved to the satisfaction of the court that the value of the company's assets is less than the amount of its liabilities, taking into account its contingent and prospective liabilities.

(3) The money sum for the time being specified in subsection (1)(a) is subject to increase or reduction by order under section 416 in part 15.

Section 123 creates six separate methods of proof

7.94 Paragraphs (a), (b), (c), (d) and (e) of IA 1986, s 123(1), and s 123(2) are six separate ways of establishing a company's inability to pay its debts: a petitioner may rely on any one or more of them.[244]

7.95 In *Re Turf Enterprises Pty Ltd*[245] the petition alleged a neglect to pay on a statutory demand. It was found that the debt demanded was not owed to the person who made the demand so that there was no neglect to comply with it. The court decided the dispute about the debt when hearing the petition[246] and heard oral evidence, during which the company's insolvency was admitted in cross-examination. It was held that this evidence was admissible to determine whether the company was unable to pay its debts. The person who was found to be the true creditor for the petition debt was substituted as petitioner and permitted to amend the petition, on which a winding-up order was made. But in *Ng Tai Tuan v Chng Gim Huat Pte Ltd*,[247] in which the petition alleged only neglect to pay on a statutory demand, the court refused to consider an affidavit alleging the company's general insolvency which had been filed too late for the company to have an adequate opportunity to rebut.

7.96 There is no requirement that a particular method of proof must be used by any particular petitioners. A petitioner with a debt presently due does not have to serve a statutory

---

[243] Paragraphs (c) and (d) of s 123(1) do not apply to a charitable incorporated organization (Charitable Incorporated Organisations (Insolvency and Dissolution) Regulations 2012 (SI 2012/3013), sch, para 1(7)).

[244] *Teck Yow Brothers Hand-Bag Trading Co v Maharani Supermarket Sdn Bhd* [1989] 1 MLJ 101; *Weng Wah Construction Co Sdn Bhd v Yik Foong Development Sdn Bhd* [1994] 2 MLJ 266.

[245] [1975] QdR 266.

[246] See 7.526.

[247] [1991] 1 MLJ 338.

demand.[248] A petitioner who is a judgment creditor does not have to levy execution.[249] A petitioner holding a dishonoured bill of exchange in Scotland does not have to protest it.[250]

A company is deemed unable to pay its debts if any one of the six circumstances is **7.97** proved and even though one or more of the other circumstances cannot be proved. In particular, a company which fails to comply with a statutory demand or is proved to be unable to pay its debts as they fall due is deemed to be unable to pay its debts even though, according to its balance sheet, its assets are larger than its liabilities.[251] This reflects the fact that failure to pay an undisputed debt when it is demanded is a more crucial test of insolvency than whether liabilities exceed assets, because there is always doubt whether assets will achieve their stated value if they have to be sold to meet liabilities.[252] In practice a company whose assets are greater than liabilities should be able to borrow money to pay debts as they fall due, and the fact that a company is able to pay its debts only with borrowed money does not show that it is unable to pay its debts.[253] In *Malayan Plant (Pte) Ltd v Moscow Narodny Bank Ltd*[254] the Privy Council (per Lord Edmund-Davies) described as 'impeccable' the following statement commenting on what is now IA 1986, s 123(1)(a)–(d) (failure to comply with statutory demand; failure of execution):

> The particular indications of insolvency mentioned in [s 123(1)(a) to (d)] are all instances of commercial insolvency, that is of the company being unable to meet current demands upon it. In such a case it is useless to say that if its assets are realized there will be ample to pay 20 shillings in the pound; this is not the test. A company may be at the same time insolvent and wealthy. It may have wealth locked up in investments not presently realisable; but although this be so, yet if it have not assets available to meet its current liabilities it is commercially insolvent and may be wound up.[255]

Discretion whether to order winding up remains

The fact that a company is deemed unable to pay its debts does not take away the court's **7.98** discretion whether to order the company to be wound up.[256] For the principles on which that discretion is exercised in relation to creditors' petitions see 7.674–7.741.

---

[248] *Teck Yow Brothers Hand-Bag Trading Co v Maharani Supermarket Sdn Bhd* [1989] 1 MLJ 101; *Taylors Industrial Flooring Ltd v M and H Plant Hire (Manchester) Ltd* [1990] BCLC 216. The contrary view in *Re Hunza Investments Ltd* [1988–9] CILR 1 is, with respect, wrong.

[249] *Re Flagstaff Silver Mining Co of Utah* (1875) LR 20 Eq 268; *Re Yate Collieries and Limeworks Co* [1883] WN 171; *Re Lyric Club* (1892) 36 SJ 801.

[250] *Gandy* 1912 2 SLT 276.

[251] *Re Gem Sapphires (Aust) Pty Ltd* (1974) 8 ACLR 225; *Re Sunshine Securities (Pte) Ltd* [1978] 1 MLJ 57; *Sri Hartamas Development Sdn Bhd v MBf Finance Bhd* [1992] 1 MLJ 313, in which the company claimed to own land worth more than M$500 million but was wound up for failure to pay a debt of M$5 million; *Re Minrealm Ltd* [2007] EWHC 3078 (Ch), [2008] 2 BCLC 141.

[252] See 7.88.

[253] *Re a Company (No 006794 of 1983)* [1986] BCLC 261.

[254] [1980] 2 MLJ 53 at p 54.

[255] *Buckley on the Companies Acts*, 14th edn (London: Butterworths, 1981), p 534. The Privy Council cited the same passage in the previous edition, but omitted the first sentence. Applied in *Sri Hartamas Development Sdn Bhd v MBf Finance Bhd* [1992] 1 MLJ 313 and *Sri Binaraya Sdn Bhd v Golden Approach Sdn Bhd* [2000] 3 MLJ 465.

[256] *Re Derrygarrif Investments Pty Ltd* (1982) 6 ACLR 751; *Re Pardoo Nominees Pty Ltd* [1987] TasR 1 at p 4.

Paragraphs with full commentary on the statutory methods of proof

7.99 Full commentary on the various statutory methods of proving the inability of a registered company to pay its debts is provided in the following paragraphs of this work:

IA 1986, section	Method	Commentary in
123(1)(a)	Statutory demand	7.125–7.247
123(1)(b)	Unsatisfied execution	7.248–7.253
123(1)(e)	Cash-flow test	7.254–7.283
123(2)	Assets less than liabilities	7.284–7.292

Is section 123 an exclusive definition of inability to pay debts?

7.100 The six methods of proving inability to pay debts provided by IA 1986, s 123, are very wide-ranging and convenient, but it is difficult to decide whether s 123 should be construed to mean that a petitioner who wishes to establish a company's inability to pay its debts can do so *only* in the ways specified in s 123 or whether any admissible evidence can be used to satisfy the court that the company is, as a matter of fact, unable to pay its debts (sometimes called 'actual insolvency' as opposed to the 'deemed insolvency' arrived at through s 123). Other provisions of IA 1986[257] treat s 123 as providing a definition of 'unable to pay its debts'. And provisions of the Companies Act 2006 concerning solvency statements by directors of private companies deliberately do not refer to IA 1986, s 123, so as to require directors to take into account more liabilities than would be taken into account in determining whether a company is unable to pay its debts for the purposes of being wound up.[258]

7.101 In *Barclays Bank Ltd v Commissioners of Inland Revenue*[259] the House of Lords considered legislation (since repealed) with a similar structure to IA 1986, s 123. The Finance Act 1940, s 55(1), stated what was to be done if a deceased person had owned shares or debentures in a company of which he or she 'had the control'; s 55(3) stated that in certain circumstances a person was to be deemed to have had control of a company; and other provisions of the Act treated s 55(3) as a definition. A majority of the House held that s 55(3) was not an exhaustive definition, and that whether or not a person had control of a company could be proved otherwise than by using s 55(3).

7.102 However, the structure of the legislation may not be enough to determine the question, for in an earlier version of IA 1986, s 123, namely, the Companies Act 1862, s 80, it was thought necessary to state expressly that inability to pay debts could be proved by any means, thus turning s 80 into an exhaustive definition. The 1862 provision stated:

A Company under this Act shall be deemed to be unable to pay its Debts, …

(4) Whenever it is proved to the Satisfaction of the Court that the Company is unable to pay its Debts.

---

[257] For example, s 240(2), s 245(4) and sch B1, para 111.
[258] Companies Act 2006, ss 643(2) and 714(4); Companies Act 2006 Explanatory Notes, para 1021. Solvency statements are required in connection with reductions of capital and payments out of capital on redemption or repurchase of shares.
[259] [1961] AC 509.

From 1908 to 1986, words were added to the provision so as to direct the court to take into **7.103**
account the company's contingent and prospective liabilities.[260]

In Canada, the Winding-up and Restructuring Act applies to a company that 'is insolvent',[261] **7.104**
and s 3 specifies 11 circumstances in which a company is deemed insolvent. The 11 deeming
provisions are not supplemented by a general provision allowing proof of insolvency to the satisfaction of the court. In early cases it was held that the circumstances listed in s 3 are the only
circumstances in which a company is insolvent.[262]

The first circumstance in which a company is deemed insolvent under s 3 is if it is unable **7.105**
to pay its debts as they become due. Section 4 specifies one circumstance (neglect to pay
on a statutory demand) in which a company is deemed to be unable to pay its debts as they
become due and there has never been an alternative provision for proof to the satisfaction of
the court like the Companies Act 1862 (United Kingdom), s 80(4). After early cases deciding that proceeding under s 4 was the only means of proving inability to pay debts, it has
subsequently been held that a finding of inability to pay debts as they become due may be
based on evidence other than evidence of failure to comply with a statutory demand:

- in British Columbia: *Re G Minerals Ltd*[263] refusing to follow *Re Anchor Investment Co
  Ltd*;[264]
- in Manitoba: *Re Milo Wheat Co Ltd*[265] (in which inability to pay debts as they became due
  was not proved) overruling *Re Rapid City Farmers' Elevator Co*;[266]
- in Nova Scotia: *Re Dominion Antimony Co*;[267]
- in Ontario: *Re Home Bank of Canada*[268] refusing to follow *Re Ewart Carriage Works
  Ltd*;[269]
- in Quebec: *MacKay v L'Association Coloniale de Construction et de Placements*;[270] *Moore
  Carpet Co Ltd v Mitchell*;[271] *Calumet Metals Co v Eldredge*;[272] *System Theatre Operating
  Co Ltd v Pulos*[273] (though the company was subsequently found not to be insolvent[274]);
- but not in Saskatchewan: *Re Outlook Hotel Co*;[275] *Re Great West Brick and Coal Co Ltd*.[276]

---

[260] See 7.259–7.263. See *Re Bond Corporation Holdings Ltd* (1990) 1 ACSR 488 and *Dikwa Holdings Pty
Ltd v Oakbury Pty Ltd* (1992) 36 FCR 274 on Australian legislation in the same form as the British legislation
from 1908 to 1986.
[261] s 6(1)(a).
[262] *Re Qu'Appelle Valley Farming Co Ltd* (1888) 5 Man R 160; *Re Grundy Stove Co* (1904) 7 OLR 252.
But *E B Eddy Manufacturing Co v Henderson Lumber Co* (1890) MLR 6 SC 137 and *H Walters and Sons Ltd v
Walters* (1920) 30 Que KB 525 are to the contrary.
[263] (1967) 10 CBR NS 281.
[264] (1912) 7 DLR 915.
[265] [1925] 2 DLR 1170.
[266] (1894) 9 Man R 574.
[267] (1908) 6 ELR 177.
[268] (1923) 54 OLR 606.
[269] (1904) 8 OLR 527. In *Re Cobalt Development Co* (1908) 12 OWR 83 Britton J also seemed to regard
s 4 as just one way of proving inability to pay debts as they become due.
[270] (1884) 6 ELR 179 n.
[271] (1908) 5 ELR 248.
[272] (1914) 23 Que KB 521.
[273] (1949) 30 CBR 232.
[274] [1953] Que QB 524.
[275] (1909) 2 Sask LR 435.
[276] (1916) 9 Sask LR 240.

7.106 In Australia the Corporations Act 2001, s 459A, provides that 'the court may order that an insolvent company be wound up in insolvency', and s 459B provides that the court may order a company to be wound up if 'satisfied that the company is insolvent'. Section 459C(2) provides six circumstances in which the court must presume a company is insolvent unless the contrary is proved, but there is no provision for insolvency to be proved in any other way. In *Deputy Commissioner of Taxation v Barroleg Pty Ltd*[277] Young J held that the insolvency of a company sought to be wound up may be proved by any admissible evidence.

7.107 In New Zealand the Companies Act 1993, s 287, provides a list of circumstances in which a company is presumed to be unable to pay its debts, but s 288(2) states that s 287 'does not prevent proof by other means that a company is unable to pay its debts'.

7.108 It is submitted that, as IA 1986, s 123, is not expressed to be an exhaustive definition, it should not be regarded as one, and so it should be possible for a petitioner to establish a company's inability to pay its debts by any admissible evidence which satisfies the court that the company is, as a matter of fact, unable to pay its debts. It seems that this was the approach taken by the learned deputy High Court judge in *Re Clemence plc*.[278]

Unregistered companies

7.109 Sections 222–224 of IA 1986 state a number of circumstances in which an unregistered company 'is deemed (for the purposes of section 221) unable to pay its debts'. The text of the sections is as follows:

222 Inability to pay debts: unpaid creditor for £750 or more

(1) An unregistered company is deemed (for the purposes of section 221) unable to pay its debts if there is a creditor, by assignment or otherwise, to whom the company is indebted in a sum exceeding £750 then due and—
   (a) the creditor has served on the company, by leaving at its principal place of business, or by delivering to the secretary or some director, manager or principal officer of the company, or by otherwise serving in such manner as the court may approve or direct, a written demand in the prescribed form requiring the company to pay the sum due, and
   (b) the company has for three weeks after the service of the demand neglected to pay the sum or to secure or compound for it to the creditor's satisfaction.
(2) The money sum for the time being specified in subsection (1) is subject to increase or reduction by regulations under section 417 in part 15; but no increase in the sum so specified affects any case in which the winding-up petition was presented before the coming into force of the increase.

223 Inability to pay debts: debt remaining unsatisfied after action brought

An unregistered company is deemed (for the purposes of section 221) unable to pay its debts if an action or other proceeding has been instituted against any member for any debt or demand due, or claimed to be due, from the company, or from him in his character of member, and—
   (a) notice in writing of the institution of the action or proceeding has been served on the company by leaving it at the company's principal place of business (or by delivering it to the secretary or some director, manager or principal officer of the company, or by otherwise serving it in such manner as the court may approve or direct), and

---

[277] (1997) 25 ACSR 167.
[278] (1992) 59 BLR 56.

(b) the company has not within three weeks after service of the notice paid, secured or compounded for the debt or demand, or procured the action or proceeding to be stayed or sisted, or indemnified the defendant or defender to his reasonable satisfaction against the action or proceeding, and against all costs, damages and expenses to be incurred by him because of it.

224 Inability to pay debts: other cases

(1) An unregistered company is deemed (for purposes of section 221) unable to pay its debts—

(a) if in England and Wales execution or other process issued on a judgment, decree or order obtained in any court in favour of a creditor against the company, or any member of it as such, or any person authorized to be sued as nominal defendant on behalf of the company, is returned unsatisfied;

(b) if in Scotland the induciae of a charge for payment on an extract decree, or an extract registered bond, or an extract registered protest, have expired without payment being made;

(c) if in Northern Ireland a certificate of unenforceability has been granted in respect of any judgment, decree or order obtained as mentioned in paragraph (a);

(d) if it is otherwise proved to the satisfaction of the court that the company is unable to pay its debts as they fall due.

(2) An unregistered company is also deemed unable to pay its debts if it is proved to the satisfaction of the court that the value of the company's assets is less than the amount of its liabilities, taking into account its contingent and prospective liabilities.

These provisions correspond to the provisions for registered companies as follows: **7.110**

Unregistered companies IA 1986, section	Registered companies IA 1986, section	Commentary in
222(1)	123(1)(a)	7.125–7.247
223	–	8.112–8.118
224(1)(a)	123(1)(b)	7.248–7.253
224(1)(b)	123(1)(c)	–
224(1)(c)	123(1)(d)	–
224(1)(d)	123(1)(e)	7.254–7.283
224(2)	123(2)	7.284–7.292

For a relevant scheme,[279] an s 222 demand is to be served by a creditor of the relevant   **7.111** scheme, each reference in s 222(1)(a) and (b) to the company is to be read as a reference to the operator, s 223 does not apply and s 224(1)(a) is modified to refer to execution or other process issued in favour of a creditor of the relevant scheme against the property subject to that scheme.[280]

---

[279] See 1.168.
[280] Collective Investment in Transferable Securities (Contractual Scheme) Regulations 2013 (SI 2013/1388), sch 2, paras 3, 5(a) and (c), and part 3.

Insolvent partnership where the petitioner is not also petitioning for the winding up or bankruptcy of a member of the partnership

7.112 On a petition under IPO 1994, art 7 or art 9, IA 1986, ss 222 and 223, are modified by IPO 1994, sch 3, paras 4 and 5, as follows:

222 Inability to pay debts: unpaid creditor for £750 or more

(1) An insolvent partnership is deemed (for the purposes of section 221) unable to pay its debts if there is a creditor, by assignment or otherwise, to whom the partnership is indebted in a sum exceeding £750 then due and—

  (a) the creditor has served on the partnership, in the manner specified in subsection (2) below, a written demand in the prescribed form requiring the partnership to pay the sum so due, and

  (b) the partnership has for three weeks after the service of the demand neglected to pay the sum or to secure or compound for it to the creditor's satisfaction.

(2) Service of the demand referred to in subsection (1)(a) shall be effected—

  (a) by leaving it at a principal place of business of the partnership in England and Wales, or

  (b) by leaving it at a place of business of the partnership in England and Wales at which business is carried on in the course of which the debt (or part of the debt) referred to in subsection (1) arose, or

  (c) by delivering it to an officer of the partnership, or

  (d) by otherwise serving it in such manner as the court may approve or direct.

(3) The money sum for the time being specified in subsection (1) is subject to increase or reduction by regulations under section 417 in part 15; but no increase in the sum so specified affects any case in which the winding-up petition was presented before the coming into force of the increase.

223 Inability to pay debts: debt remaining unsatisfied after action brought

(1) An insolvent partnership is deemed (for the purposes of section 221) unable to pay its debts if an action or other proceeding has been instituted against any member for any debt or demand due, or claimed to be due, from the company, or from him in his character of member, and—

  (a) notice in writing of the institution of the action or proceeding has been served on the company in the manner specified in subsection (2) below, and

  (b) the partnership has not within three weeks after service of the notice paid, secured or compounded for the debt or demand, or procured the action or proceeding to be stayed or sisted, or indemnified the defendant or defender to his reasonable satisfaction against the action or proceeding, and against all costs, damages and expenses to be incurred by him because of it.

(2) Service of the notice referred to in subsection (1)(a) shall be effected—

  (a) by leaving it at a principal place of business of the partnership in England and Wales, or

  (b) by leaving it at a place of business of the partnership in England and Wales at which business is carried on in the course of which the debt (or part of the debt) referred to in subsection (1) arose, or

  (c) by delivering it to an officer of the partnership, or

  (d) by otherwise serving it in such manner as the court may approve or direct.

7.113 For commentary on statutory demands generally see 7.125–7.247. For commentary on s 223 see 8.112–8.118.

IA 1986, s 123, does not apply to an art 7 or art 9 petition.[281]   **7.114**

If a winding-up or bankruptcy order has been made against a member of a partner- **7.115**
ship because of that member's inability to pay a joint debt, and the liquidator or
trustee of the member presents an art 7 petition on the ground that the partnership
is unable to pay its debts, the winding-up or bankruptcy order is proof, unless it is
proved otherwise to the satisfaction of the court, that the partnership is unable to
pay its debts.[282]

*Insolvent partnership: petition by creditor with concurrent petitions presented
against one or more members*

On concurrent petitions under IPO 1994, art 8, for the winding up of a partnership and **7.116**
the winding up or bankruptcy of a member or former member, the only method provided
by the legislation for proving that the partnership and the member are unable to pay their
debts is by statutory demand. For the partnership, IA 1986, s 222, is modified by IPO 1994,
sch 4, para 4, as follows:

222 Inability to pay debts: unpaid creditor for £750 or more

(1) An insolvent partnership is deemed (for the purposes of section 221) unable to pay
its debts if there is a creditor, by assignment or otherwise, to whom the partnership is
indebted in a sum exceeding £750 then due and—
   (a) the creditor has served on the partnership, in the manner specified in subsection (2),
   a written demand in form 4 in schedule 9 to IPO 1994 requiring the partnership to
   pay the sum so due,
   (b) the creditor has also served on any one or more members or former members
   of the partnership liable to pay the sum due (in the case of a corporate member by leaving it at its registered office and in the case of an individual member
   by serving it in accordance with the rules) a demand in form 4 in schedule 9
   to that Order, requiring that member or those members to pay the sum so
   due, and
   (c) the partnership and its members have for three weeks after the service of
   the demands, or the service of the last of them if served at different times,
   neglected to pay the sum or to secure or compound for it to the creditor's
   satisfaction.
(2) Service of the demand referred to in subsection (1)(a) shall be effected—
   (a) by leaving it at a principal place of business of the partnership in England and
   Wales, or
   (b) by leaving it at a place of business of the partnership in England and Wales at which
   business is carried on in the course of which the debt (or part of the debt) referred to
   in subsection (1) arose, or
   (c) by delivering it to an officer of the partnership, or
   (d) by otherwise serving it in such manner as the court may approve or direct.
(3) The money sum for the time being specified in subsection (1) is subject to increase or
reduction by regulations under section 417 in part 15; but no increase in the sum so
specified affects any case in which the winding-up petition was presented before the
coming into force of the increase.

---

[281] IA 1986, s 221(6), as modified by IPO 1994, sch 3, para 3 (in relation to art 7 petitions); IA 1986,
s 221(6), as modified by IPO 1994, sch 5, para 2 (in relation to art 9 petitions).
[282] IA 1986, s 221A(3), as modified by IPO 1994, sch 3, para 3.

7.117 For a corporate member, IA 1986, s 123, is modified by IPO 1994, sch 4, para 7(a), as follows:

123 Definition of inability to pay debts

(1) A corporate member or former member is deemed unable to pay its debts if there is a creditor, by assignment or otherwise, to whom the partnership is indebted in a sum exceeding £750 then due for which the member or former member is liable and—

  (a) the creditor has served on that member or former member and the partnership, in the manner specified in subsection (2) below, a written demand in form 4 in schedule 9 to IPO 1994 requiring that member or former member and the partnership to pay the sum so due, and

  (b) the corporate member or former member and the partnership have for three weeks after the service of the demands, or the service of the last of them if served at different times, neglected to pay the sum or to secure or compound for it to the creditor's satisfaction.

(2) Service of the demand referred to in subsection (1)(a) shall be effected, in the case of the corporate member or former corporate member, by leaving it at its registered office, and, in the case of the partnership—

  (a) by leaving it at a principal place of business of the partnership in England and Wales, or

  (b) by leaving it at a place of business of the partnership in England and Wales at which business is carried on in the course of which the debt (or part of the debt) referred to in subsection (1) arose, or

  (c) by delivering it to an officer of the partnership, or

  (d) by otherwise serving it in such manner as the court may approve or direct.

(3) The money sum for the time being specified in subsection (1) is subject to increase or reduction by order under section 416 in part 15.

7.118 For commentary on statutory demands generally see 7.125–7.247. Sections 223 and 224 are not available on art 8 petitions to prove that a partnership is unable to pay its debts.[283]

7.119 For an individual member, IA 1986, s 268, is modified[284] as follows:

268 Definition of 'inability to pay', etc; the statutory demand

(1) For the purposes of section 267(2)(c), an individual member or former individual member appears to be unable to pay a joint debt for which he is liable if the debt is payable immediately and the petitioning creditor to whom the insolvent partnership owes the joint debt has served—

  (a) on the individual member or former individual member in accordance with the rules a demand (known as 'the statutory demand'), in Form 4 in Schedule 9 to the Insolvent Partnerships Order 1994, and

  (b) on the partnership in the manner specified in subsection (2) below a demand (known as 'the written demand') in the same form,

    requiring the member or former member and the partnership to pay the debt or to secure or compound for it to the creditor's satisfaction, and at least 3 weeks have elapsed since the service of the demands, or the service of the last of them if served at different times, and neither demand has been complied with nor the demand against the member set aside in accordance with the rules.

---

283 IPO 1994, art 8(1).
284 By IPO 1994, sch 4, para 7(b).

(2) Service of the demand referred to in subsection (1)(b) shall be effected—
   (a) by leaving it at a principal place of business of the partnership in England and Wales, or
   (b) by leaving it at a place of business of the partnership in England and Wales at which business is carried on in the course of which the debt (or part of the debt) referred to in subsection (1) arose, or
   (c) by delivering it to an officer of the partnership, or
   (d) by otherwise serving it in such manner as the court may approve or direct.

In relation to petitions presented under IPO 1994, art 10, for the winding up of a partner-**7.120** ship and the bankruptcy or winding up of all its members, IA 1986, ss 222, 223 and 224,[285] can be used to prove that the partnership is unable to pay its debts.[286] The applied sections must be interpreted in accordance with IPO 1994, art 3 (references to companies to be construed as references to insolvent partnerships etc). IA 1986, s 123, as modified by IPO 1994, sch 4, para 7(a) (which is quoted at 7.117), applies in relation to the winding up of a corporate member on an art 10 petition.[287]

Building societies

IA 1986, s 123,[288] applies for the purposes of determining whether a building society is **7.121** unable to pay its debts with the substitution of 'building society' for 'company' and 'principal office' for 'registered office'.[289]

Incorporated friendly societies

IA 1986, s 123,[290] applies for the purposes of determining whether an incorporated friendly **7.122** society is unable to pay its debts with the substitution of 'incorporated friendly society' for 'company'.[291]

Company subject to main insolvency proceedings in another EU State (apart from Denmark)

If a company is subject to main insolvency proceedings elsewhere in the EU which are **7.123** subject to Regulation (EC) No 1346/2000,[292] secondary proceedings may be opened in England and Wales without the company's insolvency being examined in England and Wales.[293] Secondary proceedings must be winding-up proceedings listed in annex B[294] as winding up by the court is.[295]

Company subject to a foreign main proceeding in a non-EU State or Denmark

If a company is subject to a foreign main proceeding[296] in a non-EU State or Denmark, and **7.124** the proceeding has been recognized in Great Britain,[297] there is a rebuttable presumption that the company is insolvent.[298]

---

[285] See 7.109–7.110.
[286] IA 1986, s 221(5), as modified by IPO 1994, sch 6, para 4.
[287] IPO 1994, art 10(2), (3) and (6).
[288] See 7.92–7.108.
[289] Building Societies Act 1986, s 90 and sch 15, para 3(1)(a) and (d).
[290] See 7.92–7.108.
[291] Friendly Societies Act 1992, s 23 and sch 10, para 3(1)(a).
[292] See 1.361–1.407.
[293] art 27.
[294] arts 3(3) and 27.
[295] See 10.188–10.193.
[296] See 10.194–10.199.
[297] See 10.206–10.210.
[298] Cross-Border Insolvency Regulations 2006 (SI 2006/1030), sch 1, art 31.

Statutory Demand

Nature of Statutory Demand

Definition

7.125 Under IA 1986, s 123(1)(a), a registered company is deemed unable to pay its debts:

> if a creditor (by assignment or otherwise) to whom the company is indebted in a sum exceeding £750 then due has served on the company, by leaving it at the company's registered office, a written demand (in the prescribed form) requiring the company to pay the sum so due and the company has for three weeks thereafter neglected to pay the sum or to secure or compound for it to the reasonable satisfaction of the creditor.

7.126 Under s 222(1), an unregistered company is deemed unable to pay its debts:

> if there is a creditor, by assignment or otherwise, to whom the company is indebted in a sum exceeding £750 then due and—
>
> (a) the creditor has served on the company, by leaving at its principal place of business, or by delivering to the secretary or some director, manager or principal officer of the company, or by otherwise serving in such manner as the court may approve or direct, a written demand in the prescribed form requiring the company to pay the sum due, and
>
> (b) the company has for three weeks after the service of the demand neglected to pay the sum or to secure or compound for it to the creditor's satisfaction.

7.127 A notice given by a creditor of a company under IA 1986, s 123(1)(a) (if it is a registered company) or s 222(1) (if it is an unregistered company), is called a 'statutory demand'.[299] There is no requirement that a creditor should investigate whether a company is insolvent before serving a statutory demand.[300] If a company which has been served a statutory demand neglects to comply with it, a petitioner for the company's winding up may rely on the neglect to show that the company is unable to pay its debts. It does not matter that the petitioner is not the creditor whose debt was the subject of the statutory demand[301] though usually they are the same person. If the petitioner is the creditor whose debt was the subject of the statutory demand, the petitioner may rely on non-compliance with the statutory demand to show inability to pay debts despite actually being owed more than the amount demanded.[302] But if the petitioner's statutory demand for an amount less than the petitioner is actually owed has been complied with, the company is not deemed to be unable to pay its debts because of neglect to pay the whole amount owed to the petitioner within the time limited by the statutory demand.[303]

Bankruptcy statutory demands

7.128 A rather different purpose is served by statutory demands in bankruptcy. Statutory demands served on individuals are used to qualify creditors to present bankruptcy petitions. A creditor of an individual cannot petition for a bankruptcy order to be made against that individual unless either (a) a statutory demand for the debt has not been complied with

---

[299] IR 1986, r 4.4(2); form 4.1.
[300] *Dooney v Henry* [2000] HCA 44, 174 ALR 41, at [9].
[301] *Re Island of Anglesea Coal and Coke Co Ltd* (1861) 4 LT 684; *Brinds Ltd v Offshore Oil NL* (1985) 63 ALR 94 at pp 101–2.
[302] *Wichita Pty Ltd v Elders IXL Ltd* (1990) 2 ACSR 273.
[303] *De Montfort v Southern Cross Exploration NL* (1987) 17 NSWLR 327.

or (b) judgment has been obtained for the debt and execution or other process to enforce the judgment has been returned partially or wholly unsatisfied.[304] There is no statutory provision that an individual who fails to comply with a statutory demand is deemed unable to pay his or her debts. Instead, failure by an individual to comply with a statutory demand for a debt means that the individual 'appears to be unable to pay' that debt.[305] The different purposes of statutory demands in bankruptcy and in companies winding were emphasized by the Court of Appeal in *TSB Bank plc v Platts*:[306]

> The statutory demand can...be seen to be of crucial importance if a creditor, who does not have a judgment debt, is to obtain a bankruptcy order....It is accordingly quite different from a statutory demand in the field of company law which merely provides one means of establishing a company's inability to pay its debts, the usual ground on which a company is wound up compulsorily. In contrast in bankruptcy it is not the debtor's general inability to pay his debts that is crucial but the apparent inability to pay the debt in the statutory demand, and at the hearing of the bankruptcy petition the failure to pay or secure or compound for that debt.

Juridical classification

Service of a statutory demand on a company is not the bringing of an action,[307] nor is it a 'proceeding'.[308] In particular, it is not a civil proceeding in the High Court or County Court.[309] For the purposes of IR 1986, r 7.55 (insolvency proceedings not invalidated by formal defect or irregularity), service of a statutory demand is not in itself an 'insolvency proceeding',[310] but is a preliminary or incidental step in winding-up proceedings,[311] and courts in Australia and Malaysia have treated a defect or irregularity in a statutory demand as occurring in the proceedings on the subsequent petition and so covered by a provision like IR 1986, r 7.55.[312] In Australia it has been held that service of a statutory demand on a company is 'for...the purposes of the winding up' of the company.[313] **7.129**

Service of a statutory demand 'is in no sense equivalent to the institution of proceedings in the court'[314] and so cannot be attacked as an abuse of court process.[315] However, by analogy **7.130**

---

[304] IA 1986, ss 267 and 268.
[305] s 268(1).
[306] [1998] 2 BCLC 1 at pp 6–7.
[307] *Re a Debtor (No 88 of 1991)* [1993] Ch 286.
[308] *Clarke and Walker Pty Ltd v Thew* (1967) 116 CLR 465; *Bartex Fabrics Pty Ltd v Phillips Fox* (1994) 13 ACSR 667; *B and M Quality Constructions Pty Ltd v Buyrite Steel Supplies Pty Ltd* (1994) 116 FLR 218; *Cornick Pty Ltd v Brains Master Corporation* (1995) 60 FCR 565; *St George Bank v Active Property Investment Pty Ltd* [2010] NSWSC 736, 77 NSWLR 148.
[309] *Shalson v DF Keane Ltd* [2003] EWHC 599 (Ch), [2003] BPIR 1045.
[310] *Re a Debtor (No 190 of 1987)* (1988) *The Times*, 21 May 1988.
[311] *Re a Debtor (No 68/SD/97)* [1998] 4 All ER 779.
[312] *Pro-Image Productions (Vic) Pty Ltd v Catalyst Television Productions Pty Ltd* (1988) 14 ACLR 303; *Re Macro Constructions Pty Ltd* [1994] 2 QdR 31; *Pioneer Concrete (M) Sdn Bhd v Celini Corp Sdn Bhd* [1998] 3 MLJ 810. The Australian provision (now the Corporations Act (Australia) 2001, s 1322) is more widely drafted than IR 1986, r 7.55, in that it covers any proceeding whether a legal proceeding or not (Corporations Act 2001 (Australia), s 1322(1)(a)).
[313] *Re Buildmat (Australia) Ltd* (1981) 5 ACLR 459.
[314] Per McLelland J in *Altarama Ltd v Camp* (1980) 5 ACLR 513 at p 521.
[315] *Altarama Ltd v Camp*; *Chippendale Printing Co Pty Ltd v Deputy Commissioner of Taxation* (1995) 15 ACSR 682 per Lindgren J at p 696.

with the concept of abuse of court process, misuse of the statutory demand procedure for an improper purpose may be regarded as an abuse,[316] and for this purpose, it is unnecessary to treat issuing the statutory demand as a court process.[317] Winding-up proceedings are not begun by service of a statutory demand,[318] though it is a preliminary or incidental step in the winding-up proceedings.[319]

7.131 Service of a statutory demand on a company by a secured creditor of the company is not an action to enforce the security.[320]

7.132 Service of a statutory demand for a debt is not a proceeding for the recovery of the debt.[321] Service of a statutory demand for a judgment debt is not execution of the judgment.[322]

Strict adherence

7.133 It is sometimes said that inability to pay debts is not deemed by virtue of IA 1986, s 123(1)(a), unless the procedure prescribed in the paragraph is strictly adhered to.[323] The need for strict adherence means that nothing less than that which the legislation requires will suffice, but it does not preclude doing something more.[324]

7.134 However, courts have generally conceded that an error which does not prejudice the company on which a demand is served can be waived.[325] The only real point of controversy is whether an overstatement of the amount which is indisputably due can be waived.[326] In Malaysia it has been held that the statutory provision should be interpreted liberally not literally.[327] See the provisions for setting aside statutory demands in Australia and New Zealand discussed at 7.237–7.247.

Building societies

7.135 IA 1986, s 123(1)(a),[328] applies to a building society with the substitution of 'building society' for 'company' and 'principal office' for 'registered office'.[329]

---

[316] *Accordent Pty Ltd v RMBL Investments Ltd* [2009] SASC 248, 105 SASR 62, at [55]–[63], where no abuse was found. See 7.232–7.234.

[317] As was done in *Mala Pty Ltd v Johnston* (1994) 13 ACLC 100.

[318] *Thiess Peabody Mitsui Coal Pty Ltd v A E Goodwin Ltd* [1966] QdR 1 at p 5.

[319] *Re a Debtor (No 68/SD/97)* [1998] 4 All ER 779.

[320] *Australian Cherry Exports Ltd v Commonwealth Bank of Australia* (1996) 132 FLR 266.

[321] *Jarena Pty Ltd v Sholl Nicholson Pty* (1996) 136 ALR 427 at p 429; *Standard Commodities Pty Ltd v Société Socinter Département Centragel* [2005] NSWSC 294, 54 ACSR 489.

[322] *Tatlers.com.au Pty Ltd v Davis* [2006] NSWSC 1055, 203 FLR 473, at [25] (coincidentally confirming a submission made in the second edition of this work, which had not then been published).

[323] *Re Mannum Haulage Pty Ltd* (1974) 8 SASR 451 per Walters J at p 452; *General Welding and Construction Co (Qld) Pty Ltd v International Rigging (Aust) Pty Ltd* (1983) 8 ACLR 307 per McPherson J at p 309; *Collins Bros Stationers Pty Ltd v Zebra Graphics Pty Ltd* (1985) 10 ACLR 267 per Young J at p 268; *Craig v Iona Hotels Ltd* (1988) SCLR 130 per Sheriff Principal MacLeod at p 135; *Lord Advocate v Blairwest Investments Ltd* (1989) SLT (Sh Ct) 97 per Sheriff Henderson at p 98; *Racecourse Totalizators Pty Ltd v Hartley Cyber Engineering Pty Ltd* (1989) 15 ACLR 457 per O'Bryan J at p 459.

[324] *Emhill Pty Ltd v Bonsoc Pty Ltd* [2005] VSCA 239, 55 ACSR 379.

[325] See 7.202–7.230 concerning errors in statutory demands and per Ormiston J in *Re Elgar Heights Pty Ltd* [1985] VR 657 at pp 669–71 and in *Deputy Commissioner of Taxation (Vic) v Players Entertainment Network Pty Ltd* (1988) 13 ACLR 541 at pp 544–5.

[326] See 7.223–7.229.

[327] *Malaysia Air Charter Co Sdn Bhd v Petronas Dagangan Sdn Bhd* [2000] 4 MLJ 657.

[328] See 7.125.

[329] Building Societies Act 1986, s 90, and sch 15, para 3(1)(a) and (d).

Incorporated friendly societies

IA 1986, s 123(1)(a),[330] applies to an incorporated friendly society with the substitution of **7.136** 'incorporated friendly society' for 'company'.[331]

Form of Demand

Prescribed form

To lead to a registered or unregistered company being deemed unable to pay its debts, a **7.137** statutory demand must be in writing,[332] and cannot be in electronic form.[333] It must be in the prescribed form, which means the form prescribed by IR 1986,[334] and those rules prescribe that form 4.1 in sch 4 to the rules shall be used with such variations, if any, as the circumstances may require.[335]

Form 4.1 is designed to provide all the information required by rr 4.4(3), 4.5 and 4.6. Rule **7.138** 4.4(3) requires that a statutory demand must be dated, and must be signed by the creditor personally or by a person who states that he or she is authorized to make the demand on the creditor's behalf. The signature of the person signing may be written or put on the demand by another person who is authorized by the person signing.[336] Rules 4.5 and 4.6 are as follows:[337]

4.5 Form and content of statutory demand

(1) The statutory demand must state the amount of the debt and the consideration for it (or, if there is no consideration, the way in which it arises).
(2) If the amount claimed in the demand includes—
  (a) any charge by way of interest not previously notified to the company as included in its liability, or
  (b) any other charge accruing from time to time,
  (c) the amount or rate of the charge must be separately identified, and the grounds on which payment of it is claimed must be stated.
  (d) In either case the amount claimed must be limited to that which has accrued due at the date of the demand.

4.6 Information to be given in statutory demand

(1) The statutory demand must include an explanation to the company of the following matters—
(2) Information must be provided for the company as to how an officer or representative of it may enter into communication with one or more named individuals, with a view to securing or compounding for the debt to the creditor's satisfaction.

In the case of any individual so named in the demand, his address and telephone number (if any) must be given.

---

[330] See 7.125.
[331] Friendly Societies Act 1992, s 23 and sch 10, para 3(1)(a).
[332] IA 1986, ss 123(1)(a) and 222(1)(a).
[333] IA 1986, s 436B(2)(f) and (h).
[334] IA 1986, ss 123(1)(a), 222(1)(a) and 251.
[335] IR 1986, r 12A.30(2).
[336] *Re Horne* [2000] 4 All ER 550; *Deputy Commissioner of Taxation v Jetbird Holdings Pty Ltd* [2004] WASC 66, 22 ACLC 629.
[337] For a petition to wind up a relevant scheme (see 1.168), rr 4.4, 4.5 and 4.6 are modified by the Collective Investment in Transferable Securities (Contractual Scheme) Regulations 2013 (SI 2013/1388), sch 3. Form

Demand by an agent

7.139 It has been held in Australia that if solicitors are authorized to institute proceedings for the liquidation of a company, they have sufficient authority to take all necessary steps to enable those proceedings to be brought, including making a statutory demand.[338] The fact that an agent of a creditor caused the creditor to make the contract under which a debt has arisen does not in itself give the agent authority to serve a statutory demand for the debt.[339]

Insolvent partnerships

7.140 For the purposes of petitions under IPO 1994, art 8 or art 10 (concurrent petitions for the winding up of a partnership and one or more of its present or former members), the prescribed form of statutory demand to be served on both members of a partnership and (for art 8 petitions only) the partnership itself is form 4 in IPO 1994, sch 9.[340]

7.141 For an art 7 or art 9 petition, or an art 10 petition against a partnership, no form of statutory demand is prescribed in IPO 1994 and so the form prescribed by IR 1986 must be used.[341]

Method and Place of Service of Demand

Permitted methods of service

7.142 It is submitted that the plain meaning of IA 1986, s 123(1)(a), is that the only permitted method of service of a statutory demand on a registered company is by leaving it at the company's registered office. Section 123(1)(a) may be contrasted with s 222(1)(a) which states two specific methods of service on an unregistered company (first, leaving at the principal place of business; secondly, delivering to the secretary or some director, manager or principal officer) and also provides for the court to approve or direct some alternative method of service. It has been held that a statutory demand cannot be served on a registered company by telex[342] or fax.[343] The provisions of IR 1986 relating to electronic service do not apply to statutory demands.[344]

7.143 It has been held that leaving a statutory demand for a debt owed by a registered company at a place which is not the company's registered office is not effective service.[345] There may be two ways round this:

(a) It has been held that the Malaysian provision, which is in the same terms as IA 1986, s 123(1)(a), does not prescribe the only means of service, so that any form of service

---

4.1 must be varied as necessary to take account of these modifications; see IR 1986, r 12A.30, as applied and modified by SI 2013/1388, sch 3.

[338] *Metropolitan Waste Disposal Authority v Willoughby Waste Disposals Pty Ltd* (1987) 9 NSWLR 7; *Dennis Hanger Pty Ltd v Kanambra Pty Ltd* (1992) 34 FCR 242.

[339] *Agilo Ltd v Henry* [2010] EWHC 2717 (Ch), [2011] BPIR 297.

[340] IA 1986, s 123(1)(a), as modified by IPO 1994, sch 4, para 7(a) (art 8 or art 10 petition; corporate member's inability to pay its debts); IA 1986, s 222(1)(a), as modified by IPO 1994, sch 4, para 4 (art 8 petition; partnership's inability to pay its debts).

[341] See 6.4.2.1. IPO 1994, art 18 and sch 10.

[342] *Re a Company* [1985] BCLC 37.

[343] *Best Consultants Ltd v Aurasound Speakers Ltd* [2004] HKLRD 502.

[344] IR 1986, r 12A.6(3)(b).

[345] *Re Mannum Haulage Pty Ltd* (1974) 8 SASR 451; *Pac Asian Services Pte Ltd v European Asian Bank AG* [1987] SLR 1.

which brings the demand to the company's attention is effective.[346] The Malaysian court did not want a company to escape being deemed to be insolvent for not complying with a statutory demand which had in fact been brought to its attention, albeit not in the way prescribed by the legislation. It is submitted that, rather than putting a strained interpretation on the wording of s 123(1)(a), it is better to deal with such a case by deeming the company to be unable to pay its debts under s 123(1)(e), because it failed to pay the debt when it was demanded.[347]

(b) Another way of dealing with attempted service of a statutory demand at the wrong address is to treat the statutory demand as a step in the winding-up proceedings.[348] Attempted service at the wrong address would then be an 'error of procedure' within CPR, r 3.10,[349] or a formal defect or irregularity under IR 1986, r 7.55.[350] If either of those rules applies, service at the wrong address does not invalidate the proceedings unless, under CPR, r 3.10, there has been prejudice to the company or a third party,[351] or, under IR 1986, r 7.55, it has caused substantial injustice. If there has not been prejudice or substantial injustice, the court may make an order under CPR, r 3.10, or IR 1986, r 7.55, to remedy the error.

In Australia, the provision equivalent to IA 1986, s 123(1)(a),[352] now refers to a statutory **7.144**
demand being served on a company without specifying a method of service. Australian legislation makes general provision for methods of service which 'may' be used to serve documents on companies[353] or bodies corporate.[354] It has been held that these provisions do not prescribe the only methods that may be used to serve a company, so that any means of service of a statutory demand which does bring the demand to the attention of a responsible officer of the company may be used.[355]

What constitutes leaving; use of a postal carrier

IA 1986, s 123(1)(a), comes into operation only when a creditor of a registered company **7.145**
has served a statutory demand on the company 'by leaving it at the company's registered office'.[356] This contrasts with the provision of the Companies Act 2006, s 1139(1), that: 'A document may be served on a company registered under this Act by leaving it at, or sending it by post to, the company's registered office'. Accordingly, Nourse J, in *Re a Company*,[357] took the view that IA 1986, s 123(1)(a), does not operate if a statutory demand has been sent by post. The same view was taken[358] in *Craig v Iona Hotels Ltd*,[359]

---

[346] *Masboh Trading Sdn Bhd v Mejaris Builders Sdn Bhd* [2001] 5 MLJ 369 (service at a place of business of the company which was not its registered office).
[347] See 7.272–7.281.
[348] Whether this can be done is controversial. See 7.129–7.130.
[349] *Nelson v Clearsprings (Management) Ltd* [2006] EWCA Civ 1252, [2007] 1 WLR 962, at [48].
[350] *Pioneer Concrete (M) Sdn Bhd v Celini Corp Sdn Bhd* [1998] 3 MLJ 810.
[351] *Nelson v Clearsprings (Management) Ltd* at [50].
[352] Corporations Act 2001 (Australia), s 459E.
[353] Corporations Act 2001 (Australia), s 109X. The methods permitted by s 109X include leaving the document at, or posting it to, the company's registered office (s 109X(1)(a)).
[354] Acts Interpretation Act 1901 (Australia), s 28A.
[355] *Parklands Blue Metal Pty Ltd v Kowari Motors Pty Ltd* [2003] QSC 98, [2004] 1 QdR 140 (service by fax); *Polstar Pty Ltd v Agnew* [2007] NSWSC 114, 208 FLR 226 (service at a post office box); *Woodgate v Garard Pty Ltd* [2010] NSWSC 508, 239 FLR 339, at [44(iv)].
[356] IA 1986, s 123(1)(a).
[357] [1985] BCLC 37.
[358] Without reference to *Re a Company* [1985] BCLC 37.
[359] 1988 SCLR 130.

ruling that a statutory demand sent by recorded delivery was not effective. However, in *Re a Company (No 008790 of 1990)*[360] Morritt J observed that s 123(1)(a) does not specify who is to leave the demand at the registered office, and held that it can be left there by any agent of the person making the demand, including a postal carrier.[361] Morritt J's decision was not welcomed by practitioners, who prefer to employ professional process servers to deliver statutory demands so as to obtain the best evidence of service. However, it is submitted that the decision is correct. It accords with the view of Wynn-Parry J in *Stylo Shoes Ltd v Prices Tailors Ltd*[362] that the act of sending a letter by ordinary post is equivalent to leaving it for the proposed recipient at the place to which the letter is delivered.[363]

7.146 The distinction between the Companies Act 2006, s 1139(1), and IA 1986, s 123(1)(a), is that s 1139(1), by referring to serving a document on a company by sending it by post, invokes the Interpretation Act 1978, s 7 (deemed effect of service by post), whereas s 123(1)(a), by not referring at all to post, does not invoke s 7. Under s 1139(1) a person serving a document effects service by posting it, which results in deemed service of the document. Under s 123(1)(a), service can only be effected by delivery, which must be proved. Clearly a very important factor to be considered when choosing who is to serve a statutory demand is the quality of evidence of service that can be provided. The difficulty of proving that a postal item has been left at a particular place is illustrated by the cases discussed at 7.147–7.148. The English legal system has never tried to enforce standards of service by giving judicial officers the exclusive right to serve process. Even so, in Scotland, where this exclusive right does exist, it has been held not to apply to statutory demands.[364]

7.147 In *Re a Company (No 008790 of 1990)* a demand sent by registered post, which the company admitted had been delivered, was effective.[365] But in *Re Bcon Communications Ltd*[366] denial by the company that a demand sent by registered post had been received meant that it was not effective. In *Re Galaxy Electro-Plating Factory Ltd*[367] it was held that two statutory demands sent by post had not been served, because there was no evidence that they had been delivered.[368] See also *Brown v Bluestone Property Services Pty Ltd*[369] where the serving party could not even prove that the demand had been posted. In *Re Pacific Mobile Phones Pty Ltd*[370] it was proved that the demand had not been delivered.

[360] [1991] BCLC 561.
[361] The same view was taken in *South Seas Developments Ltd v Commercial Advances Nominees Ltd* [1976] 1 NZLR 679; *Re Alpina Pty Ltd* (1977) 17 SASR 528 at p 534; *Re Riviera Leisure Ltd* [2009] IEHC 183.
[362] [1960] Ch 396.
[363] See also *Kinch v Bullard* (1998) *The Times*, 16 September 1998.
[364] *Lord Advocate v Blairwest Investments Ltd* 1989 SLT (Sh Ct) 97; *Lord Advocate v Traprain Ltd* 1989 SLT (Sh Ct) 99; *Lord Advocate* 1993 SLT 1324.
[365] Service by registered post at a company's registered office was also effective in *Weng Wah Construction Co Sdn Bhd v Yik Foong Development Sdn Bhd* [1994] 2 MLJ 266. These cases were not considered in *Dayakuasa Holdings Sdn Bhd v Kayaal Holdings Sdn Bhd* [2003] 2 MLJ 263, in which it was held that a statutory demand cannot be served by registered post.
[366] [2012] IEHC 362.
[367] [2000] 1 HKLRD 876.
[368] Followed in *Best Consultants Ltd v Aurasound Speakers Ltd* [2004] HKLRD 502.
[369] [2010] NSWSC 869.
[370] [2008] QSC 210, 219 FLR 422.

A demand sent by post to a company's post office box which is actually located at a post office **7.148** and from which the company collects its mail is not served in accordance with IA 1986, s 123(1)(a), because the postal carrier does not leave it at the company's registered office.[371] Similarly, if a statutory demand for a debt to be paid by a company is sent by post and the postal carrier is unable to deliver it (for example, because no one is available to sign for it), and the demand is subsequently collected from the carrier's office by someone on behalf of the company, it will not have been left at the company's registered office as required by s 123(1)(a).[372] But in Australia it has been held that the person leaving the demand need not be an agent of the person serving it, so that a demand left in a post office box is served when an agent of the company takes it to the registered office.[373] It is submitted that this is contrary to the natural meaning of the words 'served by leaving at the company's registered office' which require the serving party (acting personally or by agents) to leave the document at the registered office. This does not encompass leaving the document at another place in the hope that someone who is under no obligation to do so may take it to the registered office.

A statutory demand is not 'left at' a registered office if the individual serving it takes it away **7.149** after service has been refused.[374]

If a statutory demand is not a document in 'proceedings',[375] it is not possible to apply to the **7.150** court under CPR, r 6.27, for an order permitting service by an alternative method or at an alternative place.[376]

Service out of office hours

It has been held in Australia that service of a statutory demand does not have to be during **7.151** office hours[377] and that a demand is left at the registered office if it is taped to the outside of the locked door of the office when the office is closed.[378]

Service at building in multiple occupancy

For service at a registered office in a building in multiple occupancy see 1.528. **7.152**

Service according to rules does not bring demand to company's attention

IA 1986, s 123(1)(a), requires only that a statutory demand be left at a registered company's **7.153** registered office and, unlike s 222, makes no provision for alternative modes of service. With two exceptions, in the reported cases courts have held that leaving a demand at a company's registered office is sufficient, even if it is known that the demand will not come to the attention of any individual connected with the company.[379]

---

[371] *South Seas Developments Ltd v Commercial Advances Nominees Ltd* [1976] 1 NZLR 679.

[372] *Re Amanatidis Holdings Pty Ltd* (1991) 4 ACSR 253.

[373] *Derma Pharmaceuticals Pty Ltd v HSBC Bank Australia Ltd* [2005] SASC 48, 188 FLR 373. There was no need to find that any prescribed method of service had been used, because in Australia any effective method is permitted (see 7.144).

[374] *Jin Xin Investment and Trade (Australia) Pty Ltd v ISC Property Pty Ltd* [2006] NSWSC 7, 196 FLR 350.

[375] See 7.129–7.130.

[376] *St George Bank v Active Property Investment Pty Ltd* [2010] NSWSC 736.

[377] *Cornick Pty Ltd v Brains Master Corporation* (1995) 60 FCR 565; *SV Steel Supplies Pty Ltd v Palwizat* [2007] QSC 24 (service when office was shut for two-week holiday); *Career Training on Line Pty Ltd v BES Training Solutions Pty Ltd* [2010] NSWSC 460.

[378] *Chains and Power (Aust) Pty Ltd v Commonwealth Bank of Australia* (1994) 15 ACSR 544 at p 555. It should be securely fastened in a waterproof envelope to protect against rain making it illegible.

[379] See *Chief Commissioner of Stamp Duties v Paliflex Pty Ltd* [1999] NSWSC 15, 17 ACLC 467, at [24] and the cases cited in 7.154, 7.155 and 7.157. The two exceptional cases are discussed at 7.159.

7.154 In *Quicksafe Freightlines Pty Ltd v Shell Co of Australia Ltd*[380] the registered address of a company's registered office was the address of a building, part of which had been occupied by the company's accountants. At the time when it was sought to serve a statutory demand the accountants had moved and the demand was left at a solicitors' office in a different part of the building. The secretary with whom the demand was left posted it back to the agents who were acting for the creditor. Waddell J described this as 'good and effective service'. Similarly in *Re Dewatering (WA) Pty Ltd*[381] leaving a statutory demand in a letter box on the site of a company's registered office, which had been redeveloped and was unoccupied, was effective service, even though the creditor whose debt was being demanded was the holding company of the debtor company and had itself sold the site of the registered office for redevelopment.

7.155 In *Re Future Life Enterprises Pty Ltd*[382] service of a statutory demand at a company's registered office, which was the office of a firm of accountants, was held to be good despite the fact that it was immediately posted back to the creditor's solicitors by the accountants with a statement that they no longer acted for the company and had no means of contacting anyone connected with it. *Re Shangri-la Cruise Pte Ltd*[383] and *Dewina Trading Sdn Bhd v Ion International Pty Ltd*[384] are similar cases.

7.156 For evidence of service in these circumstances see 1.529.

7.157 Under the Australian doctrine of fair notice which is discussed at 1.531, it may be an abuse of process for a creditor to apply for a company to be wound up on the ground of non-compliance with a statutory demand served in these circumstances[385] and in *Joe Mangraviti Pty Ltd v Lumley Finance Ltd*[386] a statutory demand was set aside for this reason.[387] However, the mere fact that a creditor knows that a statutory demand served at a company's registered office will not be brought to the attention of anyone connected with the company does not show that applying for the company to be wound up is an abuse of process.[388]

7.158 One point which was not raised in any of the cases discussed at 7.154, 7.155 and 7.157 was that even if the statutory demand was validly served, the company could not have failed to comply with a demand of which it had no knowledge.[389]

7.159 The first exceptional reported case is *FCOS Finance Ltd v Colway Farms Ltd*,[390] in which a demand served at a place which had been registered as the company's registered office by mistake, and which the creditor and the process server knew the company had no connection with, was held to be ineffective.[391] The second exceptional case is *Re Specialty*

---

[380] (1984) 10 ACLR 161.
[381] (1988) 14 ACLR 315.
[382] (1994) 33 NSWLR 559.
[383] [1990] SLR 799.
[384] (1996) 21 ACSR 535.
[385] *Woodgate v Garard Pty Ltd* [2010] NSWSC 508, 239 FLR 339, at [44(iii)].
[386] [2010] NSWSC 61.
[387] Under the Corporations Act 2001 (Australia), s 459J(1)(b).
[388] *Dewina Trading Sdn Bhd v Ion International Pty Ltd.*
[389] *CGU Workers' Compensation (Vic) Ltd v Carousel Bar Pty Ltd* [1999] VSC 227, 17 ACLC 1213, at [136].
[390] (1990) 5 NZCLC 66,888.
[391] See also 3.17–3.19.

Laboratories Asia Pte Ltd,[392] in which one man was the 'controlling mind' of both the company that was the petitioning creditor and the company sought to be wound up. He had given the Singapore Registrar of Companies and Businesses a notice of change of address of the registered office of the company sought to be wound up, without authority to do so. It was held that a statutory demand served at the false address was ineffective and that the petitioner could not rely on the registrar's records.

Unregistered companies

Under IA 1986, s 222(1)(a), a statutory demand may be served on an unregistered company   **7.160** by leaving the demand at the company's principal place of business, or by delivering it to the secretary or some director, manager or principal officer of the company, or by otherwise serving it in such manner as the court may approve or direct. Although s 221(3) provides that the principal place of business of an unregistered company within the jurisdiction of the court in which winding-up proceedings are brought is deemed to be the registered office of the company, it is respectfully submitted that it was wrong of Needham J to hold in *Re Buildmat (Australia) Ltd*[393] that the converse is true so that service of a statutory demand on an unregistered company at its registered office outside the jurisdiction amounts to service at its principal place of business within the jurisdiction.

Type of Debt for which Demand may be Served

Debt must be due and payable

A statutory demand must relate to a debt presently due, not one due in the future.[394] This   **7.161** must mean due at the time of serving the demand.[395] It follows that interest can be claimed only up to the date of the demand, not up to the date of payment.[396] A statutory demand is ineffective if the debt is contingent and the contingency has not occurred.[397] A statutory demand for a claim for unliquidated damages is ineffective.[398] A statutory demand cannot be used to seek payment before an agreed period of credit has expired.[399]

It has been held in Australia that 'due' means that it must have been possible to enforce pay-   **7.162** ment of the debt by legal proceedings at the time of service of the statutory demand.[400] It follows that it is not possible to serve a statutory demand for a debt at a time when there is a statutory prohibition[401] on bringing proceedings to enforce that debt.[402] In Australia it has

---

[392] [2001] 2 SLR 563.

[393] (1981) 5 ACLR 459.

[394] *Re Bryant Investment Co Ltd* [1974] 1 WLR 826; *Stonegate Securities Ltd v Gregory* [1980] Ch 576 per Buckley LJ at p 579.

[395] *Stonegate Securities Ltd v Gregory* at p 580; *Re Synthetic Oils Pty Ltd* (1989) 1 ACSR 187; see also *New Travellers' Chambers Ltd v Cheese and Green* (1894) 70 LT 271.

[396] IR 1986, r 4.5(2); *Deputy Commissioner of Taxation v Cye International Pty Ltd (No 2)* (1985) 10 ACLR 305; *ANZ Banking Group Ltd v Kamlock Pty Ltd* (1993) 10 ACSR 458.

[397] *JSF Finance and Currency Exchange Co Ltd v Akma Solutions Inc* [2001] 2 BCLC 307.

[398] *Odyssey Re (Bermuda) Ltd v Reinsurance Australia Corporation Ltd* [2001] NSWSC 266, 19 ACLC 987; *CGI Information Systems and Management Consultants Pty Ltd v APRA Consulting Pty Ltd* [2003] NSWSC 728, 47 ACSR 100; *Re General Healthcare Group Ltd* [2004] EWHC 3471 (Ch), LTL 13/12/2004.

[399] *Re Briton Medical and General Life Association Ltd* (1886) 11 OR 478.

[400] *Re Elgar Heights Pty Ltd* [1985] VR 657.

[401] Such as the prohibition in the Solicitors Act 1974, s 69, on bringing an action to recover a solicitor's costs until one month after delivery of a bill.

[402] *Re Elgar Heights Pty Ltd*; *Remuneration Data Base Pty Ltd v Pauline Goodyer Real Estate Pty Ltd* [2007] NSWSC 59.

been held that a statutory demand for a debt should be set aside[403] if a statutory prohibition on bringing proceedings to enforce the debt comes into effect after service of the demand.[404]

7.163 A statutory demand is ineffective if the debt is statute-barred.[405]

7.164 The holder of a dishonoured cheque drawn by a company can certainly serve a statutory demand on the company.[406]

7.165 If a debt will become due only after it has been demanded, a statutory demand should not be served until after the debt has been separately demanded and so made due;[407] but compare the decision that a statutory demand can be sufficient notice of assignment of a debt.[408] A demand is not a condition precedent to repayment of an amount borrowed with no time specified for repayment, such as an amount repayable on demand or at call,[409] and so a statutory demand for such an amount is effective without any prior demand.[410] Prior demand is, however, required for an amount owed by a bank to its customer.[411]

Debt in which more than one creditor is interested

7.166 The statutory demand procedure is available to a creditor 'by assignment or otherwise'.[412] So the legal assignee of a debt may present a statutory demand for it. A statement in the demand itself that the debt has been assigned is sufficient notice for the purposes of the Law of Property Act 1925, s 136, to perfect a legal assignment of the debt and provide the assignee with standing to serve the notice.[413]

7.167 Where the whole of a debt has been assigned in equity only, the assignor may serve a statutory demand for it.[414] In addition an equitable assignee of a whole debt may serve a statutory demand for it.[415] This is because the statutory demand procedure is available to a creditor 'by assignment or otherwise'[416] and these words have appeared in the legislation since the Companies Act 1862, s 80(1), when only equitable assignment was possible.

7.168 If only part of a debt has been equitably assigned, a statutory demand for that part must be served by or on behalf of both assignor and assignee.[417]

---

[403] Under the Corporations Act 2001 (Australia), s 459J(1)(b); see 7.240.

[404] *Olympic Holdings Pty Ltd v Interwest Investments Pty Ltd* (1998) 16 ACLC 1242; *Re Chameleon Mining NL* [2009] NSWSC 602.

[405] *Re a Debtor (No 50A-SD-1995)* [1997] Ch 310; *Re a Debtor (No 647-SD-1999)* (2000) *The Times*, 10 April 2000. It has subsequently been held that the debt in *Re a Debtor (No 50A-SD-1995)* was not statute-barred (*Ridgeway Motors (Isleworth) Ltd v ALTS Ltd* [2005] EWCA Civ 92, [2005] 1 WLR 2871).

[406] *L M and W J Taylor Pty Ltd v Armour Timber and Trading Pty Ltd* (1996) 19 ACSR 231.

[407] *Permanent Custodians Ltd v Digital Enterprises Pty Ltd* (1992) 8 ACSR 542 (which concerned an acceleration clause in a mortgage); *TS and S Global Ltd v Fithian-Franks* [2007] EWHC 1401 (Ch), LTL 25/6/2007 (bankruptcy statutory demand).

[408] See 7.166.

[409] *Re Brown's Estate* [1893] 2 Ch 300; *Bradford Old Bank v Sutcliffe* [1918] 2 KB 833.

[410] *Toskas Investments Pty Ltd v Toskas* (2000) 34 ACSR 503.

[411] *N Joachimson v Swiss Bank Corporation* [1921] 3 KB 110.

[412] IA 1986, ss 123(1)(a) and 222(1).

[413] *Clearance Nominees Pty Ltd v Discount Acceptance Corporation Pty Ltd* (1997) 25 ACSR 531 at p 533; *Bennell v Netlink Australia Pty Ltd* [2002] NSWSC 822, 42 ACSR 680, at [42]–[47]; but compare the decision that a statutory demand does not in itself make due a debt which is not due until demanded (see 7.165).

[414] *Rohan Trading Co Pty Ltd v Glengor Pastoral Co Pty Ltd* [2003] NSWSC 1265.

[415] *Re Small and Shattell (Sales) Pty Ltd* (1992) 7 ACSR 99.

[416] IA 1986, ss 123(1)(a) and 222(1).

[417] *Re Steel Wing Co Ltd* [1921] 1 Ch 349; *Manzo v 555/255 Pitt Street Pty Ltd* (1990) 21 NSWLR 1.

The prescribed form of statutory demand[418] requires a creditor who is entitled by assign- **7.169**
ment to the debt being demanded to give details of the original creditor and any intermedi-
ary assignees. In Australia it has been held that if the company has had no previous notice
of the assignment, the description in the statutory demand must be sufficient to enable
the company to verify that payment to the person making the demand will discharge the
debt.[419]

If a debt is owed to joint creditors, payment to any one of them discharges the debt. So **7.170**
in England it has been held that any one of joint creditors may serve a statutory demand
for the debt.[420] But in Australia it has been held that the demand must be served by or on
behalf of all the joint creditors.[421] In England it has been held[422] that a statutory demand
may be served by a legally aided litigant for money payable in connection with the dispute,
even though the money is subject to the statutory charge[423] so that a good discharge for the
money can be given only by the legally aided party's provider.[424]

It has been held in Australia that three separate creditors cannot serve a single statutory **7.171**
demand for the total of their debts, even though it specified the debts separately.[425]

Joint debtors

If two or more persons are jointly liable to pay a sum of money, the creditor may serve a **7.172**
statutory demand for the whole amount on any one of them.[426]

Judgment debt

A statutory demand may be served on a company for a judgment debt despite the fact that **7.173**
the company is appealing against the judgment.[427]

Service of a statutory demand for a judgment debt, like presentation of a winding-up peti- **7.174**
tion by the judgment creditor,[428] is not an execution of the judgment and so is not prevented
by a stay of execution of the judgment[429]—a judgment debt is still due despite a stay of
execution.[430] However, in Australia it has been held that a statutory demand for a judgment debt should be set aside[431] if execution of the judgment is stayed after service of the

---

[418] IR 1986, sch 4, form 4.1.
[419] *Condor Asset Management Ltd v Excelsior Eastern Ltd* [2005] NSWSC 1139, 56 ACSR 223.
[420] *Mahmood v Penrose* [2004] EWHC 1500 (Ch), [2005] BPIR 170.
[421] *115 Constitution Road Pty Ltd v Downey* [2008] NSWSC 997, 220 FLR 216.
[422] *Re a Debtor (No 68/SD/97)* [1998] 4 All ER 779.
[423] Legal Aid, Sentencing and Punishment of Offenders Act 2012, s 25.
[424] Civil Legal Aid (Statutory Charge) Regulations 2013 (SI 2013/503), reg 13. If the legally aided party
is no longer represented by a provider, only the Lord Chancellor may give a good discharge (SI 2013/503,
reg 12).
[425] *First Line Distribution Pty Ltd v Whiley* (1995) 18 ACSR 185.
[426] *Barclays Australia (Finance) Ltd v Mike Gaffikin Marine Pty Ltd* (1996) 21 ACSR 235; *Dynasty Rangers
Sdn Bhd v Perak Meat Industries Sdn Bhd* [2002] 5 MLJ 291.
[427] *Barclays Australia (Finance) Ltd v Mike Gaffikin Marine Pty Ltd* (1996) 21 ACSR 235; *Scope Data
Systems Pty Ltd v BDO Nelson Parkhill* [2003] NSWSC 137, 199 ALR 56; *Pontian United Theatre Sdn Bhd v
Southern Finance Bhd* [2006] 2 MLJ 602.
[428] See 7.60.
[429] *Scope Data Systems Pty Ltd v BDO Nelson Parkhill* [2003] NSWSC 137, 199 ALR 56.
[430] *Woodley v Woodley (No 2)* [1994] 1 WLR 1167; *Australian Beverage Distributors Pty Ltd v Evans and
Tate Premium Wines Pty Ltd* [2007] NSWCA 57, 61 ACSR 441.
[431] Under the Corporations Act 2001 (Australia), s 459J(1)(b); see 7.240.

demand, because non-compliance with the demand should not give rise to a presumption of insolvency.[432]

7.175 There is no requirement that a debt for which a statutory demand is served must be a judgment debt.[433]

Secured creditors

7.176 A statutory demand can be served by a secured creditor.[434] A secured creditor's demand may be for the whole debt, not just the amount by which the value of the security falls short.[435]

Debt in a foreign currency

7.177 IA 1986 does not prohibit a creditor serving a statutory demand for an amount in a foreign currency in which the debt is payable.[436] In the prescribed form for a statutory demand there is a £ sign before the space where the amount demanded is to be inserted, but this does not mean that the amount demanded must be in sterling.[437] But see *Re Dynamics Corporation of America*,[438] in which Oliver J said, at p 765, that a £ sign in the prescribed form of proof of debt indicated that the proof must be for a sterling sum,[439] and the earlier Australian cases of *Re Ikin*[440] (bankruptcy statutory demand must be for a sum in Australian dollars) and *Vehicle Wash Systems Pty Ltd v Mark VII Equipment Inc*[441] (winding-up statutory demand must be in Australian dollars) which were distinguished in *Daewoo Australia Pty Ltd v Suncorp Metway Ltd*.[442] In *Re a Debtor (No 51-SD-1991)*[443] Morritt J observed, at p 1301, that tendering the sterling equivalent of the amount demanded in a foreign currency would be regarded as compounding the debt in a manner which the creditor could not reasonably refuse. In *Re Ikin* the fact that the relevant rules permitted the prescribed forms to be used with such variations as the circumstances required[444] was considered insufficient to allow alteration of the currency symbol in the prescribed form.

Amount accruing

7.178 If the amount claimed in a statutory demand includes interest which has not previously been notified to the company or any other charge accruing from time to time, the amount claimed must be limited to what has accrued due at the date of the demand.[445] A demand

---

[432] *Tatlers.com.au Pty Ltd v Davis* [2006] NSWSC 1055, 203 FLR 473.

[433] *Dooney v Henry* [2000] HCA 44, 174 ALR 41, at [8].

[434] *Re Cushing Sulphite Fibre Co Ltd* (1905) 37 NBR 254; *Accordent Pty Ltd v RMBL Investments Ltd* [2009] SASC 248, 105 SASR 62, at [61].

[435] *Accordent Pty Ltd v RMBL Investments Ltd* [2009] SASC 248, 105 SASR 62, at [62].

[436] *International Factors (Singapore) Pty Ltd v Speedy Tyres Pty Ltd* (1991) 5 ACSR 250; *Re a Debtor (No 51-SD-1991)* [1992] 1 WLR 1294, which concerned a statutory demand in bankruptcy but Morritt J said, at p 1299, that there was no material difference in this respect between bankruptcy and company insolvency.

[437] *Re a Debtor (No 51-SD-1991)* [1992] 1 WLR 1294, which concerned a bankruptcy statutory demand; *Daewoo Australia Pty Ltd v Suncorp Metway Ltd* [2000] NSWCA 35, 48 NSWLR 692; *SMEC International Pty Ltd v CEMS Engineering Inc* [2001] NSWSC 459, 162 FLR 383, at [28]–[33].

[438] [1976] 1 WLR 757.

[439] At that time, there was no equivalent of the present rule that a debt in a foreign currency must be converted into sterling for the purpose of proving it (IR 1986, r 4.91).

[440] (1985) 4 FCR 582.

[441] (1997) 80 FCR 571.

[442] [2000] NSWCA 35, 48 NSWLR 692.

[443] [1992] 1 WLR 1294.

[444] A provision similar to IR 1986, r 12A.30(2).

[445] IR 1986, r 4.5(2).

must be dated.[446] The statutory demand must state separately either the amount of interest or accruing charge included or the rate of charge.[447] It must also state the grounds on which payment of interest or other accruing charge is claimed.

Rule 4.5(2) prohibits a statutory demand claiming interest or other accruing charge up to **7.179** the date of payment, specifying only the rate and leaving it to the company to calculate what the amount at the date of payment is. In Malaysia, where there is no equivalent of r 4.5(2), it has been held that a statutory demand may be worded in this way.[448]

Method of Compliance

Time for payment

A company is not deemed by IA 1986, s 123(1)(a) or s 222(1), to be unable to pay its debts **7.180** following service of a statutory demand until 21 clear days have elapsed from service of the demand without the company complying with it. This means 21 whole calendar days and the day of service does not count.[449] In a petition presented before the 21 days have elapsed the petitioner cannot claim that the company is then deemed by the operation of s 123(1)(a) or s 222(1) in relation to that demand to be unable to pay its debts: the petition will therefore be dismissed,[450] unless the petitioner can prove the company's inability to pay its debts at the time of petitioning in some other way.[451]

In Australia the provisions which came into force on 23 June 1993 apparently permit an **7.181** applicant for a winding-up order to rely on failure, after the filing of the application, to comply with a statutory demand.[452] However, the application must set out particulars of the failure to comply with the demand,[453] which cannot be done if the failure has not occurred when the application is filed. An applicant who relies on a failure occurring after the application is filed must rely on the court declaring, under s 1322, that the application is not invalid despite the failure to comply with s 459Q(a). This declaration can be made only if the court is satisfied that no substantial injustice has been or is likely to be caused to any person.[454] Failure to comply with s 459Q(a) was excused by the court in *Aizen v Essendon Travel (Vic) Pty Ltd*.[455] But in *Long Nominees Pty Ltd v Roandale Holdings Pty Ltd*[456] the company was prejudiced and the application to wind up was dismissed as an abuse of process. In *Woodgate v Garard Pty Ltd*[457] Palmer J said that, if necessary, he would hold that an applicant for winding up in insolvency cannot rely on failure, after filing the application,

[446] r 4.4(3).
[447] r 4.5(2).
[448] *Malaysia Air Charter Co Sdn Bhd v Petronas Dagangan Sdn Bhd* [2000] 4 MLJ 657.
[449] *Re Lympne Investments Ltd* [1972] 1 WLR 523 at pp 525–6.
[450] *Re Catholic Publishing and Bookselling Co Ltd* (1864) 3 De G J & S 116; *Re Lympne Investments Ltd* [1972] 1 WLR 523; *Kong Long Huat Chemicals Sdn Bhd v Raylee Industries Sdn Bhd* [1998] 6 MLJ 330.
[451] *Syd Mannix Pty Ltd v Leserv Constructions Pty Ltd* [1971] 1 NSWLR 788, affirmed (1972) 46 ALJR 548; *Comalco Aluminium Ltd v Ohtsu Tyre and Rubber Co (Aust) Pty Ltd* (1983) 8 ACLR 330; *Re Toys For Less Ltd* (1986) 3 NZCLC 99,988; *Sri Hartamas Development Sdn Bhd v MBf Finance Bhd* [1992] 1 MLJ 313.
[452] Corporations Act 2001, s 459C(2); *Aizen v Essendon Travel (Vic) Pty Ltd* (1994) 49 FCR 594; *Pinn v Barroleg Pty Ltd* (1997) 138 FLR 417.
[453] s 459Q(a).
[454] s 1322(6)(c).
[455] (1994) 49 FCR 594.
[456] [2009] NSWSC 932.
[457] [2010] NSWSC 508, 239 FLR 339.

to comply with a statutory demand, because of the conflict with s 459Q(a), but his Honour was not referred to *Aizen v Essendon Travel (Vic) Pty Ltd* or the possible use of s 1322.

7.182   Payment may be made by a person other than the company.[458]

7.183   The general rule stated by Lord Denning in *Thomson v Moyse*,[459] at p 1004, is that a payment by cheque is an actual payment at the time the payee is given the cheque, but there is a condition subsequent that if the cheque is dishonoured, the payment will not have been made. It follows that if a cheque for the sum demanded in a statutory demand is received by the creditor within three weeks after the demand is served, and is not subsequently dishonoured, there has been compliance with the statutory demand.

7.184   A creditor is not bound to present a petition immediately the 21 days have expired.[460] In *Deputy Commissioner of Taxation v Cye International Pty Ltd (No 2)*,[461] Young J thought that the deemed insolvency arising on neglect to comply with a statutory demand expired after a sufficient period of time had elapsed (in the case, six months) but this was rejected by McLelland J in *Australian Card Services Pty Ltd v JS Wallboards Pty Ltd*.[462] In Australia there is now a statutory limit of three months.[463] In England and Wales, a delay of more than four months must be explained in the statement of truth filed in support of the petition (see 2.195).

7.185   For the possibility that the deemed inability to pay debts brought about by neglect to comply with a statutory demand is brought to an end if there is subsequent compliance see 7.298–7.301.

Place of payment

7.186   It has been held in Australia that a statutory demand may require payment of the amount demanded outside the jurisdiction, provided it is feasible to communicate with the creditor for the purpose of paying, securing or compounding for the debt within the statutory three-week period.[464] Earlier, in deciding in *Re P H and J P Harding Pty Ltd*[465] that, because of the cooperative agreement for uniform companies legislation throughout Australia, the whole of Australia was one jurisdiction for this purpose, the drift of Senior Master Mahony's argument appeared to suggest that a statutory demand requiring payment outside the jurisdiction would be invalid.[466]

Payment must be unconditional

7.187   In *Re Alwinco Products Ltd*[467] a creditor presented a statutory demand for one part of its claim against the company, being a part that was undisputed. The remainder of the claim was the subject of legal action. The company tendered the amount demanded on condition

---

[458] *Deputy Commissioner of Taxation v Barroleg Pty Ltd* (1997) 25 ACSR 167 at p 172.
[459] [1961] AC 967.
[460] *Re Imperial Hydropathic Hotel Co, Blackpool, Ltd* (1882) 49 LT 147, in which the delay was nine months.
[461] (1985) 10 ACLR 305.
[462] (1991) 5 ACSR 274.
[463] Corporations Act 2001 (Australia), s 459C(2).
[464] *Re Shuttle Datacomm Pty Ltd* (1990) 2 ACSR 729 per Senior Master Mahony.
[465] (1986) 10 ACLR 365.
[466] See *Delaine Pty Ltd v Quarto Publishing plc* (1990) 3 ACSR 81 and *Re International Business Solutions Pty Ltd* (1992) 7 ACSR 753.
[467] [1985] 1 NZLR 710.

that it should be accepted in full and final settlement of the whole claim. It was held that this conditional tender was insufficient so that the company had neglected to pay the amount demanded and so was deemed unable to pay its debts.[468]

Security for sum due

Under IA 1986, ss 123(1)(a) and 222(1), a company may comply with a statutory demand by providing security for the sum due to the reasonable satisfaction (s 123(1)(a)) or satisfaction (s 222(1)) of the creditor. **7.188**

Under s 123(1)(a), if a creditor refuses to accept offered security for the debt demanded, there has not been a failure to comply with the statutory demand if the creditor's dissatisfaction with the security is unreasonable. It is submitted that the same test applies to s 222(1) even though there is no express reference to reasonableness. The wording of s 222(1) follows the equivalent provision in bankruptcy.[469] It is unnecessary to include the word 'reasonable' in the bankruptcy provision at this point because there is a separate provision that a bankruptcy petition may be dismissed if an offer has been unreasonably refused.[470] **7.189**

In *Commercial Bank of Scotland Ltd v Lanark Oil Co Ltd*[471] Lord President Inglis said, at p 149, that the true test of the sufficiency of security is whether it would command the amount of the debt if 'put into the market'. **7.190**

Security which the company has given before service of the statutory demand, and with which the creditor should be satisfied, counts as security provided to comply with the statutory demand.[472] **7.191**

A bank's unconditional performance guarantee, which the bank has secured by a charge on the company's property, is a charge on the company's property with which the creditor ought to be reasonably satisfied.[473] A bank guarantee that payment will be made if and when the creditor obtains judgment for the amount claimed is not a security with which a creditor could be reasonably satisfied.[474] **7.192**

Once the creditor is satisfied with the security the statutory demand has been complied with and the company is not deemed to be unable to pay its debts: a change of mind by the creditor on the satisfactoriness of the security cannot reactivate the deeming provision.[475] **7.193**

Composition and compromise

Under IA 1986, ss 123(1)(a) and 222(1), a company may comply with a statutory demand by compounding for the debt to the reasonable satisfaction of the creditor.[476] A composition is a promise by each of two or more creditors of a debtor that, provided the debtor pays them a specified proportion of their debts, each creditor will take no action to enforce payment of the **7.194**

---

[468] See also *Australian Mid-Eastern Club Ltd v Yassim* (1989) 1 ACSR 399; *Alcatel Australia Ltd v PRB Holdings Pty Ltd* (1998) 27 ACSR 708.

[469] IA 1986, s 268(1)(a).

[470] IA 1986, s 271(3).

[471] (1886) 14 R 147.

[472] *Covington Railways Ltd v Uni-Accommodation Ltd* [2001] 1 NZLR 272.

[473] *Covington Railways Ltd v Uni-Accommodation Ltd.*

[474] *Forsayth NL v Juno Securities Ltd* (1991) 4 WAR 376, in which it was found that there was no dispute over the debt demanded sufficient to justify preventing the creditor applying for a winding-up order.

[475] *Kema Plastics Pty Ltd v Mulford Plastics Pty Ltd* (1981) 5 ACLR 607.

[476] The adjective 'reasonable' does not appear in s 222(1); see 7.188–7.189.

remainder of their debt in return for the other creditors not enforcing payment of the remainder of their debts.[477] The consideration that makes each creditor's own promise not to require full payment of a debt contractually enforceable is the forbearance of other creditors from requiring full payment of their debts.[478]

7.195 It would seem that in ss 123(1)(a) and 222(1) 'compounding' must include what would usually be called a 'compromise', under which creditor and debtor agree that a debt will be discharged by payment of less than the total amount owed and/or by payment later than due. In *Kema Plastics Pty Ltd v Mulford Plastics Pty Ltd*[479] it was assumed without argument that this was how compounding was to be interpreted in this context.[480] A creditor's promise to a debtor not to enforce full payment of the amount owed does not bind the creditor unless it is:

(a) made in a deed; or
(b) made for consideration given by the debtor (payment, on or after the due date, of part of the debt is not consideration, because it is only what the debtor is already required to do);[481] or
(c) made binding by promissory estoppel.[482]

7.196 Once a creditor who has served a statutory demand on a company is satisfied with a compromise, the statutory demand has been complied with and the company is not deemed to be unable to pay its debts: a change of mind by the creditor on the satisfactoriness of the compromise cannot reactivate the deeming provision.[483]

7.197 When offering a composition, a company must be full, frank and open and provide all the necessary information to enable an informed decision to be made by the creditor.[484] A creditor's refusal of a company's offer to compound is unreasonable if no reasonable hypothetical creditor would have refused the offer in the actual circumstances of the case as disclosed to the court.[485] The court is not limited to considering the factors that were taken into account by the creditor when refusing to agree to the offer. The court must look at all relevant factors and decide what impact those relevant factors would have on the hypothetical reasonable creditor.[486]

Reasonable Excuse for not Complying

7.198 A company on which a statutory demand has been served by a creditor is deemed unable to pay its debts if it 'has neglected' to pay, secure or compound the sum due to the creditor. If the company has a reasonable excuse for not paying, securing or compounding, it has not 'neglected' to pay and is not deemed unable to pay its debts.[487]

---

[477] *Re Hatton* (1872) LR 7 Ch App 723 per Mellish LJ at p 726; *Slater v Jones* (1873) LR 8 Ex 186 per Bramwell B at p 193.
[478] *Norman v Thompson* (1850) 4 Ex 755.
[479] (1981) 5 ACLR 607.
[480] See also *Re a Debtor (No 32 of 1993)* [1994] 1 WLR 899.
[481] *Foakes v Beer* (1884) 9 App Cas 605.
[482] *Collier v P and M J Wright (Holdings) Ltd* [2007] EWCA Civ 1329, [2008] 1 WLR 643.
[483] *Kema Plastics Pty Ltd v Mulford Plastics Pty Ltd* (1981) 5 ACLR 607.
[484] *Commissioners of Customs and Excise v Dougall* [2001] BPIR 269.
[485] *Re a Debtor (No 32 of 1993)*; *Commissioners of Customs and Excise v Dougall*; *Nottingham City Council v Pennant* [2009] EWHC 2437 (Ch), [2010] BPIR 430.
[486] See also *Commissioners of HM Revenue and Customs v Garwood* [2012] BPIR 575.
[487] *Re London and Paris Banking Corporation* (1874) LR 19 Eq 444; *Re Imperial Hydropathic Hotel Co, Blackpool Ltd* (1882) 49 LT 147 per Cotton LJ at p 150 ('reasonable cause or excuse'); *Re Lympne Investments*

It is a reasonable excuse for a company not complying with a statutory demand that the debt **7.199**
to which the demand refers is disputed by the company.[488]

A court order forbidding the company from disposing of its assets is a reasonable excuse **7.200**
for not complying with a statutory demand.[489] The fact that the company is prohibited
by law from paying the sum due is a reasonable excuse for not complying with a statutory
demand.[490]

The fact that the company on which a statutory demand has been served by a creditor has a **7.201**
claim against that creditor which exceeds the amount claimed in the statutory demand is a
reasonable excuse for failing to comply with the demand.[491]

Error in and Dispute about the Contents of a Statutory Demand
Effect of errors

In England and Wales, it seems that if a statutory demand served on a company contains **7.202**
an error, the court will be unlikely to conclude that the error gives the company a reasonable excuse for not complying with the demand unless the company is prejudiced by the
error: this is the attitude of the court to errors in statutory demands served on individuals.[492]
It has been said, in relation to statutory demands on individuals, that although it is desirable that there should be room for flexibility in their preparation this is not to be taken as a
charter for slipshod preparation.[493]

If an erroneous statutory demand has nevertheless brought to the company's attention the **7.203**
fact that the creditor is demanding payment, neglect to pay may be evidence of the company's inability to pay its debts under IA 1986, s 123(1)(e) or s 224(1)(d).[494]

If a creditor who has served a statutory demand realizes that it may be invalid, a second **7.204**
demand for the same debt may be served, even if the time for complying with the first
demand has not expired.[495]

Effect of errors: Australia

In Australia, before there were provisions for setting aside statutory demands,[496] some courts **7.205**
took the view that an error in a statutory demand does not necessarily render it invalid: the

Ltd [1972] 1 WLR 523 per Megarry J at pp 527–8; and other cases cited at 7.198–7.201; *L and D Audio
Acoustics Pty Ltd v Pioneer Electronic Australia Pty Ltd* (1982) 7 ACLR 180; *General Welding and Construction
Co (Qld) Pty Ltd v International Rigging (Aust) Pty Ltd* (1983) 8 ACLR 307 at p 309: in the Australian legislation considered in the last two cases 'neglected' is replaced by 'failed'.
[488] See 7.198–7.201.
[489] *Eagle v New Zealand School of Advertising, Marketing and Public Relations Ltd* (1988) 4 NZCLC
64,844.
[490] *Hall v Bangor Corporation Ltd* [1993] MCLR 171.
[491] *Clem Jones Pty Ltd v International Resources Planning and Development Pty Ltd* [1970] QdR 37; *Re Clem
Jones Pty Ltd* [1970] QWN 6; *Re Jeff Reid Pty Ltd* (1980) 5 ACLR 28; *Dow Securities Pty Ltd v Manufacturing
Investments Ltd* (1981) 5 ACLR 501.
[492] *Re a Debtor (No 190 of 1987)* (1988) The Times, 21 May 1988; *Re a Debtor (No 1 of 1987)* [1989] 1 WLR
271; *Wallace LLP v Yates* [2010] EWHC 1098 (Ch), [2010] BPIR 1041, at [17].
[493] *Re a Debtor (No 1 of 1987)* at p 280.
[494] See 7.272–7.281.
[495] *Indaba Pty Ltd v Home Building Society Ltd* [2000] WASC 38, 18 ACLC 335 (first demand not signed);
James Estate Wines Pty Ltd v Widelink (Aust) Pty Ltd [2003] NSWSC 744, 47 ACSR 72 (first demand served
at wrong address).
[496] See 7.237–7.245.

question is whether the error had the effect of frustrating in some way a purpose of the statutory provisions under consideration or whether it was capable of depriving a party of a right or opportunity to exercise a right.[497] A case which occurred after the provisions for setting aside statutory demands were introduced is an example of a mistake depriving a party of an opportunity to exercise a right. In *Re Beralt*[498] a statutory demand was held to be ineffective because it omitted to state (as required by the prescribed form) that an application to set it aside had to be made within 21 days and the company's application to set it aside had failed because it was out of time. In *Re International Business Solutions Pty Ltd*[499] it was said that the question which has to be answered is whether the company is to be deemed unable to pay its debts by virtue of non-compliance with the demand.

7.206 In *Re Crust 'n' Crumb Bakers (Wholesale) Pty Ltd*[500] it was held that a statutory demand was valid despite the fact that, when referring to the legislative provision under which it was made, it mistakenly referred to a provision which had been repealed and replaced by a new law which in all material respects was indistinguishable from the one cited. There was no reason to suppose the company was misled by the notice.[501] The heading of the prescribed form of statutory demand in England and Wales[502] states that it is a 'statutory demand under section 123(1)(a) or 222(1)(a) of the Insolvency Act 1986'.

7.207 In *Re P H and J P Harding Pty Ltd*[503] a statutory demand served on a company stated that if the company did not comply with the demand, application would be made to the Supreme Court of Queensland for a winding-up order: in fact application was made to the Supreme Court of Victoria, but the demand was held to be valid: there was no requirement in the relevant legislation that the forum for winding-up proceedings had to be stated in the statutory demand. In *Re Terra Nova Pty Ltd*[504] a statutory demand was not invalidated by an erroneous statement that it had been sealed by the creditor: the error had obviously not misled the company.

7.208 In *Re International Business Solutions Pty Ltd*[505] it was said that the mere theoretical possibility that a mistake in a statutory demand served on a company will prejudice the company is not enough: the actual effect of the mistake should be assessed in the light of the information the company had about the debt being demanded. However, the onus is on the applicant for the winding-up order to show that the theoretically possible prejudice to the company has not in fact occurred. This was applied in *Re Williamsport Holdings Ltd*,[506] in which there was no admissible evidence that misnaming the creditor in a statutory demand served on a company had not prejudiced the company.

7.209 An alternative line taken by some courts in Australia is to say that a mistake in a statutory demand renders it invalid (so that neglect to pay on the demand does not in itself mean that

---

[497] *Pro-Image Productions (Vic) Pty Ltd v Catalyst Television Productions Pty Ltd* (1988) 14 ACLR 303.
[498] [1999] QSC 202, [2001] 1 QdR 232.
[499] (1992) 7 ACSR 753.
[500] (1991) 5 ACSR 70.
[501] The same was held in relation to a subsequent replacement of legislation in *Quitstar Pty Ltd v Cooline Pacific Pty Ltd* [2003] NSWCA 359, 48 ACSR 222.
[502] IR 1986, sch 4, form 4.1.
[503] (1986) 10 ACLR 365.
[504] (1990) 2 ACSR 646.
[505] (1992) 7 ACSR 753.
[506] (1993) 9 WAR 390.

the company is deemed to be unable to pay its debts) but that if the mistake has not prejudiced the company, neglect to pay may be evidence that the company is unable to pay its debts.[507]

Misnomer of the company

In Australia it has been said that if it is sought to rely on a statutory demand served on a **7.210** company as deeming the company to be unable to pay its debts but the company was mis-named in the demand, the question is whether, on a fair construction of the document, the company was not named (in which case the demand is ineffective) or whether it was named with a trivial mistake (in which case the demand is effective).[508]

In *Re Willes Trading Pty Ltd*[509] a statutory demand for a debt owed by Willes Trading Pty Ltd, **7.211** but addressed to 'Willis Trading Pty Ltd', was held to be invalid. In *Allen Properties (Qld) Pty Ltd v Encino Holding Pty Ltd* a statutory demand for a debt owed by Encino Holding Pty Ltd but addressed to 'Encino Holdings Pty Ltd' was held to be effective (the company had appeared at the hearing of a winding-up petition based on the demand). In *Pro-Image Productions (Vic) Pty Ltd v Catalyst Television Productions Pty Ltd*[510] a statutory demand for a debt owed by Catalyst TV Productions Pty Ltd was addressed to 'Catalyst Television Productions Pty Ltd'; the company was not misled, and the Full Court in Victoria held that the demand was not invalid.

In New Zealand, mistakenly naming United Homes (1988) Ltd as United Homes (1998) **7.212** Ltd could not possibly have caused any misunderstanding.[511]

Disputed debt

It is a reasonable excuse for a company not complying with a statutory demand[512] that the **7.213** debt to which the demand refers is disputed by the company[513] on the date of the demand.[514] In *Re Lympne Investments Ltd*[515] Megarry J said at pp 527–8:

> In the context of a notice requiring a person to do some act, I do not see how it can be said that the person 'neglects' to do that act if the reason for not doing it is a genuine and strenu-ous contention, based on substantial grounds, that the person is not liable to do the act at all. If there is liability, a failure to discharge that liability may well be 'neglect' whether it is due to inadvertence or obstinacy or dilatoriness: but a challenge to liability is a challenge to the foundation upon which any contention of 'neglect' in relation to an obligation must rest.

'If there is a dispute on substantial grounds there is no "neglect"'.[516] '[T]he presumption of **7.214** insolvency under [the Australian equivalent of s 123(1)(a)] will not arise if there is a genuine

---

[507] *Ataxtin Pty Ltd v Gordon Pacific Developments Pty Ltd* (1991) 29 FCR 564; *Re Vendas (Wholesale) Pty Ltd* (1991) 5 ACSR 447.

[508] *Allen Properties (Qld) Pty Ltd v Encino Holding Pty Ltd* (1985) 10 ACLR 104.

[509] [1978] 1 NSWLR 463.

[510] (1988) 14 ACLR 303.

[511] *United Homes (1988) Ltd v Workman* [2001] 3 NZLR 447.

[512] See 7.198–7.201.

[513] *Re London and Paris Banking Corporation* (1874) LR 19 Eq 444; *Securicor (M) Sdn Bhd v Universal Cars Sdn Bhd* [1985] 1 MLJ 84; *Rothwells Ltd v Nommack (No 100) Pty Ltd* (1988) 13 ACLR 421; *Re Mechanised Construction Pte Ltd* [1989] 3 MLJ 9; *Re Yap Kim Kee and Sons Sdn Bhd* [1990] 2 MLJ 108; *Brunsfield Information Technology Sdn Bhd v Masterloq Technologies Sdn Bhd* [2003] 6 MLJ 305.

[514] *Re Mechanised Construction Pte Ltd* [1989] 3 MLJ 9.

[515] [1972] 1 WLR 523.

[516] Per Needham J in *Club Marconi of Bossley Park Social Recreation Sporting Centre Ltd v Rennat Constructions Pty Ltd* (1980) 4 ACLR 883 at p 887.

dispute of substance as to the amount (and a fortiori the existence) of the debt the subject of the demand'.[517]

7.215 Therefore, according to Mervyn Davies J in *Re a Company (No 003729 of 1982)*:[518]

> [IA 1986, s 123(1)(a)] contemplates a creditor being able to point to a debt of a specified sum that cannot be seriously questioned either as to existence or quantum.

This was followed by Nourse J in *Re a Company*.[519]

7.216 Thus a claim for damages for breach of contract not quantified by judgment or by agreement cannot be the subject of a statutory demand.[520]

Mistaken statement of amount; partially disputed amount

7.217 The fact that, in a statutory demand served on a company by a creditor, there is an error in the statement of the amount owed to the creditor will not necessarily give the company an excuse for not complying with the demand. In order to comply with a statutory demand served on it, a company must pay (or secure or compound for) the amount due to the creditor, which may not be the same as the amount demanded.[521] The effect of paying an amount which is different from what is demanded will depend on whether creditor and company can agree on how much is to be paid.

7.218 If the amount of the debt demanded is erroneously stated, but the company can readily ascertain the correct amount which it accepts is payable and which the creditor will accept as full payment of the debt, the company will be deemed to be unable to pay its debts if it does not pay (or secure or compound for) the correct amount within the time limit.[522] (Though in *Re a Company*[523] Nourse J[524] was 'by no means certain' that a demand for payment of £161,000 could be relied on as a statutory demand for £83,000 because the 'discrepancy between the figures... is so enormous'.)

7.219 The cases have mostly been concerned with statutory demands which erroneously overstate the amount owed. In Australia it has been held that if a creditor's statutory demand for an amount less than the creditor is actually owed has been complied with, the company is not deemed to be unable to pay its debts because the whole amount owed to the creditor was not paid within the time limited by the statutory demand.[525]

7.220 If company and creditor cannot agree what the correct amount to be paid is, there is a dispute about the debt and the company has a reasonable excuse for not complying with the

---

[517] Per McPherson J in *National Mutual Life Association of Alasia Ltd v Oasis Developments Pty Ltd* (1983) 7 ACLR 758 at p 762.

[518] [1984] 1 WLR 1090 at p 1095.

[519] [1985] BCLC 37 at p 40. See also *Re General Exchange Bank Ltd* (1866) 14 LT 582; *Thiess Peabody Mitsui Coal Pty Ltd v A E Goodwin Ltd* [1966] QdR 1 at p 5; *Murdoch Constructions Pty Ltd v Learnton Nominees Pty Ltd* (1983) 7 ACLR 422; *Jurupakat Sdn Bhd v Kumpulan Good Earth (1973) Sdn Bhd* [1988] 3 MLJ 49.

[520] *Re Prime Link Removals Ltd* [1987] 1 NZLR 510.

[521] *Cardiff Preserved Coal and Coke Co v Norton* (1867) LR 2 Ch App 405 per Lord Chelmsford LC at p 410.

[522] *Cardiff Preserved Coal and Coke Co v Norton*; *Re a Company (No 003729 of 1982)* [1984] 1 WLR 1090 at p 1095; *Re a Debtor (No 10 of 1988)* [1989] 1 WLR 405 at p 406; *Re Trinity Insurance Co Ltd* [1990] BCC 235.

[523] [1985] BCLC 37.

[524] At p 41.

[525] *De Montfort v Southern Cross Exploration NL* (1987) 17 NSWLR 327.

demand, and it makes no difference that the company accepts liability for a certain part of the amount demanded.[526] The company may apply for an injunction against presentation of a petition based on non-compliance with the statutory demand, or, if the petition has been presented, an order striking it out. However, the court may take non-payment of any undisputed portion of the debt as evidence of inability to pay debts and allow the petition to proceed.

Where there is provision for setting aside statutory demands,[527] it is possible to make it a **7.221** condition of setting aside a demand for a partially disputed debt that the admitted part must be paid. This is the position taken in relation to bankruptcy statutory demands,[528] unless the admitted sum is less than the minimum debt in respect of which a bankruptcy petition may be presented.[529]

It is submitted that a company's failure to do anything about a statutory demand for an **7.222** amount of which part is disputed (for example, by tendering the undisputed amount and applying for an injunction to prevent presentation of a petition) may be evidence from which the court may conclude under IA 1986, s 123(1)(e), that the company is unable to pay its debts as they fall due.[530]

Validity of a statutory demand which overstates the amount indisputably due

If presentation of a petition based on a statutory demand for a partially disputed debt **7.223** is restrained, or a petition which has been presented is struck out (or, in bankruptcy, if the statutory demand is set aside), it is unnecessary to consider whether the demand itself was valid so that the company is deemed to be unable to pay its debts because of neglect to pay. If the question of validity does arise, it is submitted that the distinction drawn in *Re a Company (No 003729 of 1982)*[531] between an effective but erroneous demand for an undisputed debt and an ineffective demand for a debt which is disputed (even though the creditor is willing to admit part of it) should be maintained, even though it may be[532] a fine distinction. It is submitted, with respect, that this is better than the view expressed by the Court of Appeal in *TSB Bank plc v Platts*[533] (a bankruptcy case), at p 12, that it was doubtful whether *Re a Company (No 003729 of 1982)* was correctly decided 'having regard to the offer and subsequent payment of [the amount the company admitted owing]'. It is submitted that, while it may be true that not paying an undisputed part of a disputed debt may be evidence of inability to pay debts sufficient to justify a winding-up order, this is not relevant to the validity of a statutory demand for the disputed debt, and it seems that this confusion caused the doubts expressed in *TSB Bank plc v Platts* about the correctness of *Re a Company (No 003729 of 1982)*.

---

[526] *Re a Company (No 003729 of 1982)* [1984] 1 WLR 1090; *Re Clemence plc* (1992) 59 BLR 56.
[527] See 7.236–7.247.
[528] *Re a Debtor (No 490-SD-1991)* [1992] 1 WLR 507.
[529] *Re a Debtor (Nos 49 and 50 of 1992)* [1995] Ch 66.
[530] This was the view taken in *Ataxtin Pty Ltd v Gordon Pacific Developments Pty Ltd* (1991) 29 FCR 564; *Re Vendas (Wholesale) Pty Ltd* (1991) 5 ACSR 447; *Dikwa Holdings Pty Ltd v Oakbury Pty Ltd* (1992) 36 FCR 274; *Commonwealth Bank of Australia v Individual Homes Pty Ltd* (1994) 119 ACTR 1; and *YPJE Consultancy Service Sdn Bhd v Heller Factoring (M) Sdn Bhd* [1996] 2 MLJ 482.
[531] [1984] 1 WLR 1090.
[532] Per Warner J in *Re a Company (No 008122 of 1989)* [1990] BCLC 697 at p 697.
[533] [1998] 2 BCLC 1.

7.224   The question of the validity of a statutory demand for a partially disputed debt has been considered in other jurisdictions.

7.225   In Australia, before there were provisions for setting aside company statutory demands,[534] the states divided over the correct answer to the question. In some states it was held that a statutory demand which overstated the amount indisputably due was valid if part of the sum demanded was undisputed and the undisputed amount was not less than the minimum for which a statutory demand could be served. This was the position in Victoria,[535] Tasmania,[536] Northern Territory[537] and Western Australia,[538] and was taken in one case in Queensland.[539] The same view has been taken in India,[540] Malaysia,[541] New Zealand,[542] Papua New Guinea[543] and Singapore.[544]

7.226   The difficulty with this view is that it is unclear what a company served with such a statutory demand is to do in order to avoid being deemed unable to pay its debts. The problem of having to pay the whole amount demanded in order not to be deemed unable to pay debts was avoided by the court in *Re Fabo Pty Ltd* by saying that the deemed inability to pay debts which follows from failure to comply with a statutory demand may be rebutted,[545] and it is the failure to rebut which shows the company's inability to pay its debts and will lead to a winding-up order. The court said, at p 437:

> In our opinion, having been called upon to pay an amount including a sum undoubtedly due, the company could be reasonably called upon to pay that sum and to demonstrate the existence of genuine dispute as to its liability in respect of the balance.

7.227   In New South Wales a different view was taken: it was said there that a demand did not comply with the statutory requirement, and therefore had no effect, unless it was a demand for the amount due to the creditor[546] or for a lesser amount.[547] In the first of the cases cited, the creditor was restrained from applying for a winding-up order; in the other cases the application was dismissed when it was heard. The court was not, in any of these New South Wales cases, concerned

---

[534] See 7.237–7.245.

[535] *Re Convere Pty Ltd* [1976] VR 345 (in which the winding-up application was subsequently withdrawn); *Re Fabo Pty Ltd* [1989] VR 432.

[536] *Re Pardoo Nominees Pty Ltd* [1987] TasR 1.

[537] *Arafura Finance Corporation Pty Ltd v Kooba Pty Ltd* (1987) 52 NTR 43.

[538] *Mine Exc Pty Ltd v Henderson Drilling Services Pty Ltd* (1989) 1 ACSR 118; *Re Collinda Pty Ltd* (1991) 6 ACSR 123; *Re Newman Air Charter Pty Ltd* (1991) 5 WAR 365.

[539] *Re Great Barrier Reef Flying Boats Pty Ltd* (1982) 6 ACLR 820 (in which the applicants were no longer asking for a winding-up order), not followed in *General Welding and Construction Co (Qld) Pty Ltd v International Rigging (Aust) Pty Ltd* (1983) 8 ACLR 307.

[540] *Pfizer Ltd v Usan Laboratories P Ltd* [1986] LRC (Comm) 545.

[541] *Malaysia Air Charter Co Sdn Bhd v Petronas Dagangan Sdn Bhd* [2000] 4 MLJ 657.

[542] *Re Hart Systems Ltd* (1985) 3 NZCLC 99,504; *Re Khyber Pass Outdoor Centre Ltd* (1986) 3 NZCLC 99,756; *Commissioner of Inland Revenue v Cappucci Knitwear Ltd* (1989) 3 BCR 274; *Cockayne v Ellen Mitchell Creations Ltd* [1993] MCLR 30; though a different view was taken in another New Zealand case cited at 7.228.

[543] *Re Paradise Property and Development Pty Ltd* [1994] PNGLR 286.

[544] *Re Inter-Builders Development Pte Ltd* [1991] 3 MLJ 259; *Re Makin Nominees Pte Ltd* [1994] 3 SLR 429.

[545] See 7.302–7.306.

[546] *Processed Sand Pty Ltd v Thiess Contractors Pty Ltd* [1983] 1 NSWLR 384; *Irani v Asian Boutique Pty Ltd (No 2)* (1983) 8 ACLR 481; *Frank Hermens (Wholesale) Pty Ltd v Palma Pty Ltd* (1985) 10 ACLR 257; *Deputy Commissioner of Taxation v Cye International Pty Ltd (No 2)* (1985) 10 ACLR 305; *Re Vendas (Wholesale) Pty Ltd* (1991) 5 ACSR 447.

[547] *Wichita Pty Ltd v Elders IXL Ltd* (1990) 2 ACSR 273.

to distinguish between a mere mistake in the demand and a dispute on a substantial ground, though in the first and third cases, it is obvious that there was a substantial dispute about what was owed. Although neglect to comply with a statutory demand for a sum of which part was disputed could not be relied on to prove inability to pay debts, inability might be proved by other evidence,[548] including non-payment of the undisputed part.[549]

The view taken in New South Wales was also taken in Queensland,[550] New Zealand,[551] and in the Federal Court of Australia.[552]

7.228

Literature

Vincent Annetta, 'Statutory demands under the Companies Code: the effect of overstatement and disputed indebtedness' (1989) 7 C & SLJ 54.

7.229

Mistake in time allowed for compliance

In *Re Manda Pty Ltd*[553] it was held that a statutory demand which mistakenly gave the time limit for complying with the demand as two weeks instead of three weeks was not valid: the company (which did not appear at the hearing) might have decided not to comply because it could not do so within two weeks whereas it might have been able to within three weeks.

7.230

Withdrawal of a Statutory Demand

A person who has served a statutory demand on a company may withdraw it, either expressly or by implication.[554] There will then be no demand to be complied with, so the company cannot be deemed to be unable to pay its debts for not complying with the demand.[555] An oral statement that a demand is withdrawn is effective.[556]

7.231

Abuse of the Statutory Demand Procedure

In Australia, it has been held that, by analogy with the concept of abuse of court process, misuse of the statutory demand procedure for an improper purpose may be regarded as an abuse.[557] For this purpose, it is unnecessary to treat issuing the statutory demand as a court process.[558] It is an abuse of the statutory demand procedure to use it to enforce payment of

7.232

---

[548] *Re National Computers Systems and Services Ltd* (1991) 6 ACSR 133.

[549] See 7.539–7.540.

[550] *Thiess Peabody Mitsui Coal Pty Ltd v A E Goodwin Ltd* [1966] QdR 1; *General Welding and Construction Co (Qld) Pty Ltd v International Rigging (Aust) Pty Ltd* (1983) 8 ACLR 307, not following *General Welding and Construction Co (Qld) Pty Ltd v International Rigging (Aust) Pty Ltd* (1983) 8 ACLR 307.

[551] *Re First Fifteen Holdings Ltd* (1987) 4 NZCLC 64,108; though a different view has been taken in other New Zealand cases cited at 7.225.

[552] *Ataxtin Pty Ltd v Gordon Pacific Developments Pty Ltd* (1991) 29 FCR 564, in which Heerey J observed, at pp 569–70, 'It is probably just coincidence that this divergence [between the Supreme Courts of New South Wales and Queensland and those of other Australian States] follows the same line as that which divides Australia between different football codes, although it has to be noted that New Zealand has followed the New South Wales and Queensland line—and, what is more, in a case called *Re First Fifteen Holdings Ltd*'. His Honour was referring to varieties of football in which the ball may be handled. The predominant codes are rugby league in New South Wales and Queensland, Australian football in other parts of Australia, and rugby union in New Zealand.

[553] (1991) 6 ACSR.

[554] *Re Imperial Hydropathic Hotel Co, Blackpool Ltd* (1882) 49 LT 147 per Jessel MR at p 149.

[555] *Cempro Pty Ltd v Dennis M Brown Pty Ltd* (1994) 128 ALR 277 at p 278.

[556] *Re Chameleon Mining NL* [2009] NSWSC 602 at [13].

[557] *Accordent Pty Ltd v RMBL Investments Ltd* [2009] SASC 248, 105 SASR 62, at [55]–[63], where no abuse was found.

[558] As was done in *Mala Pty Ltd v Johnston* (1994) 13 ACLC 100. See 7.129–7.130.

a debt which the person serving the demand knows to be disputed.[559] A statutory demand containing 98 pages of complex calculations intended to swamp the recipient with information which could not be dealt with in the time available was an abuse of the statutory demand procedure.[560] It is not an abuse to serve two demands for the same debt, if there is a good reason for the duplication.[561]

7.233 It is not possible to obtain an injunction forbidding service of a statutory demand for a disputed debt.[562]

7.234 In Australia, the appropriate remedy for abuse of the statutory demand procedure is an order setting aside the demand.[563] If no application for such an order is made within the strict time limit, the question of abuse of the statutory demand procedure cannot be raised in proceedings on a winding-up application based on non-compliance with the demand unless it is material to proving that the company is solvent.[564]

Setting Aside Statutory Demands

No procedure for setting aside statutory demands served on companies

7.235 In the United Kingdom there is no procedure for setting aside a statutory demand served on a company. The only effective way to challenge a statutory demand before the hearing of a winding-up petition based on non-compliance with it is to apply for an injunction to prevent a petition being presented or, after one has been presented, to prevent it from proceeding.

Setting aside bankruptcy statutory demands

7.236 In English bankruptcy law an individual on whom a statutory demand has been served may apply under IR 1986, r 6.4, to the appropriate court for an order setting the statutory demand aside.[565] The circumstances in which the court may grant such an application are set out in r 6.5(4) as follows:

   (a) the debtor appears to have a counterclaim, set-off or cross-demand which equals or exceeds the amount of the debt or debts specified in the statutory demand; or
   (b) the debt is disputed on grounds which appear to the court to be substantial; or
   (c) it appears that the creditor holds some security in respect of the debt claimed by the demand, and either rule 6.1(5) [which requires that the statutory demand must be only for the net amount of the debt after deducting the value of the security] is not complied with in respect of it, or the court is satisfied that the value of the security equals or exceeds the full amount of the debt; or

---

[559] *Moutere Pty Ltd v Deputy Commissioner of Taxation* [2000] NSWSC 379, 34 ACSR 533; *Re Softex Industries Pty Ltd* [2001] QSC 377, 187 ALR 448; *Universal Music Australia Pty Ltd v Brown* [2003] FCA 1213, 47 ACSR 501; *Old Kiama Wharf Co Pty Ltd v Deputy Commissioner of Taxation* [2005] NSWSC 929, 55 ACSR 223; *Createc Pty Ltd v Design Signs Pty Ltd* [2009] WASCA 85, 71 ACSR 602.
[560] *Cremona Bros Pty Ltd v Chris Antico Pty Ltd* [2009] NSWSC 390.
[561] *James Estate Wines Pty Ltd v Widelink (Aust) Pty Ltd* [2003] NSWSC 744, 47 ACSR 72.
[562] *Altarama Ltd v Camp* (1980) 5 ACLR 513.
[563] Under the Corporations Act 2001 (Australia), s 459J(1)(b); see 7.240. Abuse justifying setting aside was found in *Old Kiama Wharf Co Pty Ltd v Deputy Commissioner of Taxation* [2005] NSWSC 929, 55 ACSR 223; and *Createc Pty Ltd v Design Signs Pty Ltd* [2009] WASCA 85, 71 ACSR 602.
[564] Corporations Act 2001 (Australia), s 459S; *Brown v Zomba Music Publishers Australia Pty Ltd* [2003] FCA 1214, 47 ACSR 490; see 7.243.
[565] See PD Insolvency Proceedings 2014, para 13.3.

(d) the court is satisfied, on other grounds, that the demand ought to be set aside.

See David Milman, 'Statutory demands in the courts: a retreat from formalism in bankruptcy law' [1994] Conv 289. The cases on setting aside demands served on individuals are not necessarily relevant to statutory demands served on companies.[566] In relation to a statutory demand served on a company the key question is not whether the demand can be set aside—it cannot—but whether the company will be deemed unable to pay its debts if it does not comply with the demand.

Setting aside company statutory demands in Australia

A procedure for setting aside company statutory demands has been introduced in Australia.[567] The emphasis in the scheme is on strict time limits.   **7.237**

A company on which a demand has been served may apply to the court for an order setting it aside,[568] but only within 21 days after service.[569] The court has no power to extend the time limit.[570]   **7.238**

A demand may be set aside under s 459H if there is a 'genuine dispute' between the company and the creditor about the existence or amount of the debt[571] and/or the company has an offsetting claim.[572] Section 459H requires the court to find out whether there is a 'substantiated amount' which could have been claimed in the demand. The substantiated amount is any amount which the company admits it owes the creditor less any offsetting claims. If the substantiated amount is less than the statutory minimum for which a demand may be served, the court must set aside the demand.[573] If the substantiated amount is equal to or greater than the statutory minimum, the court may vary the demand and declare it to have had effect, as so varied, as from when it was served.[574] Even if the creditor acknowledges that there is an error in the amount claimed and agrees what it should be, there is a dispute about the amount and the court has jurisdiction under s 459H(4) to amend the demand.[575] An offsetting claim may be by way of counterclaim, set-off or cross-demand, even if it does not arise out of the same transaction or circumstances as a debt to which the statutory demand relates.[576]   **7.239**

A demand may be set aside under s 459J if the court is satisfied that: **7.240**

(a) because of a defect in the demand, substantial injustice will be caused unless it is set aside;[577] or

(b) there is some other reason why the demand should be set aside.[578]

---

[566] Nicholls LJ in *Re a Debtor (No 1 of 1987)* [1989] 1 WLR 271 at p 276 said that r 6.5(4) should be interpreted without reference to previous authorities concerned with setting aside bankruptcy notices because they 'were concerned with a different scheme'.

[567] Corporations Act 2001 (Australia), ss 459G to 459N, which originally came into force on 23 June 1993.

[568] s 459G(1).

[569] s 459G(2).

[570] *David Grant and Co Pty Ltd v Westpac Banking Corporation* (1995) 184 CLR 265.

[571] s 459H(1)(a).

[572] s 459H(1)(b).

[573] s 459H(3).

[574] s 459H(4).

[575] *Besser Industries (NT) Pty Ltd v Steelcon Constructions Pty Ltd* (1995) 129 ALR 308.

[576] s 459H(5).

[577] s 459J(1)(a).

[578] s 459J(1)(b).

But the court must not set aside a statutory demand merely because of a defect.[579]

7.241   If a company on which a statutory demand is served applies for an order setting aside the demand, the period for complying with it is automatically extended to seven days after the application is finally determined or otherwise disposed of.[580]

7.242   Section 459F(2)(a)(i) contemplates that on hearing an application to set aside a statutory demand the court may extend the period for compliance with the demand: s 459H(4) empowers the court to vary a demand on finding that there is an undisputed debt.

7.243   On the hearing of an application for a company to be wound up relying on a failure to comply with a statutory demand, the company cannot, without the leave of the court, oppose the application on a ground which it relied on when applying for the demand to be set aside or which it could have relied on when making such an application but did not (whether it made an application or not).[581] The court cannot give leave to oppose unless it is satisfied that the ground on which the company seeks to base its opposition is material to proving that the company is solvent.[582] This means that a company which fails to apply for the setting aside of a statutory demand, on the ground that the debt demanded is disputed or that the company has a cross-claim, will be wound up despite the existence of the dispute or cross-claim, unless it can prove that it is solvent.[583]

7.244   The effect of these provisions has been described as entitling a creditor of a company, whose claim is disputed, to test the genuineness of that dispute by serving a statutory demand. If the dispute is genuine, the court will set aside the demand and the creditor will have to pay costs. But if the company fails to establish that there is a genuine dispute or cross-claim, the creditor may proceed to apply for the company to be wound up, and making that application cannot, on its own, be an abuse of process,[584] even if the creditor knows that the dispute is genuine.[585]

7.245   The provisions have generated an enormous quantity of reported litigation.[586]

---

[579] s 459J(2).

[580] s 459F(2)(a)(ii).

[581] s 459S.

[582] s 459S(2).

[583] *ACP Syme Magazines Pty Ltd v TRI Automotive Components Pty Ltd* (1997) 144 ALR 517, in which the company disputed the debt claimed by a substituted applicant; *State Bank of New South Wales v Tela Pty Ltd (No 2)* [2002] NSWSC 20, 188 ALR 702, in which the company had a cross-claim; *Braams Group Pty Ltd v Miric* [2002] NSWCA 417, 171 FLR 449, in which the debt was disputed; *CMA Corporation Ltd v SNL Group Pty Ltd* [2009] NSWSC 1452, in which the debt was disputed and the winding up was terminated six months later with the debt being paid into court (*Re SNL Group Pty Ltd* [2010] NSWSC 797); *Georgiou Building Pty Ltd v Perrinepod Pty Ltd* [2012] WASC 72, 261 FLR 211, in which there was both a dispute and a cross-claim.

[584] *Redglove Holdings Pty Ltd v GNE and Associates Pty Ltd* [2001] NSWSC 867, 165 FLR 72, at [29]; *State Bank of New South Wales v Tela Pty Ltd (No 2)* [2002] NSWSC 20, 188 ALR 702.

[585] *Braams Group Pty Ltd v Miric* [2002] NSWCA 417, 171 FLR 449.

[586] See Andrew Keay, 'Statutory demands in light of the Corporate Law Reform Act 1992' (1994) 12 C & SLJ 407; Andrew Keay, 'Finding a way through the maze that is the law of statutory demands' (1998) 16 C & SLJ 122.

Setting aside company statutory demands in New Zealand

In New Zealand, the court may set aside a statutory demand served on a company.[587] The company must apply within ten working days of service of the demand.[588] The court cannot extend this time limit.[589] The court may, by s 290(4), set aside a demand if satisfied that:[590]

(a) there is a substantial dispute whether or not the debt is owing or is due; or
(b) the company appears to have a counterclaim, set-off, or cross-demand and the amount specified in the demand less the amount of the counterclaim, set-off or cross-demand is less than the minimum debt for which a statutory demand may be served; or
(c) the demand ought to be set aside on other grounds.

7.246

A demand must not be set aside by reason only of a defect or irregularity, unless the court considers that substantial injustice would be caused if it were not set aside.[591] In this provision 'defect' includes a material misstatement of the amount due to the creditor and a material misdescription of the debt.[592] In order to show that there is a substantial dispute, the company must show a 'fairly arguable basis' on which it is not liable on the demand.[593] The fact that a company on which a statutory demand has been served is solvent is not a reason for setting aside the demand.[594]

7.247

Unsatisfied Execution

Under IA 1986, s 123(1)(b), a registered company is deemed unable to pay its debts:

7.248

if, in England and Wales, execution or other process issued on a judgment, decree or order of any court in favour of a creditor of the company is returned unsatisfied in whole or in part.

Under s 224(1)(a), an unregistered company is deemed unable to pay its debts:

7.249

if in England and Wales execution or other process issued on a judgment, decree or order obtained in any court in favour of a creditor against the company, or any member of it as such, or any person authorized to be sued as nominal defendant on behalf of the company, is returned unsatisfied.

What has to be proved is that execution has been levied but has failed to result in payment of the execution creditor's debt, wholly or partly. In *Re a Debtor (No 340 of 1992)*[595] (a case on the parallel provision in bankruptcy law, namely, IA 1986, s 268(1)) the sheriff visited the debtor's house to execute a writ of *fieri facias*[596] but failed to gain entry and was asked by the execution creditor's solicitors to abandon further attempts to execute the writ. It was held that s 268(1) had not come into operation because execution had not been effected. *Re Worsley, ex parte Gill*[597] is a similar case.

7.250

---

[587] Companies Act 1993 (New Zealand), ss 290 and 291.
[588] s 290(2).
[589] s 290(3).
[590] s 290(4).
[591] s 290(5).
[592] s 290(6).
[593] *United Homes (1988) Ltd v Workman* [2001] 3 NZLR 447 at [27].
[594] *AMC Construction Ltd v Frews Contracting Ltd* [2008] NZCA 389, 10 NZCLC 264,450.
[595] [1996] 2 All ER 211.
[596] The old name for a writ of control.
[597] (1957) 19 ABC 105.

7.251 The primary evidence of what happened on execution is the return to the writ. The court may conclude from the facts stated in the return whether or not the execution has been returned unsatisfied and may overrule any conclusion from the facts drawn by the person making the return.[598] A return cannot be made until the writ has been executed and it is not possible to make a return that the writ has not been executed.[599] If a return is not available, what happened on execution may be proved by any admissible evidence.[600] The view of the High Court of Australia in *King v Commercial Bank of Australia Ltd*[601] (a case on individual insolvency) that the essential point is whether the *return* showed that the execution was unsatisfied must now be regarded as wrong.

7.252 Execution wrongly issued for an amount in excess of the actual judgment debt cannot give rise to a presumption of inability to pay debts.[602]

7.253 The fact that a petitioner for the winding up of a company is a judgment creditor of the company does not mean that the petitioner is required to issue execution in order to prove the company's inability to pay its debts: any means of proof may be used.[603]

Cash Flow Test

Current Statutory Provisions

7.254 Under IA 1986, s 123(1)(e), a registered company is deemed unable to pay its debts:

> if it is proved to the satisfaction of the court that the company is unable to pay its debts as they fall due.

7.255 Paragraph (e) of s 123(1) is very different from paras (a)–(d):

> It does not treat proof of a single specific default by a company as conclusive of the general issue of its inability to pay its debts. Instead it goes to that very issue. It may open up for inquiry a much wider range of factual matters, on which there may be conflicting evidence. The range is wider because s 123(1)(e) focuses not on a single debt (which under paragraphs (a) to (d) has necessarily accrued due) but on all the company's debts 'as they fall due' (words which look to the future as well as to the present).[604]

7.256 Under IA 1986, s 224(1)(d), an unregistered company is deemed (for purposes of section 221) unable to pay its debts:

> if it is otherwise[605] proved to the satisfaction of the court that the company is unable to pay its debts as they fall due.

---

[598] *Re Worsley, ex parte Gill* (1957) 19 ABC 105.
[599] *Munk v Cass* (1841) 9 Dowl Pr Cas 332; *Re a Debtor (No 340 of 1992)* [1996] 2 All ER 211.
[600] *Ataxtin Pty Ltd v Gordon Pacific Developments Pty Ltd* (1991) 29 FCR 564; *Skarzynski v Chalford Property Co Ltd* [2001] BPIR 673.
[601] (1921) 29 CLR 141.
[602] *Downley Properties Ltd v Downsview Nominees Ltd* [1994] MCLR 19.
[603] *Re Flagstaff Silver Mining Co of Utah* (1875) LR 20 Eq 268; *Re Yate Collieries and Limeworks Co* [1883] WN 171; *Re Lyric Club* (1892) 36 SJ 801.
[604] *BNY Corporate Trustee Services Ltd v Eurosail-UK 2007-3BL plc* [2013] UKSC 28, [2013] 1 WLR 1408, per Lord Walker at [25].
[605] Meaning, otherwise than under paras (a)–(c) of s 224(1).

In Australia, since the Corporate Law Reform Act 1992 (Australia), the test set out in IA **7.257** 1986, ss 123(1)(e) and 224(1)(d), is the test which determines whether a company is 'insolvent',[606] which is the term used in the Australian winding-up provisions instead of 'unable to pay its debts'.[607]

Failure by a company to prove that it is able to pay its debts as they fall due is not necessarily **7.258** proof that it is unable to do so.[608]

History[609]

The Companies Act 1862, s 80(4), provided that a registered company was deemed unable **7.259** to pay its debts:

> Whenever it is proved to the Satisfaction of the Court that the Company is unable to pay its Debts.[610]

In *Re European Life Assurance Society*[611] it was held that, in determining, under that provi- **7.260** sion, whether a company was unable to pay its debts, the court could not take into account debts presently incurred but not due for payment until a future date.[612] The Life Assurance Companies Act 1870, s 21, was then enacted to provide that the court could order the winding up of a life assurance company if it was insolvent and in determining insolvency the court was to take into account the company's 'contingent or prospective liability' under existing contracts. Then the Companies Act 1907, s 28, was enacted to require the court, when determining whether any registered company was unable to pay its debts, to take into account the contingent and prospective liabilities of the company. This provision was in force, in various Companies Acts, from 1 July 1908 until 28 December 1986 (and so will be referred to here as the 1908–86 test), ending up as the Companies Act 1985, s 518(1)(e) as originally enacted.[613] Section 518(1)(e) provided that a registered company was deemed unable to pay its debts:

> if it is proved to the satisfaction of the court that the company is unable to pay its debts (and, in determining that question, the court shall take into account the company's contingent and prospective liabilities).

By virtue of amendments made by IA 1985, sch 6, para 27(4), which came into force on **7.261** 29 December 1986,[614] this single test was divided into the two now re-enacted as IA 1986, s 123(1)(e) ('the company is unable to pay its debts as they fall due'—the liquidity or cash-flow

---

[606] The Corporations Act 2001 (Australia), s 95A, provides that: '(1) A person is solvent if, and only if, the person is able to pay all the person's debts, as and when they become due and payable. (2) A person who is not solvent is insolvent.'

[607] Corporations Act 2001 (Australia), ss 459A to 459D.

[608] *Ace Contractors and Staff Pty Ltd v Westgarth Development Pty Ltd* [1999] FCA 728.

[609] The history of the provisions considered at 7.254–7.292 is discussed in detail in *BNY Corporate Trustee Services Ltd v Eurosail-UK 2007-3BL plc* [2013] UKSC 28, [2013] 1 WLR 1408, at [23]–[37].

[610] This form of words is still in force in the Cayman Islands (Companies Law (2013 Revision) (Cayman Islands), s 93(c)).

[611] (1869) LR 9 Eq 122.

[612] See also *Macdonell's Trustees v Oregonian Railway Co* (1884) 11 R 912; *Re a Debtor (No 17 of 1966)* [1967] Ch 590 (concerning what is now IA 1986, s 272(1)).

[613] It seems to have been considered unnecessary to continue to make separate provision for life assurance companies: the Life Assurance Companies Act 1870 was repealed by the Assurance Companies Act 1909, s 37 and sch 9.

[614] Insolvency Act 1985 (Commencement No 5) Order 1986 (SI 1986/1924), art 2.

test) and s 123(2) ('the value of the company's assets is less than the amount of its liabilities, taking into account its contingent and prospective liabilities'—the balance sheet test).[615]

7.262 The 1908–86 test (which also appears in the legislation of several Commonwealth jurisdictions) is not the same as the current ratio test (which asks whether current liabilities can be met from current assets).[616] The current ratio is a measure of liquidity rather than solvency. The 1908–86 test is concerned with the present capacity of the company to pay all its debts, including future and contingent liabilities, but future additions to its assets must be ignored.[617] Taking account of future assets had made the concept of insolvency in the Life Assurance Companies Act 1870, s 21, meaningless.[618] For cases in which the 1908–86 test was satisfied see *Re Burke Successors Ltd*[619] (company not earning enough to pay interest on large loans of working capital) and *Re HL Sensecurity Pte Ltd*.[620] Although the words 'as they fall due' are not in the statutory statement of the 1908–86 test, they were understood to be implicit in it.[621]

7.263 The wording of what is now IA 1986, s 224(1)(d), was introduced by an amendment made to the Companies Act 1985, s 669(1)(d), by IA 1985, sch 6, para 52(1).[622] Until that amendment came into force, the words 'as they fall due' were not part of the provision. In relation to unregistered companies the court was never required to take into account contingent and prospective liabilities until what is now IA 1986, s 224(2),[623] was added by IA 1985, sch 6, para 52(2), which came into force on 29 December 1986.[624] There was no equivalent provision before this.

Application of the Cash Flow Test

7.264 Amending CA 1985, s 518(1)(e) (the 1908–86 test), to produce IA 1986, s 123(1)(e) and (2),[625] has made a material difference to the wording of the provision but should be seen as making little significant change in the law.[626] IA 1986, s 123(1)(e) (the cash flow test), has replaced, in the 1908–86 test:

> one futurity requirement, namely to include contingent and prospective liabilities, with another more flexible and fact-sensitive requirement encapsulated in the new phrase 'as they fall due'.[627]

---

[615] See 7.284–7.292.

[616] *Re Great Eastern Hotel (Pte) Ltd* [1989] 1 MLJ 161; *Datuk Mohd Sari bin Datuk Hj Nuar v Idris Hydraulic (M) Bhd* [1997] 5 MLJ 377; *Wangsini Sdn Bhd v Grand United Holdings Bhd* [1998] 5 MLJ 345. Current liabilities are liabilities falling due within one year. Current assets are cash at bank and in hand, marketable securities held as temporary investments, debtors for amounts expected to be paid within one year, stocks and work in progress, and prepayments paid to purchase current assets.

[617] *Byblos Bank SAL v Al-Khudairy* [1987] BCLC 232 at p 247.

[618] See *Re London and Manchester Industrial Association* (1875) 1 ChD 466 at p 472.

[619] (1989) 26 JLR 252.

[620] [2006] SGHC 135.

[621] *BNY Corporate Trustee Services Ltd v Eurosail-UK 2007-3BL plc* [2013] UKSC 28, [2013] 1 WLR 1408, at [30] per Lord Walker citing *Re a Company (No 006794 of 1983)* [1986] BCLC 261.

[622] IA 1985, sch 6, para 52, was brought into force on 29 December 1986 by the Insolvency Act 1985 (Commencement No 5) Order 1986 (SI 1986/1924), art 2.

[623] See 7.284–7.292.

[624] Insolvency Act 1985 (Commencement No 5) Order 1986 (SI 1986/1924), art 2.

[625] See 7.259–7.263.

[626] *BNY Corporate Trustee Services Ltd v Eurosail-UK 2007-3BL plc* [2013] UKSC 28, [2013] 1 WLR 1408, at [35] and [37].

[627] Briggs J in *Re Cheyne Finance plc* [2007] EWHC 2402 (Ch), [2008] Bus LR 1562, at [56], approved by Lord Walker in *BNY Corporate Trustee Services Ltd v Eurosail-UK 2007-3BL plc* at [34].

This change underlines:

> that the 'cash flow' test is concerned, not simply with the petitioner's own presently due debt, nor only with other presently due debts owed by the company, but also with debts falling due from time to time in the reasonably near future. What is the reasonably near future, for this purpose, will depend on all the circumstances, but especially on the nature of the company's business.[628]

If the petitioner asks the court to take into account debts which fall due (or may fall due) further away than the reasonably near future, the cash flow test in IA 1986, ss 123(1)(e) and 224(1)(d), becomes completely speculative and the balance sheet test in s 123(2) or s 224(2) must be used instead.[629]   **7.265**

If a company is found to be unable to pay its debts under s 123(1)(e) or s 224(1)(d), the balance sheet test in s 123(2) or s 224(2) is irrelevant.[630] A company's inability to pay its debts as they fall due may be proved simply by the fact that it is not paying them, and non-payment of one debt may be sufficient evidence.[631]   **7.266**

If a company is paying its debts as they fall due for the time being, the court must, in an appropriate case go on to ask how this is being achieved. The balance sheet test in s 123(2) or s 224(2) is then relevant. A company which avoids cash flow insolvency by incurring more and more long-term debt which it has no prospect of repaying is unable to pay its debts.[632]   **7.267**

Future additions to the company's assets must be ignored.[633] However, a company's prospects of acquiring further assets before it will be called on to meet future liabilities will be very relevant when the court is exercising its discretion regarding the making of a winding-up order.[634]   **7.268**

In *JSF Finance and Currency Exchange Co Ltd v Akma Solutions Inc*[635] Park J refused to take into account a contingent debt under s 123(1)(e), saying, 'A contingent debt where the contingency has not happened has not fallen due'. In Australia there is an express provision that the court may take into account a contingent or prospective liability of a company when determining, for the purposes of an application for a winding-up order, whether the company is insolvent on the cash flow test.[636]   **7.269**

Admission

An admission on behalf of a company that it is unable to pay its debts is sufficient evidence of that fact and means that the company cannot pay its debts as they fall due. For example: **7.270**

- In *Re Fortune Copper Mining Co*[637] the company secretary had told the petitioners' solicitor that the company was 'deeply involved in debt' and had no money and no means.

---

[628] *BNY Corporate Trustee Services Ltd v Eurosail-UK 2007-3BL plc* at [37].
[629] *BNY Corporate Trustee Services Ltd v Eurosail-UK 2007-3BL plc* at [37].
[630] *Commissioners of HM Revenue and Customs v Bodychell Recycling Ltd* 2011 WL 4084881 at paras 4.1 and 4.9.
[631] See 7.272–7.281.
[632] *Bucci v Carman* [2014] EWCA Civ 383, [2014] BCC 269, at [29]–[31].
[633] *Byblos Bank SAL v Al-Khudairy* [1987] BCLC 232 at p 247. *Byblos Bank SAL v Al-Khudairy* was a case about ability to pay debts as they fall due (*BNY Corporate Trustee Services Ltd v Eurosail-UK 2007-3BL plc* at [34]).
[634] *Byblos Bank SAL v Al-Khudairy* [1987] BCLC 232 at p 247.
[635] [2001] 2 BCLC 307 at p 314.
[636] Corporations Act 2001 (Australia), s 459D. See *Brooks v Heritage Hotel Adelaide Pty Ltd* (1996) 20 ACSR 61.
[637] (1870) LR 10 Eq 390.

- In *Re Flagstaff Silver Mining Co of Utah*[638] the creditor, who had obtained judgment for his debt, was told by the company's solicitors that there were no assets in Britain on which execution could be levied, though the company had assets abroad.
- In *Re Yate Collieries and Limeworks Co*[639] a judgment creditor was informed by the company's solicitors that all the company's assets had been seized by a mortgagee.
- In *Re Douglas Griggs Engineering Ltd*[640] a judgment creditor was informed by the company's solicitors that the company had no assets at its premises or at the solicitors' office on which execution could be levied, though the company did have money in a bank account, and see the comments on this case by Millett LJ in *Re a Debtor (No 340 of 1992).*[641]
- In *Re SVO Limousines Pty Ltd*[642] the company's managing director had admitted that the company did not have sufficient funds to pay the petitioner's debt.

7.271 Evidence of an admission should state when and where the statement was made and who made it, and whether it was oral or in writing, and should give the actual words used, leaving the court to infer whether the words amounted to an admission of inability to pay debts.[643]

Non-payment of One Debt

7.272 The non-payment of a single undisputed debt may be sufficient to satisfy the court under IA 1986, s 123(1)(e) or s 224(1)(d), that a company is unable to pay its debts as they fall due even if no statutory demand has been served for the debt.[644] The possibility that the company just does not want to pay the debt is to be ignored.[645]

7.273 A debt is 'undisputed' unless there is a dispute on a substantial ground: 'It is not enough if a thoroughly bad reason is put forward honestly'.[646] It is not necessary for the debt to be a judgment debt. However, normally it must be shown that a demand has been made for payment of the debt. It must be shown that the company was notified of the amount of the debt and was given an opportunity to pay it.[647] In *Re a Company (No 006798 of 1995)*[648]

---

[638] (1875) LR 20 Eq 268.
[639] [1883] WN 171.
[640] [1963] Ch 19.
[641] [1996] 2 All ER 211 at p 218.
[642] (1990) 2 ACSR 367.
[643] *Re SVO Limousines Pty Ltd.*
[644] *Taylors Industrial Flooring Ltd v M and H Plant Hire (Manchester) Ltd* [1990] BCLC 216; *Re Simpson Development Investment (HK) Co Ltd* [1999] 1 HKLRD 202; *Re Dayang Construction and Engineering Pte Ltd* [2002] 3 SLR 379; *Clowes Developments (Scotland) Ltd v Whannel* 2002 SLT (Sh Ct) 6. The contrary view has been taken in Australia (*Re Redhead Coal Mining Co Ltd* (1893) 3 BC (NSW) 50; *QBE Workers Compensation (NSW) Ltd v Wandiyali ATSI Inc* [2004] NSWSC 1022, 62 NSWLR 117; *Workers Compensation Nominal Insurer v Doonside Community Activities Group Inc* [2008] NSWSC 1062) and Canada (*Re Milo Wheat Co Ltd* [1925] 2 DLR 1170).
[645] *Taylors Industrial Flooring Ltd v M and H Plant Hire (Manchester) Ltd* [1990] BCLC 216 per Dillon LJ at p 220.
[646] *Taylors Industrial Flooring Ltd v M and H Plant Hire (Manchester) Ltd* [1990] BCLC 216 per Dillon LJ at p 220.
[647] *Re Easy Letting and Leasing* [2008] EWHC 3175 (Ch), LTL 23/1/2009.
[648] [1996] 1 WLR 491.

Chadwick J said, at p 502, that 'in exceptional circumstances' the court could conclude that a company was unable to pay its debts as they fall due because of failure to pay a single debt even if there had been no demand at all for payment, but his Lordship did not give any examples of such circumstances and went on to say:

> at the least, ... the court should be slow to reach the conclusion that a company is unable to pay its debts from the mere fact of non-payment of a debt which has never been demanded of it at all.

Failure to pay a debt which became due for payment after the petition was presented may be **7.274** evidence that the company is unable to pay its debts as they fall due.[649] IA 1986, s 127, does not prevent a payment being made, it merely puts the payee in danger of having to repay it. In practice, though, after a winding-up petition has been presented against a company its bank would refuse to make payments from its account and so the company would have to seek a validation order to pay any debt that could not be paid from, for example, cash takings.

Failure to pay a debt before it is due is no evidence at all of inability to pay debts.[650]   **7.275**

It is common for a creditor petitioner to rely on the fact that the company has not paid a debt   **7.276** owed to the petitioner as proof[651] of the company's inability to pay its debts. This means of establishing that a circumstance exists in which the court has jurisdiction to make a winding-up order is comparatively straightforward.

Showing that there has been a neglect to comply with a statutory demand[652] or that there   **7.277** has been an unsatisfied execution[653] or that the company's assets are less than its liabilities[654] is sufficient for the company to be deemed to be unable to pay its debts. However, as Dillon LJ pointed out in *Taylors Industrial Flooring Ltd v M and H Plant Hire (Manchester) Ltd*:[655]

> The practice for a long time has been that the vast majority of creditors who seek to petition for the winding up of companies do not serve statutory demands. The practical reason for that is that if a statutory demand is served, three weeks have to pass until a winding-up petition can be presented. If, after the petition has been presented, a winding-up order is made, the winding up is only treated as commencing at the date of the presentation of the petition; thus, if the creditor takes the course of serving a statutory demand, it would be giving the company an extra three weeks' grace in which such assets as the company may have may be dissipated in attempting to keep an insolvent business afloat, or may be absorbed into the security of a debenture-holder bank. So there are practical reasons for not allowing extra time, particularly where commercial conditions and competition require promptness in the payment of companies' debts so that the creditor companies can manage their own cash flow and keep their own costs down.

In *Re a Company (No 003079 of 1990)*[656] Ferris J said, at pp 235–6:

> No statutory demand has been served on any of the companies [sought to be wound up by the petitions before his Lordship] nor has any judgment been obtained against them. Those

---

[649] *Re Richbell Strategic Holdings Ltd* [1997] 2 BCLC 429.
[650] *Re Easy Letting and Leasing* [2008] EWHC 3175 (Ch), LTL 23/1/2009, at [27].
[651] Under s 123(1)(e) or s 224(1)(d).
[652] s 123(1)(a).
[653] s 123(1)(b), (c) or (d).
[654] s 123(2).
[655] [1990] BCLC 216, at p 219.
[656] [1991] BCLC 235.

facts of course are in no way fatal to the petitions. In a suitable case the court will make a winding-up order on the ground of inability to pay debts if it is satisfied that there is a debt due to the petitioner which has not been paid in circumstances which indicate that the company is insolvent and unable to pay its debts.

7.278   The non-payment of a single undisputed debt was sufficient to satisfy the court of a company's inability to pay its debts under the Companies Act 1862, s 80(4). In *Re Globe New Patent Iron and Steel Co*[657] Jessel MR said, at p 338:

> It appears that the petitioners sold goods to the company, and took in part payment a bill, which was dishonoured, and continues unpaid. That is proof which ought to satisfy me, and which does satisfy me, that the company is unable to pay its debts.

7.279   Failure to pay a single debt was also sufficient to satisfy the court of a company's inability to pay its debts in *Re E M Martin (Succs) Ltd* [658] and in *Nigerian Commercial and Industrial Enterprises Ltd v Omagiafo Builders Ltd*.[659] In *Re Great Northern Copper Mining Co of South Australia*,[660] however, Lord Romilly MR appears to have regarded presentation of a bill of exchange for payment as a way of making a statutory demand (which at that time did not have to be in a prescribed form) so that dishonouring a bill on presentation for payment was equivalent to neglecting to comply with a statutory demand.

7.280   The non-payment of a single undisputed debt was sufficient to satisfy the court of a company's inability to pay its debts during the period when the court was required to take into account the company's contingent and prospective liabilities. In *Cornhill Insurance plc v Improvement Services Ltd*,[661] a company with profits of £11 million for the year failed to pay a debt of £1,154 despite repeated requests (though a statutory demand was not served). Harman J held that the creditor was entitled to infer that the company was unable to pay its debts and so was entitled to petition for the company to be wound up, apparently because non-payment of a single debt could be sufficient proof under the Companies Act 1985, s 518(1)(e), as originally enacted, of inability to pay debts. His Lordship cited *Re a Company*,[662] in which Vaisey J is reported as having said that 'Rich men and rich companies who did not pay their debts had only themselves to blame if it were thought that they could not pay them'.

7.281   In *Re Capital Annuities Ltd*[663] Slade J said, at p 187:

> A failure by the company to pay an admitted creditor within a reasonable time after demand would be likely to provide ample evidence of [the company's inability to pay its debts].

Moreover, in *Re a Company (No 006794 of 1983)*[664] Nourse J said:

> It seems to me that if a company is shown persistently and deliberately to have refused and neglected to pay its debts until it has to, then (subject to questions of degree) the court must

---

[657] (1875) LR 20 Eq 337.
[658] (1962) 5 WIR 39.
[659] 1974 (3) ALR Comm 91.
[660] (1869) 20 LT 264.
[661] [1986] 1 WLR 114.
[662] (1950) 94 SJ 369.
[663] [1979] 1 WLR 170.
[664] [1986] BCLC 261.

be able to conclude that the company is unable to pay its debts for the purposes of [the Companies Act 1985, s 518(1)(e)].

Appointment of a Receiver

In *Re Lyric Club*[665] the petitioners were judgment creditors who could not levy execution **7.282** because the court had already appointed a receiver on behalf of debenture holders. This was held to be sufficient evidence of the company's inability to pay its debts.

In *Tan Ah Teck v Coffral (Malaysia) Sdn Bhd*[666] it was held that appointment of a receiver under **7.283** a contract creating a floating charge over a company's property did not in itself prove that the company was unable to pay its debts (taking into account contingent and prospective liabilities) but showing that the receiver had taken possession of all the company's assets would.

Balance Sheet Test

Current Statutory Provisions

Under IA 1986, s 123(2), a registered company is deemed unable to pay its debts: **7.284**

> if it is proved to the satisfaction of the court that the value of the company's assets is less than the amount of its liabilities, taking into account its contingent and prospective liabilities.

The same provision is made in relation to unregistered companies by s 224(2). For the history of these provisions see 7.259–7.263 and for their relation to ss 123(1)(e) and 224(1)(d) see 7.264–7.269.

This is usually called the balance sheet test of insolvency, because a company's balance sheet **7.285** shows its assets and liabilities. But there is no limitation that the test can only be applied to the balance sheet drawn up to comply with statutory accounting requirements.[667]

Application of the Balance Sheet Test

The balance sheet test of insolvency in IA 1986, ss 123(2) and 224(2), is very far from an **7.286** exact test.[668] What has to be proved, on the balance of probabilities, is that a company has insufficient assets to be able to meet all its liabilities, including prospective and contingent liabilities.[669] Proving that depends on the available evidence of the circumstances of the particular case.[670]

> Essentially, s 123(2) requires the court to make a judgment whether it has been established that, looking at the company's assets and making proper allowance for its prospective and contingent liabilities, it cannot reasonably be expected to be able to meet those liabilities. If so, it will be deemed insolvent although it is currently able to pay its debts as they fall due. The more distant the liabilities, the harder this will be to establish.[671]

---

[665] (1892) 36 SJ 801.
[666] [1992] 1 MLJ 553.
[667] *BNY Corporate Trustee Services Ltd v Eurosail-UK 2007-3BL plc* [2011] EWCA Civ 227, at [1].
[668] *BNY Corporate Trustee Services Ltd v Eurosail-UK 2007-3BL plc* [2013] UKSC 28, [2013] 1 WLR 1408, at [37].
[669] *BNY Corporate Trustee Services Ltd v Eurosail-UK 2007-3BL plc* at [48].
[670] *BNY Corporate Trustee Services Ltd v Eurosail-UK 2007-3BL plc* at [38].
[671] *BNY Corporate Trustee Services Ltd v Eurosail-UK 2007-3BL plc* at [42], quoting with approval the words of Toulson LJ in the same case in the Court of Appeal, [2011] EWCA Civ 227, [2011] 1 WLR 2524, at [119].

7.287   As was said in the second sentence of the quotation in 7.286, it is possible for a court to find that a company's inability to pay its debts is not proved under s 123(1)(e) but is proved under s 123(2).[672] The Supreme Court has held that it had not been shown that a company, which had been (without any permanent increase in its borrowings) paying its debts as they fell due, was insolvent under s 123(2) by virtue of liabilities which could be deferred for over 30 years. The circumstances of the company over that length of time were incapable of prediction with any confidence. In particular, it could not be predicted how much would have to be paid to clear debts in foreign currencies and so the court could not be satisfied that there would eventually be a deficiency.[673] Where a company being wound up was presumed, for the purposes of reversing prior transactions, to have been, at the time of the transactions, insolvent as defined by s 123, that presumption was not rebutted by the fact that it was paying debts as they fell due at that time because it only did so by misusing money received from clients.[674]

7.288   The most significant question is how the 'proper allowance' is to be made for prospective and contingent liabilities. Future and contingent liabilities must be discounted for deferment and contingency.[675] In *Re a Company (No 006794 of 1983)*[676] Nourse J, referring to the 1908–86 test,[677] said:

> what I am required to do is 'take into account' the contingent and prospective liabilities. That cannot mean that I must simply add them up and strike a balance against assets. In regard to prospective liabilities I must principally consider whether, and if so when, they are likely to become present liabilities.

However, as pointed out by Nicholls LJ in *Byblos Bank SAL v Al-Khudairy*,[678] the way in which Nourse J applied this principle in the case before him is not revealed in the report.

7.289   Account can only be taken of existing assets. Expected profits cannot be taken into account as an asset in assessing the balance sheet test any more than in the cash flow test. However, it is submitted that, as with the cash flow test, a company's prospects of acquiring further assets before it will be called on to meet future liabilities will be very relevant when the court is exercising its discretion regarding the making of a winding-up order.[679]

7.290   Lord Neuberger of Abbotsbury MR pointed out the danger that ss 123(2) and 224(2) can deem solvent, successful and creditworthy companies to be unable to pay their debts.[680] His Lordship suggested that the way to deal with this was to adopt a rule,[681] that, on the petition

---

[672] *Bucci v Carman* [2014] EWCA Civ 383, [2014] BCC 269.

[673] *BNY Corporate Trustee Services Ltd v Eurosail-UK 2007-3BL plc* [2013] UKSC 28, [2013] 1 WLR 1408, at [42] and [49].

[674] *Bucci v Carman* [2014] EWCA Civ 383, [2014] BCC 269.

[675] *BNY Corporate Trustee Services Ltd v Eurosail-UK 2007-3BL plc* at [37].

[676] [1986] BCLC 261.

[677] See 7.260–7.262.

[678] [1987] BCLC 232 at p 249.

[679] *Byblos Bank SAL v Al-Khudairy* [1987] BCLC 232 at p 247.

[680] *BNY Corporate Trustee Services Ltd v Eurosail-UK 2007-3BL plc* [2011] EWCA Civ 227, [2011] 1 WLR 2524, at [44]–[47].

[681] *BNY Corporate Trustee Services Ltd v Eurosail-UK 2007-3BL plc* [2011] EWCA Civ 227 at [58].

of a future or contingent creditor, the court can deem a company to be unable to pay its debts under s 123(2) or s 224(2) only if the company is one:

> which has reached 'the end of the road',[682] or in respect of which the shutters should be 'put up',[683] imprecise, judgement-based and fact-specific as such a test may be.

While an appeal was pending, the 'end of the road' test was applied in two reported cases,[684] but on appeal it was held to be the wrong test. Sections 123(2) and 224(2) do not require a petitioner to do anything more than satisfy the court, on a balance of probabilities, that a company has insufficient assets to be able to meet all its liabilities, including prospective and contingent liabilities.[685] **7.291**

Contributed share capital is not a liability.[686] **7.292**

Is Deemed Inability to Pay Debts Rebuttable?

Evidentiary Purpose of Deeming

That a company is unable to pay its debts is one of the circumstances in which the court may order the winding up of the company.[687] However, even if one of those circumstances exists, the court's power to order winding up is discretionary.[688] IA 1986, s 123 (in relation to registered companies) and ss 222–224 (in relation to unregistered companies), state that if certain events have occurred, a company 'is deemed' unable to pay its debts. (The events will be called 'deeming events' in this discussion.) In ss 222–224 this is expressed to be for the purposes of s 221, but s 123 is not similarly limited, and in fact it additionally applies for the purposes of s 240 (circumstances in which an order adjusting a prior transaction may be made) and sch B1, para 11 (circumstances in which an administration order may be made).[689] **7.293**

There are two types of deeming event in ss 123 and 222–224: **7.294**

(a) Events which occur before a winding-up petition is heard and therefore before the court hears the company's evidence. These are neglect to pay on a statutory demand,[690] failure

---

[682] At [48] his Lordship had quoted Professor Sir Roy Goode's view that the provisions deal with the case of a company which has 'reached the point of no return because of an incurable deficiency in its assets' (*Principles of Corporate Insolvency Law*, 3rd edn (2005), para 4-06).

[683] This is a reference to a quotation by his Lordship, at [54], from *Insolvency Law and Practice. Report of the Review Committee* (Cmnd 8558, 1982, the Cork Report) at para 216: 'A balance has to be drawn between the right of an honest and prudent businessman, who is prepared to work hard, to continue to trade out of his difficulties if he can genuinely see a light at the end of the tunnel, and the corresponding obligation to "put up the shutters" when, by continuing to trade, he would be doing so at the expense of his creditors and in disregard of those business considerations which a reasonable businessman is expected to observe'.

[684] *Deiulemar Shipping SpA v Transfield ER Futures Ltd* [2012] EWHC 928 (Comm), LTL 25/4/2012; *Re TST Group Ltd* [2012] EWHC 4059 (Ch), LTL 1/11/2012.

[685] *BNY Corporate Trustee Services Ltd v Eurosail-UK 2007-3BL plc* [2013] UKSC 28, [2013] 1 WLR 1408, at [48].

[686] *Re Great West Brick and Coal Co Ltd* (1916) 9 Sask LR 240.

[687] IA 1986, s 122(1)(f) (registered companies) and s 221(5)(b) (unregistered companies).

[688] See 7.674–7.741.

[689] See sch B1, para 111(1), definition of 'unable to pay its debts'.

[690] ss 123(1)(a) and 222.

of execution[691] and failure of an unregistered company to indemnify a member sued for the company's debt.[692] These 'are true deeming provisions'.[693]

(b) Events which are decisions by the court on hearing the petition, after considering the company's evidence. These are a finding that the company is unable to pay its debts as they fall due[694] and a finding that liabilities exceed assets.[695] These are labelled as deeming provisions though neither is obviously of that character.[696]

7.295 Neglect to pay on a statutory demand is 'a convenient method of proof... that a company is unable to pay its debts'.[697]

> A company's non-compliance with a statutory demand, or non-satisfaction of execution of a judgment debt, is a matter that can be proved quite simply, usually by a single short witness statement. If proved, it establishes the court's jurisdiction to make a winding up order, even if the company is in fact well able to pay its debts.[698]

7.296 The odd grouping, as deeming events, of pre-hearing events with actual decisions by the court has led some courts to conclude that it is always the court which deems (in the sense of adjudges) a company to be unable to pay its debts and that the pre-hearing deeming events are set out in the sections as methods (or avenues) of proof.[699] This is the first theory.[700] The alternative, second theory[701] is that it is the occurrence of a deeming event which causes deemed inability to pay debts.

When does the Deemed Inability to Pay Debts Take Effect?

No time frame in legislation

7.297 The time frame of IA 1986, ss 123 and 222–224, is not stated. The sections do not state that the deemed inability to pay debts on the occurrence of any of the deeming events is an inability to pay at any particular time. Nor do they state any specific time at which the deeming provision takes effect. The sections neutrally say that a company 'is deemed' unable to pay its debts if one of the deeming events has occurred.[702]

---

[691] ss 123(1)(b), (c) and (d), and 224(1)(a), (b) and (c).

[692] s 223.

[693] *BNY Corporate Trustee Services Ltd v Eurosail-UK 2007-3BL plc* [2013] UKSC 28, [2013] 1 WLR 1408, at [24].

[694] ss 123(1)(e) and 224(1)(d).

[695] ss 123(2) and 224(2).

[696] *BNY Corporate Trustee Services Ltd v Eurosail-UK 2007-3BL plc* at [35].

[697] *Clarke and Walker Pty Ltd v Thew* (1967) 116 CLR 465 at p 467.

[698] *BNY Corporate Trustee Services Ltd v Eurosail-UK 2007-3BL plc* at [24].

[699] *Thiess Peabody Mitsui Coal Pty Ltd v A E Goodwin Ltd* [1966] QdR 1 at p 4 (neglect to pay etc on statutory demand causes the court to deem the company to be unable to pay its debts); *Re Pardoo Nominees Pty Ltd* [1987] TasR 1 at p 4; *Re Fabo Pty Ltd* [1989] VR 432; *Datuk Mohd Sari bin Datuk Hj Nuar v Idris Hydraulic (M) Bhd* [1997] 5 MLJ 377 at pp 399–400. All these cases were concerned with statutes which say that if a deeming event occurs, a company 'shall be deemed' unable to pay its debts, which can be more readily interpreted as a direction to a court than the words 'is deemed' in IA 1986, ss 123 and 222–224.

[700] See 7.298.

[701] See 7.299–7.301.

[702] The Companies Act 1965 (Malaysia), s 218, says 'shall be deemed', as did the Uniform Companies Act 1961 (Australia), s 222(2), and the Companies Act 1981 (Australia), s 364(2).

First theory: deeming begins with court's decision

The first theory is that the deemed inability to pay debts does not arise until the court has **7.298** decided to deem it.[703] A consequence of this is that deemed inability takes effect at the time of the court's decision, whether the deeming event occurred before or at the hearing. In *Re QBS Pty Ltd* this theory depended on holding that in IA 1986, ss 123(1)(a) and 222(1) (service of statutory demand), 'is indebted' means indebted at the time of the hearing. It follows that if a creditor presents a petition to wind up a company based on non-compliance with a statutory demand, the company will not, at the hearing of the petition, be deemed by the operation of s 123(1)(a) in relation to that demand to be unable to pay its debts if the sum due to the creditor is paid at any time before that hearing.[704] It is submitted, though, that 'is indebted' in ss 123(1)(a) and 222(1) means indebted when the statutory demand is served.[705]

Second theory: deeming begins with deeming event and may come to
an end before the hearing

The second theory is that the deemed inability to pay debts arises when the deeming event **7.299** occurs.[706]

Some judges added to the second theory the idea that the deemed inability to pay debts **7.300** can be brought to an end by a subsequent event, for example, by paying the demanded debt after the period for complying with a statutory demand has expired.[707] However, Needham J, who was the first to state the second theory in a judgment, refused to accept this idea.[708] In *De Montfort v Southern Cross Exploration NL*[709] Needham J said, at p 471, that after the debt which was the subject of the statutory demand has been paid, another creditor who is substituted as petitioner can rely on the deemed inability to pay debts arising from the original failure to pay within the time limited by the demand.

In *Deputy Commissioner of Taxation v Cye International Pty Ltd (No 2)*[710] Young J thought **7.301** that the deemed insolvency arising on neglect to comply with a statutory demand expired after a sufficient period of time had elapsed (in the case, six months) but this was rejected by McLelland J in *Australian Card Services Pty Ltd v JS Wallboards Pty Ltd.*[711] In *Deputy Commissioner of Taxation v Guy Holdings Pty Ltd*[712] Zeeman J pointed out, at pp 583–4, that Young J had really used the same argument as had been used by Needham J in *Re G Stonehenge Constructions Pty Ltd.*

---

[703] *Re QBS Pty Ltd* [1967] QdR 218 at pp 223–4; *Re Pardoo Nominees Pty Ltd* [1987] TasR 1; *Re Fabo Pty Ltd* [1989] VR 432; *Datuk Mohd Sari bin Datuk Hj Nuar v Idris Hydraulic (M) Bhd* [1997] 5 MLJ 377.

[704] *Re QBS Pty Ltd.*

[705] See 7.161–7.165.

[706] *Re G Stonehenge Constructions Pty Ltd* (1978) 3 ACLR 941; *Club Marconi of Bossley Park Social Recreation Sporting Centre Ltd v Rennat Constructions Pty Ltd* (1980) 4 ACLR 883; *Australian Card Services Pty Ltd v JS Wallboards Pty Ltd* (1991) 5 ACSR 274.

[707] *Fire and All Risks Insurance Co Ltd v Southern Cross Exploration NL* (1986) 10 ACLR 683 at p 687; *Australian Card Services Pty Ltd v JS Wallboards Pty Ltd.*

[708] *Club Marconi of Bossley Park Social Recreation Sporting Centre Ltd v Rennat Constructions Pty Ltd* at p 887, disavowing remarks made in *Re G Stonehenge Constructions Pty Ltd.*

[709] (1987) 17 NSWLR 468.

[710] (1985) 10 ACLR 305.

[711] (1991) 5 ACSR 274.

[712] (1994) 14 ACSR 580.

Evidence in Rebuttal of Deemed Inability to Pay Debts

7.302   There is controversy over whether the evidence of inability to pay debts provided by IA 1986, ss 123 and 222–224, can be rebutted. In other words, can a company in relation to which one of the deeming events has occurred persuade the court that nevertheless the circumstance that it is unable to pay its debts does not exist, so that the court cannot order it to be wound up? Or must the company accept that it is deemed to be unable to pay its debts and hope that its evidence of solvency can be admitted despite the deeming and will persuade the court to exercise its discretion against making an order?

7.303   Whether the word 'deemed' establishes an irrebuttable presumption depends on the context[713] and what appears to be the purpose of the deeming provision.[714]

7.304   It is only in relation to pre-hearing deeming events that the court may have to decide whether it can consider evidence in rebuttal. From the earliest cases, judges have adopted the first theory[715] and have held that the court is required to deem a company to be unable to pay its debts if it is proved that one of the deeming events has occurred.[716] This means that the deemed inability to pay debts is irrebuttable.[717] It has been said that failure to comply with a statutory demand 'is conclusive evidence that the company is unable to pay its debts',[718] creates 'a statutory admission that a company is unable to pay its debts'[719] and 'leads automatically to a deemed insolvency'.[720]

7.305   From the 1980s, Australian and Malaysian courts which have adopted the first theory have said that at the hearing of a petition which justifies an allegation of inability to pay debts by reference to neglect to pay on a statutory demand, the company can assert that it is able to pay its debts.[721] In Malaysia, it has been held in three reported cases that a company which has failed to comply with a statutory demand may rebut the presumption that it is unable to pay its debts. If the presumption is rebutted, the court will issue an injunction to restrain presentation of a winding-up petition grounded on failure to comply with the

---

[713]   *Inverness District Council v Highland Universal Fabrications Ltd* 1986 SLT 556.

[714]   Per Schultz JA in *Consolidated School District of St Leon Village No 1425 v Ronceray* (1960) 23 DLR (2d) 32 at p 37; *Credit Foncier Franco-Canadien v Bennett* (1963) 43 WWR NS 545; *Murphy v Ingram* [1974] Ch 363 per Russell LJ at p 370; *Anderton v Clwyd County Council (No 2)* [2002] EWCA Civ 933, [2002] 1 WLR 3174. See, for example, *Godwin v Swindon Borough Council* [2001] EWCA Civ 1478, [2002] 1 WLR 997, in which a deeming provision was held to create an irrebuttable presumption, and *Leicestershire County Council v Transco plc* [2003] EWCA Civ 1524, *The Times*, 7 November 2003, in which a different deeming provision was held to be rebuttable.

[715]   See 7.298.

[716]   *Re Imperial Hydropathic Hotel Co, Blackpool Ltd* (1882) 49 LT 147 per Cotton LJ at p 150.

[717]   *Re South East Corporation Ltd* (1915) 23 DLR 724; *Re Willes Trading Pty Ltd* [1978] 1 NSWLR 463 (irrebuttable 'so far as the ground of the petition is concerned'); *Club Marconi of Bossley Park Social Recreation Sporting Centre Ltd v Rennat Constructions Pty Ltd* (1980) 4 ACLR 883 at p 887; *Furmston* 1987 SLT (Sh Ct) 10 (an 'interim view' based on an assumption that use of the word 'deemed' always establishes an irrebuttable presumption).

[718]   *Re Catholic Publishing and Bookselling Co Ltd* (1864) 2 De G J & S 116 per Turner LJ at p 120.

[719]   *Processed Sand Pty Ltd v Thiess Contractors Pty Ltd* [1983] 1 NSWLR 384 per Waddell J at p 389.

[720]   *Re Elgar Heights Pty Ltd* [1985] VR 657 per Ormiston J at p 671.

[721]   *Re Pardoo Nominees Pty Ltd* [1987] TasR 1 at p 4; *Re Fabo Pty Ltd* [1989] VR 432; *Malaysia Air Charter Co Sdn Bhd v Petronas Dagangan Sdn Bhd* [2000] 4 MLJ 657 at p 668; *Masboh Trading Sdn Bhd v Mejaris Builders Sdn Bhd* [2001] 5 MLJ 369 at p 372; *Visage Continental Sdn Bhd v Smooth Track Sdn Bhd* [2008] 1 MLJ 101 at [30].

statutory demand,[722] strike out a petition that has been presented[723] or dismiss a petition on hearing it.[724] In all three cases the debt was also disputed on substantial grounds.

Some courts which have adopted the second theory say that the state of being deemed unable to pay debts can be terminated.[725] **7.306**

Legislative Solutions in Australia and New Zealand

The conflict between the first and second theories has been resolved in Australia by rewording the legislation so that it now provides that the court must presume that a company is insolvent if one of the deeming events has occurred within three months before the winding-up application is made.[726] This presumption operates except so far as the contrary is proved.[727] **7.307**

In New Zealand the Companies Act 1993, s 287, provides that a company is presumed to be unable to pay its debts when the events specified in the section have occurred, 'unless the contrary is proved'. **7.308**

Which Creditors may Petition?

Meaning of the Term 'Creditor'

IA 1986, s 124(1), permits 'any creditor or creditors (including any contingent or prospective creditor or creditors)' of a company to apply for the company to be wound up by the court. In IA 1986, in relation to the winding up of a company, 'creditor' means a person who is owed a 'debt' and it has been held that the definition in IR 1986, r 13.12, applies for the purposes of IA 1986, s 124(1).[728] It is established that a person who claims to be owed a debt by a company is not a creditor of the company for the purposes of s 124(1) if the claim is disputed on substantial grounds.[729] It is argued at 7.362 that a claimed debt whose existence is disputed is not a 'debt' as that term is defined in IR 1986, r 13.12. If that argument is wrong, the relevance of r 13.12 for defining 'creditor' for the purposes of IA 1986, s 124(1), would be called into question.[730] **7.309**

Another reason for doubting the application of IR 1986, r 13.12, for the purposes of IA 1986, s 124(1), is that the rule is expressed to apply to the winding up of a company and the presentation of a winding-up petition is not part of the winding up.[731] It is submitted, however, that there is no reason to exclude from the status of creditor for the purpose of IA 1986, s 124(1), any person who is owed a debt as defined in IR 1986, **7.310**

---

[722] *Molop Corp Sdn Bhd v Uniperkasa (M) Sdn Bhd* [2003] 6 MLJ 311.
[723] *Chong Chee Yan v Golden Garden Sdn Bhd* [1999] 1 MLJ 573.
[724] *Dayakuasa Holdings Sdn Bhd v Kayaal Holdings Sdn Bhd* [2003] 2 MLJ 263.
[725] See 7.299–7.301.
[726] Corporations Act 2001 (Australia), s 459C(2).
[727] s 459C(3).
[728] *Tottenham Hotspur plc v Edennote plc* [1995] 1 BCLC 65. Rule 13.12 is set out at 7.75.
[729] See 7.359–7.361.
[730] If a disputed debt claimant does have standing to petition, as has been suggested (see 7.369–7.374), the inconsistency would not arise.
[731] See 1.26 and 5.294–5.298.

r 13.12 (provided that definition excludes a claimed debt whose existence is disputed on substantial grounds[732]). The principle enunciated by Lloyd LJ,[733] that a local authority may petition in respect of unpaid council tax because it can prove for the tax in the winding up, can be extended to all debts that are made provable by r 13.12 read with r 12.3 (which specifies unprovable debts).[734] There is a fear that this will open the floodgates to petitions by persons with unresolved tort claims. But if a tort claim is unresolved because liability has not been admitted or adjudged, a petition by the claimant would be a disputed debt petition which the court would normally not allow to proceed.[735] If liability for a tort is established but damages have not been quantified, the claimant is a contingent or prospective creditor, who is expressly given standing to petition by IA 1986, s 124(1).[736]

7.311 A petition for the winding up of a relevant scheme[737] may be presented by any creditor of the scheme,[738] which means a person to whom a sum is or may become payable in respect of a debt of the relevant scheme.[739] That in turn means a debt or obligation incurred for the purposes of, or in connection with, the acquisition, management or disposal of property subject to the relevant scheme.[740]

7.312 The fact that a person with a claim against a company cannot present a statutory demand for it does not preclude that person from having standing to petition for the winding up of the company.[741]

7.313 A creditor in equity[742] of a company has standing to petition for its winding up.[743]

7.314 Before IR 1986 there was no definition of 'creditor', 'debt', 'debtor' or 'liability' in the insolvency legislation and it was suggested that these terms could mean different things in different parts of the legislation.[744] Courts were also likely to restrict the meaning of 'debt' to a monetary claim which could have been recovered in an action for debt in the days when it was necessary to take proceedings in a specific 'form of action'.[745] This resulted in cases in

---

[732] See 7.309.

[733] *Bolsover District Council v Ashfield Nominees Ltd* [2010] EWCA Civ 1129, [2011] Bus LR 492, at [10].

[734] A petition by a person with an unprovable debt will be struck out because of the petitioner's lack of interest; see 7.418–7.423.

[735] See 7.569. For examples see *Re Pen-y-Van Colliery Co* (1877) 6 ChD 477 (claimed misrepresentation); *Re Gold Hill Mines* (1883) 23 ChD 210 (claimed wrongful dismissal from employment).

[736] *Securum Finance Ltd v Camswell Ltd* [1994] BCC 434 where the court refused to strike out a petition based on a judgment for damages to be assessed for the tort of trespass to land, which was described as a prospective debt.

[737] See 1.168.

[738] Collective Investment in Transferable Securities (Contractual Scheme) Regulations 2013 (SI 2013/1388), reg 17(9)(a).

[739] SI 2013/1388, reg 17(1)(b)(i).

[740] SI 2013/1388, reg 17(1)(b)(ii).

[741] *Re Steel Wing Co Ltd* [1921] 1 Ch 349.

[742] The phrase used in the Companies Act 1862, s 80, to refer to a person with an equitable interest in a debt, such as an equitable assignee of the debt.

[743] *Re Steel Wing Co Ltd* [1921] 1 Ch 349; *Tele-Art Inc v Nam Tai Electronics Inc* (1999) 57 WIR 76.

[744] See (1949) 208 LT Jo 302 and *Government of India, Ministry of Finance (Revenue Division) v Taylor* [1955] AC 491 (meaning of 'liabilities'). See also *CCA Systems Pty Ltd v Communications and Peripherals (Australia) Pty Ltd* (1989) 15 ACLR 720 (person claiming a disputed debt not able to petition as a creditor for winding up but is a creditor bound by a scheme of arrangement).

[745] See Sir Francis Buller, *Trials at Nisi Prius*, 7th edn by Richard Whalley Bridgman (1817), part 2, ch 4; *Chitty's Treatise on Pleading and Parties to Actions*, 7th edn by Henry Greening (1844), vol 1, ch 2. The distinctions between forms of action were effectively abolished by the Common Law Procedure Act 1852.

which persons who had claims for which they could prove in a winding up were held not to be creditors with standing to petition for winding up. As it was put by Santow J in *Re Wilson Market Research Pty Ltd*:[746]

> There is no compelling logic in making the class of those who can *prove* in a liquidation identical with those who can *trigger* it. There is a procedure in the winding up itself for proof of debts and claims. This allows for the testing and ultimate quantification of, for example, an unliquidated claim. This is absent at the initial point where application for winding up is first made.

For example, the Companies Act 1862, s 82, authorized 'any one or more creditor or creditors' of a company to apply for it to be wound up by the court, but made no express reference to contingent or prospective creditors.[747] It was held that persons with future or contingent claims could not petition for winding up, even though, by s 158 of the Act, they could prove for their claims if winding up occurred.[748] **7.315**

One case which showed a different approach was *Re North Bucks Furniture Depositories Ltd*.[749] In that case it was necessary to decide whether a local authority with a claim for unpaid general rates had standing to petition as a creditor. Unpaid general rates were not a debt in the common law sense of being recoverable in an action for debt.[750] Crossman J said that in the Companies Act 1929, s 264, in the provision last re-enacted as the Companies Act 1985, s 614 and sch 19 (preferential payments), rates were described as 'debts' and, though he did not say so, his Lordship assumed that 'creditor', when used in the Companies Act 1929, s 170(1) (persons who may petition for winding up, now IA 1986, s 124(1)), meant a person owed a 'debt' in the sense in which the word was used elsewhere in the Act. **7.316**

Now, a local authority with a claim against a company for unpaid council tax, non-domestic rates or BID levy has standing to petition for it to be wound up because the claim is a debt as defined by IR 1986, r 13.12.[751] **7.317**

Contingent and Prospective Creditors

Standing of contingent and prospective creditors

IA 1986, s 124(1), permits 'any contingent or prospective creditor or creditors' to petition for the winding up of a company. Before this provision was introduced by the Companies Act 1907, s 28, contingent and prospective creditors were not permitted to petition,[752] except that, from 1870, a holder of a life assurance policy could petition for the winding-up **7.318**

---

[746] (1996) 39 NSWLR 311, at pp 322–3.

[747] Express reference to contingent and prospective creditors was added by the Companies Act 1907, s 28; see 7.318.

[748] See *Re Milford Docks Co* (1883) 23 ChD 292 (contingent creditor); *Re W Powell and Sons* [1892] WN 94 (future creditor on a bill of exchange); *Re Melbourne Brewery and Distillery* [1901] 1 Ch 453 (future creditors with a series of debentures). This is still the case in jurisdictions where there is no express reference to contingent and prospective creditors and no more inclusive definition of 'creditor': *Re Hunza Investments Ltd* 1988–89 CILR 1 (Cayman Islands); *New Hampshire Insurance Co v Magellan Reinsurance Co Ltd* [2009] UKPC 33, LTL 22/7/2009 (Turks and Caicos Islands). In relation to bankruptcy law in Canada see *Re Down* 2001 BCCA 201, 198 DLR (4th) 76.

[749] [1939] Ch 690.

[750] *Liverpool Corporation v Hope* [1938] 1 KB 751.

[751] *Bolsover District Council v Ashfield Nominees Ltd* [2010] EWCA Civ 1129, [2011] Bus LR 492, at [10] (claim is a debt for the purposes of insolvency proceedings).

[752] See 7.315.

of the company that issued the policy or was liable under it.[753] The Companies Act 1907, s 28, was enacted in response to the Report of the Company Law Amendment Committee (Cd 3052, 1906). The committee were concerned that a creditor of an insolvent company whose debt was not presently payable would have to stand by helpless until the debt became due while the company dissipated all its assets unless given a right to petition for the company to be wound up.[754]

7.319 Until 29 December 1986, the court would not hear a petition presented by a contingent or prospective creditor until the petitioner had given security for costs and established a prima facie case for winding up.[755] This meant that, after the petition was presented, there had to be a preliminary hearing to determine the amount of security required and whether a prima facie case was established.[756] In Australia, it is still the case that a contingent or prospective creditor must obtain the court's leave before applying for a company to be wound up in insolvency.[757]

7.320 From 1 July 1910 until 30 November 2001, petitions by policyholders to wind up insurance companies were subject to the requirement for security for costs and establishment of a prima facie case, and an additional restriction that a petition could only be presented by ten or more policyholders owning policies with an aggregate value of £10,000 or more.[758]

7.321 Petitions by contingent or prospective creditors have been rare, even after the repeal of the requirements to give security and show a prima facie case.[759]

Grounds

7.322 A petition by a contingent or prospective creditor may rely on any of the circumstances in which a company of its type may be wound up.[760] In particular, it may be on the ground that the company is (presently) unable to pay its debts.[761] A predicted inability to pay a debt due (or contingently due) in the future is not necessarily evidence of present inability to pay debts.[762]

---

[753] Life Assurance Companies Act 1870, s 21. There is no longer any provision to this effect since the Insurance Companies Act 1982, s 53, was repealed.

[754] See para 43 of the report.

[755] Life Assurance Companies Act 1870, s 21 (in relation to petitions by policy holders to wind up life assurance companies), which was replaced by the Assurance Companies 1909, s 15 (see 7.320); Companies Act 1907, s 28 (in relation to petitions other than by policyholders), last re-enacted in England and Wales and Scotland as the Companies Act 1985, s 519(5), which was repealed by IA 1985, sch 10, part 2 (brought into force by the Insolvency Act 1985 (Commencement No 5) Order 1986 (SI 1986/1924), art 2).

[756] *Re Fitness Centre (South East) Ltd* [1986] BCLC 518.

[757] Corporations Act 2001 (Australia), s 459P(2)(a).

[758] Assurance Companies Act 1909, s 15; last re-enacted as the Insurance Companies Act 1982, s 53, which was repealed by the Financial Services and Markets Act 2000 (Consequential Amendments and Repeals) Order 2001 (SI 2001/3649), art 3(1). See *Re British Equitable Bond and Mortgage Corporation* [1910] 1 Ch 574 at p 580; *Re Chesapeake Insurance Co Ltd* [1991] Bda LR 42 (such provisions restrict who may petition).

[759] *BNY Corporate Trustee Services Ltd v Eurosail-UK 2007-3BL plc* [2013] UKSC 28, [2013] 1 WLR 1408, at [32].

[760] *Re a Company (No 003028 of 1987)* [1988] BCLC 282 at p 294. See 2.23–2.53.

[761] IA 1986, ss 122(1)(f) (registered companies) and 221(5)(b) (unregistered companies); *Securum Finance Ltd v Camswell Ltd* [1994] BCC 434.

[762] For the purposes of IA 1986, ss 123(2) (registered companies) and 224(2) (unregistered companies); see 7.284–7.292.

If the only evidence available to a contingent or prospective petitioner relates to inabil- **7.323** ity to pay the petitioner's debt when it becomes due in the future, the petition should be on the just and equitable ground[763] and the petitioner must show that the inability to pay debts at the time when the petitioning creditor's debt becomes payable justifies winding up the company now.[764] The fact that the petitioning creditor would be better off if the company were wound up now than if it continued is not in itself a justification for winding up now.[765] In *Re Millennium Advanced Technology Ltd*[766] the justification was that the only prospect of recovering money to pay the petitioner's debt was by investigation of the company's affairs by a liquidator. On a contingent or prospective creditor's petition on the just and equitable ground, showing only that the company is presently unable to pay its debts may not be enough to justify winding up the company now,[767] though it would be sufficient to justify winding up on the ground of present inability to pay debts.[768]

Definition of contingent creditor and prospective creditor

The terms 'contingent creditor' and 'prospective creditor' are not given a statutory defin- **7.324** ition in IA 1986. The term 'contingent liability' is not a term of art and its precise meaning will depend on context.[769]

In order to have standing to petition as a creditor for winding up, the debt which a contin- **7.325** gent or prospective creditor is claiming must be a debt as that term is defined in IR 1986, r 13.12.[770] Earlier, it had been held that any person with a claim against a company in respect of any contingent or prospective liability to be taken into account in determining whether a company is unable to pay its debts[771] is entitled to petition as a contingent or prospective creditor.[772]

The term 'prospective' creditor means the same as 'future' creditor.[773] **7.326**

---

[763] IA 1986, s 122(1)(g) or s 221(5)(c).

[764] *Re a Company (No 003028 of 1987)* [1988] BCLC 282 at p 294; *Re Millennium Advanced Technology Ltd* [2004] EWHC 711 (Ch), [2004] 1 WLR 2177.

[765] *BNY Corporate Trustee Services Ltd v Eurosail-UK 2007-3BL plc* [2011] EWCA Civ 227, [2011] 1 WLR 2524, at [79].

[766] [2004] EWHC 711 (Ch), [2004] 1 WLR 2177, at [78].

[767] *Re a Company (No 003028 of 1987)* [1988] BCLC 282 at p 294; *Re Millennium Advanced Technology Ltd* [2004] EWHC 711 (Ch), [2004] 1 WLR 2177.

[768] The petitions in *Re a Company (No 003028 of 1987)* and *Re Millennium Advanced Technology Ltd* were on the just and equitable ground only. In *Re Millennium Advanced Technology Ltd* the judge invited the petitioner to amend the petition to allege present inability to pay debts, but this was not done because preparing the necessary evidence would have caused an unwanted delay (see at [61]).

[769] *County Bookshops Ltd v Grove* [2002] EWHC 1160 (Ch), [2003] 1 BCLC 479, at p 492; *R (Steele) v Birmingham City Council* [2005] EWCA Civ 1824, [2006] 1 WLR 2380, per Arden LJ, with whom May LJ agreed, at [21].

[770] *Tottenham Hotspur plc v Edennote plc* [1995] 1 BCLC 65; see 7.309–7.310. For the text of r 13.12 see 7.75.

[771] IA 1986, ss 123(2) (registered companies) and 224(2) (unregistered companies). See 7.284–7.292.

[772] *Re British Equitable Bond and Mortgage Corporation* [1910] 1 Ch 574. The result was that a holder of a bond, issued by a company, who, upon making periodical payments to the company, would at a future date become entitled to the payment of a sum of money by the company was entitled to petition, as a contingent or prospective creditor, for the company to be wound up.

[773] Per Judge Roger Cooke sitting as a High Court judge in *Burford Midland Properties Ltd v Marley Extrusions Ltd* [1995] 1 BCLC 102 at p 108.

7.327   Speaking of the provision requiring a contingent or prospective creditor to give security and establish a prima facie case,[774] Buckley LJ, in *Stonegate Securities Ltd v Gregory*,[775] said, at p 579:

> In that context, in my opinion, the expression 'contingent creditor' means a creditor in respect of a debt which will only become due in an event which may or may not occur; and a 'prospective creditor' is a creditor in respect of a debt which will certainly become due in the future, either on some date which has been already determined or on some date determinable by reference to future events.

7.328   Sometimes, as in the dictum of Buckley LJ quoted in 7.327, 'future' or 'prospective' is only used with reference to a certain debt. However, a debt described presently as a contingent debt is payable only if the contingency occurs in the future, and so could be described as a future or prospective debt, and in that sense, the category of prospective creditors would include contingent creditors.[776] For example, the liability of a lessee under an existing lease to pay rent for the remaining term of the lease has been described as 'a perfectly certain debt, a future debt but not a contingent debt'.[777] IR 1986, r 13.12(3), refers to debts being 'present or future, ... certain or contingent',[778] indicating that futurity and contingency refer to different aspects or qualities of a debt.

7.329   A contingent debt of a company is a debt to which the company may become subject, not a debt to which it is subject. So contingent debts are addressed in IR 1986, r 13.12(1)(b), not r 13.12(1)(a).[779] It follows that a contingent debt is not a debt of a company in relation to its winding up unless the company will become subject to it by reason of an obligation incurred before the company goes into liquidation or before it entered into administration immediately preceding liquidation.

7.330   Of course, there are ways in which the liability to pay a future debt may be ended, for example, by purchasing it. Liability to pay rent under a lease is ended if the lease is forfeited. In *Re Cancol Ltd*,[780] Knox J said that he thought 'defeasible' was the appropriate description for such a liability.

7.331   The fact that a creditor may not be able to pay a debt does not make it a contingent debt.[781] In particular, the fact that a debt is subordinated in a winding up does not make it a contingent debt.[782]

7.332   If liability arises only when a triggering event occurs, the liability should not be classified as contingent unless there is a reasonable possibility that the triggering event will not occur.[783] For example, a liability which will occur only after a supplier has issued an invoice is not contingent if there is no commercial reason for not raising the invoice.

---

[774] See 7.319.

[775] [1980] Ch 576.

[776] *Burford Midland Properties Ltd v Marley Extrusions Ltd* [1995] 1 BCLC 102 at p 108.

[777] *Palace Billiard Rooms Ltd and Reduced* 1911 2 SLT 324 at p 326. See also *Oppenheimer v British and Foreign Exchange and Investment Bank* (1877) 6 ChD 744.

[778] See also IA 1986, s 382(3).

[779] *Re T & N Ltd* [2005] EWHC 2870 (Ch), [2006] 1 WLR 1728, at [115]; *Re Nortel GmbH* [2013] UKSC 52, [2014] 1 AC 209, at [68]–[71].

[780] [1996] 1 BCLC 100 at p 105.

[781] *Re Maxwell Communications Corporation plc* [1993] 1 WLR 1402 at p 1418.

[782] *Re Maxwell Communications Corporation plc* at p 1418.

[783] *County Bookshops Ltd v Grove* [2002] EWHC 1160 (Ch), [2003] 1 BCLC 479.

In *Re Burke Successors Ltd*[784] a guarantor of a company's debts successfully petitioned as a **7.333** contingent creditor.

Existing obligation

Under the definition in *Stonegate Securities Ltd v Gregory*,[785] a person can be a prospective **7.334** creditor only in respect of a debt which is certain to become due in the future. This implies that the obligation under which the debt will become due must presently exist. Similarly, a person can be a contingent creditor only under a presently existing obligation to pay a debt if an event occurs in the future (such as an insurance company's obligation to pay money under an insurance policy should one of the perils insured against occur and cause loss to the insured).[786] In *Re William Hockley Ltd*[787] Pennycuick J said, at p 558:

> The expression 'contingent creditor'[788]...must, I think, denote a person towards whom under an existing obligation, the company may or will become subject to a present liability upon the happening of some future event or at some future date.

Pennycuick J applied this definition with the result that a petitioner to whom, it was held, **7.335** the company did not have a present obligation did not have standing to petition. Years later a divisional court held that the petitioner had in fact been a present creditor.[789]

The inclusion of the words 'or will' in Pennycuick J's definition shows, as Kitto J pointed **7.336** out in *Community Development Pty Ltd v Engwirda Construction Co*,[790] that this 'is perhaps rather a definition of "a contingent or prospective creditor"'.[791] Kitto J went on to say though that:

> The importance of [Pennycuick J's definition] lies in [its] insistence that there must be an existing obligation and that out of that obligation a liability on the part of the company to pay a sum of money will arise in a future event.

As Judge Roger Cooke put it in *Burford Midland Properties Ltd v Marley Extrusions Ltd*:[792]

> (1) a future prospective debt cannot include a debt that arises out of a future transaction;
> (2)...it can and will include a debt that arises out of an existing transaction as a result of which the basic liability is incurred which depends on the reaching of a future date or the happening of a future event to make it payable if it is ever to be payable.

As pointed out at 7.326, the judge was using the terms 'future' and 'prospective' (which he considered to be equivalent) to include 'contingent'.

In *Re SBA Properties Ltd*,[793] another decision of Pennycuick J, legal proceedings had been **7.337** started in a company's name against a bank but the proceedings were unauthorized; the bank said that if the company adopted the proceedings and then lost, the bank would

---

[784] (1989) 26 JLR 252.
[785] [1980] Ch 576 at p 579, quoted at 7.327.
[786] *Re SBA Properties Ltd* [1967] 1 WLR 799; *FAI Workers Compensation (NSW) Ltd v Philkor Builders Pty Ltd* (1996) 20 ACSR 592; IR 1986, r 13.12(1)(b).
[787] [1962] 1 WLR 555.
[788] In what is now IA 1986, s 124(1).
[789] *Re a Debtor (No 2 of 1977)* [1979] 1 WLR 956.
[790] (1969) 120 CLR 455, at p 459.
[791] See also per Neuberger J in *County Bookshops Ltd v Grove* [2002] EWHC 1160 (Ch), [2003] 1 BCLC 479, at p 493.
[792] [1995] 1 BCLC 102 at p 109.
[793] [1967] 1 WLR 799.

become a creditor for its costs. The court pointed out that as the company had not adopted the proceedings yet, it was under no present obligation to the bank, and therefore the bank was not a contingent creditor and did not have standing to appear on the hearing of a petition to wind up the company.

7.338 In *Federal Commissioner of Taxation v Gosstray*[794] it was held that tax assessed, on income earned in 1973 and 1974, under a retrospective statute enacted in 1982, was not a contingent debt before the statute was enacted.

7.339 A different view was taken in *Re Austral Group Investment Management Ltd*.[795] Holland J held that the distinction between contingent and prospective creditors is that a person can be a contingent creditor only in respect of an existing obligation but a person may be a prospective creditor without an existing obligation. His Honour held that in order to have standing to petition as a prospective creditor of a company for the company to be wound up it is sufficient to have 'a real prospect' of becoming a creditor of the company.[796]

Incurring an obligation

7.340 There has been difficulty in deciding what amounts to incurring an 'obligation' which may make a company subject to a contingent debt as defined in IR 1986, r 13.12(1)(b).[797] In *Winter v Commissioners of Inland Revenue*,[798] a case which was not concerned with insolvency law, Lord Reid drew on Scots law to define a contingent liability as:

> a liability which, by reason of something done by the person bound, will necessarily arise or come into being if one or more of certain events occur or do not occur.

7.341 The question before the House in *Winter v Commissioners of Inland Revenue* was whether the 'something done by the person bound' had to involve incurring an obligation under a contract or statute. A majority of the appellate committee held (in favour of a taxpayer) that a contractual or statutory obligation is not necessary. In subsequent cases it was held that this decision did not apply to the meaning of debt for the purposes of IA 1986, for which a contractual or statutory obligation was required,[799] except in relation to voluntary arrangements.[800] This has been overruled by the Supreme Court, which has held that, for the purposes of IA 1986, the obligation under which a contingent debt arises need not be contractual or statutory.[801] Lord Neuberger suggested[802] that what is required, at least normally, in order for a company to have incurred a relevant obligation under IR 1986, r 13.12(1)(b), is that the company:

(a) must have taken, or been subjected to, some step or combination of steps which had some legal effect (such as putting it under some legal duty or into some legal relationship);

---

[794] [1986] VR 876.

[795] [1993] 2 NZLR 692.

[796] See also 7.375–7.378.

[797] Which is the criterion for standing to present a creditor's winding-up petition; see 7.309.

[798] [1963] AC 235 at p 249.

[799] *Glenister v Rowe* [2000] Ch 76; *County Bookshops Ltd v Grove* [2002] EWHC 1160 (Ch), [2003] 1 BCLC 479; *R (Steele) v Birmingham City Council* [2005] EWCA Civ 1824, [2006] 1 WLR 2380. Earlier, the wide definition adopted in *Winter v Commissioners of Inland Revenue* had been applied in *Re SBA Properties Ltd* [1967] 1 WLR 799, but the alleged liability in that case was found not to be a contingent debt even under that wide test.

[800] *Re T & N Ltd* [2005] EWHC 2870 (Ch), [2006] 1 WLR 1728, at [46]–[68].

[801] *Re Nortel GmbH* [2013] UKSC 52, [2014] 1 AC 209.

[802] *Re Nortel GmbH* at [77].

(b) doing so must have resulted in it being vulnerable to the specific liability in question, such that there would be a real prospect of that liability being incurred; and

(c) it would be consistent with the regime under which the liability is imposed to conclude that the step or combination of steps gave rise to an obligation under r 13.12(1)(b).

The problem with point (c) is that the desirability of finding that a debt is within **7.342** r 13.12(1)(b) depends on context. The cases have been concerned with whether or not a debt is provable and the Supreme Court has indicated a preference for a policy of making all debts provable where possible so that bankruptcy clears all the bankrupt's liabilities.[803] But giving persons to whom a company owes no contractual obligation, and who have only a prospect (albeit a real prospect) of becoming a creditor, the power to petition for it to be wound up may be thought to be undesirably enabling nuisance litigation.[804]

In cases that are not concerned with standing to petition for winding up, it has been decided **7.343** that the following non-contractual obligations are contingent liabilities:

(a) liability in revenue law for a balancing charge arising from claiming and taking a capital allowance;[805]

(b) liability for a protective award under the Trade Union and Labour Relations (Consolidation) Act 1992, s 189, arising from a failure to consult before dismissing employees for redundancy;[806]

(c) liability to meet a financial support direction given by the Pensions Regulator arising from being, within the past two years, a member of a group of companies which included either a service company with a pension scheme, or an insufficiently resourced company with a pension scheme;[807]

(d) liability for another party's costs arising from entering into legal proceedings.[808]

It has been held that putting oneself in a position where one could be liable as a non-party for **7.344** costs does not create a contingent liability,[809] but this is now open to question. It has also been held, in relation to standing to petition for winding up, that a person who has guaranteed a company's indebtedness to its bank but has not discharged that debt is not a contingent creditor of the company if the bank has not demanded payment of the debt.[810]

IR 1986, r 13.12(2), provides that a liability in tort is a contingent liability provable in the wind- **7.345** ing up of a company if all the elements necessary to establish the cause of action, other than actionable damage, exist at the date when it went into liquidation or entered an immediately preceding administration.[811] The fact that a company has done something from which a cause of action in tort could arise if another person does something in the future (for example, if an

---

[803] *Re Nortel GmbH* at [90].
[804] Contingent creditors have no power to petition for bankruptcy.
[805] *Winter v Commissioners of Inland Revenue.*
[806] *Day v Haine* [2008] EWCA Civ 626, [2008] ICR 1102.
[807] *Re Nortel GmbH.*
[808] *Re Nortel GmbH* at [89], expressly overruling *Glenister v Rowe* [2000] Ch 76. But in Australia, the pre-*Nortel* position was affirmed by the High Court in *Foots v Southern Cross Mine Management Pty Ltd* [2007] HCA 56, 234 CLR 52.
[809] *Re Wisepark Ltd* [1994] BCC 221.
[810] *Re La Plagne Ltd* [2011] IEHC 91, [2012] 1 ILRM 203.
[811] r 13.12(2) was inserted by the Insolvency (Amendment) Rules 2006 (SI 2006/1272) and the Insolvency (Amendment) Rules 2010 (SI 2010/686), sch 1, para 498(1) and (3), so as to reverse the effect of *Re T & N Ltd* [2005] EWHC 2870 (Ch), [2006] 1 WLR 1728.

individual in the future comes into contact with the company's asbestos product) does not create a contingent liability.[812]

7.346 The Supreme Court has held that whether or not a debt is contingent does not depend on whether it is imposed by the exercise of a discretion.[813] This overrules the principle that:

> where a court or tribunal has a discretion whether or not to make an award, any sum awarded in the exercise of that discretion does not exist as a debt or liability until the award is made.[814]

7.347 See also 7.375–7.378.

Debt to be quantified

7.348 If the existence of a debt claimed from a company is not disputed but its amount is still to be quantified, it is a prospective debt to which the company is subject within IR 1986, r 13.12(1)(a).[815] This applies, for example, to an unliquidated claim for damages where liability is not disputed[816] or where liability has been established by a court.[817] It also applies to an order for costs which have not yet been assessed.[818]

7.349 In other cases it has been held that such a claimant is covered by the phrase 'contingent or prospective creditor' without needing to decide which of the alternative descriptions in the phrase is the more apt.[819]

7.350 But there are other cases in which a person claiming an amount which has yet to be settled is described as a contingent creditor.

7.351 In *Community Development Pty Ltd v Engwirda Construction Co*[820] a final payment was claimed under a building contract but the architect had declined to certify the amount claimed and arbitration had not been started. The builder was held to be a contingent creditor of the owner. The contingency was 'the making of an award in the [builder's] favour by an arbitrator'.[821]

---

[812] *Fay v Tegral Pipes Ltd* [2005] IESC 34, [2005] 2 IR 261, at [24]; *Re T & N Ltd* at [67].

[813] *Re Nortel GmbH* at [136].

[814] *Casson v Law Society* [2009] EWHC 1943 (Admin), [2010] BPIR 49, at [36], where the principle is derived from *Glenister v Rowe* [2000] Ch 76, *R (Steele) v Birmingham City Council* [2005] EWCA Civ 1824, [2006] 1 WLR 2380, and *Day v Haine* [2008] EWCA Civ 626, [2008] ICR 1102. The Supreme Court expressly overruled *Glenister v Rowe* and *R (Steele) v Birmingham City Council* (*Re Nortel GmbH* at [91] and [136]).

[815] *Re T & N Ltd* [2005] EWHC 2870 (Ch), [2006] 1 WLR 1728, at [116]–[117] and [128]. Rule 13.12(3) provides that it is immaterial whether the amount of a debt is fixed or liquidated, or is capable of being ascertained by fixed rules or as a matter of opinion.

[816] *Re T & N Ltd* [2005] EWHC 2870 (Ch), [2006] 1 WLR 1728, at [116]–[117] and [128].

[817] *Securum Finance Ltd v Camswell Ltd* [1994] BCC 434 at p 434.

[818] *Securum Finance Ltd v Camswell Ltd*. But see *Re a Company (No 001573 of 1983)* [1983] BCLC 492, in which Harman J did not seem ready to accept that a person in whose favour a costs order had been made, but not assessed, was a prospective creditor.

[819] *Re M B Coogan Ltd* [1953] NZLR 582; *Re Elgar Heights Pty Ltd* [1985] VR 657 at p 660; *United States Surgical Corporation v Ballabil Holdings Pty Ltd* (1985) 9 ACLR 904; *Ganda Holdings Bhd v Pamaron Holdings Sdn Bhd* [1989] 2 MLJ 346. See also *Re a Company (No 00315 of 1973)* [1973] 1 WLR 1566, in which it was accepted that a person who had obtained judgment against a company, in default of defence, for damages to be assessed could be a contingent or prospective creditor of the company. (The company had obtained an order setting aside the judgment but this was subject to a condition which the company refused to comply with and against which it was appealing.)

[820] (1969) 120 CLR 455.

[821] Owen J at p 462.

In *Re Hurren*[822] the Inland Revenue had instituted proceedings for tax penalties under **7.352** the Taxes Management Act 1970, part 10, but the penalties had not been determined by the general commissioners. The penalties were described as contingent debts. However, as the court thought that penalties of some amount were bound to be imposed and described them as liabilities to which the debtor was already subject, it seems that they did not depend on any contingency and would have been better classified as prospective debts.

In *Re Dollar Land Holdings Ltd*[823] the petitioner had issued proceedings against the com- **7.353** pany alleging breach of contract and claiming either specific performance of the contract or damages. Nicholls V-C found that there had been a breach of contract and described the petitioner as a contingent creditor in respect of the claim for damages—the contingency being whether or not the company performed the contract rather than whether or not the petitioner elected to proceed on the claim for specific performance rather than the claim for damages.

In *Re Butterworth Products and Industries Sdn Bhd*[824] (which was concerned with cover- **7.354** age of a court-sanctioned scheme of arrangement) the beneficiary of a guarantee given by the company who had not yet commenced proceedings to obtain payment under it was described as a contingent creditor.

It is interesting that in *Re R L Child and Co Pty Ltd*[825] McLelland J spoke[826] of 'unliquid- **7.355** ated, prospective or contingent claims' as if there were three categories.

Contingent non-monetary obligation

Another situation that is difficult to analyse is where a company has a contingent obliga- **7.356** tion to do something other than pay money. Is the person to whom that obligation is owed a contingent creditor, on the ground that if the company failed to fulfil the obligation, it would be liable to pay damages? The cases in which this question has arisen have concerned contingent obligations to issue shares on the exercise of subscription options.

In *Re BDC Investments Ltd*[827] Young J said, at p 203: 'Until the company has committed a **7.357** breach of contract, I fail to see how there is any claim against it'. However, in *Re Compañía de Electricidad de la Provincia de Buenos Aires Ltd*[828] Slade J held that persons to whom, under a scheme of arrangement, the company had an obligation to issue ordinary shares but who had not, 11 years later, claimed them, and who were now untraceable, were contingent credit- ors because if they ever did come forward and claim their shares, and the company (now in liquidation) failed to issue them, they could claim damages from the company. Similarly, in *Re Asia Oil and Minerals Ltd*[829] Cohen J decided that holders of subscription warrants were contingent creditors, because if they chose to exercise the warrants and the company failed to issue the shares, they could claim damages from the company. His Honour analysed a subscription warrant as a contract under which the company would allot shares on condition

---

[822] [1983] 1 WLR 183.
[823] [1994] 1 BCLC 404.
[824] [1992] 1 MLJ 429.
[825] (1986) 10 ACLR 673.
[826] At p 674.
[827] (1988) 13 ACLR 201.
[828] [1980] Ch 146.
[829] (1986) 5 NSWLR 42.

that a warrant holder exercised the option within the agreed time limit.[830] An alternative analysis of an option is as an offer coupled with a contract not to revoke the offer.[831] The different approaches were discussed in *Spiro v Glencrown Properties Ltd*[832] by Hoffmann J, who concluded that they are appropriate in different circumstances and that in truth an option is *sui generis*. Even if a company which has sold an option to subscribe for its shares is regarded as being bound by a contract not to revoke an offer to issue the shares at the option price, that contract would create a present obligation with a contingent liability to damages if the company refused to allot shares when the option was properly exercised. This would seem to remove the doubt expressed by Franklyn J in *Re Austamax Resources Ltd*[833] whether an option creates a present obligation and therefore whether an option holder is a contingent creditor.

7.358 Holders of subscription warrants were also held to be contingent creditors in *Re US Masters Ltd*.[834]

Dispute about the Existence of the Debt

No standing to petition if existence of debt disputed

7.359 In *Mann v Goldstein*[835] Ungoed-Thomas J said, at p 1099: 'until a creditor is established as a creditor he is not entitled to present the petition and has no *locus standi*'. This statement was approved in *Stonegate Securities Ltd v Gregory*[836] by Buckley LJ, who said, at p 580:

> In my opinion a petition founded on a debt which is disputed in good faith and on substantial grounds is demurrable for the reason that the petitioner is not a creditor of the company within the meaning of [IA 1986, s 124(1)] at all, and the question whether he is or is not a creditor of the company is not appropriate for adjudication in winding-up proceedings.

7.360 In *Re Selectmove Ltd*[837] Peter Gibson LJ said, at p 476:

> The jurisdiction of the Companies Court to wind up companies is not for the purpose of deciding a factual dispute concerning a debt which is sought to be relied on to found a petition. Until the petitioner can establish that he is a creditor, he is not entitled to present a petition based on a claimed debt.

7.361 In *Pentagin Technologies International Ltd v Express Company Secretaries Ltd*,[838] Nourse LJ said:

> the whole of the [petitioner's] claim against the [company] was [found by the judge at first instance to be] disputed in good faith and on substantial grounds. It is very well established that if that is the position the petitioner has no *locus standi*. If the petition has not yet been presented, he will be restrained from presenting it. If it has been presented, it will be struck out or dismissed.[839]

---

[830] See also his Honour's judgment in *National Companies and Securities Commission v Consolidated Gold Mining Areas NL* (1985) 1 NSWLR 454 and per Gibbs J in *Laybutt v Amoco Australia Pty Ltd* (1974) 132 CLR 57 at p 76.
[831] See, for example, *Mountford v Scott* [1975] Ch 258.
[832] [1991] Ch 537.
[833] (1985) 10 ACLR 194.
[834] (1991) 4 ACSR 462.
[835] [1968] 1 WLR 1091.
[836] [1980] Ch 576.
[837] [1995] 1 WLR 474.
[838] (1995) *The Times*, 7 April 1995.
[839] See also *Re Lympne Investments Ltd* [1972] 1 WLR 523 per Megarry J at p 527; *Holt Southey Ltd v Catnic Components Ltd* [1978] 1 WLR 630 at pp 631–2; *Re Calsil Ltd* (1982) 6 ACLR 515; *Jurupakat Sdn Bhd*

It is submitted that a claimed debt whose existence is disputed is not a 'debt' as that term is **7.362** defined in IR 1986, r 13.12, and therefore the claimant is not a 'creditor' for the purposes of IA 1986, s 124.[840] There is a provision that for the purposes of any reference to a debt or liability in the winding-up provisions of IA 1986 and IR 1986, 'it is immaterial whether the debt or liability is present or future, whether it is certain or contingent, or whether its amount is fixed or liquidated, or is capable of being ascertained by fixed rules or as a matter of opinion'.[841] It is submitted that this provision refers to disputes about the amount that is owed or when it is payable, not disputes about the existence of the debt, and the provision does not extend the meaning of 'debt' to include one whose existence is disputed. This may be contrasted with the provision that any person alleged to be a contributory is to be treated as one, for the purposes of all proceedings for determining, and all proceedings prior to the final determination of, the persons who are to be deemed contributories.[842] IR 1986 provide for the submission of a proof of debt by 'a person claiming to be a creditor',[843] rather than by 'a creditor'. It is for the liquidator to decide whether or not a person submitting a proof is a creditor by deciding whether to admit the proof for dividend, in whole or in part, or reject it.[844] The liquidator's decision is subject to appeal to the court.[845] In order to be admitted for dividend, it must be found that:

(a) the claimed pecuniary obligation exists;

(b) it is a debt as defined in IR 1986, r 13.12; and

(c) it is a provable debt as defined in rr 12.3 and 13.12(2).[846]

It is points (a) and (b) which determine whether the claimant is a creditor.

It is a unique feature of proceedings on a winding-up petition that, as a matter of practice, **7.363** the court will not usually decide a question of standing to commence the proceedings but will instead usually dismiss the petition and leave that question to be determined elsewhere.[847] There is an alternative view that a disputed debt petitioner does have standing so that there is no need to resolve a dispute about the debt in the proceedings on the petition.[848] There is another alternative view that a person claiming a disputed debt is a contingent or prospective creditor, who is expressly given standing to petition by IA 1986, s 124.[849]

---

v Kumpulan Good Earth (1973) Sdn Bhd [1988] 3 MLJ 49; *CVC Investments Pty Ltd v P and T Aviation Pty Ltd* (1989) 18 NSWLR 295 at pp 299–300; *Avery v Worldwide Testing Services Pty Ltd* (1990) 2 ACSR 834; *Re Wallace Smith and Co Ltd* [1992] BCLC 970; *Thomas v Mackay Investments Pty Ltd* (1996) 22 ACSR 294; *Angel Group Ltd v British Gas Trading Ltd* [2012] EWHC 2702 (Ch), [2013] BCC 265, at [22]. Warren J took the view that a person claiming a disputed debt does not have standing in *El Ajou v Dollar Land (Manhattan) Ltd* [2005] EWHC 2861 (Ch), [2007] BCC 953, at [8], but rejected it in *Hammonds v Pro-Fit USA Ltd* [2007] EWHC 1998 (Ch), [2008] 2 BCLC 159, at [26]–[35].

[840] See 7.309. To the contrary is an Australian decision that a person with a disputed claim against a company should be permitted to appear as a creditor at the hearing of another person's petition for the winding up of the company (*Re Gasbourne Pty Ltd* [1984] VR 801).

[841] IR 1986, r 13.12(3).

[842] IA 1986, s 79(1).

[843] IR 1986, r 4.73(1).

[844] IR 1986, r 4.82.

[845] IR 1986, rr 4.83 and 4.85.

[846] *Re Toshoku Finance UK plc* [2002] UKHL 6, [2002] 1 WLR 671, at [24]; *Re T & N Ltd* [2005] EWHC 2870 (Ch), [2006] 1 WLR 1728, at [112].

[847] See 7.364–7.368.

[848] See 7.369–7.374.

[849] See 7.375–7.378.

Winding-up court's unwillingness to determine questions of standing

7.364 Normally a court faced with an allegation that a person who has commenced proceedings before it does not have standing to do so will first determine the question of standing. If the challenge to standing succeeds, the court will dismiss the proceedings. If the challenge fails, it will hear the substantive application or claim. However, a dispute about the existence of a debt cannot be expected to be decided in proceedings on a winding-up petition, because those proceedings are particularly unsuited to determining such a question.[850] The court deals with this procedural problem in four ways:

(a) Usually, the court will dismiss a creditor's winding-up petition if there is a dispute on substantial grounds about the existence of the petitioner's debt, leaving the petitioner to establish standing in other more appropriate proceedings.[851] Dismissal is commonly anticipated by granting an injunction against presentation of a disputed debt petition or striking out one that has been presented.[852] In Australia it is commonly anticipated by setting aside a statutory demand for a disputed debt.[853]

(b) The petition may be adjourned to await the determination in the proper forum of the dispute about the debt.[854]

(c) Despite the unsuitability of the forum, the court will sometimes determine a dispute about the existence of the petitioner's debt in the proceedings on the winding-up petition.[855]

(d) Very rarely, the court will make a winding-up order despite there being a dispute about the existence of the petitioner's debt, leaving the dispute to be resolved in the winding up.[856]

7.365 Option (a) is a rule of practice, which can be departed from in appropriate cases.[857] The rule of practice exists only to deal with the procedural difficulty of resolving questions of standing in proceedings on a winding-up petition. The Privy Council has, in three cases, rejected an argument that option (a) must always be taken.[858] In each of the Privy Council cases the courts below had taken option (c) and that choice was approved by the Privy Council. In *Re Claybridge Shipping Co SA*[859] Oliver LJ said:

> It is not, in general, convenient that the very status of the petitioner to proceed with his petition [because the petitioner's debt is said to be disputed] should be fought out on a winding-up petition.... But it ought not, in my judgment, to be an inflexible rule that the Companies

---

[850] See 7.515–7.522. See per David Richards J in *Tallington Lakes Ltd v Ancasta International Boat Sales Ltd* [2012] EWCA Civ 1712, [2013] CP Rep 18, at [5].

[851] See 7.529–7.535.

[852] See 7.569–7.608.

[853] See 7.237–7.245.

[854] See 7.541–7.549.

[855] See 7.523–7.527.

[856] See 7.551–7.568.

[857] *Re Claybridge Shipping Co SA* [1997] 1 BCLC 572; *Stonegate Securities Ltd v Gregory* [1980] Ch 576 per Buckley LJ at p 580; *RWH Enterprises Ltd v Portedge Ltd* [1998] BCC 556 at p 558; *Re ICS Computer Distribution Ltd* [1996] 1 HKLR 181 at p 182; *Alipour v Ary* [1997] 1 WLR 534 at p 541; *Re MCI WorldCom Ltd* [2002] EWHC (Ch), [2003] 1 BCLC 330, at [11]; *Parmalat Capital Finance Ltd v Food Holdings Ltd* [2008] UKPC 23, [2009] 1 BCLC 274, at [9].

[858] *Bateman Television Ltd v Coleridge Finance Co Ltd* [1971] NZLR 929 at p 932; *Brinds Ltd v Offshore Oil NL* (1985) 63 ALR 94 at pp 99–100; *Parmalat Capital Finance Ltd v Food Holdings Ltd* [2008] UKPC 23, [2009] 1 BCLC 274 at [9].

[859] [1997] 1 BCLC 572 at p 579.

Court should never take upon itself the burden of determining the matter[860] on the hearing of the petition.

In the earliest cases, the court concentrated on the need to decide whether the petitioner **7.366** had standing before making any order on the petition. This meant that option (a) (dismissing the petition) was not available, because a disputed debt petition could not be dismissed unless and until it had been decided that the petitioner was not a creditor.[861] Usually a disputed debt petition was adjourned (option (b)).[862]

However, the court soon began to dismiss disputed debt petitions where it was clear that the **7.367** petitioner could not prove that the company was unable to pay its debts, because then there was no ground for a winding-up order.[863]

It was recognized that adjournment of a winding-up petition put disproportionate bur- **7.368** dens on a company that wished to continue trading.[864] Courts realized the danger of petitions based on disputed claims being presented in the hope that the claim would be settled by the company so as to avoid the practical disadvantages of being subject to a pending winding-up petition. A petition presented for that ulterior purpose would be struck out as an abuse of process.[865] An injunction could be obtained to prevent presentation of a petition with such an ulterior purpose.[866] In later cases, the need to prove that ulterior purpose was not mentioned and a practice was established of preventing presentation or continuation of a creditor's petition whenever the existence of the petition debt was disputed (option (a)).[867] It was said[868] that:

> There is no doubt as to the general rule that a disputed debt may not be the basis of a creditors' petition.

In *Mann v Goldstein*[869] Ungoed-Thomas J concluded that this applied whether or not the company was actually insolvent.[870] However, his Lordship held that a disputed debt petition should be restrained or dismissed because it is an abuse of process, because 'the winding-up jurisdiction is not for the purpose of deciding a disputed debt'.[871]

Disputed claimant as creditor

The analysis presented at 7.359–7.368 is that: **7.369**

(a) as a matter of law, a person with a disputed claim to be a creditor of a company does not have standing to petition as a creditor for the company to be wound up; but

---

[860] The 'matter' here is the disputed status of the petitioner (*Alipour v Ary* [1997] 1 WLR 534 at p 544).

[861] *Re Rhydydefed Colliery Co, Glamorganshire, Ltd* (1858) 3 De G & J 80 per Knight Bruce LJ at p 83; *Re Lundy Granite Co* (1868) 17 WR 91 per Lord Romilly MR at p 91.

[862] *Re Rhydydefed Colliery Co, Glamorganshire, Ltd*; *Re Island of Anglesea Coal and Coke Co Ltd* (1861) 4 LT 684 (petition relied on non-payment of another creditor's debt and that debt was disputed); per Turner LJ in *Re Catholic Publishing and Bookselling Co Ltd* (1864) 2 De G J & S 116 at p 121.

[863] The earliest case was *Re Brighton Club and Norfolk Hotel Co Ltd* (1865) 35 Beav 203. See 7.528.

[864] See 7.548.

[865] *Re Gold Hill Mines* (1883) 23 ChD 210. See 7.603–7.608.

[866] *Cadiz Waterworks Co v Barnett* (1874) LR 19 Eq 182; *Niger Merchants Co v Capper* (1877) 18 ChD 557 n; *John Brown and Co v Keeble* [1879] WN 173; *Cercle Restaurant Castiglione Co v Lavery* (1881) 18 ChD 555.

[867] *New Travellers' Chambers Ltd v Cheese and Green* (1894) 70 LT 271. See 7.569–7.608.

[868] *Re Russian and English Bank* [1932] Ch 663 per Bennett J at p 670.

[869] [1968] 1 WLR 1091.

[870] At pp 1094–5 and 1097–9.

[871] At pp 1098–9.

(b) as a matter of practice, the court will not decide a dispute about a petitioner's debt (and hence the petitioner's standing) in proceedings on a winding-up petition.

7.370 An alternative view is that both (a) and (b) are matters of practice only.[872] Under this alternative analysis, a person with a disputed claim to be a creditor of a company does have standing to petition for it to be wound up and it is therefore unnecessary to resolve any dispute about the existence of the debt. For discussion of whether a winding-up order would actually be made on a disputed debt petition see 7.551–7.568.

7.371 In *Re Claybridge Shipping Co SA*[873] the judge at first instance had struck out a petition, before it was advertised, on the ground that the existence of the debt claimed by the petitioner was the subject of a bona fide and substantial dispute.[874] The Court of Appeal heard further evidence from the petitioner,[875] decided that there was no substantial dispute and restored the petition. It could then have been given a substantive hearing by the High Court at which a winding-up order would have been made, but whether or not to make an order was not an issue before the Court of Appeal. Clearly the same result would have been achieved if the petition had not been struck out and it had proceeded without interruption to a substantive hearing at which the petitioner's further evidence had been adduced.

7.372 Lord Denning said that what he called 'a rule of practice . . . to the effect that' a person with a disputed claim against a company is not a 'creditor' for the purposes of what is now IA 1986, s 124, and therefore such a person's petition should be struck out, is incorrect.[876] It seemed to his Lordship that a person is a 'creditor' for the purposes of s 124, 'so long as he has a good arguable case that a debt of sufficient amount is owing to him'.[877] By extending standing to petitioners whose standing is disputed, Lord Denning would avoid the need to resolve any dispute about standing. But once it is recognized that the court applies a rule of practice about whether to resolve a dispute about standing to petition and not a rule on standing to petition, it can be seen that the rule of practice can be departed from where appropriate.[878] It is submitted that *Re Claybridge Shipping Co SA* did not involve a question of the law on standing to petition and Lord Denning's reference to a petitioner having a good arguable case is better considered only as a criterion for not striking out a petition at an early stage.[879]

---

[872] *Re Claybridge Shipping Co SA* [1997] 1 BCLC 572 per Lord Denning MR at pp 574–5; *Commissioners of Customs and Excise v Anglo German Breweries Ltd* [2002] EWHC 2458 (Ch), [2003] BTC 5021, per Lawrence Collins J at [40]; *Commissioners of HM Revenue and Customs v Rochdale Drinks Distributors Ltd* [2011] EWCA Civ 1116, [2012] 1 BCLC 748, per Rimer LJ at [79]; *Commissioners of HM Revenue and Customs v SED Essex Ltd* [2013] EWHC 1583 (Ch), [2013] BVC 314, at [4]–[5].

[873] The case was decided in 1981, before the definition of 'debt' in IR 1986, r 13.12, was introduced.

[874] See per Oliver LJ at p 576.

[875] There was no explanation of why the evidence was admitted or why it could not have been deployed at the first hearing. Compare *Capital Landfill (Restoration) Ltd v William Stockler and Co* (5 September 1991 Court of Appeal (Civil Division) Transcript No 859 of 1991), in which it only became clear that the company was insolvent when a receiver was appointed after the petition had been struck out on the company's evidence that it was solvent.

[876] At pp 574–5.

[877] At p 574.

[878] Per Shaw LJ at p 576 and Oliver LJ at p 578.

[879] It was interpreted in that way by the Court of Appeal in *Alipour v Ary* [1997] 1 WLR 534 at p 546, but the view that a person claiming a disputed debt does have standing to petition for winding up has been taken by Lawrence Collins J in *Commissioners of Customs and Excise v Anglo German Breweries Ltd* [2002] EWHC 2458 (Ch), [2003] BTC 5021, at [40], and by Judge Berens in *Corbett v NYSIR UK Ltd* [2008] EWHC 2670 (Ch), LTL 19/11/2008, at [10].

However, Lord Denning's remark has been applied[880] to hold that a person with a good arguable claim has standing as a creditor to make an administration application.[881]

As the Court of Appeal in *Re Claybridge Shipping Co SA* found that there was no dispute about the existence of the petitioner's debt,[882] the court was not concerned with whether a winding-up order was to be made without deciding whether the debt existed. Oliver LJ said at p 578:[883] **7.373**

> The question in issue in an application of this sort is not the final disposition of the proceedings. It is solely whether under the rule of practice of the Companies Court the matter should or should not proceed to a hearing at which the winding-up order may or may not be made after a full investigation of the facts.

Oliver LJ went on to say that this 'full investigation' would involve determining the dispute about the debt and the petitioner's standing.[884]

In *Re Rhydydefed Colliery Co, Glamorganshire, Ltd*,[885] Turner LJ thought that 'creditor' in the Joint Stock Companies Act 1856 included a person claiming to be a creditor because the Act included specific provisions[886] enabling the court to determine what was owed to a petitioner and to set a date on which a winding-up order would be made unless the determined amount was paid. As those provisions were not carried forward in the Companies Act 1862 and have never been re-enacted, this is not relevant to the meaning of 'creditor' in IA 1986, s 124.[887] **7.374**

Disputed claimant as contingent or prospective creditor

In some cases it has been suggested that a person with a disputed claim to be a creditor of a company or, more generally, a person making a claim in legal proceedings against a company which the company is defending, could be entitled to petition for its winding up as a contingent or prospective creditor of the company. The claimant could be classed as a contingent or prospective creditor on the basis that if the claim were to be decided in the claimant's favour, the claimant would be a creditor of the company. There has been disagreement over whether 'contingent' or 'prospective' is the appropriate adjective. **7.375**

A claim for damages for a company's breach of contract has been described as a contingent claim,[888] which is a contingent liability of the company[889] and makes the claimant a contingent creditor.[890] It has been held that any person with an arguable claim against a company is a contingent creditor of the company.[891] A person claiming to be a creditor of a company in respect of a debt which is wholly disputed by the company has been said to **7.376**

---

[880] By Warren J in *Hammonds v Pro-Fit USA Ltd* [2007] EWHC 1998 (Ch), [2008] 2 BCLC 159, at [53]; *Corbett v NYSIR UK Ltd*.

[881] Under IA 1986, sch B1, para 12(1)(c).

[882] See per Lord Denning at p 574, Shaw LJ at p 576 and Oliver LJ at pp 576–9.

[883] At p 578.

[884] At p 579. See also *Alipour v Ary* [1997] 1 WLR 534 at p 544; *Jubilee International Inc v Farlin Timbers Pte Ltd* [2005] EWHC 3331 (Ch), [2006] BPIR 765, at [62].

[885] (1858) 3 De G & J 80 at p 84.

[886] ss 70 and 71.

[887] *Re GFN Corporation Ltd* 2009 CILR 650 at [51].

[888] *Re Prime Link Removals Ltd* [1987] 1 NZLR 510 at p 512.

[889] *Unite The Union v Nortel Networks UK Ltd* [2010] EWHC 826 (Ch), [2010] 2 BCLC 674, at [25].

[890] *Re Adelaide Holdings Ltd* [1982] 1 NSWLR 167 at p 174.

[891] *Re Gasbourne Pty Ltd* [1984] VR 801.

be a contingent creditor.[892] In *Re Austral Group Investment Management Ltd*,[893] though, Holland J held that a person with 'a real prospect' of becoming a creditor of a company is a prospective creditor, so that persons claiming unliquidated damages against a company were prospective creditors entitled to petition for it to be wound up. In *Commissioner of Taxation of the Commonwealth of Australia v Simionato Holdings Pty Ltd*[894] it was held that a person with an arguable claim against a company is a contingent or prospective creditor, without needing to decide which of those terms is the more apt.

7.377   The difficulty with this analysis is the theory that the existence of a present obligation is an essential feature of a contingent or prospective debt.[895] The company's assertion that it is not liable to the claimant means that there is a dispute about whether a present obligation exists. A court's adjudication on a claim creates a judgment debt by reason of an obligation which the court finds was incurred when the claimant's cause of action arose, but the judgment debt is a present obligation only from the date of the court's order.[896] This difficulty is usually confronted by asserting that the categories of contingent creditor and prospective creditor should not be limited to persons owed present obligations.[897] But in *Re Wilson Market Research Pty Ltd*[898] Santow J said, at p 318:

> I expressly do not follow this extension of the notion of creditor or contingent creditor. The potentially fatal power to trigger winding up was not intended to be vested in those with merely arguable claims. Such claims might well turn out eventually to be without foundation, yet the company may have been destroyed or injured with no redress.

In *Mandarin International Developments Pty Ltd v Growthcorp (Australia) Pty Ltd*[899] his Honour said, at p 422:

> it is necessary for a contingent or prospective creditor to base its claim upon existing *obligations* of the company though they may not yet be due for performance. If a debt is genuinely in dispute it has yet to achieve the status of an obligation, whether contingent or prospective, and may never do so.

In *Re Wilson Market Research Pty Ltd*[900] his Honour rejected Holland J's interpretation of the term 'prospective creditor' and held that a person with an untried claim for unliquidated damages is neither a contingent nor a prospective creditor.

7.378   Classifying a person with a disputed claim against a company as a contingent or prospective creditor does not alter the fact that the claim is disputed.[901] It is submitted that a petition by a person with a disputed contingent or prospective claim against a company should be treated in the same way as a petition by a person with a disputed present claim.

---

[892] *National Mutual Life Association of Alasia Ltd v Oasis Developments Pty Ltd* (1983) 7 ACLR 758 at p 762.
[893] [1993] 2 NZLR 692.
[894] (1997) 15 ACLC 477.
[895] See 7.334–7.339.
[896] *Re Austral Group Investment Management Ltd* [1993] 2 NZLR 692.
[897] *Re Gasbourne Pty Ltd* [1984] VR 801 at p 837; *Re Austral Group Investment Management Ltd* [1993] 2 NZLR 692; *Commissioner of Taxation of the Commonwealth of Australia v Simionato Holdings Pty Ltd* (1997) 15 ACLC 477.
[898] (1996) 39 NSWLR 311.
[899] (1998) 143 FLR 408.
[900] (1996) 39 NSWLR 311 at p 323.
[901] See *Hadden Construction Ltd* 2008 SLT (Sh Ct) 12; *LSI 2013 Ltd v Solar Panel Co (UK) Ltd* [2014] EWHC 248 (Ch), LTL 16/1/2014.

Assigned Debts

An assignee of a debt has standing to petition,[902] even if only an equitable assignee (for example, **7.379** if only part of the debt has been assigned).[903] An equitable assignee of a debt is entitled, in its own right and name, to bring proceedings for the debt. An equitable assignee will usually be required to join the assignor to the proceedings so as to ensure there is no double recovery, but that is a purely procedural requirement which the court can dispense with.[904] It is unnecessary to join the assignor to a winding-up petition because payment of the debt is not made by the winding-up order, but by the liquidator in the winding up, when all interests can be taken into account.[905]

The facts of any assignment of a petition debt must be stated in the petition[906] and also in **7.380** any statutory demand for the debt.[907]

The assignor of an assigned debt also has standing to petition, at least where the assignment **7.381** is only equitable.[908] Despite the rule that after an equitable assignment the assignor cannot sue to recover the debt without joining the assignee,[909] an equitable assignor has a sufficient interest to petition for winding up without joining the assignee, and payment of the debt will be made in the liquidation with regard to the interests of both assignor and assignee.[910] Petitions in respect of assigned debts have been presented jointly by assignor and assignee.[911]

A creditor's petition may be dismissed if the petition debt has been assigned and the petition **7.382** was presented without the assignee's concurrence,[912] but not in the unusual circumstances in *Bell Group Finance (Pty) Ltd v Bell Group (UK) Holdings Ltd*.[913] In that case a petition was presented by the liquidator of a company, in the company's name, to wind up another company in the same group. All companies in the group had created floating charges over their assets in favour of the same chargees and the liquidator wished to challenge the validity of those charges. If a relevant charge had been valid, the petition debt would have been subject to it. On the day before the petition was to be heard, the chargee exercised a power under the charge contract to assign the petition debt to itself and then opposed the making of a winding-up order. It was held that the assignment should be ignored. It was valid only if the charge was valid, and that was the very question to be investigated in the winding up.

---

[902] *Re Cheshire Patent Salt Co Ltd* (1863) 1 New Rep 533; *Re Premier Permanent Building Land and Investment Association, ex parte Stewart* (1890) 16 VLR 20.

[903] *Re Montgomery Moore Ship Collision Doors Syndicate Ltd* (1903) 72 LJ Ch 624; *Re Steel Wing Co Ltd* [1921] 1 Ch 349; *Tele-Art Inc v Nam Tai Electronics Inc* (1999) 57 WIR 76; *Mitchell McFarlane and Partners Ltd v Foremans Ltd* (2002) LTL 18/12/2002.

[904] *Kapoor v National Westminster Bank plc* [2011] EWCA Civ 1083, [2012] 1 All ER 1201, at [30].

[905] *Kapoor v National Westminster Bank plc* at [41], quoting *Re Steel Wing Co Ltd* [1921] Ch 349 at p 357.

[906] *Re Ooregum Gold Mining Co* (1885) 29 SJ 204.

[907] See 7.169.

[908] *Rohan Trading Co Pty Ltd v Glengor Pastoral Co Pty Ltd* [2003] NSWSC 1265; *Parmalat Capital Finance Ltd v Food Holdings Ltd* [2008] UKPC 23, [2009] 1 BCLC 274.

[909] *Kapoor v National Westminster Bank plc* at [30].

[910] *Kapoor v National Westminster Bank plc* at [42] quoting *Parmalat Capital Finance Ltd v Food Holdings Ltd* [2008] UKPC 23, [2009] 1 BCLC 274, at [8].

[911] As in *Re London and Birmingham Flint Glass and Alkali Co Ltd* (1859) 1 De G F & J 257; *Re Paris Skating Rink Co* (1877) 5 ChD 959; *Re Ooregum Gold Mining Co* (1885) 29 SJ 204; *Re Bartitsu Light Cure Institute Ltd* (1909) *The Times*, 13 January 1909.

[912] *Re Pentalta Exploration Co* [1898] WN 55, in which it was found that the petitioner's 'real interest' in receiving the debt had been passed to another person for value received, though no actual assignment had been proved.

[913] [1996] 1 BCLC 304.

7.383 A liquidated claim may be assigned to another person for the purpose of enforcing it, for example, by petitioning for the debtor to be wound up or made bankrupt.[914] An assignment of any other right of action may be illegally champertous. In some cases the courts have refused to make a winding-up order on a petition in respect of an assigned debt if the petitioner took the assignment for the purpose of acquiring standing to petition.[915]

7.384 There is no rule that a creditor's petition will be dismissed if the petition debt is assigned after the petition is presented,[916] though that was what happened in *Re Paris Skating Rink Co*,[917] where the assignee, who was a member of the company, took the assignment for the purpose of acquiring standing to petition.

Attached Debts

Attached debt owed by a company

7.385 A person who has attached a debt owed by a company is not, by virtue of the third party debt order, a creditor of the company, and is not entitled to present a petition for the winding up of the company when the company fails to pay the attached debt.[918] The situation changes if a judgment is obtained for the attached money: this makes the person who attached the debt a judgment creditor of the company and therefore entitled to petition for its winding up.[919]

7.386 In *Re European Banking Co, ex parte Baylis*[920] it was said that the court would not make a winding-up order on the petition of a creditor whose debt had been attached. But in *Re Swiss Oil Corporation*[921] a winding-up order was made where a court had appointed a receiver of the debt due to the petitioning creditor.

Attached debt owed by a company's creditor

7.387 A person who has attached a debt owed by a creditor of a company does not have standing to petition as a creditor for the winding up of the company.[922]

Uncertainty of Amount of Claim or Time for Payment

7.388 Subject to what is said at 7.392–7.397 about small debts, if the fact that a company is indebted to a person who is petitioning as a creditor for the company to be wound up is not disputed, but the amount to be paid, and/or the time at which it is to be paid, is disputed (in particular, if only part of the petitioner's debt is disputed), then the petitioner's standing is not in question.[923]

---

[914] *Fitzroy v Cave* [1905] 2 KB 364; *Re Down* 2001 BCCA 65, 196 DLR (4th) 114.
[915] *Re Paris Skating Rink Co* (1877) 5 ChD 959; *Re People's Loan and Deposit Co* (1906) 7 OWR 253; but not in *Re Ooregum Gold Mining Co* (1885) 29 SJ 204.
[916] *Perak Pioneer Ltd v Petroliam Nasional Bhd* [1986] AC 849.
[917] (1877) 5 ChD 959.
[918] *Re Combined Weighing Machine and Advertising Co* (1889) 43 ChD 99.
[919] *Pritchett v English and Colonial Syndicate* [1899] 2 QB 428.
[920] (1866) LR 2 Eq 521.
[921] 1988–89 CILR 319.
[922] *Re Barrier Reef Finance and Land Pty Ltd* [1989] 1 QdR 252 at p 253.
[923] *Re Yniscedwyn Iron Co Ltd* (1870) 19 WR 194; *Re Tweeds Garages Ltd* [1962] Ch 406; *Tandy v Harmony House Furniture Co Ltd 1964* (1) ALR Comm 299; *Re Claybridge Shipping Co SA* [1997] 1 BCLC 572 per Lord Denning MR at pp 574–5; *L and D Audio Acoustics Pty Ltd v Pioneer Electronic Australia Pty Ltd* (1982) 7 ACLR 180; *Chapmans Ltd v Brinds Ltd* (1985) 9 ACLR 943 (dispute over time for payment); *Re R A Foulds Ltd* (1986) 2 BCC 99,269 per Hoffmann J at p 99,274; *Taylors Industrial Flooring Ltd v M and H Plant Hire (Manchester) Ltd* [1990] BCLC 216 at p 218; *Re National Computers Systems and Services Ltd* (1991) 6 ACSR

If the size of the creditor's debt is not known with certainty, a statutory demand for it can- **7.389**
not be served[924] and the petitioner must be able to prove the company's inability to pay its
debts otherwise than by neglect to comply with a statutory demand for the petitioner's debt.
Sometimes, this can be proved under IA 1986, s 123(1)(e), by non-payment of an undisputed portion of the debt. In *Clowes Developments (Scotland) Ltd v Whannel*[925] a company's
failure to fulfil a promise, given by its solicitor, that it would pay an undisputed portion of
a disputed debt was sufficient to prove its inability to pay its debts, even though it never
identified precisely what the undisputed amount was.

In two reported cases the court has made no order as to costs on a petition based on a **7.390**
debt of uncertain amount where the dispute could have been settled without resorting to a
winding-up petition.[926]

The same applies where there is uncertainty over the time at which a debt is payable. **7.391**

Small Debts

No minimum debt qualification has ever been imposed by statute on creditor petitioners **7.392**
for compulsory winding up of companies.[927] This is unlike the position in bankruptcy
law under which a creditor's petition may be presented in respect of a debt only if the debt
equals or exceeds the bankruptcy level, which is currently £750.[928] However, the court has
deprecated petitions for winding up companies presented by creditors whose debts are so
small that statutory demands could not be presented for them.[929]

In 1895 Vaughan Williams J said that, in future, where the debt was small, no winding-up **7.393**
order would be made, or if the order was made it would be without costs.[930] In 1899 Wright
J said that when the debt is small the petitioner 'should allege and make out some special
ground for making a winding-up order'.[931] In *Re W H Hyde Ltd*,[932] in which a petition by
an unpaid creditor owed £45.25 was dismissed, Buckley J expressed a 'pious hope' that the
practice of not making a winding-up order on a small debt would not be disregarded. The
practice does not apply to a petition by a creditor with a small debt which is supported by

133; *Re Clemence plc* (1992) 59 BLR 56; *Fiesta Girl of London Ltd v Network Agencies* [1992] 2 EGLR 28; *Hixgold Pty Ltd v FCT* (1992) 8 ACSR 607; *Tottenham Hotspur plc v Edennote plc* [1995] 1 BCLC 65; *Re Pendigo Ltd* [1996] 2 BCLC 64; *Truck and Machinery Sales Ltd v Marubeni Komatsu Ltd* [1996] 1 IR 12; *Re Bydand Ltd* [1997] BCC 915; *Renshaw Birch Ltd v Marquet* [1998] BPIR 399; *Corbern v Whatmusic Holdings Ltd* [2003] EWHC 2134 (Ch), LTL 1/10/2003; *Angel Group Ltd v British Gas Trading Ltd* [2012] EWHC 2702 (Ch), [2013] BCC 265.
[924] *Re a Company (No 003729 of 1982)* [1984] 1 WLR 1090.
[925] 2002 SLT (Sh Ct) 6.
[926] *Re Great Barrier Reef Flying Boats Pty Ltd* (1982) 6 ACLR 820; *Re Kingsley Monogramming Ltd* (1985) 2 NZCLC 99,420.
[927] *Re London and Birmingham Flint Glass and Alkali Co Ltd* (1859) 1 De G F & J 257.
[928] IA 1986, s 267; two or more creditors for small amounts may present a joint petition provided the aggregate debt owed to them is equal to or exceeds the bankruptcy level.
[929] *Re Wear Engine Works Co* (1875) LR 10 Ch App 188; *Re Milford Docks Co* (1883) 23 ChD 292 per Bacon V-C at p 295. Originally a statutory demand could be presented only for a debt exceeding £50; increased to £200 from 20 December 1976 by IA 1976, sch 2; increased to £750 from 1 October 1984 by the Insolvency Proceedings (Increase of Monetary Limits) Regulations 1984 (SI 1984/1199), reg 2(c); presently £750 under IA 1986, ss 123(1)(a) and 222(1).
[930] *Re Herbert Standring and Co* [1895] WN 99.
[931] *Re Fancy Dress Balls Co* [1899] WN 109.
[932] (1900) 44 SJ 731.

other creditors if the total of their debts is an amount for which a statutory demand may be served.[933]

7.394   The practice announced by Vaughan Williams J is not followed in Scotland.[934]

7.395   It is implicit in Vaughan Williams J's statement that there must be special circumstances to induce the court to make a winding-up order on the petition of a creditor for a small amount.[935]

7.396   A creditor of a company with a debt of £750 or less cannot use the statutory demand procedure to establish the company's inability to pay its debts but can rely on failure of execution[936] or adduce other evidence to prove inability to pay debts.[937] The fact that a petitioner now has to pay the court £1,530 when presenting a petition[938] makes winding-up proceedings an unattractive method of collecting small debts. Nevertheless it has been said in Australia that the fact that the probable costs of winding up a company exceed the amount of the petitioner's debt is not a reason for dismissing the petition.[939]

7.397   If a company will not pay an undisputed debt, however small, the creditor is entitled to assume that the company is unable to pay its debts and, if the debt exceeds £750, may present a petition for it to be wound up.[940] Failure to pay a small debt may actually be a good indication of insolvency.

Secured Creditors and Holders of Debt Securities

7.398   Holding security for a debt owed by a company does not disentitle the creditor from petitioning for the company to be wound up if the debt is wholly or partly unpaid.[941] A secured creditor does not have to elect between resting on the security and taking part in the liquidation until after the winding-up order is made.[942]

7.399   In *Re Exmouth Docks Co*[943] and *Re Herne Bay Waterworks Co*[944] Malins V-C held that where the method of enforcing a security given by a statutory company was limited to the appointment of a receiver, a winding-up order could not be granted. However, in *Re Borough of*

---

[933]   *Re Leyton and Walthamstow Cycle Co Ltd* (1901) 50 WR 93. In *Re Grosvenor House Property Acquisition and Investment Building Society* (1902) 71 LJ Ch 748 the petitioner was owed £31.93 and the petition was supported by two other creditors, whose debts, together with the petitioner's, amounted to £54.35; Buckley J made a winding-up order.

[934]   *J Speirs and Co v Central Building Co Ltd* (1911) SC 330.

[935]   *Re Fancy Dress Balls Co* [1899] WN 109; *Re Industrial Insurance Association Ltd* [1910] WN 245.

[936]   *Re London and Birmingham Flint Glass and Alkali Co Ltd* (1859) 1 De G F & J 257; *Re Yate Collieries and Limeworks Co* [1883] WN 171; *Re Fancy Dress Balls Co* [1899] WN 109; *J Speirs and Co v Central Building Co Ltd* (1911) SC 330.

[937]   *Re Metropolitan Fuel Pty Ltd* [1969] VR 328.

[938]   See 2.253–2.254.

[939]   *FAI Insurances Ltd v Goldleaf Interior Decorators Pty Ltd* (1988) 14 NSWLR 643.

[940]   *Cornhill Insurance plc v Improvement Services Ltd* [1986] 1 WLR 114.

[941]   *Moor v Anglo-Italian Bank* (1879) 10 ChD 681; *Commercial Bank of Scotland Ltd v Lanark Oil Co Ltd* (1886) 14 R 147; *Re Borough of Portsmouth (Kingston, Fratton and Southsea) Tramways Co* [1892] 2 Ch 362; *Re Strathy Wire Fence Co* (1904) 8 OLR 186 at pp 191–2 (worker's lien for wages); *Re Cushing Sulphite Fibre Co Ltd* (1905) 37 NBR 254; *Re Gem Sapphires (Aust) Pty Ltd* (1974) 8 ACLR 225; *Re Alexanders Securities Ltd (No 2)* [1983] 2 QdR 597; *Re Lafayette Electronics Europe Ltd* [2006] EWHC 1006 (Ch), LTL 9/10/2006.

[942]   *Re Carmarthenshire Anthracite Coal and Iron Co* (1875) 45 LJ Ch 200.

[943]   (1873) LR 17 Eq 181.

[944]   (1878) 10 ChD 42.

Portsmouth (Kingston, Fratton and Southsea) Tramways Co[945] Stirling J said that he could not quite follow the reasoning of Malins V-C, because a petition for the winding up of a company is not an enforcement of the petitioner's security.

If a company issues marketable loan securities and a person is constituted trustee for the **7.400** holders of the securities, it is a question of construction of the documents constituting the loan whether the individual security holders are creditors of the company who can petition for it to be wound up[946] or whether only the trustee is capable of petitioning.[947] In *Segenhoe v Permanent Trustee Co Ltd*[948] the trustee was entitled to petition but whether or not individual security holders could petition was not in issue.

Belief that security given by a company is inadequate to pay the debt owed is not a sufficient **7.401** reason to wind up the company under IA 1986, s 122(1)(g), the just and equitable clause.[949]

Payment by Cheque

Payment by cheque is an actual payment at the time the cheque is delivered to the payee, **7.402** but there is a condition subsequent that if the cheque is dishonoured, the payment will not have been made.[950] It follows that a creditor who has accepted payment of a debt by cheque ceases to be a creditor unless and until the cheque is dishonoured. Re-presentation of a dishonoured cheque is a fresh acceptance of payment and again ends the status of creditor unless and until there is a further dishonour.[951]

Judgment Debts and Arbitration Awards

If a creditor's petition is based on non-payment of a judgment debt, the fact that the com- **7.403** pany has appealed against the judgment does not in itself affect the petitioner's standing, because the judgment is effective until it is reversed on appeal.[952] A winding-up order may be made while the appeal is pending.[953] A stay of execution of a judgment does not prevent the judgment creditor from petitioning.[954] But in New South Wales, an application for a company to be wound up, based on non-payment of an entire judgment debt, has been dismissed as an abuse of process where the court had ordered payment by instalments,[955] which were being paid.[956]

A creditor with a default judgment has standing to petition.[957] For disputes about default **7.404** judgments see 7.509.

---

[945] [1892] 2 Ch 362.
[946] As in *Re Olathe Silver Mining Co* (1884) 27 ChD 278 and *Re Cushing Sulphite Fibre Co Ltd* (1905) 37 NBR 254.
[947] As in *Re Uruguay Central and Hygueritas Railway Co of Monte Video* (1879) 11 ChD 372.
[948] (1992) 9 ACSR 270.
[949] *Re Squashland Southport Pty Ltd* (1980) 5 ACLR 47.
[950] *Thomson v Moyse* [1961] AC 967 per Lord Denning at p 1004.
[951] *Re a Company (No 001259 of 1991)* [1991] BCLC 594.
[952] *Bank Utama (M) Bhd v GKM Amal Bhd* [2000] 5 MLJ 657, point not considered on appeal; *El Ajou v Dollar Land (Manhattan) Ltd* [2005] EWHC 2861 (Ch), [2007] BCC 953, at [9].
[953] *Re BLV Realty II Ltd* [2010] EWHC 1791 (Ch), LTL 17/9/2010, in which the company had failed to provide security for the debt as a condition of having the petition adjourned.
[954] See 7.60.
[955] Civil Procedure Act 2005 (New South Wales), s 107.
[956] *Botany Bay City Council v Parmtree Pty Ltd* [2009] NSWSC 896.
[957] *Bank Pembangunan (M) Bhd v Elgi Marka Sdn Bhd* [1998] 5 MLJ 504.

7.405 If an appeal against a petitioner's judgment is successful, the petition will be dismissed (unless some other creditor is substituted), even if a further appeal has been launched.[958] Similarly, if a creditor petitioner's debt was declared payable by a judgment obtained by default and the creditor has subsequently withdrawn the claim, the petition will be dismissed.[959]

7.406 In *Re Goldthorpe and Lacey Ltd*[960] a creditor of a company sued it but in the proceedings (in which the plaintiff was given judgment) the creditor was misnamed. It was held that the creditor was not entitled to present a winding-up petition in respect of the judgment debt unless and until it had the judgment amended.

7.407 The presentation of a petition to wind up a company based on a judgment debt is not an action upon the judgment for the purposes of the Limitation Act 1980, s 24, and so the six-year limitation period in s 24 does not apply.[961] Generally the presentation of a petition based on a judgment is not execution or enforcement of the judgment and a petition based on an arbitration award is not enforcement of the award.[962] This means that a judgment debtor does not require the permission of the court to petition for winding up when six years have elapsed since the date of the judgment.[963] It follows that a judgment debtor of a company may petition for its winding up at any time without limitation. The same applies to a local authority which has a liability order for council tax, non-domestic rates or BID levy.[964]

7.408 Presenting a petition to wind up a company based on a judgment is a proceeding for the recovery of a sum payable under the judgment.[965] So, if the judgment is a foreign judgment to which the Foreign Judgments (Reciprocal Enforcement) Act 1933, part 1, applies, the petition must not be entertained by any court in the United Kingdom unless the foreign judgment is registered under s 2 of the Act.[966] Part 1 of the Act is applied, as a result of reciprocal enforcement conventions concluded with individual countries, by Orders in Council under s 1, to judgments of recognized courts in Australia,[967] Canada,[968] Guernsey,[969] India,[970] the Isle of Man,[971] Israel,[972] Jersey,[973] Pakistan,[974] Suriname[975] and Tonga.[976] In

---

[958] *Re Anglo-Bavarian Steel Ball Co* [1899] WN 80.

[959] *Teng Foh v Liwu Realty Sdn Bhd* [1989] 2 MLJ 425.

[960] (1987) 3 BCC 595.

[961] *Ridgeway Motors (Isleworth) Ltd v ALTS Ltd* [2005] EWCA Civ 92, [2005] 1 WLR 2871, overruling *Re a Debtor (No 50A-SD-1995)* [1997] Ch 310, which had been followed in *Re a Debtor (No 647-SD-1999)* (2000) *The Times*, 10 April 2000.

[962] See 7.60–7.61. But see 2.110 for enforcement of a judgment against a company protected under the Reserve and Auxiliary Forces (Protection of Civil Interests) Act 1951.

[963] CPR, r 83.2(3)(a).

[964] *Bolsover District Council v Ashfield Nominees Ltd* [2010] EWCA Civ 1129, [2011] Bus LR 492.

[965] See 7.70.

[966] Foreign Judgments (Reciprocal Enforcement) Act 1933, s 6; *Bank of East Asia Ltd Singapore Branch v Axis Incorporation Bhd* [2009] MYMHC 109.

[967] Reciprocal Enforcement of Foreign Judgments (Australia) Order 1994 (SI 1994/1901).

[968] Reciprocal Enforcement of Foreign Judgments (Canada) Order 1987 (SI 1987/468) as amended. No provincial courts of Quebec are recognized.

[969] Reciprocal Enforcement of Foreign Judgments (Guernsey) Order 1973 (SI 1973/610).

[970] Reciprocal Enforcement of Judgments (India) Order 1958 (SI 1958/425).

[971] Reciprocal Enforcement of Foreign Judgments (Isle of Man) Order 1973 (SI 1973/611).

[972] Reciprocal Enforcement of Foreign Judgments (Israel) Order 1971 (SI 1971/1039).

[973] Reciprocal Enforcement of Foreign Judgments (Jersey) Order 1973 (SI 1973/612).

[974] Reciprocal Enforcement of Judgments (Pakistan) Order 1958 (SI 1958/141).

[975] Reciprocal Enforcement of Foreign Judgments (Suriname) Order 1981 (SI 1981/735).

[976] Reciprocal Enforcement of Foreign Judgments (Tonga) Order 1980 (SI 1980/1523).

relation to Austria, Belgium, France, Germany, Italy, the Netherlands and Norway, the reciprocal enforcement conventions were superseded by the Brussels Convention or, in relation to Norway, the Lugano Convention 1988, except for judgments which are not covered by the superseding instrument.[977] Judgments of courts of those European countries are therefore enforced in the United Kingdom under the provisions of those conventions or their successors. However, the individual reciprocal enforcement conventions and the Foreign Judgments (Reciprocal Enforcement) Act 1933, part 1, continue to apply to judgments that are within their scope but are not covered by the superseding conventions or their successors.

The general prohibition imposed by the 1933 Act on proceedings for recovery of a sum **7.409** payable under an unregistered judgment is not repeated in other legislation providing for registration in England and Wales of judgments of courts in other jurisdictions.[978] It is not necessary to register a judgment under legislation of that kind before basing a winding-up petition on the judgment debt. Similarly, a judgment for which there is no provision for registration can be the basis of a winding-up petition in England and Wales without any preliminary proceedings (such as a claim on the judgment) in this jurisdiction.[979]

The sanction for not registering a foreign judgment under the Administration of Justice **7.410** Act 1920, part 2, is that the judgment creditor cannot recover the costs of an action on the judgment.[980] But a winding-up petition is not an action on a judgment,[981] and it is submitted that the court should not apply a penal statutory provision to a situation, however analogous, which could have been specified by the legislator but was not.

---

[977] The treaties with Belgium, France, Germany, Italy and the Netherlands were superseded by the Brussels Convention when that Convention was incorporated into United Kingdom law by the Civil Jurisdiction and Judgments Act 1982 and the treaty with Austria was superseded by the Brussels Convention when the UK agreed to a revision of the Convention on the accession of Austria to it (see the Brussels Convention, art 55, as set out in sch 1 to the 1982 Act). The treaty with Norway was superseded by the Lugano Convention 1988 when that Convention was incorporated into UK law by the Civil Jurisdiction and Judgments Act 1991 (see art 55 of the 1988 Convention).

[978] Administration of Justice Act 1920, part 2 (judgments of superior courts of those parts of Her Majesty's dominions outside the UK that are specified in the Reciprocal Enforcement of Judgments (Administration of Justice Act 1920, Part II) (Consolidation) Order 1984 (SI 1984/129) as amended and as affected by the Foreign Judgments (Reciprocal Enforcement) Act 1933, s 7(2), under which the 1920 Act ceased to apply to Newfoundland (now Newfoundland and Labrador) and Saskatchewan when the 1933 Act was applied to those provinces, and as affected by Regulation (EU) No 1215/2012 which has superseded the 1920 Act's application to Cyprus and Malta); Civil Jurisdiction and Judgments Act 1982, s 18 and sch 6 (judgments of courts of other parts of the UK); Brussels Convention, arts 26 and 31 (judgments of courts of Aruba and French overseas departments), given the force of law in the UK by the Civil Jurisdiction and Judgments Act 1982, s 2, and applied to Gibraltar by the Civil Jurisdiction and Judgments Act 1982 (Gibraltar) Order 1997 (SI 1997/2602); Regulation (EC) No 44/2001, arts 33(1) and 38(2) (judgments of courts in EU States in proceedings instituted before 10 January 2015); Lugano Convention 2007, arts 33(1) and 38(2), and Civil Jurisdiction and Judgments Act 1982, s 4A (judgments of courts of Iceland, Norway and Switzerland).

[979] *Sun Legend Investments Ltd v Ho* [2013] BPIR 532, which proceeded on the basis that it is not possible to register Hong Kong judgments, without mentioning that Hong Kong has never been removed from the list in SI 1984/129 of jurisdictions to which the Administration of Justice Act 1920 applies. No provision for registration of judgments of courts in EU States may be made in relation to proceedings instituted on or after 10 January 2015 (Regulation (EU) No 1215/2012, arts 36(1) and 39).

[980] Administration of Justice Act 1920, s 9(5).

[981] See 7.64.

Execution Creditors

7.411 An execution creditor of a company may petition for it to be wound up.[982] A judgment debt is still due despite a stay of execution[983] and so a winding-up order can be made on a petition by the judgment creditor despite the stay of execution.[984]

Taxes

7.412 The basic principle is that once a charge to tax has been assessed by self-assessment, or assessed or determined by HM Revenue and Customs, it must be paid on the date specified in the relevant legislation.[985] For taxes to which the Taxes Management Act 1970 applies,[986] liability to pay is not affected by an appeal to the First-tier Tribunal, unless an amount is postponed pending determination of the appeal.[987] If there is a further appeal, tax is payable as determined on the initial appeal, despite the further appeal having been made, and there is no provision for postponement.[988] If the result of a further appeal is that more tax is payable, the extra amount is due and payable 30 days after a notice to pay is issued by HMRC.[989] There are very similar provisions for stamp duty land tax[990] and annual tax on enveloped dwellings.[991]

7.413 The Taxes Management Act 1970 states that, in the County Court or High Court, any tax may be sued for as a debt due to the Crown.[992] However, this does not create the liability to pay the tax: it only identifies a method by which the tax can be collected.[993] Submission of a VAT return showing an amount of VAT to be paid is 'at the least an admission of a statutory liability for VAT', and the amount payable is recoverable as a debt even though that is not expressly provided in the legislation.[994]

7.414 For indirect taxes, the fact that an appeal is lodged with the First-tier Tribunal (Tax) does not suspend liability for the assessment or determination appealed against.[995] An appeal shall not be entertained unless the assessed or determined amount has been paid or secured, except where this requirement is disapplied on hardship grounds.[996] Exceptionally, if that

---

[982] *Re Lake Winnipeg Transportation, Lumber and Trading Co* (1891) 7 Man R 255.

[983] *Woodley v Woodley (No 2)* [1994] 1 WLR 1167; *Australian Beverage Distributors Pty Ltd v Evans and Tate Premium Wines Pty Ltd* [2007] NSWCA 57, 61 ACSR 441.

[984] *Deputy Commissioner of Taxation (WA) v Mobile Homes of Australia Pty Ltd* (1986) 19 ATR 183.

[985] *Commissioners of Inland Revenue v Pearlberg* [1953] 1 WLR 331.

[986] Income tax, corporation tax, and capital gains tax (Taxes Management Act 1970, s 1), petroleum revenue tax (Oil Taxation Act 1975, sch 2, para 1), bank levy (Finance Act 2011, sch 19, para 52).

[987] Taxes Management Act 1970, s 55.

[988] Taxes Management Act 1970, s 56(1) and (2).

[989] Taxes Management Act 1970, s 56(3).

[990] Finance Act 2003, sch 10, paras 38–43.

[991] Finance Act 2013, sch 33, paras 47–53.

[992] Taxes Management Act 1970, ss 66(1) and 68(1). For the County Court, the reference is to 'tax due and payable'.

[993] See *R (Balding) v Secretary of State for Work and Pensions* [2007] EWCA Civ 1327, [2008] 1 WLR 564, at [25].

[994] *Commissioners of HM Revenue and Customs v Chamberlin* [2011] EWCA Civ 271, [2011] BPIR 691, at [26].

[995] *Re D and D Marketing (UK) Ltd* [2002] EWHC 660 (Ch), [2003] BPIR 539 (VAT); *Commissioners of Customs and Excise v Anglo German Breweries Ltd* [2002] EWHC 2458 (Ch), [2003] BTC 5021 (excise duty and VAT); *Commissioners of HM Revenue and Customs v Autotech Design Ltd* [2006] EWHC 1596 (Ch) (excise duty).

[996] Finance Act 1994, s 16(3) (customs and excise duties and EU agricultural levy) and s 60(4), (4A) and (4B) (insurance premium tax); Value Added Tax Act 1994, s 84(3)–(3C); Finance Act 1996, s 55(3), (3A) and

requirement has been disapplied on hardship grounds and the appeal is against a customs duty determination which is subject to Regulation 2913/92/EEC (the Community Customs Code), implementation of the decision is suspended[997] and HM Revenue and Customs ceases to be a creditor (and is not a contingent or prospective creditor).[998]

A tax authority of another EU member State may request HMRC to recover in the United **7.415** Kingdom a claim which the foreign authority has against a person for a tax, duty etc within the scope of Directive 2010/24/EU.[999] Such steps may be taken to enforce the foreign claim as might be taken to enforce a corresponding UK claim.[1000] Those steps may be taken by or on behalf of the Commissioners of HM Revenue and Customs, whether or not the Commissioners could have taken the steps in relation to the corresponding UK claim.[1001] Clearly the available steps include petitioning for winding up.

Unenforceable Claims

A person owed an unenforceable debt is not entitled to petition as a creditor. This has been **7.416** held in relation to:

(a) A claim arising from a transaction which the company did not have capacity to enter into.[1002]

(b) A statute-barred debt.[1003]

(c) A claim for the recovery of money due under an illegal contract.[1004]

In addition, taxes imposed in another State are unenforceable,[1005] unless the other State is **7.417** a fellow member of the EU.[1006]

Unprovable Claims

A claim against a company which, though it could be enforced against the company in **7.418** proceedings outside winding up, is not provable in winding up is nevertheless a debt under IR 1986, r 13.12, and so the claimant is a creditor with standing to petition for the winding

---

(3B) (landfill tax); Finance Act 2000, sch 6, para 122(2), (2A) and (2B) (climate change levy); Finance Act 2001, s 41(2), (2A) and (2B) (aggregates levy).

[997] Regulation 2913/92/EEC, art 244.

[998] *Commissioners of Customs and Excise v Broomco (1984) Ltd* (2000) *The Times*, 17 August 2000.

[999] Directive 2010/24/EU, arts 10–15. The very wide scope of the Directive is defined in art 2. The Directive is implemented in UK law by the Finance Act 2011, s 87 and sch 25, and the MARD Regulations 2011 (SI 2011/2931). The acronym 'MARD' used in the title of these Regulations is from 'mutual assistance in the recovery of debt'. The Directive is sometimes called the MARD Directive.

[1000] Finance Act 2011, sch 25, para 6(3). 'Corresponding UK claim' is defined in para 8.

[1001] Finance Act 2011, sch 25, para 6(3). If the foreign claim relates to agricultural levy, various government departments have authority concurrently with the Commissioners (para 7).

[1002] *Re National Permanent Benefit Building Society, ex parte Williamson* (1869) LR 5 Ch App 309.

[1003] *Motor Terms Co Pty Ltd v Liberty Insurance Ltd* (1967) 116 CLR 177 (in which it was held that the petitioner's debt was not statute-barred); *Re Karnos Property Co Ltd* [1989] BCLC 340, criticized by A McGee, 'Who is a creditor?' (1989) 10 Co Law 235; *Ridgeway Motors (Isleworth) Ltd v ALTS Ltd* [2005] EWCA Civ 92, [2005] 1 WLR 2871, at [35] (a person who was owed a debt that is now statute-barred is not a creditor at all).

[1004] *Re South Wales Atlantic Steamship Co* (1876) 2 ChD 763.

[1005] *Peter Buchanan Ltd v McVey* [1954] IR 89; *Government of India, Ministry of Finance (Revenue Division) v Taylor* [1955] AC 491; *QRS 1 ApS v Frandsen* [1999] 1 WLR 2169.

[1006] Directive 2010/24/EU; Finance Act 2011, s 87 and sch 25; MARD Regulations 2011 (SI 2011/2931).

up of the company.[1007] However, as a petitioner with an unprovable claim would have no interest as a creditor in having the company wound up, an order would not be made on the petition.[1008]

7.419   This applies to enforceable claims which are made unprovable by IR 1986, r 12.3.

7.420   Rule 12.3(2)(b) makes unprovable any obligation arising under a confiscation order made under the Drug Trafficking Offences Act 1986, s 1, the Criminal Justice (Scotland) Act 1987, s 1, the Criminal Justice Act 1988, s 71, or parts 2, 3 or 4 of the Proceeds of Crime Act 2002, and any obligation arising from a payment out of the social fund under the Social Security Contributions and Benefits Act 1992, s 138(1)(b), by way of crisis loan or budgeting loan.

7.421   IR 1986, r 12.3(3), preserves any enactment or rule of law under which a particular kind of debt is not provable, whether on grounds of public policy or otherwise. A claim against a company for damages arising from a cause of action accruing after the company has gone into liquidation is unprovable.[1009] At common law a debt incurred under foreign law which has been extinguished by that law is unprovable.[1010]

7.422   Rule 12.3(2A) provides that certain claims are not provable until all other claims[1011] have been paid in full with interest. It is submitted that a person with a claim against a company within r 12.3(2A) does not have a sufficient interest to be able to petition for the company to be wound up, unless it can be shown that the company's assets are sufficient for the claim to be provable. The claims covered by r 12.3(2A) are:

  (a) By r 12.3(2A)(a), any claim arising by virtue of the Financial Services and Markets Act 2000, s 382(1)(a) (court order that a person must pay to the FCA or PRA an amount representing profits which have accrued to the person as a result of contravening, or being knowingly concerned in contravening, a 'relevant requirement' as defined in s 382(9)), which does not also arise by virtue of s 382(1)(b) (order for payment of an amount representing a loss or adverse effect of the contravention). Amounts payable under s 382(1) must be paid by the regulator to such qualifying person[1012] or distributed by it among such qualifying persons, as the court may direct.[1013]

  (b) By r 12.3(2A)(c), any claim which, by virtue of IA 1986 or any other enactment, is a claim the payment of which in a bankruptcy or a winding up is to be postponed. This would include:

   (i) any sum within the Companies Act 2006, s 735(6) (which postpones any amount which a company is liable under s 735(4) to pay in respect of any shares which it (1) issued on terms that they are or are liable to be redeemed or (2) agreed to purchase);

[1007] *Levy v Legal Services Commission* [2001] 1 All ER 895; *Tottenham Hotspur plc v Edennote plc* [1995] 1 BCLC 65. In the Virgin Islands, a person with an unprovable claim is excluded from the definition of 'creditor' (Insolvency Act 2003 (Virgin Islands), s 9(1)(a)) and so does not have standing to petition (*Westford Special Situations Fund Ltd v Barfield Nominees Ltd* (HCVAP 2010/014)).

[1008] *Levy v Legal Services Commission*; see 2.127–2.141. There might be a wholly exceptional case in which an order would be made (*Levy v Legal Services Commission* at [44]).

[1009] *Re T & N Ltd* [2005] EWHC 2870 (Ch), [2006] 1 WLR 1728.

[1010] *Re Banque des Marchands de Moscou (Koupetschesky)* [1952] 1 All ER 1269; *Re Banque des Marchands de Moscou (Koupetschesky) (No 2)* [1954] 1 WLR 1108.

[1011] Apart from claims within r 12.3(2A).

[1012] Defined in s 382(8).

[1013] s 382(3).

(ii) any sum within IA 1986, s 74(2)(f) (which postpones any 'sum due to any member of the company (in his character of a member) by way of dividends, profits or otherwise');[1014]

(iii) any sum within the Partnership Act 1890, s 3 (which postpones (1) recovery by a lender of anything in respect of a loan to a person engaged or about to engage in any business on a contract with that person that the lender shall receive a rate of interest varying with the profits, or shall receive a share of the profits arising from carrying on the business and (2) recovery by a seller of goodwill in consideration of a share of the profits of the business of anything in respect of the share of profits contracted for).

The fact that the tax authorities and social security authorities of other EU member States (apart from Denmark) are expressly given the right to prove in a winding up[1015] means that such an authority may petition for winding up.[1016] **7.423**

Alternative Formulations of Claim

A person with a claim against a company which can be formulated alternatively as a claim for a debt or for damages for breach of contract may petition for the winding up of the company as a creditor without electing for the purposes of the petition how to formulate the claim.[1017] **7.424**

Debt in Receivership

If a court has appointed a receiver of a debt due from a company to a creditor, the creditor nevertheless still has the legal title to the debt and can petition as a creditor for the company to be wound up.[1018] **7.425**

Creditor Bound not to Petition

A contractual obligation of a creditor not to apply for winding up will be enforced by the court, if necessary by striking out, and is not contrary to public policy.[1019] **7.426**

A creditor who is bound by a company voluntary arrangement cannot petition and any petition presented by such a creditor will be struck out.[1020] **7.427**

If recitals to a deed made by a company and a creditor declare that the debt owed to the creditor has been paid, when both parties know that this is not the case, the creditor may be estopped from petitioning for the company to be wound up for not paying the debt.[1021] **7.428**

[1014] *Soden v British and Commonwealth Holdings plc* [1996] 2 BCLC 207 at p 223.

[1015] Regulation (EC) No 1346/2000, art 39.

[1016] *Re Cedarlease Ltd* [2005] 1 IR 470.

[1017] *Re Adelaide Holdings Ltd* [1982] 1 NSWLR 167 at p 174.

[1018] *Re Swiss Oil Corporation* 1988–89 CILR 319.

[1019] *Re Peter Dynes Esq International Ltd* (1988) 4 NZCLC 64,906; *Re a Company (No 00928 of 1991)* [1991] BCLC 514; *Re COLT Telecom Group plc* [2002] EWHC 2815 (Ch), [2003] BPIR 324. See also *Westcoast (Holdings) Ltd v Wharf Land Subsidiary (No 1) Ltd* [2012] EWCA Civ 1003, LTL 26/7/2012, in which a creditor obtained, along with judgment for its debt, a declaration that it was no longer bound not to petition for winding up. The creditor was also a member of the company and the restriction was in a shareholders' agreement.

[1020] *Beverley Group plc v McClue* [1995] BCC 751.

[1021] *Prime Sight Ltd v Lavarello* [2013] UKPC 22, [2014] AC 436.

Creditor Pursuing other Claims against Company

7.429   It is not an abuse of process for a landlord to sue for unpaid rent for some periods by an ordinary claim and present a winding-up petition based on non-payment of rent for other periods,[1022] even if the purpose is to get the claim stayed and dealt with in the winding up.[1023]

Beneficial Interest in Trust Property

7.430   A beneficial interest in property held in trust by a company does not in itself make the person with that interest a creditor of the company.[1024]

Insolvent Partnerships

7.431   The discussion so far in 7.309–7.430 applies to a petition by a creditor for the winding up of an insolvent partnership under IPO 1994, art 7 (where there is no concurrent petition for the winding up or bankruptcy of any member or former member of the partnership).[1025] However, the only type of creditor who may petition for the winding up of an insolvent partnership under IPO 1994, art 8 (concurrent petitions for the winding up of an insolvent partnership and the bankruptcy or winding up of one or more present or former members of the partnership), is a creditor to whom the partnership and the present or former member or members sought to be wound up or adjudged bankrupt are indebted in respect of a liquidated sum payable immediately.[1026] It follows that a bankruptcy petition under IPO 1994, art 8, against any individual member or former individual member of that partnership must be in respect of one or more joint debts owed by the insolvent partnership,[1027] and the petitioning creditor or each of the petitioning creditors must be a person to whom the debt or (as the case may be) at least one of the debts is owed.[1028] The following conditions apply to the debt or debts on which such a bankruptcy petition is based:

(a) the amount of the debt, or the aggregate amount of the debts, must be equal to or exceed the bankruptcy level,[1029] which is £750;[1030]

(b) the debt, or each of the debts, must be for a liquidated sum payable to the petitioning creditor, or one or more of the petitioning creditors, immediately, and must be unsecured;[1031] and

(c) the debt, or each of the debts, must be a debt for which the individual member or former member is liable and appears to be unable to pay.[1032]

7.432   The only method of proving that the individual member or former member appears to be unable to pay the petition debt or debts is by non-compliance with a written demand served on the partnership and a statutory demand served on the member or former member under

---

[1022] *Argyle Crescent Ltd v Definite Finance Ltd* [2004] EWHC 3422 (Ch), LTL 29/7/2004, at [29]–[30].

[1023] *James Dolman and Co Ltd v Pedley* [2003] EWCA Civ 1686, [2004] BCC 504, per Arden LJ at [2].

[1024] *Re Lehman Brothers International (Europe) (No 2)* [2009] EWCA Civ 1161, [2010] Bus LR 489.

[1025] IA 1986, s 124(1), is applied to the winding up of an insolvent partnership under IPO 1994, art 7, by the modified form of IA 1986, s 221(5), set out in IPO 1994, sch 3, para 3.

[1026] IA 1986, s 124(2), as modified by IPO 1994, sch 4, para 8, and applied by the modified form of IA 1986, s 221(5), set out in IPO 1994, sch 4, para 3.

[1027] Meaning a debt owed jointly by both the partnership and the individual member or former member (*Commissioners of Customs and Excise v Jack Baars Wholesale* [2004] EWHC 18 (Ch), [2004] BPIR 543, at [39]).

[1028] IA 1986, s 267(1), as modified by IPO 1994, sch 4, para 6(b).

[1029] IA 1986, s 267(2)(a), as modified by IPO 1994, sch 4, para 6(b).

[1030] IA 1986, s 267(3), as modified by IPO 1994, sch 4, para 6(b).

[1031] IA 1986, s 267(2)(b), as modified by IPO 1994, sch 4, para 6(b).

[1032] IA 1986, s 267(2)(c), as modified by IPO 1994, sch 4, para 6(b).

IA 1986, s 268.[1033] A bankruptcy petition may not be presented at a time when there is an outstanding application to set aside the statutory demand,[1034] but if this is done, it is an irregularity which does not invalidate the petition.[1035]

Disputed Debt and Cross-claim Petitions

Introduction

Disputed debt petitions

A creditor's petition for the winding up of a company will be described here as a 'disputed **7.433** debt petition' if the company disputes the existence and/or size and/or due time for payment of the debt which the petitioner claims to be owed by the company. As far as concerns the petitioner, a dispute about whether the debt is owed to the petitioner or to some other person is a dispute about the existence of the debt.

What must be paid to a person with a claim against a company which is disputed by the **7.434** company will not be known and payable until the dispute is resolved.

A dispute about the *existence* of the petitioner's debt is a dispute about standing to peti- **7.435** tion[1036] and must normally be resolved before the court can consider whether the company should be wound up. However, a dispute about the existence of a debt, or the identity of the creditor, cannot be expected to be decided in proceedings on a winding-up petition, because those proceedings are particularly unsuited to determining such a question.[1037] The usual practice of the court is to dismiss (or, sometimes, adjourn) a creditor's winding-up petition if there is a dispute on substantial grounds about the existence of the petitioner's debt, leaving the petitioner to establish standing in other more appropriate proceedings.[1038] Dismissal is commonly anticipated by granting an injunction against presentation of a disputed debt petition or striking out one that has been presented.[1039] Slade J said:[1040]

> It is the well established practice of this court to refuse to allow petitions for the winding up of companies brought at the suit of alleged creditors, whose debts are disputed bona fide on substantial grounds. It has been said in several reported cases that the procedure of a winding-up petition is not an appropriate course by which to attempt to resolve such a dispute.

In order to decide whether to dismiss a petition, or to prevent one being presented or con- **7.436** tinuing, because there is a dispute about the existence of the petitioner's debt, the court must decide whether there is a substantial ground for that dispute.[1041]

Despite the unsuitability of the forum, the court will sometimes determine a dispute about **7.437** the existence of the petitioner's debt in the proceedings on the petition.[1042] Very rarely, the

---

[1033] See 7.119.
[1034] IA 1986, s 267(2)(d), as modified by IPO 1994, sch 4, para 6(b).
[1035] IR 1986, r 7.55; *Commissioners of Customs and Excise v Jack Baars Wholesale* [2004] EWHC 18 (Ch), [2004] BPIR 543, at [39].
[1036] See 7.359–7.363.
[1037] See 7.515–7.522.
[1038] See 7.528–7.549.
[1039] See 7.569–7.608.
[1040] *Re Laceward Ltd* [1981] 1 WLR 133 at p 136.
[1041] See 7.444–7.514.
[1042] See 7.523–7.527.

court will make a winding-up order despite there being a dispute about the existence of the petitioner's debt, leaving the dispute to be resolved in the winding up.[1043]

7.438 If the fact that the company is indebted to the petitioner is not disputed, but the amount to be paid and/or the time at which it is to be paid is disputed, the petitioner's standing is not in question.[1044] However, usually the only evidence such a petitioner will have that the company is unable to pay its debts is that it has not paid the full amount of the petitioner's claim, and this will not be sufficient proof since the amount of the claim is disputed.

7.439 The existence of a dispute about a debt may become apparent only when a demand is made for payment of the debt, but the distinction between a mistaken demand and a disputed demand is a fine one.[1045]

Cross-claim petitions

7.440 The term 'cross-claim petition' will be used in this work for a creditor's petition to wind up a company filed at a time when the company has a cross-claim against the creditor. If the cross-claim exceeds the creditor's debt (or falls short of it by £750 or less), the petition will be treated in the same way as a disputed debt petition.[1046]

Arbitration agreement

7.441 A company may apply under the Arbitration Act 1996, s 9, to prevent a court making any decision about the existence of a debt claimed in a petition to wind up the company, if that is a matter which is to be referred to arbitration under an arbitration agreement between the petitioner and the company. The court will not make an order under s 9 if it finds that there are no substantial grounds for the dispute.[1047]

Customs duty determinations, excise duty and VAT assessments

7.442 A customs duty determination, or excise duty or VAT assessment, remains due and payable despite an appeal.[1048] It follows that a winding-up petition based on non-payment of a determination or assessment cannot be a disputed debt petition.[1049] However, such a petition will be treated in the same way as a disputed debt petition and will not be permitted to proceed if there is an appeal against the determination or assessment.[1050] Whether there is no reasonable prospect of the appeal succeeding is a question for the First-tier Tribunal to determine on an application to strike it out or an application for an extension of time to appeal.[1051]

Literature

7.443 Philip H Barton, 'The law relating to disputed indebtedness where the winding up of a company is sought on the ground of inability to pay debts' (1981) 9 ABLR 94.

J F Corkery, 'Winding up by the court for inability to pay debts: the court's exercise of its discretion' (1982–3) 8 Adel LR 61.

[1043] See 7.551–7.568.
[1044] See 7.388–7.391.
[1045] Per Warner J in *Re a Company (No 008122 of 1989)* [1990] BCLC 697 at p 697.
[1046] See 7.618–7.665.
[1047] *Salford Estates (No 2) Ltd v Altomart Ltd* [2014] EWCA Civ 1575, LTL 9/12/2014.
[1048] See 7.412–7.415.
[1049] *Commissioners of HM Revenue and Customs v Autotech Design Ltd* [2006] EWHC 1596 (Ch) at [5].
[1050] *Enta Technologies Ltd v Commissioners of HM Revenue and Customs* [2014] EWHC 548 (Ch), [2014] BVC 22.
[1051] *Enta Technologies Ltd v Commissioners of HM Revenue and Customs.*

Fidelis Oditah, 'Winding up recalcitrant debtors' [1995] LMCLQ 107.

Andrew Keay, 'Disputing debts relied on by petitioning creditors seeking winding-up orders' (2000) 22 Co Law 40.

Substantiality of Ground of Dispute

The test

A dispute about the existence of a debt will not justify preventing presentation or continua- **7.444**
tion of a winding-up petition for non-payment of the debt, unless the court is satisfied that
'the debt is disputed on some substantial ground (and not just on some ground which is
frivolous or without substance and which the court should, therefore, ignore)'.[1052] There has
been a great deal of litigation about how this crucial test of substantiality should be applied
in practice.[1053]

In *Delaine Pty Ltd v Quarto Publishing plc*[1054] Young J said, at p 82: **7.445**

> The view appears to be gaining currency that, so long as a debtor can think of some dispute with
> its creditor, it can force the creditor to go to law and evade winding up for a considerable period
> of time. This view is a misconception. It is only if the debtor can prove that there are substantial
> grounds for disputing the debt that relief may be given.

In *Re a Company (No 0010656 of 1990)*[1055] Harman J said, at p 466:

> it is clear that mere honest belief that payment is not due is not sufficient. There has to be a sub-
> stantial ground for disputing liability to justify non-payment.

In *Re a Company (No 006685 of 1996)*[1056] Chadwick J said, at p 645:

> the general rule under which this court refuses to entertain a petition founded on a disputed
> debt applies only where the dispute is a genuine dispute founded on substantial grounds;
> and does not preclude this court from determining—or entitle this court to decline to deter-
> mine—the question whether or not there are substantial grounds for dispute.

The test of substantiality is the same whether it is being applied to prevent presentation, to **7.446**
prevent gazetting and strike out or to dismiss a petition on hearing it.[1057] The test has been
expressed in various ways.[1058] A different test is applied in New Zealand.[1059]

If there is a substantial ground for dispute, presentation or continuation of the petition will **7.447**
be prevented even if the company's case is 'shadowy'.[1060] The court should not consider the

---

[1052] *Mann v Goldstein* [1968] 1 WLR 1091 per Ungoed-Thomas J at p 1096.
[1053] See 7.449–7.514.
[1054] (1990) 3 ACSR 81.
[1055] [1991] BCLC 464.
[1056] [1997] 1 BCLC 639.
[1057] *Re a Company (No 003079 of 1990)* [1991] BCLC 235; *Re a Company (No 0160 of 2004)* [2004]
EWHC 380 (Ch), LTL 20/2/2004, at [22].
[1058] See 7.462–7.488.
[1059] See 7.514.
[1060] *ICS Incorporation Ltd v Michael Wilson and Partners Ltd* [2005] EWHC 404 (Ch), [22005] BPIR 805,
per Lawrence Collins J at [87]. See also *Markham v Karsten* [2007] EWHC 1509 (Ch), [2007] BPIR 1109,
at [45] (defence of a creditor's bankruptcy petition). In *Re LHF Wools Ltd* [1970] Ch 27 at p 36 Harman LJ
described the cross-claim in *Re Portman Provincial Cinemas Ltd* [1999] 1 WLR 157 as 'shadowy'.

prospects of success of either party to the dispute.[1061] In order to prevent presentation or continuation of a creditor's petition, it is not necessary to prove that a claim for the petition debt must fail.[1062] In order to reject an application for an order preventing presentation or continuation, it is not necessary to prove that the company has no properly arguable defence to a claim for the petition debt.[1063] A decision not to prevent presentation or continuation of a petition is not necessarily a finding, which binds the company, that the claimed petition debt is due.[1064] However, if 'it is as plain as a pikestaff that there is no debt', the court should say so.[1065]

7.448 If there are no substantial grounds for disputing the debt claimed by the petitioner, the court will not prevent the petition proceeding, however genuine and intense the wish of the company to dispute the debt.[1066] This applies even if the dispute is the subject of an arbitration agreement.[1067]

Evidence and onus

7.449 It is not sufficient merely to allege that the debt is disputed: there must be a positive statement of the grounds of dispute with supporting relevant details to demonstrate that those grounds are substantial.[1068]

7.450 On hearing an application to prevent a disputed debt petition proceeding, the court is not normally concerned to decide the dispute,[1069] only to determine whether a dispute on substantial grounds exists.[1070] Accordingly, the court will not normally order the cross-examination of persons making witness statements to be put in evidence at the hearing.[1071]

7.451 Most courts have held that the onus is on the company to prove (on a balance of probabilities) that the debt is disputed on some substantial ground.[1072] This applies even if the petitioner alleges serious fraud.[1073] Some courts have held that the onus is on the petitioner

---

[1061] *Abbey National plc v JSF Finance and Currency Exchange Co Ltd* [2006] EWCA Civ 328, LTL 31/3/2006, at [46].

[1062] *Pembinaan Lian Keong Sdn Bhd v Yip Fook Thai* [2005] 5 MLJ 786.

[1063] *Re a Company (No 0160 of 2004)* [2004] EWHC 380 (Ch), LTL 20/2/2004, at [28] and [32].

[1064] *Tag Capital Ventures Ltd v Potter* [2013] EWHC 2338 (Ch), LTL 6/8/2013, at [5]–[6].

[1065] *Spacorp Australia Pty Ltd v Myer Stores Ltd* [2001] VSCA 89, 19 ACLC 1270, at [4].

[1066] *Forsayth NL v Juno Securities Ltd* (1991) 4 WAR 376.

[1067] *Salford Estates (No 2) Ltd v Altomart Ltd* [2014] EWCA Civ 1575, LTL 9/12/2014, overruling *Rusant Ltd v Traxys Far East Ltd* [2013] EWHC 4083 (Comm), LTL 8/1/2014.

[1068] *Re General Exchange Bank Ltd* (1866) 14 LT 582 per Lord Romilly MR at p 583; *Re Imperial Hydropathic Hotel Co, Blackpool Ltd* (1882) 49 LT 147 per Jessel MR at p 149; *Re Collinda Pty Ltd* (1991) 6 ACSR 123 at p 127; *Roy Morgan Research Centre Pty Ltd v Wilson Market Research Pty Ltd (No 2)* (1996) 20 ACSR 120; *Commissioners of HM Revenue and Customs v Rochdale Drinks Distributors Ltd* [2011] EWCA Civ 1116, [2012] 1 BCLC 748, at [80].

[1069] See 7.444–7.448 and 7.515–7.522.

[1070] *Argyle Crescent Ltd v Definite Finance Ltd* [2004] EWHC 3422 (Ch), LTL 29/7/2004, at [9].

[1071] *Re Janeash Ltd* [1990] BCC 250; *Re a Company (No 00962 of 1991)* [1992] BCLC 248.

[1072] *Re Great Britain Mutual Life Assurance Society* (1880) 16 ChD 246; *Australian Mid-Eastern Club Ltd v Elbakht* (1988) 14 ACLR 234 per Kirby P at p 241; *Morrison v Speedy Parcels Ltd* (1989) 5 NZCLC 66,203; *Derby Motorplus Pty Ltd v Swan Building Society* (1990) 2 ACSR 239; *Ocean City Ltd v Southern Oceanic Hotels Pty Ltd* (1993) 10 ACSR 483; *Re ICS Computer Distribution Ltd* [1996] 1 HKLR 181 at p 183; *Allied Leasing and Finance Corporation v Banco Econômico SA* [2000] CILR 118 at p 129; *Re TAG Capital Ventures Ltd* [2012] EWHC 1171 (Ch), LTL 17/5/2012, at [12] and [42].

[1073] *Commissioners of HM Revenue and Customs v Rochdale Drinks Distributors Ltd* [2011] EWCA Civ 1116, [2012] 1 BCLC 748, at [84].

to show that the dispute is not sufficiently substantial.[1074] The test of substantiality is sometimes expressed as if the onus were on the petitioner.[1075] It is submitted that the onus must be on the company, which is the applicant and is the party asserting the existence of a dispute.

If several grounds of dispute are advanced it is enough if one is found to be sufficiently substantial.[1076] **7.452**

The court's task

When it is asserted that there is a dispute about the debt on which a winding-up petition **7.453** is grounded, the court must decide whether the dispute is based on sufficiently substantial grounds to justify preventing presentation or continuation of the petition. The court is not required to decide the dispute, though it may do so in exceptional circumstances.[1077]

Deciding whether a company's dispute with a petitioner is based on sufficiently substantial **7.454** grounds to justify preventing presentation or continuation of the petition is 'often quite exceptionally difficult'.[1078] The Court of Appeal would be very reluctant to take a different view from a judge sitting in the Companies Court on this issue.[1079] But a more robust attitude was adopted in *Feldman v Nissim*,[1080] where it was said that a decision at first instance on whether a debt (in a bankruptcy statutory demand) is disputed is not the kind of multi-factorial or discretionary decision that should be accorded particular respect by an appeal court.[1081]

The court cannot prevent a petition proceeding simply because the company asserts that **7.455** there is a dispute about the petition debt: the issue is always whether the debt is disputed on substantial grounds.[1082] The court is entitled to refuse to take at face value a company's assertion that there is a dispute and is entitled to enquire into the basis for the alleged dispute.[1083] An assertion of facts unsupported by evidence will not provide a substantial ground for a dispute.[1084]

The court should not conduct a long and elaborate hearing, examining in minute detail **7.456** the case made on each side.[1085] The court will not normally order the cross-examination of persons who make witness statements used as evidence that the petitioner's debt is disputed on substantial grounds,[1086] and the court should not seek to resolve issues of fact

---

[1074] *Medi Services International Pty Ltd v Jarson Pty Ltd* (1978) 3 ACLR 518; *Re Beverage Holdings Pty Ltd* (1991) 5 ACSR 277 at pp 287–8; *Pembinaan Lian Keong Sdn Bhd v Yip Fook Thai* [2005] 5 MLJ 786, not following *Sri Binaraya Sdn Bhd v Golden Approach Sdn Bhd* [2000] 3 MLJ 465.

[1075] See 7.471–7.483.

[1076] *Celtech International Ltd v Dalkia Utilities Services plc* [2004] EWHC 193 (Ch), LTL 2/3/2004, at [22].

[1077] See 7.523–7.527.

[1078] *Re Ringinfo Ltd* [2002] 1 BCLC 210 per Pumfrey J at p 223.

[1079] *Pentagin Technologies International Ltd v Express Company Secretaries Ltd* (1995) *The Times*, 7 April 1995; *Marchands Associates LLP v Thompson Partnership LLP* [2004] EWCA Civ 878, LTL 28/6/2004, at [45].

[1080] [2010] EWHC 1353 (Ch), [2010] BPIR 815, at [5]–[9].

[1081] Nevertheless, the appeal was dismissed.

[1082] *Re a Company (No 006685 of 1996)* [1997] 1 BCLC 639 at pp 642 and 648 per Chadwick J; *Pacific Recreation Pte Ltd v SY Technology Inc* [2008] SGCA 1, [2008] 2 SLR 491.

[1083] *Re Easy Letting and Leasing* [2008] EWHC 3175 (Ch), LTL 23/1/2009, at [12].

[1084] *Eyota Pty Ltd v Hanave Pty Ltd* (1994) 12 ACSR 785 at p 787; *Feldman v Nissim* [2010] EWHC 1353 (Ch), [2010] BPIR 815.

[1085] *Tallington Lakes Ltd v Ancasta International Boat Sales Ltd* [2012] EWCA Civ 1712, [2013] CP Rep 18, at [41].

[1086] See 7.450.

without cross-examination where there is credible evidence on each side.[1087] The fact that cross-examination is required to resolve such issues would in itself normally indicate that there are substantial grounds of dispute.[1088] However, the evidence is not to be approached with a wholly uncritical eye.[1089] Even in the absence of cross-examination, the court may conclude from critical examination of the evidence that it does not disclose substantial grounds for dispute.[1090]

7.457 In *Re Richbell Strategic Holdings Ltd*[1091] Neuberger J said, at p 435:

> a judge, whether sitting in the Companies Court or elsewhere, should be astute to ensure that, however complicated and extensive the evidence might appear to be, the very extensiveness and complexity [are] not being invoked to mask the fact that there is, on proper analysis, no arguable defence to a claim, whether on the facts or the law.

NCK Wire Products Sdn Bhd v Konmark Corp Sdn Bhd[1092] is an example of 'copious affidavits' disguising the fact that there was no dispute at all.

7.458 The court will avoid the realms of fancy[1093] and will be wary of relying on unparticularized or unsubstantiated assertions.[1094] The court may be prepared to reject evidence tendered by the company as so obviously incredible as not to warrant being tested by cross-examination.[1095] But this should only be done in a clear case, because it is not the function of the Companies Court to adjudicate in respect of a genuinely disputed debt, particularly where it involves the rejection of sworn evidence.[1096] Whether the company's assertions are believable is a question to be answered not by taking those assertions in isolation but rather by taking them in the context of so much of the background as is either undisputed or beyond reasonable dispute.[1097]

7.459 In Hong Kong it has been said that the company must adduce sufficiently precise factual evidence to satisfy the court that it has a bona fide dispute on substantial grounds: a hypothetical case is not enough.[1098]

7.460 A 'patently feeble legal argument' will not be a substantial ground for a dispute.[1099]

[1087] *Re a Company (No 006685 of 1996)* [1997] 1 BCLC 639 at p 649 per Chadwick J; *Sykes and Son Ltd v Teamforce Labour Ltd* [2012] EWHC 883 (Ch), LTL 5/4/2012.

[1088] *Re Janeash Ltd* [1990] BCC 250.

[1089] *Re Hong Kong Construction (Works) Ltd* (07/01/2003, HCCW670/2002) per Kwan J at [6].

[1090] *Eyota Pty Ltd v Hanave Pty Ltd* (1994) 12 ACSR 785 at p 787; *Re Claybridge Shipping Co SA* [1997] 1 BCLC 572 at pp 578–9.

[1091] [1997] 2 BCLC 429.

[1092] [2001] 6 MLJ 57.

[1093] *Re Claybridge Shipping Co SA* [1997] 1 BCLC 572 at p 576 per Shaw LJ.

[1094] *Re Claybridge Shipping Co SA* [1997] 1 BCLC 572 at pp 576–9 per Shaw and Oliver LJJ; *Re ICS Computer Distribution Ltd* [1996] 1 HKLR 181; *Re Hong Kong Construction (Works) Ltd* (07/01/2003, HCCW670/2002) per Kwan J at [6]; *Re Solar Touch Ltd* [2004] 3 HKLRD 154 at p 160.

[1095] *Re a Company (No 006685 of 1996)* [1997] 1 BCLC 639 at p 649 per Chadwick J; *Re Arena Corporation Ltd* [2004] EWCA Civ 371, [2004] BPIR 415, at [88]; *Commissioners of HM Revenue and Customs v Autotech Design Ltd* [2006] EWHC 1596 (Ch) at [4]. See also, in a different context, *Lexi Holdings plc v Luqman* [2007] EWCA Civ 1501, LTL 7/8/2007.

[1096] *Re Arena Corporation Ltd* [2004] EWCA Civ 371, [2004] BPIR 415, at [91].

[1097] *Re Safe Rich Industries Ltd* (03/11/1994, CACV81/1994) per Bokhary JA at [13]; *Re a Company (No 006685 of 1996)* [1997] 1 BCLC 639; both relying on *National Westminster Bank plc v Daniel* [1993] 1 WLR 1453.

[1098] *Re ICS Computer Distribution Ltd* [1996] 1 HKLR 181 per Rogers J at p 183.

[1099] *Eyota Pty Ltd v Hanave Pty Ltd* (1994) 12 ACSR 785 at p 787.

Many first-instance cases on disputed debts and the similar topic of cross-claims[1100] have   **7.461**
been reported. They range from brief[1101] to extensive. The bulk of a judgment in these cases
is usually concerned with summing up the evidence and deciding whether it discloses a
sufficiently substantive dispute or cross-claim to justify preventing the presentation or continuation of the petition. Sometimes the question can be disposed of by ruling on a point
of law.[1102] It has not been thought necessary to cite such cases in this chapter if there is no
significant remark, or any decision on, the law and practice relating to applications to wind
up companies.

Alternative formulation of test: bona fide dispute

The test of whether a dispute about a debt will justify preventing presentation or con-   **7.462**
tinuation of a winding-up petition for non-payment of the debt was expressed at 7.444 as
whether the debt is disputed on some substantial ground (and not just on some ground
which is frivolous or without substance and which the court should, therefore, ignore).[1103]
Many other statements of the test use the words 'bona fide', but it is often difficult to know
whether this refers to:

(a) an attribute of the dispute that is to be tested, whether it is 'real' or 'genuine'; or
(b) the way in which the dispute is put forward by the company, whether it is put forward
    'in good faith' or 'honestly'.

Often, a formulation of the test uses 'bona fide' (or 'in good faith') and also refers to the   **7.463**
dispute being substantial, but it is not clear whether this means that there are two separate
elements to the test (the circumstance in which the dispute is put forward and the substance
of the dispute) or that there is one element which can be expressed in two different ways.

Some examples of the test being expressed using 'bona fide or 'in good faith' are: **7.464**

(a) In *Re Brighton Club and Norfolk Hotel Co Ltd*[1104] Romilly MR said, at p 205, that the
    company must have 'some reasonable ground' for disputing the debt, and went on to
    describe the debt in that case as 'a bona fide contested debt'.
(b) In *Stonegate Securities Ltd v Gregory*[1105] Goff LJ, at p 589, expressed the court's task as
    distinguishing 'whether there is a bona fide dispute or whether it is insubstantial or
    trumped up'.
(c) In *Re Nicholls Pty Ltd*[1106] Kearney J, at p 83, used the phrase 'bona fide dispute on good
    and substantial grounds'.
(d) In *Re a Company (No 003079 of 1990)*[1107] Ferris J, at p 238, said the test is 'whether
    there is a bona fide dispute on substantial grounds concerning the indebtedness relied
    upon [by the petitioner]'. *Re Beverage Holdings Pty Ltd*[1108] is to the same effect. In

---

[1100] See 7.618–7.665.
[1101] *Re a Company (No 6410 of 2004)* [2004] EWHC 3147 (Ch), LTL 18/11/2004, is four paragraphs.
[1102] For example, *Re Healing Research Trustee Co Ltd* [1992] 2 All ER 481; *Bank of Commerce (M) Bhd v Selangor Frits and Glazes Sdn Bhd* [1999] 5 MLJ 96.
[1103] *Mann v Goldstein* [1968] 1 WLR 1091 per Ungoed-Thomas J at p 1096.
[1104] (1865) 35 Beav 204.
[1105] [1980] Ch 576.
[1106] (1982) 7 ACLR 76.
[1107] [1991] BCLC 235.
[1108] (1991) 5 ACSR 277 at pp 287–8.

Commissioners of Customs and Excise v Jack Baars Wholesale[1109] Lindsay J said, at [22], that in his experience this was the most frequently applied test.

(e) In *Re a Company (No 008725 of 1991)*[1110] and in *Re Selectmove Ltd*[1111] the test was expressed as whether the company disputes the debt in good faith and on substantial grounds.

(f) In *Re a Company (No 0012209 of 1991)*[1112] Hoffmann J said that a petition should continue if the company's dispute 'is either not put forward in good faith or... has really no rational prospect of success'. Seeking to delay payment so as to obtain a period of credit to which it was not contractually entitled was given as an example of not putting forward a dispute in good faith,[1113] but surely it is just an example of asserting an interpretation of a contract which the court finds is not correct in law.

(g) In *Re a Company (No 4079 of 2003)*[1114] and *Corbern v Whatmusic Holdings Ltd*[1115] Hart J identified the question as whether there is a 'bona fide dispute'. The phrase 'bona fide dispute' was also used by Evans-Lombe J.[1116]

(h) In *Ross and Craig v Williamson*[1117] Park J restrained presentation of a petition to wind up an allegedly insolvent partnership, because he found, at [8], it had not been shown that, 'in disputing the debt, the firm is acting in bad faith or that its grounds are not substantial'.

(i) In *Abbey National plc v JSF Finance and Currency Exchange Co Ltd*[1118] Morritt C spoke, at [36], of there being 'a substantial ground on which [the company] bona fide disputes its liability' and, at [46], of 'substantial grounds for disputing the claim... [which] are advanced honestly'.

(j) In Northern Ireland the test is whether 'there is a genuine dispute on grounds showing a potentially viable defence requiring investigation'.[1119]

7.465 Judges who have analysed formulations of the test which include the terms 'bona fide' or 'in good faith' have concluded either that 'bona fide' (as an attribute of a dispute) means the same as 'substantial' or that whether a dispute is raised in good or bad faith is irrelevant.

7.466 In *Re Welsh Brick Industries Ltd*[1120] Lord Greene MR said, at p 198:

> I do not think that there is any difference between the words 'bona fide disputed' and the words 'disputed on some substantial ground'.

In *Re Arena Corporation Ltd*[1121] Morritt V-C said, at [53], that 'bona fide disputed on substantial grounds' is, for all practical purposes, synonymous with 'real as opposed to frivolous'.

[1109] [2004] EWHC 18 (Ch), [2004] BPIR 543.
[1110] [1992] BCLC 633 per Hoffmann J at p 634.
[1111] [1995] 1 WLR 474 per Peter Gibson LJ.
[1112] [1992] 1 WLR 351 at p 354.
[1113] [1992] 1 WLR 351 at p 354. At least, that is how the remark was interpreted by Norris J in *Angel Group Ltd v British Gas Trading Ltd* [2012] EWHC 2702 (Ch), [2013] BCC 265, at [22].
[1114] [2003] EWHC 1879 (Ch), LTL 1/10/2003, at [10].
[1115] [2003] EWHC 2134 (Ch), LTL 1/10/2003, at [4].
[1116] *Re Javelin Promotions Ltd* [2003] EWHC 1932 (Ch), LTL 30/9/2003.
[1117] [2006] EWHC 880 (Ch), LTL 9/3/2006.
[1118] [2006] EWCA Civ 328, LTL 31/3/2006.
[1119] *Sheridan Millennium Ltd v Odyssey Property Co* [2003] NICh 7, [2004] NI 117, at [8].
[1120] [1946] 2 All ER 197.
[1121] [2004] EWCA Civ 371, [2004] BPIR 415.

In *Nickel Rim Mines Ltd v Horizon Pacific Ltd*[1122] Rolfe J said, at pp 752–3, that the for- **7.467**
mulation 'bona fide dispute on substantial grounds' does not require the proof of two elements, namely, bona fides and substantial grounds. Rather, once substantial grounds are
established, there is a bona fide dispute. On the other hand a bona fide belief that there
is a dispute is not enough in itself because it does not prove that there is substance in the
dispute.[1123] In *Re a Company (No 001946 of 1991)*[1124] Harman J criticized the formulation 'bona fide dispute on substantial grounds', emphasizing Lord Greene's equation of
the two phrases 'bona fide disputed' and 'disputed on substantial grounds' and saying, at
p 739: 'There is but one proposition of law which can be expressed in either of the forms of
words'. His Lordship went on to say, at p 740:

> for a man to raise substantial grounds of dispute must be enough to prevent a petition being
> properly presented to this court, notwithstanding that he does so with the utmost malice
> toward the other side. 'Bona fides', in the sense of good faith, has nothing to do with the
> matter… the true question is, and always is: Is there a substantial dispute as to the debt upon
> which the petition is allegedly founded?

Another case which suggests that the bona fide element of the formulation is not essential **7.468**
is *ICS Incorporation Ltd v Michael Wilson and Partners Ltd*,[1125] in which Lawrence Collins J
restrained presentation of a petition on the ground that there was a substantial dispute, but
said that whether it was a bona fide dispute depended on the credibility of the company's
witnesses to be tested at trial.[1126]

It has also been said that a dispute must be: **7.469**

> bona fide in both its subjective and objective senses. So the reason for not paying the debt
> must be honestly believed to be in existence and must be based on substantial or reasonable
> grounds.[1127]

If the facts alleged to give rise to a dispute are untrue, there will be no substance in the dispute, **7.470**
and this will be so whether the untrue facts are put forward dishonestly or mistakenly.

Alternative formulation of test: company's defence has no rational prospect of success

In *Re a Company (No 0012209 of 1991)*[1128] Hoffmann J said, at p 354, that in order to con- **7.471**
clude that a disputed debt petition should proceed the court would have to conclude that
the dispute was either not put forward in good faith[1129] or that it has really no rational prospect of success.[1130] In *Re a Company (No 0013734 of 1991)*[1131] the learned deputy High Court
judge expanded on the second of these alternatives, saying that it is not necessary to decide the

[1122] (1991) 4 ACSR 750.
[1123] *Westpac Banking Corporation Ltd v Leichhardt Development Co Pty Ltd* (1989) 99 FLR 323 at p 337.
[1124] [1991] BCLC 737.
[1125] [2005] EWHC 404 (Ch), [2005] BPIR 805.
[1126] At [120].
[1127] Abdul Malik Ishak J in *Pembinaan Purcon v Entertainment Village (M) Sdn Bhd* [2004] 1 MLJ 545
at [31].
[1128] [1992] 1 WLR 351.
[1129] See 7.462–7.470.
[1130] Taken to be the test in *Angel Group Ltd v British Gas Trading Ltd* [2012] EWHC 2702 (Ch), [2013]
BCC 265. Hoffmann J had, just a month before *Re a Company (No 0012209 of 1991)*, used the 'good faith or
substantial grounds' formula in *Re a Company (No 008725 of 1991)* [1992] BCLC 633 at p 634 (see 7.464(e)).
See also per Neuberger J in *Re Richbell Strategic Holdings Ltd* [1997] 2 BCLC 429 at p 450.
[1131] [1993] BCLC 59.

arguments over a petitioner's debt: the petition will be allowed to continue if the arguments 'afford the company no really rational prospect of success or … the argument of the petitioner cannot be seriously questioned'. Mere doubts that the company's case will succeed are not enough to satisfy this test.[1132]

7.472 The 'really no rational prospect of success' formulation seems to approach from the wrong direction. The question is not whether the petitioner can show that the petition should be allowed to proceed: the question is whether the company can show that the petition should be prevented from proceeding.[1133] If the test is turned round to provide a standard that the company must meet, it would require the company to show, on a balance of probabilities, that its defence to the petitioner's claim is one that has a rational prospect of success.

7.473 There was a similar focus on the merits of the petition in *Clandown Ltd v Davis*[1134] where Morris J said that, on a company's application to prevent a disputed debt petition proceeding, the question for the court is whether it is 'satisfied that the amount of the [petitioner's] claim is clear and incapable of dispute'.

Alternative formulation of test: analogy with summary judgment

7.474 In *Mitchell McFarlane and Partners Ltd v Foremans Ltd*[1135] the parties agreed that the test of whether a petition could proceed is whether, if the debt had been claimed in common law proceedings, the claimant would have been entitled to summary judgment.[1136] The test for giving summary judgment to a claimant is that the defendant 'has no real prospect of successfully defending' the claim,[1137] and there is no other compelling reason why the case or issue should be disposed of at a trial.[1138] 'Real prospect' means a realistic as opposed to a fanciful prospect,[1139] but it is not necessary to show that the defence cannot succeed or is bound to fail.[1140]

7.475 Like the 'really no rational prospect of success' formulation,[1141] this formulation seems to approach from the wrong direction, but it may be turned round to state what the company must prove. The company must show, on the balance of probabilities, that it would have a real prospect of successfully defending the claim. As 'real' ('not fanciful') seems to have the same meaning as 'rational', this is the same as the 'really no rational prospect of success' formulation.

7.476 In *Re a Company (No 0160 of 2004)*[1142] the learned deputy judge made the analogy with summary judgment by saying, at [24]:

> Any claimant or petitioner must be permitted to proceed with his claim or petition unless he has no real prospect of success in obtaining the relief sought. A petition to wind up a company will fail if the court hearing the petition concludes that the company has a substantial

---

[1132] *Quarry Products Ltd v Austin International Inc* 2000 CILR 265.
[1133] See 7.449–7.452.
[1134] [1994] 2 ILRM 536.
[1135] (2002) LTL 18/12/2002.
[1136] Under CPR, Part 24. See *Blackstone's Civil Practice 2015*, ch 34.
[1137] CPR, r 24.2(a)(ii).
[1138] CPR, r 24.2(b). This means that notwithstanding the absence of a real prospect of success, nevertheless there is some compelling reason why the case or issue should go to trial (*Miller v Garton Shires* [2006] EWCA Civ 1386, [2007] RTR 24, at [3]).
[1139] *Swain v Hillman* [2001] 1 All ER 91.
[1140] *Swain v Hillman*.
[1141] See 7.471–7.473.
[1142] [2004] EWHC 380 (Ch), LTL 20/2/2004.

defence to the creditor's claim, ie would have a real prospect of defeating that claim, for in such a case it is entitled to have that substantial dispute resolved in ordinary proceedings.

That a dispute being on a substantial ground is the same criterion as having a real prospect of success has also been suggested in relation to setting aside a bankruptcy statutory demand.[1143] But Briggs J has said[1144] that the test of substantiality of a ground for a dispute about a winding-up petition debt sets a threshold (for the company to cross) 'similar to or possibly slightly higher than the threshold for obtaining permission to defend under CPR, Part 24'.[1145] **7.477**

In relation to defending a creditor's bankruptcy petition it has been said[1146] that there is no reason to make a bankruptcy order where, had the petitioner issued a claim for the debt and applied for summary judgment,[1147] the court would have dismissed the application or, if the defence was regarded as shadowy, made a conditional order.[1148] **7.478**

Before the CPR, summary judgment was given under the Rules of the Supreme Court 1965, ord 14, and it was said that the test of whether there was a ground for disputing a winding-up petitioner's debt which was sufficiently substantial to halt proceedings on the petition was whether the company had an arguable case which would have been sufficient to resist an application for summary judgment under ord 14.[1149] **7.479**

Summary judgment was given under ord 14 unless there was an issue or question in dispute which ought to be tried or there ought for some other reason to be a trial.[1150] **7.480**

However, it was also held that a winding-up court was not bound by a failure of the petitioner to obtain summary judgment under ord 14 for the petition debt and could make its own assessment of whether there was a substantial ground of dispute.[1151] This was because an application for summary judgment could be refused if there was a fair probability that the company had a bona fide defence,[1152] which was a lower standard than the substantial ground for dispute required to prevent presentation or continuation of a winding-up petition.[1153] In particular, in *Re Claybridge Shipping Co SA*[1154] Lord Denning MR said, at p 575: **7.481**

> If [the defence to the petitioner's claim] is obviously a 'put-up job'—or if it is so insubstantial that a Queen's Bench master would only give conditional leave to defend[1155]—then I should think the petition to wind up should stand.

[1143] See 7.484–7.488.
[1144] *Re a Company* [2007] EWHC 2137 (Ch), LTL 28/4/2008, at [2].
[1145] 'Permission to defend' is, more formally, dismissal of a claimant's application for summary judgment.
[1146] *Markham v Karsten* [2007] EWHC 1509 (Ch), [2007] BPIR 1109, at [45].
[1147] Under CPR, Part 24.
[1148] PD 24, paras 4, 5.1 and 5.2.
[1149] *Re Amadeus Trading Ltd* (1997) *The Times*, 1 April 1997; *London and Global Ltd v Sahara Petroleum Ltd* (1998) *The Times*, 3 December 1998.
[1150] ord 14, r 3(1).
[1151] *Re Welsh Brick Industries Ltd* [1946] 2 All ER 197.
[1152] *Ward v Plumbley* (1890) 6 TLR 198.
[1153] *Re Welsh Brick Industries Ltd* [1946] 2 All ER 197 per Lord Greene MR at p 198 and Morton LJ at p 200.
[1154] [1997] 1 BCLC 572.
[1155] Under ord 14, r 4(3). Now, the probability that a conditional order would be made under CPR, Part 24, and PD 24, paras 4, 5.1 and 5.2, is sufficient to justify preventing presentation or continuation of the petition. See *ICS Incorporation Ltd v Michael Wilson and Partners Ltd* [2005] EWHC 404 (Ch), LTL 29/3/2005, at [87], and *Markham v Karsten* [2007] EWHC 1509 (Ch), [2007] BPIR 1109, at [45].

But in *Atlantic and General Investment Trust Ltd v Richbell Information Services Inc*[1156] it was said that the test of substantiality of grounds of dispute for the purposes of preventing a winding-up petition proceeding was the same as under ord 14, namely, whether there was 'a probability of a bona fide genuine defence being established'.

7.482 The Court of Appeal in *Re Welsh Brick Industries Ltd* held that it is for the winding-up court to decide whether there is a substantial ground for disputing a petitioner's debt, and that this question is not decided by the fate of an application for summary judgment on the petitioner's claim for that debt. It found that at that time (1946) the tests for those two questions were different. This meant that it was harder for a company to have a winding-up petition halted because of doubts over the petitioner's standing than it was to require a defence to be tried which, if successful, would prove that the petitioner did not have standing. It is perhaps odd that the petitioner in *Atlantic and General Investment Trust Ltd v Richbell Information Services Inc* conceded that the easier test could be applied to the petition in that case.

7.483 The Court of Appeal in *Re Welsh Brick Industries Ltd* was unconcerned with the fact that different civil courts applied different criteria when deciding to bring proceedings to an end before trial. But the need for civil courts to apply the same standard when deciding that question appealed to the learned deputy judge in *Re a Company (No 0160 of 2004)*.[1157] However, unlike giving summary judgment, preventing a creditor's winding-up petition proceeding, because of a dispute about the petitioner's debt, does not finish litigation over the debt: it merely requires the claim to be pursued in a more appropriate forum. So it may be appropriate to use different tests for these different purposes.

Alternative formulation of test: question to be tried

7.484 The test of whether a dispute over a petitioner's debt is sufficiently substantial to halt proceedings on the petition has sometimes been expressed in terms of having a question to be tried. This was very probably influenced by the test for summary judgment which used to apply under the Rules of the Supreme Court 1965, ord 14.[1158] In *Re General Exchange Bank Ltd*[1159] Lord Romilly MR said, at p 583, that:

> where there is so much doubt and question about the liability to pay the debt as that the court sees there is a question to be decided, the alleged debtor may reasonably require the matter to be decided in a court of justice.

In *Re King's Cross Industrial Dwellings Co*[1160] Malins V-C said, at p 151, 'the Court is bound...to see that the question is a substantial one before directing an action to be brought'. In *Re Great Britain Mutual Life Assurance Society*[1161] Jessel MR said, at p 253:

> it is not sufficient for the respondents, upon a petition of this kind, to say, 'We dispute the claim'. They must bring forward a prima facie case which satisfies the court that there is something which ought to be tried.

[1156] [2000] 2 BCLC 778, decided four months before the RSC were replaced by the CPR.

[1157] [2004] EWHC 380 (Ch), LTL 20/2/2004. See also *De Montfort University v Stanford Training Systems Pte Ltd* [2005] SGHC 202, [2006] 1 SLR 218, at [28]; *Pacific Recreation Pte Ltd v SY Technology Inc* [2008] SGCA 1, [2008] 2 SLR 491, at [23].

[1158] See 7.479–7.483. The connection is made explicitly in *Pacific Recreation Pte Ltd v SY Technology Inc* [2008] SGCA 1, [2008] 2 SLR 491, at [23].

[1159] (1866) 14 LT 582.

[1160] (1870) LR 11 Eq 149.

[1161] (1880) 16 ChD 246.

In *Argyle Crescent Ltd v Definite Finance Ltd*[1162] Park J said, at [9], that the test is whether **7.485**
the dispute 'has sufficient substance to justify it being determined in a normal civil action'.

The test for setting aside a bankruptcy statutory demand,[1163] when the debtor claims to **7.486**
have a counterclaim, set-off or cross-demand, or disputes the debt, is whether, in the court's
opinion, the debtor has raised a 'genuine triable issue'.[1164] In *Kellar v BBR Graphic Engineers
(Yorks) Ltd*[1165] the learned deputy judge said that it was 'generally thought' that this was
a 'lower threshold' than the 'real prospect of success' criterion based on the test for summary judgment in CPR, Part 24.[1166] The deputy judge cited *Alpine Bulk Transport Co Inc
v Saudi Eagle Shipping Co Inc*,[1167] but the comparison which the Court of Appeal made
in that case[1168] was not with the 'genuinely triable issue' test, but with the criterion of 'an
arguable case', which, the court observed, was commonly used in relation to the Rules of
the Supreme Court 1965, ord 14. The Court of Appeal said that a real prospect of success
is a higher standard than an arguable case and indicates that the arguable case must carry
some degree of conviction.[1169] As the learned deputy judge said in *Union Bank (UK) plc v
Pathak*[1170] it is:

> inherent in the phrase 'genuine triable issue' that the applicant [for the setting aside of
> a statutory demand] must produce material which raises an objection to the statutory
> demand which cannot be determined without a trial, ie which cannot be summarily
> determined.

In *Ashworth v Newnote Ltd*,[1171] Lawrence Collins LJ said that debating whether there is a **7.487**
distinction between 'genuine triable issue' and 'real prospect of success' 'involves a sterile
and largely verbal question' because there is no practical difference between them. Shortly
afterwards, Arden LJ said[1172] that the court cannot find that a triable issue is 'genuine',
or that the grounds of a dispute appear to be 'substantial',[1173] simply by finding that the
debtor's case is arguable. There has to be something to suggest that the debtor's assertion
is sustainable, and this may mean that the 'genuine triable issue' criterion is the same as
having a real prospect of success.[1174] For Lord Denning MR, 'genuine' and 'triable' were
synonymous:

> I have used the word 'genuine'[1175] because I prefer not to use the words 'prima facie case'
> or 'a cross-claim with a reasonable possibility of success'. Suffice it that there is a triable
> issue.[1176]

[1162] [2004] EWHC 3422 (Ch), LTL 29/7/2004.
[1163] On an application under IR 1986, r 6.4. See 7.236.
[1164] PD Insolvency Proceedings 2014, para 13.3.4; *Kellar v BBR Graphic Engineers (Yorks) Ltd* [2002]
BPIR 544; *Crossley-Cooke v Europanel (UK) Ltd* [2010] EWHC 124 (Ch), [2010] BPIR 561.
[1165] [2002] BPIR 544. Followed in *Wilson v Edwards* [2006] BPIR 367 at [17].
[1166] See 7.474–7.478.
[1167] [1986] 2 Lloyd's Rep 221.
[1168] [1986] 2 Lloyd's Rep 221 at p 223.
[1169] See also *E D and F Man Liquid Products Ltd v Patel* [2003] EWCA Civ 472, [2003] CP Rep 51, at [8].
[1170] [2006] BPIR 1062 at [32].
[1171] [2007] EWCA Civ 793, [2007] BPIR 1012, at [33].
[1172] *Collier v P and M J Wright (Holdings) Ltd* [2007] EWCA Civ 1329, [2008] 1 WLR 643, at [21].
[1173] IR 1986, r 6.5(4)(b).
[1174] See 7.471–7.483.
[1175] To describe the kind of cross-claim that would justify not complying with a bankruptcy notice under
the Bankruptcy Act 1914, s 1(1)(g) (now repealed).
[1176] *Re a Debtor (No 991 of 1962)* [1963] 1 WLR 51 at pp 55–6.

7.488 In *Abernethy v Hotbed Ltd*[1177] Newey J concluded that the 'genuine triable issue' test is not less stringent than a real prospect of success.

Dispute must be rational

7.489 A foolish belief that borrowed money is not repayable is not a substantial dispute.[1178] A lay person's mistaken belief about the law is not a substantial dispute.[1179]

7.490 Disinclination to accept liability for a debt is not a dispute about liability.[1180]

Dispute must be about the company's liability to the petitioner

7.491 An assertion that a third party has an obligation to indemnify or reimburse the company for payment of its debt to the petitioner is not a dispute about the petitioner's debt.[1181] However, a cross-claim against the petitioner, provided it is of sufficient size, is treated in the same way as a disputed debt petition.[1182]

Playing for time

7.492 If the company debtor has previously requested time to pay the debt, its sudden assertion that the debt is disputed will be regarded with acute suspicion.[1183] In *Re a Company (No 006341 of 1992)*[1184] the learned judge, deciding that there was a dispute which was sufficiently serious to prevent a petition proceeding, mentioned, at pp 230–1, that it did not seem to him that the company was playing for time.

7.493 In *Stephen*[1185] the company claimed it disputed the petitioner's debt despite having had an action for recovery of the debt adjourned by undertaking to pay the debt by a certain date. When the debt was not paid on the due date, judgment was given against the company which then launched an appeal which was dismissed because the company failed to appear. A winding-up order was made and the company's defence of the action was described as 'a mere sham from the beginning'.

7.494 In *Re Mobitel (International) Pty Ltd*[1186] the petitioner was a judgment creditor. The company had obtained a master's order setting aside the judgment, provided it paid the claimed sum into court by a certain date. The money was not paid into court by that date, and the company appealed against the master's order, seeking unconditional leave to defend. The petition was adjourned but the company's appeal against the master's order was unsuccessful. The company then launched a further appeal against the master's order, claiming that the judge who heard the previous appeal should have recused himself on the ground of bias though he had not in fact been asked to do so. White J allowed the petitioner's appeal against the latest adjournment of the petition and made a winding-up order, observing that

---

[1177] [2011] EWHC 1476 (Ch), [2011] BPIR 1547, at [8].
[1178] *Re General Exchange Bank Ltd* (1866) 14 LT 582 per Lord Romilly MR at p 583.
[1179] *Re Imperial Hydropathic Hotel Co, Blackpool Ltd* (1882) 49 LT 147.
[1180] *Emibarb Pty Ltd v Schipp* [2001] NSWSC 761 at [42]; *Expile Pty Ltd v Jabb's Excavations Pty Ltd* [2003] NSWCA 163, 45 ACSR 711, at [10].
[1181] *Reale Bros Pty Ltd v Reale* [2003] NSWSC 666, 179 FLR 427, at [60].
[1182] See 7.618–7.665.
[1183] *Delaine Pty Ltd v Quarto Publishing plc* (1990) 3 ACSR 81 per Young J at p 82. For an example, see *Re Record Tennis Centres Ltd* [1991] BCC 509.
[1184] [1994] 1 BCLC 225.
[1185] (1884) 21 SLR 764.
[1186] (1984) 8 ACLR 695.

the company was obviously insolvent and was 'merely manipulating the processes of the law to buy time to trade out of grave financial difficulties'.

In *Banfoong Sydney (JM) Sdn Bhd v MIFC Credit and Leasing Sdn Bhd*[1187] an application   **7.495**
to prevent a petition being presented by a judgment creditor was dismissed. The judgment had been obtained in default of appearance and the company claimed the debt which was the subject of the judgment was disputed on substantial grounds but it had failed in its first attempt to have the judgment set aside though a further application was pending.

In *Re Ban Hong Co Ltd*[1188] Rigby J described the company's dispute as 'an ingenious   **7.496**
afterthought arrived at for the sole purpose of resisting these proceedings' and made the winding-up order asked for.

Relevance of company's solvency

The solvency of a company claiming to dispute a petitioner's debt may be a relevant factor   **7.497**
in determining whether the debt is disputed on a substantial ground: 'A court would more readily conclude that the dispute is bona fide when it is shown that the [company] is manifestly solvent than would otherwise be the case'.[1189] Although it is easy to think of reasons why a solvent company might want to delay or frustrate payment to a creditor, it is unlikely to want to suffer winding-up proceedings. The fact that the company has in the past disputed previously admitted debts may also be relevant.[1190]

Relevance of other proceedings concerning the petitioner's debt; going behind a judgment

It is for the court that is hearing a creditor's winding-up petition to decide whether the   **7.498**
ground for disputing the petitioner's debt is substantial enough to justify dismissing the petition: the question is not decided by the continuance of other proceedings brought by the petitioner to recover the debt, even if an application by the petitioner for summary judgment in those proceedings has failed.[1191] Similarly, a decision whether or not a creditor's winding-up petition should go ahead does not determine an application for summary judgment in a claim for the debt.[1192] The second court to consider an application should pay very great regard to the first court's decision and should be slow to differ from it.[1193] Of course, in many cases the evidence which persuaded the court to dismiss the petitioner's application for summary judgment on a claim for the petition debt will also persuade the winding-up court that the debt is disputed on substantial grounds so that the petition should be prevented from proceeding.[1194] The rules stated in this paragraph were established on the basis that different tests were being applied in applications for summary judgment and applications to halt proceedings on a winding-up petition. They may need to be re-examined if it is clearly established that the same test is involved[1195] so that the first court's decision will be binding on the parties as *res judicata*.

[1187] [1990] 2 MLJ 120.
[1188] (1959) 25 MLJ 100.
[1189] Per Ipp J in *Mine Exc Pty Ltd v Henderson Drilling Services Pty Ltd* (1989) 1 ACSR 118 at p 121; *Re Juson Pty Ltd* (1992) 8 WAR 13 at p 16.
[1190] *Re Juson Pty Ltd* (1992) 8 WAR 13 at p 16.
[1191] *Re Welsh Brick Industries Ltd* [1946] 2 All ER 197.
[1192] *Wilson v Edwards* [2006] BPIR 367 at [12].
[1193] *Wilson v Edwards* [2006] BPIR 367 at [12] and [17].
[1194] For example, *Ansa Teknik (M) Sdn Bhd v Cygal Sdn Bhd* [1989] 2 MLJ 423.
[1195] See 7.487–7.488.

7.499 The fact that a creditor petitioner and the company sought to be wound up have agreed that a court outside England and Wales is to have exclusive jurisdiction to decide disputes about the debt on which the petition is based does not preclude the English court from deciding whether there is a dispute about the debt sufficient to prevent the winding-up petition proceeding.[1196]

7.500 If the petitioner's claim arises from a judgment against the company in legal proceedings, the fact that the company has appealed against the judgment, without needing permission to appeal, does not necessarily mean that there is a dispute on substantial grounds.[1197] The court must consider the grounds for the appeal to judge whether they disclose substantial grounds for disputing the debt. This applies, for example, to an appeal, for which permission is not required, against a tax assessment.[1198] In England and Wales, permission is always required to appeal against a money judgment.[1199] It is likely that if permission to appeal has been given there will be substantial grounds for disputing the judgment. This is because a court can give permission to appeal only where it considers that the appeal would have a real prospect of success, or where there is some other compelling reason why the appeal should be heard.[1200] Separate consideration by the winding-up court of whether grounds for appeal disclose substantial grounds for disputing the debt is required where an application for permission to appeal has been refused by the court below but is being renewed before the appeal court.[1201] However, the winding-up court should be slow to differ from the court which has refused permission to appeal.[1202]

7.501 The fact that the company has applied for a stay of execution of the petitioner's judgment does not affect the petitioner's standing and does not in itself make the petition an abuse of process.[1203] The winding-up court may, however, consider that the reasons for ordering a stay of execution disclose substantial grounds for disputing the judgment debt.[1204]

[1196] *BST Properties Ltd v Reorg-Aport Pénzügyi Rt* [2001] EWCA Civ 1997, LTL 13/12/2001; *Citigate Dewe Rogerson Ltd v Artaban Public Affairs SPRL* [2009] EWHC 1689 (Ch), [2011] 1 BCLC 625.

[1197] *Re Amalgamated Properties of Rhodesia* (1913) Ltd [1917] 2 Ch 115; *Re British Liquid Air Co Ltd* (1908) 126 LT Jo 7; *LKM Investment Holdings Pte Ltd v Cathay Theatres Pte Ltd* [2000] 1 SLR 692; *Bank Utama (M) Bhd v GKM Amal Bhd* [2000] 5 MLJ 657; *Scope Data Systems Pty Ltd v BDO Nelson Parkhill* [2003] NSWSC 137, 199 ALR 56; *SBSK Plantations Sdn Bhd v Dynasty Rangers (M) Sdn Bhd* [2002] 1 MLJ 326. In *Re Amalgamated Properties of Rhodesia (1913) Ltd* the petitioner was the successful defendant in proceedings brought by the company and petitioned because of non-payment of costs. A winding-up order would have been granted despite the company's pending appeal against the judgment but the company gave satisfactory security for the costs. *Re British Liquid Air Co Ltd* is a similar case in which the petition was subsequently dismissed by consent on terms agreed between the parties (*Re British Liquid Air Co Ltd* (1908) 126 LT Jo 77).

[1198] *Commissioners of HM Revenue and Customs v Rochdale Drinks Distributors Ltd* [2011] EWCA Civ 1116, [2012] 1 BCLC 748, at [85].

[1199] CPR, r 52.3.

[1200] r 52.3(6).

[1201] *Society of Lloyd's v Bowman* [2003] EWCA Civ 1886, [2004] BPIR 324, at [11].

[1202] *Society of Lloyd's v Bowman* at [13]. Although the Court of Appeal thought that the solution was for the appeal court to hear appeals (or at least applications for permission to appeal) from both courts together (as happened in the case it was considering), that would depend on the routes of appeal available. For discussion of whether a bankruptcy petition should be adjourned because of an application to appeal against the petition judgment debt see *Society of Lloyd's v Beaumont* [2006] BPIR 1021.

[1203] *Australian Beverage Distributors Pty Ltd v Evans and Tate Premium Wines Pty Ltd* [2007] NSWCA 57, 61 ACSR 441, not referring to the contrary opinion of Barrett J in *Scope Data Systems Pty Ltd v BDO Nelson Parkhill* [2003] NSWSC 137, 199 ALR 56.

[1204] *LKM Investment Holdings Pte Ltd v Cathay Theatres Pte Ltd* [2000] 1 SLR 692. A stay which is imposed automatically by statute is irrelevant to whether there are substantial grounds for disputing the judgment debt (*Scope Data Systems Pty Ltd v BDO Nelson Parkhill* [2003] NSWSC 137, 199 ALR 56).

On the other hand, the fact that a judgment for the petition debt has been set aside has been treated as showing that the debt is disputed.[1205] **7.502**

In *Re Mosbert Finance (Australia) Pty Ltd*[1206] a stay of execution of the petitioner's judgment had been granted and the petition was adjourned (indicating that the dispute was considered substantial enough to justify dismissing the petition had adjournment not been more appropriate[1207]), but in *Ataxtin Pty Ltd v Gordon Pacific Developments Pty Ltd*[1208] a stay of execution had been refused and the company's application for an adjournment of the petition was refused. **7.503**

Unless there is an outstanding appeal or a stay of execution, the winding-up court will not consider whether there are grounds for disputing a judgment debt (colloquially, it will not go behind the judgment), unless: **7.504**

(a) it is shown that the judgment is tainted by fraud, collusion or miscarriage of justice, or that the court which gave the judgment or issued the order did not have jurisdiction to do so; or

(b) there are other truly compelling circumstances.[1209]

The same applies to a tax assessment or determination.[1210] **7.505**

The procedure for making a liability order for non-domestic rates, BID levy or council tax is not inherently unfair so as to justify an insolvency court examining whether an order was rightly made.[1211] But a local authority must be prepared to prove the existence and currency of any liability order relied on in a petition.[1212] **7.506**

The restriction on going behind judgments does not apply to a construction contract adjudication for which an enforcement order has not been obtained.[1213] **7.507**

In *Re Derrygarrif Investments Pty Ltd* (1982) 6 ACLR 751 the court was invited to find that the petitioner's debt was disputed despite the fact that the petitioner had obtained judgment for it. The company's defence of the action in which that judgment had been obtained had been 'hopelessly mismanaged'. Nevertheless it had already obtained adjournments of the petition in order to appeal unsuccessfully against the judgment and had not submitted any evidence that it was solvent. A winding-up order was made. **7.508**

A judgment obtained by default or consent may in fact be for a disputed, unenforceable or even non-existent debt, on which a winding-up order should not be made.[1214] If the court **7.509**

[1205] *Re Vivre Boutique Pty Ltd* (1981) 30 SASR 475; *Re Holcon Pty Ltd* (1990) reported with *Yore Contractors Pty Ltd v Holcon Pty Ltd* (1990) 2 ACSR 663 at pp 674–5.

[1206] (1976) 2 ACLR 5.

[1207] See 7.541–7.549.

[1208] (1991) 29 FCR 564.

[1209] *Re Bydand Ltd* [1997] BCC 915 per Lindsay J at p 918; *Dawodu v American Express Bank* [2001] BPIR 983 per Etherton J at p 990; *Re Menastar Finance Ltd* [2002] EWHC 2610 (Ch), [2003] 1 BCLC 338, per Etherton J at [51]; *Re Phoon Lee Piling Co Ltd* [2003] 2 HKLRD 391.

[1210] *Lam v Commissioners of Inland Revenue* [2005] EWHC 592 (Ch), [2006] STC 893, at [13].

[1211] *Dias v Havering London Borough Council* [2011] EWHC 172 (Ch), [2011] BPIR 395.

[1212] *Lambeth London Borough Council v Simon* [2007] BPIR 1629 at [45].

[1213] *Towsey v Highgrove Homes Ltd* [2013] BLR 45.

[1214] *Bowes v Hope Life Insurance and Guarantee Co* (1865) 11 HL Cas 389; *Re United Stock Exchange Ltd* (1884) 51 LT 687. See also the bankruptcy cases of *Re Onslow, ex parte Kibble* (1875) LR 10 Ch App 373; *Re Hawkins, ex parte Troup* [1895] 1 QB 404; and the discussion in *McCourt v Baron Meats Ltd* [1997] BPIR 114.

has before it all material necessary to determine the question, it will investigate whether, despite the judgment, the petitioner is not a creditor of the company.[1215] In *Bowes v Hope Life Insurance and Guarantee Co*[1216] the court did not have sufficient material and adjourned the petition to allow the company to take proceedings to have the judgment set aside.

7.510 In *Cowan v Scottish Publishing Co*[1217] the petitioner had obtained a judgment in respect of an arbitration award. The company disputed liability for £15 of the amount awarded, but had taken no steps to set aside the judgment or the arbitration and the Lord President said that he could not see a 'high or immediate probability' that a court would set aside either of them. The court announced it would make a winding-up order, at which point the company paid the debt and costs.

7.511 Exceptionally, the Malaysian Court of Appeal has held that the fact that an appeal has been lodged against an arbitration award is sufficient to justify an injunction against presenting a petition based on the award.[1218]

Relevance of creditor's attitude to the debt

7.512 The fact that the creditor might release the debt does not mean that it is disputed.[1219]

Extreme examples of insubstantial disputes

7.513 In *Re a Company (No 001913 of 1983)*[1220] an allegation that a petition was an abuse of process was rejected as there was 'no possible dispute on any grounds, substantial or mythical' about the debt owed to the petitioner. In *Re Cayman Islands Television and Video Production Co Ltd*[1221] the company's dispute was described as 'preposterous'. In *Re General Healthcare Group Ltd*[1222] a statutory demand had been issued for unliquidated damages, which had already been claimed in three previous proceedings which had all been struck out. An injunction was granted restraining presentation of a winding-up petition.

Alternative views in New Zealand

7.514 In New Zealand, it has been said in some cases that the test of whether a dispute is substantial enough to justify intervention by the court is 'whether [the company seeking to prevent a petition proceeding] has established a strong prima facie case of the existence of a genuine dispute, on substantial grounds, as to the present existence of a debt to the [petitioner] sufficient to found a winding-up petition'.[1223] In other cases, though, this test has not been

[1215] *Re United Stock Exchange Ltd* (1884) 51 LT 687, in which the judgment was a consent judgment which was disputed by an opposing contributory; *Re Gasbourne Pty Ltd* [1984] VR 801.
[1216] (1865) 11 HL Cas 389.
[1217] (1892) 19 R 437.
[1218] *Mobikom Sdn Bhd v Inmiss Communications Sdn Bhd* [2007] 3 MLJ 316.
[1219] *Re Tune Masters Pty Ltd* (1990) 108 FLR 440.
[1220] (1983) 1 BCC 98,941.
[1221] 1992–93 CILR 332.
[1222] [2004] EWHC 3471 (Ch), LTL 13/12/2004.
[1223] Per Eichelbaum J in *Pink Pages Publications Ltd v Team Communications Ltd* [1986] 2 NZLR 704 at p 711; followed in *Lockwood Buildings Ltd v Hunter Douglas Coilcoaters Ltd* (1988) 4 NZCLC 64,295; *Tracy Properties Ltd v Tracy* (1988) 3 BCR 1; *Churchill Group Holdings Ltd v Abel* (1988) 4 NZCLC 64,830; *National Mutual Finance v Mckillop Cars Ltd* (1989) 3 BCR 460; *Hewlett-Packard (NZ) Ltd v Compusales Software and Hardware Ltd* (1990) 5 NZCLC 66,281; *Cameron Distributors Ltd v Nashua Australia Pty Ltd* (1990) 5 NZCLC 66,907; *Hollands Printing Ltd v San Michele Ltd* [1992] 3 NZLR 469; and *Forms First Ltd v Front Page Marketing Ltd* [1993] MCLR 199—in all these cases the test was not satisfied. See also *Trilogy Corporation v Cashel Holdings Ltd* (1988) 4 NZCLC 64,514; *Auto Instrument Services Ltd v Thomas G Faria Corporation* (1988) 3 BCR 12; *New Zealand Factors Ltd v Farmers Trading Co Ltd* [1992] 3 NZLR 703; and

used. In *Microage Holdings Ltd v Powell Hutton McRea Advertising Ltd*[1224] and *Re Profcom Systems Ltd*[1225] the court prevented petitions from proceeding saying merely that the debts were bona fide disputed. In *Proconsult Associates Ltd v Graham Ilich Ltd*[1226] Robertson J concentrated on the dictum in the joint judgment of Woodhouse P and McMullin J in *Anglian Sales Ltd v South Pacific Manufacturing Co Ltd*[1227] that the question whether a winding-up petition should not be heard: 'ought not to rest simply on the balance of convenience considerations which may be relevant for an interim injunction. Something more than that is required.' In *Ngati Kahu Trust Board v Southern Lights Floral Exports Ltd*[1228] it was said, at p 452, that the test is 'whether there is a reasonably arguable bona fide defence to the claim'.

Determination of Disputes about Petition Debts

Generally disputes about petition debts will not be resolved in proceedings on the petition

Proceedings on a creditor's winding-up petition are not suited to determining a dispute **7.515** about the debt on which the petition is based. A dispute about a debt should be tried as an ordinary claim. The CPR procedures applying to claims are designed for trying such questions and the company will not be subject to the unfavourable publicity and legal disabilities[1229] which attend a company subject to a winding-up petition but which are irrelevant to trying a dispute about a debt.[1230] In *Re Catholic Publishing and Bookselling Co Ltd*[1231] Turner LJ said:

> I do not say that the Legislature has not given the court power to decide upon a winding-up petition the question whether a debt which the company disputes is owing or not, but I think that such an application is a most inconvenient mode of trying that question.

In *Re Inventors' Association Ltd*[1232] Kindersley V-C said, at p 558:

> But the question is whether a person claiming to be a creditor of a company (there being no question whatever except whether he is a creditor or not, and for how much, if at all, he is a creditor) can come to this court upon a petition for an order to wind up the company. It appears to me that it cannot be necessary or proper that he should come to this court upon a petition for a winding-up order for the mere purpose of trying whether he is a creditor or not.

In argument in *Re Imperial Guardian Life Assurance Society*[1233] James V-C said, at p 450, 'A **7.516** winding-up petition is not to be used as machinery for trying a common law action'. In *New Travellers' Chambers Ltd v Cheese and Green*[1234] Kekewich J said, at p 272:

> it has been said over and over again, that the presentation of a winding-up petition is not a convenient, and often not a proper method of trying a disputed debt.

Daily Freightways Ltd v Rio Beverages Ltd [1994] MCLR 289, in which the test was satisfied and winding-up proceedings were prevented.

[1224] (1986) 3 NZCLC 100,060.
[1225] (1988) 4 NZCLC 64,505.
[1226] (1989) 4 NZCLC 65,421.
[1227] [1984] 2 NZLR 249 at p 252.
[1228] [1994] MCLR 450.
[1229] For example, under IA 1986, s 127.
[1230] See 7.519–7.522. See per David Richards J in *Tallington Lakes Ltd v Ancasta International Boat Sales Ltd* [2012] EWCA Civ 1712, [2013] CP Rep 18, at [5].
[1231] (1864) 2 De G J & S 116 at p 121.
[1232] (1865) 2 Dr & Sm 553.
[1233] (1869) LR 9 Eq 447.
[1234] (1894) 70 LT 271.

In *Re Laceward Ltd*[1235] Slade J said, at p 136:

> It has been said in several reported cases that the procedure of a winding-up petition is not an appropriate course by which to attempt to resolve [a disputed debt].

In *Re Selectmove Ltd*[1236] Peter Gibson LJ said, at p 476, 'The jurisdiction of the Companies Court to wind up companies is not for the purpose of deciding a factual dispute concerning a debt which is sought to be relied on to found a petition'. In *John Holland Construction and Engineering Pty Ltd v Kilpatrick Green Pty Ltd*[1237] Young J, in the New South Wales Supreme Court, referred, at p 251, to the basic and continuing principle that 'the Companies Court is not to be the court which deals with disputed debts', because:

> The Companies List is designed to wind up insolvent companies in the public interest, not as a way of getting a dispute between companies in the marketplace on before a court quickly.

Unsuitability of petition procedure

7.517 Proceedings on a creditor's winding-up petition are especially ill-suited to the determination of disputed questions of fact.[1238] There are no pleadings, no disclosure and no oral evidence.[1239] In *Re Lympne Investments Ltd*[1240] Megarry J said, at p 527: 'A real dispute, turning to a substantial extent on disputed questions of fact which require viva voce evidence, and involving charges of fraud or near fraud, cannot properly be decided on petition'. In *Re Arena Corporation Ltd*[1241] Morritt V-C said, at [91]:

> It is not the function of the Companies Court to adjudicate in respect of a genuinely disputed debt, particularly where it involves the rejection of sworn evidence.

7.518 Winding-up proceedings are not suitable for determining whether a company does or does not owe an amount claimed by a petitioner or whether its liability is immediate or only prospective or contingent.[1242]

Detriment to the company

7.519 In *Re Lympne Investments Ltd*[1243] Megarry J said:

> The effects on a company of the presentation of a winding-up petition against it are such that it would be wrong to allow the machinery designed for such petitions to be used as a means of resolving disputes which ought to be settled in ordinary litigation.

7.520 In *Re a Company (No 006685 of 1996)*[1244] Chadwick J said that the court does not allow proceedings on a winding-up petition to be used to determine a dispute about a debt:

> because the effect of presenting a winding-up petition and advertising that petition is to put upon the company a pressure to pay (rather than to litigate) which is quite different in nature

---

[1235] [1981] 1 WLR 133.
[1236] [1995] 1 WLR 474.
[1237] (1994) 14 ACSR 250.
[1238] *Re Horizon Pacific Ltd* (1977) 2 ACLR 495; *Re Amadeus Trading Ltd* (1997) *The Times*, 1 April 1997.
[1239] *Alipour v Ary* [1997] 1 WLR 534 at p 541.
[1240] [1972] 1 WLR 523.
[1241] [2004] EWCA Civ 371, [2004] BPIR 415.
[1242] *Stonegate Securities Ltd v Gregory* [1980] Ch 576, especially per Buckley LJ at p 587. See also *F J Reddacliffe and Associates Pty Ltd v Arc Engineering Pty Ltd* (1978) 3 ACLR 426; *Re Allco Newsteel Pty Ltd* (1990) 2 ACSR 609 ('highly undesirable' for 'what is not much more than an ordinary building case to be tried on affidavit in the Companies Court' (at p 613)); *Arundel v Designers International Ltd* [1994] MCLR 433.
[1243] [1972] 1 WLR 523 at p 527.
[1244] [1997] 1 BCLC 639 at p 642.

from the effect of an ordinary writ action. The pressure arises from the fact that once the existence of the petition is known amongst those having dealings with the company, they are likely to withdraw credit or refuse to continue to trade with the company on the ground that, if the company is wound up on the petition, their dealings with it will be subject to the provisions in IA 1986, s 127. In those circumstances it may well be commercially necessary for the company to pay a debt which is disputed on substantial grounds rather than to run the risk that the whole of the company's business will be destroyed.

The fact that the company has already made public its reasons for opposing the winding-up **7.521** petition does not lessen the damage that would be done by giving notice of it, and is not a reason for departing from the practice of not allowing such a petition to proceed.[1245]

Preventing a disputed debt petition proceeding forces the person petitioning or threatening to **7.522** petition either to use the proper forum for determining the dispute, or to abandon the claim.[1246]

Exceptional cases

The court may, exceptionally, and at its discretion, decide that it would be proper and just **7.523** to determine a dispute concerning a creditor petitioner's debt in the course of proceedings on the petition.[1247]

In *Bateman Television Ltd v Coleridge Finance Co Ltd*[1248] a company ordered to be wound up **7.524** claimed that the petitioner's debt was unenforceable for illegality, but it was held that the trial judge was right to dispose of this question on the application to wind up, even though the question was sufficiently uncertain to justify appeal to the Privy Council.

In *Bulk Chartering and Consultants Australia Pty Ltd v T and T Metal Trading Pty Ltd*[1249] **7.525** the applicant for the winding-up order claimed payment of an arbitration award which the company said was unenforceable. At the hearing of the application it was held that the award was enforceable, and a winding-up order was made. On appeal, Kirby P (dissenting) said that the question had been too difficult to decide in winding-up proceedings, but the other two members of the New South Wales Court of Appeal simply affirmed the judge's decision.

A dispute about the petitioner's debt may be determined on an application for a winding up **7.526** in an appropriate case, for example:

(a) If (i) the dispute is sufficiently simple and straightforward, and (ii) all the evidence necessary to resolve the dispute is before the court;[1250] in particular, if there is a short

---

[1245] *Mutual Home Loan Fund of Australia Ltd v Smith* (1978) 3 ACLR 589.

[1246] *Fortuna Holdings Pty Ltd v Deputy Federal Commissioner of Taxation* [1978] VR 83; *F J Reddacliffe and Associates Pty Ltd v Arc Engineering Pty Ltd* (1978) 3 ACLR 426; *Dow Securities Pty Ltd v Manufacturing Investments Ltd* (1981) 5 ACLR 501; *Re a Company* (1983) 1 BCC 98,901; *Re a Company (No 003079 of 1990)* [1991] BCLC 235; *Re a Company (No 0012209 of 1991)* [1992] 1 WLR 351; *Re a Company (No 006341 of 1992)* [1994] 1 BCLC 225.

[1247] *Re Imperial Silver Quarries Co Ltd* (1868) 16 WR 1220; *Re United Stock Exchange Ltd* (1884) 51 LT 687; *Bateman Television Ltd v Coleridge Finance Co Ltd* [1971] NZLR 929; *Re Gasbourne Pty Ltd* [1984] VR 801; *Brinds Ltd v Offshore Oil NL* (1985) 63 ALR 94; *Kuehne and Nagel (New Zealand) Ltd v Ellison Trading Ltd* (1990) 5 NZCLC 66,499; *Re Arena Corporation Ltd* [2004] EWCA Civ 371, [2004] BPIR 415, in which Morritt V-C said, at [91], that this should not be followed in 'less clear' cases—compare the more cautious approach in *Commissioners of Customs and Excise v Anglo Overseas Ltd* [2004] EWHC 2198 (Ch), [2005] BPIR 137.

[1248] [1971] NZLR 929.

[1249] (1993) 114 ALR 189.

[1250] *Re Imperial Silver Quarries Co Ltd* (1868) 16 WR 1220; *Re Newcastle Permanent Investment and Building Society* (1897) 18 LR (NSW) Eq 76; *Re Turf Enterprises Pty Ltd* [1975] QdR 266; per Buckley LJ

point of law or the construction of documents on agreed facts.[1251] In Australia, although it has been said that it would be appropriate to determine a dispute if all the evidence is before the court, without restricting to cases which are sufficiently simple and straight-forward,[1252] it has also been emphasized that only short points should be dealt with in this way.[1253] In *Re United Stock Exchange Ltd*[1254] hearing the evidence relating to the dispute occupied the court for several days and Pearson J said he regretted having 'to waste the time of the court upon such a case as this'. In *Re Kentucky Homes (NZ) Ltd*,[1255] even though the question had been argued, it was inappropriate to determine the disputes between the parties because of the complexity of the legal and factual issues which were not clearly thought through before the hearing, partly because of the lack of pleadings, so that the evidence was inadequately presented and the issues inadequately argued.

(b) If the question of whether there is a dispute is difficult to determine without determining the merits of the dispute itself.[1256] In *Westpark Marina Ltd v Deepat Investments Ltd*,[1257] when determining whether there was a dispute, the court heard all the evidence which the parties were willing to adduce about the dispute and was able to determine it. In *Re Datadeck Ltd*[1258] determining whether there was a dispute involved rejecting the company's contention that the petitioner's debt was payable by a different company because of a novation.

(c) If the evidence necessary to determine the dispute must be heard anyway in order to decide other questions arising on the petition.[1259]

(d) If the position of the company is such that the likely result of refusing to determine the dispute so that the winding-up petition can go forward is that 'the creditor, if he established his debt, would lose his remedy altogether'.[1260] For example, if it appears that the company's assets may be disposed of or removed from the jurisdiction by the company,[1261] or if the company's solvency is doubtful.[1262]

See also *Yassim v Australian Mid-Eastern Club Ltd*,[1263] in which the factual background to the dispute was not complex, there had already been lengthy litigation in which the company had failed to produce evidence it claimed to have to rebut the claim of the person applying for winding up, and the applicant was supported by a large number of other

---

in *Stonegate Securities Ltd v Gregory* [1980] Ch 576 at p 587; *Kuehne and Nagel (New Zealand) Ltd v Ellison Trading Ltd* (1990) 5 NZCLC 66,499.

[1251] *Delnorth Pty Ltd v State Bank of New South Wales* (1995) 17 ACSR 379 at p 384. See, for example, *Re Healing Research Trustee Co Ltd* [1992] 2 All ER 481 (point of law); *Bank of Commerce (M) Bhd v Selangor Frits and Glazes Sdn Bhd* [1999] 5 MLJ 96 (point of law); *Tatlers.com.au Pty Ltd v Davis* [2007] NSWSC 835, 213 FLR 109 (point of law); *Pacific Recreation Pte Ltd v SY Technology Inc* [2008] SGCA 1, [2008] 2 SLR 491 (construction of documents).

[1252] *Re Horizon Pacific Ltd* (1977) 2 ACLR 495; and see *Bateman Television Ltd v Coleridge Finance Co Ltd* [1971] NZLR 929 discussed at 7.524.

[1253] *Wellnora Pty Ltd v Fiorentino* [2008] NSWSC 483, 66 ACSR 229.

[1254] (1884) 51 LT 687.

[1255] (1988) 4 NZCLC 64,803.

[1256] Per Gibbs J in *Re QBS Pty Ltd* [1967] QdR 218 at p 225, approved by the Privy Council in *Brinds Ltd v Offshore Oil NL* (1985) 63 ALR 94.

[1257] [1992] MCLR 219.

[1258] [1998] BCC 694.

[1259] *Brinds Ltd v Offshore Oil NL* (1985) 63 ALR 94.

[1260] Per Oliver LJ in *Re Claybridge Shipping Co SA* [1997] 1 BCLC 572 at p 579.

[1261] *Re Claybridge Shipping Co SA*. It would usually be more appropriate to deal with this problem by applying for a freezing injunction under CPR, r 25.1(1)(f).

[1262] *Re Allco Newsteel Pty Ltd* (1990) 2 ACSR 609.

[1263] (1989) 15 ACLR 449.

creditors owed substantial amounts. The dispute was determined in the applicant's favour and a winding-up order made. The winding-up order was affirmed on appeal.[1264]

If the court has determined a dispute about the petitioner's debt at the hearing of the peti-   **7.527**
tion and decided that a winding-up order should be made, it may adjourn the hearing or delay perfection of the order for a short time to allow the company an opportunity to pay the debt, at least if it appears that the company is solvent.[1265]

Treatment of Disputed Debt Petition at Substantive Hearing

Principle

The court has jurisdiction to wind up a company if the company is unable to pay its debts.   **7.528**
However, the fact that a company and a petitioner are disputing whether, or to what extent, the company is indebted to the petitioner is no evidence that the company is unable to pay its debts. If, at the substantive hearing of the petition, such a petitioner does not bring other evidence sufficient to show the company's inability to pay its debts, the petition will nor- mally be dismissed.[1266] Whether the petitioner will be permitted to present other evidence depends on whether the dispute is about the existence of the petitioner's debt,[1267] or is about the amount or timing of an otherwise admitted debt,[1268] or is about only part of the peti- tioner's debt.[1269] In *Kolot Property Services Ltd v Rightop Investment Ltd*[1270] the petitioner was ordered to pay the company's costs on the indemnity basis as it 'had not begun to make out a prima facie case of the alleged indebtedness'.

Disputed existence of debt

If the *existence* of a creditor petitioner's debt (rather than its size or timing) is disputed, on   **7.529**
substantial grounds,[1271] that dispute cannot normally be resolved in proceedings on the petition[1272] and the court's usual practice is to dismiss the petition.[1273] In *Alipour v Ary*[1274] the Court of Appeal (per Peter Gibson LJ) said:

> It has long been the practice of the Companies Court when faced with a creditor's petition based on a disputed debt to dismiss the petition, insisting that the dispute be determined

---

[1264] Sub nom *Australian Mid-Eastern Club Ltd v Yassim* (1989) 1 ACSR 399.
[1265] *Re Imperial Silver Quarries Co Ltd* (1868) 16 WR 1220; *Re King's Cross Industrial Dwellings Co* (1870) LR 11 Eq 149; *Re Newcastle Permanent Investment and Building Society* (1897) 18 LR (NSW) Eq 76; *Re Concrete Pipes and Cement Products Ltd* [1926] VLR 34; *Re Mittagong RSL Club Ltd* (1980) 4 ACLR 897; *Re Borley Holdings Ltd* (1987) 4 NZCLC 64,489.
[1266] *Re Brighton Club and Norfolk Hotel Co Ltd* (1865) 35 Beav 203 (disputed amount); *Re London Wharfing and Warehousing Co Ltd* (1865) 35 Beav 37; *Re General Exchange Bank Ltd* (1866) 14 LT 582; *Re London and Paris Banking Corporation* (1874) LR 19 Eq 444; *Re Positive Government Security Life Assurance Co* [1877] WN 23; *Re British Alliance Assurance Corporation* [1877] WN 261; *Re Queensland Steam Shipping Co* (1887) 3 TLR 377; *Re Martin, Wallis and Co Ltd* (1893) 37 SJ 822, 38 SJ 112; *Re Anglo-Bavarian Steel Ball Co* [1899] WN 80; *Re Rhodesian Properties Ltd* [1901] WN 130; *Re Cobalt Development Co* (1908) 12 OWR 83; *Re Meaford Manufacturing Co* (1919) 46 OLR 282; *Re Tanganyika Produce Agency Ltd* [1957] EA 241; *Re Pageboy Couriers Ltd* [1983] ILRM 510; *Re Nima Travel Sdn Bhd* [1986] 2 MLJ 374; *Ng Ah Kway v Tai Kit Enterprise Sdn Bhd* [1986] 1 MLJ 58; *Re First Fifteen Holdings Ltd* (1987) 4 NZCLC 64,108; *Re Mechanised Construction Pte Ltd* [1989] 3 MLJ 9; *Kemayan Construction Sdn Bhd v Prestara Sdn Bhd* [1997] 5 MLJ 608.
[1267] See 7.529–7.535.
[1268] See 7.536–7.538.
[1269] See 7.539–7.540.
[1270] [2003] 2 HKLRD 13 at [17].
[1271] See 7.444–7.514.
[1272] See 7.515–7.522.
[1273] *Re Welsh Brick Industries Ltd* [1946] 2 All ER 197 at p 198; *Mann v Goldstein* [1968] 1 WLR 1091 at p 1094.
[1274] [1997] 1 WLR 534 at p 541.

outside the petition.... The reason for the practice has been essentially pragmatic. The vast majority of petitions to wind up [companies] are creditors' petitions. The Companies Court procedure on such petitions is ill-equipped to deal with the resolution of disputes of fact. There are no pleadings, there is no [disclosure] and there is no oral evidence normally tolerated on such petitions.

But in *Parmalat Capital Finance Ltd v Food Holdings Ltd*[1275] the Privy Council (per Lord Hoffmann) said:

The main reason for this practice is the danger of abuse of the winding up procedure. A party to a dispute should not be allowed to use the threat of a winding up petition as a means of forcing the company to pay a bona fide disputed debt.[1276]

7.530 There is no need to wait until the substantive hearing of the petition. At any time after the presentation of a creditor's petition to wind up a company which is based on a debt whose existence is disputed, the court will normally, on an application by the company, prevent the petition proceeding.[1277] It is also possible to obtain an injunction to prevent presentation of such a petition.[1278]

7.531 The juridical basis for this treatment of disputed debt petitions has often been said to be that a person claiming a disputed debt from a company does not have standing to petition for its winding up.[1279] But it is often argued that the better explanation is the one given in the quotation from *Alipour v Ary* at 7.529, namely, that it is the usual practice of the court, which has been adopted to deal with the procedural problem that a dispute about a debt cannot normally be adjudicated on in proceedings on a winding-up petition.[1280]

7.532 Exceptions may be made to the court's usual practice:

(a) The court may, exceptionally, determine a dispute about the existence of a petitioner's debt in proceedings on the petition.[1281]

(b) In some circumstances a petition may be adjourned instead of dismissed.[1282]

(c) In rare cases, a winding-up order may be made without resolving a dispute about the petitioner's standing.[1283]

7.533 It has been said that whether or not the company is insolvent is irrelevant to the court's practice of dismissing a disputed debt petition if the dispute is about the existence of the debt.[1284] But this ignores the exceptional cases in which showing that the company is, or

---

[1275] [2008] UKPC 23, [2009] 1 BCLC 274, at [9].

[1276] See also per Oliver LJ in *Re Claybridge Shipping Co SA* [1997] 1 BCLC 572 at pp 578–9 and 7.519–7.522.

[1277] See 7.569–7.608.

[1278] See 7.569–7.608.

[1279] See 7.359–7.363.

[1280] See 7.364–7.368. *Re Claybridge Shipping Co SA* [1997] 1 BCLC 572; *Stonegate Securities Ltd v Gregory* [1980] Ch 576 per Buckley LJ at p 580; *Re ICS Computer Distribution Ltd* [1996] 1 HKLR 181 at p 182; *RWH Enterprises Ltd v Portedge Ltd* [1998] BCC 556 at p 558; *Re MCI WorldCom Ltd* [2002] EWHC (Ch), [2003] 1 BCLC 330, at [11]; *Parmalat Capital Finance Ltd v Food Holdings Ltd* [2008] UKPC 23, [2009] 1 BCLC 274, at [9].

[1281] See 7.523–7.527.

[1282] See 7.541–7.549.

[1283] See 7.551–7.568.

[1284] *Mann v Goldstein* [1968] 1 WLR 1091 at pp 1094–5; *Holt Southey Ltd v Catnic Components Ltd* [1978] 1 WLR 630 at p 631; *Re Wilson Market Research Pty Ltd* (1996) 39 NSWLR 311; *Brunsfield Information Technology Sdn Bhd v Masterloq Technologies Sdn Bhd* [2003] 6 MLJ 305; *Portsmouth City Football Club Ltd v Commissioners of HM Revenue and Customs* [2010] EWHC 75 (Ch), [2011] STC 683, at [13].

probably is, insolvent may persuade the court to adjourn the petition or make a winding-up order instead of dismissing the petition.

A petitioner whose own debt is disputed cannot rely on non-payment of that disputed debt to show that the company is unable to pay its debts. Such a petitioner cannot rely on non-compliance with a statutory demand for that disputed debt as deeming that the company is unable to pay its debts because the non-compliance is not a 'neglect' to comply.[1285]   **7.534**

A further reason which is often given for dismissing a disputed debt petition where the dispute is about the existence of the debt is that the petition is an abuse of process.[1286] The following reasons for characterizing such a petition as an abuse of process have been identified: **7.535**

(a) Obtaining a decision on whether or not a debt exists is not a legitimate purpose for which a winding-up petition may be presented.[1287] Other, more appropriate proceedings should be used.[1288]

(b) The petitioner lacks standing.[1289] This is irrelevant if the idea that a petitioner whose standing is in question does not have standing is rejected.

(c) In at least some cases, the petition is being used for the improper purpose of pressurizing a company to abandon a dispute over a debt and pay it.[1290] Dismissal of a disputed debt petition does not depend on it being shown to be used for this improper purpose, and this may not in fact be the petitioner's purpose.[1291] Even if it is not the petitioner's purpose, the petition may have that effect in practice.[1292]

Disputed amount or timing

If a petitioner's status as a creditor is not disputed, but the amount of the petitioner's debt is disputed, the petitioner may show by evidence other than the non-payment of the total amount claimed that the company is unable to pay its debts.[1293]   **7.536**

In *Re Swiss Oil Corporation*[1294] the company had already lost one appeal against the foreign arbitral award for which the petitioner was a judgment creditor. Evidence was given that a further appeal might reduce the amount of the award but would be very unlikely to extinguish it altogether: the appeal process might take many years and waiting for it to end before winding up the company would delay misfeasance proceedings against company officers.   **7.537**

[1285] *Re General Exchange Bank Ltd* (1866) 14 LT 582; *Re London and Paris Banking Corporation* (1874) LR 19 Eq 444; *Re a Company (No 003729 of 1982)* [1984] 1 WLR 1090; *Brunsfield Information Technology Sdn Bhd v Masterloq Technologies Sdn Bhd* [2003] 6 MLJ 305; and see the discussion at 7.213–7.216.

[1286] *Mann v Goldstein* [1968] 1 WLR 1091 at p 1099.

[1287] *Mann v Goldstein* [1968] 1 WLR 1091 at p 1099; *Re a Company (No 006685 of 1996)* [1997] 1 BCLC 639 at p 642 per Chadwick J; *Re Ringinfo Ltd* [2002] 1 BCLC 210 at p 220; *Camulos Partners Offshore Ltd v Kathrein and Co* 2010 (1) CILR 303 per Chadwick P at [59]–[61].

[1288] See 7.515–7.522.

[1289] *Holt Southey Ltd v Catnic Components Ltd* [1978] 1 WLR 630 at p 632; *CVC Investments Pty Ltd v P and T Aviation Pty Ltd* (1989) 18 NSWLR 295 at p 302.

[1290] See 7.603–7.608 and the quotation at 7.529 from *Parmalat Capital Finance Ltd v Food Holdings Ltd* [2008] UKPC 23, [2009] 1 BCLC 274, at [9].

[1291] *Argyle Crescent Ltd v Definite Finance Ltd* [2004] EWHC 3422 (Ch), LTL 29/7/2004, at [6].

[1292] See 7.519–7.522.

[1293] *Re Tweeds Garages Ltd* [1962] Ch 406; *Tandy v Harmony House Furniture Co Ltd 1964* (1) ALR Comm 299; *Re Metropolitan Fuel Pty Ltd* [1969] VR 328 (see at p 330); *Just Juice Corporation Pty Ltd v Murrayland Fruit Juice Pty Ltd* (1990) 2 ACSR 541; *Tottenham Hotspur plc v Edennote plc* [1995] 1 BCLC 65, in which inability to pay debts was conceded.

[1294] 1988–89 CILR 319.

An application to adjourn the petition to await the outcome of the appeal was refused and a winding-up order was made.

7.538　If the dispute about the petitioner's claim relates only to whether it is payable presently or at some time in the future, the petitioner has standing to petition either as a creditor or as a future creditor, and may show by evidence other than the non-payment of the total amount claimed that the company is unable to pay its debts. In *Aristes Trading Ltd v Interlink Overseas Trading LLC*,[1295] exceptionally, the court resolved, on hearing a winding-up petition, a dispute about whether the petition debt was presently payable or not.

Partially disputed debt

7.539　If only part of a creditor petitioner's claim is disputed, the court may find that non-payment of the undisputed part proves inability to pay debts.[1296] In *Re James Vallentine and Co Ltd*[1297] part of the petitioner's debt was disputed: the report says that Kennedy J concluded that the company was unable to pay its debts but does not say what led him to that conclusion. On the other hand, in *Re Brighton Club and Norfolk Hotel Co Ltd*[1298] the petition was dismissed though the company had not paid any part of the petitioner's claim but had admitted that it was indebted to him for some amount: the report does not make it clear that any specific amount was admitted. In *Re Alderney Dairy Co Ltd*[1299] the petitioner claimed £73, the company admitted (but had apparently not paid) only £36 and the petition was dismissed because of the dispute. In *Re Bydand Ltd*[1300] the court refused to rescind a winding-up order made on a creditor's petition despite accepting that part of the debt claimed was disputed: non-payment of the undisputed debt of about £2,723 was sufficient justification for the winding-up order. In *TSB Bank plc v Platts*[1301] the Court of Appeal said, at p 11, 'we find it hard to see why a petition should be dismissed if based on a debt part of which is undisputed and exceeds the statutory minimum without payment by the company of the undisputed part'.[1302]

7.540　If it is found that only part of the petitioner's claim is disputed, the petition may be adjourned for a short time to allow the company to pay the undisputed debt if it can.[1303]

[1295]　[2005] EWHC 3250 (Ch), LTL 4/11/2005.

[1296]　*Re Gem Exports Pty Ltd* (1984) 36 SASR 571, in which the dispute related only to the interest payable on the principal debt and would have affected less than 5 per cent of the amount claimed; *Arafura Finance Corporation Pty Ltd v Kooba Pty Ltd* (1987) 52 NTR 43; *Westpac Banking Corporation Ltd v Leichhardt Development Co Pty Ltd* (1989) 99 FLR 323, in which the dispute was held to be without substance; *Ataxtin Pty Ltd v Gordon Pacific Developments Pty Ltd* (1991) 29 FCR 564; *Dikwa Holdings Pty Ltd v Oakbury Pty Ltd* (1992) 36 FCR 274; *Morshead Management Ltd v Capital Entertainment Establishment* (1999) LTL 28/3/2000.

[1297]　(1893) 37 SJ 823.

[1298]　(1865) 35 Beav 204.

[1299]　(1885) 9 VLR 628.

[1300]　[1997] BCC 915.

[1301]　[1998] 2 BCLC 1.

[1302]　The case before the Court of Appeal concerned a bankruptcy order and the court overlooked the fact that, unlike the position in bankruptcy, there is no statutory minimum debt for which a creditor may petition for a company to be wound up (see 7.392–7.397).

[1303]　*Re James Vallentine and Co Ltd* (1893) 37 SJ 823, adjournment for three weeks; *Arafura Finance Corporation Pty Ltd v Kooba Pty Ltd* (1987) 52 NTR 43, adjournment for seven days but the debt was not paid—see *Arafura Finance Corporation Pty Ltd v Kooba Pty Ltd (No 2)* (1987) 52 NTR 52; *Westpac Banking Corporation Ltd v Leichhardt Development Co Pty Ltd* (1989) 99 FLR 323, settled after adjournment; *Re Javelin Promotions Ltd* [2003] EWHC 1932 (Ch), LTL 30/9/2003, adjournment for 14 days.

Adjournment of a Disputed Debt Petition

Circumstances in which a disputed debt petition may be adjourned

Instead of dismissing a disputed debt petition, the court may adjourn it to await the outcome of proceedings to establish liability for the debt.[1304] But this should be done only if it appears: **7.541**

(a) that if the debt were to be established, the company would be unable to pay it;[1305] or

(b) there is a real possibility that the company has been involved in fraud;[1306] or

(c) adjournment is required by the particular circumstances of the case.[1307]

Although an appeal to the First-tier Tribunal (Tax) does not suspend liability for the assess- **7.542** ment or determination appealed against,[1308] if there is a real doubt about the propriety of an appealed assessment or determination, a petition to wind up the taxpayer should be adjourned to await the outcome of the appeal.[1309]

Where company would be unable to pay the petition debt

The court may adjourn a disputed debt petition to await the outcome of proceedings to **7.543** establish liability for the debt where it appears that if the debt were to be established, the company would be unable to pay it in full.[1310]

As a condition of granting an adjournment, the company may be required to pay into court **7.544** the sum in dispute.[1311] In *Bowes v Hope Life Insurance and Guarantee Co*[1312] the petitioner had obtained judgment for his debt and the company was required to give an undertaking to bring proceedings to have the judgment set aside. In *Re Horizon Pacific Ltd*[1313] the company was required to give an undertaking to assist in obtaining a speedy hearing of proceedings to establish the petitioner's debt. In *Patrick Carr Investments Pty Ltd v P E Marosszeky Pty Ltd*[1314] the company was required to give security for the petitioner's claim

---

[1304] IA 1986, s 125(1); per Turner LJ in *Re Catholic Publishing and Bookselling Co Ltd* (1864) 2 De G J & S 116 at p 121.

[1305] *Re London Wharfing and Warehousing Co Ltd* (1865) 35 Beav 37 per Romilly MR at p 40. See 7.543–7.547.

[1306] *Commissioners of Customs and Excise v Jack Baars Wholesale* [2004] EWHC 18 (Ch), [2004] BPIR 543.

[1307] *Landauer and Co v W H Alexander and Co Ltd* 1919 SC 492 (court unable to decide whether the dispute was substantial enough to justify dismissal of the petition); *Re QBS Pty Ltd* [1967] QdR 218 (petitioning company and company sought to be wound up both had the same directors and the disputed petition debts were alleged preferences); *Re Jeff Reid Pty Ltd* (1980) 5 ACLR 28 (dispute only raised after presentation of the petition; not possible to determine whether the company could pay the debt; company had ceased carrying on business).

[1308] See 7.412–7.415.

[1309] *Re Arena Corporation* [2004] EWCA Civ 371, [2004] BPIR 415, at [52] and [74].

[1310] *Re Imperial Guardian Life Assurance Society* (1869) LR 9 Eq 447; *Re Mosbert Finance (Australia) Pty Ltd* (1976) 2 ACLR 5; *Re Horizon Pacific Ltd* (1977) 2 ACLR 495; *Re Vivre Boutique Pty Ltd* (1981) 30 SASR 475; *Patrick Carr Investments Pty Ltd v P E Marosszeky Pty Ltd* (1982) 7 ACLR 59; *Re D J and S R Campbell Building Contractors Pty Ltd* (1983) 7 ACLR 696; *Irani v Asian Boutique Pty Ltd* (1983) 7 ACLR 755; *General Welding and Construction Co (Qld) Pty Ltd v International Rigging (Aust) Pty Ltd* (1983) 8 ACLR 307; *Avery v Worldwide Testing Services Pty Ltd* (1990) 2 ACSR 834; *Commonwealth Bank of Australia v Begonia Pty Ltd* (1993) 11 ACSR 609; *Jubilee International Inc v Farlin Timbers Pte Ltd* [2005] EWHC 3331 (Ch), [2006] BPIR 765. See also *Re LHF Wools Ltd* [1970] Ch 27, in which the company had a cross-claim against the petitioner (see 7.688).

[1311] *Re Compagnie Générale des Asphaltes de Paris, ex parte Neuchatel Asphalte Co* [1883] WN 17.

[1312] (1865) 11 HL Cas 389.

[1313] (1977) 2 ACLR 495.

[1314] (1982) 7 ACLR 59.

and to undertake to commence arbitration or cooperate with arbitration proceedings brought by the petitioner.

7.545   A petition should not be adjourned without hearing the views of any supporting creditors.[1315]

7.546   In *Re Universal Non-tariff Fire Assurance Co, ex parte Peter Forbes and Co*[1316] Peter Forbes and Co had petitioned for the winding up of the insurance company and the petition was adjourned for the debt to be established in separate proceedings. Meanwhile the insurance company went into voluntary winding up and a supervision order was granted on the petition of another creditor. Peter Forbes and Co's proof of debt was rejected by the liquidator but accepted on appeal to the court, which ordered that the costs of Peter Forbes and Co's petition should be paid in priority to all other debts.

7.547   In *Bicoastal Corporation v Shinwa Co Ltd*[1317] the petition of a judgment creditor was adjourned until determination of an appeal against the petitioner's judgment: the company was a non-trading holding company and the petitioner would have been prejudiced by losing the date of commencement of winding up established by the presentation of the present petition because it wanted to question prior transactions.

Where company active

7.548   Adjournment is deprecated where a company is to continue in any business activity because:

(a) it is difficult for it to do so with a winding-up petition hanging over its head;
(b) if a winding up is ordered, it will be deemed to have commenced when the petition was presented, which creates difficulties over validation of transactions; and
(c) its effect is that another creditor with an undisputed unpaid debt is, in practice, prevented from petitioning.[1318]

Where company solvent

7.549   A disputed debt petition will be dismissed rather than adjourned if the dispute is about the existence of the debt and it appears that the company would be able to pay the debt if it were to be established.[1319] In *Re Inventors' Association Ltd*[1320] a disputed debt petition was presented by a Mr Chefferiel against a company which was in voluntary liquidation and would apparently have been able to pay the debt if it were to be established. The voluntary liquidator had led Mr Chefferiel to believe that if he sued for the debt, the liquidator would have the action stayed.[1321] Mr Chefferiel therefore believed his only course was to have the company wound up by the court. In fact, as Kindersley V-C pointed out, the court would be most unlikely to order a stay of an action against a solvent company.

[1315]   *Re Allco Newsteel Pty Ltd* (1990) 2 ACSR 609.
[1316]   (1875) 23 WR 464.
[1317]   [1994] 1 HKLR 65.
[1318]   *Re Meaford Manufacturing Co* (1919) 46 OLR 282; *Re Lympne Investments Ltd* [1972] 1 WLR 523; *Re Boston Timber Fabrications Ltd* [1984] BCLC 328; *Commissioners of Customs and Excise v Anglo Overseas Ltd* [2004] EWHC 2198 (Ch), LTL 6/10/2004.
[1319]   *Re Brighton Club and Norfolk Hotel Co Ltd* (1865) 35 Beav 203; *Re London Wharfing and Warehousing Co Ltd* (1865) 35 Beav 37.
[1320]   (1865) 2 Dr & Sm 553.
[1321]   By applying under what is now IA 1986, s 112, for the court to exercise its power under s 130(2), as applied by s 112(1), to stay the action.

Short adjournments to give the company a chance to pay a debt, after the court has deter- **7.550**
mined a dispute or established an undisputed part of a partially disputed debt, are discussed
at 7.527 and 7.540.

Making a Winding-up Order on a Disputed Debt Petition

Principle

In three cases[1322] the Privy Council has held that where there is a dispute about the existence **7.551**
of the debt on which a creditor's winding-up petition is grounded, the court has a discretion
to hear the petition, instead of dismissing or adjourning it. If, on hearing the petition, the
court is satisfied that one of the statutory circumstances in which a winding-up order may
be made exists, it may, at its discretion, make a winding-up order. The discretion to make a
winding-up order is correctly exercised where the court has decided, after full consideration
of the question, that the petitioner is a creditor[1323] or that there is no substantial dispute.[1324]

The Privy Council has not discussed the circumstances in which it would be a correct **7.552**
exercise of the discretion to make a winding-up order without determining the dispute
about the petitioner's standing.[1325] According to Saville LJ, it is only 'perhaps in a wholly
exceptional case' that a court will make a winding-up order without being satisfied that the
petitioner has standing to apply for it.[1326] Much earlier, Malins V-C had denied the possibility completely:

> on a [creditor's] petition to wind up no order can be made until the debt is proved where there
> is a bona fide dispute as to its existence.[1327]

Even if a company is ordered to be wound up on the petition of a person whose claim to **7.553**
be a creditor is disputed by the company, without resolving that dispute, nothing will be
paid to the petitioner in the winding up unless the petitioner's proof of debt is admitted
by the liquidator or, on appeal, by the court. As the learned deputy judge said in *Jubilee
International Inc v Farlin Timbers Pte Ltd*,[1328] it would be a very unusual circumstance
where the court would leave it to the liquidator to resolve the issue whether or not the
petitioner had the standing to petition. It is plain from what was said by Oliver LJ in *Re
Claybridge Shipping Co SA*[1329] that the issue of standing should normally be decided by the
court before making a winding-up order.[1330]

[1322] *Bateman Television Ltd v Coleridge Finance Co Ltd* [1971] NZLR 929 at p 932; *Brinds Ltd v Offshore Oil NL* (1985) 63 ALR 94 at pp 99–100; *Parmalat Capital Finance Ltd v Food Holdings Ltd* [2008] UKPC 23, [2009] 1 BCLC 274, at [9].

[1323] *Bateman Television Ltd v Coleridge Finance Co Ltd*; *Brinds Ltd v Offshore Oil NL*.

[1324] *Parmalat Capital Finance Ltd v Food Holdings Ltd*.

[1325] *Parmalat Capital Finance Ltd v Food Holdings Ltd* at [9].

[1326] *Re MTI Trading Systems Ltd* [1998] BCC 400 at p 403. Warren J dropped the 'wholly' in *Lacontha Foundation v GBI Investments Ltd* [2010] EWHC 37 (Ch), [2010] 2 BCLC 624, at [85]. Warren J has also held that there is no such restriction in relation to administration applications (*Hammonds v Pro-Fit USA Ltd* [2007] EWHC 1998 (Ch), [2008] 2 BCLC 159).

[1327] *Cadiz Waterworks Co v Barnett* (1874) LR 19 Eq 182 at p 193. See also *Re Imperial Silver Quarries Co Ltd* (1868) 16 WR 1220 at p 1221, where his Lordship said: 'It is against the principles of this court to wind up a company either (1) upon a disputed debt, or (2) if it is clear that on the debt being established it will be paid.'

[1328] [2005] EWHC 3331 (Ch), [2006] BPIR 765, at [62].

[1329] [1997] 1 BCLC 572 at pp 578–9.

[1330] *Jubilee International Inc v Farlin Timbers Pte Ltd* at [62].

7.554   Winding-up orders have been made on disputed debt petitions in a small number of reported cases, which are discussed at 7.556–7.568. In some of these cases, winding up is justified because the process of admitting a proof for dividend is seen as the only, or only practicable, way of deciding whether the petitioner is a creditor and, if so, obtaining payment of the debt.[1331] In another group of cases, winding up has been justified by the need to assist the petitioner, summed up by saying that otherwise the petitioner would be without a remedy.[1332] In other cases, it has been said that once the court has found that a company is insolvent, the company should be wound up whether or not any person before the court has standing to apply for a winding-up order.[1333]

7.555   In recent times, two English High Court judges (one sitting in the Cayman Islands Court of Appeal) have come to very different conclusions about when it is right to make a winding-up order without deciding whether the petitioner is a creditor. In England, Warren J has decided that this may be done in various circumstances, including where there is a danger that the company's assets will be dissipated so that the petitioner's claim cannot be met.[1334] In the Cayman Islands, Vos JA has decided that the court cannot wind up a company on a creditor's petition unless it is proved, on a balance of probabilities that the petitioner actually is a creditor.[1335] The 'very special situation' discussed at 7.557 may be the only legitimate exception.[1336] Vos JA gave four reasons for his conclusion:[1337]

(a)   it would be remarkable if the court were prepared to exercise a statutory jurisdiction to put into effect a process of collective execution against the assets of the company for the benefit of all the creditors at the behest of someone who had no legitimate interest in the affairs of the company;

(b)   since the legislature has laid down that only a creditor or contributory (or, in some cases, other specified persons) can present a petition to wind up, one would expect that creditor to establish his status before any final order is made at his instigation;

(c)   if it were to be held that a petitioning creditor could proceed to obtain a winding-up order without establishing his debt, companies would be at greater risk and have less protection from those wishing to damage them than the legislature can, it seems to me, have possibly intended; and

(d)   as I have shown, on a proper analysis, the authorities provide no significant support for the proposition that a winding-up order can be made without the petitioning creditor establishing his standing as a creditor.

Vos JA went on to say:[1338]

> In my view, the point can be tested by considering what would happen if a disputed debt were decided at the hearing of a petition, but it was concluded that there was in fact no indebtedness to the petitioner at all. In that situation, I think it is inconceivable for the reasons I have

---

[1331]   See 7.556–7.557.

[1332]   See 7.558–7.561.

[1333]   See 7.562–7.568.

[1334]   *Hammonds v Pro-Fit USA Ltd* [2007] EWHC 1998 (Ch), [2008] 2 BCLC 159, at [26]–[35]; *Lacontha Foundation v GBI Investments Ltd* [2010] EWHC 37 (Ch), [2010] 2 BCLC 624, at [80]–[84] and [136]–[169].

[1335]   *Re GFN Corporation Ltd* 2009 CILR 650. Vos JA expressed (at [87] and [97]) disagreement with what Warren J had said in *Hammonds v Pro-Fit USA Ltd* but this disagreement was not cited to Warren J in *Lacontha Foundation v GBI Investments Ltd*.

[1336]   *Re GFN Corporation Ltd* at [94(f)] and [96].

[1337]   *Re GFN Corporation Ltd* at [101].

[1338]   *Re GFN Corporation Ltd* at [102].

given that the court would make a winding-up order at the behest of that 'non-creditor', even if it were established that the company was insolvent, or even that it was just and equitable that it be wound up.[1339]

It is submitted that Vos JA's conclusion is correct, for those reasons, in English as well as Cayman Islands law.

Where a winding-up order is made on a concurrent petition

In *Re Lundy Granite Co*[1340] a creditor's petition to wind up the Granite Co was presented **7.556** by the National Bank. Two months later a group of shareholders in the Granite Co presented a contributories' petition which alleged that the National Bank had promoted the Granite Co as a fraud on shareholders. The allegation seems to have been that it was a 'bubble company' with no real business. The Granite Co, which was said to be controlled by the Bank, supported the Bank's petition. The contributories' petition alleged that the Bank's petition was a collusive one based on a non-existent debt. At that time it was crucial to have the carriage of a winding-up order so as to be able to nominate a liquidator (who, in those days, was not necessarily an independent professional). Lord Romilly MR held that he could not dismiss the Bank's petition, because there was not sufficient evidence to hold that the Bank was not a creditor.[1341] There was no point in adjourning the Bank's petition to await determination of the dispute about the debt in other proceedings because it was clear that the company, under the Bank's control, would not defend such proceedings. So his Lordship made a winding-up order on both petitions but gave carriage of the order to the contributories. This seems to be an example of a case in which proof of debt in winding up is the only practical way of deciding whether the petitioner is a creditor. However, this practical problem was caused by the procedure used at that time.[1342] Nowadays, the shareholders would be substituted as petitioners on the creditor's petition.

Revival of dissolved unregistered company

IA 1986 allows for the winding up of a dissolved unregistered company, even though it has **7.557** ceased to exist as a juristic entity capable of being sued for debt.[1343] An order made on such a petition commences a procedure for settling debts that were owed by the company before it was dissolved. It seems that anticipation of this gives any person owed such a debt standing to petition as a creditor for the winding up. It has been held that standing can be extended to a person with a disputed claim against a dissolved foreign corporation.[1344] The justification is that winding up is the only way of creating an entity against which a claim for the disputed debt can be asserted and adjudicated.[1345] Under this procedure, the existence of the petitioner's debt is not settled on the application for the winding-up order and the making

---

[1339] Australian courts have contemplated making a winding-up order in this circumstance. See 2.68 and 7.742.

[1340] (1868) 17 WR 91.

[1341] See 7.364–7.368.

[1342] And the fraudulent promotion of companies was caused by the complete absence of regulation of securities marketing at that time.

[1343] IA 1986, ss 221(5)(a) and 225.

[1344] All the reported cases were concerned with companies incorporated in Russia, but it would seem that the approach could also be applied to a dissolved unregistered English company.

[1345] *Re Russian and English Bank* [1932] 1 Ch 663; *Re Russian Bank for Foreign Trade* [1933] Ch 745; *Re Tovarishestvo Manufactur Liudvig-Rabenek* [1944] Ch 404.

of that order does not establish that the petitioner is a creditor.[1346] In two of the three reported cases there were also undisputed creditors who wanted the companies wound up, and the court said that no harm could be done to anyone by ordering winding up.[1347] In the third case, the only other person interested in the company's English assets was the Crown if the assets were *bona vacantia* and the court added words to the winding-up order saving the Crown's rights in that respect.[1348]

Where the petitioner would be without a remedy

7.558 In *Re Russian and English Bank*,[1349] counsel said that, because the bank had been dissolved and had ceased to exist as a juristic entity capable of being sued, persons with disputed claims against the bank: 'have now no way of asserting their claim except by means of this petition'.[1350] In his judgment, Bennett J significantly altered this by saying that the petitioners 'will be without remedy unless they can proceed by way of a winding-up petition'.[1351] In fact, in all the cases discussed in 7.557, a winding-up order provided only an opportunity to assert the petitioners' disputed claims and have them adjudicated. Whether they were entitled to any remedies depended on whether their claims were eventually upheld. The 'without a remedy' idea was further tweaked by the learned editors of *Buckley on the Companies Acts* who said:

> The circumstances may in the case of a foreign company[1352] warrant a departure from the general rule that a disputed debt may not form the basis of a creditor's petition, for in these circumstances the petitioner will probably be without any other remedy.[1353]

In *Re Claybridge Shipping Co SA* Lord Denning MR said that this 'is a very wise and sensible statement', which 'should also apply to English companies if the special circumstances of the case so demand'.[1354] In *Alipour v Ary*,[1355] the Court of Appeal further developed the statement, saying that:

> A creditor's petition based on a disputed debt . . . will not be dismissed if the petitioning creditor has a good arguable case that he is a creditor[1356] and the effect of dismissal would be to deprive the petitioner of a remedy or otherwise injustice would result or for some other sufficient reason the petition should proceed.

Thus a statement about the particular circumstances of dissolved foreign corporations became a general rule about all companies, without actually winding up anything other than a dissolved foreign company.

[1346] Per Bennett J in *Re Russian and English Bank* at p 670.

[1347] *Re Russian and English Bank* at p 670; *Re Russian Bank for Foreign Trade* at p 770.

[1348] *Re Tovarishestvo Manufactur Liudvig-Rabenek* at p 413.

[1349] [1932] 1 Ch 663. See 7.557.

[1350] *Re Russian and English Bank* [1932] 1 Ch 663 at p 664.

[1351] *Re Russian and English Bank* at p 670.

[1352] There is no reference to the company being dissolved.

[1353] 12th edn (1949), p 739; 13th edn (1957), p 736; 14th edn (1981), p 850.

[1354] *Re Claybridge Shipping Co SA* [1997] 1 BCLC 572 at p 575. In *Re Claybridge Shipping Co SA* the Court of Appeal held that there was no dispute about the existence of the petitioner's debt. The case was not concerned with whether a winding-up order should be made.

[1355] [1997] 1 WLR 534 at p 546. The case was not concerned with whether a winding-up order should be made, only whether the court should decide whether a petitioner had standing.

[1356] The condition that the petitioner should have a good arguable case is also taken from *Re Claybridge Shipping Co SA* per Lord Denning MR at p 574. See 7.369–7.374.

In *Lacontha Foundation v GBI Investments Ltd*[1357] Warren J held that the statement in *Alipour* **7.559**
v Ary quoted at 7.558 must define the circumstances in which a winding-up order may be
made against any company on a disputed debt petition without deciding that the petitioner is
a creditor. In this case, Warren J held that the petitioner was a creditor and made a winding-up
order on that basis.[1358] His lordship also found that the petitioner was owed another, undisputed debt (for costs), on which the petition could have been based.[1359] However, he also stated
that he would have ordered the company to be wound up even if he had considered that there
was a bona fide dispute on substantial grounds about the existence of the debt on which the
petition was based but had not decided that dispute.[1360] Warren J gave five reasons for this:

(a) Even if the petition debt was ignored, the company was insolvent.[1361]
(b) The other undisputed debt should be taken into account, though there might have been
    difficulties with amending the petition to refer to that debt.[1362]
(c) A winding-up order would not prejudice the company, which was effectively dormant.
(d) Most importantly, the petitioner 'is without an adequate remedy unless a winding-up
    order is made'. This was because the company's assets would be dispersed if the petition
    was dismissed so that there ceased to be a provisional liquidator. Also the company's
    claims in other jurisdictions would not be pursued.
(e) A liquidator would be able to deal with another significant legal dispute involving the
    company and governed by Dutch law.

His Lordship thought that adjourning the petition and leaving the provisional liquidator **7.560**
in office, which might have been thought to be the obvious 'remedy' for the danger of dissipation of assets, did not have 'any advantage for any party or any merit as compared with
an immediate winding up'.[1363]

It is difficult to see what is 'exceptional' about these circumstances. It remains to be seen **7.561**
whether other petitioners in similar circumstances will take this case as a precedent for inviting the court to make a winding-up order without resolving a dispute about the petition debt.

Where the company is insolvent

In 1877, Jessel MR[1364] mentioned the possibility of ordering a company to be wound up on **7.562**
a creditor's petition without deciding a dispute about the petitioner's debt if it is proved that
the company is unable to pay its debts:

> It is plain there is no reasonable ground in this case for presenting a petition to wind up the
> company.

[1357] [2010] EWHC 37 (Ch), [2010] 2 BCLC 624, at [85]–[89].

[1358] At [135].

[1359] At [161].

[1360] At [167]. His Lordship did not say why he might not have decided it.

[1361] For insolvency as a justification for winding up a company regardless of the standing of the petitioner
see 7.562–7.568.

[1362] The difficulties are not specified. Clearly a petitioner who has a choice between relying on an undisputed
debt and relying on a disputed one, should petition on the undisputed debt so as to save all the costs of arguing a
disputed debt petition, even if those costs were reduced by persuading the court not to resolve the dispute.

[1363] At [166]. His Lordship did not go into detail about why a provisional liquidator could not pursue
necessary litigation to protect or get in the company's property. There was no mention of the effect on the
petitioner's undertaking in damages given on appointment of the provisional liquidator.

[1364] *Niger Merchants Co v Capper* (1877) 18 ChD 557 n at p 559 n. The case was concerned with restraining presentation of a disputed debt petition.

There is a bona fide dispute whether there is anything due from the company. When a company is solvent, the right course is to bring an action for the debt: where a company is insolvent, no doubt it is reasonable to wind up the company, even where the debt is disputed.

7.563 In *Mann v Goldstein*[1365] Ungoed-Thomas J commented on this as follows:

But this statement is tentatively phrased in an apparently unreserved judgment unreported at the time in the early period of the development of the jurisdiction, and, so far as I know, stands alone.... there is no authority, so far as I have been able to ascertain, to support the suggestion that a company might be wound up on a creditor's petition where the company is insolvent though the debt upon which the petition is founded is disputed. It seems to me neither in accordance with the requirements of the [IA 1986] nor the practice [of dismissing disputed debt petitions] recognised by Lord Greene MR [in *Re Welsh Brick Industries Ltd*[1366]] and I do not consider it justifiable to treat Sir George Jessel's observation as other than the incidental and tentative observation which it appears to me to be.

7.564 In New Zealand, North P in the Court of Appeal[1367] said that he was prepared to accept Ungoed-Thomas J's view and preferred it to an obiter statement in an earlier New Zealand case at first instance[1368] that an insolvent company may be wound up by the court on a creditor's application, even if the creditor's debt is disputed.

7.565 In Australia, before the provisions for setting aside statutory demands[1369] came into force on 23 June 1993, Ungoed-Thomas J's view was followed in one case in Queensland.[1370] But some judges in Australia took a view similar to that expressed by Jessel MR, quoted at 7.562, that an insolvent company may be wound up by the court on a creditor's application, even if the creditor's debt is disputed.[1371] That view has now been affirmed by the High Court of Australia.[1372]

7.566 In Australia, the provisions for setting aside statutory demands introduced in 1993 are intended to prevent an application being made to wind up a company by a person whose claimed debt is disputed by the company. If a creditor serves a statutory demand, an assertion that the debt does not exist must be made on an application to set aside the demand. If the assertion is not made in that way, it cannot be made in proceedings on an application for the company to be wound up unless it is material to proving that the company is solvent. As a result, an insolvent company which fails to get a statutory demand for a debt which it

---

[1365] [1968] 1 WLR 1091 at p 1095.
[1366] [1946] 2 All ER 197.
[1367] *Bateman Television Ltd v Coleridge Finance Co Ltd* [1969] NZLR 794 at pp 808–10.
[1368] *Re a Private Company* [1935] NZLR 120. The statement was obiter, as there was found to be no dispute in the case.
[1369] Corporations Act 2001 (Australia), ss 459G to 459N; see 7.237–7.245.
[1370] *Re Calsil Ltd* (1982) 6 ACLR 515.
[1371] In New South Wales: Young J in *Tecma Pty Ltd v Solah Blue Metal Pty Ltd* (1988) 14 ACLR 358 at p 361 (though, before making a winding-up order, his Honour found that there was no substantial ground for dispute in the case). Subsequent judges at first instance in New South Wales said that Young J's view was wrong. See Cohen J in *CVC Investments Pty Ltd v P and T Aviation Pty Ltd* (1989) 18 NSWLR 295 at p 302; Santow J in *Re Wilson Market Research Pty Ltd* (1996) 39 NSWLR 311 at p 320; White J in *Tokich Holdings Pty Ltd v Sheraton Constructions (NSW) Pty Ltd* [2004] NSWSC 527, 185 FLR 130. In Western Australia: Master White in *Re Synthetic Oils Pty Ltd* (1989) 1 ACSR 187 at pp 189–90 (also no substantial ground for dispute in the case before him). Master White's view was said to be wrong in a subsequent case in Western Australia (Master Ng in *Taylor Bryant Pty Ltd v Wright Critical Care Pty Ltd* (1995) 15 ACSR 564).
[1372] *Australian Securities and Investments Commission v Lanepoint Enterprises Pty Ltd* [2011] HCA 18, 244 CLR 1. The High Court did not comment on any of the cases mentioned in n 1371.

disputes set aside can be wound up on the application of the creditor despite the existence of the dispute.[1373] It even means that a company can be wound up for failing to comply with a statutory demand and failing to apply for it to be set aside where that debt is paid but another creditor is substituted whose debt is disputed.[1374] This statutory scheme provides no basis for an assumption in favour of a dismissal or stay of an application to wind up a company by reason of a dispute about whether the applicant is a creditor.[1375]

In Australia, it has also sometimes been said that it is the court's duty to wind up a company **7.567** which it has found to be insolvent. For example, in *ACP Syme Magazines Pty Ltd v TRI Automotive Components Pty Ltd*[1376] Spender J said:

> My understanding of the fundamental policy of [the Corporations Act 2001 (Australia), part 5.4] is that, where there is a company that is insolvent in the 'cash-flow' sense, that company should, as a matter of general application, apart from any special circumstances to the contrary, be wound up in the interests of the creditors and in the interests of equity between creditors.

In *Georgiou Building Pty Ltd v Perrinepod Pty Ltd*[1377] Allanson J said:

> It is neither in the public interest nor in the interest of creditors other than [the disputed creditor applying for winding up] for a company to continue to trade while insolvent: see, for example, *Emanuele v Australian Securities Commission*.[1378]

See further 7.742–7.749. **7.568**

Preventing Presentation or Continuation of a Disputed Debt Petition

Principle

If there is a dispute, on substantial grounds,[1379] about the existence of the debt on which a cred- **7.569** itor's winding-up petition is grounded, that dispute cannot normally be resolved in proceedings on the petition[1380] and the court's usual practice is to dismiss the petition.[1381] Because of this practice, on the company's application:

(a) The court will restrain presentation of a creditor's winding-up petition if it finds that the existence of the intending petitioner's claimed debt is disputed.[1382]

(b) If a creditor's petition is presented based on non-payment of a debt and the existence of the debt is disputed, the court will restrain gazetting of the petition and strike it out.[1383]

[1373] *State Bank of New South Wales v Tela Pty Ltd (No 2)* [2002] NSWSC 20, 188 ALR 702; *Braams Group Pty Ltd v Miric* [2002] NSWCA 417, 171 FLR 449; *CMA Corporation Ltd v SNL Group Pty Ltd* [2009] NSWSC 1452; *Georgiou Building Pty Ltd v Perrinepod Pty Ltd* [2012] WASC 72, 261 FLR 211.

[1374] *ACP Syme Magazines Pty Ltd v TRI Automotive Components Pty Ltd* (1997) 144 ALR 517. This decision was criticized by White J in *Tokich Holdings Pty Ltd v Sheraton Constructions (NSW) Pty Ltd* [2004] NSWSC 527, 185 FLR 130.

[1375] *Australian Securities and Investments Commission v Lanepoint Enterprises Pty Ltd* [2011] HCA 18, 244 CLR 1, at [30].

[1376] (1997) 144 ALR 517 at p 526.

[1377] [2012] WASC 72, 261 FLR 211, at [73].

[1378] (1995) 188 CLR 114.

[1379] See 7.444–7.514.

[1380] See 7.515–7.522.

[1381] See 7.529–7.535.

[1382] *New Travellers' Chambers Ltd v Cheese and Green* (1894) 70 LT 271; see 2.165–2.166.

[1383] See 3.60–3.76. *Re Gold Hill Mines* (1883) 23 ChD 210; *Re a Company (No 0013734 of 1991)* [1993] BCLC 59; *Re a Company (No 4079 of 2003)* [2003] EWHC 1879 (Ch), LTL 1/10/2003.

7.570   A dispute about the existence of a contingent debt is treated in the same way as a dispute about the existence of a present debt.[1384]

7.571   A dispute about which person is to be paid a debt is treated in the same way as a dispute about the existence of a debt.[1385]

7.572   The court prevents presentation or continuation of a disputed debt petition, where the dispute is about the existence of the debt, because the petition is an abuse of process[1386] and is bound to fail, because the petitioner lacks standing[1387] and the court's usual practice is to dismiss such a petition rather than determine the question of standing.[1388] Saying that it is an abuse of process does not necessarily mean that the petitioner is acting objectionably or improperly.[1389] In particular it does not necessarily mean that the petition has been presented for the wrongful collateral purpose of exerting pressure on the company to pay a disputed debt.[1390] The abuse of process may be unintentional if the petitioner does not know or believe that the debt is disputed on a substantial ground.[1391]

7.573   The test of whether a disputed debt petition should be prevented from proceeding is whether, at the time of hearing the application to restrain or strike out, the court can see that the petition, if it came on for a substantive hearing, would be bound to be dismissed because of a dispute about the petitioner's standing.[1392] It does not matter that the petitioner was unaware of the dispute at the time of presenting the petition.[1393] A disputed debt petition will not be dismissed unless the grounds for the dispute are sufficiently substantial.[1394] Using the test of substantiality discussed at 7.475, the test for preventing presentation or continuation of a petition has been expressed as whether the creditor has no real prospect of persuading the court at any substantive hearing that the company has no real prospect of successfully defending the creditor's claim.[1395] A petition is not bound to be dismissed at a substantive hearing, because of a dispute about the petition debt, if there is a real prospect that it will not be dismissed.[1396]

[1384]   *Re QBS Pty Ltd* [1967] QdR 218.

[1385]   *Tower Bank Ltd v Jamaica Broilers Group Ltd* (1996) 33 JLR 250; *Re a Company (No 2634 of 2002)* [2002] EWHC 944 (Ch), [2002] 2 BCLC 591.

[1386]   *Mann v Goldstein* [1968] 1 WLR 1091 at pp 1093–4 and 1098–9; *Holt Southey Ltd v Catnic Components Ltd* [1978] 1 WLR 630 at pp 631–2; *CVC Investments Pty Ltd v P and T Aviation Pty Ltd* (1989) 18 NSWLR 295 at p 302; *Permanent Custodians Ltd v Digital Enterprises Pty Ltd* (1992) 8 ACSR 542; *Pentagin Technologies International Ltd v Express Company Secretaries Ltd* (1995) *The Times*, 7 April 1995; *Re Wilson Market Research Pty Ltd* (1996) 39 NSWLR 311 at p 318; *Re Ringinfo Ltd* [2002] 1 BCLC 210 at p 220; *Re MCI WorldCom Ltd* [2002] EWHC 2436 (Ch), [2003] 1 BCLC 330, at [11]; *Argyle Crescent Ltd v Definite Finance Ltd* [2004] EWHC 3422 (Ch), LTL 29/7/2004, at [5]–[7].

[1387]   *Mann v Goldstein* [1968] 1 WLR 1091 at p 1094 (petition of a petitioner without standing is bound to fail); *Jurupakat Sdn Bhd v Kumpulan Good Earth (1973) Sdn Bhd* [1988] 3 MLJ 49 (petition of a petitioner without standing is bound to fail).

[1388]   See 7.529–7.535. For inevitable failure as an aspect of abuse of process see 2.148–2.152.

[1389]   *Argyle Crescent Ltd v Definite Finance Ltd* at [6].

[1390]   See 7.603–7.608.

[1391]   *Jacob v Vockrodt* [2007] EWHC 2403 (QB), [2007] BPIR 1568.

[1392]   *Re a Company (No 003079 of 1990)* [1991] BCLC 235 at p 237; *Greenacre Publishing Group v The Manson Group* [2000] BCC 11; *Re a Company (No 0160 of 2004)* [2004] EWHC 380 (Ch), LTL 20/2/2004.

[1393]   *Re a Company (No 003079 of 1990)* [1991] BCLC 235.

[1394]   See 7.444–7.514.

[1395]   *Re a Company (No 0160 of 2004)* [2004] EWHC 380 (Ch), LTL 20/2/2004, at [25] and [29].

[1396]   *Citigate Dewe Rogerson Ltd v Artaban Public Affairs SPRL* [2009] EWHC 1689 (Ch), [2011] 1 BCLC 625, at [43]–[44].

The petitioner may be able to persuade the court that it should, exceptionally, determine the dispute about the debt in the proceedings on the petition,[1397] in which case the petition will be allowed to proceed.[1398] Sometimes, a disputed debt petition is allowed to proceed in the expectation that another creditor may be substituted as petitioner.[1399] **7.574**

It has been said that a disputed debt petition will be allowed to proceed to a substantive hearing if there is a good arguable case that the petitioner is a creditor and the effect of dismissal would be to deprive the petitioner of a remedy or otherwise result in injustice or there is some other sufficient reason why the petition should proceed.[1400] An example is where there is a danger that the company's assets may be removed from the jurisdiction.[1401] Another example is where, if a winding-up order were to be made, the date of presentation of the petition would determine whether a suspect prior transaction could be reversed.[1402] **7.575**

If the court has already rejected an application to restrain presentation of a petition, made on the ground that the debt claimed by the petitioner is disputed, an application, on the same ground, to strike out the petition after it has been presented essentially repeats the previous proceedings and will be dismissed if the only additional evidence is material which could, with reasonable diligence, have been presented on the first application.[1403] **7.576**

In *Re Par Excellence Co Ltd*[1404] the court struck out a disputed debt petition, apparently of its own motion, on an application (at which the company was not represented) for an adjournment of the hearing. **7.577**

If a creditor of a company cannot petition for the company to be wound up, because of a dispute or cross-claim, the creditor also cannot petition for the winding up or bankruptcy of a guarantor of the debt.[1405] **7.578**

In Australia, if a statutory demand is served for a debt, an assertion that the debt is disputed, or that there is a cross-claim, must be made in an application to set aside the demand. It cannot be made after a winding-up application has been presented unless it is material to proving that the company is solvent.[1406] It follows that if such an assertion has not been raised in an application to set aside the demand, the court will not prevent a winding-up application proceeding if the company is insolvent.[1407] **7.579**

[1397] See 7.523–7.527.

[1398] *Re Claybridge Shipping Co SA* [1997] 1 BCLC 572; *Success Sea Tours Pty Ltd v Wallo Pty Ltd* [1988] WAR 41; *Ocean City Ltd v Southern Oceanic Hotels Pty Ltd* (1993) 10 ACSR 483.

[1399] See 7.587–7.590.

[1400] *Alipour v Ary* [1997] 1 WLR 534 at p 546, interpreting what was said by Lord Denning MR in *Re Claybridge Shipping Co SA* [1997] 1 BCLC 572 at pp 574–5.

[1401] *Re Claybridge Shipping Co SA* per Lord Denning at p 575. His Lordship did not identify how the pendency of a winding-up petition would help in this respect. Appointment of a provisional liquidator might be considered.

[1402] *Capital Landfill (Restoration) Ltd v William Stockler and Co* (5 September 1991 Court of Appeal (Civil Division) Transcript No 859 of 1991) (setting aside a floating charge under IA 1986, s 245).

[1403] *Re Portedge Ltd* [1997] BCC 23; [1998] BCC 556 sub nom *RWH Enterprises Ltd v Portedge Ltd*.

[1404] [1990] 2 HKLR 277.

[1405] *Remblance v Octagon Assets Ltd* [2009] EWCA Civ 581, [2010] Bus LR 119.

[1406] Corporations Act 2001 (Australia), s 459S.

[1407] *Macks v Valamios Produce Pty Ltd* [2003] NSWSC 993, 47 ACSR 583.

7.580   In *Club Marconi of Bossley Park Social Recreation Sporting Centre Ltd v Rennat Constructions Pty Ltd*[1408] (in which the argument was about the size rather than existence of the debt) the *company* was required, as a condition of the court restraining a disputed creditor from petitioning for the winding up of the company, to undertake to commence proceedings within 14 days to have the dispute determined unless the creditor started proceedings before then.

Other ways of treating disputed debt petitions

7.581   It is not usually appropriate to adjourn a disputed debt petition with liberty to apply, for the reasons set out at 7.548,[1409] though this was done in *Bank of New Zealand v Rada Corporation Ltd*.[1410]

7.582   Restraint of gazetting only may be an appropriate temporary measure. For example, in *Re a Company (No 007020 of 1996)*[1411] a winding-up petition had been presented by a person who had obtained a default judgment against the company in proceedings after having a stay on the proceedings under the Arbitration Act 1950, s 4 (now the Arbitration Act 1996, s 9), lifted. Chadwick J indicated that, as the company had obtained a stay of execution of the judgment, he would have restrained advertisement of the petition while the company sought leave to appeal against removal of the stay on the proceedings in which the judgment had been obtained.

7.583   If the court only restrains gazetting of the petition, the injunction will not be lifted merely because the petitioner amends the petition to add another ground for a winding-up order.[1412]

7.584   If the court finds that there is no substantial dispute concerning a petition which has been presented, it must not restrain gazetting.[1413]

7.585   If the court finds that there is no substantial dispute, but the petition has not yet been presented, it may restrain presentation for a short time to allow the company to pay the debt, at least where the court is satisfied that the company can pay.[1414]

7.586   In some cases the court has allowed a petition to continue so that another creditor can be substituted as petitioner.[1415]

Solvency of company normally irrelevant

7.587   A disputed debt petition, where the dispute is about the existence of the debt, is prevented from proceeding even if the company sought to be wound up may be insolvent.[1416] This reflects the practice which would be followed at a substantive hearing of the petition of dismissing it without hearing evidence from the petitioner of the company's insolvency.[1417]

[1408] (1980) 4 ACLR 883.
[1409] *Re GSA Controls Pty Ltd* (1990) 1 ACSR 773.
[1410] (1989) 5 NZCLC 66,221.
[1411] [1998] 2 BCLC 54.
[1412] *Mutual Home Loan Fund of Australia Ltd v Smith* (1978) 3 ACLR 589.
[1413] *James Dolman and Co Ltd v Pedley* [2003] EWCA Civ 1686, [2004] BCC 504.
[1414] *Orion Media Marketing Ltd v Media Brook Ltd* [2002] 1 BCLC 184 at [12] and [36], a cross-claim case.
[1415] See 7.587–7.590.
[1416] *Mann v Goldstein* [1968] 1 WLR 1091; *Re Record Tennis Centres Ltd* [1991] BCC 509 at p 514; *Re a Company (No 00212 of 1995)* (1995) *The Times*, 7 April 1995; *Mobikom Sdn Bhd v Inmiss Communications Sdn Bhd* [2007] 3 MLJ 316 at [13]. But see *Re R A Foulds Ltd* (1986) 2 BCC 99,269 discussed at 7.588.
[1417] See 7.529–7.535.

If a company is seeking to prevent presentation or continuation of a disputed debt petition, there is no onus on it to prove its solvency, if the dispute is about the existence of the petition debt.[1418] If the company is insolvent, it is a matter for a creditor, established as such, or one of the other persons who have standing to petition, to bring the matter to court. Hoffmann J expressed unease about this in *Re R A Foulds Ltd*.[1419] For alternative views in Australia, see 7.609–7.612. **7.588**

In some cases the court has allowed a disputed debt petition to continue, where the dispute is about the existence of the debt, because the company appears to be insolvent and it is assumed that another creditor will wish to be substituted as petitioner.[1420] The company's application to prevent the petition proceeding may be dismissed[1421] or, perhaps better, adjourned to the hearing of the petition.[1422] In *Robinson Cox v Woodings*[1423] the court refused to validate[1424] expenditure by an insolvent company on legal fees in connection with opposing a disputed debt petition after another creditor was substituted as petitioner and a winding-up order was made. **7.589**

If a company's application to prevent a disputed debt petition proceeding is dismissed, without deciding the dispute about the debt, the company is not prevented, through issue estoppel, from disputing the debt in other proceedings.[1425] It may be different if the court dismissing the company's application to prevent the petition proceeding makes express findings relating to the disputed debt.[1426] It seems, for example, that in *Re Adelaide Holdings Ltd*,[1427] in which the court allowed the petitioner to proceed, the court determined the question of law in the dispute (though it did not make an order requiring payment of the debt as would have been the result of determining the dispute in an action). **7.590**

Neglect to comply with statutory demand irrelevant

If the existence of a debt is disputed, it is irrelevant to an application to prevent a petition based on the debt from being presented or proceeding that the company has not complied with a statutory demand for the disputed amount claimed. The fact that the claim is disputed means that the company has a reasonable excuse for not complying with the statutory **7.591**

[1418] *Stonegate Securities Ltd v Gregory* [1980] Ch 576 at pp 584–5; *CVC Investments Pty Ltd v P and T Aviation Pty Ltd* (1989) 18 NSWLR 295; *Mine Exc Pty Ltd v Henderson Drilling Services Pty Ltd* (1989) 1 ACSR 118; *Re Bond Corporation Holdings Ltd* (1990) 1 WAR 465; *Avery v Worldwide Testing Services Pty Ltd* (1990) 2 ACSR 834; *Re Wilson Market Research Pty Ltd* (1996) 39 NSWLR 311; see also *Re Kolback Group Ltd* (1991) 4 ACSR 165 where the petition was by a contributory.

[1419] (1986) 2 BCC 99,269 at pp 99,274–5.

[1420] *Community Development Pty Ltd v Engwirda Construction Co* [1968] QdR 541; *Re R A Foulds Ltd* (1986) 2 BCC 99,269; *Vertex Trading Sàrl v Infinity Holdings Ltd* [2009] EWHC 461 (Ch), LTL 30/10/2009; see also *Commissioners of Customs and Excise v Anglo German Breweries Ltd* [2002] EWHC 2458 (Ch), [2003] BTC 5021, at [73] and [107].

[1421] As in *Re R A Foulds Ltd* and *Vertex Trading Sàrl v Infinity Holdings Ltd*.

[1422] *Re Allco Newsteel Pty Ltd* (1990) 2 ACSR 609.

[1423] (1993) 11 ACSR 351.

[1424] Under the Australian equivalent of IA 1986, s 127.

[1425] *Brinds Ltd v Chapmans Ltd* (1985) 10 ACLR 97; *Exchange Finance Co Ltd v Lemmington Holdings Ltd (No 2)* [1984] 2 NZLR 247; *Australian Mid-Eastern Club Ltd v Elbakht* (1988) 13 NSWLR 697; *Nickel Rim Mines Ltd v Horizon Pacific Ltd* (1991) 4 ACSR 750.

[1426] *Australian Mid-Eastern Club Ltd v Yassim* (1989) 1 ACSR 399 at p 402; *Just Juice Corporation Pty Ltd v Murrayland Fruit Juice Pty Ltd* (1990) 2 ACSR 541 at p 543.

[1427] [1982] 1 NSWLR 167.

demand and so has not 'neglected' to comply with it, and so is not deemed to be unable to pay its debts.[1428] It appears to be unnecessary to say[1429] that the statutory demand is invalid.

Disputed amount or timing; partially disputed debt

7.592 If the fact that a company is indebted to a creditor is not disputed, but there is a dispute about the amount to be paid and the creditor can prove the company's inability to pay its debts otherwise than by virtue of non-payment of the whole sum claimed by the creditor, then the creditor will not be restrained from petitioning.[1430] If a company does not dispute its potential liability, but alleges it is a future liability, the creditor will not be restrained from presenting a petition to wind up the company.[1431] But a petition which claims that a debt is presently due when in fact the time for payment is disputed will be prevented from proceeding because the court will not determine the dispute in the proceedings on the petition.[1432]

7.593 In practice it may be difficult to distinguish between a dispute about existence and a dispute about quantum. In *Re a Company (No 003729 of 1982)*[1433] the amount that the company owed the petitioner was in dispute at the time of presentation of the petition. Six weeks after the petition was presented the company paid to the petitioner an amount which the company claimed was all that was owed to the petitioner but the petitioner claimed that over £10,000 was still owing. On the company's application, the petition was struck out. Mervyn Davies J noted that the petitioner's only evidence of the company's inability to pay its debts was its non-compliance with a statutory demand for the whole of the petitioner's alleged debt but it had been deposed on behalf of the company that it was solvent. In *Re R A Foulds Ltd*[1434] the company had various cross-claims against the petitioner which totalled less than the petitioner's debt and had offered to pay the undisputed balance. Evidence produced for the purpose of obtaining a validation order for continuation of the company's business showed that it was insolvent. Hoffmann J allowed the petition to continue on the assumption that another creditor would wish to be substituted as petitioner.

7.594 In *Re Javelin Promotions Ltd*,[1435] the court quantified the undisputed part of the petition debt and adjourned the petition for ten days to allow the company to pay the undisputed amount.

7.595 *Chip Yew Brick Works Sdn Bhd v Chang Heer Enterprise Sdn Bhd*[1436] seems to be inconsistent with these cases. In it, the petitioner claimed M$127,159 from the company; the company admitted owing M$60,580 and said that it was ready and willing to pay this sum and was

---

[1428] *Re London and Paris Banking Corporation* (1874) LR 19 Eq 444; *Re a Company (No 003729 of 1982)* [1984] 1 WLR 1090.

[1429] As was said in *Processed Sand Pty Ltd v Thiess Contractors Pty Ltd* [1983] 1 NSWLR 384.

[1430] *New Travellers' Chambers Ltd v Cheese and Green* (1894) 70 LT 271 per Kekewich J at p 272; *Hixgold Pty Ltd v FCT* (1992) 8 ACSR 607; *Re Pendigo Ltd* [1996] 2 BCLC 64; *Truck and Machinery Sales Ltd v Marubeni Komatsu Ltd* [1996] 1 IR 12; *Renshaw Birch Ltd v Marquet* [1998] BPIR 399; *Angel Group Ltd v British Gas Trading Ltd* [2012] EWHC 2702 (Ch), [2013] BCC 265.

[1431] *Chapmans Ltd v Brinds Ltd* (1985) 9 ACLR 943.

[1432] *Stonegate Securities Ltd v Gregory* [1980] Ch 576 per Buckley LJ at pp 586–7 disapproving *Holt Southey Ltd v Catnic Components Ltd* [1978] 1 WLR 630.

[1433] [1984] 1 WLR 1090.

[1434] (1986) 2 BCC 99,269.

[1435] [2003] EWHC 1932 (Ch), LTL 30/9/2003.

[1436] [1988] 2 MLJ 447.

solvent. Nevertheless it was held that the petition should be allowed to proceed because the undisputed amount had not in fact been paid.

Cheque given for disputed debt dishonoured

In *Re a Company (No 0010656 of 1990)*[1437] a cheque was given for a disputed petition debt, **7.596** but dishonoured. The court refused to treat the petition as one based on an undisputed debt under the principle that a court hearing a claim for payment of a cheque must not consider a cross-claim or defence, apart from a defence concerning the validity of the cheque (the autonomy principle).[1438] The petition debt was payment for printing work and it was found that the cheque had been given 'carelessly' before discovering defects in the work which gave rise to the dispute about the debt.[1439] However, in *Re Javelin Promotions Ltd*[1440] the court approached a petition based on dishonoured cheques as if the autonomy principle applied, though this did not make any difference to the outcome, because it found that the debt was only partially disputed.

Costs

Orders as to costs of proceedings for preventing a petition being presented or proceeding **7.597** are at the discretion of the court but will normally follow the event.[1441] The court should not order that the costs of the application are to be costs in the proceedings in which the claim to the petition debt is determined, or reserved to a hearing in that claim, because that would encourage persons who claim disputed debts from companies to treat a winding-up petition as a first stage in litigating the claim.[1442] This principle should not be affected by the likelihood that in subsequent proceedings evidence given on the application will be disbelieved.[1443] The principle will not apply if the application would have been dismissed but for the potentially false evidence and that evidence was not revealed until after the petition was presented.[1444]

A person who has threatened to present a winding-up petition which would be an abuse **7.598** of process is adopting a 'high risk strategy' and may be ordered to pay the company's costs of restraining presentation of the petition on the indemnity basis.[1445] In *Re a Company (No 00751 of 1992)*[1446] an indemnity costs order was made though there was no evidence whether the company was solvent or not.[1447] The indemnity basis is not appropriate where

---

[1437] [1991] BCLC 464.

[1438] See 7.638–7.641.

[1439] See also *Vecta Software Corporation Ltd v Despec Supplies Ltd* [2004] EWHC 3151 (Ch), LTL 19/7/2004.

[1440] [2003] EWHC 1932 (Ch), LTL 30/9/2003.

[1441] *Cannon Screen Entertainment Ltd v Handmade Films (Distributors) Ltd* (1988) 5 BCC 207; *Re Pendigo Ltd* [1996] 2 BCLC 64; *Re a Company (No 007356 of 1998)* [2000] BCC 214.

[1442] *Re Fernforest Ltd* [1990] BCLC 693; *GlaxosmithKline Export Ltd v UK (Aid) Ltd* [2003] EWHC 1383 (Ch), [2004] BPIR 528.

[1443] *Re a Debtor (No 620 of 1997)* [1999] BPIR 89; *GlaxosmithKline Export Ltd v UK (Aid) Ltd* [2003] EWHC 1383 (Ch), [2004] BPIR 528. See also *Papanicola v Sandhu* [2011] EWHC 1431 (QB), [2011] 2 BCLC 811.

[1444] *Sykes and Son Ltd v Teamforce Labour Ltd* [2012] EWHC 1005 (Ch), [2013] Bus LR 106, in which costs were reserved until after the conclusion of proceedings for determining the petitioner's debt.

[1445] *Re a Company (No 0012209 of 1991)* [1992] 1 WLR 351; *Baillieu Knight Frank (NSW) Pty Ltd v Ted Manny Real Estate Pty Ltd* (1992) 30 NSWLR 359; *Re a Company (No 2597 of 2003)* [2003] EWHC 1484 (Ch), [2003] 2 BCLC 346; *Re Sat-Elite Ltd* [2003] EWHC 2990 (Ch), LTL 17/11/2003; *Baker Hughes Ltd v CCG Contracting International Ltd* 2005 SC 65.

[1446] [1992] BCLC 869.

[1447] See P Friedman, 'Countering the abuse of the winding-up petition' (1992) 136 SJ 999.

both parties have acted bona fide.[1448] The court may refuse to order assessment on the indemnity basis if warning of the application was not given to the petitioner or potential petitioner.[1449] In *Re a Company (No 003689 of 1998)*[1450] (in which a claimant was ordered not to petition on the basis of a statutory demand for a disputed debt), the court ordered the claimant to pay the company's costs, which were to be assessed forthwith. A similar order was made in *London Bridge Software Ltd v Anite Group plc*.[1451]

7.599 Usually the crucial question is whether the creditor was, or should have been, aware of the dispute and whether, on being made aware of the dispute, offered an adequate undertaking. If there is a dispute on substantial grounds about the existence of the debt, the claimant should undertake not to present a petition at all until the dispute is resolved: an undertaking to give the company 14 days' notice of intention to present a petition is not adequate.[1452] If a petition has been presented, an undertaking to give the company notice before gazetting it, so that the company may apply for an injunction if so advised, is not adequate.[1453]

7.600 In *Cannon Screen Entertainment Ltd v Handmade Films (Distributors) Ltd*[1454] Warner J rejected the idea that when a company is served with a statutory demand for a debt which it disputes, it must give the creditor notice of the grounds of the dispute before applying to restrain presentation of a petition. It would not necessarily be possible to do this in the 21 days before a petition can be presented. Nevertheless it was pointed out in *Re Merc Property Ltd*[1455] (a wasted costs application; see 7.671–7.672) that a company cannot claim that a disputed debt petition has been pursued unreasonably if it has not promptly informed the petitioner that the debt is disputed and set out the nature of the dispute.

7.601 The court has made no order as to costs in cases where the creditor was not aware of the dispute until after serving a statutory demand and offered an undertaking not to present a petition on becoming aware.[1456]

7.602 If a creditor of a company is ordered to pay the company's costs of opposing a disputed debt petition and subsequently takes other proceedings to recover the debt, the court in which those other proceedings are taken may order them to be stayed until the winding-up costs are paid, so as to prevent a further abuse of process.[1457]

Alternative basis for preventing presentation or continuation of a petition:
improper pressure to pay a disputed debt

7.603 It is an abuse of process to petition for the compulsory winding up of a company for the improper purpose of pressurizing the company to abandon a dispute over a debt and

---

[1448] *Re a Company* [2005] EWHC 1622 (Ch), LTL 29/6/2005.
[1449] *Re Realstar Ltd* [2007] EWHC 2921 (Ch), [2008] BPIR 1391.
[1450] (1998) *The Times*, 7 October 1998.
[1451] [2002] EWHC 297 (Ch), LTL 5/4/2002.
[1452] *Sleetree Ltd v Reston Ltd* [2006] EWHC 2489 (Ch), LTL 3/11/2006.
[1453] *Re a Company (No 2597 of 2003)* [2003] EWHC 1484 (Ch), [2003] 2 BCLC 346.
[1454] (1988) 5 BCC 207.
[1455] [1999] 2 BCLC 286.
[1456] *Re Druce and Co* [1993] BCLC 964; *Sleetree Ltd v Reston Ltd* [2006] EWHC 2489 (Ch), LTL 3/11/2006.
[1457] *Investment Invoice Financing Ltd v Limehouse Board Mills Ltd* [2006] EWCA Civ 9, [2006] 1 WLR 985.

pay it[1458] or provide security for it.[1459] A winding-up petition must not be used to force a company to pay a debt without having its liability to do so properly established.[1460] 'The Companies Court must not be used . . . as a means of bringing improper pressure to bear on a company.'[1461]

The court will restrain threatened presentation of a petition brought for such an improper **7.604** purpose.[1462]

In *Re Gold Hill Mines*[1463] the petitioner claimed to be owed a debt of £15 which the company **7.605** disputed. The petitioner had no evidence that the company was unable to pay its debts. Jessel MR said, at p 213: 'this petition can only be correctly described as a scandalous abuse of the process of the court'.

The mere fact that a company disputes the debt on which a creditor's petition to wind up the **7.606** company is based does not show that the petition was presented for the improper purpose of pressurizing the company to abandon the dispute and pay the debt.[1464]

The fact that the petitioner has offered to abandon the petition and instead issue a claim to **7.607** recover the debt from the company, provided it is assured that the company is solvent and able to pay the debt, does not show that the petition is an abuse of process.[1465]

The fact that the petitioner has already sued for payment of the debt and has been refused **7.608** summary judgment may show that the petition is an abuse of process.[1466]

Alternative views in Australia

In Australia, dicta in *Cadiz Waterworks Co v Barnett*;[1467] *Niger Merchants Co v Capper*[1468] **7.609** and *Cercle Restaurant Castiglione Co v Lavery*[1469] have been taken to mean that the jurisdiction to prevent a disputed debt petition proceeding is based on the irreparable injury which such a petition might do to a solvent company.[1470] On this view, if it appears to the court

---

[1458] *Re London Wharfing and Warehousing Co Ltd* (1865) 35 Beav 37; *Cadiz Waterworks Co v Barnett* (1874) LR 19 Eq 182; *Re Gold Hill Mines* (1883) 23 ChD 210; *Re Scott Plumbers Ltd* (1984) 2 NZCLC 99,184; *Re a Company (No 0012209 of 1991)* [1992] 1 WLR 351. For examples see *Re Bond Corporation Holdings Ltd* (1990) 1 WAR 465; *Pacific Communication Rentals Pty Ltd v Walker* (1993) 12 ACSR 287; *Daily Freightways Ltd v Rio Beverages Ltd* [1994] MCLR 289; *Datuk Mohd Sari bin Datuk Hj Nuar v Idris Hydraulic (M) Bhd* [1997] 5 MLJ 377; *Re a Company (No 004601 of 1997)* [1998] 2 BCLC 111.
[1459] *Moose Holdings Ltd v Kendall and Waller Ltd* (1985) 3 NZCLC 99,520.
[1460] *Re Public Works and Contract Co Ltd* (1888) 4 TLR 670.
[1461] *Re Lympne Investments Ltd* [1972] 1 WLR 523 per Megarry J at p 527.
[1462] *Cadiz Waterworks Co v Barnett* (1874) LR 19 Eq 182; *Niger Merchants Co v Capper* (1877) 18 ChD 557 n; *John Brown and Co v Keeble* [1879] WN 173; *Cercle Restaurant Castiglione Co v Lavery* (1881) 18 ChD 555; *Soverina Pty Ltd v Jackson and Associates Pty Ltd* (1987) 12 ACLR 693; *Pembinaan Lian Keong Sdn Bhd v Yip Fook Thai* [2005] 5 MLJ 786.
[1463] (1883) 23 ChD 210.
[1464] *Liverpool Cement Renderers (Aust) Pty Ltd v Landmarks Constructions (NSW) Pty Ltd* (1996) 19 ACSR 411; *Re Lummus Agricultural Services Ltd* [2001] 1 BCLC 137.
[1465] *London Bridge Software Ltd v Anite Group plc* [2002] EWHC 297 (Ch), LTL 5/4/2002.
[1466] *Ansa Teknik (M) Sdn Bhd v Cygal Sdn Bhd* [1989] 2 MLJ 423.
[1467] (1874) LR 19 Eq 182. Cited in *Charles Forte Investments Ltd v Amanda* [1964] Ch 240 (which concerned a contributory's petition) by Willmer LJ at pp 251–2.
[1468] (1877) 18 ChD 557 n.
[1469] (1881) 18 ChD 555.
[1470] *Community Development Pty Ltd v Engwirda Construction Co* [1968] QdR 541 at p 547; *Fortuna Holdings Pty Ltd v Deputy Federal Commissioner of Taxation* [1978] VR 83; *Altarama Ltd v Camp* (1980) 5 ACLR 513 at p 519; *L and D Audio Acoustics Pty Ltd v Pioneer Electronic Australia Pty Ltd* (1982) 7 ACLR

that the company is insolvent, the petition will be allowed to proceed.[1471] Some Australian courts have said that 'there should be evidence that the company is solvent' before the court will prevent a petition from proceeding.[1472] Others have said that the company's proof of its solvency is a 'strong factor to take into account' but that neither party has an obligation to prove solvency or insolvency and, in the absence of evidence, the court should presume the company to be solvent.[1473] It has also been said that if the company raises a dispute about the petitioner's debt, the court has a duty to decide whether or not the dispute should be determined in the winding-up proceedings.[1474]

7.610 Then in *CVC Investments Pty Ltd v P and T Aviation Pty Ltd*[1475] Cohen J in the Supreme Court of New South Wales said that the underlying reason for the court preventing a disputed debt petition proceeding against a company is that such a petition is an abuse of process, which the court will prevent regardless of the solvency of the company involved. In the Supreme Court of Western Australia, Ipp J said that not all disputed debt petitions are an abuse of process, and the principles governing the grant of an injunction to prevent a disputed debt petition proceeding if it is not an abuse of process are the same as those governing interim injunctions generally.[1476] In Australia (where the approach to interim injunctions set out in *American Cyanamid Co v Ethicon Ltd*[1477] has not been adopted) those principles include a rule that the applicant for the injunction must show that it will suffer substantial and irreparable damage if the action sought to be restrained proceeds. An insolvent company is unlikely to be able to show that presenting and giving notice of an application for its winding up will cause it the requisite degree of damage. Accordingly there is an onus on the company to prove its solvency.[1478]

7.611 In *Jingellic Minerals NL v Beach Petroleum NL*,[1479] on appeal it was found that the company sought to be wound up by an applicant whose debt was disputed was solvent and an order dismissing the winding-up application was substituted for an order adjourning it which had been made at first instance on the basis that the company was insolvent.

---

180 at pp 182–3; *Rothwells Ltd v Nommack (No 100) Pty Ltd* (1988) 13 ACLR 421. Irreparable damage was also mentioned in the Malaysian case of *Ng Kong You v MBf Property Services Sdn Bhd* [2001] 5 MLJ 122. In Singapore, irreparable harm was said to be 'only one factor, albeit a significant factor' that a court takes into account (*Metalform Asia Pte Ltd v Holland Leedon Pte Ltd* [2007] SGCA 6, [2007] 2 SLR 268, at [59]).

[1471] *Community Development Pty Ltd v Engwirda Construction Co*; *Fortuna Holdings Pty Ltd v Deputy Federal Commissioner of Taxation*.

[1472] *General Welding and Construction Co (Qld) Pty Ltd v International Rigging (Aust) Pty Ltd* (1983) 8 ACLR 307 per McPherson J at p 308; see also *Metal Protectives Co Pty Ltd v Site Welders Pty Ltd* [1968] 1 NSWR 106 and *Grant Matich and Co Pty Ltd v Toyo Menka Kaisha Ltd* (1978) 3 ACLR 375.

[1473] *Transport and Property Holdings Pty Ltd v Buntine* (1982) 63 FLR 67; *Westeq Ltd v Challenger Mining Corp NL* (1988) 13 ACLR 627.

[1474] *Detroit Finance Corporation Ltd v Camillo* (1979) 4 ACLR 509.

[1475] (1989) 18 NSWLR 295.

[1476] *Mine Exc Pty Ltd v Henderson Drilling Services Pty Ltd* (1989) 1 ACSR 118; *Re Bond Corporation Holdings Ltd* (1990) 1 WAR 465; *Forsayth NL v Silver* (1990) 2 ACSR 595; *Kopai Holdings Pty Ltd v R and I Bank of Western Australia Ltd* (1993) 12 ACSR 193. See also *Alperin Technical Pty Ltd v ACI Australia Ltd* (1990) 2 ACSR 234 (Victoria); *United Reefs NL v Cooks Construction Pty Ltd* [1995] 1 QdR 96 (Queensland); *Mooloolaba Development Corporation Ltd v Evans Harch Constructions Pty Ltd* (1992) 33 FCR 524 (Federal Court); *Re WU Investments Pty Ltd* (1993) 10 ACSR 636 (Western Australia), in which only advertisement of the petition was restrained; *Argyll Park Thoroughbreds Pty Ltd v Glen Pacific Pty Ltd* (1993) 11 ACSR 1 (Federal Court).

[1477] [1975] AC 396.

[1478] *Argyll Park Thoroughbreds Pty Ltd v Glen Pacific Pty Ltd* (1993) 11 ACSR 1.

[1479] (1991) 56 SASR 532.

In Australia, the disagreements about the correct approach to disputed debt petitions have **7.612** become less important since the introduction of the system for applying to set aside statutory demands.[1480]

Alternative views in New Zealand

The practice of not allowing a disputed debt petition to proceed merely because the exist- **7.613** ence of the petitioner's debt is disputed is not followed in New Zealand. There, it has been said that a disputed debt petition should be prevented from proceeding only if 'presenting or proceeding with a petition savours of unfairness or undue pressure'.[1481] This would seem to be the same as the abuse of process concept considered at 7.603–7.608, with the addition of unfairness.

In *Taxi Trucks Ltd v Nicholson*, the Court of Appeal added[1482] that the company also had **7.614** to show that it would be 'unfair' to allow the dispute over the debt to be determined in the winding-up proceedings rather than by action. In *Monaco Motors (Auckland) Ltd v Burrett and Veitch Ltd*[1483] presentation of a petition by a person whose claim was disputed was described as improper pressure to pay the disputed debt and was restrained. In *Re Profcom Systems Ltd*[1484] there was a bona fide dispute about the debt and no evidence apart from non-compliance with a statutory demand for the disputed debt that the company was in any financial difficulty: it seems that this was considered to be a case of improper pressure.

In other New Zealand cases on disputed debt petitions, the court has said that the reason for **7.615** preventing the petition before it from proceeding was simply that the dispute about the debt should be resolved by action rather than in the winding-up proceedings, and the unfairness or undue pressure test was not mentioned.[1485]

In New Zealand, if the fact that a company is indebted to a creditor is not disputed but there is **7.616** a dispute about the amount to be paid, the creditor will not be restrained from petitioning even if the only means of proving the company's inability to pay its debts is by virtue of non-payment of the sum claimed by the creditor.[1486]

[1480] See 7.237–7.245. See M Dorney, 'Injunction to restrain the filing of a summons to wind up a company' (1992) 10 C & SLJ 131.

[1481] *Exchange Finance Co Ltd v Lemmington Holdings Ltd* [1984] 2 NZLR 242; see, for example, *New Plymouth Hotels Holdings Ltd v Fletcher Development and Construction Ltd* (1986) 3 NZCLC 99,627; *Scantech Corporation Ltd v Designforces Holdings Ltd* (1986) 3 NZCLC 99,860; *H H Brandon Ltd v Laker* (1986) 3 NZCLC 99,908; *Goldcorp Holdings Ltd v Greedus* (1988) 2 BCR 468; *Auto Instrument Services Ltd v Thomas G Faria Corporation* (1988) 3 BCR 12; *Taxi Trucks Ltd v Nicholson* [1989] 2 NZLR 297; *Chow Mein Fashions v Farry's Ltd* (1989) 3 BCR 425; *Bank of New Zealand v Rada Corporation Ltd* (1989) 5 NZCLC 66,221; *Hewlett-Packard (NZ) Ltd v Compusales Software and Hardware Ltd* (1990) 5 NZCLC 66,281; *Booth v Walker Foods International Ltd* [1992] MCLR 226; *Plumbing and Heating Services Ltd v J H Willson Ltd* (1992) 6 NZCLC 67,674; *Devon Cottages Ltd v P and P Savage Ltd* [1993] MCLR 49; *Forms First Ltd v Front Page Marketing Ltd* [1993] MCLR 199.

[1482] At p 299.

[1483] (1976) 1 BCR 69.

[1484] (1988) 4 NZCLC 64,505.

[1485] *Binmasta Disposals (1976) Ltd v Cameron* (1977) 1 BCR 116; *Provincial Steel Merchants Ltd v Fletcher Industries Ltd* (1984) 2 NZCLC 99,081, which was decided before *Exchange Finance Co Ltd v Lemmington Holdings Ltd*; *Microage Holdings Ltd v Powell Hutton McRea Advertising Ltd* (1986) 3 NZCLC 100,060; *Ngati Kahu Trust Board v Southern Lights Floral Exports Ltd* [1994] MCLR 450.

[1486] *Re Hart Systems Ltd* (1985) 3 NZCLC 99,504; *Re Khyber Pass Outdoor Centre Ltd* (1986) 3 NZCLC 99,756.

7.617 In New Zealand the rules of court specifically provide for staying proceedings on a winding-up application.[1487] See, for example, *McNeil v Blockley Transport (1990) Ltd*,[1488] in which it was found that there was no bona fide dispute. A stay can be lifted if it is shown that circumstances have changed.[1489]

Cross-claim against Petitioner

Cross-claim greater than petitioner's claim

7.618 If a creditor of a company presents a petition for the compulsory winding up of the company, but the company claims from the petitioner a sum which is greater than or equal to the petitioner's debt, or falls short of it by £750 or less,[1490] the petition will be treated in the same way as a disputed debt petition.[1491]

7.619 Unless there are special circumstances,[1492] the petition will be prevented from proceeding[1493] or, at the hearing of the petition, it will be dismissed,[1494] or, possibly,[1495] adjourned.[1496] It is wrong to order adjournment for a fixed period to give time for payment of the petitioner's debt:[1497] there must either be adjournment until the company's cross-claim is settled or dismissal of the petition.

7.620 If presentation of a cross-claim petition is threatened, it will be restrained.[1498]

7.621 No restrictions have been imposed on what circumstances, provided they are material, are capable of being special circumstances justifying making a winding-up order despite a cross-claim.[1499] A court which finds that there are special circumstances must explain what those circumstances are and why they justify making a winding-up order despite a cross-claim.[1500]

[1487] Judicature Act 1908 (New Zealand), sch 2 (High Court Rules), r 31.11 (formerly r 700K).

[1488] [1991] MCLR 145.

[1489] *Australian Guarantee Corporation (NZ) Ltd v Frater Williams and Co Ltd* [1994] MCLR 1.

[1490] See 7.392–7.397.

[1491] *Re Portman Provincial Cinemas Ltd* [1999] 1 WLR 157; *Re LHF Wools Ltd* [1970] Ch 27; *Re Bayoil SA* [1999] 1 WLR 147; *Malta Timber Products Sdn Bhd v N and P Constructions Sdn Bhd* [2004] 1 MLJ 119; *Metalform Asia Pte Ltd v Holland Leedon Pte Ltd* [2007] SGCA 6, [2007] 2 SLR 268; *Re WMG (Toughening) Ltd* [2003] IESC 4, [2003] 1 IR 389.

[1492] See 7.631–7.643.

[1493] *Re a Company* (1983) 1 BCC 98,901.

[1494] *Re Portman Provincial Cinemas Ltd* [1999] 1 WLR 157; *Re Humberstone Jersey Ltd* (1977) 74 LS Gaz 711; *Cruisair Ltd v CMC Aviation Ltd 1978* (2) ALR Comm 47; *Re Goode Concrete* [2012] IEHC 439; see 7.528–7.540.

[1495] See 7.541–7.549.

[1496] *Re LHF Wools Ltd*, in which the company had ceased to be a going concern; *Ng Tai Tuan v Chng Gim Huat Pte Ltd* [1991] 1 MLJ 338; *Australian Telephone Distributors Pty Ltd v Golden Always Ltd* [1996] 2 HKLR 325.

[1497] *Cruisair Ltd v CMC Aviation Ltd* 1978 (2) ALR Comm 47.

[1498] *Re a Company (No 002272 of 2004)* [2005] EWHC 422 (Ch), [2005] BPIR 1251, in which permission to apply was given in case the cross-claim was not prosecuted; *Re Pan Interiors Ltd* [2005] EWHC 3241 (Ch), LTL 14/7/2005, at [37]; *Metalform Asia Pte Ltd v Holland Leedon Pte Ltd* [2007] SGCA 6, [2007] 2 SLR 268; *Moorside Investments Ltd v DAG Construction Ltd* [2007] EWHC 3490 (Ch), LTL 18/12/2007.

[1499] *Atlantic and General Investment Trust Ltd v Richbell Information Services Inc* [2000] 2 BCLC 778 at p 791 per Judge Weeks QC sitting as a High Court judge. See 7.631–7.643.

[1500] *Re Bayoil SA* [1999] 1 WLR 147 at p 156.

As with a disputed debt petition, a cross-claim petition may be restrained, struck out or **7.622**
dismissed if it is an abuse of process.[1501]

What the company must prove
The company has the burden of proving:[1502]   **7.623**

(a) that its cross-claim is larger than the admitted debt of the petitioner, or falls short of it
    by £750 or less;[1503]
(b) that its cross-claim is either undisputed or is based on substantial grounds.[1504] It is
    unnecessary to prove that the cross-claim must succeed.[1505]

The fact that there has been delay in taking steps to establish a cross-claim by arbitration or **7.624**
litigation may show that the cross-claim is not based on substantial grounds.[1506]

The point made at 7.624 was put in a different way by Nourse LJ in *Re Bayoil SA*,[1507] where **7.625**
his Lordship said that it is necessary for the company to show that it has been unable to
litigate the cross-claim.[1508] Nourse LJ may well have taken this condition from the headnote to *Re LHF Wools Ltd*.[1509] In that case, the company had been unable to litigate a
cross-claim in the Belgian courts until a related criminal case was concluded. The headnote
included inability to litigate the cross-claim in a list of general conditions for not allowing
a cross-claim petition to proceed, whereas it was actually just one of the facts in the case.[1510]
Following expressions of considerable doubt about whether the court should require a company to meet the condition formulated by Nourse LJ,[1511] it is now established that the court
should not impose that requirement.[1512]

The amount of a cross-claim is not to be diminished by the value of any security held **7.626**
for it.[1513]

[1501] *Southern Cross Group plc v Deka Immobilien Investment GmbH* [2005] BPIR 1010 at [29] and [30];
repeated in *Re Pan Interiors Ltd* at [36].
[1502] *Re Bayoil SA* [1999] 1 WLR 147 per Nourse LJ at p 155.
[1503] *Re a Company* (1983) 1 BCC 98,901 citing *Re Flagbrook Hotels Ltd* (18 November 1969 unreported);
Greenacre Publishing Group v The Manson Group [2000] BCC 11.
[1504] See 7.627–7.630.
[1505] *Metalform Asia Pte Ltd v Holland Leedon Pte Ltd* [2007] SGCA 6, [2007] 2 SLR 268.
[1506] *Re a Debtor (No 544/SD/98)* [2000] 1 BCLC 103 per Robert Walker LJ at p 114; *Guardi Shoes Ltd v
Datum Contracts* [2002] CILL 1934; *Southern Cross Group plc v Deka Immobilien Investment GmbH* [2005]
BPIR 1010; *Bolsover District Council v Dennis Rye Ltd* [2009] EWCA Civ 372, [2009] 4 All ER 1140.
[1507] [1999] 1 WLR 147 at p 155.
[1508] The condition formulated by Nourse LJ was found to have been satisfied in *Re Environmental Services
Ltd* (2001) LTL 18/1/2002 and *Alstom Transport v Elequip Projects Ltd* [2004] EWHC 2897 (Ch), LTL
20/12/2004. The condition was not satisfied in *Re a Company (No 1299 of 2001)* [2001] CILL 1745 (in which
it was held that the question is whether the company could have obtained judgment for its cross-claim) and
Re SY Engineering Co Ltd (20/02/2002, CACV1896/2001).
[1509] [1970] Ch 27.
[1510] The headnote writer may have been recalling a requirement of bankruptcy law at that time. In order
to show that failure to comply with a bankruptcy notice founded on a judgment debt was not an act of bankruptcy because there was a cross-claim, it had to be shown that the cross-claim could not have been set up in
the action in which the judgment was obtained (Bankruptcy Act 1914, s 1(1)(g)).
[1511] See *Re a Debtor (No 87 of 1999)* [2000] BPIR 589; *Montgomery v Wanda Modes Ltd* [2002] 1 BCLC 289;
Re Keen Lloyd Resources Ltd (23/07/2003, HCCW1134/2002); *Re Project Global Ltd* [2005] 4 HKLRD 185.
[1512] *Bolsover District Council v Dennis Rye Ltd* [2009] EWCA Civ 372, [2009] 4 All ER 1140, at [23];
Accessory People Ltd v Rouass [2010] EWCA Civ 302, LTL 13/4/2010.
[1513] *Metalform Asia Pte Ltd v Holland Leedon Pte Ltd* [2007] SGCA 6, [2007] 2 SLR 268, at [56].

Test of substantiality

7.627 As with disputed debt petitions,[1514] the test of whether a disputed cross-claim is based on sufficiently substantial grounds to justify restraining, striking out or dismissing a petition has been expressed in various ways. The cross-claim must:

- be based on a substantial ground;[1515]
- have substance;[1516]
- be genuine and serious;[1517] in *Re a Company (No 002272 of 2004)*[1518] Sir Francis Ferris said that 'the test for deciding' this 'is very much the same as the test for deciding whether a debt is disputed in good faith and on substantial grounds';
- be genuine and substantial;[1519]
- be genuine, serious and of substance.[1520]

7.628 In Singapore, it has been held that the test of substantiality when considering an application for an injunction against presentation of a petition is whether there is a distinct possibility that the company's cross-claim may exceed the intending petitioner's debt.[1521]

7.629 As with a disputed debt petition,[1522] it is not sufficient merely to allege that there is a cross-claim: there must be a positive statement of the grounds for the cross-claim with supporting relevant details to demonstrate that those grounds are substantial.[1523] For example, it is not enough to provide just the particulars of claim which have been prepared for proceedings on the cross-claim: such particulars are evidence of nothing other than the making of, or intention to make, the claim.[1524] The statement of truth of the particulars is only a statement of belief that they are true, not evidence that they are true.[1525]

7.630 The court may be particularly cautious about deciding that a cross-claim is insubstantial where it is to be heard by a tribunal with which the court is unfamiliar, such as one concerned with professional discipline.[1526]

Special circumstances: company not trading

7.631 In *Atlantic and General Investment Trust Ltd v Richbell Information Services Inc*[1527] the company had already arranged that its cross-claim was to be financed by others. It was held that winding up could not be ordered unless it was also shown that it would not be unfair to creditors who did not actively support the petition, and to the company's members, to stop

---

[1514] See 7.444–7.514.
[1515] *Re KL Tractors Ltd* [1954] VLR 505 at p 509. This condition was not satisfied in the case.
[1516] Per Lord Denning MR in *Re Portman Provincial Cinemas Ltd* [1999] 1 WLR 157; *Fortuna Holdings Pty Ltd v Deputy Federal Commissioner of Taxation* [1978] VR 83 at p 101.
[1517] *Re Bayoil SA* [1999] 1 WLR 147 per Nourse LJ at p 155 and Ward LJ at p 156; *Re Pan Interiors Ltd* [2005] EWHC 3241 (Ch), LTL 14/7/2005, at [40].
[1518] [2005] EWHC 422 (Ch), [2005] BPIR 1251, at [12].
[1519] *Alstom Transport v Elequip Projects Ltd* [2004] EWHC 2897 (Ch), LTL 20/12/2004, at [10]; *Moorside Investments Ltd v DAG Construction Ltd* [2007] EWHC 3490 (Ch), LTL 18/12/2007, at [63].
[1520] *Orion Media Marketing Ltd v Media Brook Ltd* [2002] 1 BCLC 184 at p 191.
[1521] *Metalform Asia Pte Ltd v Holland Leedon Pte Ltd* [2007] SGCA 6, [2007] 2 SLR 268, at [82].
[1522] See 7.449.
[1523] *Pontian United Theatre Sdn Bhd v Southern Finance Bhd* [2006] 2 MLJ 602.
[1524] *Re Foster, ex parte Basan* (1885) 2 Morr 29.
[1525] *Earthwave Corporation Pty Ltd v Starcom Group Pty Ltd* [2011] NSWSC 694.
[1526] *Re a Company (No 002272 of 2004)* [2005] EWHC 422 (Ch), LTL 24/2/2005.
[1527] [2000] 2 BCLC 778.

it trading when there is a genuine dispute about what, if anything, is owed to the petitioner. In this case the company was not trading and so a winding-up order was made. But in *Re LHF Wools Ltd*,[1528] discussed at 7.688, the petition was adjourned.

Special circumstances: company unable to pay petitioner's costs of cross-claim

The petitioner's fear of being involved in litigation on a cross-claim with a company which **7.632** the petitioner believes to be insolvent should be dealt with by applying for security for costs, not by having the company wound up.[1529]

Special circumstances: reverse cross-claim

The court must take into account other claims which a creditor petitioner has against the **7.633** company besides the petition debt. If other claims, together with the petition debt, exceed the company's cross-claim, the petition may be allowed to proceed, but not if the other claims are disputed on substantial grounds.[1530]

Special circumstances: judgment on petitioner's claim

The fact that the petitioner's debt has been established definitively in legal or arbitration **7.634** proceedings from which there is no appeal and the fact that the company appears to be incapable of paying it are not special circumstances which would justify the petition proceeding despite a cross-claim.[1531]

If the petitioner's debt is a judgment debt, preventing the petition proceeding because of the **7.635** company's cross-claim might be seen as equivalent to staying execution of the petitioner's judgment. However, a stay of execution of a judgment against a company does not prevent the judgment creditor petitioning for the winding up of the company, because the petition is not an execution of the judgment,[1532] and dismissal of a winding-up petition based on a judgment debt does not prevent execution of the judgment. So stay of execution of the petitioner's judgment against the company and preventing the winding-up petition proceeding are different matters. In *Ng Tai Tuan v Chng Gim Huat Pte Ltd*[1533] the petition was stayed even though the court which had given judgment on the petitioner's debt had refused a stay of execution.

In *Marchands Associates LLP v Thompson Partnership LLP*[1534] Peter Gibson LJ said, at [46]: **7.636**

> It matters not that the debt is one for which summary judgment would have been obtained or on which execution could be levied notwithstanding the cross-claim. A winding-up order has more serious consequences and the Companies Court is entitled to adopt a different approach.[1535]

[1528] [1970] Ch 7.
[1529] *De Montfort University v Stanford Training Systems Pte Ltd* [2005] SGHC 202, [2006] 1 SLR 218.
[1530] *Montgomery v Wanda Modes Ltd* [2002] 1 BCLC 289; *To Kwan Chak v City Top Engineering Ltd* [2006] 2 HKLRD 562.
[1531] *Re Bayoil SA* [1999] 1 WLR 147; *Re a Company (No 1299 of 2001)* [2001] CILL 1745; *Re Environmental Services Ltd* (2001) LTL 18/1/2002. The second and third of these cases involved claims governed by the Housing Grants, Construction and Regeneration Act 1996, part 2.
[1532] See 7.60.
[1533] [1991] 1 MLJ 338.
[1534] [2004] EWCA Civ 878, LTL 28/6/2004.
[1535] It is the same in bankruptcy: see *White v Davenham Trust Ltd* [2011] EWCA Civ 747, [2011] Bus LR 1443, per Lloyd LJ at [33], citing *Remblance v Octagon Assets Ltd* [2009] EWCA Civ 581, [2010] Bus LR 119.

7.637   A cross-claim which is actually an attempt to re-litigate the petitioner's judgment will not justify preventing the petition from proceeding.[1536]

Special circumstances: autonomy of petitioner's claim (pay now, argue later)

7.638   The fact that the petitioner's claim is autonomous, so that it must be paid regardless of a dispute or cross-claim, which must be dealt with in separate proceedings (pay now, argue later), is not a special circumstance which would justify a petition proceeding despite a cross-claim against the petitioner. This applies, for example, where the petitioner's claim is for freight or for an unpaid cheque or bill of exchange.[1537] So the principle of autonomy, which requires a court hearing a claim for payment of a negotiable instrument not to consider a cross-claim or defence, apart from a defence concerning the validity of the instrument,[1538] does not apply to a winding-up petition based on non-payment of the instrument.

7.639   Similarly, the fact that the petitioner's debt is a sum due under a construction contract, and the company has not given an effective notice of intention to withhold payment,[1539] is not a special circumstance which would justify the petition proceeding despite a cross-claim against the petitioner.[1540]

7.640   The same applies to contractual requirements to pay now, argue later.[1541]

7.641   The fact that a withholding notice has not been served, coupled with other delays in establishing a cross-claim, may show that the cross-claim is not based on substantial grounds.[1542]

Special circumstances: company voluntary arrangement

7.642   The fact that a voluntary arrangement has effect in relation to a company is not a special circumstance which would justify a creditor's winding-up petition proceeding despite a cross-claim by the company against the petitioner.[1543]

Special circumstances: company's hands not clean

7.643   In *Dow Securities Pty Ltd v Manufacturing Investments Ltd*[1544] the defendant company's claim was for repayment of a loan which was alleged to be illegal, because a director of the defendant company had a substantial shareholding in the borrowing company. The borrowing company had an unrelated counterclaim against the defendant company. It was held that the borrowing company's want of clean hands would not be a ground for winding it up and did not prevent it from pursuing its counterclaim. So the want of clean hands was not a reason for refusing to grant an injunction restraining the defendant company from petitioning for the winding up of the borrowing company.

[1536] *Chauhan v Commissioners of Inland Revenue* [2004] EWHC 1304 (Ch), [2004] BPIR 862.

[1537] *Re Bayoil SA* [1999] 1 WLR 147; *Marchands Associates LLP v Thompson Partnership LLP* [2004] EWCA Civ 878, LTL 28/6/2004. The contrary view in *Golden City Electronic Industries Co Ltd v RCR Electronics Manufacturing Ltd* [1996] 2 HKLR 257 must be reconsidered in the light of *Re Bayoil SA*. See also *Re a Company (No 0010656 of 1990)* [1991] BCLC 464; *Vecta Software Corporation Ltd v Despec Supplies Ltd* [2004] EWHC 3151 (Ch), LTL 19/7/2004.

[1538] *Cebora SNC v SIP (Industrial Products) Ltd* [1976] 1 Lloyd's Rep 271.

[1539] Housing Grants, Construction and Regeneration Act 1996, s 111.

[1540] *Re a Company (No 1299 of 2001)* [2001] CILL 1745; *Medlock Products Ltd v SCC Construction Ltd* [2006] CILL 2384.

[1541] *Marchands Associates LLP v Thompson Partnership LLP* [2004] EWCA Civ 878, LTL 28/6/2004.

[1542] *Guardi Shoes Ltd v Datum Contracts* [2002] CILL 1934.

[1543] *Re VP Developments Ltd* [2005] EWHC 259 (Ch), [2005] 2 BCLC 607.

[1544] (1981) 5 ACLR 501.

Company's cross-claim falls short of the petitioner's debt by more than £750

If, on hearing a winding-up petition, it is found that the company has a cross-claim against the petitioner which falls short of the petitioner's debt by more than £750, and it is shown that the company is unable to pay its debts, a winding-up order will be made.[1545] **7.644**

If such a finding is made on hearing an application to restrain gazetting of and strike out a petition, the court may adjourn the petition to allow the company to pay the undisputed part of the petition debt, but did not do so in *Alexander Sheridan Ltd v Beaujersey Ltd*,[1546] because the amount was large (about £61,600) and there was no evidence of the company's solvency. **7.645**

In *Celtech International Ltd v Dalkia Utilities Services plc*[1547] it was found that of £3,648,367.29 demanded, all but £26,013 was disputed. Richards J said, at [34], that he would not have thought it right to allow presentation of a petition when the undisputed amount was so much smaller than the demanded amount, but he also found that the £26,013 was disputed. **7.646**

In *Imbar Maritima SA v Republic of Gabon*[1548] the republic had obtained judgment for a foreign arbitral award against Swiss Oil Corporation and had filed a petition to wind up that corporation. Opposing creditors brought an action seeking (a) a declaration that the republic had agreed not to pursue the petition until proceedings concerning a cross-claim by the corporation had ended and (b) an injunction to enforce that agreement. (The cross-claim was for significantly less than the republic's judgment debt.) This action was dismissed but an appeal was launched and the appellants asked for an interim injunction restraining pursuit of the winding-up petition pending determination of the appeal: they claimed that this would preserve the status quo. The interlocutory injunction was refused because even if the cross-claim were decided in the corporation's favour it would not prevent the corporation being wound up. **7.647**

For other examples of cases where the company was unable to show that its claim was larger than the petitioner's see *Re ICS Computer Distribution Ltd*;[1549] *Greenacre Publishing Group v The Manson Group*.[1550] **7.648**

Mutuality

The reason why a cross-claim petition is treated in the same way as a disputed debt petition is that the cross-claim may reduce what the company owes the petitioner to less than £750. Accordingly a cross-claim can be taken into account only if it is a claim by the company against the petitioner.[1551] **7.649**

The following claims have been held to be not cross-claims that may be relied on to halt a petition to wind up a company, because of lack of mutuality: **7.650**

(a) a claim by the company sought to be wound up against a subsidiary of the petitioner;[1552]

[1545] *Re Exchange Finance Co Ltd* (1984) 2 NZCLC 99,247; *Re Futile Pty Ltd* (1988) 13 ACLR 412; *Blue Star Security Services (Scotland) Ltd* 1992 SLT (Sh Ct) 80.
[1546] [2004] EWHC 2072 (Ch), LTL 12/8/2004.
[1547] [2004] EWHC 193(Ch), LTL 2/3/2004.
[1548] 1988–89 CILR 286.
[1549] [1996] 1 HKLR 181.
[1550] [2000] BCC 11.
[1551] *Re The Sun's Group (HK) Ltd* [2004] 3 HKLRD 65.
[1552] *Tottenham Hotspur plc v Edennote plc* [1995] 1 BCLC 65.

(b) a claim against the petitioner by a subsidiary of the company sought to be wound up;[1553]

(c) a claim against the petitioner by a person who was jointly and severally liable with the company for the petitioner's debt.[1554]

7.651   The fact that a company's cross-claim is held in trust, for example, because there is a voluntary arrangement in force in relation to the company, does not destroy its mutuality.[1555]

Set-off

7.652   Some cross-claims by a company against a creditor may be characterized as set-offs. A set-off may be an independent set-off (also known as a legal set-off) or a transaction set-off.[1556] Set-off of two monetary claims results in only one amount being recoverable, which is the net amount remaining after the smaller claim has been deducted from the larger. In the case of a transaction set-off this occurs when the set-off arises,[1557] but in the case of an independent set-off it does not occur until a court gives judgment on both claims.[1558]

7.653   If C brings legal proceedings against D for a liquidated sum, D can assert an independent set-off (legal set-off) of any liquidated debt or money demand claimed by it from C, provided both C's claim and D's claim are liquidated at the time of filing a defence.[1559] A claim is liquidated for this purpose even if there is a dispute about its amount.[1560] If the court finds that both debts are owing, its order will be for the payment only of the balance owed when the smaller debt is deducted from the larger.[1561] When the court gives judgment, but not before,[1562] the debts will cease to be separate debts and will become a single judgment debt. It follows that legal set-off of one debt cannot be asserted against another debt which cannot be claimed in the same court, for example, because the court must stay a claim for it in favour of arbitration or in favour of a court in a different jurisdiction.[1563] The rule that it must be possible to litigate both claim and cross-claim in the same court does not apply to transaction set-offs.[1564]

7.654   A transaction set-off can be either an equitable set-off or a common law abatement of price.

7.655   A person A from whom money is claimed by another person B can assert an equitable set-off of a claim against B if it arises out of the same transaction or is closely connected with that transaction and 'is so closely connected with B's demands that it would be manifestly unjust

---

[1553]   *Landune International Ltd v Cheung Chung Leung Richard* [2006] 1 HKLRD 39.

[1554]   *Tatlers.com.au Pty Ltd v Davis* [2007] NSWSC 835, 213 FLR 109.

[1555]   *Re VP Developments Ltd* [2005] EWHC 259 (Ch), [2005] 2 BCLC 607.

[1556]   See *Aectra Refining and Marketing Inc v Exmar NV* [1994] 1 WLR 1634.

[1557]   Though the amount recoverable may remain to be determined (*S L Sethia Liners Ltd v Naviagro Maritime Corporation* [1981] 1 Lloyd's Rep 18 at pp 25–7; *Fearns v Anglo-Dutch Paint and Chemical Co Ltd* [2010] EWHC 2366 (Ch), [2011] 1 WLR 366).

[1558]   *Glencore Grain Ltd v Agros Trading Co* [1999] 2 Lloyd's Rep 410. But an assignment of a debt is subject to any right to claim an independent set-off that arose before notice of the assignment was received by the debtor (*Roxburghe v Cox* (1881) 17 ChD 520; *Glencore Grain Ltd v Agros Trading Co*).

[1559]   See *Hanak v Green* [1958] 2 QB 9 per Morris LJ at p 17; *Axel Johnson Petroleum AB v MG Mineral Group AG* [1992] 1 WLR 270; *B Hargreaves Ltd v Action 2000 Ltd* [1993] BCLC 1111; CPR, r 16.6.

[1560]   *Aectra Refining and Marketing Inc v Exmar NV* [1994] 1 WLR 1634.

[1561]   CPR, r 40.13.

[1562]   *Re Hiram Maxim Lamp Co* [1903] 1 Ch 70; *Glencore Grain Ltd v Agros Trading Co* [1999] 2 Lloyd's Rep 410.

[1563]   *Aectra Refining and Marketing Inc v Exmar NV* [1994] 1 WLR 1634.

[1564]   *Aectra Refining and Marketing Inc v Exmar NV* [1994] 1 WLR 1634 at pp 1649–50; *Prekons Insaat AS v Rowlands Castle Contracting Group Ltd* [2006] EWHC 1367 (QB), [2007] 1 Lloyd's Rep 98.

to allow B to enforce payment without taking A's claim into account'.[1565] Whether there is a sufficiently close connection, in any particular case, is a question of fact and degree on which the judge must form an impression.[1566] Equitable set-off is not restricted to liquidated claims.[1567] Equitable set-off is not restricted to claims arising from the same contract.[1568]

If an application by a company to prevent a creditor presenting a winding-up petition because **7.656** of the company's cross-claim has failed and the company has been ordered to pay the creditor's costs, the liability to pay those costs is not so closely connected to the cross-claim itself that there can be an equitable set-off of the costs against the cross-claim.[1569]

Common law abatement of price is the right to reduce the amount paid for goods or services **7.657** to reflect a breach of warranty by the seller.[1570]

It is possible for the contract governing payment of a debt to prevent the debtor from exercis- **7.658** ing a right of set-off, whether independent or transaction, against the creditor even in legal proceedings brought to enforce payment of the debt.[1571]

From the time that a transaction set-off arises, it provides a defence against a claim for any **7.659** amount other than the balance owing when the smaller debt is deducted from the larger. So, where a creditor's petition is presented to wind up a company and the company claims a transaction set-off against the petitioner's debt, the petition should be classified as a disputed debt petition rather than a cross-claim petition,[1572] but this is now[1573] not important as the two are treated in the same way.

Petitioner's standing not affected by cross-claim

A cross-claim is different from a disputed debt petition in that a cross-claim, if it is not a **7.660** transaction set-off, does not affect the petitioner's standing to petition as a creditor. If the company's cross-claim cannot be asserted as a transaction set-off,[1574] the company is not entitled to deduct the amount of its claim when tendering payment for the petitioner's debt,[1575] and so cannot dispute the petitioner's standing to petition as a creditor. Even if the company could plead its cross-claim as an independent set-off, the company's claim and the petitioner's claim would be two separate debts until judgment in the proceedings in which set-off is asserted. Thus the petitioner has standing to petition as a creditor despite

---

[1565] Per Lord Denning MR in *Federal Commerce and Navigation Co Ltd v Molena Alpha Inc* [1978] QB 927 at pp 974–5 and Goff LJ at p 987, point not considered on appeal; *Geldof Metaalconstructie NV v Simon Carves Ltd* [2010] EWCA Civ 667, [2010] 4 All ER 847; *Autoweld Systems Ltd v Kito Enterprises LLC* [2010] EWCA Civ 1469, [2011] TCLR 1, at [25].

[1566] *Addax Bank BSC v Wellesley Partners LLP* [2010] EWHC 1904 (QB), LTL 26/7/2010, at [45].

[1567] *Bim Kemi v Blackburn Chemicals Ltd* [2001] EWCA Civ 457, [2001] 2 Lloyd's Rep 93.

[1568] *Bim Kemi v Blackburn Chemicals Ltd* [2001] EWCA Civ 457, [2001] 2 Lloyd's Rep 93, at [29].

[1569] *Re Portedge Ltd* [1997] BCC 23; [1998] BCC 556 sub nom *RWH Enterprises Ltd v Portedge Ltd*.

[1570] Sale of Goods Act 1979, s 53(1)(a); *Mondel v Steel* (1841) 8 M & W 858; *Gilbert-Ash (Northern) Ltd v Modern Engineering (Bristol) Ltd* [1974] AC 689.

[1571] *Coca-Cola Financial Corporation v Finsat International Ltd* [1998] QB 43; *Re Kaupthing Singer and Friedlander Ltd* [2009] EWHC 740 (Ch), [2009] 2 Lloyd's Rep 154.

[1572] *McDonald's Restaurants Ltd v Urbandivide Co Ltd* [1994] 1 BCLC 306.

[1573] Since *Re Bayoil SA* [1999] 1 WLR 147. See 7.663–7.665.

[1574] See 7.652–7.659.

[1575] Per Lord Denning MR in *Federal Commerce and Navigation Co Ltd v Molena Alpha Inc* [1978] QB 927 at p 974.

the existence of the cross-claim.[1576] This means that the petitioner can rely on evidence of inability to pay debts other than the non-payment of the debt which is subject to the cross-claim.[1577] Nevertheless, it may be an abuse of process to petition for the winding up of a company which has a larger cross-claim against the petitioner for which the company is entitled to claim an independent set-off, if the petition is for the improper collateral purpose of pressurizing the company to pay the petitioner's claim free of the set-off.[1578]

Similarities between disputed debt and set-off

7.661 The English practice of treating cross-claim petitions in the same way as disputed-debt petitions recognizes that the effect of both a dispute about the existence of the petitioner's debt and a cross-claim equal to or greater than the petitioner's debt is to question whether the company must pay anything to the petitioner and so whether the petitioner has any interest in having the company wound up, beyond the hope that it might cause the company to abandon its dispute or cross-claim. This similarity between cross-claim and disputed-debt petitions is more significant than the difference in standing to petition.[1579] In *Malayan Plant (Pte) Ltd v Moscow Narodny Bank Ltd*[1580] Lord Edmund-Davies said, at p 55, 'There is no distinction in principle between a cross-claim of substance (such as in *Re LHF Wools Ltd*[1581]) and a serious dispute regarding the indebtedness imputed against a company'. The distinction between a cross-claim against the petitioner and a dispute about the petitioner's debt was described by Hoffmann J in *Re R A Foulds Ltd*[1582] as 'somewhat technical'. His Lordship said that 'on the face of it it is hard to see the difference between a disputed debt and a dispute which consists of alleging that by virtue of a set-off nothing is in fact owing'.[1583]

7.662 The similarity between cross-claim and disputed-debt petitions is now recognized in the provisions for setting aside statutory demands in bankruptcy in England and Wales, and in companies winding up in Australia and New Zealand, which are discussed at 7.236–7.247.

History: England and Wales

7.663 Although the practice of treating cross-claims in the same way as disputes was declared by the Court of Appeal in 1964 in *Re Portman Provincial Cinemas Ltd*, that case was not fully reported until 1999[1584] and it was not appreciated that it laid down a rule of practice. Until the Court of Appeal reconsidered the question in *Re Bayoil SA*,[1585] courts tended to base their consideration of cross-claim petitions on the fully reported case of *Re LHF Wools Ltd*[1586] and seized upon Edmund Davies LJ's statement in that case[1587] that the discretion of a court of

---

[1576] *Re Euro Hotel (Belgravia) Ltd* [1975] 3 All ER 1075; *Re Jeff Reid Pty Ltd* (1980) 5 ACLR 28; *Dow Securities Pty Ltd v Manufacturing Investments Ltd* (1981) 5 ACLR 501 at p 504; *Re Julius Harper Ltd* [1983] NZLR 215 at p 221; *Anglian Sales Ltd v South Pacific Manufacturing Co Ltd* [1984] 2 NZLR 249; *Re R A Foulds Ltd* (1986) 2 BCC 99,269; *Innes* 2004 SCLR 789; *Equity Australia Corporation Pty Ltd v Falgat Constructions Pty Ltd* [2005] NSWSC 918, 54 ACSR 813 at [13]–[16].
[1577] *Innes* 2004 SCLR 789.
[1578] *Equity Australia Corporation Pty Ltd v Falgat Constructions Pty Ltd* [2005] NSWSC 918, 54 ACSR 813.
[1579] See 7.660.
[1580] [1980] 2 MLJ 53.
[1581] [1970] Ch 27.
[1582] (1986) 2 BCC 99,269 at p 99,275.
[1583] See also per Ward LJ in *Re Bayoil SA* [1999] 1 WLR 147 at p 156.
[1584] [1999] 1 WLR 157.
[1585] [1999] 1 WLR 147.
[1586] [1970] Ch 27.
[1587] At p 42.

first instance was not to be rigidly constrained by the Court of Appeal. This was interpreted as meaning that it is a matter of discretion whether a claim against a petitioner which equals or exceeds the petitioner's debt will be treated in the same way as a dispute about the existence of the petitioner's debt.[1588] In *Re Leasing and Finance Services Ltd*[1589] and *Re a Company (No 006273 of 1992)*[1590] applications to restrain presentation of petitions were refused. In *Re a Company (No 009080 of 1992)*[1591] an application for an order restraining advertisement of the petition and a temporary stay of proceedings was refused.

In *Re Bayoil SA*[1592] Nourse LJ said: **7.664**

> The correct view is that the practice in cross-claim cases was established by the actual decision in *Re Portman Provincial Cinemas Ltd*.[1593] In *Re LHF Wools Ltd*[1594] Harman LJ, with whose judgment Danckwerts LJ agreed, recognised and affirmed its existence. So too did Edmund Davies LJ, his only reservation being that there was still a residual discretion in the court and that the petition ought not to be rejected out of hand. The reservation was clearly correct. It is met by the exception for special circumstances.

Nourse LJ went on to say that as Warner J in *Re FSA Business Software Ltd* and Millett J in   **7.665**
Re a Company (No 006273 of 1992) had not seen full transcripts of *Re Portman Provincial Cinemas Ltd*, weight could not be given to their views on the question. This would clearly also apply to the other first-instance cases cited in 7.663, which were not referred to in *Re Bayoil SA*.

Former position in Australia

In Australia, before statutory provisions were introduced for setting aside a statutory   **7.666**
demand served on a company where the company has a sufficient cross-claim,[1595] a petition based on a debt less than or equal to a cross-claim could be treated, as in England and Wales, in the same way as a disputed debt petition.[1596] However, the Australian courts have, as explained at 7.609–7.612, a slightly different attitude to disputed debt petitions. In Australia it has been said that it is unnecessary to consider the technical legal nature of the company's cross-claim—whether it may be asserted as a set-off or not and, if it can be, whether it is a legal or equitable set-off.[1597] However, the view of Yeldham J in *Re Glenbawn*

[1588] Per Megarry J in *Re Euro Hotel (Belgravia) Ltd* [1975] 3 All ER 1075 at p 1079; Hoffmann J in *Re RA Foulds Ltd* (1986) 2 BCC 99,269 at p 99,275; Warner J in *Re FSA Business Software Ltd* [1990] BCC 465 at p 470; Morritt J in *Re Leasing and Finance Services Ltd* [1991] BCC 29 at p 31; *Re Pendigo Ltd* [1996] 2 BCLC 64; *Re Finbo Engineering Co Ltd* [1998] 2 HKLRD 695 at p 703; *Greenacre Publishing Group v The Manson Group* [2000] BCC 11.

[1589] [1991] BCC 29.

[1590] [1993] BCLC 131.

[1591] [1993] BCLC 269.

[1592] [1999] 1 WLR 147 at p 154.

[1593] [1999] 1 WLR 157.

[1594] [1970] Ch 27.

[1595] See 7.237–7.245.

[1596] See, for example, *Clem Jones Pty Ltd v International Resources Planning and Development Pty Ltd* [1970] QdR 37; *Fortuna Holdings Pty Ltd v Deputy Federal Commissioner of Taxation* [1978] VR 83 at pp 96–7; *Re Glenbawn Park Pty Ltd* (1977) 2 ACLR 288; *Altarama Ltd v Camp* (1980) 5 ACLR 513; *Re Jeff Reid Pty Ltd* (1980) 5 ACLR 28; *Dow Securities Pty Ltd v Manufacturing Investments Ltd* (1981) 5 ACLR 501; *Transport and Property Holdings Pty Ltd v Buntine* (1982) 63 FLR 67; *Alperin Technical Pty Ltd v ACI Australia Ltd* (1990) 2 ACSR 234.

[1597] *Fortuna Holdings Pty Ltd v Deputy Federal Commissioner of Taxation* [1978] VR 83 per McGarvie J at p 96; *Re Glenbawn Park Pty Ltd* (1977) 2 ACLR 288 per Yeldham J at p 291; *Dow Securities Pty Ltd v Manufacturing Investments Ltd* (1981) 5 ACLR 501 per Wootten J at p 504.

Park Pty Ltd, at p 291, that if the company has a cross-claim against the petitioner, the petitioner's debt actually is disputed, even if the cross-claim is not a transaction set-off, goes too far—it would imply that the petitioner does not have standing to petition as a creditor if the cross-claim exceeds his debt, but this is not so—see 7.660.[1598]

Former position in New Zealand

7.667   In New Zealand, before statutory provisions were introduced for setting aside a statutory demand served on a company where the company has a sufficient cross-claim,[1599] cross-claim petitions were treated like disputed debt petitions if the company's cross-claim could be asserted as a set-off.[1600] But a cross-claim which could not be asserted as a set-off was normally not a reason for preventing a petition proceeding unless proceeding with the petition would be oppressive or unfair.[1601] This included a case where the company was contractually bound to pay the petitioner's debt without raising any set-off, counterclaim or defence.[1602]

7.668   The former rule in New Zealand was that a cross-claim that was not a set-off was not even a reason for dismissing the petition on hearing it.[1603] But in *Wilsons (NZ) Portland Cement Ltd v Gatx-Fuller Australasia Pty Ltd (No 2)*[1604] it was held to be an abuse of process for a creditor of a company to present a petition for the compulsory winding up of the company where the company had a large cross-claim against the creditor and the parties had a binding agreement to submit all differences between them to arbitration. Accordingly, an injunction was issued to prevent the creditor presenting a petition. In *Re A J and B A Chatfield Ltd*[1605] the petition was stayed on the company undertaking to prosecute its cross-claim with the utmost diligence, because this was considered just. A similar order was made in *Race Industries (NZ) Ltd v Kitchen Time Ltd*.[1606] In *Taupo Auto Machinists v Kennedy*[1607] the members of a company were taking action to obtain a share in the estate of a deceased creditor of the company and the company applied to restrain presentation by the deceased's executor of a petition to wind it up, suggesting that extinction of the debt would settle the claim against the estate. The application was adjourned on condition that the company gave security for the debt and the members pursued their claim with due dispatch.

[1598] See per McLelland J in *Re Jeff Reid Pty Ltd* (1980) 5 ACLR 28 at p 31 and per Wootten J in *Dow Securities Pty Ltd v Manufacturing Investments Ltd* (1981) 5 ACLR 501 at p 504.

[1599] See 7.246–7.247.

[1600] *Nemisis Holdings Ltd v North Harbour Industrial Holdings Ltd* (1989) 4 NZCLC 65,084; *Bean Supreme Ltd v ASDA Wholesale Ltd* (1989) 4 NZCLC 65,134 and *New Zealand Factors Ltd v Farmers Trading Co Ltd* [1992] 3 NZLR 703, the latter two refusing to follow *Re K McDougall Ltd* (1985) 3 NZCLC 99,607.

[1601] *Anglian Sales Ltd v South Pacific Manufacturing Co Ltd* [1984] 2 NZLR 249; *Fletcher Development and Construction Ltd v New Plymouth Hotels Holdings Ltd* [1986] 2 NZLR 302; *Re Reawood Orchards Ltd* (1987) 3 NZCLC 100,261; *Markline Boats Ltd v Tauranga Fibreglass Services Ltd* (1988) 4 NZCLC 64,601; *Forbes and Davies (Auck) Ltd v Blue Wing Honda Ltd* (1989) 4 NZCLC 64,874; *Commissioner of Inland Revenue v Cappucci Knitwear Ltd* (1989) 3 BCR 274; *Hewlett-Packard (NZ) Ltd v Compusales Software and Hardware Ltd* (1990) 5 NZCLC 66,281; *Bank of New Zealand v Packer and Jones Ltd* (1990) 5 NZCLC 66,485; *Stewart Scott Cabinetry Ltd v Wallace and Bryant Ltd* [1992] MCLR 258; *Devon Cottages Ltd v P and P Savage Ltd* [1993] MCLR 49; *ASB Bank Ltd v Irdoss Computer Systems Ltd* [1993] MCLR 145.

[1602] *Liapis v Vasey* (1989) 4 NZCLC 64,959.

[1603] *Re Rosbro Holdings Ltd* (1987) 3 NZCLC 100,131.

[1604] [1985] 2 NZLR 33.

[1605] (1985) 2 NZCLC 99,379.

[1606] (1990) 5 NZCLC 66,441.

[1607] (1988) 3 BCR 21.

Substitution of a Disputed Creditor as Petitioner

A person who does not have standing to petition will not be substituted as petitioner.[1608] In **7.669**
particular, the court will not permit a disputed creditor to be substituted as petitioner.[1609]
The onus is on the company to prove that the dispute is sufficiently substantial to refuse
substitution.[1610] In *Re Invicta Works Ltd*[1611] the court did permit a disputed creditor to be
substituted, but adjourned the petition for the substituted petitioner to produce evidence
of his debt.

A disputed creditor may be substituted as applicant for the winding up of a company if the **7.670**
court has found that the company is insolvent and adopts the view that it can order the
company to be wound up without resolving the dispute about the petitioner's debt.[1612]

Wasted Costs Orders

In some cases in which a company has been the subject of a disputed debt petition the com- **7.671**
pany has sought a wasted costs order[1613] against the petitioner's legal representative. Wasted
costs are defined[1614] as costs incurred by a party:

(a) as a result of any improper, unreasonable or negligent act or omission on the part of any
    legal or other representative or any employee of such a representative; or
(b) which, in the light of any such act or omission occurring after they were incurred, the
    court considers it is unreasonable to expect that party to pay.

Advising a client to use a winding-up petition as a means of pressurizing a company into **7.672**
paying or compromising the client's claim is an unreasonable act which may justify a wasted
costs order.[1615] The fact that the client refuses to authorize the legal representative to give an
undertaking not to present a petition does not mean that the representative must cease to act for
the client.[1616] A company cannot claim that a disputed debt petition has been pursued unreasonably if it has not promptly informed the petitioner that the debt is disputed and set out the
nature of the dispute.[1617]

[1608] *Perak Pioneer Ltd v Petroliam Nasional Bhd* [1986] AC 849 at p 857.
[1609] *Re Calsil Ltd* (1982) 6 ACLR 515; *Fire and All Risks Insurance Co Ltd v Southern Cross Exploration NL* (1986) 10 ACLR 683; *Commissioner of Inland Revenue v Bemelman Engineering Ltd* (1990) 5 NZCLC 66,494; *Beverage Holdings Pty Ltd v Greater Pacific Investments Pty Ltd* (1990) 3 ACSR 743, in which it was found that the dispute was not sufficiently substantial to refuse the substitution and, on hearing the petition (*Re Beverage Holdings Pty Ltd* (1991) 5 ACSR 277), the dispute was found to be not sufficiently substantial to dismiss the petition; *South East Water Ltd v Kitoria Pty Ltd* (1996) 21 ACSR 465; *Tokich Holdings Pty Ltd v Sheraton Constructions* (NSW) Pty Ltd [2004] NSWSC 527,185 FLR 130; *Cadura Investments v Rototek Pty Ltd* [2004] WASC 249, 51 ACSR 390.
[1610] *Beverage Holdings Pty Ltd v Greater Pacific Investments Pty Ltd* (1990) 3 ACSR 743 per Wallace J at p 747.
[1611] [1894] WN 39.
[1612] *ACP Syme Magazines Pty Ltd v TRI Automotive Components Pty Ltd* (1997) 144 ALR 517. See 7.562–7.568.
[1613] Under the Senior Courts Act 1981, s 51(6).
[1614] Senior Courts Act 1981, s 51(7).
[1615] *Philex plc v Golban* (reported with *Ridehalgh v Horsefield*) [1994] Ch 205, in which the Court of Appeal found that there was no evidence of misconduct by the solicitor; *Daily Freightways Ltd v Rio Beverages Ltd* [1994] MCLR 289; *Re a Company (No 006798 of 1995)* [1996] 1 WLR 491, in which a wasted costs order was made.
[1616] *Philex plc v Golban*.
[1617] *Re Merc Property Ltd* [1999] 2 BCLC 286.

Sufficient Interest of Petitioner

7.673 A petition may be dismissed if it is shown that the petitioner does not have a 'sufficient interest' in having a winding up ordered.[1618]

Exercise of Court's Discretion

Principles on which the Discretion is Exercised

Existence of the discretion

7.674 The court's power to make a winding-up order is discretionary.[1619] The discretion whether or not to order the winding up of a company exists even when it is proved that the company is unable to pay its debts.[1620] In relation to a creditor's petition, even if the creditor's debt is undisputed and unpaid, the court nevertheless has a discretion whether or not to make a winding-up order.[1621] Under the statutory scheme now in force in Australia the court has a discretion whether or not to order a company to be wound up in insolvency, even where insolvency is established[1622] or is deemed by statute.[1623]

7.675 Like any discretion, this must be exercised in a principled way.

Petition of unpaid admitted creditor

7.676 The basic rule is that where a creditor petitioner's debt is undisputed and not satisfied and there are no exceptional circumstances, the creditor is entitled to expect the court to exercise its jurisdiction in the way of making a winding-up order.[1624] As Park J put it in *Re Lummus Agricultural Services Ltd*:[1625]

> if a creditor with standing to make the application wants to have the company wound up, and if the court is satisfied that the company is unable to pay its debts, a winding-up order will follow unless there is some special reason why it should not.

7.677 This basic rule must be modified to take account of the views of other creditors.[1626] Also, if an administration application has been made, the court may make an administration order instead of a winding-up order.[1627]

[1618] See 2.127–2.141.

[1619] See 5.71–5.99.

[1620] *Re Pardoo Nominees Pty Ltd* [1987] TasR 1 at p 4; *Laucke Flour Mills (Stockwell) Pty Ltd v Fresjac Pty Ltd* (1992) 58 SASR 110 at p 113; *Re Minrealm Ltd* [2007] EWHC 3078 (Ch), [2008] 2 BCLC 141.

[1621] *Re Greta Collieries Ltd* (1894) 4 BC (NSW) 47; *Re Strathy Wire Fence Co* (1904) 8 OLR 186; *Marsden v Minnekahda Land Co Ltd* (1918) 40 DLR 76; *Re P and J Macrae Ltd* [1961] 1 WLR 229; *Re Southard and Co Ltd* [1979] 1 WLR 1198.

[1622] *Hamilhall Pty Ltd v A T Phillips Pty Ltd* (1994) 15 ACSR 247 at p 249; *Ace Contractors and Staff Pty Ltd v Westgarth Development Pty Ltd* [1999] FCA 728; *Crema (Vic) Pty Ltd v Land Mark Property Developments (Vic) Pty Ltd* [2006] VSC 338, 58 ACSR 631.

[1623] *Re Derrygarrif Investments Pty Ltd* (1982) 6 ACLR 751; *Deputy Commissioner of Taxation v Guy Holdings Pty Ltd* (1994) 14 ACSR 580 at p 584.

[1624] Per Buckley LJ in *Re Southard and Co Ltd* [1979] 1 WLR 1198 at p 1203. This statement quoted and the following discussion cited by Sales J in *Re Hellas Telecommunications (Luxembourg) II SCA* [2011] EWHC 3176 (Ch), [2013] 1 BCLC 426, at [88].

[1625] [2001] 1 BCLC 137 at p 141.

[1626] See 7.683–7.684.

[1627] See 7.734–7.738.

The method by which the petitioner proves the company's inability to pay its debts, whether **7.678**
by service of a statutory demand or otherwise, is not a factor affecting the discretion.[1628] For
the position where the petitioner's debt is disputed, see 7.433–7.672.

It is not wrongful for a company's bank to demand immediate repayment of a substantial **7.679**
overdraft which the company is using as working capital, and a petition based on failure to meet such a demand will be treated like any other petition by an unpaid admitted
creditor.[1629]

Ex debito justitiae

In the early years of the winding-up jurisdiction, the rule stated at 7.676 was expressed in **7.680**
terms even more favourable to the petitioning creditor. In *Bowes v Hope Life Insurance and
Guarantee Co*[1630] Lord Cranworth said, at p 402:

> it is not a discretionary matter with the court when a debt is established, and not satisfied,
> to say whether the company shall be wound up or not; that is to say, if there be a valid debt
> established, valid both at law and in equity. One does not like to say positively that no case
> could occur in which it would be right to refuse it; but, ordinarily speaking, it is the duty of
> the court to direct the winding up.

This view was linked with the early attitude of the courts that a creditor's winding-up peti- **7.681**
tion was an individual remedy provided by statute to enable an unpaid creditor of a company to obtain payment.[1631] So in *Re Imperial Guardian Life Assurance Society*[1632] counsel
asserted that 'An unpaid creditor is entitled to a winding-up order *ex debito justitiae*'.[1633] In
Re Western of Canada Oil, Lands and Works Co[1634] Jessel MR said, at p 7:

> a creditor of a company who cannot get paid, and presents a petition for winding up, is entitled
> *ex debito justitiae* to a winding-up order; but at the same time it is not to be said that this is a
> rule without exception, or that the court has not power to direct the petition to stand over.

In *Re Pritchard*[1635] Upjohn LJ, explaining the meaning of '*ex debito justitiae*', said, at pp 520–1: **7.682**

> The right to wind up a company is by statute a discretionary right. Yet the books and authori-
> ties point out that in many cases as against the company an unpaid creditor on a winding-up
> petition is entitled to a winding-up order *ex debito justitiae*. This means no more than that, in
> accordance with settled practice, the court can only exercise its discretion one way, namely,
> by granting the order sought.

Class benefit

The *ex debito justitiae* principle[1636] was modified by recognizing that, as Malins V-C pointed **7.683**
out in *Re Brighton Hotel Co*,[1637] Parliament has provided in what is now IA 1986, s 195,[1638]

[1628] *Marsden v Minnekahda Land Co Ltd* (1918) 40 DLR 76 per Macdonald CJA at p 77.
[1629] *Malayan Plant (Pte) Ltd v Moscow Narodny Bank Ltd* [1980] 2 MLJ 53.
[1630] (1865) 11 HL Cas 389.
[1631] See 7.33–7.39.
[1632] (1869) LR 9 Eq 447 at p 450.
[1633] As a matter of right. The debt of the petitioner in the case was disputed and the petition was adjourned
until an action on the debt had been determined.
[1634] (1873) LR 17 Eq 1.
[1635] [1963] Ch 502.
[1636] See 7.680–7.682.
[1637] (1868) LR 6 Eq 339.
[1638] First enacted as the Companies Act 1862, s 91.

that in all matters relating to the winding up of a company the court may have regard to the wishes of the creditors or contributories.[1639] It became accepted that a winding-up order on a creditor's petition should be for the benefit of creditors generally so that the court will consider the views of creditors other than the petitioner.[1640] In *Re Crigglestone Coal Co Ltd*[1641] Buckley J said, at pp 331–2, in relation to a creditor's petition:

> the order which the petitioner seeks is not an order for his benefit, but an order for the benefit of a class of which he is a member. The right *ex debito justitiae* is not his individual right, but his representative right. If a majority of the class are opposed to his view, and consider that they have a better chance of getting payment by abstaining from seizing the assets, then, upon general grounds and upon s 91 of the Companies Act 1862,[1642] the court gives effect to such right as the majority of the class desire to exercise.

In *Re Southard and Co Ltd*,[1643] Buckley LJ, at p 1203, commented as follows on the dictum of Lord Cranworth quoted at 7.680:

> [Lord Cranworth] was not saying that the jurisdiction is not discretionary; what he was saying was that where the debt is established and not satisfied and there are no exceptional circumstances, the creditor is entitled to expect the court to exercise its jurisdiction in the way of making a winding-up order.

See also *Re Concrete Pipes and Cement Products Ltd*[1644] per Irvine CJ at p 39.

7.684 Reasons for not making a winding-up order on a creditor's petition may be put forward by the company itself, by its contributories or its directors[1645] or by other creditors.[1646] Any of these parties (though it is usually the directors) may, by making an administration application, assert that administration is preferable to winding up.[1647]

Disfavour of ex debito justitiae *limitations to discretion*

7.685 Recently, it has been emphasized that a discretion to make an order given by rules of court cannot be excluded by a judicial rule that, in certain circumstances, the order will be made *ex debito justitiae*.[1648]

Opposition by Contributories or by the Company itself or its Directors

7.686 The views of contributories or of the company itself, or its directors, will normally carry little weight when considering the petition of an undisputed creditor whose debt is due

---

[1639] See also *Re Lonsdale Vale Ironstone Co* (1868) 16 WR 601; *Re Langley Mill Steel and Iron Works Co* (1871) LR 12 Eq 26.
[1640] *Re St Thomas' Dock Co* (1876) 2 ChD 116; *Re Uruguay Central and Hygueritas Railway Co of Monte Video* (1879) 11 ChD 372; *Re Chapel House Colliery Co* (1883) 24 ChD 259; *Re Strathy Wire Fence Co* (1904) 8 OLR 186; *Re Crigglestone Coal Co Ltd* [1906] 2 Ch 327 per Buckley J; *Re Belmont Land Co* (1913) 32 NZLR 864; *Marsden v Minnekahda Land Co Ltd* (1918) 40 DLR 76.
[1641] [1906] 2 Ch 327.
[1642] Now IA 1986, s 195.
[1643] [1979] 1 WLR 1198.
[1644] [1926] VLR 34.
[1645] See 7.686–7.697.
[1646] See 7.698–7.733.
[1647] See 7.734–7.738.
[1648] *Raja v Van Hoogstraten (No 9)* [2008] EWCA Civ 1444, [2009] 1 WLR 1143.

and unpaid.[1649] As Master Seaman put it in *Re DTX Australia Ltd*:[1650] 'The shareholders of this insolvent company cannot expect to trade with the capital of the company's creditors'. This applies whether the company has only one member or is a listed public company.[1651] In *Hamilhall Pty Ltd v A T Phillips Pty Ltd*[1652] the court ordered the winding up of a company on the application of an unpaid creditor despite the company's contention that, as it operated only as the trustee of a family trust, there was less cause for the court to be concerned about the irregular conduct of its affairs than if it had been a public company. The fact that there is evidence that the company is solvent is an exceptional circumstance which may justify not making a winding-up order.[1653]

Persuasive argument by a company sought to be wound up by a creditor that it would be in **7.687** its creditors' interests for the petition to be dismissed or adjourned will not outweigh the petitioner's considered view that the company should be wound up.[1654]

If a company's principal asset is a claim against a third party, the view of its directors, that **7.688** they, rather than a liquidator, should conduct the claim, is unlikely to persuade the court not to make a winding-up order.[1655] However, in *Re LHF Wools Ltd*,[1656] where the company's only asset was a cross-claim in another jurisdiction against the petitioning creditor, the Court of Appeal adjourned the petition having accepted that a liquidator would be no better able to pursue the cross-claim than the directors, who had arranged financing for it.

In *El Ajou v Dollar Land (Manhattan) Ltd*[1657] a creditor's winding-up petition was heard **7.689** together with the company's application for an administration order. The administration application was dismissed and a winding-up order made because the court did not consider that an administration would give any significant economic advantage to creditors, and the petitioner was entitled to the complete independence and objectivity of the official receiver as liquidator rather than administrators nominated by the company.

If a secured creditor of a company has appointed a receiver, who is deemed to be an agent of **7.690** the company, the receiver's views may be taken to be those of the company rather than the creditor, especially if they are presented by counsel for the company.[1658]

The whole idea of having a company to conduct a business is that it separates the business **7.691** and personal affairs of the individuals involved: it is no defence to a winding-up petition to claim that a company is merely a 'vehicle' for an individual's business interests and that

---

[1649] *Re General Rolling Stock Co Ltd* (1865) 34 Beav 314; *Re Consolidated Bank* [1866] WN 232; *Re International Contract Co Ltd, ex parte Spartali and Tabor* (1866) 14 LT 726; *Re Heyes Brothers Ltd* (1915) 8 OWN 390; *Re Melbourne Carnivals Pty Ltd (No 1)* [1926] VLR 283 at p 290; *Re Camburn Petroleum Products Ltd* [1980] 1 WLR 86; *Re Stafford Mall Ltd* (1987) 3 NZCLC 100,258; *Re Consumers Co-operative Society (Manawatu) Ltd* (1988) 4 NZCLC 64,605; *Re Leigh Estates (UK) Ltd* [1994] BCC 292 at p 295.
[1650] (1987) 11 ACLR 444 at p 451.
[1651] *Re DTX Australia Ltd* at p 451.
[1652] (1994) 15 ACSR 247.
[1653] *Re Surplus Properties (Huddersfield) Ltd* [1984] BCLC 89 per Harman J at p 92. See also 7.43–7.45.
[1654] *Re Lummus Agricultural Services Ltd* [2001] 1 BCLC 137 at pp 141–2.
[1655] *Re Oryx Natural Resources* 2007 CILR N6. The court may be more willing to accept the views of creditors on this point, see 7.728.
[1656] [1970] Ch 27.
[1657] [2005] EWHC 2861 (Ch), [2007] BCC 953.
[1658] *Genting Sanyen Industrial Paper Sdn Bhd v WWL Corrugators Sdn Bhd* [2000] 5 MLJ 33.

the individual and the company taken together would not be insolvent even if the company cannot pay its own debts.[1659]

7.692 Occasionally the court is persuaded to adjourn a petition for a short time, or delay perfection of a winding-up order, to allow the company an opportunity to pay the petitioner's debt,[1660] especially if it appears that the company is solvent.[1661] But in *Re Avon Security Ltd*[1662] an offer by the company's principal shareholder to pay the company's debts over an unspecified period was not enough to persuade the court to adjourn the petition. In *Dubolo Pty Ltd v Codrington Investment Corporation Pty Ltd*[1663] the company's offer to assign its future earnings to the petitioner and its complaint that winding it up would prevent it earning money to pay the petitioner's debt were both dismissed, especially as the debt was already 18 months overdue. In *Fuji Photo Film Co Ltd v Jazz Photo (Hong Kong) Ltd*[1664] a winding-up order was made despite the company's assertion that it would recover enough in damages from a pending legal action, which the court described as 'speculative', to pay the petitioner's debt. Payment proposals supported by a majority of independent creditors may, however, justify not making a winding-up order, see 7.710–7.719.

7.693 A petition which is supported by other creditors will not be dismissed if only the petitioner's debt is paid.[1665]

7.694 The fact that the financial difficulties of a company sought to be wound up have been caused by a war being fought by its country is not a special circumstance which will persuade the court not to make a winding-up order on the petition of an unpaid admitted creditor.[1666] Similarly, the fact that there is a general economic recession is not a reason for not making a winding-up order.[1667]

7.695 It is unlikely that a court today would follow the view taken in *Re Redhead Coal Mining Co Ltd*[1668] that a company should not be wound up for not paying for construction works which had to be completed before it could start its operations.

7.696 In *Re British Widows Assurance Co*[1669] the company had sold life assurance with no regard to whether its business was actuarially sound. Two policyholders petitioned for it to be wound up. The Court of Appeal accepted an undertaking by the company that it would conduct its business in future in accordance with a scheme which independent actuaries had found acceptable and discharged the winding-up order made by Buckley J.

7.697 For disputed debt petitions, see 7.433–7.672.

[1659] *Re Hanamoa Pty Ltd* (1982) 7 ACLR 30.

[1660] *Re General Rolling Stock Co Ltd* (1865) 34 Beav 314 per Romilly MR at pp 315–16 (but not, as in the case before him, where it was obvious that the company was insolvent); *Re East Coast Shipping Co Ltd* [1925] GLR 326; *Re Regent Street Ltd* [1933] GLR 329.

[1661] *Re Kieran Byrne and Associates Geotechnical Consultants Pty Ltd* (1987) 12 ACLR 367; *Re Barrier Reef Finance and Land Pty Ltd* [1989] 1 QdR 252.

[1662] (1986) 3 NZCLC 99,931.

[1663] (1998) 26 ACSR 723.

[1664] [2005] 1 HKLRD 530.

[1665] *Re Pavy's Patent Felted Fabric Co Ltd* (1875) 24 WR 91, decided before substitution of petitioners was allowed.

[1666] *Re Globe Trust Ltd* (1915) 84 LJ Ch 903.

[1667] *Re Hong Huat Realty (M) Sdn Bhd* [1987] 2 MLJ 502.

[1668] (1893) 3 BC (NSW) 50.

[1669] [1905] 2 Ch 40.

Opposition by other Creditors

Importance of other creditors' views

On a winding-up petition presented by a creditor of a company, the views of other creditors **7.698** of the company are of considerable importance. A winding-up order on a creditor's petition should be for the benefit of the company's creditors generally and so the court will consider the views of other creditors.[1670] A judge who hears a creditor's winding-up petition without giving other creditors the opportunity of stating their views will not be in a position properly to exercise discretion to make a winding-up order.[1671]

Other creditors are informed of the petition and the date of the initial hearing by gazet- **7.699** ting.[1672] The notice that is gazetted informs creditors that they may state their opposition to or support for the petition by informing the petitioner or the petitioner's solicitor by 4 pm on the business day before the initial hearing.[1673] The petitioner's solicitor must prepare for the court a list of persons intending to appear, stating whether each appears in opposition to or support of the petition.[1674]

Usually, it is unsecured, not secured, creditors whose views are important: secured creditors **7.700** are protected by their security and usually uninterested in whether or not the company is wound up.[1675] The views of unsecured creditors may be considered even if the company's assets are subject to charges to secure amounts exceeding the value of the assets (so that there is no likelihood of the unsecured creditors receiving anything), for that fact is not in itself a reason for refusing a winding-up order.[1676] The court is not bound to accede to the wishes of creditors.[1677]

For proof of the wishes of other creditors, see 5.58–5.60. **7.701**

Principle on which discretion is exercised

The rule stated at 7.676, that an unpaid admitted creditor will normally be granted a **7.702** winding-up order unless there are exceptional circumstances, must be qualified by saying that, as between the company and an unpaid admitted creditor, the creditor is entitled to a winding-up order as a matter of course, but, as between the petitioning creditor and the other creditors, the majority's opposition to compulsory liquidation may prevail.[1678] Majority means a majority in value,[1679] where the value of a creditor's debt is the amount claimed, not the amount likely to be realized in the winding up.[1680] But the court may discount the views of creditors connected to the company.[1681]

[1670] *Re Uruguay Central and Hygueritas Railway Co of Monte Video* (1879) 11 ChD 372; *Re Chapel House Colliery Co* (1883) 24 ChD 259.
[1671] *Adebayo v Official Receiver of Nigeria* [1954] 1 WLR 681.
[1672] See 3.117–3.134.
[1673] IR 1986, rr 4.11(5)(g) and 4.16, and sch 4, form 4.6.
[1674] See 5.37.
[1675] *Re Demaglass Holdings Ltd* [2001] 2 BCLC 633 per Neuberger J at p 639.
[1676] IA 1986, s 125(1); *Re Leigh Estates (UK) Ltd* [1994] BCC 292.
[1677] *Re Cushing Sulphite Fibre Co Ltd* (1905) 37 NBR 254; *Re George Downs and Co Ltd* [1943] IR 420.
[1678] See *Re Great Western (Forest of Dean) Coal Consumers' Co* (1882) 21 ChD 769 per Fry J at p 773; *Re Chapel House Colliery Co* (1883) 24 ChD 259 per Baggallay LJ at pp 265–6.
[1679] IA 1986, s 195(2).
[1680] *Re Manakau Timber Co Ltd* (1895) 13 NZLR 319.
[1681] See 7.732.

7.703 Those who oppose the petition of an unpaid admitted creditor must actually produce reasons to persuade the court to vary its normal practice of making a winding-up order on such a petition; the court does not simply abide by a majority decision that there should not be a compulsory liquidation.[1682] Opposition for which no reason is given will be ignored.[1683] In *Re J D Swain Ltd*[1684] Diplock LJ said, at p 915:

> if the only circumstances which are available are that the petitioner seeks a compulsory winding up and the majority of the creditors seek that there should be no winding up at all, then prima facie the petitioning creditor is entitled to a winding up unless there are some additional reasons for deciding to the contrary.

7.704 It is not a question of weighing up advantages to those who want a winding up against disadvantages to those who oppose it. It is more an exercise of saying: Do the matters raised by the opponents outweigh the normal rule of policy?[1685]

7.705 Much earlier, Turner LJ said in *Re Northumberland and Durham District Banking Co*:[1686]

> I think that the Legislature, not having thought proper to provide that the majority of creditors should have the power to bind the minority in the choice of proceedings..., I should not be disposed to give any decided weight to the opinion of the majority of the creditors against the minority upon the question as to the choice of proceedings, without being fully satisfied not merely by the votes of the majority, but by the facts of the case, that there would be secured to the minority the full dividend which they might obtain if the course of proceeding they desired was adopted.

7.706 Opposing creditors should have their case ready at the first hearing of the petition: they must not assume that an adjournment will be granted for them to organize their case.[1687] In *Re Don Agricultural Machinery Pty Ltd*[1688] the court had brought forward the hearing of a winding-up petition but adjourned it until the date originally set because opposing creditors had not been able to prepare their case properly.

7.707 The principles which are applied to cases in which opposing creditors seek the dismissal of a winding-up petition are also applied when opposing creditors seek adjournment of the petition against the wishes of the petitioner.[1689] The court may be less reluctant to adjourn than to dismiss because of the views of creditors other than the petitioner, especially if the adjournment is for a relatively short period.[1690]

7.708 The fact that a majority of a company's creditors take the view that a compulsory winding up of the company applied for by one creditor is not in the best commercial

---

[1682] *Re Great Western (Forest of Dean) Coal Consumers' Co* (1882) 21 ChD 769; *Re Charles H Davis Co Ltd* (1907) 9 OWR 993; *Re Vuma Ltd* [1960] 1 WLR 1283; *Re P and J Macrae Ltd* [1961] 1 WLR 229; *Re Restaurant Chevron Ltd* [1963] NZLR 225; *Re Television Parlour plc* (1987) 4 BCC 95; *Laucke Flour Mills (Stockwell) Pty Ltd v Fresjac Pty Ltd* (1992) 58 SASR 110.
[1683] *Re Phoon Lee Piling Co Ltd* [2003] 2 HKLRD 391.
[1684] [1965] 1 WLR 909.
[1685] *New South Wales Rugby League v United Telecasters Sydney Ltd* (1991) 4 ACSR 510 per Young J at p 512.
[1686] (1858) 2 De G & J 357, at p 379.
[1687] *Southern World Airlines Ltd v Auckland International Airport Ltd* [1992] MCLR 210.
[1688] (1976) 7 ACLR 897.
[1689] *Re D W Crompton and Co Ltd* (1975) 1 BCR 51; *Re Airfast Services Pty Ltd* (1976) 11 ACTR 9; *Re Nationwide Air Ltd* (1978) 1 BCR 208; *Re DTX Australia Ltd* (1987) 11 ACLR 444; see also *Re Leonard Spencer Pty Ltd* [1963] QdR 230 in which a provisional liquidator had been appointed.
[1690] *Re Demaglass Holdings Ltd* [2001] 2 BCLC 633 per Neuberger J at p 640.

interests of the creditors is not a sufficient reason for ordering that the petition is not to be gazetted.[1691]

An opposing creditor may seek to rely on any circumstances of justice which may affect it **7.709** in its relations with the company or the petitioner.[1692]

Carrying on the company's business

The most common reason for other creditors' opposition to a winding-up petition has been **7.710** that it will be advantageous for the company's business to be carried on otherwise than only for the beneficial winding up of the company (which is the only purpose for which a compulsory liquidator may be authorized to carry on the company's business under IA 1986, s 167(1)(a) and sch 4, para 5). Opposing creditors have wanted trading to be continued, not for winding up, but:

(a) so that earnings could pay debts;[1693] or
(b) so that a reconstruction could be attempted.[1694]

In *Re Tudhope Motor Co*[1695] the opposing creditors would have accepted a compromise, **7.711** which apparently involved an external reconstruction, but the judge said that the petitioner could not be forced to accept the compromise and made the winding-up order. In *Re D W Crompton and Co Ltd*[1696] the petition was adjourned for two months to enable meetings to be convened to consider a court-sanctioned arrangement. In *Re Nationwide Air Ltd*[1697] the petition was adjourned for six weeks while the company formulated proposals for a court-sanctioned scheme.

[1691] *Cambridge Clothing Co Ltd v Hire Suits Ltd* (1991) 5 NZCLC 67,486.
[1692] *Re Allobrogia Steamship Corporation* [1978] 3 All ER 423 at p 431. See 7.710–7.731.
[1693] Accepted in *Re St Thomas' Dock Co* (1876) 2 ChD 116; *Re Uruguay Central and Hygueritas Railway Co of Monte Video* (1879) 11 ChD 372; *Re Great Western (Forest of Dean) Coal Consumers' Co* (1882) 21 ChD 769; *Re Chapel House Colliery Co* (1883) 24 ChD 259 (in which the company's business was being carried on by a mortgagee in possession); *Re Bryan Construction Co Ltd* [1957] NZLR 748; *Re ABC Coupler and Engineering Co Ltd* [1961] 1 WLR 243 (though a winding-up order was made on a creditor's petition 18 months later — see *Re ABC Coupler and Engineering Co Ltd (No 2)* [1962] 1 WLR 1236 at p 1245); *Re JRS Garage Ltd* [1961] NZLR 632 and *Kim Wah Theatre Sdn Bhd v Fahlum Development Sdn Bhd* [1990] 2 MLJ 511. Rejected in *Re International Commercial Co Ltd* (1897) 75 LT 639; *Re Melbourne Carnivals Pty Ltd (No 1)* [1926] VLR 283; *Re Ithaca Shipping Co Ltd* (1950) 84 Ll L Rep 507; *Re Jacobs River Sawmilling Co Ltd* [1961] NZLR 602; *Re Leonard Spencer Pty Ltd* [1963] QdR 230 (in which a provisional liquidator had been appointed and only a minority of creditors opposed compulsory winding up); *Re Restaurant Chevron Ltd* [1963] NZLR 225 (in which an administrative receiver had been appointed); *Re Airfast Services Ltd* (1976) 11 ACTR 9; *Wei Giap Construction Co (Pte) Ltd v Intraco Ltd* [1979] 2 MLJ 4; *Re Thames Freightlines Ltd* (1981) 1 NZCLC 98,112 (in which an administrative receiver had been appointed and it was expected to be two years before debts would be paid); *Cetico Sdn Bhd v Tropical Veneer Co Bhd* [1988] 2 MLJ 665 (in which administrative receivers had been appointed and it was expected to be four years before debts would be paid); *Tanco Holdings (NZ) Ltd v T S and L A Davies Ltd* (1989) 4 NZCLC 64,879; *Laucke Flour Mills (Stockwell) Pty Ltd v Fresjac Pty Ltd* (1992) 58 SASR 110; and *Commissioner of Inland Revenue v Roadmark Systems Ltd* [1997] 3 NZLR 744, [1998] 3 NZLR 139 (in which creditors of the company other than the petitioner were bound by a compromise which contemplated the company taking three to five years to pay its debts and was thought to be of doubtful benefit to them).
[1694] Accepted in *Re East Kent Colliery Co Ltd* (1914) 30 TLR 659; *Re Ohau Ski Area Ltd* (1983) 1 BCR 555; *Re DTX Australia Ltd* (1987) 11 ACLR 444; *Re Bank of Credit and Commerce International SA* [1992] BCLC 570 (in which the adjournment was for four months); *Southern World Airlines Ltd v Auckland International Airport Ltd* [1992] MCLR 210; *Re UDL Holdings Ltd* [1999] 2 HKLRD 817. Rejected in *Bell's Trustees v Holmes Oil Co* (1900) 3 F 23.
[1695] (1914) 5 OWN 865.
[1696] (1975) 1 BCR 51.
[1697] (1978) 1 BCR 208.

7.712 If the advantage will be only for the creditors opposing winding up, the court is unlikely to accept their argument.[1698] If there is simply a disagreement between the business judgments of creditors whose interests are qualitatively the same, the court is likely to follow the view of the majority if they have provided a good reason for not making a winding-up order.[1699]

7.713 In *Kim Wah Theatre Sdn Bhd v Fahlum Development Sdn Bhd*[1700] the company sought to be wound up was a property development company. The opposing creditors, with debts amounting to M$36 million, had paid deposits for flats which the company was building. The petitioner, which had a judgment for its debt, and the supporting creditors were owed M$5 million and were presumably trade creditors. The petition was adjourned for ten months to enable the development to be completed so that the opposing creditors would not lose both their deposits and their flats. It was expected that on completion of the development, the company would be able to pay all its debts.[1701]

7.714 In *Re St Thomas' Dock Co*[1702] and *Re Great Western (Forest of Dean) Coal Consumers' Co*[1703] the petitions were adjourned for six months but in *Re Chapel House Colliery Co*[1704] this was said to be because of the peculiar circumstances of the cases[1705] and lengthy adjournment of petitions is now generally deprecated.[1706]

7.715 A company may be put into administration to achieve the objectives of rescuing it as a going concern or achieving a better result for the company's creditors as a whole than would be likely if the company were wound up without first being in administration.[1707] In the Republic of Ireland it has been said that a lengthy period of protection from winding up should be by means of a formal rescue procedure which can only be obtained by providing an independent assessment of the company's prospects and which includes safeguards for creditors (administration in the UK, examinership in the Republic) rather than by a lengthy adjournment of a winding-up petition.[1708]

More advantageous realization of assets

7.716 Other creditors may oppose making a winding-up order on the ground that a more advantageous realization of the company's assets can be achieved outside of compulsory liquidation.[1709]

[1698] *Re Clandown Colliery Co* [1915] 1 Ch 369; *Re SOS Motors Ltd* [1934] NZLR s 129; *Re Thames Freightlines Ltd* (1981) 1 NZCLC 98,112; *Re Flooks of Bristol (Builders) Ltd* [1982] Com LR 55; *Genting Sanyen Industrial Paper Sdn Bhd v WWL Corrugators Sdn Bhd* [2000] 5 MLJ 33.

[1699] *Re Uruguay Central and Hygueritas Railway Co of Monte Video* (1879) 11 ChD 372; *Re East Kent Colliery Co Ltd* (1914) 30 TLR 659; *Re ABC Coupler and Engineering Co Ltd* [1961] 1 WLR 243; *Re DTX Australia Ltd* (1987) 11 ACLR 444.

[1700] [1990] 2 MLJ 511.

[1701] See also the similar cases of *Pilecon Engineering Bhd v Remaja Jaya Sdn Bhd* [1997] 1 MLJ 808 and *Wong Thai Kuai v Kansas Corp Sdn Bhd* [2007] 4 MLJ 33.

[1702] (1876) 2 ChD 116.

[1703] (1882) 21 ChD 769.

[1704] (1883) 24 ChD 259.

[1705] Per Baggallay LJ at p 267.

[1706] *Re Boston Timber Fabrications Ltd* [1984] BCLC 328.

[1707] See 1.38–1.39 and 7.734–7.738.

[1708] *Re Heatsolve Ltd* [2013] IEHC 399.

[1709] Accepted in *Re Planet Benefit Building and Investment Society* (1872) LR 14 Eq 441; *Re Brendacot Ltd* (1986) 2 BCC 99,164; *Re Stafford Mall Ltd* (1987) 3 NZCLC 100,258; *Re Dallhold Estates (UK) Pty Ltd* (1991) 6 ACSR 378; *Re Dallhold Estates (UK) Pty Ltd* [1992] BCC 394. Rejected in *Re General Rolling Stock*

A company may be put into administration with the objective of achieving a better result **7.717**
for the company's creditors as a whole than would be likely if the company were wound up
without first being in administration.[1710]

In Canada, a creditor's winding-up petition has been refused where the majority of creditors **7.718**
wished the company's assets to be realized under an assignment for the benefit of creditors
generally controlled by statutory provisions which do not exist in England[1711] unless the
court doubted whether the assignment was bona fide.[1712]

A suggestion that liquidation should be delayed because it was not an opportune time to **7.719**
realize the company's assets was rejected in *Re South East Corporation Ltd*[1713] but accepted
in *Re Edmonton Brewing and Malting Co Ltd*.[1714]

Administrative receivership preferred

Other creditors may oppose making a winding-up order on the ground that realization of **7.720**
the company's assets should be left to an incumbent administrative receiver.[1715] In some
cases this has been conceded to be a good reason for not making a winding-up order.[1716]

If there is simply a disagreement between the business judgments of unsecured creditors **7.721**
about the expediency of allowing the administrative receiver to continue, the majority view
will prevail.[1717]

On a petition by an unsecured creditor, if the other unsecured creditors do not oppose **7.722**
and the opposition is from creditors for whom the receiver is acting, the court may make
a winding-up order so that a liquidator can represent the interests of the unsecured creditors.[1718] In *Re Joseph Bull Sons and Co*[1719] an adjournment for six months was allowed on
condition that a joint receiver be appointed to represent the unsecured creditors' interests.

Co Ltd (1865) 34 Beav 314 (in which the majority of creditors wanted the company to go into voluntary
liquidation); *Re South East Corporation Ltd* (1915) 23 DLR 724; *Re Metropolitan Fuel Pty Ltd* [1969] VR 328;
Field v Egmont Contractors Ltd [1992] MCLR 91.

[1710] See 1.38–1.39 and 7.734–7.738.
[1711] *Wakefield Rattan Co v Hamilton Whip Co Ltd* (1893) 24 OR 107; *Re Maple Leaf Dairy Co* (1901) 2 OLR
590; *Re Strathy Wire Fence Co* (1904) 8 OLR 186; *Re Olympia Co* (1915) 25 DLR 620; *Marsden v Minnekahda
Land Co Ltd* (1918) 40 DLR 76; though *Re William Lamb Manufacturing Co of Ottawa* (1900) 32 OR 243
was apparently to the contrary.
[1712] *Re International Trap Rock Co Ltd* (1915) 8 OWN 461 in which a winding-up order was made; *Re
British American Feldspar Ltd* (1920) 18 OWN 313 in which the petition was adjourned.
[1713] (1915) 23 DLR 724.
[1714] [1918] 2 WWR 350.
[1715] *Re Ocean Falls Co* (1913) 13 DLR 265; *Re Rubber Improvement Ltd* (1962) *The Times*, 5 June 1962;
Re Northern Developments (Holdings) Ltd (1977) 128 NLJ 86; *Re Bonaparte Licensed Restaurant Ltd* (1988) 4
NZCLC 64,421; *Re Leigh Estates (UK) Ltd* [1994] BCC 292; *Re Demaglass Holdings Ltd* [2001] 2 BCLC 633
(adjournment for ten weeks); see also *Re Clutha Leathers Ltd* (1987) 4 NZCLC 64,160 discussed at 3.205.
[1716] *Re R W Sharman Ltd* [1957] 1 WLR 774; *Re A E Hayter and Sons (Porchester) Ltd* [1961] 1 WLR 1008;
Re Sklan Ltd [1961] 1 WLR 1013.
[1717] *Re Rubber Improvement Ltd* (1962) *The Times*, 5 June 1962.
[1718] *Re Cushing Sulphite Fibre Co Ltd* (1905) 37 NBR 254; *Re Crigglestone Coal Co Ltd* [1906] 2 Ch 327;
Re SOS Motors Ltd [1934] NZLR s 129; *Re Marlborough Sealink Ltd* (1985) 3 NZCLC 99,501; *Cetico Sdn
Bhd v Tropical Veneer Co Bhd* [1988] 2 MLJ 665; *Re Consumers Co-operative Society (Manawatu) Ltd* (1988) 4
NZCLC 64,605; *City Realties (Holdings) Ltd v Investment Finance Corporation Ltd* (1989) 4 NZCLC 65,417;
New South Wales Rugby League v United Telecasters Sydney Ltd (1991) 4 ACSR 510; but not in *Re Northern
Developments (Holdings) Ltd* (1977) 128 NLJ 86.
[1719] (1892) 36 SJ 557.

7.723   If the assets charged to the secured creditors will not pay their debts, they can also be counted as unsecured creditors.[1720]

7.724   In Scotland this reason is not strong enough to justify summary dismissal and refusal of the first order for intimation, advertisement and service.[1721]

7.725   A floating charge created on or after 15 September 2003 cannot be enforced by the appointment of an administrative receiver.[1722] Instead the chargee may appoint an administrator.[1723]

Voluntary winding up preferred

7.726   Other creditors may oppose making a winding-up order on the ground that the company should go into voluntary liquidation.[1724]

Miscellaneous reasons for opposing a winding-up order

7.727   In *Re Vuma Ltd*[1725] the opposing creditors (who were the majority in value) had received an offer of payment of their debts from an undisclosed source but the petitioning creditor had not received any offer and the company appeared to have no assets: a winding-up order was made. The fact that opposing creditors will be able to retain property seized in execution, taking control of goods, attachment or sequestration if no winding-up order is made[1726] is not a good reason for not making an order.[1727] On the other hand, in *Re Bula Ltd*[1728] it was admitted that the petition was presented for the purpose of preventing the opposing creditor from gaining priority by registering a charge on the company's only asset; the petitioners had already appointed a receiver who was attempting to sell that asset; the values of the petitioners' and opponents' claims were approximately equal; the Irish Supreme Court allowed an appeal against the making of a winding-up order.

7.728   The view of a majority of creditors that the directors of a company would be better able than a liquidator to conduct its litigation may be accepted as a reason for not making a winding-up order.[1729] In *Re OJSC ANK Yugraneft*,[1730] though, both the petitioning creditor and the company's Russian liquidator wanted an English liquidator appointed to manage the company's claim against an English defendant, and the court rejected the view of a much smaller opposing creditor that such an appointment was unnecessary.

[1720]   *Re Leigh Estates (UK) Ltd* [1994] BCC 292.

[1721]   *Foxhall and Gyle (Nurseries) Ltd* 1978 SLT (Notes) 29.

[1722]   IA 1986, s 72A; Insolvency Act 1986, Section 72A (Appointed Date) Order 2003 (SI 2003/2095). Exceptions are specified in IA 1986, ss 72B to 72H.

[1723]   IA 1986, sch B1, para 14.

[1724]   *Re Langley Mill Steel and Iron Works Co* (1871) LR 12 Eq 26, in which the resolution for voluntary winding up had been adopted while the petition was pending and was supported by nearly all creditors; rejected in *Bell's Trustees v Holmes Oil Co* (1900) 3 F 23, because there would have been a delay in convening the necessary meetings which would have meant that a particular prior transaction questioned by the petitioner would have become immune from adjustment; also rejected in *Re Television Parlour plc* (1987) 4 BCC 95, which was a petition by the company's administrative receivers (see 10.68–10.70); accepted in *Re Fitness Centre (South East) Ltd* [1986] BCLC 518.

[1725]   [1960] 1 WLR 1283.

[1726]   Because those processes will not become invalid under IA 1986, ss 128 and 183, as they would if a winding-up order were made.

[1727]   *Mercantile Credits Ltd v Foster Clark (Australia) Ltd* (1964) 112 CLR 169; *Re Irish Shipping Ltd* [1985] HKLR 437; *Teck Yow Brothers Hand-Bag Trading Co v Maharani Supermarket Sdn Bhd* [1989] 1 MLJ 101; *Re Griffin Securities Corporation* [1999] 3 SLR 346.

[1728]   [1990] 1 IR 440.

[1729]   *Re Polynesia Co, ex parte Detmold* (1873) 4 AJR 47.

[1730]   [2008] EWHC 2614 (Ch), [2009] 1 BCLC 298.

In *Re Allobrogia Steamship Corporation*[1731] the opposing creditor alleged that the petitioner's **7.729** purpose was to institute legal proceedings against the opposing creditor which would be struck out as an abuse of process, but could not establish that the proposed legal proceedings were bound to fail.

In *Re Greta Collieries Ltd*[1732] a petition presented in New South Wales to wind up a foreign **7.730** company was adjourned for two months to allow for proceedings in its country of incorporation (England) to recover unpaid calls on shares. It was also relevant that the company's principal asset was a lease which would have been forfeited on the making of a winding-up order.

In *Re Federal Bank of Australia Ltd*[1733] an order to wind up a foreign company was made **7.731** even though creditors would have preferred adjournment of the petition while the company's affairs were wound up by the voluntary liquidator appointed in the jurisdiction of incorporation (Victoria) because they wanted to save the expense of liquidation in England.

Discounted views of creditors connected with the company

The court will not pay so much regard to the views of creditors who are connected with the **7.732** company—for example, as directors, shareholders or subsidiaries—as to genuine outside creditors, even if the outsiders' debts are smaller.[1734] This principle was not taken into consideration in *Re Sairs Pty Ltd*,[1735] but the reasons which creditors connected with the company put forward for not making a winding-up order (that the individual who had founded the company and was in sole control of it should be permitted to continue settling its affairs) were clearly based on their connection and were rejected by the court.

Accepting the views of a minority opposed to a winding-up order

Just as the court is not bound to accede to the views of the majority against a winding-up **7.733** order so it may, in principle, accede to the views of a *minority against* an order if their reasons are convincing.[1736] Normally, however, if the majority in value of creditors are in favour of compulsory liquidation on the petition of an unpaid creditor, the court does not need any further reason to make a winding-up order.[1737]

Choice between Winding Up and Administration

Some of the reasons for not making a winding-up order in cases before 1986 would **7.734** now be dealt with by putting the company into administration.[1738] When a petition has been presented for a company to be wound up, the company and its directors cannot appoint an administrator,[1739] but they can make an administration application, as can

---

[1731] [1978] 3 All ER 423.
[1732] (1894) 4 BC (NSW) 47.
[1733] (1893) 62 LJ Ch 561.
[1734] *Ross T Smyth and Co v Salem (Oregon) Flour Mills Co Ltd* (1887) 14 R 441; *Re Oilfields Finance Corporation Ltd* (1915) 59 SJ 475; *Re Melbourne Carnivals Pty Ltd (No 1)* [1926] VLR 283; *Re ABC Coupler and Engineering Co Ltd* [1961] 1 WLR 243 at p 245; *Re Jacobs River Sawmilling Co Ltd* [1961] NZLR 602; *Re D W Crompton and Co Ltd* (1975) 1 BCR 51 (opposition of relatives of a director ignored); *Re Roma Industries Pty Ltd* (1976) 1 ACLR 296 at pp 298–9; *Re Holiday Stamps Ltd* (1985) 82 LS Gaz 2817; *Re Lowerstoft Traffic Services Ltd* [1986] BCLC 81 per Hoffmann J at p 84; *Brinds Ltd v Offshore Oil NL* (1985) 63 ALR 94.
[1735] [1969–70] P&NGLR 293.
[1736] *Re Oilfields Finance Corporation Ltd* (1915) 59 SJ 475.
[1737] *Re Belmont Land Co (No 2)* (1913) 32 NZLR 1017.
[1738] See 1.38–1.39.
[1739] IA 1986, sch B1, para 25(a). See 3.106–3.109.

one or more of the company's creditors.[1740] If the court makes an administration order, it must dismiss the winding-up petition.[1741] The holder of a qualifying floating charge in respect of the company's property is entitled to appoint an administrator out of court[1742] (unless a provisional liquidator has been appointed[1743]) and the appointment suspends the winding-up petition.[1744]

7.735 An administration application is entitled to serious consideration by the court as an alternative to winding up, even if it is made by the company or its directors, because it must be accompanied by a statement by the proposed administrator that, in his or her opinion, the purpose of administration is likely to be achieved,[1745] as well as a statement of the company's financial position.[1746] But the court may find that the proposed administrator's statement is so flawed that it cannot be relied on.[1747] It may also find that the directors' evidence in their application does not disclose the true position.[1748]

7.736 If the statutory conditions for making an administration order are fulfilled,[1749] the court may exercise its discretion in favour of making an administration order rather than a winding-up order.[1750] Of course, a winding-up order will be made if it is not shown to be reasonably likely that the purpose of administration will be achieved.[1751]

7.737 If the affairs of the company require investigation which could lead to recovery of money, the winding-up petitioner and other creditors are entitled to the complete independence and objectivity of the official receiver as liquidator rather than administrators nominated by the company.[1752] Winding up may be preferred if it appears that money could be recovered in proceedings which can only be taken in liquidation, for example, for fraudulent or wrongful trading,[1753] or recovery of post-petition dispositions.[1754] If there is a significant interval between presenting a winding-up petition and filing an administration application, this may affect which prior transactions can be adjusted.[1755]

[1740] IA 1986, sch B1, para 12(1).

[1741] IA 1986, sch B1, para 40(1)(a). See 3.99–3.102.

[1742] IA 1986, sch B1, para 14.

[1743] IA 1986, sch B1, para 17(a)).

[1744] IA 1986, sch B1, para 40(1)(b). See 3.103–3.105.

[1745] IR 1986, r 2.8(5).

[1746] IR 1986, r 2.4(2)(a).

[1747] As in *Re Integeral Ltd* [2013] EWHC 164 (Ch), LTL 11/2/2013, at [69]–[72].

[1748] As in *Re Bowen Travel Ltd* [2012] EWHC 3405 (Ch), [2013] BCC 182; *Re Brown Bear Foods Ltd* [2014] EWHC 1132 (Ch), LTL 15/4/2014.

[1749] The company is, or is likely to become, unable to pay its debts and the order is reasonably likely to achieve the purpose of administration: IR 1986, sch B1, para 11 (see 1.38–1.39).

[1750] *Re Redman Construction Ltd* (2004) LTL 16/6/2004; *Re Logitext.UK Ltd* [2004] EWHC 2899 (Ch), [2005] 1 BCLC 326; *DKLL Solicitors v Commissioners of HM Revenue and Customs* [2007] EWHC 2067 (Ch), [2008] 1 BCLC 112.

[1751] See, for example, *Re Ace Telecom Ltd* [2007] EWHC 2272 (Ch), LTL 14/5/2008; *EPIS Services Ltd v Commissioners of HM Revenue and Customs* [2007] EWHC 3534 (Ch), LTL 30/4/2010; *Re Integeral Ltd* [2013] EWHC 164 (Ch), LTL 11/2/2013.

[1752] *El Ajou v Dollar Land (Manhattan) Ltd* [2005] EWHC 2861 (Ch), [2007] BCC 953; *Re Integeral Ltd* [2013] EWHC 164 (Ch), LTL 11/2/2013, at [75].

[1753] IA 1986, ss 213 and 214. *Re Integeral Ltd* [2013] EWHC 164 (Ch), LTL 11/2/2013, at [57] and [58].

[1754] *Re UK Steelfixers Ltd* [2012] EWHC 2409 (Ch), [2012] BCC 751; *Re Brown Bear Foods Ltd* [2014] EWHC 1132 (Ch), LTL 15/4/2014 (in which a provisional liquidator was appointed).

[1755] IA 1986, ss 238–241, 245 and 246; *Re Integeral Ltd* [2013] EWHC 164 (Ch), LTL 11/2/2013, at [59]–[63].

In *Re Logitext.UK Ltd*[1756] an administration order was made because the applicant for that order indicated that funding for investigations by the administrator to recover assets would be made available but there was no evidence that there would be similar funding in a winding up. But evidence from the owner of the company sought to be wound up that funding for a claim against another company would be available only if there was administration and not winding up was not accepted in *Re Integeral Ltd*.[1757]   **7.738**

Company's COMI in another Jurisdiction

If an English registered company's centre of main interests (COMI) is in another jurisdiction outside the United Kingdom, a request by a court in that jurisdiction for the dismissal of a petition to wind up the company in England, because the pendency of that petition jeopardizes a rescue plan in the COMI jurisdiction, is 'an almost overwhelming consideration' in favour of dismissal.[1758]   **7.739**

Interests of Employees

When a creditor of a company petitions for its compulsory liquidation, the court does not consider the interests of the company's employees other than as creditors.[1759] The opposite view has been adopted in India because the country's constitution prescribes that it shall be a socialist democratic republic and requires the State to secure the participation of workers in the management of undertakings.[1760]   **7.740**

Interests of the Public Revenue

In *Deputy Commissioner of Taxation (Vic) v Avram Investments Pty Ltd*[1761] the petitioner said that if the views of objecting creditors were accepted and winding up was not ordered, the public revenue would lose because the company could offset its past trading losses against its future taxable profits, but the court refused to take into account this collateral advantage to the petitioner. Similarly, in *Re Leigh Estates (UK) Ltd*[1762] the court refused to take into account the supposed advantage of the local authority petitioner that if the company were to be wound up its incumbent administrative receiver would become liable to pay rates on property the company occupied.   **7.741**

Payment of Petitioner's Debt

Payment before the Hearing

If, after presentation of a creditor's winding-up petition, the petition debt and costs are paid, the petition will still be before the court unless and until it is withdrawn.[1763] Any other   **7.742**

[1756] [2004] EWHC 2899 (Ch), [2005] 1 BCLC 326.

[1757] *Re Integeral Ltd* [2013] EWHC 164 (Ch), LTL 11/2/2013, at [51].

[1758] *Re Integrated Medical Solutions Ltd* [2012] BCC 215.

[1759] *Re Craven Insurance Co Ltd* [1968] 1 WLR 675; *Re DTX Australia Ltd* (1987) 11 ACLR 444 at p 451; *Commissioner of Inland Revenue v Cappucci Knitwear Ltd* (1989) 3 BCR 274 at p 277.

[1760] *National Textile Workers' Union v Ramakrishnan* [1980–84] LRC (Comm) 729. See K Arjunan, 'Locus standi of employees in companies winding up' (1993) 11 C & SLJ 141.

[1761] (1992) 9 ACSR 580.

[1762] [1994] BCC 292.

[1763] *Re Western Welsh International System Buildings Ltd* (1984) 1 BCC 99,296 at p 99,297.

person who would have a right to present a petition may be substituted as petitioner.[1764] Even if there is no substitution the petition will still be heard if it is not withdrawn.[1765] In Australia, it has been said that the petition ought to be dismissed, unless a positive reason for making a winding-up order is established.[1766] This is on the basis that, even if the petitioner no longer has standing to petition, the court still has power to make a winding-up order on the petition and whether it does so or not is a matter of discretion.[1767] However, it is submitted that if a court has decided that the person who presented a winding-up petition no longer has standing to do so, and no other person has been substituted as petitioner, the only order the court can make is to dismiss the petition,[1768] unless it is one of the thoroughly exceptional cases in which the court may make a winding-up order on its own initiative.[1769] A winding-up order may be made if it is proved that the company owes the petitioner another unpaid debt at the time the petition is heard.[1770]

7.743 If only part of the petitioner's debt is paid before the hearing, the petitioner may still obtain a winding-up order, though the petition may have to be amended and other evidence of inability to pay debts presented,[1771] and if a winding-up order is made, the part-payment will be void under IA 1986, s 127, unless the court orders otherwise.[1772]

7.744 If the petitioner's costs are not paid, the petition may be heard for the purpose of making a costs order.[1773]

7.745 If payment has very recently been made by cheque, even if it is a banker's draft, the petition should be adjourned to allow the cheque to clear.[1774]

7.746 If a creditor of a company petitions for its winding up and is then paid the debt, but some other creditor is substituted and obtains a winding-up order, the payment to the original petitioner

---

[1764] See 3.181–3.206; *Re Bostels Ltd* [1968] Ch 346; *DMK Building Materials Pty Ltd v C B Baker Timbers Pty Ltd* (1985) 10 ACLR 16.
[1765] *Motor Terms Co Pty Ltd v Liberty Insurance Ltd* (1967) 116 CLR 177 per Menzies J at pp 194–5; *Morgan Guaranty Trust Co of New York v Lian Seng Properties Sdn Bhd* [1991] 1 MLJ 95.
[1766] *Motor Terms Co Pty Ltd v Liberty Insurance Ltd* at pp 194–5; *Deputy Commissioner of Taxation v Guy Holdings Pty Ltd* (1994) 14 ACSR 580; *Bidald Consulting Pty Ltd v Miles Special Builders Pty Ltd* [2005] NSWSC 397, 54 ACSR 228, at [15].
[1767] *Motor Terms Co Pty Ltd v Liberty Insurance Ltd* at pp 194–5; *Deputy Commissioner of Taxation v Guy Holdings Pty Ltd* (1994) 14 ACSR 580; *Deputy Commissioner of Taxation v Visidet Pty Ltd* [2005] FCA 830 at [5]–[6]; *Australian Beverage Distributors Pty Ltd v The Redrock Co Pty Ltd* [2007] NSWSC 966, 213 FLR 450, at [33]. There is no reported case in which a winding-up order has been made in these circumstances.
[1768] See 2.68.
[1769] See 2.20–2.22.
[1770] *Deputy Commissioner of Taxation v Guy Holdings Pty Ltd* (1994) 14 ACSR 580; *Bidald Consulting Pty Ltd v Miles Special Builders Pty Ltd* [2005] NSWSC 397, 54 ACSR 228, at [15]. But in *De Montfort v Southern Cross Exploration NL* (1987) 17 NSWLR 327 Needham J thought a winding-up order should not be made in those circumstances, and in New Zealand it has been held that a petitioner who loses standing because the petition debt is paid cannot be substituted for itself so as to proceed, as a substituted petitioner, on the basis of non-payment of another debt (*Re Mercantile Developments Ltd* (1980) Butterworths Current Law Digest 1979–1983 216). In Australia, substitution of the original petitioner is now expressly allowed by the Corporations Act 2001 (Australia), s 465B(3).
[1771] *Re Liverpool Civil Service Association, ex parte Greenwood* (1874) LR 9 Ch App 511; *Re Western Welsh International System Buildings Ltd* (1984) 1 BCC 99,296 at p 99,297; *Kampat Timber Industries Sdn Bhd v Bensa Sdn Bhd* [1990] 2 MLJ 46; *Re Ritecast (S) Pte Ltd* [1996] 2 SLR 65.
[1772] *Re Liverpool Civil Service Association, ex parte Greenwood* (1874) LR 9 Ch App 511.
[1773] See 5.192–5.193.
[1774] *Deputy Commissioner of Taxation v B K Ganter Holdings Pty Ltd* [2008] FCA 1730, 172 FCR 385.

is void under s 127, unless the court orders otherwise.[1775] Accordingly a creditor petitioner is entitled to refuse a tender of payment[1776] but there is no legal obligation to do so.[1777]

If the petitioner refuses a tender of payment of the petition debt, that debt will still be outstanding and it has been said that a winding-up order could still be made,[1778] even if the money is paid into court to show the company's continuing willingness to pay the debt.[1779] However, payment into court would be a complete defence to any claim for the debt, and so, it is submitted, is equivalent to the company having a transaction set-off equal to the petition debt—that is, the petition should be treated as a disputed debt petition.[1780] Alternatively, it has been said that the court would exercise its discretion not to make a winding-up order if the refusal of tender was unreasonable.[1781]   **7.747**

In *Re Concrete Pipes and Cement Products Ltd*[1782] it was said that if payment of a petitioner's debt was tendered and refused before the hearing of the petition, the petitioner should no longer be regarded as being entitled to a winding-up order *ex debito justitiae* but the court would have to consider the position of other creditors. As the company in the case appeared to be solvent, the court adjourned the petition to allow for payment to be made.[1783]   **7.748**

In *Rocks v Brae Hotel (Shetland) Ltd*[1784] a provisional liquidator was appointed. A director of the company, without the provisional liquidator's permission, drew a cheque on the company's bank account for the amount of the petitioner's debt and, without the petitioner's authority, paid it into her bank account. It was held that this was not a 'valid repayment of the debt',[1785] so that the petitioner still had the status of creditor when the petition was heard.   **7.749**

Payment at, or Soon after, the Hearing

If, at the hearing of a creditor's petition to wind up a company, the company tenders payment of the petitioner's debt and costs, and there is no supporting creditor willing to be substituted as petitioner, the court will usually adjourn the petition for 14 days with a view to dismissing it when payment has cleared.[1786] A petition which is supported by other creditors   **7.750**

[1775] *Re Western Welsh International System Buildings Ltd* (1984) 1 BCC 99,296.
[1776] *Re Bostels Ltd* [1968] Ch 346; *Australian Mid-Eastern Club Ltd v Yassim* (1989) 1 ACSR 399; *Occidental Life Insurance Co of Australia Ltd v Life Style Planners Pty Ltd* (1992) 111 ALR 261. Contrast *Re Times Life Assurance and Guarantee Co* (1869) LR 9 Eq 382 and *Re Adjustable Horse Shoe Syndicate Ltd* [1890] WN 157, which were decided before substitution of petitioners was allowed. The position where gazetting the petition has been prohibited so that no other creditor will apply to be substituted is uncertain.
[1777] See *Nationwide Produce Holdings Pty Ltd v Franklins Ltd* [2001] NSWSC 1120, 20 ACLC 309, at [9] (no legal obligation to refuse payment by a company of a debt which would be repayable if it were found to be a preference).
[1778] *Australian Mid-Eastern Club Ltd v Yassim* (1989) 1 ACSR 399; *Deputy Commissioner of Taxation v Barroleg Pty Ltd* (1997) 25 ACSR 167.
[1779] *Australian Beverage Distributors Pty Ltd v The Redrock Co Pty Ltd* [2007] NSWSC 966, 213 FLR 450.
[1780] See 7.652–7.659.
[1781] *Australian Beverage Distributors Pty Ltd v The Redrock Co Pty Ltd* [2007] NSWSC 966, 213 FLR 450, at [33].
[1782] [1926] VLR 34.
[1783] See also *Re Kieran Byrne and Associates Geotechnical Consultants Pty Ltd* (1987) 12 ACLR 367.
[1784] 1997 SLT 474.
[1785] At p 481.
[1786] There should be an adjournment even if a banker's draft is tendered (*Deputy Commissioner of Taxation v B K Ganter Holdings Pty Ltd* [2008] FCA 1730, 172 FCR 385).

will not be dismissed if only the petitioner's debt is paid,[1787] but a petition which is opposed by other creditors may be dismissed if those other creditors pay the petitioner's debt.[1788]

7.751 In Australia, if on an unpaid creditor's petition it appears that the company is solvent, the court may be prepared to adjourn the hearing for a short time to allow the debt to be paid.[1789] In *Re General Rolling Stock Co Ltd*[1790] Romilly MR said that if, on an unpaid creditor's petition, the company asked for time to pay the debt, he was 'disposed to grant that indulgence' provided it was clear that funds were available (normally, in those days, by making a call on members).

7.752 A supporting creditor who intends to apply to be substituted as petitioner if the original petitioning creditor is paid should object to an adjournment for the purpose of paying or agreeing a compromise with the petitioner so that the winding-up proceedings are not prolonged unnecessarily and no void disposition of the company's assets is made to the original petitioner.[1791]

Company Member of Insolvent Partnership

7.753 A company which is in partnership with other persons is liable jointly with the other partners for all debts and obligations of the firm incurred while it is a partner.[1792] Accordingly a creditor of the firm is a creditor of the company and has standing to petition for the company's compulsory winding up.[1793] IPO 1994, art 19(5), authorizes a creditor of an insolvent partnership to petition for a bankruptcy or winding-up order to be made against one member, or for orders against some but not all members, of the firm without petitioning for orders against the other members and without petitioning for the winding up of the firm.[1794]

7.754 IPO 1994, art 8, provides a special procedure by which a creditor can petition for the winding up of a present or former corporate member of an insolvent partnership, in its capacity as such, and the partnership itself. An application to wind up a corporate member under art 8 is, by art 8(4), (8) and (9), governed by the provisions of IA 1986, part 4, in so far as they relate to winding up of companies by the court in England and Wales on a creditor's petition and as modified by IPO 1994, sch 4, part 2.

7.755 The court has jurisdiction to wind up a corporate member of an insolvent partnership on an art 8 petition if it has jurisdiction in respect of the partnership.[1795]

[1787] *Re Pavy's Patent Felted Fabric Co Ltd* (1875) 24 WR 91, decided before substitution of petitioners was allowed.

[1788] *Re Baker Tucker and Co* (1894) 38 SJ 274.

[1789] *Re Concrete Pipes and Cement Products Ltd* [1926] VLR 34; *Re Mittagong RSL Club Ltd* (1980) 4 ACLR 897; *Re Barrier Reef Finance and Land Pty Ltd* [1989] 1 QdR 252; *Ace Contractors and Staff Pty Ltd v Westgarth Development Pty Ltd* [1999] FCA 728.

[1790] (1865) 34 Beav 314.

[1791] *Re Ron Winters Glazing Services Ltd* (1988) 4 NZCLC 64,294.

[1792] Partnership Act 1890, s 9.

[1793] *Schooler v Commissioners of Customs and Excise* [1995] 2 BCLC 610.

[1794] *Schooler v Commissioners of Customs and Excise* [1995] 2 BCLC 610.

[1795] See 1.457–1.459. IA 1986, s 117(5), as modified by IPO 1994, sch 4, para 5.

The only circumstance in which a winding-up order may be made against a corporate mem- **7.756**
ber or former corporate member on an art 8 petition is if the member or former member
is unable to pay its debts.[1796] The only method provided by the legislation for proving that
a corporate member or former corporate member is unable to pay its debts is by statutory
demand under IA 1986, s 123, as modified by IPO 1994, sch 4, para 7(a).[1797] The only type
of creditor who may petition under art 8 is a creditor to whom the corporate member or
former corporate member and the partnership are indebted in respect of a liquidated sum
payable immediately.[1798]

[1796] IA 1986, s 122, as modified by IPO 1994, sch 4, para 6(a).
[1797] See 7.117.
[1798] IA 1986, s 124(2), as modified by IPO 1994, sch 4, para 8.

8

PETITIONS BY CONTRIBUTORIES

Standing of Contributories to Petition and Circumstances in which they may Petition

Standing

General rule

A petition to the court for the winding up of a registered or unregistered company may be **8.1** presented by any contributory[1] or contributories,[2] but this is subject to restrictions which are discussed at 8.29–8.38. The same applies to building societies,[3] incorporated friendly

---

[1] For the definition of 'contributory' see 8.18–8.50.

[2] IA 1986, s 124(1), applied to unregistered companies by s 221(1), but not to relevant schemes (see 1.168), as they do not have contributories (Collective Investment in Transferable Securities (Contractual Scheme) Regulations 2013 (SI 2013/1388), reg 17(9) and sch 2, para 5(d)).

[3] Building Societies Act 1986, s 89(2)(d).

societies,[4] and any other entity that may be wound up as a registered company.[5] For an insolvent partnership, the equivalent of a contributory's petition is a member's petition under IPO 1994, art 9 or art 10. Only an insolvent partnership can be wound up on a member's petition under IPO 1994, but, in practice, almost all contributories' petitions to wind up registered companies relate to solvent companies, which are the main concern of this chapter.

Resolution of a dispute about standing

8.2 If it is disputed that a person petitioning as a contributory for the winding up of a company has standing to do so, that dispute must be resolved before the petition can be heard. Formerly the attitude of the court was that, as with a dispute about a creditor's standing,[6] a dispute about the standing of a person to petition as a contributory should not be resolved in the proceedings on the petition. It was said that such a dispute should be tried in an ordinary action, or an application for rectification of the company's register of members, in which the procedures would be more suited to trying such a question and the company would not be subject to the unfavourable publicity and legal disabilities[7] which attend a company subject to a winding-up petition but which are irrelevant to trying a dispute over whether or not a person is a contributory. A winding-up petition should not be used as a means of putting pressure on a company to meet the petitioner's demands in relation to allotment of shares.[8] As a matter of practice the court would usually dismiss a contributory's petition if there was a dispute about the petitioner's standing.[9] It was not appropriate for a person who had applied for the winding up of a company, claiming to be a contributory, to apply in the winding-up proceedings for rectification of the company's register of members,[10] so as to establish status as a contributory.[11]

8.3 The Court of Appeal pointed out in *Alipour v Ary*[12] that changes in procedure on contributories' winding-up petitions have removed many of the arguments for dismissing a petition because of a dispute over the petitioner's standing. A contributory's petition is not normally advertised and dispositions of the company's property are routinely validated in advance so that the company is not unnecessarily damaged by the existence of the petition. The court expects to deal with complex factual questions when hearing a contributory's petition, and there are no procedural difficulties in resolving the petitioner's standing as a preliminary point. The court said, at pp 545–6:

> It is hard to see why the Companies Court now should normally refuse to determine such a dispute, even if it does relate to the petitioner's *locus standi*, if the existence of the petition is not likely to cause substantial damage or inconvenience to the company.

[4] Friendly Societies Act 1992, s 22(2)(d).
[5] Charitable incorporated organizations (see 1.122), European cooperative societies (see 1.123), European public limited-liability companies (see 1.124), limited liability partnerships (see 1.126) and registered societies (see 1.127–1.129).
[6] See 7.515–7.522.
[7] For example, under IA 1986, s 127.
[8] *Re a Company (No 0089 of 1894)* [1894] 2 Ch 349.
[9] *Re Bambi Restaurants Ltd* [1965] 1 WLR 750; *Re Leon Needham Ltd* (1966) 110 SJ 652; *Higgins v Brock and Higgins Insurance Agencies Ltd* (1976) 22 CBR NS 248 (in which the petitioner also claimed a disputed debt); *Re JN2 Ltd* [1978] 1 WLR 183; *Bital Holdings Ltd v Middleditch* [1992] MCLR 323 at pp 330–1.
[10] Companies Act 2006, s 125.
[11] *Re Fan Bostic Construction Ltd* (1982) 17 Barb LR 84.
[12] [1997] 1 WLR 534.

However, we would not go so far as to say that the court cannot take into account the factor that there is a genuine dispute as to the *locus standi* of the petitioner. There may be evidence of damage or inconvenience caused to the company through the continued existence of the petition, and the circumstances may indicate that the appropriate course is to require the dispute to be determined outside the petition.

The fact that a provisional liquidator has been appointed, on unchallenged evidence that **8.4** the company's assets were in jeopardy, is not damage or inconvenience to the company justifying dismissal of a contributory's petition because of the disputed standing of the petitioner.[13] The fact that the petitioner would probably be left without an effective remedy if the winding-up court dismissed the petition rather than dealing with the dispute about the petitioner's standing is a reason for not dismissing the petition.[14]

Grounds

A contributory cannot petition on the ground that a moratorium has not resulted in an **8.5** approved voluntary arrangement, which is a ground that is only available for a creditor's petition.[15] Apart from this, a contributory may petition on any of the grounds listed in IA 1986, s 122(1)[16] (in relation to a registered company) or s 221(5)[17] (in relation to an unregistered company).[18] The same applies to the separate lists of circumstances set out for some entities that can be wound up as registered companies[19] or the additional circumstances available for some other entities.[20] Any provision in a company's constitution purporting to limit the circumstances in which a member may petition as a contributory is void.[21]

Petition by a Member of a Partnership or a Member's Insolvency Office-holder

Petition by a member of a partnership

A member of a partnership may petition under IPO 1994, art 9 or art 10, for the partner- **8.6** ship to be wound up as an unregistered company. A petition is presented under art 9 if the petitioner does not also petition for the winding up or bankruptcy of any member or former member of the partnership. A petition is presented under art 10 if the petitioner also petitions for the winding up or bankruptcy of all members of the partnership.

If the partnership has eight or more members, any member may petition under art 9.[22] If the **8.7** partnership has fewer than eight members, by IA 1986, s 221A(2) inserted by IPO 1994, sch 5, para 2, a member may, with the leave of the court, obtained on an application

---

[13] *Alipour v Ary* [1997] 1 WLR 534.

[14] *Alipour v Ary.*

[15] IA 1986, ss 122(1)(fa) and 124(3A); IA 1986, ss 122(1)(da) and 124(3A), as modified by the Limited Liability Partnerships Regulations 2001 (SI 2001/1090), sch 3; IA 1986, ss 122(1)(d) and 124(3A), as modified by the Charitable Incorporated Organisations (Insolvency and Dissolution) Regulations 2012 (SI 2012/3013), sch, para 1(5) and (7).

[16] See 2.27.

[17] See 2.37.

[18] *Re Shelbourne Cheese Manufacturing and Produce Co Ltd* (1888) 14 VLR 294 per Webb J at pp 296–7.

[19] Building societies (see 2.29–2.30), charitable incorporated organizations (see 2.31), incorporated friendly societies (see 2.34) and limited liability partnerships (see 2.35).

[20] European cooperative societies (see 2.32) and European groupings of territorial cooperation (see 2.50–2.51). For European economic interest groupings see 8.12.

[21] *Re Peveril Gold Mines Ltd* [1898] 1 Ch 122.

[22] IA 1986, s 221A(1) inserted by IPO 1994, sch 5, para 2.

by the member, petition for the winding up of the partnership, but only if the court is satisfied that:

(a) a written demand in form 10 in IPO 1986, sch 9, has been served on the partnership in respect of a joint debt or debts exceeding £750 then due from the partnership but paid by the member, other than out of partnership property;

(b) the partnership has for three weeks after the service of the demand neglected to pay the sum or to secure or compound for it to the member's satisfaction; and

(c) the member has obtained a judgment, decree or order of any court against the partnership for reimbursement of the amount of the joint debt or debts so paid; and

(d) all reasonable steps (other than insolvency proceedings) have been taken by the member to enforce that judgment, decree or order.

Form 10 must be served by leaving it at a principal place of business of the partnership in England and Wales, or by delivering it to an officer of the partnership, or in such manner as the court may approve or direct.

8.8 Petitions can be presented under art 10 for the winding up of a partnership and the winding up or bankruptcy of every one of its members only by a member of the partnership and only if all the members consent to orders being made against them.[23]

Petition by member's insolvency office-holder

8.9 By IA 1986, s 221A(1), as modified by IPO 1994, sch 3, para 3, a petition to wind up an insolvent partnership may be presented under IPO 1994, art 7 (where there is no concurrent petition for the winding up or bankruptcy of any member or former member of the partnership), by:

(a) the liquidator or administrator of a corporate member or of a former corporate member, or

(b) the trustee of an individual member's, or of a former individual member's, estate, or

(c) the supervisor of a voluntary arrangement approved under IA 1986, part 1, in relation to a corporate member, or under part 8 in relation to an individual member.

8.10 An insolvency practitioner who presents a petition under this provision may be appointed provisional liquidator and, if the winding-up order is made, liquidator of the partnership.[24]

8.11 If a winding-up or bankruptcy order has been made against a member of a partnership because of that member's inability to pay a joint debt, and the liquidator or trustee of the member presents an art 7 petition on the ground that the partnership is unable to pay its debts, the winding-up or bankruptcy order is proof, unless it is proved otherwise to the satisfaction of the court, that the partnership is unable to pay its debts.[25]

European Economic Interest Groupings

8.12 A member of a European economic interest grouping (EEIG) may apply for the grouping to be wound up by the court 'on just and proper grounds'.[26] It is submitted that the scope of 'just and proper grounds' is at least as extensive as the just and equitable clause in IA 1986,

---

[23] IA 1986, s 124(2), as modified by IPO 1994, sch 6, para 2. Unfortunately IA 1986, s 221(6), as modified by IPO 1994, sch 6, para 4, accidentally provides that s 124(2) does not apply to an art 10 petition; see 1.229.

[24] See 5.143–5.150. IA 1986, s 221A(4) and (5), inserted by IPO 1994, sch 3, para 3.

[25] IA 1986, s 221A(3), as modified by IPO 1994, sch 3, para 3.

[26] Regulation (EEC) No 2137/85, art 32(2), which is applied in the winding up of an EEIG by IA 1986, s 221(1), as modified by the European Economic Interest Grouping Regulations 1989 (SI 1989/638), reg 8(1).

s 221(5)(c). A member of an EEIG would also probably be a 'person concerned' who may apply for winding up under Regulation (EEC) No 2137/85, art 32(1).[27]

Nature of Contributories' Petitions

The members of a registered company may decide that it is to be wound up by passing a special resolution under IA 1986, s 84(1)(b) (voluntary winding up) or s 122(1)(a) (winding up by the court). A petition by a member for winding up by the court is necessary only if the member cannot persuade fellow members to join in passing a special resolution, and the court must be persuaded that, nevertheless, the company must be wound up. **8.13**

A member of a registered company does not have an unqualified right to the dissolution of the association: one of the circumstances in which the court has jurisdiction to make a winding-up order must be established.[28] **8.14**

In relation to a choice between winding up and not winding up, a member must make a 'very strong case' for the court to take the decision away from the domestic forum established for the management of the company's affairs.[29] **8.15**

For the choice between voluntary and compulsory liquidation of a registered company, see 10.122–10.129. **8.16**

Proceedings on a contributory's petition for the winding up of a company are inevitably concerned with the competing interests of the company's members, but the court must also bear in mind the wider interests of the public and in particular the interests of the company's creditors.[30] **8.17**

Which Contributories may Petition

Definition of Contributory

Registered companies

Any person liable to contribute to the assets of a registered company in the event of its being wound up is one of the company's 'contributories'.[31] Until final determination of who is and who is not a contributory of a registered company, a person who is alleged to be a contributory is treated as one.[32] A person may be described as a contributory of a company before the company is wound up even though the person's liability as contributory of the company is not a present liability until the commencement of the company's winding up.[33] Liability, of a person to contribute to the assets of a company, which is created by a declaration of the **8.18**

---

[27] See 2.47–2.49.

[28] See 8.153–8.154.

[29] Per James LJ in *Re Langham Skating Rink Co* (1877) 5 ChD 669 at p 685; see also per Jessel MR in the same case at p 684; per Chisholm J in *Re British Empire Steel Corp Ltd* [1927] 2 DLR 964 at p 968; per Plowman J in *Re Surrey Garden Village Trust Ltd* [1965] 1 WLR 974 at p 981.

[30] *Yuanta Securities Asia Financial Services Ltd v Core Pacific Investment Holdings (BVI) Ltd* [2005] 3 HKLRD 636 per Ma CJHC at [12].

[31] IA 1986, s 79(1); Companies Act 2006, s 1170B(1).

[32] IA 1986, s 79(1); Companies Act 2006, s 1170B(2). See also 8.2–8.4.

[33] Per Wynn-Parry J in *Re H L Bolton Engineering Co Ltd* [1956] Ch 577 at p 584.

court under IA 1986, s 213 (fraudulent trading) or s 214 (wrongful trading), does not make the person a contributory of the company.[34] As in the case of an unregistered company,[35] liability imposed on a person under IA 1986, s 212 (misfeasance proceedings), does not make the person a contributory.[36]

8.19 This definition focuses on contributories as persons liable to contribute to the assets of a company in winding up. In the discussion here, the focus is on contributories as persons sufficiently closely connected to a company to have standing to petition for it to be wound up by the court. The class of contributories eligible to petition for a company's compulsory liquidation is not entirely the same as the class of contributories liable to contribute to its assets in the event of it being liquidated, and cases on liability to contribute are not necessarily good guides to eligibility to petition.[37] IA 1986, s 124(2), imposes qualifying conditions which generally mean that a transferee of shares in a company must be registered as a member for at least six months before being able to petition for it to be wound up.[38]

8.20 The most significant practical difference between being a contributory for the purposes of petitioning and being a contributory for the purposes of liability to contribute to the assets of the company in winding up is that a person whose liability to contribute is nil may nevertheless have standing to petition as a contributory.[39]

8.21 The equivalent of IA 1986, s 79(1), in the Companies Act 1862, was s 74, which defined 'contributory' as meaning 'every person liable to contribute to the assets of a company under this Act, in the event of the same being wound up'. In *Re National Savings Bank Association*[40] Turner LJ said, at p 551, that this 'may well mean every person liable under this Act to contribute'. The drafter of the next consolidation, the Companies (Consolidation) Act 1908, seems to have decided that 'under this Act' merely described 'company' (there being a separate definition of contributory of an unregistered company in the Companies Act 1862, s 200, now IA 1986, s 226) and omitted the words 'under this Act' from the definition of contributory in s 124 of the 1908 Act. Nevertheless, Turner LJ's interpretation is clearly correct so that, as with unregistered companies,[41] a person such as a simple contract debtor of a company whose liability does not depend on it being wound up is not a contributory. This has been held in Canada[42] in relation to the definition of 'contributory' in the Winding-up and Restructuring Act, s 2, as 'a person liable to contribute to the assets of a company under this Act' (the Act being concerned only with contribution in the event of winding up), and so a contributory of a company can owe a debt to the company otherwise than as a contributory.[43]

---

34 IA 1986, s 79(2); Companies Act 2006, s 1170B(3).
35 See *Re Cardiff Savings Bank, Davies's Case* (1890) 45 ChD 537.
36 *Re AMF International Ltd* [1996] 1 WLR 77.
37 *Re a Company (No 003160 of 1986)* [1986] BCLC 391.
38 See 8.29–8.38.
39 See 8.52 and 8.57.
40 (1866) LR 1 Ch App 547.
41 See 8.49.
42 *Re Central Bank of Canada, Yorke's Case* (1888) 15 OR 625.
43 *Ings v Bank of Prince Edward Island* (1885) 11 SCR 265.

The classes of persons liable under IA 1986 to contribute to the assets of a registered **8.22**
company in the event of its being wound up, and who are, by s 79, the company's
contributories, are:

(a) Present and past members.[44] This includes any person to whom shares in the company
have been transferred, or transmitted by operation of law,[45] but who is not registered as a
member.[46]
(b) Persons whose shares in the company were purchased or redeemed by the company with
a payment out of capital within the preceding year and directors who signed the statutory declaration made in accordance with the Companies Act 2006, s 714(1)–(3).[47]

Contributories include members whose shares are fully paid.[48] The argument that fully paid **8.23**
shareholders are contributories only for certain purposes was expressly rejected by Turner LJ in
Re National Savings Bank Association at pp 549–50: that argument was accepted by Maugham
J in *Re Aidall Ltd*[49] without having been referred to the earlier case.

In the case of a company registered but not formed under the Companies Act 2006,[50] contribu- **8.24**
tories are listed in IA 1986, s 83.

Registered companies: members under 18
A contributory who is a child under 18 may petition[51] by a litigation friend,[52] though the court **8.25**
may permit the child to conduct proceedings without a litigation friend.[53]

Registered companies: joint members
In Australia it has been held that where a share in a company is held jointly, each of the **8.26**
joint holders is a contributory and so entitled to present a contributory's petition for the
company's winding up, provided the conditions stated at 8.29 are satisfied.[54] In England
it has been pointed out that the nature of the joint holding may require the holders to act
unanimously. This applies if:

(a) the joint owners are trustees who must act unanimously;[55] or
(b) the holding is a joint tenancy.[56]

---

[44] s 74.
[45] As personal representative of a deceased member or as trustee of a bankrupt member.
[46] s 250.
[47] IA 1986, s 76.
[48] *Re National Savings Bank Association* (1866) LR 1 Ch App 547; *Re Anglesea Colliery Co* (1866) LR 1 Ch App 555; *Re Phoenix Oil and Transport Co Ltd* [1958] Ch 560; see also on the Canadian legislation *Christie v Edwards* [1939] 1 DLR 158.
[49] [1933] Ch 323 at pp 328–30.
[50] See 1.4.2.2.
[51] *Dennison v Jeffs* [1896] 1 Ch 611 per North J at p 617.
[52] CPR, r 21.2(2).
[53] r 21.2(3).
[54] *Re Peerless Engineering Co Pty Ltd* [1955] VLR 170.
[55] See 8.39–8.40.
[56] *Re Exchange Travel (Holdings) Ltd* [1991] BCLC 728 at p 735. For the rule that joint tenants must act unanimously see *Leek and Moorlands Building Society v Clark* [1952] 2 QB 788; *Newman v Keedwell* (1977) 35 P & CR 393. But as joint tenants must act unanimously to renew a periodic tenancy, a notice of refusal to renew given by one of them only is effective: see *Leek and Moorlands Building Society v Clark*; *Hammersmith and Fulham London Borough Council v Monk* [1992] 1 AC 478; *Sims v Dacorum Borough Council* [2014] UKSC 63, [2014] 3 WLR 1600.

8.27 The cases also refer to whether the liability of joint shareholders is joint only[57] or joint and several.[58]

8.28 However, in another English case it was held that joint shareholders must act unanimously without any reference to, or investigation of, the nature of the shareholding.[59]

Registered companies: conditions relating to acquisition of shares

8.29 Standing of a contributory of a registered company to petition for it to be wound up is restricted by IA 1986, s 124(2)(b),[60] which provides that a contributory's petition may be presented only if[61] shares which give the petitioner the status of contributory:

(i)   were originally allotted to the petitioner, or

(ii) have been registered in the petitioner's name for at least six of the 18 months preceding presentation of the petition; or

(iii) have devolved on the petitioner through the death of a former holder.

This restriction does not apply if the number of members of a company has been reduced below two[62] or to a past member in the circumstances described at 8.58.

8.30 It is sufficient if some of the shares by virtue of which the petitioner is a contributory satisfy one of the conditions in s 124(2)(b). One of the conditions must be satisfied at the time of petitioning, in particular, a petitioner seeking to qualify by condition (ii) must have been registered for six months by the time of presenting the petition.[63]

8.31 A contributory's petition will not be dismissed merely because there is no statement in it of how the petitioner has complied with s 124(2)(b), but the court must be satisfied that the petitioner has complied with it before making a winding-up order.[64]

8.32 It would seem that joint petitioners must each satisfy s 124(2)(b). It is submitted that if a share was originally allotted to, or has been held by, and registered in the names of, or has devolved on two or more persons jointly, then the relevant qualification has been gained by each of them.[65]

Number of members reduced below two

8.33 If the number of members of a company is reduced below two, a contributory may petition for it to be wound up despite not qualifying under IA 1986, s 124(2)(b).[66] It would seem that the number of members includes persons who are regarded as members by virtue of s 250, that is, persons to whom shares in the company have been transferred, or transmitted

---

[57] *Re Exchange Travel (Holdings) Ltd* [1991] BCLC 728 at p 735. Joint liability is the default position (*Re Maria Anna and Steinbank Coal and Coke Co, Hill's Case* (1875) LR 20 Eq 585 at 595).

[58] As it was under the articles of the company in *Re Peerless Engineering Co Pty Ltd* [1955] VLR 170 and is under the Model Articles for Public Companies, art 55(2), in the Companies (Model Articles) Regulations 2008 (SI 2008/3229), sch 3.

[59] *Dennison v Jeffs* [1896] 1 Ch 611.

[60] Introduced by the Companies Act 1867, s 40.

[61] s 124(2)(b).

[62] s 124(2)(a); see 8.33–8.34.

[63] *Bital Holdings Ltd v Middleditch* [1992] MCLR 323 at p 330.

[64] *Re City and County Bank* (1875) LR 10 Ch App 470; *Re Glendower Steamship Co Ltd* (1899) 43 SJ 657; *Re a Company (No 007936 of 1994)* [1995] BCC 705.

[65] See *Re Peerless Engineering Co Pty Ltd* [1955] VLR 170.

[66] IA 1986, s 124(2)(a).

by operation of law,[67] but have not been registered as members. This would mean that the death of one of two members would not reduce the number of members below two.

In *Re Pimlico Capital Ltd*[68] the applicant argued that if a company had only ever had one **8.34** member, it could not be said that the number of its members has been 'reduced' below two, so as to permit a contributory to petition despite not qualifying under s 124(2)(b).[69] However, Lawrence Collins J held, at [31]–[32], that the person whose compliance with s 124(2) was in question was not a contributory at all, so s 124(2) was irrelevant. (Although the point is perhaps ambiguously expressed in the judgment, it is submitted that the headnote is erroneous in saying that it was held that the person could petition because the number of members had not been reduced below two.)

Original allottee

The fact that the court has ordered specific performance of a contract to allot shares to a person **8.35** and has ordered rectification of the register of members accordingly is sufficient to prove that the person is an original allottee[70] and an original allottee may petition despite never having been entered on the register of members.[71] A person who has entered into an 'agreement to agree' about terms on which he is to become a member of a company does not have standing to petition as a contributory.[72]

In *Re Littlehampton, Havre and Honfleur Steamship Co Ltd*[73] a transferee of a 'provisional scrip **8.36** certificate' (a document akin to a renounceable letter of allotment but transferable by delivery) was held to have standing to petition, on his undertaking to submit to be a contributory, but in *Re Littlehampton, Havre and Honfleur Steamship Co Ltd, Ormerod's Case*[74] it was held that an allottee of scrip certificates in the company had no liability to contribute in respect of the scrip.

Registered for six months

Condition (ii) in 8.29 is satisfied only if there has been actual registration for six months. An **8.37** entitlement to be registered is not enough.[75] The existence of an estoppel by representation precluding the company from denying that the petitioner is a shareholder is not enough.[76] Registration is sufficient to satisfy condition (ii): provided the contributory has been registered as holder of the shares for the requisite period it does not matter that the contributory was not the beneficial owner of them throughout the period.[77]

Non-shareholding member

IA 1986, s 124(2),[78] is irrelevant to a contributory whose liability to contribute arises other- **8.38** wise than by virtue of a shareholding. This is the case, for example, with a contributory liable as a director, or a contributory of a company without a share capital (a company

---

[67] As personal representative of a deceased member or as trustee of a bankrupt member.
[68] [2002] EWHC 878 (Ch), [2002] 2 BCLC 544.
[69] See at [30].
[70] *Re Patent Steam Engine Co* (1878) 8 ChD 464.
[71] *Re JN2 Ltd* [1978] 1 WLR 183.
[72] *Wallace v Fisher* (1986) 75 NSR (2d) 183.
[73] (1865) 2 De G J & S 521.
[74] (1867) LR 5 Eq 110.
[75] *Re Gattopardo Ltd* [1969] 1 WLR 619.
[76] *Re UOC Corporation* [2003] EWHC 530 (Ch), LTL 13/3/2003.
[77] *Re Wala Wynaad Indian Gold Mining Co* (1882) 21 ChD 849. See further 8.51–8.63.
[78] See 8.29–8.37.

without a share capital must be either a guarantee company or an unlimited company). In a case concerning a guarantee company[79] the Hong Kong equivalent of s 124(2)[80] was not mentioned, and the court held that members of the company had standing to petition because they were entitled to have their names entered in the register of members, even though their names had not been registered, which is not the case under IA 1986, s 124(2).[81]

Trustee shareholder

8.39 If a company share is held in trust jointly by two or more trustees, they must act unanimously in presenting a contributories' petition for the winding up of the company, unless the terms of the trust provide otherwise.[82]

8.40 In the Cayman Islands it has been held that if a share in a company is held on trust for a beneficiary and the trustee refuses to act on a request by the beneficiary to petition for the company to be wound up, the court should not authorize the beneficiary to petition as a derivative claimant.[83]

Building societies and incorporated friendly societies

8.41 The definition of 'contributory' in IA 1986, s 79, does not apply to building societies or incorporated friendly societies.[84] The definitions of 'contributory' given in the Building Societies Act 1986, sch 15, para 9(2) and the Friendly Societies Act 1992, sch 10, para 9(2), are identical. As with the definition of a contributory of a registered company,[85] a contributory of a society is defined as every person liable to contribute to the assets of the society in the event of its being wound up but excluding persons liable to contribute under IA 1986, ss 213 and 214. In relation to a society, 'contributory' includes persons who are liable to pay or contribute to the payment of:

(a) any debt or liability of the society being wound up, or
(b) any sum for the adjustment of rights of members among themselves, or
(c) the expenses of the winding up.

8.42 A contributory of a building society may not present a petition unless either:[86]

(a) the number of members is reduced below ten, or
(b) the share in respect of which the petitioner is a contributory has been held by the petitioner, or has devolved to the petitioner on the death of a former holder and between them been held, for at least six months before the commencement of the winding up.

8.43 A contributory of an incorporated friendly society may not present a petition unless either:[87]

(a) the number of members is reduced below seven, or
(b) the petitioner has been a contributory for at least six months before the winding up.

---

[79] *Mak Sik Bun v Mak Lei Wun* [2005] 4 HKLRD 328.
[80] Companies Ordinance (Hong Kong), s 179(1)(a).
[81] *Re Gattopardo Ltd* [1969] 1 WLR 619. See 8.37.
[82] *Re Exchange Travel (Holdings) Ltd* [1991] BCLC 728. For the rule that trustees must act unanimously unless the terms of the trust provide otherwise, see *Luke v South Kensington Hotel Co* (1879) 11 ChD 121. This point was not raised in *Re Peerless Engineering Co Pty Ltd* [1955] VLR 170, where shares had devolved on two executors but it was held that a petition could be presented by just one of them.
[83] *Hannoun v R Ltd* 2009 CILR 124.
[84] Building Societies Act 1986, sch 15, para 9(1); Friendly Societies Act 1992, sch 10, para 9(1).
[85] See 8.18.
[86] Building Societies Act 1986, s 89(3).
[87] Friendly Societies Act 1992, s 22(3).

Limited liability partnerships

Any past or present member of a limited liability partnership liable to contribute to its **8.44** assets in the event of its being wound up is one of the LLP's 'contributories'.[88] This does not include a person liable by virtue of a declaration by the court under IA 1986, s 213 (liability for fraudulent trading), s 214 (liability for wrongful trading) or s 214A (adjustment of withdrawals).[89]

The provisions of IA 1986, s 124(2)[90] and (3),[91] do not apply to a contributory's petition to **8.45** wind up an LLP.[92]

Charitable incorporated organizations

The provisions of IA 1986, s 124(2)[93] and (3),[94] do not apply to a petition by a member of a **8.46** charitable incorporated organization to wind up the CIO.[95]

Unregistered companies

IA 1986, s 226, contains provisions relating to contributories of unregistered companies. **8.47** The text is as follows:

> **226 Contributories in winding up of unregistered company**
> (1) In the event of an unregistered company being wound up, every person is deemed a contributory who is liable to pay or contribute to the payment of any debt or liability of the company, or to pay or contribute to the payment of any sum for the adjustment of the rights of members among themselves, or to pay or contribute to the payment of the expenses of winding up the company.
> (2) Every contributory is liable to contribute to the company's assets all sums due from him in respect of any such liability as is mentioned above.
> (3) In the case of an unregistered company engaged in or formed for working mines within the stannaries, a past member is not liable to contribute to the assets if he has ceased to be a member for two years or more either before the mine ceased to be worked or before the date of the winding-up order.

It is submitted that, by virtue of s 221(1) the restrictions in s 124(2)[96] apply to petitions by **8.48** contributories of unregistered companies. The contrary was argued in *Re Pimlico Capital Ltd*,[97] but it was held, at [31]–[32], that the person whose compliance with s 124(2) was in question was not a contributory at all, so s 124(2) was irrelevant. In *Re London, Bristol and South Wales Direct Railway Co, ex parte Capper*[98] a holder of scrip certificates for shares in a company provisionally registered under the Joint Stock Companies Act 1844 who had not

---

[88] IA 1986, s 79(1), as modified by the Limited Liability Partnerships Regulations 2001 (SI 2001/1090), reg 5 and sch 3.
[89] IA 1986, s 79(2), as modified by SI 2001/1090, reg 5 and sch 3.
[90] See 8.29.
[91] See 8.58.
[92] SI 2001/1090, sch 3.
[93] See 8.29.
[94] See 8.58.
[95] Charitable Incorporated Organisations (Insolvency and Dissolution) Regulations 2012 (SI 2012/3013), sch, para 1(7).
[96] See 8.29.
[97] [2002] EWHC 878 (Ch), [2002] 2 BCLC 544.
[98] (1849) 3 De G & Sm 1.

signed the subscribers' agreement or subscription contract was held to be entitled to present a winding-up petition under the Joint Stock Companies Winding-up Act 1848. It may be that, because of IA 1986, s 124(2), such a person would not have standing to petition under IA 1986, part 5.

8.49 A person who is liable to an unregistered company is a contributory only if the liability is 'a legal or equitable liability to contribute in the character of a partner'.[99] A mere debtor to a company is not a contributory.[100] Liability imposed on a person under IA 1986, s 212 (misfeasance proceedings), does not make the person a contributory.[101]

Partnerships

8.50 The provisions of IA 1986, s 124(2)[102] and (3),[103] do not apply to a petition by a member of a partnership to wind up the partnership. In relation to petitions under IPO 1994, art 9, the subsections are excluded by IA 1986, s 221(6), as modified by IPO 1994, sch 5, para 2. In relation to art 10 petitions, the modified version of s 124 set out in para 2 of sch 6 to the Order does not include the provisions, though the situation is confused by a drafting error.[104]

Present Members

Registered companies

8.51 Any person liable to contribute to the assets of a registered company in the event of its being wound up is one of the company's 'contributories'.[105] Accordingly a person may petition as a contributory for the winding up of a company if, at the time of presenting the petition, that person is a member of the company, because in the event of the company being ordered to be wound up on the petition, IA 1986, s 74(1), will make the petitioner, as a 'present' member (meaning a member at the time winding up commenced[106]) 'liable to contribute to its assets'. This is subject to the restriction in IA 1986, s 124(2), which is discussed at 8.29–8.38.

8.52 The fact that the shares of a present member of a company limited by shares are fully paid up (so that, by s 74(2)(d), the member's liability to contribute to the assets of the company is nil) does not affect the member's standing to petition as a contributory.[107] (Before the question was settled on appeal in *Re National Savings Bank Association*, Kindersley V-C in *Re Cheshire Patent Salt Co Ltd*[108] thought it very doubtful that a holder of fully paid shares could petition while Romilly MR seems to have taken the view that although a fully paid

---

[99] Per James LJ in *Ex parte British Nation Life Assurance Association* (1878) 8 ChD 679 at p 708.
[100] *Re Shields Marine Insurance Association, Lee and Moor's Case* (1868) LR 5 Eq 368; *Re Hoylake Railway Co, ex parte Littledale* (1874) LR 9 Ch App 257; *Ex parte British Nation Life Assurance Association* (1878) 8 ChD 679.
[101] *Re Cardiff Savings Bank, Davies's Case* (1890) 45 ChD 537.
[102] See 8.29–8.32.
[103] See 8.58.
[104] See 1.229.
[105] IA 1986, s 79(1); Companies Act 2006, s 1170B(1).
[106] *Re National Bank of Wales, Taylor, Phillips and Rickards's Cases* [1897] 1 Ch 298.
[107] *Re National Savings Bank Association* (1866) LR 1 Ch App 547; *Re Macdonald and Noxon Brothers Manufacturing Co Ltd* (1888) 16 OR 368; *Walker* (1894) 2 SLT 397; *Re Timbers Ltd* (1917) 35 DLR 431; *Re Pe Ben Pipelines Ltd* (1978) 7 Alta LR (2d) 174.
[108] (1863) 1 New Rep 533.

shareholder had standing to petition, the petition would succeed only in exceptional circumstances,[109] though his Lordship made an order on a fully paid contributory's petition in *Re Constantinople and Alexandria Hotels Co Ltd*;[110] however, in *Re Patent Bread Machinery Co Ltd*[111] his Lordship is reported as saying that a holder of fully paid-up shares is not a contributory.)

A member of a company with partly paid shares will not be precluded from petitioning **8.53** for the company to be wound up just because of being in arrears with calls,[112] but the arrears must be paid or at least paid into court.[113] Before the Court of Appeal's decision in *Re Diamond Fuel Co*, a contributory in arrears with calls was held not to be entitled to petition in *Re European Life Assurance Society*;[114] *Re Steam Stoker Co*;[115] and *Re Petersburgh and Viborg Gas Co, ex parte Hartmont*,[116] but such a contributory had been granted a winding-up order in *Re York and London Assurance Co, ex parte Hodsell*[117] (where the contributory was being sued for payment of calls) and *Re Birch Torr and Vitifer Co, ex parte Lawton*.[118]

A provision in a company's constitution relieving members of liability to contribute in the **8.54** event of liquidation is void because IA 1986, ss 88 and 127, make void any alteration in the status of a company's members after commencement of liquidation without the sanction of the court.[119]

Building societies and incorporated friendly societies

A present member of a building society or incorporated friendly society is a contributory by **8.55** virtue of IA 1986, s 74(1), and the Building Societies Act 1986, sch 15, para 9(2), and the Friendly Societies Act 1992, sch 10, para 9(2). A present member of a society can petition for its winding up subject to the restrictions discussed at 8.41–8.43.

Unregistered companies

In *Re Welsh Highland Railway Light Railway Co*[120] Vinelott J said, obiter, at p 353, that **8.56** a member of an unregistered share company who held only fully paid shares and so had none of the liabilities mentioned in IA 1986, s 226(1),[121] was not a contributory. In *Re Greater Beijing Region Expressways Ltd*,[122] however, Le Pichon J came to the opposite conclusion.

---

[109] *Re Patent Artificial Stone Co Ltd* (1864) 34 LJ Ch 330; *Re Lancashire Brick and Tile Co* (1865) 34 LJ Ch 331; *Re London Armoury Co Ltd* (1865) 11 Jur NS 963.
[110] (1865) 13 WR 851.
[111] (1866) 14 LT 582.
[112] *Re Diamond Fuel Co* (1879) 13 ChD 400.
[113] *Re Crystal Reef Gold Mining Co* [1892] 1 Ch 408; *Re Gee Floor Scrubbing Machine Co Ltd* (1898) 42 SJ 819; *Re West African Rubber, Oil, Gold and Stores Syndicate Ltd* (1914) *The Times*, 14 October 1914.
[114] (1870) LR 10 Eq 403.
[115] (1875) LR 19 Eq 416.
[116] (1875) 33 LT 637.
[117] (1849) 19 LJ Ch 234.
[118] (1854) 1 Kay & J 204.
[119] *Re National Bank of Wales, Taylor, Phillips and Rickards's Cases* [1897] 1 Ch 298 per Lindley LJ at p 306.
[120] [1993] BCLC 338.
[121] See 8.47.
[122] [2000] 2 HKLRD 776.

Past Members

Registered companies

8.57 A person who is a past member of a registered company may, in principle, petition as a contributory for its winding up because, in the event of the company being ordered to be wound up on the petition, the person is, under IA 1986, s 74(1), 'liable to contribute to its assets'. Although the cases in which a member holding only fully paid shares has been held to be a contributory[123] have concerned only present members, it is submitted that the same reasoning must apply to past members. In *Re Consolidated Goldfields of New Zealand Ltd*[124] it was held that a past member holding only fully paid shares is a 'member' for the purposes of s 74(2)(f), which provides that a sum due from a company being wound up to one of its members, qua member, is not payable in competition with money due to a creditor who is not a member. The paragraph goes on to provide that such a sum can be taken into account 'for the purpose of the final adjustment of the rights of the contributories among themselves'. In *Re Anglesea Colliery Co*[125] (in which a present member holding only fully paid shares was held to be a contributory) Turner LJ said, at p 560, that the terms 'member' and 'contributory' are used interchangeably in this provision. Roxburgh J in *Re Consolidated Goldfields of New Zealand Ltd* rejected the argument that a past member who had held only fully paid shares could not be a member for the purposes of s 74(2)(f) because such a person could not be a contributory, holding that, following *Re Anglesea Colliery Co*, such a person is a contributory. However, the restrictions on contributories' standing to petition contained in IA 1986, s 124(2),[126] apply, and it may be very difficult for a past member of a company to demonstrate a tangible interest in having it wound up.[127]

8.58 The restrictions in s 124(2) do not apply to a petition to wind up a company presented by a person whose shares in the company were purchased or redeemed by the company with a payment out of capital within the preceding year.[128] However, such a contributory is restricted to petitioning only in the circumstances specified in s 122(1)(f) (company's inability to pay its debts) or s 122(1)(g) (just and equitable).[129]

Building societies and incorporated friendly societies

8.59 Past members of building societies are not contributories[130] nor are past members of incorporated friendly societies.[131]

Unregistered companies

8.60 In *Re Times Fire Assurance Co*[132] four past members of a company incorporated by registration under the Joint Stock Companies Act 1844 were granted a winding-up order. Under the Act they had personal unlimited liability for the debts of the company even before winding up and had already been compelled to pay some of its debts.

---

[123] See 8.52.
[124] [1953] Ch 689.
[125] (1866) LR 1 Ch App 555.
[126] See 8.29–8.38.
[127] See 8.83–8.85.
[128] IA 1986, s 124(3).
[129] IA 1986, s 124(3).
[130] Building Societies Act 1986, sch 15, para 7(2).
[131] Friendly Societies Act 1992, sch 10, para 7(2).
[132] (1861) 30 Beav 596.

Personal Representatives and Trustees in Bankruptcy of Members

If the shares in respect of which a person is a contributory of a company, or some of them, **8.61** have devolved on that person through the death of a former holder then the person has, under IA 1986, s 124(2)(b), standing to petition for the company's compulsory winding up. This provision permits a personal representative of a deceased member to petition even if not entered as a member on the company's register.[133] The provision in IA 1986, s 81, that if a contributory of a company dies then his or her personal representatives become contributories in his or her place, operates only after the company has gone into liquidation.[134] However, where legislation has not included a provision like IA 1986, s 124(2)(b), courts have concluded that unregistered personal representatives of deceased members are contributories who have standing to petition as such.[135]

The shares of a member of a company who is bankrupt will have vested in the trustee in **8.62** bankruptcy in accordance with IA 1986, s 306, but the trustee does not become a contributory ex officio unless the company goes into liquidation, in which case s 82 makes the trustee of a bankrupt a contributory in place of the bankrupt. So, except where the company is already in voluntary liquidation, the trustee has no standing to petition for the company to be wound up by the court unless he or she has been registered as the holder of the shares in the company's register of members and the registration has been for at least six months as required by s 124(2).[136] If the trustee in bankruptcy is not registered in place of the bankrupt (and the company has not gone into voluntary liquidation), a petition can be presented by the bankrupt, provided the bankrupt is within the restrictions imposed by s 124(2).[137] The provision in s 82 that a bankrupt contributory of a company is replaced as contributory by his or her trustee operates only after the company has gone into liquidation.[138]

In Scotland, in *Cumming's Trustee v Glenrinnes Farms Ltd*[139] it was held that the power to **8.63** petition for the winding up of a company in which a bankrupt holds shares is part of the 'whole estate of the debtor' which vests in the trustee under the Bankruptcy (Scotland) Act 1985, s 31, because it falls within the category, 'the capacity to exercise and to take proceedings for exercising, all such powers in, over, or in respect of any property as might have been exercised by the debtor for his own benefit as at, or on, the date of sequestration or might be exercised on [a date after the date of sequestration and before the date on which the debtor's discharge becomes effective]'.[140] Accordingly the trustee is entitled to petition for the winding up of the company. In the bankruptcy law of England and Wales, the provision corresponding to s 31 of the Bankruptcy (Scotland) Act 1985 is IA 1986, s 283, in which s 283(4) refers to 'any power exercisable by [a bankrupt] over or in respect of property [with some exceptions]', but this has always been taken to refer to powers of appointment.

---

[133] *Re Bayswater Trading Co Ltd* [1970] 1 WLR 343.
[134] *Re H L Bolton Engineering Co Ltd* [1956] Ch 577 per Wynn-Parry J at p 582; *Re Bayswater Trading Co Ltd* [1970] 1 WLR 343.
[135] *Re Norwich Yarn Co* (1850) 12 Beav 366; *Re Great West Permanent Loan Co* [1927] 2 WWR 15.
[136] *Re Fox Johnson and Co Ltd* (1941) 23 CBR 205; *Re H L Bolton Engineering Co Ltd* [1956] Ch 577.
[137] *Re K/9 Meat Supplies (Guildford) Ltd* [1966] 1 WLR 1112; *Ng Yat Chi v Max Share Ltd* [1998] 1 HKLRD 866.
[138] *Re H L Bolton Engineering Co Ltd* [1956] Ch 577.
[139] 1993 SLT 904.
[140] s 31(8).

Transferor or Beneficial Owner of Shares

8.64 If shares of a member of a company have been transferred but the transferee has not been registered in the company's register of members as the new holder of the shares, the transferee may require the transferor to petition for the company to be wound up.[141] If the transfer is contractual, the transferee could probably obtain an injunction to prevent the transferor petitioning without the transferee's consent, so as to prevent a breach of contract by delivering shares in a company subject to a winding-up petition instead of the promised shares in a company not so subject.[142] A transferee who has breached the contract of sale loses any right to halt the transferor's petition.[143]

8.65 If a share in a company is held by a bare trustee, the trustee's power to petition for the winding up of the company is part of the property held on trust for the beneficial owner and must be exercised at the direction of the beneficial owner, provided a proper indemnity is offered.[144]

8.66 In *Miharja Development Sdn Bhd v Tan Sri Datuk Loy Hean Heong*[145] it was held that persons who had mortgaged their shares in a company could petition for it to be wound up despite the fact that the shares had been registered in the name of a nominee for the mortgagee. The mortgagee had not taken any steps to enforce the security. This decision seems very doubtful. The petitioners were not contributories or even members of the company: their standing to petition could only arise as past members.

Tangible Interest

Requirement

8.67 A winding-up order will not be made on a contributory's petition unless the petitioner has a sufficient interest in having the company wound up.[146] This rule does not apply only to petitions on the just and equitable ground: it applies whatever circumstance the petitioner alleges gives the court jurisdiction to wind up the company.[147] The interest that a contributory must have is known as a 'tangible interest', a phrase used by Jessel MR in *Re Rica Gold Washing Co* at p 43. A tangible interest is also required of a contributory who wishes to be heard on some other person's petition.[148] The petitioner's tangible interest must be alleged in the petition. For the way in which this may be done see *Re W R Willcocks and Co Ltd.*[149]

---

[141] *Ng Yat Chi v Max Share Ltd* [1998] 1 HKLRD 866, in which the transferor was bankrupt and it was held that it made no difference that his trustee had disclaimed the shares.

[142] Cf *Kells Investments Pty Ltd v Industrial Equity Ltd* (1984) 9 ACLR 507, in which a transferor was prohibited from voting in favour of the company's voluntary liquidation.

[143] *Re Bond Street Development Co Ltd* [1965–70] 2 LRB 398; *Re Commercial Pacific Lumber Exports Pty Ltd* [1971–72] P&NGLR 178.

[144] *Kelly v Mawson* (1982) 6 ACLR 667.

[145] [1995] 1 MLJ 101.

[146] See 2.127–2.141. *Re Great Munster Railway Co, ex parte Inderwick* (1850) 3 De G & Sm 231; *Re Patent Artificial Stone Co Ltd* (1864) 34 LJ Ch 330; *Re Lancashire Brick and Tile Co Ltd* (1865) 34 LJ Ch 331; *Re London Permanent Benefit Building Society* (1869) 21 LT 8; *Re Rica Gold Washing Co* (1879) 11 ChD 36; *Re Italcomm (Western Nigeria) Ltd* 1972 (2) ALR Comm 293; *Win-Doors Ltd v Bryan* (1990) 27 JLR 292; *O'Connor v Atlantis Fisheries Ltd* 1998 SCLR 401; *Re GATX Flightlease Aircraft Co Ltd* 2004–05 CILR N-38.

[147] *O'Connor v Atlantis Fisheries Ltd* 1998 SCLR 401.

[148] *Re Rodencroft Ltd* [2004] EWHC 862 (Ch), [2004] 1 WLR 1566.

[149] [1974] Ch 163.

Disputes about whether a petitioner has a tangible interest can usually be resolved in the winding-up proceedings and so only prima facie evidence of a tangible interest is required to give standing to petition.[150]

Dismissing a contributory's petition because of the petitioner's lack of tangible interest does **8.68** not infringe IA 1986, s 125(1), because, apparently, the court is not dismissing the petition *only* because of the company's lack of free assets.[151]

There is no equivalent of the tangible interest rule in relation to unfair prejudice petitions.[152] **8.69** For criticism of the tangible interest rule see G Pitt, 'Winding up on the "just and equitable" ground' (1977) 127 NLJ 619. The rule has been rejected in the Republic of Ireland[153] and abolished by statute in Australia,[154] Malaysia and Singapore.[155]

A contributory's tangible interest may be an interest in receiving something[156] or an interest **8.70** in limiting a liability.[157] A member of a limited company whose shares are fully paid up has no further liability to limit. It follows that a fully paid-up shareholder in a limited company does not have standing to petition for it to be wound up unless it can be shown that there would be a surplus for contributories.[158]

Interest in Receiving

Type of receipt

It seems that the only tangible interest in receiving something which can be claimed by **8.71** a contributory of a registered company is the probability of receiving a dividend in the winding up.[159] It seems that this may be a dividend on a debt owed by the company to the petitioner,[160] but it is submitted that if the only interest of a petitioner is as a creditor then the petition is a creditor's not a contributory's even if the petitioner is a member of the company.

---

[150] *CVC/Opportunity Equity Partners Ltd v Demarco Almeida* [2002] UKPC 16, [2002] 2 BCLC 108, at [13].
[151] See 2.135. *Re Kaslo-Slocan Mining and Financial Corporation Ltd* [1910] WN 13; *Re Taranaki Amusements (Hawera) Ltd* [1935] NZLR s 33; *Re Othery Construction Ltd* [1966] 1 WLR 69.
[152] *Re Martin Coulter Enterprises Ltd* [1988] BCLC 12.
[153] *Re Connemara Mining Co plc* [2013] IEHC 225.
[154] *Re Campbell's Corporation Ltd* (1978) 3 ACLR 519. Nevertheless, a member's application to wind up a company will be dismissed if winding up will not confer any benefit on the applicant (*Joint v Stephens (No 2)* [2008] VSC 69).
[155] *Miharja Development Sdn Bhd v Tan Sri Datuk Loy Hean Heong* [1995] 1 MLJ 101.
[156] See 8.71–8.79.
[157] See 8.80–8.82.
[158] *CVC/Opportunity Equity Partners Ltd v Demarco Almeida* [2002] UKPC 16, [2002] 2 BCLC 108, at [13].
[159] Per Baggallay LJ in *Re Gold Co* (1879) 11 ChD 701 at p 716; *Re Rica Gold Washing Co* (1879) 11 ChD 36; *Re Nation Building, Land and Investment Co Ltd* (1895) 6 BC (NSW) 14; *Re Tangier Amalgamated Mining Co Ltd* (1906) 39 NSR 373; *Re Cruickshank and Co Ltd* (1910) 13 GLR 307; *Re Taranaki Amusements (Hawera) Ltd* [1935] NZLR s 33; *Re Bellador Silk Ltd* [1965] 1 All ER 667; *Re Othery Construction Ltd* [1966] 1 WLR 69; *Re Expanded Plugs Ltd* [1966] 1 WLR 514; *Re Chesterfield Catering Co Ltd* [1977] Ch 373; *Re a Company (No 002470 of 1988)* [1991] BCLC 480.
[160] *Re Ah Yee Contractors (Pte) Ltd* [1987] SLR 383 (in which the abolition of the tangible interest rule in Singapore was not drawn to the court's attention, see Belinda Ang J in *Summit Co (S) Pte Ltd v Pacific Biosciences Pte Ltd* [2006] SGHC 190, [2007] 1 SLR 46, at [45]); *Culross Global SPC Ltd v Strategic Turnaround Master Partnership Ltd* [2010] UKPC 33, 2010 (2) CILR 364, at [42] (the Privy Council left open the question whether the petitioner could be both a member of the company in respect of shares which it had elected to redeem and a creditor for the unpaid redemption money).

8.72 A contributory of an unregistered company who has been compelled to pay debts of the company may have an interest in obtaining from the other contributories their share of what has been paid.[161]

Showing probability of a distribution to contributories

8.73 The probability that a distribution to contributories will be made in the winding up of a company may be demonstrated by proving:

(a) that the company is presently solvent or at least that it is solvent on the balance sheet test even if it is unable to pay its debts as they fall due,[162] or

(b) that a liquidator would be able to recover assets for the company,[163] or

(c) that the petitioner will receive a share of calls made on other contributories who have paid up a smaller amount on their shares than the petitioner has;[164] the articles may prevent such a call being made.[165]

8.74 The burden of proof is on the petitioner.[166] In *Walker*[167] a winding-up order was made on the petition of a contributory who alleged that there would be a surplus though the company (which had also presented its own petition) denied it. Circumstance (b) is difficult to prove in winding-up proceedings.[168] As circumstance (b) is difficult to prove and circumstance (c) would very rarely occur nowadays, the position may be summarized by saying that an insolvent company will not be wound up on a contributory's petition.[169]

Insufficient amount

8.75 In *Re Rica Gold Washing Co*[170] Jessel MR said that a winding-up order would not be made on the petition of a contributory who could expect only a negligible amount from the liquidation (his Lordship mentioned a figure of £5) but it would seem that the expectation of only a few pence per share would be enough to constitute a tangible interest to a holder of a large number of shares.

8.76 £358 to be divided between three joint petitioners was considered sufficient in *Re S A Hawken Ltd.*[171] In *Bryanston Finance Ltd v De Vries (No 2)*[172] a member's interest in his company had been valued at £4.34 by a takeover bidder. Buckley LJ said, at p 75, that if the member wanted to present a contributory's petition for the company's winding up he would

---

[161] See, for example, *Re Times Fire Assurance Co* (1861) 30 Beav 596.

[162] *Re Pioneers of Mashonaland Syndicate* [1893] 1 Ch 731.

[163] *Re Diamond Fuel Co* (1879) 13 ChD 400; *Re Haycraft Gold Reduction and Mining Co* [1900] 2 Ch 230; *Re Othery Construction Ltd* [1966] 1 WLR 69.

[164] *Re Lancashire Brick and Tile Co* (1865) 34 LJ Ch 331; *Re Lucky Hit Silver Mining Co Ltd* (1890) 1 BC (NSW) 8; this seems to have been the position in *Re National Savings Bank Association* (1866) LR 1 Ch App 547.

[165] *Re Eclipse Gold Mining Co* (1874) LR 17 Eq 490; *Re Kinatan (Borneo) Rubber Ltd* [1923] 1 Ch 124; *Re Taranaki Amusements (Hawera) Ltd* [1935] NZLR s 33.

[166] *Re Lancashire Brick and Tile Co Ltd* (1865) 34 LJ Ch 331.

[167] (1894) 2 SLT 397.

[168] See *Re Rica Gold Washing Co* (1879) 11 ChD 36; *Re National Company for the Distribution of Electricity by Secondary Generators Ltd* [1902] 2 Ch 34; *Re Othery Construction Ltd* [1966] 1 WLR 69, in all of which petitions failed.

[169] For example, *Re Chase Plastics Ltd* (1966) 110 SJ 564.

[170] (1879) 11 ChD 36.

[171] [1950] 2 All ER 408.

[172] [1976] Ch 63.

have to show a prima facie probability that he would receive more than that in the winding up (the member expected to be able to show that).

In *Re Kolback Group Ltd*[173] the petitioner held 1,000 out of 35,686,880 issued ordinary 25c **8.77** shares in the company and petitioned on the ground that the company was unable to pay its debts. The petitioner's shares were all fully paid. Bryson J said, at p 172, that:

> The protection of the plaintiff's $250 of share capital is unlikely in any imaginable circumstances to move the court to wind the company up: everything would depend on other interests such as any interest of creditors or other contributories who took part in the proceedings, and in weighing those persons' views the size and nature of their interests would be material.

In *Re Greenhaven Motors Ltd*[174] in the context of an application under IA 1986, s 167(3) **8.78** (application by a contributory etc in respect of exercise of powers by a liquidator in a compulsory winding up), Harman J said, at p 744, that the £5 mentioned by Jessel MR in *Re Rica Gold Washing Co* would be something more like £1,000 now.

A contributory does not have a tangible interest in winding up a company if all of its assets **8.79** are held as trustee for a person other than the petitioner, because the petitioner could not participate in any distribution of the company's assets.[175]

Preventing Increase in Liability

Principle

According to Oliver J in *Re Chesterfield Catering Co Ltd*,[176] preventing an increase in a con- **8.80** tributory petitioner's liability may be enough to satisfy the court that the petitioner has a tangible interest in having the company wound up.

Examples

An interest in preventing an increase in liability may arise, for example, because: **8.81**

(a) The petitioner holds partly paid shares,[177] though it might be argued that if the company's position is already such that the whole amount unpaid on the petitioner's shares must be called up, the petitioner has no tangible interest in preventing the situation getting worse.
(b) The company is an unlimited company.[178]
(c) The company is a guarantee company, though it might be argued that if the company's position is already such that the whole amount guaranteed by the petitioner must be called up, the petitioner has no tangible interest in preventing the situation getting worse.
(d) The petitioner is a person with liability under IA 1986, s 76, in respect of a payment out of capital for the purchase or redemption of shares.
(e) The petition is for the winding up of an insolvent partnership and the petitioner is not a limited partner.

---

[173] (1991) 4 ACSR 165.
[174] [1997] 1 BCLC 739.
[175] *Guerinoni v Argyle Concrete and Quarry Supplies Pty Ltd* (1999) 34 ACSR 469.
[176] [1977] Ch 373 at p 380.
[177] As in *Re Bristol Joint Stock Bank* (1890) 44 ChD 703; *Re Florida Mining Co Ltd* (1902) 9 BCR 108; *Re Pacific Fisheries Ltd* (1909) 26 WN (NSW) 127.
[178] See *Re Electric Telegraph of Ireland* (1856) 22 Beav 471, which concerned a statutory company whose members had unlimited liability.

8.82 However, if the company is dormant and has no liabilities, no order will be made if the petition is opposed by the other contributories.[179] (An abandoned company may be struck off the register by the registrar using a power introduced by the Companies Act 1880, s 7, and now in the Companies Act 2006, s 1000.)

Tangible Interest of Past Members

8.83 A past member of an insolvent registered company who transferred shares when they were partly paid may have difficulty in showing a tangible interest in having it wound up because there is no liability to contribute in respect of any debt or liability of the company contracted after ceasing to be a member[180] and such a person would have to show a probability of being liable for a call to pay prior debts.

8.84 It follows that a past member of a company limited by shares who held only fully paid shares, and who has no liability under either s 76 or s 77(2) of IA 1986, has no tangible interest and therefore no standing to petition.

8.85 A person who ceased to be a member of an insolvent registered company more than a year past cannot have a tangible interest in having the company wound up because such a person cannot receive any dividend in the winding up of the company and cannot have any liability to contribute to its assets.[181] (In the case of a company that was an unlimited company which has re-registered as limited, IA 1986, s 77(2), imposes liability on past members for up to three years but only in respect of debts incurred before re-registration.)

Striking Out for Lack of Tangible Interest

8.86 The court will not strike out a contributory's petition for absence of tangible interest unless it is plain and obvious that the petitioner does not have a tangible interest. So a petition will not be struck out where the company's financial position is not known because the company has not produced accounts[182] or where the amounts of assets and liabilities are disputed[183] or require investigation[184] or where the petitioner is prevented from ascertaining the present position.[185] However, the company's true financial position should be established before the petition is heard.[186] In *Re Delip Singh and Moody Shingles Ltd*,[187] on an appeal against the making of a winding-up order on a contributory's petition, it was argued that the petitioner had not shown a tangible interest but this argument was rejected because in fact the company had never kept proper accounting records and had never produced any annual accounts: indeed this was one of the reasons for making the winding-up order.

---

[179] *Re New Gas Generator Co* (1877) 4 ChD 874; though in *Re Caementium (Parent) Co Ltd* [1908] WN 257 a winding-up order was made, apparently because there was a danger that the dormant company could have been confused with an overseas company with the same name.

[180] IA 1986, s 74(2)(b).

[181] IA 1986, s 74(2)(a).

[182] *Re Newman and Howard Ltd* [1962] Ch 257.

[183] *Re Martin Coulter Enterprises Ltd* [1988] BCLC 12.

[184] *Re Wessex Computer Stationers Ltd* [1992] BCLC 366; *Re Pimlico Capital Ltd* [2002] EWHC 878 (Ch), [2002] 2 BCLC 544.

[185] *Re a Company (No 007936 of 1994)* [1995] BCC 705.

[186] *Re Commercial and Industrial Insulations Ltd* [1986] BCLC 191.

[187] [1947] 1 WWR 480.

Alternative Dispute Resolution

Arbitration Agreement

On the application of a party to an arbitration agreement, a court must stay legal proceed- **8.87**
ings brought against that party (whether by way of claim or counterclaim) so far as the
proceedings concern a matter which, under the arbitration agreement, is to be referred to arbitration.[188] A stay will not be granted if the court finds that the arbitration agreement is null and
void.[189] An agreement is null and void in so far as it purports to refer to arbitration the question
whether a company is to be wound up.[190] Nevertheless, a contributory's petition to wind up a
company may be stayed in favour of arbitration so far as the petition concerns a dispute which
is covered by an arbitration agreement.[191] The same applies to an unfair prejudice petition.[192]
The arbitrator may find that winding up is the appropriate remedy and if so an application may
be made to lift the stay so that the court may consider whether to make a winding-up order.

In earlier cases, courts took the view that the only question raised on an application to wind up **8.88**
a company is whether or not the company should be wound up. It was considered that disputes
are mentioned in a petition as evidence to justify winding up, the question being whether it is
just and equitable to wind up the company because the disputes exist.[193] On this view, it was
common to find that the question whether the company should be wound up was not one
covered by the wording of an arbitration agreement so that no stay could be granted.[194]

In a very early case it was held that an agreement to submit differences between members of a **8.89**
company and the company to arbitration, which does not bind all contributories and does not
provide the arbitrator with powers equal to those of the court in winding up a company, cannot preclude a contributory from petitioning for the company to be wound up by the court.[195]

Discretionary Stay in Favour of ADR

The court has a discretion to stay proceedings in favour of alternative dispute resolution.[196] **8.90**
It is widely thought that many of the disputes which lead to contributories' winding-up petitions and members' unfair prejudice petitions could be dealt with by ADR. The Company

---

[188] Arbitration Act 1996, s 9. The term 'arbitration agreement' is defined in s 6. Section 9 applies only
if the agreement is in writing (s 5). A winding-up petition is neither a claim nor a counterclaim and so s
9 does not apply to a winding-up petition (*Best Beat Ltd v Rossall* [2006] EWHC 1494 (Comm), [2006]
BPIR 1357; *Salford Estates (No 2) Ltd v Altomart Ltd* [2014] EWCA Civ 1575, LTL 9/12/2014).

[189] Arbitration Act 1996, s 9(4).

[190] *A Best Floor Sanding Pty Ltd v Skyer Australia Pty Ltd* [1999] VSC 170; *ACD Tridon Inc v Tridon
Australia Pty Ltd* [2002] NSWSC 896; *Fulham Football Club (1987) Ltd v Richards* [2011] EWCA Civ 855,
[2012] Ch 333, at [76] and [83]. In Northern Ireland, *Re Wine Inns Ltd* [2000] NIJB 343 is to the contrary.

[191] *ACD Tridon Inc v Tridon Australia Pty Ltd*; *Fulham Football Club (1987) Ltd v Richards* at [76] and [83].

[192] *Re Vocam Europe Ltd* [1998] BCC 396; *Re Via Net Works (Ireland) Ltd* [2002] 2 IR 47; *Fulham Football
Club (1987) Ltd v Richards*, overruling *Exeter City Association Football Club Ltd v Football Conference Ltd*
[2004] EWHC 2304 (Ch), [2004] 1 WLR 2910. In Northern Ireland, *Re Wine Inns Ltd* is to the contrary.

[193] *Re Seed Coating Services Ltd* (1977) 1 BCR 109 citing the partnership case of *Olver v Hillier* [1959] 1
WLR 551; *Four Pillars Enterprises Co Ltd v Beiersdorf AG* [1999] 1 SLR 737; *Re Wine Inns Ltd*.

[194] *De Cruyenaere v Green Acres Memorial Gardens Ltd* (1961) 30 DLR (2d) 627; *Four Pillars Enterprises
Co Ltd v Beiersdorf AG*; *Re Wine Inns Ltd*.

[195] *Re Lancaster and Newcastle-upon-Tyne Railway Co* (1849) 5 Ry & Can Cas 632.

[196] *Exeter City Association Football Club Ltd v Football Conference Ltd* [2004] EWHC 2304 (Ch), [2004]
1 WLR 2910, at [14]. CPR, rr 1.4(2)(e) and 26.4.

Law Review Steering Group made quite elaborate suggestions for an arbitration scheme to deal with disputes which might otherwise be the subject of unfair prejudice petitions.[197] For discussion of how ADR could be used see James Corbett and Rosalind Nicholson, 'Mediation and section 459 petitions' (2002) 23 Co Law 274.

Grounds other than Just and Equitable

Special Resolution that a Registered Company be Wound Up by the Court

8.91 By IA 1986, s 122(1):

> A company may be wound up by the court if—
>
> (a) the company has by special resolution resolved that the company be wound up by the court.

8.92 If the members of a registered company have adopted a special resolution under s 122(1)(a) that the company be wound up by the court, normally the petition will be presented in the company's name and so this ground is discussed at 11.4–11.6.

Public Company's Failure to Obtain a Trading Certificate

8.93 By IA 1986, s 122(1):

> A company may be wound up by the court if—
>
> ...
>
> (b) being a public company which was registered as such on its original incorporation, the company has not been issued with a trading certificate under section 761 of the Companies Act 2006 (requirement as to minimum share capital) and more than a year has expired since it was so registered.

8.94 A company registered as a public company on its original incorporation (as opposed to a private company which re-registers as public) may not do business or exercise any power to borrow money unless the registrar has issued it with a trading certificate under the Companies Act 2006, s 761. If a public company has failed to obtain a trading certificate one year after incorporation, members may be justified in thinking they have wasted the capital they contributed. IA 1986, s 122(1)(b), gives them an opportunity to have the company wound up so that what is left of the share capital can be returned to them.

8.95 IA 1986, s 122(1)(b), does not apply to a public company which has been converted from a European public limited-liability company (SE) under Regulation 2157/2001, art 66.[198]

Old Public Companies

8.96 By IA 1986, s 122(1):

> A company may be wound up by the court if—
>
> ...

---

[197] *Modern Company Law for a Competitive Economy: Developing the Framework* (URN 00/656) (London: Department of Trade and Industry, 2000), paras 7.44 to 7.69; *Modern Company Law for a Competitive Economy: Final Report*, vol 1 (URN 01/942) (London: Department of Trade and Industry, 2001), paras 4.10 to 4.12.

[198] European Public Limited-Liability Company Regulations 2004 (SI 2004/2326), sch 4, para 9(b).

(c) it is an old public company, within the meaning of Schedule 3 to the Companies Act 2006 (Consequential Amendments, Transitional Provisions and Savings) Order 2009.[199]

During a transitional period that lasted until 22 March 1982, every company limited by shares, and every guarantee company with a share capital, that was in existence or in course of registration on 22 December 1980 and which was not (or was not in course of being registered as) a 'private company' as that term was defined by the Companies Act 1948, s 28,[200] had to apply to be re-registered as a public company or apply for a certificate from the registrar of companies that it was a private company as defined by the Companies Act 1980, s 1(1).[201] Any such company not re-registered as a public company and not certified as being a private company is called an 'old public company', and the company and its officers are committing an offence for failure to acquire a new status for the company[202] (though presumably some such companies are already in course of liquidation). Under IA 1986, s 122(1)(c), the fact that a company is an old public company is a circumstance in which its compulsory liquidation may be ordered. **8.97**

Registered Company's Failure to Commence Business or Suspension of Business

By IA 1986, s 122(1): **8.98**

A company may be wound up by the court if—

…

(d) the company does not commence its business within a year from its incorporation or suspends its business for a whole year.

Winding up will be ordered in these circumstances only if the court is convinced that there is no intention to commence or recommence business.[203]

Formal business such as allotting shares, or the exercise of mere ancillary powers, such as depositing money received for shares at the bank, does not count as carrying on business for the purposes of s 122(1)(d).[204] But carrying on business outside England and Wales, unless it is not allowed by the company's constitution, does count as carrying on business for the purposes of s 122(1)(d) even if business is not conducted in England and Wales.[205] **8.99**

In *Re Eastern Telegraph Co Ltd*[206] the company had transferred its telegraph business in 1930 to another telegraph company in exchange for shares in the transferee company and had done nothing since then except collect dividends. However, subscribing for shares in **8.100**

---

[199] SI 2009/1941. Because of an error in SI 2009/1941, its provisions relating to old public companies in England and Wales and Scotland had to be re-enacted and the relevant definition is now in the Companies Act 2006 (Consequential Amendments and Transitional Provisions) Order 2011 (SI 2011/1265), sch 1, para 1.

[200] Which was repealed on 22 December 1980 by the Companies Act 1980, sch 4, and the Companies Act 1980 (Commencement No 2) Order 1980 (SI 1980/1785).

[201] Companies Act 1980, ss 8 and 9, re-enacted as SI 2011/1265, sch 1, paras 1 to 6. The definition of 'private company' in the Companies Act 1980, s 1(1), is re-enacted in the Companies Act 2006, s 4.

[202] SI 2011/1265, sch 1, para 6.

[203] *Re Metropolitan Railway Warehousing Co Ltd* (1867) 36 LJ Ch 827 (failure to commence within one year); *Re Middlesborough Assembly Rooms Co* (1880) 14 ChD 104 (suspension of business for a year).

[204] *Re Metropolitan Railway Warehousing Co Ltd* (1867) 36 LJ Ch 827; *Re South Luipaards Vlei Gold Mines Ltd* (1897) 13 TLR 504.

[205] *Re Capital Fire Insurance Association* (1882) 21 ChD 209.

[206] [1947] 2 All ER 104.

other telegraph companies was found to be one of the main objects for which the company was formed so that it had not ceased business. *Re National Finance Co*[207] seems to have been a similar case.

8.101 From *Re Metropolitan Railway Warehousing Co Ltd*,[208] *Re Heaton's Steel and Iron Co*,[209] *Re Petersburg and Viborg Gas Co*,[210] *Re Middlesborough Assembly Rooms Co*[211] and *Re Tomlin Patent Horse Shoe Co Ltd*,[212] it appears that normally the court will decide *not* to order a winding up where business has not been commenced or has been suspended if all of the following three factors are present:

(a) there is an adequate explanation of the company's inactivity;
(b) the company is solvent; and
(c) the majority of shareholders wish the company to continue.

8.102 In *Re South Luipaards Vlei Gold Mines Ltd*[213] there was no adequate explanation of the delay in commencing business and the court doubted the bona fides of the shareholders who wanted to carry on: compulsory liquidation was ordered.

8.103 In *Re Southland Woollen-Mills Ltd*[214] the delay in commencing business was not satisfactorily explained and a majority of members were in favour of winding up: compulsory liquidation was ordered.

8.104 In *Re Tumacacori Mining Co*[215] the company had transacted no business since being registered four years previously, and Malins V-C was satisfied that the company would never commence business.[216] The majority of the shareholders were opposed to compulsory liquidation and wished the directors to carry out an external reconstruction (contributing the company's entire undertaking to a new company in return for shares in the new company to be distributed to the existing company's members). However, Malins V-C held that such a transaction would not be authorized by the company's constitution, and decided that the only way of dealing with the company's property was to make a winding-up order. The statement in the headnote to the report in the *Law Reports* that it was held that the court had no discretion to refuse a winding-up order if a company had not commenced business within a year is not accurate. The point that the Vice-Chancellor seemed to be making in the judgment was that he was not able to refuse jurisdiction despite his view that it was not convenient that this company should be wound up by the court. To the extent that it followed that inaccurate headnote, *Re Shelbourne Cheese Manufacturing and Produce Co Ltd*[217] is of doubtful authority.[218]

---

[207] [1866] WN 243.
[208] (1867) 36 LJ Ch 827.
[209] [1870] WN 85.
[210] [1874] WN 196.
[211] (1880) 14 ChD 104.
[212] (1886) 55 LT 314.
[213] (1897) 13 TLR 504.
[214] [1929] NZLR 289.
[215] (1874) LR 17 Eq 534.
[216] At p 540.
[217] (1888) 14 VLR 294.
[218] Junior counsel for the company in *Re Tumacacori Mining Co* subsequently said that the winding-up order was never perfected: see *Re New Gas Generator Co* (1877) 4 ChD 874 at p 876 and per Bacon V-C at p 877.

Inability to Pay Debts

Inability to pay debts as ground for winding up

In relation to a registered company, IA 1986, s 122(1), provides:　　**8.105**

> A company may be wound up by the court if—
>
> …
>
> (f) the company is unable to pay its debts.

The same provision is made in relation to an unregistered company by s 221(5)(b) and, in relation to a petition under IPO 1994, art 9, to wind up an insolvent partnership, by IA 1986, s 221(7), as modified by IPO 1994, sch 5, para 2.

In relation to petitions under IPO 1994, art 10, for the winding up of an insolvent partner-　**8.106**
ship and the winding up or bankruptcy of all its members IA 1986, s 221(8), as modified by IPO 1994, sch 6, para 4, provides, ungrammatically:

> The circumstances in which an insolvent partnership may be wound up as an unregistered company are that the partnership is unable to pay its debts.

And IA 1986, s 122, as modified by IPO 1994, sch 4, para 6(a), and applied by art 10(2), (3) and (6), provides:

> A corporate member … may be wound up by the court if it is unable to pay its debts.

Inability to pay debts is considered fully in relation to creditors' petitions at 7.74–7.308.　**8.107**

If a limited company is unable to pay its debts, a member with fully paid shares would not have　**8.108**
a tangible interest in having it wound up and a petition by such a member would be dismissed. However, a member with partly paid shares would have a tangible interest in preventing the company incurring further liabilities for which a call would be made, and so such a member's petition would be heard. A member of an unlimited company or a partnership will have a tangible interest in preventing the financial position of the company or partnership getting worse.

On hearing a contributory's petition that a company should be wound up because of its　**8.109**
inability to pay its debts, the court does not apply any *ex debito justitiae* principle as it would on a creditor's petition:[219] the court will consider the views of the other contributories and the creditors.[220] A winding-up order will not be made if the company's financial difficulties have been contrived by the petitioner.[221]

Loss of capital

Inability to return share capital contributed by members does not count as inability to pay　**8.110**
debts.[222] The Joint Stock Companies Act 1856 permitted a contributory of a registered

---

[219] See 7.680–7.682. Per James V-C in *Re European Life Assurance Society* (1869) LR 9 Eq 122 at pp 126–7; per Mellish LJ in *Re London Suburban Bank* (1871) LR 6 Ch App 641 at p 643 and in *Re Professional, Commercial and Industrial Benefit Building Society* (1871) LR 6 Ch App 856.

[220] *Re Professional, Commercial and Industrial Benefit Building Society*; *Re City and County Bank* (1875) LR 10 Ch App 470; *Re Hudson's Steam Biscuit Co* (1886) 2 TLR 833 (presumably: the report does not actually state the ground of the petition); *Fortin v La Compagnie Électrique Dorchester* (1915) 48 Que SC 258; *Re Shipway Iron Bell and Wire Mfg Co Ltd* [1926] 2 DLR 887.

[221] *Re La Plagne Ltd* [2011] IEHC 91, [2012] 1 ILRM 203.

[222] *Re United Canneries of British Columbia Ltd* (1903) 9 BCR 528; *Re Great West Brick and Coal Co Ltd* (1916) 9 Sask LR 240.

company to petition for it to be wound up if three quarters of the capital had 'been lost or become unavailable'[223] but this provision was omitted from the Companies Act 1862[224] and has never reappeared in the British legislation. However, there is now a provision requiring the directors of a public company to convene an extraordinary general meeting of its members if its net assets fall to half or less of its called-up share capital.[225]

8.111 In Canada, under the Winding-up and Reconstruction Act, s 10(d), a winding-up order in respect of a company may be made 'when the capital stock of the company is impaired to the extent of 25 per cent thereof,[226] and when it is shown to the satisfaction of the court that the lost capital will not likely be restored within one year'. For examples of companies being wound up under this provision see *Re Base-O-Lite Products Ltd*;[227] *Re Eastern Fur Finance Corp Ltd*.[228] The provision does not apply where the loss of capital has been reflected in a duly authorized reduction of capital.[229]

Failure of unregistered company or partnership to indemnify member

8.112 A contributory of an unregistered company against whom legal proceedings may be taken for a debt of the company may invoke IA 1986, s 223,[230] which deems an unregistered company to be unable to pay its debts if it fails to relieve a member from legal proceedings which have been instituted against the member for a debt or demand due (or claimed to be due) from the company or from the member qua member.

8.113 A company will not be deemed to be unable to pay its debts under s 223 unless a notice of the institution of the action or proceeding has been served on it and, within three weeks after service of the notice, the company has not:

(a) paid, secured or compounded for the debt or demand; or
(b) procured the action or proceeding to be stayed or sisted; or
(c) indemnified the defendant to his reasonable satisfaction against the action or proceeding, and against all costs, damages and expenses to be incurred by him because of it.

8.114 The notice must be in writing, but not in electronic form.[231] It must be served:

(a) by leaving it at the company's principal place of business; or
(b) by delivering it to the secretary, or some director, manager or principal officer of the company; or
(c) in such other manner as the court may approve or direct.[232]

8.115 Section 223 is derived from the Joint Stock Companies Winding-up Act 1848, s 5, case 5.

8.116 A member of a partnership petitioning under IPO 1994, art 9 (where no concurrent petition is presented for the winding up or bankruptcy of any member of the partnership), may rely on

---

[223] ss 67(5) and 69.
[224] See s 79.
[225] Companies Act 2006, s 656.
[226] That is, if one quarter of the capital is lost.
[227] [1933] OR 156.
[228] [1934] 1 DLR 611.
[229] *Re Canada Nat'l Fire Ins Co* [1930] 4 DLR 572; [1931] 1 DLR 751.
[230] Set out at 7.112.
[231] IA 1986, ss 223(a) and 436B(2)(i).
[232] IA 1986, s 223(a).

IA 1986, s 223, as modified by IPO 1994, sch 3, para 5,[233] though if the partnership has fewer than eight members the petitioner must have actually paid a partnership debt and obtained judgment against the partnership for it.[234]

For examples of a winding-up order made under the 1848 Act on the petition of **8.117** contributories who had been sued for the company's debts see *Re Tretoil and Messer Mining Co*[235] and *Re South Lady Bertha Mining Co*.[236] Under the 1848 Act it was held that if the company's debt claimed from the petitioner was less than the arrears of calls owed by the petitioner to the company then the petitioner would not be entitled to a winding-up order.[237]

It seems that under the 1848 Act a threat of proceedings against a contributory was suf- **8.118** ficient ground for a winding-up order.[238]

Unregistered Company Dissolved or Ceased to be a Going Concern

By IA 1986, s 221(5): **8.119**

The circumstances in which an unregistered company may be wound up are as follows—

(a) if the company is dissolved, or has ceased to carry on business, or is carrying on business only for the purpose of winding up its affairs.

As far as insolvent partnerships are concerned the same provision is made by IA 1986, **8.120** s 221(7)(a), as modified by IPO 1994, sch 3, para 3 (in relation to petitions under art 7 of the Order) and IA 1986, s 221(7)(a), as modified by IPO 1994, sch 5, para 2 (in relation to art 9 petitions).

IA 1986, s 221(5)(a), specifies three independent, not cumulative, conditions: an unregis- **8.121** tered company may be wound up if it is dissolved; it may be wound up if it has ceased to carry on business; it may be wound up if it is carrying on business only for the purpose of winding up its affairs.[239]

In the law of companies and other associations the term 'dissolution' can have two different **8.122** meanings:

(a) It may mean the decision to end the association and commence winding up—the term is usually used in this sense in Britain in relation to partnerships and other unincorporated associations.
(b) It may mean the ending of the existence of a company as a juridical entity, for example, by striking a registered company off the register.

---

[233] Set out at 7.112.
[234] IA 1986, s 221A, as modified by IPO 1994, sch 5, para 2; see 2.87.
[235] (1862) 2 John & H 421.
[236] (1862) 2 John & H 376.
[237] *Re Birch Torr and Vitifer Co, ex parte Lawton* (1854) 1 Kay & J 204.
[238] *Re Patent Concentrated Tea Co* (1850) 16 LT OS 189, in which one of two joint petitioners had also paid money for the company; *Re Court Grange Silver-Lead Mining Co* (1856) 2 Jur NS 949, in which a contributory who had accepted bills of exchange in order to raise money which he had lent to the company was granted a winding-up order when endorsees of the bills threatened to sue him.
[239] *Re Russian Bank for Foreign Trade* [1933] Ch 745 per Maugham J at p 765; *Banque des Marchands de Moscou (Koupetschesky) v Kindersley* [1951] Ch 112 per Evershed MR at p 125; *Inland Revenue v Highland Engineering Ltd* 1975 SLT 203 per Lord Grieve at p 205.

8.123 In relation to foreign companies, at least, IA 1986, s 225, makes it clear that a company which has been dissolved in sense (b) may nevertheless be the subject of a winding-up order in Great Britain. For commentary on this provision, see 1.213–1.220.

8.124 An unregistered company is capable of being wound up under s 221(5)(a) as a dissolved company even if it was dissolved before IA 1986 came into force.[240] This is because the words 'is dissolved' in the first clause of para (a) are equivalent to 'has been dissolved'.[241]

8.125 In *Re Agriculturist Cattle Insurance Co, ex parte Spackman*[242] it was held that the company had not been dissolved despite the fact that a significant number of members had been permitted to forfeit their shares.

8.126 For an example of an unregistered company wound up by the court because it had ceased to carry on business see *Re Bradford Navigation Co*,[243] in which the petition was presented by the company itself.

8.127 IA 1986, s 221(5)(a), is derived from the Joint Stock Companies Winding-up Act 1848, s 5, case 7. To obtain an order to wind up a company under that case it was unnecessary to show that the company was unable to pay its debts[244] or that it had any creditors at all.[245] However, the court would refuse to make a winding-up order under that case if it appeared that everything practicable had been done bona fide to wind up the company's affairs[246] and the court would adjourn a petition to allow the petitioner to inspect accounts so as to ascertain whether winding up was complete.[247] In *Re Larne, Belfast and Ballymena Railway Co*[248] a winding-up order was made because the company refused to allow the petitioner to inspect its accounts. In *Re Ipswich, Norwich and Yarmouth Railway Co*[249] and *Re Cambrian Junction Railway Co*[250] winding-up orders were discharged when it was discovered that the petitions had omitted to reveal that the companies' affairs were already wound up (the petitioners had presumably hoped to take unclaimed funds as costs).

8.128 For cases under the 1848 Act in which winding-up orders were made see *Re Borough of St Marylebone Joint Stock Banking Co, ex parte Walker*;[251] *Re London and Westminster Insurance*

---

[240] See *Re Family Endowment Society* (1870) LR 5 Ch App 118, in which an unregistered English company dissolved in 1861 was wound up under the Companies Act 1862; *Re Russian and English Bank* [1932] 1 Ch 663 and *Re Russian Bank for Foreign Trade* [1933] Ch 745, in which foreign companies dissolved in their country of incorporation in 1918 were wound up in England under the Companies Act 1929.

[241] *Re Russian and English Bank* [1932] 1 Ch 663 per Bennett J at pp 668–9; *Banque des Marchands de Moscou (Koupetschesky) v Kindersley* [1951] Ch 112 per Evershed MR at p 125.

[242] (1849) 1 Mac & G 170.

[243] (1870) LR 10 Eq 331.

[244] *Re Larne, Belfast and Ballymena Railway Co* (1849) 14 Jur 996.

[245] *Re Borough of St Marylebone Joint Stock Banking Co, ex parte Walker* (1848) 1 H & Tw 100.

[246] *Re Direct London and Manchester Railway Co, ex parte Pocock* (1849) 1 De G & Sm 731; *Re London, Bristol and South Wales Direct Railway Co, ex parte Capper* (1849) 3 De G & Sm 1; *Re London and South Essex Railway Co, ex parte Murrell* (1849) 3 De G & Sm 4; *Re Narborough and Watlington Railway Co, ex parte James* (1850) 1 Sim NS 140 (in which it seems the petitioner did not have standing anyway).

[247] *Re Direct London and Manchester Railway Co, ex parte Pocock* (1849) 1 De G & Sm 731; *Re London, Bristol and South Wales Direct Railway Co, ex parte Capper* (1849) 3 De G & Sm 1.

[248] (1849) 14 Jur 996.

[249] (1849) 1 De G & Sm 744.

[250] (1849) 3 De G & Sm 139.

[251] (1848) 1 H & Tw 100.

Co, ex parte Phillips[252] (in which there was a fund to be divided); *Re Direct London, Portsmouth and Chichester and Direct Portsmouth and Chatham Railway Co, ex parte Goldsmith*;[253] *Re Birch Torr and Vitifer Co, ex parte Lawton*;[254] and *Re Cheltenham and Gloucestershire Joint Stock Bank*.[255] The fact that the petitioner assented to the dissolution of the company is not a bar to petitioning for its compulsory winding up.[256]

In *Re Chester and Manchester Direct Railway Co, ex parte Phillipps*[257] a winding-up order **8.129** under case 7 was refused because it was said that the relief claimed in a suit which had already been brought by the petitioner against the company's ex directors would have the same effect as a winding up. But in *Re Borough of St Marylebone Joint Stock Banking Co, ex parte Walker*[258] the fact that the petitioner was a defendant in such a suit was not a reason for not making a winding-up order.

In *Re Anglo-Australian and Universal Family Life Assurance Co, ex parte Smith*[259] the under- **8.130** taking of the company had been transferred to another company which had agreed to pay the taken-over company's debts, and shareholders of the taken-over company were invited to exchange their shares for shares in the acquiring company, though not all did. A person who had exchanged his shares petitioned under case 7 for the taken-over company to be wound up but the court refused saying that this was just a device by which the acquiring company could obtain contribution from the remaining shareholders in the taken-over company for the debts of the taken-over company which it had promised to pay.

The Just and Equitable Clause

Principle

Statutory provisions

In relation to a registered company, IA 1986, s 122(1), provides: **8.131**

A company may be wound up by the court if—

…

(g) the court is of the opinion that it is just and equitable that the company should be wound up.

Section 221(5) provides:

The circumstances in which an unregistered company may be wound up are as follows—

…

(c) if the court is of the opinion that it is just and equitable that the company should be wound up.

---

[252] (1849) 3 De G & Sm 3.
[253] (1850) 19 LJ Ch 235.
[254] (1854) 1 Kay & J 204.
[255] (1856) 4 WR 624.
[256] *Re Cheltenham and Gloucestershire Joint Stock Bank.*
[257] (1851) 1 Sim NS 605.
[258] (1848) 1 H & Tw 100.
[259] (1860) 1 Drew & Sm 113.

8.132 In relation to insolvent partnerships, the same provision is made by s 221(7)(c) as modi-fied by IPO 1994, sch 3, para 3 (petitions under art 7 of the Order), and by s 221(7)(c) as modified by IPO 1994, sch 5, para 2 (art 9 petitions). The same provision is made by the Building Societies Act 1986, s 89(1), and the Friendly Societies Act 1992, s 22(1), with respect to the societies which they cover. A member of an EEIG may apply for the group-ing to be wound up by the court 'on just and proper grounds'.[260] It is submitted that the scope of 'just and proper grounds' is at least as extensive as the just and equitable clause in IA 1986, s 221(5)(c).

Nature

8.133 The just and equitable clause is most often considered in the context of contributories' peti-tions. However, it is also the only one under which the court can consider a public interest petition by the Secretary of State[261] and it may be invoked by creditors.[262]

8.134 A contributory's petition under the just and equitable clause 'is not in truth hostile litiga-tion by a shareholder against a company. It is in truth a claim by a shareholder based upon wrongful acts by other shareholders or directors which have amounted to some equitable mal-doing.'[263]

History

8.135 The just and equitable clause was first introduced in the Joint Stock Companies Winding-up Act 1848, s 5. It was not included in the Joint Stock Companies Act 1856 but reappeared in the Companies Act 1862, s 79 (in relation to registered companies) and s 199 (in relation to unregistered companies).

Literature

8.136 'The winding up of companies by the court—where just and equitable' (1950) 84 ILT & SJ 213, 219.

H Batshaw, 'Involuntary liquidation of solvent companies' (1953) 13 RduB 157.

B H McPherson, 'Winding up on the "just and equitable" ground' (1964) 27 MLR 282.

D Huberman, 'Compulsory winding up—the "just and equitable" rule' (1966–7) 5 Alta L Rev 135.

F H Callaway, *Winding up on the Just and Equitable Ground* (Sydney: Law Book Co, 1978).

N Furey, 'The statutory protection of minority shareholders in the United Kingdom' (1987) 22 Wake Forest L Rev 81.

Teng Kam Wah, 'Power to the minority shareholder' [1997] 2 MLJ xxxvii.

---

[260] Regulation (EEC) No 2137/85, art 32(2), which is applied in the winding up of an EEIG by IA 1986, s 221(1), as modified by the European Economic Interest Grouping Regulations 1989 (SI 1989/638), reg 8(1).
[261] See 9.19.
[262] See 7.5, 8.149, 8.301 and 8.424.
[263] Per Harman J in *Re Hydrosan Ltd* [1991] BCLC 418 at p 421.

The Court's Approach

Inference from facts

Whether it is just and equitable that a company should be wound up is an inference of law from the facts of the situation.[264] '[T]he equity must be founded on facts alleged in the petition'.[265]

8.137

For a contributory to show that it is just and equitable to wind up a solvent company is not so simple and uncomplicated as for an unpaid creditor to show that a winding up should be ordered because the company is unable to pay its debts.[266]

8.138

> That question as to its being just and equitable has reference, of course, to what is just and equitable in a judicial point of view, regard being had to all the circumstances of the case.[267]
>
> …grounds must be given which can be examined and justified.[268]

Whether or not it is just and equitable to wind up a company must be decided in the light of the circumstances which exist at the time of the hearing.[269] In *Re Hillcrest Housing Ltd* the petitioners and the other shareholders had resolved their disputes about the day-to-day management of the company by an agreement embodied in a consent judgment and had operated under that agreement for more than six years. MacDonald CJTD said, at p 233:

8.139

> The principle set forth in *Re Fildes Bros Ltd*, that it is the facts existing at the time of the hearing which are relevant, prevents the regurgitation of past ills. To wind up a company is a drastic measure and to do so based on past complaints would certainly not be an equitable decision.

In relation to public interest petitions, though, it may be right to order winding up because of past wrongdoing.[270]

8.140

Whole picture

In *Re Dominion Steel Corp Ltd*[271] Graham J said, at p 362: 'The court cannot accumulate circumstances, which taken separately might not justify action, and act upon a general indefinite ground'. But in *Entreprises M Canada Abitibi Inc v Maurice Canada Construction Ltée*[272] Bergeron J said, at p 73:

8.141

> Nous avons décidé qu'il y avait lieu de prononcer la liquidation de l'intimée non parce que chacun des actes reprochés à l'un ou l'autre des acteurs principaux … pouvait donner ouverture à cette mesure, mais en raison de l'atmosphère générale qui imprégnait cette compagnie.[273]

---

[264] Per Jessel MR during argument in *Re Rica Gold Washing Co* (1879) 11 ChD 36.

[265] *Re Wear Engine Works Co* (1875) LR 10 Ch App 188 per James LJ at p 191.

[266] Per Danckwerts LJ in *Re Davis Investments (East Ham) Ltd* [1961] 1 WLR 1396 at pp 1398–9.

[267] Per Lord Hatherley LC in *Princess of Reuss v Bos* (1871) LR 5 HL 176 at p 193.

[268] Per Lord President Clyde in *Baird v Lees* 1924 SC 83 at p 90.

[269] *Re Fildes Bros Ltd* [1970] 1 WLR 592; *Re Deep Sea Trawlers Ltd* (1984) 2 NZCLC 99,137 at p 99,146; *Re Hillcrest Housing Ltd* (1998) 165 Nfld & PEIR 181 at pp 229 and 231–3; *Jenkins v Supscaf Ltd* [2006] 3 NZLR 264 at [100]–[108].

[270] See 9.34–9.37.

[271] [1927] 4 DLR 337.

[272] (1979) 34 CBR NS 68.

[273] We have decided that it would be right to order the winding up of the respondent not because every one of the acts blamed on one or other of the principal actors could be a ground for that step, but because of the general atmosphere which permeated this company.

And formerly, under the Companies Act 1948, s 210, the court was asked to consider whether it was just and equitable that a company should be wound up because its affairs were 'being conducted in a manner oppressive to some part of the members'. In *Re H R Harmer Ltd*[274] Jenkins LJ, at pp 84–5, accepted the reasoning of Roxburgh J at first instance, who had said (as quoted by Jenkins LJ):

> I think [s 210] invites attention not to events considered in isolation, but to events considered as part of a consecutive story. . . . It remains, in my view, a question for the court to decide on the whole story, as revealed in the evidence, whether the affairs of the company are being . . . conducted in a manner oppressive to some part of the members.

8.142 Similarly, in *Re Co-operative Development Funds of Australia Ltd (No 3)*[275] Sangster J said:

> although I am concerned to consider both the whole canvas, and each brush mark, consideration of each brush mark is not a separate exercise but only a step towards considering the whole canvas: in the end I must step back and say what I think of the whole canvas as I see it.

Balancing exercise

8.143 In *Re Walter L Jacob and Co Ltd*[276] Nicholls LJ said, at pp 351–2:

> In considering whether or not to make a winding-up order under IA 1986, s 122(1)(g), the court has regard to all the circumstances of the case as established by the material before the court at the hearing. Normally that will involve the court, faced with a petition presented by a creditor or a contributory, considering primarily the conflicting interests and wishes of the opposing parties to the petition, whether creditors or contributories or the company itself. The court will consider those matters which constitute reasons why the company should be wound up compulsorily, and those which constitute reasons why it should not. The court will carry out a balancing exercise, giving such weight to the various factors as is appropriate in the particular case.

In *Jenkins v Supscaf Ltd*[277] Heath J said:

> [The Companies Act 1993 (New Zealand), s 241(4)(d)] places no fetter upon the discretion of the court, either in relation to the factors that would justify an order, or in relation to circumstances in which an order must be refused. Therefore, I proceed on the basis that I must balance all relevant factors available for consideration at the present time to determine whether an order ought to be made.

List of factors

8.144 The principal factors affecting the court's decision on a contributory's petition under the just and equitable clause include:

(a) The circumstances of the company as they affect the petitioner.[278]
(b) The petitioner's interest in the company.[279]
(c) The opposition of other members.[280]

---

[274] [1959] 1 WLR 62.
[275] (1978) 3 ACLR 437 at p 476; see also *John J Starr (Real Estate) Pty Ltd v Robert R Andrew (A'asia) Pty Ltd* (1991) 6 ACSR 63 at pp 64–5 and 69.
[276] [1989] BCLC 345.
[277] [2006] 3 NZLR 264 at [134], where the reference to the wrong subsection has been corrected in the quotation.
[278] See 8.147–8.188.
[279] See 8.193.
[280] See 8.194–8.199.

(d) The drastic character of the remedy.[281]

(e) The availability of alternative remedies.[282]

(f) The petitioner's own responsibility for the company's circumstances.[283]

This list is adapted from a list provided, in a slightly different context, by Lord Wilberforce in *Re Kong Thai Sawmill (Miri) Sdn Bhd*,[284] where his Lordship said that in exercising its discretion whether or not to make a winding-up order:

> the court will have in mind the drastic character of this remedy, if sought to be applied to a company which is a going concern; it will take into account (a statement which is not exhaustive) the gravity of the case made out...; the possibility of remedying the complaints proved in other ways than by winding the company up; the interest of the applicant in the company; the interests of other members of the company not involved in the proceedings.

The wishes of the company's creditors, though not immaterial,[285] are by comparison of **8.145** minor importance.[286] See 8.109 for the position where the company is insolvent.

Petitioner's previous acquiescence

In *Re Lowes Park Pty Ltd*[287] it was said to be relevant that, before applying for the com- **8.146** pany to be wound up, the applicant had never complained of the way the company was conducted, which he said made it just and equitable to wind up the company, though the conduct had continued for the 28 years that he had been a member.

Circumstances of the Company as they Affect the Petitioner

From ejusdem generis *to wide generality*

Paragraphs (a) to (fa) of IA 1986, s 122(1), define specific circumstances in which the court **8.147** has jurisdiction to order the winding up of a company. Paragraph (g), on the other hand, allows a petitioner to invite the court to find that there are other circumstances making it just and equitable that the company should be wound up. At first the courts took the view that a petitioner had to show that there was a circumstance analogous to those specified in the other paragraphs.[288] Later there was a considerable relaxation of this application of

---

[281] See 8.200–8.208.
[282] See 8.209–8.247.
[283] See 8.248–8.257.
[284] [1978] 2 MLJ 227, at p 233.
[285] *Re Vehicle Buildings and Insulations Ltd* [1986] ILRM 239 at p 244.
[286] *Re Modern Retreading Co Ltd* [1962] EA 57 at p 60.
[287] (1994) 62 FCR 535.
[288] *Re Agriculturist Cattle Insurance Co, ex parte Spackman* (1849) 1 Mac & G 170 per Lord Cottenham LC at p 174; *Re National and Provincial Live Stock Insurance Co* (1858) 31 LT OS 277 per Turner LJ at p 278; and see, for example, per Lord Romilly MR in *Re Anglo-Greek Steam Co* (1866) LR 2 Eq 1 at pp 5–6 and in *Re Great Northern Copper Mining Co of South Australia* (1869) 20 LT 264 at p 265; per Lord Cairns LJ in *Re Suburban Hotel Co* (1867) LR 2 Ch App 737 at pp 740–1; per James V-C in *Re European Life Assurance Society* (1869) LR 9 Eq 122 at pp 127–8; per Gwynne PJ in *Re Golden Reef Mining Co Ltd* (1874) 8 SALR 241 at p 253; per James LJ in *Re Wear Engine Works Co* (1875) LR 10 Ch App 188 at p 191; per Bacon V-C in *Re New Gas Co* (1877) 36 LT 364 at p 366; per Baggallay LJ in *Re Diamond Fuel Co* (1879) 13 ChD 400 at p 408; *Re Mason Brothers Ltd* (1891) 12 LR (NSW) Eq 183 at pp 189–90; *Re Horsham Industrial and Provident Society Ltd* (1894) 70 LT 801 at p 802.

the *ejusdem generis* rule of statutory construction[289] or a recognition that it did not apply at all.[290]

> The words 'just and equitable' are words of the widest significance, and do not limit the jurisdiction of the court to any case. It is a question of fact, and each case must depend on its own circumstances.[291]

> It seems to me that, in deciding whether it is just and equitable that the company should be wound up, I am left really to consider in the widest possible terms what justice and equity require: and it is with due regard to that consideration that I must form an opinion of what was being and what is being done.[292]

> The words 'just and equitable' are wide general words to be construed generally and taken at their face value.[293]

8.148 A contributory petitioning under s 122(1)(g) may rely:

> upon any circumstances of justice or equity which affect him in his relations with the company, or . . . with the other shareholders.[294]

8.149 Similarly, a creditor (specifically a contingent creditor) has a right to invoke the jurisdiction 'where for reasons arising out of the relationship between the contingent creditor and the company it is just and equitable that the company should be wound up'.[295]

8.150 This indicates a wider scope for s 122(1)(g) than the earlier remark by Lord Shaw of Dunfermline[296] that:

> It is undoubtedly true that at the foundation of applications for winding up, on the 'just and equitable' rule, there must lie a justifiable lack of confidence in the conduct and management of the company's affairs.

Limits: overlap with the unfair prejudice jurisdiction

8.151 The breadth of the discretion to order winding up on the just and equitable ground does not mean that there are no cases in which winding up will not be ordered. Various circumstances which have been found not, in themselves, to justify winding up are discussed at 8.153–8.154 and 8.173–8.192.

8.152 In *Re Guidezone Ltd*[297] Jonathan Parker J considered what Lord Hoffmann had said in *O'Neill v Phillips*[298] (a case about an unfair prejudice petition) and concluded, at p 357, that winding up on the just and equitable ground cannot be ordered unless the situation

---

[289] Per Vaughan Williams J in *Re Sailing Ship 'Kentmere' Co* [1897] WN 58 and in *Re Amalgamated Syndicate* [1897] 2 Ch 600 at p 607; per Lord President Clyde in *Baird v Lees* 1924 SC 83 at p 90.

[290] *Symington v Symingtons' Quarries Ltd* (1905) 8 F 121 per Lord M'Laren at pp 129–30; *Re Newbridge Sanitary Steam Laundry Ltd* [1917] 1 IR 67; *Re Upper Hutt Town Hall Co Ltd* [1920] NZLR 125; *Loch v John Blackwood Ltd* [1924] AC 783; *Davis and Co Ltd v Brunswick (Australia) Ltd* [1936] 1 All ER 299 at p 309; *Ebrahimi v Westbourne Galleries Ltd* [1973] AC 360.

[291] Per Neville J in *Re Blériot Manufacturing Aircraft Co Ltd* (1916) 32 TLR 253 at p 255.

[292] Per Crossman J in *Re Davis and Collett Ltd* [1935] Ch 693 at p 701.

[293] Per Dillon J in *Re St Piran Ltd* [1981] 1 WLR 1300 at p 1307.

[294] Per Lord Wilberforce in *Ebrahimi v Westbourne Galleries Ltd* [1973] AC 360 at p 375.

[295] Per Scott J in *Re a Company (No 003028 of 1987)* [1988] BCLC 282 at p 294.

[296] *Loch v John Blackwood Ltd* [1924] AC 783 at p 788.

[297] [2000] 2 BCLC 321.

[298] [1999] 1 WLR 1092.

would justify relief for unfairly prejudicial conduct of the company's affairs.[299] This was wholly unexpected and would have limited the well-established wide discretion described at 8.147–8.150. The Court of Appeal has held that the judgment of Jonathan Parker J on this point is not correct and should not be followed.[300] Stanley Burnton LJ pointed out[301] that the winding-up and unfair prejudice jurisdictions are parallel, not coterminous. The statutory provisions are differently worded and they ask the court to consider different questions: on a winding-up petition, the question is whether the company's existence should be ended; on an unfair prejudice petition, the question is how the company's existence should be continued. In many, if not most, cases, conduct of a company's affairs may justify relief under both jurisdictions. However, the unfair prejudice provisions were enacted specifically to provide remedies for situations which do not justify winding up,[302] and it is not necessary to show that the circumstances justify winding up a company in order to succeed with a petition for the relief of unfairly prejudicial conduct of its affairs.[303] There have been cases in which it was held that winding up could be ordered but no unfairly prejudicial conduct was proved,[304] and at least one case in which it was not possible to devise any relief for unfairly prejudicial conduct which would meet the justice of the case and be more advantageous than winding up.[305] Deadlock in a company may justify winding up[306] but is unlikely to be unfairly prejudicial.[307]

No no-fault winding up

One important limit on the discretion to order winding up on the just and equitable ground **8.153** is that it cannot be used to obtain a winding up simply because the petitioner wants it—what Lord Hoffmann called 'no-fault divorce'.[308] In particular:

(a) winding up will not be ordered so that the petitioner's investment in the company can be realized;[309] and

---

[299] See 8.454–8.460.

[300] *Hawkes v Cuddy* [2009] EWCA Civ 291, [2009] 2 BCLC 427, at [107]. Earlier, it had been held not to apply in Singapore (*Sing Yong Kim v Evenstar Investments Pte Ltd* [2006] SGCA 23, [2006] 3 SLR 827).

[301] *Hawkes v Cuddy* [2009] EWCA Civ 291, [2009] 2 BCLC 427, at [104]–[105].

[302] See 8.433–8.434.

[303] *Re a Company (No 00314 of 1989)* [1991] BCLC 154; *O'Neill v Phillips* [1999] 1 WLR 1092 per Lord Hoffmann at pp 1099–1100.

[304] *Re R A Noble and Sons (Clothing) Ltd* [1983] BCLC 273 (the doubts about that case expressed by Jonathan Parker J in *Re Guidezone Ltd* [2000] 2 BCLC 321 at p 357 were overruled in *Hawkes v Cuddy* [2009] EWCA Civ 291, [2009] 2 BCLC 427, at [104]–[107]); *Oakley v McDougall* (1987) 14 BCLR (2d) 128; *Jesner v Jarrad Properties Ltd* 1993 SC 34; *Safarik v Ocean Fisheries Ltd* (1995) 12 BCLR (3d) 342; *Nassar v Innovative Precasters Group Pty Ltd* [2009] NSWSC 342, 71 ACSR 343; *Maresca v Brookfield Development and Construction Ltd* [2013] EWHC 3151 (Ch), LTL 5/11/2013. Stanley Burnton LJ in *Hawkes v Cuddy* at [104] gave the example of cases in which the company's substratum has gone: see 8.260–8.277.

[305] *Re Full Cup International Trading Ltd* [1995] BCC 682, affirmed sub nom *Antoniades v Wong* [1997] 2 BCLC 419.

[306] See 8.278–8.292.

[307] *Fexuto Pty Ltd v Bosnjak Holdings Pty Ltd* [2001] NSWCA 97, 37 ACSR 672, at [89]; *Amin v Amin* [2009] EWHC 3356 (Ch), LTL 5/1/2010, at [613] (complete breakdown in relations between two families with equal shareholdings in company could justify winding up but no unfair prejudice proved).

[308] *O'Neill v Phillips* [1999] 1 WLR 1092 at pp 1104–5. See also *Re John While Springs (S) Pte Ltd* [2001] 2 SLR 248 at [12].

[309] See 8.186–8.188.

(b) the petitioner's unjustified unilateral cessation of trust and confidence in a quasi-part-nership company does not justify winding up[310] and does not constitute unfairly preju-dicial conduct of the company's affairs.[311]

As Aronovitch J said in *Western Quebec Investment Ltd v J G Bisson Construction and Engineering Ltd:*[312]

> nous ne pouvons souscrire à la théorie que tout actionnaire non satisfait de la bonne marche des affaires de la compagnie ou de son administration, ou qui désire mettre un terme à ses responsabilités, peut en demander la dissolution.[313]

8.154   Unless the articles of association of a registered company provide otherwise, a member cannot get it to wind up voluntarily other than by persuading members to pass a special resolution. A person must accept, on joining a company, that leaving the company is subject to this fundamental restriction. A contributory presenting a just and equitable petition is claiming that it is just and equitable to waive this restriction. The essential question on a contributory's petition is whether members who do not desire to stay in a company should be entitled to be released.[314] A member of a registered company does not have an unquali-fied right to the dissolution of the association: one of the circumstances in which the court has jurisdiction to make a winding-up order must be established, for example, that it is just and equitable to wind up the company.[315]

Collateral purpose

8.155   In *Re Tober Enterprises Ltd*[316] a contributory of an insolvent company petitioned for its winding up under the just and equitable clause in a British Columbia statute apparently for the purpose of obtaining a tax advantage for itself. The provincial statute under which the application was made does not give jurisdiction to wind up an insolvent company, because in Canada insolvency is a matter for federal legislation exclusively. So the petition was presented under the just and equitable clause. The court refused to make the winding-up order because to do so would circumvent the policy of not winding up insolvent companies under the provincial statute, and because it had not been shown that an order would benefit members of the company in their capacity as members.

8.156   In *Re J E Cade and Son Ltd*[317] the petitioner sought to have the company put into liquidation so that he would be entitled to give it notice to quit land which he owned which the com-pany occupied for the purposes of its farming business. The petitioner alleged an agreement with other shareholders that he would be given possession of the land unless they exercised an option to purchase the land and his shares in the company within a period of five years which had expired. The petition was struck out as bound to fail because the petitioner was

---

[310] See 8.388–8.390.
[311] *O'Neill v Phillips* [1999] 1 WLR 1092.
[312] [1972] Que SC 331, at pp 337–8.
[313] We are unable to subscribe to the theory that every shareholder who is not satisfied that the affairs of the company or its administration are running smoothly, or who wishes to put an end to his liabilities, may claim dissolution.
[314] Per Harman J in *Re a Company (No 00370 of 1987)* [1988] 1 WLR 1068 at p 1075.
[315] *Western Quebec Investment Ltd v J G Bisson Construction and Engineering Ltd* [1972] Que SC 331 per Aronovitch J at pp 337–8; *Re a Company (No 002567 of 1982)* [1983] 1 WLR 927 per Vinelott J at pp 935–6.
[316] (1980) 109 DLR (3d) 184.
[317] [1992] BCLC 213.

seeking to protect, not his interests as a member of the company, but his interests as free-holder of the farm—indeed those interests were directly opposed.[318]

Company in voluntary liquidation

For the position where the company is already in voluntary liquidation, see 10.122–10.129. **8.157**

Examples of Just and Equitable Winding Up on Contributory's Petition

Categorization deprecated

In *Ebrahimi v Westbourne Galleries Ltd*[319] Lord Wilberforce said, at pp 374–5: **8.158**

> there has been a tendency to create categories or headings under which cases must be brought if the [just and equitable] clause is to apply. This is wrong. Illustrations may be used, but general words should remain general and not be reduced to the sum of particular instances.

In *Re Straw Products Pty Ltd*[320] Mann CJ said, at p 223:

> Facts rendering it just and equitable that a company should be wound up cannot be resolved into categories. Cases upon the subject are to be read with this always in mind. They merely illustrate the diversity of the circumstances calling for an exercise of the court's discretion in winding up a company because it is just and equitable to do so.

Commenting on this remark, Smith J in *Re Wondoflex Textiles Pty Ltd*[321] said, at p 464:

> This, however, does not, of course, mean that the court should reject the assistance provided by the illustrations contained in the decided cases.

See also *Re Rogers and Agincourt Holdings Ltd*[322] per Lacourcière JA at p 156.

In *Thomas v Mackay Investments Pty Ltd*[323] Owen J said at p 302: **8.159**

> Counsel for the respondents submitted that this case did not fall within any of the recognised areas in which the just and equitable ground is usually employed. It must be recognised that there is no necessary limit to the generality of the words 'just and equitable'. They are to be applied in their ordinary meaning as calling for the exercise of judgment in the conventional way.

Lines of cases identified in this work

Despite what is said at 8.158–8.159 courts regularly refer to earlier cases as precedents **8.160** and this has created well-recognized lines of cases. For the purposes of discussion of cases decided so far it is convenient to group them. Some cases must be treated as in a class of their own while others form important and well-recognized lines of cases.

The following lines of cases are treated in separate sections, as indicated: **8.161**

(a) Cases in which the company was promoted fraudulently.[324]
(b) Cases in which the company's substratum has gone.[325]

---

[318] For criticism of this case see S Griffin, 'Defining the scope of a membership interest' (1993) 14 Co Law 64.
[319] [1973] AC 360.
[320] [1942] VLR 222.
[321] [1951] VLR 458.
[322] (1976) 74 DLR (3d) 152.
[323] (1996) 22 ACSR 294.
[324] See 8.258–8.259.
[325] See 8.260–8.277.

(c) Cases in which there is a 'deadlock'.[326]

(d) Cases in which there is a constitutional and administrative vacuum.[327]

(e) Cases in which the management and conduct of the company are such that it is unjust and inequitable to require the petitioner to continue as a member.[328]

(f) Cases in which the company is a quasi-partnership company and the circumstances described in 8.339–8.414 exist.

(g) Other cases are in a class of their own or a small group.[329]

Judicial classifications

8.162 B H McPherson submitted[330] that the cases could be reduced to three classes:

(a) where initially it is, or later becomes, impossible to achieve the objects for which the company was formed;[331]

(b) where it has become impossible to carry on the business of the company;[332]

(c) where there has been serious fraud, misconduct or oppression in regard to the affairs of the company.[333]

This statement was approved and adopted in *International Hospitality Concepts Pty Ltd v National Marketing Concepts Inc (No 2)*[334] (by which time Mr McPherson was a judge of the Queensland Court of Appeal), in *Smith v French*[335] and in *Gregor v British-Israel-World Federation (NSW).*[336] Mr McPherson's article was written before the cases in 8.161(d) and before *Ebrahimi v Westbourne Galleries Ltd*[337] transformed the importance of the line of cases in 8.161(f) (which Mr McPherson did acknowledge could constitute a separate class[338]). Mr McPherson said that he did not have space to deal with the miscellaneous cases in 8.161(a) and (g).[339]

8.163 In Canada courts often say that the cases can be put in four categories. For example, in *Coutu v San Jose Mines Ltd*,[340] Pitfield J, at [21], said that there are four broad sets of circumstances which make it just and equitable to order a winding up:

(a) the substratum, or purpose for which the company was formed, has been exhausted;[341]

(b) there is a justifiable lack of confidence in management;[342]

(c) deadlock prevents or inhibits corporate action;[343] and

---

[326] See 8.278–8.292.
[327] See 8.293–8.297.
[328] See 8.298–8.338.
[329] See 8.418–8.431.
[330] B H McPherson, 'Winding up on the "just and equitable" ground' (1964) 27 MLR 282, at p 285.
[331] (b) in the list in 8.161.
[332] 8.161(c).
[333] 8.161(e).
[334] (1994) 13 ACSR 368 at p 371.
[335] [2000] VSC 381.
[336] [2002] NSWSC 12, 41 ACSR 641, at p 666.
[337] [1973] AC 360.
[338] McPherson (1964) 27 MLR 282 at p 285, n 19.
[339] McPherson (1964) 27 MLR 282 at p 297, n 97.
[340] 2005 BCSC 453, 3 BLR (4th) 22.
[341] 8.161(b).
[342] 8.161(e).
[343] 8.161(c).

(d) the shareholders agreed from the outset that the corporation would carry on business in a manner similar to a partnership.[344]

In *Palmieri v AC Paving Co Ltd*[345] the same four grounds are quoted from textbooks. They are similar to the four grounds on which winding up was claimed in the Alberta case of *Keho Holdings Ltd v Noble*:[346] (a) deadlock in management, (b) loss of confidence in management, (c) loss of substratum, and (d) a partnership analogy. They seem to derive from an article by David Huberman.[347] In *Baxted v Warkentin*[348] a slightly different four-category analysis, in which oppression replaces justifiable lack of confidence in management, is quoted from another textbook.   **8.164**

Legislative Definitions of Circumstances

Introduction

Legislatures have sometimes defined specific circumstances in which the court is to have jurisdiction to wind up companies as a remedy for members.[349] These are sometimes seen as examples of when it would be just and equitable to wind up a company, but it may be that they also extend the jurisdiction to situations where winding up would not otherwise be possible.   **8.165**

Oppressive or unfairly prejudicial conduct (Australia, Canada)

In some jurisdictions (but not in any part of the United Kingdom), oppressive or unfairly prejudicial conduct of a company's affairs is a ground for winding up. For example, the Canada Business Corporations Act, s 214(1), provides: **8.166**

> A court may order the liquidation and dissolution of a corporation or any of its affiliated corporations on the application of a shareholder,
>
> (a) if the court is satisfied that in respect of a corporation or any of its affiliates
>   (i) any act or omission of the corporation or any of its affiliates effects a result,
>   (ii) the business or affairs of the corporation or any of its affiliates are or have been carried on or conducted in a manner, or
>   (iii) the powers of the directors of the corporation or any of its affiliates are or have been exercised in a manner
>
> that is oppressive or unfairly prejudicial to or that unfairly disregards the interests of any security holder, creditor, director or officer.

Similar provisions are made in provincial Corporations Acts[350] and in Australia.[351]

Under these provisions, winding up is the only remedy. However, both Australia and Canada also have specific provisions for oppression or unfair prejudice which make available a wide range of remedies, including winding up.[352]   **8.167**

---

[344] 8.161(f).
[345] (1999) 48 BLR (2d) 130 at [26] and [31].
[346] (1987) 38 DLR (4th) 368 at p 378.
[347] David Huberman, 'Compulsory winding up—the "just and equitable" rule' (1966–7) 5 Alta L Rev 135 at p 139.
[348] 2006 MBQB 214, [2007] 3 WWR 531, at [27].
[349] See also 8.287 ('deadlock' under Quebec law).
[350] See, for example, *Keho Holdings Ltd v Noble* (1987) 38 DLR (4th) 368 (Alberta); *Meltzer v Western Paper Box Co Ltd* [1978] 1 WWR 451 (Manitoba).
[351] Corporations Act 2001 (Australia), s 461(1)(f).
[352] See 8.461–8.463.

8.168   Oppression has long been recognized as a ground for winding up.[353]

Directors acting in their own interests (Australia, Malaysia, Singapore)

8.169   In Australia, the Corporations Act 2001 provides that the court may order the winding up of a company if: 'Directors have acted in affairs of the company in their own interests rather than in the interests of the members as a whole, or in any other manner whatsoever that appears to be unfair or unjust to other members'.[354] The same provision is made in Malaysia and Singapore.

8.170   In *Re G Jeffery (Mens Store) Pty Ltd*[355] this provision was treated as stating examples of circumstances in which it would be just and equitable to wind up a company. See also *Re William Brooks and Co Ltd*[356] (in which a winding-up order was made) and *Cumberland Holdings Ltd v Washington H Soul Pattinson and Co Ltd*[357] (in which the Privy Council set aside a winding-up order on appeal, saying that the petitioners had failed to show that directors had acted in their own interests rather than the interests of the members as a whole). In *Re National Discounts Ltd*,[358] a winding-up order was made where this circumstance was proved, but the court made no mention of the just and equitable clause. In *Re Weedmans Ltd*[359] (in which the court indicated that a winding-up order should be made but the matter was settled), Lucas J said that the provision is wider in scope than the just and equitable clause. But in *Re Johnson Corporation Ltd*,[360] Needham J said that evidence which might fail to justify a winding-up order under what is now s 461(1)(e) might, when considered with other evidence, justify an order under the just and equitable clause. In *Re Kornblums Furnishings Ltd*[361] the petitioner failed to make out this ground and the petition failed. In *Re City Meat Co Pty Ltd*[362] this ground was proved and it was held that it was also just and equitable to wind up the company.

8.171   For Malaysian cases see *Foo Yin Shung v Foo Nyit Tse and Brothers Sdn Bhd*,[363] in which the allegations were either unproved or too trivial to justify winding up; *Fairview Schools Bhd v Indrani a/p Rajaratnam (No 2)*,[364] in which the petitioners' case was described as a non-starter because it was not shown that the directors had made any secret profit or personal gain and their actions had been approved by special resolutions of the members; and *Chloride Eastern Industries Pte Ltd v Premium Vegetables Oils Sdn Bhd*,[365] in which this ground was made out, but no winding-up order was made: instead, alternative relief asked for in the petition, including redemption of the petitioner's shares, was granted.

8.172   For a case in Singapore see *Re HL Sensecurity Pte Ltd*,[366] in which the winding-up order was made on this ground, on the just and equitable ground, and because the company was

---

[353] See 8.320–8.337.
[354] s 461(1)(e).
[355] (1984) 9 ACLR 193.
[356] (1961) 79 WN (NSW) 354.
[357] (1977) 13 ALR 561.
[358] (1951) 52 SR (NSW) 244.
[359] [1974] QdR 377.
[360] (1980) 5 ACLR 227 at p 234.
[361] (1981) 6 ACLR 456.
[362] (1983) 8 ACLR 673.
[363] [1989] 2 MLJ 369.
[364] [1998] 1 MLJ 110.
[365] [2002] 2 MLJ 43.
[366] [2006] SGHC 135.

unable to pay its debts. A false claim by a director that he had transferred his shares in the company to its employees, made so as to persuade other shareholders to do the same, was held to be acting in his interests rather than the interests of the company.

Factors not Sufficient to Justify Winding Up

Wrong done to company

The fact that a wrong has been done to a company is not in itself sufficient to justify winding **8.173** up the company on a contributory's petition if suing the wrongdoer would be an adequate remedy.[367] The court will not put a company into liquidation merely because a liquidator might be more sympathetic than those presently in control of the company's litigation to taking legal action favoured by a contributory petitioner. In this situation, a derivative claim might be possible.

If, however, the majority's refusal to sue the wrongdoer is part of a continuing oppression of **8.174** the minority, it may be just and equitable to make a winding-up order.[368]

Similarly the fact that a company has acted, or is about to act, *ultra vires* is not in itself a **8.175** reason for winding it up.[369]

In all the cases cited in 8.173–8.175 the court was not required by IA 1986, s 125(2),[370] **8.176** to consider whether the petitioner was being unreasonable in not pursuing the alternative remedy.

In *Re Co-operative Development Funds of Australia Ltd (No 3)*[371] (which concerned public **8.177** interest petitions presented by the State Attorney General) Sangster J said that it would be just and equitable to wind up a company which had been wronged by a person in control of the company if there was no practical possibility of members taking a derivative action (the case concerned industrial and provident societies whose members were all individuals in modest circumstances who could not be expected to take on the enormously complex case against the controllers—there had been eight weeks of hearings on the winding-up petitions alone). In *Re Blériot Manufacturing Aircraft Co Ltd*[372] a winding-up order was made because of loss of the company's substratum. It was also alleged that there had been misconduct by a director. Neville J, at p 255, described the company as 'so constituted that it is deprived of its usual remedies' against the director, but it is not clear what his Lordship meant by this statement. His Lordship said that this absence of remedy would in itself have been sufficient for it to be just and equitable to wind up the company, had there not been loss of substratum.

---

[367] *Re National and Provincial Live Stock Insurance Co* (1858) 31 LT OS 277; *Re Anglo-Greek Steam Co* (1866) LR 2 Eq 1; *Re Great Cobar Copper Mining Co Ltd* (1902) 2 SR (NSW) Eq 94; *Re Jury Gold Mine Dev Co* [1928] 4 DLR 735; *Re Mutual Enterprises Inc* (1938) 19 CBR 170; *Re Kitson and Co Ltd* [1946] 1 All ER 435 per Lord Greene MR at p 441; *Idugboe v Oilfield Supply Ltd* 1979 (1) ALR Comm 1; *Win-Doors Ltd v Bryan* (1990) 27 JLR 292; *RCB v Thai Asia Fund Ltd* 1996 CILR 9.
[368] See 8.320–8.338.
[369] *Re Irrigation Co of France, ex parte Fox* (1871) LR 6 Ch App 176; *Re Pioneers of Mashonaland Syndicate* [1893] 1 Ch 731.
[370] See 8.216–8.247.
[371] (1978) 3 ACLR 437.
[372] (1916) 32 TLR 253.

Need to investigate company

8.178   A need to investigate a company's affairs does not in itself justify winding up on a contributory's petition.[373] *Re Berlin Great Market and Abattoirs Co*[374] is to the contrary and so is *Re Manchester and Liverpool Transport Co Ltd*,[375] though the judge in the latter case emphasized that there were very peculiar circumstances. A need to investigate a company may be a sufficient reason for ordering a winding up by the court on a public interest petition.[376]

Dispute which should be solved internally

8.179   A dispute which is a mere domestic quarrel between groups of shareholders, which should be settled by majority vote under the company's constitution, will not justify winding up.[377] In *Loch v John Blackwood Ltd*[378] Lord Shaw of Dunfermline said, at p 788, that a contributory could not ground a winding-up petition on 'dissatisfaction at being outvoted on the business affairs or on what is called the domestic policy of the company'. In *Re Harris Maxwell Larder Lake Gold Mining Co Ltd*[379] Middleton J said, at p 986: 'A winding-up petition cannot be resorted to merely because there is dissension within the company. The majority must govern.' In *Re Imperial Steel and Wire Co Ltd*[380] Kelly J is reported, at p 325, as having said that:

> These shareholders were in the position in which minority shareholders frequently find themselves—bound to submit to the ruling and management of the majority; but that in itself was not a justification for a winding-up at the instigation of the minority.

His Lordship made a similar remark in *Re Noden Hallitt and Johnson Ltd*.[381] In *Re Jury Gold Mine Development Co*[382] Middleton JA said, at p 736:

> [The applicant for winding up] is a minority shareholder and must endure the unpleasantness incident to that situation. If he choose to risk his money by subscribing for shares, it is part of his bargain that he will submit to the will of the majority. In the absence of fraud or transactions *ultra vires*, the majority must govern, and there should be no appeal to the courts for redress.

8.180   Strong dissension from the course pursued by the majority, or directors elected by the majority, does not justify winding up, even if the petitioner is a substantial shareholder.[383]

---

[373] *Re British Asahan Plantations Co Ltd* (1892) 36 SJ 363 (in which the company was in voluntary liquidation); *Re Nation Building, Land and Investment Co Ltd* (1895) 6 BC (NSW) 14; *Re Great Cobar Copper Mining Co Ltd* (1902) 2 SR (NSW) Eq 94 per Owen J at p 109; *Black v United Collieries Ltd* (1904) 7 F 18; *Re Othery Construction Ltd* [1966] 1 WLR 69; *Walter L Jacob and Co Ltd v Financial Intermediaries, Managers and Brokers Regulatory Association* 1988 SCLR 184.

[374] (1871) 24 LT 773.

[375] (1903) 19 TLR 227.

[376] *Re Lubin, Rosen and Associates Ltd* [1975] 1 WLR 122; *Securities and Investments Board v Lancashire and Yorkshire Portfolio Management Ltd* [1992] BCLC 281; see also *Re a Company (No 7151 of 2000)* (2000) LTL 27/11/2000, in which one of the purposes of appointing a provisional liquidator on a public interest petition was investigation of the company's affairs.

[377] Per Lord President Dunedin in *Symington v Symingtons' Quarries Ltd* (1905) 8 F 121 at p 129; *Fairview Schools Bhd v Indrani a/p Rajaratnam (No 2)* [1998] 1 MLJ 110 at p 148.

[378] [1924] AC 783.

[379] (1910) 1 OWN 984.

[380] (1919) 17 OWN 324.

[381] (1924) 26 OWN 269.

[382] [1928] 4 DLR 735.

[383] *Re Hugh-Pam Porcupine Mines Ltd* [1942] OWN 544.

In *Re Grimm's Foods Ltd*,[384] a battle for control of the company, which was won by one faction without illegality or lack of probity, was described as 'an internal corporate matter with which the court should not interfere'.[385]

Saying that opposing factions in a company merely have a domestic quarrel is another **8.181** way of saying that it is not unjust and inequitable to leave the petitioner to submit to the exercise by an opposing faction in the company of their legal rights rather than invoke equitable considerations to release the petitioner. Whether it is just and equitable to subject the exercise of legal rights in a company to equitable considerations depends on the nature of the company. Companies in which equitable considerations should be superimposed on legal rights are known as 'quasi-partnership' companies.[386] The companies in *Re Harris Maxwell Larder Lake Gold Mining Co Ltd, Re Jury Gold Mine Dev Co, Re Imperial Steel and Wire Co Ltd, Re Noden Hallitt and Johnson Ltd* and *Re Hugh-Pam Porcupine Mines Ltd* were apparently not quasi-partnership companies[387] and the company in *Re Grimm's Foods Ltd* was explicitly found not to be one. It is noticeable that all the Canadian cases cited in 8.179–8.181 have been in Ontario and may reflect reluctance of the Ontario courts at that time to use the just and equitable clause to assist minorities in companies.[388]

Feared future events

Events the petitioner fears may happen in the future will usually not, by themselves, justify **8.182** winding up,[389] such as a proposal that the company should enter into a transaction which the petitioner believes would be improvident.[390] But winding up may be ordered to relieve the petitioner from a continuing course of conduct of the company's affairs.[391]

Petitioner cannot get voluntary winding up

The fact that the petitioner cannot secure a three quarters majority for a resolution for **8.183** voluntary winding up will not by itself justify a winding up by the court, even if winding up is desired by members who have more than 50 per cent of the votes.[392] However, winding up may be ordered if the blocking minority also want the company to be wound up but are delaying putting the company into voluntary liquidation to the prejudice of the petitioner.[393] In *Re Global Opportunity Fund Ltd*[394] a petition presented by the directors of a company authorized by only an ordinary resolution was successful: all members wanted

---

[384] (1979) 99 DLR (3d) 377.

[385] At p 384.

[386] See 8.339–8.414.

[387] See per Lacourcière JA in *Re Rogers and Agincourt Holdings Ltd* (1976) 74 DLR (3d) 152 at p 157 commenting on the last three of those cases.

[388] David Huberman, 'Compulsory winding up—the "just and equitable" rule' (1966–7) 5 Alta L Rev 135 at pp 162–3.

[389] *Re James Lumbers Co* [1926] 1 DLR 173 at p 186; *Re British Empire Steel Corp Ltd* [1927] 2 DLR 964; *Re Anglo-Continental Produce Co Ltd* [1939] 1 All ER 99 at p 103.

[390] *Shillingford v The Penn Syndicate* (1958) 1 WIR 58.

[391] *Re Newbridge Sanitary Steam Laundry Ltd* [1917] 1 IR 67 at p 92; *Re Merchants and Shippers' Steamship Lines Ltd* (1917) 17 SR (NSW) 146; *Re Martello and Sons Ltd* [1945] OR 453 at pp 458 and 466; *Kokotovich Constructions Pty Ltd v Wallington* (1995) 17 ACSR 478.

[392] *Re Langham Skating Rink Co* (1877) 5 ChD 669 per James LJ at pp 685–6; *Re Wilkinson (No 2)* [1924] SASR 156; *Re Anglo-Continental Produce Co Ltd* [1939] 1 All ER 99.

[393] *Baird v Lees* 1924 SC 83; *Re Coast Quarries Ltd* (1956) 18 WWR NS 47; *Bernhardt v Beau Rivage Pty Ltd* (1989) 15 ACLR 160; *Re Perfectair Holdings Ltd* [1990] BCLC 423.

[394] 1997 CILR N-7.

a winding up of some kind and it seems that the minority's refusal to support a special resolution was based mainly on objections to the liquidator whom the majority wished to appoint.[395]

Petitioner's wish to be relieved of a bad investment

8.184 The fact that the petitioner has taken the view that the company's undertaking is a bad speculation from which the petitioner wishes to salvage whatever is left of capital invested in shares, or stop the company from calling for further contributions on partly paid shares, does not in itself justify winding up.[396]

8.185 Similarly, the fact that, because of changed circumstances, the company's constitution is not as financially advantageous to the petitioner as it was thought to be on joining the company, does not justify winding up.[397]

Petitioner's desire to realize investment

8.186 The petitioner's desire to realize an investment in the company does not in itself justify winding up.[398] The fact that the petitioner is insolvent makes no difference.[399] The fact that the petitioner and other shareholders cannot agree the terms on which the petitioner is to leave the company does not justify a winding-up order.[400]

8.187 In *Re Pioneers of Mashonaland Syndicate*[401] a winding-up order was refused because the petitioner's prime reason for asking for a winding up seemed to be that he hoped that a liquidator would be able to make calls on other shareholders (whose shares had been issued at a discount) to produce a surplus in which he could share. A winding-up order was refused in *Re Eastern Telegraph Co Ltd*,[402] in which holders of preference stock entitled only to a fixed dividend out of annual profits sought a winding up so as to participate in the surplus which would result when compensation was paid on the nationalization of the company's assets: if the compensation were paid before winding up it could

---

[395] See 1997 CILR N–7–8. See also 8.194–8.199.

[396] *Re Patent Artificial Stone Co Ltd* (1864) 34 LJ Ch 330; *Re Hop and Malt Exchange Co* [1866] WN 222; *Re Suburban Hotel Co* (1867) LR 2 Ch App 737; *Re Langham Skating Rink Co* (1877) 5 ChD 669; *Re Horsham Industrial and Provident Society Ltd* (1894) 70 LT 801; *Re Jury Gold Mine Dev Co* [1928] 4 DLR 735; *Re Winnipeg Saddlery Co Ltd* (1934) 42 Man R 448; *International Hospitality Concepts Pty Ltd v National Marketing Concepts Inc (No 2)* (1994) 13 ACSR 368 (in which minority shareholders in the company started to compete with it).

[397] *Re Empire Building Ltd* [1973] 1 NZLR 214; *Hadfield v Kawarra Chambers Pty Ltd* (1991) 4 ACSR 225.

[398] *Re Anglo-Continental Produce Co Ltd* [1939] 1 All ER 99; *Buckner v Bourbon Farming Co Ltd* (1955) 14 WWR 406; *Shacket v Universal Factors Corporation* [1967] Que SC 131; *Gattuso Investments Inc v Gattuso Corporation Ltd* (1969) 14 CBR NS 161, in which the petitioners held redeemable preference shares and could not persuade the company to exercise its right to redeem; *Federal Commissioner of Taxation v Coppleson* (1981) 39 ALR 30, in which it was held that redeemable preference shares should be valued on the basis that the holders could not obtain a just and equitable winding up merely by reason of the company's inability, because of statutory rules on maintenance of capital, to fulfil its obligation to redeem the shares at the holder's option; *Alldrew Holdings Ltd v Nibro Holdings Ltd* (1996) 91 OAC 241, in which the Ontario Court of Appeal said, at p 248: 'There must be much more than a mere desire of one shareholder or group of shareholders to be bought out to trigger the winding-up provisions of the [Ontario Business Corporations] Act'; *Re Guidezone Ltd* [2000] 2 BCLC 321; *Summit Co (S) Pte Ltd v Pacific Biosciences Pte Ltd* [2006] SGHC 190, [2007] 1 SLR 46.

[399] *Re K/9 Meat Supplies (Guildford) Ltd* [1966] 1 WLR 1112; *Re Burgess Homes Ltd* [1987] 1 NZLR 513. In *Ebrahimi v Westbourne Galleries Ltd* [1973] AC 360 Lord Cross of Chelsea suggested, at p 387, that the judge in *Re K/9 Meat Supplies (Guildford) Ltd* had failed to take account of other factors which justified winding up.

[400] *Summit Co (S) Pte Ltd v Pacific Biosciences Pte Ltd* [2006] SGHC 190, [2007] 1 SLR 46.

[401] [1893] 1 Ch 731.

[402] [1947] 2 All ER 104.

be distributed to the ordinary shareholders. *Re Lowes Park Pty Ltd*[403] concerned a family company in which the applicant for winding up held only non-voting shares on which no dividend was paid but which entitled him to a share in the company's considerable assets on winding up. He had been given his shares by his late father. He claimed to be locked in to the company but had not in fact tried to use the share sale provisions in the company's articles, which provided for independent valuation. The court refused to order winding up.

See also 8.353 (there is no right to a no-fault winding up of a quasi-partnership company).   **8.188**

Removal of petitioner from directorship

Removal of the petitioner from office as a director of the company does not justify winding   **8.189**
up the company, unless it is a quasi-partnership company in which there is an understanding that the petitioner will participate in management.[404]

Refusal to appoint petitioner a director

In *Re Kornblums Furnishings Ltd*[405] winding up was not justified by the refusal by the direct-   **8.190**
ors of a public company to make the petitioner a director. The petitioner was a substantial minority shareholder, but the directors knew they would not be able to work with him, and they acted bona fide in what they believed to be the interests of the company.

Connection with another company sought to be wound up

Winding up of a company is not justified by the fact that it has the same shareholders as, and   **8.191**
is connected in business with, another company which the petitioner has applied to have wound up,[406] unless the companies' affairs are so much connected that it would be difficult to wind up one without the other.[407]

Change of company's constitution

In *Re Bulawayo Market and Offices Co Ltd*[408] the company's members had altered its articles   **8.192**
by special resolution to provide that it would no longer have any directors but that its business was to be controlled and managed by a manager or managers, who in the first place would be another limited company. A member alleged that it would be just and equitable to wind up the company, because the members would no longer be able to hold individual directors, with unlimited liability, responsible for breach of duty to the company, but this was rejected by Warrington J. A requirement was introduced by the Companies Act 1928, s 28, that every public company should have at least two directors and by the Companies Act 1947, s 26(1), that every other company should have at least one director.[409] The Companies Act 2006, s 155, introduced the present requirement that every company must have at least one director who is a natural person.

---

[403] (1994) 62 FCR 535.
[404] *Re a Company (No 00314 of 1989)* [1991] BCLC 154. See 8.398–8.411.
[405] (1981) 6 ACLR 456.
[406] *Re Chase Plastics Ltd* (1966) 110 SJ 564; *Re Omega Legal Services (Worldwide) Ltd* (2001) LTL 29/6/2001.
[407] *Re Nefertiti Estates Ltd* [2003] EWHC 1709 (Ch), LTL 25/6/2003.
[408] [1907] 2 Ch 458.
[409] See now the Companies Act 2006, s 154.

Petitioner's Interest in the Company

8.193   A petitioner for the compulsory liquidation of a company must satisfy the tangible interest rule.[410] In *Bryanston Finance Ltd v De Vries (No 2)*[411] it was held that the fact that a member of a company who wished to petition for its compulsory liquidation held only 62 of the company's 7,414,938 shares did not mean that a petition presented by him was bound to fail.

Opposition of other Members

8.194   A contributory petitioner will almost always be opposed by fellow contributories, for otherwise the company would wind up voluntarily. If there is simply a disagreement between the petitioner and the majority of members about whether the company should be wound up compulsorily or voluntarily, the court will not make a winding-up order.[412] If there is simply a disagreement between the petitioner and a majority of the members about the company's commercial viability, the court will not make a winding-up order.[413] In *Re Rock Investment Trust Ltd*[414] North J dismissed a petition brought by five contributories who held a total of 50 fully paid shares who were opposed by 2,700 other shareholders. The petitioners alleged that the company was recklessly speculating with shareholders' capital which had been contributed mainly by 'small holders, chiefly working and uneducated men'.

8.195   Usually a contributory petitioning under the just and equitable clause for the winding up of a company is, in essence, asking the court for relief from a situation that is unjust and inequitable to that contributory alone or principally to that contributory, and it is almost inevitable that if winding up is ordered it will be against the wishes of the majority of members. The view of Crockett J in *Re G Jeffery (Mens Store) Pty Ltd*[415] that '[i]f an order is made because it is just and equitable to do it must be just and equitable not just for the applicant but for all' is, with respect, misconceived. It may be compared with the view of Cormack J in *Upton v Weimann*:[416]

> Counsel for the appellant [a member appealing against the making of a winding-up order]...suggested...that the respondent [the applicant for the winding-up order] was required to demonstrate that liquidation would benefit the shareholders as a whole in order to succeed in his application for dissolution. In my opinion [this factor] might possibly have some bearing on an application were it not [for the finding at first instance] that 'the parties are at loggerheads'.

This does not, however, mean that an order cannot be made unless those opposing it have been unjust or inequitable.[417]

8.196   If the substratum of the company has gone, winding up will usually be ordered despite the opposition of a majority of members.[418]

---

[410]   See 8.67–8.86.
[411]   [1976] Ch 63.
[412]   *Re Beaujolais Wine Co* (1867) LR 3 Ch App 15 at pp 19–20.
[413]   *Re Factage Parisien Ltd* (1864) 34 LJ Ch 140; *Re Bwlch y Plwm Co Ltd* (1867) 17 LT 235.
[414]   (1891) 35 SJ 447.
[415]   (1984) 9 ACLR 193 at p 201.
[416]   (1985) 61 AR 16 at p 18.
[417]   Per Lord Cross of Chelsea in *Ebrahimi v Westbourne Galleries Ltd* [1973] AC 360 at p 383.
[418]   *Re Haven Gold Mining Co* (1882) 20 ChD 151; *Re Baku Consolidated Oilfields Ltd* [1944] 1 All ER 24.

In *Re National Savings Bank Association*[419] Turner LJ said the court would not be guided by **8.197** what he described[420] as a 'packed' meeting of members which had resolved that the company should be wound up voluntarily (but without the necessary formalities to constitute a resolution for voluntary winding up under what is now IA 1986, s 84). In *Re Neath Harbour Smelting and Rolling Works Ltd*[421] the Court of Appeal discounted the views of contributories who wanted a bubble company to continue.

In *Re British Oil and Cannel Co*[422] Stuart V-C said he would order the winding up of the **8.198** company, despite the opposition of 29 out of 42 shareholders, unless the members adopted a resolution for voluntary winding up. He is reported as saying that he came to this decision because 'the assets and the way in which the company had been managed were both unsatisfactory' but the report gives little further information.

If opposition to a contributory's petition to wind up a company arises from a personal dis- **8.199** pute between the members of the company, it is a misapplication of the company's money to finance the opposition, except so far as is necessary for the representation in the proceedings of the company as a separate person.[423]

Drastic Character of Winding Up as a Remedy

The drastic character of winding up as a remedy for an unjust and inequitable situation is often **8.200** commented on.

Lord President Cooper pointed out in *Elder v Elder and Watson Ltd*[424] that in many cases wind- **8.201** ing up a company as a cure for a member's unjust and inequitable position is worse than the disease 'owing to the prejudice likely to be inflicted upon the applicant for relief as a result of a compulsory liquidation of the company'.

In *Re R J Jowsey Mining Co Ltd*[425] Laskin JA said, at p 552: **8.202**

> The remedy is drastic, and hence must be addressed to a serious condition affecting the proper conduct or management of the company's affairs.

Lord Wilberforce said in *Cumberland Holdings Ltd v Washington H Soul Pattinson and Co* **8.203** *Ltd*:[426] 'to wind up a successful and prosperous company and one which is properly managed must clearly be an extreme step and must require a strong case to be made'.

In *Re Walter L Jacob and Co Ltd*[427] Nicholls LJ agreed, at p 354:

> that to wind up an active company compulsorily is a serious step, and he who asserts that it is just and equitable for the court to take that step must put forward and establish reasons which have a weight justifying the court taking that step.

---

[419] (1866) LR 1 Ch App 547.
[420] At p 553.
[421] (1886) 2 TLR 336.
[422] (1867) 15 LT 601.
[423] See 8.508–8.512.
[424] 1952 SC 49 at p 54.
[425] [1969] 2 OR 549.
[426] (1977) 13 ALR 561 at pp 566–7.
[427] [1989] BCLC 345.

8.204 In *Bernhardt v Beau Rivage Pty Ltd*[428] Young J said, at p 164: 'the court should be slow to wind up a solvent company and such an order is not lightly made'.

8.205 It has been said in Canada that winding up a company is so drastic a remedy that it is not ordered if the wrong may be adequately repaired by milder relief,[429] but in Britain this may be subject to IA 1986, s 125(2).[430]

8.206 The effect of the compulsory winding up of a company on its members and creditors is a factor which the court should take into account when deciding whether or not it is just and equitable to order winding up.[431]

8.207 The effect of winding up a solvent company on the petition of a minority shareholder will be proportionally worse for the majority than for the petitioner, but usually the majority can avoid this by buying out the petitioner.[432] Having decided that it is appropriate to order the winding up of a company which is a going concern, the court may give the parties time to agree that one side will buy out the other,[433] or even attempt to solve serious disputes about the running of the company.[434]

8.208 The court may feel less compunction about ordering the winding up of a company that has ceased to be a prosperous going concern[435] or is only a holding company with no trading activities[436] or does nothing but own and rent out a single piece of land.[437]

Buying Out Petitioner

8.209 What the minority shareholder in cases of this sort really wants is not to have the company wound up—which may prove an unsatisfactory remedy—but to be paid a proper price for his shareholding.[438]

It is not an abuse of process to present a petition with this in mind.[439]

8.210 In practice it is expected that on the court finding that a minority shareholder of a company is entitled to have the company wound up, the other members will buy out the petitioner. Sometimes the court has made a winding-up order but has rescinded it before it was drawn up on being informed that there has been an agreement to buy out the petitioner.[440]

---

[428] (1989) 15 ACLR 160.

[429] Per O'Connor J in *Gattuso Investments Inc v Gattuso Corporation Ltd* (1969) 14 CBR NS 161 at p 163 and in *Raicevic v Nancy G Dress Corporation* (1969) 15 CBR NS 149.

[430] See 8.216–8.247.

[431] *Western Quebec Investment Ltd v J G Bisson Construction and Engineering Ltd* [1972] Que SC 331; *91436 Canada Inc v Evalyne Sales Corp* (1984) 54 CBR NS 87; *Re Lowes Park Pty Ltd* (1994) 62 FCR 535 at pp 552–3; *Re Hillcrest Housing Ltd* (1998) 165 Nfld & PEIR 181 at pp 303–4. But *Varusay Mohamed Shaik Abdul Rahman v SVK Patchee Bros (M) Sdn Bhd* [2002] 3 MLJ 674 is to the contrary.

[432] See 8.209–8.215.

[433] See 8.210.

[434] *Haselgrove v Lavender Estates Pty Ltd* [2009] NSWSC 1076.

[435] *Re R J Jowsey Mining Co Ltd* [1969] 2 OR 549 per Laskin JA at p 557; *Re Humberbank Investment and Development Ltd* (1972) 17 CBR NS 220.

[436] *91436 Canada Inc v Evalyne Sales Corp* (1984) 54 CBR NS 87 at p 109.

[437] *Kokotovich Constructions Pty Ltd v Wallington* (1995) 17 ACSR 478.

[438] Per Lord Cross of Chelsea in *Ebrahimi v Westbourne Galleries Ltd* [1973] AC 360 at p 385.

[439] *Tench v Tench Bros Ltd* [1930] NZLR 403; *CVC/Opportunity Equity Partners Ltd v Demarco Almeida* [2002] UKPC 16, [2002] 2 BCLC 108; see also *Cumberland Holdings Ltd v Washington H Soul Pattinson and Co Ltd* (1977) 13 ALR 561 per Lord Wilberforce at p 574.

[440] *Re Crown Bank* (1890) 44 ChD 634 at pp 647–9; *Re XL Petroleum Pty Ltd* [1971] VR 560.

The court may announce that it is minded to make a winding-up order but will adjourn to allow the parties to agree a settlement.[441] The court cannot, of course, decide to make an order on the basis that the order will not be acted on.

The court has no power in winding-up proceedings to order other members of the company, or the company itself, to purchase the petitioner's shares[442] though it would have such a power[443] if the petitioner applied for protection against unfair prejudice under the Companies Act 2006, s 994.[444] A different view has been taken in cases cited at 8.221. **8.211**

In *Lusk v Archive Security Ltd*[445] a controller of one of two equal shareholders in a company applied for it to be wound up and the other applied for relief in respect of oppressive, unfairly discriminatory or unfairly prejudicial conduct of the company's affairs. It was held that there had been oppression and that winding up was inappropriate because the oppressed shareholder regarded the company as his life's work. The applicant for winding up was ordered to sell its shares to the oppressed shareholder. **8.212**

In some cases a contributory's petition has clearly been prompted by a campaign by those in control of the company to force the petitioner to sell shares to them at an undervalue.[446] This is sometimes described as an attempt to 'freeze out' the petitioner[447] or 'squeeze out'.[448] **8.213**

Any transfer of shares after the presentation of a winding-up petition will, by virtue of IA 1986, s 127, be void if a winding-up order is made. In *Caratti Holding Co Pty Ltd v Zampatti*[449] an interim injunction was issued restraining one shareholder in a company from activating his right under the company's articles to compulsorily purchase the shares of another shareholder who had presented a petition for the company to be wound up. Part of the petitioner's case was that the compulsory purchase procedure valued his shares at less than one per cent of their true value. **8.214**

See also 8.230–8.239. **8.215**

Alternative Remedies

Effect of petitioner's failure to seek another remedy

A court hearing a contributory's petition for winding up on the just and equitable ground must decide whether the company should be wound up, *ignoring* the possibility of other **8.216**

---

[441] See, for example, *Re Wondoflex Textiles Pty Ltd* [1951] VLR 458 at p 469; *Re National Drive-In Theatres Ltd* [1954] 2 DLR 55 at p 65; *Re Tivoli Freeholds Ltd* [1972] VR 445 at p 480; *Re Humber Valley Broadcasting Co Ltd* (1978) 19 Nfld & PEIR 230 at pp 259–62; *Re Gerard Nouvelle Cuisine Ltd* (1981) 1 BCR 311; *Re R A Noble and Sons (Clothing) Ltd* [1983] BCLC 273 at p 292; *Re City Meat Co Pty Ltd* (1983) 8 ACLR 673 at pp 674–5 and 682; *Re Deep Sea Trawlers Ltd* (1984) 2 NZCLC 99,137 at p 99,148; *Re Rongo-ma-tane Farms Ltd* (1987) 3 NZCLC 100,145; *Bernhardt v Beau Rivage Pty Ltd* (1989) 15 ACLR 160 at p 166; *Jesner v Jarrad Properties Ltd* 1993 SC 34; *Kay v Nipissing Twin Lakes Rod and Gun Club* (1993) 7 BLR (2d) 225; *Amin v Amin* [2009] EWHC 3356 (Ch), LTL 5/1/2010, at [613].

[442] *Re Humber Valley Broadcasting Co Ltd* (1978) 19 Nfld & PEIR 230; *Rafuse v Bishop* (1979) 34 NSR (2d) 70 at pp 82–3; *Re Hillcrest Housing Ltd* (1998) 165 Nfld & PEIR 181 at p 185.

[443] Under the Companies Act 2006, s 996(2)(e).

[444] In Canada and the Cayman Islands, powers to order alternative remedies when hearing petitions by shareholders have been provided by statute—see 8.223.

[445] (1990) 5 NZCLC 66,979.

[446] *Loch v John Blackwood Ltd* [1924] AC 783; *Re Wondoflex Textiles Pty Ltd* [1951] VLR 458.

[447] *Re James Lumbers Co Ltd* [1926] 1 DLR 173 at p 189.

[448] M Chesterman, *Small Businesses* (London: Sweet & Maxwell, 1977), ch 6.

[449] [1975] WAR 183.

forms of relief.[450] If the court comes to the conclusion that in the absence of any other remedy it would be just and equitable that the company should be wound up, it *must* make a winding-up order *unless* it is of opinion that the petitioner is acting unreasonably in seeking a winding-up order rather than pursuing some alternative remedy.[451] Under this statutory provision, making a winding-up order is mandatory,[452] subject to a discretion not to make the order if the petitioner is acting unreasonably.[453] It follows that if there is no alternative remedy, a winding-up order must be made.[454] As originally proposed by the Cohen committee,[455] the provision would not have limited the court's discretion. The Jenkins committee recommended amending the provision so as to remove its limitations on the court's discretion,[456] but this has never been implemented.

8.217 The formation by a judge of an opinion that a petitioner is acting unreasonably is not an exercise of judicial discretion and so the opinion can be reviewed on appeal.[457] It cannot be unreasonable of the petitioner not to pursue an alternative remedy that has already been refused.[458]

8.218 Three particularly significant alternative remedies are:

(a) where the essential complaint is that a person has harmed the company, taking legal action against that person;[459]

(b) a petition for relief in respect of unfairly prejudicial conduct of the company's affairs;[460]

(c) a sale of the petitioner's shares.[461]

History

8.219 In *Re Pioneers of Mashonaland Syndicate*[462] Vaughan Williams J said, at pp 733–4:

> It was very fairly admitted in argument that it would not be just and equitable that I should make the order if the petitioner was complaining of a matter which could be dealt with by the ordinary tribunals, on ordinary process, at his instance.

It seems that this was regarded as founding a rule that winding up would not be ordered if another remedy was available, regardless of whether winding up was just and equitable, and reversing this rule was the reason for introducing what is now IA 1986, s 125(2), which was first enacted as the Companies Act 1947, s 90, in response to a recommendation of the Cohen committee.[463] In fact Vaughan Williams J held that the petitioner in *Re Pioneers of Mashonaland*

---

[450] 1986, s 125(2).

[451] s 125(2) as interpreted in *Re a Company (No 002567 of 1982)* [1983] 1 WLR 927 per Vinelott J at p 932; *Vujnovich v Vujnovich* [1990] BCLC 227 at p 232.

[452] IA 1986, s 125(2), and the New Zealand legislation considered in *Vujnovich v Vujnovich* state that the court 'shall' make a winding-up order. The Corporations Act 2001 (Australia), s 467(4), uses 'must'.

[453] *Vujnovich v Vujnovich.*

[454] *Johnny Oceans Restaurant Pty Ltd v Page* [2003] NSWSC 952.

[455] See 8.219.

[456] Report of the Company Law Committee (Cmnd 1749, 1962), para 503(i).

[457] *Virdi v Abbey Leisure Ltd* [1990] BCLC 342.

[458] *Vujnovich v Vujnovich.*

[459] See 8.173–8.177.

[460] See 8.227–8.229.

[461] See 8.230–8.239.

[462] [1893] 1 Ch 731.

[463] Report of the Committee on Company Law Amendment (Cmd 6659, 1945), paras 60 and 152, and p 95, recommendation I.

Syndicate[464] did not have an alternative remedy, and it is clear that the reason for refusing the winding-up order in that case was simply that winding up was not just and equitable.

Insolvent partnerships

IA 1986, s 125(2), applies on a petition by a member of an insolvent partnership under IPO **8.220** 1994, art 9, for the winding up of the partnership where there is no concurrent petition for the winding up or bankruptcy of any member of the partnership,[465] but it does not apply to petitions under art 10 of the 1994 Order where there are concurrent petitions against all the members of the partnership (as the modified form of s 125 which is applied to such petitions by IPO 1994, sch 6, para 3, does not include the provision).

Ordering an alternative remedy

In cases in 2013 in the Republic of Ireland[466] and England[467] a court, which had found **8.221** that there was a suitable alternative remedy to winding up, ordered,[468] or held that it could order,[469] that alternative remedy without requiring the petitioner to bring separate proceedings. In the Irish case it was held that this could be done under the power to make 'any other order' on hearing a winding-up petition, though earlier cases not considered by the court had ruled that was not possible[470] without the express statutory authority that is provided in some jurisdictions.[471] In the English case, it seems that dismissal of the winding-up application was made conditional on implementation of the alternative remedy decided by the court, though the precise wording of the order is not reported. Conditional dismissal has also previously been held to be illegitimate.[472]

Any remedy (other than winding up) for unfairly prejudicial conduct of a company's affairs **8.222** may be obtained by petitioning under CA 2006, s 994,[473] and the rather awkward compromise in England and Wales is that a petitioner for relief in respect of unfairly prejudicial conduct may formulate the petition as alternatively a petition for winding up. But this should not be done unless winding up is the relief which the petitioner prefers or it is thought that it may be the only relief to which the petitioner is entitled.[474]

Statutory powers to order alternative remedy on winding-up petition

In most provinces of Canada,[475] and under Canadian Federal corporations law,[476] a court **8.223** hearing a winding-up application by a shareholder under the just and equitable clause may order the same remedies as it can on an application for protection against unfairly prejudicial

---

[464] [1893] 1 Ch 731.
[465] IA 1986, s 221(5), as modified by IPO 1994, sch 5, para 2.
[466] *Re Dublin Cinema Group Ltd* [2013] IEHC 147.
[467] *Maresca v Brookfield Development and Construction Ltd* [2013] EWHC 3151 (Ch), LTL 5/11/2013.
[468] *Maresca v Brookfield Development and Construction Ltd.*
[469] *Re Dublin Cinema Group Ltd*, in which the parties settled without the court making an order.
[470] See 5.127–5.134.
[471] See 8.223.
[472] See 5.104.
[473] For the overlap of the unfair prejudice and winding-up jurisdictions see 8.152.
[474] PD 49B, para 1. See 8.432–8.468.
[475] For example, in British Columbia the Business Corporations Act, s 324(3)(b).
[476] Canada Business Corporations Act, s 214(2).

conduct.[477] Conversely, a court hearing an application for relief in respect of oppressive or unfairly prejudicial conduct can order winding up.[478] In the Cayman Islands, there is provision for alternative remedies on a contributory's winding-up petition.[479] Alternative remedies under these Canadian and Caymanian provisions can only be granted where winding up would otherwise be ordered,[480] which is the same position as it was in Great Britain under the Companies Act 1948, s 210.[481]

Striking out for failure to seek an alternative remedy

8.224 The court will strike out a winding-up petition if it is plain and obvious that the petition will fail because of IA 1986, s 125(2).[482] However, 'it is a very strong thing to say, on an application to strike out, that it is plain and obvious that a petitioner is behaving unreasonably in seeking a winding-up order'.[483] The onus is on the person applying for the petition to be struck out to show that it is plain and obvious that the petition will fail.[484]

8.225 IA 1986, s 125(2), was given as the reason for striking out in *Re a Company (No 002567 of 1982)*[485] and *Re a Company (No 003096 of 1987)*,[486] and the Hong Kong equivalent was one of the reasons for striking out in *Re Trocadero Ltd*.[487] In *Re a Company (No 003843 of 1986)*[488] and *Re a Company (No 004377 of 1986)*[489] the court simply cited *Re a Company (No 002567 of 1982)*.

8.226 In Singapore there is no equivalent to IA 1986, s 125(2), and it has been held that, in that jurisdiction, a contributory's winding-up petition cannot be struck out because of the petitioner's failure to pursue an alternative remedy.[490] However, this has been done in Malaysia[491] and the Cayman Islands,[492] where there is also no equivalent of s 125(2).

Striking out for failure to seek unfair prejudice remedy

8.227 If it is plain and obvious that if the allegations in a winding-up petition were proved, they would show unfairly prejudicial conduct of the company's affairs, for which the court would make an order under the Companies Act 2006, s 996 (relief in respect of unfairly prejudicial

---

[477] See, for example, *Jarman v Brown* [1979] 5 WWR 673; *Morton v Asper* (1989) 62 Man R (2d) 1; *Lamoureux v Golden Flooring Accessories Ltd* [1991] 4 WWR 452; *Clarfield v Manley* (1993) 14 BLR (2d) 295; *Wittlin v Bergman* (1995) 25 OR (3d) 761, in which it was emphasized that the court must first find that winding up is justified before deciding that one of the alternative remedies is preferable; *Belman v Belman* (1995) 26 OR (3d) 56; *Safarik v Ocean Fisheries Ltd* (1995) 12 BCLR (3d) 342, (1996) 17 BCLR (3d) 354; *Mroz v Shuttleworth* (1996) 30 OR (3d) 205; *Palmieri v AC Paving Co Ltd* (1999) 48 BLR (2d) 130.
[478] See 8.461–8.463.
[479] Companies Law (2013 Revision) (Cayman Islands), s 95(3) to (6).
[480] *Wittlin v Bergman*; *Camulos Partners Offshore Ltd v Kathrein and Co* 2010 (1) CILR 303.
[481] See 8.320–8.325.
[482] *Charles Forte Investments Ltd v Amanda* [1964] Ch 240.
[483] Per Warner J in *Re a Company (No 001363 of 1988)* [1989] BCLC 579 at p 586.
[484] *Fuller v Cyracuse Ltd* [2001] 1 BCLC 187.
[485] [1983] 1 WLR 927.
[486] (1987) 4 BCC 80.
[487] [1988] 2 HKLR 443.
[488] [1987] BCLC 562 at p 571.
[489] [1987] 1 WLR 102 at p 112.
[490] *Tang Choon Keng Realty (Pte) Ltd v Tang Wee Cheng* [1992] 2 SLR 1114 at p 1137.
[491] *Eng Man Hin v King's Confectionery Sdn Bhd* [2006] 4 MLJ 421.
[492] *Camulos Partners Offshore Ltd v Kathrein and Co* 2010 (1) CILR 303.

conduct of a company's affairs), the court will strike out the winding-up petition.[493] This contrasts with the position in Canada where the court would be able to hear the winding-up petition and grant the appropriate relief.[494]

In *Re a Company (No 001363 of 1988)*[495] it was claimed that IA 1986, s 125(2), applied **8.228** because, it was alleged, the contributories would have been more likely to obtain relief on a petition for relief in respect of unfairly prejudicial conduct of the company's affairs than under a winding-up petition, but Warner J said that this depended on the view formed by the judge at the hearing of the petition and was not plain and obvious at the time of hearing the application to strike out, and so refused to strike out the winding-up petition.[496] See also *Chong Choon Chai v Tan Gee Cheng*,[497] in which the mere possibility that a winding-up petitioner could have made an application under the Singapore equivalent of the British provisions for relief in respect of unfairly prejudicial conduct was not a reason for striking out the winding-up petition.

An unfair prejudice petition is not necessarily a suitable alternative remedy because there **8.229** are cases in which the situation of the company does not justify relief under the unfair prejudice provisions but does justify winding up under the just and equitable clause.[498] It is also possible that, although unfairly prejudicial conduct is proved, the only appropriate remedy is winding up.[499]

Offer to buy the petitioner's shares

When there is a contributory's petition to wind up a company, a reasonable offer to buy the **8.230** petitioner's shares is an alternative remedy.[500] If a reasonable offer is made, presentation of a petition will be restrained.[501]

An offer may be made at any stage of proceedings, though there may be a costs penalty **8.231** for a late offer.[502] An offer may be amended to cater for objections properly made.[503]

---

[493] *Re Forbes Enterprises (1975) Ltd* (1978) 1 BCR 178; *Re Copeland and Craddock Ltd* [1997] BCC 294; *Re a Company (No 004415 of 1996)* [1997] 1 BCLC 479; *Eng Man Hin v King's Confectionery Sdn Bhd* [2006] 4 MLJ 421; *Man Po Lo Paul v Cheung Kang Wah* [2007] 1 HKLRD 751; *Re Woven Rugs Ltd* [2008] BCC 903. *Re Copeland and Craddock Ltd*, *Re a Company (No 004415 of 1996)* and *Man Po Lo Paul v Cheung Kang Wah* concerned alternative unfair prejudice and winding-up petitions (see 8.432–8.468). In *Re Copeland and Craddock Ltd* the prayer for winding up was not struck out; in *Re a Company (No 004415 of 1996)* and *Man Po Lo Paul v Cheung Kang Wah* it was.
[494] See 8.223.
[495] [1989] BCLC 579.
[496] *Re Botherill Builders* (2001) LTL 12/10/2001 is a similar case.
[497] [1993] 3 SLR 1.
[498] See, for example, *Re R A Noble and Sons (Clothing) Ltd* [1983] BCLC 273 and other cases cited at 8.152.
[499] See *Antoniades v Wong* [1997] 2 BCLC 419 and 8.461 and 8.465.
[500] *Meltzer v Western Paper Box Co Ltd* [1978] 1 WWR 451; *Re a Company (No 002567 of 1982)* [1983] 1 WLR 927; *Re a Company (No 003843 of 1986)* [1987] BCLC 562; *Re a Company (No 003096 of 1987)* (1987) 4 BCC 80; *Virdi v Abbey Leisure Ltd* [1990] BCLC 342; *CVC/Opportunity Equity Partners Ltd v Demarco Almeida* [2002] UKPC 16, [2002] 2 BCLC 108. A contrary view has been expressed in New South Wales by Young J in *Bernhardt v Beau Rivage Pty Ltd* (1989) 15 ACLR 160 at p 164.
[501] *CVC/Opportunity Equity Partners Ltd v Demarco Almeida* [2002] UKPC 16, [2002] 2 BCLC 108, in which presentation was not restrained because the offer was not reasonable.
[502] *Fuller v Cyracuse Ltd* [2001] 1 BCLC 187 at pp 192–3; *Re CVC/Opportunity Equity Partners Ltd* 2002 CILR 531.
[503] *Fuller v Cyracuse Ltd* [2001] 1 BCLC 187 at pp 192–3.

If a reasonable offer is made after a petition is presented but before it is heard, the court will strike out the petition.[504] If, however, there may be difficulties in determining the price or other details, the court will stay proceedings instead of striking out.[505] Proceedings were also stayed in *Re a Company (No 003843 of 1986)*.[506] If the value of the shares depends on the answer to a question of law, the question should be left for the court to decide.[507] In *Yeung Bun v Brio Technology International Ltd*,[508] though, the court decided that allegations of misappropriation and misfeasance which affected share valuation could not be dealt with by negotiation and ordered winding up so that a liquidator could decide whether to take proceedings.

8.232 Similarly, the court may restrain presentation of, or strike out, an unfair prejudice petition if a reasonable offer has been made to buy the petitioner's shares.[509]

8.233 A reasonable offer is one that puts an objectively fair value on the petitioner's shares, as would be awarded by the court in proceedings for relief in respect of oppressive or unfairly prejudicial conduct of the company's affairs, even in a jurisdiction where no such proceedings are available.[510] This is not necessarily the same as the amount which the petitioner would receive in a winding up.

8.234 An offer is not reasonable if the offeror cannot finance it.[511] It is not unreasonable for a petitioner to refuse to accept an offer until the shares have been valued so as to assess whether it is affordable and whether to make a counter-offer.[512] It is not unreasonable to refuse an offer which does not specify the price to be paid and essentially leaves the price to be determined by the offeror.[513]

8.235 In many cases the petitioner contends that the value of the shares has been diminished by the conduct complained of in the petition and some way has to be found for a valuer to take this into account. In *Todd v Todd*[514] winding up was ordered because a liquidator would be best placed to recover misappropriated funds. In *Re Wessex Computer Stationers Ltd*[515] an application to stay proceedings following an offer to buy out the petitioner was refused because it would not have been possible, given the state of the company's accounts, for the two sides to agree on the basis of valuation, though it was thought that a stay could be granted later when auditors completed investigations into the company's affairs.

---

[504] *Re a Company (No 003096 of 1987)* (1987) 4 BCC 80.
[505] *Re a Company (No 002567 of 1982)* [1983] 1 WLR 927; *Fuller v Cyracuse Ltd* [2001] 1 BCLC 187.
[506] [1987] BCLC 562.
[507] *North Holdings Ltd v Southern Tropics Ltd* [1999] 2 BCLC 625. See also *Joint v Stephens (No 2)* [2008] VSC 69, where the offeror's view that the shares were worth only a nominal amount depended on the answer to a question of law. The court found in the offeror's favour on that question but nevertheless held that the offer was unreasonable.
[508] [2000] 2 HKLRD 218.
[509] *Re a Company (No 006834 of 1988)* [1989] BCLC 365.
[510] *CVC/Opportunity Equity Partners Ltd v Demarco Almeida* [2002] UKPC 16, [2002] 2 BCLC 108.
[511] *West v Blanchet* [2000] 1 BCLC 795.
[512] *Apcar v Aftab* [2003] BCC 510.
[513] *Harding v Edwards* [2014] EWHC 247 (Ch), LTL 27/3/2014.
[514] 2008 SLT (Sh Ct) 26.
[515] [1992] BCLC 366.

It is not unreasonable of a petitioner to refuse an offer to buy shares if there is any risk that **8.236** the valuation procedure provided by the articles will undervalue them.[516] This risk may be present, for example, if:

(a) The articles provide for some arbitrary or artificial method of valuation.[517]
(b) There has been some impropriety in the management of the company which has significantly affected the value of the shares.[518]
(c) The valuer will apply a discount to reflect the fact that the shareholding is not large enough to give control of the company.[519]
(d) There is no procedure for making representations to the valuer and the valuer has inadequate means of evaluating claims against the company.[520]
(e) The valuer is not, or cannot be seen to be, wholly independent.[521]

The person valuing the shares should be given complete access to the company's books and **8.237** papers and should be able to call for information and investigate the way in which the company's affairs have been conducted. The valuer should take into account any claims he or she thinks the company has for misappropriation or misapplication of the company's assets against those who are to buy the shares.[522]

It is not unreasonable of a petitioner to refuse an offer to be bought out if the petitioner **8.238** wishes to have the opportunity of bidding for the company's business on winding up.[523] Similarly, on an unfair prejudice petition, it is not unreasonable for the petitioner to refuse an offer to be bought out if the petitioner wishes to buy out the other members.[524]

In *Re a Company (No 001363 of 1988)*[525] it was not unreasonable of the petitioner to refuse **8.239** an offer to buy the one share registered in his name because one of the claims of his petition was that he was entitled to 3,250 shares.

Should the petitioner invite other members to buy shares?

In the case of a private company, inviting other members of the company to purchase **8.240** the petitioner's shares is not an alternative remedy, even if the articles set out a procedure for valuing shares being offered by one member to others.[526] In *Re Rongo-ma-tane Farms Ltd*[527] it was argued that the petitioners could have invited the other members to buy their shares. Wylie J said that even if this was a remedy for the petitioners, they were not acting

[516] *Re a Company (No 00330 of 1991)* [1991] BCLC 597.
[517] *Re a Company (No 004377 of 1986)* [1987] 1 WLR 102.
[518] *Re a Company (No 006834 of 1988)* [1989] BCLC 365, in which allegations of such impropriety were rejected as they were in *Re a Company (No 003843 of 1986)* [1987] BCLC 562.
[519] *Virdi v Abbey Leisure Ltd* [1990] BCLC 342.
[520] *Virdi v Abbey Leisure Ltd* [1990] BCLC 342; *Re a Company (No 00330 of 1991)* [1991] BCLC 597.
[521] *Re Boswell and Co (Steels) Ltd* (1988) 5 BCC 145.
[522] *Re a Company (No 002567 of 1982)* [1983] 1 WLR 927 at p 934; *Re a Company (No 003843 of 1986)* [1987] BCLC 562 at p 571.
[523] *Re Copeland and Craddock Ltd* [1997] BCC 294.
[524] *Amin v Amin* [2009] EWHC 3356 (Ch), LTL 5/1/2010, at [422].
[525] [1989] BCLC 579.
[526] *Virdi v Abbey Leisure Ltd* [1990] BCLC 342; per Harman J in *Re a Company (No 00330 of 1991)* [1991] BCLC 597 at p 602. This calls into question the correctness of the decisions to strike out winding-up petitions in *Re a Company (No 004377 of 1986)* [1987] 1 WLR 102 and *Re Trocadero Ltd* [1988] 2 HKLR 443. See also *Re Belfield Furnishings Ltd* [2006] EWHC 183 (Ch), [2006] 2 BCLC 705.
[527] (1987) 3 NZCLC 100,145.

unreasonably in seeking a winding up instead, because the articles fixed an artificially low price for the transfer of shares between members.

Other alternative remedies

8.241 In *Re Gerard Nouvelle Cuisine Ltd*[528] it was found that although the petitioners could deal with some of their complaints by using their majority voting power to adopt resolutions favourable to themselves, acting in that way would be considered oppression of the minority shareholder and entitle him to petition for the company to be wound up, so the petitioners were not unreasonable in seeking a winding up themselves.

8.242 In Canada, where there is no provision equivalent to IA 1986, s 125(2), it has been held that an order to wind up a company will not be made on the just and equitable ground merely on an allegation that the company is trading illegally or outside its objects or is contravening company law, because all such transgressions can be remedied in other ways, even though some of those remedies can be invoked only by public officials and not by the petitioner.[529] But the fact that directors of a company have allowed it to break the law may show that it is just and equitable to wind up the company because of the directors' lack of probity.[530] See also *Bermuda Cablevision Ltd v Colica Trust Co Ltd*,[531] in which it was held that the principle that the criminal law should not be enforced by civil proceedings does not apply to petitions for relief in respect of prejudicial conduct of companies' affairs.

8.243 In *Shillingford v The Penn Syndicate*,[532] where there was no provision equivalent to s 125(2), the petitioners claimed a proposed transaction would be outside the objects of the company, but the court said that this should be the subject of proceedings for an injunction not winding up.

8.244 For voluntary winding up as an alternative to compulsory liquidation, see 10.122–10.129.

Relitigation of member's complaints

8.245 In two cases, *McCain v McCain Foods Group Inc*[533] and *Roberts v Walter Developments Pty Ltd*,[534] a member of a company brought proceedings for relief in respect of unfairly prejudicial conduct of the company's affairs and subsequently applied for an order winding up the company.

8.246 In *McCain v McCain Foods Group Inc*[535] it was held that a claim for relief in respect of prejudicial conduct of a company's affairs and a claim that it is just and equitable that the company should be wound up are different causes of action so that rejection of the first claim does not create a cause-of-action estoppel to bar the second claim. However, in this case the winding-up application depended on proving that the company was a quasi-partnership, but it had been held in the unfair prejudice proceedings that the

[528] (1981) 1 BCR 311.
[529] *La Société des Arts du Canada v Prévost* (1910) 20 Que KB 227; *Shacket v Universal Factors Corporation* [1967] Que SC 131.
[530] As in *Re Maritime Asphalt Products Ltd* (1965) 52 DLR (2d) 8.
[531] [1998] AC 198.
[532] (1958) 1 WIR 58.
[533] (1995) 157 NBR (2d) 321.
[534] (1995) 16 ACSR 544.
[535] (1995) 157 NBR (2d) 321.

company was not a quasi-partnership. Issue estoppel prevented the point being argued again in the winding-up application, which therefore could not succeed and was dismissed. In *Roberts v Walter Developments Pty Ltd*[536] the first claim for relief in respect of unfairly prejudicial conduct had resulted in an order altering the company's articles of association and requiring one shareholder to pay compensation to the claimant. Two years later the same claimant claimed that it was just and equitable that the company be wound up and it was held that he was not restricted to relying on events since the previous judgment: there had been an escalating conflict between the claimant and other shareholders and the quality of the events since the previous judgment depended to some extent on events before it.

Literature

Say Hak Goo, 'The Companies Act 1985, s 459 and the Insolvency Act 1986, s 122(1)(g)' (1994) 15 Co Law 184. **8.247**

Petitioner's Contribution to the Situation

The courts have generally taken the view that it is not just and equitable to wind up a company on a contributory's petition if the petitioner is to blame for the situation which is claimed to be unjust and inequitable.[537] In *Re F Hall and Sons Ltd*[538] the New Zealand Court of Appeal ruled that 'the petitioner is not entitled to a winding-up order based upon an impasse which it has itself created'.[539] **8.248**

In the case of a breakdown of business relationship[540] the rule of partnership law, embodied in the Partnership Act 1890, s 35(d), and in the passage from *Lindley on the Law of Partnership* relied on in *Re Yenidje Tobacco Co Ltd*,[541] is that a partner is not allowed to obtain a dissolution on the ground that it is impossible to work with fellow partners where that impossibility has been created by the partner claiming the dissolution. This rule is applied to winding up companies. See, for example, *Guerinoni v Argyle Concrete and Quarry Supplies Pty Ltd*,[542] in which winding up was applied for on the ground that the applicant shareholder-director, Michael, could not work with his fellow shareholder-director, and brother, Steven. It was found that Michael simply refused to work with Steven, whom he had loathed since childhood, and that Steven had attempted to find ways of resolving the problem. Winding up was refused. In *Re John While Springs (S) Pte Ltd*[543] the petitioners were minority shareholders in two related companies. They had diverted business from those companies to one that they had set up themselves. They then petitioned for the companies to be wound up on the ground **8.249**

---

[536] (1995) 16 ACSR 544.

[537] *Re Wilkinson (No 2)* [1924] SASR 156.

[538] [1939] NZLR 408.

[539] At p 423. See also *Re James Lumbers Co Ltd* [1926] 1 DLR 173 at pp 186–7; *Re Toronto Finance Corp* [1930] 3 DLR 882 at p 885; *Re Sovereign Oil Co Ltd* [1934] 3 WWR 317; *Ng Eng Hiam v Ng Kee Wei* (1964) 31 MLJ 238; *Bleau v Le Perruquier Français Inc* (1967) 10 CBR NS 296; *Western Quebec Investment Ltd v J G Bisson Construction and Engineering Ltd* [1972] Que SC 331; *Re Kiwitea Sawmilling Co Ltd* (1978) 1 BCR 193; *Dato' Ibrahim bin Hj Ismail v Onstream Marine Sdn Bhd* [1998] 4 MLJ 86; *Eng Man Hin v King's Confectionery Sdn Bhd* [2006] 4 MLJ 421.

[540] See 8.382–8.397.

[541] [1916] 2 Ch 426. See 8.384.

[542] (1999) 34 ACSR 469.

[543] [2001] 2 SLR 248.

that they could not work with the majority shareholder, who had successfully sued them. It was held that they could not be allowed to wind up the companies that they had tried to destroy. In *Harrison v Tennant*[544] Romilly MR said, at pp 493–4:

> no party is entitled to act improperly, and then to say the conduct of the partners, and their feelings towards each other, are such that the partnership can no longer be continued, and certainly this court would not allow any person so to act, and thus to take advantage of his own wrong.

However, the rule did not apply in the case before his Lordship because the situation complained of had been caused by the conduct of both partners and this exception (which was also mentioned by Lord Cross of Chelsea in *Ebrahimi v Westbourne Galleries Ltd*[545]) is applicable in the winding up of companies.[546] Commenting on it in *Re Lundie Brothers Ltd*,[547] Plowman J said that he understood the rule to be that if a partner asks the court to dissolve a partnership on the ground that it is impossible for the partners to place that confidence in each other which each has a right to expect, it must be shown that this state of affairs 'has not been caused exclusively by the person seeking to take advantage of it'. In *Re R A Noble and Sons (Clothing) Ltd*[548] the petitioner's conduct, though 'not above reproach',[549] was not a bar to a winding-up order, because the other member's conduct 'was the substantial cause of the destruction of the mutual confidence involved in the personal relationship' between them.[550]

8.250 Two other reasons have been advanced for dismissing this kind of petition:

(a) A petitioner who cannot show that those in control of the company are to blame is unable to show a justifiable lack of confidence in the conduct and management of the company's affairs, which, in *Loch v John Blackwood Ltd*,[551] Lord Shaw of Dunfermline, at p 788, saw as being 'at the foundation of applications for winding up, on the "just and equitable" rule'.[552]

(b) The equitable maxim, He who comes to equity must come with clean hands.[553] In *Re Martello and Sons Ltd*[554] the petition was on the basis of the lack of probity of the controlling director who had diverted the company's revenues into his own pocket. It was alleged that the petitioner participated in this wrongdoing and therefore that a winding-up order should not be made, but the Ontario Court of Appeal found that the allegation against the petitioner was not proved, and made a winding-up order.

---

[544] (1856) 21 Beav 482.
[545] [1973] AC 360 at pp 383–4.
[546] *Re Balfour Fashions Ltd* [1957] OWN 91; *DiRisio v DeLorenzo* (1981) 38 CBR NS 154, in which Boland J said, at p 162, 'one gets the distinct impression that what has happened here is merely that three rogues have fallen out of bed with one another'; *Morgan v 45 Flers Avenue Pty Ltd* (1986) 10 ACLR 692 at p 708 per Young J; *Khamo v XL Cleaning Services Pty Ltd* [2004] NSWSC 1134, 51 ACSR 397.
[547] [1965] 1 WLR 1051 at p 1056.
[548] [1983] BCLC 273.
[549] At p 291.
[550] At p 291.
[551] [1924] AC 783.
[552] See, for example, *Re Florentine Co Ltd* (1926) 31 OWN 70.
[553] *Re George Coles Ltd* (1949) 30 CBR 50 at p 57.
[554] [1945] 3 DLR 626.

In *Ebrahimi v Westbourne Galleries Ltd*[555] Lord Cross of Chelsea said, at p 387:   **8.251**

> A petitioner who relies on the 'just and equitable' clause must come to court with clean hands, and if the breakdown in confidence between him and the other parties to the dispute appears to have been due to his misconduct he cannot insist on the company being wound up if they wish it to continue.

In *Vujnovich v Vujnovich*[556] Lord Oliver of Aylmerton said, at p 231:

> It is quite clear that Lord Cross was considering the position in which the petitioner's misconduct (and thus the relative uncleanliness of his hands) was causative of the breakdown in confidence on which the petition was based.

If the petitioner caused the breakdown of relationship, winding up will be refused.[557]   **8.252**
Misconduct by the petitioner which did not cause the breakdown on which the petition is based does not necessarily prevent the court making a winding-up order.[558] The fact that the petitioner has refused to agree to a reconciliation is not a reason for refusing a winding-up order if continuing distrust is reasonable.[559] If, however, it is unreasonable of the petitioner not to agree to fellow members' suggestions of ways to work together, winding up will be refused.[560] Typically a finding of unreasonable refusal to be reconciled will be coupled with a finding that the petitioner contributed to the breakdown.

In *Re Trocadero Ltd*[561] it was held that a petition was bound to fail, and so was struck out,   **8.253**
because the petitioner had caused the situation he complained of, and he was described as not coming to the court with clean hands. In *Cairney v Golden Key Holdings Ltd* (*No 2*)[562] a petition for relief in respect of oppressive conduct of the company's affairs was dismissed because the petitioner had caused the conduct complained of.

In *Morgan v 45 Flers Avenue Pty Ltd*[563] Young J said, at p 708, that rather than treat a   **8.254**
petitioner's unclean hands as a defence to a winding-up petition (so that it is necessary to consider the petitioner's conduct after it has been decided to make a winding-up order) it would probably be better to say that the petitioner's conduct was one of the factors to be taken into consideration in deciding whether it is just and equitable to wind up a company.

Whether or not the business relationship in a company has broken down irretrievably is a   **8.255**
question of fact. In *Re Modern Retreading Co Ltd*[564] Windham CJ said, at p 60:

> The material point is the very existence of the quarrel, which has made it impossible for the company to be run in the manner in which it was designed to be run, or for the parties' disputes to be resolved in any other way than by a winding up.

---

[555] [1973] AC 360.
[556] [1990] BCLC 227.
[557] *Re Quiet Moments Ltd* [2013] EWHC 3806 (Ch), LTL 18/12/2013, at [241]–[243].
[558] *Yeung Bun v Brio Technology International Ltd* [2000] 2 HKLRD 218.
[559] *Belman v Belman* (1995) 26 OR (3d) 56.
[560] *Guerinoni v Argyle Concrete and Quarry Supplies Pty Ltd* (1999) 34 ACSR 469; *Belgiorno-Zegna v Exben Pty Ltd* (2000) 35 ACSR 305.
[561] [1988] 2 HKLR 443.
[562] (1988) 40 BLR 289.
[563] (1986) 10 ACLR 692.
[564] [1962] EA 57.

8.256 In some cases courts have regarded the objective fact of breakdown of business relation-ship as sufficient to justify winding up and have refused to go into allegations about the petitioner's conduct.[565] In *Re Humberbank Investment and Development Ltd*[566] the court emphasized that the company had ceased to be a prosperous going concern. In *Re Vehicle Buildings and Insulations Ltd*[567] the court emphasized that it could not, on the evidence before it, determine who was to blame for the undoubted breakdown of the business rela-tionship in the company. In *Suleiman v Saffuri*[568] the court thought it would be meaning-less to attempt to sort out who was originally at fault. *Re Central Realty Co (Pte) Ltd*[569] is another case in which it was not possible to conclude from the evidence who was responsible for the breakdown.

8.257 In *Re Phoneer Ltd*[570] winding up on the ground of deadlock was ordered, despite acknow-ledgment of the petitioner's responsibility for the deadlock, because the company was no longer a going concern and because the only other shareholder also wanted a winding up (though he petitioned, unsuccessfully, for other relief in respect of unfairly prejudicial conduct of the company's affairs). *Malos v Malos*[571] and *Pham Thai Duc v PTS Australian Distributor Pty Ltd*[572] are similar cases.

Fraudulent Promotion

8.258 It is just and equitable to wind up a company on a contributory's petition if the company was promoted fraudulently, for example, for the purpose of taking money from subscribers for shares without any intention of carrying on any substantial business.[573] Such companies are usually described as 'bubbles'[574] or 'shams'. The entire scheme of the company must be fraudulent in order to justify compulsory liquidation: the fact that the company has been defrauded is not sufficient because normally action should be taken in the name of the com-pany against persons such as promoters who have defrauded it.[575] The appropriate remedy for a person who has been misled into subscribing for shares is rescission of the allotment of the shares.[576]

8.259 In *Re Neath Harbour Smelting and Rolling Works Ltd*[577] the Court of Appeal discounted the views of contributories who wanted a bubble company to continue.

---

[565] See, for example, *Entreprises M Canada Abitibi Inc v Maurice Canada Construction Ltée* (1979) 34 CBR NS 68; *Re Rongo-ma-tane Farms Ltd* (1987) 3 NZCLC 100,145.
[566] (1972) 17 CBR NS 220.
[567] [1986] ILRM 239.
[568] (2004) 48 BLR (3d) 286.
[569] [1999] 1 SLR 559.
[570] [2002] 2 BCLC 241.
[571] [2003] NSWSC 118, 44 ACSR 511.
[572] [2005] NSWSC 98.
[573] *Re London and County Coal Co* (1866) LR 3 Eq 355; *Re Neath Harbour Smelting and Rolling Works Ltd* (1886) 2 TLR 336; *Re Thomas Edward Brinsmead and Sons* [1897] 1 Ch 406.
[574] See also *Mahony v East Holyford Mining Co Ltd* (1875) LR 7 HL 869 per Lord Cairns LC at p 886 and Lord Chelmsford at p 889.
[575] *Foss v Harbottle* (1843) 2 Hare 461; *Re Anglo-Greek Steam Co* (1866) LR 2 Eq 1; *Re Haven Gold Mining Co* (1882) 20 ChD 151; *Re Nylstroom Co Ltd* (1889) 60 LT 477; *Re Othery Construction Ltd* [1966] 1 WLR 69.
[576] *Re Bwlch y Plym Co Ltd* (1867) 17 LT 235.
[577] (1886) 2 TLR 336.

Failure of Substratum

Principle

It is just and equitable for the court to order the winding up of a company if 'that which the **8.260**
company was formed to do can no longer be done'[578] or if the company has ceased to carry
on its business and the carrying on of the business has become, in a practical sense, impossible.[579] It is usually said in such a case that the company's 'substratum' has gone, using
terminology apparently coined by Lord Cairns LJ in *Re Suburban Hotel Co*.[580] In *Baird v
Lees*[581] Lord President Clyde, at p 90, described this class of case as one 'in which circumstances occur which have the effect of knocking the bottom out of the company's business'.
It is just and equitable to wind up a company whose substratum has gone if members of a
company take shares in it and contribute capital to it on the basis that it will use its money to
pursue particular objects.[582] However, when considering whether a company's substratum
has failed, the court is not concerned with when or how the petitioner became a member of
the company, provided the petitioner meets the conditions of IA 1986, s 124(2).[583]

At first, failed substratum cases were dealt with on the basis that they were *ejusdem generis* **8.261**
with suspension of business for a year or failure to commence business within a year of
incorporation.[584] However, it is now established that the *ejusdem generis* rule does not apply
to IA 1986, s 122(1)(g).[585]

Types of Case

The court may conclude that a company's substratum has gone if: **8.262**

(a) There is no reasonable hope of achieving the object of trading at a profit.[586] In *Re Suburban
Hotel Co*[587] Lord Cairns LJ thought that the court could not make a winding-up order
against a solvent company which had no prospect of making a profit and had not suspended business, because the company's circumstances would not be *ejusdem generis*
with the other circumstances in which the court may order winding up.[588] However, it
is now established that the *ejusdem generis* rule does not apply to IA 1986, s 122(1)(g).[589]

---

[578] Per Kekewich J in *Re Bristol Joint Stock Bank* (1890) 44 ChD 703 at p 712.
[579] *Re Diamond Fuel Co* (1879) 13 ChD 400 per James LJ at p 408.
[580] (1867) LR 2 Ch App 737 at p 750.
[581] 1924 SC 83.
[582] Until 30 September 2009, a registered company's objects had to be stated in its memorandum
(Companies Act 1985, s 2(1)(c)). As from 1 October 2009, provisions of the memorandum of an existing
company are treated as provisions of its articles (Companies Act 2006, s 28) and restrictions on objects are
optional (s 31).
[583] *Galbraith v Merito Shipping Co Ltd* 1947 SC 446; cf *Re Dominion Steel Corp Ltd* [1927] 4 DLR 337,
in which the successful petitioner had acquired one share in the company for the purpose of petitioning.
[584] *Re New Gas Co* (1877) 36 LT 364 per Bacon V-C at p 366; *Re Diamond Fuel Co* (1879) 13 ChD 400
per Baggallay LJ at pp 408–10.
[585] See 8.147–8.149.
[586] *Re Factage Parisien Ltd* (1864) 34 LJ Ch 140 (MR), 11 LT 556 (LC); *Re Hamilton Ideal Manufacturing
Co Ltd* (1915) 23 DLR 640; *Davis and Co Ltd v Brunswick (Australia) Ltd* [1936] 1 All ER 299, in which this
was not proved; *Ng Sing King v PSA International Pte Ltd (No 2)* [2005] SGHC 5, [2005] 2 SLR 56.
[587] (1867) LR 2 Ch App 737.
[588] Followed in *Re Joint Stock Coal Co* (1869) LR 8 Eq 146.
[589] See 8.147–8.149.

(b) The company's business is no longer viable, for example:

   (i) where its business cannot be pursued without further capital which the members will not contribute;[590]

   (ii) where a mutual fund's asset value has declined so far that it cannot continue to function as a mutual fund;[591]

   (iii) where a non-profit-making company has no realistic prospect of being able to fund the services it was formed to provide.[592]

But if a company can pursue another business, the mere fact that its assets have declined in value and are at present unsaleable because of market conditions does not mean that its substratum has gone.[593]

(c) The company was formed to pursue a specific opportunity which has proved to be worthless.[594] For cases in which the petition was dismissed because the petitioner did not succeed in proving that the opportunity which the company was formed to pursue was worthless see *Re Patent Artificial Stone Co Ltd*;[595] *Re Electric Arms and Ammunition Syndicate Ltd*[596] and *Re Kronand Metal Co.*[597] For cases in which the petition was dismissed because the court was not satisfied that pursuing the opportunity which had proved to be worthless was the company's sole purpose see *Re Patent Bread Machinery Co Ltd*;[598] *Re New Gas Co*[599] and *Re M'Donald Gold Mines Ltd.*[600] In *Re Suburban Hotel Co*[601] the company had so far pursued only one opportunity which had not been successful but the court was not satisfied either that it was entirely worthless or that pursuing that opportunity was the company's only purpose and refused to make a winding-up order. In *Re Columbia Gypsum Co*[602] winding up was refused because there was merely a disagreement between different factions in the company about the value of its mining claims and this disagreement was not a matter for the court to adjudicate on.

---

[590] *Re Diamond Fuel Co* (1879) 13 ChD 400; *Re Bristol Joint Stock Bank* (1890) 44 ChD 703; *Re Fromm's Extract Co Ltd* (1901) 17 TLR 302; *Pirie v Stewart* (1904) 6 F 847; *Re Dominion Steel Corp Ltd* [1927] 4 DLR 337.

[591] *Re Belmont Asset Based Lending Ltd* 2010 (1) CILR 83; *Re Wyser-Pratte Eurovalue Fund Ltd* 2010 (2) CILR 194, disagreeing with *Citco Global Custody NV v Y2K Finance Inc* (BVIHCV 2009/0020A). In all the cases, the directors were conducting a 'soft wind down', as permitted by the companies' articles of association. In *Citco Global Custody NV v Y2K Finance Inc* the court held that it could not interfere with a process which was in accordance with the articles, but in *Re Wyser-Pratte Eurovalue Fund Ltd* it was said that the shareholders could not have anticipated that this would happen in the ordinary course of business (at [23]).

[592] *Re Bankstown Students Association Inc* [2005] NSWSC 700; *Macquarie University v Macquarie University Students' Council Inc* [2007] NSWSC 510; *Macquarie University v Macquarie University Union Ltd (No 2)* [2007] FCA 844.

[593] *Re Toronto Finance Corp* [1930] 3 DLR 882, in which the directors wanted to pursue a new line of business within the company's objects and it was not proved that the company was unable to pay its debts.

[594] *Re Red Rock Gold Mining Co Ltd* (1889) 61 LT 785; *Re Coolgardie Consolidated Gold Mines Ltd* (1897) 76 LT 269.

[595] (1864) 34 LJ Ch 330.

[596] (1891) 35 SJ 818.

[597] [1899] WN 14.

[598] (1866) 14 LT 582.

[599] (1877) 36 LT 364, affirmed 5 ChD 703.

[600] (1898) 14 TLR 204.

[601] (1867) LR 2 Ch App 737.

[602] (1958) 17 DLR (2d) 280.

(d) The company was formed to pursue a specific opportunity not in fact available to the company.[603] In *Re International Cable Co*[604] the court was not satisfied on the evidence then before it that the opportunity had become unavailable to the company and adjourned the petition for three months. However, after the three-month adjournment, a winding-up order was made.[605] In *Marsden v Tower Taxi Technology LLP*[606] the company had been formed to acquire the right to use certain software and had entered into a contract for that purpose with two other parties, one of which had failed to perform its part of the contract and the other had cancelled the contract. The petitioners argued that the company had been formed to exploit the particular contract which had failed, but it was held that the substratum was acquisition of the software rights and, as negotiations were still continuing to achieve that acquisition, the substratum had not failed.

(e) The company was formed to pursue a specific opportunity which has never materialized.[607]

(f) The company was formed to carry on a specific business which it then sold.[608]

(g) The company was formed to pursue a specific business which has come to an end.[609]

(h) The regulatory authority for the business operated by the company has withdrawn its authorization and it is unlikely that the company can regain authorization.[610]

Mere withdrawal from business does not count as failure of substratum justifying winding **8.263** up under the just and equitable clause.[611] In *Re Kitson and Co Ltd*[612] Lord Greene MR said, at p 438, that whether or not the board of directors intend to re-enter a business from which they have withdrawn is irrelevant to the question of whether the company's substratum has failed. There is a failure of a company's substratum if it has abandoned its business

---

[603] *Re Haven Gold Mining Co* (1882) 20 ChD 151, in which the company was formed to work a mine but could not obtain possession of it; *Re Palace Restaurants Ltd* (1909) 127 LT Jo 430, in which the company was formed to take over the business of another company but the business was sold elsewhere; *Re Pacific Fisheries Ltd* (1909) 26 WN (NSW) 127, in which the company was formed to work a particular patent method of food processing which in fact was never available for purchase by the company; *Re Blériot Manufacturing Aircraft Co Ltd* (1916) 32 TLR 253, in which the company was formed to acquire a business which the owner refused to sell to it; *Re Baku Consolidated Oilfields Ltd* [1944] 1 All ER 24, in which the company was formed to purchase the undertakings of four companies whose undertakings were expropriated without compensation shortly after the company was formed—compensation was finally agreed in 1990, see *Re Baku Consolidated Oilfields Ltd* [1994] 1 BCLC 173.

[604] (1890) 2 Meg 183.

[605] (1892) 8 TLR 307 at p 308.

[606] [2005] EWCA Civ 1503, LTL 14/10/2005.

[607] *Re German Date Coffee Co* (1882) 20 ChD 169, in which the company was formed to work a patent which was not granted; *Re The Varieties Ltd* [1893] 2 Ch 235, in which the company was formed to build a theatre on a site that was too small.

[608] *Re Edison Telephone Co of London* (1881) 25 SJ 240; *Re Florida Mining Co Ltd* (1902) 9 BCR 108; *Re Stratton's Independence Ltd* (1916) 33 TLR 98; *Re Dominion Trust Co Ltd* (1918) 26 BCR 302 affirmed sub nom *MacPherson v Boyce* (1919) 59 SCR 691. Compare *Re Norwegian Titanic Iron Co Ltd* (1865) 35 Beav 223; *Re Kitson and Co Ltd* [1946] 1 All ER 435; *Re Columbia Gypsum Co* (1958) 17 DLR (2d) 280 and *Re Community Press Pty Ltd* (1980) 4 ACLR 782, in which winding up was not ordered because it was found that the company was not formed to pursue only the specific business that was sold.

[609] *Re Amalgamated Syndicate* [1897] 2 Ch 600, in which the company was formed to provide facilities for celebrations during Queen Victoria's jubilee in 1897.

[610] *Canada (Attorney General) v Security Home Mortgage Corporation* (1996) 45 Alta LR (3d) 98, which was a public interest petition.

[611] *Galbraith v Merito Shipping Co Ltd* 1947 SC 446, in which the company had withdrawn from its business for many years but had adequate resources to re-enter the business if a suitable opportunity should arise.

[612] [1946] 1 All ER 435.

permanently with the intention of winding up.[613] Also it has been held to be just and equitable to wind up a company which has withdrawn from the business it was formed to pursue if those in control of the company are using it for purposes beyond those for which it was incorporated.[614]

8.264   It may not be just and equitable to wind up a parent company because of a subsidiary's loss of substratum, if it is found that the principal purpose of the parent company is to hold shares in the subsidiary which still have a value.[615]

Opposition of other Members

8.265   In cases of types (d), (e), (f) and (g) in 8.262, where it is logically impossible for the company to continue operating within its objects, winding up will usually be ordered despite the fact that more contributories oppose compulsory liquidation than support it.[616]

8.266   Winding-up proceedings 'cannot be used, and ought not to be used, as a means of evoking a judicial decision as to the probable success or non-success of a company as a commercial speculation'[617] so in cases of type (a) the court will leave it to the members to decide whether, as a matter of business, the company should continue or not.[618] A resolution against compulsory liquidation is not, however, a decision that the company should continue.[619]

8.267   The court may order a compulsory winding up in a case of type (a) where the majority are preventing the company winding up for a purpose of their own in fraud of the minority, for example, because they earn salaries which are paid out of calls on the minority's shares.[620] In *Davis and Co Ltd v Brunswick (Australia) Ltd,*[621] the company sought to be wound up had been formed by the petitioner, D Davis and Co Ltd, and an American company, Brunswick Balke Collender Co (the 'Brunswick Company'). The petitioner held all the preference shares in the company and 10,000 ordinary shares, giving a total of 16,000 votes. The Brunswick Company held 20,000 ordinary shares, giving it 20,000 votes, and had guaranteed to pay to the petitioner the nominal value of its preference shares if the company should go into liquidation during the first two years of its existence. Because of the Great Depression, the company traded at a loss from its inception and the petition for compulsory liquidation was presented 14 months after the company started. The petitioner claimed that the Brunswick Company was resisting voluntary liquidation in order to avoid being liable on its guarantee. The Privy Council found that there was no fraud on the minority: both

---

[613] *Thomas v Mackay Investments Pty Ltd* (1996) 22 ACSR 294.

[614] *Re Crown Bank* (1890) 44 ChD 634; *Re Tivoli Freeholds Ltd* [1972] VR 445; *Marzitelli v Verona Construction Ltd* (1979) 33 CBR NS 180; see also *Re Johnson Corporation Ltd* (1980) 5 ACLR 227.

[615] *Coutu v San Jose Mines Ltd* 2005 BCSC 453, 3 BLR (4th) 22; see also *Re Eastern Telegraph Co Ltd* [1947] 2 All ER 104 discussed at 8.100.

[616] *Re Haven Gold Mining Co* (1882) 20 ChD 151; *Re Palace Restaurants Ltd* (1909) 127 LT Jo 430; *Re Baku Consolidated Oilfields Ltd* [1944] 1 All ER 24.

[617] Per Lord Cairns LJ in *Re Suburban Hotel Co* (1867) LR 2 Ch App 737 at p 750.

[618] *Re Factage Parisien Ltd* (1864) 34 LJ Ch 140 (MR), 11 LT 556 (LC); *Re Patent Artificial Stone Co Ltd* (1864) 34 LJ Ch 330; *Re Patent Bread Machinery Co Ltd* (1866) 14 LT 582; *Re Suburban Hotel Co*; *Re New Zealand Quartz Crushing Co* [1873] WN 174; *Re Langham Skating Rink Co* (1877) 5 ChD 669; *Re Buzolich Patent Damp-Resisting and Anti-Fouling Paint Co Ltd* (1884) 10 VLR (E) 276; *Re Canada Nat'l Fire Ins Co* [1930] 4 DLR 572, affirmed [1931] 1 DLR 751.

[619] *Re General Phosphate Corporation Ltd* (1893) 37 SJ 683.

[620] Per Romilly MR in *Re Factage Parisien Ltd* (1864) 34 LJ Ch 140 at p 141.

[621] [1936] 1 All ER 299.

the petitioner in seeking winding up and the Brunswick Company in resisting it were motivated by the existence of the guarantee and 'These motives were natural and in the circumstances not improper'.[622] Accordingly the only question in the case was whether there was any reasonable hope of the company trading at a profit: the guarantee of the preference shares should be ignored except insofar as it might have biased the evidence on either side. The Privy Council found that there was a reasonable hope of trading at a profit and so held, affirming the decision of the Full Court of the New South Wales Supreme Court, that a winding-up order should not be made.

As voluntary liquidation is the natural response to failure of substratum, it has been held in Scotland that a petition for compulsory liquidation for failure of substratum should not be presented before the members have considered whether to wind up voluntarily.[623]   **8.268**

What is the Company's Substratum?

In determining whether what can no longer be done is that which the company was formed to do, the court must consider the provision of its articles which restricts its objects (if there is such a provision). When this provision is considered for the purpose of deciding whether it is just and equitable to wind up a company (a question of equity between the company and its shareholders) the court's approach will not be the same as the approach that is appropriate for considering whether the company is bound by a particular contract with a third party, which is a question of law.[624] Accordingly the fact that a company's capacity is no longer limited by its objects[625] is not relevant to the question whether its substratum has gone.[626] To determine whether a company's substratum has gone the court may extract from a statement of objects what it considers to be the company's 'main object' (or 'paramount object' or 'dominant object').[627] The court may apply what has become known as the 'main objects rule'. This was described by Salmon J in *Anglo-Overseas Agencies Ltd v Green*[628] as follows: **8.269**

> where a memorandum of association expresses the objects of the company in a series of paragraphs, and one paragraph, or the first two or three paragraphs, appear to embody the 'main object' of the company, all the other paragraphs are treated as merely ancillary to this 'main object', and as limited or controlled thereby.

The court recognizes that there is a difference between a company formed to deal with some specific subject matter and one formed with wider and more comprehensive objects.[629] Identification of the main object of a company has also been considered in cases on   **8.270**

---

[622] At p 308.

[623] *Cox v 'Gosford' Ship Co* (1894) 21 R 334; *Scobie v Atlas Steel Works Ltd* (1906) 8 F 1052.

[624] *Cotman v Brougham* [1918] AC 514 per Lord Parker of Waddington at p 520; *H A Stephenson and Son Ltd v Gillanders, Arbuthnot and Co* (1931) 45 CLR 476 per Dixon J at p 487; *Re Tivoli Freeholds Ltd* [1972] VR 445 at pp 470–1.

[625] Companies Act 2006, s 39(1).

[626] *Re Tivoli Freeholds Ltd* at p 471.

[627] *Re German Date Coffee Co* (1882) 20 ChD 169; *Re Coolgardie Consolidated Gold Mines Ltd* (1897) 76 LT 269; *Re Amalgamated Syndicate* [1897] 2 Ch 600.

[628] [1961] 1 QB 1 at p 8.

[629] Per Lord Greene MR in *Re Kitson and Co Ltd* [1946] 1 All ER 435 at p 438.

restraining an act by a company alleged to be outside its objects, where it may be sufficient to show that the act is outside the company's main object.[630]

8.271 To decide what it is that the company was formed to do, the court may take into account the company's articles,[631] name[632] and prospectus,[633] though the prospectus may be taken into account only to confirm the court's view of the company's constitution.[634]

8.272 In *H A Stephenson and Son Ltd v Gillanders, Arbuthnot and Co*[635] Dixon J, at p 487, said, obiter, that where the question is whether it is just and equitable to wind up a company, 'general intention and common understanding among the members of the company may be important'.

8.273 In the case of a quasi-partnership company the court may go beyond the company's constitution to determine the members' general intention and common understanding.[636]

8.274 In *Re Tivoli Freeholds Ltd*,[637] Menhennitt J expressed the view, at p 469, that it was not only in the case of quasi-partnership companies that the court could go beyond the constitution, but this statement was obiter, and his Honour admitted, at p 472, 'that the material being looked at must establish something general or common to all members'. It may be that it is only in a quasi-partnership company that one would find intentions and understandings common to all members. The opinions of the petitioner which are not shared by other members are not relevant.[638] In *Egyptian Salt and Soda Co Ltd v Port Said Salt Association Ltd*[639] the Privy Council refused to accept that the express words of the appellant company's objects clause ought to be modified by the intention of the company's promoters, because the shareholders did not have access to this additional source of information. The question was regarded as still open by Needham J in *Re Johnson Corporation Ltd*.[640]

Miscellaneous Cases

8.275 In *Thomas v Mackay Investments Pty Ltd*[641] it was said that there was a failure of corporate substratum where the companies had sold all assets of any value and all members were agreed that there should be a winding up, subject to resolution of a dispute between them.

---

[630] *Stephens v Mysore Reefs (Kangundy) Mining Co Ltd* [1902] 1 Ch 745; *Pedlar v Road Block Gold Mines of India Ltd* [1905] 2 Ch 427; *Butler v Northern Territories Mines of Australia Ltd* (1906) 96 LT 41.

[631] *Re Capital Fire Insurance Association* (1882) 21 ChD 209.

[632] *Re Crown Bank* (1890) 44 ChD 634; *Re Blériot Manufacturing Aircraft Co Ltd* (1916) 32 TLR 253; *Cotman v Brougham* [1918] AC 514 per Lord Parker of Waddington at p 521.

[633] *Re Crown Bank*; *Re International Cable Co* (1890) 2 Meg 183; *Re Blériot Manufacturing Aircraft Co Ltd*.

[634] Per Jessel MR in *Re German Date Coffee Co* (1882) 20 ChD 169 at pp 184–5; *Re Electric Arms and Ammunition Syndicate Ltd* (1891) 35 SJ 818; *Re Pacific Fisheries Ltd* (1909) 26 WN (NSW) 127.

[635] (1931) 45 CLR 476.

[636] *Virdi v Abbey Leisure Ltd* [1990] BCLC 342; *Bernhardt v Beau Rivage Pty Ltd* (1989) 15 ACLR 160.

[637] [1972] VR 445.

[638] *International Hospitality Concepts Pty Ltd v National Marketing Concepts Inc (No 2)* (1994) 13 ACSR 368.

[639] [1931] AC 677.

[640] (1980) 5 ACLR 227 at p 235. For examples of cases in which what failed was found not to be the whole substratum, see *Re Suburban Hotel Co* (1867) LR 2 Ch App 737; *Re M'Donald Gold Mines Ltd* (1898) 14 TLR 204; *Re Wickham and Bullock Island Coal Co Ltd* (1905) 5 SR (NSW) 365; *Re Taldua Rubber Co Ltd* [1946] 2 All ER 763; *Re Kitson and Co Ltd* [1946] 1 All ER 435.

[641] (1996) 22 ACSR 294.

In *Alldrew Holdings Ltd v Nibro Holdings Ltd*[642] a company whose objects were the manu- **8.276**
facture, purchase and sale of starch in Canada abandoned manufacturing in Canada and
turned to importing and marketing starch made elsewhere. The Ontario Court of Appeal,
reversing the judge at first instance, held that this did not justify winding up. The petitioners did not dispute the business efficacy of the decision to cease manufacturing, which had
been taken by the board after careful consideration.

In *Re Eastern Telegraph Co Ltd*[643] the company's principal assets had been nationalized but **8.277**
compensation had not been negotiated and the court decided that it was in the company's
interests for the compensation to be negotiated by the directors, who knew the business,
rather than by a liquidator. The fact that the petition was primarily an opportunist move to
secure a financial advantage to the petitioners was also an important reason for dismissing
the petition. In *Idugboe v Oilfield Supply Ltd*,[644] *Re Eastern Telegraph Co Ltd* was treated
as authority for the proposition that nationalization of a company's assets cannot create a
failure of substratum,[645] but, with respect, this reads too much into the decision.

Deadlock

Principle

It has been said several times that it is just and equitable to order the winding up of a com- **8.278**
pany where there is a 'deadlock'.[646]

In *Ng Eng Hiam v Ng Kee Wei*[647] Lord Donovan said, at p 240: **8.279**

> The principle is clear that if the court is satisfied that complete deadlock exists in the man-
> agement of a company the jurisdiction [to wind up a company if the court thinks it just and
> equitable to do so] will be exercised…. It may be that the jurisdiction will be more readily
> exercised where…although the business is carried on by means of a private limited com-
> pany, the case is not unlike one of a partnership.

Deadlock in a quasi-partnership company inevitably involves cessation of trust and con- **8.280**
fidence among the quasi-partners, which is in itself a recognized ground for winding up a
quasi-partnership company.[648]

What Constitutes Deadlock?

There is no precise definition of 'deadlock' for the purpose of winding up on the just and **8.281**
equitable ground. Lord Donovan in *Ng Eng Hiam v Ng Kee Wei*[649] said, at p 240: 'The

---

[642] (1996) 91 OAC 241.
[643] [1947] 2 All ER 104.
[644] 1979 (1) ALR Comm 1.
[645] At pp 30 and 37.
[646] *Re Sailing Ship 'Kentmere' Co* [1897] WN 58 per Vaughan Williams J; *Re Fromm's Extract Co Ltd* (1901)
17 TLR 302; *Symington v Symingtons' Quarries Ltd* (1905) 8 F 121 per Lord President Dunedin at p 129 and
Lord Kinnear at p 131; *Re Sydney and Whitney Pier Bus Service Ltd* [1944] 3 DLR 468 per Doull J at p 471
(where the reference is to 'deadlock or anything which prevents the company from properly functioning');
Re Bondi Better Bananas Ltd [1952] 1 DLR 277 at p 281; *Ng Eng Hiam v Ng Kee Wei* (1964) 31 MLJ 238; *Re
Deep Sea Trawlers Ltd* (1984) 2 NZCLC 99,137; *Re Vehicle Buildings and Insulations Ltd* [1986] ILRM 239.
[647] (1964) 31 MLJ 238.
[648] See 8.382–8.397.
[649] (1964) 31 MLJ 238.

question whether such a deadlock exists as makes it just and equitable to wind the company up is a question predominantly of fact in each case'. It seems that deadlock involves a division of the membership and directors into two opposed and uncooperative factions inhibiting decisions on matters crucial to the company's prosperity. Deadlock has been described as 'an impasse in the corporate decision-making process'.[650] In *Re Deep Sea Trawlers Ltd*[651] Jeffries J said, at p 99,148:

> Deadlock is an interesting word in sound and meaning. It appealed to Charles Dickens as an appropriate name for leading characters in a novel concerning a suit in Chancery.[652] The dictionary meaning is that of a standstill, or inaction, resulting from the opposing aims of different people. The impasse is the result of clash.... An impasse can arise without the presence of exact equality.

8.282 The writer of the headnote of *Re Motor Accessories Repair Co Pty Ltd*[653] referred to '[i]nsoluble dissension and differences... between the directors'. In *Ng Sing King v PSA International Pte Ltd (No 2)*[654] the court used the phrase 'irretrievable breakdown in the relationship amongst the shareholders'. In *Re Fromm's Extract Co Ltd*[655] 'deadlock' seemed to mean that it was impossible for the company to carry on business. But the word 'deadlock' was not used at all in the judgment in *Re Upper Hutt Town Hall Co Ltd*,[656] in which a winding-up order was made because, it was said (at p 126), that 'there are two factions in the company. Neither will coalesce with the other, and the continuance of the company has become impossible.' In *Re Mataia Ltd*[657] the petitioner held one quarter of the company's shares and another man held the remainder; the two were the company's only directors. Adams J summarized the position at p 808: 'it is hopeless to expect these two persons to work together... Neither of them can carry on the business of the company alone.' His Honour described this as 'a complete deadlock' and made a winding-up order citing *Re Sailing Ship 'Kentmere' Co*,[658] *Re Fromm's Extract Co Ltd*[659] and *Re Upper Hutt Town Hall Co Ltd*.[660] In *Scozzafava v Prosperi*[661] Read J said, at [50]:

> It is apparent... that there are two equal factions of shareholders and that they are at odds. This is a classic case of deadlock.

8.283 However, in *Keho Holdings Ltd v Noble*,[662] in which the company was not a quasi-partnership company, the fact that the applicants for the company's winding up controlled sufficient votes to block a special resolution was held not to constitute a deadlock. See further the discussion in 8.382–8.397 of just and equitable winding up of quasi-partnership companies in which there has been a failure of cooperation.

[650] J O'Donovan and G W O'Grady, 'Company deadlocks: prevention and cure' (1982) 1 C & SLJ 67 at p 67.
[651] (1984) 2 NZCLC 99,137.
[652] Sir Leicester and Lady Dedlock in *Bleak House*, published in instalments 1852–3.
[653] [1956] QWN 46.
[654] [2005] SGHC 5, [2005] 2 SLR 56.
[655] (1901) 17 TLR 302.
[656] [1920] NZLR 125.
[657] [1921] NZLR 807.
[658] [1897] WN 58.
[659] (1901) 17 TLR 302.
[660] [1920] NZLR 125.
[661] 2003 ABQB 248, [2003] 6 WWR 351.
[662] (1987) 38 DLR (4th) 368.

In *Re Quality International Ltd*[663] Blair-Kerr J said that it seemed that 'there exists at the **8.284** moment the sort of deadlock which can best be resolved by [the company being wound up by the court]'. The petitioner owned 90 of the company's 400 shares and had offered to buy out another shareholder which owned 220 shares but the board refused to register the transfer. The vendor shareholder had indicated its support for the petition.

In *McGinn v Carrathool Hotel Pty Ltd*[664] the only two members and directors of the com- **8.285** pany had been husband and wife, but at the time of hearing the winding-up application there was such hostility between them that an apprehended violence order[665] had been made. The court ordered the company to be wound up.[666]

In *Gregor v British-Israel-World Federation (NSW)*,[667] the word 'deadlock' was not used at **8.286** all. The company was not for profit. It promoted a particular interpretation of the Bible. Its board of directors comprised bitterly opposed factions who clearly could not work together and make sensible decisions for the company's future, in particular, how to deal with a recent legacy of AU$0.5 million. Its register of members was so unreliable that there was no practical possibility of holding elections to the board. Winding up was ordered.

From 1958 to 1963, a Quebec statute provided that 'deadlock' in a company was a circum- **8.287** stance in which the court would have jurisdiction to order winding up, provided there was no other effective and appropriate remedy. For the provision to be applicable there had to be two groups of shareholders sharing capital and control; serious and persistent disagreement over choice of directors or officers or over important questions respecting the management and functioning of the company; resulting deadlock; and paralysis or serious interference with the normal operations of the company. The provision was examined in two reported cases: *Lefebvre v Lefebvre Frères Ltée*,[668] in which it was found that the conditions of the section had not been met, and *Re Prussin and Park Distributors Inc*,[669] in which they were.

Possibility of Resolution

In *Ng Eng Hiam v Ng Kee Wei*[670] deadlock was alleged but the Privy Council refused to dis- **8.288** turb the decision of the courts below not to wind up the company because 'there seems to be reasonable hope of reconciliation and cooperation if ordinary good sense is employed'.[671] In *Re Goodwealth Trading Pte Ltd*[672] Yong Pung How CJ said, at pp 318–19, that this was an 'extraordinary opinion…which was against the evidence'. The Chief Justice thought that the evidence showed there was 'what can only be described as a Chinese family feud of considerable intensity'.

It has been said that there is no deadlock if there is any procedure under the company's **8.289** constitution or the general law by which one faction could get decisions made (for example,

---

[663] [1964] HKLR 669.
[664] [2008] NSWSC 197.
[665] Restraining violent, harassing or intimidating behaviour.
[666] Apprehended violence also showed the degree of hostility that justified winding up in *Johnny Oceans Restaurant Pty Ltd v Page* [2003] NSWSC 952.
[667] [2002] NSWSC 12, 41 ACSR 641.
[668] (1960) 4 CBR NS 38.
[669] (1963) 6 CBR NS 31.
[670] (1964) 31 MLJ 238.
[671] At p 240, quoting the words of Hill JA in the Malaya Court of Appeal (1962) 29 MLJ 73 at p 77.
[672] [1991] 2 MLJ 314.

by appointing additional directors, using casting votes, going to arbitration, dismissing directors or asking the court to summon a general meeting and directing that one member may be a quorum).[673] If a company is a quasi-partnership company, the court will recognize that it may be unjust and inequitable for one faction to exercise its legal rights to overrule the petitioner[674] and in a case involving a quasi-partnership company the situation may be described as a deadlock even if one of these procedures could be used to make decisions.[675] The factor determining whether it is just and equitable to wind up a company may be whether it is just and equitable to leave the petitioner to submit to the exercise by an opposing faction in the company of their legal rights rather than invoke equitable considerations to release the petitioner.[676] This accounts for the fact that, as Lord Donovan pointed out in the passage from *Ng Eng Hiam v Ng Kee Wei* quoted in 8.279, a company is more likely to be wound up for deadlock if it is a quasi-partnership company than if it is not.

8.290 In both *Re Michael P Georgas Co Ltd*[677] and *Bleau v Le Perruquier Français Inc*[678] the court suggested that with the exercise of tolerance and good sense by all parties concerned there was no reason for a continuance of the alleged deadlock.

Petitioner's Responsibility

8.291 The fact that difficulties in the company were brought about by the petitioner's own behaviour may be a reason for refusing to make a winding-up order.[679]

Literature

8.292 'Deadlock' (1954) 217 LT Jo 120.

J O'Donovan and G W O'Grady, 'Company deadlocks: prevention and cure' (1982) 1 C & SLJ 67.

Constitutional and Administrative Vacuum

8.293 It is just and equitable to wind up a company which has no officers, if there is no practical possibility of officers being appointed, and it is clear that no one wishes the company to continue. The fact that no one wishes to reactivate the company may be apparent from no one applying under the Companies Act 2006, s 306, for the court to summon a meeting. The phrase 'constitutional and administrative vacuum' was used for this state of affairs in *Lunn v Cardiff Coal Co (No 3)*.[680] In that case the man applying for winding up was the only member who could

---

[673] *Re Furriers' Alliance Ltd* (1906) 51 SJ 172; *Re Dewey and O'Heir Co* (1908) 13 OWR 32; *Re National Drive-In Theatres Ltd* [1954] 2 DLR 55 at p 64; *Re Expanded Plugs Ltd* [1966] 1 WLR 514 at p 519; per Lord Cross of Chelsea in *Ebrahimi v Westbourne Galleries Ltd* [1973] AC 360 at p 383; *Jaksi v ADD Human Resources Consultants Inc* [1975] Que SC 691.

[674] *Re Citizen's Coal and Forwarding Co Ltd* [1927] 4 DLR 275; *Re White Castle Inn Ltd* [1946] OWN 773; *Ebrahimi v Westbourne Galleries Ltd*.

[675] *Re Dunham and Apollo Tours Ltd (No 2)* (1978) 86 DLR (3d) 595 at p 600.

[676] *Ebrahimi v Westbourne Galleries Ltd*.

[677] [1948] OR 708.

[678] (1967) 10 CBR NS 296.

[679] *Re Toronto Finance Corp* [1930] 3 DLR 882 at p 885; *Re Michael P Georgas Co Ltd* [1948] OR 708 at 710; *Ng Eng Hiam v Ng Kee Wei* (1964) 31 MLJ 238; *Bleau v Le Perruquier Français Inc* (1967) 10 CBR NS 296; see also 8.248–8.257.

[680] [2003] NSWSC 789, 177 FLR 411.

be traced of a company incorporated by an Act of the New South Wales Parliament in 1863, before it was possible to incorporate companies by registration in New South Wales. The company was being administered by a court-appointed receiver and its only asset was cash.

In *Re Kapunda United Tradesmen's Prospecting Co Ltd*[681] it was held to be just and equitable **8.294** to wind up a company because it was impracticable to hold meetings of members because a quorum could not be assembled (the report does not state who petitioned). *Re Outram Societies Hall Co Ltd*[682] is a similar case in which a contributory petitioned.

In *CIC Insurance Ltd v Hannan and Co Pty Ltd*[683] both the company's directors had resigned, **8.295** a provisional liquidator had been appointed of its sole shareholder and there was no realistic possibility of anyone agreeing to act as director because of the company's insolvency. See also *Phelan v Ambridge Corporation Pty Ltd*[684] (one member, who was the only director, was bankrupt and untraceable, and the other member was a company, now in receivership, with the same man as its only director) and *Official Trustee in Bankruptcy v Buffier*[685] (all shares in the company owned by a bankrupt individual; only director of the company not validly appointed; no one willing to take office as director because of no knowledge of the state of the company's affairs).

It is just and equitable to wind up a company which has been restored to the register after **8.296** dissolution, if there is no prospect of any directors being appointed,[686] for example, if the sole purpose of restoration is to make the company a party to legal proceedings which will be dealt with by an insurer.[687]

Even if there are directors in office, it may be just and equitable to wind up a company if its **8.297** directors neglect it and fail to file annual returns or to comply with other statutory obligations so that the company is in danger of being struck off.[688]

Management and Conduct of Company: Oppression

Principle

It may be just and equitable to order the winding up of a company if the petitioner shows **8.298** what Lord Shaw of Dunfermline described as 'a justifiable lack of confidence in the conduct and management of the company's affairs'.[689] However, his Lordship went on to say that:

> this lack of confidence must be grounded on conduct of the directors, not in regard to their private life or affairs, but in regard to the company's business. Furthermore the lack of confidence must spring not from dissatisfaction at being outvoted on the business affairs or on what is called the domestic policy of the company.

---

[681] (1874) 8 SALR 55.
[682] (1914) 33 NZLR 1249.
[683] [2001] NSWSC 437, 38 ACSR 245.
[684] [2005] NSWSC 875, 55 ACSR 136.
[685] [2005] NSWSC 839, 54 ACSR 767.
[686] *Re Sparad Ltd* (1993) 12 ACSR 12 (in which it was also obvious that the company would be insolvent when restored); *Deputy Commissioner of Taxation v Action Workwear Pty Ltd* (1996) 132 FLR 345.
[687] *Shaw v Goodsmith Industries Pty Ltd* [2002] NSWSC 406, 41 ACSR 556.
[688] *Re Fuerta Ltd* [2014] IEHC 12 (a creditor's petition).
[689] *Loch v John Blackwood Ltd* [1924] AC 783 at p 788.

8.299   Unless a company is a quasi-partnership company,[690] a winding-up order will not be made if the only substantial reason for the petitioner's lack of confidence in the directors is dissension from the course they are pursuing.[691] Animosity between directors does not justify winding up a company that is not a quasi-partnership.[692] The fact that one member with about 6 per cent of the shares in a company whose shares are publicly traded has lost confidence in the company's directors cannot justify winding it up.[693]

8.300   If the shares of a member of a company can be sold at a reasonable price, the member will normally be unable to have the company wound up compulsorily on the ground of mismanagement or misconduct of its affairs. So, for example, a contributory will not succeed in such a case if the company's shares are publicly traded,[694] unless the share price has been depressed by the mismanagement and misconduct complained of.[695] Similarly, a contributory's petition to wind up a company whose shares are not publicly traded will not succeed if other shareholders or the company itself are willing to buy out the petitioner at a fair price.[696]

8.301   Justifiable lack of confidence in the conduct and management of a company's affairs has been held to justify winding up on the just and equitable ground not only on the petition of a contributory but also on the petition of a creditor[697] and even the company itself.[698]

Factors which Justify Winding Up

Introduction

8.302   Winding up a company because of the way it is managed or its affairs are conducted is usually justified by an overall picture of what has been happening. Some commonly occurring factors are discussed at 8.303–8.338. It is common for several of them to occur in the same case, and many of them are just different aspects of the same forms of maladministration.

Directors' lack of probity

8.303   It may be just and equitable to wind up a company if directors whom the petitioner cannot remove appear to have shown a lack of probity in the conduct of the company's affairs.[699] A petitioner is entitled to continue to lack confidence in directors who have misappropriated

---

[690]   See 8.382–8.397.

[691]   *Re Hugh-Pam Porcupine Mines Ltd* [1942] OWN 544.

[692]   *Re Hillcrest Housing Ltd* (1998) 165 Nfld & PEIR 181 at pp 226–30; *Cassegrain v Gerard Cassegrain and Co Pty Ltd* [2012] NSWSC 403 at [335]–[339] (numerous other allegations of oppression were dismissed by the court at [269]–[334]).

[693]   *Re Connemara Mining Co plc* [2013] IEHC 225.

[694]   *Re Wondoflex Textiles Pty Ltd* [1951] VLR 458 at p 465.

[695]   *Re William Brooks and Co Ltd* (1961) 79 WN (NSW) 354; *Re Johnson Corporation Ltd* (1980) 5 ACLR 227 at p 236.

[696]   *Re Hillcrest Housing Ltd* (1998) 165 Nfld & PEIR 181 at pp 220–1 (paras 145 and 153).

[697]   *Re Millennium Advanced Technology Ltd* [2004] EWHC 711 (Ch), [2004] 1 WLR 2177; *Deputy Commissioner of Taxation v Casualife Furniture International Pty Ltd* [2004] VSC 157, 55 ATR 599; *Macquarie Bank Ltd v TM Investments Pty Ltd* [2005] NSWSC 608, 223 ALR 148.

[698]   *Re Trans Pacific Insurance Corporation* [2009] NSWSC 554, 72 ACSR 327.

[699]   *Re Yue Hing Co Ltd* (1916) 11 HKLR 53; *Re Newbridge Sanitary Steam Laundry Ltd* [1917] 1 IR 67; *Loch v John Blackwood Ltd* [1924] AC 783; *Re Straw Products Pty Ltd* [1942] VLR 272; *Re Martello and Sons Ltd* [1945] OR 453; *Re W A Swan and Sons Ltd* [1962] SASR 310; *Re Concrete Column Clamps Ltd* [1953] 4 DLR 60 (in which the controlling director had systematically stolen a vast sum of money from the company

the company's property despite their restoring the property and promising not to make further misappropriations.[700] In *Re St Piran Ltd*[701] Dillon J, at p 1307, suggested that a listed
company would be wound up if its directors caused trading in its securities to be suspended
by flouting the City Code on Takeovers and Mergers.

Where interlocking companies are controlled by a common director, lack of confidence **8.304**
in that director may be justified by his or her conduct in managing the affairs of companies other than the one sought to be wound up.[702] A petitioner may rely on conduct
that occurred before the petitioner became a member of the company sought to be
wound up.[703]

The fact that directors are unwise, inefficient and careless in the performance of their duties **8.305**
may well inspire lack of confidence in them but it does not show lack of probity and does
not justify winding up.[704]

The lack of probity factor may be relevant whether or not the company is a quasi-partnership **8.306**
company:[705]

> Lack of confidence rested on a lack of probity in the conduct of a company's affairs seems to
> me to be something quite different from a mutual lack of confidence between partners in the
> management of partnership affairs.[706]

The burden of proving lack of probity is on the petitioner.[707]   **8.307**

---

over many years and had sold its principal revenue-earning assets to a new company owned by himself and
his son); *Re Waipuna Investments Pty Ltd* [1956] VLR 115; *Re William Brooks and Co Ltd* (1961) 79 WN
(NSW) 354; *Re Maritime Asphalt Products Ltd* (1965) 52 DLR (2d) 8 (in which the company and its control-
ling directors had been fined for numerous tax offences); *Re R J Jowsey Mining Co Ltd* [1969] 2 OR 549 (in
which the way in which the director engineered his takeover of the company was considered significant); *Re
Investment Properties International Ltd* (1973) 41 DLR (3d) 217, affirmed (1974) 43 DLR (3d) 684; *91436
Canada Inc v Evalyne Sales Corp* (1984) 54 CBR NS 87; *Sound Advice Inc v 358074 Ontario Ltd* (1984) 5
OAC 288; *Mammone v Doralin Investments Ltd* (1985) 54 CBR NS 171; *Hyndman v R C Hyndman Ltd* 1989
SCLR 294; *Chong Choon Chai v Tan Gee Cheng* [1993] 3 SLR 1; *Re Worldhams Park Golf Course Ltd* [1998]
1 BCLC 554 (in which one director had got his position by lying about his qualifications and had stolen the
company's retail takings: this was characterized, at p 556, as 'gross misconduct'); *Mak Sik Bun v Mak Lei Wun*
[2005] 4 HKLRD 328 (in which the criterion was expressed, at [76], as lack of integrity in the conduct of the
company's affairs); *Todd v Todd* 2008 SLT (Sh Ct) 26.

[700]   *Todd v Todd* 2008 SLT (Sh Ct) 26 at [54].
[701]   [1981] 1 WLR 1300.
[702]   *Sound Advice Inc v 358074 Ontario Ltd* (1984) 5 OAC 288.
[703]   *Sound Advice Inc v 358074 Ontario Ltd*.
[704]   *Re William Dawe and Sons Ltd* (1950) 25 MPR 30; *Re Five Minute Car Wash Service Ltd* [1966] 1
WLR 745, especially at p 752; see also per Baggallay J in *Re Diamond Fuel Co* (1879) 13 ChD 400 at p 408;
Middleton J in *Re Harris Maxwell Larder Lake Gold Mining Co Ltd* (1910) 1 OWN 984 and Plowman J in
Re Surrey Garden Village Trust Ltd [1965] 1 WLR 974 at p 981; compare, however, *Pirie v Stewart* (1904) 6
F 847, in which a winding-up order was made where the mismanagement of the company thus far had been
disastrous.
[705]   *Re Wondoflex Textiles Pty Ltd* [1951] VLR 458 at p 465; *Re National Drive-In Theatres Ltd* [1954] 2 DLR
55 at p 64; *Sound Advice Inc v 358074 Ontario Ltd* (1984) 5 OAC 288.
[706]   Per Lord Keith in *Elder v Elder and Watson Ltd* 1952 SC 49 at p 59.
[707]   *Re Hillcrest Housing Ltd* (1998) 165 Nfld & PEIR 181 at p 220. For examples of cases in which allegations of lack of probity were not proved and so petitions were dismissed, see *Menard v Horwood and Co
Ltd* (1922) 31 CLR 20; *Re James Lumbers Co Ltd* [1926] 1 DLR 173; *Re Sydney and Whitney Pier Bus Service
Ltd* [1944] 3 DLR 468; *Re R C Young Insurance Ltd* [1955] 3 DLR 571; *Re Columbia Gypsum Co* (1958) 17
DLR (2d) 280; *Shacket v Universal Factors Corporation* [1967] Que SC 131; *Mitha v Mitha* [1967] EA 575;

8.308 In *Re Saul D Harrison and Sons plc*[708] it was alleged that, following a fire which had destroyed the company's premises, the directors had irrationally decided to move into new premises and continue the company's business not in the interests of the company but so as to provide themselves with a continuing income from salaries. The petition contained no evidence from which it could be inferred that the directors had acted in bad faith and it was struck out.

8.309 Misconduct by directors is not enough to justify winding up if it could be remedied by a claim brought by the company against the directors, or a derivative claim brought by a member.[709] In *Re Blériot Manufacturing Aircraft Co Ltd*[710] a winding-up order was made because of loss of the company's substratum. It was also alleged that there had been misconduct by a director. Neville J, at p 255, described the company as 'so constituted that it is deprived of its usual remedies' against the director, but it is not clear what his Lordship meant by this statement. His Lordship said that this absence of remedy would in itself have been sufficient for it to be just and equitable to wind up the company, had there not been loss of substratum.

Actions not in the company's interests

8.310 Lack of probity[711] may be shown by a persistent disregard of an obligation to act in the interests of the company.[712]

8.311 In *Scottish Co-operative Wholesale Society Ltd v Meyer*[713] the majority shareholder diverted essential raw materials, which were in short supply, to its own plant as part of a policy of running down the company, and directors of the company which it had nominated acquiesced in this. On the application of minority shareholders this was found to be oppressive conduct justifying winding up.

8.312 In *Fedoruk v Fedoruk Holdings Ltd*,[714] the applicant for winding up held one-third of the shares in a company and her brothers-in-law held the other two-thirds. The men owned a retail business which leased shop premises from the company. As the shop was doing badly they used their control of the company to reduce the rent payable and indicated that they would continue to sacrifice the company's interests to ensure the continuation of their retail business. Winding up was ordered.

Cumberland Holdings Ltd v Washington H Soul Pattinson and Co Ltd (1977) 13 ALR 561; *Re Kong Thai Sawmill (Miri) Sdn Bhd* [1978] 2 MLJ 227; *B Love Ltd v Bulk Steel and Salvage Ltd* (1982) 38 OR (2d) 691; *Re Ah Yee Contractors (Pte) Ltd* [1987] 2 MLJ 590; *RCB v Thai Asia Fund Ltd* 1996 CILR 9 (in which the petitioner's allegations were characterized as mere disagreements over business affairs); *Alldrew Holdings Ltd v Nibro Holdings Ltd* (1996) 91 OAC 241; *Three Point Oils Ltd v Glencrest Energy Ltd* (1997) 200 AR 184; *Re Hillcrest Housing Ltd* (1998) 165 Nfld & PEIR 181.

[708] [1995] 1 BCLC 14.

[709] *Re National and Provincial Live Stock Insurance Co* (1858) 31 LT OS 277; *Re Anglo-Greek Steam Co* (1866) LR 2 Eq 1 per Lord Romilly MR at p 5; *Re Diamond Fuel Co* (1879) 13 ChD 400 per Baggallay LJ at p 408; *Re Great Cobar Copper Mining Co Ltd* (1902) 2 SR (NSW) Eq 94; *Re Kitson and Co Ltd* [1946] 1 All ER 435 per Lord Greene MR at p 441; *Re Surrey Garden Village Trust Ltd* [1965] 1 WLR 974 per Plowman J at p 981; *Win-Doors Ltd v Bryan* (1990) 27 JLR 292; *RCB v Thai Asia Fund Ltd* 1996 CILR 9.

[710] (1916) 32 TLR 253.

[711] See 8.303–8.309.

[712] *Thomson v Drysdale* 1925 SC 311; *Re Wondoflex Textiles Pty Ltd* [1951] VLR 458; *Re W A Swan and Sons Ltd* [1962] SASR 310; *Re William Brooks and Co Ltd* (1961) 79 WN (NSW) 354.

[713] [1959] AC 324.

[714] [1978] 6 WWR 40.

Diversion of company assets

It is just and equitable to wind up a company if its administration is fraudulent with the result **8.313**
that its property is imperilled or might be transferred into the pockets of its directors.[715]

In *Cossgrove v Cossgrove*,[716] it was held to be just and equitable to order the winding up of a com- **8.314**
pany 'Where there was a danger that substantial assets would disappear into some unrealisable
securities or investments for the benefit of the majority shareholder...and where there was a
lack of confidence on the part of the minority shareholder in the conduct and management of
the affairs of the company with its deteriorating financial condition'.

In *Rafuse v Bishop*,[717] Mr Rafuse (the petitioner) and Mr Bishop had set up two companies **8.315**
in which they were equal shareholders. Mr Rafuse had an alcohol problem and had to stop
working for the companies. Negotiations for the sale of his shares to other members dragged
on for many months. Mr Bishop organized the sale of the companies' assets to another company in which he was principal shareholder but in which Mr Rafuse had no interest because
Mr Bishop did not want the continuing trading of the companies to increase the value of
Mr Rafuse's shares. Glube J said, at p 82, that in doing this, Mr Bishop 'stepped beyond the
bounds of propriety' and[718] found a lack of confidence in the conduct of the management of
the two companies by Mr Bishop. This and the 'freeze-out' of the petitioner made it just and
equitable to order the winding up of the two companies.

Ignoring statutory safeguards for members

A factor which may justify winding up is that procedures laid down by the Companies Act and/ **8.316**
or the company's constitution have been ignored so that the petitioner has been unlawfully
denied the safeguards provided by those procedures.[719]

In *Baird v Lees*[720] Lord President Clyde said, at p 92: **8.317**

> I have no intention of attempting a definition of the circumstances which amount to a 'just
> and equitable' cause. But I think I may say this. A shareholder puts his money into a company
> on certain conditions. The first of them is that the business in which he invests shall be limited
> to certain definite objects. The second is that it shall be carried on by certain persons elected
> in a specified way. And the third is that the business shall be conducted in accordance with
> certain principles of commercial administration defined in the statute, which provide some
> guarantee of commercial probity and efficiency. If shareholders find that these conditions or
> some of them are deliberately and consistently violated and set aside by the action of a member
> and official of the company who wields an overwhelming voting power, and if the result of
> that is that, for the extrication of their rights as shareholders, they are deprived of the ordinary
> facilities which compliance with the Companies Acts would provide them with, then there
> does arise, in my opinion, a situation in which it may be just and equitable for the court to
> wind up the company.

---

[715] *Loch v John Blackwood Ltd* [1924] AC 783 at p 789.

[716] (1977) 24 CBR NS 172.

[717] (1979) 34 NSR (2d) 70.

[718] At p 83.

[719] *Baird v Lees* 1924 SC 83; *Thomson v Drysdale* 1925 SC 311; *Re Kurilpa Protestant Hall Pty Ltd* [1946]
StR Qd 170; *Re Fish and Game League (Regina)* (1967) 63 DLR (2d) 47, which concerned a non-profit company; *Re Pre-Delco Machine and Tool Ltd* (1973) 36 DLR (3d) 50; *Strickland v Tricom Associates (1979) Ltd*
(1982) 38 Nfld & PEIR 451.

[720] 1924 SC 83.

In *Thomson v Drysdale*[721] his Lordship said, at p 315:

> [I]n any case in which the shareholders who hold a preponderating interest in a company make it manifest that they intend to set at naught the security provided by company procedure, and to treat the company and its affairs as if they were their own property, it is impossible that the minority should retain any confidence in the impartiality or probity of the company's administration, and—according to the circumstances of each particular case—it becomes a question whether the minority are not entitled, as a matter of 'justice and equity' within the meaning of [IA 1986, s 122(1)(g)], to have the company wound up.

8.318 Informal conduct of a company's affairs which the petitioner has previously acquiesced in will not be enough to justify winding up.[722]

Directors not providing information

8.319 A factor which may justify winding up is that directors whom the petitioner cannot remove have failed to provide information to shareholders to enable them to assess the value of the company and whether the directors are doing a good job.[723] This factor was not sufficient in *Buckner v Bourbon Farming Co Ltd*,[724] which the court said was not a case of concealment in connection with attempted fraud, unlike *Loch v John Blackwood Ltd*.[725] Refusal to allow the petitioner to inspect accounting records which the petitioner does not have a right to inspect cannot be a ground for complaint.[726]

Oppression

8.320 In Great Britain, the Companies Act 1948, s 210 (repealed), provided that if a member of a company could prove that its affairs were being conducted in a manner oppressive to some part of the members, and the court found that the oppression justified the making of a winding-up order, then the court could instead make other orders (the most useful of which was an order that the other shareholders buy out the petitioner).[727] Similar provisions were enacted in other Commonwealth jurisdictions. Oppressive conduct justifying winding up was found in *Scottish Co-operative Wholesale Society Ltd v Meyer*;[728] *Re H R Harmer Ltd*;[729] *Re Associated Tool Industries Ltd*;[730] *Re British Columbia Electric Co Ltd*;[731] *Re National Building Maintenance Ltd*;[732] *Re Ingleburn Horse and Pony Club Ltd*;[733] *Re Federated Fashions*

---

[721] 1925 SC 311.

[722] *Shillingford v The Penn Syndicate* (1958) 1 WIR 58, in which steps to rectify previous informalities were taken immediately the petition was launched; *Re Lowes Park Pty Ltd* (1994) 62 FCR 535.

[723] *Re Merchants and Shippers' Steamship Lines Ltd* (1917) 17 SR (NSW) 146; *Loch v John Blackwood Ltd* [1924] AC 783; *Re Delip Singh and Moody Shingles Ltd* [1947] 1 WWR 480, in which the company had never kept proper accounting records and had never produced any annual accounts; *Re Earley Mead Investments Ltd* [1989] LRC (Comm) 601, in which audited accounts were not produced for 20 years.

[724] (1955) 14 WWR 406.

[725] [1924] AC 783.

[726] *Murray's Judicial Factor v Thomas Murray and Sons (Ice Merchants) Ltd* 1992 SLT 824.

[727] See A B Afterman, 'Statutory protection for oppressed minority shareholders: a model for reform' (1969) 55 Va L Rev 1043; H Rajak, 'The oppression of minority shareholders' (1972) 35 MLR 156. The provision was first enacted as the Companies Act 1947, s 9, following a recommendation by the Cohen Committee (Report of the Committee on Company Law Amendment (Cmd 6659, 1945), paras 60 and 152, and p 95, recommendation II).

[728] [1959] AC 324.

[729] [1959] 1 WLR 62.

[730] [1964] ALR 73.

[731] (1964) 47 DLR (2d) 754.

[732] [1971] 1 WWR 8, [1972] 5 WWR 410.

[733] [1973] 1 NSWLR 641.

(NZ) Ltd;[734] and *Re East West Promotions Pty Ltd*.[735] Cases in which the factors discussed at 8.303–8.309 (directors' lack of probity) or 8.316–8.318 (ignoring statutory safeguards for members) were present would probably have been considered cases of oppressive conduct had they been brought under the Companies Act 1948, s 210.[736]

Oppression as a statutory ground for winding up was alleged but not proved in *Re Kornblums Furnishings Ltd*.[737]　**8.321**

In *Re Fish and Game League (Regina)*[738] Tucker J, in Saskatchewan, having considered the British Companies Act 1948, s 210 (of which there was no equivalent in Saskatchewan at the time), specifically described the conduct of the officers of the company in the case before him as 'oppressive' to the petitioners.　**8.322**

Some Commonwealth statutes empowered the courts to remedy oppressive conduct without having to find that it justified winding up. In petitions under such statutes, oppression was found in *Re Bright Pine Mills Pty Ltd*,[739] *Re Anticorrosive Treatments Ltd*,[740] *Re Federated Fashions (NZ) Ltd*[741]and *Butler v Butler*,[742] but not in *Re Great Eastern Hotel (Pte) Ltd*.[743]　**8.323**

Provisions for remedying oppression were held to apply only to oppression of members qua members and therefore could not apply to exclusion of members from management, which was thought to affect them only as directors or employees.[744]　**8.324**

The Companies Act 1948, s 210, was repealed by the Companies Act 1980 and replaced by the provisions for protection of members against unfair prejudice which are now in the Companies Act 2006, ss 994 to 999.[745] To obtain relief under ss 994 to 999 it is not necessary to show that the prejudicial conduct would justify winding up the company.[746] There is no longer any reference to oppression in United Kingdom companies legislation. In other Commonwealth countries, the scope of legislation providing remedies for oppressive conduct has been expanded to cover unfairly prejudicial or unfairly discriminatory conduct[747] but the expanded legislation continues to be referred to as providing a remedy for oppression.[748]　**8.325**

---

[734] (1981) 1 BCR 297.
[735] (1986) 10 ACLR 222.
[736] Per Lord Keith in *Elder v Elder and Watson Ltd* 1952 SC 49 at pp 59–60.
[737] (1981) 6 ACLR 456.
[738] (1967) 63 DLR (2d) 47.
[739] [1969] VR 1002.
[740] (1980) 1 BCR 238.
[741] (1981) 1 BCR 297, in which it was held that the oppression would have justified winding up, but the petitioner preferred to be bought out.
[742] (1993) 30 JLR 348.
[743] [1989] 1 MLJ 161.
[744] *Elder v Elder and Watson Ltd* 1952 SC 49; *Re BC Aircraft Propeller and Engine Co Ltd* (1968) 66 DLR (2d) 628.
[745] See 8.432–8.468.
[746] *Re a Company (No 00314 of 1989)* [1991] BCLC 154; *O'Neill v Phillips* [1999] 1 WLR 1092 per Lord Hoffmann at pp 1099–1100.
[747] See the legislation discussed at 8.461–8.463.
[748] See *Fexuto Pty Ltd v Bosnjak Holdings Pty Ltd* [2001] NSWCA 97, 37 ACSR 672, at [300].

What amounts to oppression?

8.326 Conduct of a company's affairs in disregard of the interests of members of the company as members is oppressive to those members.[749] Persistent disregard of members' interests in receiving dividends may justify winding up.[750]

8.327 In *Kokotovich Constructions Pty Ltd v Wallington*[751] the action of the governing director in allotting shares to himself so as to dilute the petitioner's shareholding was described as oppression, and winding up was ordered because of a real risk of further oppression, and because the two shareholders had equal votes at members' meetings so that there was deadlock.

8.328 In *Re Jermyn Street Turkish Baths Ltd*,[752] in which oppression was alleged but not proved, Buckley LJ, delivering the judgment of the Court of Appeal, said at pp 1059–60:

> In our judgment, oppression occurs when shareholders, having a dominant power in a company, either (1) exercise that power to procure that something is done or not done in the conduct of the company's affairs or (2) procure by an express or implicit threat of an exercise of that power that something is not done in the conduct of the company's affairs; and when such conduct is unfair or, to use the expression adopted by Viscount Simonds in *Scottish Co-operative Wholesale Society Ltd v Meyer*,[753] 'burdensome, harsh and wrongful' to the other members of the company or some of them, and lacks that degree of probity which they are entitled to expect in the conduct of the company's affairs: see *Scottish Co-operative Wholesale Society Ltd v Meyer* and *Re H R Harmer Ltd*.[754] We do not say that this is necessarily a comprehensive definition of the meaning of the word 'oppressive' in section 210 [of the Companies Act 1948], for the affairs of life are so diverse that it is dangerous to attempt a universal definition.... Oppression must, we think, import that the oppressed are being constrained to submit to something which is unfair to them as the result of some overbearing act or attitude on the part of the oppressor.

8.329 In Australia, two modifications to this summary have been suggested. In *Re Tivoli Freeholds Ltd*,[755] Menhennitt J, at p 452, thought that it was unnecessary for both lack of probity and unfairness to be present, as the quotation at 8.328 would suggest: either one of them on its own would be sufficient. Nevertheless his Honour found that the alleged oppression in the case before him had not been proved. In *John J Starr (Real Estate) Pty Ltd v Robert R Andrew (A'asia) Pty Ltd*[756] Young J said, 'we all know that in many situations it is a combination of factors which leads to oppression, rather than the action of one particular person'. His Honour found that there was oppression on the part of the majority but, if he was wrong on that, he would find that the whole of the circumstances of the company were oppressive.[757]

---

[749] *Re H R Harmer Ltd* [1959] 1 WLR 62; per Lord Wilberforce in *Re Kong Thai Sawmill (Miri) Sdn Bhd* [1978] 2 MLJ 227 at p 229.
[750] *Re City Meat Co Pty Ltd* (1983) 8 ACLR 673; *Re a Company (No 00370 of 1987)* [1988] 1 WLR 1068; but not in *Re Lowes Park Pty Ltd* (1994) 62 FCR 535.
[751] (1995) 17 ACSR 478.
[752] [1971] 1 WLR 1042.
[753] [1959] AC 324 at p 342.
[754] [1959] 1 WLR 62.
[755] [1972] VR 445.
[756] (1991) 6 ACSR 63 at p 73.
[757] See also 8.141–8.142.

Deadlock and loss of trust and confidence between directors of a quasi-partnership com- **8.330**
pany do not in themselves mean that there is oppression.[758]

In *Re Empire Building Ltd*[759] the petitioners thought that the articles of the company could **8.331**
be altered so as to be more advantageous to them and alleged that the company's failure to
alter the articles in their favour was oppression, but this was rejected by the court.

Mere disagreement not enough

The mere fact that a minority in a company disagree with decisions taken by those in the **8.332**
majority does not mean that the minority are oppressed: 'in a company…the minority
must bow to the will of the majority'.[760] Accordingly, the fact that the majority have elected
directors with whom the minority disagree does not amount to oppression of the minority,[761] though it has also been said that an appointment of a director must be made for the
benefit of the company as a whole and not for any ulterior purpose.[762]

In *Re Kong Thai Sawmill (Miri) Sdn Bhd*[763] Lord Wilberforce said, at p 229: **8.333**

> The mere fact that one or more of those managing the company possess a majority of the vot-
> ing power and, in reliance upon that power, make policy or executive decisions, with which
> the complainant does not agree, is not enough. Those who take interests in companies lim-
> ited by shares have to accept majority rule. It is only when majority rule passes over into rule
> oppressive of the minority, or in disregard of their interests, that [the court can provide a rem-
> edy]. As was said in [*Elder v Elder and Watson Ltd*[764]] there must be a visible departure from
> the standards of fair dealing and a violation of the conditions of fair play which a shareholder
> is entitled to expect before a case of oppression can be made: their lordships [of the Privy
> Council] would place the emphasis on 'visible'. And similarly 'disregard' involves something
> more than a failure to take account of the minority's interest: there must be awareness of that
> interest and an evident decision to override it or brush it aside or to set at naught the proper
> company procedure (per Lord Clyde in *Thomson v Drysdale*[765]). Neither 'oppression' nor
> 'disregard' need be shown by a use of the majority's voting power to vote down the minor-
> ity: either may be demonstrated by a course of conduct which in some identifiable respect, or
> at an identifiable point in time, can be held to have crossed the line.

Can a minority oppress the majority?

In *Cairney v Golden Key Holdings Ltd*,[766] on a striking-out application, it was held that it is **8.334**
possible for a minority to oppress a majority if the minority is exercising control over the
financial management of the company (though the petition was dismissed when heard
because the situation complained of had been caused by the petitioner's own fraud[767]). But
in *Re Sin Lee Sang Sawmill Sdn Bhd*[768] Abdul Malek J could not see how the petitioners,

---

[758] *Jarman v Brown* [1979] 5 WWR 673.
[759] [1973] 1 NZLR 214.
[760] Per Doull J in *Re Sydney and Whitney Pier Bus Service Ltd* [1944] 3 DLR 468 at p 472.
[761] *Re Sydney and Whitney Pier Bus Service Ltd*.
[762] *Re H R Harmer Ltd* [1959] 1 WLR 62 per Jenkins LJ at p 82; *Re Broadcasting Station 2GB Pty Ltd*
[1964-5] NSWR 1648 per Jacobs J at p 1662; see also *Theseus Exploration NL v Mining and Associated
Industries Ltd* [1973] QdR 81.
[763] [1978] 2 MLJ 227.
[764] 1952 SC 49.
[765] 1925 SC 311.
[766] (1987) 40 BLR 263.
[767] *Cairney v Golden Key Holdings Ltd (No 2)* (1988) 40 BLR 289.
[768] [1990] 1 MLJ 250.

who, as managing director and executive director, were in control of the management of the company, could suggest that its affairs were being conducted by its chairman and another director in a manner oppressive to the petitioners. Similarly, in *Win-Doors Ltd v Bryan*[769] the three petitioners, though minority shareholders, formed a majority of the board of directors and their complaints about the company's management were held insufficient to justify winding up, because they could have dealt with them at board meetings. In *Re Baltic Real Estate Ltd (No 2)*[770] Knox J held that the provisions for protection of members against unfair prejudice now in the Companies Act 2006, ss 994 to 999, are not available to a petitioner who can 'readily rid himself' of the prejudice by exercising voting control.[771] In *Re Polyresins Pty Ltd*[772] the petitioner held the majority of shares in the company which he was seeking to have wound up, but he had played little active part in its affairs, and claimed to have been oppressed by the shareholder-directors who actually managed the company. Chesterman J held that the concepts of oppression and unfair prejudice had no relevance to this situation, as the petitioner had the right to remove the alleged oppressors from their directorships.

8.335   In *Watson v James*,[773] which concerned the oppression remedy, Bergin J said, at [72]:

> Notwithstanding Chesterman J's compelling analysis I do not agree that [what is now the Corporations Act 2001 (Australia), s 232] is only available for the protection of minorities.... Although one would not expect that a controlling shareholder would need recourse to the section the complexities of shareholders' and/or directors' relationships within corporate structures are such that I am not willing to rule out the possibility of such an event.

8.336   In *Goozee v Graphic World Group Holdings Pty Ltd*[774] it was alleged that the conduct of the affairs of wholly owned subsidiaries was oppressive or unfairly prejudicial to their holding company, because their affairs were conducted for the benefit of the holding company's majority shareholder. A minority shareholder in the holding company applied for permission to bring a derivative claim for the winding up of the subsidiaries (and their subsidiaries and sub-subsidiaries) under ss 232 and 233(1)(a). The application was refused because there was no evidence of oppressive or unfairly prejudicial conduct.

Controller treating the company as his or her own

8.337   In several of the cases in which minority shareholders have been ignored, oppressed or defrauded the situation has been summarized by saying that one individual in *de facto* control of a company has treated the company as his own.[775]

Directors' failure to take account of relevant matters in decision-making

8.338   It is possible that persistent failure by directors, when making decisions, to consider matters which they ought to consider, or to ignore matters which they ought not to consider, would

---

[769] (1990) 27 JLR 292.
[770] [1993] BCLC 503.
[771] See also *Re Legal Costs Negotiators Ltd* [1999] 2 BCLC 171.
[772] (1998) 28 ACSR 671.
[773] [1999] NSWSC 600.
[774] [2002] NSWSC 640, 42 ACSR 534.
[775] *Baird v Lees* 1924 SC 83; *Thomson v Drysdale* 1925 SC 311; *Loch v John Blackwood Ltd* [1924] AC 783 at p 794; *Shimelman v Ste-Marie Snack Bar of Quebec Inc* [1968] Que SC 149; *Nieforth v Nieforth Bros Ltd* (1985) 69 NSR (2d) 10.

justify winding up.[776] Although this is an administrative law concept, it has been applied in company law to invalidate a directors' decision.[777]

Just and Equitable Winding Up of Quasi-partnership Companies

Recognition of Legitimate Expectations outside the Company's Constitution

Legitimate expectations and quasi-partnership companies

In some cases the court recognizes that members of a company have understood and accepted that the company's affairs will be conducted in a particular way, even though there is nothing to that effect in the company's constitution or company law. In such a case, it may be just and equitable to wind up the company on the petition of a member who has been adversely affected by a failure to run the company in the accepted way. The common acceptance and understanding may be said to have given the petitioner a legitimate expectation that the company's affairs will be conducted in a particular way.[778] Companies in which such expectations will be taken into account are known as 'quasi-partnership companies'. This term is only 'a useful shorthand label', and the real question is: **8.339**

> whether the circumstances surrounding the conduct of the affairs of a particular company are such as to give rise to equitable constraints upon the behaviour of other members going beyond the strict rights and obligations set out in the Companies Act and the articles of association.[779]

The equitable restraints on behaviour which the courts have recognized in this context are of two types: **8.340**

(a) a company's member-directors may be required to act in a way that maintains their mutual trust and confidence as in a partnership firm;[780]
(b) limits may be placed on the exercise by members or directors of their powers even though the limits are not expressed in the company's constitution.[781]

In *O'Neill v Phillips*[782] Lord Hoffmann emphasized that the term 'legitimate expectation' refers to an expectation that the company's affairs will be conducted in the manner agreed by all the members, not a personal hope of the petitioner that other members will do something which they have not in fact agreed to do. His Lordship approved the following statement by Jonathan Parker J in *Re Astec (BSR) plc*:[783] **8.341**

---

[776] *Re a Company (No 00370 of 1987)* [1988] 1 WLR 1068 per Harman J at pp 1076–7.

[777] *Hunter v Senate Support Services Ltd* [2004] EWHC 1985 (Ch), [2005] 1 BCLC 175.

[778] *Re Posgate and Denby (Agencies) Ltd* [1987] BCLC 8 at p 14 per Hoffmann J; *Re Saul D Harrison and Sons plc* [1995] 1 BCLC 14 at pp 19–20 per Hoffmann LJ. In his final pronouncement on the subject, Lord Hoffmann regretted introducing the term, which he thought had led to misunderstanding (*O'Neill v Phillips* [1999] 1 WLR 1092 at p 1102). However, previous misunderstanding should not prevent the term, for which there is no convenient alternative, being used correctly now and in the future (*Fexuto Pty Ltd v Bosnjak Holdings Pty Ltd* [2001] NSWCA 97, 37 ACSR 672, at [421]).

[779] *Fisher v Cadman* [2005] EWHC 377 (Ch), [2006] 1 BCLC 499, at [84]. Arden LJ has said that the term 'quasi-partnership' is not always helpful (*Strahan v Wilcock* [2006] EWCA Civ 13, [2006] 2 BCLC 555, at [17]). In New South Wales, Spigelman CJ has said that it is 'often misleading' and preferred the phrase 'a majority-controlled business requiring mutual cooperation and a level of trust' (*MMAL Rentals Pty Ltd v Bruning* [2004] NSWCA 451, 63 NSWLR 167, at [71]).

[780] See 8.382–8.397.

[781] See 8.346–8.350 and 8.398–8.414.

[782] [1999] 1 WLR 1092.

[783] [1998] 2 BCLC 556 at p 588.

[I]n order to give rise to an equitable constraint based on 'legitimate expectation' what is required is a personal relationship or personal dealings of some kind between the party seeking to exercise the legal right and the party seeking to restrain such exercise, such as will affect the conscience of the former.

Lord Hoffmann in *O'Neill v Phillips* went on to say:[784]

This is putting the matter in very traditional language, reflecting in the word 'conscience' the ecclesiastical origins of the long-departed Court of Chancery.... I think that one useful cross-check in a case like this is to ask whether the exercise of the power in question would be contrary to what the parties, by word or conduct, have actually agreed. Would it conflict with the promises which they appear to have exchanged?...In a quasi-partnership company, [these promises] will usually be found in the understandings between the members at the time they entered into association. But there may be later promises, by words or conduct, which it would be unfair to allow a member to ignore. Nor is it necessary that such promises should be independently enforceable as a matter of contract. A promise may be binding as a matter of justice and equity although for one reason or another (for example, because in favour of a third party) it would not be enforceable in law.

8.342 The fact that members of a company have formulated arrangements between themselves in detailed documentation, such as a shareholders' agreement, does not exclude the possibility that some other arrangements or understandings between them exist.[785]

8.343 The court will only take into account understandings between the members, not a belief by some members that others will be externally constrained to act in a particular way.[786]

8.344 The court will take account of an understanding between all the members, but not an understanding between some members and the directors, where there are other members who are not directors: the directors cannot be regarded as entering into an understanding on behalf of the non-director members.[787]

8.345 The fact that a petitioner's complaint is that members of the company have stopped conducting its affairs on a quasi-partnership basis does not mean that the court cannot apply remedies appropriate to a quasi-partnership because it is no longer one.[788]

Subjecting legal rights to equitable considerations

8.346 The normal rule of company law is that members of a company do not have to cooperate with each other. For example, at a general meeting, a member's vote may be cast in such a way as to favour the member's own interest even if that conflicts with the company's interest.[789] Likewise, the majority in a company have a statutory right to remove any director.[790] But the just and equitable clause enables the court:

to subject the exercise of legal rights to equitable considerations; considerations, that is, of a personal character arising between one individual and another, which may make it unjust, or inequitable, to insist on legal rights, or to exercise them in a particular way.[791]

---

[784] [1999] 1 WLR at p 1101.
[785] *Re a Company (No 002015 of 1996)* [1997] 2 BCLC 1.
[786] *Re Carrington Viyella plc* (1983) 1 BCC 98,951.
[787] *Re Benfield Greig Group plc* [2001] BCC 92, point not considered on appeal.
[788] *Shah v Shah* [2010] EWHC 313 (Ch), LTL 2/3/2010, at [104].
[789] *North-West Transportation Co Ltd v Beatty* (1887) 12 App Cas 589 per Sir Richard Baggallay at p 593.
[790] Companies Act 2006, s 168.
[791] Per Lord Wilberforce in *Ebrahimi v Westbourne Galleries Ltd* [1973] AC 360 at p 379.

Lord Wilberforce, at p 378, quoted with approval a passage from the judgment of Smith J **8.347**
in *Re Wondoflex Textiles Ltd*[792] including the following words:

> Acts which, in law, are a valid exercise of powers conferred by the articles may nevertheless
> be entirely outside what can fairly be regarded as having been in the contemplation of the
> parties when they became members of the company; and in such cases the fact that what has
> been done is not in excess of power will not necessarily be an answer to a claim for winding
> up. Indeed it may be said that one purpose of [the just and equitable provision] is to enable
> the court to relieve a party from his bargain in such cases.

If the articles specifically provide a procedure to deal with a breakdown of the business **8.348**
relationship in the company or the removal of the petitioner from management (typically by providing for the petitioner to be bought out at a fair price), it is not just and
equitable to wind up the company if the petitioner unjustifiably refuses to follow that
procedure.[793] But it may be unjust and inequitable to insist that the petitioner must be
confined to following that procedure.[794] In *Virdi v Abbey Leisure Ltd*[795] Balcombe LJ
said, at p 350:

> The House of Lords in *Ebrahimi v Westbourne Galleries Ltd* [1973] AC 360, made it clear that
> on a petition for the winding up of a company on just and equitable grounds, the legal rights
> and obligations conferred or imposed on shareholders by the constitution of the company
> may be subjected to equitable considerations. If in the present case it may be equitable to
> ignore the provisions of the company's constitution which prima facie entitle the directors
> to carry on the business of the company after the sale of [what the petitioner alleged was the
> only business the company was formed to carry on], I do not see why it would not be equally
> equitable, if this had been a case where [the petitioner] was bound by [a provision of the
> company's articles] to sell his shares to the majority at whatever price the accountant might
> fix, to ignore those provisions also.

It is the members' legitimate expectations which the court takes into account, not its **8.349**
own view of what would be fair. In *Re J E Cade and Son Ltd*[796] Warner J commented
at p 227 on the passage just quoted from Balcombe LJ's judgment in *Virdi v Abbey
Leisure Ltd*:

> What [Balcombe LJ] said…was based on the fact that in the *Westbourne Galleries* case
> the House of Lords had held that, on a petition for winding up on the just and equitable
> ground, equitable considerations might override the legal rights and obligations conferred
> or imposed on the shareholders by the constitution of the company, including of course its
> articles. Balcombe LJ did not say, and cannot be taken to have meant to say, that, where such
> equitable considerations arise from agreements or understandings between the sharehold-
> ers dehors the constitution of the company, the court is free to superimpose on the rights,
> expectations and obligations springing from those agreements or understandings further
> rights and obligations arising from its own concept of fairness. There can in my judgment be
> no such third tier of rights and obligations. The court, exercising its jurisdiction to wind up
> a company on the just and equitable ground…, has a very wide discretion, but it does not
> sit under a palm tree.

---

[792] [1951] VLR 458 at p 467.
[793] See *Re a Company (No 004377 of 1986)* [1987] 1 WLR 102.
[794] *Virdi v Abbey Leisure* Ltd [1990] BCLC 342.
[795] [1990] BCLC 342.
[796] [1992] BCLC 213.

Principal types of case

8.350 If a company is a quasi-partnership company, it may be just and equitable to order its compulsory liquidation on a contributory's petition if:

(a) There is a legitimate expectation that the company would be conducted on the basis of a personal business relationship between members involving mutual confidence and that relationship has irretrievably broken down.[797] The leading case is *Re Yenidje Tobacco Co Ltd*.[798]

(b) The petitioner had a legitimate expectation of participating in managing the company while a member of it but has been unjustifiably excluded from its management.[799] The leading case is *Ebrahimi v Westbourne Galleries Ltd*.[800]

(c) Despite what is said in the objects clause of the constitution, there was an understanding that the company would engage in one venture only, which venture has now been completed or abandoned.[801]

(d) The petitioner has been denied pre-emption rights.[802]

(e) There has been disregard of the heir of a member.[803]

In many of these cases, one or more of the other factors listed in 8.303–8.338 as justifying winding up are also present. For example, in *Re National Drive-In Theatres Ltd*,[804] a winding-up order was justified both by the breakdown of cooperation between the two factions in the company and the lack of probity shown in the management of the company by the faction with de facto control.

The petitioner's contribution to the situation

8.352 The court may regard the petitioner's own responsibility for the situation as a particularly important factor against making a winding-up order in cases of this type.[805]

No right to a no-fault winding up

8.353 The fact that a company is a quasi-partnership company does not give a member a right to have the company wound up at will: it must be just and equitable to order the winding up.[806] This may be contrasted with the position in partnership law, where a partnership that is not for a fixed term (a partnership at will) may be brought to an end at any time by notice given by any of the partners to the others.[807]

---

[797] See 8.382–8.397.

[798] [1916] 2 Ch 426.

[799] See 8.398–8.411.

[800] [1973] AC 360.

[801] *Virdi v Re Abbey Leisure Ltd* [1990] BCLC 342; *Bernhardt v Beau Rivage Pty Ltd* (1989) 15 ACLR 160 (see 8.412).

[802] See 8.413.

[803] See 8.414.

[804] [1954] 2 DLR 55.

[805] See 8.248–8.257.

[806] *Western Quebec Investment Ltd v J G Bisson Construction and Engineering Ltd* [1972] Que SC 331; *Kok Fook Sang v Juta Vila (M) Sdn Bhd* [1996] 2 MLJ 666. See 8.153.

[807] Partnership Act 1890, ss 26(1) and 32(c), codifying the rule stated by Parke J in *Heath v Sansom* (1832) 4 B & Ad 172 at p 175; *Lawfund Australia Pty Ltd v Lawfund Leasing Pty Ltd* [2008] NSWSC 144, 66 ACSR 1.

History

The earlier view, taken in the context of cases involving irretrievable breakdown of business **8.354** relationship, was that if a private company was 'in substance…a partnership' then it would be just and equitable to order it to be wound up in circumstances which would justify the dissolution of a partnership. This view was expressed in *Re Yenidje Tobacco Co Ltd*[808] by Lord Cozens-Hardy MR at p 432 and by Warrington LJ at p 434. It was stated as a rule in several succeeding cases, for example, *Re Davis and Collett Ltd*;[809] *Re Wondoflex Textiles Pty Ltd*;[810] *Re National Drive-In Theatres Ltd*;[811] *Re R C Young Insurance Ltd*;[812] *Re Expanded Plugs Ltd*.[813] It is sometimes known as the 'partnership analogy'.[814]

In *Ebrahimi v Westbourne Galleries Ltd*[815] the law was substantially developed. Lord **8.355** Wilberforce said, at p 379, that he thought the courts in earlier cases might be criticized for being 'too timorous in giving [the words "just and equitable"] full force'. It is not always easy to align the previous cases with *Ebrahimi v Westbourne Galleries Ltd*. The Law Lords disapproved of earlier suggestions that there could not be a situation of injustice and inequity in a company where members were merely insisting on their legal rights. For example, *Re Cuthbert Cooper and Sons Ltd*[816] 'should no longer be regarded as of authority'.[817] Lord Wilberforce, at p 377, disagreed with the statement of Plowman J in *Re Expanded Plugs Ltd*[818] that a contributory petitioning under the just and equitable clause could not complain of acts done in accordance with the articles unless they were not done bona fide in the interests of the company.[819]

Lord Wilberforce pointed out, at pp 379–80, that although the idea that it is just and equit- **8.356** able to wind up a company where probity, good faith and mutual confidence are absent is taken from partnership law, it must be adapted and applied in the context of company law, for companies are wound up in accordance with company law, not partnership law. Thus it cannot be expected that there will be a precise analogy between partnership dissolution and company winding up.

Courts in Australia have adopted and developed the reasoning in *Ebrahimi v Westbourne* **8.357** *Galleries Ltd*, but in Canada, though the case is often cited, courts have been slow to depart from the more restrictive view stated by the Ontario Court of Appeal in *Re R C Young Insurance Ltd*,[820] in which a winding-up order was refused.[821] However, a wider

---

[808] [1916] 2 Ch 426.
[809] [1935] Ch 693 at p 701.
[810] [1951] VLR 458 at p 465.
[811] [1954] 2 DLR 55 at p 63.
[812] [1955] 3 DLR 571 at p 573.
[813] [1966] 1 WLR 514 at p 519.
[814] D Huberman, 'Compulsory winding up—the "just and equitable" rule' (1966–7) 5 Alta L Rev 135.
[815] [1973] AC 360.
[816] [1937] Ch 392.
[817] Per Lord Wilberforce in *Ebrahimi v Westbourne Galleries Ltd* [1973] AC 360 at p 377, see also per Lord Cross of Chelsea at pp 384–5.
[818] [1966] 1 WLR 514 at p 523.
[819] The same view had been taken in *Mitha v Mitha* [1967] EA 575 and by Lord Fraser in *Lewis v Haas* 1971 SLT 57.
[820] [1955] 3 DLR 571.
[821] See, for example, *Re Pre-Delco Machine and Tool Ltd* (1973) 36 DLR (3d) 50, in which a winding-up order was made, and *Re Grimm's Foods Ltd* (1979) 99 DLR (3d) 377, in which winding up was not ordered.

view was urged by the Ontario Court of Appeal in *Re Rogers and Agincourt Holdings Ltd.*[822]

Literature

8.358 'Winding up of "family" companies' (1937) 71 ILT & SJ 1.

M R Chesterman, 'The "just and equitable" winding up of small private companies' (1973) 36 MLR 129.

L H Leigh, 'Just and equitable winding up' (1972) 88 LQR 468.

K Polack, 'Companies—winding up on the just and equitable ground' [1972A] CLJ 225.

D D Prentice, 'Winding up on the just and equitable ground: the partnership analogy' (1973) 89 LQR 107.

Determining whether a Company is a Quasi-Partnership Company

Partnership analogy

8.359 The idea that in relation to some companies, called 'quasi-partnership companies', it is just and equitable to take into consideration the legitimate expectations of members about how the company will be run, even though those expectations are not expressed in the company's constitution or the Companies Acts, developed from cases in which it was considered just and equitable to wind up a company in circumstances which would justify the dissolution of a partnership. It was considered appropriate to apply this partnership analogy to a company if, in the words of Lord Cozens-Hardy MR in *Re Yenidje Tobacco Co Ltd*,[823] 'in substance it is a partnership in the form or the guise of a private company'. This will clearly be so if the company was incorporated to carry on the business of a pre-existing partnership and the members of the company are the members of the former partnership.[824] A joint-venture company may be a partnership in corporate form.[825] At the other extreme, offering a company's shares to the general public will show that it is not a quasi-partnership.[826] In *Re Kwong On Co Ltd*,[827] the company had originally carried on business as a partnership but had too many members to be legal. When it registered as a company, several of the members could not be traced because of wartime conditions and their shares were allotted to one individual. When the winding-up petition was presented, the company had 14 members and seven directors and was held not to be a quasi-partnership company.

8.360 It is not necessary that a company should have been a quasi-partnership company from its formation. It is sufficient if it has become one by the time that events occurred which are claimed to be wrongful because the company was a quasi-partnership.[828]

---

[822] (1976) 74 DLR (3d) 152. See *Re Jordan and McKenzie* (1980) 117 DLR (3d) 751 and *DiRisio v DeLorenzo* (1981) 38 CBR NS 154 at p 160; and in *Re Hillcrest Housing Ltd* (1990) 87 Nfld & PEIR 40 in Prince Edward Island.

[823] [1916] 2 Ch 426 at p 432.

[824] As in *Strickland v Tricom Associates (1979) Ltd* (1982) 38 Nfld & PEIR 451.

[825] *Lawfund Australia Pty Ltd v Lawfund Leasing Pty Ltd* [2008] NSWSC 144, 66 ACSR 1.

[826] *Re Sydney and Whitney Pier Bus Service Ltd* [1944] 3 DLR 468; *Re Hillcrest Housing Ltd* (1998) 165 Nfld & PEIR 181.

[827] [1949] SLR 20.

[828] *Croly v Good* [2010] EWHC 1 (Ch), [2010] 2 BCLC 569, at [88].

Lord Wilberforce's factors

In *Ebrahimi v Westbourne Galleries Ltd*[829] the partnership analogy adopted in cases such **8.361**
as *Re Yenidje Tobacco Co Ltd*[830] was treated as an example of the principle that in relation
to some companies—quasi-partnership companies—it is appropriate to subject the legal
rights of the members of the company to equitable considerations. In many companies it
is not appropriate to look beyond the legal rights of members. Lord Wilberforce said, at p
379, that it was impossible, and wholly undesirable, to define the circumstances in which it
is appropriate. His Lordship went on to say:

> Certainly the fact that a company is a small one, or a private company, is not enough. There
> are very many of these where the association is a purely commercial one, of which it can
> safely be said that the basis of association is adequately and exhaustively laid down in the
> articles. The superimposition of equitable considerations requires something more, which
> typically may include one, or probably more, of the following elements: (i) an association
> formed or continued on the basis of a personal relationship, involving mutual confidence—
> this element will often be found where a pre-existing partnership has been converted into
> a limited company; (ii) an agreement, or understanding, that all, or some (for there may
> be 'sleeping' members), of the shareholders shall participate in the conduct of the business;
> (iii) restriction upon the transfer of the members' interest in the company—so that if con-
> fidence is lost, or one member is removed from management, he cannot take out his stake
> and go elsewhere.

> It is these, and analogous, factors which may bring into play the just and equitable clause.

Without the 'something more' mentioned by Lord Wilberforce there is no basis for a legiti- **8.362**
mate expectation that limits not expressed in the company's constitution will apply to the
exercise by the board and the company in general meeting of whatever powers they are given
by that constitution.[831] In a petition for the winding up of a company it is not enough to
allege without explanation that the company is a quasi-partnership company: facts must be
alleged to show that it is appropriate for the court to take account of the petitioner's legitimate expectations not expressed in the company's constitution.[832] This involves showing
the 'something more' referred to by Lord Wilberforce. It may be possible to do this without
showing all of the three 'elements' mentioned by his Lordship or, indeed, any one of them,[833]
but the three elements are the usual means of demonstrating that a quasi-partnership exists.
In relation to the third element, it does not matter that there is no restriction on transfer in
the company's constitution if in practice it would be extremely difficult for the petitioner to
realize shares in the company at a fair and reasonable price.[834]

Members who do not take part in management

If a company has some members who have managed it and a minority who have not taken **8.363**
part in management, the minority shareholders cannot be ignored in determining whether

---

[829] [1973] AC 360.

[830] [1916] 2 Ch 426.

[831] *Re Saul D Harrison and Sons plc* [1995] 1 BCLC 14 per Hoffmann LJ at p 20; *RCB v Thai Asia Fund Ltd* 1996 CILR 9.

[832] *Re a Company (No 007936 of 1994)* [1995] BCC 705.

[833] *Tien Ik Enterprises Sdn Bhd v Woodsville Sdn Bhd* [1995] 1 MLJ 769. In *Loh Eng Leong v Lo Mu Sen and Sons Sdn Bhd* [2000] 5 MLJ 529 the petitioners asserted that the company was a quasi-partnership but it was found that none of the three elements was present and that the company was not a quasi-partnership.

[834] *Re Iniaga Building Supplies (S) Pte Ltd* [1994] 3 SLR 359.

it is a quasi-partnership. As Lord Wilberforce said in the passage quoted in 8.361, there may be 'sleeping' members who do not destroy the quasi-partnership nature of the company.[835] However, if it cannot be shown that the members who did not take part in management understood that the company was to be conducted by the principal shareholders on a quasi-partnership basis, the company will probably be found not to be a quasi-partnership.[836]

Equality of shareholding not required

8.364 For a company to be a quasi-partnership company it is not necessary that its members should have equal shareholdings.[837] A quasi-partnership has been recognized where the petitioner has held as little as 10 per cent of the shares compared with 90 per cent held by the controlling shareholder and his wife.[838] The proportions of shares held by the members may simply reflect their different financial resources.

Shareholders' agreements

8.365 It is not necessary for there to be a shareholders' agreement from which the court can infer that the company is a quasi-partnership company.[839] The fact that there is a shareholders' agreement between the members which expressly provides that it is not to be construed as constituting a partnership between them does not mean that the company cannot be a quasi-partnership company.[840]

Extension to different company structures

8.366 A company may be a quasi-partnership company even though members are companies rather than individuals.[841]

8.367 The concept of the quasi-partnership involves looking past the technical company structure.[842] So it can be applied to an application to wind up the holding company of two quasi-partnership companies as in *Re Norvabron Pty Ltd (No 2)*. In *Lamoureux v Golden Flooring Accessories Ltd*[843] there were three companies. Two men each held half of the shares in each of the companies and they were both directors of each company. They met daily to discuss business but in fact one man ran one company and the other ran the other two companies. It was held that the relationship between the men 'was tantamount to partnership' and it was just and equitable to wind up all three companies because of the cessation of cooperation between the two men.[844]

---

[835] As in *Re Planet Organic Ltd* [2000] 1 BCLC 366, where the 'sleeping' members held only preference shares.

[836] *Re Sharon Golf and Country Club Ltd* (1975) 20 CBR NS 159; *Re Grimm's Foods Ltd* (1979) 99 DLR (3d) 377; *Yai Yen Hon v Lim Mong Sam* [1997] 2 MLJ 190; *Re Hillcrest Housing Ltd* (1998) 165 Nfld & PEIR 181.

[837] *Re Modular Furniture Pty Ltd* (1981) 5 ACLR 463.

[838] *Richards v Lundy* [2000] 1 BCLC 376.

[839] *Re Modular Furniture Pty Ltd* (1981) 5 ACLR 463.

[840] *Re a Company (No 003028 of 1987)* [1988] BCLC 282 at pp 294–5.

[841] See, for example, *Re Pe Ben Pipelines Ltd* (1978) 7 Alta LR (2d) 174, in which the members were a public company, an individual, and a private company which was the petitioner; *Re R A Noble and Sons (Clothing) Ltd* [1983] BCLC 273; but in *Yai Yen Hon v Lim Mong Sam* [1997] 2 MLJ 190 at p 198 the Malaysian Court of Appeal said, 'We wonder how one individual shareholder can establish a personal relationship or quasi-partnership with a corporate shareholder'.

[842] *Re Norvabron Pty Ltd (No 2)* (1986) 11 ACLR 279 per Derrington J at p 295.

[843] [1991] 4 WWR 452.

[844] See 8.382–8.397.

In *Re National Drive-In Theatres Ltd*[845] the 'partnership' was between two families, one of **8.368** which held shares in the company indirectly through a family holding company. In finding that the company was a quasi-partnership company, Wilson J, at p 63, emphasized that it is the essential nature of the relationship that is important. *Re Central Realty Co (Pte) Ltd*[846] is another case in which the relationship was between families.

Non-business companies

In *Kay v Nipissing Twin Lakes Rod and Gun Club*[847] a non-business company without a **8.369** share capital, which had been formed on the basis of cooperation between, and participation of, all members in the management of the company, was treated as a quasi-partnership company.

Death of a quasi-partner

A company which has been a quasi-partnership may continue to be one after the death of a **8.370** member-director whose shares are retained by an heir,[848] but not if the heir's shares are sold to outsiders.[849] In *Murray's Judicial Factor v Thomas Murray and Sons (Ice Merchants) Ltd*[850] the court focused on the fact that the original members of the company had no expectation that an heir would take part in management as a reason for denying quasi-partnership status to the company after a founder's death. In *Fisher v Cadman* it was the fact that the heir had accepted continuance of the original legitimate extra-constitutional expectations which persuaded the court that the company continued to be a quasi-partnership.[851]

See also 8.395. **8.371**

Family company requiring mutual trust and confidence

A company which is founded to hold assets for the benefit of the founder's family, members **8.372** of which are to be directors, may be a quasi-partnership company. The inherent assumption in forming the company may be that directors will work together for the good of the family and this will impose a duty on directors to maintain mutual trust and confidence.[852]

Companies that are not quasi-partnerships

For cases in which it was decided that the petitioner did not establish that the company was **8.373** a quasi-partnership company see *Morgan v 45 Flers Avenue Pty Ltd*[853] (nearly all shares in the company held in trust for the founder members' families with no evidence of the role of the trustees in the affairs of the company or their attitude to the petition); *Keho Holdings Ltd v Noble*[854] (company originally formed by 20 persons with equal shareholdings, some of whom had left, with no understanding that all should participate in management); *Re a Company (No 003096 of 1987)*.[855]

---

[845] [1954] 2 DLR 55.
[846] [1999] 1 SLR 559.
[847] (1993) 7 BLR (2d) 225.
[848] *Fisher v Cadman* [2005] EWHC 377 (Ch), [2006] 1 BCLC 499.
[849] *Re Lo Siong Fong* [1994] 2 MLJ 72.
[850] 1992 SLT 824.
[851] See also 8.414.
[852] *Chow Kwok Chuen v Chow Kwok Chi* [2008] SGCA 37, [2008] 4 SLR 362; *Harding v Edwards* [2014] EWHC 247 (Ch), LTL 27/3/2014.
[853] (1986) 10 ACLR 692.
[854] (1987) 38 DLR (4th) 368.
[855] (1987) 4 BCC 80.

8.374   A shareholder director of a company whose service agreement includes a term requiring him or her to resign if asked to do so by the rest of the board cannot claim that the company is a quasi-partnership.[856] In *Re Warrick Howard (Aust) Pty Ltd*[857] the company was found not to be 'in effect . . . a partnership of three working partners closed in a corporate entity' to which the principles appropriate to the dissolution of partnerships should apply, because in the past, members, including the petitioner, had summarily dismissed a director-shareholder when he had been in the company only a few months.

8.375   A company with a constitution drafted on the assumption that there is *no* mutual trust and confidence between the participants and providing for each of them to have a deadlocking veto is not a quasi-partnership company.[858]

8.376   The fact that an employee of a small private company becomes a shareholder in the company does not necessarily mean that a quasi-partnership relationship exists: the shares may be no more than an incentive or reward.[859] A quasi-partnership may be formed if the employee contributes capital and guarantees the company's bank loan.[860] It is important to ask whether, if the company had been formed at the time when the employee became a shareholder, it would have been formed as a quasi-partnership company.[861] In *Strahan v Wilcock*[862] five factors were considered significant in showing that a quasi-partnership was created when an employee became a shareholder (one of only two members of the company):

(a) the significant size (5 per cent) of the shareholding;
(b) the employee contributed capital, which was paid out of previously agreed bonuses;
(c) he took management decisions and the other member ceased to do so;
(d) he was a signatory, possibly the only signatory, on the company's bank account;
(e) the arrangements were never committed to writing;
(f) he received more in dividends than in salary.

See also *Croly v Good*.[863]

8.377   In *Re Ah Yee Contractors (Pte) Ltd*[864] the company had been incorporated to take over a business previously conducted by one Boey Chun Heng as sole proprietor (and before him, by his stepfather). 30,000 shares were held by Boey and his family; 10,000 were held by the petitioner who had been general manager of the business while it was a sole proprietorship and after its incorporation. Thean J held that the company was formed for the benefit of Boey and his family and that the petitioner had been given a minority stake only as recognition of his loyal service—there was never meant to be a partnership between Boey and the petitioner. Accordingly the company was not a quasi-partnership company.

---

[856]   *Third v North East Ice and Cold Storage Co Ltd* 1997 SLT 1177.
[857]   (1982) 7 ACLR 441.
[858]   *Korogonas v Andrew* (1992) 1 Alta LR (3d) 316.
[859]   *Re Kiwitea Sawmilling Co Ltd* (1978) 1 BCR 193; *Re Graham and Technequip Ltd* (1981) 121 DLR (3d) 640; *Re D and D Holdings Ltd* [1981] 4 WWR 13; *Re John While Springs (S) Pte Ltd* [2001] 2 SLR 248.
[860]   *O'Neill v Phillips* [1999] 1 WLR 1092 at pp 1102–3.
[861]   *Strahan v Wilcock* [2006] EWCA Civ 13, [2006] 2 BCLC 555, at [21].
[862]   [2006] EWCA Civ 13, [2006] 2 BCLC 555, at [23].
[863]   [2010] EWHC 1 (Ch), [2010] 2 BCLC 569.
[864]   [1987] 2 MLJ 590.

Canadian adherence to the partnership analogy

Many recent Canadian cases have continued to express the test in the earlier terms of **8.378**
whether the company was 'a partnership in the guise of a private company'.[865]

In *Re Dunham and Apollo Tours Ltd (No 2)*[866] the company was found to be a quasi-part- **8.379**
nership company. Two men had equal shareholdings in the company and it was found that
they considered it a joint venture. In *DiRisio v DeLorenzo*[867] and *Suleiman v Saffuri*,[868] the
company was found to be a partnership in the guise of a private company.

However, in *Re Humber Valley Broadcasting Co Ltd*,[869] Mifflin CJ said, at p 237, that it is the **8.380**
presence of a close relationship between the parties which would make it unjust or inequitable to insist on legal rights or the exercise of them in a particular way, and it is unnecessary
to consider whether there is in substance a partnership, though in the case before him, his
Lordship found that 'One could almost say that [the members of the company] are partners
carrying on business under the cloak of incorporation'.[870]

In *Re Hillcrest Housing Ltd*[871] MacDonald CJTD said, at pp 202–3: **8.381**

> In summary, the following elements have been found to exist in the case of companies not
> found to be partnerships in the guise of a corporation:
>
> (1) a lack of any previous business association between members of the corporation;
> (2) the company not having existed previously as a partnership;
> (3) where the shareholders are sophisticated people and know the difference between cor-
>   porate and partnership structure;
> (4) the lack of a shareholders' agreement that might provide evidence of an expression of a
>   partnership;
> (5) where the petitioner held a minority position from the outset of the company's business;
> (6) where the business was set up to be used for tax purposes or for financial protection;
> (7) where the present owners of the shares are not the original shareholders;
> (8) where there are many shareholders;
> (9) situations where there is nothing to show that the persons involved in the company, or
>   the original petitioners, understood that the acquisition of shares would subject them
>   to the law of partnership;
> (10) where there is an agreement establishing that the corporation was to be treated as a
>   separate entity;
> (11) situations where there is no equality of control among the principal shareholders of the
>   corporations;
> (12) situations where there were obvious reasons for the formation of a corporation in con-
>   trast to a partnership, ie the principals lacked mutual confidence;
> (13) where the company is in a strong financial position and is thriving.

---

[865] See, for example, *Re Marmel and Burshtein* (1973) 36 DLR (3d) 745; *Re Sharon Golf and Country Club Ltd* (1975) 20 CBR NS 159; *Re Levine Developments (Israel) Ltd* (1978) 5 BLR 164; *Re Grimm's Foods Ltd* (1979) 99 DLR (3d) 377 (in which Montgomery J quoted the section of Lord Wilberforce's speech quoted in 8.361); *B Love Ltd v Bulk Steel and Salvage Ltd* (1982) 38 OR (2d) 691 and *Burnett v Tsang* (1985) 37 Alta LR (2d) 154. In all of these cases the companies were found not to be quasi-partnerships.
[866] (1978) 86 DLR (3d) 595.
[867] (1981) 38 CBR NS 154.
[868] (2004) 48 BLR (3d) 286.
[869] (1978) 19 Nfld & PEIR 230.
[870] At p 247.
[871] (1998) 165 Nfld & PEIR 181.

The above list of factors that have been used by the courts to arrive at a finding that a corporation is not in actual fact a partnership is not an exhaustive list.

Item (13) in the list is a reason for not winding up any company at all, not a reason for finding it not to be a quasi-partnership.

Cessation of Trust and Confidence

Principle

8.382 In *Symington v Symingtons' Quarries Ltd*,[872] Lord M'Laren, at p 129, referred to the principle of partnership law that 'incompatibility between the views or methods of the partners' justifies a decree of dissolution, and said that this was applicable by analogy to divisions amongst shareholders of a quasi-partnership company. In that case there was continual quarrelling 'directed . . . to points not only of substance, but to points of an absolutely trivial description'.[873]

8.383 In *Re Yenidje Tobacco Co Ltd*[874] the company had two shareholders, Mr Weinberg and Mr Rothman, who had equal votes as members and who were both directors for life. At board meetings, by the articles of the company, no casting vote could be exercised. The two were not on speaking terms. Rothman had sued Weinberg alleging fraudulent misrepresentation. Disagreement between the two over the dismissal of a factory manager had been referred to a lengthy and expensive arbitration but Rothman had refused to accept the result of that arbitration. The Court of Appeal affirmed Astbury J's decision to make a winding-up order on Weinberg's petition. Lord Cozens-Hardy MR said, at p 432:

> I think that in a case like this we are bound to say that circumstances which would justify the winding up of a partnership between these two by action are circumstances which should induce the court to exercise its jurisdiction under the just and equitable clause and to wind up the company.

8.384 The relevant circumstance was identified by his Lordship at p 430, quoting a passage from the work latterly known as *Lindley on the Law of Partnership*. In the 15th edition of that work,[875] the passage was on pp 704–5 and was as follows (omitting footnotes):

> [R]efusal to meet on matters of business, continued quarrelling, and such a state of animosity as precludes all reasonable hope of reconciliation and friendly cooperation, have been held sufficient to justify a dissolution. It is not necessary, in order to induce the court to interfere, to show personal rudeness on the part of one partner to the other, or even any gross misconduct as a partner. All that is necessary is to satisfy the court that it is impossible for the partners to place that confidence in each other which each has a right to expect, and that such impossibility has not been caused by the person seeking to take advantage of it.[876]

8.385 This is a commentary on para (d) of the Partnership Act 1890, s 35, which provides:

> On application by a partner the court may decree a dissolution of the partnership in any of the following cases:
>
> . . .

---

[872] (1905) 8 F 121.
[873] Per Lord President Dunedin at p 128.
[874] [1916] 2 Ch 426.
[875] London: Sweet & Maxwell, 1984.
[876] In *Lindley & Banks on Partnership*, 19th edn (London: Sweet & Maxwell, 2010), a slightly abbreviated version of the quotation is divided between 24-82 and 24-83.

(d) When a partner, other than the partner suing, wilfully or persistently commits a breach of the partnership agreement, or otherwise so conducts himself in matters relating to the partnership business that it is not reasonably practicable for the other partner or partners to carry on the business in partnership with him.

The same passage from *Lindley on the Law of Partnership* was applied in *Re Bondi Better* **8.386** *Bananas Ltd*[877] in a case in which the Ontario Court of Appeal described the two owners of the company as 'mutually openly hostile, mistrustful and abusive'.[878]

Impropriety not required

In many cases where there has been a breakdown of business relationship between a major- **8.387** ity and a minority in a company there has also been a lack of probity in the conduct of the company by the majority, which would be in itself a reason for ordering winding up whether or not the company was a quasi-partnership company.[879] But, in order to show that cessation of trust and confidence justifies winding up, it is not necessary to show that the breakdown was caused by fraud or actual wrongdoing[880] or by lack of good faith, want of probity or other improper conduct.[881]

Unilateral loss of confidence

It is not necessary for the loss of confidence to be mutual: in *Belman v Belman*[882] one of two **8.388** owners of a company petitioned, saying she had lost confidence in the other, but the other claimed that as he had not lost confidence in her there was no justification for winding up the company. However, as Spence J said, at p 73:

> Obviously, if a party opposed to a winding up could defend on the basis that the loss of confidence was only on the part of the other party seeking the winding up, that could render the remedy useless.

The petitioner's loss of confidence is a sufficient reason for winding up, provided the court **8.389** is satisfied that the loss of confidence is justified. In *Belman v Belman* Mr and Mrs Belman between them owned all the shares in two companies, which had been set up by Mrs Belman and depended on her talents. Mr and Mrs Belman had had marital difficulties and had agreed to separate, but continue to work together. Mr Belman was then informed that Mrs Belman was having an affair with a married man, the informant being that man's wife. Mrs Belman denied the affair, but Mr Belman denounced her, declared that he could no longer work with her—indeed he did not wish to see her again—and broke off nego-tiations for a financial settlement in the break-up of their marriage. However, he claimed that he later forgave her and was willing to continue to work with her. He then petitioned for divorce and Mrs Belman petitioned that it was just and equitable that the company be wound up (though she sought alternative relief available under the Canadian legislation). The court heard that after a period of great difficulty the two were working together in the

---

[877] [1952] 1 DLR 277 at p 282.
[878] At p 280. See also *Re Purvis Fisheries Ltd* [1955] 1 DLR 93; *Re Cappuccitti Potato Co Ltd* (1972) 17 CBR (NS) 213; *Re Rogers and Agincourt Holdings Ltd* (1976) 74 DLR (3d) 152 at p 159.
[879] See 7.12; *Re National Drive-In Theatres Ltd* [1954] 2 DLR 55; *Strickland v Tricom Associates (1979) Ltd* (1982) 38 Nfld & PEIR 451; *Mammone v Doralin Investments Ltd* (1985) 54 CBR NS 171; *Stapp v Surge Holdings Pty Ltd* (1999) 31 ACSR 35.
[880] *Re Welport Investments Ltd* (1985) 31 BLR 232 at p 247.
[881] *Belman v Belman* (1995) 26 OR (3d) 56.
[882] (1995) 26 OR (3d) 56.

business, but concluded that this was only a temporary truce anticipating the hearing of the petitions, that Mrs Belman had no confidence in being able to work satisfactorily with Mr Belman and that her lack of confidence was not unfounded. The fact that someone else might have accepted Mr Belman's expressions of forgiveness did not mean that Mrs Belman was being unreasonable in not accepting. It was just and equitable to wind up the company, but, using the powers available to Canadian courts to order alternative relief, the court ordered Mrs Belman to buy out Mr Belman's interest.

8.390 If it is unreasonable of the petitioner not to agree to fellow members' suggestions of ways to work together, winding up will be refused.[883] Typically a finding of unreasonable refusal to be reconciled will be coupled with a finding that the petitioner contributed to the breakdown.

Examples

8.391 In *Morton v Asper*[884] Morse J described the situation in companies run by the partnership of Messrs Asper, Epstein and Morton in the following words:[885]

> I have no doubt whatever that the affairs of Ventures and of Global [a company operating a television station] are effectively deadlocked. There is a complete lack of trust and confidence between Mr Asper and CanWest [a company controlled by Asper] on the one hand and Messrs Morton and Epstein on the other. The atmosphere at Global and Ventures board meetings is very unpleasant and unproductive. Meetings are taped because neither side trusts the other to produce accurate minutes, and lawyers are in attendance. Both Mr Morton and Mr Epstein have indicated that they do not trust Mr Asper. Mr Epstein has stated that Mr Asper has lied, and Mr Morton has gone so far as to make disparaging remarks in the business community and to friends with respect to Mr Asper's sobriety, veracity and reliability as a businessman. For a number of years the CanWest and Morton/Epstein groups have been unable to agree upon the election of independent directors for Global, a requirement of the [regulator], and the so-called independent directors continue in office even though CanWest has lost confidence in them. Nor have the two groups been able to agree on the appointment of auditors and the approval of financial statements or on the holding of annual meetings.

8.392 In *Re Pre-Delco Machine and Tool Ltd*,[886] which was decided after but without reference to *Ebrahimi v Westbourne Galleries Ltd*,[887] the applicant for winding up held 49 per cent of the company's issued common shares and was a director of the company; the company's only other director, Harold Schoenhardt, held the remaining shares. The company had been formed to acquire Mr Schoenhardt's business with cash put up by the applicant. Both men worked in the business: Mr Schoenhardt as general manager, the applicant in charge of sales and estimating. The company got into financial difficulties. Mr Schoenhardt refused to discuss these difficulties with the applicant and dismissed him from his employment with the company. The result was described by Henry J as 'a complete breakdown of relations between the two partner-shareholders' and winding up was ordered.[888]

---

[883] *Guerinoni v Argyle Concrete and Quarry Supplies Pty Ltd* (1999) 34 ACSR 469; *Belgiorno-Zegna v Exben Pty Ltd* (2000) 35 ACSR 305.

[884] (1989) 62 Man R (2d) 1.

[885] At p 25.

[886] (1973) 36 DLR (3d) 50.

[887] [1973] AC 360.

[888] For other examples of breakdown of business relationships see *Re Hughes and Co* [1911] 1 Ch 342 (a limited partnership wound up as an unregistered company): *Re Timbers Ltd* (1917) 35 DLR 431; *Re American Pioneer Leather Co Ltd* [1918] 1 Ch 556; *Re Mataia Ltd* [1921] NZLR 807 (discussed in 8.282); *Re Citizen's*

Deadlock

Breakdown of the business relationship in a quasi-partnership company manifested by **8.393** refusal to cooperate in managing the company (at least in relation to developing business policy) is often described as a 'deadlock'. In several of the cases it has been observed that, despite the breakdown of the business relationship, decisions can still be carried by one party which has more votes, or more directors, or can exercise a casting vote, or has some other advantage under the company's constitution or the Companies Acts. Sometimes it is doubted whether it is correct to describe such a situation as a 'deadlock': see, for example, *Re White Castle Inn Ltd*,[889] in which Smily J described the company's situation as 'to all intents and purposes' and 'in substance' a deadlock. In principle, if it is still possible for decisions to be taken, the company could be allowed to continue in operation with one party continually overruling the other.[890] It is a characteristic of a quasi-partnership company that the court finds it unjust and inequitable that the petitioner should have to submit to the majority's exercise of its legal rights. If it is not appropriate to subject the exercise of legal rights to equitable considerations it may be said that there is deadlock only when decision-making in a company fails because two opposing parties who have exactly equal power refuse to agree,[891] and then the court may be content to allow one party to use any means under the company's constitution (casting votes, right to dismiss directors, court-summoned meetings) to carry on the company's business without the cooperation of the other party.[892] In a case involving a quasi-partnership company the situation may be described as a deadlock even if one of these procedures could be used to make decisions.[893]

Other means of dispute resolution

The nature of the quarrel is a factor to be considered. If the quarrel is of a type which it is **8.394** just and equitable to leave to be solved by the company's internal procedures, winding up is not justified.[894] It may be just and equitable to leave the quarrel to be solved by other

---

Coal and Forwarding Co Ltd [1927] 4 DLR 275; *Re White Castle Inn Ltd* [1946] OWN 773; *Bonar v Toth* [1957] OWN 268; *Re Modern Retreading Co Ltd* [1962] EA 57; *Re Medipharm Publications (Nigeria) Ltd* 1970 (2) ALR Comm 287; *Re XL Petroleum Pty Ltd* [1971] VR 560; *Re North End Motels (Huntly) Ltd* [1976] 1 NZLR 446; *Re Dunham and Apollo Tours Ltd (No 2)* (1978) 86 DLR (3d) 595; *Re Pe Ben Pipelines Ltd* (1978) 7 Alta LR (2d) 174; *Re Johnson and W S Johnson and Sons Ltd* (1979) 95 DLR (3d) 495; *DiRisio v DeLorenzo* (1981) 38 CBR NS 154; *Strickland v Tricom Associates (1979) Ltd* (1982) 38 Nfld & PEIR 451; *Re Cravo Equipment Ltd, ex parte Cramaro* (1982) 44 CBR NS 208; *Re R A Noble and Sons (Clothing) Ltd* [1983] BCLC 273; *Kapeluck v Pro Industries Ltd* (1983) 25 Sask R 58; *Re Dalkeith Investments Pty Ltd* (1984) 9 ACLR 247; *Upton v Weimann* (1985) 61 AR 16; *Re Vehicle Buildings and Insulations Ltd* [1986] ILRM 239; *Re Norvabron Pty Ltd (No 2)* (1986) 11 ACLR 279; *Vujnovich v Vujnovich* [1990] BCLC 227; *Re Inter-Builders Development Pte Ltd* [1991] 3 MLJ 259; *Lamoureux v Golden Flooring Accessories Ltd* [1991] 4 WWR 452; *Hurler v MLE Industries Ltd* (1991) 122 AR 358; *Chua Kien How v Goodwealth Trading Pte Ltd* [1992] 2 SLR 296; *Jesner v Jarrad Properties Ltd* 1993 SC 34; *Clarfield v Manley* (1993) 14 BLR (2d) 295; *Tien Ik Enterprises Sdn Bhd v Woodsville Sdn Bhd* [1995] 1 MLJ 769; *Mroz v Shuttleworth* (1996) 30 OR (3d) 205; *Lawfund Australia Pty Ltd v Lawfund Leasing Pty Ltd* [2008] NSWSC 144, 66 ACSR 1; *Chow Kwok Chuen v Chow Kwok Chi* [2008] SGCA 37, [2008] 4 SLR 362.

[889] [1946] OWN 773.
[890] As in *Re Furriers' Alliance Ltd* (1906) 51 SJ 172.
[891] *Re Furriers' Alliance Ltd* (1906) 51 SJ 172; *Re National Drive-In Theatres Ltd* [1954] 2 DLR 55.
[892] *Re Furriers' Alliance Ltd* (1906) 51 SJ 172.
[893] *Re Dunham and Apollo Tours Ltd (No 2)* (1978) 86 DLR (3d) 595 at p 600.
[894] *Re Grimm's Foods Ltd* (1979) 99 DLR (3d) 377, in which there was a battle for control of the company which was won by one faction without illegality or lack of probity; *Re Jordan and McKenzie* (1980) 117 DLR (3d) 751, in which the petitioner was said to have over-reacted to trivial incidents.

legal proceedings, as in *Re Balfour Fashions Ltd*,[895] in which the only dispute concerned the failure by the applicant for winding up to carry out a contract to purchase the shares of the other members: no winding-up order was made and the matter was left to be dealt with in a claim for specific performance of the contract.

Death of a quasi-partner

8.395 It may be just and equitable to order the winding up of a company which was founded as a quasi-partnership company if the family of a deceased founder member refuse to work with the remaining founder member.[896]

Extension of the concept of breakdown of business relationship to non-business companies

8.396 In *Kay v Nipissing Twin Lakes Rod and Gun Club*[897] it was accepted that the concept of a breakdown of the business relationship between the members of a quasi-partnership company could be extended to a breakdown of the relationship between the members of a non-business company without a share capital which had been formed on the basis of cooperation between, and participation of, all members in the management of the company.

Petitioner's contribution to the situation

8.397 In cases on breakdown of business relationship the court often has to consider whether to refuse relief because of the petitioner's own actions.[898]

Exclusion from Management

Principle

8.398 It is just and equitable to order the compulsory liquidation of a quasi-partnership company on a contributory's petition if the petitioner has been unjustifiably excluded from management of the company contrary to a legitimate expectation of participating in that management.[899] These cases are sometimes called 'expulsion' cases. Lord Hoffmann has referred to:

> the standard case in which shareholders have entered into association upon the understanding that each of them who has ventured his capital will also participate in the management of the company. In such a case it will usually be considered unjust, inequitable or unfair for a majority to use their voting power to exclude a member from participation in the management without giving him the opportunity to remove his capital upon reasonable terms.[900]

8.399 There will not be injustice and inequity if there is a reasonable offer to purchase the petitioner's shares or to make some other fair arrangement.[901] There are helpful discussions of

---

[895] [1957] OWN 91.

[896] *Re Broadway Enterprise Ltd* [1972] 6 WWR 673; *Thomas v Mackay Investments Pty Ltd* (1996) 22 ACSR 294.

[897] (1993) 7 BLR (2d) 225.

[898] See 8.248–8.257.

[899] *Re Davis and Collett Ltd* [1935] Ch 693; *Re Wondoflex Textiles Pty Ltd* [1951] VLR 458; *Re Lundie Brothers Ltd* [1965] 1 WLR 1051; *Ebrahimi v Westbourne Galleries Ltd* [1973] AC 360; *Re Rogers and Agincourt Holdings Ltd* (1976) 74 DLR (3d) 152; *Re Humber Valley Broadcasting Co Ltd* (1978) 19 Nfld & PEIR 230; *Re Murph's Restaurants Ltd* [1979] ILRM 141; *Kapeluck v Pro Industries Ltd* (1983) 25 Sask R 58; *Tay Bok Choon v Tahansan Sdn Bhd* [1987] 1 WLR 413; *Re Lai Kan Co Ltd* [1988] 1 HKLR 257; *Rivers v Denton* (1992) 5 BLR (2d) 212; *Chong Choon Chai v Tan Gee Cheng* [1993] 3 SLR 1; *Harding v Edwards* [2014] EWHC 247 (Ch), LTL 27/3/2014.

[900] *O'Neill v Phillips* [1999] 1 WLR 1092 at p 1102.

[901] *O'Neill v Phillips* [1999] 1 WLR 1092 per Lord Hoffmann at p 1107; *CVC/Opportunity Equity Partners Ltd v Demarco Almeida* [2002] UKPC 16, [2002] 2 BCLC 108.

what counts as a reasonable offer to purchase a petitioner's shares in *O'Neill v Phillips* at pp 1107–8 and in *CVC/Opportunity Equity Partners Ltd v Demarco Almeida* at [36]–[41].

In *Ebrahimi v Westbourne Galleries Ltd*[902] Mr Ebrahimi and Mr Nazar had carried on business in partnership dealing in Persian and other carpets. They shared equally in management and profits. In 1958 they formed a private company carrying on the same business and were appointed its first directors. Shortly after the company's incorporation, Mr Nazar's son, George, became a director. Mr Nazar and his son between them held the majority of votes exercisable at general meetings. The company made good profits which were all distributed as directors' remuneration: no dividends were ever paid. In 1969 Mr Ebrahimi was removed from his directorship by a resolution of a general meeting under what is now the Companies Act 2006, s 168, and a provision of the company's articles. The House of Lords upheld Plowman J's decision to order the company to be wound up on Mr Ebrahimi's petition, because of his inability after his dismissal to participate in the company's management and profits. **8.400**

The fact that the petitioner has been excluded from management may be connected with a breakdown in the business relationship between the petitioner and other members of the company, as in *Re Citizen's Coal and Forwarding Co Ltd*[903] and *Re Modern Retreading Co Ltd*.[904] **8.401**

Legitimate expectation

An obligation to allow the petitioner to participate in management of the company may be implied or inferred from the conduct of the parties.[905] It is not necessary for the members to have the kind of relationship of trust and confidence characteristic of the cases discussed in 8.382–8.397.[906] **8.402**

In *Re Chetal Enterprises Ltd*[907] the applicant for winding up could not rely on exclusion from management because he failed to persuade the court that there was an understanding that he should participate in the conduct of the business. Presumably the same applied in *Scott v Northland Beverages (1956) Ltd*.[908] **8.403**

In *Three Point Oils Ltd v Glencrest Energy Ltd*[909] an application to wind up a company was made by companies which were minority shareholders. Their owner had been a director of (but did not himself hold shares in) the company sought to be wound up, but had resigned after disagreements with other directors. The remaining directors had offered to appoint another representative of his companies to the board. The court said that the company's initial business plan did not provide evidence of a legitimate expectation that this man would participate in the management of the company (which it thought was not a quasi-partnership anyway) and it refused to characterize what had happened as exclusion from management in contravention of legitimate expectations. **8.404**

---

[902] [1973] AC 360.
[903] [1927] 4 DLR 275.
[904] [1962] EA 57.
[905] *Tay Bok Choon v Tahansan Sdn Bhd* [1987] 1 WLR 413.
[906] *Mopeke Pty Ltd v Airport Fine Foods Pty Ltd* [2007] NSWSC 153, 61 ACSR 395.
[907] (1973) 39 DLR (3d) 116.
[908] (1959) 31 WWR NS 287.
[909] (1997) 200 AR 184.

8.405 In *Gammack v Mitchells (Fraserburgh) Ltd*[910] the petitioners were not allowed to rely on exclusion from management because they had never been involved in the day-to-day running of the company and their expectation was only to be appointed directors without executive positions in the company.

8.406 In *Re a Company (No 007936 of 1994)*[911] it was alleged that a man who had been a shareholder in and managing director of a company had a legitimate expectation of participating in its management. He had transferred all his shares to trustees and ceased to be a member of the company but continued as managing director until he was summarily dismissed. It was held that on ceasing to be a member he could no longer have legitimate expectations which the trustees could rely on in their petition to wind up the company.

8.407 In *Dosike Pty Ltd v Johnson*[912] it was found that the company had been set up to provide a tax-efficient channel for the earnings of partners in a firm of solicitors. All the partners were directors of the company. When one of them left the partnership, the fact that the company ceased to remunerate him as a director was in accordance with the understandings on which the company had been founded and could not justify winding up.

Resignation

8.408 In *Re Iniaga Building Supplies (S) Pte Ltd*[913] the petitioners had fallen out with their fellow directors but, rather than wait to be dismissed, they had resigned their directorships, set up their own rival business and agreed to sell their shares to another member of the company: it was held that this did not amount to exclusion of them from management justifying winding up. The real complaint of the petitioners was that the proposed buyer had reneged on the agreement so that they were unable to realize their investment in the company, but this was also not a sufficient reason for winding up the company.

Justified removal

8.409 Winding up of a company will not be ordered if the petitioner's exclusion from management is justified by the petitioner's own misconduct.[914]

8.410 In *Re Jordan and McKenzie*[915] the applicant's exclusion from management was held to be justifiable because he walked off the job unjustifiably at a crucial time. This was one of many reasons for refusing to make a winding-up order in the case. By contrast, in *Strickland v Tricom Associates (1979) Ltd*,[916] although the dismissal of the petitioner was justified by his failure to pull his weight and failure to earn his salary by proper work habits, winding-up was justified because of the subsequent failure of the other members to hold proper meetings or provide the petitioner with information about the company and their general attitude that the petitioner had no rights in relation to the company and they could do what they liked with the company.

---

[910] 1983 SC 39.
[911] [1995] BCC 705.
[912] (1996) 16 WAR 241.
[913] [1994] 3 SLR 359.
[914] *Re a Company (No 003028 of 1987)* [1988] BCLC 282 at p 295.
[915] (1980) 117 DLR (3d) 751.
[916] (1982) 38 Nfld & PEIR 451.

Justified removal of a director has also been held not to be unfairly prejudicial conduct of   **8.411**
a company's affairs. Dismissal will not be unfair if it was caused by the director's own misconduct which threatened the company's viability.[917] A breach of an otherwise enforceable
mutual understanding is not unfair if it is to protect the company from conduct which is
detrimental to the company or its assets.[918] A director who is justifiably dismissed is not
unfairly prejudiced by more lenient treatment of a fellow director who is equally culpable.[919]

Failure of Substratum

It may be just and equitable to order the winding up of a quasi-partnership company if it was   **8.412**
originally the common understanding of its members that the company should undertake
one project only but, on completion of that project, a member who wants the company
wound up cannot get a special resolution for voluntary winding up adopted because some
members wish to go on to another project. Winding up may be ordered in these circumstances even if the restriction to one project is not provided for in the company's constitution.[920] More generally, winding up may be ordered where the majority use their powers 'to
maintain the association in circumstances to which the minority can reasonably say it did
not agree: *non haec in foedera veni*'.[921]

Pre-emption Rights

In *Re Humber Valley Broadcasting Co Ltd*[922] the petitioner had wished to buy some of a   **8.413**
departing member's shares so that his shareholding would not be diluted but had not complied with time limits set in the provisions of the company's articles relating to pre-emption
rights on sale of members' shares. The other members took all of the departing member's
shares for themselves and refused to allow the petitioner to have any. Mifflin CJ held, at
p 251, that this was an unreasonable exercise of the other shareholders' legal rights which
would make it just and equitable to order the winding up of the company.

Disregard of the Heir of a Member

If one of the principal members of a quasi-partnership company dies and the survivors   **8.414**
disregard the individual who inherits the deceased member's shares, it may be just and
equitable to order the winding up of the company.[923] In *Murray's Judicial Factor v Thomas
Murray and Sons (Ice Merchants) Ltd*[924] it was held that, after the death of a member of a
quasi-partnership company and inheritance of some of his shares by two of his brothers,
who had not previously had any financial or occupational interest in the company, the company was no longer a quasi-partnership company. But in similar circumstances (widow who

---

[917] *Woolwich v Milne* [2003] EWHC 414 (Ch), LTL 14/2/2003; *Joint v Stephens* [2007] VSC 145, 62
ACSR 309.
[918] *Grace v Biagioli* [2005] EWCA Civ 1222, [2006] 2 BCLC 70, at [64].
[919] *Mears v R Mears and Co (Holdings) Ltd* [2002] 2 BCLC 1.
[920] *Virdi v Abbey Leisure Ltd* [1990] BCLC 342; *Bernhardt v Beau Rivage Pty Ltd* (1989) 15 ACLR 160;
Chua Kien How v Goodwealth Trading Pte Ltd [1992] 2 SLR 296, in which the company was a shelf company.
[921] *O'Neill v Phillips* [1999] 1 WLR 1092 per Lord Hoffmann at pp 1101–2. The Latin may be translated
as 'I did not enter into this alliance' and is taken, with a slight adaptation, from Virgil, *The Aeneid*, book 4,
lines 336–9.
[922] (1978) 19 Nfld & PEIR 230.
[923] *Kelly v Condon* (1986) 62 Nfld & PEIR 196; *Reznick v Bilecki* (1986) 49 SaskR 232; but not in *Re
Halcyon Heights Estates Ltd* [1980–84] LRC Comm 583.
[924] 1992 SLT 824.

had not previously taken part in management inheriting shareholding of deceased member of quasi-partnership company) in *Gallelli Estate v Bill Gallelli Investments Ltd*[925] McMahon J said, at p 225, that there was 'no reason why the devolution of the shares should prevent the application of the just and equitable principle'.

Principle Underlying the Substratum and Quasi-partnership Cases

8.415 In Australia, it has been pointed out that there is a more basic concept underlying the substratum and quasi-partnership cases considered at 8.260–8.277 and 8.339–8.414, namely, that where persons have become members of a company on certain understandings and it is not possible or likely that the circumstances underlying those understandings will continue to exist then it is just and equitable to wind up the company.[926] In *Re Wondoflex Textiles Pty Ltd*,[927] Smith J said, at p 467, that in considering whether it would be just and equitable to wind up a company:

> it is necessary to consider whether the situation which has arisen is not quite outside what the parties contemplated by the arrangement they entered into, and whether what has been done is not contrary to the assumptions which were the foundation of their agreement.

8.416 In *Re Tivoli Freeholds Ltd*,[928] Menhennitt J referred, at p 468, to winding up a company which engaged in acts 'which are entirely outside what can fairly be regarded as having been within the general intention and common understanding of the members when they became members'. His Honour, at p 469, observed that this more basic concept is not confined to quasi-partnership companies, though Young J, cited at 8.415, did confine his remarks to such companies. In *Re Gerard Nouvelle Cuisine Ltd*[929] Holland J said, at p 317:

> In every reported case to which I have been referred, circumstances have arisen which could not have been in contemplation of the parties at the time the company was incorporated, and those circumstances have rendered it unjust and inequitable to bind the parties together for the future.

8.417 For an extended discussion see F H Callaway, *Winding up on the Just and Equitable Ground*.[930]

Miscellaneous Cases in which it is Just and Equitable to Wind Up a Company

8.418 The following cases, which are not in the lines of cases discussed in 8.258–8.414, are approximately in chronological order.

8.419 In *Re Great Northern Copper Mining Co of South Australia*[931] it was said to be just and equitable to wind up the company because it appeared that it was insolvent and it seemed to have suspended business for at least six months.

---

[925] [1994] 5 WWR 217.
[926] Per Young J in *Bernhardt v Beau Rivage Pty Ltd* (1989) 15 ACLR 160 at p 161.
[927] [1951] VLR 458.
[928] [1972] VR 445.
[929] (1981) 1 BCR 311.
[930] Sydney: Law Book Co, 1978.
[931] (1869) 20 LT 264.

In *Re European Life Assurance Society* [932] James V-C said, at p 128: **8.420**

> [I]t would be just and equitable to wind up a company like this assurance company if it were made out to my satisfaction that it is, not in any technical sense but, plainly and commercially insolvent—that is to say, that its assets are such, and its existing liabilities are such, as to make it reasonably certain—as to make the court feel satisfied—that the existing and probable assets would be insufficient to meet the existing liabilities.

Re European Life Assurance Society (in which insolvency was not proved) was decided at a **8.421**
time when it was not possible to take future and contingent debts into consideration when deciding whether a company should be wound up under what is now IA 1986, s 122(1)(f) or s 221(5)(b), for being unable to pay its debts. As explained at 7.259–7.263, this has since been changed so now a company that is insolvent because of future and/or contingent debts would be wound up for being unable to pay its debts rather than under the just and equitable clause. James V-C's opinion was, however, applied in *Insurance Commissioner v Associated Dominions Assurance Society Pty Ltd* [933] in which the petitioner was a public official and the petition was under legislation under which winding up could be ordered only if it was just and equitable to do so.

It was found to be just and equitable that a company should be wound up when it had issued **8.422**
partly paid bearer shares. [934] In *Re Florida Mining Co Ltd* [935] it was just and equitable to order the winding up of a company which had issued shares at a discount.

In *Re Mason Brothers Ltd* [936] a winding-up order was made because it was said that 'it is not **8.423**
unfair to describe the state of affairs as one of chaos, and entirely beyond the power of the company itself to set right in time to save the credit of the company'. [937]

In *Re Australian Joint-Stock Bank Ltd* [938] it was held to be just and equitable to wind up a **8.424**
company on a creditor's petition so that the company could take advantage of the provisions for court-sanctioned arrangements with creditors in the Joint Stock Companies Arrangement Act 1870, which applied only to companies being wound up (its provisions were extended to companies not being wound up by the Companies Act 1907, s 38; see now the Companies Act 2006, ss 895 to 901).

It is just and equitable that a company be wound up if it was formed for an illegal purpose [939] **8.425**
or if its business is illegal. [940]

In *Re A and BC Chewing Gum Ltd* [941] the petitioner had purchased a one-third shareholding **8.426**
in the company from one of its three founder members and the articles had been altered to

---

[932] (1869) LR 9 Eq 122.
[933] (1953) 89 CLR 78.
[934] *Princess of Reuss v Bos* (1871) LR 5 HL 176 as explained in *Re Capital Fire Insurance Association* (1882) 21 ChD 209 by Chitty J.
[935] (1902) 9 BCR 108.
[936] (1891) 12 LR (NSW) Eq 183.
[937] At p 190.
[938] (1897) 41 SJ 469.
[939] *Re International Securities Corporation Ltd* (1908) 24 TLR 837, affirmed (1908) 25 TLR 31.
[940] *Re Sentinel Securities plc* [1996] 1 WLR 316; *Secretary of State for Trade and Industry v Hasta International Ltd* 1998 SLT 73; *Re Market Wizard Systems (UK) Ltd* [1998] 2 BCLC 282; *Re Delfin International (SA) Ltd* [2000] 1 BCLC 71.
[941] [1975] 1 WLR 579.

provide the petitioner with the right to appoint a director of the company and to remove any director so appointed. The other two founder members, the brothers Douglas and Anthony Coakley, continued as directors of the company. They and the petitioner and the company signed and sealed a shareholders' agreement governing the future running of the company. The petitioner agreed to appoint Douglas Coakley as its director but when it attempted to remove him and appoint someone else in his place, the Coakleys claimed that the petitioner had agreed with them to abandon its contractual right to do so and they refused to recognize the change. Plowman J found that 'the relationship between [the petitioner] and the Coakleys [has been] destroyed, and I am satisfied that it cannot be restored'[942] and that 'the Coakleys have repudiated the relationship established by the shareholders' agreement and the articles'.[943] His Lordship saw the case as analogous to the expulsion cases discussed in 8.398–8.411 and made a winding-up order.

8.427   In *Sobrinho v Oakville Portuguese Canadian Club*[944] it was held to be just and equitable to order the winding up of an incorporated non-profit-making social club because of violent disagreements between different factions of members.

8.428   In *Re Dublin and Eastern Regional Tourism Organisation Ltd*[945] the company had been set up by a public body, Bord Failte Éireann, to assist it in carrying out its statutory duties. Bord Failte Éireann was a member of the company. The company was bound by its constitution to cooperate with the policies of Bord Failte Éireann and follow its directions. The company was ordered to be wound up on the petition of Bord Failte Éireann because disagreements among the members of the company and its chairman led to it failing to cooperate with Bord Failte Éireann.

8.429   In *Safarik v Ocean Fisheries Ltd*[946] it was held to be just and equitable to wind up a family company on the petition of a family member who was unjustifiably dismissed from his employment in the company (he had never been a director), leaving him without an income from the company, because of its policy of paying low dividends. Southin JA emphasized, at pp 384–5, that winding up was appropriate only because this was a family company, which the petitioner had joined because his father had assured him he would be treated fairly and equitably. At a subsequent hearing,[947] under Canadian statutory provisions which enable the court to grant alternative relief instead of winding up,[948] the court made an order which effectively required the other members to purchase the petitioner's shares.

8.430   It should be emphasized that any case decided so far can only be an illustration of the circumstances in which it is just and equitable to wind up a company. In *Re G Jeffery (Mens Store) Pty Ltd*[949] Crockett J said, at pp 199–200:

> The court has a wide discretion and if, in its view, there is present some aspect to justify its exercise then the power to wind up exists despite such aspect's not having been treated before as justification for a winding-up order.

---

[942] At p 590.
[943] At p 591.
[944] (1982) 37 OR (2d) 581.
[945] [1990] 1 IR 579.
[946] (1995) 12 BCLR (3d) 342.
[947] *Safarik v Ocean Fisheries Ltd* (1996) 17 BCLR (3d) 354.
[948] See 8.223.
[949] (1984) 9 ACLR 193.

In *Re Goodwealth Trading Pte Ltd*[950] Yong Pun How CJ said, at p 317:   **8.431**

> There is now a practically unlimited range of circumstances within which a winding-up
> order can justifiably be made on this ground. Judicial interpretation has added steadily to
> the categories of cases which may be brought under this ground, and it is inevitable that still
> more categories will be added by the courts in the future.

Alternative Unfair Prejudice and Winding-up Petition

Unfair Prejudice Petitions with Alternative Prayer for Winding Up

The Companies Act 2006, s 994, entitles a member of a company registered under the   **8.432**
Act[951] to apply to the court by petition for an order giving relief in respect of conduct of the
company's affairs which is unfairly prejudicial to the interests of its members generally or
of some part of its members (including at least the petitioner), or any actual or proposed act
which is or would be so prejudicial. If the court is satisfied that the petition is well founded,
it may make such order as it thinks fit for giving relief in respect of the matters complained
of.[952] Orders which the court may make are listed in s 996(2), which does not (unlike much
equivalent Commonwealth legislation, see 8.461–8.463) include a winding-up order.[953]
This restriction can be circumvented by drawing up a petition so as to seek relief in respect
of unfairly prejudicial conduct or, in the alternative, for winding up on the just and equitable ground in IA 1986, s 122(1)(g).[954] This practice is acknowledged, but deprecated, in
PD 49B, para 1, which says:

> Attention is drawn to the undesirability of asking as a matter of course for a winding-up
> order as an alternative to an order under the Companies Act 2006, s 994. The petition should
> not ask for a winding-up order unless that is the relief which the petitioner prefers or it is
> thought that it may be the only relief to which the petitioner is entitled.

Provision for relief of unfairly prejudicial conduct was first made in the Companies Act   **8.433**
1980, s 75,[955] which replaced the Companies Act 1948, s 210.[956] The 1980 Act implemented
recommendations made by the Jenkins committee 18 years earlier.[957]

In order to succeed with a petition for the relief of unfairly prejudicial conduct of a com-   **8.434**
pany's affairs it is not necessary to show that the circumstances justify winding up the company.[958] The Jenkins committee regarded this as dealing with the most significant defect of
the Companies Act 1948, s 210.[959]

---

[950] [1991] 2 MLJ 314.

[951] See 1.87–1.104.

[952] Companies Act 2006, s 996(1).

[953] Except under s 758 where it is shown that the company has contravened the prohibition on private
companies making public offers of their securities; see 8.519–8.521.

[954] *Todd v Todd* 2008 SLT (Sh Ct) 26 at [44]. This is also done under similar legislation in Hong
Kong (Companies Ordinance (Hong Kong), ss 168A (unfair prejudice) and 177(1)(f) (just and equitable
winding up)).

[955] Brought into force on 22 December 1980 by the Companies Act 1980 (Commencement No 2) Order
1980 (SI 1980/1785).

[956] Companies Act 1980, s 75(11). The Companies Act 1948, s 210, is discussed at 8.320–8.325.

[957] Report of the Company Law Committee (Cmnd 1749, 1962), paras 199–212.

[958] *Re a Company (No 00314 of 1989)* [1991] BCLC 154; *O'Neill v Phillips* [1999] 1 WLR 1092 per Lord
Hoffmann at pp 1099–1100.

[959] Report of the Company Law Committee (Cmnd 1749, 1962), para 201.

8.435 If it is plain and obvious that if the allegations in an unfair prejudice petition were proved, they would show unfairly prejudicial conduct of the company's affairs, for which the court would make an order under s 996 and not a winding-up order, the court will strike out an alternative prayer for winding up.[960]

8.436 If the relief sought for unfair prejudice is purchase of the petitioner's shares, it is not necessary to include an alternative prayer for winding up in the petition from the start to deal with the possibility that neither the other shareholders nor the company itself will comply with a share-purchase order. If, after a share-purchase order is made on an unfair prejudice petition, it turns out that the order will not be complied with, the petition can be amended to pray for winding up.[961] However, if an alternative prayer for winding up is included from the beginning to deal with this possibility, the alternative prayer will not be struck out unless it can be shown that it is unnecessary because there would be compliance with a share-purchase order.[962]

8.437 Although amendment of a pure unfair prejudice petition to add a prayer for winding up may be permitted after the substantive hearing of the petition,[963] in Hong Kong such an amendment has not been permitted before the substantive hearing.[964]

8.438 The Companies Act 2006, ss 994 to 997, apply in modified form to limited liability partnerships.[965] The members of an LLP may agree to exclude the right to petition for relief of unfairly prejudicial conduct of the LLP's affairs, either indefinitely or for a specified period.[966] The agreement must be unanimous and recorded in writing.[967]

8.439 The winding-up and unfair prejudice jurisdictions overlap, but are not identical.[968]

Standing to Petition

Principle

8.440 Under the Companies Act 2006, s 994(1), a petition for relief in respect of unfairly prejudicial conduct of a company's affairs may be presented by a member of the company in respect of conduct which unfairly prejudices the interests of: (a) the members generally, or (b) a section of the membership which includes at least the petitioner (in many petitions the petitioner is the only member claiming to have been prejudiced).

---

[960] *Re Copeland and Craddock Ltd* [1997] BCC 294; *Re a Company (No 004415 of 1996)* [1997] 1 BCLC 479; *Man Po Lo Paul v Cheung Kang Wah* [2007] 1 HKLRD 751. In *Re Copeland and Craddock Ltd* the prayer for winding up was not struck out; in *Re a Company (No 004415 of 1996)* and *Man Po Lo Paul v Cheung Kang Wah* it was.

[961] *Re Full Cup International Trading Ltd* [1995] BCC 682; *Re Central Coating Ltd* [2004] EWHC 3472 (Ch), LTL 7/5/2004.

[962] *Re Central Coating Ltd* [2004] EWHC 3472 (Ch), LTL 7/5/2004.

[963] *Re Full Cup International Trading Ltd* [1995] BCC 682.

[964] *Cheung Hon Wah v Cheung Kam Wah* [2005] 2 HKLRD 599.

[965] Limited Liability Partnerships (Application of Companies Act 2006) Regulations 2009 (SI 2009/1804), regs 48 and 49.

[966] Companies Act 2006, s 994(3), as applied and modified by SI 2009/1804 reg 48.

[967] Companies Act 2006, s 994(3), as applied and modified by SI 2009/1804 reg 48.

[968] *Hawkes v Cuddy* [2009] EWCA Civ 291, [2009] 2 BCLC 427, at [107], overruling *Re Guidezone Ltd* [2000] 2 BCLC 321. See 8.152.

A petition for relief in respect of unfairly prejudicial conduct of a company's affairs may be **8.441** presented by a person who joined the company in the knowledge that its affairs were being conducted in the manner complained of.[969]

Transferee or transmittee

A person to whom shares in a company have been transferred, or have been transmitted **8.442** by operation of law, but who is not a member of the company (because of not being on the register of members) is treated as a member for the purposes of the Companies Act 2006, s 994(1), and references to a member or members must be construed accordingly.[970] This means that both transferor and transferee may petition.[971]

The word 'transferred' in s 994(2) requires at least that a proper instrument of transfer **8.443** should have been executed and delivered to the transferee or the company in respect of the shares in question. It is not sufficient that there is an agreement for transfer.[972]

The phrase 'transmitted by operation of law' in s 994(2) refers to a legal process by which **8.444** the legal title passes on death or bankruptcy and does not cover the creation of an equitable interest, for example, under a trust.[973]

Nominee

A nominee shareholder, holding shares as a bare trustee, may petition under the Companies **8.445** Act 2006, s 994, because the interests of such a shareholder include the economic and contractual interests of the beneficial owners of the shares.[974]

Former member

A former member does not have standing to petition under the Companies Act 2006, **8.446** s 994.[975] In *Re a Company (No 00330 of 1991)* an injunction was granted to prevent the other members of the company operating a provision in the company's articles entitling them to compulsorily purchase the petitioner's shares and thus deprive him of his standing before the petition was heard.

Disputed standing

As with contributories' petitions for winding up,[976] the present attitude of the court is that **8.447** an unfair prejudice petition need not be dismissed because of a dispute about the petitioner's standing.[977] The question may be dealt with as a preliminary issue or the petition may be stayed to await a determination in other proceedings.[978] Formerly, dismissal was usual.[979]

---

[969] *Bermuda Cablevision Ltd v Colica Trust Co Ltd* [1998] AC 198.
[970] s 994(2).
[971] *Re McCarthy Surfacing Ltd* [2006] EWHC 832 (Ch), LTL 24/4/2006.
[972] *Re a Company (No 003160 of 1986)* [1986] BCLC 391; *Re Quickdome Ltd* [1988] BCLC 370.
[973] *Re a Company (No 007828 of 1985)* (1985) 2 BCC 98,951.
[974] *Atlasview Ltd v Brightview Ltd* [2004] EWHC 1056 (Ch), [2004] 2 BCLC 191; *Re McCarthy Surfacing Ltd* [2006] EWHC 832 (Ch), LTL 24/4/2006.
[975] *Re a Company (No 00330 of 1991)* [1991] BCLC 597.
[976] See 8.2–8.4.
[977] *Re Starlight Developers Ltd* [2007] EWHC 1660 (Ch), [2007] BCC 929, which does not mention *Alipour v Ary* [1997] 1 WLR 534.
[978] *Re Starlight Developers Ltd* [2007] EWHC 1660 (Ch), [2007] BCC 929.
[979] *Re Quickdome Ltd* [1988] BCLC 370.

Time limits

8.448 No limitation period applies to a petition for relief in respect of unfairly prejudicial conduct of a company's affairs. However, the court has a discretion whether to grant relief and it was held in *Re Grandactual Ltd*,[980] that no court would grant relief for events which happened nine years ago and which the petitioner had cooperated in.

Meaning of 'Interests of Members'

8.449 The interests of members which are claimed to be unfairly prejudiced in a petition under CA 2006, s 994, need not necessarily be interests in their capacity as members, though they must be sufficiently connected with membership.[981] It has been held, for example, that a loan by a member of a company to the company, to provide it with working capital, is an interest of the member which may be the subject of an unfair prejudice petition,[982] but a lease of farmland is not.[983] In *Gamlestaden Fastigheter AB v Baltic Partners Ltd* the company was a joint venture and the Privy Council said (at [34]) that what distinguished the case from *Re J E Cade and Son Ltd* was that the loans were made pursuant to and for the purposes of the joint venture.[984] Lord Hoffmann has said:

> As cases like *R and H Electric Ltd v Haden Bill Electrical Ltd*[985] show, the requirement that prejudice must be suffered as a member should not be too narrowly or technically construed.[986]

8.450 Disputes among members of a company about dealings in their shares cannot normally involve unfairly prejudicial conduct of the company's affairs.[987]

8.451 The rights of a member of a company are defined by the company's constitution and the Companies Acts but the word 'interests' is wider than the term 'rights'[988] and members may have different interests even if their rights as members are the same.[989]

8.452 Conduct that affects all members may be prejudicial to the interests of some of them only.[990] However, until an amendment was made by the Companies Act 1989, sch 19, para 11, the court did not have jurisdiction under what is now the Companies Act 2006, s 994, to deal with conduct that was indiscriminately prejudicial to the interests of all the members of a company.[991] It may be that the court in *Re a Company (No 00370 of 1987)* was mistaken

---

[980] [2005] EWHC 1415 (Ch), [2006] BCC 73.

[981] *Gamlestaden Fastigheter AB v Baltic Partners Ltd* [2007] UKPC 26, [2007] Bus LR 1521.

[982] *Gamlestaden Fastigheter AB v Baltic Partners Ltd.*

[983] *Re J E Cade and Son Ltd* [1992] BCLC 213; see also *Brown v Scottish Border Springs Ltd* 2002 SLT 1213.

[984] For criticism of *Re J E Cade and Son Ltd* see S Griffin, 'Defining the scope of a membership interest' (1993) 14 Co Law 64.

[985] [1995] 2 BCLC 280.

[986] *O'Neill v Phillips* [1999] 1 WLR 1092 at p 1105.

[987] *Re Unisoft Group Ltd (No 3)* [1994] 1 BCLC 609.

[988] *Re a Company (No 00477 of 1986)* [1986] BCLC 376.

[989] *Re Sam Weller and Sons Ltd* [1990] Ch 682.

[990] As in *Re Cumana Ltd* [1986] BCLC 430, in which it was known that a rights issue on apparently favourable terms could not be taken up by a minority shareholder because of his financial position and would have had the desired effect of squeezing him out of the company—see also the earlier proceedings in the same case [1985] BCLC 80.

[991] *Re a Company (No 00370 of 1987)* [1988] 1 WLR 1068; cf *Re Carrington Viyella plc* (1983) 1 BCC 98,951 at p 98,959.

in not recognizing that the conduct complained of affected different members in different ways and could have been found to have been unfairly prejudicial to some of them.[992]

In *Jaber v Science and Information Technology Ltd*[993] a number of persons claimed that they **8.453** had been wrongfully excluded from membership of a company. They could not petition under what is now s 994 in respect of that wrong because they were not members. An individual who supported them and was actually a member could not petition in respect of that wrong because it was held that a member of a company does not have an interest in the recognition of voting rights of other persons claiming to be members. Disputes about membership must be resolved by other means, for example, an application for rectification of the register of members.

Meaning of 'Unfairly Prejudicial'

In *Re Saul D Harrison and Sons plc*[994] Neill LJ said, at pp 30–1: **8.454**

> The words 'unfairly prejudicial' are general words and they should be applied flexibly to meet the circumstances of the particular case…. The conduct [being complained of] must be both prejudicial (in the sense of causing prejudice or harm to the relevant interest) and also unfairly so: conduct may be unfair without being prejudicial or prejudicial without being unfair, and it is not sufficient if the conduct satisfies only one of these tests.

The prejudice must be 'harm in a commercial sense, not in a merely emotional sense'.[995] **8.455** However, the Companies Act 2006, s 994, cannot be limited to cases in which the value of members' shareholdings has been seriously diminished or jeopardized.[996] Not receiving a full entitlement may be prejudicial.[997]

In *O'Neill v Phillips*[998] Lord Hoffmann emphasized that equitable jurisdiction must be **8.456** exercised in a principled way, saying, at p 1098:

> In [s 994] Parliament has chosen fairness as the criterion by which the court must decide whether it has jurisdiction to grant relief. It is clear…that it chose this concept to free the court from technical considerations of legal right and to confer a wide power to do what appeared just and equitable. But this does not mean that the court can do whatever the individual judge happens to think fair. The concept of fairness must be applied judicially and the content which it is given by the courts must be based upon rational principles…. Although fairness is a notion which can be applied to all kinds of activities, its content will depend upon the context in which it is being used.

It is not easy to agree with Lord Hoffmann that a court's concept of fairness should vary **8.457** from context to context, and the examples which his Lordship gave of contexts in which he asserted that concepts of fairness differ (business, family, cricket, love and war) do not seem to be relevant to the content of judicial fairness. Lord Hoffmann went on to say that the

---

[992] See *Re Sam Weller and Sons Ltd*; *McGuiness v Black* 1990 SC 21 at p 24.
[993] [1992] BCLC 864.
[994] [1995] 1 BCLC 14.
[995] Per Harman J in *Re Unisoft Group Ltd (No 3)* [1994] 1 BCLC 609 at p 611.
[996] Per Nourse J in *Re R A Noble and Sons (Clothing) Ltd* [1983] BCLC 273 at p 291; *Re Elgindata Ltd* [1991] BCLC 959.
[997] *Gowanbrae Properties Ltd* [2008] CSOH 106 at [20].
[998] [1999] 1 WLR 1092.

context in which an evaluation of the fairness of prejudicial conduct of a company's affairs must be made is that:

> a company is an association of persons for an economic purpose, usually entered into with legal advice and some degree of formality.

This:

> leads to the conclusion that a member of a company will not ordinarily be entitled to complain of unfairness unless there has been some breach of the terms on which he agreed that the affairs of the company should be conducted.

However:

> there will be cases in which equitable considerations make it unfair for those conducting the affairs of the company to rely upon their strict legal powers. Thus unfairness may consist in a breach of the rules or in using the rules in a manner which equity would regard as contrary to good faith.

8.458 In *Re Guidezone Ltd*[999] Jonathan Parker J said, at p 355, that it has been established by *O'Neill v Phillips* that:

> 'unfairness' for the purposes of [s 994] is not to be judged by reference to subjective notions of fairness, but rather by testing whether, applying established equitable principles, the majority has acted, or is proposing to act, in a manner which equity would regard as contrary to good faith.

In the Court of Session in Scotland Lord Coulsfield has expressed agreement with Jonathan Parker J's summary.[1000]

8.459 A situation which a member can get rid of immediately by exercising voting control (for example, by dismissing a director) cannot be unfairly prejudicial to that member's interests.[1001]

8.460 An infringement of a member's rights under the articles may not in itself be unfairly prejudicial.[1002] Section 994 was not intended to cover trivial or technical infringements of the articles.[1003]

Winding Up as a Statutory Oppression Remedy outside the UK

8.461 In some jurisdictions the statutory provisions under which applications can be made to the court for relief in respect of oppressive, unfairly discriminatory or unfairly prejudicial conduct of a company's affairs provide that winding up the company is one of the remedies that can be granted. See, for example:

- In Alberta, *Stech v Davies*.[1004]
- In Australia, the Corporations Act 2001, s 233(1)(a) and (2); *John J Starr (Real Estate) Pty Ltd v Robert R Andrew (A'asia) Pty Ltd*,[1005] in which Young J said[1006] that the court

---

[999] [2000] 2 BCLC 321.
[1000] *Anderson v Hogg* 2002 SC 190 at p 198.
[1001] *Re Baltic Real Estate Ltd (No 2)* [1993] BCLC 503. See also *Re Legal Costs Negotiators Ltd* [1999] 2 BCLC 171.
[1002] *Re Carrington Viyella plc* (1983) 1 BCC 98,951.
[1003] Per Hoffmann LJ in *Re Saul D Harrison and Sons plc* at p 19.
[1004] [1987] 5 WWR 563.
[1005] (1991) 6 ACSR 63.
[1006] At p 76.

should turn against winding up if there is any viable way forward; *Raymond v Cook*,[1007] in which winding up as a remedy was considered but rejected by the court; *Belgiorno-Zegna v Exben Pty Ltd*,[1008] in which it was held that there had been no unfair prejudice; *Shum Yip Properties Development Ltd v Chatswood Investment and Development Co Pty Ltd*,[1009] in which it was held that there was an overwhelming case of oppression, unfair prejudice, unfair discrimination, and action contrary to the interests of members, for which winding up was the only suitable remedy; *Nutectime International Pty Ltd v Timentel Pty Ltd*,[1010] in which it was held that there had been no oppression or unfair prejudice.

- In Canada, the Canada Business Corporations Act, s 241(3)(l). The fact that the Act also provides[1011] that oppressive or unfairly prejudicial conduct is a ground on which a winding-up application may be presented does not mean that winding up is the primary remedy for oppressive or unfairly prejudicial conduct.[1012]
- In Malaysia, *Re Kong Thai Sawmill (Miri) Sdn Bhd*.[1013]
- In Manitoba, the Corporations Act, s 234(3)(l); *Chartrand v De La Ronde*,[1014] in which a winding-up order was reversed on appeal; *Cohen v Jonco Holdings Ltd*.[1015]
- In New Zealand, the Companies Act 1993, s 174(2)(g).
- In Ontario, the Business Corporations Act, s 248; *Murphy v Phillips*,[1016] in which a winding-up order was refused.
- In Singapore, the Companies Act s 216(2)(f); *Re Great Eastern Hotel (Pte) Ltd*,[1017] in which a winding-up order was asked for but refused; *Re Gee Hoe Chan Trading Co Pte Ltd*;[1018] *Kumagai Gumi Co Ltd v Zenecon Pte Ltd*,[1019] in which a winding-up order was made; *Lim Swee Khiang v Borden Co (Pte) Ltd*,[1020] in which it was held that winding up should be ordered only if, having taken into account all the circumstances of the case, it is the best solution for all the parties involved.

In Malaysia a member of a company may present both a winding-up petition and a petition for relief of oppressive or unfairly prejudicial conduct which asks for winding up as a remedy, and both petitions may be heard together.[1021] In Singapore it has been held that proceedings for relief of oppressive or unfairly prejudicial conduct which ask for winding up as a remedy are not winding-up proceedings and cannot be commenced by a winding-up petition.[1022] **8.462**

[1007] (1998) 29 ACSR 252.
[1008] (2000) 35 ACSR 305.
[1009] [2002] NSWSC 13, 166 FLR 451.
[1010] [2011] NSWCA 257, 85 ACSR 570.
[1011] s 214(1)(a).
[1012] *Westfair Foods Ltd v Watt* (1991) 79 DLR (4th) 48.
[1013] [1978] 2 MLJ 227.
[1014] (1996) 113 Man R (2d) 12.
[1015] 2005 MBCA 48, [2005] 7 WWR 212.
[1016] (1993) 12 BLR (2d) 58.
[1017] [1989] 1 MLJ 161.
[1018] [1991] SLR 837.
[1019] [1995] 2 SLR 297.
[1020] [2006] SGCA 33, [2006] 4 SLR 745.
[1021] *Teh Chin Chuan v Chuan Hong Co* [1999] 5 MLJ 459; *Lau Man Hing v Eramara Jaya Sdn Bhd* [2007] 2 MLJ 578 at [23].
[1022] *Kuah Kok Kim v Chong Lee Leong Seng Co (Pte) Ltd* [1991] 2 MLJ 129.

8.463 In the United Kingdom, winding up is not one of the remedies for unfairly prejudicial conduct listed in the Companies Act 2006, s 996, but a petition under s 994 may include an alternative prayer for winding up by the court under IA 1986, s 124.[1023] The Law Commission recommended that winding up be added to the remedies available for unfair prejudice, subject to a requirement to obtain the court's permission to ask for it as a remedy.[1024] This recommendation was not taken up in the Companies Act 2006.

Interaction of Unfair Prejudice and Winding-up Remedies

8.464 On hearing an unfair prejudice petition which asks alternatively for winding up, unfair prejudice should be considered first, because of the wide range of remedies available under the Companies Act 2006, s 996, which are preferable to the drastic remedy of winding up.[1025]

8.465 In *Re Full Cup International Trading Ltd*[1026] the petition was under what is now s 994, but, although unfairly prejudicial conduct of the company's affairs was proved, Ferris J decided that it was not possible to devise any relief under what is now s 996 which would meet the justice of the case and be more advantageous than a winding up, and so adjourned the petition so that it could be amended to seek a winding-up order. His Lordship's refusal to grant any relief under s 996 was affirmed by the Court of Appeal.[1027]

8.466 Unfairly prejudicial conduct of a company's affairs by its directors is brought to an end by the appointment of a provisional liquidator[1028] or liquidator.[1029]

8.467 If a company is insolvent, a petitioner for relief of unfairly prejudicial conduct of its affairs must, in general, show that the petitioner's shares would have had a value but for the unfairly prejudicial conduct.[1030] If a company is ordered to be wound up because it is unable to pay its debts, the interests of creditors are entitled to consideration in priority to the interests of members.[1031]

8.468 In *Campbell v Backoffice Investments Pty Ltd*[1032] a provisional liquidator was appointed while an application for relief of unfairly prejudicial conduct of the company's affairs was pending. With the agreement of all members of the company, the provisional liquidator sold its business. It was held that, in these circumstances, an order could not be made in the unfair prejudice jurisdiction for purchase of one member's share by the other member.

[1023] See 8.432–8.439.
[1024] *Shareholder Remedies* (Law Com No 246, Cm 3769) (1997), 4.24–4.49.
[1025] *Re Norvabron Pty Ltd (No 2)* (1986) 11 ACLR 279 at p 289; see also *Re Eng Cheong Peng Kee Pte Ltd* [1998] 3 SLR 1 and *Re Eng Cheong Peng Kee Pte Ltd (No 2)* [1998] 3 SLR 61, in which a full trial was held and a share purchase order made despite the offer by those opposing the application to put the company into voluntary winding up and, when that was refused, their request for a winding-up order.
[1026] [1995] BCC 682.
[1027] Sub nom *Antoniades v Wong* [1997] 2 BCLC 419.
[1028] *Campbell v Backoffice Investments Pty Ltd* [2009] HCA 25, 238 CLR 304, at [180].
[1029] *Webb v Stanfield* [1991] 1 QdR 593 at pp 598–9.
[1030] *Maidment v Attwood* [2012] EWCA Civ 998, [2013] BCC 98, per Arden LJ at [11].
[1031] *Webb v Stanfield* [1991] 1 QdR 593 at p 599.
[1032] [2009] HCA 25, 238 CLR 304.

Procedure

Applicable Rules

Contributories' winding-up petitions

Most of the procedures described in chapters 2 and 3 do not apply to contributories' wind- **8.469**
ing-up petitions. This is because IR 1986, r 4.2(4), provides that rr 4.7–4.21B do not apply
to contributories' petitions, but instead rr 4.22–4.24 apply. However, r 4.24 provides that
the following rules apply, with the necessary modifications, to contributories' petitions:

(a) r 4.16 (notice of appearance),
(b) r 4.17 (list of appearances),
(c) r 4.20 (notice and settling of winding-up order),
(d) r 4.21 (transmission and advertisement of order),
(e) r 4.21A (expenses of voluntary arrangements).

For these purposes, a petition to wind up a company presented at the instance of a com- **8.470**
pany's voluntary arrangement supervisor or administrator is treated as a contributories'
petition.[1033] For special rules governing petitions by these officers see 10.6–10.10, 10.31–
10.34 and 10.51–10.58.

Members' unfair prejudice petitions with an alternative prayer for winding up

IR 1986 do not apply at all to an unfair prejudice petition, because it is not an insolvency **8.471**
proceeding. An unfair prejudice petition with an alternative prayer for winding up is
not a winding-up petition.[1034] Instead the Companies (Unfair Prejudice Applications)
Proceedings Rules 2009[1035] apply to all petitions presented under the Companies Act 2006,
part 30 (ss 994–999),[1036] but the procedure provided by these rules follows the procedure
for contributories' petitions for winding up.

The CPR apply to proceedings under the Companies Act 2006, part 30 (ss 994–999), with **8.472**
any necessary modifications, except so far as they are inconsistent with the Companies Act
2006 or SI 2009/2469.[1037]

Presentation of a Petition

Contributories' winding-up petitions

A contributory's petition for the compulsory liquidation of a company must be in form 4.14 **8.473**
in IR 1986, sch 4: it must specify the grounds on which it is presented and must be filed in
court with one copy for service on the company.[1038]

[1033] IR 1986, r 4.7(9).
[1034] *Re United Iron Mining Co Ltd* [1970] 1 MLJ 105.
[1035] SI 2009/2469.
[1036] SI 2009/2469, r 2(1).
[1037] SI 2009/2469, r 2(2).
[1038] IR 1986, r 4.22(1).

8.474 Despite the fact that the rules make provision for particulars of claim to be delivered,[1039] the petition itself must set out the petitioner's case:

> with clarity, substance and precision so that the respondent company knows, and the court knows, what case the company has to meet. The petition must, either in its original form or as amended, therefore contain all the material averments or, to use the words specified in r 4.22(1), 'the grounds' upon which it is based.[1040]

8.475 As a company which is sought to be wound up on a contributory's petition is almost inevitably a solvent company, it is normally in the interest of all concerned that the company should continue in business as usual. Accordingly, a contributory's petition is required by PD 49B, para 2, to state whether the petitioner consents, or objects, to an order under IA 1986, s 127, in the standard form set out in PD 49B, para 7. If the petitioner objects, the written evidence in support must contain a short statement of the petitioner's reasons for objecting. Failure to set out in a petition the petitioner's attitude to validation orders is 'quite a bad error' which may give the impression that the petition is not genuine.[1041]

8.476 If a contributory petitioner will not consent to an order in this standard form but will consent to a modified form, the petition must set out the form of order which is acceptable, and the written evidence in support must contain a short statement of the reasons for seeking the modification.[1042]

8.477 If a contributory's petition contains a statement that the petitioner consents to an anticipatory validation order, whether in the standard or a modified form, but the petitioner has a change of mind before the first hearing of the petition, the petitioner must notify the respondents. In this situation the petitioner may apply on notice to a judge for an order directing that no validation order shall be made by the registrar (or, as the case may be, that a modified order be made), but validating dispositions made without notice of the judge's order.[1043]

8.478 If a contributory's petition contains a statement that the petitioner consents to an anticipatory validation order, whether in the standard or a modified form, the registrar will without further inquiry make an order in such form at the first hearing unless an order to the contrary has been made by the judge in the meantime.[1044]

8.479 If a contributory's petition contains a statement that the petitioner objects to an anticipatory validation order in the standard form, the company may apply (in cases of urgency, without notice to the petitioner or other parties) to the judge for an order.[1045]

8.480 The provision of IR 1986 requiring verification of a winding-up petition by a statement of truth[1046] does not apply to a contributory's petition[1047] and a petition is not a statement of

---

[1039] See 8.494–8.500.

[1040] Roger Kaye QC sitting as a deputy High Court judge in *Re a Company (No 007936 of 1994)* [1995] BCC 705 at p 709.

[1041] *Re Whitchurch Insurance Consultants Ltd* [1993] BCLC 1359.

[1042] PD 49B, para 3.

[1043] PD 49B, para 4.

[1044] PD 49B, para 5.

[1045] PD 49B, para 6.

[1046] IR 1986, r 4.12.

[1047] r 4.2(4).

case,[1048] but the provisions of the CPR concerning verification of a statement of case by a statement of truth[1049] apply to winding-up petitions with any necessary modifications.[1050] Paragraph 7 of the prescribed form of contributory's petition[1051] requires 'the statement of truth … filed in support hereof' to give the same evidence of the application of Regulation (EC) No 1430/2000 (the EC Regulation) as is required by the prescribed form for petitions other than by contributories.[1052]

Members' unfair prejudice petitions with an alternative prayer for winding up

8.481 The requirement that an application under the Companies Act 2006, s 994, must be made by petition is imposed by statute and so the court has no power under the CPR to waive a failure to comply with it.[1053]

8.482 The prescribed form for an unfair prejudice petition is set out in the schedule to SI 2009/2469 and is to be used with such variations, if any, as the circumstances may require.[1054] The petition must specify the grounds on which it is presented and the nature of the relief which is sought by the petitioner.[1055] The extensive powers of the court to make orders on an unfair prejudice petition are set out in the Companies Act 2006, s 996. The relief sought must be appropriate to the conduct of which the petition complains,[1056] though it need not be directed solely towards remedying the particular things that have happened.[1057] The court is required to make the order that is appropriate at the time of the hearing.[1058]

8.483 If a winding-up order is asked for, the petition must comply with PD 49B, paras 2–7, on orders under IA 1986, s 127, sanctioning transactions by the company while the petition is pending.[1059]

8.484 The petition must state the names of persons on whom it is intended to serve the petition (known as the 'respondents'), one of whom will be the company itself.

8.485 The provisions of the CPR concerning verification of a statement of case by a statement of truth[1060] apply to unfair prejudice petitions with any necessary modifications.[1061]

8.486 An unfair prejudice petition must be delivered to the court for filing with copies for service on all the respondents (including the company itself) named in the petition.[1062]

8.487 If a petitioner wishes to claim relief in respect of unfairly prejudicial conduct of two or more companies, there must be a separate petition for each company, however much they have in common.[1063]

[1048] See 2.9.
[1049] CPR, Part 22, and PD 22.
[1050] IR 1986, r 7.51A(2).
[1051] IR 1986, sch 4, form 4.14.
[1052] See 2.234–2.237.
[1053] *Re Osea Road Camp Sites Ltd* [2004] EWHC 2437 (Ch), [2005] 1 WLR 760.
[1054] SI 2009/2469, r 3(1).
[1055] SI 2009/2469, r 3(2).
[1056] *Re J E Cade and Son Ltd* [1992] BCLC 213 at p 223.
[1057] *Re Hailey Group Ltd* [1993] BCLC 459 at p 472.
[1058] *Re Hailey Group Ltd* at p 472.
[1059] See 8.475–8.479.
[1060] CPR, Part 22 and PD 22.
[1061] SI 2009/2469, r 2(2).
[1062] SI 2009/2469, rr 3(2) and 4.
[1063] *Re a Company* [1984] BCLC 307; *Tam Shuk Yin Anny v Choi Kwok Chan* [2005] 4 HKLRD 375.

Fee and Deposit

8.488   The court fee on entering a petition, either for winding up or for relief in respect of unfairly prejudicial conduct, is £280.[1064] If winding up is asked for, a deposit for the official receiver's administration fee is required.[1065]

Fixing a Return Day

8.489   The court will fix a hearing for a day (called the 'return day') on which, unless the court otherwise directs, the petitioner and the company must attend before the registrar or district judge for directions to be given in relation to the procedure on the petition.[1066]

8.490   On the return day for a winding-up petition presented at the instance of the company's administrator or voluntary arrangement supervisor, the court may hear the petition, rather than give directions, if the court considers it just in all the circumstances.[1067]

8.491   On fixing the return day, the court returns to the petitioner sealed copies of the petition for service, endorsed with the return day and time of hearing.[1068]

Service of the Petition

Contributories' winding-up petitions

8.492   The petitioner must, at least 14 days before the return day, serve a sealed copy of the petition on the company.[1069] If a member State liquidator has been appointed in main proceedings in relation to the company, the petitioner must send a copy of the petition to him or her.[1070] Service must be effected in accordance with CPR, Part 6.[1071] A petition is a claim form for the purposes of CPR, Part 6.[1072]

Members' unfair prejudice petitions with an alternative prayer for winding up

8.493   The petitioner must, at least 14 days before the return day, serve a sealed copy of the petition on all respondents named in the petition (including the company itself).[1073] The applicable rules on service are those of CPR, Part 6.[1074]

Directions

Matters on which directions will be given

8.494   On the return day, or at any time after it, the court must give such directions as it thinks appropriate with respect to the following matters:[1075]

[1064]   Civil Proceedings Fees Order 2008 (SI 2008/1053), sch 1, fee 3.3.
[1065]   IR 1986, r 4.22(1A); see 2.254–2.256.
[1066]   IR 1986, r 4.22(2); SI 2009/2469, r 3(3).
[1067]   IR 1986, r 4.22(2)(b).
[1068]   IR 1986, r 4.22(3); SI 2009/2469, r 3(4).
[1069]   IR 1986, r 4.22(4).
[1070]   r 4.22(5).
[1071]   The provisions of the CPR apply, by IR 1986, r 7.51A(2), because the provisions of IR 1986 relating to service do not apply, see rr 4.2(4), 12A.1(2)(a) and 12A.16(2)(a).
[1072]   CPR, r 6.2(c).
[1073]   SI 2009/2469, r 4.
[1074]   SI 2009/2469, r 2(2).
[1075]   IR 1986, r 4.23(1); SI 2009/2469, r 5. For a winding-up petition presented at the instance of the company's administrator or voluntary arrangement supervisor, giving directions on the return day is optional, because the court may instead hear the petition then (IR 1986, rr 4.22(2)(b) and 4.23(1)).

(a) service of the petition, whether in connection with the venue for a further hearing, or for any other purpose (for a winding-up petition the court must consider whether any of the persons specified in IR 1986, r 4.10,[1076] should be served with a copy of the petition[1077]);

(b) whether particulars of claim and defence are to be delivered;[1078]

(c) whether, and if so by what means, the petition is to be advertised;[1079]

(d) the manner in which any evidence is to be adduced at any hearing before the judge[1080] and in particular:

    (i) the taking of evidence wholly or in part by witness statement or orally;

    (ii) the cross-examination of any persons authenticating witness statements;[1081]

    (iii) the matters to be dealt with in evidence;

(e) any other matter affecting the procedure on the petition or in connection with the hearing and disposal of the petition.

For a contributory's winding-up petition, the court must also give directions generally as **8.495** to the procedure on the petition.[1082] For an unfair prejudice petition, the court must make such orders, if any, including a stay for any period, as the court thinks fit, with a view to mediation or other form of alternative dispute resolution.[1083]

Particulars or points of claim and defence

Before the CPR, directions usually referred to 'points' of claim and defence rather than **8.496** 'particulars', adopting the terminology then used in the Commercial Court.[1084] Under the CPR, the term generally used is 'particulars of claim'[1085] and that is the term used in IR 1986, r 4.23(1)(b). However, SI 2009/2469, r 5(b), uses 'points of claim'. Particulars or points of claim must contain a concise statement of the facts on which the petitioner relies.[1086] They should be as brief as possible.[1087] They must comply with CPR, r 16.4, and PD 16.

A defence must comply with CPR, r 16.5, and PD 16. **8.497**

Particulars or points of claim and defence are statements of case[1088] and so must be verified **8.498** by a statement of truth.[1089]

[1076] See 3.46–3.47.

[1077] IR 1986, r 4.23(2).

[1078] See 8.496–8.500.

[1079] See 8.502–8.503.

[1080] See 8.501.

[1081] In SI 2009/2469, r 5, the phrase 'persons making a witness statement' is used instead of 'persons authenticating witness statements'.

[1082] IR 1986, r 4.23(1)(b).

[1083] SI 2009/2469, r 5(f).

[1084] See per Harman J in *Re Unisoft Group Ltd (No 3)* [1994] 1 BCLC 609 at p 612.

[1085] CPR, r 16.4; PD 16; Admiralty and Commercial Courts Guide, C1.

[1086] CPR, r 16.4(1)(a).

[1087] Per Harman J in *Re Unisoft Group Ltd (No 3)* at p 612; Admiralty and Commercial Courts Guide, para C1.1(a).

[1088] CPR, r 2.3(1).

[1089] CPR, r 22.1(a).

8.499 Under the procedure before the CPR it was said that points of claim were a pleading to which 'the whole practice of the High Court in relation to pleadings will apply'.[1090] Under the CPR pleadings are now known as statements of case.

8.500 A petition may be drafted in such a way that it can stand as particulars or points of claim.[1091]

Evidence

8.501 Unfairly prejudicial conduct may be proved by documentary and/or oral evidence. There is no rule that a petitioner must give oral evidence if the case can be proved by documents and/or the evidence of other parties.[1092]

Advertisement of Petition

8.502 A contributory's winding-up petition or an unfair prejudice petition is advertised only if the court directs.[1093] A contributory's winding-up petition usually relates to a solvent company whose creditors would be uninterested in appearing at the hearing of the petition but who could be unnecessarily alarmed by the announcement of a petition which they would assume was a creditor's petition on the ground of inability to pay debts.

8.503 No notification may be given of a petition to, for example, the company's creditors, unless the court has directed that it is to be advertised.[1094]

Certificate of Compliance

8.504 IR 1986, r 4.14, requiring the filing of a certificate of compliance with the rules[1095] does not apply to contributories' winding-up petitions.[1096] There is no equivalent provision for unfair prejudice petitions.

Permission to Withdraw a Petition

8.505 IR 1986, r 4.15, specifying circumstances in which a winding-up petition may be withdrawn, does not apply to contributories' petitions.[1097] The relevant rules for contributories' winding-up petitions and unfair prejudice petitions are in CPR, Part 38 (discontinuance).[1098]

Substitution of Petitioner

8.506 IR 1986, r 4.19, allowing the substitution of petitioners[1099] does not apply to contributories' petitions.[1100] There is no equivalent provision for unfair prejudice petitions.

[1090] *Re Unisoft Group Ltd (No 3)* [1994] 1 BCLC 609 at p 613.

[1091] *Re a Company (No 007936 of 1994)* [1995] BCC 705 at p 708.

[1092] *Cassegrain v Gerard Cassegrain and Co Pty Ltd* [2012] NSWSC 403 at [196].

[1093] IR 1986, r 4.23(1)(c); SI 2009/2469, r 5(c). See 8.494.

[1094] *Re a Company (No 00687 of 1991)* [1992] BCLC 133; *Re Doreen Boards Ltd* [1996] 1 BCLC 501, in which the petition was struck out after the petitioner had telephoned the company's bank, invoice factors and local Inland Revenue office to inform them of the petition; *Re a Company (No 002015 of 1996)* [1997] 2 BCLC 1.

[1095] See 3.156–3.162.

[1096] r 4.2(4).

[1097] IR 1986, r 4.2(4).

[1098] Applied to contributories' winding-up petitions by IR 1986, r 7.51A(2). Applied to unfair prejudice petitions by SI 2009/2469, r 2(2).

[1099] See 3.181–3.206.

[1100] r 4.2(4).

Notice of Appearance or Permission to be Heard

On the hearing of a contributories' winding-up petition, the rules on notice of appearance and **8.507** permission to be heard[1101] apply. There are no equivalent rules for unfair prejudice petitions.

Costs of Defending Petition

Where a petition for the compulsory winding up of a company arises from a personal dis- **8.508** pute between members of the company, it is a misapplication of the company's money to pay any costs of the proceedings (other than as ordered by the court) except for those necessarily incurred in representing the company as a separate person.[1102] An injunction will be granted to prevent the company paying such costs.[1103] An anticipatory validation order[1104] for payment of costs of an unfair prejudice petition will not be made unless it is shown that it is bona fide for the purposes of the company.[1105]

The same applies to unfair prejudice petitions.[1106] The court may also restrain expenditure **8.509** on other proceedings started against the petitioner which concern the same issues, if they were started in response to the petition.[1107]

In *Re a Company (No 001126 of 1992)*[1108] Lindsay J considered an application to the court to **8.510** sanction in advance the directors' expenditure of the company's money on proceedings on an unfairly prejudicial conduct petition. His Lordship reviewed earlier cases cited so far at 8.508–8.509 and concluded, at p 156, that the test of whether such expenditure would be a misapplication of funds is 'whether it is necessary or expedient in the interests of the company as a whole' and held that advance approval is very unlikely in the absence of the most compelling circumstances proved by cogent evidence. It is respectfully submitted that the phrase 'the interests of the company as a whole' is best avoided, because its meaning is so uncertain, and that the phrase 'bona fide for the purposes of the company', used at p 153 of the judgment, is a preferable formulation of the test to be applied. It may be that under Lindsay J's test more expenditure would be allowed than under the test expressed in the first sentence of 8.508 (that is, necessarily incurred in representing the company as a separate person). In *Mavromatis v Haspaz Pty Ltd*[1109] the company's expenditure on defending an application to wind it up was held to be necessary, and an order preventing the expenditure was refused.

[1101] See 5.32–5.40.

[1102] *Re A and BC Chewing Gum Ltd* [1975] 1 WLR 579 at p 592; *Re Kenyon Swansea Ltd* [1987] BCLC 514; *Re Elgindata Ltd* [1991] BCLC 959; *Re C G and L Investment Ltd* [1993] 1 HKLR 107; *Cassegrain v CTK Engineering Pty Ltd* [2005] NSWSC 495, 54 ACSR 249.

[1103] *Re Milgate Developments Ltd* [1991] BCC 24; *Re a Company (No 004502 of 1988)* [1992] BCLC 701; *Dato' Tan Toh Hua v Tan Toh Hong* [2001] 1 MLJ 369. See S Griffin, 'A company's inability to fund disputes between shareholders' (1992) 13 Co Law 137.

[1104] IA 1986, s 127.

[1105] *Re Crossmore Electrical and Civil Engineering* Ltd [1989] BCLC 137; *Re a Company (No 001126 of 1992)* [1993] BCC 325.

[1106] *Re Crossmore Electrical and Civil Engineering Ltd* [1989] BCLC 137; *Corbett v Corbett* [1998] BCC 93, in which it was said that the matters on which the company can properly spend its money are disclosing documents to the other parties and allowing inspection, attending the hearing to learn of the court's decision, and presenting its view on any order which affects it, such as, in the context of an unfair prejudice petition, an order that it should purchase a member's shares.

[1107] *Pollard v Pollard* (2007) 151 SJLB 1260.

[1108] [1994] 2 BCLC 146.

[1109] (1993) 10 ACSR 473.

8.511 It is proper to use the company's money to defend an application for it to be wound up because of exclusion from management where the exclusion was justified by the petitioner's misbehaviour which threatened the company's viability.[1110]

8.512 The view taken in *Re Ibo Investment Trust Ltd*,[1111] that on a contributory's petition to wind up a company, other shareholders should not be given the costs of defending charges made against them by the petitioner, because it is the company which should defend the petition, would probably not be followed now in relation to contributories' petitions, which the court now recognizes to be litigation between members which the company itself should not pay for.

Representation of the Company

8.513 Where two equal factions in a company refuse to cooperate, the result may be that solicitors and/or counsel cannot be appointed to represent the company as a separate person, and the court must refuse to recognize legal representatives who have in fact been appointed only by one faction.[1112]

Disclosure and Inspection of Legal Advice to Company

8.514 In proceedings to which a company and one of its members are parties, the company cannot claim legal professional privilege for communications with its legal advisers, unless:

(a) the communications were for the purpose of the proceedings in which inspection is sought, and

(b) as between the company and the member, those proceedings are hostile.[1113]

8.515 For the purposes of this rule a petition of a member of the company, as a contributory, for the company to be wound up on the just and equitable ground is not hostile litigation between the member and the company, so privilege cannot be claimed.[1114]

Use of Investigative Material in Evidence

8.516 Investigative material which can be adduced as evidence by the Secretary of State on a public interest petition[1115] is admissible to the same extent on a contributory's petition, at least where the statutory purpose of the investigation includes providing information to members.[1116]

Consent Order

8.517 Even if all parties to proceedings on a contributory's winding-up petition agree to the making of a winding-up order, the court cannot make the order unless satisfied that it

---

[1110] *Joint v Stephens (No 2)* [2008] VSC 69.

[1111] [1904] 1 Ch 26.

[1112] *Re Rothlish Investments Ltd* (1953) 61 Man R 195; *Re Tak Ming Co Ltd (No 2)* [1960] HKLR 389, in which contributories claimed there was a deadlock in the company, it was held that the solicitors claiming to represent the company did not have authority to do so and the court refused to convene a general meeting to decide on the conduct of the litigation because the deadlock would make such a meeting a waste of time.

[1113] *Woodhouse and Co Ltd v Woodhouse* (1914) 30 TLR 559; *W Dennis and Sons Ltd v West Norfolk Farmers' Manure and Chemical Co-operative Co Ltd* [1943] Ch 220; *CAS (Nominees) Ltd v Nottingham Forest plc* [2001] 1 All ER 954.

[1114] *Re Hydrosan Ltd* [1991] BCLC 418.

[1115] See 9.27–9.32.

[1116] *Re St Piran Ltd* [1981] 1 WLR 1300.

should be made.[1117] If the parties can compromise their dispute in some other way, the court may make a consent order.[1118] In proceedings on a petition which asks alternatively for winding up or relief in respect of unfairly prejudicial conduct the court should not make a Tomlin order (a consent order in the form of a stay of proceedings on agreed terms recorded in a schedule).[1119] This is because, if a winding-up order is made because the agreed terms have been breached, the winding up will be deemed by IA 1986, s 129(2), to have commenced when the petition was presented. It is suggested that this difficulty may be overcome by obtaining permission to amend the petition to remove the prayer for winding up.

Petitioner's Costs of Successful Petition

If a contributory's winding-up petition is successful, the court may order that the petitioner's costs are to be paid by the other contributories who defended the petition.[1120] They may also have to indemnify the company for its costs.[1121]

8.518

Public Offer of Securities by Private Company

A private company limited by shares, or limited by guarantee and having a share capital, must not offer any of its securities to the public.[1122] This prohibition cannot be evaded by allotting, or agreeing to allot, securities with a view to their being offered to the public.[1123] Contravention of this prohibition may be brought to the court's attention in proceedings on an unfair prejudice petition or by an application specifically for that purpose under the Companies Act 2006, s 758. If it appears to the court, on such a petition or application, that a company has contravened the prohibition, the court must order the company to re-register as a public company,[1124] unless the company does not meet the requirements for re-registration[1125] or it is impractical or undesirable to require the company to take steps to re-register.[1126] If the court does not order re-registration, it may make a remedial order[1127] and/or 'an order for the compulsory winding up of the company'.[1128]

8.519

The following may make an application under s 758:

8.520

(a) a member of the company who—
   (i) was a member at the time the offer was made (or, if the offer was made over a period, at any time during that period), or

---

[1117] *J and M Jankar Pty Ltd v Dellmain Pty Ltd* [2009] NSWSC 766 at [3]; *Re Belmont Asset Based Lending Ltd* 2010 (1) CILR 83 at [11].

[1118] *Lee Teng Siong v Lee Geok Thye Holdings Sdn Bhd* [2004] 5 MLJ 13.

[1119] *Re a Company (No 003324 of 1979)* [1981] 1 WLR 1059.

[1120] *Re Tan Eng Seng Holdings Sdn Bhd* [2003] 2 MLJ 233; *Jenkins v Supscaf Ltd* [2006] 3 NZLR 264.

[1121] *J and M Jankar Pty Ltd v Dellmain Pty Ltd* [2009] NSWSC 766.

[1122] Companies Act 2006, s 755(1)(a).

[1123] s 755(1)(b).

[1124] Under ss 90 to 96.

[1125] There is a list of conditions in s 90(2).

[1126] s 758(1) and (2).

[1127] A remedial order is an order for the purpose of putting a person affected by anything done in contravention of s 755 in the position that person would have been in if it had not been done. (s 759(1)).

[1128] s 758(3).

      (ii) became a member as a result of the offer,

    (b) a creditor of the company who was a creditor at the time the offer was made (or, if the offer was made over a period, at any time during that period), or

    (c) the Secretary of State.

8.521 An application under s 758 is governed by the CPR, in particular, PD 49A, and must be commenced by Part 8 claim form.[1129]

[1129] PD 49A, para 5(1).

9

PUBLIC INTEREST PETITIONS

Public Interest Petitions

Winding Up in the Public Interest

Standing to petition

9.1   A petition for a company to be wound up by the court in the public interest can only be presented by a person who is authorized to do so by statute.[1]

9.2   Two statutory provisions authorize public interest petitions against companies of all kinds, though only in certain circumstances. See 9.5–9.8 (Secretary of State as petitioner) and 9.9 (Director of Public Prosecutions, Director of the Serious Fraud Office as petitioner).

9.3   Other provisions authorize public interest petitions in respect of particular types of company. See 9.10 (Secretary of State, Financial Conduct Authority (FCA), Prudential Regulation Authority (PRA) as petitioner).

9.4   In addition, the Secretary of State, the Attorney General, the Welsh Ministers, the FCA, the PRA, the Charity Commission, the Regulator of Community Interest Companies and the Office for Tenants and Social Landlords (the Regulator of Social Housing) have statutory powers to petition for winding up, which are discussed in 9.87–9.146. These powers are not expressed in terms of public interest, but they are given to persons or bodies who must exercise their powers in the public interest.

Secretary of State's general power to petition in the public interest

9.5   If it appears to the Secretary of State, from the results of any of various investigatory processes,[2] that it is expedient in the public interest that a company should be wound up, the Secretary of State may, under the Insolvency Act 1986 (IA 1986), s 124A, petition for that company to be wound up by the court.[3] This provision does not apply if the company is already being wound up by the court.[4] The fact that another winding-up petition has been presented does not in itself mean that the company is being wound up by the court.[5] A petition under s 124A is on the just and equitable ground.[6]

9.6   Section 124A applies to registered and unregistered companies,[7] building societies,[8] incorporated friendly societies[9] and any other entity that may be wound up as a registered company[10]

---

[1] *Re Millennium Advanced Technology Ltd* [2004] EWHC 711 (Ch), [2004] 1 WLR 2177. This is not the position in Australia (*Deputy Commissioner of Taxation v Casualife Furniture International Pty Ltd* [2004] VSC 157).

[2] See 9.11.

[3] IA 1986, s 124(4)(b), also lists this as one of the circumstances in which the Secretary of State may petition.

[4] s 124A(2).

[5] *Secretary of State for Business, Innovation and Skills v Top Choice Wholesale Ltd* [2012] EWHC 1262 (Ch), BAILLI.

[6] Last words of s 124A.

[7] It is applied to unregistered companies by IA 1986, s 221(1); *Re a Company (No 007946 of 1993)* [1994] Ch 198. It is applied to relevant schemes (see 1.168) by the Collective Investment in Transferable Securities (Contractual Scheme) Regulations 2013 (SI 2013/1388), sch 2, paras 3, 5(a) and part 3.

[8] See 1.120.

[9] See 1.125.

[10] European cooperative societies (see 1.123), European public limited-liability companies (see 1.124), limited liability partnerships (see 1.126) and registered societies (see 1.127–1.129).

apart from charitable incorporated organizations.[11] It also applies to a petition[12] to wind up an insolvent partnership as an unregistered company.[13] IA 1986, s 124(4)(b), applies to all these types of entity except building societies[14] and incorporated friendly societies.[15]

Whereas creditors and contributories petition in their own interests as members of a class, the Secretary of State necessarily acts not in his or her own interest but in the interests of the public at large.[16] **9.7**

After receiving a report under an investigatory process in respect of a company, the Secretary of State may, in addition to, or instead of, petitioning for the company to be wound up, petition for protection of its members from unfairly prejudicial conduct of its affairs.[17] The relevant investigatory processes listed in the Companies Act 2006, s 995(1), are almost the same as those listed in IA 1986, s 124A(1). **9.8**

Failure to comply with a serious crime prevention order

If a company has been convicted of an offence under the Serious Crime Act 2007, s 25, in relation to a serious crime prevention order, the Director of Public Prosecutions or the Director of the Serious Fraud Office may petition for the company to be wound up, provided the Director considers that winding up would be in the public interest.[18] The court may make a winding-up order only if the company has been convicted under s 25 and the court considers it is just and equitable for the company to be wound up.[19] A petition cannot be presented, or a winding-up order made, under this provision against a company if an appeal against conviction for the offence concerned has been made and not finally determined, or the period during which such an appeal may be made has not expired.[20] A petition cannot be presented, or a winding-up order made, under this provision against a company already being wound up by the court.[21] This provision applies to companies registered under the Companies Act 2006 in England and Wales or Scotland, and unregistered companies as defined in IA 1986, s 220, building societies, incorporated friendly societies, limited liability partnerships (LLPs), partnerships and registered societies.[22] **9.9**

---

[11] Charitable Incorporated Organisations (Insolvency and Dissolution) Regulations 2012 (SI 2012/3013), sch, para 1(7).

[12] Under IPO 1994, art 7.

[13] IA 1986, s 124A, is applied to such a petition by the modified form of s 221(5) set out in IPO 1994, sch 3, para 3.

[14] Building Societies Act 1986, sch 15, para 16.

[15] Friendly Societies Act 1992, sch 10, para 20.

[16] Per Megarry J in *Re Lubin, Rosen and Associates Ltd* [1975] 1 WLR 122 at pp 128–9; per Harman J in *Re Xyllyx plc (No 2)* [1992] BCLC 378 at p 380; per Finn J in *Australian Securities Commission v AS Nominees Ltd* (1995) 133 ALR 1 at p 59.

[17] Companies Act 2006, s 995, which is applied in modified form to limited liability partnerships by the Limited Liability Partnerships (Application of Companies Act 2006) Regulations 2009 (SI 2009/1804), reg 48. Unfair prejudice petitions are discussed at 8.432–8.518.

[18] Serious Crime Act 2007, s 27(1) and (3).

[19] s 27(4).

[20] s 27(9). Any power to appeal out of time is to be ignored (s 27(11)).

[21] s 27(10).

[22] s 27(12).

Powers relating to particular types of company

9.10 The following legislative provisions mention the public interest as a reason for presenting a winding-up petition:

(a) The Secretary of State may, if it is expedient in the public interest, petition for the winding up of a European economic interest grouping which has its official address in Great Britain if the grouping has acted contrary to the public interest.[23]

(b) The FCA or the PRA may petition for the winding up of a credit union if it appears to be in the public interest.[24]

(c) The FCA or the PRA may petition for the winding up of an unincorporated registered friendly society, if it appears to be in the public interest following a report on an investigation into the state and conduct of its activities.[25]

Secretary of State's Decision to Present a Public Interest Petition

Investigatory processes

9.11 By IA 1986, s 124A(1), the opinion of the Secretary of State that it is expedient in the public interest that a company should be wound up may be based on:

(a) By s 124A(1)(a), any report made under the Companies Act 1985, part 14.[26] Reports are made under part 14 by inspectors, who may be appointed by the Secretary of State under s 431 (investigation of affairs of a company on application by the company or its members), s 432 (investigation of affairs of a company at request of the court or on Secretary of State's initiative) or s 442 (investigation of ownership of a company). Inspectors must make a final report to the Secretary of State at the end of an investigation; they may also make interim reports and must do so if the Secretary of State directs them to.[27] For the use of an inspectors' report as evidence see 9.27–9.32.

(b) By IA 1986, s 124A(1)(a), any information obtained under the Companies Act 1985, part 14,[28] except s 448A (information provided by a whistle-blower). Information may be obtained under the following provisions of part 14 other than s 448A:

   (i) Under s 437(1A), inspectors appointed under s 431 or s 432 may, at any time, inform the Secretary of State of any matters coming to their knowledge as a result of their investigations, and must give such information if the Secretary of State directs them to do so.

   (ii) Under s 444, the Secretary of State has power to obtain information about the ownership of shares in or debentures of a company. The Secretary of State cannot base an unfair prejudice petition on information obtained under s 444.[29]

   (iii) Under s 447 (confidential investigation of a company) an investigator who is authorized by the Secretary of State may require production of documents or provision of information in relation to a company, or the Secretary of State may direct production of documents or provision of information. Information obtained in

---

[23] European Economic Interest Grouping Regulations 1989 (SI 1989/638), reg 7(2) and (2A), exercising the member State option provided in Regulation (EEC) No 2137/85, art 32(3).
[24] Credit Unions Act 1979, s 20(2); see 9.110–9.111.
[25] Friendly Societies Act 1974, s 87(1); see 9.142.
[26] ss 431–453C.
[27] ss 437(1), applied to an investigation under s 442 by s 443(1).
[28] ss 431–453C.
[29] Companies Act 2006, s 995(1).

pursuance of a requirement imposed under s 447 may be disclosed, without offending against s 449, to the Secretary of State under s 449(2)(a) and sch 15C, para 1,
or, under s 449(2)(b) and sch 15D, para 9(c), for the purpose of enabling or assisting
the Secretary of State to exercise any of his or her functions under IA 1986.

(iv) Under s 448 (entry and search of premises) documents whose production has been
or could be required under part 14 can be seized by a constable executing a warrant
issued by a justice of the peace. The constable may also be authorized to require any
person named in the warrant to provide an explanation of the documents.

(c) By IA 1986, s 124A(1)(b)(i), any report made by an investigator appointed by the FCA,
PRA or Secretary of State under the Financial Services and Markets Act 2000, s 167 or
s 168; by the FCA or PRA under s 169; or by the FCA or the Secretary of State under
s 284. An investigator appointed under s 167, s 168 or s 284 is required by s 170(6)
to report to whichever investigating authority (the FCA, PRA or Secretary of State: s
170(10)) made his or her appointment. By s 169(2) an investigator appointed under s 169
has the same powers as an investigator appointed under s 168(3) and it may be that this
makes such an investigator subject to the requirement in s 170(6) to make a report to
the appointing regulator. A person appointed under s 167, s 168, s 169 or s 284 is called
an investigator in the Financial Services and Markets Act 2000 but an inspector in IA
1986. For confidentiality considerations see 9.13–9.14. This basis is not available in the
case of a limited liability partnership.[30]

(d) By IA 1986, s 124A(1)(b)(ii), any report made by an investigator appointed by the FCA
or the Secretary of State under the Open-Ended Investment Companies Regulations
2001,[31] reg 30.[32] The requirement to report to the appointing regulator imposed by the
Financial Services and Markets Act 2000, s 170(6), is applied to such an investigator by
SI 2001/1228, reg 30(4). For confidentiality considerations see 9.13–9.14. This basis is
not available in the case of a limited liability partnership.[33]

(e) By IA 1986, s 124A(1)(bb), any information or documents obtained under the Financial
Services and Markets Act 2000, s 165 (FCA's and PRA's power to obtain information
and documents), s 171 (power of investigator appointed by the FCA, PRA or Secretary
of State under s 167 to obtain information and documents), s 172 (power of investigator
appointed by the FCA, PRA or Secretary of State as a result of s 168(1) or by the FCA or
PRA as a result of s 168(4) to obtain information and documents), s 173 (power of investigator appointed by the FCA, PRA or Secretary of State as a result of s 168(2) to obtain
information and documents) or s 175 (powers conferred by ss 165, 171, 172 and 173 also
give power to require documents held by third persons and to require person producing
documents to explain them). For confidentiality considerations see 9.13–9.14. This basis
is not available in the case of a limited liability partnership.[34]

(f) By IA 1986, s 124A(1)(c), any information obtained under the Criminal Justice Act 1987,
s 2, or the Criminal Justice (Scotland) Act 1987, s 52.

---

[30] IA 1986, s 124A, as modified by the Limited Liability Partnerships Regulations 2001 (SI
2001/1090), sch 3.

[31] SI 2001/1228.

[32] Which regulation is made under the Financial Services and Markets Act 2000, s 262(2)(k).

[33] IA 1986, s 124A, as modified by the Limited Liability Partnerships Regulations 2001 (SI
2001/1090), sch 3.

[34] IA 1986, s 124A, as modified by the Limited Liability Partnerships Regulations 2001 (SI
2001/1090), sch 3.

(g) By IA 1986, s 124A(1)(d), any information obtained under the Companies Act 1989, s 83 (powers of Secretary of State to require information and documents for the purpose of assisting overseas regulatory authorities). By s 87(1)(b) and (4), information obtained by virtue of the powers conferred by s 83 may be disclosed, without offending against s 86, for the purpose of enabling or assisting the Secretary of State to discharge functions under 'the enactments relating to companies or insolvency', including functions in relation to proceedings.

9.12 There is no requirement that the Secretary of State's opinion be based on a report limited only to the affairs of the company sought to be wound up.[35]

Confidentiality of information obtained under the Financial Services and Markets Act 2000

9.13 In the Financial Services and Markets Act 2000, restrictions on the use of confidential information obtained by the FCA, the PRA, the Secretary of State, or investigators they appoint[36] are imposed by s 348, and 'confidential information' is defined for this purpose in s 348(2). But confidential information may be disclosed for the purpose of facilitating the carrying out of a public function if the disclosure is in accordance with regulations made under s 349. Public functions include functions conferred by or in accordance with any provision contained in any enactment or subordinate legislation.[37] The Financial Services and Markets Act 2000 (Disclosure of Confidential Information) Regulations 2001[38] permit a primary recipient (defined in the Financial Services and Markets Act 2000, s 348(5), to include the FCA, the PRA and an investigator) of confidential information, or a person obtaining such information directly or indirectly from a primary recipient, to disclose such information to the Secretary of State:

(a) for the purpose of enabling or assisting the Secretary of State to discharge any of his or her public functions;[39] or

(b) for the purpose of initiating proceedings to which SI 2001/2188, reg 5, applies, or of facilitating a determination of whether they should be initiated. Regulation 5(6) applies reg 5 to (among many other proceedings) winding-up proceedings under IA 1986, part 4 or part 5, but only in respect of an authorized person, former authorized person or former regulated person. An authorized person is a person who is authorized for the purposes of the Financial Services and Markets Act 2000.[40] The term 'former regulated person' is defined in SI 2001/2188, reg 2. Disclosure for the purpose of winding-up proceedings is subject to protection for confidential information about a person who attempted to rescue the company which is the subject of the proceedings.[41]

Disclosure under either of these provisions must not contravene any of the 'single market restrictions' defined in SI 2001/2188, reg 2.[42]

---

[35] *Re Testro Bros Consolidated Ltd* [1965] VR 18 at p 22.
[36] (c), (d) and (e) in 9.11.
[37] s 349(5)(a).
[38] SI 2001/2188.
[39] SI 2001/2188, reg 3(2).
[40] By ss 31(2) and 417(1) of the Act. The definition applies to subordinate legislation made under the Act by the Interpretation Act 1978, s 11.
[41] SI 2001/2188, reg 5(4).
[42] SI 2001/2188, regs 3(3) and 5(5).

A person who is conducting or has conducted an investigation under the Financial Services **9.14** and Markets Act 2000, s 167, s 168, s 169 or s 284, or the Open-Ended Investment Companies Regulations 2001,[43] reg 30, may disclose non-confidential information, which he or she has received for the purposes of, or in discharge of, his or her functions, to the FCA or the PRA, for the purpose of enabling or assisting either regulator to discharge any of its public functions.[44]

Who may make the decision

The Secretary of State has standing under IA 1986, s 124(4)(b) and s 124A, to present a **9.15** petition for the compulsory winding up of a company only if the Secretary of State has formed and holds the opinion that it is expedient in the public interest that the company be wound up. In accordance with general principles of constitutional law, it is competent for an official of the Department for Business, Innovation and Skills to form that opinion and decide to present a petition: the matter does not have to be considered by the Secretary of State personally.[45]

Judicial review of decision

A decision to present or not present a public interest petition is subject to judicial review. In **9.16** *Re Walter L Jacob and Co Ltd*[46] Nicholls LJ observed, at p 352, that judicial review of a decision to present a petition would probably be pointless because if no reasonable Secretary of State could have formed the opinion that it was in the public interest that the company be wound up, the petition would presumably fail.

Alternative proceedings

The Secretary of State may seek the winding up of a company if it is in the public interest **9.17** to do so, even if there are alternative ways of dealing with the misbehaviour that is contrary to the public interest, such as through director disqualification proceedings under the Company Directors Disqualification Act 1986, s 8,[47] or by seeking a declaration of the company's unlawfulness.[48] The fact that a regulatory authority has acted to prevent continuation of a company's objectionable behaviour is not a reason for refusing a winding-up order in the public interest.[49]

Where an industry-specific administration regime is available, though, the legislation **9.18** requires an order to be made under that regime instead of for winding up.[50]

The Court's Approach to Public Interest Petitions

Just and equitable

IA 1986, s 124A, defines cases in which the Secretary of State has standing to present a **9.19** public interest petition. Section 124A requires that a petition presented under its provisions

---

[43] SI 2001/1228.
[44] Financial Services and Markets Act 2000 (Disclosure of Information by Prescribed Persons) Regulations 2001 (SI 2001/1857).
[45] *Re Golden Chemical Products Ltd* [1976] Ch 300.
[46] [1989] BCLC 345.
[47] *Re Equity and Provident Ltd* [2002] EWHC 186 (Ch), [2002] 2 BCLC 78, at [65].
[48] *Secretary of State for Trade and Industry v Bell Davies Trading Ltd* [2004] EWCA Civ 1066, [2005] 1 BCLC 516, at [112].
[49] *Re Walter L Jacob and Co Ltd* [1989] BCLC 345; *Re UK-Euro Group plc* [2006] EWHC 2102 (Ch), [2007] 1 BCLC 812, at [9].
[50] See 9.77.

for the winding up of a company by the court can allege only one circumstance giving the court jurisdiction to order winding up, namely, that the court is of opinion that it is just and equitable to do so, as specified in IA 1986, s 122(1)(g) (registered companies) or s 221(5)(c) (unregistered companies). As Saville LJ said in *Re Senator Hanseatische Verwaltungsgesellschaft mbH*:[51]

> Parliament... decided to leave the Secretary of State to form a view as to what was expedient in the public interest and the court then to decide on the material before it whether the justice and equity of the case dictated that the company concerned should be wound up.

9.20 It has been said that '[t]he power of the court to wind up companies on public interest grounds needs to be exercised sparingly and with care'.[52]

Public interest

9.21 Before making a winding-up order on a public interest petition, the court must be satisfied that it is in the public interest to do so.[53] The court must be satisfied of that even if the petition is undefended.[54]

9.22 The fact that a company is insolvent may mean that it is just and equitable to wind it up.[55] The facts that the regulatory authority for the business operated by the company has withdrawn its authorization and it is unlikely that the company can regain authorization may mean that it is just and equitable for the company to be wound up because its substratum has gone.[56] However, the basis for the exercise of the court's jurisdiction on a public interest petition is whether or not winding up is in the public interest, not insolvency or failure of substratum.[57] A company may be wound up in the public interest even though it is solvent.[58]

9.23 Australian courts have emphasized justifiable lack of confidence in the conduct and management of the company's affairs[59] as a criterion for winding up on the just and equitable ground in public interest cases.[60]

Balancing exercise

9.24 As with any petition under IA 1986, s 122(1)(g):

> the court has regard to all the circumstances of the case as established by the material before the court at the hearing.... The court will consider those matters which constitute reasons why the company should be wound up compulsorily, and those which constitute reasons

---

[51] [1997] 1 WLR 515 at p 523.

[52] *Re Equity and Provident Ltd* [2002] EWHC 186 (Ch), [2002] 2 BCLC 78, per Patten J at [62].

[53] *Re Walter L Jacob and Co Ltd* [1989] BCLC 345 at p 354; *Re Titan International plc* [1998] 1 BCLC 102; *Re Atlantic Property Ltd* [2006] EWHC 610 (Ch), LTL 13/3/2006 at [12].

[54] *Secretary of State for Trade and Industry v Driscoll Management Facilities Ltd* (2001) LTL 18/9/2001.

[55] *Re European Life Assurance Society* (1860) LR 9 Eq 122; *Insurance Commissioner v Associated Dominions Assurance Society Pty Ltd* (1953) 89 CLR 78.

[56] *Canada (Attorney General) v Security Home Mortgage Corporation* (1996) 45 Alta LR (3d) 98.

[57] *Re Marann Brooks CSV Ltd* [2003] BCC 239 at [26]; *Re UK-Euro Group plc* [2006] EWHC 2102 (Ch), [2007] 1 BCLC 812, at [30]. Earlier legislation in Victoria specifically permitted a public interest petition where a company was unable to pay its debts: see *Re Producers Real Estate and Finance Co Ltd* [1936] VLR 235 and *Re Chemical Plastics Ltd* [1951] VLR 136.

[58] *Re ForceSun Ltd* [2002] EWHC 443 (Ch), [2002] 2 BCLC 302.

[59] *Loch v John Blackwood Ltd* [1924] AC 783 per Lord Shaw of Dunfermline at p 788. See 8.303–8.309.

[60] *Australian Securities and Investments Commission v ABC Fund Managers* Ltd [2001] VSC 383, 39 ACSR 443; *Official Trustee in Bankruptcy v Buffier* [2005] NSWSC 839, 54 ACSR 767; *Australian Securities and Investments Commission v Kingsley Brown Properties Pty Ltd* [2005] VSC 506.

why it should not. The court will carry out a balancing exercise, giving such weight to the various factors as is appropriate in the particular case.[61]

[M]atters have to be looked at as at the time of the hearing of the petition and as a whole.[62]

In *Re Senator Hanseatische Verwaltungsgesellschaft mbH*[63] Millett LJ said, at p 526:

> the decision to wind up the company is not left to the Secretary of State but to the court, which must consider whether it is just and equitable to do so. In reaching its decision the court will take into account the interests of all parties, present members and creditors of the company..., as well as the interests of the public who may hereafter have dealings with the company.

Because of the diversity of the circumstances of different cases and the subtlety of the con- **9.25** siderations which the court must balance, dicta in particular cases must be applied recognizing the qualifications built into them, the factual contexts of the cases in which they were pronounced, and the individual circumstances of any case in which they are to be applied.[64]

One factor against making a winding-up order is that it is a drastic remedy which is capable **9.26** of causing hardship to employees as well as creditors and members of the company and may reflect badly on those running the company's business.[65] This is likely to be less significant where the company has ceased its operations.[66]

Secretary of State's evidence

The court must be careful not to be influenced too much by the very fact that a public **9.27** interest petition is presented by a person of such significance as the Secretary of State.[67] This fact means that it is highly unlikely that the petition has been presented frivolously or vexatiously but it does not mean that the court is relieved of its function of determining judicially whether or not a winding-up order should be made. That is still a question within the court's discretion.[68] Nicholls LJ in *Re Walter L Jacob and Co Ltd*[69] said, at p 353:

> the court will take note that the source of the submissions that the company should be wound up is a government department charged by Parliament with wide-ranging responsibilities in relation to the affairs of companies. The department has considerable expertise in these matters and can be expected to act with a proper sense of responsibility when seeking a winding-up order. But the cogency of the submissions made on behalf of the Secretary of State will fall to be considered and tested in the same way as any other submissions. His submissions are not *ipso facto* endowed with such weight that those resisting a winding-up petition presented by him will find the scales loaded against them.

---

[61] Nicholls LJ in *Re Walter L Jacob and Co Ltd* [1989] BCLC 345 at pp 351–2; see also per Patten J in *Re Equity and Provident Ltd* [2002] EWHC 186 (Ch), [2002] 2 BCLC 78, at [62].

[62] *Secretary of State for Business, Enterprise and Regulatory Reform v Amway (UK) Ltd* [2009] EWCA Civ 32, [2011] 2 BCLC 716, at [63].

[63] [1997] 1 WLR 515.

[64] *Secretary of State for Business, Enterprise and Regulatory Reform v Amway (UK) Ltd* [2009] EWCA Civ 32, [2011] 2 BCLC 716, at [75] and [77].

[65] *Re Derek Colins Associates Ltd* (2002) LTL 12/8/2002 at [46].

[66] *Re TAG World Services Ltd* [2008] EWHC 1866 (Ch), LTL 6/8/2008, at [39].

[67] *Re Alpha Club (UK) Ltd* [2002] EWHC 884 (Ch), [2002] 2 BCLC 612, at [5]–[6].

[68] *Re Co-operative Development Funds of Australia Ltd (No 3)* (1978) 3 ACLR 437. See 9.19–9.26.

[69] [1989] BCLC 345.

9.28   Equally the court should not indulge a prejudice against civil servants as being incapable of understanding the realities of business life, though, regrettably, such a lack of understanding seems to have occurred in *Re a Company (No 5669 of 1998)*[70] with disastrous consequences.

9.29   The mere fact that complaints have been made against a company by members of the public, even in significant numbers, is unlikely to justify winding up the company if no evidence is given of the substance of the complaints.[71] If evidence of the substance of complaints cannot be given because it is confidential, the complaints should not be mentioned at all.[72]

9.30   Parliament has established investigatory processes for providing the Secretary of State with reports, information or documents on which an opinion may be based that it is expedient in the public interest that a company should be wound up[73] or that a disqualification order should be made against a person.[74] It follows that the Secretary of State may use the relevant report etc as evidence in support of a petition to wind up the company or an application for a disqualification order despite the former rule against hearsay[75] or the continuing rule against evidence of findings of fact, conclusions and evaluative judgments.[76] However, other evidence of findings of fact, conclusions and evaluative judgments, such as findings by a court, may not be adduced.[77]

9.31   A report by inspectors appointed under CA 1985, part 14,[78] is admissible evidence of the opinion of the inspectors in relation to any matter contained in the report, provided the copy tendered to the court is properly certified by the Secretary of State.[79] However, this is of very limited help to a party seeking to use the report to persuade the court, because the court acts on its own opinion, not someone else's.[80] Where a person properly before the court challenges the basis for the opinion of inspectors, the court is put on inquiry and must consider whatever relevant facts those opposing the winding up wish to put forward.[81] However, an insubstantial challenge, such as a mere assertion by those attacked in a report

---

[70] [2000] 1 BCLC 427.

[71] *Re Derek Colins Associates Ltd* (2002) LTL 12/8/2002 at [12].

[72] *Re Derek Colins Associates Ltd* at [13].

[73] IA 1986, s 124A(1). See 9.11.

[74] Company Directors Disqualification Act 1986, s 8.

[75] *Re Travel and Holiday Clubs Ltd* [1967] 1 WLR 711; *Re SBA Properties Ltd* [1967] 1 WLR 799 at p 804; *Re Allied Produce Co Ltd* [1967] 1 WLR 1469; *Re Rex Williams Leisure plc* [1994] Ch 350; *Re Barings plc (No 2)* [1998] 1 BCLC 590. See per Dillon J in *Re St Piran Ltd* [1981] 1 WLR 1300 at p 1306. In *Secretary of State for Trade and Industry v Ashcroft* [1998] Ch 71 Millett LJ pointed out, at p 79, that there is no difference in this respect between an application by the Secretary of State for a director disqualification order and an application for a winding-up order: 'The two cases are merely two different regulatory responses to the same process'. In civil proceedings in England and Wales, the rule against hearsay was abolished by the Civil Evidence Act 1995, s 1.

[76] *Secretary of State for Business, Enterprise and Regulatory Reform v Aaron* [2008] EWCA Civ 1146, [2009] Bus LR 809. The opposite view has been taken in Australia (*Re Chemical Plastics Ltd* [1951] VLR 136; *Re Co-operative Development Funds of Australia Ltd (No 3)* (1978) 3 ACLR 437). The rule against evidence of findings of fact, conclusions and evaluative judgments was established in *Hollington v F Hewthorn and Co Ltd* [1943] KB 587.

[77] *Secretary of State for Trade and Industry v Bairstow* [2003] EWCA Civ 321, [2004] Ch 1.

[78] See 9.11(a).

[79] Companies Act 1985, s 441.

[80] *Re Walter L Jacob and Co Ltd* [1989] BCLC 345 per Nicholls LJ quoted at 9.27; *Secretary of State for Business, Enterprise and Regulatory Reform v Aaron* [2008] EWCA Civ 1146, [2009] Bus LR 809, at [32], per Thomas LJ. See *Re Mutual Home Loans Management Co (Qld) Ltd* [1974] QdR 111.

[81] *Re Co-operative Development Funds of Australia Ltd* (1977) 2 ACLR 284.

that it is wrong, would not be sufficient to cause the court to doubt the value of the report as material on which it may make a winding-up order.[82]

Where an investigator's report is used as evidence in support of a petition, the passages sup-   **9.32**
porting each allegation should be identified.[83]

Wrongdoing need not be that of the company's directing mind

The jurisdiction to wind up a company in the public interest is not restricted to cases in which   **9.33**
the wrongdoing contrary to the public interest is that of the company's directing mind.[84]

Deterrence and disapproval

It may be in the public interest to wind up a company as a matter of punishment for past   **9.34**
misbehaviour and setting an example to others, and to mark the court's disapproval of that
misbehaviour.[85] In *Re Alpha Club (UK) Ltd*, at [38], the learned deputy judge said that the
court should disapprove of behaviour because it was not in the public interest rather than
because the court thought it morally wrong. In *Re ForceSun Ltd*, at [26], Neuberger J said
that 'the court has to be careful of being priggish'.

Even the fact that a company is no longer able to continue its former business, because, for   **9.35**
example, of the withdrawal of a licence, should not persuade the court that a winding-up
order is not required in order to express disapproval and serve as an example.

The wishes of the company's controllers, that the company should remain extant for other   **9.36**
purposes, should normally carry little weight.[86]

The likelihood that past misbehaviour will continue may be a reason for ordering   **9.37**
winding up.[87]

Recent reform of objectionable behaviour

The court may dismiss a public interest petition to wind up a company as a sanction   **9.38**
for its past misbehaviour, if the court is satisfied that the company has implemented
effective reforms and can operate in future in a way that is not contrary to the public interest.[88] The company's reformed business methods may be set out in undertakings. The court will need to be satisfied that acting against the public interest is neither
an essential feature of the company's business nor a characteristic behaviour of the

---

[82] *Re Armvent Ltd* [1975] 1 WLR 1679; *Re St Piran Ltd* [1981] 1 WLR 1300 per Dillon J at p 1307.
[83] *Re Abacrombie and Co* [2008] EWHC 2520 (Ch), LTL 20/11/2008, at [65]–[67].
[84] *Secretary of State for Business, Enterprise and Regulatory Reform v Amway (UK) Ltd* [2008] EWHC 1054 (Ch), [2008] BCC 713, at [54(m)]. For the concept of the directing mind and will of a company see *Mayson, French and Ryan on Company Law*, 31st edn (Oxford: Oxford University Press, 2014), 19.8.1 and 19.8.3.
[85] *Re Walter L Jacob and Co Ltd* [1989] BCLC 345; *Australian Securities Commission v AS Nominees Ltd* (1995) 133 ALR 1 at p 62; *Re Equity and Provident Ltd* [2002] EWHC 186 (Ch), [2002] 2 BCLC 78, at [64]; *Re ForceSun Ltd* [2002] EWHC 443 (Ch), [2002] 2 BCLC 302; *Re Alpha Club (UK) Ltd* [2002] EWHC 884 (Ch), [2002] 2 BCLC 612, at [38]; *Re The Inertia Partnership LLP* [2007] EWHC 539 (Ch), [2007] Bus LR 879.
[86] *Re Walter L Jacob and Co Ltd* [1989] BCLC 345 per Nicholls LJ at p 360.
[87] *Deputy Commissioner of Taxation v Casualife Furniture International Pty Ltd* [2004] VSC 157; *Re TAG World Services Ltd* [2008] EWHC 1866 (Ch), LTL 6/8/2008, at [48].
[88] *Re Derek Colins Associates Ltd* (2002) LTL 12/8/2002; *Re Portfolios of Distinction Ltd* [2006] EWHC 782 (Ch), [2006] 2 BCLC 261; *Secretary of State for Business, Enterprise and Regulatory Reform v Amway (UK) Ltd* [2009] EWCA Civ 32, [2011] 2 BCLC 716.

company's controllers. In many cases the court is not satisfied on these points and the pervasive fraudulence of a company's operations and the character of its controllers show that it must be wound up.[89]

Undertakings

9.39 A company which is the subject of a public interest winding-up petition may offer undertakings to the court that its objectionable behaviour will cease. The court has a discretion whether or not to accept undertakings and whether or not to make dismissal of the petition conditional on the giving of undertakings.[90] Breach of an undertaking to the court is a civil contempt of court.[91] But punishment of a breach depends on an application being made to the court by the party in whose favour the undertaking was given and it is not the function of the Secretary of State to monitor undertakings by companies which have been the subject of public interest winding-up proceedings.[92] In practice, therefore, undertakings are used only as a formal record of what the company must do and are only accepted where the company has convinced the Secretary of State and/or the court that the undertakings can be implemented without supervision by the Secretary of State.[93]

9.40 The Secretary of State and the court have the following options for dealing with proffered undertakings:[94]

(a) The Secretary of State and the court may accept the undertakings, on which the court will dismiss the petition.

(b) The court may dismiss the petition on undertakings, even if that course is opposed by the Secretary of State,[95] although that will be unusual.[96] The court may act in this way where it would have dismissed the petition without the undertakings.[97]

(c) The Secretary of State and the court may refuse to accept undertakings and a winding-up order will be made if, for example, the court is not satisfied that those in control of the company can be trusted.[98]

---

[89] See, for example, *Re Equity and Provident Ltd* [2002] EWHC 186 (Ch), [2002] 2 BCLC 78; *Re Supporting Link Ltd* [2004] EWHC 523 (Ch), [2004] 1 WLR 1549; *Re UK-Euro Group plc* [2006] EWHC 2102 (Ch), [2007] 1 BCLC 812.

[90] *Secretary of State for Trade and Industry v Bell Davies Trading Ltd* [2004] EWCA Civ 1066, [2005] 1 BCLC 516, at [110].

[91] See *Blackstone's Civil Practice 2015*, 81.25.

[92] *Re Bamford Publishers Ltd* (1977) 74 LS Gaz 711.

[93] *Secretary of State for Business, Enterprise and Regulatory Reform v Amway (UK) Ltd* [2009] EWCA Civ 32, [2011] 2 BCLC 716, at [79].

[94] *Secretary of State for Trade and Industry v Bell Davies Trading Ltd* [2004] EWCA Civ 1066, [2005] 1 BCLC 516, at [111].

[95] *Secretary of State for Business, Enterprise and Regulatory Reform v Amway (UK) Ltd* [2009] EWCA Civ 32, [2011] 2 BCLC 716. See also *Re Secure and Provide plc* [1992] BCC 405; *Re Derek Colins Associates Ltd* (2002) LTL 12/8/2002 at [48].

[96] *Secretary of State for Trade and Industry v Bell Davies Trading Ltd* [2004] EWCA Civ 1066, [2005] 1 BCLC 516, at [111]; *Secretary of State for Business, Enterprise and Regulatory Reform v Charter Financial Solutions Ltd* [2009] EWHC 1118 (Ch), [2011] 2 BCLC 788, at [61].

[97] *Secretary of State for Business, Enterprise and Regulatory Reform v Amway (UK) Ltd* [2009] EWCA Civ 32, [2011] 2 BCLC 716, at [79].

[98] For example, *Re Abacrombie and Co* [2008] EWHC 2520 (Ch), LTL 20/11/2008, at [63]; *Secretary of State for Business, Enterprise and Regulatory Reform v Charter Financial Solutions Ltd* [2009] EWHC 1118 (Ch), [2011] 2 BCLC 788, at [61]–[62]; *Re Corvin Construction Ltd* (2012) LTL 8/1/2013 at [88].

In *Re Forrester and Lamego Ltd*[99] an application by the Secretary of State for the appoint- **9.41**
ment of a provisional liquidator was refused on the company giving undertakings which the
court considered adequate to deal with the only allegations in the petition that it considered
were unarguable, but it did not dismiss the petition. In *Secretary of State for Trade and
Industry v Bell Davies Trading Ltd*[100] the Secretary of State had agreed to dismissal of a public interest petition on the giving of undertakings: it was held that this did not imply that
the Secretary of State should have brought proceedings aimed solely at securing the undertakings without seeking winding up. Undertakings were accepted on a creditors' petition
in *Re British Widows Assurance Co.*[101] On a petition to wind up a foreign company alleged
to be conducting an illegal pyramid trading scheme and lottery, the court initially granted
an injunction forbidding the company from trading in England, but made a winding-up
order three months later when it was clear that the controller of the company would ignore
the injunction.[102]

Cessation of the company's operations

The fact that the company's operations have practically ceased is not a reason for refusing to **9.42**
make a winding-up order on a public interest petition.[103]

For the effect of the company being in voluntary winding up see 10.130–10.133. **9.43**

Associated companies

Having ordered the winding up of a company because its controller's use of it was contrary **9.44**
to the public interest, it may be necessary to wind up an associated company to prevent it
being used in the same way, even if it has so far been dormant.[104] However, a case must be
made for winding up an associated company. A winding-up order cannot be made simply
because of the association.[105]

Aspects of Public Interest Protected

Protection from inevitable financial loss

In the reported cases the public interest which is most often invoked is the protection of **9.45**
those who deal with companies from financial loss caused by those companies' activities. In
Re Senator Hanseatische Verwaltungsgesellschaft mbH[106] Millett LJ said, at p 526:

> The Secretary of State has a right, and some would say a duty, to apply to the court to protect
> members of the public who deal with the company from suffering inevitable loss, whether
> this derives from illegal activity or not. A common case in which he intervenes is where
> an insolvent company continues to trade by paying its debts as they fall due out of money
> obtained from new creditors. The insolvency is the cause of the eventual loss, but it is the
> need to protect the public, not the insolvency, which grounds the Secretary of State's applica-
> tion for a winding-up order in such cases.

---

[99] [1997] 2 BCLC 155.
[100] [2004] EWCA Civ 1066, [2005] 1 BCLC 516.
[101] [1905] 2 Ch 40.
[102] *Re Delfin International (SA) Ltd* [2000] 1 BCLC 71.
[103] *Re Walter L Jacob and Co Ltd* [1989] BCLC 345; *Re TAG World Services Ltd* [2008] EWHC 1866 (Ch),
LTL 6/8/2008.
[104] *Secretary of State for Business, Innovation and Skills v PGMRS Ltd* [2010] EWHC 2864 (Ch), [2011] 1
BCLC 443.
[105] *Re TAG World Services Ltd* [2008] EWHC 1866 (Ch), LTL 6/8/2008, at [51].
[106] [1997] 1 WLR 515.

In *Re North West Holdings plc*,[107] Charles J said, at [51]–[52]:

> [T]he allegations which found [the conclusion of the Secretary of State that it appears to be expedient in the public interest that the company should be wound up] and the application to wind up will often include allegations that amount to an assertion that the directors (or others who have been in control of the company and caused it to trade) have abused the privilege of trading with limited liability. Such an abuse can be, but does not have to be, based on allegations of dishonesty....

> There are a wide range of business activities that can found a public interest petition to wind up a company but the conclusion of the Secretary of State upon which the petition is based means that it will often assert that the activities of the company are such that the members of the public who deal with it are exposed to unacceptable risks which are different in kind to the risks flowing simply from the advantages of limited liability.

9.46 The key factor justifying winding up appears to be the virtual inevitability of loss because of an essential feature of the company's business, product or way of doing business. A company may be wound up if its business is inherently objectionable.[108] Even if a company's business is entirely conventional, the company may be wound up because of the way that business is conducted. Winding up may be in the public interest whether or not the company's business or business methods are illegal[109] or dishonest.[110] The test that is often applied is whether a company has fallen below generally accepted minimum standards of commercial behaviour.[111] However, this does not mean that every company that falls below the acceptable standard must be wound up: it is possible for a company to reform itself.[112] Another test is that a company has been run with a lack of commercial probity,[113] a phrase often used in director disqualification proceedings.[114] The persons whose dealings with companies may require protection include consumers,[115] investors (whether in the company's own securities[116] or in other investments marketed by the company[117]), other businesses[118] and the Crown.[119]

---

[107] [2001] EWCA Civ 67, [2001] 1 BCLC 468.

[108] *Re Alpha Club (UK) Ltd* [2002] EWHC 884 (Ch), [2002] 2 BCLC 612. See 9.47–9.48.

[109] *Re Senator Hanseatische Verwaltungsgesellschaft mbH* per Saville LJ at pp 522–3 and Millett LJ at p 526.

[110] *Re North West Holdings plc* [2001] EWCA Civ 67, [2001] BCLC 468, at [51].

[111] *Re Walter L Jacob and Co Ltd* [1989] BCLC 345 per Nicholls LJ at p 359; *Secretary of State for Trade and Industry v Driscoll Management Facilities Ltd* (2001) LTL 18/9/2001; *Re Marann Brooks CSV Ltd* [2003] BCC 239; *Deputy Commissioner of Taxation v Casualife Furniture International Pty Ltd* [2004] VSC 157, 55 ATR 599.

[112] *Secretary of State for Business, Enterprise and Regulatory Reform v Amway (UK) Ltd* [2009] EWCA Civ 32, [2011] 2 BCLC 716, at [64].

[113] For example, *Re UK-Europe Group plc* [2006] EWHC 2102 (Ch), [2007] 1 BCLC 812, at [2], [62] and [63]; *Secretary of State for Business, Enterprise and Regulatory Reform v Charter Financial Solutions Ltd* [2009] EWHC 1118 (Ch), [2011] 2 BCLC 788, at [62]; *Secretary of State for Business, Innovation and Skills v PGMRS Ltd* [2010] EWHC 2864 (Ch), [2011] 1 BCLC 443, at [4] and [79].

[114] For example, *Re Lo-Line Electric Motors Ltd* [1988] Ch 477 at p 486.

[115] See 9.52–9.59.

[116] See 9.60–9.61.

[117] See *Re Liquid Acquisitions Ltd* [2002] EWHC 180 (Ch), LTL 31/1/2002, and *Re Walter L Jacob and Co Ltd* [1989] BCLC 345, discussed at 9.53.

[118] See 9.62.

[119] See 9.63.

Money circulation schemes: pyramids, snowballs and lotteries

The court has wound up several companies whose business was the recruitment of people **9.47** to pay money to be shared among existing members so as to recoup what the existing members had paid to join. Such schemes are often found to be illegal lotteries.[120] Such schemes were also considered in *Re Senator Hanseatische Verwaltungsgesellschaft mbH*,[121] which was concerned with steps to protect the public pending the hearing of a winding-up petition. They may now also be illegal under the Fair Trading Act 1973, part 11, which came into force after *Secretary of State for Trade and Industry v Hasta International Ltd* and *Re Senator Hanseatische Verwaltungsgesellschaft mbH* were decided.[122]

It is in the public interest to protect the public from such schemes, which are pernicious and **9.48** inherently objectionable.[123] It is in their nature that people are likely to lose money when they come to an end, which is why they are illegal and why it is necessary to stop them sooner rather than later.[124]

Breach of regulatory requirements

Courts have mentioned that mere technical infringement of regulatory requirements is **9.49** not sufficient to justify winding up. See, for example, *Re Omega Legal Services (Worldwide) Ltd*,[125] in which some instances of carrying on an ancillary credit business without a licence under the Consumer Credit Act 1974 were not sufficient to justify winding up; *Re Liquid Acquisitions Ltd*,[126] in which failures to comply with the Companies Act 1985 and the Consumer Protection (Distance Selling) Regulations 2000[127] would not in themselves justify winding up; *Re TAG World Services Ltd*,[128] in which breaches of the Consumer Protection (Cancellation of Contracts Concluded away from Business Premises) Regulations 1987[129] would not in isolation have justified a winding-up order. However, the attitude of a company's management to regulatory requirements may demonstrate their disregard of, for example, consumers' interests[130] and may be taken into account in deciding to make a winding-up order. For example, total failure to maintain accounting records was a significant factor in justifying a winding-up order in *Re Get Me Tickets Ltd*,[131] *Australian Securities and Investments Commission v Kingsley Brown Properties Pty Ltd*[132] and *Secretary of State for Business, Innovation and Skills v PGMRS Ltd*.[133]

---

[120] See *Secretary of State for Trade and Industry v Hasta International Ltd* 1998 SLT 73; *Re Vanilla Accumulation Ltd* (1998) *The Times*, 24 February 1998; *Re Delfin International (SA) Ltd* [2000] 1 BCLC 71; *Re Alpha Club (UK) Ltd* [2002] EWHC 884 (Ch), [2002] 2 BCLC 612; *Re Treasure Traders Corporation Ltd* [2005] EWHC 2774 (Ch), LTL 8/12/2005.
[121] [1997] 1 WLR 515.
[122] *Re Delfin International (SA) Ltd*; *Re Alpha Club (UK) Ltd*.
[123] *Re Alpha Club (UK) Ltd* at [35].
[124] *Re Treasure Traders Corporation Ltd* at [31].
[125] (2001) LTL 29/6/2001.
[126] [2002] EWHC 180 (Ch), LTL 31/1/2002.
[127] SI 2000/2334. Now replaced by the Consumer Contracts (Information, Cancellation and Additional Charges) Regulations 2013 (SI 2013/3134).
[128] [2008] EWHC 1866 (Ch), LTL 6/8/2008, at [41].
[129] SI 1987/2117. Now replaced by SI 2013/3134.
[130] *Re TAG World Services Ltd* [2008] EWHC 1866 (Ch), LTL 6/8/2008, at [41].
[131] [2006] EWHC 1058 (Ch), LTL 25/5/2006.
[132] [2005] VSC 506.
[133] [2010] EWHC 2864 (Ch), [2011] 1 BCLC 443.

9.50   Public interest petitions failed in *Re Secure and Provide plc*;[134] *Re a Company (No 007923 of 1994) (No 2)*;[135] *Re a Company (No 007816 of 1994)*.[136] In all these cases the companies had broken the law regulating insurance business but the court refused to accept that the breaches were serious enough to justify winding up. In *Re Sentinel Securities plc*[137] and *Re Digital Satellite Warranty Cover Ltd*,[138] on the other hand, companies were wound up for carrying on insurance business without being authorized to do so. Similarly, in *Re OTC Network Ltd*,[139] actual or potential breach of the general prohibition against carrying on regulated financial services activities except as an authorized or exempt person[140] would not in itself have justified winding up. But in *Re Digital Satellite Warranty Cover Ltd*[141] it was said that it is in the public interest to wind up a company if its entire business is in breach of the general prohibition, especially if there have been clear warnings from the relevant regulator that the business was illegal.[142] Clearly each case depends on its own facts.

9.51   In *Re Market Wizard Systems (UK) Ltd*[143] a company was wound up for giving investment advice without being authorized under the Financial Services Act 1986.

Deceitful or misleading selling to consumers

9.52   To justify winding up for mis-selling, it must be shown there has been intentional and dishonest deceit of the public, and any deliberate misstatement or omission must be of some significance.[144]

9.53   In *Re Liquid Acquisitions Ltd*,[145] winding up was ordered of a company selling, by unsolicited telephone calls, fine wines as investments. The company acted as a retailer with a very large mark-up, but pretended to be a broker acting in customers' interests and charging only commission. Lloyd J found that the 'company's whole approach to customers involved deceit' and that 'mis-selling is endemic to the company's manner of business'. *Re Walter L Jacob and Co Ltd*[146] is a similar case in which the company had sold shares in three failing American companies in which its sole director and his associates were interested, using promotional material in the form of a broker's research recommendation.

9.54   In *Re Equity and Provident Ltd*,[147] winding up was ordered of a company which sold a so-called 'motor vehicle warranty' on the internet. However, in order to avoid controls on insurance business, the 'warranty' merely required the company to consider any claim, and

---

[134]   [1992] BCC 405.

[135]   [1995] 1 BCLC 594.

[136]   [1997] 2 BCLC 685.

[137]   [1996] 1 WLR 316.

[138]   [2011] EWHC 122 (Ch), [2011] Bus LR 981. The subsequent appeals were concerned only with whether the business was a regulated insurance business, which the Supreme Court held it was (*Re Digital Satellite Warranty Cover Ltd* [2013] UKSC 7, [2013] 1 WLR 605).

[139]   (2011) LTL 22/7/2011 at [43].

[140]   Financial Services and Markets Act 2000, s 19.

[141]   [2011] EWHC 122 (Ch), [2011] Bus LR 981, at [91]–[96]. See also *Re Sky Land Consultants plc* [2010] EWHC 75 (Ch), LTL 23/3/2011, at [81].

[142]   *Re Digital Satellite Warranty Cover Ltd* [2011] EWHC 122 (Ch), [2011] Bus LR 981, at [91].

[143]   [1998] 2 BCLC 282.

[144]   *Re Company (No 5669 of 1998)* [2000] 1 BCLC 427 at p 441.

[145]   [2002] EWHC 180 (Ch), LTL 31/1/2002.

[146]   [1989] BCLC 345.

[147]   [2002] EWHC 186 (Ch), [2002] 2 BCLC 78.

no prominence had been given to this feature on the website where the product was sold. The controller of the company had not cooperated at all with a confidential investigation under the Companies Act 1985, s 447, and no reliance could be placed upon him to ensure that the company's business would be properly run in the future.

In *Re a Company (No 6494 of 2003)*,[148] the company invited investments in buy-to-rent   **9.55** properties which it managed, using grossly misleading promises of the returns which would be achieved. This 'went to the core of the business'[149] and justified winding up. However, in another case concerning a company in the same line of business the Secretary of State failed to obtain a winding-up order.[150]

In *Re Get Me Tickets Ltd*,[151] the company was a secondary ticket agent (selling tickets to   **9.56** events but not as an agent of the venue) which led customers to believe that it had tickets available for resale to them, whereas its usual practice was to try to acquire tickets to meet orders and often failed to do so.

In *Re Abacrombie and Co*[152] the company advised insolvent individuals who shared owner-   **9.57** ship of a house or flat to transfer that interest to the co-owner for a consideration which was mostly paid to the company as a fee for the advice. The court found that clients obtained no financial or commercial benefit from these transactions, which were detrimental to the clients' creditors and undermined the proper administration of their bankruptcies.

Deliberate misrepresentation of a company's resources and/or track record so as to deceive   **9.58** customers about its ability to provide the goods or services it is selling justifies winding up in the public interest.[153] '[T]he prevention of the dissemination of false and misleading information with a view to winning customers is an aspect of the public interest which amply justifies the making of a winding-up order'.[154]

It is also in the public interest to protect business customers against deceitful selling; see 9.62.   **9.59**

Investor protection

In *Australian Securities and Investments Commission v Pegasus Leveraged Options Group Pty*   **9.60** *Ltd*[155] a company carried on a managed investment scheme (a collective investment scheme in United Kingdom law) without the authorization required by Australian securities legislation. Its sole director, Mr Craig McKim, promised investors ludicrously high rates of return from vaguely specified investments and took from them about AU$3.7 million, most of which he spent at betting shops. It was said, at [98], to be appropriate to wind up the company for investor protection, particularly because of repeated contraventions of securities legislation, and mismanagement of, and misconduct in the conduct of the affairs of, the company.

In *Re UK-Euro Group plc*[156] the court ordered the winding up of a company which had, in   **9.61** contravention of the Financial Services and Markets Act 2000, s 21, used a team of telephone

---

148 [2004] EWHC 126 (Ch), LTL 28/1/2004.
149 At [33].
150 *Re Portfolios of Distinction Ltd* [2006] EWHC 782 (Ch), [2006] 2 BCLC 261.
151 [2006] EWHC 1058 (Ch), LTL 25/5/2006.
152 [2008] EWHC 2520 (Ch), LTL 20/11/2008.
153 *Re OTC Network Ltd* (2011) LTL 22/7/2011.
154 *Re OTC Network Ltd* at [43].
155 [2002] NSWSC 310, 41 ACSR 561.
156 [2006] EWHC 2102 (Ch), [2007] 1 BCLC 812.

salespersons to seek subscriptions for its own shares, taking in £5 million, of which about a third had been spent on the telephone campaign itself or given as a commission to the man who organized it. In the campaign the company never told the truth about itself.[157] Although the company had a genuine product under development, it never sold anything. 'The way in which the affairs of the company were conducted, from start to finish, was a fraud on the public.'[158]

Deceitful selling to business customers

9.62 It is in the public interest to protect business customers against deceitful selling. In *Re Drivertime Recruitment Ltd*,[159] it was in the public interest to order the winding up of a franchising company which systematically failed to reveal the very high failure rate of its franchisees and which did not provide the support services it advertised. *Secretary of State for Business, Enterprise and Regulatory Reform v Charter Financial Solutions Ltd*[160] is another franchising case, in which projected income from franchises was greatly exaggerated and the company was falsely represented as being part of a group which had been established for over 22 years. In *Re Derek Colins Associates Ltd*[161] and *Re Supporting Link Ltd*[162] companies were wound up which sold advertising space, in publications which would have no likelihood of influencing the advertisers' potential customers, on the misrepresentation that the money paid for the advertisements would support charities. In *Re ForceSun Ltd*[163] the company overcharged for directories and credit card terminals, invoiced for unsolicited goods and impersonated genuine suppliers.

Causing loss to the Crown

9.63 In *Secretary of State for Business, Innovation and Skills v PGMRS Ltd*[164] Mrs Shekiluwa had, for nearly six years, conducted a staff recruitment business through four successive companies. Each company had failed to pay Crown debts, become insolvent and then sold its business to the next company in the sequence. By the time the fourth company, Lakewest Associates Ltd, began operating, Mrs Shekiluwa had given a director disqualification undertaking but nevertheless took part in the management of the company. Lakewest was ordered to be wound up in the public interest. The pattern of trading companies at the expense of HMRC until they were insolvent represented a lack of commercial probity.

Other reckless, dishonest or unsatisfactory business practice

9.64 In *Australian Securities Commission v AS Nominees Ltd*[165] the court ordered the winding up of three companies which acted as trustees of pension schemes and unit trusts after finding misconduct and mismanagement, reckless and improvident investment, inadequate record keeping, regular breaches of companies legislation, and ignorance of the duties of trusteeship.

9.65 Winding up of two companies was ordered in *Secretary of State for Trade and Industry v Leyton Housing Trustees Ltd*.[166] They were providing social housing but had failed to keep

---

[157] At [61].
[158] At [64].
[159] [2004] EWHC 1637 (Ch), [2005] 1 BCLC 411.
[160] [2009] EWHC 1118 (Ch), [2011] 2 BCLC 788.
[161] (2002) LTL 12/8/2002.
[162] [2004] EWHC 523 (Ch), [2004] 1 WLR 1549.
[163] [2002] EWHC 443 (Ch), [2002] 2 BCLC 302.
[164] [2010] EWHC 2864 (Ch), [2011] 1 BCLC 443.
[165] (1995) 133 ALR 1.
[166] [2000] 2 BCLC 808.

adequate records and accounts and were part of a group of companies which made false statements relating to housing benefit, misrepresented the terms and effect of leases, and failed to meet obligations under their head leases.

In *Re Marann Brooks CSV Ltd*[167] it was held to be in the public interest to wind up a com- **9.66** pany which offered to make claims for reduction of business rates and took fees for doing so, but rarely if ever actually made the claims and did not employ anyone qualified to do so.

In *Re Atlantic Property Ltd*[168] it was held to be in the public interest to wind up a property **9.67** rental agency, operating on a substantial scale, which systematically failed to repay tenants' deposits when tenancies ended, apparently kept no records of receipts from tenants, and paid all receipts into the bank accounts of its owners, who failed to cooperate with a confidential investigation under the Companies Act 1985, s 447.

In *Re Corvin Construction Ltd*[169] six building companies under common control were **9.68** wound up because the 'hallmark of their operations' was a 'litany of complaints concerning invoicing for monies not due, persistent substandard workmanship, disregard of health and safety requirements, evasiveness with customers and general irresponsible behaviour'. Two of the companies had 'just disregarded' their obligations to file accounts. A director had continued to act as such while bankrupt. There had been no cooperation with an investigation under the Companies Act 1985, part 14.

Advising or enabling clients to act unlawfully

It is in the public interest to order the winding up of a company conducting an unlawful **9.69** scheme.[170]

In *Secretary of State for Trade and Industry v Driscoll Management Facilities Ltd*[171] the court **9.70** concluded that it was in the public interest to order the winding up of 14 companies controlled by Mr Kevin Sykes and used in his business as a debt management consultant (or 'creditor resistance strategist'). At the time Mr Sykes was undischarged from two bankruptcy orders, was subject to three director disqualification orders (the most recent for the maximum of 15 years) and was under a suspended prison sentence. In advising his clients to evade their debts, his business involved the systematic deception of their creditors, including the use of bogus winding-up petitions to prevent debt enforcement, deceptive proposals for voluntary arrangements and failure to pay employees' tax and national insurance contributions.[172]

In *Re London Citylink Ltd*,[173] Mr Weigt ran a business incorporating companies in England **9.71** and Wales for other persons (called beneficial owners) in such a way that the names of the

---

[167] [2003] BCC 239.

[168] [2006] EWHC 610 (Ch), LTL 13/3/2006.

[169] (2012) LTL 8/1/2013.

[170] *Secretary of State for Trade and Industry v Bell Davies Trading Ltd* [2004] EWCA Civ 1066, [2005] 1 BCLC 516, in which companies were incorporated to make unlawful applications for import licences. See also 9.47–9.48.

[171] (2001) LTL 18/9/2001.

[172] The suspended prison sentence was activated in 2004 when Mr Sykes was sentenced to six and a half years for his part in a conspiracy to steal nearly £3 million from a pension fund. Mr Sykes subsequently pleaded guilty to a charge of fraudulent trading based on the use of bogus winding-up petitions and was given another prison sentence and disqualified yet again for the maximum 15 years (Serious Fraud Office Press Release, 2 November 2005).

[173] [2005] EWHC 2875 (Ch), LTL 20/12/2005.

beneficial owners, who actually ran the company's businesses, were never associated with their companies in Companies House records. Mr Weigt was the sole director of the hundreds of companies involved. It was held that the purpose and effect of these companies were not in the public interest, and the two companies which nominally held their shares and held office as secretary were ordered to be wound up.

Interaction with Moratorium and Administration

Preparation of a voluntary arrangement of a company or LLP

9.72   The Secretary of State may present a public interest petition under IA 1986, s 124A, for the winding up of a company despite the fact that a moratorium under IA 1986, s 1A (moratorium when directors propose a voluntary arrangement), is in force in relation to the company.[174] A winding-up order may be made on such a petition, while a moratorium is in force, whether the petition was presented before or since the moratorium started.[175]

9.73   All these provisions apply to limited liability partnerships.[176]

Preparation of a voluntary arrangement of a partnership

9.74   The Secretary of State may present a public interest petition under IA 1986, s 124A, for the winding up of an insolvent partnership despite the fact that a moratorium under IA 1986, s 1A, as modified by the Insolvent Partnerships Order 1994 (IPO 1994), sch 1, part 1 (moratorium when members of an insolvent partnership propose a voluntary arrangement), is in force for the partnership.[177] The investigatory processes on which a petition may be based, if it is to be eligible for presentation while a moratorium is in force, are limited[178] to those listed in IA 1986, s 124A(1)(b), (c) and (d).[179] Such a petition is presented under IPO 1994, art 7. A winding-up order may be made on such a petition, while a moratorium is in force, whether the petition was presented before or since the moratorium started.[180]

Companies in or preparing for administration

9.75   The Secretary of State does not need the court's permission to present a petition under IA 1986, s 124A, while an interim moratorium preceding administration is in force for a company.[181] The administrator's consent or the court's permission is required to present such a petition while a company is in administration.[182] A winding-up order may be made on such a petition (whenever it was presented) while an interim moratorium is in force or while the company is in administration.[183]

9.76   The same applies to partnerships[184] and to limited liability partnerships.[185]

---

[174]   sch A1, para 12(1)(a), (4) and (5)(a).

[175]   sch A1, para 12(1)(c), (4) and (5)(a).

[176]   Limited Liability Partnerships Regulations 2001 (SI 2001/1090), reg 5.

[177]   IA 1986, sch A1, para 12(1)(a), (3) and (4)(a), as modified by IPO 1994, sch 1, part 2.

[178]   By IA 1986, sch A1, para 12(4)(a), as modified by IPO 1994, sch 1, part 2.

[179]   Items (c), (d), (f) and (g) in 9.11.

[180]   IA 1986, sch A1, para 12(1)(c), (3) and (4)(a), as modified by IPO 1994, sch 1, part 2.

[181]   IA 1986, sch B1, paras 42(4)(a) and 44(7)(a).

[182]   paras 43(1) and (6).

[183]   sch B1, para 42(1), (3) and (4)(a), applied to an interim moratorium by para 44(5).

[184]   sch B1, paras 42(1), (2) and (5)(a), 43(1) and (5) and 44(1)–(5) and (7)(a), as applied by IPO 1994, art 6, and modified by IPO 1994, sch 2, paras 17 and 18.

[185]   Limited Liability Partnerships Regulations 2001 (SI 2001/1090), reg 5.

These exemptions for the Secretary of State do not apply to the industry-specific admin- **9.77**
istration regimes discussed at 1.245–1.294.[186] But some of those regimes[187] provide for an
administration order to be made (on an appropriate petition or application) instead of a
winding-up order if:

(a) the Secretary of State has certified that it would be appropriate to petition under IA
1986, s 124A; and
(b) the court is satisfied that it would be just and equitable for the company to be wound up.

The appropriateness of petitioning and the justice and equity of winding up must be assessed
disregarding, as relevant, the prohibition on winding up water companies and air traffic
services licence companies, or the objective of energy administration, energy supply company administration, postal administration or FMI administration. These provisions are
made in the Water Industry Act 1991, s 24(1), (1A) and (2)(d); the Railways Act 1993,
s 60(2); the Greater London Authority Act 1999, s 221(1) and (2)(b); the Transport Act 2000,
s 28(1) and (3); the Energy Act 2004, s 157(2)(c) and (3);[188] the Postal Services Act 2011,
s 71(2)(b) and (3); and the Financial Services (Banking Reform) Act 2013, s 117(1)(c) and (2).

Publicizing Public Interest Petitions

The fact that a company is of importance to a large number of customers, creditors, depos- **9.78**
itors or shareholders has sometimes persuaded the courts to prevent proceedings on public
interest petitions being publicized generally for fear of a disastrous loss of business to the
company sought to be wound up. See *Re Golden Chemical Products Ltd*[189] (public interest petition should not be advertised until the latest practical time); *Morgan Roche Ltd v
Registrar of Companies*[190] (on dismissing the company's application to have a public interest
petition struck out, the court ordered that the petition must not be advertised, the judgment was not to be published, and the court file was not to be searched without the leave of
the court); *Re London and Norwich Investment Services Ltd*[191] (application to strike out public interest petition and revoke order appointing provisional liquidator heard in camera); *Re
a Company (No 007130 of 1998)*.[192] This attitude was described as 'somewhat paternalistic'
in *Australian Securities Commission v AS Nominees Ltd*,[193] where it was pointed out that not
advertising a public interest petition prevented persons who were interested in the proceedings from knowing about them.

In *Re a Company (No 007946 of 1993)*[194] the Secretary of State opposed a company's appli- **9.79**
cation that a public interest petition should not be advertised, saying that as the petition
had been presented in the public interest it should be brought to the attention of the public.
Morritt J thought that an advertisement in the *London Gazette* would not alert the public
but, of course, advertisement there would give financial journalists an opportunity to make

---

[186] See 10.39.
[187] Water industry special administration, railway administration, PPP administration, air traffic admin-
istration, energy administration, energy supply company administration, postal administration, and FMI
administration.
[188] Applied to energy supply companies by the Energy Act 2011, s 96.
[189] [1976] Ch 300.
[190] (1987) 3 NZCLC 100,189.
[191] [1988] BCLC 226.
[192] [2000] 1 BCLC 582.
[193] (1995) 18 ACSR 358 at p 361.
[194] [1994] Ch 198.

the company's position known to the public. In *Applied Data Base Ltd v Secretary of State for Trade and Industry*[195] Lightman J accepted that a public interest petition should be notified to the public and refused the company's application for an order that one presented against it should not be advertised.

9.80 In *Secretary of State for Trade and Industry v North West Holdings plc*[196] the Court of Appeal was told that official policy is to issue a press release when a provisional liquidator is appointed on a public interest petition, even if the petition has not been gazetted, provided the provisional liquidator agrees. It was held that, as in the instant case, this would normally be unobjectionable, because the provisional liquidator would have to inform everyone dealing with the company of his or her appointment anyway, and because:

> The public is entitled to know that the Secretary of State has taken the view that it is expedient in the public interest to present a petition; and that the court, on the application of the Secretary of State, has been satisfied that the case was a proper case in which to appoint a provisional liquidator.[197]

But his Lordship went on to say:

> In any case where the Secretary of State or the provisional liquidator [is] uncertain whether it is appropriate to issue an immediate press notice directions can be sought from the court, either on the hearing of an *ex parte* application [(without notice to other parties)] or by the provisional liquidator following his or her appointment. It would be open to the court in a suitable case to restrain the issue of a press notice for a short period so as to give the company an opportunity to make representations as to why no advertisement should take place. Whether or not the court would think it right to do so will, of course, depend on the circumstances. But those advising the Secretary of State will need to bear in mind that, if there is no compelling reason to issue an immediate press notice without seeking the directions of the court at the time of the appointment of the provisional liquidator, the court may subsequently be concerned to enquire why directions were not sought.

9.81 In *Re a Company (No 007946 of 1993)*[198] and *Re Dollar Land Holdings Ltd*[199] the mere fact that advertising a petition would have the same adverse effect on those companies as it would on any other company was not enough to persuade the court to order that the petitions should not be advertised.

9.82 In *Re a Company (No 007923 of 1994)*[200] the Secretary of State petitioned for the winding up of an insurance company alleging that it was conducting business without necessary authorization. The Court of Appeal directed that the petition should not be advertised. Nourse LJ observed that there was no allegation that the company was insolvent; the company had undertaken that until the hearing of the petition it would not conduct any insurance business that it was alleged not to be authorized to conduct; an anticipatory validation order had been made under IA 1986, s 127; all contributories were aware of the petition; and existing policyholders would not be prejudiced. These were necessary conditions for directing that the petition should not be advertised but they were not sufficient. The petition would have to be advertised unless the companies showed that advertisement would

---

[195] [1995] 1 BCLC 272.
[196] [1999] 1 BCLC 425.
[197] Per Chadwick LJ at p 431.
[198] [1994] Ch 198.
[199] [1994] 1 BCLC 404.
[200] [1995] 1 WLR 953.

'cause serious damage to the reputation and financial stability of the companies',[201] which they were able to show.

If a petition has not been gazetted by the time the court decides to make a winding-up order, **9.83** it should, in principle, adjourn the hearing for gazetting so that it can consider the views of creditors. However, in *Re Liquid Acquisitions Ltd*,[202] advertisement of a public interest petition was waived, because the company had undertaken to cease trading as a condition of the court not appointing a provisional liquidator and the petition was said to be known to the public through the Internet and publication of the court's cause list.

Third Party Costs Orders

In proceedings on a public interest petition, the power to order a non-party, who caused a **9.84** company to defend proceedings, to pay costs[203] can be exercised if, in all the circumstances, it is just to do so.[204] A third party costs order may be made against a person who caused a company to defend a winding-up petition unsuccessfully if that person did not believe bona fide (a) that the company had an arguable case and (b) that it was in the interests of the company (or if the company was insolvent, its creditors) to pursue that case to the extent that it did.[205]

In *Re North West Holdings plc* Charles J said, at [54]–[55], that when the court is asked to **9.85** make a non-party costs order against a non-party who has caused a company to defend, unsuccessfully, a public interest winding-up petition, it should take into consideration:

(a) the nature and extent of the risks to which the public have been exposed by the activities of the company and the non-party's responsibility for creating those risks;
(b) any abuse by the non-party of the privilege of trading with limited liability;
(c) failure by the non-party to show that the company's activities were bona fide and should not be ended by winding up, bearing in mind that it might be financially impracticable or imprudent to fund such a defence.

Literature

Clare Campbell, 'Protection by elimination: winding up of companies on public interest **9.86** grounds' (2001) 17 Insolv L & P 129.

Other Petitions by the Secretary of State

Defunct Public Companies

IA 1986, s 124(4)(a), empowers the Secretary of State to petition for a company to be wound **9.87** up by the court if the ground of the petition is that:

(a) It is a company which was registered as a public company but, more than a year after its registration, has failed to obtain its trading certificate under the Companies Act 2006, s 761. This is a circumstance in which the company may be wound up by the court.[206]

---

[201] At p 959.
[202] [2002] EWHC 180 (Ch), LTL 31/1/2002.
[203] See *Mayson, French and Ryan on Company Law*, 31st edn (Oxford: Oxford University Press, 2014), 19.9.2.
[204] *Re Aurum Marketing Ltd* [2000] 2 BCLC 646 at p 654; *Dymocks Franchise Systems (NSW) Pty Ltd v Todd* [2004] UKPC 39, [2004] 1 WLR 2807, at [25].
[205] *Re Aurum Marketing Ltd*; *Re North West Holdings plc* [2001] EWCA Civ 67, [2001] 1 BCLC 468; *Secretary of State for Trade and Industry v Liquid Acquisitions Ltd* [2002] EWHC 180 (Ch), [2003] 1 BCLC 375.
[206] IA 1986, s 122(1)(b); see 8.93–8.95.

(b) It is an old public company that has failed to re-register. This is a circumstance in which the company may be wound up by the court.[207]

European Economic Interest Groupings

9.88 The Secretary of State has power to apply under Regulation (EEC) No 2137/85, art 32(1), for a European economic interest grouping (EEIG) to be wound up if it infringes Regulation (EEC) No 2137/85, art 3, 12 or 31(3).[208] This because the Secretary of State is the 'competent authority' referred to in art 32(1), unless the EEIG's official address is in Northern Ireland, in which case the competent authority is the Department of Enterprise, Trade and Investment in Northern Ireland.[209]

9.89 The Secretary of State also has a power to petition for the winding up of an EEIG if the grouping has acted contrary to the public interest.[210]

European Public Limited-Liability Companies

9.90 The Secretary of State has power to petition for the winding up, on the just and equitable ground,[211] of a European public limited-liability company (SE) whose registered office is in Great Britain, if it is not in compliance with Regulation (EC) No 2157/2001, art 7, which requires an SE's head office to be in the same European Economic Area (EEA) member State as its registered office.[212] This power cannot be exercised if the SE is already being wound up by the court.[213]

9.91 A petition may be presented under IA 1986, s 124B, despite the fact that a moratorium under s 1A (moratorium when directors propose a voluntary arrangement) is in force in relation to the SE.[214] A winding-up order may be made on such a petition, while a moratorium is in force, whether the petition was presented before or since the moratorium started.[215]

9.92 The Secretary of State does not need the court's permission to present a petition under IA 1986, s 124B, while an interim moratorium preceding administration is in force for an SE.[216] The administrator's consent or the court's permission is required to present such a petition while an SE is in administration.[217] A winding-up order may be made on such a petition (whenever it was presented) while an interim moratorium is in force[218] or while the SE is in administration.[219]

Enemy Companies

9.93 If an order has been made by the Board of Trade[220] or the Secretary of State under the Trading with the Enemy Act 1939, s 3A(1), in respect of a business carried on by a company,

---

207 s 122(1)(c); see 8.96–8.97.
208 See 2.47–2.49.
209 European Economic Interest Grouping Regulations 1989 (SI 1989/638), reg 7(1).
210 SI 1989/638, reg 7(2) and (2A); see 9.10.
211 IA 1986, s 122(1)(g).
212 IA 1986, ss 124(4)(b) and 124B, implementing Regulation (EC) No 2157/2001, art 64.
213 IA 1986, s 124B(2).
214 IA 1986, sch A1, para 12(1)(a), (4) and (5)(a).
215 IA 1986, sch A1, para 12(1)(c), (4) and (5)(a).
216 IA 1986, sch B1, para 43(1) and (6) applied by para 44(1)–(5); para 42(4)(aa) applied by para 44(7)(a).
217 IA 1986, sch B1, para 43(1) and (6).
218 IA 1986, sch B1, para 44(7)(a).
219 IA 1986, sch B1, para 42(1), (3) and (4)(aa).
220 For the role of the Board of Trade see 9.97.

the Board of Trade or the Secretary of State may present a petition for the winding up of the company.[221] For an example see *Re Polack Tyre and Rubber Co Ltd.*[222] No other person may present a petition without the consent of the Board of Trade or the Secretary of State.[223]

9.94 The fact that an order has been made by the Board of Trade or the Secretary of State under the Trading with the Enemy Act 1939, s 3A(1), and SI 1970/1537, arts 2(1) and 7(4), in respect of a business carried on by a company is prescribed in s 3A(8) of the 1939 Act as 'a ground on which the company may be wound up by the court'.

9.95 An order under s 3A(1) may be either:

(a) a restriction order, prohibiting the carrying on of the business either absolutely or except for such purposes and subject to such conditions as may be specified in the order, or
(b) a winding-up order, requiring the business to be wound up.

9.96 A winding-up order under s 3A(1) directs 'a winding up not by a court of law carrying out statutory provisions, but by the Board of Trade performing the duties imposed upon it by the [Act] as an act of State'.[224] It is a winding up of the business as a separate entity,[225] but the process does not invest that entity with legal personality.[226]

9.97 A State is an enemy for the purposes of the law on trading with the enemy only if there has been a formal declaration of war against it by Her Majesty's Government.[227] As there has been no declaration of war since the Second World War, the law on trading with the enemy has become obsolescent. Until the creation of the Department of Trade and Industry (DTI, now the Department for Business, Innovation and Skills) in 1970, ministerial functions under the Trading with the Enemy Act 1939 were exercisable by the Board of Trade (in practice by the President of the Board as no quorum was ever set for the Board's meetings). From 20 October 1970, those functions have been exercisable concurrently by the Secretary of State and the Board,[228] and successive Secretaries of State for the DTI and its successor departments have held concurrent appointments as President of the Board. Unless and until HM Government makes a new declaration of war, all applications under the Act at the present time will concern surviving matters from before 1970, so they are likely to be dealt with in the name of the Board. After a declaration of war, new matters will be in the name of the Secretary of State.

Particular Types of Company: Winding Up in Public Interest

Introduction

9.98 The powers to petition for the winding up of a company to be considered in 9.99–9.146 are available only in relation to particular types of company. Most of the powers are only

---

[221] Trading with the Enemy Act 1939, s 3A(8); Secretary of State for Trade and Industry Order 1970 (SI 1970/1537), arts 2(1) and 7(4). The Secretary of State's functions are exercisable concurrently with the Board of Trade.
[222] [1918] WN 17.
[223] Trading with the Enemy Act 1939, s 3A(8); SI 1970/1537, arts 2(1) and 7(4).
[224] *Re Banca Commerciale Italiana* [1943] 1 All ER 480 per Bennett J at p 482.
[225] *Re Banca Commerciale Italiana* per Bennett J at p 482.
[226] *Meyer and Co v Faber (No 2)* [1923] 2 Ch 421.
[227] *Amin v Brown* [2005] EWHC 1670 (Ch), [2005] NPC 104.
[228] SI 1970/1537, arts 2(1) and 7(4).

available in certain defined circumstances. The circumstances are not necessarily defined in the same terms as the definitions of the circumstances in which the court may make a winding-up order. Often the circumstances in which these special powers arise are circumstances in which it will be just and equitable for a company to be wound up. In other cases the power to petition arises when a company is unable to pay its debts.

Building Societies

9.99 The FCA or the PRA may petition for the winding up of a building society[229] on any of the grounds set out in the Building Societies Act 1986, s 89(1).[230] Before either regulator presents a petition for the winding up of a building society, it must consult the other regulator.[231] If a building society is not a PRA-authorized person,[232] the PRA cannot petition for it to be wound up[233] and the FCA is not required to consult the PRA before petitioning.[234]

9.100 Under s 36, the 'appropriate authority' may give directions to a building society which is in financial difficulties. In relation to a building society which is a PRA-authorized person, the appropriate authority is the PRA. Otherwise it is the FCA.[235] The PRA must consult the FCA before giving a direction under s 36.[236] If a society fails to carry out a direction given under s 36, the appropriate authority may exercise its power under s 37(1)(a) to present a winding-up petition.[237] A winding-up petition under s 37 can be presented only to the High Court or, if the society's principal office is in Scotland, the Court of Session.[238]

9.101 If the appropriate authority directs a building society to carry out a restructuring plan but the plan fails to achieve its objectives, the appropriate authority may issue an order prohibiting the society from carrying on activities specified in the order.[239] If a society contravenes a prohibition order, the appropriate authority may exercise its power under s 37(1)(b) to petition for the winding up of the society.[240]

9.102 Section 5(1) of the 1986 Act requires the purpose or principal purpose of a building society to be that of making loans which are secured on residential property and are funded substantially by its members.[241] It also requires the principal place of business of the society to be in the United Kingdom.[242] Section 5(4A) provides that if, after being established, a building society fails to comply with either of these requirements, the powers conferred on the appropriate authority by s 36 or s 37 shall become exercisable. Section 37 empowers the appropriate authority to petition for the winding up of a building society, but s 37(1)(c)

---

[229] Building Societies Act 1986, ss 89(2)(a) and (aa) and 119(1).
[230] See 2.29–2.30.
[231] Building Societies Act 1986, s 89(2)(a) and (aa).
[232] See 9.114.
[233] Building Societies Act 1986, s 89(2)(aa).
[234] Building Societies Act 1986, s 89(2)(a).
[235] Building Societies Act 1986, s 119(1).
[236] Building Societies Act 1986, s 36(17).
[237] Building Societies Act 1986, s 36(13).
[238] s 37(6).
[239] s 36A.
[240] s 36A(12).
[241] s 5(1)(a).
[242] s 5(1)(b).

confers this power only where the appropriate authority has reason to believe that the purpose or principal purpose of a building society has ceased to be that required by s 5(1)(a). By s 89(1)(f) and (4)(b) this is one of the circumstances in which the court may make a winding-up order.[243] The court must not make a winding-up order on a petition presented under s 37(1)(c) unless it is satisfied that the purpose or principal purpose of a building society has ceased to be that required by s 5(1)(a) of the Act.[244] It seems that if a building society ceases to have a principal office in the United Kingdom, the appropriate authority can only give directions under s 36 and cannot petition for winding up until the society fails to comply with those directions.

These provisions are modified in the case of a building society which is receiving, or has agreed to receive, or has been offered, financial assistance from the Treasury, the Bank of England, another EEA central bank or the ECB.[245] **9.103**

Charitable Companies

The Attorney General may petition for the winding up of any charity which may be wound up by the High Court under IA 1986.[246] An unincorporated charitable trust cannot be wound up under IA 1986 as an unregistered company.[247] **9.104**

The Charity Commission for England and Wales may petition for the winding up of any charity which may be wound up by the High Court under IA 1986 if,[248] after instituting an inquiry,[249] the Commission has become satisfied: **9.105**

(a) that there is or has been any misconduct or mismanagement in the administration of the charity;[250] or
(b) that it is necessary or desirable to act for the purpose of:[251]
   (i) protecting the property of the charity, or
   (ii) securing that the charity's property or property coming to the charity is properly applied for the purposes of the charity.

The reference to 'misconduct or mismanagement' extends[252] (regardless of anything in the trusts of the charity) to using excessive amounts of money (in relation to the property which is or is likely to be applied or applicable for the charity's purposes): **9.106**

(a) for the remuneration or reward of persons acting in the affairs of the charity, or
(b) for other administrative purposes.

The Commission cannot present a petition under this provision unless it has the agreement of the Attorney General.[253] **9.107**

---

[243] See 2.29–2.30.
[244] s 37(5).
[245] Building Societies (Financial Assistance) Order 2010 (SI 2010/1188).
[246] Charities Act 2011, s 113(1) and (2).
[247] *Gilbert Deya Ministries v Kashmir Broadcasting Corporation Ltd* [2010] EWHC 3015 (Ch), LTL 11/11/2010.
[248] Charities Act 2011, s 113(1) and (3).
[249] Under the general power to institute inquiries in s 46.
[250] s 76(1)(a).
[251] s 76(1)(b).
[252] s 76(2).
[253] s 113(4).

9.108   The Charities Act 2011 does not apply to a charity established outside England and Wales under the law of a foreign jurisdiction.[254]

Community Interest Companies

9.109   The Regulator of Community Interest Companies has a power to petition for a community interest company to be wound up if the court is of the opinion that it is just and equitable to do so.[255] This power is not available if the company is already being wound up by the court.[256]

Credit Unions

9.110   Under the Credit Unions Act 1979, s 20(2), the FCA or the PRA may petition for the winding up of a credit union if it appears to the regulator concerned that:

(a)   the credit union is unable to pay sums due and payable to its members, or is able to pay such sums only by obtaining further subscriptions for shares or by defaulting in its obligations to creditors; or

(b)   there has been, in relation to that credit union, a failure to comply with any provision of, or of any direction given under, the Credit Unions Act 1979 or the Co-operative and Community Benefit Societies Act 2014; or

(c)   the rules of the credit union provide for one or more common bonds involving a connection with a locality and the requirements of the Credit Unions Act 1979, s 1B,[257] are no longer met; or

(d)   the winding up of the credit union is in the public interest; or

(e)   the winding up of the credit union is just and equitable having regard to the interests of all the members of the credit union.

9.111   Before either regulator presents a petition under s 20(2), it must consult the other regulator.[258]

European Cooperative Societies

9.112   The FCA has standing under IA 1986, ss 124(4AA) and 124C, to petition for the winding up of a European cooperative society (SCE) on the just and equitable ground[259] if it appears to the FCA that the SCE should be wound up, and it is not already being wound up by the court,[260] and:

(a)   there has been a breach of Regulation (EC) No 1435/2003, art 2(1) (which defines the ways in which an SCE may be formed), and/or art 3(2) (which requires an SCE's subscribed capital to be at least €30,000);[261] or

(b)   the SCE was formed by merger without scrutiny of legality;[262] or

---

[254] *Gaudiya Mission v Brahmachary* [1998] Ch 341.

[255] IA 1986, s 124(4A); Companies (Audit, Investigations and Community Enterprise) Act 2004, s 50(1).

[256] s 50(2).

[257] Those requirements are that: (a) the number of potential members of the society does not exceed two million or such higher figure as may be specified by the Treasury and it is reasonably practicable for every potential member to participate in votes of the society, serve on the society's committee and have access to all the services offered by the society; or (b) extraordinary circumstances exist justifying registration of the society as a credit union.

[258] Credit Unions Act 1979, s 20(3).

[259] s 122(1)(g).

[260] s 124C(3).

[261] art 73(1).

[262] arts 34 and 73(1).

(c) the SCE is not in compliance with art 6 (head office must be located in the UK).[263]

Regulation (EC) No 1435/2003, art 73(1), specifies (a) and (b) as in themselves grounds for winding up and also permits 'any person with a legitimate interest' to petition on those grounds.

Financial Services Companies and Partnerships

Authorized, PRA-authorized and PRA-regulated persons

The Financial Services and Markets Act 2000 controls the carrying on of what it calls 'regu- **9.113** lated activities'[264] in the United Kingdom. Regulation of these activities is entrusted to the FCA and the PRA. The PRA supervises 'PRA-regulated activities'.[265] The FCA is responsible for other regulated activities. The Act provides that only authorized persons[266] and exempt persons[267] may carry on (or purport to carry on) regulated activities in the UK.[268] The following are authorized persons for the purposes of the Act:[269]

(a) a person who has a part 4A permission[270] to carry on one or more regulated activities;
(b) an EEA firm qualifying for authorization under sch 3;
(c) a Treaty firm qualifying for authorization under sch 4;
(d) a person who is otherwise authorized by a provision of, or made under, the Act.

A 'PRA-authorized person' is an authorized person who has permission, given under **9.114** part 4A or resulting from another provision of the Act, to carry on regulated activities that consist of or include one or more PRA-regulated activities.[271]

The term 'PRA-regulated person' means[272] a person who: **9.115**

(a) is or has been a PRA-authorized person,
(b) is or has been an appointed representative[273] whose principal (or one of whose principals) is, or was, a PRA-authorized person, or
(c) is carrying on or has carried on a PRA-regulated activity in contravention of the general prohibition.

---

[263] art 73(3).
[264] Defined in the Financial Services and Markets Act 2000, s 22 and sch 2, the Financial Services and Markets Act 2000 (Regulated Activities) Order 2001 (SI 2001/544) and the Financial Services and Markets Act 2000 (Carrying on Regulated Activities by Way of Business) Order 2001 (SI 2001/1177).
[265] Defined in the Financial Services and Markets Act 2000, s 22A, and the Financial Services and Markets Act 2000 (PRA-regulated Activities) Order 2013 (SI 2013/556).
[266] Defined in the next sentence.
[267] Identified in the Financial Services and Markets Act 2000, ss 38 (exemption by order), 39 (appointed representatives), 285 (recognized investment exchanges, recognized clearing houses and central counterparties) and 327 (members of professions), and the Financial Services and Markets Act 2000 (Exemption) Order 2001 (SI 2001/1201). See also the Financial Services and Markets Act 2000 (Appointed Representatives) Regulations 2001 (SI 2001/1217) and the Financial Services and Markets Act 2000 (Professions) (Non-Exempt Activities) Order 2001 (SI 2001/1227).
[268] Financial Services and Markets Act 2000, s 19(1). This is 'the general prohibition' (s 19(2)).
[269] s 31.
[270] Permission, to carry on one or more regulated activities, given by the FCA or the PRA under the Financial Services and Markets Act 2000, part 4A, or having effect as so given (s 55A(5)).
[271] s 2B(5).
[272] s 355(1).
[273] Defined in s 39(2).

Power to petition

9.116 Under the Financial Services and Markets Act 2000, s 367, the FCA may petition for the winding up of what the section refers to as a 'body' (see 9.121) which:[274]

(a) is, or has been, an authorized person or recognized investment exchange;

(b) is, or has been, an authorized representative; or

(c) is carrying on, or has carried on, a regulated activity in contravention of the general prohibition.[275]

9.117 The PRA may petition for the winding up of such a body if it is a PRA-regulated person.[276]

9.118 There is no power to petition for the winding up of a body which is only purporting to carry on a regulated activity in contravention of the general prohibition.[277]

9.119 Under the Financial Services and Markets Act 2000, s 367, as applied and modified by the Payment Services Regulations 2009[278] and the Electronic Money Regulations 2011,[279] the FCA may petition for the winding up of a body which:

(a) is, or has been, an authorized payment institution[280] or an EEA authorized payment institution;[281]

(b) is providing, or has provided, payment services in contravention of SI 2009/209, reg 110(1);

(c) is, or has been, an electronic money institution[282] or an EEA electronic money institution;[283] or

(d) is issuing, or has issued, electronic money in contravention of SI 2011/99, reg 63(1).

---

[274] s 367(1). The terminology is explained in 9.113–9.115.

[275] The expenses which the FCA incurs in the exercise, or consideration of the possible exercise, of its power to petition because of contravention of the general prohibition are 'enforcement costs' which it may deduct from the penalty receipts which it must remit to the Treasury (Financial Services and Markets Act 2000, sch 1ZA, para 20(1)–(3) and (4)(d); Payment to Treasury of Penalties (Enforcement Costs) Order 2013 (SI 2013/418), para 2(1)(b)).

[276] Financial Services and Markets Act 2000, s 367(1A).

[277] *Financial Services Authority v European Property Investments (UK) Ltd* [2013] EWHC 4340 (Ch), LTL 7/12/2012, at [9]. In this case the company was found to be at least carrying on the regulated activity of establishing a collective investment scheme (Financial Services and Markets Act 2000 (Regulated Activities) Order 2001 (SI 2001/544), art 51ZE).

[278] SI 2009/209, sch 5, para 6.

[279] SI 2011/99, sch 3, para 7. SI 2009/209, sch 5, para 6, and SI 2011/99, sch 3, para 7, have been inconsistently amended by the Financial Services Act 2012 (Consequential Amendments and Transitional Provisions) Order 2013 (SI 2013/472), sch 2, paras 155(1) and (6)(f) and 196(1) and (5)(g). It appears that the amendments set out in para 155(6)(f) should also appear in para 196(5)(g) and vice versa.

[280] Defined in SI 2009/209, reg 2(1), as a person included in the FCA's register of authorized payment institutions (reg 4(1)(a)) or a person deemed to have been granted authorization by the FCA by virtue of reg 121 (transitional arrangements for United Kingdom financial institutions which lawfully provided payment services in the UK before 25 December 2007).

[281] Defined in SI 2009/209, reg 2(1), as a person authorized in an EEA State other than the United Kingdom to provide payment services in accordance with Directive 2007/64/EC.

[282] Defined in SI 2011/99, reg 2(1), as a person included in the FCA's register of authorized electronic money institutions (reg 4(1)(a)) or small electronic money institutions (reg 4(1)(b)) or a person deemed to have been granted authorization by the FCA by virtue of reg 74 (transitional arrangements for persons authorized to issue electronic money before 30 April 2011).

[283] Defined in SI 2011/99, reg 2(1), as a person authorized in an EEA State other than the United Kingdom to issue electronic money and provide payment services in accordance with Directive 2009/110/EC.

Also, the PRA may petition for the winding up of a body in category (c) or (d) if it is a PRA-regulated person.[284]   **9.120**

'Body' means a body of persons over which the court has jurisdiction under any provision   **9.121**
of, or made under, IA 1986, apart from a building society, friendly society, or registered
society[285] (for which there are separate provisions[286]), but including any partnership.[287] So
the one respect in which 'body' implies a wider jurisdiction than the court normally has
over winding up is that the jurisdiction is extended to include solvent partnerships. The
Financial Services and Markets Act 2000, s 367, applies to limited liability partnerships[288]
and references to a 'body' include references to a limited liability partnership.[289]

If a company or partnership is authorized to carry on a regulated activity in the United   **9.122**
Kingdom by virtue of being authorized to do so in another EEA State, neither the FCA nor
the PRA may petition for it to be wound up unless one of them has been asked to do so by
the firm's home State regulator or, in the case of a payment or electronic money institution,
the company's home State competent authority. This applies to:

(a) an EEA firm[290] which qualifies for authorization under the Financial Services and
    Markets Act 2000, sch 3;[291]
(b) a Treaty firm[292] which qualifies for authorization under the Financial Services and
    Markets Act 2000, sch 4;[293]
(c) an EEA authorized payment institution;[294]
(d) an EEA electronic money institution.[295]

If one UK regulator receives a request to petition for the winding up of a body from that   **9.123**
body's home State regulator (or home State competent authority), it must notify the other
UK regulator and provide the other regulator with such information relating to the request
as it thinks fit.[296]

In this work, the entities against which a petition may be presented under the Financial   **9.124**
Services and Markets Act 2000, s 367, are called financial services companies and

---

[284] Financial Services and Markets Act 2000, s 367(1A), as applied by SI 2011/99, reg 62 and sch 3, para 7.
[285] Financial Services and Markets Act 2000, s 355(1).
[286] See 9.99–9.103 (building societies), 9.141–9.142 (friendly societies) and 9.145–9.146 (registered societies).
[287] s 367(2). This does not apply to s 367 as applied by SI 2009/209, sch 5, para 6 (payment services), or SI 2011/99, sch 3, para 7 (electronic money).
[288] Limited Liability Partnerships Regulations 2001 (SI 2001/1090), reg 6.
[289] SI 2001/1090, reg 6(2)(b).
[290] Defined in the Financial Services and Markets Act 2000, sch 3, para 5. The relevant definition of 'home State regulator' is in sch 3, para 9.
[291] Financial Services and Markets Act 2000, s 368(1).
[292] Defined in the Financial Services and Markets Act 2000, sch 4, para 1(1). The relevant definition of 'home State regulator' is also in sch 4, para 1(1).
[293] Financial Services and Markets Act 2000, s 368(1).
[294] Financial Services and Markets Act 2000, s 368(1), as applied and modified by SI 2009/209, sch 5, para 6(d). The relevant definition of 'home State competent authority' is in SI 2009/209, reg 2(1).
[295] Financial Services and Markets Act 2000, s 368(1), as applied and modified by SI 2011/99, sch 3, para 7(d), which refers to petitioning by the FCA only. The reference to 'home State competent authority' (relevantly defined in SI 2011/99, reg 2(1)) has been accidentally removed.
[296] Financial Services and Markets Act 2000, s 368(2). In relation to an EEA electronic money institution, this applies only to the FCA (s 368(2) as applied and modified by SI 2011/99, sch 3, para 7(d); the modification does not change 'home State regulator' to 'home State competent authority').

partnerships. In IA 1986, sch A1, para 44, they are called regulated companies.[297] In the Cross-Border Insolvency Regulations 2006,[298] an entity which the FCA can petition to be wound up is called a 'debtor who is of interest to the Financial Conduct Authority',[299] and an entity which the PRA can petition to be wound up is called a 'debtor who is of interest to the Prudential Regulation Authority'.[300]

Circumstances in which a winding-up order may be made

9.125 The only circumstances in which a winding-up order may be made on a petition presented under the Financial Services and Markets Act 2000, s 367, are:[301]

(a) the company or partnership is unable to pay its debts within the meaning of IA 1986, s 123 (registered companies, see 7.92–7.108) or s 221 (unregistered companies, see 7.109–7.111)—this is the ground specified in s 122(1)(f) for registered companies and s 221(5)(b) for unregistered companies; or
(b) it is just and equitable that the company or partnership should be wound up—this is the ground specified in s 122(1)(g) for registered companies and s 221(5)(c) for unregistered companies.

9.126 A company or partnership is to be treated as unable to pay its debts if it is in default on an obligation to pay a sum due and payable under an agreement, the making or performance of which constitutes or is part of the regulated activity which it carries on.[302] In the application of these provisions to payment services, a company is to be treated as unable to pay its debts if it is in default on an obligation to pay a sum due and payable under a contract for payment services.[303] In the application of these provisions to electronic money, a company is to be treated as unable to pay its debts if it is in default on an obligation to pay a sum due and payable under a contract for electronic money issuance or payment services.[304]

9.127 It was just and equitable to wind up a land banking company carrying on business, in breach of the general prohibition, which was shown to have consistently used 'the kind of high-pressure selling techniques, gross exaggerations and false representations that all too often dupe people into parting with large sums of money that they cannot afford to lose'.[305]

9.128 There is a close analogy between an application by the FCA or the PRA under the Financial Services and Markets Act 2000, s 367, to wind up a company on the just and equitable ground and an application by the Secretary of State under IA 1986, s 124A, and both jurisdictions are to be exercised with a view to protecting the public interest.[306] It is just and equitable to order the winding up of a company so as to satisfy a regulator's regulatory objectives.[307]

---

[297] IA 1986, sch A1, para 44(18).
[298] SI 2006/1030.
[299] SI 2006/1030, sch 2, para 1(6), and sch 3, para 1(3).
[300] SI 2006/1030, sch 2, para 1(6A), and sch 3, para 1(3A).
[301] Financial Services and Markets Act 2000, s 367(3).
[302] Financial Services and Markets Act 2000, s 367(4) and (5).
[303] Financial Services and Markets Act 2000, s 367(4), as applied and modified by SI 2009/209, sch 5, para 6(c)(i) and (iii).
[304] Financial Services and Markets Act 2000, s 367(4), as applied and modified by SI 2011/99, sch 3, para 7(c)(i) and (iii).
[305] *Financial Services Authority v European Property Investments (UK) Ltd* [2013] EWHC 4340 (Ch), LTL 7/12/2012, at [17].
[306] *Re The Inertia Partnership LLP* [2007] EWHC 539 (Ch), [2007] Bus LR 879, at [51].
[307] *Re The Inertia Partnership LLP* at [53].

In two past Commonwealth cases a challenge to an allegation of inability to pay debts **9.129** has threatened protracted litigation. In *Re Advocate General Insurance Co of Canada*[308] the Attorney General of Canada petitioned for the winding up of an insurance company, claiming that the company was insolvent and that it was just and equitable to order winding up. The company admitted that it was not in compliance with the statutory capital adequacy rules. Its licence to carry on insurance business had been withdrawn. However, it denied that it was actually insolvent. It was held that the court would not delay hearing the winding-up application to determine the difficult question of the company's solvency. It was just and equitable that the company be wound up immediately in the interests of policyholders and claimants, whose interests prevailed over the interests of shareholders.

A different approach was taken by the Hong Kong Court of Appeal in *Re Armour Insurance* **9.130** *Co Ltd*.[309] When the Hong Kong Insurance Authority petitioned for the winding up of the company its directors denied that it was insolvent and claimed that accounts showing it to be insolvent were inaccurate. The provisional liquidator had refused them access to the company's accounting records. At the hearing of the petition the provisional liquidator gave evidence that the company was insolvent and the judge refused to adjourn the hearing and direct the provisional liquidator to allow the directors to inspect the accounting records. He made a winding-up order saying that the directors had not presented any evidence to support their claim that the company was not insolvent. The Hong Kong Court of Appeal held that this was in breach of the rules of natural justice. Clough JA said, at p 185, that the Insurance Authority would not be prejudiced by an adjournment, because the company was under the control of the provisional liquidator.

Moratorium for preparation of a voluntary arrangement of a company
or limited liability partnership

The FCA or the PRA may present a petition, on the just and equitable ground, under the **9.131** Financial Services and Markets Act 2000, s 367, for the winding up of a company despite the fact that a moratorium under IA 1986, s 1A (moratorium when directors propose a company voluntary arrangement), is in force in relation to the company.[310] A winding-up order may be made on such a petition, while a moratorium is in force, whether the petition was presented before or since the moratorium started.[311] IA 1986, sch A1, para 12(5)(b) and (c), also permits petitions under previous financial services legislation.

All these provisions are applied to limited liability partnerships by the Limited Liability **9.132** Partnerships Regulations 2001,[312] reg 5.

Companies in or preparing for administration

The FCA and the PRA do not need the court's permission to present a petition under the **9.133** Financial Services and Markets Act 2000, s 367, while an interim moratorium preceding administration is in force for a company.[313] The administrator's consent or the court's permission is required to present such a petition while a company is in administration.[314]

---

[308] (1989) 60 Man R (2d) 186.
[309] [1993] 1 HKLR 179.
[310] sch A1, para 12(1)(a), (4) and (5)(d).
[311] sch A1, para 12(1)(c), (4) and (5)(d).
[312] SI 2001/1090.
[313] IA 1986, sch B1, para 43(1) and (6) applied by para 44(1)–(5); para 42(4)(b) applied by para 44(7)(a).
[314] para 43(1) and (6).

A winding-up order may be made on such a petition (whenever it was presented) while an interim moratorium is in force[315] or while the company is in administration.[316]

9.134 All these provisions are applied to limited liability partnerships by the Limited Liability Partnerships Regulations 2001,[317] reg 5.

Partnerships

9.135 IPO 1994, art 19(4), provides that nothing, except the provisions for a moratorium for preparation of a voluntary arrangement,[318] in IPO 1994 is to be taken as preventing a petition being presented under the Financial Services and Markets Act 2000, s 367, against an insolvent partnership. Section 367(6) and (7) provide that in Scotland, where there is no provision equivalent to IPO 1994 for winding up insolvent partnerships as unregistered companies, winding up on an s 367 petition will be as an unregistered company under IA 1986, part 5, whether the ground for the petition is inability to pay debts or that winding up is just and equitable. But for England and Wales, this is provided only in relation to the just and equitable ground. The assumption seems to be that in England and Wales a petition under s 367 on the ground of insolvency can be presented for winding up as an unregistered company under IPO 1994, whereas the winding up of a solvent partnership on the just and equitable ground can be under IA 1986, part 5, as applied by the Financial Services and Markets Act 2000, s 367(7). The only article of IPO 1994 which may be construed as providing for a petition by the FCA or the PRA is art 7, which provides for the petition 'of any other person other than a member'. A petition under art 7 is for the winding of the partnership with no concurrent insolvency petition against any member.[319]

9.136 A petition may be presented under the Financial Services and Markets Act 2000, s 367, while a moratorium under IA 1986, s 1A, as modified by IPO 1994, sch 1, part 1 (moratorium when members of an insolvent partnership propose a voluntary arrangement), is in force for an insolvent partnership, provided the petition is on the just and equitable ground.[320] A winding-up order may be made on such a petition, while a moratorium is in force, whether the petition was presented before or since the moratorium started.[321] IA 1986, sch A1, para 12(4)(b) and (c), as so modified, also permits petitions under previous financial services legislation.

9.137 The court is given jurisdiction to wind up a partnership, on a petition presented under the Financial Services and Markets Act 2000, s 367 on the just and equitable ground, as if the partnership were an unregistered company.[322] In proceedings on such a petition in respect of a partnership, IA 1986 applies as if the partnership were an unregistered company.[323]

---

[315] para 44(7)(a).
[316] para 42(1), (3) and (4)(b).
[317] SI 2001/1090.
[318] See 9.136.
[319] It is very difficult to make sense of this legislation. *Lindley & Banks on Partnership*, 19th edn (London: Sweet & Maxwell, 2010), 27-04, says that winding up on the ground of insolvency is not as an unregistered company, but does not identify the jurisdiction under which such winding up would proceed. Clearly it cannot be as a registered company. The only possibility seems to be under the Partnership Act 1890, but that does not require a petition, as specified by the Financial Services and Markets Act 2000, s 367. Also it would make no sense to require insolvent winding up to be under the Partnership Act 1890 in England but under IA 1986 in Scotland.
[320] IA 1986, sch A1, para 12(1)(a), (3) and (4)(d), as modified by IPO 1994, sch 1, part 2.
[321] IA 1986, sch A1, para 12(1)(c), (3) and (4)(d), as modified by IPO 1994, sch 1, part 2.
[322] Financial Services and Markets Act 2000, s 367(6) and (7).
[323] Financial Services and Markets Act 2000, s 367(6) and (7).

Residual banks and building societies

The PRA or the FCA must give notice to the Bank of England before petitioning for the **9.138**
winding up of a residual bank or building society.[324] The Bank of England may participate
in the winding-up proceedings.[325]

Feeder UCITS

The legislation[326] regulating undertakings for collective investment in transferable secur- **9.139**
ities (UCITS)[327] contemplates the existence of master-feeder structures. The term 'feeder
UCITS' is defined[328] to mean a UCITS, or a sub-fund of a UCITS, which has been
approved by the FCA, or (where relevant) by its home State regulator, to invest 85 per cent
or more of the total property which is subject to the collective investment scheme constituted by the UCITS in units of another UCITS or UCITS sub-fund (the 'master UCITS').
Where a feeder UCITS is an open-ended investment company and its master UCITS is
wound up, the FCA must petition for the winding up of the feeder UCITS unless the FCA
approves:

(a) the investment by the feeder UCITS of at least 85 per cent of its assets in the units of
another UCITS or master UCITS; or
(b) the conversion of the feeder UCITS into a UCITS which is not a feeder UCITS.[329]

It is provided that the FCA can petition only if it considers that the feeder UCITS may **9.140**
be wound up under IA 1986, s 221.[330] However, it is submitted that this does not affect
the position that the FCA's only power to petition for winding up is under the Financial
Services and Markets Act 2000, s 367, which provides for winding up only under IA 1986,
s 122(1)(f) (inability to pay debts) or (g) (just and equitable).[331]

Friendly Societies

The FCA or the PRA may petition for the winding up of an incorporated friendly society[332] **9.141**
on any of the grounds specified in the Friendly Societies Act 1992, s 22(1).[333] Before either
regulator presents a petition for the winding up of an incorporated friendly society, it must
consult the other regulator.[334] If an incorporated friendly society is not a PRA-authorized
person,[335] the PRA cannot petition for it to be wound up[336] and the FCA is not required to
consult the PRA before petitioning.[337]

---

[324] Banking Act 2009, s 157. Applied to building societies by the Building Societies Act 1986, s 90C. For
the meaning of 'residual' in this context see 1.265.
[325] Banking Act 2009, s 157(1); Building Societies Act 1986, s 90C.
[326] Financial Services and Markets Act 2000, part 17 (ss 235–84).
[327] The term 'UCITS' is defined for this purpose in Directive 2009/65/EC, art 1.2, which is applied by the
Financial Services and Markets Act 2000, s 237(3).
[328] Financial Services and Markets Act 2000, s 237(3).
[329] Open-Ended Investment Companies Regulations 2001 (SI 2001/1228), reg 33A.
[330] SI 2001/1228, reg 33A(2).
[331] See 9.125.
[332] Friendly Societies Act 1992, ss 22(2)(a) and 119(1).
[333] See 2.34.
[334] Friendly Societies Act 1992, s 22(2A) and (2B).
[335] See 9.114.
[336] Friendly Societies Act 1992, s 22(2B).
[337] Friendly Societies Act 1992, s 22(2A).

9.142 The FCA or the PRA may, under the Friendly Societies Act 1992, s 65, appoint one or more competent persons to investigate and report to it on the state and conduct of the activities of a friendly society. If a report under s 65 on an unincorporated registered friendly society is received by a regulator and it appears to that regulator from the report that it is in the interests of the society's members or of the public that the society should be wound up, that regulator may, after consulting the other regulator, petition for the society to be wound up under IA 1986 if the court thinks it just and equitable.[338] The petition must be presented to the High Court and cannot be presented if the society is already being wound up by the court.[339]

Registered Providers of Social Housing and Social Landlords

9.143 In England, if a registered provider of social housing is a non-profit organization[340] and is a registered society or a registered company, the Regulator of Social Housing may present a petition for it to be wound up on any of the following grounds:[341]

(a) that it is failing properly to carry out its objects;
(b) that it is unable to pay its debts within the meaning of IA 1986, s 123;
(c) that the regulator has directed it[342] to transfer all its land to another person.

9.144 In Wales, if a registered social landlord[343] is a registered company (including a company which is also a registered charity) or a registered society, the Welsh Ministers may present a petition for it to be wound up on either of the following grounds:[344]

(a) that the landlord is failing properly to carry out its purposes or objects, or
(b) that the landlord is unable to pay its debts within the meaning of IA 1986, s 123.

Registered Societies

9.145 Under the Co-operative and Community Benefit Societies Act 2014, sch 3, para 15, the FCA or the PRA may petition for the winding up of a society registered, or deemed to be registered, under the Industrial and Provident Societies Act 1893 before 26 July 1938 if it appears to the regulator concerned:

(a) that the society meets neither of the conditions in s 2(2)(a) of the 2014 Act for registration under the Act (the society is a bona fide cooperative society or the business of the society is being, or is intended to be, conducted for the benefit of the community); and
(b) that the winding up of the society would be in the interests of persons who have invested or deposited money with the society or any other person.

---

[338] Friendly Societies Act 1974, s 87(1). Section 87(1) applies in relation to a registered branch of a registered friendly society as it applies in relation to such a society (s 87(2)).
[339] s 87(1).
[340] Provision for registration with the Office for Tenants and Social Landlords (the Regulator of Social Housing) is made in the Housing and Regeneration Act 2008, ss 110–121. Each entry in the register must designate the body registered as either a non-profit organization or a profit-making organization (s 115, in which those terms are defined).
[341] Housing and Regeneration Act 2008, s 166.
[342] Under s 253 following an inquiry or audit.
[343] Provision for registration of social landlords in Wales is made in the Housing Act 1996, ss A1–6.
[344] Housing Act 1996, sch 1, para 14.

The PRA must consult the FCA before presenting a petition under this provision.[345] The **9.146**
FCA must consult the PRA before presenting a petition under this provision in respect of
a PRA-authorized person.[346] For the background to this provision, see *Re First Mortgage
Co-operative Investment Trust Ltd*.[347]

---

[345] Co-operative and Community Benefit Societies Act 2014, sch 3, para 15(3).
[346] para 15(2). PRA-authorized person is defined in 9.114.
[347] [1941] 2 All ER 529.

10

COMPANY SUBJECT TO ANOTHER INSOLVENCY PROCEEDING

Introduction

10.1 Where a company is already subject to an insolvency procedure, this chapter sets out who can apply for a winding-up order. For all the insolvency procedures where there is an insolvency office-holder, that office-holder is given standing to apply for winding up.[1] For many insolvency procedures, no person other than the office-holder can apply except the Secretary of State and financial regulators acting in the public interest. These restrictions do not apply to a receivership or administrative receivership (neither of which is ended by a winding up) or a voluntary arrangement.

10.2 This chapter deals first with insolvency procedures under the law of England and Wales, then insolvency procedures in other parts of the United Kingdom, and then insolvency procedures outside the UK.

Voluntary Arrangements

Company Voluntary Arrangements

Moratorium for preparation of company voluntary arrangement

10.3 While a moratorium under the Insolvency Act 1986 (IA 1986), s 1A (moratorium when directors propose a company voluntary arrangement), is in force for a company,[2] no petition

---

[1] There is no office-holder for a moratorium while a voluntary arrangement is prepared or for an interim moratorium before administration.

[2] For the scope of the provisions on company voluntary arrangements see 1.238–1.241.

may be presented for the company to be wound up,[3] except[4] by:

(a) the Secretary of State as a public interest petition under s 124A;[5]
(b) the Secretary of State in respect of a European public limited-liability company (SE) under s 124B;[6] or
(c) the Financial Conduct Authority (FCA) or the Prudential Regulation Authority (PRA) on the just and equitable ground under the Financial Services and Markets Act 2000, s 367.[7]

While a moratorium is in force for a company, an order for it to be wound up can be made only **10.4** on petitions of kinds (a), (b) and (c), whether presented before or after the moratorium started.[8]

Failure of moratorium to produce voluntary arrangement

The circumstance that when a moratorium for a company under IA 1986, s 1A, comes to an **10.5** end, no approved voluntary arrangement has effect in relation to the company is a circumstance in which the company may be wound up by the court.[9] A petition for winding up on this ground may be presented only by a creditor or creditors.[10]

Petition by supervisor of a company's voluntary arrangement for the company to be wound up

A supervisor of a company's voluntary arrangement approved under IA 1986, part 1, may **10.6** petition for the compulsory winding up of the company,[11] and the court may appoint the supervisor to be liquidator of the company.[12] Such a petition must be presented to the court to which the nominee's report under s 2 was submitted.[13]

A supervisor's petition is presented in the supervisor's own name, not in the company's **10.7** name. It is treated as a contributories' petition.[14] If the court considers it just in all the circumstances, it may hear the petition on the return day rather than give directions.[15]

In *Re Carman Construction Ltd*[16] the supervisor of a company's voluntary arrangement successfully petitioned for a winding-up order after the company had been put into voluntary **10.8** winding up without his agreement, contrary to the terms of the arrangement.

A company's voluntary arrangement is ended by an order for the company's compulsory **10.9** winding up, if the order was made on a petition by the supervisor of the arrangement,[17] but not if the petition was by the company's directors or by a creditor who is not bound by the arrangement.[18]

---

[3] IA 1986, sch A1, para 12(1)(a).
[4] para 12(4) and (5).
[5] See 9.72–9.73.
[6] See 9.90–9.92.
[7] See 9.131–9.132.
[8] IA 1986, sch A1, para 12(1)(c), (4) and (5).
[9] IA 1986, s 122(1)(fa).
[10] s 124(3A).
[11] s 7(4)(b).
[12] s 140(2); for procedure see 5.143–5.150.
[13] IR 1986, r 4.7(8).
[14] r 4.7(9); see 8.469–8.518.
[15] r 4.22(2)(b).
[16] (1999) LTL 16/12/99.
[17] *Re Arthur Rathbone Kitchens Ltd* [1997] 2 BCLC 280.
[18] *Re Excalibur Airways Ltd* [1998] 1 BCLC 436.

10.10   IA 1986, s 7(3) (which provides for the court to make orders controlling a supervisor's conduct on the application of a creditor or any other person dissatisfied by any act, omission or decision of the supervisor), does not empower the court to order the supervisor of a company's voluntary arrangement not to petition for the company to be wound up.[19]

Limited Liability Partnerships

10.11   All the provisions of IA 1986 and IR 1986 mentioned in 10.3–10.10 are applied to limited liability partnerships.[20] The provisions of IA 1986 are modified.[21] In the version of s 122(1) which applies to limited liability partnerships (LLPs), the circumstance that when a moratorium for an LLP under s 1A comes to an end, no approved voluntary arrangement has effect in relation to the LLP, is a circumstance in which the LLP may be wound up by the court.[22]

Charitable Incorporated Organizations

10.12   All the provisions of IA 1986 and IR 1986 mentioned in 10.3–10.10 are applied to charitable incorporated organizations.[23] IA 1986, sch A1, para 12(5), is substituted[24] to provide that the only petition which may be presented, or on which a winding-up order may be made, while a moratorium is in force is one presented by the Attorney General or the Charity Commission.[25] In the version of IA 1986, s 122(1), which applies to charitable incorporated organizations (CIOs), the circumstance that when a moratorium for a CIO under s 1A comes to an end, no approved voluntary arrangement has effect in relation to the CIO, is a circumstance in which the CIO may be wound up by the court.[26]

Building Society Voluntary Arrangements

10.13   IA 1986, part 1, is applied with modifications to building societies by the Building Societies Act 1986, sch 15A, without provision for a moratorium. What is said in 10.6–10.10 about company voluntary arrangements also applies to building society voluntary arrangements.[27] The exception is that, unfortunately, IA 1986, s 140, was prevented from applying to building societies by the Building Societies Act 1986, sch 15, para 22, when voluntary arrangements and administration were not available to building societies, and was not reinstated when those procedures became available.

Insolvent Partnerships

Moratorium for preparation of partnership voluntary arrangement

10.14   While a moratorium under IA 1986, s 1A, as applied by the Insolvent Partnerships Order (IPO 1994), art 4, and modified by IPO 1994, sch 1, part 1 (moratorium when members of an

---

[19] *Re Leisure Study Group Ltd* [1994] 2 BCLC 65.
[20] Limited Liability Partnerships Regulations 2001 (SI 2001/1090), regs 5 and 10(1)(b) and sch 6, part 2. IR 1986, r 4.7, applies by virtue of r 4.2(1) and (2).
[21] By SI 2001/1090, sch 3.
[22] IA 1986, s 122(1)(da), as substituted by SI 2001/1090, sch 3. The cross-reference in IA 1986, s 124(3A), is modified accordingly.
[23] Charitable Incorporated Organisations (Insolvency and Dissolution) Regulations 2012 (SI 2012/3013), sch.
[24] By SI 2012/3013, sch, para 1(7).
[25] Under the Charities Act 2011, s 113.
[26] IA 1986, s 122(1)(d), as substituted by SI 2012/3013, sch 1, para 1(5). The cross-reference in IA 1986, s 124(3A), is modified accordingly by SI 2012/3013, sch 1, para 1(7).
[27] The rules in IR 1986, r 4.7, apply by virtue of r 4.2(1) and (2).

insolvent partnership propose a voluntary arrangement), is in force for an insolvent partnership, no petition may be presented for the partnership to be wound up,[28] except[29] by:

(a) the Secretary of State as a public interest petition under s 124A(1)(b), (c) or (d);[30] or
(b) the FCA or the PRA on the just and equitable ground under the Financial Services and Markets Act 2000, s 367.[31]

While a moratorium is in force for a partnership, an order for it to be wound up can be made **10.15** only on petitions of kinds (a) and (b), whether presented before or after the moratorium started.[32]

Failure of moratorium to produce voluntary arrangement

The circumstance that when a moratorium for an insolvent partnership under IA 1986, **10.16** s 1A, as applied by IPO 1994, art 4, comes to an end, no approved voluntary arrangement has effect in relation to the partnership is a circumstance in which the partnership may be wound up by the court.[33] This ground is available only for a petition under IPO 1994, art 8, and an art 8 petition may be presented only by a creditor or creditors.[34]

If a partnership moratorium fails and a corporate member, or former corporate member, is **10.17** liable for a partnership debt, this is a circumstance in which the corporate member may be wound up on an art 8 petition.[35]

Petition by a partnership's voluntary arrangement supervisor for its winding up

The supervisor of a partnership voluntary arrangement may apply to the court, under IPO **10.18** 1994, art 7, for the winding up of the partnership as an unregistered company (with no concurrent petition for the winding up or bankruptcy of any member or former member of the partnership).[36] The supervisor may be appointed provisional liquidator and, if the winding-up order is made, liquidator of the partnership.[37]

The provisions of IR 1986, r 4.7, relating to a petition by the supervisor of a voluntary **10.19** arrangement[38] apply to a petition by the supervisor of a partnership voluntary arrangement.[39]

A supervisor of a voluntary arrangement of a member of an insolvent partnership may apply **10.20** to the court, under IPO 1994, art 7, for the winding up of the partnership as an unregistered company.[40] The supervisor may be appointed provisional liquidator and, if the winding-up order is made, liquidator of the partnership.[41]

---

[28] IA 1986, sch A1, para 12(1)(c), as modified by IPO 1994, sch 1, part 2.
[29] IA 1986, sch A1, para 12(3) and (4), as modified by IPO 1994, sch 1, part 2.
[30] See 9.74.
[31] See 9.136.
[32] IA 1986, sch A1, para 12(1)(c), (3) and (4), as modified by IPO 1994, sch 1, part 2.
[33] IA 1986, s 221(8)(b), as modified by IPO 1994, sch 4, para 3.
[34] See 2.86.
[35] IA 1986, s 122, as modified by IPO 1994, sch 4, para 6(a), and applied by art 8(4), (5) and (8).
[36] IA 1986, s 221A(1)(d), inserted by IPO 1994, sch 3, para 3; IA 1986, s 7(4)(b), as applied by IPO 1994, art 4(1), and modified by sch 1, part 1.
[37] See 5.143–5.150. IA 1986, s 221A(4) and (5), inserted by IPO 1994, sch 3, para 3.
[38] See 10.6–10.10.
[39] IR 1986, r 4.2(1) and (2).
[40] IA 1986, s 221A(1)(d), inserted by IPO 1994, sch 3, para 3.
[41] See 5.143–5.150. IA 1986, s 221A(4) and (5), inserted by IPO 1994, sch 3, para 3.

Conversion from Voluntary Arrangement to Winding-up Proceedings

10.21   If a company or other entity for which a voluntary arrangement is in force in England and Wales is subject to main insolvency proceedings elsewhere in the EU which are subject to Regulation (EC) No 1346/2000,[42] the liquidator in the main proceedings is entitled, under art 37, to request the court to convert the voluntary arrangement into winding-up proceedings, if this proves to be in the interests of the creditors in the main proceedings. A procedure for dealing with applications for a conversion order is set out in IR 1986, rr 1.31–1.33, in which the liquidator in the main proceedings is referred to as a member State liquidator.[43] There is a virtually identical procedure for converting administration into winding-up proceedings.[44]

10.22   The court's order is described as being for conversion into winding-up proceedings.[45] It is an order under Regulation (EC) No 1346/2000, art 37, that the voluntary arrangement is converted into:

(a) administration proceedings whose purposes are limited to the winding up of the company through administration and are to exclude the purpose contained in IA 1986, sch B1, para 3(1)(a) (rescuing the company as a going concern);

(b) a creditors' voluntary winding up; or

(c) a winding up by the court.

10.23   An application[46] for conversion of a voluntary arrangement into winding-up proceedings must be supported by a witness statement, which must be filed with the court, giving the information required by IR 1986, r 1.32(1).[47] The application and written evidence must be served on the company and the supervisor.[48] For rules on service see 3.249–3.251. The court fee is £160.[49]

10.24   The witness statement must be made by, or on behalf of, the liquidator in the main proceedings.[50] It must state:[51]

(a) that main proceedings have been opened in relation to the company in a member State other than the United Kingdom or Denmark;

(b) the belief of the person making the statement that the conversion of the voluntary arrangement into winding-up proceedings would prove to be in the interests of the creditors in the main proceedings;

(c) the opinion of the person making the statement on whether the company ought to go into voluntary liquidation or be wound up by the court; and

(d) all other matters that, in the opinion of the liquidator in the main proceedings, would assist the court:

---

[42] See 1.361–1.407.
[43] IR 1986, r 13.13(11).
[44] See 10.62–10.66.
[45] IR 1986, r 1.31(1A).
[46] See 3.233–3.263.
[47] r 1.31(1).
[48] r 1.31(3).
[49] Civil Proceedings Fees Order 2008 (SI 2008/1053), sch 1, fee 3.6.
[50] IR 1986, r 1.32(2).
[51] IR 1986, r 1.32(1).

    (i) in deciding whether to make an order converting the voluntary arrangement into winding-up proceedings; and

    (ii) if the court were to do so, in considering the need for any consequential provision that would be necessary or desirable.

On hearing an application for conversion of a voluntary arrangement into winding-up proceedings, the court may make such order as it thinks fit.[52] An order for conversion may contain whatever consequential provisions the court deems necessary or desirable.[53] If the court orders conversion into a creditors' voluntary winding up, it may provide that the company is to be wound up as if a resolution for voluntary winding up had been passed on the day the order is made.[54] **10.25**

Administration

Schedule B1 Administration

Interim moratorium

While an interim moratorium under IA 1986, sch B1, para 44, is in force for a company, no petition may be presented for the company to be wound up without the court's permission,[55] except: **10.26**

(a) by the Secretary of State as a public interest petition under s 124A;[56]

(b) by the Secretary of State in respect of a European public limited-liability company under s 124B;[57]

(c) by the FCA or the PRA under the Financial Services and Markets Act 2000, s 367;[58] or

(d) for the purpose of proceedings under the default rules of exchanges and clearing houses in financial markets described in 10.67.[59]

While an interim moratorium is in force for a company, an order for it to be wound up can be made only on petitions of kinds (a), (b), (c) and (d), whether presented before or after the moratorium started.[60] **10.27**

In the application of these provisions to a charitable incorporated organization, the petitions of kinds (a), (b) and (c) are replaced by a petition presented by the Attorney General or the Charity Commission under the Charities Act 2011, s 113.[61] **10.28**

---

  [52] r 1.33(1).
  [53] r 1.33(2).
  [54] r 1.33(3).
  [55] IA 1986, sch B1, para 43(6), applied and modified by para 44(5); *Re Arucana Ltd* [2009] EWHC 3838 (Ch), LTL 21/6/2012.
  [56] paras 42(4)(a) and 44(7)(a); see 9.75–9.77.
  [57] paras 42(4)(aa) and 44(7)(a); see 9.90–9.92.
  [58] IA 1986, sch B1, paras 42(4)(b) and 44(7)(a); see 9.133–9.134.
  [59] Companies Act 1989, s 161(4).
  [60] IA 1986, sch B1, para 42(3) and (4) applied by para 44(5); Companies Act 1989, s 161(4).
  [61] Charitable Incorporated Organisations (Insolvency and Dissolution) Regulations 2012 (SI 2012/3013), sch, para 1(7).

Companies in administration

10.29 When a company is in administration, no petition for it to be wound up may be presented without the administrator's consent or the court's permission,[62] unless it is presented for the purpose of proceedings under the default rules of exchanges and clearing houses in financial markets described in 10.67.[63] No order may be made to wind up a company in administration,[64] except on a petition presented:

(a) by the Secretary of State as a public interest petition under IA 1986, s 124A;[65]

(b) by the Secretary of State in respect of a European public limited-liability company under s 124B;[66]

(c) by the FCA or the PRA under the Financial Services and Markets Act 2000, s 367;[67] or

(d) for the purpose of proceedings under the default rules of exchanges and clearing houses in financial markets described in 10.67.[68]

10.30 In the application of these provisions to a charitable incorporated organization, the petitions of kinds (a), (b) and (c) are replaced by a petition presented by the Attorney General or the Charity Commission under the Charities Act 2011, s 113.[69]

Petition by a company's administrator for it to be wound up

10.31 A petition for the compulsory winding up of a company may be presented at the instance of the company's administrator.[70] Such a petition must be presented to the court having jurisdiction for the administration.[71] An administrator of a company is deemed to act as the company's agent[72] and an administrator's petition must be expressed to be the petition of the company by its administrator.[73] It must state the name of the administrator, the court case number and the date that the company entered administration.[74]

10.32 A petition presented at the instance of an administrator must contain, where applicable, an application under IA 1986, sch B1, para 79, requesting that the administrator's appointment shall cease to have effect from a specified time,[75] because of the restrictions on making a winding-up order when a company is in administration.[76] An administrator's petition is treated as a contributories' petition.[77] If the court considers it just in all the circumstances, it may hear the petition on the return day rather than give directions.[78]

---

[62] IA 1986, sch B1, para 43(1) and (6); *Re BTR (UK) Ltd* [2012] EWHC 2398 (Ch), [2012] BCC 864, at [73].

[63] Companies Act 1989, s 161(4).

[64] IA 1986, sch B1, para 42(3).

[65] sch B1, paras 42(4)(a) and 44(7)(a); see 9.75–9.77.

[66] paras 42(4)(aa) and 44(7)(a); see 9.90–9.92.

[67] IA 1986, sch B1, paras 42(4)(b) and 44(7)(a); see 9.133–9.134.

[68] Companies Act 1989, s 161(4).

[69] Charitable Incorporated Organisations (Insolvency and Dissolution) Regulations 2012 (SI 2012/3013), sch, para 1(7).

[70] IA 1986, sch B1, para 60, and sch 1, para 21.

[71] IR 1986, r 4.7(8).

[72] IA 1986, sch B1, para 69.

[73] IR 1986, r 4.7(7)(a).

[74] r 4.7(7)(b).

[75] IR 1986, r 4.7(7)(c).

[76] See 10.29.

[77] IR 1986, r 4.7(9); see 8.469–8.518.

[78] IR 1986, r 4.22(2)(b).

If a winding-up order is made immediately upon the appointment of an administrator ceasing to have effect, the court may appoint the former administrator (but no one else) instead of the official receiver as liquidator.[79]   **10.33**

An administrator of a company may also personally petition for it to be wound up as a creditor in respect of unpaid charges.[80]   **10.34**

Moving from administration to dissolution

If the administrator of a company has sent to the registrar of companies notice that, in the administrator's opinion, the company has no property which might permit a distribution to its creditors,[81] the administrator's appointment will cease to have effect on registration of the notice.[82] Normally the company would be dissolved three months after registration of the notice.[83] However, an application may be made to the court for an order disapplying automatic dissolution[84] coupled with a petition for the company to be wound up by the court.[85] The applicant must be 'the administrator or another interested person'[86] and must have standing to petition for winding up.[87] A winding-up order may be made in these circumstances so that there can be further investigation of the company's affairs.[88]   **10.35**

Failure to obtain approval of administrator's proposals

If an administrator of a company reports to the court that a creditors' meeting has failed to approve the administrator's proposals for achieving the purpose of administration,[89] or a revision of previously approved proposals,[90] the administrator must apply to the court to exercise its powers under IA 1986, sch B1, para 55(2).[91] That sub-paragraph includes provisions under which the court may: **10.36**

(a) provide that the administrator's appointment shall cease to have effect from a specified time;[92]

---

[79] IA 1986, s 140(1); for procedure see 5.143–5.150.

[80] *Re Lafayette Electronics Europe Ltd* [2006] EWHC 1006 (Ch), LTL 9/10/2006.

[81] IA 1986, sch B1, para 84(1).

[82] IA 1986, sch B1, para 84(3). For a charitable incorporated organization, the notice is sent to the Charity Commission and the administrator's appointment ceases when the Commission publishes the notice (Charitable Incorporated Organisations (Insolvency and Dissolution) Regulations 2012 (SI 2012/3013), sch, para 1(3)(e) and (7)).

[83] IA 1986, sch B1, para 84(6).

[84] IA 1986, sch B1, para 84(7)(c).

[85] *Re Hellas Telecommunications (Luxembourg) II SCA* [2011] EWHC 3176 (Ch), [2013] 1 BCLC 426, at [85].

[86] IA 1986, sch B1, para 84(7). Registration of the para 84(1) notice terminates the administrator's appointment, so 'the administrator' here must mean the former administrator (*Re People's Restaurant Group Ltd* (2012) LTL 6/2/2013 at [30]–[31]).

[87] In *Re Hellas Telecommunications (Luxembourg) II SCA* [2011] EWHC 3176 (Ch), [2013] 1 BCLC 426, at [85] it was said that a creditor could make the application and file the petition, though the former administrators undertook to do so after the court directed that the company should be wound up by the court (at [95]).

[88] *Re Hellas Telecommunications (Luxembourg) II SCA* [2011] EWHC 3176 (Ch), [2013] 1 BCLC 426, at [86]–[95].

[89] See IA 1986, sch B1, paras 49–53.

[90] IA 1986, sch B1, para 54.

[91] *Re BTR (UK) Ltd* [2012] EWHC 2398 (Ch), [2012] BCC 864, at [64] and [69]. A creditor may apply if the administrator does not (*Re BTR (UK) Ltd* at [64]).

[92] IA 1986, sch B1, para 55(2)(a).

(b) if the administrator was appointed by the holder of a qualifying floating charge when a winding-up petition was pending, make an order on that petition;[93]

(c) in any other case, direct the administrator to petition for winding up by the court,[94] or make a winding-up order of its own motion.[95]

10.37 A winding-up order may be made of the court's own motion only in thoroughly exceptional circumstances,[96] for example, where it is plain that an order should be made, no persons not before the court will be prejudiced, the creditors should not be put to the expense of petitioning, and there is an urgent need for the company's affairs to be investigated.[97]

Limited liability partnerships

10.38 All the provisions of IA 1986 and IR 1986 mentioned in 10.26–10.37 are applied to limited liability partnerships.[98] The Companies Act 1989, s 161(4), disapplies those provisions whenever they would otherwise apply.

Industry-specific Administration Regimes

Protection from winding up

10.39 In the industry-specific administration regimes discussed at 1.245–1.294, petitions by the Secretary of State, the FCA and the PRA are not exempted from the need to obtain permission to present a petition and the ban on making a winding-up order as they are in administration proceedings in relation to other companies.[99] But in some of the regimes there are provisions for putting a company into administration when there would otherwise be a winding up in the public interest.[100]

Interim moratorium

10.40 While a petition is pending for an administration order to be made in respect of a company under any of the industry-specific administration regimes based on IA 1986, part 2, without the amendments made by the Enterprise Act 2002, s 248,[101] a petition to wind up the company may be presented by any person without the court's permission,[102] but no winding-up order may be made,[103] except in relation to a company incorporated outside Great Britain if it is a protected railway company[104] or a PPP company.[105]

---

[93] IA 1986, sch B1, para 55(2)(d). The petition will have been suspended under para 40(1)(b); see 3.103–3.105.

[94] IA 1986, sch B1, para 55(2)(e); *Re BTR (UK) Ltd* at [73].

[95] IA 1986, sch B1, para 55(2)(e); *Re BTR (UK) Ltd*.

[96] *Lancefield v Lancefield* [2002] BPIR 1108 (see 2.20–2.22); *Re BTR (UK) Ltd* at [74]–[75].

[97] *Re BTR (UK) Ltd* at [83].

[98] Limited Liability Partnerships Regulations 2001 (SI 2001/1090), regs 5 and 10 and sch 6. The provisions of IR 1986, r 4.7, also apply by virtue of r 4.2(1) and (2).

[99] See 10.26–10.30. But petitions for the purpose of proceedings under the default rules of exchanges and clearing houses in financial markets (CA 1989, s 161(4); see 10.67) are exempt.

[100] See 9.77.

[101] See 1.248–1.261.

[102] IA 1986, s 10(2)(a), as applied by the provisions cited in 10.41.

[103] s 10(1)(a), as applied by the provisions cited in 10.41.

[104] Railways Act 1993, s 65(4)(a).

[105] Greater London Authority Act 1999, s 224(4)(a).

The relevant provisions of IA 1986, part 2,[106] are continued in force by the Enterprise Act **10.41**
2002, s 249, and applied:

(a) to water industry special administration by the Water Industry Act 1991, s 24(5);
(b) to railway administration by the Railways Act 1993, s 60(5);
(c) to administration of building societies by the Building Societies Act 1986, sch 15A, paras 1, 2 and 12;
(d) to PPP administration by the Greater London Authority Act 1999, s 221(5);
(e) to air traffic administration by the Transport Act 2000, s 30(3).

While an application is pending for an administration order to be made in respect of a **10.42**
company under any of the industry-specific administration regimes based on schedule B1
administration,[107] the court's permission is required for the presentation of any winding-up
petition.[108]

The relevant provisions of IA 1986, sch B1,[109] are applied: **10.43**

(a) to energy administration and energy supply company administration by the Energy Act 2004, sch 20, paras 1–4 and 8;[110]
(b) to bank administration, building society special administration and special administration (bank administration) by the Banking Act 2009, s 145(2), (3), (4) and table 1;[111]
(c) to investment bank special administration and special administration (bank insolvency) by the Investment Bank Special Administration Regulations 2011 (SI 2011/245), reg 15(4), (5) and table 1;[112]
(d) to postal administration by the Postal Services Act 2011, sch 10, paras 1, 2 and 6;
(e) to FMI administration by the Financial Services (Banking Reform) Act 2013, sch 6, paras 2 and 3 and table 1.

In some administration regimes, when deciding whether to give permission, the court must **10.44**
have regard to the following objectives:

(a) in bank administration and building society special administration, the objectives set out in the Banking Act 2009, s 137;[113]
(b) in special administration (bank administration), objective A and the special administration objectives;[114]
(c) in special administration (bank insolvency), objective A.[115]

---

[106] IA 1986, s 10(1)(a) and (2)(a).
[107] See 1.262–1.287 and 1.291–1.294.
[108] IA 1986, sch B1, para 43(1) and (6), as applied by para 44(1) and (5), and applied by the provisions cited in 10.43.
[109] paras 43(1) and (6) and 44(1) and (5).
[110] Applied to energy supply company administration by the Energy Act 2011, s 96.
[111] Applied to building society special administration by the Building Societies Act 1986, s 90C. Applied to special administration (bank administration) by the Investment Bank Special Administration Regulations 2011 (SI 2011/245), sch 2, para 6.
[112] Applied to special administration (bank insolvency) by SI 2011/245, sch 1, para 5(1).
[113] IA 1986, sch B1, para 43, as modified by the Banking Act 2009, s 145, table 1.
[114] IA 1986, sch B1, para 43, as modified by the Banking Act 2009, s 145, table 1, and further modified by SI 2011/245, sch 2, para 6(2)(f). For the objectives of special administration (bank administration) see 1.279.
[115] SI 2011/245, sch 1, para 5(2). For the objectives of special administration (bank insolvency) see 1.276.

During administration

10.45 While an administration order made under any of the industry-specific administration regimes based on IA 1986, part 2, without the amendments made by the Enterprise Act 2002, s 248,[116] is in force in relation to a company, no winding-up order may be made on any person's petition,[117] except for the purpose of proceedings under the default rules of exchanges and clearing houses in financial markets described in 10.67[118] or in relation to a company incorporated outside Great Britain if it is in railway administration[119] or PPP administration.[120] While such an administration order is in force, no petition for the company to be wound up may be presented without the administrator's consent or the court's leave,[121] except for the purpose of proceedings under the default rules of exchanges and clearing houses in financial markets.[122]

10.46 The relevant provisions of IA 1986, part 2,[123] are continued in force by the Enterprise Act 2002, s 249, and applied:

(a) to water industry special administration by the Water Industry Act 1991, sch 3, paras 1 and 2;

(b) to railway administration by the Railways Act 1993, sch 6, paras 1 and 2;

(c) to administration of building societies by the Building Societies Act 1986, sch 15A, paras 1, 2 and 13;

(d) to PPP administration by the Greater London Authority Act 1999, sch 14, paras 1 and 2;

(e) to air traffic administration by the Transport Act 2000, sch 1, paras 1–4.

10.47 While an administration order made under any of the industry-specific administration regimes based on schedule B1 administration,[124] is in force in relation to a company, no winding-up petition may be presented without the administrator's consent or the court's permission, and no order may be made for the winding up of the company,[125] except for the purpose of proceedings under the default rules of exchanges and clearing houses in financial markets described in 10.67.[126]

10.48 The relevant provisions of IA 1986, sch B1,[127] are applied:

(a) to energy administration and energy supply company administration by the Energy Act 2004, sch 20, paras 1, 2 and 7;[128]

---

[116] See 1.248–1.261.

[117] IA 1986, s 11(3)(a), as applied by the provisions cited in 10.46.

[118] Companies Act 1989, s 161(4), without the amendment made by the Enterprise Act 2002; Enterprise Act 2002, s 249.

[119] Railways Act 1993, sch 6, para 13(4)(a).

[120] Greater London Authority Act 1999, sch 14, para 13(4)(a).

[121] IA 1986, s 11(3)(d), as applied by the provisions cited in 10.46.

[122] Companies Act 1989, s 161(4), without the amendment made by the Enterprise Act 2002; Enterprise Act 2002, s 249.

[123] s 11(3)(a) and (d).

[124] See 1.262–1.287 and 1.291–1.294.

[125] IA 1986, sch B1, paras 42(1) and (3) and 43(1) and (6), as applied by the provisions cited in 10.48.

[126] Companies Act 1989, s 161(4).

[127] paras 42(1) and (3) and 43(1) and (6).

[128] Applied to energy supply company administration by the Energy Act 2011, s 96.

(b) to bank administration, building society special administration and special administration (bank administration) by the Banking Act 2009, s 145(2), (3), (4) and table 1;[129]

(c) to investment bank special administration and special administration (bank insolvency) by the Investment Bank Special Administration Regulations 2011 (SI 2011/245), reg 15(4), (5) and table 1;[130]

(d) to postal administration by the Postal Services Act 2011, sch 10, paras 1, 2 and 5;

(e) to FMI administration by the Financial Services (Banking Reform) Act 2013, sch 6, paras 2 and 3 and table 1.

10.49 In bank administration, building society special administration or special administration (bank administration), if there has been a transfer to a bridge bank,[131] consent of the administrator cannot be given without the approval of the Bank of England, unless the Bank has given an objective 1 achievement notice (objective A achievement notice in special administration (bank administration)).[132]

10.50 In some administration regimes, when deciding whether to give permission, the court must have regard to the following objectives:

(a) In bank administration or building society special administration, the court must have regard to the objectives set out in the Banking Act 2009, s 137, but this does not apply if the administration follows transfer to a bridge bank and the Bank of England has given an objective 1 achievement notice.[133]

(b) In special administration (bank administration), the court must have regard to objective A and the special administration objectives, but this does not apply if the administration follows transfer to a bridge bank and the Bank of England has given an objective A achievement notice.[134]

(c) In special administration (bank insolvency), until the objective A committee has passed a full payment resolution, any decision by the court must have regard to the achievement of objective A.[135]

---

[129] Applied to building society special administration by the Building Societies Act 1986, s 90C. Applied to special administration (bank administration) by the Investment Bank Special Administration Regulations 2011 (SI 2011/245), sch 2, para 6.

[130] Applied to special administration (bank insolvency) by SI 2011/245, sch 1, para 5(1).

[131] A company wholly owned by the Bank of England to which all or part of the business of a bank, building society or investment bank is transferred in accordance with the Banking Act 2009, ss 12 and 136 (applied to building society special administration by the Building Societies Act 1986, s 90C). For special administration (bank administration) see SI 2011/245, sch 2, para 17.

[132] IA 1986, sch B1, para 43, as modified by the Banking Act 2009, s 145, table 1; applied to building societies by the Building Societies Act 1986, s 90C; applied to special administration (bank administration) and further modified by SI 2011/245, sch 2, para 6. 'Objective 1 achievement notice' is defined in 1.266, 'objective A achievement notice' in 1.279.

[133] IA 1986, sch B1, para 43, as modified by the Banking Act 2009, s 145, table 1; applied to building societies by the Building Societies Act 1986, s 90C.

[134] IA 1986, sch B1, para 43, as modified by the Banking Act 2009, s 145, table 1, and further modified by SI 2011/245, sch 2, para 6(2)(f). For the objectives of special administration (bank administration) see 1.279.

[135] SI 2011/245, sch 1, para 5(2). For the objectives of special administration (bank insolvency) see 1.276.

Petition by a company's administrator for its winding up

10.51 The industry-specific administration regimes described at 1.245–1.294 all have the same provision for an administrator to apply:

(a) for the administration to end;

(b) for the winding up of the company; and

(c) to be appointed its liquidator,[136]

as in schedule B1 administration.[137] In the industry-specific administration regimes based on IA 1986, part 2, without the amendments made by the Enterprise Act 2002, s 248,[138] the administrator's power to petition for winding up is in IA 1986, s 14(1) and sch 1, para 21; the deemed agency of an administrator is provided by s 14(5); and an application to discharge an administration order is made under s 18. All these provisions are applied:

(a) to special administration of water companies by the Water Industry Act 1991, sch 3, paras 1, 4 and 7 (the company must have ceased to be appointed as a water or sewerage undertaker or ceased to be a qualified licensed water supplier, otherwise it cannot be wound up: s 25);

(b) to railway administration by the Railways Act 1993, sch 6, paras 1, 4, 7, 12 and 15;

(c) to administration of building societies by the Building Societies Act 1986, sch 15A, paras 1, 2 and 16;

(d) to PPP administration by the Greater London Authority Act 1999, sch 14, paras 1, 4 and 7;

(e) to air traffic administration by the Transport Act 2000, sch 1, paras 1, 2, 3, 6 and 9 (the company must have ceased to hold a licence under part 1, chapter 1, of the Act, otherwise it cannot be wound up: s 27).

10.52 For industry-specific administration regimes based on schedule B1 administration,[139] the provisions of IA 1986, sch B1, paras 60, 69 and 79 and sch 1, para 21, discussed in 10.31–10.32, are applied, with some of the provisions modified:

(a) to energy administration and energy supply company administration by the Energy Act 2004, sch 20, paras 1, 2, 12 and 18;[140]

(b) to bank administration, building society special administration and special adminis-tration (bank administration) by the Banking Act 2009, s 145(2), (3), (4) and table 1;[141]

(c) to investment bank special administration and special administration (bank insolv-ency) by the Investment Bank Special Administration Regulations 2011 (SI 2011/245), reg 15(4), (5) and table 1;[142]

(d) to postal administration by the Postal Services Act 2011, sch 10, paras 1, 2, 10 and 17;[143]

---

[136] Except for building societies, see 10.13.

[137] See 10.31–10.34.

[138] See 1.248–1.261.

[139] See 1.262–1.287 and 1.291–1.294.

[140] Applied to energy supply company administration by the Energy Act 2011, s 96. IA 1986, sch B1, para 69, is replaced by the Energy Act 2004, s 158(1)(b).

[141] Applied to building society special administration by the Building Societies Act 1986, s 90C. Applied (apart from IA 1986, sch B1, para 79) to special administration (bank administration) by the Investment Bank Special Administration Regulations 2011 (SI 2011/245), sch 2, para 6.

[142] Applied to special administration (bank insolvency) by SI 2011/245, sch 1, para 5(1).

[143] IA 1986, sch B1, para 69, is replaced by the Postal Services Act 2011, s 72(1)(b).

(e) to FMI administration by the Financial Services (Banking Reform) Act 2013, sch 6, paras 2 and 3 and table 1.

In bank administration, building society special administration and special administration **10.53** (bank administration), exercise of the power to present a winding-up petition is subject to the need to prioritize objective 1 of bank or building society administration or objective A of special administration (bank administration).[144] Also, if there has been a transfer to a bridge bank, a winding-up petition cannot be presented without the approval of the Bank of England, unless the Bank has given an objective 1 achievement notice (objective A achievement notice in special administration (bank administration)).[145]

In special administration (bank administration), an administrator does not have express **10.54** power to apply for his or her appointment to cease to have effect[146] unless:[147]

(a) the Bank of England has given an objective A achievement notice; and
(b) the administrator has pursued the first part of objective 3 (to rescue the investment bank as a going concern) and thinks that it has been sufficiently achieved.

In relation to industry-specific administration regimes based on IA 1986, part 2, without **10.55** the amendments made by the Enterprise Act 2002, s 248[148] (other than building society administration), IA 1986, s 140(1), discussed in 10.33, is applied as originally enacted.[149] In that form, the references to an administration order and an administrator include references to

(a) a special administration order and a special administrator;[150]
(b) a railway administration order and a railway administrator;[151]
(c) a PPP administration order and a special PPP administrator;[152] and
(d) an air traffic administration order and an air traffic administrator.[153]

In its application to energy administration, energy supply company administration or **10.56** postal administration, the reference to an administrator in IA 1986, s 140(1) as currently in force, includes a reference to, as appropriate, an energy administrator, energy supply company administrator or postal administrator.[154]

IA 1986, s 140(1), is not applied to building society administration, bank administration, **10.57** building society special administration, investment bank special administration, special administration (bank insolvency) or special administration (bank administration).

---

[144] IA 1986, sch B1, para 60, and sch 1, para 21, as modified by the Banking Act 2009, s 145, table 1, and further modified by SI 2011/245, sch 2, para 6.

[145] IA 1986, sch B1, para 60, and sch 1, para 21, as modified by the Banking Act 2009, s 145, table 1, and further modified by SI 2011/245, sch 2, para 6. 'Objective 1 achievement notice' is defined in 1.266, 'objective A achievement notice' in 1.279.

[146] IA 1986, sch B1, para 79.

[147] SI 2011/245, sch 2, para 15.

[148] See 1.248–1.261.

[149] Enterprise Act 2002, s 249.

[150] Water Industry Act 1991, sch 3, para 11(1).

[151] Railways Act 1993, sch 6, para 20(1).

[152] Greater London Authority Act 1999, sch 14, para 20(1).

[153] Transport Act 2000, sch 1, para 13(1).

[154] Energy Act 2004, sch 20, para 41, applied to energy supply company administration by the Energy Act 2011, s 96; Postal Services Act 2011, sch 10, para 40.

10.58   The provisions of IR 1986, r 4.7, apply to a petition by an administrator in any industry-specific administration regime by virtue of r 4.2(1) and (2).

Partnership Administration

10.59   IA 1986, sch B1, is applied to insolvent partnerships, by IPO 1994, art 6, with the modifications set out in sch 2. The effect is that what is said in 10.26–10.27 about an interim moratorium for a company applies to an interim moratorium for a partnership, except that IA 1986, s 124B, is irrelevant and the reference to it is omitted from the modified sch B1, para 42. Also, references to sch B1, para 42(4), have to be read as references to para 42(5), as modified by IPO 1994, sch 2, para 17. Unfortunately, it has been forgotten to modify sch B1, para 44(7)(a), so that it refers to para 42(5) instead of 42(4).

10.60   Similarly, what is said in 10.29 about a company in administration applies to a partnership in administration and what is said in 10.31–10.34 about an administrator of a company applying for it to be wound up applies to an administrator of a partnership. The power of an administrator of a partnership to present a petition for its winding up, under IPO 1994, is in IA 1986, sch B1, para 60, and sch 1, para 19, as modified by IPO 1994, sch 2, para 43.

10.61   A petition by the administrator of a partnership for its winding up is presented under IPO 1994, art 7.[155] The power to appoint the administrator as the partnership's liquidator is in IA 1986, s 221A(5), which is inserted by IPO 1994, sch 3, para 3. The provisions of IR 1986, r 4.7, apply by virtue of r 4.2(1) and (2) and IPO 1994, art 18 and sch 10. But IR 1986, r 4.7(7)(a) (administrator's petition is to be company's petition), is overruled by the prescribed form 3,[156] which makes it clear that it is the administrator's petition.

Conversion of Administration into Winding-up Proceedings

10.62   If a company in administration in England and Wales is subject to main insolvency proceedings elsewhere in the EU which are subject to Regulation (EC) No 1346/2000,[157] the foreign liquidator in the main proceedings is entitled, under art 37, to request the court to convert the administration into either a creditors' voluntary winding up with confirmation by the court or a winding up by the court, if this proves to be in the interests of the creditors in the main proceedings. A procedure for dealing with applications for a conversion order is set out IR 1986, rr 2.130–2.132, in which the liquidator in the main proceedings is referred to as a member State liquidator.[158]

10.63   The court's order is described as being for conversion into winding-up proceedings.[159] It is an order under Regulation (EC) No 1346/2000, art 37, that:

(a)   the purposes of the administration are to be limited to the winding up of the company through administration and are to exclude the purpose contained in IA 1986, sch B1, para 3(1)(a) (rescuing the company as a going concern);

(b)   the administration is converted into a creditors' voluntary winding up; or

---

[155]   IA 1986, s 221A(1)(b), inserted by IPO 1994, sch 3, para 3.
[156]   IPO 1994, sch 9.
[157]   See 1.361–1.407.
[158]   IR 1986, r 13.13(11).
[159]   IR 1986, r 2.130(1A).

(c) the administration is converted into a winding up by the court.

An application[160] for conversion of administration into winding-up proceedings must be **10.64**
supported by a witness statement, which must be filed with the court, giving the information required by r 2.131(1).[161] The application and written evidence must be served on the
company and the administrator.[162] For rules on service see 3.249–3.251.

The witness statement must be made by, or on behalf of, the liquidator in the main proceed- **10.65**
ings.[163] It must state:[164]

(a) that main proceedings have been opened in relation to the company in a member State
other than the United Kingdom or Denmark;
(b) the belief of the person making the statement that the conversion of the administration
into winding-up proceedings would prove to be in the interests of the creditors in the
main proceedings;
(c) the opinion of the person making the statement on whether the company ought to go
into voluntary liquidation or be wound up by the court; and
(d) all other matters that, in the opinion of the liquidator in the main proceedings, would
assist the court:
(i) in deciding whether to make an order converting the administration into
winding-up proceedings; and
(ii) if the court were to do so, in considering the need for any consequential provision
that would be necessary or desirable.

On hearing an application for conversion of an administration into winding-up proceed- **10.66**
ings, the court may make such order as it thinks fit.[165] An order for conversion may contain
whatever consequential provisions the court deems necessary or desirable.[166] If the court
orders conversion into a voluntary winding up, it may provide that the company is to be
wound up as if a resolution for voluntary winding up had been passed on the day the order
is made.[167]

Default Rules of Exchanges and Clearing Houses

Restrictions on winding-up petitions against a company in or preparing for **10.67**
administration[168] do not apply to a petition by a recognized investment exchange or recognized clearing house for the purpose of proceedings under its default rules.[169] The 'default
rules' of a recognized investment exchange or clearing house are its rules which provide for
action to be taken when a person[170] appears to be unable (or likely to become unable) to
meet obligations in respect of one or more market contracts connected with the exchange or

---

[160] See 3.233–3.263.
[161] IR 1986, r 2.130(1).
[162] r 2.130(3).
[163] r 2.131(2).
[164] IR 1986, r 2.131(1).
[165] IR 1986, r 2.132(1).
[166] r 2.132(2).
[167] r 2.132(3).
[168] See 3.102, 3.103, 10.26, 10.29, 10.39, 10.45, 10.47.
[169] Companies Act 1989, ss 161(4) and 188(3).
[170] Including another recognized investment exchange or recognized clearing house.

clearing house.[171] The default procedures for a recognized central counterparty referred to in Regulation (EU) No 648/2012, art 48, are default rules.[172] 'Recognized clearing house' and 'recognized investment exchange' have the same meaning as in the Financial Services and Markets Act 2000.[173]

Administrative Receivership

10.68 A petition for the compulsory winding up of a registered company, LLP or SE may be presented at the instance of its administrative receiver.[174] An administrative receiver of a company is deemed to act as the company's agent.[175]

10.69 The power of an administrative receiver of a company to present the company's petition for its winding up was introduced by IA 1985, s 48 and sch 3, para 21. In the absence of the statutory power, a receiver of a company may not present a petition in the company's name.[176]

10.70 By analogy with the situation where a creditor's petition is opposed by other creditors,[177] creditors opposing a petition presented at the instance of a company's administrative receiver must give reasons for their opposition.[178] In *Re Television Parlour plc* all the directors of the company had resigned. A member, who was also formerly managing director of the company and was defending a claim brought against him by the company for damages for breach of fiduciary duty and breach of contract, applied for an order under what is now the Companies Act 2006, s 306, calling a general meeting of the company to consider adopting a resolution for voluntary winding up. His application was heard together with a petition presented by the company's administrative receivers for the compulsory winding up of the company, which he opposed as a creditor. Peter Gibson J dismissed the application and made the winding-up order. His Lordship did not accept that compulsory liquidation would either delay dealing with the company's affairs or be more expensive. It was better that the claim against the former managing director be conducted by a compulsory liquidator, who would do so as an officer of the court and so would be seen to be independent.

Receivership

10.71 A receiver appointed under a charge on a company's property, who is not an administrative receiver, may present a petition for the winding up of the company,[179] but only on the ground that it is unable to pay its debts.[180] Two conditions must be satisfied before this power can be exercised:[181]

(a) the charge must have been created as a floating charge;

---

171 Companies Act 1989, s 188.
172 Companies Act 1989, s 188(1).
173 Companies Act 1989, s 190(1).
174 IA 1986, s 42(1) and (2), and sch 1, para 21. For the definition of administrative receiver see 1.295–1.296.
175 s 44(1).
176 *Re Emmadart Ltd* [1979] Ch 540.
177 See 7.698–7.733.
178 *Re Television Parlour plc* (1987) 4 BCC 95.
179 IR 1986, r 3.40(a).
180 IA 1986, s 122(1)(f).
181 r 3.39(1).

(b) IA 1986, s 176A (share of assets for unsecured creditors), must apply. The circumstances in which s 176A applies are set out in that section and the Insolvency Act 1986 (Prescribed Part) Order 2003.[182]

If those two conditions are satisfied, the receiver must notify creditors whether he or she **10.72** proposes to petition for winding up.[183] This notification (with notice of the receiver's appointment and a report on the share of assets for unsecured creditors) must be given within three months of the date of the receiver's appointment, or such longer period as the court may allow.[184]

Lloyd's Reorganization

Winding Up of Member or Former Member of Lloyd's

While a Lloyd's market reorganization order is in force, a reorganization controller may **10.73** present a petition for the winding up of a company which is an underwriting member or former member of Lloyd's.[185] 'Former member' is defined in reg 2(1) as a person who has ceased to be an underwriting member, whether by resignation or otherwise, in accordance with the Lloyd's Act 1982 or whichever of its predecessors was in force at the time of ceasing to be a member. A petition may be presented in respect of a registered company or a company incorporated outside Great Britain.[186] The petition will be treated as made under IA 1986, s 124.[187]

A reorganization controller may allege any of the circumstances listed in IA 1986, s 122(1), **10.74** in which the court may make a winding-up order, but also has available two extra circumstances,[188] which apply only to a petition by a reorganization controller. They are:

(a) that the member is in default of an obligation to pay an insurance market debt which is due and payable, and the court thinks that winding up the member is necessary or desirable for achieving the objectives of the Lloyd's market reorganization order;
(b) the court considers that the member is, or is likely to be, unable to pay insurance market debts as they fall due, and the court thinks that winding up the member is necessary or desirable for achieving the objectives of the Lloyd's market reorganization order.

In this context, the term 'insurance market debt' means an insurance debt under, or in con- **10.75** nection with, a contract of insurance written at Lloyd's.[189]

'Insurance debt' means a debt to which an underwriting member or former member is, or **10.76** may become, liable, pursuant to a contract of insurance, to a policyholder or to any person who has a direct right of action against that member or former member, and includes any

---

[182] SI 2003/2097.
[183] IR 1986, r 3.39(2)(c).
[184] r 3.39(2).
[185] Insurers (Reorganisation and Winding Up) (Lloyd's) Regulations 2005 (SI 2005/1998), reg 25(1).
[186] SI 2005/1998, reg 2(1) definition of 'company'.
[187] SI 2005/1998, reg 25(2).
[188] Added to s 122(1) by SI 2005/1998, reg 25(3).
[189] reg 2(1).

premium paid in connection with a contract of insurance (whether or not that contract was concluded) which the member or former member is liable to refund.[190]

10.77 Other terms used in the definitions of insurance debt and insurance market debt have lengthy technical definitions in financial services law, primarily for the purpose of defining what activities are subject to regulation. So, 'contract of insurance' is defined in the Financial Services and Markets Act 2000 (Regulated Activities) Order 2001,[191] reg 3(1), which must be read with the Financial Services and Markets Act, s 22 and sch 2, but does not include a reinsurance contract.[192] 'Policyholder' is defined in the Financial Services and Markets Act 2000 (Meaning of 'Policy' and 'Policyholder') Order 2001,[193] art 3, applied by SI 2004/353, reg 2(1), and SI 2005/1998, reg 2(2).

Winding Up of Lloyd's

10.78 A reorganization controller has standing to petition for the winding up, as an unregistered company, of Lloyd's, alleging any of the circumstances listed in IA 1986, s 221(5).[194] IA 1986, s 221(1), will apply to the petition.[195]

Voluntary Winding Up

Voluntary Winding Up no Bar to Winding Up by the Court

Standing to petition not affected by voluntary winding up

10.79 IA 1986, s 124(5), provides that any person given standing to petition for the winding up of a registered company by the other provisions of s 124 may do so if the company is in voluntary liquidation. The fact that the company is in voluntary liquidation does not affect the standing of persons to petition for its compulsory winding up and does not prevent the court making a winding-up order.

Choice between voluntary and compulsory winding up

10.80 In *Re James McHale Automobiles Ltd*[196] Robert Walker J said, at p 276:

> As a broad generalisation more draconian courses are open in the case of a compulsory winding up than in the case of a voluntary winding up and it is of course possible, and quite frequently does happen in practice, that a creditors' voluntary winding up is succeeded by a compulsory winding-up order precisely in order to obtain the more severe regime of winding up by the court.

10.81 It is commonly thought that suspicious past dealings will be more thoroughly investigated in compulsory than in voluntary winding up.[197] One advantage of compulsory over

---

[190] Insurers (Reorganisation and Winding Up) Regulations 2004 (SI 2004/353), reg 2(1), as applied by SI 2005/1998, reg 2(2) and (3).
[191] SI 2001/544.
[192] SI 2004/353, reg 2(4), applied by SI 2005/1998, reg 2(2).
[193] SI 2001/2361.
[194] See 2.37. Insurers (Reorganisation and Winding Up) (Lloyd's) Regulations 2005 (SI 2005/1998), reg 29(1)).
[195] SI 2005/1998, reg 29(2).
[196] [1997] 1 BCLC 273.
[197] See *Re Zirceram Ltd* [2000] 1 BCLC 751; *Re Internet Investment Corporation Ltd* [2009] EWHC 2744 (Ch), [2010] 1 BCLC 458. In *Colson v Infill Construction (1992) Ltd* [1994] MCLR 439 a winding-up order was made, despite the company going into voluntary liquidation the day before the hearing, because the

voluntary winding up is that in a winding up by the court the official receiver has a duty, under IA 1986, s 132, to investigate the causes of the company's failure and its promotion, formation, business, dealings and affairs.[198] The official receiver may make a report to the court on these matters.[199] A disadvantage is that the fees payable to the official receiver may make a winding up by the court more expensive than a voluntary liquidation.

From 1857 until 1986, an alternative to the compulsory winding up of a registered company in voluntary liquidation was winding up under supervision.[200] **10.82**

Replacing voluntary liquidator suitable alternative remedy

If a petitioner's only reason for converting a voluntary liquidation into a winding up by the court is dissatisfaction with the incumbent voluntary liquidator, an application to the court to replace the liquidator[201] is an adequate alternative remedy and the court will not make a winding-up order.[202] But a winding-up order is appropriate if the real complaint is that the conduct of the liquidation so far shows that past suspicious dealings require investigation in a compulsory winding up.[203] If a petition criticizes the liquidator's conduct of the voluntary winding up, the liquidator should answer the criticisms fully.[204] A petition for the compulsory winding up of a company in voluntary liquidation cannot ask alternatively for removal and replacement of the voluntary liquidator.[205] **10.83**

In Australia a winding-up order has been made in respect of a company in voluntary liquidation so as to bring into operation the provision for avoidance of a floating charge,[206] which in Australia does not apply in voluntary winding up.[207] Also in Australia a winding-up order has been made because it appeared that a claim could be made on an insurance policy by a court-appointed liquidator but not any other liquidator.[208] **10.84**

Official receiver's standing to petition

IA 1986, s 124(5), confers standing on the official receiver to petition for the compulsory winding up of a company being wound up voluntarily in England and Wales, but introduces a condition—that the court must not make a winding-up order on an official receiver's petition unless satisfied that the voluntary liquidation cannot be continued with due regard to the interests of the creditors or contributories.[209] **10.85**

company's dealings with the petitioner, itself a company being wound up by the court, needed to be 'looked at independently and in a way which would give a measure of supervision of the winding up by the court'.

[198] *Re a Company (No 007070 of 1996)* [1997] 2 BCLC 139.

[199] s 132.

[200] See 10.152–10.165.

[201] IA 1986, s 108(2).

[202] *Re Inside Sport Ltd* [2000] 1 BCLC 302; *Re AB (Handling) Ltd* (1999) LTL 5/2/99.

[203] *Re Zirceram Ltd* [2000] 1 BCLC 751. See 10.81.

[204] *Re Arthur Rathbone Kitchens Ltd* [1997] 2 BCLC 280; *Re Leading Guides International Ltd* [1998] 1 BCLC 620.

[205] *Re Cork Shipping and Mercantile Co Ltd* (1879) 7 LR Ir 148.

[206] Corporations Act 2001 (Australia), s 588FJ. The equivalent provision in IA 1986, s 245, applies in both voluntary winding up and winding up by the court.

[207] *Carter v New Tel Ltd* [2003] NSWSC 128, 44 ACSR 661.

[208] *Re Green* [2004] NSWSC 1095, 52 ACSR 452. This was also a further reason for making the order in *Carter v New Tel Ltd* [2003] NSWSC 128, 44 ACSR 661.

[209] See 10.134–10.138.

10.86 Although the drafting of the subsection is ambiguous, it has been held that the condition is applied by the subsection only to a petition by the official receiver.[210] The same has been held in relation to equivalent legislation in New Zealand.[211] In Australia the equivalent legislative provision has been repealed, but see the discussion by J S Lockhart, 'Winding up companies in voluntary liquidation'[212] and *Re North Western Fruitgrowers Pty Ltd*.[213] A similar condition is imposed on contributories' petitions by s 116[214] and used to be imposed on creditors' petitions.[215]

Voluntary liquidator

10.87 While a petition for the compulsory winding up of a company in voluntary liquidation is pending, the voluntary liquidator should be seen to be disinterested, and should not canvass support for continuation of the voluntary liquidation.[216] The liquidator should also be neutral at the hearing of the petition.[217] This will not apply where the petition is by the company at the instigation of the voluntary liquidator.

Literature

10.88 Abbas Mithani, 'The voluntary liquidator and the compulsory petitioner' (1987) 84 LS Gaz 1808.

Superfluous provision

10.89 IA 1986, s 116, states that:

> The voluntary winding up of a company does not bar the right of any creditor or contributory to have it wound up by the court; . . .

10.90 Since the Companies (Consolidation) Act 1908, s 137(2), there has been express provision that any person with standing to petition for the winding up of a registered company may do so if the company is being wound up voluntarily,[218] so this part of s 116 is superfluous.

10.91 This part of s 116 is also confusing in that it seems to restrict to creditors and contributories standing to petition for the compulsory winding up of a company in voluntary liquidation. But that apparent restriction has always been ignored. Before 1908 this provision referred only to creditors[219] though the Companies Act 1862, s 82, permitted creditors, contributories and the company itself to petition for winding up without referring to what was to happen if the company was in voluntary liquidation. It was accepted that contributories of a company in voluntary liquidation were also not barred from petitioning for its compulsory winding up.[220]

---

[210] *Re Lubin, Rosen and Associates Ltd* [1975] 1 WLR 122 at pp 126–7.

[211] *Re E E McCurdy Ltd* [1958] NZLR 135, which seems to have been misunderstood by the learned master in *Sayer v Capital Aviation Ltd* (1993) 6 NZCLC 68,372.

[212] (1960) 34 ALJ 171.

[213] [1965] VR 306.

[214] See 10.122–10.124.

[215] See 10.114–10.121.

[216] *Re Lubin, Rosen and Associates Ltd* [1975] 1 WLR 122.

[217] See 5.20.

[218] Now IA 1986, s 124(5).

[219] Compare the Companies Act 1862, s 145, and the Companies (Consolidation) Act 1908, s 197.

[220] *Re Irrigation Co of France, ex parte Fox* (1871) LR 6 Ch App 176; *Re Gold Co* (1879) 11 ChD 701; *Re Union Fire Insurance Co* (1882) 7 OAR 783; *Re Haycraft Gold Reduction and Mining Co* [1900] 2 Ch

Validity of voluntary winding up

On a petition for the winding up of a company in voluntary liquidation, if the court finds **10.92** that the resolution for voluntary winding up is invalid, it can ignore the voluntary liquidation and determine the petition on its merits.[221] On a creditor's petition, it may be found that a majority of the creditors still prefer a voluntary winding up if one can be properly constituted.[222]

If the court orders the compulsory winding up of a company in voluntary liquidation, **10.93** all proceedings taken in the voluntary winding up are deemed to have been validly taken unless the court, on proof of fraud or mistake, directs otherwise.[223] The winding up by the court is deemed to have commenced when the resolution for voluntary winding up was adopted, if that was before the presentation of the petition on which the winding-up order is made; otherwise it commences with the presentation of the petition.[224]

In *Re Empire Preserving Co Ltd*[225] a general meeting of the company had adopted a resolution **10.94** for voluntary winding up and appointed a liquidator, but it was found that the meeting had not been properly summoned so that the resolution was invalid. This in itself was held to be a reason for making a winding-up order on a creditor's petition. The proceedings in the supposed voluntary winding up could not be adopted by the court because of the irregularity.

A creditor may appear at the hearing of a contributory's petition for the compulsory wind- **10.95** ing up of a company in voluntary liquidation for the purpose of objecting to adoption of the proceedings in the voluntary winding up.[226]

Unregistered companies

Voluntary winding up under IA 1986, part 4, is not available to unregistered companies, **10.96** except in accordance with Regulation (EC) No 1346/2000.[227] However, in many cases it is possible to wind up an unregistered company voluntarily under its own constitution or under legislation governing it. The fact that an unregistered company is being wound up voluntarily is no bar to the making of an order for it to be wound up by the court[228] and indeed is expressly mentioned as a circumstance in which an unregistered company may be wound up.[229]

Building societies

If an order is made to wind up a building society and, before the petition was presented, **10.97** an instrument of dissolution under the Building Societies Act 1986, s 87, was placed in the society's public file, any proceedings taken in the course of the dissolution are deemed to have been validly taken, unless the court, on proof of fraud or mistake, directs otherwise.

230; *Re National Company for the Distribution of Electricity by Secondary Generators Ltd* [1902] 2 Ch 34; *Re Australasian Pictures Productions Ltd* [1925] StR Qd 249; though earlier doubted by Turner LJ in *Re Bank of Gibraltar and Malta* (1865) LR 1 Ch App 69 at pp 73–4.
[221] *Re Imperial Bank of China, India, and Japan* (1866) LR 1 Ch App 339; *Re State of Wyoming Syndicate* [1901] 2 Ch 431.
[222] *Re Fitness Centre (South East) Ltd* [1986] BCLC 518. See 7.726.
[223] IA 1986, s 129(1).
[224] IA 1986, s 129(1).
[225] [1901–3] SASR 157.
[226] *Re Cumberland Black Lead Mining Co Ltd, ex parte Bell* (1862) 6 LT 197.
[227] IA 1986, s 221(4); see 1.298.
[228] *Re Irish Mercantile Loan Society* [1907] 1 IR 98.
[229] IA 1986, s 221(5)(a); see 8.119–8.130.

The winding up by the court is deemed to have commenced on the date on which the instrument was placed in the file.[230]

Incorporated friendly societies

10.98 If an order is made to wind up an incorporated friendly society and, before the petition was presented, an instrument of dissolution under the Friendly Societies Act 1992, s 20, was placed in the society's public file, any proceedings taken in the course of the dissolution are deemed to have been validly taken unless the court, on proof of fraud or mistake, directs otherwise. The winding up by the court is deemed to have commenced on the date on which the instrument was placed in the file.[231]

Creditor's Petition

Standing of creditors to petition

10.99 A creditor of a company may petition for its compulsory winding up despite it being in voluntary liquidation.[232] This provision applies whether the creditor's debt was incurred before or after commencement of the voluntary winding up.[233]

No objection by other creditors

10.100 If no other creditors object to a winding up by the court on a creditor's petition, the usual rule applies that a winding-up order will be made on the petition of an unpaid admitted creditor,[234] subject to the rule that an order will not be made if an application to the court to replace the liquidator[235] is an adequate alternative remedy.[236] But a winding-up order is appropriate if the real complaint is that the conduct of the liquidation so far shows that past suspicious dealings require investigation in a compulsory winding up.[237] Otherwise, the fact that the company is in voluntary liquidation is normally not a factor which weighs either way when deciding whether to make a winding-up order,[238] nor does it matter whether the voluntary winding up commenced before or after the petition for compulsory winding up was presented.[239]

10.101 The fact that a declaration of solvency has been made and the company is in members' voluntary liquidation[240] will be weighed as a 'serious factor'.[241] A declaration of solvency is a declaration that the company's debts will be paid in full, with post-liquidation interest, in at most 12 months, so a creditor petitioner should not be prejudiced by not having a winding

---

[230] Building Societies Act 1986, sch 15, para 20.

[231] Friendly Societies Act 1992, sch 10, para 23.

[232] IA 1986, s 124(5); see also s 116 discussed at 10.89–10.91.

[233] *Re Bank of South Australia (No 2)* [1895] 1 Ch 578 per Lindley LJ at p 595; *Re Greenwood and Co* [1900] 2 QB 306.

[234] See 7.676. *Re James Millward and Co Ltd* [1940] Ch 333; *Re A and N Thermo Products Ltd* [1963] 1 WLR 1341.

[235] IA 1986, s 108(2).

[236] *Re Inside Sport Ltd* [2000] 1 BCLC 302; *Re AB (Handling) Ltd* (1999) LTL 5/2/99. See 10.83–10.84.

[237] *Re Zirceram Ltd* [2000] 1 BCLC 751. See 10.81.

[238] *Re James Millward and Co Ltd* [1940] Ch 333; *Re J D Swain Ltd* [1965] 1 WLR 909 per Diplock LJ at p 914.

[239] *Re J D Swain Ltd* [1965] 1 WLR 909.

[240] IA 1986, ss 89 and 90.

[241] Per Harman J in *Re Surplus Properties (Huddersfield) Ltd* [1984] BCLC 89 at p 91.

up by the court. In *Re Surplus Properties (Huddersfield) Ltd*[242] a winding-up order was made in respect of a company which had gone into members' voluntary winding up after the petition was presented. The debts of the petitioner and a supporting creditor had not been paid; it was doubtful that the assets would realize the value given to them in the declaration of solvency; and no evidence was given of how a winding up by the court would be detrimental to the contributories. In *Re Leading Guides International Ltd*[243] the company was in members' voluntary winding up but a winding-up order was made because the company produced no evidence to refute the petitioner's view that it would not in fact be able to pay its debts within the 12-month period referred to in the directors' declaration of solvency.

Views of other creditors

If, on a creditor's petition for a company in voluntary liquidation to be wound up by the court, there is opposition by other creditors, the court must balance several factors in exercising its discretion whether to make a winding-up order. Accordingly it is incorrect to speak of an 'onus' on a petitioner to justify the making of an order (or, presumably, on those opposing the order to show that it should not be made).[244] If there is opposition at the hearing of the petition, the petitioner must be prepared to give reasons for preferring compulsory to voluntary liquidation.[245]   **10.102**

In determining whether there is a majority of creditors in favour of or opposing compulsory winding up, the court may discount the views of persons connected with the company, for example, as directors, shareholders or associated companies.[246] In *Re H J Tomkins and Son Ltd*[247] Hoffmann J referred, at p 78, to taking into account only the views of 'ordinary outside creditors, taking a purely commercial view of how best the company should be wound up'. Normally the decisive factor is the view of the majority in value of the creditors who are independent of the company—'It is after all their money'.[248]   **10.103**

Besides counting debts, the court is entitled to have regard to the general principles of fairness and commercial morality which underlie the details of the insolvency law as applied to companies.[249]   **10.104**

Majority opposing winding up by the court

The fact that the majority in value of creditors of a company in voluntary winding up prefer the voluntary liquidation to continue rather than having a compulsory winding up is normally a sufficient reason for not making an order, though it may be outweighed by other factors.[250]   **10.105**

---

[242] [1984] BCLC 89.
[243] [1998] 1 BCLC 620.
[244] Per Hoffmann J in *Re Lowerstoft Traffic Services Ltd* [1986] BCLC 81 at pp 83–4.
[245] *Re Riviera Pearls Ltd* [1962] 1 WLR 722; per Hoffmann J in *Re William Thorpe and Son Ltd* (1988) 5 BCC 156 at p 159.
[246] *Re R and H Grossmark Ltd* (1968) 112 SJ 416; *Re Falcon RJ Developments Ltd* (1987) 3 BCC 146; and see *Re Lowerstoft Traffic Services Ltd* [1986] BCLC 81 per Hoffmann J at p 84 and *Re MCH Services Ltd* [1987] BCLC 535.
[247] [1990] BCLC 76.
[248] Per Hoffmann J in *Re William Thorpe and Son Ltd* (1988) 5 BCC 156 at p 158. See 10.105–10.113.
[249] *Re Palmer Marine Surveys Ltd* [1986] 1 WLR 573 per Hoffmann J at p 578; *Sysma Construction Pte Ltd v EK Developments Pte Ltd* [2007] SGHC 36, [2007] 2 SLR 742.
[250] *Re Langley Mill Steel and Iron Works Co* (1871) LR 12 Eq 26; *Re J D Swain Ltd* [1965] 1 WLR 909; *Re MCH Services Ltd* [1987] BCLC 535. See also *Re Empire Timber Lumber and Tie Co Ltd* (1920) 55 DLR 90;

10.106   A winding-up order was made in *Re M and P Woodware Ltd*[251] despite the opposition of a majority of creditors but the report is too brief to explain why.

Need for investigation and doubts about voluntary liquidator's impartiality: suitable alternative remedy

10.107   In the reported cases up to *Re Inside Sport Ltd*,[252] the factor that has outweighed a majority view opposing compulsory winding up on a creditor's petition[253] has been the desirability of replacing the incumbent liquidator, not because of any impropriety on his part but because, in the circumstances, creditors had reasonable cause to doubt his impartiality, often leading to reasonable doubt about whether past suspicious dealings with the company would be fully investigated.[254] In cases before *Re Inside Sport Ltd*, there was perhaps not enough attention paid to the distinction between:

(a)   the need to replace the voluntary liquidator, which can be achieved by an application under IA 1986, s 108(2),[255] without a winding-up order; and

(b)   the need for further investigation, which may justify an order.[256]

10.108   In *Re Inside Sport Ltd* it was made clear that a winding-up order will not be made if an application under s 108(2) is an adequate remedy.[257] But a winding-up order is appropriate if the real complaint is that the conduct of the liquidation so far shows that past suspicious dealings require investigation in a compulsory winding up.[258]

10.109   Formerly the attitude of the court was that there was no presumption that a liquidator of an insolvent company appointed by a controlling shareholder could not be regarded by creditors as impartial: the court had to hear the views of the creditors.[259] Now, in principle, impartiality should be assured when a liquidator is a qualified insolvency practitioner. However, the courts have recognized that creditors who are not linked to a company in voluntary liquidation will feel aggrieved if, at the initial creditors' meeting, an insolvency practitioner chosen by those in control of the company is appointed liquidator instead of one nominated by the creditors. Before *Re Inside Sport Ltd*, this grievance was seen as a reason

---

E Green and Sons v Frasers (Aberdeen) Ltd (1938) 55 Sh Ct Rep 133; *Re Home Remedies Ltd* [1943] Ch 1; *Re B Karsberg Ltd* [1956] 1 WLR 57; *Re Riviera Pearls Ltd* [1962] 1 WLR 722. For factors which may outweigh the majority's view see 10.107–10.111.

[251]   (1953) 103 LJ 518.

[252]   [2000] 1 BCLC 302.

[253]   See 10.105–10.106.

[254]   *G A Coles and Co Ltd v KK Footwear Ltd* [1943] GLR 64; *Re Britton and Millard Ltd* (1957) 107 LJ 601; *Re R and H Grossmark Ltd* (1968) 112 SJ 416; *Re Palmer Marine Surveys Ltd* [1986] 1 WLR 573; *Re H J Tomkins and Son Ltd* [1990] BCLC 76, in which the balance between those supporting and those opposing compulsory liquidation was roughly equal; *Re Magnus Consultants Ltd* [1995] 1 BCLC 203; *Re Gordon and Breach Science Publishers Ltd* [1995] 2 BCLC 189; *Citrix Systems Inc v Telesystems Learning Pty Ltd* (1998) 28 ACSR 529.

[255]   Or under s 100(3) if the members and the creditors at their initial meetings nominate different persons to be liquidator. An application under s 100(3) must be made within seven days of the nomination by the creditors.

[256]   In *Re Palmer Marine Surveys Ltd* [1986] 1 WLR 573 an application for replacement of the voluntary liquidator had already been rejected by the court (see at p 577).

[257]   See also *Re AB (Handling) Ltd* (1999) LTL 5/2/99.

[258]   *Re Zirceram Ltd* [2000] 1 BCLC 751. This factor was not present in *Re Permanent Formwork Systems Ltd* [2007] IEHC 268 and no winding-up order was made.

[259]   *Adebayo v Official Receiver of Nigeria* [1954] 1 WLR 681.

for making a winding-up order.[260] See also *Re Leading Guides International Ltd*,[261] in which the incumbent liquidator had not sought to meet criticism of the conduct of the liquidation.

In the Republic of Ireland most cases on compulsory winding up of a company in volun- **10.110** tary liquidation are concerned with replacing a voluntary liquidator with a liquidator nominated by the petitioner and each case has depended very much on its own facts. In *Re Gilt Construction Ltd*[262] the court did not accept the allegation that the voluntary liquidator lacked impartiality and a winding-up order was refused. In *Re Balbradagh Developments Ltd*[263] the court considered there were sufficient safeguards in place, including a committee of inspection of which the petitioner was a member and the Directorate of Corporate Enforcement which had been established since *Re Gilt Construction Ltd*, to render it unnecessary to make a winding-up order so as to replace the liquidator. But in *Re Fencore Services Ltd*[264] and *Re Marcon Developments*[265] the need for investigation of the company's affairs persuaded the court to make a winding-up order. In both cases the court was suspicious of the company going into voluntary liquidation after the winding-up petition was presented despite it being obvious for some time that the companies were hopelessly insolvent. In *Re Hayes Homes Ltd*[266] the court attached 'a great deal of weight' to the petitioner's offer to finance an investigation by his nominated liquidator. But in *Re Larkin Partnership Ltd*[267] the court decided that the necessary investigation could be conducted in the voluntary liquidation.

In Australia, a need to replace an incumbent voluntary liquidator is still a proper reason **10.111** for ordering winding up by the court.[268] The court will approach an application for a winding-up order for that reason in the same way as it would an application for replacement of a liquidator.[269]

Majority support for winding up by the court

If the majority in value of ordinary outside creditors, taking a purely commercial view of **10.112** how best the company should be wound up, support compulsory winding up, an order will normally be made,[270] unless it appears that:

(a) replacement of the incumbent liquidator would be an adequate remedy;[271] or

---

[260] *Re Lowerstoft Traffic Services Ltd* [1986] BCLC 81, in which Hoffmann J referred, at p 84, to a public interest that the liquidator should not only be independent but seen to be independent; *Re Palmer Marine Surveys Ltd* [1986] 1 WLR 573; *Re Falcon RJ Developments Ltd* [1987] BCLC 437; *Re MCH Services Ltd* [1987] BCLC 535; *Re Magnus Consultants Ltd* [1995] 1 BCLC 203.
[261] [1998] 1 BCLC 620.
[262] [1994] 2 ILRM 456.
[263] [2008] IEHC 329, [2009] 1 IR 597.
[264] [2010] IEHC 358.
[265] [2010] IEHC 373.
[266] [2004] IEHC 124.
[267] [2010] IEHC 163.
[268] *Donmastry Pty Ltd v Albarran* [2004] NSWSC 632, 49 ACSR 745.
[269] *Neha Impex International Pty Ltd v Mintz and Co Pty Ltd* [2003] WASC 196; *Re Evcorp Grains Pty Ltd (No 2)* [2014] NSWSC 155.
[270] *Re Manchester Queensland Cotton Co* (1867) 16 LT 583; *Re David Jones and Co Ltd* (1897) 41 SJ 748; *Re E Bishop and Sons Ltd* [1900] 2 Ch 254; *Re AB Cycle Co Ltd* (1902) 19 TLR 84; *Re Wellington Farmers' Meat and Manufacturing Co Ltd* [1924] NZLR 623; *Re Lowerstoft Traffic Services Ltd* [1986] BCLC 81; *Re Palmer Marine Surveys Ltd* [1986] 1 WLR 573; *Re Falcon RJ Developments Ltd* (1987) 3 BCC 146; *Re MCH Services Ltd* [1987] BCLC 535; *Re William Thorpe and Son Ltd* (1988) 5 BCC 156; *Re Goldcone Properties Ltd* [2000] 2 HKLRD 16.
[271] See 10.108.

(b) the majority are acting unreasonably or are seeking a special advantage to the detriment of the minority.

10.113 In *Re Medisco Equipment Ltd*[272] a winding-up order was not made because the liquidation was very nearly complete and would have been delayed if a compulsory order had been made, and a compulsory winding up would have involved substantial additional costs. The petitioning creditor seemed to be perverse or even masochistic in pursuing a compulsory liquidation.[273] In *Re Southard and Co Ltd*,[274] although a majority in value of creditors supported compulsory winding up, no criticism was made of the independence, integrity or ability of the voluntary liquidator[275] and the petition was dismissed: the majority of creditors supporting a compulsory winding up were in fact associated with the company's members and former management. In *Re Rhine Film Corporation (UK) Ltd*[276] an order was not made because the petitioning creditor would have gained a special advantage, to the detriment of other unsecured creditors, if an order had been made. In *Re Greenwood and Co*[277] the petitioning creditor would have had a special advantage but it is not clear that it would have been to the detriment of the other unsecured creditors; at first instance the petition was dismissed and on appeal the court would not interfere with the judge's exercise of discretion.

Former requirement to show prejudice to petitioner

10.114 From 1862 until 1929, the statement in the legislation that the court could order the winding up of a company in voluntary liquidation on a creditor's petition was followed by the words, 'if the court is of opinion that the rights of such creditor will be prejudiced by a voluntary winding up'.[278] This applied where the voluntary winding up was under supervision of the court[279] and even if the resolution for voluntary winding up was adopted after presentation of the creditor's petition.[280] The words were repealed by an amendment to the Companies (Consolidation) Act 1908, s 197, made by the Companies Act 1928, sch 2.

10.115 In *Re E Bishop and Sons Ltd*[281] it was held that the Companies Act 1862, s 145, did not mean that the only circumstance in which a company in voluntary liquidation would be wound up by the court on a creditor's petition was when it was shown that the creditor would be prejudiced: a winding-up order could be made in other circumstances, in particular, if the majority of creditors supported compulsory winding up. This was followed in *Re Hermann Lichtenstein and Co Ltd*;[282] *Re Seremban General Agency Ltd*;[283] and, it seems, in *Re Wicklow Textile Industries Ltd*.[284] See also *Re Gilbert Machinery Co (No 2)*,[285] in which a supervision

---

[272] [1983] BCLC 305.
[273] Per Vinelott J in *Re Falcon RJ Developments Ltd* (1987) 3 BCC 146 at p 150.
[274] [1979] 1 WLR 1198.
[275] Per Buckley LJ at p 1201.
[276] (1985) 2 BCC 98,949.
[277] [1900] 2 QB 306.
[278] Companies Act 1862, s 145; Companies (Consolidation) Act 1908, s 197.
[279] *Re National Debenture and Assets Corporation* [1891] 2 Ch 505.
[280] *Re New York Exchange Ltd* (1888) 39 ChD 415; *Re Medical Battery Co* [1894] 1 Ch 444; *Re Pulsator Milking Co Ltd* (1898) 1 GLR 51; *Re Whangarei Daily News Ltd* [1929] GLR 269; *Re Snowdrift Lime Co Ltd* [1934] GLR 2.
[281] [1900] 2 Ch 254.
[282] (1907) 23 TLR 424.
[283] (1922) 3 FMSLR 3.
[284] (1952) 87 ILTR 72.
[285] (1906) 26 NZLR 53.

order was made on the petition. So the position was that it had to be proved that a creditor petitioning for the compulsory winding up of a company in voluntary liquidation would be prejudiced by the continuation of the voluntary winding up, unless there were circumstances in which the court would make the winding-up order without proof of prejudice to the petitioner.

Prejudice to the petitioning creditor was proved, and winding-up orders were made: **10.116**

(a) Where the conduct of the voluntary liquidator was suspicious.[286]
(b) Where the voluntary liquidator was not sufficiently independent of persons from whom assets might be recovered.[287]
(c) Where the conduct of the company's affairs before winding up commenced required investigation which would be carried out better in a compulsory winding up.[288]
(d) Where there had been serious frauds in the conduct of the voluntary winding up.[289]
(e) Where the voluntary winding up was agreed to for the purposes of a reconstruction which did not materialize.[290]

In three early cases in which winding-up orders were made the reports do not mention any **10.117**
consideration of whether the creditor petitioners' interests would be prejudiced by continuation of the voluntary winding up. In *Re Barned's Banking Co Ltd*[291] a compulsory order was made because of the enormity of the crash of the company involved and the need for a thorough investigation. In *Re London and Provincial Starch Co*[292] (in which the resolution for voluntary winding up was adopted after the petition was presented) a winding-up order was made because the company's affairs required investigation. In *Re Manchester Queensland Cotton Co*[293] the company had been in voluntary liquidation under supervision for some time but a winding-up order was made because the liquidator had prevaricated over paying the petitioners' debts and the petitioners were a majority of the creditors. Prejudice to the petitioner's interests was also not mentioned in *Drysdale and Gilmour v Liquidator of International Exhibition of Electrical Engineering and Inventions*,[294] in which the company had gone into voluntary liquidation after presentation of the petition and the court made a supervision order asked for by the voluntary liquidator.

---

[286] *Re Caerphilly Colliery Co* (1875) 32 LT 15.
[287] *Re Root Hog Gold Mining Co Ltd* (1890) 1 BC (NSW) 32, in which the liquidator was a shareholder and treated shares as fully paid which the petitioner argued were not; *Re Johnston, Dunster and Co* (1891) 17 VLR 100, in which the liquidator was a creditor who admitted his own claim though other creditors disputed it; *Re Medical Battery Co* [1894] 1 Ch 444, in which the liquidator was also receiver for debenture holders who were associated with the company's principal shareholder and managing director; *Great Fingall Associated Gold Mining Co v Harness* (1906) 4 CLR 223, in which the liquidator was a shareholder and treated shares as fully paid which the petitioner argued were not; *Re McLeod and Co (India) Ltd* (1925) 25 SR (NSW) 319, in which the liquidator was a shareholder and treated shares as fully paid which the petitioner argued were not.
[288] *Re National Debenture and Assets Corporation* [1891] 2 Ch 505; and see *Re J H Evans and Co Ltd* (1892) 36 SJ 648; *Re David Jones and Co Ltd* (1897) 41 SJ 748; *Re J H Selkirk Ltd* (1906) 50 SJ 802; *Re Wellington Farmers' Meat and Manufacturing Co Ltd* [1924] NZLR 623; *Bouboulis v Mann, Macneal and Co Ltd* 1926 SC 637; *Re George Downs and Co Ltd* [1943] IR 420.
[289] *Re Inecto Ltd* (1922) 38 TLR 797.
[290] *Re George Downs and Co Ltd* [1943] IR 420.
[291] (1866) 14 LT 451.
[292] (1867) 16 LT 474.
[293] (1867) 16 LT 583.
[294] (1890) 18 R 98.

10.118   Creditor petitioners failed to show that continuing the voluntary winding up would prejudice them in *Re Universal Drug Supply Association*,[295] where the company was solvent and no other creditors supported the petitioner; *Re Brixton Cycle Co*;[296] *Re New York Exchange Ltd*;[297] *Re Russell, Cordner and Co*,[298] in which a supervision order was made on another petition; *Re City Avenue Co Ltd*,[299] where the petitioner's position was adequately protected by orders made in other proceedings; *Re Pulsator Milking Co Ltd*;[300] *George Elsmie and Son v Tomatin Spey District Distillery Ltd*,[301] in which a supervision order was made at the company's request; *Re E H Bennett and Co Ltd*,[302] in which the petition was adjourned and the court directed a meeting of creditors to be summoned; *Re Belfast Tailors' Co-partnership Ltd*;[303] *Re New Zealand Wholesale Club Ltd*,[304] in which a majority of creditors favoured continuation of the voluntary winding up; *Re Londonderry Ltd*;[305] *Re Whangarei Daily News Ltd*.[306]

10.119   Where the court was not completely satisfied that voluntary winding up would prejudice the petitioner but also remained doubtful about the voluntary winding up, it could make a supervision order, as in *Re Simon's Reef Consolidated Gold Mining Co*;[307] *Re Regent's Park Co Ltd*;[308] *Re Acetylene Gas Co of Australasia Ltd*;[309] *Re Gilbert Machinery Co (No 2)*.[310]

10.120   In three early cases, the company adopted a resolution for voluntary winding up while rival creditors' petitions were pending, one asking for a winding-up order and one for a supervision order, and a supervision order was made because it was favoured by a large majority of creditors,[311] but the reports do not mention any consideration of whether there would be prejudice to the other creditor who wanted a winding-up order. In *Re Langley Mill Steel and Iron Works Co*[312] a resolution for voluntary winding up was adopted while the petition was pending and a vast majority of creditors preferred voluntary to compulsory winding up, and this was considered sufficient reason to dismiss the petition.

10.121   In *Re AB Cycle Co Ltd*[313] it was said that there were three reasons for ordering compulsory winding up of the company, which was already in voluntary liquidation, on a creditor's petition: (a) the resolution for voluntary winding up was not passed in good faith, (b) a large

---

[295] (1874) 22 WR 675.
[296] (1885) 1 TLR 254.
[297] (1888) 39 ChD 415.
[298] [1891] 3 Ch 171.
[299] (1891) 2 BC (NSW) 41.
[300] (1898) 1 GLR 51.
[301] (1906) 8 F 434.
[302] (1907) 9 GLR 355.
[303] [1909] 1 IR 49.
[304] (1911) 14 GLR 166.
[305] (1921) 21 SR (NSW) 263.
[306] [1929] GLR 269.
[307] [1882] WN 173.
[308] (1898) 24 VLR 420.
[309] (1901) 1 SR (NSW) Eq 102.
[310] (1906) 26 NZLR 53.
[311] *Re Inns of Court Co* [1866] WN 348; *Re Owen's Patent Wheel, Tire and Axle Co Ltd* (1873) 29 LT 672; *Re West Hartlepool Ironworks Co* (1875) LR 10 Ch App 618.
[312] (1871) LR 12 Eq 26.
[313] (1902) 19 TLR 84.

majority of the creditors asked for a compulsory order, (c) circumstances in carrying on the company required investigation.

Contributory's Petition

Prejudice to rights of contributories must be shown

A contributory of a company may petition for its compulsory winding up despite it being **10.122** in voluntary liquidation,[314] but the court must be satisfied that the rights of the contributories will be prejudiced by a voluntary winding up.[315] A similar statutory test was imposed on creditors' petitions from 1862 until 1929.[316] The test was imposed on contributories' petitions by the Companies (Consolidation) Act 1908, s 197, apparently without having been enacted in any previous legislation. It reflected the position already arrived at by the courts.[317] In *Re Oro Fino Mines Ltd*,[318] even though the test was not imposed by the relevant Canadian legislation, the court applied it to a contributory's petition, by analogy with English cases on creditors' petitions (but in *Re Empire Timber Lumber and Tie Co Ltd*,[319] under the same legislation, the test was not applied to a creditor's petition).

In *Re Oro Fino Mines Ltd*[320] it was held that the test must be satisfied even if the voluntary **10.123** winding up commenced after the contributory's petition was presented. This was decided by analogy with cases on creditors' petitions.[321] In *Re Internet Investment Corporation Ltd*[322] it was assumed that the test had to be satisfied even though the resolution for voluntary winding up was passed after the winding-up petition had been presented. See also cases on a similar New Zealand provision which applied to both creditors' and contributories' petitions: *Re Pulsator Milking Co Ltd*;[323] *Re Snowdrift Lime Co Ltd*.[324] See also *Re Whangarei Daily News Ltd*;[325] *Re North Western Fruitgrowers Pty Ltd*.[326] All the New Zealand cases involved creditors' petitions except *Re Whangarei Daily News Ltd*, which was a joint petition by creditors and contributories.

The statutory test in IA 1986, s 116, was held to have been satisfied in *Re Peruvian Amazon* **10.124** *Co Ltd*;[327] *Re Zinotty Properties Ltd*;[328] and *Re Internet Investment Corporation Ltd*.[329]

Cases before the statutory condition was introduced

Before the statutory test in IA 1986, s 116, was introduced in 1908 the Court of Appeal had **10.125** arrived at the position that the winding up of a company in voluntary liquidation could be

---

[314] IA 1986, s 124(5).
[315] IA 1986, s 116.
[316] See 10.114–10.121.
[317] See 10.125–10.129.
[318] (1900) 7 BCR 388.
[319] (1920) 55 DLR 90.
[320] (1900) 7 BCR 388.
[321] *Re New York Exchange Ltd* (1888) 39 ChD 415; *Re Medical Battery Co* [1894] 1 Ch 444. See 10.114.
[322] [2009] EWHC 2744 (Ch), [2010] 1 BCLC 458.
[323] (1898) 1 GLR 51.
[324] [1934] GLR 2.
[325] [1929] GLR 269.
[326] [1965] VR 306 at pp 308–9.
[327] (1913) 29 TLR 384.
[328] [1984] 1 WLR 1249.
[329] [2009] EWHC 2744 (Ch), [2010] 1 BCLC 458.

ordered on a contributory's petition if the circumstances of the voluntary winding up were likely to prejudice the contributories.[330]

10.126 Before this position was arrived at, more restrictive criteria had been suggested. It was said, for example, that the question whether there should be a voluntary or a compulsory winding up is essentially one for the discretion of the members,[331] unless the company is insolvent in which case the view of the majority of creditors should normally prevail.[332] The members of a company should be bound by a resolution of the members for voluntary winding up, so a contributory had to show that the resolution for voluntary winding up was a fraud on the minority.[333]

10.127 Before the introduction of the statutory test in s 116, winding-up orders were made on contributories' petitions where:

(a) It appeared that the liquidator appointed by the majority of members would not pursue an investigation of their conduct in relation to the company because of his association with them, and their conduct appeared to warrant investigation.[334]

(b) The voluntary liquidation was agreed to for the purposes of a reconstruction which did not materialize.[335]

(c) It appeared that a public examination of persons connected with the company was necessary.[336] It seems now that where a company is in voluntary liquidation, its liquidator or any creditor or contributory may apply under IA 1986, s 112(1), for the court to exercise its power under s 133 to order a public examination as if the company were in compulsory liquidation.[337]

(d) The voluntary liquidator had neglected his duties.[338]

(e) There was 'so much danger of irregularity and want of efficient supervision under a voluntary winding up' as to justify a compulsory liquidation.[339]

(f) The company's affairs should be investigated and this could be better done under a compulsory than a voluntary liquidation.[340]

---

[330] *Re National Company for the Distribution of Electricity by Secondary Generators Ltd* [1902] 2 Ch 34 at p 40.

[331] *Re Beaujolais Wine Co* (1867) LR 3 Ch App 15 at pp 19–20; *Re Madras Coffee Co Ltd* (1869) 17 WR 643; *Re British Asahan Plantations Co Ltd* (1892) 36 SJ 363.

[332] *Re Lonsdale Vale Ironstone Co* (1868) 16 WR 601.

[333] *Re London and Mercantile Discount Co* (1865) LR 1 Eq 277; *Re St David's Gold Mining Co Ltd* (1866) 14 LT 539; *Re Imperial Mercantile Credit Association, Coleman's, M'Andrew's, Figdor's and Doyle's Cases* (1866) 12 Jur NS 739; *Re Petersburgh and Viborg Gas Co, ex parte Hartmont* (1875) 33 LT 637. In all the cases cited the petition was dismissed, as were the petitions in *Re Cab Company of Graham and Co Ltd* (1884) 1 TLR 46 and *Re Goldfields of Matabeleland Ltd* (1906) 50 SJ 773, in which suggestions of fraud on the minority were not accepted.

[334] *Re West Surrey Tanning Co* (1866) LR 2 Eq 737; *Re London Flour Co* (1868) 17 LT 636; *Re The Varieties Ltd* [1893] 2 Ch 235; *Re Haycraft Gold Reduction and Mining Co* [1900] 2 Ch 230; *Re Gutta Percha Corporation* [1900] 2 Ch 665.

[335] *Re Gutta Percha Corporation* [1900] 2 Ch 665.

[336] *Re Gutta Percha Corporation.*

[337] *Re Campbell Coverings Ltd (No 2)* [1954] Ch 225; *Bishopsgate Investment Management Ltd v Maxwell* [1993] Ch 1 per Dillon LJ at p 24 and Stuart-Smith LJ at p 46.

[338] *Re Fire Annihilator Co* (1863) 32 Beav 561.

[339] *Re Littlehampton, Havre and Honfleur Steamship Co Ltd* (1865) 2 De G J & S 521 per Knight Bruce LJ at p 525.

[340] *Re Anglo-Austrian Printing and Publishing Union Ltd* (1891) 35 SJ 469, in which the petition was supported by a majority of creditors and the judge thought the incumbent voluntary liquidator, though

In *Re Star and Garter Ltd*,[341] a contributory's petition was refused because all the matters it **10.128** raised could have been dealt with in applications under what is now IA 1986, s 112.

In relation to unregistered companies, in *Re Second Commercial Benefit Building Society*[342] **10.129** the petition was refused because the company could be satisfactorily wound up by its officials and the petitioner could sue for what was owed to her. A contrary view was taken in *Re Anglo-Mexican Mint Co.*[343]

Public Interest Petitions

When considering a public interest petition for the compulsory winding up of a company, **10.130** the fact that the company is already in voluntary liquidation is a factor to be considered, as is the opposition of creditors to compulsory winding up, but the opposition of even a majority of creditors will not be of such significance as it would be on a petition by another creditor on the ground of the company's inability to pay its debts where the question is essentially between the creditors only.[344]

In *Re Lubin, Rosen and Associates Ltd*[345] it appeared to the Secretary of State from infor- **10.131** mation obtained under what is now the Companies Act 1985, s 447, that it was expedient in the public interest that the company be wound up by the court. The petition was presented a fortnight after the company had gone into creditors' voluntary winding up, but was prompted by information obtained before the members adopted their resolution for voluntary winding up. The petition was opposed by a large number of creditors, but it appeared that there were conflicts of interest between those creditors and others, and the support of creditors had been improperly canvassed by the incumbent voluntary liquidator. Megarry J held that it was just and equitable that there should be a compulsory liquidation because of the suspicion that offences had been committed which required investigation.

The fact that a winding up by the court will involve more extensive investigation of the com- **10.132** pany's affairs than a voluntary winding up, which will increase the expenses of the liquidation, should not deter the court from making a winding-up order if a proper investigation of the company is required in the public interest.[346]

It may be in the public interest to order the compulsory winding up of a company in vol- **10.133** untary liquidation so as to make clear that the court will act to stop the kind of business conducted by the company.[347]

Official Receiver's Petition

An official receiver may petition for the compulsory winding up of a company that is being **10.134** wound up voluntarily in England and Wales, but the court must not make a winding-up

---

independent of the directors, was not properly appointed; *Re Australasian Pictures Productions Ltd* [1925] StR Qd 249.

[341] (1873) 42 LJ Ch 374.
[342] (1879) 48 LJ Ch 753.
[343] [1875] WN 168.
[344] *Re Lubin, Rosen and Associates Ltd* [1975] 1 WLR 122.
[345] [1975] 1 WLR 122.
[346] *Securities and Investments Board v Lancashire and Yorkshire Portfolio Management Ltd* [1992] BCLC 281; *Re ForceSun Ltd* [2002] EWHC 443 (Ch), [2002] 2 BCLC 302.
[347] *Re Alpha Club (UK) Ltd* [2002] EWHC 884 (Ch), [2002] 2 BCLC 612, at [39].

order on the petition unless it is satisfied that the voluntary liquidation cannot be continued with due regard to the interests of the creditors or contributories.[348] The court needs to be satisfied only on a balance of probabilities.[349] Section 124(5) says that a petition may be presented by 'the official receiver attached to the court', which must, it is submitted, mean the court to which the petition is presented (that is, the court mentioned in s 124(1)). In other words an official receiver can present a winding-up petition only to the court to which he or she is attached.

10.135   The views of creditors are relevant on a petition by an official receiver[350] and the court will normally accept the view of the majority against compulsory liquidation if they have sound reasons for their opposition.[351] However, a petition by the official receiver will usually be presented because of grave concern with the conduct of the voluntary liquidation, and the need for investigation is likely to outweigh opposing creditors' views, as it did in *Re Hewitt Brannan (Tools) Co Ltd*, in which it was observed that creditors could have done something themselves through the creditors' committee to discipline the voluntary liquidator.

10.136   In *Re Ryder Installations Ltd*[352] the official receiver petitioned in November 1965 for the compulsory winding up of a company that had commenced creditors' voluntary liquidation in March 1958 but had never held a creditors' meeting. The voluntary liquidator had already been convicted five times for failing to submit returns to Companies House. Compulsory winding up was ordered.

10.137   In *Re J Russell Electronics Ltd*[353] the official receiver's petition was dismissed on the incumbent voluntary liquidator undertaking (a) to repay money which he admitted misapplying and (b) to complete the liquidation (which was virtually finished) with all due dispatch.

10.138   In *Re 1897 Jubilee Sites Syndicate*[354] Wright J said that an order ought to be made on an official receiver's petition 'where the powers of the voluntary liquidator are proved, in the opinion of the court, to be insufficient for the purposes of the winding up in so far as the interests of creditors or contributories are concerned'. Accordingly a compulsory winding up was ordered so that an application could be made to the court for the public examination of a man who had been concerned in the promotion of the company. It seems now that where a company is in voluntary liquidation, its liquidator or any creditor or contributory may apply under IA 1986, s 112(1), for the court to exercise its power under s 133 to order a public examination as if the company were in compulsory liquidation.[355]

Other Petitioners

10.139   The liquidator of a company being wound up voluntarily is empowered to bring legal proceedings in the name and on behalf of the company,[356] and so, it is submitted, may petition

---

[348] IA 1986, s 124(5).
[349] *Re J Russell Electronics Ltd* [1968] 1 WLR 1252.
[350] *Adebayo v Official Receiver of Nigeria* [1954] 1 WLR 681.
[351] *Re Hewitt Brannan (Tools) Co Ltd* [1991] BCLC 80.
[352] [1966] 1 WLR 524.
[353] [1968] 1 WLR 1252.
[354] [1899] 2 Ch 204.
[355] *Re Campbell Coverings Ltd (No 2)* [1954] Ch 225; *Bishopsgate Investment Management Ltd v Maxwell* [1993] Ch 1 per Dillon LJ at p 24 and Stuart-Smith LJ at p 46.
[356] IA 1986, s 165(3) and sch 4, para 4.

for the compulsory winding up of the company (such a petition being a proceeding, see 2.12).[357] In Australia a liquidator has a statutory power to petition in his or her own right.[358]

In *Re British Alliance Assurance Corporation*[359] an insurance company in voluntary liquid- **10.140** ation was wound up on the petition of two policyholders under the Life Assurance Companies Act 1870, s 21,[360] because the company's affairs required investigation, which could not be carried out effectively by the voluntary liquidator, who had previously been the secretary of the company.

In *Re Arthur Rathbone Kitchens Ltd*[361] a petition for the winding up by the court of a com- **10.141** pany in voluntary liquidation which was presented by the supervisor of the company's voluntary arrangement succeeded because it was necessary to replace the incumbent voluntary liquidator, who had failed to cooperate with the supervisor, had not demonstrated the necessary qualities of independence and impartiality, and had failed to respond to criticisms of his conduct of the liquidation. Since this case was decided, the court has indicated that a winding-up order will not be made if a petitioner's only reason for converting a voluntary liquidation into a winding up by the court is dissatisfaction with the incumbent voluntary liquidator.[362]

Confirmation by the Court

Voluntary winding up is not listed in Regulation (EC) No 1346/2000, annex A, among **10.142** insolvency proceedings. In order to obtain recognition under the Regulation a voluntary winding up must be confirmed by the court, and confirmation is available only if the winding up is a creditors' voluntary winding up. The procedure for applying for confirmation is set out in IR 1986, rr 7.62 and 7.63. The procedure may be used if a creditors' voluntary winding up was initiated:

(a) by resolution of the members under IA 1986, s 84(1); or
(b) by an administrator sending a notice to the registrar of companies under sch B1, para 83.[363]

An application for court confirmation of a creditors' voluntary winding up must be made **10.143** by the liquidator[364] using form 7.20 in IR 1986, sch 4.

Confirmation is given only for the purposes of Regulation (EC) No 1346/2000,[365] and **10.144** the application must state that the Regulation applies to the company, and whether the winding-up proceedings will be main proceedings, territorial proceedings or secondary proceedings.[366]

---

[357] See *Re Hooker's Cream Milk Co Ltd* (1879) 23 SJ 231, in which the voluntary liquidator of a company successfully petitioned in the company's name for the voluntary winding up to be continued under the supervision of the court.
[358] Corporations Act 2001 (Australia), ss 459P(1)(e) and 462(2)(d).
[359] (1878) 9 ChD 635.
[360] See 7.318.
[361] [1997] 2 BCLC 280.
[362] *Re Inside Sport Ltd* [2000] 1 BCLC 302; *Re AB (Handling) Ltd* (1999) LTL 5/2/99. See 10.83–10.84.
[363] IR 1986, r 7.62(8).
[364] IR 1986, r 7.62(1).
[365] IR 1986, r 7.62(1).
[366] r 7.62(2)(e).

10.145   The application must be supported by a witness statement.[367]

10.146   Two copies of the application must be filed in court together with one copy of:[368]

(a) the resolution for voluntary winding up;

(b) evidence of the applicant's appointment as liquidator of the company; and

(c) the statement of affairs prepared by the directors for the creditors;[369] or

(d) in a move from administration to creditors' voluntary winding up,[370] a copy of the administrator's notice of moving from administration to creditors' voluntary liquidation[371] and the statement of affairs of the company prepared for the administrator.[372]

It is not necessary to serve the application on, or give notice of it to, any other person.[373] The court fee is £50.[374]

10.147   On an application under IR 1986, r 7.62, the court may confirm the creditors' voluntary winding up.[375] This makes it clear that the court's decision is discretionary,[376] even though most cases are so routine that an application may be dealt with by a member of the court staff.[377] An application which requires fuller consideration may be referred to the registrar or the judge.[378]

10.148   The form of the confirmation order is included in form 7.20.

10.149   If a confirmation order is made, the liquidator must notify it to any liquidator of the company in another EU State (apart from Denmark) in the list of insolvency office-holders in Regulation (EC) No 1346/2000, annex C, and known creditors in other member States in accordance with art 40.[379]

10.150   The procedure can also be used to provide confirmation of a creditors' voluntary winding up of a UK credit institution[380] for the purposes of Directive 2001/24/EC, arts 10 and 28 (which define the law applicable to winding up and provide for proof of a liquidator's appointment).[381]

10.151   A similar provision was made for UK insurers[382] by the Insurers (Reorganisation and Winding Up) Regulations 2003,[383] reg 7, but was repealed by the Insurers (Reorganisation

---

[367]   IR 1986, r 7.62(2).

[368]   IR 1986, r 7.62(3).

[369]   IA 1986, s 99.

[370]   IR 1986, r 7.62(8).

[371]   IA 1986, sch B1, para 83(3) and (4).

[372]   sch B1, para 47.

[373]   IR 1986, r 7.62(4).

[374]   Civil Proceedings Fees Order 2008 (SI 2008/1053), sch 1, fee 3.7.

[375]   r 7.62(5).

[376]   *Re TXU Europe German Finance BV* [2005] BCC 90 at [7].

[377]   r 7.62(7).

[378]   *Re TXU Europe German Finance BV* at [21].

[379]   IR 1986, r 7.63.

[380]   Defined at 1.323.

[381]   Credit Institutions (Reorganisation and Winding Up) Regulations 2004 (SI 2004/1045), reg 6, which provides a modified version of IR 1986, r 7.62, for the purposes of SI 2004/1045.

[382]   Defined at 1.320.

[383]   SI 2003/1102.

and Winding Up) Regulations 2004,[384] reg 53. Instead of re-enacting the provision, SI 2004/353, reg 7, attempted to amend it, apparently in the belief that IR 1986, r 7.62, had actually been amended instead of just modified for the purposes of SI 2003/1102. The attempted amendment is therefore of no effect and the result is that there is now no provision for confirmation of a creditors' voluntary winding up of a UK insurer.

Voluntary Winding Up Subject to Supervision of Court

Availability of supervision orders

From 1857 until 1986, under a provision last re-enacted as the Companies Act 1985, s 606, **10.152** when a registered company had passed a resolution for voluntary winding up, the court could make an order that the voluntary winding up should continue but subject to such supervision of the court, and with such liberty for creditors, contributories or others to apply to the court, and generally on such terms and conditions, as the court thought just. This was known as a supervision order. Winding up subject to supervision was abolished by IA 1985, s 88 and sch 10, part 2, which was brought into force on 29 December 1986 by the Insolvency Act 1985 (Commencement No 5) Order 1986,[385] art 2. The equivalent Northern Ireland provision was repealed on 11 October 1991.[386] Abolition implemented a recommendation by the Jenkins committee, which said that the provisions on winding up subject to supervision served no useful purpose.[387]

An unregistered company could not be wound up subject to supervision.[388]   **10.153**

Winding up subject to the supervision of the court has been included by the UK in annexes   **10.154** A (insolvency proceedings) and B (winding-up proceedings) of Regulation (EC) No 1346/2000, because winding up subject to supervision is available in Gibraltar,[389] though it will be abolished by the reform of company law currently in progress there.[390] Regulation (EC) No 1346/2000 does not apply to any winding up under the supervision of the court in the UK, because all such proceedings were opened before the Regulation came into force on 31 May 2002, and the Regulation does not apply to proceedings opened before it entered into force.[391] If it is correct that art 3 of the Regulation means that a UK court must make available all proceedings listed for the UK in annex A to every debtor whose centre of main interests is in the UK, the court will have to find a way of making supervision orders again, but it is submitted at 1.394–1.406 that this argument is not correct. Winding up subject to the supervision of the court is also available in the Cayman Islands[392] and the Isle of Man.[393]

---

[384] SI 2004/353.
[385] SI 1986/1924.
[386] By the Insolvency (Northern Ireland) Order 1989 (SI 1989/2405 (NI 19)), sch 10.
[387] *Report of the Company Law Committee* (Cmnd 1749, 1962), para 503(v).
[388] Companies Act 1985, s 666(4), repealed by IA 1985, sch 10, part 2.
[389] Companies Act (1930-07) (Gibraltar), ss 298–302.
[390] Insolvency Act 2011 (Gibraltar); Companies Bill 2014 (Gibraltar).
[391] Regulation (EC) No 1346/2000, art 43.
[392] Companies Law (2013 Revision) (Cayman Islands), ss 131–133.
[393] Companies Act 1931 (Isle of Man), ss 243–246A; Companies Act 2006 (Isle of Man), s 182.

Supervision and winding up by the court compared

10.155 In *Re Manual Work Services (Construction) Ltd* [394] Megarry J said, at pp 343–4:

> The differences between winding up by the court and winding up subject to supervision are, of course, very great. . . . In general, winding up under supervision is a voluntary liquidation with some important but not very extensive safeguards for those concerned, such as the requirement of quarterly reports to the court, protection against actions against the company, and the opportunity to make applications to the court. The two processes are in substance, very different indeed.

10.156 Nevertheless it was said in an early case that if a company was in voluntary liquidation under supervision, there would normally be no reason for making an order for compulsory winding up of the company, because the court's control of the winding up under supervision would be adequate protection for all interests. [395] But winding up under supervision was superseded by compulsory winding up in *Re Manchester Queensland Cotton Co* [396] and *Re Caerphilly Colliery Co, ex parte Dolling.* [397]

Application procedure

10.157 Application for a supervision order was by petition following the same procedure as a petition for a winding-up order. The company itself could petition for a supervision order at the instance of its voluntary liquidator. [398] The advertisement for a petition for a supervision order was required to state expressly that it was a petition for the company to be wound up subject to the supervision of the court. [399]

Petition asking only for supervision order

10.158 At the hearing of a petition for a supervision order the court could not make a winding-up order, despite the wishes of other creditors for one, unless the petitioner consented. [400]

Petition asking for winding-up order or such other order as would be just

10.159 On a petition for a winding-up order or such other order as would be just, the court could make a supervision order if the company was in voluntary liquidation. [401]

10.160 Until the procedure for substitution of petitioner was introduced in 1893, a petitioner whose petition had asked for a compulsory winding up or such other order as would be just could, at the hearing of the petition, ask for a supervision order despite the opposition of creditors who wanted a winding-up order. [402] In these circumstances the petition would have been advertised as a petition for the winding up of the company by the court, and so had to be

---

[394] [1975] 1 WLR 341.
[395] *Re London and Mediterranean Bank Ltd* (1866) 15 LT 153.
[396] (1867) 16 LT 583.
[397] (1875) 32 LT 15.
[398] *Re Hooker's Cream Milk Co Ltd* (1879) 23 SJ 231.
[399] Companies (Winding-up) Rules 1949 (SI 1949/330), form 6.
[400] *Re Electric and Magnetic Co* (1881) 50 LJ Ch 491, in which, however, Fry J adjourned the petition, indicating that if the opposing creditors presented their own petition, a winding-up order would be made.
[401] *Re Simon's Reef Consolidated Gold Mining Co* (1882) 31 WR 238; *Re Russell, Cordner and Co* [1891] 3 Ch 171; *Re New Oriental Bank Corporation* [1892] 3 Ch 563; *Re Regent's Park Co Ltd* (1898) 24 VLR 420; *Re Acetylene Gas Co of Australasia Ltd* (1901) 1 SR (NSW) Eq 102; *Re Gilbert Machinery Co (No 2)* (1906) 26 NZLR 53.
[402] *Re Chepstow Bobbin Mills Co* (1887) 36 ChD 563; *Re New Oriental Bank Corporation* [1892] 3 Ch 563.

adjourned to be amended and advertised again.⁴⁰³ Adjournment for re-advertising became the normal practice sometime in the 1890s. Previously, amendment and re-advertisement were normally not required in these circumstances.⁴⁰⁴ Amendment and adjournment for re-advertising were also required (at least from the 1890s) if the petition asked for, and had been advertised as asking for, a supervision order only, but at the hearing the petitioner asked for a winding-up order⁴⁰⁵ or if the petition had asked for a winding-up order or alternatively a supervision order but the petitioner abandoned the claim for a winding-up order.⁴⁰⁶

Court's discretion

The court's power to make a supervision order was discretionary.⁴⁰⁷ In *Re Bank of Gibraltar*   **10.161**
*and Malta*⁴⁰⁸ Turner LJ said, at p 73, that it was necessary to show that it was proper to put in force provisions of the legislation which did not apply in a voluntary winding up but would in a winding up under supervision. In *Crawford v A R Cowper Ltd*⁴⁰⁹ it was said that cause had to be shown for a supervision order 'such as the danger of preferences being created, or some impropriety—actual or threatened—in the conduct of the liquidation'.⁴¹⁰ In Practice Note [1901] WN 14 Wright J said that he would not allow the costs of a petition for a supervision order unless it could be shown that there was some sufficient reason for making it.

Views of creditors and contributories

The Companies Act 1862, s 149, expressly provided that in determining whether a company   **10.162**
was to be wound up altogether by the court or subject to the supervision of the court, the court might have regard to the wishes of the creditors or contributories.

On a contributory's petition, the court's attitude was that every member of a company   **10.163**
should abide by a majority decision in favour of a voluntary winding up⁴¹¹ so that a supervision order would not be made unless it was shown that the resolution for voluntary winding up was a fraud on the minority.⁴¹² But a need to bring into operation the provision preventing proceedings against the company being commenced or proceeded with except by leave

---

⁴⁰³ *Re New Oriental Bank Corporation* [1892] 3 Ch 563; Practice Note [1902] WN 77; *Re Manual Work Services (Construction) Ltd* [1975] 1 WLR 341.
⁴⁰⁴ *Re United Bacon Curing Co* [1890] WN 74 (in which amendment was required but not re-advertisement); per Kekewich J in *Re National Whole Meal Bread and Biscuit Co* [1891] 2 Ch 151 at p 153; *Re Civil Service Brewery Co* [1893] WN 5; and *Re Gilbert Machinery Co (No 2)* (1906) 26 NZLR 53 followed the earlier English practice.
⁴⁰⁵ *Re National Whole Meal Bread and Biscuit Co* [1891] 2 Ch 151; though *Re Electric and Magnetic Co* (1881) 50 LJ Ch 491 apparently shows the earlier practice of not requiring amendment or re-advertisement.
⁴⁰⁶ *Re New Morgan Gold Mining Co* [1893] WN 79.
⁴⁰⁷ *Re Bank of Gibraltar and Malta* (1865) LR 1 Ch App 69 per Turner LJ at pp 72–3; *Re Beaujolais Wine Co* (1867) LR 3 Ch App 15; *Re Owen's Patent Wheel, Tire and Axle Co Ltd* (1873) 29 LT 672.
⁴⁰⁸ (1865) LR 1 Ch App 69.
⁴⁰⁹ (1902) 4 F 849.
⁴¹⁰ At p 851.
⁴¹¹ *Re Bank of Gibraltar and Malta* (1865) LR 1 Ch App 69 per Turner LJ at p 73.
⁴¹² *Re London and Mercantile Discount Co* (1865) LR 1 Eq 277; *Re St David's Gold Mining Co Ltd* (1866) 14 LT 539; *Re Beaujolais Wine Co* (1867) LR 3 Ch App 15; *Re Irrigation Co of France, ex parte Fox* (1871) LR 6 Ch App 176.

of the court[413] was a good reason for making a supervision order.[414] On a contributory's petition a supervision order was considered to be the wrong way of dealing with an allegation of misconduct by voluntary liquidators.[415]

10.164   On a petition by creditors in *Re New Zealand Wholesale Club Ltd*[416] a supervision order was refused because a majority of creditors had voted against it. The petitioners wanted an investigation of the actions of promoters and directors of the company, but did not claim that this would add to the company's assets.

Voluntary winding up void

10.165   A supervision order could not be made if the company's resolution for voluntary winding up was void.[417]

Company being Wound Up by the Court

10.166   A second winding-up order cannot be made against a company which is already being wound up by a court in the same jurisdiction.[418] It is, however, possible to order the compulsory winding up of a company in voluntary winding up[419] or, subject to Regulation (EC) No 1346/2000, a company which is being wound up by a court in another jurisdiction.[420]

10.167   There are express prohibitions against presenting a petition for the winding up of a company which is already being wound up by the court in:

(a)   the Friendly Societies Act 1974, s 87(1) (FCA's or PRA's petition to wind up unincorporated registered friendly society);

(b)   IA 1986, s 124A(2) (Secretary of State's petition to wind up a company in the public interest);

(c)   s 124B(2) (Secretary of State's petition to wind up a European public limited-liability company);

(d)   s 124C(3) (FCA's petition to wind up a European cooperative society);

(e)   Companies (Audit, Investigations and Community Enterprise) Act 2004, s 50(2) (Regulator of Community Enterprise Companies' petition to wind up a CIC);

(f)   Serious Crime Act 2007, s 27(10) (failure to comply with a serious crime prevention order).

---

[413] Now IA 1986, s 130(2). It came into operation because a supervision order was deemed to be a winding-up order—see the provision last enacted as the Companies Act 1985, s 610(3).

[414] *Re Zoedone Co Ltd (No 1)* (1883) 53 LJ Ch 465.

[415] *Re London Bank of Scotland* (1867) 15 WR 1103; *Re Star and Garter Ltd* (1873) 42 LJ Ch 374.

[416] (1911) 14 GLR 166.

[417] *Re Bridport Old Brewery Co* (1867) LR 2 Ch App 191; *Re Patent Floor-Cloth Co* (1869) LR 8 Eq 664.

[418] *Re British and Foreign Generating Apparatus Co Ltd* (1865) 12 LT 368 at 369 (MR); *Commonwealth of Australia v Emanuel Projects Pty Ltd* (1996) 21 ACSR 36; *Dewina Trading Sdn Bhd v Ion International Pty Ltd* (1996) 141 ALR 317.

[419] See 10.79–10.141.

[420] See 1.114 and 10.185–10.187.

Bank Insolvency

No order may be made for the winding up of a building society which is in building society **10.168**
insolvency.[421] But a bank in bank insolvency may be ordered to be wound up on a public
interest petition.[422]

Insolvency Proceedings Elsewhere in United Kingdom

Jurisdiction of English Court to Order Winding Up

The rules on allocation of jurisdiction to wind up companies within the United Kingdom **10.169**
are discussed at 1.419–1.432. Those rules ensure that a registered company can be wound up
by the court only in the part of the United Kingdom in which it is registered. A winding-up
order made by a court in Scotland or Northern Ireland takes effect in England and Wales
under the provisions discussed at 10.171–10.177. In relation to a registered company, this
means that the protection from applications and orders for winding up provided by a moratorium for preparation of a voluntary arrangement,[423] an interim moratorium in preparation for administration,[424] or administration,[425] need apply only in the part of the United
Kingdom in which the company is registered. In England and Wales and Scotland, this is
achieved because the protection is invoked by filing documents with, or making an application to, the court, which means a court having jurisdiction to wind up the company.[426] In
Northern Ireland, it is because the legislation applies to registered companies only if they
are registered in Northern Ireland.[427]

It is possible for an unregistered company or an insolvent partnership to be wound up by the **10.170**
court in more than one part of the United Kingdom, if it has principal places of business in
more than one part,[428] or if it has no principal place of business in the United Kingdom but
has sufficient connections with two or more parts of the UK. An unregistered company may
obtain a moratorium for preparation of a voluntary arrangement or go into administration,
if it is incorporated in a European Economic Area (EEA) State other than the UK or is not
incorporated in an EEA State but has its centre of main interests in an EU member State
other than Denmark.[429] As the relevant provisions of IA 1986 apply in both England and
Wales and Scotland, any restriction on winding up an unregistered company by virtue of
a moratorium or administration in Scotland is directly enforceable in England and Wales.

---

[421] Building Societies (Insolvency and Special Administration) Order 2009 (SI 2009/805), sch 1, para
20(1) and (3).
[422] IA 1986, sch B1, para 42, applied by the Banking Act 2009, s 119.
[423] See 10.3–10.4.
[424] See 10.26–10.28.
[425] See 10.29–10.30.
[426] IA 1986, s 251.
[427] Insolvency (Northern Ireland) Order 1989 (SI 1989/2405, NI 19), art 14(4)(a) (voluntary arrangement) and sch B1, para 1(1A)(a) (administration).
[428] See 1.427–1.432.
[429] IA 1986, s 1(4)(b) and (c) (voluntary arrangement) and sch B1, para 111(1A)(b) and (c) (administration); SI 1989/2405, art 14(4)(b) and (c) (voluntary arrangement) and sch B1, para 1(1A)(b) and
(c) (administration).

Restrictions on winding up an insolvent partnership by virtue of insolvency procedures in Scotland or on winding up an unregistered company or insolvent partnership by virtue of procedures in Northern Ireland arise under local legislation which is not directly applicable in England and Wales, but the restrictions would be an important factor for the English court to take into account in exercising its discretion, for example, whether or not to make a winding-up order.

Enforcing Orders Made in Scotland and Northern Ireland

10.171 An order made by a court in Scotland or Northern Ireland in the exercise of jurisdiction in relation to insolvency law shall be enforced in England and Wales as if it were made by a court exercising the corresponding jurisdiction in England and Wales.[430] This does not require a court in England and Wales to enforce another court's order in relation to property situated in England and Wales.[431]

Assisting Courts in Scotland and Northern Ireland

10.172 The courts of England and Wales which have jurisdiction in relation to insolvency law must assist the courts which have the corresponding jurisdiction in Scotland and Northern Ireland.[432]

10.173 A request made to a court in England and Wales by a court in Scotland or Northern Ireland is authority for the English court to apply, in relation to any matters specified in the request, the insolvency law which is applicable by either court in relation to comparable matters falling within its jurisdiction.[433]

10.174 If an unregistered company being wound up in one part of the United Kingdom has extensive interests in another part, it may be useful to conduct an ancillary winding up there. After the English High Court ordered the winding up in England and Wales of Bank of Credit and Commerce International SA, which was a Luxembourg company, an ancillary winding up was ordered by the Court of Session in Scotland in response to letters of request for assistance issued by the High Court.[434]

Meaning of 'Insolvency Law'

10.175 In relation to England and Wales, 'insolvency law' means[435] provision extending to England and Wales made by or under IA 1986 or various provisions of the Company Directors Disqualification Act 1986[436] and provisions of or by virtue of the Banking Act 2009, part 2[437] and part 3.[438]

---

[430] IA 1986, s 426(1). Proceedings under s 426 are subject to the CPR, not IR 1986 (*Fourie v Le Roux* [2005] EWHC 922 (Ch), [2005] BPIR 779, at [61]).

[431] s 426(2).

[432] IA 1986, s 426(4). Proceedings under s 426 are subject to the CPR, not IR 1986 (*Fourie v Le Roux* [2005] EWHC 922 (Ch), [2005] BPIR 779, at [61]).

[433] IA 1986, s 426(5).

[434] See *Liquidator of Bank of Credit and Commerce International SA* [2007] CSOH 165, 2007 SLT 1149.

[435] IA 1986, s 426(10)(a).

[436] Sections 1A, 6–10, 12–15, 19(c), 20 and sch 1, and ss 1–17 as they apply for the purposes of those provisions.

[437] Banking Act 2009, s 129.

[438] Banking Act 2009, s 165.

In relation to Scotland, 'insolvency law' means[439] provision extending to Scotland made **10.176** by or under IA 1986, various provisions of the Company Directors Disqualification Act 1986,[440] the Companies Act 1985, part 18, or the Bankruptcy (Scotland) Act 1985, and provisions of or by virtue of the Banking Act 2009, part 2[441] and part 3.[442]

In relation to Northern Ireland, 'insolvency law' means[443] provision made by or under the **10.177** Insolvency (Northern Ireland) Order 1989[444] or the Company Directors Disqualification (Northern Ireland) Order 2002[445] and provisions of or by virtue of the Banking Act 2009, part 2[446] and part 3.[447]

Assisting Foreign Courts

Assisting Foreign Courts: Common Law

The principle of universality of insolvency proceedings is given effect at common law by **10.178** recognizing that a person appointed under a foreign jurisdiction's insolvency law to act for a company is entitled to act for it in England and Wales.[448] The English court will actively assist such a person, or the court which made the appointment, so far as it properly can, subject to English law and public policy and acting within the limits of its own statutory and common law powers.[449] In English common law, only an insolvency proceeding in the jurisdiction where the company was incorporated can be recognized and assisted, not, for example, a proceeding in another jurisdiction where the company's COMI is located.[450]

In relation to the proceedings to which they apply, the legislative provisions discussed at **10.179** 10.180–10.184 and 10.188–10.210 provide the court with further powers of assistance.

Assisting the Courts of Relevant Countries and Territories

Under IA 1986, s 426(4), the courts of England and Wales which have jurisdiction in rela- **10.180** tion to insolvency law shall assist the courts which have the corresponding jurisdiction in

---

439 IA 1986, s 426(10)(b).
440 Sections 1A, 6–10, 12–15, 19(c), 20 and sch 1, and ss 1–17 as they apply for the purposes of those provisions.
441 Banking Act 2009, s 129.
442 Banking Act 2009, s 165.
443 IA 1986, s 426(10)(c).
444 SI 1989/2405 (NI 19).
445 SI 2002/3150 (NI 4).
446 Banking Act 2009, s 129.
447 Banking Act 2009, s 165.
448 *Cambridge Gas Transport Corporation v Official Committee of Unsecured Creditors of Navigator Holdings plc* [2006] UKPC 26, [2007] 1 AC 508, at [20]. It may be possible to recognize a person appointed by a court established by a government which Her Majesty's Government does not recognize: see *Chen Li Hung v Ting Lei Miao* (2000) 3 HKCFAR 9 (recognition in Hong Kong of trustee in bankruptcy appointed by court in Taiwan).
449 *Cambridge Gas Transport Corporation v Official Committee of Unsecured Creditors of Navigator Holdings plc* at [20]–[22]; *Singularis Holdings Ltd v PricewaterhouseCoopers [2014]* UKPC 36, [2014] 2 BCLC 597, at [15] and [19].
450 *Rubin v Eurofinance SA* [2012] UKSC 46, [2013] 1 AC 236. The Supreme Court held that the contrary decision of the Privy Council (on an appeal from the Isle of Man) in *Cambridge Gas Transport Corporation v Official Committee of Unsecured Creditors of Navigator Holdings plc* [2006] UKPC 26, [2007] 1 AC 508, was wrong. This also throws into doubt *Re Dickson Group Holdings Ltd* [2008] Bda LR 34 (assistance would be given by Bermuda court to insolvency proceedings in the USA concerning a Bermuda company), which followed the *Cambridge Gas Transport* case.

any relevant country or territory.[451] This is a general direction to English courts, not an instruction that they must comply with every request for assistance.[452] The relevant countries and territories are:[453] Anguilla, Australia, The Bahamas, Bermuda, Botswana, Brunei Darussalam,[454] Canada, Cayman Islands, any of the Channel Islands,[455] Falkland Islands, Gibraltar, Hong Kong, Republic of Ireland, Isle of Man,[456] Malaysia,[457] Montserrat, New Zealand, Republic of South Africa,[458] St Helena, Turks and Caicos Islands, Tuvalu, Virgin Islands.

10.181 A request made to a court in England and Wales by a court in a relevant country or territory is authority for the English court to apply, in relation to any matters specified in the request, the insolvency law which is applicable by either court in relation to comparable matters falling within its jurisdiction.[459] In exercising its discretion to apply either English or foreign law, the court shall have regard, in particular, to the rules of private international law.[460]

10.182 When asked for assistance, a court in England and Wales may apply:

(a) its own general jurisdiction and powers and either (b) the insolvency law of England and Wales as provided for in the Insolvency Act 1986, the specified sections of the Company Directors Disqualification Act 1986 and the subordinate legislation made under any of those provisions or (c) so much of the law of the relevant country as corresponds to that comprised in (b).[461]

The court must consider whether, in accordance with these sources of law, the requested assistance may properly be granted. If it may be granted, it should be, so as to fulfil the obligation to assist the foreign court. If the requested assistance is discretionary, the obligation to assist is a weighty factor in favour of granting the assistance but this does not constrain the court's discretion. A request to apply a foreign law must be decided in accordance with the principles and practice by which that law is administered, not the principles and practice governing the corresponding English provision.[462] The English court may apply the law of the requesting court to a person who is not within that court's jurisdiction.[463] If the

---

[451] IA 1986, s 426(4). For interaction with Regulation (EC) No 1346/2000 and the UNCITRAL Model Law see Paul J Omar, 'Cross-border insolvency law in the UK: an embarrassment of riches' (2006) 22 Insolv L & P 132. Proceedings under s 426 are subject to the CPR, not IR 1986 (*Fourie v Le Roux* [2005] EWHC 922 (Ch), [2005] BPIR 779, at [61]). The history of s 426(4) is discussed in *Hughes v Hannover Rückversicherungs-AG* [1999] BPIR 224 and *Al Sabah v Grupo Torras SA* [2005] UKPC 1, [2005] 2 AC 333.
[452] *Hughes v Hannover Rückversicherungs-AG* [1999] BPIR 224 at p 243.
[453] Except where otherwise noted, these countries and territories are designated by the Co-operation of Insolvency Courts (Designation of Relevant Countries and Territories) Order 1986 (SI 1986/2123).
[454] Co-operation of Insolvency Courts (Designation of Relevant Country) Order 1998 (SI 1998/2766).
[455] IA 1986, s 426(11)(a).
[456] IA 1986, s 426(11)(a).
[457] Co-operation of Insolvency Courts (Designation of Relevant Countries) Order 1996 (SI 1996/253).
[458] Co-operation of Insolvency Courts (Designation of Relevant Countries) Order 1996 (SI 1996/253).
[459] IA 1986, s 426(5). In relation to England and Wales, 'insolvency law' is defined in s 426(10)(a); see 10.175–10.177. In relation to a relevant country or territory, s 426(10)(d) defines 'insolvency law' as 'so much of the law of that country or territory as corresponds to provisions falling within any of [paragraphs (a), (b) and (c) of s 426(10)]'. Those paragraphs define respectively the insolvency law of England and Wales, Scotland and Northern Ireland; see 10.175–10.177.
[460] IA 1986, s 426(5). There is some discussion of this 'obscure and ill thought-out provision' by Lawrence Collins J in *Re Television Trade Rentals Ltd* [2002] EWHC 211 (Ch), [2002] BCC 807, at [17].
[461] *Hughes v Hannover Rückversicherungs-AG* [1999] BPIR 224 at p 243.
[462] *England v Smith* [2001] Ch 419.
[463] *Fourie v Le Roux* [2005] EWHC 922 (Ch), [2005] BPIR 779.

requested assistance may not be granted, the court should consider whether it can assist in some other way.[464]

Assistance is given to a court in another jurisdiction, under IA 1986, s 426(4), in response **10.183** to a letter of request from that court. It is not necessary for the request to relate to insolvency proceedings in the requesting court: a request may, for example, be for the English court to commence insolvency proceedings of a kind that is not available in the requesting court.[465]

The English court's jurisdiction is extended by IA 1986, s 426(5), so that it may apply **10.184** English insolvency law to a foreign entity over which it would not normally have jurisdiction. In particular, it may apply an English insolvency procedure which would not normally apply to a foreign entity.[466] It would seem that this would enable the English court to wind up a foreign company over which it would normally not have jurisdiction, for example, a non-business association.

Insolvency Proceedings outside United Kingdom

Jurisdiction to Wind Up a Company being Wound Up outside the United Kingdom

Subject to the rules on allocation of jurisdiction,[467] a foreign company may be wound up **10.185** by the court in England and Wales even if it is being wound up in the place where it was incorporated,[468] or, it is submitted, in any other jurisdiction outside the United Kingdom. The fact that a foreign company is being wound up under the law of its domicile does not mean that it is being wound up for the purposes of IA 1986.[469]

The stay of actions and proceedings on the recognition of a foreign main proceeding under **10.186** the Great Britain version of the UNCITRAL Model Law[470] does not affect the right to request or otherwise initiate the commencement of a proceeding under British insolvency law or the right to file claims in such a proceeding.[471]

For factors affecting the exercise of the court's discretion to wind up a foreign company see **10.187** 1.209–1.212.

---

[464] *Hughes v Hannover Rückversicherungs-AG* [1999] BPIR 224 at pp 243–4.

[465] *Re Tambrook Jersey Ltd* [2013] EWCA Civ 576, [2014] Ch 252.

[466] *Re Dallhold Estates (UK) Pty Ltd* [1992] BCLC 621 (administration order made in respect of a Western Australian company); *Re Television Trade Rentals Ltd* [2002] EWHC 211 (Ch), [2002] BCC 807 (an Isle of Man company could enter into a company voluntary arrangement).

[467] See 1.347–1.432.

[468] *Re Oriental Bank Corporation* (1884) 10 VLR (E) 154; *Re Matheson Brothers Ltd* (1884) 27 ChD 225; *Re Commercial Bank of South Australia* (1886) 33 ChD 174; *Queensland Mercantile and Agency Co Ltd v Australasian Investment Co Ltd* (1888) 15 R 935 at p 939; *Re North Australian Territory Co Ltd* (1889) 23 SALR 163 (in which the company was in voluntary winding up); *Re Breakwater Co* (1914) 33 OLR 65; *Re Norske Lloyd Insurance Co Ltd* (1922) 10 Ll L Rep 43 (in which the company was described as 'undergoing in [its country of incorporation] a process analogous to a voluntary winding up'); *Re Hibernian Merchants Ltd* [1958] Ch 76.

[469] *Primary Producers Bank of Australia Ltd v Hughes* (1931) 32 SR (NSW) 14, in which there was a voluntary winding up under the supervision of the court.

[470] Cross-Border Insolvency Regulations 2006 (SI 2006/1030), sch 1, art 20(1) and (2).

[471] SI 2006/1030, sch 1, art 20(5).

Main Proceedings in another EU State (apart from Denmark)

10.188   If, in an EU State other than the UK and Denmark, a company is subject to main insolvency proceedings which are subject to Regulation (EC) No 1346/2000,[472] the liquidator in the main proceedings is entitled to request the opening of secondary proceedings in the UK.[473] For that purpose, the company must be taken to be insolvent.[474] Secondary proceedings must be winding-up proceedings listed in annex B to the Regulation.[475] The right of a liquidator in main proceedings to request the opening of secondary proceedings is recognized in IA 1986 by giving a liquidator in main proceedings standing to petition for winding up by the court.[476] If a voluntary arrangement is in force for the company, or it is in administration, in England and Wales, the liquidator in the main proceedings may request the court to convert the voluntary arrangement or administration into winding-up proceedings.[477] In this context, 'liquidator' means any of the office-holders listed in annex C to the Regulation, and main proceedings must be insolvency proceedings, as listed in annex A, but do not have to be winding-up proceedings.[478] In IR 1986 a liquidator in main proceedings covered by Regulation (EC) No 1346/2000 is referred to as a member State liquidator.[479]

10.189   When main proceedings are opened which are subject to Regulation (EC) No 1346/2000, courts in other EU States (apart from Denmark) with jurisdiction in insolvency matters have a duty to cooperate with the court that is seized with the main proceedings.[480]

10.190   If a company is subject to main proceedings under the Regulation in another EU State (apart from Denmark), a court in England and Wales will have jurisdiction under Regulation (EC) No 1346/2000, art 3, to open secondary proceedings only if the company has an establishment[481] in the United Kingdom and the courts of England and Wales would otherwise have jurisdiction over the company.[482] For a company incorporated outside the UK, this would normally be the case if the company's UK establishment is in England and Wales and constitutes a principal place of business here.[483] Secondary proceedings will not be opened unless they will serve some useful purpose and will add something to the main proceedings.[484]

10.191   The appointment of a liquidator in main proceedings is evidenced by a certified copy of the original decision appointing him or her, or by any other certificate issued by the court

---

[472] See 1.361–1.407.

[473] Regulation (EC) No 1346/2000, arts 27 and 29.

[474] Regulation (EC) No 1346/2000, art 27. *Bank Handlowy w Warszawie SA v Christianapol sp z oo* (case C-116/11) [2013] Bus LR 956.

[475] arts 3(3) and 27. In the United Kingdom, in relation to companies, the winding-up proceedings listed in annex B are: winding up by the court, winding up through administration, and creditors' voluntary winding up with confirmation by the court. In Gibraltar there is also winding up subject to the supervision of the court.

[476] IA 1986, s 124(1).

[477] See 10.21–10.25 and 10.62–10.66.

[478] *Bank Handlowy w Warszawie SA v Christianapol sp z oo* (case C-116/11) [2013] Bus LR 956.

[479] IR 1986, r 13.13(11).

[480] *Re Nortel Networks* [2009] EWHC 206 (Ch), [2009] BCC 343.

[481] See 1.387–1.389.

[482] See 1.172–1.178 and 1.419–1.432.

[483] See 1.427–1.430.

[484] *Re Office Metro Ltd* [2012] EWHC 1191 (Ch), [2012] BPIR 1049, at [34].

which has jurisdiction.[485] Another member State may require a translation into its official language.[486]

The court which has jurisdiction over the main proceedings may appoint a temporary **10.192** administrator in order to ensure preservation of the company's assets. Such a temporary administrator is empowered by art 38 to request any measures to secure and preserve any of the company's assets situated in another member State. Although art 38 refers to this preservation being for the period between the request to open proceedings and the judgment opening the proceedings, the appointment of the temporary administrator is itself a judgment opening insolvency proceedings.[487] A temporary administrator of a company has standing to petition for its winding up under IA 1986.[488]

A liquidator or temporary administrator in main proceedings concerning a company is **10.193** entitled to petition if any one or more of the circumstances in which a company of its type may be wound up[489] exists.

Great Britain Version of the UNCITRAL Model Law

Scope of the Great Britain version of the UNCITRAL Model Law

The Great Britain version of the UNCITRAL Model Law, which is in the Cross-Border **10.194** Insolvency Regulations 2006,[490] sch 1, is concerned with foreign proceedings. The term 'foreign proceeding' is defined as:[491]

> a collective judicial or administrative proceeding in a foreign State, including an interim proceeding, pursuant to a law relating to insolvency in which proceeding the assets and affairs of the debtor are subject to control or supervision by a foreign court, for the purpose of reorganisation or liquidation.

The appointment of a receiver, to prevent detriment to a particular class of creditors, in **10.195** proceedings which have nothing to do with insolvency, is not a foreign proceeding for this purpose.[492] But a creditors' voluntary winding up is.[493] The different parts of the United Kingdom are not foreign States and the Cross-Border Insolvency Regulations 2006 have no application, for example, to the effect in Scotland of a bankruptcy in England.[494]

A foreign proceeding is a foreign main proceeding if it is taking place in the State where **10.196** the debtor has the centre of its main interests.[495] A foreign proceeding, which is not a main proceeding, is a foreign non-main proceeding if it is taking place in a State where the debtor has an establishment.[496]

---

[485] Regulation (EC) No 1346/2000, art 19.
[486] Regulation (EC) No 1346/2000, art 19.
[487] *Re Eurofood IFSC Ltd* (case C-341/04) [2006] Ch 508.
[488] IA 1986, s 124(1).
[489] See 2.23–2.53.
[490] SI 2006/1030.
[491] SI 2006/1030, sch 1, art 2(i).
[492] *Re Stanford International Bank Ltd* [2010] EWCA Civ 137, [2011] Ch 33.
[493] *Re New Paragon Investments Ltd* [2012] BCC 371.
[494] *Hynd's Trustee* [2009] CSOH 76, 2009 SC 593.
[495] art 2(g).
[496] art 2(h).

10.197 An entity which is the subject of a foreign proceeding is a 'debtor' even if proceedings could not be taken against it in Great Britain, for example, because it does not have legal personality.[497]

10.198 The term 'centre of main interests' is not defined in the Model Law, though, for the purposes of recognition of a foreign proceeding in relation to a company, it is presumed, in the absence of proof to the contrary, to be the registered office.[498] For the use of the term in Regulation (EC) No 1346/2000 see 1.376–1.386.

10.199 'Establishment' is defined[499] as:

> any place of operations where the debtor carries out a non-transitory economic activity with human means and assets or services.

This is practically the same as the definition in Regulation (EC) No 1346/2000.[500]

Companies excluded

10.200 The Great Britain version of the UNCITRAL Model Law does not apply to proceedings concerning the following types of company:

(a) all companies for which pre-2003 industry-specific administration regimes[501] are available[502] and protected energy companies;[503]

(b) Scottish Water;[504]

(c) UK credit institutions, EEA credit institutions, branches of UK and EEA credit institutions,[505] and third country credit institutions,[506] which means a person who has permission under the Financial Services and Markets Act 2000 to accept deposits or issue electronic money and whose head office is not in an EEA State (including the UK);[507]

(d) insurers, being:

    (i) persons who have permission under, or by virtue of, the Financial Services and Markets Act 2000, part 4A or part 19, to effect or carry out contracts of insurance;[508]

    (ii) EEA insurers;[509]

    (iii) persons (other than those in (d)(i)) pursuing the activity of reinsurance who have received authorization for that activity from a competent authority in an EEA State;[510]

(e) the Concessionaires, as defined in the Channel Tunnel Act 1987, s 1;[511]

---

[497] *Rubin v Eurofinance SA* [2010] EWCA Civ 895, [2011] Ch 133, at [24] (point not considered on appeal).

[498] art 16(3).

[499] SI 2006/1030, sch 1, art 2(e).

[500] See 1.387–1.389.

[501] See 1.248–1.261.

[502] Cross-Border Insolvency Regulations 2006 (SI 2006/1030), sch 1, art 1(2)(a), (c), (d), (e) and (g).

[503] See 1.262–1.264. SI 2006/1030, sch 1, art 1(2)(f).

[504] art 1(2)(b).

[505] See 1.323–1.325. SI 2006/1030, sch 1, art 1(2)(h).

[506] art 1(2)(i).

[507] Credit Institutions (Reorganisation and Winding Up) Regulations 2004 (SI 2004/1045), reg 36.

[508] SI 2006/1030, sch 1, art 1(2)(j).

[509] See 1.318–1.322. SI 2006/1030, sch 1, art 1(2)(k).

[510] art 1(2)(l).

[511] SI 2006/1030, sch 1, art 1(2)(m).

(f) owners of asset pools from which the claims attaching to regulated covered bonds are to be paid.[512]

Interaction with Regulation (EC) No 1346/2000

The Great Britain version of the UNCITRAL Model Law is overridden by Regulation **10.201**
(EC) No 1346/2000[513] and so does not apply to any proceedings which are subject to the Regulation. However, it does apply to proceedings in another EU State (apart from Denmark) which are not subject to the Regulation, if they are 'foreign proceedings' for the purposes of the UNCITRAL Model Law.[514]

Foreign Representative's Standing to Petition

A 'foreign representative' is defined as a person or body, including one appointed on an **10.202**
interim basis, authorized in a foreign proceeding[515] to administer the reorganization or the liquidation of the debtor's assets or affairs or to act as a representative of the foreign proceeding.[516]

If a company is subject to a foreign main or non-main proceeding[517] in a non-EU **10.203**
State or Denmark, a foreign representative is entitled by the Great Britain version of the UNCITRAL Model Law to commence a proceeding under British insolvency law (including winding up by the court) if the conditions for commencing the proceeding are otherwise met.[518] This does not apply if the company's centre of main interests is in an EU State (other than Denmark), because in that case Regulation (EC) No 1346/2000 applies[519] instead of the Great Britain version of the UNCITRAL Model Law.[520]

If a foreign main proceeding in relation to a company is recognized in Great Britain,[521] **10.204**
there is a rebuttable presumption that the company is insolvent.[522]

The sole fact that an application, pursuant to the Great Britain version of the UNCITRAL **10.205**
Model Law, is made to a court in Great Britain by a foreign representative does not subject the foreign representative, or the foreign assets and affairs of the company, to the jurisdiction of the courts of Great Britain, or any part of it, for any purpose other than the application.[523]

---

[512] Regulated Covered Bonds Regulations 2008 (SI 2008/346), sch, para 11.
[513] SI 2006/1030, sch 1, art 3. See Paul J Omar, 'Cross-border insolvency law in the UK: an embarrassment of riches' (2006) 22 Insolv L & P 132.
[514] *Re Bud-Bank Leasing sp z oo* [2010] BCC 255.
[515] See 10.194–10.199.
[516] Cross-Border Insolvency Regulations 2006 (SI 2006/1030), sch 1, art 2(j).
[517] See 10.194–10.199.
[518] Cross-Border Insolvency Regulations 2006 (SI 2006/1030), sch 1, art 11.
[519] See 10.188–10.193.
[520] SI 2006/1030, sch 1, art 3.
[521] See 10.206–10.210.
[522] SI 2006/1030, sch 1, art 31.
[523] art 10.

Recognition of a Foreign Proceeding

Principle

10.206 A foreign representative[524] may apply to the court for recognition of the foreign proceeding in which the representative has been appointed.[525]

Court

10.207 The High Court, Chancery Division, makes recognition orders in England and Wales, the Court of Session in Scotland.[526]

10.208 The part of Great Britain whose court has jurisdiction to make a recognition order in relation to a company is the part in which the company has a place of business or assets situated.[527] A court may also assume jurisdiction if it considers, for any other reason, that it is the appropriate forum to consider making the order.[528] In considering whether it is the appropriate forum a court must take into account where any other proceedings under British insolvency law concerning the company are taking place, or likely to take place.[529]

Form of recognition order

10.209 The form of a recognition order is form ML 2 in the Cross-Border Insolvency Regulations 2006,[530] sch 5. It specifies whether the proceeding is recognized as a foreign main proceeding or a foreign non-main proceeding, as required by SI 2006/1030, sch 1, art 17(2).

Effects of recognition

10.210 Recognition of a foreign proceeding has the effects set out in the Cross-Border Insolvency Regulations 2006,[531] sch 1, arts 20–24 (protection of company's assets, entitlement of foreign representative to intervene in any proceedings to which the company is a party), and arts 28–32 (presumption of insolvency; restriction of British non-main proceedings to British assets; coordination of British and foreign proceedings).

Foreign Winding-up Application and Related English Proceedings: Election

10.211 If a claimant in English proceedings is also applying for the winding up of a company in a foreign jurisdiction, and there are issues common to both proceedings, the English court may require the claimant to choose which proceeding to pursue first.[532] But an election will not be required if it is unnecessary for efficient case management (ignoring the possibility of an appeal) or to prevent inconvenience in the foreign winding-up application.[533]

---

[524] See 10.202.

[525] Cross-Border Insolvency Regulations 2006 (SI 2006/1030), sch 1, art 15(1); Sharif A Shivji, 'The Cross-Border Insolvency Regulations 2006—a practical guide' (2007) 23 Insolv L & P 37; *Re Rajapakse* [2007] BPIR 99.

[526] SI 2006/1030, sch 1, art 4(1).

[527] art 4(2)(a).

[528] art 4(2)(b).

[529] art 4(3).

[530] SI 2006/1030.

[531] SI 2006/1030.

[532] *Racy v Hawila* [2004] EWCA Civ 209, 2004 WL 62175.

[533] *Citicorp International Ltd v Shiv-Vani Oil and Gas Exploration Services Ltd* [2014] EWHC 245 (Comm), LTL 18/2/2014.

11

OTHER PETITIONERS

Company's Petition for its Own Winding Up

Power to Petition

A company (registered or unregistered) may petition for itself to be wound up by the court.[1] **11.1**
The same applies to a building society,[2] an incorporated friendly society,[3] a limited liability
partnership,[4] and any other entity that may be wound up as a registered company.[5] But it is
submitted that an unregistered company without legal personality is incapable of petitioning.[6] Service, and proof of service, of a company's own petition on itself are not required.[7]

A company's power to petition for its own winding up may be exercised by its directors, **11.2**
at least if the company has passed a special resolution that the company be wound up by
the court, that being a circumstance in which the court may make a winding-up order.[8]
There is controversy over whether directors may exercise the power without the authority
of such a resolution.[9] However, the directors may petition in their own names.[10] If there

---

[1] IA 1986, s 124(1), applied to unregistered companies by s 221(1).

[2] Building Societies Act 1986, s 89(2)(b).

[3] Friendly Societies Act 1992, s 22(2)(b).

[4] IA 1986, s 124(1) as modified by the Limited Liability Partnerships Regulations 2001 (SI 2001/1090), reg 5(2)(a).

[5] Charitable incorporated organizations (see 1.122), European cooperative societies (see 1.123), European public limited-liability companies (see 1.124), registered societies (see 1.127–1.129).

[6] Thus there is no provision for a petition by an insolvent partnership in IPO 1994 or for a petition by a relevant scheme in the Collective Investment in Transferable Securities (Contractual Scheme) Regulations 2013 (SI 2013/1388), reg 17(9).

[7] IR 1986, r 4.8(1).

[8] IA 1986, s 122(1)(a).

[9] See 11.7–11.11.

[10] IA 1986, s 124(1). See 11.14–11.17.

are no directors, the members may, by ordinary resolution, exercise the company's power to litigate.[11] Some insolvency office-holders may exercise the company's power to petition.[12]

Grounds

Available grounds

11.3 A company cannot petition on the ground that a moratorium has not resulted in an approved voluntary arrangement, which is a ground that is only available for a creditor's petition.[13] Apart from this, a company may petition on any of the grounds listed in the Insolvency Act 1986 (IA 1986), s 122(1)[14] (in relation to a registered company) or s 221(5)[15] (in relation to an unregistered company). The same applies to the separate lists of circumstances set out for some entities that can be wound up as registered companies[16] or the additional circumstances available for some other entities.[17]

Resolution to be wound up

11.4 A petition by a company for its own compulsory winding up will usually rely on the circumstance that a special resolution has been adopted that the company be wound up by the court.[18] For a limited liability partnership there is a determination rather than a special resolution.[19] For a charitable incorporated organization there is a resolution for court winding up.[20] This procedure is appropriate, for example, where the company sought to be wound up is a wholly owned subsidiary of a company that is itself being wound up by the court or is subject to some other form of external administration.[21]

11.5 When a resolution for compulsory winding up has been adopted, the court retains a discretion whether or not to make a winding-up order. It should refuse to do so only if it is shown that the majority were acting fraudulently or in bad faith in adopting the resolution[22] or the court accepts the view of creditors that there should not be a compulsory winding up.[23]

---

[11] *Alexander Ward and Co Ltd v Samyang Navigation Co Ltd* [1975] 1 WLR 673.

[12] See 11.12.

[13] IA 1986, ss 122(1)(fa) and 124(3A); IA 1986, ss 122(1)(da) and 124(3A), as modified by the Limited Liability Partnerships Regulations 2001 (SI 2001/1090), sch 3; IA 1986, ss 122(1)(d) and 124(3A), as modified by the Charitable Incorporated Organisations (Insolvency and Dissolution) Regulations 2012 (SI 2012/3013), sch, para 1(5) and (7).

[14] See 2.27.

[15] See 2.37.

[16] Building societies (see 2.29–2.30), charitable incorporated organizations (see 2.31), incorporated friendly societies (see 2.34) and limited liability partnerships (see 2.35).

[17] European cooperative societies (see 2.32), European economic interest groupings (see 2.45–2.49) and European groupings of territorial cooperation (see 2.50–2.51).

[18] IA 1986, s 122(1)(a); Building Societies Act 1986, s 89(1)(a); Friendly Societies Act 1992, s 22(1)(a). This circumstance is not available to an unregistered company or an insolvent partnership.

[19] IA 1986, s 122(1)(a), as substituted by the Limited Liability Partnerships Regulations 2001 (SI 2001/1090), reg 5 and sch 3.

[20] IA 1986, ss 84 and 122, as substituted by the Charitable Incorporated Organisations (Insolvency and Dissolution) Regulations 2012 (SI 2012/3013), sch, para 1(1), (4) and (5).

[21] *CIC Insurance Ltd v Hannan and Co Pty Ltd* [2001] NSWSC 437, 38 ACSR 245 (provisional liquidation); *Hillig v Darkinjung Local Aboriginal Land Council* [2006] NSWSC 1371, 205 FLR 450 (special form of administration in public interest for a local aboriginal land council).

[22] *Re United Fuel Investments Ltd* (1961) 31 DLR (2d) 331 at p 349, affirmed (1963) 40 DLR (2d) 1; *Re Comtowell Ltd* [1998] 2 HKLRD 463.

[23] *Hillig v Darkinjung Local Aboriginal Land Council* [2006] NSWSC 1371, 205 FLR 450, at [35]. See 7.698–7.733.

Unless otherwise provided by legislation, the fact that voluntary winding up is available to a company is not a reason for refusing to order the company to be wound up by the court.[24]

In *Re Lemay Ltd*[25] a petition for an order winding up a company was presented citing a members' resolution, but the notice of the meeting at which the resolution was adopted had not specified that winding up was to be discussed and a subsequent meeting had rescinded the resolution. It seemed that the registered holder of nearly all the shares wanted a winding up and so the petition was adjourned to enable matters to be put in order. In *Belanger v Union Abitibi Mining Co*[26] an appeal was allowed against a winding-up order based on a members' resolution when the court heard that the notice of the meeting at which the resolution was adopted had not specified that winding up was to be discussed, an action was pending for a declaration that the resolution was void and the company had taken proceedings to rescind the allotment of shares to the members who had voted for the resolution. In *Re Fernlake Pty Ltd*[27] the court refused to order the winding up of a company on the unanimous resolution of its two registered shareholders, because those shareholders had sold half their shares to a purchaser who did not agree to the winding up. W C Lee J described voting the sold shares as a breach of trust. Alternatively, it may be said that there is an implied term in a contract of sale of shares in a company that the vendor will not vote them in favour of a resolution for the winding up of the company without the purchaser's agreement.[28] **11.6**

Authority of Directors to Present Company's Petition

In Great Britain, under IA 1986, s 124(1), the directors of a company are empowered to present their own petition for the company to be wound up.[29] The directors of a company do not have power to cause a petition to be presented in the company's name for its own compulsory winding up without being authorized to do so by the members, unless they are given an express power to do so by the company's constitution. A general power of management conferred, for example, by art 3 of the model articles of association for private companies limited by shares and for public companies[30] is a power to carry on the company's business as a going concern and does not give authority to end the business.[31] If directors present a petition without authority, their action may be ratified by the members.[32] **11.7**

In New South Wales a different view has been taken: there it has been held that the directors of a company may present a petition in the company's name.[33] In *Re Compaction Systems Pty Ltd*[34] Bowen CJ in Eq argued at p 492 that a decision to present a petition to wind up a company is not a decision to terminate the affairs of the company because it is for the court **11.8**

---

[24] *Hillig v Darkinjung Local Aboriginal Land Council* at [35].
[25] (1924) 26 OWN 443.
[26] (1916) 32 DLR 700.
[27] [1995] 1 QdR 597.
[28] *Kells Investments Pty Ltd v Industrial Equity Ltd* (1984) 9 ACLR 507.
[29] See 11.2.
[30] Companies (Model Articles) Regulations 2008 (SI 2008/3229), sch 1 and sch 3.
[31] *Re Standard Bank of Australia Ltd* (1898) 24 VLR 304; *Re Galway and Salthill Tramways Co* [1918] 1 IR 62; *Re Birmacley Products Pty Ltd* [1943] VLR 29; *Re Woulfe and Son Pty Ltd* [1972] QWN 50; *Re Emmadart Ltd* [1979] Ch 540; *Re United Uranium NL* [1990] VR 121; *Re Giant Resources Ltd* [1991] 1 QdR 107.
[32] *Re Galway and Salthill Tramways Co.*
[33] *Re Inkerman Grazing Pty Ltd* (1972) 1 ACLR 102; *Re New England Agricultural Corporation Ltd* (1982) 7 ACLR 231; *Spicer v Mytrent Pty Ltd* (1984) 8 ACLR 711; *Re T and L Trading (Aust) Pty Ltd* (1986) 10 ACLR 388.
[34] [1976] 2 NSWLR 477.

to decide whether the company should be wound up, and the company's affairs will continue until it is wound up. See also the discussion in *Strong v J Brough and Son (Strathfield) Pty Ltd*.[35] The New South Wales position has been followed in Malaysia[36] and Bermuda.[37]

11.9 The conflict between New South Wales and other Australian jurisdictions seems to have been resolved in *Re Interchase Management Services Pty Ltd*[38] and *Re United Medical Protection Ltd*,[39] by treating presentation by the directors of a company, in the name of the company, of a petition to wind it up, as being done under a provision in a company's articles that the directors 'may exercise all such powers of the company as are not hereby or by statute required to be exercised by the company in general meeting'. This may be construed as not subject to the limitation that the powers must be used in the management of the company.[40] The same applies to a power to control the company's affairs and property.[41]

11.10 It used to be thought that a general meeting of a company could, by ordinary resolution, instruct directors to commence legal proceedings in the company's name.[42] Accordingly it was thought that a simple majority of the members of a company could require the directors to present a petition for the compulsory winding up of the company.[43] A petition was presented in these circumstances in *Re Anglo-Continental Produce Co Ltd*[44] but was dismissed because those supporting the petition had failed to show that it was just and equitable for the court to intervene when a bare majority of members were unable to persuade their fellow members to adopt a special resolution for either voluntary or compulsory liquidation. The theory of members' control of litigation has now, however, been abandoned,[45] so there is no doubt that members can get a winding up only by passing a special resolution.[46]

11.11 In *Re Global Opportunity Fund Ltd*[47] a petition presented by the directors of a company authorized by only an ordinary resolution was successful. All members wanted a winding up and it seems that the minority's refusal to support a special resolution was based mainly on objections to the liquidator whom the majority wished to appoint.[48]

---

[35] (1991) 5 ACSR 296.

[36] *Miharja Development Sdn Bhd v Tan Sri Datuk Loy Hean Heong* [1995] 1 MLJ 101; see Choong Yeow Choy, 'Who has the right to terminate the life of a company—the shareholders or the board of directors?' (1996) 17 Co Law 61.

[37] *Re First Virginia Reinsurance Ltd* (2003) 66 WIR 133.

[38] (1992) 11 ALR 561.

[39] [2002] NSWSC 413, 41 ACSR 623. Applied in *Re Trans Pacific Insurance Corporation* [2009] NSWSC 308, 71 ACSR 569, and *Re Trans Pacific Insurance Corporation* [2009] NSWSC 554, 72 ACSR 327, in which it was assumed that the law is the same in the Cayman Islands.

[40] *Campbell v Rofe* [1933] AC 91.

[41] *Re University of Newcastle Union Ltd* [2008] NSWSC 1361.

[42] *Marshall's Valve Gear Co Ltd v Manning Wardle and Co Ltd* [1909] 1 Ch 267.

[43] *Re Langham Skating Rink Co* (1877) 5 ChD 669 per Jessel MR at p 684.

[44] [1939] 1 All ER 99.

[45] *Breckland Group Holdings Ltd v London and Suffolk Properties Ltd* [1989] BCLC 100; *Mitchell and Hobbs (UK) Ltd v Mill* [1996] 2 BCLC 102. See *Mayson, French and Ryan on Company Law*, 31st edn (Oxford: Oxford University Press, 2014), 15.10.3.

[46] Unless the articles provide that the company is to be dissolved after a fixed period of time or on the happening of a certain event, in which case an ordinary resolution is sufficient for a voluntary winding up under IA 1986, s 84(1)(a).

[47] 1997 CILR N-7.

[48] See 1997 CILR N-7–8.

Insolvency Office-holders

Various insolvency office-holders have powers to petition for the winding up of the company to which they are appointed. A petition may be presented in the company's name by its administrator,[49] administrative receiver[50] or voluntary liquidator.[51] A member State liquidator or temporary administrator,[52] a foreign representative,[53] a supervisor of a voluntary arrangement[54] or an insolvency office-holder of a partnership[55] can only petition in his or her own name. **11.12**

Corporate Member of Insolvent Partnership

If a registered company which is a member of an insolvent partnership (a 'corporate member', see 1.115–1.119) petitions under Insolvent Partnerships Order 1994 (IPO 1994), art 10, for the winding up of the partnership and the winding up or bankruptcy of all its members, the petitioning member must petition for its own winding up.[56] The only possible ground for the member's petition for its own winding up is that it is unable to pay its debts.[57] **11.13**

Directors' Petition

Registered and Unregistered Companies

The directors of a company (registered or unregistered) may petition for it to be wound up by the court.[58] The same applies to the directors of a building society,[59] an incorporated friendly society,[60] or any other entity that may be wound up as a registered company and which has directors.[61] For entities that do not have directors, their role is performed by the charity trustees of a charitable incorporated organization,[62] the committee of management of an incorporated friendly society[63] and the members of a limited liability partnership.[64] The decision to present a petition must be taken at a properly constituted board meeting[65] or agreed to by all the directors without meeting.[66] A petition may be presented by all of a company's directors even if, under the company's constitution, there are too few of them to form a quorum.[67] A winding-up order has been made on the court's own initiative where **11.14**

---

[49] See 10.31–10.35, 10.38, 10.51–10.58 and 10.60–10.61.
[50] See 10.68–10.70.
[51] See 10.139.
[52] See 10.188–10.193.
[53] See 10.202–10.205.
[54] See 10.6–10.11 and 10.18–10.20.
[55] See 10.61.
[56] IA 1986, s 124(2)(a), as modified by IPO 1994, sch 6, para 2.
[57] IA 1986, s 122, as modified by IPO 1994, sch 4, para 6(a), and applied by art 10(2), (3) and (6).
[58] IA 1986, s 124(1), applied to unregistered companies by s 221(1).
[59] Building Societies Act 1986, s 89(2)(b).
[60] Friendly Societies Act 1992, s 22(2)(b).
[61] European cooperative societies (see 1.123), European public limited-liability companies (see 1.124), registered societies (see 1.127–1.129).
[62] IA 1986, s 124(1), as applied by the Charitable Incorporated Organisations (Insolvency and Dissolution) Regulations 2012 (SI 2012/3013), sch, para 1(1) and (2), and modified by para 1(3)(i).
[63] Friendly Societies Act 1992, s 22(2)(b).
[64] Limited Liability Partnerships Regulations 2001 (SI 2001/1090), reg 5(2)(b).
[65] *Re Equiticorp International plc* [1989] 1 WLR 1010.
[66] *Re Instrumentation Electrical Services Ltd* [1988] BCLC 550.
[67] *Re Coleraine Football and Sports Club Ltd* [2005] NICh 4, [2006] NI 159, at [5].

it was urgently necessary to wind up an insolvent credit union but a board meeting could not be properly constituted because notice of it could not be given to a director who had disappeared following discovery of his embezzlement which had caused the insolvency.[68]

11.15 The provision allowing the directors of a company to petition for its winding up was introduced by IA 1985, sch 6, para 28.

11.16 In *Re Minrealm Ltd*[69] the company's directors decided by majority to petition for the company to be wound up on the ground of inability to pay its debts. The company was found to be unable to pay its debts as they fell due, but this would be cured if directors met their own obligations to the company, some of which were the subject of other proceedings. As no creditor supported the petition, it was adjourned to await the outcome of the other proceedings.

Open-Ended Investment Companies

11.17 An open-ended investment company is incorporated by an authorization order made by the Financial Conduct Authority (FCA). The FCA has the power to give a direction requiring any director of an open-ended investment company to present a petition to the court to wind up the company.[70] This power may be exercised[71] if it appears to the FCA that:

(a) one or more requirements for the making of an authorization order are no longer satisfied;

(b) the company, any of its directors or its depositary:
  (i) has contravened or is likely to contravene any relevant provision (meaning any requirement imposed by or under the Financial Services and Markets Act 2000); or
  (ii) has, in purported compliance with any such provision, knowingly or recklessly given the FCA information which is false or misleading in a material particular; or

(c) it is desirable to give a direction in order to protect the interests of shareholders or potential shareholders in the company.

Fine Collection

11.18 The designated officer for a magistrates' court may petition for a registered or unregistered company to be wound up by the court.[72] The same applies to a limited liability partnership,[73] any other entity that may be wound up as a registered company[74] (except a charitable incorporated organization[75]), and an insolvent partnership where there is no

---

[68] *Re Marches Credit Union Ltd* [2013] EWHC 1731 (Ch), LTL 2/7/2013.

[69] [2007] EWHC 3078 (Ch), [2008] 2 BCLC 141.

[70] Open-Ended Investment Companies Regulations 2001 (SI 2001/1228), reg 25(2) (for the definition of 'the Authority' see reg 2).

[71] SI 2001/1228, reg 25(1).

[72] IA 1986, s 124(1), applied to unregistered companies by s 221(1).

[73] IA 1986, s 124(1), as modified by the Limited Liability Partnerships Regulations 2001 (SI 2001/1090), reg 5(2)(a).

[74] European cooperative societies (see 1.123), European public limited-liability companies (see 1.124), registered societies (see 1.127–1.129).

[75] IA 1986, s 124(1), as modified by the Charitable Incorporated Organisations (Insolvency and Dissolution) Regulations 2012 (SI 2012/3013), sch, para 1(7).

concurrent petition against a member.[76] A designated officer does not have authority to petition for the winding up of a building society, an incorporated friendly society, or a CIO. The only circumstance in which a magistrates' court's designated officer may petition is where:[77]

(a) the court has, or is treated by any enactment as having, adjudged the company by a conviction to pay a sum; and
(b) the court has issued a warrant of control[78] for the purpose of levying the sum; and
(c) it appears on the return to the warrant that the company's money and goods are insufficient to pay the amount outstanding.[79]

The designated officer does not need any further specific authorization to petition and no court hearing is required. **11.19**

---

[76] IPO 1994, art 7. It is submitted that the designated officer is 'any other person other than a member' referred to in art 7(1). IA 1986, s 124(1), as applied by the modified form of s 221(5) set out in IPO 1994, sch 3, para 3.

[77] Magistrates' Courts Act 1980, s 87A.

[78] Under the Magistrates' Courts Act 1980, s 76(1).

[79] The 'amount outstanding' is defined in the Tribunals, Courts and Enforcement Act 2007, sch 12, para 50(3).

INDEX